THE WORKS
OF
GEOFFREY CHAUCER
AND OTHERS

THE WORKS
OF
GEOFFREY CHAUCER
AND OTHERS

BEING A REPRODUCTION IN FACSIMILE OF
THE FIRST COLLECTED EDITION 1532
FROM THE COPY IN THE
BRITISH MUSEUM

WITH AN INTRODUCTION BY WALTER W. SKEAT, Litt.D., F.B.A.

KALPAZ

ISBN: 978-93-5128-545-8

First Published in 1905
Indian Reprint in 2017

Published by

Kalpaz Publications
C-30, Satyawati Nagar,
Delhi – 110052
E-mail: kalpaz@hotmail.com
Website: kalpazpublications.com
Ph.: +91-9212142040

Cataloging in Publication Data—DK
Courtesy: D.K. Agencies (P) Ltd. <docinfo@dkagencies.com>

Chaucer, Geoffrey, -1400., author.
[Works]
The works of Geoffrey Chaucer and others : being a reproduction in facsimile of the first collected edition 1532, from the copy in the British Museum / with an introduction by Walter W. Skeat (Lirr.D., F.B.A.).
pages cm
"First published in 1905"—Title page verso.
ISBN 9789351285458

1. English poetry—Middle English, 1100-1500. I. Lydgate, John, 1370?-1451?, author. II. Hoccleve, Thomas, 1370?-1450?, author. III. British Museum. IV. Title. V. Title: Geoffrey Chaucer.

PR1850.C43 2017 DDC 821.1 23

LIST OF SUBSCRIBERS

A

Abraham & Strauss.
Adam, Peter.
Adam, William.
Allen, Edward George.
Amherst of Hackney, Lord.
Anderson, J. F.
Andrews, Emile.
Angus & Robertson.
Army & Navy Co-operative Society.
Asher, A., & Co.
Athenaeum Club.

B

Bain, J.
Bangs, L. W.
Barrett, Thomas.
Bartlett, A.
Bates, E. B.
Bennett, Miss Frances E.
Berlin, Englisches Seminar.
Berlin, Königliche Bibliothek.
Bickers & Son.
Billson, Charles James.
Birkenruth, W. S.
Birmingham University.
Blackwell, B. H.
Bland, F. M.
Boston Athenaeum, Mass., U.S.A.
Boston Public Library, Mass., U.S.A.
Brainerd, Ira H.
Brentano's.
Brophy, Michael M.
Brown, G. B.
Brown, S. C., Langham & Co.
Bruce, Alex.
Bumpus, J. & E.
Burdick, Leon D.

C

Cardiff Free Library.
Carlton Club.
Carswell, R.
Carter, A. H.
Carter, T. A.
Cecil, Charles.
Chawner, G.
Chew, Beverley.
Chicago Public Library, Ill., U.S.A.
Chicago University, Ill., U.S.A.
Chivers, Cedric.
Clark, D. R.
Clarke, Sir Ernest.
Clarke Co., W. B.
Clay, William F.
Cleghorn, William.
Clements, H. J. B.
Cobbold, Felix T.
Commin, Horace G.
Commin, James G.
Congress Library, Washington, U.S.A.
Cornell University, Ithaca, U.S.A.
Cornish, J. E.
Cornish Bros.
Crooks, R. Fleming.

D

Daubuz, J. C.
Davidson, W. E.
Davis, Joseph.
Dawes, Charles Reginald.
Dawson, William, & Sons.
Deighton, Bell & Co.
Denny, A. & F.
Derry, William.
Dodd, Mead & Co.
Dooley, Henry.

E

Edinburgh Public Library.
Edinburgh University Library.
Edwards, Francis.
Elder, Paul & Co.
Elliot, Andrew.
Ellis & Elvey.
Ellsworth, J. W.
Engelbach, G. F.

F

Farrer, Lord.
Fenwick, G. J.
Fergusson, Robert M.
Forbes Library, Mass., U.S.A.
Fowler, Thos. P.
Fowler, The Rev. Canon W. W.
Fox, W. H.
Frost, William Spatchett.
Fyers, Evan.

G

Gardner, A.
Gardner, John.
George's Sons, William.
Gosset, Maj.-Genl. M.
Göttingen, Königliche Universitäts-Bibliothek.
Graham, Daniel.
Grant, W.
Gray, W.
Green, Charles.
Grolier Club, New York.

H

Hall, W. H.
Hammond, Miss Eleanor P.
Hampstead Public Library.
Hargreave, James.
Harris, W. F.
Harrison & Sons.
Hart, H. C.
Hartshorne, Robert.
Harvard University Library, Camb., U.S.A.
Hatchards.
Heffer & Sons.
Henderson, J. B. S.
Heywood, Miss Monica M.
Hillier, J. J.
Hodson, Lawrence W.

Holliday

Holliday, J. R.
Hollis, W. E.
Howell, Edward.
Howell, James, Jun.
Howell, T. Francis.
Humphries, Sydney.

I

Iowa State Library, U.S.A.

J

Jago-Trelawny, Maj.-Genl. J.
Johnson, Sydney.
Johnson, W.
Johnston, George P.
Johnston, Walter.
Jones, E. Peter.
Jones, F. R.
Jones & Evans.

K

Kansas University, Lawrence, U.S.A.
Kerr, William Smith.
Knox, D. J.

L

Lamley & Co.
Lauriat Co., Charles E.
Lehmann & Stage.
Leon, G.
Levi, Phin H.
Lewis, Walter.
Lichtenstadt, M. V.
Linnell, Charles.
Luyster, S. B.

M

Macan, C. Reginald Walter.
McCormick, W. S.
MacGregor, The Rev. William.
McLaughlin, The Rev. C. L.
MacLehose, James, & Sons.
Macmillan & Bowes.
McNicol, R. S.
Macniven & Wallace.
McVitie, Robert.
Maggs, Bros.
Matthews, John.
Meek, W. A.
Melbourne Public Library.
Michigan University, U.S.A.
Midland Educational Co.
Mills, W. Stead.
Minards, W. A.
Mitchell Library, Glasgow.
Morrison, Hubert Peter.
Mynott, A.

N

National Library of Ireland.
Neale, W. G.
Newberry Library, U.S.A.
New York Public Library, U.S.A.
Nutt, David.

O

Oliver, Mrs. George Carter.
Orrock, G. D.
Osborn, Douglas.
Oxford and Cambridge University Club.

P

Parker, C. C.
Parker & Son.
Payne, Mrs.
Peabody Institute, Baltimore, U.S.A.
Pearce, W. R.
Penfold, Hugh.
Penfold, Oliver.
Pinsent, R. A.
Pocock, Arthur F.
Poor, Henry W.
Power, D'Arcy.
Price, Rees.
Purves, James.
Putnam, W. C.
Putnam's Sons, G. P.

Q

Quaritch, Bernard.

R

Raymond, Alfred.
Ross, J. W.
Rothschild'sche, Freiherrlich Carl von, öffentliche Bibliothek, Frankfurt a/M.
Rowe, The Rev. George Stringer.
Rundell, T. W.
Rylands Library, Manchester.

S

St. Andrews University Library.
Sawers, J.
Scribner, A. H.
Scribner, Charles.
Scribner's Sons, Charles.
Seligsberg, Frank W.
Sewell, J. Sefton.
Sharp, The Rev. J. Alfred.
Shaw-Stewart, Lady Alice.
Shepard, Charles E.
Shillaber, W. G.
Shillington, J. M.
Signet Library, Edinburgh.
Simpkin, Marshall, Hamilton, Kent & Co.
Slater, James A.
Smith, H. L.
Smith, John, & Son.
Smith, Judge Lumley.
Smith, W. J.
Smith Book Co.
Sotheran, Henry, & Co.
Southgate, Herbert.
Speight, E. E.
Spiers, Lionel.
Squance, H. S.
Stechert, G. E., & Co.
Stevens, B. F., & Brown.
Stewart, C. J.
Stilling, H.
Stucken, E.
Symon, J. H.
Syracuse Public Library, U.S.A.

T

Taylor, J. S.
Taylor, T. G.
Thatcher, Edward H.
Thin, James.
Thornton, Joseph, & Son.
Toronto Public Library.
Truslove & Hanson.
Twietmeyer, A.

V

Van Wyck, Stephen.
Veitch, George T.
Venables, William H.
Victoria University, Manchester.
Vienna, K. K. Hofbibliothek.
Von Sobbe, T. A.

W

Walker, T. Sydney.
Warrington, E. M.
Warwick, William Deeping.
Waters, A. C.
Webster, Isaac.
Whitworth Institute, Manchester.
Wigan Free Public Library.
Wilcocks, H. S.
Wilkinson, Norman.
Williams College Library.
Willis, Judge W.
Wilson, J.
Wood, Humphrey.
Woodward, The Rev. G. R.
Worthington, J. V.
Wright, W. Aldis.

Y

Young, Harold Edgar.

Z

Zaehnsdorf, J.

TABLE OF CONTENTS OF THE FOLIO EDITION (1532)

*** The numbers refer to the present pages.

TABLE OF CONTENTS

*** Exclusive of The Romaunt of the Rose, part of which is by Chaucer, and Surigon's Latin Epitaph, the Folio includes 40 pieces. Of these, 18 are by Chaucer; 8 (apparently) by Lydgate; 2 by Hoccleve; 1 apiece by Henryson, Ros, Usk, Gower, Clanvowe, and Scogan (6 in all); and 6 are anonymous. To these we may add 1 more piece by Chaucer, viz. his Balade on Gentilesse, introduced into the midst of the piece by Scogan. Out of these 41 pieces, 19 are by Chaucer, and 22 by others. Even if we reckon by pages, the genuine works occupy less than three-fourths of the volume.

INTRODUCTION

§ 1. WILLIAM THYNNE

THE credit of being the first to print a collected edition of the Works of Chaucer (and others) belongs to William Thynne, Chief Clerk of the Kitchen to Henry VIII, who published the First Folio edition (here reproduced) in 1532, just a century before the appearance, in 1632, of the Second Folio edition of Shakespeare's Plays. A sufficient account of him is given in the Dictionary of National Biography, which is indebted for many particulars to the short accounts of the lives of William and Francis Thynne, by Dr. G. H. Kingsley, prefixed to his edition (in 1865), for the Early English Text Society, of Francis Thynne's 'Animadversions' upon a new edition of Chaucer issued by Thomas Speght in 1598. A later edition of F. Thynne's 'Animadversions' was printed in 1875 for the same Society, edited by Dr. Furnivall, which contains many additional particulars, and is of much value in connexion with the present subject. This edition was of course also consulted by the writer of the above-named article.

We thus learn that 'the family name of Thynne occurs in records in the West of England as early as Edward II'; and that 'a certain Walter or Thomas Botfield about 1388 was the root of several branches, some of which retained the name, with the variety of Botevyle; but the eldest branch obtained that of Thynne [i.e. of th' Ynne], from the circumstance of its inheriting the freeholds and mansion-house or Inn, the copyholds being given to another. The term Inn was used in the sense which has given us "Lincoln's Inn," "Gray's Inn," or "Furnival's Inn," merely meaning a place of residence of the higher class, though in this case inverted, the Inn giving its name to its owner.'

William Thynne was the son of John de la Inne and Jane Bowdler; and in 1532 was Chief Clerk of the Kitchen to Henry VIII, the appointment being one of trust and value. Subsequently, he was made one of the Masters of the Household. He lived to publish the Second Folio edition of Chaucer in 1542; and died on the 10th of August, 1546. He was buried in the church of Allhallows, Barking, near the Tower of London, where there is a brass to his memory which has been restored in recent times by the Marquis of Bath, a descendant of Thomas Thynne, who was William's brother.

§ 2. FRANCIS THYNNE

By marriage with Anne Bond, whose father William was Clerk of the Green Cloth, William Thynne had a son named Francis, and some daughters. Francis Thynne was born in Kent in or before 1546, the year of his father's death. He inherited his father's tastes, and had a good reputation as an antiquary. Being so fortunate as to obtain a good position in the Herald's office, perhaps as Blanch Lyon pursuivant, but at any rate (in 1602) as Lancaster Herald, he was enabled to pursue the study of antiquities, and to take a special interest in the Works of Chaucer. He was distinguished as an author, and the long list of his works in Dr. Furnivall's edition of his 'Animadversions' (see § 1) fills nine pages. The only one that we are here concerned with is entitled 'Animaduersions vppon the Annotacions and Corrections of some imperfections of impressiones of Chaucers workes (sett downe before tyme, and nowe) reprinted in the

the yere of oure lorde 1598; sett downe by Francis Thynne. Soortee pur bien ou ne sortee rien. 1599.' This work was not printed at the time, but the autograph MS. was carefully preserved among the treasures of the Bridgewater Library, where it still remains; and it was from this copy that Dr. Kingsley's edition was prepared for press[1]. I shall have occasion to refer again to this interesting treatise below; and for this purpose I employ the later edition by Dr. Furnivall.

§ 3. EARLIER EDITIONS OF SOME OF CHAUCER'S WORKS

Though Thynne was the first to issue Chaucer's Works in a collected form, several of the poems and one prose work had already been printed before 1532; and Pynson, in 1526, had already gathered some of these into one collection. The Canterbury Tales, in particular, had already been printed no less than five times.

The following is a list of genuine works printed before 1532. The figure 1 denotes *first* edition; and so of the rest.

Canterbury Tales. 1. Caxton, about 1477–8, from a poor MS.; 2. Caxton, ab. 1483, from a better MS.; 3. Pynson, ab. 1493; 4. Wynkyn de Worde, 1498; 5. Pynson, 1526.

Boethius. 1. Caxton, before 1479.

Book [or *House*] *of Fame.* 1. Caxton, ab. 1483; 2. Pynson, 1526.

Troilus. 1. Caxton, ab. 1483; 2. Wynkyn de Worde, 1517; 3. Pynson, 1526.

Parliament of Foules. 1. Caxton, ab. 1477–8; 2. Pynson, 1526; 3. Wynkyn de Worde, 1530.

Gentilesse (included in Scogan's poem). 1. Caxton, ab. 1477–8.

Truth (The good counceyl of Chawcer). 1. Caxton, ab. 1477–8; 2. Wynkyn de Worde (before 1519), in a book entitled Proverbs of Lydgate; 3. Pynson, 1526.

Fortune (Balade of the vilage (*sic*) without peyntyng). 1. Caxton, ab. 1477–8; 2. Wynkyn de Worde (before 1519), in a book entitled Proverbs of Lydgate.

Envoy to Scogan. 1. Caxton, ab. 1477–8 (all lost after the third stanza).

Anelida and Arcite. 1. Caxton, ab. 1477–8.

Purse (The Compleynt of Chaucer vnto his empty purse). 1. Caxton, ab. 1477–8.

Mars; Venus; Marriage (Lenvoy to Bukton). 1. Julian Notary, 1499–1502.

Pynson's edition of 1526 also included La Belle Dame sans Merci and The Lamentation of Mary Magdaleyn. Neither of these is by Chaucer, but both appear again in Thynne.

§ 4. CHRONOLOGICAL ORDER OF EARLIER EDITIONS

I here repeat the above list in a strictly chronological form, in order to show what had been done from time to time.

1477–8. Caxton. 1. *Canterbury Tales.*

1477–8. Caxton. 1. *Parliament of Foules*; 1. A poem by Scogan, including Chaucer's *Gentilesse*; a stanza of seven lines, beginning—'Wyth empty honde men may no hawkes lure' [not by Chaucer]; 1. *Truth*; 1. *Fortune*; 1. *Envoy to Scogan* (first three stanzas). (The two extant copies of the book are both imperfect at the end.)

1477–8. Caxton. 1. *Anelida and Arcite*; 1. *Purse*; some Sayings [not by Chaucer].

1478 (or earlier). Caxton. 1. *Boethius.*

[1] It had previously been printed in 1810, by the Rev. H. J. Todd, in his Illustrations of the Lives and Writings of Gower and Chaucer, pp. 1–83.

1483 (?). Caxton. 1. *Troilus.*

1483 (?). Caxton. 2. *Canterbury Tales.*

1483 (?). Caxton. 1. *Book of Fame.*

1493. Pynson. 3. *Canterbury Tales.*

1498. Wynkyn de Worde. 4. *Canterbury Tales.*

1502 (?). Julian Notary. 1. *Mars*; 1. *Venus*; 1. *Envoy to Bukton.*

1517. Wynkyn de Worde. 2. *Troilus.*

Before 1519. Wynkyn de Worde. 2. *Truth*; 2. *Fortune.*

1526. Pynson. Part I; 3. *Troilus.* Part II; 2. *Book of Fame*; 2. *Parliament of Foules*; 1. *La Belle Dame sans Merci* [not by Chaucer, but reprinted by Thynne]; 3. *Truth*; *Morall Proverbes of Cristyne* [not by Chaucer, and *not* reprinted by Thynne; they had already been printed by Caxton in 1478]; 1. *The Lamentation of Mary Magdaleyn* [not by Chaucer, but reprinted by Thynne]; *The Letter of Dydo to Eneas* [not by Chaucer, and *not* reprinted by Thynne]; *Like thine audience* [by Lydgate, and *not* reprinted by Thynne]. Part III; 5. *Canterbury Tales.* The order of the Parts is indifferent, as they could be sold separately.

1530. Wynkyn de Worde. 3. *Parliament of Foules.*

It thus appears that Thynne's design of collecting Chaucer's Works into one volume may very well have been suggested by Pynson's reprints in 1526, which dealt with no less than *five* of Chaucer's more important works, and further included La Belle Dame sans Merci and The Lamentation of Mary Magdaleyn, both of which he reprinted. We see, moreover, that it was Pynson who introduced the lamentable precedent of mixing up the works of Chaucer with those of others; and Thynne unfortunately followed his example with an almost unbounded recklessness, as will appear hereafter.

§ 5. THE FIRST EIGHT EDITIONS OF THE COLLECTED WORKS OF CHAUCER

1. By William Thynne; London, 1532. Folio. Printed by Thomas Godfray. (Here reproduced.) 'It is an edition of great importance. Its text remained for two centuries and a half the standard text of the Canterbury Tales. For the remaining poems, it has been until a comparatively late period the best text'; Lounsbury, Studies in Chaucer, i. 265.

2. Reprinted, in Thynne's lifetime, with the addition of the spurious Plowman's Tale, inserted after the Parson's Tale; London, 1542. Folio. Printed by John Reynes.

3. Reprinted, with the addition of the spurious Plowman's Tale, but now inserted *before* the Parson's Tale; London, no date. Folio. Printed by or for the booksellers, Wm. Bonham, R. Kele, T. Petit, or R. Toye [1].

4. Reprinted, with the addition of three stanzas at fol. cccxxxii, back, and considerable additions at the end by John Stowe; London, 1561. Folio. Printed by Jhon Kyngston.

5. Reprinted, with additions and alterations, by Thomas Speght; London, 1598. Folio.

6. Reprinted, with further additions and alterations by Thomas Speght; London, 1602. Folio.

[1] I possess a copy, 'Imprinted at London by Wyllyam Bonham, dwellyng in Paules churcheyarde at the sygne of the reed Lyon.' Other copies have the name of Rychard Kele, or Thomas Petit, or Robart Toye.

7. Reprinted,

7. Reprinted, with slight additions; London, 1687. Folio.

8. Reprinted, with additions and great alterations in spelling, by John Urry; London, 1721. Folio.

These editions are all that depend mainly upon Thynne's first edition. Tyrwhitt's edition of the Canterbury Tales in 1775–8, in 5 vols., 8vo, was largely corrected by reference to MSS. But all editions are indebted to Thynne for the texts of some of the pieces which the editors include.

§ 6. FULLER ACCOUNT OF THE FIRST FOUR EDITIONS

Of the above editions, the first four are the most closely connected with Thynne, and deserve somewhat fuller treatment. They might fairly be called the first four Folio editions, as in the case of the Plays of Shakespeare. Thynne himself gives a 'first' Table of Contents at p. 5, and a 'second' or more expanded Table at p. 6, but both are inaccurate and misleading. Thus he describes The Legend of Good Women, followed by a spurious and wholly unconnected piece, as 'The lege*n*de of good women, *with* a balade. v.' He joins together The Book of the Duchess and the Envoy to Bukton under the title 'The dreame of Chaucer, with a balade. vii.' After 'The Cuckowe and the Nightyngale' he omits a Ballad; and some pieces at the end are inadequately accounted for. He also entirely ignores the poems which he subjoined, at the last moment, to his Table of Contents; see pp. 7, 8. Dr. Furnivall's list of Thynne's collection, at p. 7 of his edition of F. Thynne's 'Animadversions,' likewise ignores the same, and, in separating the Genuine from the Spurious works, disturbs the order. I therefore take the present opportunity of numbering the pieces separately. References to the *pages* are given in § 7, in the appended Table of Contents, as well as at p. ix.

§ 7. CONTENTS OF THE FIRST FOLIO OF 1532

The Works here printed *for the first time* are denoted by an asterisk. Note that Fol. ccxxxiv includes p. 494 as well as p. 493; and so of the rest.

Register: Signatures marked A–Z (exclusive of J, V, W), Aa–Zz, Aaa–Uuu, in sixes, except A and Qq, which have, respectively, 4 and 9 leaves. In all, 64 quires of 6 leaves, and 13 leaves more; i.e. 397 leaves or 794 pages, the last page being blank.

Foliation: Folios 1–10 (pp. 1–20) are not counted at all; and Fol. i begins on p. 21, as indicated by the appearance of Fol. xiii on p. 45, the preceding folios being unmarked. Fol. lxxxiv is wrongly marked as lxxxv, but lxxxv itself is correct. Between Foll. ccxix and ccxx are three leaves not numbered. Fol. ccxlvii is wrongly marked ccxliiii, by a misprint of ii for v. Fol. ccc is wrongly repeated. Fol. ccclxxxiii is the last. Thus the whole number of leaves is 383, together with 13 uncounted, and 1 number repeated; i.e. 397, as before. A few folios are not marked, viz. xviii, cxxvii, clxix, ccxxxv, cclxxxv, cccxxiv.

Titles: All with the same border; at pp. 1, 9, 273, 357, 495, 568, 595, 622, 675.

*a. Eight goodly questyons, &c. (Spurious). Pref., p. 7.

*b. To the kynges most noble grace, &c. (By Hoccleve.) Pref., p. 8.

c. Sayings (14 lines, copied from the lines at the end of Caxton's edition of *Anelida* and *Purse*). Pref., p. 8.

1. Canterbury Tales. (Page 11. Pages 21 and 22 are counted as Fol. i.)

*2. The Romaunt of the Rose. Fol. cxxvii. (273).

3. Troilus and Creseyde. Fol. clxix. (357).

*4. The Testament of Creseyde. Fol. ccxix. (457).
*5. The Legend of Good Women. Fol. ccxx. (465).
*6. A Ballad—'Mother of norture, &c.' Fol. ccxxxiv. (494).
7. Translation of Boethius. Fol. ccxxxv. (495).
*8. The Dream of Chaucer [i.e. The Book of the Duchess]. Fol. cclxxi. (568).
9. Begins—'My master, &c.' [i.e. Lenvoy to Bukton]. Fol. cclxxviii. (582).
10. The Assembly [or Parliament] of Foules. Fol. cclxxix. (583).
*11. The Flour of Curtesy. Fol. cclxxxiii. (591).
*12. How Pity is dead [Complaint unto Pity]. Fol. cclxxxv. (595).
13. La Belle Dame sans Mercy. Fol. cclxxxvi. (598).
14. Annelida and false Arcite. Fol. cclxxxxi. (608).
*15. The Assembly of Ladies. Fol. cclxxxxiv. (613).
*16. The Conclusions of the Astrolabe. Fol. cclxxxxviii. (622).
17. The Complaint of the Black Knight. Fol. cccvii. (642).
*18. A Praise of Women. Fol. cccxi. (650).
19. The House of Fame. Fol. cccxii. (652).
*20. The Testament of Love. Fol. cccxxiv. (675).
21. The Lamentation of Mary Magdaleyn. Fol. ccclxi. (749).
*22. The Remedy of Love. Fol. ccclxv. (758).
23. The Complaint of Mars. Fol. ccclxviii. (764).
24. The Complaint of Venus. Fol. ccclxx. (768).
*25. The Letter of Cupid. Fol. ccclxxi. (769).
*26, *27. A Ballad in Commendation of Our Lady (775). A Ballad to my Lady (776). Fol. ccclxxiiii. [Two different poems, run together into one.]
*28. John Gower to King Henry IV. Fol. ccclxxv. (778).
*29. The Cuckoo and the Nightingale. Fol. ccclxxviii. (783).
*30. A Ballad. Fol. ccclxxix. (786). [Quite distinct from no. 29.]
31. Scogan to the Lords, &c. Fol. ccclxxx. (787). [This poem, by H. Scogan, quotes Chaucer's *Gentilesse* in full on p. 788.]
*32. Lack of Steadfastness. Fol. ccclxxxi. (789).
33. Good Counsel of Chaucer. [Truth.] Fol. ccclxxxi. (789).
34. Ballad of the Village [Visage] without Painting. [Fortune.] Fol. ccclxxxi. (790).
35. Lenvoy to Scogan. Fol. ccclxxxii. (791).
36. Go forth, King. Fol. ccclxxxii. (791).
37. Chaucer to his empty Purse. Fol. ccclxxxii. (791).
*38. Ballad :—'Consider well, &c.' Fol. ccclxxxii. (792).
39. Epitaphium Galfridi Chaucer. Fol. ccclxxxiii. (793).

Of the twenty-two pieces here printed by Thynne for the first time, it is unfortunately true that only *six* have any claim to be Chaucer's, viz. The Romaunt of the Rose (partly)[1], The Legend of Good Women, The Book of the Duchess, The Complaint to Pity, Lack of Steadfastness, and The Treatise on the Astrolabe[2].

Each of these 42 pieces (including those marked *a*, *b*, and *c*) are separately discussed below. See §§ 13–54.

[1] Only *part* of the extant translation of the Romaunt can be claimed for Chaucer, viz. ll. 1–1705.

[2] Dr. Furnivall also reckons six such pieces; but he omits the Romaunt, and includes the translation of Boethius, which had previously been printed by Caxton.

§ 8. CONTENTS OF THE SECOND FOLIO OF 1542

The Second Folio (1542) contains the same pieces as the First, in the same order; viz. *a*, *b*, *c* at the end of the Table of Contents, and nos. 1–39 in the body of the book. But it further includes the spurious piece entitled The Plowman's Tale, thrust in at the end of the Canterbury Tales, and preceding the Romaunt.

There can be little doubt that Thynne had a special object in introducing this Tale into the volume, quite irrespective of any claim it might have to be considered as one of the Canterbury Tales. For it was doubtless under his direction that Thomas Godfray (printer of the First Folio) printed The Plowman's Tale *separately*, in folio, about 1533–5. Of this edition only one copy now remains, viz. at Britwell, having formerly been in the possession, successively, of Askew, Farmer, and Heber (F. Thynne, 'Animadversions,' ed. Furnivall, p. 101). On account of its attacks upon the clergy, it was naturally objected to by them; but Thynne nevertheless persisted in his design of introducing it into his second edition, thrusting it in at the *end* of the Canterbury Tales, because no other place could be found for it; a silent acknowledgement that he knew it to be spurious. Strange as this proceeding may appear to be, there can be little doubt about it, from the fact that he actually wished to go much further, and was anxious to introduce among the Canterbury Tales, with the title of The Pilgrim's Tale, a still more direct and outspoken attack upon 'our papists rooted in malice [1],' though he must have known perfectly well that it was contemporaneous with himself, for the plain reason that, as Tyrwhitt pointed out, it contained references both to Perkin Warbeck and to Captain Cobler [2]! He went so far as to consult no less a person than the king himself as to this matter; and the rest of the story is so curious that it must be told in his son's own words.

'This tale, when kinge henrye the eighte had redde, he called my father unto hym, sayinge, "Williame Thynne! I do[u]bte this will not be allowed [i.e. approved of]; for I suspecte the Byshoppes will call the in questione for yt"; to whome my father, beinge in great fauore with his prince, (as manye yet lyvinge canne testyfye), sayed, "yf your grace be not offended, I hoope to be protected by you"; wherevppon the kinge bydd hym goo his waye, and feare not. All whiche not-withstandinge, my father was called in questione by the Byshoppes, and heaved at by cardinall Wolseye, his olde enymye, for manye causes, but mostly for that my father had furthered Skelton to publishe his "Collen Cloute" againste the Cardinall, the moste parte of whiche Booke was compiled in my fathers howse at Erithe in Kente [3]. But for all my fathers frendes, the Cardinalls perswadinge auctorytye was so greate withe the kinge, that thoughe by the kinges fauor my father escaped bodelye daunger, yet the Cardinall caused the kinge so muche to myslyke of that tale, that chaucer must be newe printed and that discourse of the pilgrymes tale lefte oute [4]; and so beinge printed agayne [5], some thynges were forsed to be omitted, and the *plowmans tale* (supposed, but vntrulye, to be made by olde Sir Thomas Wyat, father to hym which was executed in the firste yere of Quene Marye, and not by Chaucer) *with muche ado permitted to passe with the reste.*'

No doubt Francis Thynne has told this story honestly, and as well as he knew how,

[1] 'Thes be our papystes rotyd in malis'; Pilgrim's Tale, 509 (see F. Thynne, 'Animadversions,' ed. Furnivall, p. 91).

[2] 'Perkyn werbek and Iak straw
And now of lat[e] owr cobler the dawe.'
Pilgrim's Tale, 447 (id. p. 89).

Captain Cobler was a leader of the Lincolnshire rebels in 1536, so that The Pilgrim's Tale is later in date than our First Folio (1532)!

[3] As Dyce points out, Colin Clout is mentioned here by mistake for Why Come Ye not to Court, written about A.D. 1522.

[4] i. e. it was to be omitted from the 'new print' or second edition of 1542.

[5] i. e. in 1542.

but

but we cannot accept all the details, because The Pilgrim's Tale was not written till after Wolsey's death in 1530. We must take him to mean that Thynne had often met with opposition from Wolsey, and that after his death he continued to be opposed by 'the Byshoppes,' who opposed The Pilgrim's Tale successfully, but were unable to prevent him from inserting The Plowman's Tale in the Second Folio. But the really significant point of this amazing story is the obvious admission of all parties concerned—the editor, the king, and the bishops—that the question as to the admission of an extra tale or two amongst the series told by the Canterbury Pilgrims in no way depended upon the date at which such tale was composed! They all knew perfectly well that the two tales[1] to which they objected on the ground of their contents had some references to events and opinions of their own time, but they were in no way influenced by such knowledge. Nothing can more clearly emphasize the fact that the inclusion of any given piece in the present volume furnishes no *a priori* evidence of its genuineness; though it has formerly been a common habit of some thoughtless critics to assert that it does so. Perhaps it is well to add that, as Tyrwhitt pointed out long ago, the date of The Pilgrim's Tale does not depend solely upon the mention of Perkin Warbeck and Captain Cobler; for there is a further reference in it to a printed edition of The Romaunt of the Rose, which is no other than Thynne's own first print of it in 1532, as here reproduced!

The lines of The Pilgrim's Tale run thus (ll. 722–746):—

> [He] bad me reyd the 'romant of the rose,'
> *The thred leafe, Iust from the end;*
> *To the secund page* ther he dyd me send; . . .
> He prayd me thes .vi. stauis for to marke,
> *Which be chaucers awn hand wark*[2] :—
> ¶ 'Thus moche woll our boke syngnify,
> That whyle peter hath mastery,
> May neuer Iohn show well his myght.
> Now haue I declaryd right
> The meyning of the bark and rynd
> That makis the ententions blynd[3].'

We thus see that Thynne was prepared to attribute to Chaucer a poem in which the author referred to his, i.e. Thynne's, own edition of that poet.

The Second Folio may be briefly described by saying that (with the exception of The Plowman's Tale) it is a mere reprint of the First Folio; with slight variations in spelling, which are not usually improvements. Its authority is therefore less.

§ 9. CONTENTS OF THE THIRD FOLIO OF (ABOUT) 1550

As to the Third Folio, the only undated edition, the first and most important business is to determine its date. In the Appendix to his Preface to the Canterbury Tales, Tyrwhitt says: 'However, this Edition of 1532, with all its imperfections, had the luck, as I have said, to be considered as *the standard edition*, and to be copied, not only by the Booksellers, in their several editions of 1542, 1546, 1555, and 1561, but also by Mr. Speght (the first Editor in form, after Mr. Thynne, who set his name to his work)

[1] The Plowman's Tale contains much that is perhaps as old as the fourteenth century; but there are interpolations in it which seem to belong to the sixteenth.

[2] Meaning, of course, that The Pilgrim's Tale itself is *not* 'Chaucer's own hand-work.' It was not the author himself who wished his work to be taken for Chaucer's.

[3] See Rom. Rose, ll. 7165–7170; for which see the present volume, p. 352. That is, the six lines quoted occur (as stated above) on the *second page* (or *back*) of the *third leaf from the end* of the poem. In the *second* edition (1542) they occur on the *front* of the leaf.

work) in 1597 and 1602.' The dates 1546 and 1555, here mentioned, are both conjectural, and really refer to the *same* edition, i.e. the undated one now under discussion. The British Museum Catalogue suggests about 1545. Whether we take the date to be 1545, 1546, 1550, or 1555, is really of no consequence, so long as we keep it in the place of *third*, between 1542 and 1561. I merely adopt 1550 for the sake of a round number, keeping the editions nearly ten years apart, as 1532, 1542, 1550 (?), and 1561.

Unfortunately, on some occasion when this undated edition was in the market, some enterprising bookseller suggested a date *before* 1542, with the obvious object of making it a second edition and increasing its value; and this insinuation has been zealously repeated on every possible occasion. But, fortunately, there is no doubt about the matter. The form of the volume is *intermediate* between that of the Second Folio and that of the Fourth, as can be irrefragably proved. Three considerations which point in this direction may be briefly indicated; to elaborate them is needless.

1. The Plowman's Tale is here *prefixed* to The Parson's Tale, as in the Fourth Folio, not *appended* to it, as in the Second Folio. It is absurd to suppose that it was first prefixed, then appended, and then prefixed again. This is not evolution, but disturbance. Besides, the prefixing involved a wilful alteration of the text (from 'Manciple' to 'Ploweman') in the first line of the Parson's Prologue, against the authority of all the MSS. and all the earlier editions down to that of 1542; and it is absurd to suppose that this alteration was first made, then rescinded, and then re-made.

2. A comparison of the woodcuts shows that the woodcuts used for the edition of 1542 are mostly copied from those of Thynne's first edition; whereas the undated edition has only two woodcuts, one of which differs from that edition. Hence the undated edition comes *third*. Many other features of the three books indicate the same result. Thus the picture of the Knight, as it first appears in the undated edition, occurs again in that of 1561. The tendency, at that date, was to copy from the edition which had last preceded the new one.

3. The testimony of the spellings in The Plowman's Tale gives the same incontrovertible order. It is more than sufficient to consult the reprint of The Plowman's Tale in Dr. Furnivall's edition of F. Thynne's 'Animadversions,' at p. 101. Thus, in l. 2, the order of the editions is correct, if we date our book in 1550; for we find the spellings:—*mydsommer mone* (1542); *mydsomer mone* (1550); *Midsomer Moone* (1561). But if we date it 1540, i.e. *before* 1542, we have this incorrect result:—*mydsomer mone* (1540); *mydsommer mone* (1542); *Midsomer Moone* (1561). A word is not first spelt *mydsomer* (with one *m*); then *mydsommer* (with two *m*'s); and thirdly altered back again to its first form. This is (purposely) a very small point, but then there are thousands of similar examples; and matters are much more serious when we come to line 8, where we are told that the Plowman 'honge his harneys on a pynne,' i.e. hung up his gear (harness) upon a pin or peg. For here the later editions (of about 1550 and 1561) say that he 'honged his harnys on a pynne' (1550); or 'honged his harnis on a pinne' (1561). That is, they not only turn the strong past tense plural *honge* into *honged*, but they substitute *harnys* or *harnis* (meaning 'brains') for *harneys* (meaning 'harness'). Of course *harnys* is also found as a *later form* of *harneys*, but that is just the point; the later edition has the later spelling.

As any one with moderate intelligence, with these hints, can now settle the question for himself, no more need be said. All the same, we shall probably again be told, whenever a copy of this undated edition is for sale, that 'some people say that this edition preceded that of 1542.' Nevertheless, it is quite true that the printer of this edition *did* frequently follow the First Folio rather than the Second, where it was convenient

convenient to do so; and he was quite right in so doing, as it was usually a better guide. Thus in the first line of the Prologue, he has *Whanne* and *with* and *his* (as in ed. 1532), instead of *When* and *wyth* and *hys* (as in ed. 1542). Hence the right description of the Third Folio is, that it depends upon the First Folio as well as upon the Second; and its comparative value rests rather upon this circumstance than upon priority of date. Thus, in the course of the first fifty lines of the Prologue, this edition only varies from the First Folio twice; once in l. 38, where it has *condycion* for *condycyon*; and in l. 48, where it wrongly has *so farre* instead of *farre*. But the error in the latter instance (also found in ed. 1561) does not occur in the Second Folio.

This Third Folio may be briefly described by saying that it follows the Second Folio throughout The Plowman's Tale, but alters the position of it; and that otherwise it frequently follows the First Folio, though it also exhibits some mistakes from which the Second Folio is free.

§ 10. CONTENTS OF THE FOURTH FOLIO OF 1561

This Folio really consists of two parts. The former, down to the end of Fol. cccxxxvii, back, is almost wholly a reprint of the preceding one, with further changes of spelling in the direction of later forms; and is (so far) the least valuable of the four.

But at the back of Fol. cccxxxii, between Gower's Balade to King Henry IV and The Cuckoo and the Nightingale, the three following pieces, each consisting of seven lines only, occur, viz. (1) A saiyng of dan Jhon; (2) Yet of the same; (3) Balade de Bon Consail. They are printed in my 'Chaucerian and other Pieces,' Oxford, 1897, p. 297.

The latter part of the volume consists of additional poems edited by John Stowe, with which we are not here concerned. They are enumerated and discussed in my six-volume edition of Chaucer's Works, Oxford, 1894, vol. i. p. 33.

§ 11. THE ORIGINAL PREFACE (see pp. 3-5)

This is the most convenient place for a notice of the Preface at pp. 3-5, which, strangely enough, was not written by Thynne himself, but by his friend Sir Brian Tuke. The discovery of this interesting point in literary history was made by Mr. Bradshaw, late librarian of the Cambridge University Library; and I cannot do better than explain the matter in his own words, as already printed at p. xxvi of Dr. Furnivall's edition of Francis Thynne's 'Animadversions.'

'We know that Wm. Thynne was "Chief Clerk of the Kitchin," that is, as we should now say, that he held an appointment in the Royal Household (the Board of Green Cloth) at Greenwich. Sir Brian Tuke was Postmaster, then an appointment in the same office. When Leland tells us that Sir Brian Tuke wrote a *limatissima præfatio* to the edition of Chaucer published by Berthelet [1], we are all puzzled; and when Leland tells us that Thynne edited the edition, we are still more puzzled, because no such edition is known. Now the woodcut frame round the title in Godfray's edition (Thynne, 1532) [2] is that which, having belonged to Pynson, the King's Printer, was transferred to Berthelet, his successor as King's Printer; and this is enough to show that there were printing relations between Berthelet and Godfray, quite enough to allow this to be the copy meant. Curiously enough, there is a copy of Godfray's [i.e. the present] edition in one of the College Libraries here [that of Clare College], in its original binding, in which, at the top of Thynne's dedication, Sir Brian Tuke has written with his own hand:

[1] See Lounsbury, Studies in Chaucer, i. 138, 139, 146.

[2] See p. 1; it appears again at pp. 9, 273, 357, 495, 568, 595, 622, 675.

'"This

'"This p*re*face I sir Bryan Tuke knight wrot at the request of Mr Clarke of the Kechyn then being / tarying for the tyde at Grenewich."

'It would be difficult to find a prettier coincidence in all points—the tarrying for the tide at Greenwich, when we learn from quite other sources (1) that Thynne's office was at Greenwich, and (2) that he lived down the Thames at Erith. You will allow that it is not often one has the pleasure of hitting off things so prettily. Observe the words *then being*. In 1532 Thynne describes himself to the king as "Wylliam Thynne, chefe clerke of your kechyn." In 1536 Tuke died. On the monument to Wm. Thynne in All-hallows Barking Church in London, he is described as "M. William Thinne esquire, one of the masters of the honourable houshold to king Henry the 8. our soveraigne Lord" (I quote from the *Stemmata Botevilliana*, and M. Botfield probably quotes from Stowe's *London*)[1]. The monument says he died August 10, 1546. It is possible that Thynne's position was raised between 1532 and 1536 when Tuke died.'

§ 12. SIR BRIAN TUKE'S PREFACE

I here print the whole of the Preface in roman type, as given at pp. 3–5, retaining the spelling of the original.

¶ To the kynges hyghnesse / my most gratious soueraygne lorde He*n*ry the eight / by the grace of god kyng of Englande and of Fraunce / defensor of the fayth / and lorde of Irlande, &c.

AMonges all other excellencyes / most gratious souerayn lord / wher-*with* almightye god hath endowed ma*n*kynde / aboue ye resydue of erthly creatures / as an outwarde declaration of reason or resonablenesse / wherin consysteth the symylitude of man vnto aungels / and the differe*n*ce betwene the same & brute beestes / I verayly suppose / that speche or langage is nat to be reputed amonges the smallest or inferiours. For therby is exp*re*ssed the conceite of one to another in open and playne sentence / whiche in the resydue of lyuely creatures / lacketh and is nat shewed amonges them / but by certayn couert and derke signes / and that in fewe thyng*es* hauyng course and operation onely of nature. This speche or langage / after the confusyon of tonges / sente by goddes punysshment for pride and arrogance of people / hath ben by a certayne instyncte & dysposytion naturall diuysed and inuented in sundry partes of the worlde / as felowshippes or companyenges of folkes one with another chaunced / moche to the outwarde expressyng of the thyng in worde or sou*n*de / accordyng to that wherof it had meanyng or sygnification. But in processe of tyme / by dilygence or polycy of people / after dyuers fourmes / figures / and impressyons in metall / barkes of trees / and other mater vsed for memorie and knowlege of thyng*es* than present or passed / sondry letters or carectes were first amo*n*ges the Phenices diuysed and founde / with suche knyttynges and ioynynges of one to another by a marueylous subtylyte and crafte / as counterueyled was and is equiualent to the same langages. So as the conceite of ma*n*nes mynde / whiche at ye begynnyng was vsed to be declared by mouthe onely / came to such poynt / that it was as sensibly and viuely expressed in writynge. Hervpon ensewed a great occasion & corage vnto them that shulde write / to compone and adorne the rudenesse and barbariete of speche / and to forme it to an eloquent and ordynate p*er*fectyon / whervnto many and many great poet*es* and oratours haue highly employed their studies & corages / leauyng therby notable

[1] Stowe, speaking of the monuments in the church of Allhallows, Barking, has:—'William Thinne, esq., one of the clerks of the Green Cloth, and master of the household to king Henry VIII., 1546.' See 'Survey of London,' ed. Thoms, p. 50.

renoume of themselues / and example perpetuell to their posterite. Amonges other / the Grekes in all kyndes of sciences / semed so to preuayle and so to ornate their tonge / as yet by other of right noble langages can nat be perfitely ymitated or folowed. The Latyns by example of the grekes / haue gotten or wonne to them no small glorie / in the fourmynge / order / and vttrynge of that tonge. Out of the whiche two / if it be well sertched / that is to saye Greke and Latyn (though by corruptyon of speche it shulde seme moche otherwyse) haue ben deryued the resydue of the langages that be written with the letters or carectes of either of them bothe : But of all speches / those whiche most approche to the latinite / be the Italyan and Spaynysshe tonges / of whom the one by corruption of the Gothes and Longobardes had her begynnynge / as latyn spoken by straungers of a barbare vnderstandyng / The other being also latyn was by Vandales / Gothes / Moores / Sarracenes / and other so many tymes blemysshed / as marueyle it is to se now vnto what perfection these two formed out of the latyn and barbare speches be reduced. Next vnto them / in symilytude to the latyn is the Frenche tonge / whiche by dilygence of people of the same / is in fewe yeres passed so amended / as well in pronunciation as in writynge / that an Englysshman by a small tyme exercised in that tonge hath nat lacked grounde to make a grammer or rule ordinary therof. Though of trouthe [*fol. A ii, back*] (whiche some shall scarsely beleue) the Germayns haue so fourmed the order of their langage / that in the same / is bothe as moche plentie and as nere concordaunce to the phrase of the latyn / as the French tong hath. And verayly / lyke as all these and the rest haue ben thus vigilant & studyous to meliorate or amende their langages : so hath there nat lacked amonges vs Englisshmen / whiche haue right well and notably endeuoyred and employed them selues / to the beautifyeng and bettryng of thenglysh tonge. ¶ Amonges whom moost excellent prynce / my moost redoubted and gracious soueraygne lorde / I your most humble vassall / subiecte and seruaunt Wylliam Thynne / chefe clerke of your kechyn / moued by a certayne inclynacion & zele / whiche I haue to here of any thyng soundyng to the laude and honour of this your noble realme / haue taken great delectacyon / as the tymes and laysers might suffre / to rede and here the bokes of that noble & famous clerke Geffray Chaucer / in whose workes is so manyfest comprobacion of his excellent lernyng in all kyndes of doctrynes and sciences / suche frutefulnesse in wordes / wel accordynge to the mater and purpose / so swete and plesaunt sentences / suche perfectyon in metre / the composycion so adapted / suche fresshnesse of inuencion / compendyousnesse in narration / suche sensyble and open style / lackyng neither maieste ne mediocrite couenable in disposycion / and suche sharpnesse or quycknesse in conclusyon / that it is moche to be marueyled / howe in his tyme / whan doutlesse all good letters were layde a slepe throughout ye worlde / as the thynge whiche either by the disposycion & influence of the bodies aboue / or by other ordynaunce of god / semed lyke and was in daunger to haue vtterly perysshed / suche an excellent poete in our tonge / shulde as it were (nature repugnyng) spryng and aryse. For though it had ben in Demosthenes or Homerus tymes / whan all lernyng and excellency of sciences florisshed amonges the Grekes / or in the season y^t Cicero prince of eloquence amonges latyns lyued / yet had it ben a thyng right rare & straunge and worthy perpetuall laude / y^t any clerke by lernyng or wytte coulde than haue framed a tonge before so rude and imperfite / to suche a swete ornature and composycion / lykely if he had lyued in these dayes / being good letters so restored & reuyued as they be / if he were nat empeched by the enuy of suche as may tollerate nothyng / whiche to vnderstonde their capacite doth nat extende / to haue brought it vnto a full and fynall perfection. Wherfore gracious soueraygne lorde / takynge suche

suche delyte and pleasure in the workes of this noble clerke (as is afore mencioned) I haue of a longe season moch vsed to rede and visyte the same: and as bokes of dyuers imprintes came vnto my handes / I easely and without grete study / might and haue deprehended in them many errours / falsyties / and deprauacions / whiche euydently appered by the contrarietees and alteracions founde by collacion of the one with the other / wherby I was moued and styred to make dilygent sertch / where I might fynde or recouer any trewe copies or exemplaries of the sayd bookes / wheruunto in processe of tyme / nat without coste and payne I attayned / and nat onely vnto such as seme to be very trewe copies of those workes of Geffray Chaucer / whiche before had ben put in printe / but also to dyuers other neuer tyll nowe imprinted / but remaynyng almost vnknowen and in oblyuion / wherupon lamentyng with myselfe / the neglygence of the people / that haue ben in this realme / who doutlesse were very remysse in the settyng forthe or auauncement either of the histories therof / to the great hynderaunce of the renoume of such noble princes and valyant conquerours & capitayns as haue ben in the same / or also of the workes or memory of yͤ famous and excellent clerkes in all kyndes of scyences that haue florisshed therin / Of whiche bothe sortes it hath pleased god as highly to nobilytate this yle as any other regyon of christendome: I thought it in maner ap[*fol. A iij*]pertenant vnto my dewtie / and that of very honesty and loue to my countrey I ought no lesse to do / than to put my helpyng hande to the restauracion and bringynge agayne to lyght of the said workes / after the trewe copies and exemplaries aforesaid. And deuisyng *with* my selfe / who of all other were most worthy / to whom a thyng so excellent and notable shulde be dedicate / whiche to my conceite semeth for the admiracion / noueltie / and strangnesse that it myght be reputed to be of in the tyme of the authour / in comparison / as a pure and fyne tryed precious or polyced iewell out of a rude or indigest masse or mater / none coulde to my thynkyng occurre / that syns / or in the tyme of Chaucer / was or is suffycient / but onely your maieste royall / whiche by discrecyon and iugement / as moost absolute in wysedome and all kyndes of doctryne / coulde & of his innate clemence & goodnesse / wolde adde or gyue any authorite hervnto.

For this cause most excellent and in all vertues most prestant prince / I as humbly prostrate before your kyngly estate / lowly supply and beseche the same / that it wol vouchsafe to take in good parte my poore studye and desyrous mynde / in reducynge vnto lyght this so precious and necessary an ornament of the tonge of this your realme / ouer pytous to haue ben in any poynt lost / falsifyed / or neglected: So that vnder the shylde of your most royall protectyon and defence it may go forthe in publyke / & preuayle ouer those that wolde blemysshe / deface / and in many thynges clerely abolyssh the laude / renoume / and glorie hertofore compared / and meritoriously adquired by dyuers princes / and other of this said most noble yle / wheruunto nat onely straungers vnder pretexte of highe lernyng & knowlege of their malycious and peruers myndes / but also some of your owne subiectes / blynded in foly & ignorance / do with great study contende. Most gracious / victorious / and of god most electe and worthy prince / my most dradde soueraygne lorde / in whom of very merite / dewtie / and successyon / is renewed the glorious tytell of Defensor of the christen faithe / whiche by your noble progenytour / the great Constantyne / somtyme kyng of this realme / & emperour of Rome was nexte god and his apostels / chefely maynteyned / corroborate and defended / almighty Iesu sende to your highnesse the contynuall and euerlastynge habundaunce of his infynite grace. Amen.

§ 13. I shall now briefly indicate the value, for the student of literature, of each of of the pieces in the present volume, considering every one of them separately and in order[1].

THE THREE PIECES APPENDED TO THE PREFACE

The first of these, at p. 7, bears the title:—

EIGHT GOODLY QUESTYONS, WITH THEIR AUNSWERS.

This poem, consisting of nine stanzas, is obviously of no great value, and it certainly has no claim to be Chaucer's, though it may be Lydgate's. It is, apparently, an expansion of part of a poem by Ausonius, entitled Septem Sapientum Sententiæ.

The Latin lines are as follows:

Quænam summa boni? Mens quæ sibi conscia recti.
Pernicies homini quæ maxima? Solus homo alter.
Quis dives? Qui nil cupiat. Quis pauper? avarus.
Quæ dos matronæ pulcherrima? Vita pudica.
Quæ casta est? De qua mentiri fama veretur.
Quod prudentis opus? Cum possit, nolle nocere.
Quid stulti proprium? Non posse, et velle nocere.

The order of the questions differs; the questions in the English paraphrase answer, respectively, to lines 1, 2, 4, 5, 3, 7, 6 of the Latin. Of this poem there are two MS. copies, viz. (1) in the Trinity MS. (Cambridge), marked R. 3. 15; (2) in the Bannatyne MS., printed by the Hunterian Club in 1873, p. 123. The latter instructs us to alter *tree* (l. 19) to *cofre*. See The Chaucer Canon, p. 115.

The second piece (p. 8) is entitled TO THE KYNGES MOST NOBLE GRACE; AND TO THE LORDES AND KNYGHTES OF THE GARTER.

This piece, also found in MS. Phillipps 8151, was written by Hoccleve about 1415. It consists really of *two* Balades, both containing four stanzas. The former is addressed to King Henry V, and the latter to the Knights of the Garter. See Chaucerian Pieces, p. 233; The Chaucer Canon, p. 101.

The third piece (p. 8), consisting of fourteen lines, is really made up of Three Sayings, the first of six lines, and the second and third of four lines each. Thynne copied them from Caxton, who printed them at the end of his print of 'Anelida' and 'Purse' merely to fill up a blank page. They have, of course, no claim to be Chaucer's, and similar lines are found elsewhere. See F. Thynne, 'Animadversions,' ed. Furnivall, p. xlvi; The Chaucer Canon, p. 115; Chaucer's Works, Oxford, vol. i. p. 46; Chaucerian Pieces, pp. 450, lxxxi.

§ 14. THE CANTERBURY TALES

Unfortunately, this is the least satisfactory portion of Thynne's edition. Tyrwhitt remarks, in the Appendix to his Preface:—'With respect to the Canterbury Tales, I am under a necessity of observing that, upon the whole, they received no advantage from the edition of 1532. Its material variations from Caxton's *second* edition [his better one] are all, I think, for the worse. It confounds the order of the Squire's and the Frankelein's tales, which Caxton, in his *second* edition, had set right[2]. It gives the Frankelein's Prologue to the Merchant, in addition to his own proper Prologue. It produces for the first time two Prologues, one to the Doctor's [p. 167] and the other to

[1] Several of the remarks below will be found also in my book entitled The Chaucer Canon; Oxford, 1890.

[2] The Franklin's Tale ought to follow the Squire's; but in the present volume the Merchant's Tale occupies its place; see p. 84. The Franklin's Tale is at p. 140.

the Shipman's Tale [p. 178], which are both evidently spurious; and it brings back the [spurious] lines of ribaldry in the Merchant's Tale, which Caxton, in his second edition, had rejected upon the authority of his good MS.'

It is impossible to say upon what authorities Thynne founded this edition, because we know that, as he tells us, he had access to manuscripts. Still, it is to be suspected that he made very little use of these, and followed Caxton's *first* (and worse) edition only too implicitly, apparently with the object of saving himself trouble. The order of the Tales is the same as in that edition; but it is right to add that the same order (that denoted by 'D' in vol. iv. p. xxiii of my six-volume edition of Chaucer) is also found in many MSS. But it is amazing to find that, in only too many places, no attempt seems to have been made to secure an intelligible reading. A few examples will show this clearly enough.

In the Prologue, l. 2 (p. 11, col. 1), we have—

The drought of Marche had perced the rote.

Here the absence of the preposition *to* before *the rote* ruins the sense. (It also ruins the metre; but none of the printed editions pay any regard to the metre, as the editors were all alike ignorant of Middle English Grammar.) It seems material to observe that *to* is likewise omitted in both editions of Caxton and both of Pynson.

Line 6 runs thus:—

Enspired hath euery holte and heth.

The word *in* is required before *euery*, and actually occurs in Caxton (1).

In l. 10, *the* should be supplied before *night*; but is likewise omitted by Caxton and Pynson.

To take an instance of another kind, I would call attention to l. 1179 in Group A (The Knight's Tale), where the MSS. agree in reading—'Ther cam a *kytë*, whil that they were wrothe.' It is remarkable that the early editions by Caxton, Wynkyn de Worde, and Pynson have the inferior reading *curre* for *kyte*; and Thynne has the same, spelt *cur* (p. 25, col. 1, l. 13). Tyrwhitt was the first to give the right reading.

It will thus be seen that Thynne made but little use of his MSS., and cannot be depended upon for the text of the Canterbury Tales.

§ 15. SOME PECULIARITIES OF THYNNE'S TEXT

We are told by Hazlitt that the present text is 'the only known book from Godfray's press with a *date* to it.' Each page (if full) usually contains 94 lines in the two columns (47 in each column). Rarely a page contains 96 lines (48 in each column). P. 41, for example, has 48 lines in the first column; but, as there is a blank line in the second column, the whole page contains only 95 lines. Blank lines are not uncommon; see pp. 32, 34, 35, 36, &c. In the Prologue, A 252 *b* and A 252 *c*, Thynne retains the lines:—

And gaue a certayn ferme for the graunte
None of his brethern came [ther] in his haunte.

If we consult the MSS. in the Six-text edition and MS. Harl. 7334, we shall find that these lines occur in the Hengwrt MS. only. Tyrwhitt retains them also, counting them as ll. 253, 254. See p. 13, col. 2, near the end.

N.B.—As the columns are long, I shall here adopt a plan which I have used privately for more than thirty years, of dividing every column (by eye) into four parts, which I call *a*, *b*, *c*, *d*. Thus *a* means 'near the top'; *b*, 'above the middle'; *c*, 'below the middle'; and

and *d*, 'near the bottom.' Thus the two lines just referred to occur at p. 13, col. 2, *d*; or, briefly, p. 13 *b d*; where *b* (in this case) means 'column 2.' The general introduction of this system would greatly facilitate reference.

In the Miller's Prologue, Thynne omits two lines (A 3155, 3156) after *There ben ful good wyues many oon.* Tyrwhitt also omits them; and so do several MSS. But they occur in the Ellesmere, Cambridge, and Harleian MSS. See p. 46 *a d.*

In the Miller's Tale, Thynne retains two lines which Tyrwhitt omits, as do also many MSS.; but they occur in the Ellesmere MS. These are A 3721, 3722, after the line ending *I come anon*; see p. 53 *a b.*

At p. 76, col. 2, what is here called 'The Squiers prologue' is really the Shipman's. The true Squire's Prologue (only eight lines long) is wholly omitted. This is noticeable, for the Shipman's Prologue ought certainly to succeed (as here) the Man of Law's Tale. See my Chaucer, vol. iv. p. 165. The Harleian MS. also has here the same Prologue, but with the reading *Sompnour* for *Shipman* or *Squier*; see Six-text ed., B 1179.

At p. 84, col. 2, the 'wordes of the Marchaunt to the Squyer' are really the words of the *Franklin*; and the 'Wordes of the Host to the Marchaunt' are really the words to the *Franklin*; but 'the Marchauntes prologue,' at the bottom of the column, is the true Merchant's Prologue, out of its true place. It ought to follow the Clerk's Tale.

At p. 97, Thynne has fourteen spurious lines (as Tyrwhitt notes); they also occur in Caxton (1). See § 14 (above).

At p. 98, the Epilogue to the Merchant's Tale (E 2419–2440) does not appear.

At p. 139, the six stanzas in the Clerk's Envoy are in an unusual order, viz. 1, 2, 3, 5, 6, 4.

At p. 139, col. 2, 'the wordes of our hoste' are genuine, but seem to have been afterwards suppressed by the author; see my Chaucer, vol. iv. p. 424, note. But 'the wordes of the Frankelin to the Squier, and the wordes of the Host to the Frankelin,' for which see my Chaucer, vol. iv. p. 480, do not appear here in Thynne; having already appeared at p. 84, as noted above.

At p. 147 *b b*, Thynne omits two lines after *it is best for me*; and two more below after *Nichanore.*

At the bottom of the same column, Thynne retains two lines which are omitted by Tyrwhitt and by most (perhaps all) of the MSS. except the Ellesmere. These are:—

> The same thing I saye of Bilia,
> Of Rodogone / and eke Valeria.

At p. 148 *a d*, after the line *She nolde no wight tel*[*len*] *her entent*, Thynne omits six lines which appear to be in the Ellesmere MS. only.

At p. 156 *b d*, Thynne (by a misprint) repeats the line at the bottom of col. 2 at the top of p. 157. The catchword *Howe* is correct.

At p. 167, 'the doctour of Physikes prologue,' consisting of fourteen lines, is spurious. See my Chaucer, vol. iv. p. 289, note.

At p. 178, 'the Shipma*ns* prologue,' of twelve lines, is spurious. The true Prologue has already appeared above (but assigned to the Squire) at p. 76, col. 2.

At p. 188, Thynne omits the line B 1995, for which see my Chaucer, vol. iv. p. 193. The line near the bottom of col. 1—*Or euer I go out of this place*—seems to be spurious.

At p. 216, the story of Nero follows that of Zenobia, as in Tyrwhitt.

At p. 220, the stories of the two Peters, Barnabo, and Ugolino come at the end of the Monk's Tale, as in Tyrwhitt.

At p. 228, col. 2 *c*, the Epilogue to the Nun's Priest's Tale ends with the line—

'Sayd to a-nother man / as ye shal here.' And the Manciple's Prologue follows immediately, beginning '¶ Wote ye not where, &c.'; though there is nothing to connect it with what precedes.

§ 16. ARRANGEMENT OF THE TALES

The arrangement of the Tales in Thynne follows a type not unusual in MSS., which is nevertheless irregular and differs in several respects from any arrangement that can have been finally intended by Chaucer, as it involves several contradictions. The same arrangement is found, e.g., in MSS. Harl. 7333 and 1758, Sloane 1685, Royal 17 D XV and 18 C II, Barlow 20, Laud 739, New College (Oxford), and the Lichfield MS.; as well as in Caxton (1), as already said. A few notes on this arrangement may be useful.

The Order of Tales, &c., appears as follows:

Prologue, Knight, Miller, Reeve, Cook—Man of Law—Squire (with a Prologue which is really the Shipman's Prologue)[1], Words of the Merchant [it should be the Franklin] to the Squire and of the Host to the Merchant [i.e. the Franklin]—Merchant (without the Epilogue)—Wife of Bath, Friar, Sompnour—Clerk (followed by Chaucer's Envoy of six stanzas [arranged in the order 1, 2, 3, 5, 6, 4] and a stanza containing Words of the Host)[2]—Franklin (of course *without* the Words of the Franklin to the Squire, and the Words of the Host to the Franklin, already noticed)—Second Nun, Canon's Yeoman—Doctor of Physic (preceded by a *spurious* Prologue), Pardoner—Shipman (preceded by a *spurious* Prologue), Prioress, Sir Thopas, Melibeus, Monk (with the stories of the two Peters, Barnabo, and Ugolino *at the end*), Nun's Priest (with an Epilogue of 16 lines)—Manciple, Parson.

The corresponding lines in the Ellesmere MS. are (neglecting minute details) as follows: Group A, 1–4422; B 1–1190; F 9–708[3]; E 1213–2418[4]; D 1–2294; E 1–1212[5]; F 709–1624; G 1–1481; C 1–968; B 1191–3564; B 3653–3956; B 3565–3652; B 3957–4652; H 1–*end*. The references to the Six-text edition are noted at the foot of every page.

The corresponding lines in Tyrwhitt's edition are as follows: 1–5582; 12903–12930; 10323[6]–11020; 9089–10292[7]; 5583–9088; 11021–11928; 15469–16949; 11929–12902; 12931–15468; 16950–*end*. The references to Tyrwhitt's text (denoted by T.) are noted at the foot of every page.

The numerous dislocations which the text has suffered can, I think, be partly explained. But the matter is too tedious to be here discussed at length.

§ 17. ILLUSTRATIVE WOODCUTS

In addition to the ornamental border of the various title-pages, there are twenty woodcuts representing Canterbury pilgrims; but, as some of these make their appearance more than once, the number of independent ones is only fifteen. They appear at the following pages:—

P. 21, Knight; 47, Miller; 55, Reeve; 61, Cook; 63, Man of Law; 77, Squire; 85, Merchant; 98, Wife of Bath; 113, Friar; 117, Sompnour; 125, Clerk; 140,

[1] It is possible that, in his first draught, Chaucer meant to put the Squire's Tale here, and made the Prologue at first for the Squire (or some one else), though it is not very suitable. The true Squire's Prologue (of eight lines only) does not appear in Thynne at all.

[2] The stanza may be genuine; if so, it was afterwards suppressed. But it appears in the Ellesmere MS.

[3] Lines 1–8 of F are missing in Thynne.

[4] Lines 2419–2440 of E are missing in Thynne.

[5] With an extra stanza after E 1212.

[6] Lines 10315–10322 are missing in Thynne.

[7] Lines 10293–10314 are missing in Thynne.

Franklin;

Franklin; 151, Second Nun; 158, Canon's Yeoman; 167, Doctor; 172, Pardoner; 178, Shipman; 184, Prioress; 230, Manciple; 234, Parson.

Three of these appear more than once. The most useful one is the representation of the Merchant, which also does duty for the Sompnour, the Franklin, and the Manciple. The Clerk (oddly depicted with a bow) reappears as the Canon's Yeoman; and the Second Nun reappears as the Prioress.

The Knight and Squire, for all I know to the contrary, appear here for the first time. The Squire (but not the Knight) reappears in the reprint of (about) 1550. But the other figures are not new; for they may also be found in the second edition of the Canterbury Tales by Caxton. In The Biography and Typography of W. Caxton, by W. Blades, 2nd ed., London, 1882, at p. 293, is a copy of 'The Wife of Bath,' which will be seen to be identical with the figures of the Second Nun and Prioress in the present volume; pp. 151, 184. Caxton used most of his woodcuts twice; once in the Prologue, and once at the beginnings of the Tales. The Merchant, Franklin, and Sompnour, as they appear in the Prologue, are all alike; but the Manciple differs. This different figure of the Manciple also does duty, however, for the Franklin at the head of the Tale; which accounts for Thynne's promiscuous use of the figure of 'the Merchant.' We thus see that Thynne made some use of *both* the editions by Caxton.

§ 18. THE ROMAUNT OF THE ROSE (p. 275)

For this piece, Thynne's edition is of the highest service, as it is the only copy which gives us the whole of the poem. Indeed, there is but one other copy, viz. the MS. at Glasgow, which has unfortunately lost no less than eleven leaves, viz. the first, the eighth, and nine others. Hence Thynne is the sole authority for ll. 1–44, 333–380, 1387–1482, 2395–2442, 3595–3690, and 7385–7576. He also gives the concluding lines more correctly. The MS. ends abruptly in the following unsatisfactory manner:—

Ne half so lettred as am I
I am licenced boldely
To Reden in Diuinite
And longe haue red
Explicit.

But (at p. 356) Thynne gives us:—

Ne halfe so lettred (as am I)
I am lycensed boldely
In diuynite for to rede
And to confessen out of drede
If ye wol you nowe confesse
And leaue your synnes more and lesse
Without abode / knele downe anon
And you shal haue absolucion.
Finis.

I append, for comparison, the original French text:—

Ne si letré de trop com gie;
J'ai de divinité congié;
Voire par Dieu pieça l'eü.
Por confessier m'ont esleü.
Li meillor qu'en puisse savoir
Par mon sens et par mon savoir.

Se vous volés ci confessier,
Et ce pechié sans plus lessier,
Sans faire en james mencion,
Vous aurés m'asolucion.

In almost all other passages, however, the Glasgow MS. agrees with Thynne's text so closely that it is obvious that both were derived from a common source, viz. a MS. now lost, which may have been, and probably was, the very MS. which Thynne used as his authority. In any case, their common original had one defect, the contents of that MS. being curiously misarranged. This fact was first noted by Tyrwhitt, who at the very end of his Notes to the Canterbury Tales has this remark: 'In the latter part [of Thynne's Romaunt of the Rose] we have a strong proof of the negligence of the first editor, who did not perceive that two leaves in his MS. were misplaced. The passage from verse 7013 to verse 7062 inclusive [1] and the passage from verse 7257 to verse 7304 inclusive should be inserted after verse 7160. The later Editors have all copied this, as well as many other blunders of less consequence, which they must have discovered, if they had consulted the French original.' In fact, it is easily calculated that in one of the quires of eight leaves (or sixteen pages), the pair of middle leaves, containing its seventh, eighth, ninth, and tenth pages, were subtracted from the middle of the quire, and so placed that the seventh page followed the second, whilst the tenth page came to precede the fifteenth. The resulting order of the pages of that quire was, necessarily, 1, 2, 7, 8, 3, 4, 5, 6, 11, 12, 13, 14, 9, 10, 15, 16; as may easily be seen by help of a small paper model. The resulting order of the lines in Thynne (if rightly numbered [2]) is accordingly: 1–7012, 7110–7158, 7013–7109, 7209–7304, 7159–7208, 7305–*end*.

In other words, the passage beginning:—'To the copye / if him talent toke' (p. 349, col. 1, l. 5 from the bottom) down to—'Right soone he shal his lyfe for-go' (same page, col. 2, l. 2 from the bottom) is out of place, and should follow the line—'That they ne myght the booke by' (p. 351, col. 1, l. 2). Besides which, the last three words in the line last mentioned ought to run 'by the booke,' in order to preserve the rime with 'if him talent toke'; and it is clear that Thynne made an alteration here in order to force a rime with 'trewly' in the line below, viz. 'The sentence pleased hem wel trewly,' which happens to be spurious, and also perhaps due to him. Moreover, a second passage, beginning:—'But I wol stynte of this matere' (p. 351, col. 1, l. 4) and ending—'Ye sir / from hence forwardes' (p. 352, col. 1, l. 5) is likewise out of place, and should follow the line—'And ben brought to confusyoun' (p. 352, col. 2, l. 8).

This is not the place for discussing the somewhat difficult question as to the authorship of this English version. It is fully discussed in my Chaucer Canon, pp. 65–93. I only record here my conclusions, viz. that lines 1–1705 exhibit Chaucer's own work; that from line 1706 (beginning with a false rime and inconsecutive in sense) down to l. 5810 is the work of another writer, who was fond of Northumbrian forms and rimes; and that from l. 5811 to the end is in a dialect and style much more nearly resembling Chaucer's usage than those of the second fragment. Between lines 5810 and 5811 there is, in any case, a huge gap, as lines 5171–10716 of the French text are wholly ignored. See also my edition of Chaucer, vol. i. p. 1.

[1] According to the old numbering; now set aside as being incorrect. For the exact account see below.

[2] This is not easily done; for after l. 7172, the E. version omits two lines that are absolutely necessary to the sense. I call these ll. 7173–4; but Kaluza does not count them in, so that for the rest of the poem his numbers are less by 2.

§ 19. TROILUS

§ 19. TROILUS AND CRESSIDA (pp. 359-457)

As has been already noted, this genuine poem had been thrice printed previously to 1532; first, by Caxton (ab. 1483); secondly, by Wynkyn de Worde (1517); and thirdly, by Pynson (1526). But I think that, in this instance, Thynne was not much indebted to his predecessors. His text seems to have followed a MS. of a good type, and is by no means a bad one. It is much superior in quality to his text of the Canterbury Tales. See my Introduction to Troilus in the six-volume edition of Chaucer, vol. ii, especially p. lxxvi. I here repeat the description there given.

'Thynne's edition of Troilus was printed from so good a MS. as to render it an excellent authority. In a few places, I fear he has altered the text for the worse, and his errors have been carefully followed and preserved by succeeding editors. Thus he is responsible for altering *io* (=*jo*) into *go*, III. 33 [see p. 393, st. 4, l. 5]; for creating the remarkable "ghost-word" *gofysshe*, III. 584 [see p. 399, col. 2, st. 5, l. 3][1]; and for a few similar curiosities. But I found it worth while to collate it throughout; and readings from it are marked "Ed.' The later black-letter copies are mere reproductions of it.'

Briefly, the reader has here a fairly good authority for the text of Troilus, a poem which has always been ascribed to Chaucer without hesitation.

§ 20. THE TESTAMENT OF CRESEYDE (pp. 457-464)

That this poem was not written by Chaucer is quite certain, because its real author is known. It was written by Robert Henryson, of Dunfermline, a Scottish poet of no mean ability, who is supposed to have been born about 1425–1430, and to have died about 1506 or earlier; so that the poem may be dated near the middle of the fifteenth century. See the new edition (1901) of Chambers's Cyclopædia of English Literature, i. 189, where the poem is spoken of as being 'a sequel to Chaucer's Troilus and Cressida, which contains some admirable descriptive writing, and is in general both vigorous and poetic in feeling.' It is almost certain that Thynne intentionally included it as illustrating Chaucer's Troilus, well knowing that it was not Chaucer's[2]. The reference in st. 6, l. 41, is enough to show this; for Henryson there tells us how he amused himself by reading Troilus, 'written by worthy Chaucer glorious.' Again, the first line of the tenth stanza (l. 64) says—'Who wot if al that Chaucer wrate was trewe?'

Further, it is clear that the MS. used by Thynne was written in Lowland Scotch; for it could hardly have been otherwise. Thynne rather injudiciously endeavoured to turn it into Southern English, doubtless in order to render it more acceptable to his readers. But he would have done better to let it alone. However, he could not but leave several Scottish forms and words unaltered. In the first stanza, we have such non-Chaucerian words as *doly*, i.e. dool-y, full of dool, sorrowful; the Northern *tyl* for *to* (which Chaucer sometimes allowed himself to employ before a following vowel); and the use of the auxiliary verb *can* with the sense of *did*.

Thynne's text of this Poem is of considerable value; for there is but one other authority, sixty-one years later in date. Fortunately, however, it gives Scottish spellings.

[1] The third letter is indistinct, but I think it is meant for *f*; compare the *f* in *fully* in the stanza above (first line). At any rate, it is an *f* in later editions. It should rather have been *gosisshe*, i. e. goose-ish, goose-like.

[2] That its insertion was due to an afterthought is obvious, for the three leaves next to fol. ccexix are not counted in; showing that Thynne cancelled the original fol. cccxix, and substituted four leaves in its place. Cf. Lounsbury, Studies in Chaucer, i. 458.

This

This is the edition printed at Edinburgh by H. Charteris in 1593, with the author's name—'M. Robert Henrysone, Sculemaister in Dunfermeling.'

The editions by Thynne and Charteris mutually assist each other; and my own edition was compiled by carefully collating them. See the text in my Chaucerian Pieces, Oxford, 1897, pp. 327–346; and the Preface to the same, pp. lv–lvii.

Of all the non-Chaucerian pieces in the present volume, The Testament of Creseyde is the best.

The Complaynt of Creseyde, at p. 462, is a sad lament, in seven stanzas of nine lines each; but Thynne has mangled them, by omitting ten lines in various places. The rimes are arranged as in Chaucer's Complaynt of Anelida, similarly introduced into the poem of Anelida and Arcite. At the end of this Complaynt, the author resumes his first metre, adding twenty-one more stanzas of seven lines each.

§ 21. THE LEGEND OF GOOD WOMEN (pp. 465–493)

Thynne's text of this genuine poem by Chaucer is of great interest, since no other text was known to readers, or was generally accessible to them, for upwards of three hundred and fifty years. The first revised edition of it was edited by myself in 1889, chiefly from the invaluable prints of the MSS. issued by the Chaucer Society. In the Preface to that edition, I first enunciated the following facts:—

(1) That the MSS. may be roughly divided into two distinct classes, which may be called the First Class and the Second Class.

(2) That the readings of the MSS. of the First Class are, on the whole and generally, superior to those of the Second Class.

(3) That Thynne's text (like all subsequent ones previously to 1889) follows a MS. of the Second Class. Hence it is, for example, that in l. 1396 Thynne has *Ouyde* (p. 479 *b c*) instead of the correct reading *Guydo*, i.e. Guido delle Colonne.

For further information see the Preface to my edition of 1889, and the six-volume edition of Chaucer's Works, vol. iii.

§ 22. A GOODLY BALADE (p. 494)

For this Balade, Thynne is the sole authority, as no MS. is known. He calls it 'A Goodly Balade of Chaucer'; but it is plainly *not* Chaucer's, and almost certainly Lydgate's. And he evidently introduced it to fill up a blank page, viz. the page preceding the 'title' to Boethius.

It is really a triple Balade, with an Envoy, on the model of Chaucer's Fortune and Complaint of Venus. Each of such Balades should consist of *three* stanzas, but one stanza is missing, viz. the third stanza of the second Balade; and it was doubtless missing in the MS. from which Thynne took it. He did not leave it out for want of space; for there is plenty of room on the page. Observe the refrains in the final lines of each stanza.

The internal evidence strongly suggests Lydgate as the author; and no one now claims it as Chaucer's. The fifth stanza is too clumsy and obscure, both in metre and expression, to be looked upon as being in Chaucer's manner. It does not satisfy the rime-tests. In the first Balade, for example, the words *al-le*, *cal-le*, *apal-le*, *befal-le*, are shortened to *al*, *cal*, *apal*, *befal*, in order to rime with *shal* and *smal*.

The first Balade employs the rimes *-al*, *-ende*, *-aunce*. The second (imperfect) has *-orte*, *-ede*, *-ere*. The third has *-oseth*, *-ence*, *-able*; so that the line ending in *ryseth* should end in *roseth*, i.e. grows rosy or red. See my edition of this poem in Chaucerian Pieces, pp. 405–407, and the Notes; and The Chaucer Canon, p. 109.

It

It seems to have been addressed to a lady named Margaret; hence the address to the daisy in l. 22. It is hardly worth much discussion.

§ 23. BOETHIUS (pp. 497-568)

This genuine version, by Chaucer, of the Consolatio Philosophiæ by Boethius, had already been printed by Caxton before 1479; see the description of Caxton's book in Blades' Life of Caxton, ed. 1882, p. 213. At the end of this volume Caxton added a short notice of Boethius, remarking that Chaucer translated it 'oute of latyn in-to oure vsual and moder tonge.' He goes on to say:—'Atte requeste of a singuler frende and gossib of myne. I william Caxton haue done my debuoir & payne tenprynte it in fourme as is here afore made.' He concludes by referring to the 'Epitaphium Galfridi Chaucer,' which he gives at length. This Epitaphium Thynne has also reprinted, not at the end of the 'Boethius,' but at the end of his volume; and I therefore defer the discussion of it for the present. See § 54.

I cannot find that Thynne did more than simply reprint Caxton's text, which he has followed very closely, even in the spelling, though some words appear in a form a little less archaic. Thus in col. 1 of p. 497, Caxton has *matere* in l. 2 of the English; *writen* in l. 6; *yongthe* in l. 10; *arn schadde* in l. 15; and *emptid* in l. 17.

Caxton's text is of great value, as it represents an excellent MS. now lost; and Thynne's reprint is so close that it is likewise of much value, and not unfrequently corrects some of the best extant MSS. In my six-volume edition of Chaucer, vol. ii. p. xlv, I give several examples of good readings as found in Caxton, all but one of which appear in Thynne also. The exception is in Book V. pr. 1. 9, 10, where Caxton has 'assoilen to the the dette,' i.e. absolve to thee the debt, so that the repetition of *the* is correct; but Thynne does not repeat it.

In a few places, Thynne has introduced an error which he did not find in Caxton. There is an instance very near the beginning. Thus in col. 1 of p. 497, l. 6 of the English text, he has:—'endyten to me thynges to be written / & drery teeres.' But Caxton has:—'endyten to me thynges to be writen / And drery *vers of wretchidnes weten my face with very* teeris'; so that Thynne has accidentally omitted the words here printed in italics, by mistaking the *-ery* in *drery* for the *-ery* in *very*. As only sixteen copies of Caxton's 'Boethius' are known, it is clear that the present reproduction of Thynne's reprint of it is of much interest.

§ 24. THE DREAM OF CHAUCER; OR THE BOOK OF THE DUCHESS (pp. 569-582)

The usual title is The Book of the Duchesse, in allusion to Chaucer's own statement in the Legend of Good Women, l. 418, that he made 'the deeth of Blaunche the Duchesse.' The poem has always been accepted as genuine, as the internal evidence likewise shows. As only three MSS. are known, and none of them is very good, Thynne's text is hardly inferior to them. Moreover, the three MSS. are derived from an earlier one that had lost a leaf, containing ll. 31-96. It is true that in one of these MSS., viz. MS. Fairfax 16, the missing lines have been supplied in a later hand, but they were obviously copied from Thynne's edition, as there are none but very slight variations, all for the worse. Hence for these lines, beginning with—'I may not slepe/ and what me is' in col. 1 of p. 569, and ending exactly with the page, Thynne's text (as here given) is really the *sole* authority. All through the poem it is worth collating.

 'The

'The Dreame of Chaucer' seems to have been a title of Thynne's devising, though it is not inappropriate. But it is best to avoid it, in order that it may not be confused with the spurious piece entitled 'Chaucer's Dream,' first printed by Speght (with that title) in 1598. A more suitable title for the latter is 'The Ile [Isle] of Ladies'; and an excellent edition of this metrical romance (for such it really is) was printed by Dr. Jane B. Sherzer at Berlin, in 1903. It evidently belongs to the fifteenth century, and it is proposed to date it about 1420. It is certainly no earlier.

§ 25. THE ENVOY TO BUKTON (pp. 582, 583)

This poem, in four eight-line stanzas, has here no title, and is only recognized in the Table of Contents as 'a balade,' which, strictly speaking, it is not. Only one MS. copy is known, viz. MS. Fairfax 16, in which the title is 'Lenvoy de Chaucer a Bukton.' It is obviously genuine, and the allusion to 'The wyfe of Bathe' in l. 29 is most interesting. Besides the MS., the only authorities are a printed copy by Julian Notary (about 1499-1502), and the text here printed by Thynne.

Thynne's text is fairly correct, though some of the spellings are not those of Chaucer's time. The errors are as follows. In l. 1, for 'My mayster Bukton,' he oddly gives us 'My mayster, &c.,' as if the name had been suppressed. In l. 23, 'Take the way leuer' ought to be 'That thee were leuer,' as in the MS. In l. 25, *fygures* should be *figure*, as the rime shows. And in the last line *foule* is a mistake for *ful hard*. Yet in l. 13 Thynne alone has the correct reading *eft*; and in l. 24 he alone correctly inserts *to*.

§ 26. THE PARLEMENT OF FOULES (pp. 583-591)

Thynne calls it 'The Assemble of Foules,' but 'The Parlement of Foules' is the title assigned to it by Chaucer himself in the Legend of Good Women, l. 419. It had already been thrice printed, viz. by Caxton, ab. 1477-8; by Pynson, in 1526; and by Wynkyn de Worde, in 1530. There are more than a dozen MSS. still extant; so that the printed text of this piece would seem to be of no great interest. Yet it is by no means a bad one, and seems to be something more than a mere reprint of Caxton or Pynson. Thus it retains the Roundel beginning at l. 680, which Caxton and Pynson omit. And again, in l. 26 (in the fourth stanza) it preserves the word *as* in the phrase 'as of this matere,' which Caxton omits, to the ruin of the line. When all is considered, I believe it will be found that Thynne is a respectable authority for the text of this interesting and genuine poem.

In Caxton's print of this poem, the colophon is:—'Explicit the temple of bras.' This is in allusion to l. 231:—'I saw a temple of bras y-founded stronge.' No doubt the same line suggested to Lydgate the title of his poem named The Temple of Glass.

§ 27. THE FLOUR (FLOWER) OF COURTESY (pp. 591-594)

This piece bears no author's name in the first three editions; but in the fourth edition by Stowe (1561) the title is: 'The Floure of Curtesie made by Ihon lidgate'; for which he may well have found some authority.

Few poems bear Lydgate's impress more clearly; there can be no doubt as to its authorship. Schick dates it about 1400-2; see his edition of Lydgate's Temple of Glass, p. cxii. It was probably written soon after Chaucer's death; observe the statement 'Chaucer is deed' in l. 236. We ought to be much obliged to Thynne for preserving this

this poem, as no MS. copy of it seems to be known. See The Chaucer Canon, p. 102; Chaucerian Pieces, pp. xlv, 266.

§ 28. THE COMPLAINT UNTO PITY (pp. 595-598)

This is a genuine poem, and perhaps one of Chaucer's earliest efforts. There are at least nine MS. copies of it still extant. The MS. followed by Thynne seems to have been neither very good nor very bad.

§ 29. LA BELLE DAME SANS MERCY (pp. 598-608)

We know that this poem cannot have been written by Chaucer, because it is mainly a translation from a French poem by Alan Chartier, who was only fourteen years old at the time of Chaucer's death. Moreover, we know the author's name, as MS. Harl. 372 tells us that it was 'translatid out of Frenche by Sir Richard Ros.' This Sir Richard was the second son of Sir Thomas Ros of Leicestershire, and was born on March 8, 1428-9. The poem seems to have been written soon after 1450. See Chaucerian Pieces, p. li. Besides the copy printed by Thynne, four MSS. are known. Two of these resemble Thynne's text in presenting the lines of the poem in the correct order; the other two misplace many of the stanzas. It further appears by collation that Thynne's copy is nearly as good as any of the rest. Perhaps in some respects the best authority is the MS. marked Ff. 1. 6 in the Cambridge University Library.

Of this poem, only ten stanzas are original, viz. four at the beginning and six at the end; which, unlike the rest of the poem, contain seven lines only. The rest of the stanzas, translated from Chartier, consist of eight lines each.

It must not be forgotten that Thynne was not the first to print this poem. It had been previously printed by Pynson in 1526, who introduced it with the following title: 'This boke called la bele Dame Sauns mercy / was translate out of Frenche in-to Englysshe by Geffray Chaucer / flour of peotes (*sic; read* poetes) in our mother tong.' We know that this attribution of it to Chaucer is certainly wrong; but Thynne may well have been unaware of this, and it accounts for his inclusion of this poem in his volume. In many other cases he had less excuse.

Thynne seems to have followed Pynson's text for the most part, as the two texts are very much alike. Thus, in the first two stanzas, Thynne's sole alterations are these. In l. 3, *wel* for *well*; in l. 5, *leuynge* for *leauyng*; in l. 7, *hem* for *them*, and *whiche* for *the whiche*; in l. 10, *bel* for *bell*; in l. 12, *secratarie* for *secratorie*; in l. 13, *musynge* for *musyng*; and in l. 14, *ymagenynge* for *ymaginyng*. But he must have had access to some other authority as well, for he gives the *Envoy* of six stanzas at the end. Pynson, on the other hand, presents us with an Envoy of his own, also in six stanzas, which he calls: 'Lenuoy de limprimeur,' and is quite different. It begins—'O ye lusty galondes of hote corage,' and ends—'Loue god aboue althing / & than do ye well.' This 'printer's' Envoy is much inferior to Sir Richard Ros's own, and the substitution of it was ill-advised. See p. 608.

§ 30. ANELIDA AND ARCITE (pp. 608-612)

This is one of Chaucer's Minor Poems; but was left unfinished. It had previously been printed by Caxton, in the now unique quarto volume described in my Chaucer, vol. i. p. 27.

In this case it is quite clear how Thynne made up his text. He had before him

a copy

a copy of Caxton's print, and corrected it by means of a certain MS. which is still preserved at Longleat in the collection of the Marquis of Bath. It is so instructive to see him at work that I give some account of what he has done.

In l. 1, he has supplied *O* from the MS.; and he misprints Caxton's *fiers* as *feirs*. The MS. has *fers*.

In l. 2, Caxton has *the frosty*; he alters it to *thy frosty*, as in the MS.

In l. 3, Caxton has *temple*, correctly; the MS. has *temples*, which Thynne adopts.

In l. 5, Caxton has *thy* before *bellona*; the MS. has *the*, which Thynne adopts.

In l. 9, Caxton has *for tendyte*; the MS. and Thynne have *to endyte*.

In l. 10, Cx. *that*; Thynne and MS. *whiche*. So also in l. 12.

In l. 13, Cx. and all MSS. but the Longleat one correctly have *As it*; the Longleat MS. absurdly has *And it*, which Thynne adopts.

In l. 14, Cx. *my*; Thynne and MS. *our*.

In l. 16, Cx. *that with* (correctly); Thynne and MS. *that hath*.

In l. 17, Cx. *cirrea*, as in most MSS. But the Longleat MS. alone has the astonishing spelling *Cirsa*, which Thynne unwisely adopts. After this, it is needless to proceed. We have already learnt that the alterations which he made were by no means always necessary or judicious.

Caxton omits the second stanza on p. 612 (col. 1); and here Thynne follows the MS. pretty closely. But in the fourth line the MS. (like the rest) has *I wepe, I wake*; and Thynne alters *wake* to *wayle*. In the sixth line, he has *flye* for *flee*. In the seventh line, the MS. has—'Who may avaunt his bet of heuynesse'; and here he corrects *his* (an obvious slip) to *her*. But he need not have altered *bet* to *better*.

Finally, Caxton omits the last stanza of the poem (p. 612, col. 2), and again Thynne follows the MS., which concludes the poem with the words *may plainly here* (as in Thynne); whereas the other copies have *shal after here*. But he had access to some other authority for this stanza, since he gives the usual *she gan to rise* in the fourth line, where the Longleat MS. has *began to rise*; and in the sixth line he has the usual reading *sorouful*, where the Longleat MS. has *woful*. Still there can be no doubt that, for most of this poem, he follows Caxton's print, with numerous alterations from the Longleat MS.

§ 31. THE ASSEMBLY OF LADIES (pp. 613-621)

No one seems ever to have claimed this poem for Chaucer; and it is obviously not his; as the language is that of the fifteenth, not the fourteenth century. But it is a gain that Thynne should have printed it, as only two MSS. are known; see the account in Chaucerian Pieces, p. lxix; and The Chaucer Canon, p. 110.

I have once before given the history of l. 61 (p. 613, col. 2, st. 3, l. 4); but it is so extraordinary that it is worth repeating.

The authoress (for the poet so describes herself) is here alluding to the abundance of the flowers which she beheld around her, and she says: 'With marguerites [i. e. daisies] growing in due order, to show themselves, as people went to and fro, so that it was a great pleasure to behold them; and [to behold] how they were accompanied by more *ne momblysnesse and souenesse also.* [And] the poor pansies were not dislodged thence; no! no![1] God knows their place was everywhere [about].'

Required—the sense of the words in italics.

[1] So in the better MS.; Thynne has *Ne*.

The

The explanation formerly given was that *momblysnesse* was derived from *mumble*, and meant 'talk' or 'muttering'; see Speght, Skinner, Coles, and others. At the same time, *souenesse* was supposed to be an error for *sonesse*, which was said to mean 'noise'; from F. *son*, sound. In this way, the apparent sense of the line was:—'nor muttering and noise also,' which not only makes no good sense, but is quite out of keeping with the context.

Fortunately, the Additional MS. no. 34360 in the British Museum has a different reading, viz. 'Ne-moubliemies and souenez also,' which makes perfect sense; for *Ne-moubliemie* is an Old French name of the 'forget-me-not,' and *souenez* means 'remember,' evidently the same as 'remember-me,' which is a name for the germander speedwell in the North of England; see the Eng. Dial. Dictionary. Then the passage becomes:—'how they were accompanied by more forget-me-nots and germanders; and the poor pansies were not absent.' This is an excellent instance of the kind of mistake that may occur in an old printed text, when the editor failed to understand what he had before him.

§ 32. THE CONCLUSIONS OF THE ASTROLABE (p. 623)

This is a genuine treatise by Chaucer, composed by him for the use of his 'little son Lewis,' of whom nothing further is known. There are nearly two dozen MSS. of this piece, so that Thynne's text is of no very great importance; neither is it very correct. The MSS. usually have figures to illustrate the text, but Thynne has omitted them. Some of the material is out of place, so that section 12 of Part II (p. 632) is succeeded by sections 19, 20, and 21. The omitted sections 13–18 follow section 21, and are thus preserved; but the misarrangement produces some confusion. The treatise properly ends with section 40 on p. 640. The detached sections on *Umbra recta* and *Umbra versa* (the latter of which really consists of two sections run together) are probably genuine, though practically detached from the sections preceding; but the sections on p. 641 (from 'Umbra recta: If thy rule,' &c., to the end) are certainly spurious, as they merely repeat the preceding sections on the same subject.

33. THE COMPLAINT OF THE BLACK KNIGHT (p. 642)

It had been printed, no doubt previously, in an undated quarto edition of twelve leaves, of which the title was:—'The Complaynte of a Louers Lyfe. Imprynted at London in the flete strete at the sygne of the Sonne, by Wynkyn de Worde.' It has been ascertained, both from external and internal evidence, that this poem is certainly one of Lydgate's; and it deserves to be added that it is better than some others of his, and composed probably as early as 1402, when his work was more carefully executed than it was at a later date. There are at least seven MSS., but Thynne's text is as good as any of them, and I took it for the basis of the text printed in my Chaucerian Pieces. For further information, see the Introduction to that volume, p. xliii; and The Chaucer Canon, p. 102.

§ 34. A PRAISE OF WOMEN (p. 650)

It was long ago pointed out by Tyrwhitt that this poem cannot reasonably be attributed to Chaucer. It may perhaps be Lydgate's, but if so, it is not particularly good, even for him. Line 140—'Is this goodly angelyke creature' resembles l. 268 of his

his Temple of Glass—'a creature So aungellike, so goodli on to se'; and there is a similar eulogy of womankind in the same poem, ll. 729–763. But I have not reprinted it among the 'Chaucerian Pieces,' as it hardly seemed to deserve a place amongst them. The poem is only known from this print by Thynne, and one MS. copy, which exists in the Bannatyne MS., fol. 25, printed by the Hunterian Club in 1873–9, at p. 799. See my edition of Chaucer, vol. i. p. 37; Chaucerian Pieces, p. x; and The Chaucer Canon, p. 111. It is noteworthy that Lydgate, in his Temple of Glass, l. 1379, intimated his intention of writing a poem 'in pris [i. e. praise] of women.'

§ 35. THE HOUSE OF FAME (p. 652)

This is well known to be a genuine poem; indeed, Chaucer expressly claimed it, and he introduced at l. 729 his own name of 'Geffrey.' As there are but three MSS. of this poem, and none of them is of a wholly satisfactory character, Thynne's text, to say the least, is worth collating.

It had already been previously printed twice; once by Caxton, about 1483; and again by Pynson, in 1526. Pynson's text is a mere reprint of Caxton's, and Thynne's text is, apparently, a copy of one or the other of these. But Thynne must have consulted some MS. copy as well, as he inserts a considerable number of lines in various places, which Caxton had omitted; as, e.g., ll. 65, 66, 280–283, 793–796, 827–864, 1541, 1542, 2095–2158, at which point the poem suddenly ends. But Caxton added twelve lines of his own, to give it a kind of finish, and these Thynne has reproduced with slight alterations in the first three lines, which in Caxton stand thus :—

> And wyth the noyse of them wo[1] (*sic*)
> I Sodeynly awoke anon tho
> And remembryd what I had seen, &c.

For these Thynne has (see p. 674, col. 2):

> And therwithal I abrayde
> Out of my slepe halfe a-frayde
> Remembri[n]g wel what I had sene, &c.

§ 36. THE TESTAMENT OF LOVE (p. 677)

For this rather important piece, Thynne's text, as here reproduced, is the *sole* authority; which gives it a peculiar interest. Though somewhat dull and prolix, it is nevertheless one of our earliest specimens of well-ordered prose of the more modern type and of original composition; for Chaucer's Boethius and Tale of Melibeus are practically translations, and The Parson's Tale is to a great extent copied from a French original. In my Chaucerian Pieces I have given a considerably emended version of it, as it is quite clear that Thynne's text is (as I have already said) shamefully corrupt and careless.

The piece is chiefly remarkable as having been accepted as a composition of Chaucer's till quite a recent date; it was even accepted by Tyrwhitt without suspicion, though he was highly successful in pointing out the spuriousness of many of the pieces in Thynne's volume. The autobiographical details were carefully fitted into the life of Chaucer, with singular results. However, it was not Chaucer who was mixed up with the political intrigues of John of Northampton, twice Lord Mayor of London, and was imprisoned for his pains. Neither was it Chaucer who says of the author of 'Troilus,' that 'certaynly,

[1] But Pynson has 'two'; correctly.

his

his noble sayenges can I not amende'; p. 746 *b d*. Nor was it Chaucer who stole a long passage out of The House of Fame, for the purpose of turning it into inferior prose! See this explained in Chaucerian Pieces, p. xxvi, § 12.

Not only are we sure that this production was not one of Chaucer's, but we are enabled to say definitely that the author was Thomas Usk, who, according to Rastell, was 'a seriant of armes,' though he seems rather to have been a theologian, and whose doings have been rather minutely recorded by John of Malverne, in his continuation of Higden's Polychronicon[1]. As the history of the recovery of the author's name is somewhat curious, I beg leave to repeat here a short account of it. It is especially in place here, because it was from the present volume that the clue was obtained.

In the course of perusing this treatise with some care, I was struck by the frequent occurrence of the name 'Margarite,' whom the author describes as being 'ful of vertue, and able to be actyue in goodnesse' (p. 722, col. 1, l. 10 from the bottom); and he elsewhere explains that he uses the name allegorically, and that it represents Holy Church. Then, in turning over the pages, I was much struck by observing that the prologue at p. 677 begins with a capital M, the first chapter at p. 679 with A, the next, at p. 681, with R, and the next, at p. 683, with G. With this idea of MARG . . in my mind, it seemed worth while to go on; and I was not a little astonished to find (as any reader can see for himself) that the initial letters of the chapters in the first book and of the first five chapters of the second (noted at the bottom of each page where they occur) give the three words—MARGARETO OF VIRTW—answering to the expression 'Margarite . . ful of vertue,' as quoted above. The only difficulty is, of course, that MARGARETO should rather have been MARGARETE. But when we look at the source of this O, at p. 693, it is obvious that it is merely due to one of Thynne's almost countless errors. He has printed 'Ofte gan Loue to sterne me these wordes,' when he obviously should have printed 'Efte gan Loue to steren me [with] these wordes.' There is no point in the use of 'Ofte,' if we compare the whole context; but 'Eft,' with its usual sense of 'again,' or 'once more,' gives the very sense which we want. At the same time, in the very same sentence, Thynne has actually turned *steren* (i.e. to stir, excite) into *sterne*, and has omitted the necessary preposition *with*; which is quite enough to show that we must not trust him overmuch. But when this necessary correction has been made, it becomes perfectly clear that the expression thus obtained, viz. MARGARETE OF VIRTW, is intentional; and it becomes our plain duty to go further.

Proceeding as far as the end of the second book, we obtain the words—HAUE MCTRCI; where it is obvious that the second word should be MERCI. This shows that Thynne did not possess the clue, and has begun some of the chapters in the wrong place. The missing E will be found at p. 720, col. 1, l. 8 from the bottom, where Thynne (either disregarding his MS., or having before him an imperfect copy) actually prints a *small letter*, viz. in the line:—'euery soule of reason hath two thynges of steryng lyfe,' &c. That this should have been not merely a capital letter, but a large capital, appears from the sense of the context, as will best appear from reading the whole of p. 87 in my printed edition. The author is arguing with Love, who first of all answers one of his questions. This so pleases him that he exclaims:—'In good trouth, *here is a good beginnyng; yeve us more* of this way.' To this Love replies:—'I said to the[e] nat longe sithen, that resonable lyfe was one of thre thynges; and it was proued to the soule.' This is the prelude to a rather long and close argument, into which Love immediately plunges; and this argument is surely deserving of a new chapter. We can verify the true position of this

[1] See the account of Usk (Thomas) in the Dictionary of National Biography.

E by another process; for it ought to be (as indeed it is) approximately halfway between the M and the R.

Proceeding to the third book, we obtain the words:—ON THSKNVI, which is an enigma. The whole sentence now stands thus:—MARGARETE OF VIRTW, HAUE MERCI ON THSKNVI. The result is extremely disappointing, as the last seven letters, which obviously ought to yield the author's name, make no intelligible sense. It occurred to me to transpose these letters; but, even so, I failed to obtain the right answer. It never occurred to me that the seven letters do not compose *one* word, but *two*!

Here, then, the matter rested, till it was finally solved by help of a brilliant surmise that occurred to Mr. Henry Bradley, that perhaps the last leaves of the original MS. (as sometimes happens) had been disturbed so as to be displaced from their original order; and that Thynne was unaware of the fact.

With this idea, Mr. Bradley set to work, and before long discovered that the *sense* of the reasoning is actually broken in several places towards the end of Book III, producing absolute disconnexions in the argument. A complete account of the whole matter was given by Mr. Bradley in his letter to The Athenæum, no. 3615, Feb. 6, 1897.

The result is that several passages near the end of Book III require transposition in order to restore the sense. When this is done, and the right order of chapters has been thus obtained, the mysterious THSKNVI is at once presented in its true form, and becomes THIN VSK; i.e. thine Usk. This at once identifies the writer with the Thomas Usk already mentioned above.

Now that we know the true answer, we can go further, and readily understand how Usk came to think of this curious device. It is probable, from the account of Usk given by John of Malverne, that the latter may have known him personally. We may feel sure that Usk must have been acquainted with Higden's Polychronicon, the work which John of Malverne continued. But this very device, of indicating the name of the author of a work by means of the initial letters of the chapters had already been adopted by Higden. The initial letters of the chapters of Book I of that work produce the sentence—'Presentem cronicam compilavit Frater Ranulphus Cestrensis monachus.' (I may observe here, by way of parenthesis, that in vol. i of Higden, p. xvii, the editor gives this with four errors, viz. 'Pr*æ*sentem c*h*ronicam co*n*pilavit,' and 'monachus Cestrensis,' where the order of the words is strangely inverted.) We see then that Usk simply copied Higden's device.

Mr. Bradley has since kindly pointed out to me that Usk's first design seems to have been to make his sentence end with THOMAS VSK instead of THIN VSK. There is a conspicuous O in Chapter IV of Book III, and a conspicuous M in Chapter V; see my edition, p. 120, l. 159, and p. 124, l. 27. The A at p. 128, l. 154, and the S at p. 131, l. 114, are less certain, and the reading THIN certainly sounds better, and is more convincing.

For further information, see The Chaucer Canon, p. 97, and my Chaucerian Pieces, pp. xviii–xxxi. I show, at p. xxi of the latter, the exact manner in which the pages of the MS. were transposed so as to produce the order in which the material appears in Thynne.

§ 37. THE LAMENTATION OF MARY MAGDALEYN (p. 749)

This appears to be a mere reprint from Pynson's earlier edition of 1526, with a few unimportant variations. Thynne probably printed it merely because he had a copy at hand

hand, for it has no claim to be considered as Chaucer's[1]. In a dissertation by Bertha M. Skeat, Ph.D. (Zürich), printed at Cambridge in 1897, it is shown that it does not resemble Chaucer's work either in metre or grammar. Such a rime as that of *disgysed*, *to-ryued* (l. 171) is enough to condemn it. She concludes:—'There seems every reason to suppose that this poem was written by a woman, who was also a nun'; and suggests 'the period 1460–80 as the approximate date of the poem.' No MS. copy is known. See The Chaucer Canon, p. 112; Lounsbury's Studies in Chaucer, i. 478.

§ 38. THE REMEDY OF LOVE (p. 758)

The language is very late, the probable date being about 1530. It must have been written in Thynne's own lifetime, like The Pilgrim's Tale; and Thynne certainly ought not to have printed it in such company. No MS. copy is known. See The Chaucer Canon, p. 113.

§ 39. THE COMPLAINT OF MARS (p. 764)

This genuine poem had been previously printed by Julian Notary (1499–1501). But it is obvious that Thynne did not mainly follow this text. He founded it rather upon the MS. still existing at Longleat, no. 258, which he collated with Julian Notary's print, accepting some of the corrections which the latter occasionally afforded. I think these two sources, taken together, are sufficient to account for his text. Besides the copy in the Longleat MS., seven others are known. See my edition of Chaucer, vol. i. pp. 64, 323.

§ 40. THE COMPLAINT OF VENUS (p. 768)

This genuine poem has no connexion with the preceding, but must have been written at a much later date; so that Thynne's title at p. 764, viz. 'The Complaynt of Mars and Venus,' is misleading. It was doubtless copied from Julian Notary, who printed the two poems together in 1499–1501, with the title: 'The loue and complayntes bytwene Mars and Venus.' But Thynne's text of the latter Complaint was not taken from Notary; he seems to have followed a MS. copy not now known, which did not much differ (as I think) from MS. Fairfax 16.

§ 41. THE LETTER OF CUPID (p. 769)

This poem is known to have been imitated by Hoccleve from the French original by Christine de Pisan. It was written in 1402, two years after Chaucer's death, as appears from the last line of the poem. There are nine MSS. Thynne's text seems to have followed a MS. not greatly differing from MS. Fairfax 16. See Hoccleve's Poems, ed. Furnivall, p. 72; Chaucerian Pieces, p. 217; The Chaucer Canon, p. 101.

§ 42. A BALADE IN COMMENDATION OF OUR LADY; TO MY SOVERAIN LADY (p. 775)

Here Thynne has printed, as one, two distinct poems, one addressed to the Virgin Mary, and the other to an earthly mistress; both composed by Lydgate. The latter begins with the line—'I haue none englysshe conuenyent and digne'; p. 776, col. 2, st. 5.

[1] Some have thought that Pynson may have imagined it to be Chaucer's lost poem entitled 'Origenes upon the Magdaleyn.'

Of the former, there are two MS. copies; but the latter is known from Thynne's text only. MS. Sloane 1212 supplies an additional stanza to the former, and suggests several emendations. We cannot tell what has become of the original copy which Thynne followed. See Chaucerian Pieces, p. 275; The Chaucer Canon, p. 104.

§ 43. GOWER UNTO KING HENRY IV (p. 778)

Thynne's text is a good one, and does not greatly differ from that in the Trentham MS., which contains the only other copy. The writer, John Gower, is the well-known author of the Confessio Amantis. See Chaucerian Pieces, p. 205; The Chaucer Canon, p. 100.

§ 44. THE CUCKOO AND THE NIGHTINGALE (p. 783)

Thynne's text of this piece is a fairly good one; but ten lines are missing. There are five MS. copies. One of them gives the author's name as Clanvowe. See Chaucerian Pieces, p. 347; The Chaucer Canon, p. 106; Lounsbury's Studies in Chaucer, i. 486. It is decidedly one of the best of the poems in the present volume which have been wrongly associated with the name of Chaucer.

§ 45. ENVOY TO ALISON (p. 786)

To this piece Thynne assigns no title, but (as I was the first to point out) the first letters in the lines of the final Envoy spell out the name of ALISON. It has no connexion with the preceding piece, as the Fairfax MS. shows; and there are but two MS. copies, whereas of the preceding piece there are five. It evidently was intended to form the epilogue to some 'booke,' for the loss of which we can hardly express regret, if it at all resembled the present specimen. Certainly the line—'Suspires whiche I effunde in scilence' can hardly be suspected of having been written in imitation of Chaucer. See Chaucerian Pieces, p. 359; The Chaucer Canon, p. 113. I think it is certainly imitated from the Envoy to Hoccleve's De Regimine Principum, the first stanza of which begins with—'O litell booke, who yafe the hardynesse'; and the third stanza with—'Beseche hym, of his gracious noblesse.' We may safely date it after 1412.

§ 46. SCOGAN UNTO THE LORDS, &c., OF THE KING'S HOUSE (p. 787)

The right title is A Moral Balade, as in MS. Ashmole 59. It is also found in MS. Harl. 2251, but Thynne's copy seems better than either of these. It had been previously printed by Caxton, in a very rare volume, of which there is a copy in Cambridge, and another in the British Museum; both imperfect. See my Chaucer, vol. i. p. 27; William Caxton, by W. Blades, 2nd ed., p. 211. But Thynne's text does not follow it, so that he may have had access to a good MS. In fact, Thynne has all the stanzas in the right order; whereas Caxton has them in the order following, viz. 1–5, 11–13, Chaucer's Gentilesse, 6–10, 14–21. The most valuable part of this piece is, of course, the complete copy of Chaucer's 'Gentilesse,' which Scogan has inserted into his poem after the 13th stanza, distinguished by its being in seven-line stanzas, whereas the rest of the poem is in eight-line stanzas. Throughout these three stanzas Caxton gives a fairly good text, and Thynne has followed him rather closely. There are at least seven MS. copies of this Chaucerian poem, most of which are independent of Scogan's Moral Balade.

§ 47. LACK OF STEADFASTNESS (p. 789)

Thynne omits the title, beginning it immediately after the 'Explicit' in col. 1. He was the first to print this genuine poem. There are nine MS. copies still extant.

§ 48. GOOD COUNSEL OF CHAUCER; OR, TRUTH (p. 789)

Of this famous and genuine poem we possess many copies. Before Thynne's text appeared, it had already been printed thrice: (1) by Caxton; (2) by Wynkyn de Worde; and (3) by Pynson. Eighteen MS. copies are extant; and a printed copy (of no great value) appeared in Tottell's Miscellany in 1557 (ed. Arber, p. 194). Thynne follows Caxton very closely; his chief emendation being to read *folke shal rede* in l. 6, where Caxton wrongly has *folk rede*.

Pynson's reprint is closely copied from the print issued by Wynkyn de Worde, which has some truly comic readings. Of these, the most startling is in l. 12, where Chaucer's advice—'Strive not, as doth a crock (or earthen pitcher) against a wall'—assumes the original shape—'Stryve not, as doth a *cocle with a whall*,' meaning, I suppose, a cockle with a whale! It is a fine picture.

§ 49. BALADE OF THE VISAGE WITHOUT PAINTING; OR, FORTUNE (p. 790)

This genuine poem had been printed previously both by Caxton and Wynkyn de Worde. There are nine MS. copies extant. Caxton's print is a fair one, and Thynne follows it closely, though he seems to have accepted an emendation, in a few cases, from another source. In the title of the poem, Caxton unluckily misprinted *visage* as *vilage*, which Thynne has 'improved' into *vyllage*. Wynkyn de Worde's text is much worse than Caxton's, and exhibits several mistakes, such as *hen* for *hyene* (hyena) in l. 35; where, indeed, Thynne has unluckily printed *hyne* in place of Caxton's *biene*.

§ 50. LENVOY TO SCOGAN (p. 791)

Here Thynne has omitted the title, though his catchword, on the previous page, appears as *Lenuoye*. This genuine piece had been previously printed by Caxton, as we learn from two imperfect copies still extant, both of which have lost all but the first three stanzas. But there is enough to show that Thynne took his text from Caxton. There are only three MSS. extant.

§ 51. GO FORTH, KING (p. 791 *bb*)

This piece of fourteen lines is almost certainly Lydgate's, as it was printed along with his Temple of Glass no less than four times, viz. thrice by Wynkyn de Worde, about 1498–1500, and once by Berthelet. See Lydgate's Temple of Glass, ed. Schick, pp. xxvi–xxx, and p. 68. Schick shows that Wynkyn de Worde's third edition was reprinted from his second, and his second from his first. Thynne seems to have made up his text from the third of these editions and the edition by Berthelet, who alone has the spelling *rightous* in l. 6 instead of *rightuous* or *ryghtwyse*.

§ 52. CHAUCER AND HIS EMPTY PURSE (p. 791 *bc*)

This genuine piece had already been printed by Caxton; and there are seven MS. copies extant. The copies agree rather closely. I think Thynne took his text from Caxton.

§ 53. A BALADE OF GOOD COUNSEL (p. 792)

The above title rests on the authority of Stowe, who assigns it to Lydgate; and this ascription can hardly be wrong, as it exhibits his manner very plainly. There are two MS. copies, which show that Thynne has omitted two stanzas. Of these, the former (ll. 71–77) is in MS. Harl. 2251 only; the latter (ll. 106–112) is in both, the other MS. being one in the Cambridge University Library, marked Ff. 1. 6. Thynne's text appears to be a fairly good one, and I adopted it as the basis of my text. See Chaucerian Pieces, p. 285; The Chaucer Canon, p. 105.

§ 54. EPITAPHIUM GALFRIDI CHAUCER (p. 793)

These Latin verses had been previously printed by Caxton, at the end of his edition of Chaucer's translation of Boethius. They were written by Stephan Surigon of Milan, Licentiate in Decrees, and (according to Leland) at Caxton's request. See W. Blades, Biography of Caxton, 2nd ed., p. 214; Lounsbury, Studies in Chaucer, pp. 141, 441.

The last four lines make mention of Caxton himself; and it is fitting that Caxton's name should thus accidentally appear at the end of the present volume, as it is evident that Thynne was indebted to his illustrious predecessor in no small degree.

The workes of
Geffray Chau
cer newly printed/ with
dyuers workes whi
-che were neuer in
print before:
As in the table more playnly
dothe appere.

Cum priuilegio.

¶ To the kynges hyghnesse/ my most gratious soueraygne lorde Henry the eight/ by the grace of god kyng of Englande and of Fraunce/ defensor of the fayth/ and lorde of Irlande. &c.

AMonges all other excellencyes/ most gratious souerayn lord/ wher wt almightye god hath endowed mākynde/ aboue ẏ resydue of erthly creatures/ as an outwarde declaration of reason or resonablenesse/ wherin consysteth the symylitude of man vnto aungels/ and the differēce betwene the same & brute beestes/ I veraply suppose/ that speche or langage is nat to be reputed amonges the smallest or inferiours. For therby is exp̄ssed the conceite of one to another in open and playne sentence/ whiche in the resydue of lyuely creatures/ lacketh and is nat shewed amonges them/ but by certayn couert and derke signes/ and that in fewe thynges hauyng course and operation onely of nature. This speche or langage/ after the confusyon of tonges/ sente by goddes punysshment for pride and arrogance of people/ hath ben by a certayne instyncte & dysposytion naturall diuysed and inuented in sundry partes of the worlde/ as felowshippes or companyenges of folkes one with another chaunced/ moche to the outwarde expressyng of the thyng in worde or soūde/ accordyng to that wherof it had meanyng or sygnification. But in processe of tyme/ by dilygence or polycy of people/ after dyuers fourmes/ figures/ and impressyons in metall/ barkes of trees/ and other mater vsed for memorie and knowlege of thynges than present or passed/ sondry letters or caractes were first amōges the Phenices diuysed and founde/ with suche knyttynges and ioynynges of one to another by a marueylous subtylyte and crafte/ as counterueyled was and is equiualent to the same langages. So as the conceite of mānes mynde/ whiche at ẏ begynnyng was vsed to be declared by mouthe onely/ came to such poynt/ that it was as sensibly and viuely expressed in wrytynge. Hervpon ensewed a great occasion & corage vnto them that shulde wryte/ to compone and adorne the rudenesse and barbariete of speche/ and to forme it to an eloquent and ordynate ꝑfectyon/ wherunto many and many great poetes and oratours haue highly employed their studies and corages/ leauyng therby notable renoume of them selues/ and example perpetuell to their posterite. Amonges other/ the Grekes in all kyndes of sciēces/ semed so to preuayle and so to ornate their tonge/ as yet by other of right noble langages can nat be perfitely ymitated or folowed. The Latyns by example of the grekes/ haue gotten or wonne to thē no small glorie/ in the fourmynge/ order/ and vtterynge of that tonge. Out of the whiche two/ if it be well serched/ that is to saye Greke and Latyn (though by corruptyon of speche it shulde seme moche otherwyse) haue ben deryued the resydue of the langages that be written with the letters or caractes of either of them bothe: But of all speches/ those whiche most approche to the latinite/ be the Italyan and Spaynysshe tonges/ of whom the one by corruption of the Gothes and Longobardes had her begynnynge/ as latyn spoken by straungers of a barbare vnderstādyng/ The other beyng also latyn was by Wandales/ Gothes/ Moores/ Sarracenes/ and other so many tymes blemysshed/ as marueyle it is to se now vnto what ꝑfection these two formed out of the latyn and barbare speches be reduced. Next vnto them/ in symilytude to the latyn is the Frenche tonge/ whiche by dilygence of people of the same/ is in fewe yeres passed so amended/ as well in prōnūciation as in wrytynge/ that an Englysshman by a small tyme excercised in that tōge hath nat lacked groūde to make a grāmer or rule ordinary therof. Though of trouth

A. ii. (whiche

(whiche ſome ſhall ſcarſely beleue) the Germayns haue ſo fourmed the order of their langage/ that in the ſame/ is bothe as moche plentie and as nere concordaunce to the phraſe of the latyn/ as the Frenche tong hath. And veraply/ lyke as all theſe and the reſt haue ben thus vigilant & ſtudyous to meliorate or amende their langages: ſo hath there nat lacked amōges vs Engliſſhmen/ whiche haue right well and notably endeuoyred and employed them ſelues/ to the beautifyeng and bettryng of thenglyſſh tonge. ¶ Amonges whom mooſt excellent prynce/ my mooſt redoubted and gracious ſoueraygne lorde/ I your moſt humble vaſſall/ ſubiecte and ſeruaunt Wylliam Thynne/ chefe clerke of your kechyn/ moued by a certayne inclynacion & zele/ whiche I haue to here of any thyng ſoundyng to the laude and honour of this your noble realme/ haue taken great delectacyon/ as the tymes and layſers might ſuffre/ to rede and here the bokes of that noble & famous clerke Geffray Chaucer/ in whoſe workes is ſo manyfeſt comprobacion of his excellent lernyng i all kyndes of doctrynes and ſciences/ ſuche frutefulneſſe in wordes/ wel accordynge to the mater and purpoſe/ ſo ſwete and pleſaunt ſentences/ ſuche perfectyon in metre/ the cōpoſycion ſo adapted/ ſuche freſſhneſſe of inuencion/ compendyouſneſſe in narration/ ſuche ſenſyble and open ſtyle/ lackyng neither maieſte ne mediocrite couenable i diſpoſycion/ and ſuche ſharpneſſe or quyckneſſe in cōcluſyon/ that it is moche to be marueyled/ howe in his tyme/ whā doutleſſe all good letters were layde a ſlepe throughout ŷ worlde/ as the thynge whiche either by the diſpoſycion & influēce of the bodies aboue/ or by other ordynaunce of god/ ſemed lyke and was in daunger to haue vtterly peryſſhed/ ſuche an excellent poete in our tonge/ ſhulde as it were (nature repugnyng) ſpryng and aryſe. For though it had ben in Demoſthenes or Homerus tymes/ whan all lernyng and excellency of ſciences floriſſhed amonges the Grekes/ or in the ſeaſon ŷ Cicero prince of Eloquēce amonges latyns lyued/ yet had it ben a thyng right rare & ſtrāūge and worthy perpetuall laude/ ŷ any clerke by lernyng or wytte coulde than haue framed a tonge before ſo rude and imperfite/ to ſuche a ſwete ornature and cōpoſycion/ lykely if he had lyued in theſe dayes/ beīg good letters ſo reſtored & reuyued as they be/ if he were nat empeched by the enuy of ſuche as may tollerate nothyng/ whiche to vnderſtōde their capacite doth nat extēde/ to haue brought it vnto a full and fynall perfection. Wherfore gracious ſouerayne lorde/ takynge ſuche delyte and pleaſure in the workes of this noble clerke (as is afore mencioned) I haue of a longe ſeaſon moch vſed to rede and viſyte the ſame: and as bokes of dyuers imprītes came vnto my handes/ I eaſely and without grete ſtudy/ might and haue deprehended in the many errours/ falſyties/ and deprauaciōs/ whiche euydently appered by the contrarietees and alteracions founde by collacion of the one with the other/ wherby I was moued and ſtyred to make dilygent ſertch/ where I might fynde or recouer any trewe copies or exemplaries of the ſayd bookes/ wherunto in proceſſe of tyme/ nat without coſte and payne I attayned/ and nat onely vnto ſuch as ſeme to be very trewe copies of thoſe workes of Geffray Chaucer/ whiche before had ben put in prynte/ but alſo to dyuers other neuer tyll nowe imprinted/ but remaynyng almoſt vnknowen and in oblyuion/ wherupon lamentyng with my ſelfe/ the neglygence of the people/ that haue ben in this realme/ who doutleſſe were very remyſſe in the ſettyng forthe or auaūcement either of the hiſtories therof/ to the great hynderaunce of the renoume of ſuch noble princes and valyant conquerours & capitayns as haue ben in the ſame/ or alſo of the workes or memory of ŷ famous and excellent clerkes in all kyndes of ſcyences that haue floriſſhed therin/ Of whiche bothe ſortes it hath pleaſed god as highly to nobilytate this yle as any other regyon of chriſtendome: I thought it in maner appertenant

pertenant vnto my dewtie/ and that of very honesty and loue to my countrey I ought no lesse to do/ than to put my helpyng hande to the restauracion and bryngynge agayne to lyght of the said workes/ after the trewe copies and exemplaries aforesaid. And deuisyng wt my selfe/ who of all other were most worthy/ to whom a thyng so excellent and notable shulde be dedicate/ whiche to my conceite semeth for the admiracion/ noueltie/ and strangnesse that it myght be reputed to be of in the tyme of the authour/ in comparison/ as a pure and fyne tryed precious or polyced iewell out of a rude or indigest masse or mater/ none coulde to my thynkyng occurre/ that syns/ or in the tyme of Chaucer/ was or is suffycient/ but onely your maieste royall/ whiche by discrecyon and iugement/ as moost absolute in wysedome and all kyndes of doctryne/ coulde & of his innate clemence & goodnesse/ wolde adde or gyue any authorite hervnto.

For this cause most excellent and in all vertues most prestant prince/ I as humbly prostrate before your kyngly estate/ lowly supply and beseche the same/ that it wol vouchsafe to take in good parte my poore studye and desyrous mynde/ in reducynge vnto lyght this so precious and necessary an ornament of the tonge of this your realme/ ouer pytous to haue ben in any poynt lost/ falsifyed/ or neglected: So that vnder the shylde of your most royall protectyon and defence it may go forthe in publyke/ & preuayle ouer those that wolde blemysshe/ deface/ and in many thynges clerely abolyssh the laude/ renoume/ and glorie hertofore compared/ and meritoriously adquired by dyuers princes/ and other of this said most noble yle/ wherevnto nat onely straungers vnder pretexte of highe lernyng & knowlege of their malycious and peruers myndes/ but also some of your owne subiectes/ blynded in foly & ignorance/ do with great study contende. Most gracious/ victorious/ and of god most electe and worthy prince/ my most dradde soueraygne lorde/ in whom of very merite/ dewtie/ and succession/ is renewed the glorious tytell of Defensor of the christen faithe/ whiche by your noble progenytour/ the great Constantyne/ somtyme kyng of this realme/ & emperour of Rome was nexte god and his apostels/ chefely maynteyned/ corroborate/ and defended/ almighty Iesu sende to your highnesse the contynuall and euerlastynge habundaunce of his infynite grace. Amen.

¶ Thus endeth the preface.

¶ A table of all the names of the workes contayned in this volume.

¶ Thus endeth the fyrst table and here foloweth the seconde.

A. iii.

Preface — Brief Table of Contents

The table

¶ In this table ye maye fynde any thynge that ye woll haue in this volume by the Folio/ as foloweth.

The

The table

¶ Eight goodly questyōs/ with
their aunswers.

Somtyme in Grece that noble region
There were eight clerkes of grete sciēce
Philosophers of notable discretion
Of whom was asked/ to proue their prudence
Eight questions/ of derke intellygence
To whiche they answered after their entent
As here dothe appere playne and euydent

¶ The fyrst questyon/ what erthly thyng
Is best/ and to god moost cōmendable
The first clerke answered without tarying
A mannes soule/ euer ferme and stable
In right/ from trouthe nat varyable
But nowe alas ful sore may we wepe
For couetyse hath brought trouthe a slepe

The seconde/ what thyng is moost odious
A double man sayd the philosophre
With a virgyn face and a tayle venomous
With a fayre viewe/ and a false profre
A corrupte caryen in a golden cofre
It is a monster in natures lynage
One man to haue a double vysage

The thirde/ what is the best dower
That maye be to a wyfe appropriate
A clene lyfe/ was the clerkes aunswer
Without synne/ chast/ and inuyolate
From al disceytes/ and speches inornate
Or countenaunce/ whiche shal be to dispyse
No fyre make/ and no smoke wol aryse

The fourth questyon/ what mayden may
Be called clene in chastyte
The fourth clerke answered/ whiche alway
Euery creature is a shamed on to lye
Of whom euery man reporteth great honeste
Good maydens kepe your chastyte forthe
And remēbre that good name is golde worthe

Who is a poore man euer ful of wo
A couetouse man/ whiche is a nygon
He that in his herte can neuer saye ho
The more good/ the lesse distribucyon
The richer / the worse of condityon
Men in this cost/ clepen hym a nygarde
Sir Guy the bybour is his stewarde

Whiche is a riche man withouten fraude
He that can to his good suffyse
What soeuer he hath/ he yeueth god the laude
And kepeth him clene from al couetyse
He desyreth nothyng in vngoodly wyse
His body is here/ his mynde is aboue
He is a riche man/ for god dothe him loue

Who is a foole/ is the seuenth demaunde
He that wolde hurte/ and hath no powere
Myght he mykel / moche wolde he cōmaunde
His malyce great/ his myght nought were
He threteth ful faste/ ful lytel may he dere
Thynketh nat howe men haue sayd beforne
God sendeth a shrewde cowe a shorte horne

Who is a wyse man/ is the eight question
He that myght noye/ and dothe no noyaunce
Myght punysshe/ and leaueth punysshion
A man mercyful without vengeaunce

A wyse

Table of Contents — Eight Goodly Questions

A wyse man putteth in remembraunce
Sayeng/ had I venged al myne harme
My cloke had nat be furred halfe so warme.
¶ Explicit.

¶ To the kynges most noble grace/
and to the lordes and knygh-
tes of the garter.

To you welle of honour and of worthynesse
Our christen kyng/ the heire and successour
Unto Iustinians devout tendernesse
In faithe of Iesu our redemptour
And to you lordes of the garter floure
Of chevalry/ as men you clepe and cal
The lorde of vertue/ and of grace authour
Graunt the frute of your lose never appal

O liege lorde that have eke the lykenesse
Of Constantyne/ thensample and myrrour
To princes al/ in humble buxumnesse
To holy churche o veray sustaynour
And pyller of our faith/ and werryour
Agayne the heresyes bytter galle
Do forthe do forthe/ contynue your socour
Holde up Christes baner lette it nat falle

This yle or this had ben but hethnesse
Nad be of your faith the force and vigour
And yet this day the fendes crabbydnesse
Weneth fully to catche a tyme and hour
To have on us your lieges a sharpe shoure
And to his servytude us knytte and thralle
But aye we trust in you our protectour
On your constaunce we awayten alle

Commaundeth that no wight have hardynesse
O worthy kyng/ our christen emperour
Of the faith to dispute more or lesse
Openly amonge peple: Her errour
Springeth al day/ and engendreth rumour
Maketh such lawe/ and for ought may befal
Observe it wele/ there to be ye dettour
Dothe so/ and god in glorie shal you stal

Ye lordes eke/ shynyng in noble fame
To whiche appropred is the mayntenaunce
Of Christes cause/ in honour of his name
Shove on/ and put his foes to utteraunce
God wolde so/ so wolde eke your legiaunce
To tho two precketh you your duite
Who so nat kepeth this double observaunce
Of merite and honour naked is he

Your style sayth/ ye be foes to shame
Nowe kyth of your sayth the perseveraunce
In whiche an heape of us be halte and lame
Our christen kyng of Englande & of Fraunce
And ye my lordes with your alyaunce
And other faithful peple that there be
Trust I to god/ shal quenche al this noysaunce
And this lande sette in highe prosperite

Conquest of highe prowesse is for to tame
The wylde woodnesse of these myscreaunce
Right to the rote rype ye that same
Slepe nat this/ but for goddes plesaunce
And his mother/ and in sygnifyaunce
That ye ben of saynt Georges lyvere
Dothe him servyce and knightly obeysaunce
For Christes cause is his/ wel knowen ye

Stiffe stande in that/ & ye shal greve & grame
The foe to peace/ the norice of distaunce
That nowe is ernest/ tourne it in to game
Nowe kythe of your beleve the constaunce
Lorde liege/ & lordes have in remembraunce
Lorde of al is the blyssful Trinyte
Of whose vertue the mighty habundaunce
You herte and strength in faithful unyte.
¶ Explicit.

When faithe fayleth in preestes sawes
And lordes hestes are holden for lawes
And robbery is holden purchace
And lechery is holden solace
Than shal the londe of Albyon
Be brought to great confusyon

It falleth for every gentylman
To saye the best that he can
In mannes absence
And the sothe in his presence
It cometh by kynde of gentyl blood
To caste away al hevynesse
And gader togider wordes good
The werke of wysedome beareth wytnesse.
¶ Finis.

Balade by Hoccleve

Sayings (from Caxton)

The Caunter bury tales.

The prologues.

Whanne that Aprill
with his shoures sote
The drought of Marche
had perced the rote
And bathed euery vayne
in suche lycoure
Of whiche vertue/ engen-
dred is the floure
Whan zephirus eke with his sote breth
Enspired hath euery holte and heth
The tendre croppes/and the yonge sonne
Hath in the Ram halfe his course yronne
And smale foules maken melodye
That slepen al nyght with open eye
So prycketh hem nature in her courage
Than longen folke to go on pylgrymage
And palmers to seken straunge strondes
To serue halowes couthe in sondry londes
And specyally fro euery shyres ende
Of Englonde to Caunterbury they wende
The holy blyssful martyr for to seke
That hem hath holpen/ whan they were seke.

It befel that season on a day
In Southwarke at ye taberde as I lay
Redy to go in my pylgrymage
To Caunterbury with deuoute courage
That nyght was come in to that hostelrye
Wel nyne and twenty in a companye
Of sondry folke by auenture yfal
In felyshyp/and pylgrymes were they al
That towardecased nterbury wo
The chambres and stables weren
And wel weren they eased at the best
And shortly whan the sonne was at rest
So had I spoken with hem euerychone
That I was of her felyshyp anone
And made forwarde erly for to ryse
To take our way there as I you deuyse
But natheles/ whyle I haue tyme and space
Or that I ferther in this tale pace
Me thynke it accordaunt to reason
To tel you al the condycyon
Of eche of hem so as it semed me
And whiche they were/and of what degre
And eke in what aray that they were in
And at a knyght than wyl I fyrst begyn.

¶ The knyght. i.

A knyght there was/ and ye a worthy man
That fro the tyme that he fyrst began
To ryden out/he loued cheualrye
Trouthe/honour/fredom/and curtesye
Ful worthy was he in his lordes warre
And therto had he rydden no man farre
As wel in chrystendome as in hethenesse
And euer had honour for his worthynesse
At Alysaundre he was/ whan it was won
Ful ofte tyme he had the bourde begon
Abouen al nacyons in Pruce
In Lettowe had he rydden and in Ruce
No crysten man so ofte of his degre
In Garnade at the syege had he be
At Algezer/and rydden in Belmarye
At Leyes was he/and also at Satalye
Whan they were wonne/and in the great see
At many a noble armye had he be
At mortal batayles had he ben fyftene
And foughten for our fayth at Tramyssene
In lystes thries/and aye slayne his fo
This ilke worthy knyght had ben also
Somtyme with the lorde of Palathye
Ayenst another hethen in Turkye
And euermore he had a souerayne pryse
And though he was worthy he was wise
And of his porte as meke as is a mayde
He neuer yet no vilanye ne sayde
In al his lyfe/vnto no maner wight
He was a very perfyte gentyl knyght
For to tel you of his aray
His hors were good/but he was nothyng gay
Of fustyan he wered a gyppon
Al besmottred with his haubergion
For he was late come fro his vyage
And wente for to don his pylgrymage.

¶ The Squyer. ii.

With hym there was his sone a yong squyre
A louer and a lusty bachelere
Wt his lockes crul as they were layde in presse
Of twenty yere of age he was I gesse
Of his stature he was of euen length
And wonderly delyuer/and of great strength
b.ii. And

And he had be somtyme in chyuauchye
In Flaundres/ in Artoys/ and in Picardye
And borne hym wel/as of so lytel space
In hope to stande in his ladyes grace
  Enbrouded was he/as it weren a mede
Al ful of fresshe floures/ whyte and rede
Syngyng he was/ or floytynge al the day
He was fresshe as is the month of May
Short was his gowne/ wt sleues long & wide
Wel coude he syt on an horse/and fayre ryde
He coude songes make/and wel endyte
Iuste and eke daunce/ portray and wel write
So hote he loued/that by nyghter tale
He slepte no more than dothe the nyghtyngale
  Curteys he was/lowly and seruysable
And kerfte before his fader at the table.

The Squyers yoman iii.

A Yoman had he and seruauntes no mo
At that tyme/for hym lyst to ryde so
And he was clad in cote and hode of grene
A shefe of pecocke arowes bryght and shene
Under his belt he bare ful thriftely
Wel coude he dresse his tackle yomanly
His arowes drouped not with fethers lowe
And in his hande he bare a myghty bowe
  A not heed had he/ with a browne vysage
Of wodde crafte wel couth he al the usage
Upon his arme he bare a gay bracer
And by his syde a swerde and a bokeler
And on that other syde a gay daggere
Harneysed wel/and sharpe as poynte of spere
A chustofer on his brest of syluer shene
An horne he bare/ the bauderike was of grene
A foster was he sothly as I gesse

The Prioresse. iiii.

There was also a Nonne a Prioresse
That of her smylynge was symple and coye
Her grettest othe was by saynt Loye
And she was called dame Eglentyne
Ful wel she songe tho seruyce deuyne
Entewned in her voyce ful semely
And Frenche she spake ful fetously
After the schole of Stratforde at Bowe
For frenche of Parys was to her unknowe
At meate was she wel ytaught withal
She lete no morsel fro her lyppes fal
Ne wete her fyngers in her sauce depe
Wel couth she carp a morsel and wel kepe
That no drop ne fel upon her brest
In curtesy was set ful moche her lest
Her ouerlyp wyped she so clene
That in her cup was no ferthynge sene
Of grece/ whan she dronken had her draught
Ful semely after her meate she raught
And sykerly she was of great dysporte
And ful plesaunt/and amyable of porte
And payned her to counterfete chere
Of courte/and to be statelyche of manere
And to ben holden dygne of reuerence
  But for to speke of her conscyence
She was so charitable and so pytous
She wolde wepe if that she sawe a mous
Caught in a trappe/ if it were deed or bledde
Of smale houndes had she that she fedde
With roste flesshe/ mylke/ or wastel breed
But sore wepte she if any of hem were deed
Or if men smote hem with a yarde smerte
And al was conscience and tender herte
  Ful semely her wymple pynched was
Her nose tretes/her eyen gray as glas
Her mouth smale/and therto softe and reed
But sykerly she had a fayre forheed
It was almost a span brode I trowe
For hardly she was n It was almost
It was almost s her It was almost ware
It was almost aboute her arme she bare
A payre of bedes/gauded al with grene
And theron honge a broche of golde ful shene
On which ther was fyrst write a crowned. A
And after that (Amor vincit omnia)
  Another Nonne with her hath she
That was her chapeleyn/and preestes thre

The Monke. V.

A Monke there was/fayre for the maystry
An out ryder/that loued venery
A manly man to ben an abbot able
Ful many a deynte horse had he in stable
And whan he rode men myght his brydle here
Gynge.

Gyngelyng in a whystelyng wynde as clere
And eke as loude/ as dothe the chapel bel
  There as this lorde was keper of the cel
The rule of saynt Maure and of saynt Benet
Bycause it was olde and somdele strept
This ylke monke lete olde thynges pace
And helde after the newe worlde the space
He yaue not of the texte a pulled henne
That sayth/ that hunters be not holy men
Ne that a monke whan he is rechelesse
Is lykened to a fysshe that is waterlesse
This is to say/a monke out of his cloystre
This ylke texte helde he not worth an oystre
And I say his opynyon was good
wherto shuld he study/& make him selfe wood
Vpon a boke alway in cloystre to powre
Or swynke with his handes/or labowre
As Austyn byd/howe shul yͤ worlde be serued
Let Austyn haue his swynke to hym reserued
Therfore he was a pryckesour a right
Greyhoundes he had as swyft as foule of flizt
Of prickynge and of huntynge for the hare
Was al his lust/for no cost wolde he spare
  I sawe his sleues purfled at the hande
With Grice/and that the fynest in a lande
And for to faste his hoode vnder the chynne
He had of golde wrought a curious pynne
A loue knot in the greater ende there was
His heed was balde/and shone as any glas
And eke his face/as he had ben anoynte
He was a lorde ful fat and in good poynte
His eyen stepe rollynge/lynge in his heed
That stemed as a furneys of a leed
His bootes so wyle/his hors in great estate
Nowe certaynly he was a fayre prelate
He was not pale as a forpyned ghost
A fatte swan loued he best of any rost
His palfray was as browne as is a bery

¶ The Frere. vi.

  A Frere there was a wanton and a mery
A lymytour/a ful solempne man
In al the ordres foure is none that can
So moche of daliaunce and fayre langage
He had made ful many a maryage
Of yonge women at his owne cost
Vntyl his order he was a noble post
Ful wel byloued and famylyer was he
With frankeleyns ouer al in his countre
And with worthy women of the toun
For he had power of confessyoun
As he sayd hym selfe/ more than a curate
For of his ordre he was lycenciate
Ful swetely herde he confessyon
And plesaunt was his absolucyon
He was an easy man to gyue penaunce
There as he wyst to haue a good pytaunce
For vnto a poore ordre for to gyue
Is sygne that a man is wel yshryue
For if he gaue/he durst make auaunt
He wyst that a man was repentaunt
For many a man is so harde of herte
That he may not wepe though hym smerte
Therfore in stede of wepynge and prayres
Men mote gyue syluer to the poore freres
  His typpet was aye farsed ful of knyues
And pynnes/ for to gyue fayre wyues
And certaynly he had a mery note
Wel coude he synge and playen on a rote
Of yeddynge he bare vtterly the price
His necke was whyte as the floure delyce
Therto stronge he was as a champyoun
And knewe the tauerns wel in euery toun
And euery hosteler and tapstere
Bet than a lazer or a beggere
For vnto suche a worthy man as he
Accordeth nought/as by his faculte
To haue with lazers suche acqueyntaunces
It is not honest/ it maye not auaunce
For to dele with suche porayle
But al with riche/and sellers of vitayle
  And ouer al there as profyte shulde arise
Curteys he was/and lowly of seruyse
There nas no man no where so vertuous
He was the best begger in his hous
And gaue a certayn ferme for the graunte
None of his brethern came in his haunte
For thoughe a wydowe had but a shoo
(So plesaunt was his In principio)
Yet wolde he haue a ferthynge er he wente
His purchace was better than his rente
And rage he couth as it were a whelpe
In louedayes there coude he mykel helpe

B.iii. For

For there he was not lyke a cloysterere
With a threde bare cope/ as a poore frere
But he was lyke a maystert or a pope
Of double worstede was his semy cope
So rounded was as a bel out of presse
Somwhat he lysped for his wantonnesse
To make his Englysshe swete vpon his tong
And in harpynge/ whan he had songe
His eyen twynkeled in his heed aright
As done the sterres in a frosty nyght
This worthy frere was called Huberde

¶ The Marchaunt vii.

A marchaunt was there with a forked berde
In motley/ on hygh on his horse he sat
Vpon his heed a Flaundres beuer hat
His botes clasped fayre and fetously
His reasons he spake ful solempnely
Shewyng alway yͤ encrease of his wynnyng
He wolde the see were kepte for any thynge
Bytwyxe Myddelborough and Orewel
Wel coude he in eschaunge sel
This worthy man ful wel his wyt bysel
There wyst no wyght that he was in det
So stately was he of his gouernaunce
With his bargeyns/ and with his cheuysaunce
Forsothe he was a worthy man withal
But sothly to sayn/ I not what men him cal.

¶ The clerke of Oxenforde. viii.

A clerke there was of Oxenforde also
That vnto logyke had longe ygo
As leane was his horse as a rake
And he was nothyng fatte I vndertake
But loked holowe/ and therto soberly
Ful thredebare was his ouer courtpy
For he had yet getten him no benefyce
Ne was nought worthy to haue none offyce
For him was leuer to haue at his beddes heed
Twenty bookes/ cladde with blacke or reed
Of Aristotle/ and of his phylosophye
Than robes ryche/ or fyddel/ or gay sautrye
But al be that he was a phylosophre
Yet had he but lytel golde in cofre
But al that he myght of his frendes hente
On bookes and on lernyng he it spente
And besily gan for the soules praye
Of hem that helpen hym to scholaye
Of study toke he moste cure and hede
Not a worde spake he more than nede
And that was sayd in fourme and reuerence
And shorte and quicke/ and of hye sentence
Sownyng in moral vertue was his speche
And gladly wolde lerne/ and gladly teche.

¶ The sergiante at lawe ix.

A sergiaunt of lawe/ ware and wyse
That often had ben at the peruyse
That was also ful ryche of excellence
Discrete he was/ and of great reuerence
He semed suche/ his wordes were so wyse
Iustyce he was ful often in assyse
By patent/ and by playne commyssyoun
For his scyence/ and his hye renoun
Of fees and robes had he many one
So great a purchasour was no where none
Al was fee symple to hym in effecte
His purchasyng might not be to him suspecte
No where so besy a man as he there nas
And yet he semed besyer than he was
In termes had he case and domes al
That fro the tyme of kyng Wylliam was fal
Therto he coude endyte/ and maken a thyng
There coude no wight pynche at his wrytyng
And euery statute coude he playne by rote
He rode but homely in a m[illegible]y cote
Gy[illegible] a seynt of sylke/ with barres smale
Of his array/ tel I no lenger tale.

¶ The Frankeleyn. x.

A Frankeleyn there was in his companye
Whyte was his berde/ as is the deyse
And of his complexion he was sanguyne
Wel loued he by the morowe a soppe in wyne
To lyuen in delyte was euer his wonne
For he was Epycures owne sonne
That helde opinyon/ that playne delyte
Was very felycite perfyte
An housholder/ and that a great was he
Saynt Iulian he was in his countre

His

His breed/his ale/was alway after one
A better viended man was no where none
Without bake meate was neuer his house
Of fysshe and flesshe/and that so plentous
It snewed in his house of meate and drinke
Of al deyntes that men coude thynke
After the sondrie seasons of the yere
So chaunged he his meate/and his suppere
Ful many a fatte partryche had he in mewe
And many a breme/and many a luce in stewe
Wo was his coke/but his sauce were
Poynante & sharpe/and redy al his gere
His table dormaunt in his hal alway
Stode redy couered al the longe day
At cessyons there was he lorde and syre
Ful ofte tyme he was knyght of the shyre
An anelace and a gypsere al of sylke
Hyng at his gyrdel/ whyte as morowe mylke
A sheryfe had he ben/and a countour
Was no where suche a worthy vauesour.

¶ The Haberdassher. xi.

An Haberdassher there was/ & a carpenter
A webbe/a dyer/and a tapyser
Al they were yclothed in o lyuere
Of a solempne and a great fraternyte
Ful fresshe and newe her geare ipyked was
Her knyues ychaped were not with bras
But al with syluer wrought ful clene & wele
Her gyrdels and her pouches euerydele
Wel semed eueryche of hem a fayre burgeys
To sytten at a yelde hal/on the hye deys
Eueryche for the wysdome that he can
Was shape lyche for to ben an alderman
For catayle had they right ynough and rent
And eke her wyues wolde it wel assent
And els certayne they were to blame
It is ful fayre to ben ycleped madame
And gon to vigylles al before
And haue a mantel royallyche ybore.

¶ The Coke. xii.

A Coke they had with hem for the nones
To boyle the chykens and the mary bones
And pouder merchaunt/tarte/and galyngale
Wel coude he know a draught of London ale
He couthe roste/sethe/boyle/and frye
Make mortreys/and wel bake a pye
But great harme was it/ as it thought me
That on his shynne a mormal had he
And blanke manger made he with the beste

¶ The Shypman. xiii.

A Shipman was ther/wõnyng fer by west
For aught I wote/he was of Derthemouthe
He rode vpon a rownsy/as he couthe
In a gowne of faldyng to the kne
A dagger hangyng vp a lace had he
Aboute his necke/vnder his arme downe
The hote sõmer had made his hewe al browne
And certayne he was a good felawe
Ful many a draught of wyne had he drawe
Frõ Burdeux ward/whiles ye chapmen slepe
Of nyce conscience toke he no kepe
If that he faught/and had the hygher honde
By water he sent hem home to euery londe
But of his crafte/to recken wel his tydes
His streames and his daungers him besydes
His herbrough/his moone/& his lodemanage
There was none suche from Hul to Cartage
Hardy he was/and wyse to vndertake
With many a tempest had his berde be shake
He knewe al the hauens as there were
Fro Scotlande to the Cape de fenestere
And euery creke in Britayne & in Spayne
His barge was called the Maudelayne.

¶ The doctour of phisyke. xiiii.

With vs there was a doctour of phisyke
In al this worlde ne was there none him lyke
To speke of phisyke/and of surgerye
For he was grounded in astronomye
He kepte his pacient a ful great del
In houres/by his magyke naturel
Wel couthe he fortune the assendent
Of his ymage for his pacyent
He knewe the cause of euery maladye
Were it of colde/hete/moyste/or drie
And wherof engendred what humour
He was a very perfyte practysour

The

The cause yknowe/ and of his harme the rote
Anone he gaue to the sycke man his bote
Ful redy had he his apotecaries
To sende hym drugges and his lectuaries
For eche of hem made other for to wynne
Her frendshyp nas not newe to begynne
Wel knewe he the olde Esculapius
And Dioscorides/ and eke Rufus
Olde Hippocrates/ Haly/ and eke Gallen
Serapion/ Rasis/ and also Auicen
Auerroys/ Damascene/ and Constantyn
Bernarde/ Gatisden/ and Gylbertyn
Of his dyete mesurable was he
For it was of no superfluyte
But of great nourysshynge/ and digestyble
His study was but lytel on the Byble
In sangwyne and in perce he clad was al
Lyned with Taffata/ and with sendal
And yet he was but easy of dispence
He kepte that he wanne in tyme of pestylence
For golde in Physyke is a cordyal
Therfore he loued golde in specyal.

¶ The wyfe of Bathe. xv.

A good wyfe there was besyde Bathe
But she was somdel defe/ & that was scathe
Of clothe makyng she had suche an haunte
She passed hem of Ypre/ or of Gaunte
In al the parysshe wyfe ne was there none
That to the offrynge before her shulde gone
And if there dyd/ certayn ryȝt wrothe was she
That she was al out of charite
Her kerchers ful fyne were of grounde
I durst swere they wayden ten pounde
That on a Sonday were vpon her heed
Her hosen were of fyne scarlet reed
Ful strayte ystrayned/ and shoes ful newe
Bolde was her face/ and reed was her hewe
She was a worthy woman al her lyue
Husbandes at the chirche dore had she fyue
Withouten other company in youthe
But therof nedeth not to speke as nouthe
And thryse had she ben at Hierusalem
She had passed many a stronge streme
At Rome had she ben/ and at Boloyne
In Galys at saynt James/ and at Coloyne
She couth moche of wandrynge by the waye
Gat tothed was she sothely for to saye
Vpon an ambler easely she sat
Ywympled wel/ and on her heed an hat
As brode as is a bokeler or a targe
A foot mantel aboute her hyppes large
And on her fete a payre of spurres sharpe
In felyshyp wel couth she laughe and carpe
Of remedyes of loue she coude perchaunce
For she couth of that arte the olde daunce.

¶ The Person. xvi.

A Good man there was of relygyoun
And was a poore person of a toun
But ryche he was of holy thought and werke
He was also a lerned man/ and a clerke
That Christes gospels truely wolde preche
His parisshens deuoutly wolde he teche
Benygne he was and wonder dilygent
And in aduersyte ful pacyent
And suche he was proued ofte sythes
Ful lothe were hym to curse for his tythes
But rather wolde he yeuen out of doute
Vnto his poore parysshens aboute
Of his offrynge/ and of his substaunce
He couth in lytel thynge haue suffysaunce
Wyde was his parisshe/ & houses ferre asondre
But he ne lefte neyther for rayn ne thondre
In sycknesse ne in myschefe for to vysyte
The ferrest in his parysshe/ moche or lyte
Vpon his fete/ and in his hande a staf
This noble ensample to his shepe he yaf
That first he wrought/ & afterwarde taught
Out of the gospel he the wordes caught
And this fygure he added eke therto
That if golde ruste/ what shulde yron do
For if a preest be foule/ on whom we trust
No wonder is a lewde man to rust
And shame it is/ if a preest take kepe
To se a shytten shepherde/ and a clene shepe
Wel ought a preest ensample for to yeue
By his clennesse/ howe his shepe shulde lyue
He sette not his benefyce to hyre
And lette his shepe acombre in the myre
And renne to London to saynt Poules
To seken hym a chauntry for soules

Or with

General Prologue (A 423–510; T. 425–512)

Or with a brotherhede to be with holde
But dwelte at home/and kept wel his folde
So that the wolfe ne made hem not miscarye
He was a shepeherde/and not a mercenarye
And though he holy were and vertuous
He was not to synful men dispytous
Ne of his speche daungerous ne digne
But in his techyng discrete and benigne
To drawen folke to heuen with fayrnesse
By good ensample/this was his besynesse
But if it were any person obstynate
Whether he were of hye or lowe estate
Hym wolde he snybbe sharply for the nonis
A better preest I trowe nowhere none is
He wayted after no pompe ne reuerence
Ne maked him no spyced conscience
But Christes lore/and his apostels twelue
He taught/ but first he folowed it hym selue.

¶ The Plowman xvii.

Wt him there was a Plowman his brother
That had ladde of donge many a fother
A trewe swynker and a good was he
Lyuyng in peace/ and parfyte charyte
God loued he best with al his herte
At al tymes/thoughe hym gamed or smerte
And than his neyghbours right as him selfe
He wolde thresshe/and therto dyke and delfe
For Christes sake/for euery poore wyght
Withouten hyre/if it lay in his myght
His tythes payde he ful fayre and wel
Bothe of his propre swynke/and of his catel
In a tabarde he rode/ vpon a mare
There was also a Reue/and a Myllare
A Sompnour/and a Pardoner also
A Manciple/and my selfe/there was no mo.

¶ The Myller xviii.

The Myller was a stoute carle for ye nones
Ful bygge he was of brawne/& eke of bones
That proued wel/for ouer al there he cam
At wrastlyng/ he wolde haue away the Ram
He was shorte sholdred/a thicke gnarre
Ther nas no dore/but he wold heue of ye bar
Or breke it/at a rennyng with his heed
His berde as any sowe or foxe was reed
And therto brode/ as it were a spade
Vpon the coppe right of his nose he hade
A werte/and theron stode a tufte of herres
Reed as the brustels of a sowes eeres
His nostrels blacke were and wyde
A swerde and a bokeler bare he by his syde
His mouthe as great was as a furneys
He was a iangler and a golyerdeys
And that was moste of synne & of harlotryse
Wel couthe he steale corne/ and tolde it thrise
And yet he had a thombe of golde parde
A whyte cote and a blewe hoode weared he
A bagge pype wel couthe he blowe & sowne
And therwithal brought he vs out of towne.

¶ The Manciple xix.

A gentle Manciple there was of the temple
Of whiche al catours might taken ensemple
For to ben wyse/in byeng of vitayle
For whether he payde/or toke by tayle
Algate he wayted so in his asshate
That he was aye before/ in good estate
Nowe is not that of god a ful fayre grace
That suche a leude mans wyt shal pace
The wysdome of an heape of lerned men
Of maysters had he mo than thrise ten
That were of lawe experte/and curyouse
Of whiche there was a doseyn in that house
Worthy to ben stewardes of rente and lande
Of any lorde that is in Englande
To maken him lyue by his propre good
In honour detbelesse/but if he were woode
Or lyue as scarsly as him lyste desyre
And able to helpen al a shyre
In any case that might fallen or happe
And yet the Manciple set al her cappe.

¶ The Reue xx.

The Reue was a sclender colerike man
His berde was shaue as nye as euer he can
His heere was by his eeres rounde yshorne
His toppe was docked lyke a preest byforne
Ful longe were his legges and ful lene
Ylyke a staffe/there was no calfe ysene

Wel

Wel couth he kepe a garner and a bynne
There was non auditour coude on hym wyn
Wel wyst he by the drought/and by the rayne
The yeldynge of his seed/and of his grayne
His lordes shepe/his neet/and his deyrie
His swyne/his hors/his store/ and his pultrie
Were hooly in his Reuys gouernynge
And by his conenaunt yaue he rekenynge
Sithe his lorde was twenty yere of age
There coude no man brynge hym in a rerage
There nas baylly/heerd/ne none other hyne
That he ne knewe his sleyght and his coupne
They were a drad of hym as of the dethe
His dwellynge was ful fayre vpon an hethe
With grene trees shadowed was his place
He couth better than his lorde purchace
Ful riche he was astored pryuely
His lorde he coude wel please subtylly
To yeue and lene hym of his owne good
And haue a thanke/and yet a cote and hode
In youthe he had lerned a good mystere
He was a wel good wryght/a carpentere
This Reue sat vpon a right good stot
That was al pomel grey/and hight Scot
A longe surcote of perce vpon he hade
And by his syde he bare a rusty blade
Of Norfolke was this Reue/of which I tel
Besyde a towne/men clepen it Baldeswel
Tucked he was/as is a frere aboute
And euer he rode hyndrest of the route.

The Somnpnour. xxi.

A Somnpnour was there with vs in ye place
That had a fyre redde cherubyns face
For sausfleme he was/with eyen narowe
Al hote he was/and lecherous as a sparowe
With skaled browes blacke/ and pylled berde
Of his vysage chyldren were sore aferde
There nas quicksyluer/lytarge/ne brymstone
Borace/ceruse/ne oyle of tarter none
Ne oyntement that wolde clense or byte
That him myght helpe of his whelkes white
Ne of his knobbes syttynge on his chekes
Wel loued he garlyke/onyons/and eke lekes
And for to drinke stronge wyne reed as blood
Then wolde he speke & crye as he were wood
And whan he had wel ydronke the wyne
Than wolde he speke no worde but latyne
A fewe termes had he/two or thre
That he had lerned out of some degre
No wonder is/he herde it al the daye
And ye knowen wel eke howe that a iaye
Can clepe watte/as wel as can the pope
But who so couthe in other thyng him grope
Than had he spent al his philosophye
(A questio quid iuris) wolde he crye
He was a gentle harlot and a kynde
A better felawe shulde a man not fynde
He wolde suffre for a quarte of wyne
A good felawe to haue his concubyne
A twelue monthe/and excuse hym at the ful
Ful priuely eke a fynche couthe he pul
And if he fonde owhere a good felawe
He wolde teche hym to haue none awe
In suche case/of the archedekyns curse
But if mans soule were in his purse
For in his purse he shulde ypunysshed be
Purse is the archedekens hel/sayd he
But wel I wote he lyed right in dede
Of cursyng ought eche synful man drede
For cursyng wol slee/rizt as assoylyng saueth
And also ware him of a Significauit
In daunger had he at his owne gyse
The yonge gyrles of the diocyse
And knew her counsayle/and was of her reed
A garlonde had he set vpon his heed
As great as it were for an alestake
A buckeler had he maked him of a cake.

The Pardoner. xxii.

With him there rode a gentle Pardonere
Of Rounceual/ his frende and his compere
That streight was come fro ye court of Rome
Ful loude songe he/ come hyder loue tome
This Somnpnour bare him a styffe burdoun
Was neuer trompe of halfe so great a soun
This Pardoner had heere as yelowe as wexe
But smothe it hynge/as doth a strike of flexe
By ounces hynge his lockes that he had
And therwith he his sholders ouerspread
But thynne it lay by culpons one and one
But hode for iolyte weared he none

For

For it was trussed vp in his walet
Him thought he rode al of the newe iet
Disshevylde saue his cappe he rode al bare
Suche glaryng eyen had he as an hare
A vernacle had he sowed vpon his cappe
His walet beforne him in his lappe
Bretle ful of pardone come from Rome al hote
A voice he had as smale as hath a gote
No berde had he/ ne neuer shulde haue
As smoth it was as it were newe shaue
I trowe he were a geldyng or a mare
But of his crafte fro Berwyke vnto Ware
Ne was there suche another pardonere
For in his male had he a pylowe bere
Whiche as he sayd/ was our ladyes veyle
He sayd he had a gobbet of the seyle
That saynt Peter had whan that he went
Vpon the see tyl Iesu Christ him hent
  He had a crosse of laten ful of stones
And in a glasse he had pygges bones
But with these relykes whan that he fonde
A poore person dwellyng vplonde
Vpon a day he gate him more money
Than that person gate in monthes twey
And thus with fayned flateryng and iapes
He made the person and the peple his apes
  But trewly to tellen at the laste
He was in churche a noble ecclesyast
Wel couthe he rede a lesson or a storie
But alderbest he sange an offertorie
For wel he wyst/ whan that songe was songe
He muste preche/ and wel afyle his tonge
To wynne syluer as he wel coude
Therfore he songe so merely and loude.

  Nowe haue I tolde you sothly in a clause
The state/ the aray/ eche nombre/ & eke the cause
Why that assembled was this company
In Suthwerke at this gentyl hostelry
That hyght the Tabarde fast by the Belle
But nowe is tyme to you for to telle
Howe that we baren vs that ylke nyght
Whan we weren in that hostry alyght
And after wol I tel of our vyage
And al the remenaunt of our pylgrymage
  But firste I pray you of your curtesy
That ye ne arette it nat my folly
Though that I playnly speke in this matere
To tellen you her wordes and eke her chere
Ne though I speke her wordes properly
For this ye knowen as wel as I
Who shal tellen a tale after a manne
He mote reherce as nye as euer he canne
Euerych worde/ if it be in his charge
Al speke he neuer so rudely ne large
Or els he mote tellen his tale vntrewe
Or feyne thynges/ or fynde wordes newe
He may nat spare al tho he were his brother
He mote as wel saye o worde as another
Christ spake him selfe ful brode in holy writte
And wel I wotte no vyllany is itte
  Eke Plato sayth/ who so can him rede
The wordes mote ben cosyn to the dede
  Also I pray you for yeue it me
Al haue I nat sette folke in her degree
Here in this tale as they shulde stande
My wytte is shorte ye may wel vnderstande.

GReat chere made our host vs euerychon
And to the supper sette he vs anon
And serued vs with vitayle at the best
Strong was the wyne/ & wel drynke vs lest
A semely man our host was with al
For to ben a marshal in a lordes hal
A large man he was with eyen stepe
A fayrer burgeys is there none in chepe
Bolde of his speche/ wyse and wel ytaught
And of manhode him lacked right naught
Eke therto he was a right mery man
And after supper playen he began
And spake of myrthe among other thynges
Whan that we had made our rekenynges
And sayd thus/ nowe lordynges trewly.
Ye ben to me welcome right hertely
For by my trouthe if I shulde nat lye
I sawe nat this yere so mery a company
Atones/ in this herborowe as is nowe
Fayne wolde I don you myrth & I wyst how
And of a myrthe I am right nowe bethought
To done you ease/ and it shal coste nought
Ye gone to Canterbury god mote you spede
The blyssful martyr quyte you your mede
And wel I wote as ye gone by the way
Ye shapen you to talken and to play

For

For trewly comforte ne myrthe is there none
To ryden by the waye as dombe as a stone
And therfore wolde I maken you disporte
As I sayd erst/ and done you some comforte
And if you lyketh al by one assent
For to stonden at my iugement
And for to worchen as I shal you say
To morowe whan we ryden on the way
Nowe by my fathers soule that is deed
But ye be mery I wol gyue you myne heed
Holde vp your handes without more speche.
Our counsayle was nat longe for to seche
Vs thought it was nat worth to make it wise
And graunted him without more auyse
And badde him say his verdit as him lest
Lordiges (q̄d he) nowe herkeneth for ẏ best
But take it nat I praye you in disdayne
This is the poynt to speke it platte & playne
That eche of you to shorte with others way
In this vyage/ shal tel tales tway
To Caunterbery warde I meane it so
And homwardes he shal tel tales other two
Of auentures whilom that han befal
And whiche of you that beareth him best of al
That is to sayne/ that tellen in this case
Tales of best sentence and most solace
Shal haue a supper at our alder cost
Here in this place syttyng by this post
Whan that we comen ayen from Canterbery
And for to make you the more mery
I wol my seluen goodly with you ryde
Right at myne owne coste and be your gyde
And who that wol my iugement withsay
Shal paye al that we spende by the way
And if ye vouchsafe that it be so
Telle me anon without wordes mo
And I wol early shape me therfore
This thyng was graunted & our othes swore
With ful gladde herte/ and prayden him also
That he wolde vouchsafe for to do so
And that he wolde ben our gouernour
And of our tales iuge and reportour
And sette a supper at a certayne prise
And we wolden ben demed at his deuyse
In hye and lowe/ and thus by one assent
We ben accorded to the iugement
And therupon the wyne was fette anone
We dronken/ and to rest wente ylke one
Withouten any lenger taryeng
A morowe whan the day gan to spryng
Vp rose our host/ and was our alder cocke
And gadered vs al in a flocke
And forthe we ryden a lytel more than paas
Vnto the wateryng of saynt Thomas
And there our host began his horse arest
And sayd: lordes herkeneth if you lest
Ye wote your forwarde/ and I it recorde
If eue songe and morowe songe acorde
Lette se nowe who shal tel the first tale
As euer I mote drynke wyne or ale
Who so is rebel to my iugement
Shal paye for al that by the way is spent
Nowe draweth cutte or that ye farther twyn
The whiche that hath the shortest shal begyn.

Sir knyght (q̄d he) my maister & my lorde
Nowe draweth cutte/ for that is myne acorde
Cometh nere (q̄d he) my lady prioresse
And ye sir clerke/ lette be your shamefastnesse
Ne studyeth nat/ lay hande therto euery man
Anone to drawe euery wight began
And shortely for to tellen as it was
Were it by auenture/ or by shorter caas
The sothe is this/ the cutte fyl to the knyght
Of whiche ful blyth & glad was euery wight
And tellen he must his tale as it was reason
By forwarde/ and by composytion
As ye han herde/ what nedeth wordes mo
And whan this good man sawe ẏ it was so
As he that wyse was and obedyent
To kepen his forwarde by his free assent
He sayd/ sithen I shal begyn the game
What welcome cutte a goddesname
Nowe let vs ryde/ and herkeneth what I say
And with that worde we ryden forth our way
And he began with right a mery chere
His tale anone/ right as ye shal here.

¶ Thus endeth the prologues of the Caunterbury tales/ and here foloweth the knyghtes tale.

The knyghtes tale.

¶ Here begynneth the knyghtes tale.

WHylom/ as olde stories tellen vs
There was a duke yͭ hight Theseus
Of Athenes he was lorde & gouernour
And in his tyme suche a conquerour
That greatter was non vnder the son
Full many a riche countrey had he won
What with his wysedom/ & his cheualry
He conquered all the reigne of Feminy
That whylom was icleped Cythea
And wedded the quene Ipolita
& brought her home with him/ i to his contre
With mykell glory and solempnyte
And eke her yonge suster Emely.
And thus with victory and melody
Let I this worthy duke to Athenes ryde
And all his host/ in armes hym be syde
And certes / if it nere to longe to here
I wolde haue tolde fully the manere
Howe wonnen was the reigne of Feminy
By Theseus/ and by his cheualry
And of the great batayle for the nones
Betwene Athenes and Amasones
And howe beseged was Ipolyta
The yonge hardy quene of Cithea
And of the feest/ yͭ was at her weddynge
And of the tempest at her home cōmyng
But all yͭ thyng/ I mote as nowe forbere
I haue god wotte/ a large felde to ere
And weked ben the oxen in the plowe
The remenant of my tale is long ynowe
I wyll nat letten eke / non of this rout

¶ Let

Let euery felowe tell his tale about
And let se nowe/ who shall the supper wyn
And there I lefte/ I wyll agayne begyn.

This duke/ of whom I make mencyoune
Whan he was come/ almost to the towne
In all his wele and his most pride
He was ware/ as he cast his eye asyde
Where that there kneled in the highe wey
A company of ladys/ twey and twey
Eche after other/ cladde in clothes blake
But suche a crye/ ⁊ suche a wo they make
That in this worlde/ nys creature lyuinge
That euer herde suche a waymentynge
And of this crye/ they nolde neuer stynten
Tyll they the reynes of his bridell henten
What folke be ye/ y at myn home comyng
Perturben so my feest with cryeng
Quod Theseus: haue ye so great enuy
Of myn honour/ that thus cõplayne ⁊ cry:
Or who hath you mysbode/ or offended:
Nowe telleth me/ if it may be amended.
And why that ye be clothed thus in blake:
The oldest lady of them all spake
Whan she had swowned wt a dedly chere
That it was ruthe for to se and here
She said lorde/ to whom fortune hath yeue
Vyctory/ ⁊ as a conquerour to lyue
Nought greueth vs your glory ⁊ honour
But we beseke you of mercy ⁊ socour.
And haue mercy on our wo and distresse
Some drope of pyte/ through thy gẽtylnesse
Vpon vs wretched wymen/ let thou fall
For certes lorde/ there nys none of vs all
That she ne hath be a duchesse or a quene
Nowe be we caytyfes/ as it is well isene
Thanked be fortune/ and her false whele
That non estate assureth for to be wele.
Nowe certes lorde/ to abyde your presẽce
Here in this temple of the goddesse Clemẽce
We haue be waytyng all this fourtenyght
Helpe vs lorde/ sythe it lyeth in thy myght.

I Wretche/ that wepe and wayle thus
Whylom wyfe to kyng Campaneus
That starfe at Thebes/ cursed be y day
And all we that ben in this aray
And maken all this lamentacyon
We losten all our husbondes at that town
Whyle that the siege there aboute laye
And yet the olde Creon (wel a waye)
That lorde is nowe of Thebes cyte
Fulfylled of yre and of iniquite
He for dispyte/ and for his tyranny
To done the deed bodyes vyllanye
Of all our lordes/ whiche that ben slawe
Hath all the bodyes on an heape ydrawe
And wyll nat suffre hem/ by none assent
Neyther to be buryed/ ne to be brent
But maketh houdes to eate hem in dispyte
And wt that worde/ without more respite
They fallen grofly/ and cryen pytously
Haue on vs wretched wymen some mercy
And let our sorowe synke in thyn hert.
This gentle duke down frõ his hors stert
With hert pytous/ whã he herde hem speke
Hym thought that his herte wolde breke
Whan he sawe hem so pytous ⁊ so mate
That whylom were of so great astate
And in his armes/ he hem all vp hent
And hem comforted in full good entent
And swore his othe/ as he was true knyght
He wolde don so ferforthly his myght
Vpon the tyrante Creon hem to wreake
That all the people of Grece shulde speake
Howe Creon was of Theseus ysterued
As he that had his dethe full well deserued
And ryght anon withouten more abode
His baner he displayed/ and forthe rode
To Thebes warde/ and al his hoost besyde
No nere Athenes nolde he go ne ryde
Ne take his ease fully halfe a day
But onward on his way that nyght he lay
And sent anone Ipolita the quene
And Emely her yonge syster shene
Vnto the towne of Athenes to dwell
And forth he rydeth/ ther nys no more to tel.

The red statu of Mars wt spere ⁊ targe
So shyneth in his whyte baner large
That all the feldes glytteren vp ⁊ down
And by his baner/ borne is his penon
Of golde ful rych/ i which there was ybete
The mynotaure/ that he wan in Crete
Thus

The Knight's Tale (A 890–980; T. 892–982)

Thus rydeth this duke/this conquerour
And in his hoste of chyualry the flour
Tyll that he came to Thebes/ & alyght
Fayre in a felde/ther as he thought to fyght
But shortly for to speken of this thyng
With Creon/whiche was of Thebes kyng
He faught/& slewe him manly as a knyght
In playne batayle/& put his folke to flyght
And at a saute he wan the cyte after
And rente adowne wall/ sparre/ & rafter
And to the ladyes/he restored agayn
The bodyes of her husbandes ẏ were slayn
To done obsequies/ as tho was the gyse
 But it were all to longe for to deuyse
The great clamour/and the weymentyng
That the ladyes made at the brennyng
Of the bodyes/and the great honour
That Theseus/the noble conquerour
Doth to ẏ ladies/whan they from hym wēt
But shortly to tellen is myne entent
 Whan ẏ this worthy duke/this Theseus
Hath Creon slayne/and wan Thebes thus
Styll in the felde he toke all nyght his rest
And dyd with all the countre as hym lest
To ransake in the taas of bodyes dede
(Hem for to strype of harneys & of wede)
The pyllours dyd her busynesse and cure
After the batayle and the disconfyture.
And so befell/that in the taas they founde
Through gyrt wᵗ many a greuous woūde
Two yonge knyghtes lyeng by and by
Bothe in armes same/wrought full richely
Of whiche two/Arcyte hyght that one
And that other hyght Palamon
Not fully quycke/ne fully deed they were
But by her cote armours/ and by her gere
The haraudes knewe hem best in specyall
As tho that weren of the bloode ryall
Of Thebes/and of systren two yborne
Out of the taas ẏ pyllours hath hem torne
And han hem caryed softe in to the tent
Of Theseus/and he full sone hem sent
To Athenes/ to dwellen there in prison
Perpetuell/he nolde hem not raunson
And whan this worthy duke had thus idon
He toke his hoost/and home he gothe anon
With laurer crowned / as a conquerour

And there he lyueth in ioye and honour
Terme of his lyfe/ what nedeth wordes mo:
And in a towre/in anguysse and in wo
Dwelleth Palamon/ & his felowe Arcyte
For euermore/ther may no gold hem quite.

 Thus passeth yere by yere/& day by day
T Tyll it fell ones in a morowe of May
 That Emely/that fayrer was to sene
Than is the lylly/vpon the stalke grene
And fressher than May/with floures newe
For with the rose colour strofe her hewe
I not whiche was the fayrer of hem two
 Er it was day/ as was her won to do
She was arysen/and all redy dyght
For May woll haue no slogardy a night
The season pricketh euery gentell herte
And maketh it out of her slepe sterte
And sayth arise/ and do May obseruaūce
 This maketh Emely to haue remēbraūce
To don honour to May/and for to ryse
I clothed was she fresshe for to deuyse
Her yelowe heare was broyded in a tresse
Behynde her backe/a yerde longe I gesse
And in the gardyn at sonne vpryst
She walketh vp and downe as her lyst
She gadreth floures/party whyte & reed
To make a subtell garlande for her heed
And as an angell/heuenly she songe
The great tour/ ẏ was so thicke & stronge
Whiche of the castell was ẏ chefe dungeon
Wherin the knyghtes were in prison
Of whiche I tolde you/and tell shall
Was euyn ioynaunt to the garden wall
There as this Emely had her playeng
 Bright was the son / & clere the mornynge
And Palamon/this wofull prisoner
As was his won/by leaue of his gayler
Was rysen/& romed in a chambre on hyghe
In whiche he all the noble cyte syghe
And eke the gardyn/ful of braunches grene
There as this fresshe Emely the shene
Was in her walke/ & romed vp and down.
 This sorowfull prisoner/this Palamon
Gothe in his chambre romyng to and fro
And to him selfe complaynyng of his wo
That he was borne/full ofte sayd alas

And so befell by auenture or caas
That thrugh a widow thick of many a bar
Of yren gret/ & square as any spar
He caste his eyen vpon Emelia
And therwith he blent and cryed/ ha.
As though he stongen were to the herte
And with that crye Arcite anon vp sterte
And sayd/ Cosyn myn/ what eyleth the
That arte so pale and deedly for to se:
Why cryest thou: who hath do the offence:
For goddes loue/ take all in pacience
Our prison/ for it may none other be
Fortune hath yeuen vs this aduersyte.
Some wycked aspect or disposycion
Of Saturne/ by some constellacion
Hath yeuen vs this / altho we had it sworn
So stode the heuen/ whan yt we were born
We mote endure/ this is short and playn.
This Palamon answerde/ & said agayn:
Cosyn forsoth/ of this opinyon
Thou hast a vayne ymagynacion
This prison caused me nat to crye
But I was hurt right now thrugh myn ey
Into myn herte/ that woll my bane be
The fayrnesse of a lady that I se
Yonde in the gardyn/ romyng to and fro
Is cause of all my cryeng and wo
I not wher she be woman or goddesse
But Venus it is / sothly as I gesse
And therwith all on knees down he fyll
And sayd: Venus/ if it be thy wyll
You in this gardyn/ thus to transfygure
Beforne me/ sorowfull wretched creature
Out of this prison helpe that we may scape
And if our desteny be so ishape
By eterne worde/ to dyen in prison
Of our lynage haue some compassyon
That is so lowe ybrought by tyranny.
And with that worde Arcyte gan espy
Where as the lady romed to and fro
And with that sight her bewte hurt him so
That if that Palamon were wounded sore
Arcite was hurt as moche as he/ or more
And with a syghe he said pitously
The fresshe beutie sleeth me sodenly
Of her that rometh in the yonder place
And but I haue her mercy and her grace
That I may seen her at the leste way
I nam but deed/ there nys no more to say.

This Palamon/ whā he these wordes herd
Dispytously he loked/ and answerd:
Whether sayest thou this i ernest or in play
Nay quod Arcite/ in ernest by my fay
God helpe me so/ me lyst full puell to pley
This Palamō gan knyt his browes twey
It were (quod he) to the no great honour
To be false, ne for to be traytour
To me/ that am thy cosen & thy brother
Isworne full depe/ and eche of vs to other
That neuer for to dyen in the payne
Tyll that the dethe departe vs twayne
Neyther of vs in loue to hyndre other
Ne in none other case my leue brother
But that thou shuldest truly further me
In euery case/ as I shulde further the
This was thyn othe/ and myn also certayn
I wote it well/ thou darst it not withsayn
Thus arte thou of my counsell out of doute
And nowe thou woldest falsly ben aboute
To loue my lady/ whom I loue and serue
And euer shall/ tyll that myn herte sterue.
Nowe certes false Arcite thou shalt not so
I loued her first/ and tolde the my wo
As to my counsell/ & to my brother sworne
To further me/ as I haue tolde beforne
For whiche thou art ibounden/ as a knyght
To helpen me/ if it lye in thy myght
Or els arte thou false/ I dare well sayne
This Arcite full proudly spake agayne.
Thou shalt (quod he) be rather fals than I
And thou arte false I tell the vtterly.
For paramour I loued her first or thou
What wilt yu sayn/ thou wist it nat or now
Whether she be woman or goddesse
Thyn is affection of holynesse
And myn is loue/ as to a creature
For whiche I tolde the myn auenture
As to my cosyn/ and my brother sworne
Suppose that thou louedst her byforne
Wost thou not well the olde clerkes sawe:
That/ who shall gyue a louer any lawe:
Loue is a gretter lawe by my pan
Than may be yeuen to any erthly man

And therfore posityfe lawe/ & suche decre
Is broken all day for loue in eche degre
A man mote nedes loue maugre his heed
He may nat fleen it though he shuld be deed
All be she mayde/ wydowe/ or wyfe
  And eke it is not lykely all thy lyfe
To stonden in her grace/ nomore shall I
For well thou wost thy selfe verely
That thou and I be dampned to prison
Perpetuell/ vs gayneth no raunson
  We stryuen/ as dyd the houndes for ẏ bone
That faughte al day/ & yet her pte was non
Ther cam a cur/ whise ẏ they wer so wroth
And bare away the bone from hem bothe
And therfore/ at kynges court my brother
Eche man for him selfe/ there is non other
Loue if thou lyst/ for I loue and ay shall
And sothly lefe brother this is all
Here in this prison mote we endure
And eueryche of vs taken his auenture.
  Gret was the strife betwixe hem twey
If that I had leyser for to sey
But to theffect/ It happed on a day
To tell it you shortly as I may.
  A worthy duke that hyght Perithous
    That felowe was to duke Theseus
Syth thylke day ẏ they were chyldren lyte
Was come to Athenes/ his felow to visyte
And for to play/ as he was wonte to do
For in this worlde he loued no man so
And he loued hym as tenderly agayne
So well they loued/ as olde bokes sayne
That whan ẏ one was deed/ sothly to tell
His felow went & sought him down in hell
But of that story lyst me not to write
  Duke Perithous loued well Arcite
And had him know at Thebes yere by yere
And fynally at request and prayere
Of Perithous/ withouten any raunson
Duke Theseus set him out of prison
Frely to gon/ whither him lyst ouer all
In suche a gyse/ as I you tellen shall.
  This was ẏ forwarde/ playnly to endyte
Betwyx duke Theseus and hym Arcyte
That if so were/ that Arcite were yfounde
Euer in his lyfe/ by day/ night or stounde
In any countre of this duke Theseus
And he were caught/ it was acorded thus
That with a swerde he shulde lese his heed
There nas none other remedy ne reed
But taketh his leaue/ & homward him sped
Let him beware/ his necke lyeth to wedde
  Howe great sorowe suffreth now Arcite:
The dethe he feleth through his herte smyte
He wepeth/ wayleth/ & cryeth pitously
To sleen him selfe he wayteth priuely
And said/ alas the day that I was borne
Nowe is my prison worse than beforne
Nowe is me shappen eternally to dwell
Nought in purgatory/ but in hell
  Alas that euer I knewe Perithous
For els had I dwelt with Theseus
Ifetered in his prison euer mo
Then had I be in blysse/ and nat in wo
Onely the syght of her/ whom that I serue
Though ẏ I neuer her grace may deserue
Wolde haue suffysed ryght ynough for me
  O dere cosyn Palamon (quod he)
Thyn is the victory of this auenture
Full blyssfull in prison mayst thou endure
In prison/ Nay certes but in paradyse
Well hath fortune to the tourned the dyse
That hast the syght of her/ and I thabsence
For possible is/ sythnes thou hast her presẽce
And arte a knyght/ a worthy man & able
That by sõe case/ syn fortune is chaũgeable
Thou mayst somtyme to thy desyre attayne
  But I that am exiled/ and barayne.
Of all grace/ and in so great dispeyre
That ther nys water/ erthe/ fyre/ ne eyre
Ne creature/ that of hem maked is
That may me heale/ or don comfort in this
Wel ought I sterue in wanhope & distresse
Farwell my lyfe/ my lust/ & my gladnesse
  Alas/ why playnen men so in comune
Of puruepaunce of god/ or of fortune
That yeueth hem full ofte in many agyse
Well bette than hem selfe can deuyse
Some man desyreth to haue rychesse
That cause is of her murdre or sickenesse
And som man wold out of his prison fayn
That in his house/ is of his meyne slayne
Infinyte harmes ben in this matere
We wote not what thyng we prayen here

C.iii. We

We faren as he, that dronke is as a mouse
A dronken man wote well, he hath an house
But he wot nat, which the right way thider
And to a dronken man the way is slyder
And certes in this worlde so faren we
 We seken fast after felicite
But we go wronge full ofte truly
Thus may we say all, and namely I
That wenden, and had a great opinion
That if I might scape fro prison
Than had I ben in ioye and parfite hele
There nowe I am exiled fro my wele
Sithe that I may nat seen you Emely
I nam but deed, there nys no remedy.
¶ Upon that other syde Palamon
Whan that he wist Arcite was gon
Such sorowe he maketh, ẏ the great tour
Resowned of his yellyng and clamour
The pure fetters on his shynnes grete
Were of his bytter salte teares wete
 Alas (quod he) Arcite cosyn myne
Of all our strife, god wot ẏ frute is thyne
Thou walkest nowe in Thebes at large
And of my wo, thou yeuest lytel charge
Thou maist, sith yͧ hast wysdōe ⁊ māhede
Assemble all the folke of our kynrede
And make werre so sharpe in this countre
That by some auenture, or by some treate
Thou maist haue her to lady and to wyfe
For whom I must nedes lese my lyfe
For as by way of possibilite
Sithe thou arte at thy large of prison fre
And art a lorde, great is thyne auauntage
More than is myn, ẏ sterue here in a cage
For I may wepe ⁊ wayle, whiles ẏ I lyue
With all the wo that prison may me yeue
And eke with payne, ẏ loue yeueth me also
That doubleth all my tourment ⁊ my wo
 Therwith the fyre of ielousy up stert
Within his brest, and hent hym by the hert
So woodly, that he lykely was to beholde
The boxe tree, or the asshen deed and colde
Than said he. O cruell goddes, ẏ gouerne
This worlde with your worde eterne
And writen in the table of Athamant
Your parliament and eterne graunt
What is mankynde more unto you yholde
Than is the shepe, that rouketh in the folde?
For slayne is man, right as a nother beest
And dwelleth eke in prison, and in arrest
And hath sickenesse, and great aduersyte
And oft tyme gyltlesse parde.
 What gouernance is in this prescience
That gyltlesse turmenteth innocence?
And encreaseth thus all my penaunce
That man is bounden to his obseruaunce
For goddes sake, to leten of his wyll
There as a beest may all his lustes fulfyll
And whan a beest is deed, he hath no payn
But after his deth mā mote wepe ⁊ playn:
Though in this worlde he haue care ⁊ wo
Without doute it may stonden so.
 The answere of this lete I to diuynes
But wel I wote, in this world gret pyne is
Alas I se a serpent or a thefe
That many a true man hath do mischefe
Gon at his large, ⁊ wher him list may turn
But I mote ben in prison through Saturn
And eke through Juno, ialous ⁊ eke wood
That hath stroyed well nye all the blood
Of Thebes, with his waste walles wyde
And Venus sleeth me on that other syde
For ielousye, and feare of him Arcite
 Nowe wyll I stynte of Palamon alyte
And let him in his prison styll dwell
And of Arcite forth woll I you tell.
 The sōmer passeth, ⁊ the nightes longe
Encreseth double wyse the paynes stronge
Bothe of the louer, and of the prisoner
I not whiche hath the wofuller myster
For shortly to saye, this Palamon
Perpetuell is dampned to prison
In chaynes and feters to the deed
And Arcite is exiled on his heed
For euermore as out of that countre
Ne neuer more shall his lady se
 You louers aske I nowe this questyon
Who hath the worse, Arcite or Palamon?
That one may se his lady day by day
But in prison mote he dwell alway
That other where him lyst may ryde or go
But sene his lady shall he neuer mo
 Nowe demeth as ye lyst, ye that can
For I woll tell forthe my tale as I began.
¶ Whan

¶ Whan that Arcite to Thebes comen was
Full ofte a day he swelte and sayd alas
For sene his lady shall he neuer mo
And shortly to conclude/ all his wo
So mykell sorowe made neuer creature
That is or shalbe/ whyle ỷ world may dure
His slepe/ his meate/ his drike is him byraft
That leane he waxeth/ ⁊ drie as a shaft
His eyen holowe/ and grisly to beholde
His hewe pale/ and falowe as asshen colde
And solitary he was/ and euer alone
And waylyng all the night/ makyng mone
And if he herde songe or instrument
Then wolde he wepe/ he might not stent
So feble were his spirytes/ and so lowe
And chaunged so/ ỷ no mā coude him knowe
His speche ne his voyce/ though mē it herde
As in his gyre/ for all the worlde it ferde
Nought comly lyke to louers maladye
Of Hereos/ but rather lyke manye
Engendred of humours melancolyke
Beforne his selfe fantastyke
And shortly was turned all vp so down
Bothe habyte and disposycion
Of him/ this wofull louer Arcyte
What shulde I all day of his wo endyte
Whan he endured had a yere or two
This cruell torment/ ⁊ this payne and wo
At Thebes in his countre/ as I sayde
Upon a night in slepe as he him layde
Him thought howe ỷ the wynged Mercury
Beforne him stode/ ⁊ bade him to be mery
His slepy yerde in hande he bare vpright
An hatte he wered vpon his heares bright
Arayed was this god/ as he toke kepe
As he was/ whan Argus toke his slepe
And said hī thus: to Athenes shalt yu wend
There is the shapen of thy wo an ende
And with that worde Arcite awoke ⁊ stert
Nowe truely howe sore that me smerte
Quod he/ to Athenes right now wol I fare
Ne for no drede of dethe shall I spare
To se my lady/ that I loue and serue
In her presence recke I not to sterue
And wt that word he caught a gret myrrour
And sawe that chaūged was all his colour
And sawe his visage all in a nother kynde
And right anon it ran him in his mynde
That sythe his face was so dissfygured
Of maladye/ the whiche he had endured
He might well/ if that he bare him lowe
Lyue in Athenes euermore vnknowe
And sene his lady well nyghe day by day
And right anon he chaunged his aray
And clad him as a poore labourer
And all alone/ saue onely a squier
That knewe his priuyte and all his caas
Whiche was disgysed poorely as he was
To Athenes is he gon the next way
And to the courte he went vpon a day
And at the gate he profered his seruyce
To druge ⁊ drawe/ what so mē wold deuise
And shortly of this mater for to sayne
He fell in offyce with a chamberlayne
The whiche was dwellyng with Emelye
For he was wyse/ and sone couth espye
Of euery seruaunt/ whiche that serued here
Well couthe he hewen wodde/ ⁊ water bere
For he was yong and mighty for the nones
And therto he was strong ⁊ bygge of bones
To done that any wight can him deuyse.
A yere or two he was in this seruyse
Page of the chambre/ of Emely the bright
And Phylostrate he said that he hyght.
But halfe so well beloued man as he
Ne was there none in court/ of his degre
He was so gentyll of condycion
That through al the court was his renoun
They sayd that it were a charyte
That Theseus wolde enhaūcen his degre
And put him in a worshypfull seruyse
There as he might his vertue exercyse
And thus wtin a whyle his name is spronge
Bothe of his dedes/ and of his good tonge
That Theseus hath taken him so nere
That of his chambre he made hym squyere
And yafe him golde to maynteyn his degre
And eke men brought him out of his coūtre
Fro yere to yere full priuely his rent
But honestly and slyly he it spent
That no man wondred howe he it had
And thre yere in this wyse his lyfe he ladde
And bare him so in peace ⁊ eke in werre
Ther was no man that Theseus hath derre.
¶ And

The Knight's Tale (A 1355–1448; T. 1357–1450)

And in this blysse lete I nowe Arcyte
And speke I woll of Pasamon a lyte.
In derknesse horryble and stronge prison
This seuen yere hath sytten this Pasamon
Forpyned/ what for wo and distresse
Who feleth double sore and heuynesse
But Palamon: that loue distrayneth so
That wode out of his wit/ he gothe for wo
And eke therto he is a prisonere
Perpetuell/and not onely for a yere.
Who coude ryme in englysshe proprely
His martyrdom? forsoth it am nat I
Therfore I passe as lyghtly as I may.
It befell that in the seuenth yere in May
The thirde nyght/as olde bokes sayne
(That all this story tellen more playne)
Were it by auenture or by destyne
As whan a thyng is shapen / it shall be
That soon after mydnight/Palamon
By helpyng of a frende brake his prison
And fleethe the cyte/as fast as he may go
For he had yeue his gayler drinke so
Of a clarrey/made of certen wyne
With narcotise and opye / of Thebes fyne
That al ẏ night/thogh mē wold him shake
The gayler slept/he mighe nat awake
And thus he fleeth as fast as he may.
The nyght was short/ & fast by the day
That nedes cost he mote him selfe hyde
And to a groue faste there besyde
With dredful foote than stalketh Palamon
For shortly this was his opinyon
That in ẏ groue he wolde him hyde all day
And in the night then wold he take his way
To Thebes warde/ his frendes for to prey
On Theseus to helpe hym to warrey
And shortly/eyther he wolde lese his lyfe
Or wynne Emelye vnto his wyfe
This is theffecte/and his entent playne.
¶ Nowe woll I torne to Arcite agayne
That lytell wyst howe nye was his care
Tyl ẏ fortune had brought him ĩ her snare
The mery larke/messanger of day
Saleweth in her songe the morowe gray
And firy Phebus aryseth vp so bright
That all the orisont laugheth of the syght
And with his streames/drieth in the greues
The syluer dropes/hangyng in the leues
And Arcite/that in the courte ryall
With Theseus his squier principall
Is rysen/ and loketh on the mery day
And for to don his obseruaunces to May
Remembring on the poynt of his desyre
He on his courser/startlyng as the fyre
Is ryden in to the feldes him to play
Out of the court/ were it a myle or twey
And to the groue/of whiche I you tolde
By auenture/his way he gan holde
To maken him a garlonde of the greues
Were it of wodbynde/or of hauthorn leues
And loude he songe ayenst the sonne shene.
May/ with all thy floures and thy grene
Welcom be thou/ fayre fresshe May
I hope that I some grene get may
And from his courser/with a lusty herte
In to the groue full hastely he sterte
And in a pathe he romed vp and doun
There/ as by auenture this Palamon
Was in a busshe/that no man might hi[m] se
For sore aferde of his dethe was he
Nothyng ne knewe he, that it was Arcite
God wote he wolde haue trowed full lyte
But sothe is said/go sythen many yeres
That felde hath eyen / and wodde hath eres
It is full fayre a man to beare him euyn
For al day men mete at vnset steuyn
Full lytell wote Arcite of his felawe
That was so nighe to herken of his sawe
For in the busshe sytteth he nowe full styll
Whan that Arcyte had rome[d] all his fyll
And songen all the roundell lustely
In to a study he fell sodenly
As don these louers in their queynt gyres
Now in the croppe/ & now down in ẏ bires
Nowe vp nowe downe/ as boket in a well
Right as the friday/sothly for to tell
Nowe it rayneth/nowe it shyneth fast
Right so gan gery Venus ouer cast
The hertes of her folke/right as her day
Is gerysull/ right so chaungeth she aray
Selde is the friday all the weke ilyke
Whan ẏ Arcite had songe/he gan to syke
And set him downe withouten any more
Alas (quod he) the day that I was bore

Nowe

Howe longe Juno through thy crueltee
Wylt thou werren Thebes the citee
Alas ybrought is to confusyon
The blode ryall of Cadmus & Amphyon
  Of Cadmus / whiche was the first man
That Thebes buylt/or first the town began
And of the cyte first was crowned kyng
Of his lynage am I/and of his offspring
By very lyne/as of the stocke ryall
And nowe I am so caytife and so thrall
That he that is my mortall enemy
I serue him/as his squire poorly
And yet dothe me Juno well more shame
For I dare nat be knowe myn own name
But there as I was wont to hyght Arcyte
Now hight I Philostrat nat worth a myte
Alas thou fell Mars/ alas thou Juno
Thus hath your yre our lynage all fordo
Saue onely me/and wretched Palamon
That Theseus martreth in prison
And ouer all this/to sleen me utterly
Loue hath his firy darte so brenningly
I stycked through my true carefull herte
That shapen was my deth erst my sherte
Ye sleen me with your eyen Emelye
Ye ben the cause wherfore I dye
Of all the remenaunt of myn other care
Ne set I nat the mountaunce of a tare
So y I coude do ought to your plesaunce
And with y worde he fell down in a traūce
A longe tyme/ and afterwarde he up stert
  This Palamon thought y thrugh his hert
He felte a colde swerde sodenly glyde
For yre he quoke/no lenger wolde he abyde
And whan that he had herde Arcites tale
As he were wood/with face deed and pale
He sterte him up/out of the busshes thycke
And said: Arcyte false traytour wycke
Nowe art thou hent/that louest my lady so
For whom that I haue this payne and wo
And art my bloode/& to my counsell sworn
As I haue full ofte tolde the here beforn
And hast be iaped here duke Theseus
And falsly hast chaunged thy name thus
I wyll be deed/or els thou shalt dye
Thou shalt nat loue my lady Emelye
But I woll loue her onely and no mo
For I am Palamon thy mortall foe
Though y I haue no weapen in this place
But out of prison am astert by grace
I drede not/that eyther thou shalt dye
Or thou ne shalt not louen Emelye
Chese which thou wilt/or yͧ shalt not astert
  This Arcite/ with full dispytous hert
Whan he him knewe/ & had his tale herde
As fiers as a lyon/pulled out his swerde
And sayd: By god that sytteth aboue
Ne were it y thou art sicke/& wood for loue
And eke y thou no wepen hast in this place
Thou shuldest neuer out of this groue pace
That thou ne shuldest dyen of myn honde
For I defye the suretie & the bonde
Whiche y thou sayst y I haue made to the
What very fole/ thinke wel that loue is fre
And I wyl loue her maugre all thy myght
But for as moche as thou arte a knyght
And wylnest to darrayne here by batayle
Haue here my trouth/to morow I wyl nat
without wetyng of any other wight (fayle
That here I woll be founden as a knyght
And bringen harneys/right ynough for the
And chese the best/& leaue the worst for me.
And meate & drinke/this night wyl I bring
Inough for the/& clothes for thy beddyng
And if so be that thou my lady wyn
And slee me in this wodde ther I am in
Thou mayst wel haue thy lady as for me.
  This Palamon answerde: I graūt it the
And thus they ben departed tyll a morowe
Whā ech of hem had laid his faith to borow
¶ O Cupyde out of all charyte
O regne/y woldest haue no felowe wͭ the
Full sothe is sayd/that loue ne lordshyp
Woll not his thankes haue any felyshyp
We fynde that of Arcite and of Palamon
  Arcyte is rydden anon in to the toun
And on the morowe or it were day lyght
Full priuely two harneys hath he dyght
Bothe suffycient and mete to darreygne
The batayle in y felde betwyx hem tweyne
And on his horse/a lone as he was borne
He caryeth all his harneys him beforne
And in the groue/at tyme and place ysette
This Arcyte & this Palamon ben mette

To

To chaungen gan the colour in her face
Ryght as the hunter/in yͤ regne of Trace
That ſtandeth at a gappe with a ſpeare
Whan hunted is the lyon or the beare
And hereth him ruſſhyng in the leaues
And breaketh the bowes in the greaues
And thiketh/here cometh my mortal enemy
Without fayle/he muſt be deed or I
For eyther I mote ſlee hym at the gappe
Or he mote ſlee me/if me myſhappe
So ferden they/ in chaungyng of her hewe
As farre as eueryche of other knewe
There nas no good day/ne no saluyng
But ſtreyght/ without worde or rehersyng
Eueryche of hem helpeth for to arme other
As frendly/as he were his owne brother
And after that/with ſharpe ſpeares ſtronge
They foynen eche at other wonder longe
Thou myghteſt wene/ that this Palamon
In his fyghtyng/were a woode lyon
And as a cruell tygre was Arcyte
As wylde bores gan they fyght ɫ ſmyte
That frothen whyte as fome for yre woode
Vp to the ancle foughten they in her bloode
And in this wiſe/ I let hem fightyng dwell
And forthe I woll of Theſeus you tell.
The deſtenye and the mynyſter generall
That executeth in the worlde ouer all
The purueyaunce/ yͭ god hath ſayd byforne
So ſtrõg it is/ yͭ thogh yͤ world had ſworn
The contrary of thyng by ye or nay
Yet ſomtyme it ſhall fall on a day
That fell neuer yet in a thouſande yere
For certaynly our appetytes here
Be it of warre/peace/hate/ or loue
All is ruled by the ſyght aboue.
This meane I nowe by mighty Theſeus
That for to hunte is ſo deſyrous
And namely at the great harte in May
That in his bed there daweth him no day
That he nys clad/and redy for to ryde
With hunt ɫ horne/ɫ houndes him beſyde.
For in his huntyng hath he ſuche delyte
That it is all his ioye and appetyte
To ben him ſelfe the great hartes bane
For after Mars/he ſerueth nowe Dyane
Clere was the day/as I haue tolde or this
And Theſeus/with all ioye and blys
With his Ypolita/the fayre quene
And Emely/ yclothen all in grene
An huntyng ben they rydden ryally.
And to the groue/that ſtode there faſt by
In which ther was an harte/as mẽ him told
Duke Theſeus the ſtreyght way hath hold
And to the launde/ he rydeth him full ryght
For thyd̃ was yͤ hart wõt to haue his flight
And ouer a broke/ɫ ſo forthe on his wey
This duke wol haue a cours at him or twey
With hoũdes/ſuche as him lyſt cõmaunde
And whan yͤ duke was comen into yͤ laũde
Vnder the ſonne he loked/ and that anon
He was ware of Arcyte and Palamon
That foughtẽ breme/ as it were bulles two
The bright ſwordes wenten to and fro
So hydouſly/that with the leſte ſtroke
It ſemed/that it wolde haue fellen an oke
But what they weren/ nothyng he ne wote
This duke wᵗ his ſporꝭ his courſer ſmote
And at a ſterte he was bytwyxt hem two
And pulled out his ſworde/and cryed/ho
Nomore/on payne of leſyng of your heed
By mighty Mars/he ſhall anon be deed
That ſmyteth any ſtroke/ that I may ſeen
But telleth me/ what myſter men ye ben
That ben ſo hardy for to fyghten here
Without iuge/or other offycere
As though it were in lyſtes rially.
This Palamon anſwerde haſtely
And ſayd: ſyr/ what nedeth wordes mo?
We haue the dethe deſerued bothe two
Two woful wretches ben we ɫ captiues
That ben encombred of our owne lyues
And as thou arte a rightfull lorde ɫ iuge
Ne yeue vs neyther mercy ne refuge
But ſlee me firſt/ for ſaynt charite
But ſlee my felowe as well as me
Or ſle him firſt / for though yͧ knowe it lite
This is thy mortall foe/ this is Arcite
That fro thy lande is baniſſhed on his heed
For whiche he hath deſerued to be deed
For this is he/that came vnto thy yate
And ſaid/ that he hight Philoſtrate
Thus hath he iaped full many a yere
And thou haſt made him thy chefe ſquiere

And

And this is he/that loueth Emely.
  For sythe the day is come that I shall dye
I make playnly my confessyon
I am thylke wofull Palamon
That hath thy prison broke wyckedly
I am thy mortall foe/and he am I
That loueth so hotte Emelye the bright
That I woll dye here present in her syght
wherfore I aske dethe and my iewyse
But slee my felowe in the same wyse
For bothe we haue deserued to be slayn.
  This worthy duke answerde anon agayn
And sayd/this is a shorte conclusyon
Your owne mouthe/ by your confessyon
Hath dampned you/and I woll it recorde
It nedeth not to pyne you with a corde
Ye shall be deed by myghty Mars the reed
  The quene anone/for very womanheed
Gan for to wepe/and so dyd Emelye
And all the ladyes in the companye
Great pyte was it/as thought hem all
That euer suche a chaunce shulde befall
For gentylmen they were of great estate
And nothyng but for loue was this debate
And sawe her blody woundes wyde & sore
And all cryden bothe lesse and more
Haue mercy lorde vpon vs wymen all
And on her bare knees downe they fall
And wolde haue kyst his fete there he stode
Tyl at the last/ a slaked was his mode
For pyte renneth sone in gentle herte
And though he first for yre quoke & sterte
He hath consydred shortly in a clause
The trespas of hem bothe/ & eke the cause
And al though his yre her gylt accused
Yet in his reason he hem bothe excused
As thus: he thought well that euery man
Woll helpe hym selfe in loue all that he can
And eke delyuer himselfe out of prison
And eke his herte had compassyon
Of wymen/for they wepen euery in one
And in his gentle herte he thought anone
And softe vnto hymselfe he sayd: fy
Vpon a lorde, that woll haue no mercy
But be a lyon/bothe in worde and dede
To hem that ben in repentaunce & in drede
As well as to a proude dispytous man
That wyll maynteyne that he first began.
  That lorde hath lytell of discretyon
That in suche case can no diffynition
But wayeth pride and humblesse after one
And shortly/whan his yre was thus agone
He gan to loken vp with eyen lyght
And spake these wordes all on hyght.
  The god of loue/ ah/ benedicite
Howe myghty/& howe great a lorde is he
Agayn his might ther gayneth no obstacles
He may be cleaped a god for his myracles
For he can maken at his owne gyse
Of euerych hert/as him lyst deuyse
  Lo here this Arcyte/and this Palamon
That quitely were out of my prison gon
And myght haue lyued in Thebes ryally
And knowen I am her mortall enemy
And that her dethe is in my power also
And yet hath loue/maugre her eyen two
Brought hem hyther bothe for to dye
Nowe loketh/is not this a great folye?
Who may be a fole/ but if he loue?
Beholde for goddes sake/that sytteth aboue
Se howe they blede/be they nat wel arayde
Thus hath her lord/y god of loue hem payd
Her wages/& her fees for her seruyse
And yet they wenen to be full wyse
That serue loue/for aught that may befall
But yet is this the best game of all
That she/ for whom they haue this iolyte
Can hem therfore / as moche thanke as me
She wotte nomore of all this hote fare
By god/than wotte a cokowe or an hare
But all mote ben assayed hote & colde
A man mote ben a foole other yong or olde
I wote it by my selfe full yore agone
For in my tyme/a seruante was I one
And therfore syth I knowe of loues payne
I wote howe sore it can a man distrayne
As he that ofte hath be caught in her laas
I you foryeue all hooly this trespaas
At the request of the quene/y kneleth here
And eke of Emely/my syster dere
And ye shall bothe anon vnto me swere
That ye shall neuer more my countre dere
Ne make warre vpon me nyght ne day
But ben my frendes in all that ye may

I you

I you foryeue this trespas euery dele
And they hym sware his askyng fair & wele
And hym of lordshyp & of mercy prayde
And he hem graunted grace/ & thus he sayde.

To speake of worthy lynage & ryches
Though yͤ she were a quene/ or a princesse
Ilke of you bothe is worthy doutles
To wedde whan tyme is/ but netheles
I speke/ as for my syster Emely
For whom ye haue this stryfe & ielowsy
Ye wote your selfe/ she may not wedde two
At ones/ though ye fyghten euer mo
But one of you/ all be hym lothe or lefe
He mote go pype in an yue lefe
This is to say/ she may not haue bothe
Ne ben ye neuer so ielous/ ne so wrothe
And therfore/ I you put in this degre
That eche of you shall haue his destyne
As hym is shape/ and herken in what wyse
Lo here your ende/ of that I shall deuyse.
My wyll is this/ for plat conclusyon
Without any replycation
If that you lyketh/ taketh it for the best
That euerich of you shall go where hym lest
Frely/ without raunsome or daungere
And this day fyfty wekes/ ferre ne nere
Euerich of you shall bring an. C. knightes
Armed for the lystes vp all rightes
All redy to darreyne here by batayle
And this behote I you withouten fayle
Vpon my trouthe/ as I am true knyght
That wheder of you both/ hath that might
That is to say/ that wheder he or thou
May with his hũdred/ as I spake of nowe
Slee his contrary/ or out of lystes dryue
Hym shall I yeue Emely to wyue
To whom yͤ fortune yeueth so faire a grace
The lystes shall I maken in this place
And god so wisely on my soule rewe
As I shall euyn iuge be and trewe
Ye shall non other ende with me make
That one of you shalbe deed or take
And if ye thynken/ this is well sayd
Saith your auise/ & holde you well apayde
This is your ende/ and your conclusion.
Who loketh lightly now but Palamon?
Who springeth vp for ioye but Arcite?
Who coude tell/ or who coude endite?
The ioye that is made in this place
Whan Theseus had don so fayre a grace
But doun on knees wẽt euery maner wight
And thanked hym/ with all her hert & myght
And namely these Thebans many sithe
And thus with good hope and hert blythe
They take her leue/ & hõward gan they ride
To Thebes warde/ with olde walles wyde
I trowe men wolde deme it neglygence
Yf I foryetten to tell the dispence
Of Theseus/ that gothe so busely
To maken vp the lystes royally
That suche a noble Theatre/ as it was
I dare well say/ in this worlde there nas
The circute a myle was about
Walled with stone/ and diched all about
Rounde was the shape/ in maner of a cõpas
Full of degrees/ the height of sixty paas
That whan a man was set on one degre
He letted nat his felowe for to se
Estward there stode a gate of marble white
Westwarde right suche another ī thopposite
And shortly to conclude/ suche a place
Was non in erthe/ as in so lytell space
For in the londe/ there nas no craftes man
That gemetry/ or arsmetrike can
Ne portrepture/ ne caruer of ymages
That Theseus ne gaue hym mete & wages
The theatre for to make and deuyse.
And for to do his rite and sacrifyce
He estwarde hath vpon the yate aboue
In worship of Venus/ goddes of loue
Do make an auter/ and an oratory
And on the westsyde/ in memory
Of Mars/ he hath maked suche another
That cost of golde largely a fother
And northwarde/ in a turret in the wall
Of alabastre white/ and redde corall
An oratory/ riche for to se
In worship of Diane/ goddes of chastite
Hath Theseus do wrought in noble wyse.
But yet had I foryetten to deuyse
The noble caruynges and the portratures
The shap/ the countenaunce/ & the fygures
That weren in the oratories thre

Fyrst

The Knight's Tale (A 1825–1917; T. 1827–1919)

The knyghtes tale.

First in the temple of Venus thou mayst se
Wrought on the wal/ful pitously to beholde
The broken slepes/and the syghes colde
The saulte teares/and the waymentyng
The fyre strokes/and the despyring
That loues seruauntes in this lyfe enduren
The othes/that her couenauntes assuren
Plesaunce & hope/desyre/foolehardynesse
Beauty and youthe/baudry and rychesse
Charmes and sorcery/leasynges & flaterye
Dispence/busynesse/ and ielousye
That weared of yelowe goldes a garlonde
And a cokowe syttyng on her honde.
Feestes/instrumentes/carolles/ & daunces
Lustes and aray/and all the cyrcumstaũces
Of loue/whiche I reken and reken shall
By ordre / were paynted on the wall
And mo than I can make of mencyon
For sothly all the mounte of Cytheron
Wher Venus hath her princypall dwellyng
Was shewed on the wall in portreyng
With all the ioye/and the lustynesse
Nought was forgeten the porteresse ydlenesse
Ne Narcissus the fayre of yore agon
Ne yet the folye of kyng Salomon
Ne yet the great strength of Hercules
Thenchauntement of Medea and Circes
Ne of Turnus/ with his hardy fyers corage
The ryche Cresus captife in seruage
Thus may ye sen/that wysdom ne rychesse
Beaute ne sleyght/strength ne hardynesse
Ne may with Venus holde champartye
For as her lyst the worlde may she gye
Lo/all these folke so caught were in her laas
Tyll they for wo full ofte sayd alas
Suffyseth here one ensample or two
And though I coude reken a thousande mo
  The statue of Venus glorious to se
Was naked fletyng in the large see
And fro the nauyll downe all couered was
With wawes grene/& bright as any glas
A cytriole in her ryght hande had she
And on her heed/full semely for to se
A rose garlande/fresshe and well smellyng
Aboue her heed doues flytteryng
Beforne her stode her sonne Cupido
Vpon his shoulders wynges had he two
And blynde he was/as it is ofte sene
A bowe he had/& arowes bright and kene
Why shulde I not as well tellen all
The purgatory that was ther about ouer all
Within the temple of mighty Mars the rede:
Al paynted was the wall in lenght & in brede
Lyke to the Estris of the grysly place
That hyght yͤ gret temple of Mars in Trace
In thylke colde frosty regyon
Ther Mars hath his soueraygne mancyon
  First on the wall was paynted a forest
In whiche ther wonneth nother man ne best
With knotty and knarry trees olde
Of stubbes sharpe/and hydous to beholde
In whiche there was a romble & a showe
As though a storme shulde breke euery bowe
And downward vnder an hyll vnder a bent
Ther stode the temple of Mars armypotent
Wrought al of burned stele/of which thentre
Was longe and streyght/ & gastly for to se
And therout came suche a rage & such a vyse
That it made all the gates for to ryse
The northern lyght in at the dores shone
For wyndowe on the wall was there none
Through which mẽ might any light discerne
The dores were all of athamant eterne
Yclenched ouerthwarte and endlonge
With yren toughe/for to maken it stronge
Euery pyller/the temple to sustene
Was tonne great/of yren bright and shene
  There sawe I first the derke ymaginyng
Of felony/and eke the compassyng:
The cruell yre/redde as any glede
The pyckpurse/and eke the pale drede
The smyler/with the knyfe vnder the cloke
The shepen brennyng with the blacke smoke
The treason of the murdring in the bedde
The open warre/with woundes al be bledde
Cõtecke with blody knyues/ & sharpe manace
All full of chyrkyng was that sory place
  The sleer of hym selfe yet sawe I there
His herte blood hath bathed all his here
The nayle ydriuen in the shode on hyght
With colde deth/ wͭ mouth gapyng vpright
  Amyddes of the temple sate Myschaunce
With discomfort/and sory countenaunce
  yet sawe I wodnesse/laughyng in his rage

Armed complaynte on thest ⁊ fyers courage
The carrayne in the busshe/ Wt throte ycorue
A thousande slayne/ ⁊ nat of qualme ystorue
The tyraunt/ With the pray by force yraft
The town distroyed/ ther was nothyng laft
 yet sawe I brent the shyppes hoppesteres
The hūter ystrangled With ẏ Wylde beares
The sowe frettyng the chylde in the cradyll
The coke yscaulded/ for al his longe ladyll
Naught Was foryeten ẏ infortune of Marte
The carter ouer rydden by his owne carte
Vnder the whele/ full lowe he laye a down
 There Were allso of Martes diuysyon
The barbour/ the boucher/ and the smyth
That forgeth sharpe swordes on the styth
 And all aboue depaynted in a toure
Sawe I Cōquest/ syttyng in great honoure
With the sharpe sworde ouer his heed
Hangyng by a subtyll twyned threde
 Depaynted Was ther/ ẏ slaughter of Iulius
Of great Nero/ and of Anthonius
Al be that thylke tyme they Were vnborne
yet was her dethe depaynted there beforne
By manacyng of Mars/ right by fygure
So Was it shewed in that portreture
As is depaynted in the certres aboue
Who shall be deed or els slayne for loue
Suffyseth one ensample in storyes olde
I may not reken them al/ though I Wolde
The statue of Marce vpon a carte stode
Armed/ and loked grym as he Were wode
And ouer his heed there shynen two fygures
Of sterres/ that ben cleped in scryptures
That one (Puella) hight/ ẏ other (Rubeus)
This god of armes Was araped thus
A wolfe there stode beforne him at his fete
With eyen redde/ and of a man he ete
With subtyll pensyll Was paynted this story
In redoutyng of Marce and of his glory.
 Nowe to the temple of Dyane the chaste
As shortly as I can I Woll me haste
To tell you al the discripcyon
Depaynted ben the walles vp and down
Of huntyng and of shamfast chastyte
There sawe I howe Wofull Calistope
Whan that Dyane greued Was With her
Was turned fro a Woman to a bere
And afterwarde was she made the lode sterre
Thus was it paynted/ I can say no ferre
Her sonne is eke a sterre/ as men may se
 There sawe I Dane turned vnto a tre
I meane nat the goddesse Dyane
But Venus doughter/ whiche ẏ hyght Dane
 There sawe I Athcon an herte ymaked
For vengeaunce ẏ he sawe Dyane al naked
I sawe how ẏ his houndes haue him caught
And freten hym/ for they knewe him nought
Yet ypaynted was a lytel ferthermore
Howe Athalant hunted the wylde bore
And Meliager/ and many other mo
For Whiche Dyane Wrought hym care ⁊ Wo
There sawe I many a nother wonder story
Whiche me lyst not to drawe in memory
This goddesse ful Wel vp an hatte she is sete
With smale houndes al aboute her fete
And vnderneth her fete/ she had a moone
Wexyng it Was/ and shulde Wane soone
In gaudy grene/ her statue clothed was
With bowe in hande/ and arowes in a caas
Her eyen cast she ful lowe adown
There Pluto hath his darke regyoun
A Woman trauelyng was her before
But for her chylde/ so longe Was vnbore
Full pytously Lucyna gan she call
And sayd helpe/ for thou mayst best of all
Well coude he paynte lyuely that it Wrought
With many a floryn he the hewes bought.

 Nowe ben these lystes made/ and Theseus
That at his great cost hath araped thus
The temples/ and the theatre euerydell
Whan it Was done/ it liked him wonder wel.
 But stynte I woll of Theseus alyte
And speke of Palamon and of Arcyte
 The day aprocheth of her returnyng
That euerych shuld an hūdred knightes bring
The batayle to darreyne/ as I you tolde
And to Athenes/ her couenaūtes to holde
Hath euerich of hem brought an. C. knightes
Well armed for the warre/ at al ryghtes
And sykerly/ there trowed many a man
That neuer sythnes the worlde began
As for to speke of knyghthode/ of her honde
As farre as god hath made see or londe

Nas

Nas of so fewe so noble a company
For euery wight that loued chyualry
And wolde his thankes haue a passyng name
Hath prayed/that he might be of that game
And wel was him that therto chosen was
For if there fel to morowe suche a caas
ye knowe wel/that euery lusty knyght
That loueth paramours/ & hath his myght
Were it in Englande/or els where
They wolde fayne wyllen to be there
To fyght for a lady/ah/Benedicite
It were a lusty syght for to se
And right so farden they with Palamone
With him there went knyghtes many one
Some wolde ben armed in an habergion
And in a brest plate/with a lyght gyppion
And some wolde haue a payre of plates large
And some wolde haue a pruce sheld or a targe
Some wolde be armed on his legges wele
And haue an axe/& some a mace of stele
There nas non newe gyse/ that it nas olde
Armed were they/as I haue you tolde
Euerych after his opinyon
¶ Ther mayst thou se comyng wt Palamon
Lygurge him selfe/the great kyng of Trace
Blacke was his berde/& manly was his face
The sercles of his eyen in his heed
They glouden bytwyxte yelowe and reed
And lyke a lyon loked he aboute
With kemped heares on his browes stoute
His lymmes great/his brawnes stronge
His sholders brode/his armes rounde & longe
And as the gyse was in his countre
Full hye vpon a chare of golde stode he
With foure whyte bulles in the traps
In stede of a cote armure/ouer his harnaps
With nayles yelowe/& bright as any golde
He hath a beares skyn/cole blacke for olde
His longe heare was kempt behynd his backe
As any rauens fether it shone for blacke
A wrethe of golde arme gret/of huge weight
Vpon his heed/set full of stones bright
Of fyne rubyes and of dyamandes
Aboute his chare ther went whyte allaundes
Twenty and mo/as great as any stere
To hunten at the lyon/or at the wylde bere
And folowed him/with mosel faste ybounde
Collers of golde/and torrettes fyled rounde
An hundred lordes had he in his route
Armed ful wel/with hertes sterne & stoute

With Arcyte/in stories as men fynde
The great Emetrius the kyng of Ynde
Vpon a stede bay/trapped in stele
Couered with a clothe of golde diapred wele
Came rydyng lyke the god of armes Marce
His cote armure was of clothe of Trace
Couched with perle/whyte/rounde & great
His sadell was of brent golde newe ybet
A mantel vpon his sholders hongyng
Brette ful of rubyes/reed as fyre sparklyng
His crypse heare lyke rynges was yronne
And yͤ was yelowe/& gleteryng as the sonne
His nose was hye/his eyen bright cytren
His lyppes ruddy/his colour was sanguen
A fewe frekles in his face yspreynte
Betwyxt yelowe/& somedele blacke ymeynte
And as a lyon he his eyen keste
Of fyue and twenty yere his age I geste
His berde was wel begonne for to spryng
His voyce was as a trompet sownyng
Vpon his heed he weared of laurer grene
A garlande fresshe and lusty for to sene
Vpon his honde he bare for his delyte
An egle tame/as any lylly whyte
An hundred lordes had he with hym there
All armed saue her heedes in her gere
Full rychely in all maner thinges
For trusteth wel/that erles/dukes/& kynges
Were gathered in this noble companye
For loue/and for encreace of chyualrye
Aboute this kyng there ran on euery parte
Ful many a tame lyon and lyberde
And in this wise/these lordes al & some
Ben on the sonday to the cyte come
Aboute prime/and in the towne a lyght
¶ This These9/this duke/this worthy knight
Whan he had brought hem in to his cyte
And inned hem/euerych after his degre
He feesteth hem/and dothe so great laboure
To easen hem/and don hem al honoure
That yet men wenen that no mannes wyt
Of none estate coude amende it
The mynstralcye/the seruyce at the feest

O.ii. Th

The great yestes to the moste and leest
The riche array/throughout Theseus paleys
Ne who sate first ne laste upon the deys
What ladyes fayrest ben or best dauncyng
Or whiche of hem can best daunce or syng
Ne who moste felyngly speketh of loue
Ne what haukes sytten or prechen aboue
Ne what houndes lyggen on the flour adoun
 Of al this nowe make I no mencioun
But al the effecte/that thynketh me the beste
Now cometh yͤ poynt/harkeneth if you leste

 The soday at night/or day began to springe
Whan Palamon the larke herde synge
Al though it were nat day by houres two
Yet songe the larke/& Palamon right tho
With holy herte/and with an hye corage
He rose up/to wenden on his pylgrimage
Unto the blyssful Cytherea benygne
I meane Venus/honorable and dygne
And in her hour/he walketh forth apaas
Unto the lystes/there the temple was
And downe he kneleth/& with humble chere
And harte sore/he sayd as ye shal here.
 Fayrest of fayre: O lady myn Venus
Doughter of Ioue/and spouse to Vulcanus
Thou glader of the mounte of Cytheron
For thylke loue thou haddest to Adon
Haue pyte of my bytter teares smerte
And take my humble prayer at thyn herte
 Alas/I ne haue no langage to tell
The effecte/ ne the tourment of myne hel
Myne herte may nat myne harmes bewray
I am so confused that I can nat say
But mercy lady bright that woste wele
My thought/ and seest what harmes yͭ I fele
Consyder al this/ and rewe upon my sore
As wysely as I shal for euermore
Emforth my might thy trewe seruaunt to be
And holde warre alwaye with chastyte
That make I myne auowe so ye me helpe
I kepe nat of armes for to yelpe
Ne I ne aske to morowe to haue victory
Ne renoume in this case/ ne vayne glory
Of pryse of armes to blowen up and downe
But wolde haue fully possessyoun
Of Emely/ and dye in her seruyce
Fynde thou the maner howe & in what wyse
I recche nat/ but it maye better be
To haue victory of hem or they of me
So that I haue my lady in myne armes
For though so be that Mars is god of armes
Your vertue is so great in heuen aboue
That if you lyste I shal wel haue my loue
Thy temple shal I worshippe euermo
And on thyne auter where I ryde or go
I wol done sacrifyce and fyres bete
And if ye wol nat so my lady swete
Than pray I you/ to morowe with a spere
That Arcyte me through the herte bere
Than recke I nat whan I haue lost my lyfe
Though Arcyte wynne her to wyfe
This is theffecte and ende of my prayere
Yeue me my lady thou blyssful lady dere
 Whan the orison was done of Palamon
His sacrifyce he dyde and that anon
Ful pitously with al circumstaunces
Al tel I nat as nowe his obseruaunces.
 But at the last the statue of Venus shoke
And made a signe/ wherby that he toke
That his prayere accepted was that day
For though the signe shewed a delay
Yet wyst he wel that graunted was his bone
And with glad hert he went him hom ful sone

 The thirde hour in equal that Palamon
Began to Venus temple for to gone
Up rose the sonne and up rose Emely
And unto the temple of Diane gan hye
Her maydens/ the whiche thider were ladde
Ful redely with hem the fyre they hadde
The ensence/ the clothes/ & the remenaunt al
That to the sacrifyce longen shal
The hornes ful of meeth as was the gyse
There lacked nought to done her sacrifyce
Smokyng the temple ful of clothes faire
This Emely with herte debonaire
Her body wysshe with water of a wel
But howe she dyde right I dare nat tel
But it be any thyng in general
And yet it were a game to here it al
To him that meaneth wel it were no charge
But it is good a man be at his large
Her bright heer was unkempte & untressed al
A crowne

A crowne of a grene oke vnseryall
Vpon her heed set ful fayre and mete
Two fyres on the auter gan she bete
And dyd her thynges/as men may beholde
In Stace of Thebes/ and these bookes olde
Whan kendled was the fyre/ wt pitous chere
Vnto Dyane she spake as ye may here.
¶O chaste goddesse of the woddes grene
To whom both heuen & erthe and see is sene
Quene of the reygne of Pluto/derke & lowe
Goddesse of maydēs/ þ myn hert hath know
Ful many a yere/and woste what I desyre
As kepe me fro the vengeaunce of thyn yre
That Atteon abought cruelly
Chaste goddesse/wel woste thou that I
Desyre to ben a mayde al my lyfe
Ne neuer wol I be loue ne wyfe
I am thou (woste wel) of thy company
A mayde/and loue huntyng and venery
And for to walken in the woddes wylde
And not for to ben a wyfe/ & ben with chylde
Nought wyl I knowe companye of man
Nowe helpe me lady sythe ye may and can
For tho thre formes that thou haste in the
And Palamon/ þ hath suche a loue to me
And eke Arcite/that loueth me so sore
This grace I pray the/withouten more
And sende loue and peace bytwyxt hem two
And fro me turne away her hertes so
That al her hotte loue/and her desyre
And al her busy turment/and al her fyre
Be queynt/or turned in an other place
And if so be thou wolte not do me that grace
Or if so be my desteny be shapen so
That I shal nedes haue one of hem two
As sende me hym that moste desyreth me
Beholde goddesse of clene chastyte
The bytter teares/that on my chekes fall
Syn thou arte a mayde/and keper of vs all
My maydenhede thou kepe/& wel conserue
And whyle I lyue/a mayden wol I þ serue.
¶The fyres brenne vpon the auter clere
Whyle Emely was thus in her prayere
But sodenly she sawe a thyng queynte
For right anon/one of the fyres queynte
And quycked agayn/and after that anon
That other fyre was queynte/ and al agon
And as it queynte it made a whystlyng
As don these wete brondes in her brennyng
And at the brondes ende/out ran anone
As it were bloddy droppes many one
For whiche so sore agaste was Emelye
That she was wel nye madde/& gan to crye
For she ne wyste what it signyfyed
But onely for the feare thus she cryed.
And wepte/that it was pyte for to here
And therwithal Dyane gan to apere
With bowe in honde/ right as an hunteresse
And sayd doughter/stynte thyn heuynesse
Amonge the goddes hye it is affyrmed
And by eterne worde/wrytten & confyrmed
Thou shalt ben wedded to one of tho
That haue for the so moche care and wo
But vnto whiche of hem I may not tell
Farwell/for I may no lenger dwell
The fyres/whiche on myn auter brenne
Shal declaren/er that thou gon henne
This auenture of loue/as in this case
And with that worde/ the arowes in þ case
Of the goddesse/clateren faste and ryng
And forthe she went/and made vanysshyng
For whiche this Emelye astonyed was
And sayd: what mounteth this/alas
I put me vnder thy protection
Dyane/and vnder thy disposycion
And home she gothe the next way
This is the effecte/there is no more to say.

The next houre of Mars folowyng this
Arcite vnto the temple walked is
Of fyers Mars/to done his sacryfyse
With al the myght of his paynem wyse
With pytous herte/and hye deuocion
Right thus to Mars he sayd his orison.
¶O stronge god/that in the regnes colde
Of Trace honoured arte/and lorde yholde
And haste in euery reigne and euery londe
Of armes/al the brydle in thyn honde
And hem fortunest/as the lyste deuyse
Accepte of me my pytous sacrifyce
If so be my thought may deserue
And that my myght be worthy for to serue
Thy godhede/that I may ben one of thyne
Than pray I the/that thou rue on my pyne

D.iii. For

For thylke payne/and thylke hotte fyre
In whiche thou brentest whylom for desyre
Whan thou usedest the fayre beaute
Of fayre yonge fresshe Venus fre
And haddest her in thyn armes/at thy wyll
Al though thou ones on a tyme missyll
Whan Vulcanus had caught the in his laas
And founde the lyggyng by his wyfe alas
For thylke sorowe/ that was in thyn herte
Haue ruthe as wel on my paynes smerte
  I am yonge and unconnyng / as thou wost
And as I trowe/with loue offended moste
That euer was any lyues creature
For she that dothe me al this wo endure
Ne retcheth neuer/where I synke or flete
And wel I wote/or she me mercy hete
I mote with strength wyne her in this place
And wel I wote/without helpe or grace
Of the/ ne may my strength not auayle
Thā helpe me lorde to morow in my batayle
For thylke fyre/that whylom brent the
As wel as the fyre nowe brenneth me
And do/that I to morowe haue the victory
Myn be the trauayle/ and thyn be the glory
Thy souerayne tēple wol I most honouren
Of any place/and alway moste labouren
In thy plesaunce/and in thy craftes stronge
And in thy temple/ I wol my baner honge
And al the armes of my companye
And euermore/untyl the day I dye
Eterne fyre I wol beforne the fynde
And eke to this auowe I wol me bynde
My berde/my heare/yͭ hongeth lowe adoun
That neuer yet felte offensyoun
Of rasour ne of shere/I wol the yeue
And ben thy true seruaunt whyle I lyue
Now lorde haue ruthe upon my sorowes sore
Yeue me the victory/ I aske the nomore.
¶ The prayer stynte of Arcite the stronge
The rynges on the temple dore they ronge
And eke the dores clatren ful faste
Of whiche Arcite somwhat him agaste.
  The fyres brennen upon the auter bright
That it gan al the temple lyght
A swete smell anon the grounde up yafe
And Arcita anon his honde up hafe
And more ensence in to the fyre he caste
With other rytes mo/and at the laste
The statu of Mars began his hauberke ryng
And with that sounde he herde a murmuring
Ful lowe and dyin/ that sayd thus: victory
For whiche he yafe to Mars honour ⁊ glory
  And thus with ioye/⁊ hope wel to fare
Arcite anon in to his inne is fare
As fayne as foule is of the bright sonne
  And right anon, suche a stryfe is bygonne
For thylke grauntyng/in the heuen aboue
Bytwyxt Venus/the goddesse of loue
And Mars the sterne god armypotent
That Jupiter was busy it to stynte
Tyl that the pale Saturnus the colde
That knewe so many auentures olde
Founde in his experyence and arte
That he ful sone hath pleased euery parte
And sothe is sayd/elde hath great auaūtage
In elde is bothe wysdom and usage
Men may the olde out ren/ but not out rede
  Saturne anon/to stynten stryfe ⁊ drede
Al be it that it be agayne his kynde
Of al this stryfe he can remedye fynde
  My dere doughter Venus/quod Saturne
My course that hath so wyde for to turne
Hath more power than wote any man
Myn is the drenchyng in the see so wan
Myn is the prison in the derke cote
Myn is yͤ strāglyng ⁊ the hōgyng by yͤ throte
The murmure/and the churles rebellyng
The groynyng/ and the priuy enpoysonyng
I do vengeaunce and playne correction
Whyle I dwell in the sygne of the lyon
Myn is the ruyne of the hye halles
The fallyng of the toures ⁊ of the walles
Upon the mynor/or upon the carpenters
I slewe Sampson/ shakyng the pyllers
And myn ben the maladyes colde
The derke treasons/and the castels olde
My lokyng is the father of pestylence
Nowe wepe no more/I shal do my dylygence
That Palamon/that is thyne owne knyght
Shal haue his lady/as thou him behyght
Though Mars shal helpe his knight natheles
Betwyxt you it mote somtyme be pees
Al be ye not of one complection
That causeth al day suche deuysion

I am

The Knight's Tale (A 2383–2476; T. 2385–2478)

I am thyn ayle/redy at thy wyll
Wepe no more/ I wol thy luste fulfyll.
¶ Nowe wol I stynten of these goddes aboue
Of Mars/and of Venus goddesse of loue
And playnly I wol tellen you as I can
The great effecte/of whiche that I began.

Great was the feest in Athenes that day
And eke that lusty season in May
Made euery wyght to ben in suche plesaunce
That al that day iusten they and daunce
And spenten it in Venus hye seruyce
But bycause that they shulden aryse
Erly/for to se the great syght
Unto her rest went they at nyght
And on the morowe whan day gan spring
Of horse and harneys/noyse and clateryng
There was in the hostelryes al aboute
And to the palays rode there many a route
Of lordes/upon stedes and palfreys
There mayste thou se deuysing of harneys
So uncouthe/so riche/& wrought so wele
Of goldsmythry/of braudry/and of stele
The sheldes bright/testers/and trappers
Gold hewen helmes/hauberkes & cot armers
Lordes in paramentes/ on her coursers
Knyghtes of retenue/and eke squyers
Nayling the speares/and helmes bokelyng
Gyggyng of sheldes with layners lacynge
There as nede is/they were nothyng ydell
The fomyng stedes on the golden brydell
Gnawyng/and faste the armurers also
With fyle and hammer/ryding to and fro
Yemen on fote/and communes many one
With shorte staues/ thicke as they may gone
Pypes/trompes/nakoners/and clarions
That in the batayle blowen blody sowns
The palays ful of people up and down
Here thre/there ten/ holdyng her questyon
Deuinyng of these theban knightes two
Some said thus/some said it shulde be so
Some helde with him with the blacke berde
Some with ye balled/some with ye thick herde
Some said he loked grym/and wolde fight
He hath a sparth of twenty poũde of weight.
Thus was the hall ful of deuinyng
Longe after the sonne gan to spring

The great Theseus of his slepe gan wake
With mynstralcye & noyse that they make
Helde yet the chambre of his palays riche
Tyl that the Theban knightes/bothe yliche
Honoured weren/and in to the place ifette.
¶ Duke Theseus is at the wyndowe sette
Arayed right as he were a god in trone
The people preased thyderwarde ful sone
Him for to sene/and done him hye reuerence
And eke for to here his hest & his sentence.
An heraude on a scaffolde made an oo
Tyl al the noyse of the people was ydo
And whan he sawe the people of noyse styll
Thus shewed he the mighty dukes wyll.
¶ The lorde hath of his hye discretion
Considred/ that it were distruction
To gentle bloode/to fighten in this gyse
Of mortal batayle/nowe in this emprise
Wherfore to shapen/that they shal not dye
He woll his first purpose modifye
No man therfore/upppayne of losse of lyfe
No maner shotte/polaxe/ne shorte knyfe
In to the lystes sende/or thyder bring
Ne short sworde to sticke with poynt byting
No man ne drawe/ne beare it by his syde
Ne no man shal to his felowe ryde
But one course/with a sharpe groũden spere
Foyne if him lyst on fote/him selfe to were
And he that is at mischefe/shal be take
And not slayne/but brought to the stake
That shal ben ordayned on eyther syde
But thyder he shal byforce/and there abyde
And if so fal/that the chieftayne be take
On eyther syde/or els sleen his make
No lenger shal the turnament laste
God spede you/gothe and layeth on faste
With swordes & long mases fighten your fyll
Goth now your way/this is the lordes wyl.
¶ The voyce of the people touched heuen
So loude cryed they with mery steuen
God saue suche a lorde/that is so good
He wylleth no distruction of blood.
Up gothe the trompes and the melodye
And to the lystes/rideth so the companye
By ordynaunce/throughout the cyte large
Honged with cloth of golde/& not with sarge
Ful lyke a lorde this noble duke gan ryde
These

The Knight's Tale (A 2477–2569; T. 2479–2571)

These two Thebans on euery syde
And after rode the quene and Emelye
And after that an other companye
Of one and other/after her degre
And thus they passen throughout the cyte
And to the lystes comen they be by tyme
It nas not of the day yet fully prime
Whan set was Theseus ful ryche and hye
Ipolita the quene/and Emelye
And other ladyes in degrees aboute
Unto the setes preaseth al the route
And westward/thrugh ye yates under Marte
Arcite/and eke an hundred of his parte
With baner reed/is entred right anon
And in the selue momet entred Palamon
Is/under Venus/estwarde in that place
With baner whyte/and hardy chere & face
And in al the worlde/to seken up and doun
So euen without varyacion
There nas suche companyes twey
For there nas none so wyse that coude sey
That any had of other auauntage
Of worthynesse/ne of estate/ne age
So euen were they chose to gesse
And in to the renges fayre they hem dresse
Whan ye her names redde were euerychone
That in her nombre/gyle were there none
Tho were the gates shyt/& cryed was loude
Do nowe your deuer yong knyghtes proude
¶ The heraudes left her prickyng up & doun
Nowe ryngen trompes loude and claryoun
There is no more to say/este and weste
In gothe the sharpe speres sadly in the arrest
In gothe the sharpe spurres into the syde
There se men who can iust/& who can ryde
There shyueren shaftes/upon sheldes thicke
He feleth through the herte spoune the pricke
Up sprungeth ye speres/ twety foote on hyght
Out gothe the swordes/as the syluer bright
The helmes they to heawe/and to shrede
Out burst ye bloode/ with sterne stremes rede
With mighty maces/the bones they tobreke
He through the thickest of ye throge gan threke
Ther stomblen stedes stronge/& doun gon al
He rolled under the foote as dothe a ball
He foyneth on his fete with a tronchoun
And he hurleth with his horse adoun
He through the body is hurte/and sythe ytake
Maugre his heed/& brought unto the stake
As forwarde was/right there he must abyde
An other is ladde on that other syde
And somtyme dothe hem Theseus to reste
Hem to refresshe/and drinke if hem leste
Ful ofte a day haue these Thebans two
To gyther met/and don eche other wo
Unhorsed hath eche other of hem twey
Ther was no tygre/in the vale of Galaphey
Whan her whelpe is stole/whan it is lyte
So cruell on the hunte/as is Arcyte
For ielous herte/upon this Palamon
Ne in Belmarye/there is no fel lyon
That hunted is/or for his hungre woode
Ne of his prey/desyreth so the bloode
As Palamon to slee his foe Arcite
The ielous strokes on her helmes byte
Out renneth the bloode on both her sydes rede
Somtyme an ende there is of euery dede
For er the sonne unto the rest wente
The stronge kyng Emetryus gan hente
This Palamon/ as he faught wt this Arcite
And made his sworde depe in his flesshe byte
And by force of twenty is he take
Unyolden/and drawen to the stake
And in the rescous of this Palamon
The stronge kyng Lygurge is borne adoun
And kyng Emetrius/for al his strength
Is borne out of his sadle a swordes length
So hurte him Palamon or he were take
But al for naught/ he was broght to ye stake
His hardy herte might him helpe naught
He must abyde/whan that he was caught
By force/and eke by composycion
Who soroweth now but woful Palamon:
That mote no more gon agayne to fyght.
¶ And whan ye Theseus had sene ye syght
He cryed hoe: no more/for it is don.
Ne none shal lenger to his felowe gon
I wol be true iuge/and not partye
Arcite of Thebes shal haue Emelye
That by his fortune hath her fayre ywonne
Anon there is a noyse of people bygonne
For ioye of this/so loude & hye withall
It semed that the lystes shulde fall.

¶ Whan

What can nowe fayre Venus done aboue?
What sayth she now: what doth ye quene of lo-
But wepeth so/for wantyng of her wyl (ue
Tyl that her teares on the lystes fyl
She sayd: I am a shamed doutles
Saturne sayd: doughter holde thy pees
Mars hath al his wil/ his knizt hath his bone
And by myn heed/thou shalt be eased sone.
¶ The trompes with the loude mynstralcye
The heraudes/that so loude yel and crye
Ben in her wele/for loue of dan Arcyte
But herkeneth me/& stynteth noyse a lyte
Whiche a myracle there byfel anon
The fyers Arcite hath his helme of ydon
And on a courser/for to shewe his face
He pricketh endlonge the large place
Lokyng upwarde upon Emelye
And she ayen him cast a frendely eye
(For women/as to speke in comune
They folowen al the fauour of fortune)
And was al his chere/as in his herte
Out of the grounde a fyre infernal sterte
From Pluto sent/at the request of Saturne
For whiche his horse for feare gan to tourne
And lepe a syde/and foundred as he lepe
And er that Arcite may taken kepe
He pyght him on the pomel of his heed
That in the place he lay as he were deed
His brest tobrosten with his sadel bowe
As blacke he lay as any cole or crowe
So was the bloode ronne in his face
Anon he was brought out of the place
With herte sore/to Theseus paleys
Tho was he coruen out of his harneys
And in a bedde ybrought ful fayre and blyue
For he was yet in memorye/and on lyue
And alway cryeng after Emely.
¶ Duke Theseus/with al his companye
Is comen home to Athenes his cyte
With al blysse and great solempnyte
Al be it that this auenture was fal
He wolde not discomforte hem al
Men said eke/that Arcite shulde not dye
He shuld ben yhealed of his maladye
And of an other thyng they were as fayne
That of hem al there was none slayne
Al were they sore hurte/and namely one
That wt a spere was thronled his brest bone

Two other woundes and two broken armes
Some had salues and some had charmes
Fermaces of herbes and eke saue
They dronken/ for they wolde her lyues haue
For whiche this noble duke as he wel can
Comforteth and honoureth euery man
And made reuel al the longe night
Unto the straunge lordes as it was right
Ne there nas holde no discomfortyng
But as iustes/ or a tourneyng
For sothly there nas no discomfyture
For fallyng is holde but an auenture
Ne to be ladde by force unto a stake
Unyolden/ and with twenty knightes take
One persone alone withouten any mo
And haried forthe by arme/ fote/ and toe
And eke his stede driuen forthe with staues
With footemen/bothe yemen and knaues
It was aretted him no vilanye
There may no man clepe it cowardye
For whiche anon/duke Theseus dyd crye
To stynten al rancour and enuye
The grete as wel of one syde as of other
And eyther syde ylyke/as others brother
And yaue hem yyftes after her degre
And fully helde a feest dayes thre
And conueyed the knyghtes worthyly
Out of his towne/a dayes iourney largely
And home went euery man the right way
Ther was no more/but farwel & haue good (day.
Of this batayle/I wol no more endyte
But speke of Palamon and Arcyte
Swelleth the brest of Arcite/and the sore
Encreaseth at his herte more and more
The clotered bloode/for any leche crafte
Corrumped/and is in his body lafte
That neyther veynbloode/ne ventousyng
Ne drinke of herbes/may be helpyng
By vertue expulsed/or anymal
For thylke vertue cleaped natural
Ne may the venym voyde/ne expel
The pypes of his longes began to swel
And euery lacerte/ in his brest adown
Is shent with venym and corrupcion
Him gayneth neyther/for to get his lyfe
Vomyte upwarde/ne downwarde laxatyfe
Al is to brust thylke regyoun
Nature

Nature hath no dominatioun
And certainly/ ther as nature wol nat wirche
Farwel phisyke/ go beare the corse to chirche
This is al and some/ that Arcite must dye
For whiche he sendeth after Emelye
And Palamon his cosyn dere
Than said he thus/ as ye shal after here.

Nought may my woful spirite in my herte
Declare a poynt of al my sorowes smerte
To you my lady that I loue moste
But I bequeth the seruyce of my goste
To you/ abouen any creature
Sithe that my lyfe may no lenger dure
Alas the wo/ alas my paynes stronge
That I for you haue suffred/ and so longe
Alas the dethe/ alas myne Emely
Alas departyng of our company
Alas my hertes quene/ alas my lyues wyfe
Myne hertes lady/ ender of my lyfe
What is the worlde/ what asken men to haue?
Nowe with his loue/ nowe in his colde graue
Alone withouten any company
Farwel my swete foe/ myne Emely
And softe take me in your armes tway
For the loue of god herkeneth what I say.

I haue here with my cosyn Palamon
Had stryfe and rancour many day agon
For loue of you/ and for my ielousye
And Jupiter so wisely my soule gye
To speken of a seruaunt proprely
With circumstaunces al trewly
That is to say/ trouth/ honour/ & knighthede
Wysedome/ humblesse/ estate/ & hye kynrede
Fredome/ and al that longeth to that arte
So Jupiter haue of my soule parte
As in this worlde/ right nowe knowe I none
So worthy to be loued as is Palamone
That serueth you and wol done al his lyfe
And if that ye shal euer ben a wyfe
Foryet nat Palamon the gentylman
And with that worde his speche faylen began
For from his fete vnto the brest was come
The colde of dethe that had him nome
And yet moreouer for in his armes two
The vital strength is loste and al ago
Saue onely the intellecte without more
That dwelled in his herte sycke and sore
Gan faylen/ whan the herte felte dethe
Dusked his eyen two/ and fayled brethe
But on his lady/ yet caste he his eye
His laste worde was/ mercy Emelye
His spyrit chaunged/ and out went there
Whyther warde I can not tel/ ne where
Therfore I stynte I am no diuynistre
Of soule fynde I not in this regestre
Ne me lyst not thylke opinion to tell
Of hem/ though they writen wher thy dwel
Arcite is colde/ that Mars his soule gye
Nowe wol I speke forthe of Emelye.
¶ Shright Emely/ and howlen Palamon
And Theseus his suster vp toke anon
Swounyng/ & bare her fro his corse away
What helpeth it to tarry forthe the day
To tellen how she wept bothe euen & morowe
For in suche case women haue suche sorowe
Whan that her husbandes ben fro hem go
That for the more parte they sorowen so
Or els fallen in suche maladye
That at the laste/ certaynly they dye
Infinyte ben the sorowes and the teres
Of olde folke/ and folke of tender yeres
In al the towne/ for dethe of this Theban
For him there wepeth bothe chylde and man
So great wepyng was there not certayne
Whan Hector was brought/ al fresshe yslayn
To Troy alas/ the pyte that was there
Cratchyng of chekes/ rentyng eke of here
Why woldest thou be deed/ thus women crye
And haddest golde ynoughe/ and Emelye?
No man might glade Theseus
Sauyng his olde father Egeus
That knewe this worldes transmutacioun
As he had sene it/ bothe vp and doun
Joye after wo/ and wo after gladnesse
And shewed him ensamples and lykenesse
Right as there dyed neuer man (quod he)
That he ne lyued in erthe in some degre
Right so there lyued neuer man/ he sayde
In al this world/ that somtyme he ne deyde
This world is but a thorowfare ful of wo
And we ben pylgrymes passyng to and fro
Dethe is an ende of euery worldes sore.
And ouer al this yet sayd he moche more
To this effecte/ ful wysely to exhorte

Th

The knyghtes tale.

The people/that they shulde hem recomfort
  Duke Theseus with all his busy cure
Casteth nowe/ where that the sepulture
Of good Arcite/shal best ymaked be
And eke moste honorable of degre
And at the laste he toke conclusyon
That there as Arcite and Palamon
Had for loue/the batayle hem bytwene
That in the same selue groue/swete ⁊ grene
There as he had his amerous desyres
His complaynte/⁊ for loue his hotte fyres
He wolde make a fyre/in whiche the offys
Funeral he myght hem al accomplys
He hath anon cōmaunded to hacke ⁊ hewe
The okes olde/and lay hem al on arewe
In culpons/wel arayed for to brenne.
  His offycers with swyfte foote they renne
And right anon at his cōmaundement.
And after Theseus hath ysente
After a beere/and it al ouer spradde
With clothe of gol[de]/the rychest that he had
And of the same sute he clothed Arcyte
Upon his handes his gloues whyte
Eke on his heed a crowne of laurer grene
And in his hande a sworde ful bright ⁊ kene
He layde hum bare the visage on the bere
Therwith he wepte/that pyte was to here
And for the people shulde sene hum all
Whan it was day/ he brought hum to ye hall
That roreth of the crye ⁊ of the sorowes soun
  Tho gan this wofull theban Palamon
With glytering berde/⁊ ruddy shynyng heres
In clothes blacke/dropped al with teres
And passyng other of wepyng Emely
The rufullest of al the company.
  And in as moche as the seruyce shulde be
The more noble/and ryche in his degre
Duke Theseus let forthe the stedes bring
That trapped were in stele all glyteryng
And couered with the armes of dan Arcyte
Upon these stedes great and whyte
Ther saten folke/of which one bare his sheld
Another his speare/ in his hande helde
The thirde bare with hym a bowe turkes
Of brent golde was the case ⁊ eke the harnes
And ryden forthe a pace with sory chere
Towarde the groue/as ye shal after here.

¶ The noblest of the grekes/that there were
Upon her shuldres caryed the bere
With slacke pace/and eyen reed and wete
Throughout the cyte/by the mayster strete
That sprad was al wt blak/⁊ that wōder hye
Right of the same is the strete ywrye
Upon the right hande wente Egeus
And on the other syde duke Theseus
With vessels in her hande/of golde ful fyne
Al ful of hony/mylke/bloode/and wyne
Eke Palamon/with full great company
And after that/came wofull Emely
With fyre in hande/as was ye tyme the gyse
To don the offyce of funeral seruyse
  Hye labour/and ful great apparaylyng
Was at seruyce/and at fyre makyng
That with his grene toppe the heuen raught
And twenty fadome of brede armes straught
This is to sayn/the bowes were so brode
Of strawe first ther was layde many a lode.
  But how the fyre was maked vp on height
And eke the names/ howe the trees heyght
As oke/fyrre/beche/aspe/elder/elme/poplere
Wyllow/holm/plane/boxe/chesteyn/laurere
Maple/thorne/beche/ewe/hasel/ whipultre
How they were felde/shal nat be tolde for me
Ne howe the goddes ronne vp and down
Disherited of her abytacioun
In whiche they wonned in rest and pees
Nymphes/Fauny/and Amadriades
Ne howe the beestes/ne the byrdes all
Fledden for feare/whan the trees fall
Ne how the grounde agast was of the syght
That was nat wonte to se the sonne bright
Ne howe the fyre was couched first with stre
And than with drye styckes clouen a thre
And than with grene wodde/and spicery
And than with clothe of golde and perry
And garlondes hãgyng with many a floure
The myrre/the ensence/with swete odoure
Ne howe Arcite lay amonge al this
Ne what rychesse aboute his body is
Ne howe that Emely/as was the gyse
Put in the fyre of funeral seruyse
Ne how she swouned/whã maked was ye fyre
Ne what she spake/ ne what was her desyre
Ne what iewelles men in the fyre caste

Whan

Whan that the fyre was great ⁊ brent faste
Ne how some cast her shelde/ ⁊ some her spere
And of her vestementes/ whiche yͭ they were
And cuppes full of wyne/ mylke/ ⁊ bloode
In to the fyre/ that brent as it were woode
Ne howe the grekes with a huge route
Thryse rydden all the fyre aboute
Upon the lefte hande/ with a loude showting
And thryse with her speares clateryng
And thryse howe the ladyes gan crye
Ne howe that ladde was homwarde Emelye
Ne howe that Arcite is brent to asshen colde
Ne howe the lyche wake was holde
All that nyght/ ne howe the grekes play
The wake playes/ kepe I nat to say
Who wrestled best naked/ with oyle anoynt
Ne who bare hym best in euery poynt
I woll not tellen howe they gone
Whom to Athenes/ whan the play is done
But shortly to the poynt than woll I wende
And make of my longe tale an ende.

By processe and by length of yeres
All styntch is the mornyng and the teres
Of grekes/ by one generall assent
Than semed me there was a parlement
At Athenes/ vpon a certayne poynt and caas
Amonge the whiche poyntes yspoken was
To haue with certayne countrees alyaunce
And haue of Thebans fully obeysaunce
For whiche this noble Theseus anon
Let sende after this gentyll Palamon
Unwyste of him what was the cause ⁊ why:
But in his blacke clothes sorowfully
He came at his comaundement on hye
Tho sent Theseus after Emelye.
Whan they were set/ ⁊ hushte was yͤ place
And Theseus abydden hath a space
Or any worde came from his wyse brest
His eyen sette he there hym lest
And with suche a sadde vysage/ he syked styll
And after that/ right thus he sayd his wyll.
¶ The first mouer of the cause aboue
Whan he first made the fayre chayne of loue
Great was theffecte/ ⁊ hye was his entente
Well wyste he why/ ⁊ what therof he mente
For with that fayre chayne of loue he bonde
The fyre/ the eyre/ the water/ and the londe
In certayne bondes/ that they may nat fle
That same prince and that mouer/ quod he
Hath stablisshed i this wretched world adoun
Certen dayes and duracion
To all that are engendred in this place
Ouer the whiche day they may not pace
All mowe they yet the dayes abredge
There nedeth none auctorite to ledge
For it is proued by experyence
But that me lyst declaren my sentence
Than may men by this ordre discerne
That thylke mouer stable is and eterne
Well may men knowe/ but he be a fole
That euery party is deryued from his hole
For nature hath not taken his begynnyng
Of one parte or cantell of a thyng
But of a thyng that perfyte is and stable
Discendyng so/ tyll it be corrumpable
And therfore of his wyse puruepaunce
He hath so well vyset his ordynaunce
That spaces of thynges and progressyons
Shullen endure by successyons
And not eterne/ without any lye
Thus mayst thou vnderstande ⁊ se at eye.
Lo the oke/ that hath so longe a norisshyng
Fro the tyme yͭ it begynneth first to spring
And hath so longe a lyfe/ as ye may se
Yet at the last/ wasted is the tre
Consydreth eke/ howe that the harde stone
Under our fete/ on whiche we treade ⁊ gone
Yet wasteth it/ as it lyeth in the wey
The brode ryuer somtyme weyeth drey
The great townes/ se we wane and wende
Than ye se that all this thyng hath ende
And man and woman se shall we also
That nedeth in one of the termes two
That is to sayne/ in youthe or els in age
He mote be deed/ a kyng as well as a page
Some in his bedde, some in the depe see
Some in the large felde/ as ye may se
It helpeth not/ all gothe that ylke wey
Than may ye se that al thyng mote dey
What maketh this/ but Jupiter the kyng:
That is prince/ and cause of all thyng
Conuertyng all to his propre wyll
From whiche it is deryued sothe to tell
And

And here agayne/no creature on lyue
Of no degre/auayleth for to stryue
Than is it wysdome/as thynketh me
To make vertue of necessyte
And take it wel/that we may not eschewe
And namely that to vs al is dewe
And who so grutcheth aught/he dothe folye
And rebel is to him that al may gye
And certaynly/a man hath moste honour
To dyen in his excellence and flour
Whan he is lyker of his good name
Than hath he don his frẽdes ne him no sham
And gladder ought his frendes be of his deth
Whan with honour ẏ yolde is vp the breth
Than whan his name apalled is for age
For al forgeten is his vassellage
Than is it best/as for a worthy fame
To dyen/whan he is best of name
The contrarye of al this is wylfulnesse
Why grutchen we? why haue we heuynesse
That good Arcite/of cheualry the floure
Departed is/with dutye and with honoure
Out of this foule prison/of this lyfe?
Why grutchen here his cosyn and his wyfe
Of his welfare/that loueth him so wele?
Can he hem thãke? nay god wot neuer a dele
That bothe his soule/& eke hem offende
And yet they mowe not her lustes amende?
¶ What may conclude of this longe story
But after sorowe/I rede vs be mery
And thanke Iupiter of al his grace
And er we departen from this place
I rede we maken of sorowes two
One perfyte ioye/lastyng euer mo
And loke nowe where most sorowe is herin
There wol I first amende and begyn.
Suster quod he/this is my ful assent
With al the people of my parlement
That gentle Palamon/your owne knyght
That serueth you with wyl/herte/& myght
And euer hath done/sythe ye first him knewe
That ye shal of your grace vpon him rewe
And take him for husbonde and for lorde
Lene me your honde/for this is our acorde.
Let se nowe of your womanly pyte
He is a kynges brother sonne parde
And though he were a poore bachelere
Syn he hath serued you so many a yere
And had for you so great aduersyte
It muste ben consydred/leueth me
For gentle mercy ought to passen right.
Than sayd he thus to Palamon ẏ knight
I trowe there nede lytel sarmonyng
To make you to assenten to this thyng
Cometh nere/& taketh your lady by the honde
Bytwyxt hem was maked anon the bonde
That hyght matrimony or maryage
By al the counsayle of the baronage
And thus with al blysse and melodye
Hath Palamon ywedded Emelye.
¶ And god that al this worlde hath wrought
Sende him his loue/ẏ it hath so dere bought
For nowe is Palamon in al wele
Lyuyng in blysse, in richesse/and in hele
And Emely him loueth so tenderly
And he her serueth so gentelly
That neuer was ther no worde hem bytwene
Of ielousye/or of any other tene
Thus endeth Palamon and Emelye
And god saue al this fayre companye.

¶ Here endeth the knyghtes tale/ and here foloweth the Myllers prologue.

WHan ẏ the knight had thus his tale ytolde
In al the company nas ther yong ne olde
That he ne sayd/it was a noble story
And worthy to be drawen in memory
And namely the gentyls euerychone
Our hoste loughe and sware/so mote I gone
This gothe a right/vnbokled is the male
Let se nowe who shal tel a nother tale
For truely/the game is wel begonne
Nowe telleth sir monke if ye conne
Somwhat/to quyte with the knyghtes tale
¶ The myller for dronken was al pale
So that vnnethes vpon his horse he satte
Ne nolde auale neyther hoode ne hatte
Ne abyde no man for his curtesye
But in Pylates voyce he began to crye
And swore by armes/bloode/and bones
E. I can

The Myllers prologue.

I can a noble tale for the nones (tale
With whiche I wol nowe quite the knight his
¶ Our hoste sawe that he was dronken of ale
And sayd: abyde Robyn leue brother
Some better man shal tel vs first an other
Abyde/ and let vs wirche thriftely.
¶ By goddes soule (quod he) that wol not I
For I wol speke/ or els go my way
Our hoste answerde: tel on a dyuel way
Thou arte a foole/ thy wytte is ouercome
Nowe herkeneth quod the myller/ al a some
But first I make protestacion
That I am dronke/ I knowe it by my soun
And therfore if I mispeke or say
Wyte it the ale of Sothwarke/ I you pray
For I wol tel a legende and a lyfe
Bothe of a carpenter and his wyfe.
Howe that a clerke set a wrightes cappe.
¶ The Reue answerde a said/ stynte thy clap
Let be thy leude dronken harlottry
It is a synne/ and eke a great folye
To apayren any man/ or hym defame
And eke to bring wyues in suche blame
Thou mayst ynoughe of other thinges sayn.
This dronken myller spake ful sone agayn
And said: leue brother Oswolde
Who hath no wyfe is no cokolde
But I say not therfore that thou arte one
There ben ful good wyues many one
Why arte thou angry with my tale now
I haue a wyfe parde/ as wel as thou
Yet nolde I for al the oxen in my plough
Take vpon me more than ynough
To demen of my selfe that I am one
I wol beleue that I am none
An husbonde shulde not ben inquisytyfe
Of goddes priuete/ ne of his wyfe
For so he fynde goddes foyson there
Of the remenaunt/ nedeth nat to enquere.
What shulde I more say/ but this Myllere
He nolde his wordes for no man forbere
But tolde his chorles tale in this manere
Me forthinketh I shal reherce it here
And therfore/ euery gentle wight I pray
Demeth not for goddes loue/ that I say
Of yuel entent/ but that I mote reherce
Her tales al/ ben they better or werse
Or els falsen some of my matere
And therfore/ who so lyst it not to here
Turne ouer the lefe/ and chose another tale
For ye shal fynde ynowe great and smale
Of historial thyng/ that toucheth gentylnesse
And eke moralite/ and holynesse
Blame not me/ if that ye chose amys
The Myller is a chorle/ ye knowe wel this
So was the Reue eke/ and other mo
And harlotry they tolde eke bothe two
Auyse you/ and put me out of blame
And eke men shuld not make ernest of game.

¶ Here endeth the Myllers pro-
logue: and here after fol-
loweth his tale.

The Miller's Prologue (A 3126–3186; T. 3128–3186)

Hylom ther was dwellyng i Oxenforde
W A riche gnoffe/ yͭ gestes helde to borde
And of his crafte he was a carpenter
With him there was dwellyng a poore scoler
Had ylerned arte/ but al his fantasye
Was turned to lerne astrologye
And coude a certayne of conclusyons
To demen by interogacions
If that men asked him in certayne houres
Whan yͭ men shulde haue drought or shoures
Or if men asked him what shulde befall
Of euery thyng/ I may not reken al.
This clerke was cleped hende Nycholas
Of derne loue he coude and of solas
And therto he was slye and right priue
And lyke to a mayden meke to se
A chambre had he in that hostelry
Alone/ withouten any company
Ful fetously dight with herbes sote
And he him selfe as swete as is the rote
Of lycores/ or of any sytuwale
His almagiste/ and bokes great and smale
His asterlagour/ longyng for his arte
His augrym stones lyeng fayre a parte
On shelues couched at his beddes heed
His presse ycouered with a foldyng reed
And al aboue there lay a gay sautrye
On whiche he made on nyghtes melodye
So swetely/ that al the chambre ronge
And Angelus ad virginem he songe
And after that he songe the kynges note
Ful ofte blyssed was his mery throte
And thus the swete clerke his tyme spente
After his frendes fyndyng and his rente.
¶ This carpenter had wedded newe a wyfe
Whiche that he loued more than his lyfe
Of eyghtene yere she was of age
Jelous he was/ and kept her strayte in cage
For she was wylde/ and yonge: & he was olde
And demed him selfe to ben a cokewolde
He knewe not Cato: for his wytte was rude
That bade men wedde her symplitude
Men shulde wedde after her astate
For youthe and elde is often at debate
But sythe he was fallen in the snare
He must enduren/ as other folke his care.
Fayre was this yonge wyfe/ & therwithall
As any wysele her body gentle and smale
A seynte she weared/ barred al with sylke
A barme clothe/ as whyte as morowe mylke

The Miller's Tale (A 3187–3236; T. 3187–3236)

Upon her lendes/ ful of many a gore
Whyte was her smocke/& embrouded al byfore
And eke behynde on her colere aboute
Of cole blacke sylke/ within and eke without
The tapes of her whyte volypere
Were of the same sute of her colere
Her sylet brode of sylke/and set ful hye
And sikerly/ she had a lykerous eye
Ful smale ypulled were her browes two
And tho were bent/ and blacke as any slo
She was moche more blyssful for to se
Than is the newe Perienet tre
And softer than the wol is of a wether
  And by her gyrdel honge a purse of lether
Tassed with sylke/ and persed with latoun
In al this worlde/to seken up and doun
There nys no man so wyse/ ẏ couthe thenche
So gay a popelote/or so gay a wenche
Ful brighter was the shynyng of her hewe
Than in the towre the noble forged newe
But of her songe/it was so loude & yerne
As any swalowe syttyng on a berne
Therto she couthe skyppe/& make a game
As any kyde or calfe folowyng his dame
Her mouth was swete/as braket or the methe
Or horde of apples/lyeng in hey or hethe
Wynsyng she was/as is a ioly colte
Longe as a maste/and upright as a bolte
A broche she bare on her lowe collere
As brode as the bosse of a bokelere
Her shoes were lased on her legges hye
She was a primrose/and a pyggesnye
For any lorde to lyggen in his bedde
Or yet for any good yoman to wedde.
¶ Nowe sir and efte sire/so byfel the caas
That on a day this hende Nycholas
Fel with this yonge wyfe to rage and pley
Whyle that her husbonde was at Oseney,
As clerkes ben ful sotel and queynte
And priuely he caught her by the queynte
And sayd: I wys but I haue my wyll
For derne loue of the lemman I spyll
And helde her faste by the haunche bones
And said: lemman loue me wel at ones
Or I wol dyen also god me saue
  And she spronge as a colte in a trave
And with her heed she wrieth faste away
And said: I wol not kysse the by my fay
Why let be quod she/let be Nicholas
Or I wol crye out harrowe and alas
Do way your hondes for your curtesye.
  This Nicholas gan mercy for to crye
And spake so fayre/& profered him so faste
That she her loue graunted him at laste
And swore her oth/by seynt Thomas of Kent
That she wolde ben at his cōmaundement
Whan that she may her leyser wel aspye
My husbonde is so ful of ielousye
That but ye wayte wel/and be priue
I wotte right wel I nam but deed/quod she
Ye mote ben ful derne as in this caas.
  Nay therof care ye not/quod Nycholas
A clerke had lytherly byset his whyle
But if he couthe a carpenter begyle
And thus they were acorded/and ysworne
To awayten a tyme/as I haue sayd byforne
  And whā Nicholas had don thus euery dele
And thacked her aboute the lendes wele
He kyssed her swete/ than taketh his sautrye
And playeth faste/and maketh melody
  Than fel it thus/that to the parisshe cherche
(Christes owne workes for to werche)
This good wyfe went upon an holyday
Her forheed shone as bright as any day
So was it wasshe/whan she lete her werke.
¶ Now was ther of ẏ chirche a parish clerke
The whiche that was cleaped Absolon
Croulle was his heare/ & as golde it shon
And strouted as a fanne large and brode
Ful streyght & euen lay his ioly shode
His rode was redde/ his eyen gray as goos
With Poules wyndowes coruen on his shoos
In hosen redde he went fetously
Gyrde he was ful small and properly
Al in a kyrtell of lyght waget
Ful fayre and thicke ben the poyntes set
And therupon he had a gay surplyse
As whyte as is the blosome on the ryse
  A mery chylde he was/so god me saue
Wel coude he let bloode/clyppe/and shaue
And make a chartre of londe/& a quytaunce
In twenty manere coude he tryp & daunce
After the skole of Oxenforde tho
And with his legges casten to and fro
And

The Miller's Tale (A 3237–3330; T. 3237–3330)

And play songes on a smale ribyble
Therto he songe somtyme a loude quinyble
And as wel couth he play on a geterne
In al the towne nas brewhouse ne tauerne
That he ne visyted with his solas
There any gay tapstere was
But soth to say he was somwhat squaymous
Of fartyng/and of speche daungerous.
¶ This Absolon/that was ioly and gay
Gothe with a censer on the sonday
Censyng the wyues of the parisshe faste
And many a louely loke on hem he caste
And namely on this carpenters wyfe
To loke on her him thought a mery lyfe
She was so propre/and swete as lycorous
I dare wel sayne if she had ben a mous
And he a catte/he wolde haue her hente anon.
This parysshe clerke/this ioly absolon
Hath in his herte suche a loue longyng
That of no wyfe toke he none offeryng
For curtesye he said he wolde none
The moone/whan it was nyght bright shone
And Absolon his geterne hath ytake
For paramoures he thought for to wake
And forthe he gothe/ielous and amerous
Tyl he came to the carpenters hous
A lytel after the cockes had ycrowe
And dressed him by a shot wyndowe
That was vpon the carpenters wall
He syngeth in his voyce gentle and small
Nowe dere lady/if thy wyl be
I pray you that ye wolde rewe on me
Ful wel acordyng to his geternyng.
¶ This carpenter awoke/& herde him syng
And spake vnto his wyfe anon
What Alyson/heres thou not Absolon
That chaunteth thus vnder our boures wal?
And she answerde her husbonde ther withal
yes god wot/I here him euery dele
This passeth forth/what wol ye bet thā wele
Fro day to day/this ioly Absolon
So woeth her/that him was wo bygon
He waketh al the nyght/and al the day
He kembeth his lockes brode/& made him gay
He woeth her by meanes and brocage
And swore/he wolde ben her owne page
He syngeth brokkyng as a nyghtyngale
He sent her pyment/methe/and spyced ale
And wafres pypyng hotte out of the glede
And for she was of town/he profered her mede
For some folke wol be wonne for rychesse
And some for strokes/& some with gētlenesse.
Somtyme to shew his lightnesse & mastrye
He playeth Heraudes on a skaffolde hye
But what anayleth him/as in this caas?
So loueth she this hende Nycholas
That Absolon may blowe the buckes horne
He ne had for his labour but a skorne
And thus she maketh Absolon her ape
And al his request turneth to a iape
Forsothe this prouerbe it is no lye
Men say thus alway/the nye slye
Maketh the ferre loue to be lothe
For though yͭ Absolon be woode or wrothe
Bycause that he ferre was from her syght
Thus nye Nycholas stode in his syght.
But nowe beare the wel hende Nycholas
For Absolon may wayle and syng alas
And so byfel it on a saterday
This carpenter was gon to Osnay
And hende Nicholas and Alyson
Acorded were to this conclusyon
That Nycholas shulde shapen hem a wyle
This sely ielous carpenter to begyle
And if so be the game went a ryght
She shulde slepe in his armes al nyght
For this was his desyre/and hers also
And right anon/without wordes mo
This Nycholas no lenger wolde tarye
But doth ful softe vnto his chambre carye
Bothe meate and drinke/for a day or twey
And to her husbonde bade her for to say
yf that he asked after Nycholas
She shulde say she nyste where he was
Of al that day she sawe him not with eye
She trowed he was in some maladye
For no crye that her mayde coude call
He nolde answere/ for naught yͭ might befal.
¶ Thus passeth forthe al the ylke saterday
That Nycholas styl in his chambre lay
And ete/ dranke/& slept/ & dyd what him liste
Tyl sonday/ that the sonne gothe to reste.
¶ This sely carpenter hath great maruayle
Of Nycholas/ or what thing might him eyle

E.iii. And

And said: I am a drad by saynte Thomas
It stondeth not aright with Nycholas
God shylde that he dyed sodaynly
This worlde is nowe ful tykel sekerly
I sawe to day a corse borne to cherche
That now on mōday last I sawe him werche
  Go vp (quod he vnto his knaue) anone
Cleape at his dore/ & knocke fast with a stone
Loke howe it is/ and tel me boldely.
¶ This knaue wente vp ful sturdely
And at the chambre dore/ whyle that he stode
He cryed and knocked as he were woode
What howe? What do ye mayster Nicholay?
Howe may ye slepe al this longe day?
But al for naught/ he herde not a worde.
An hole he founde ful lowe vpon a borde
There as the catte was wonte in to crepe
And at that hole he loked in ful depe
And at the laste he had of him a syght.
¶ This Nycholas sate euer gapyng vpright
As he had keyked on the newe mone
  A downe he gothe/ & tolde his mayster sone
In what aray he sawe this ylke man.
¶ This carpenter to blyssen him began
And said: nowe helpe vs seynt Frideswyde
A man wot lytel what shal him betyde
This man is fallen/ with his Astronomye
In some woodnesse/ or in some agonye
I thought aye wel howe it shulde be
Men shulden not knowe of goddes priuete
Ye blessed be alway the lewde man
That naught but onely his byleue can.
  Right so ferde another clerke wt astronomy
He walked in to the feldes for to pry
Vpon the sterres/ to wete what shulde befall
Tyl he was in a marlpyt yfall
He sawe not that/ yet by saynte Thomas
Me reweth sore on hende Nycholas
He shal be rated out of his studyeng
If that I may/ by Iesus heuen kyng.
  Get me a staffe/ that I may vnderspore
Whyle that thou Robyn heuest vp the dore
He shal out of his studyeng/ as I gesse
And to the chambre dore he gan him dresse
His knaue was a stronge carle for the nones
And by the haspe hare vp the dore at ones
In to the flore the dore fel anone.

¶ This Nicholas sate as styl as any stone
And euer gaped vpwarde into the eyre.
  This carpenter wende he were in dispeyre
And hente him by the shulders mightyly
And shoke him harde/ and cryed spytously
What Nycholas/ what how loke adowne
Awake/ and thynke on Christes passyon
I crouche ye from elues & fro wicked wightes
Therwith the nyghtspel he said anonrightes
On foure halues of the house aboute
And on the dresshfolde of the dore without
Iesu Christ/ and saynt Benedight
Blysse this house from euery wycked wight
Fro the nyghtes mare the wyte Pater noster
Where wonnest thou saynt Peters suster?
¶ And at the laste this hende Nycholas
Gan for to syke sore/ and said alas
Shal al this worlde be loste eftsones nowe?
  This carpēter answerde: what sayst thou?
What thinke on god/ as we do men ye swynke
  This Nycholas answerde: fetche me drinke
And after wol I speke in priuete
Of certayne thinges/ that toucheth the & me
I wol tellen it none other man certayne.
  This carpēter goth downe/ & cometh agayn
And brought of mighty ale a large quarte
And whan that eche of hem had dronken his (parte
This Nycholas/ his dore faste shette
And downe the carpenter by him sette
And sayd: Iohā hoste myne lefe and dere
Thou shalte vpon thy trouthe swere me here
That to no wight thou shalt my coūsel wrey
For it is Christes counsayle that I say
And if thou tel it any man/ thou arte forlore
For this vengeaūce thou shalte haue therfore
That if thou wray me/ thou shalt be woode.
¶ Nay Christ it forbyd for his holy bloode
Quod tho this sely man/ I am no blabbe
Ne though I say it/ I am not lefe to gabbe
Say what thou wolte/ I shal it neuer tell
To childe ne wyfe/ by him that harowed hell.
  Nowe Iohn (quod Nicholas) I wol nat lye
I haue yfounden in myn astrologye
As I haue loked in the moone bright
That now on monday next/ at quarter night
Shal fal a rayne/ & that so wylde & woode
That halfe so great was neuer Noes floode
This

This world (he said) in lesse than in an houre
Shal al be dreynte/ so hydous is the shoure
Thus shal mankynde drenche/ & lese her lyfe.
This carpẽter answerd & said: alas my wife
And shal she drenche? Alas myn Alyson
For sorowe of this he fel almoste adoun
And said: Is there no remedye in this caas?
Yes yes ful good (quod hende Nycholas)
If thou wolt werche after lore and rede
Thou maist not werchẽ after thyn own hede
For thus sayth Salomon/ ỹ was ful trewe
Worke al by coũsayle/ & thou shalt not rewe.
And if thou wylt werken by good counsayle
I undertake/ without maste or sayle
Yet shal I saue her/ and the and me.
Hast thou not herde howe saued was Noee?
Whan ỹ our lorde had warned him byforne
That al the worlde with water shuld be lorne
Yes (quod the carpenter) ful yore a go.
¶ Hast thou not herde (quod Nicholas) also?
The sorowe of Noe with his felashyp
Or that he myght gete his wife to shippe
Him had leuer/ I dare wel undertake
At thilke tyme/ than al his wethers blake
That she had a shyp her selfe alone
And therfore wost thou what is best to done?
This asketh haste/ and of an hasty thyng
Men may not preche ne make taryeng
Anon go get us faste in to this inne
A knedyng trowe or els a kemelyn
For eche of us/ but loke that they ben large
In which men mowe swymmẽ as in a barge
And haue therin vitayles suffyciante
But for a day/ fye on the remenante
The water shal aslake and gon away
Aboute prime upon the next day
But Robyn may not weten of this thy knaue
Ne eke thy mayde Gylle/ I may not saue
Aske not why: for though thou aske me
I wol not tel goddes priuete
Suffyseth the/ but if thy wyttes be madde
To haue as great a grace as Noe hadde
Thy wyfe shal I wel saue out of doute
Go nowe thy way/ and spede the here aboute
But whan thou haste for her/ & the/ and me
Ygetten us these knedyng tubbes thre
Than shalt thou hange hem in ỹ rofe ful hye
That no man of our purueyaunce espye
And whã thou hast don thus as I haue saide
And haste our vitayle fayre in hem ylayde
And eke an axe to smyte the corde a two
Whan that the water cometh/ ỹ we may go
And breake an hole on hye upon the gable
Unto the garden warde/ ouer the stable
That we may frely passen forthe our way
Whan that the great shoure is gon away
Thã shalt thou swym as mery I undertake
As dothe the whyte ducke after her drake
Than wol I clepe/ how Alyson/ how John
Be mery: for the floode wol passe anon
And thou wolt sayn/ hayle maister Nicholay
Good morowe: for I se wel that it is day
And than we shul be lordes al our lyfe
Of al the worlde/ as was Noe and his wyfe
But of one thyng I warne the ful ryght
Be wel auysed on that ylke nyght
That we ben entred into the shyppes borde
That none of us ne speke not a worde
Ne clepe ne crye/ but ben in his prayere
For it is goddes owne heste dere.
¶ Thy wyfe & thou mot hãge ferre a twynne
For that bytwyxt you shal be no synne
No more in lokyng than there shal in dede
This ordynaunce is sayd/ go god the spede
To morowe at night/ whã men ben al a slepe
In to our knedyng tubbes wol we crepe
And sytten there/ abydyng goddes grace
Go nowe thy way/ I haue no lenger space
To make of this no lenger sermonyng
Men sayn thus: sende the wyse/ & say nothyng
Thou arte so wyse/ it nedeth the not to teche
Go saue our lyues/ and that I the beseche.
¶ This sely carpenter gothe forth his way
Ful ofte he sayd/ alas and welaway
And to his wyfe he tolde his priuete
And she was ware/ and knewe it bet than he
What al this queynte caste was for to sey
But natheles/ she ferde as she wolde dey
And sayd: alas/ go forthe thy way anone
Helpe us to skape/ or we be deed echone
I am thy trewe very wedded wyfe
Go dere spouse/ and helpe to saue our lyfe.
Lo/ whiche a great thyng is affection
Men may dye of ymagynacion

So

So depe may impꝛeſſyon be take.
 This ſely carpenter begynneth to quake
Him thynketh verily that he may ſe
Noes floode come waltryng as the ſee
To dꝛenchen Alyſon/his hony dere
He wepeth/wayleth/and maketh ſoꝛy chere
He ſyketh/with many a ſoꝛy thought
He gothe/⁊ getteth him a knedyng trough.
And after a tubbe, and a kemelyn
And priuely he ſent hem to his in
And hynge hem in the rofe ful pꝛiuely
His owne honde/he made him ladders thꝛe
To clymben by the ronges/⁊ by the ſtalkes
Into the tubbes hongyng by the balkes
And hem vitayled/bothe trough and tubbe
With breed and cheſe/⁊ good ale in a tubbe
Suffiſyng right ynowe/as foꝛ a day
 But er that he had made al this array
He ſent his knaue/and eke his wenche alſo
Vpon his nede to London foꝛ to go
And on the monday/ whan it dꝛowe to nyght
He ſhette his dooꝛe/without candel lyght
And dꝛeſſed al thyng/ as it ſhulde be
And ſhoꝛtly clomben vp al thꝛe
They ſeten ſtyll not fully a foꝛlonge way
Nowe pater noſter cloum/ſayd Nycolay
And clum qd Iohan/⁊ clum ſaid Alyſon
This carpenter ſaid his deuocion
And ſtyl he ſytte/and byddeth his prayere
Awaytyng on the rayne/ if he it here.
¶ The deed ſlepe/foꝛ wery beſyneſſe
Fel on this carpenter/ right as I geſſe
Aboute curſewe tyme/oꝛ lytel moꝛe
Foꝛ trauayle of his goſte he groneth ſoꝛe
And efte he routeth/foꝛ his heed myſlay
And down of ẏ ladder thā ſtalketh Nycholay
And Alyſon ful ſofte after ſhe ſpedde
Without wordes mo they went to bedde
There as the carpenter was woned to lye
There was the reuel/and the melodye
And thus lyeth Alyſon and Nycholas
In beſyneſſe of myꝛthe and ſolas
Tyl that the bel of laudes gan to rynge
And freres in the chaunſel gon to ſynge.
¶ This pariſſh clerke/this amerous Abſolon
That is foꝛ loue alway ſo wo bygon
Vpon the monday was at Oſenay
With company/ him to diſpoꝛte and play
And aſked vpon a caſe a cloiſtrere
Ful priuely/ after Iohn the carpentere
And he dꝛewe him a parte out of the chirche
And ſayd I not : I ſawe him nat here wirche
Sithe ſaturday/I trowe that he be went
Foꝛ tymbꝛe/ there our Abbot hath him ſent
Foꝛ he is wont foꝛ tymbꝛe foꝛ to go
And dwellen at the Grange a day oꝛ two
Oꝛ els he is at his houſe certayne
Where that he be/I can nat ſothly ſayne.
 This Abſolon/ full ioly was and lyght
And thouȝt/now is my tyme to wake al nyght
Foꝛ ſekerly/I ſawe him nat ſteryng
About his doꝛe/ſith day began to ſpringe
 So mote I thꝛyue/ I ſhall at cockes crowe
Ful priuely knocke at his wyndowe
That ſtant ful lowe vpon his boures wall
To Alyſon wol I nowe tellen all
My loue longyng : foꝛ yet I ſhal nat myſſe
That at the leeſt way I ſhal her kyſſe
Some maner comfoꝛte ſhal I haue parfaye
My mouthe hath itched al this longe day
That is a ſigne of kyſſyng at the leeſt
Al nyght me mette eke/ that I was at a feeſt
Therfoꝛe I wol go ſlepe an hour oꝛ twey
And al the night than wol I wake ⁊ pley.
¶ Whan that the firſt cocke hath crowe anon
Vp ryſte this ioly louer Abſolon
And him arayeth gay/ and in queynte deuyce
But firſt he cheweth greyns and lycoꝛice
To ſmellen ſote/oꝛ he had kempt his here
Vnder his tonge a trueloue he bere
Foꝛ therby he wende to ben graciouſe
He cometh to the carpenters houſe
And ſtyl he ſtante vnder the ſhot wyndowe
Vnto his bꝛeſt it raught/it was ſo lowe
And ſofte he knocked/ with a ſemly ſoun.
 What do ye honycombe/ſwete Alyſoun:
My fayꝛe birde/my ſwete ſynamome
Awaketh lemman myn/and ſpeketh to me
Ful lytel thinken ye vpon my wo
That foꝛ your loue I ſwelt there as I go
No wonder is though I ſwelte and ſwete
I mourne as dothe the lambe after the tete
Iwys lemman/I haue ſuche loue longyng
That lyke a turtle trewe is my mournyng

I may

I may not eaten no more than may a mayde
  Go fro the wyndowe Jacke foole/she sayde
As helpe me god and swete saynte Jame
I loue a nother/or els I were to blame
Wel bet than the (by Jesu) Absolon
Go forthe thy way/or I wol caste a ston
And let me slepe/a twenty dyuel way.
¶ Alas quod Absolon/and welaway
That trewe loue was euer so yuel bysette
Than kysse me/syn it may be no bette
For Jesus loue/and for the loue of me.
  Wylt thou thā go thy way therwith qd she?
¶ Ye certes lemman/quod this Absolon
Than make the redy (quod she) I come anon
And vnto Nycholas she said styll
Nowe peace/and thou shalt laughe thy fyll.
  This Absolon down set him vpō his knees
And sayde: I am a lorde at al degrees
For after this/ I hope there cometh more
Lemman thy grace/⁊ swete byrde thy nore.
  The wyndowe she vndothe/ ⁊ that in haste
Haue do (quod she) and spede the faste
Let not our neyghbours the aspye.
  This Absolon gan wype his mouth ful drye
Derke was the nyght/as pytche or cole
And at the wyndowe she put out her ers hole
And Absolon him felte/neyther bet ne wers
But with his mouthe he kyste her bare ers
Ful sauorly/or he were ware of this.
  A backe he sterte/⁊ thought it was amys
For wel he wyste/a woman had no berde
He felte a thyng al rowe/and longe herde
And sayd: fye/ alas what haue I do?
¶ Te he quod she/⁊ clapte the wyndowe to
And Absolon gothe forthe a sory paas
  A berde a berde/said hende Nycholas
By goddes corpus/this gothe fayre ⁊ wele.
  This sely Absolon herde it euery dele
And on his lyppe he gan for angre byte
And to him selue he sayd/ I shal the quyte.
Who rubbeth now/who froteth now his lyps
With dust/ wt sonde/with strawe/with chyps
But Absolon? that sayth ful often alas
My soule betake I to Sathanas
But me were leuer thā al this town/ quod he
Of this dispyte auenged for to be.
¶ Alas (quod he) alas ẏ I ne had yblent
His hotte loue is colde/and al yqueynt
For fro the tyme that he had kyste her ers
Of paramours he set not a kers
For he was heled of his maladye
Ful ofte paramoures he gan defye
And wepe as dothe a chylde that is ybete
A softe pace he wente ouer the strete
Vnto a smythe/ men callen dan Gerueys
That in his forge smyteth plowe harneys
He sharpeth shares/ and culters besyly
This Absolon knocketh al easily
And said vndo Gerueys/and that anon
¶ What who arte thou? It am I Absolon
What Absolon/what for Cristes swete tre
Why ryse ye so rathe? ey benedicite
What eyleth you? some gay gyrle god it wote
Hath brought you thus on the berytote
By saynte note/ye wote wel what I mene.
¶ This Absolon ne raught not a bene
Of al his play/no worde agayne he gaffe
He had more towe on his distaffe
Than Geruays knewe/ ⁊ said frende so dere
The hote cultre/ in the chymeney here
As lene it me/ I haue therwith to done
I wol bring it the agayne ful sone.
¶ Gerueys answerde: certes were it golde
Or in a poke nobles al vntolde
Thou shuldest it haue / as I am trewe smyth
Ey cristes fote/what wol ye done therwith?
  Therof (quod Absolon) be as be may
I shal wel tellen the by to morowe day
And caught the culter by the colde stele
Ful softe out at the dore gan he stele
And went vnto the carpenters wall
He coughed first/⁊ knocked ther withall
Vpon the wyndowe/right as he dyd ere.
¶ This Alyson answerde: Who is there
That knocketh so? I warante he is a thefe.
  Why nay (quod he) god wot my swete lefe
I am thyn Absolon/thyn owne derlyng
Of golde (quod he) I haue ẏ brought a ryng
My mother yaue it me/so god me saue
Ful fyne it is/and therto wel ygraue
This wol I yeue the/if thou me kysse.
  This Nycholas was rysen for to pysse
And thought he wolde amenden al the iape
He shulde kysse his ers er that he skape
And vp the wyndowe dyd he hastely
And out his ers he put ful priuely

And

And ouer the buttocke/to the haunche boon
And therwith spake this clerke/ this Absolon
Speke swete birde/I not where thou arte.
¶ This Nycholas anon let fleen a farte
As great as it had ben a thunder dent
That with the stroke he was wel ny yblent
And he was redy with his yron hote
And Nycholas in the arse he smote.
Of gothe the skyn an hondbrede about
The hotte cultor brende so his toute
And for the smerte he wende for to dye
As he were woode/he gan for to crye
Helpe/water/water/for goddes herte
This carpenter out of his slomber sterte
And herde one crye water/as he were woode
And thought/alas nowe cometh Noes floode
And sette him vp without wordes mo
And with an axe/he smote the corde a two
And downe gothe al/he foūde neyther to sell
Breed ne ale/but downe shortly he fell
Upon the flore/and there a swowne he lay.
¶ Up sterte than Alyson & hende Nycholay
And cryed out/and harrowe in the strete
The neyghbours/ bothe small and grete
In ronne/for to gauren on this man
That a swowne lay/palysshe and wan
For with that fall broken hath he his arme
But stonden he muste vnto his owne harme
For whan he spake/he was yborne adoun
With hende Nycholas/and Alisoun
They tolde euery man/that he was woode
He was agaste so of Noyes floode
Throughe fantasye/that of his vanyte
He had getten him knedyng tubbes thre
And had hem honged in the rofe aboue
And that he prayed hem for goddes loue
To sytten in the roofe par companye
The folke gan laughen at his fantasye
And in to the roofe they kyken and they gape
And turned al his ernest in to a iape
For what so this carpenter answerde
It was for naught/ no man his reason herde
With othes great/he was yswore adowne
That he was holden woode in al that towne
For euery clerke anon helde with other
They said ŷ man was wood/my leue brother
And euery wyght gan laughen at this stryfe.
¶ Thus swyued was the carpenters wyfe
For al his kepyng/and his ielousye
And Absolon hath kyst her nether eye
And Nicholas is skalded in the toute
This tale is done/& god saue al the route.

¶ Here endeth the Myllers tale: and herafter foloweth the Reues prologue.

Whan folke had laughed at this nyce caas
Of Absolon and hende Nycolas
Dyuers folke dyuersly they sayde
But for the more parte they loughe & playde
Ne at this tale I sawe no man him greue
But it were onely Oswolde the reue
Bycause he was of carpenters crafte
A lytel yre in his herte ylafte
He gan to grutchen and blamen it a lyte
Sothly quod he/ful wel couthe I ŷ quyte
With blerying of a proude myllers eye
If that me lyst to speke of rybaudrye
But eke I am olde/me lust not play for age
Grasse tyme is done/my fodder is forage
This whyte toppe writeth myn olde yeres
For somtyme yolow was/ now white ben myn
But yet I fare as doth an open ers (heres
That ylke frute is euer lenger the wers
Tyl it be rotten in molloke/or in stre
We olde men/I dreden so fare we
Tyl we be rotten can we not be rype
We hoppen alway/ while the world wol pype
For in our wyl there styketh euer a nayle
To haue an hore heed and a grene tayle
As hath a leke/for though our might be gone
Our wyl desyreth folye euer in one
For whā we may not don/thā wol we speken
Yet in our asshen olde/is fyre yreken.
¶ Four gledes han we/ whiche I shal deuyse
Auauntyng/lyeng/angre/and couetyse
These four sparkles longen on to elde
Our olde lymmes mowe wel ben vnwelde
But wyl ne shal not fayle/that is sothe
And yet haue I alway a coltes tothe
As many a yere as it is passed henne
Syn that my tappe of lyfe began to renne
For sikerly/whan I was borne anone
Dethe

The Reues prologue.

Or he drowe the tappe of lyfe/ and let it gone
And euer syns hath the tappe ronne
Tyl that almost al empty is the tonne
The streme of lyfe now droppeth on ỷ chymbe
The sely tonge may wel rynge and clymbe
Of wretcheonesse/ that passed is ful yore
With olde folke saue dotage is no more.
¶ Whan ỷ our host had herde this sermoning
He gan to speke as lordly as a kyng
And said: What amounteth al this wytte ?
What shal we speke al day of holy writte ?
The dyuel made a Reue to preche
Or a souter a shypman/ or a leche.
Say forthe thy tale/ and tary nat the tyme
Lo Depforde/ and it is halfe way prime
Lo Grenewyche/ that many a shrewe is in
It were tyme thy tale for to begyn
¶ Nowe sirs quod this Oswolde the Reue
I pray you al/ that ye not you greue
That I answere/ & somdele set his houſe
For leful it is with force/ force of shouſe
This dronken myller hath tolde vs here
Howe that begyled was a carpentere
Parauenture in skorne/ for I am one
And by your leaue/ I shal hym quite anone
Right in his cherles termes wol I speke
I pray to god his necke mote breke
He can wel in myn eye sene a stalke
But in his owne he can not sene a balke.

¶ Here endeth the Reues prologue.

¶ Here begynneth the Reues tale.

AT Trompyngton/ not far fro Cābridge
Ther gothe a broke/ & ouer that a bridge
Upon ỷ whiche broke ther stant a mell
And this is very sothe/ as I you tell
A myller was there dwellyng many a day
As any pecocke he was proude and gay
Pypen he couthe/ and fysshen/ & nettes bete
And turne cuppes/ & wel wrastle and shete
Aye by his belte he bare a longe pauade
And of a sworde ful trenchaūt was the blade
A ioly popere bare he in his pouche
Ther was no mā for peryll durst him touche
A Shefelde thwytel bare he in his hose

Rounde

Roūde was his face/ & campysed was his nose
As pylled as an ape was his skull.
He was a market beater at the full
There durst no wyght honde on him ledge
But he ne swore he shulde abedge
A these he was for sothe/ of corne and mele
And that a slye/and usaunt for to stele
His name was hoten deynous Symkyn
A wyfe he had/comen of noble kyn
The parson of the towne her father was
With her he yafe ful many a panne of bras
For that Symkyn shulde in his bloode alye
She was yfostred in a nonnerye
For Symken wolde no wyfe/as he sayde
But she were wel ynourisshed/and a mayde
To sauen his astate of yomanrye
And she was proude/and perte as a pye
A ful fayre syght was it upon hem two
On holy dayes byforne her wolde he go
With his typet wounden aboute his heed
And she came after in a gyte of reed
And Symken had hosen of the same
There durst no wyght clepen her but dame
Was none so hardy/that wente by the way
That with her ones durst rage or play
But if he wolde be slayne of Symkyn
With pauade/or with knyfe/or bodkyn
For ielous folkes ben perillous euermo
Algates they wolde her wyues wende so
And eke for she was somdele smoterlyche
She was as dygne as water in a dyche
And as ful of hoker/and of besmare
As thoughe that a lady shulde her spare
What for her kyndred/and her nortelrye
That she had lerned in the nonnerye.
¶ A doughter had they bytwyxt hem two
Of twenty yere/withouten any mo
Sauyng a chylde ẏ was of halfe yere of age
In cradell it lay/and was a propre page
This wenche thicke and wel ygrowen was
With campsed nose/and eyen gray as glas
With buttockes brode/ & brestes rounde & hye
But right fayre was her heare/I wol not lye
The parson of ẏ town/for she was so fayre
In purpose was to maken her his heyre
Bothe of his catell/and his mesuage
And straunge he made it of her maryage
His purpose was to be stowen her hye
Into some worthy blode of auncetry
For holy churches good mote ben dispended
On holy churches blode that is discended
Therfore he wolde/ his holy blode honour
Though that he holy churche shulde deuour.
¶ Great soken hath this Myller out of dout
With whete and malte/ of al the londe about
And namely there was a great college
Men clepen it the Solere hall of Cambrege
There was her whete/ & eke her malt igrounde
And on a day it happed in a stounde
Sicke lay the Maunciple/on a malady
Men wenden wisely that he shulde dye
For which this myller stale both whete & corn
An hundred tyme more than beforn
For there before/he stale but curteisly
But nowe he was a thefe outrageously
For whiche the warden chydde and made fare
But therof sette the Myller nat a tare
He craked/bosted/ and swore it nas nat so
Than were there yonge poore scholers two
That dwellen in the hall/ of whiche I say
Testife they were/ and lusty for to play
And onely for her myrthe/and her reuelrye
Upon the warden besily they crye
To yeue hem leaue/but a lytel stounde
To gon to myll/to sene her corne ygrounde
And hardely they durst lay her necke
The myller shuld not steale hem halfe a pecke
Of corne by sleyght/ne by force hem reue.
And at the last the warden yaue hem leue
Iohan hyght that one/ & Aleyn hight ẏ other
Of o town they were both/ ẏ hyght Strother
Farre in the northe/can I not tel where.
This Aleyn maketh al redy his gere
And on a horse/the sacke he caste anon
Forthe gothe Aleyn the clerke/and also Iohn
With good sworde & bockeler by her syde
Iohan knewe the way/him nedeth no gyde
And at the myll dore the sacke down he layth
¶ Aleyn spake first: alhayle Symkē in fayth
Howe fares thy fayre doughter/ & thy wyfe?
Aleyn welcom (quod Symken) by my lyfe
And Iohan also: how now? what do ye here?
By god Simōd (qd Iohn) nede has no pere
Him behoueth serue him selfe ẏ has no swayn
Or els

Or els he is a fole/ as clerkes sayne
Our Manciple I hope he wyl be deed
Swa werkes aye the wanges in his heed
And therfore is I come/ and eke Alayne
To grynde our corne & cary it home agayne
We pray you spede us heme in that ye may
 It shalbe don /quod Symkin/ be my fay
What wol ye don/ while it is in hande
By god / right by the hopper wol I stande
Qd Johan: & sen how gates the corne goth in
Yet sawe I neuer by my father kyn
Howe that the hopper wagges to and fra
 Alayne answerd: Johan wylte thou sa
Than wol I be byneth by my crowne
And se howe the mele falles adowne
Into the troughe/that shalbe my disporte
Qd John/in fay I may ben one of your sorte
I is as yll a myllere as is ye.
 This Miller smyleth at her nycite
And thought al nys done but for a wyle
They wene that no man may hem begyle
But by my thryfte/yet shal I blere her eye
For al the sleyght in her philosofye
The more queynte clerkes that they make
The more wol I steale whan I take
In stede of floure yet wol I gyue hem brenne
The greatest clerkes ben not the wysest men
As whilom to the wolfe spake the Mare
Of al her arte counte I not a tare.
¶ Out at the dore he gothe ful priuely
Whan that he sawe his tyme/subtelly
He loked up & downe/tyl he had yfounde
The clerkes horse/there as he stode ybounde
Behynde the Mylle/under a lessel
And to the horse he gothe him fayre and wel
He stryppeth of the bridel ryght anon.
 And whan ye horse was lose/ he gan to gon
Towarde the fen/there wylde mares rynne
And forth/with wehe/through thicke & thynne
The myller gothe agayne/ no worde he sayde
But doth his note/ & with these clerkes playde
Tyl that her corne was fayre & wel ygroūde
And whan the meale was sacked & ybounde
This Johan goth out/ & fonde her hors away
And gan to crye/harowe and welaway
Our horse is loste Aleyne for goddes banes
Steppe on thy fete man/come forth al atanes
Alas our wardeyn has his palfray lorne.
 ¶ This Aleyn al forgate bothe mele & corne
Al was out of mynde his husbondrye
What/whylke way is he gon: he gan to crye.
 The wyfe came leapyng inwarde at a renne
She sayd alas/he gothe to the fenne
With wylde mares/as faste as he may go
Unthāke come on his honde/ yt bonde him so
And he ye better shulde haue knyt the reyne.
 Alas qd Johan/Aleyn for Christes peyne
Lay downe thy swerde/ & I shal myn alswa
I is ful swyfte god wate as is a raa
By goddes sale he shal not skape us bathe:
Why ne haddest thou put the capel in ye lathe:
Il heyle Aleyn by god thou is a fonne.
¶ These sely clerkes han ful faste ronne
Towarde the fenne/ Aleyn and eke John
And whan the myller sawe yt they were agon
He halfe a bussshel of her floure hath take
And bade his wyfe knede it in a kake
He said/ I trowe the clerkes were a ferde
Yet can a myller make a clerkes berde
For al her arte/ yet let hem gon her way
Lo where they gon/let the chyldren play
They get him not so lightly by my crowne
 These sely clerkes rennen up and downe
With kepe kepe/ iossa Warderere
Ga whystle thou/and I sal kepe him here
 But shortly/tyll it was very nyght
They couth not/though they dyd al her might
Her caple catche/he ran away so faste
Tyl in a dyche they caught him at the laste.
¶ Wery and wete/as beestes in the rayne
Cometh sely John/ & with him cometh Alayn
Alas (quod Johan) the day that I was borne
Nowe are we driuen to hethen and to skorne
Our corne is stole/men wol us fooles call
Bothe the warden/and our felowes all
And namely the myller/ wayla way
Thus playneth Johan/as he gothe by ye way
Towarde the myll/ & bayarde in his honde
The myller syttyng by the fyre he fonde
For it was night/ & ferther might they nought
But for the loue of god they him besought
Of herbrough and ease/as for her peny.
¶ The myller said agen/if there ben any
Suche as it is/yet shal ye haue your parte

F My

My house is strayte/but ye haue lerned arte
Ye can by argument make a place
A myle brode/ of twenty foote of space
Let se nowe if this place may suffyse
Or make it rōmer wt speche/ as is your gyse
Now Symōd (said John) by saint Cutberde
Aye is thou mery/ & that is fayre answerde
I haue herd say/ mē shuld take of twa thīges
Swylke as he fyndes or swilke as he bringes
But specially I pray the hoste dere
Get vs some meate & drinke/ & make vs chere
And we wyl pay trewly at the ful
With empty honde/men may no haukes tull
Lo here our syluer redy for to spende.
 The myller to the towne his doughter sēde
For ale and breed/and rosted hem a goos
And bōde her hors he shuld no more go loos
And in his owne chambre he made a bedde
With shetes & with chalons fayre yspredde
Not from his owne bedde/ten fote or twelue
His doughter had a bedde al by her selue
Right in the same chambre/by and by
It myght be no bette/and the cause why.
Ther was no rowmer herbrowe in yͤ place.
They soupen/ & they speken of myrth & solace
And dronken euer stronge ale at beste
Aboute mydnight went they to reste.
¶ Wel hath this myller vernysshed his heed
Ful pale he was for dronken/ & nothyng reed
He galpeth/ & he speketh through his nose
As he were in the quacke/or in the pose
To bedde he gothe/and with him his wyfe
As any Iay was she lyght and iolyfe
So was her ioly whystell wel ywette
The cradell at the beddes fete was sette
To rocken/ & to yeue the chylde to souke
And whan yͤ dronken was al in the crouke
To bedde went the daughter ryght anon
To bedde gothe Aleyn and eke John
There nas no more/hem neded no dwale
This myller hath so wisely bybbed ale
That as an horse he snorteth in his slepe
Ne of his tayle behynde he toke no kepe
His wyfe bare to him a bordon wel strong
Men might hem here route a forlonge
The wenche routeth eke par company.
¶ Aleyn the clerke/that herde this melody
He poked on Iohan/ & said: slepest thou?
Herdest thou euer swylke a sange er nowe?
Lo swylke a couplyng is ytwyxt hem all
A wylde fyre on her bodyes fall.
Who herde euer swylke a ferly thyng?
ye/they shal haue the floure of yuel endyng
Al this lange nyght tydes me no reste
But yet na force/al shal be for the beste
For Iohan (sayd he) as euer mote I thriue?
If that I may/yon wenche wol I swyue
Some esement hath lawe shapen vs
For Iohan, there is a lawe that saythe thus
That if a man in one poynte ben a greued
That in an other he shal be releued
Our corne is stolne/sothly it is no nay
And we haue had an yuel fyt to day
And syn I shal haue none amendement
Agayne my losse I wyl haue myn esement
By goddes sale/it shal none other be.
¶ This Iohan answerde: Aleyn/auyse the
The myller is a perillous man/he sayde
And if that he out of his slepe abrayde
He myght don vs bathe a vilonye.
 Aleyn answerd: I coūt him not worth a fly
And vp he ryste/and by the wenche he crept.
 This wenche lay vpright/and faste slept
Tyl he so nye was/er she myght aspye
That it had ben to late for to crye
And shortly for to sayne/they were at on
Nowe play Aleyn/for I wol speke of John.
 This Iohan lay styl a forlonge way or two
And to him selfe he maketh routh and wo
 Alas (quod he) this is a wicked iape
Nowe may I say/I is but an ape
yet hath my felowe somwhat for his harme
He hath the myllers doughter in his arme
He auntreth him/and hath his nede ysped
And I lye as a draffe sacke in my bedde
And whan this iape is tolde a nother dey
I shal be holde a daffe/or a cokeney
I wol aryse/ and auntre me it by my fay
Unhardy is vnsely/thus men say.
 And vp he rose/and softely he wente
Unto the cradell/ and in his arme it hent
And bare it softly to his beddes fete
Sone after the wyfe her routyng lete
And gan awake/and went her out to pysse

And

And came agayn/ & gan the cradell mysse
And groped here & there/ but she founde none
Alas (quod she) I had almoste mysgone
I had almost gone to the clerkes bedde
Eye benedycite/ than had I foule yspedde
And forthe she gothe/ tyl she the cradel fonde
She gropeth alway further with her honde
And founde the bedde/ & thought nat but good
Bycause that the cradel by it stode
And nyste where she was/ for it was derke
But fayre & wel she crepte in by the clerke
And lyeth ful styl/ & wold haue caught a slepe
Within a whyle this Iohan the clerke vp lepe
And on this good wyfe he layde ful sore
So mery a fyt had she nought ful yore
And pricked harde & depe/ as he were madde
  This ioly lyfe haue these two clerkes ladde
Tyl that the thirde cocke began to syng.
¶ Aleyn waxe wery in the dawnyng
For he had swonken al the longe nyght
And sayd/ farwel Malyn swete wyght
The day is comen/ I may no lenger byde
But euermo/ where so I go or ryde
I am thyn owne clerke/ so haue I hele.
  Nowe dere lemman (quod she) go/ farwele
But or thou go/ one thyng I wol the tell
Whan thou wendest homwarde by the Mell
Right at the entre of the dore behynde
Thou shalt a cake of halfe a busshel fynde
That was ymaked of thyn owne mele
Whiche that I helpe my syre to stele
And good lemman god the saue and kepe
And with ye worde she gan almoste to wepe.
¶ Aleyn vprist/ and thought er it dawe
He wolde go crepen in by his felawe
And founde the cradel with his honde anon
By god thought he/ al wronge haue I gon
My heed is totty of my swynke to nyght
That maketh me that I go not aryght
I wot wel that by ye cradel I haue mysse go
Here lyeth the Myller and his wyfe also
And forthe he gothe on twenty dyuels way
Vnto the bedde/ there as the myller lay
He wende haue cropen by his felowe Iohn
And by the myller he crepte in anon
And caught hym by the necke/ & soft he spake
And sayd: Iohan/ thou swynesheed awake
For Christes soule/ and here a noble game
For by that lorde that called is saynt Iame
As I haue thryse in this shorte nyght
Swyued the myllers doughter bolte vpright
Whyles thou haste/ as a cowarde ben agaste.
  Ye false harlot (quod the myller) haste
A false traytour/ false clerke (quod he)
Thou shalte be deed by goddes dignyte
Who durste be so bolde to disparage
My doughter/ that is come of suche lynage
And by the throte bolle he caught Alayn
And he hym hente dispytously agayn
And on the nose he smote him with his fest
Downe ran the bloode streme vpon his brest
And in the flore/ with mouthe & nose ybroke
They walowen/ as dothe pygges in a poke
And vp they gon/ and downe ayen anone
Tyl that the myller spurnde on a stone
And downe he fyl backwarde vpon his wyfe
That wyste nothyng of this nyce stryfe
For she was fal a slepe a lytel wyght
With Iohan the clerke/ ye waked had al nyght
And with the fall/ out of her slepe she brayde
Helpe holy crosse of Bromholme she sayde
In manus tuas/ lorde to the I call
A wake Symonde/ the fende is on me fall
My herte is broken/ helpe I am but deed
There lyeth one on my wombe & on my heed
Helpe Symkyn/ for these false clerkes fyght.
  This Iohn stert vp/ as fast as euer he myght
And graspeth by the walles to and fro
To fynde a staffe/ and she stert vp also
And knewe the estres bet than dyd this Iohn
And by the wal she founde a staffe anon
And sawe a lytel shemeryng of a lyght
For at an hole in shone the moone bryght
And by that lyght she sawe hem bothe two
But lykerly she nyste who was who
But as she sey a whyte thyng in her eye
And whan she gan this whyte thyng aspye
She wende the clerke had weared a voluper
And with ye staffe she drowe alway ner & ner
And wende haue hyt this Aleyn at full
And smote the myller on the pylled skull
That downe he gothe/ & cryed/ harrowe I dye
These clerkes bete hym wel/ and let hym lye
And arayeth hem/ and toke her horse anon

And eke her meale/ and on her way they gon
And at the mylle dore they toke her cake
Of halfe a bussher floure/wel ybake.
¶Thus is the proude myller wel ybete
And hath ylost the gryndyng of the whete
And payde for the supper everydele
Of Aleyn and of Johan/that bete him wele
His wyfe is swyved/and his doughter als
Lo suche it is a Myller to be fals
And therfore this proverbe is ful sothe
Hym dare not wel wene that yvel dothe
A gylour shal him selfe begyled be
And god that sytte hye in maieste
Save al this company/great and smale
Thus have I quyt the myller in his tale.

¶Here endeth the Reves tale/ and here foloweth the Cokes prologue.

The Coke of London/whyle ȳ Reve spake
For ioy him thought he claude him on ȳ bake
A ha (quod he) for Christes passyon
This myller hath a sharpe conclusyon
Upon his argument of herbygage
Wel said Salomon in his langage
Ne bring not every man in to thyn hous
For herbrowyng by nyght is perelous
Wel ought a man avysed for to be
Whom that he brought in to his privete
I pray to god so yeve me sorowe and care
If ever sythen I hyght Hodge of Ware
Herde I myller bette ysette awerke
He had a iape of malyce in the derke.
But god forbyd that we stynten here
And therfore if ye vouche safe to here
A tale of me/that am a poore man
I wol you tel as wel as I can
A lytel iape/that fel in our cyte.
¶Our host sayd/sir I graunte it the
Nowe tel on Rodger/loke that it be good
For many a pasty haste thou letten bloode
And many a Iacke of Dover hast thou solde
That hath be twyse hotte and twyse colde
Of many a pilgrym hast thou Christes curse
For of thy parsle yet fare they the worse
That they have eaten with thy stobel goos
For in thy shoppe is many a flye loos
Nowe tel on gentle Rogere by thy name
But yet I pray the be not wrothe for game
A man may say ful sothe in game ⁊ play.
¶Thou sayst ful soth (qd̄ Roger) by my fay
But soth play/quade play/ as ȳ flemig saith
And therfore Henry Baylly by thy fayth
Be thou not wrothe/or we departen here
Though that my tale ben of an hostelere
But nathelesse/I wol not tellen it yet
But er we parte/ywys thou shalte be quyt
And therwithal he lough and made chere
And sayd his tale/as ye shullen after here.

¶Here endeth the Cokes prologue/ and here foloweth his tale.

A Prentise whilom dwelte in our cyte
And of the crafte of Vitaplers was he
Galiard he was/as goldfinch in ye shaw
Browne as a bery/ a proper shorte felawe
With lockes blake/kempt ful fetously
Daunce he couthe ful wel and iolily
He was called Perkyn Reuelour
He was as ful of loue and paramour
As is the hyue ful of hony swete
Wel was the wenche with hym might mete
At euery bridal wolde he syng and hoppe
He loued bette the tauernes than the shoppe
For whan any ridyng was in chepe
Out of the shoppe thider wolde he lepe
Tyl that he had al the sight iseyn
And daunced wel/ he wolde not come ageyn
And gather hym a meyny of his sorte
To hop and syng/ and make suche disporte
And there they sette steuyn for to mete
To playen at the dise in suche a strete
For in the cyte nas there no prentise
That fayrer couthe casten a payre of dise
Than Perken couthe/ and therto he was free
Of his dispence/ in place of priuyte
That founde his maister wele in his chafare
For oftymes he founde his boye ful bare
For sikerly/ a prentise reuelour
That haunteth dise/ riotte/ or paramour
His maister shal it in his shoppe abye
Al haue he no parte of the mynstralcy
For thefte and riotte/ they ben conuertible
Al can he play on gettron or on ribible
Reuel and trouthe/ as in lowe degre
They ben ful wrothe al day / as men may se
This ioly prentise/ with his maister abode
Tyl he were nye out of his prentishode
Al were he snybbed bothe early and late
And somtyme ledde with reuel to Newgate
But at the last / his maister him bethought
Vpon a day/ whan he his paper sought
Of a prouerbe/ that saith this same worde
Welbette is rotten apple out of horde
Than that it rote al the remenaunt
So fareth it by a riottous seruaunt
It is moche lesse harme to let hym passe
Than he shende al the seruauntes in the place
Therfore his maistrr gaue him a quitaunce
And badde him go/ with sorowe & myschaũce
And thus this ioly prentise had his leue
Nowe lette him riot al the night or leue

F.iii. And

The man of lawes prologue.

And for there is no thefe without a louke
That helpeth him to waste or to souke
Of that he brybe can/or borowe may
Anon he sent his bedde and his array
Unto a compere of his owne sorte
That loued dyce/reuel/and disporte
And had a wyfe/ that helde for countenaunce
A shoppe/⁊ swyued for her sustenaunce.

¶ Here endeth the Cokes tale/ and here foloweth the man of lawes prologue.

Our hoste sawe wel/ that the bright sonne
O The arke of his artifycial day hath ronne
The fourthe parte/⁊ halfe an hour more
And though he were not depe expert in lore
He wyste it was the eyghtene day
Of April/that is the messanger to May
And sawe wel/ that the shadowe of euery tre
Was as in lengthe/the same quantyte
As was the body erecte/that caused it
And therfore by the shadowe he toke his wyt
That Phebus/whiche ỹ shone clere ⁊ bright
Degrees was fourty clomben of hyght
And for that daye/as in latytude
It was ten of the clocke/he gan conclude
And sodaynly he plyght his horse aboute.
¶ Lordynges (qd he) I warne you al ỹ route
The fourthe parte of this day is gon
Nowe for the loue of god and of saynt John
Leseth no tyme/as ferforth as ye may
Lordynges the tyme wasteth both night ⁊ day
And stealeth from vs/what priuely slepyng
And what through negligēce in our wakyng
As doth the streme/that turneth neuer agayn
Discendyng fro the moūtayne in to ỹ playn
Wel can Senecke/and many a phylosofre
Bywaylen tyme/more than golde in cofre
For losse of catel may recouered be
But losse of tyme shendeth vs (quod he)
It wol not come ayen withouten drede
No more than wol Malkyns maydenhede
Whan she hath loste it in her wantonnesse
Let vs not mawlen thus in ydelnesse.
Syr man of lawe (quod he) so haue I blys
Tel vs a tale anon/as forwarde is
ye ben submytted/through your fre assent
To stonden in this case at my iudgement
Acquyteth you nowe of your behestе
Than haue ye done your deuer at the leste.
¶ Hoste (quod he) de pardeux ieo assent
To breke forwarde is not myn entent
Byheste is dette/ and I wol holde fayne
Al my behest/I can no better sayne
For such lawe as a mā yeueth an other wight
He shulde him selue vsen it by ryght
Thus wol our text: But natheles certayne
I can right nowe no thrifty tale sayne
That Chaucer (though he can but lewdly
On metres and in rymyng craftely)
Hath sayd hem/in suche englysshe as he can
Of olde tyme/as knoweth many a man
And if he haue not sayd hem leue brother
In one boke/he hath sayd hem in a nother
For he hath tolde of louers vp and down
Mo than Ouyde made of mencioun
In his epystels/ that ben ful olde
What shuld I telle hem/ sythen they ben tolde:
In youthe he made of Ceyx and Alcyone
And sythen he hath spoken of euerychone
These noble wyues/and these louers eke
Who so that woll his large volume seke
Cleped the sayntes legende of Cupyde
There may he se the large woundes wyde
Of Lucresse/ and of Babylon Thisbe
The swerde of Dydo for the false Enee
The tre of Phillis for her Demophoon
The playnte of Dianire/ and of Hermyon
Of Adriane/and of Hypsiphilee
The barayne yle stondyng in the see
That dreynte Leandre for his Hero
The teares of Heleyn/ and eke the wo
Of Briseis/and of Laodomia
The crueltie of quene Media
The lytel children hongyng by the hals
For the Jason/that was of loue so fals
Of Hypermistra/ Penelope/and Alceste
Your wyfehode he cōmendeth with the beste
But certaynly no worde ne writeth he
Of thylke wycked ensample of Canace
That loued her owne brother synfully
Of suche cursed stories I say fy
Or els of Tyro Appollonius

Howe

Howe that the cursed kyng Antyocus
Byrafte his doughter of her maydenhede
That is so horrible a tale for to rede
Whan he her drewe vpon the pament
And therfore he of ful auisement
Nolde neuer write in non of his sermons
Of suche vnkynde abhominations
Ne I ne wol non reherce/ yef that I may
But of my tale howe shal I don this day
Me were lothe be lykened doutles
To Muses/that men clepeth Pieryades
Methamorphoseos wotte what I mene
But nathelees I recche not a bene
Though I come after him with haubake
I speke in prose/and let him rymes make
And with that worde/he with a sobre chere
Began his tale/as ye shullen after here.

¶ Here endeth the man of lawes prologue/ & here foloweth his tale.

O Hateful harme/condycion of pouert
With thurst/wt colde/with hugre so cōfounded
To asken helpe / the shameth in thyn hert
If thou non aske/wt nede thou art so wounded
That very nede vnwrapeth al thy woūdz hyd
Maugry thyn hed/thou must for indygēce
Or stele/or begge/or borowe thy dispence

Thou blamest Christ/and sayest ful bytterly
He misdeparteth rychesse temporall
Thy neyghbour thou wytest synfully
And sayest/thou haste to lytel/& he hath all
Parfay (sayst thou) somtyme he reken shall
Whan that his tayle shal brenne in glede
For he nought helpeth nedeful in her nede.

¶ Herken what is the sentence of the wyse
Better is to dyen/than to haue indygence
Thyn selfe neyghbour wol the dispyse
If thou be poore/farwel thy reuerence
Yet of the wyse man take this sentence
Al the dayes/poore men ben wycke
Beware therfore or thou come to the prycke

If thou be poore/thy brother hateth the
And al thy frendes fleeth fro the/alas
O ryche marchauntes ful of wele be ye
O noble prudent folke/as in this caas
Your bagges ben not fylde with ambes aas
But wt syse synke/y renneth for your chaunce
At Christenmasse/ mery may ye daunce

Ye seken

The man of lawes tale.

¶ Ye seken londe ⁊ see for your wynnynges
As wise folke ye knowen al the state
Of regnes/ ye ben fathers of tidynges
And tales/ bothe of peace and debate
I was right nowe of tales desolate
Nere that a marchaunt/ goue is many a yere
Me taught a tale/ whiche ye shullen here.

IN Surrey whilom dwelte a company
Of chapmen rich/ and therto sad ⁊ trewe
That wydewhere senten her spicery
Clothes of golde/ and satten ryche of hewe
Her chafare was so thrifty and so newe
That euery wight hath deyntie to chafare
With hem/ and eke to sellen hem her ware

Nowe fel it/ that the maisters of that sorte
Han shapen hem/ to Rome for to wende
Were it for chapmanhode/ or for disporte
Non other messãgere wolde they thyder sende
But comen hem selfe to Rome/ this is yͤ ende
And in suche place as thought hem auãtage
For her entent/ they taken her herbygage

Soiourned han these marchaũtes in yͤ towne
Certayne tyme/ as fel to her plesaunce
But so byfel/ that the excellent renowne
Of the emperours doughter dame Custãce
Reported was/ with euery circumstaunce
Unto these surreyn marchaũtes/ in suche wise
Fro day to day/ as I shal you deuyse

¶ This was the comen voyce of euery man
Our emperour of Rome/ god him se
A doughter hath/ yͤ sythen the worlde began
To reken as wel her goodnesse as her beaute
Nas neuer suche a nother as is she
I pray to god in honour her sustene
And wolde she were of al Europe yͤ quene

In her is hye beautie/ without pride
Youthe/ without grenhede or folye
To al her werkes vertu is her gyde
Humblesse hath slayne in her al tyrannye
She is a myrrour of al curtesye
Her herte is very chambre of holynesse
Her honde mynistre of fredom ⁊ almesse

¶ And al this voyce was soth/ as god is trew
But now to our purpose let vs turne agayn
These marchãtes han don fret her shyps new
And whã they han this blysful mayden seyn
Home to Surrey ben they went ageyn
And done her nedes/ as they han done yore
And lyuen in welth/ I can say no more.

Now fel it/ yͤ these marchãtes stoden in grace
Of him that was the Soudon of Surrye
For whã yͤ they came from any straũge place
He wolde of his benygne curtesye
Maken hem good chere/ ⁊ besyly aspye
Tydynges of sondry realmes for to lere
The wonders that they might seen or here

Amonge other thynges specially
These marchãtes haue him tolde of dãe Custaũce
So gret noblesse/ in ernest ceryously
That this Soudon hath caught so gret plesãce
To han her fygure in his remembraunce
And al his luste/ and al his besy cure
Was for to loue her/ while his lyfe may dure

¶ Parauenture in that ylke large boke
Whiche yͤ cleped is the heuen/ ywritten was
With sterres/ whan that he his byrthe toke
That he for loue shulde han his dethe/ alas
For in the sterres/ clerer than is the glas
Is written god wot/ who so coude it rede
The dethe of euery man withouten drede

¶ In sterres many a wynter there byfore
Was written the deth of Hector ⁊ of Achylles
Of Pompey and Iulyus/ or they were bore
The stryfe of Thebes/ and of Hercules
Of Sampson/ Turnus/ and of Socrates
The dethe: but that mens wyttes ben so dull
That no wyght can wel rede it at the full

¶ This Soudon for his priue coũsayle sent
And shortly of this mater for to pace
He hath to hem declared al his entent
And said hem certain/ but if he might haue grace
To haue Custaũce/ within a lytel space
He nas but deed/ and charged hem to hye
To shapen for his lyfe some remedye.

Dyuers

The Man of Law's Prologue and Tale (B 127–210; T. 4547–4630)

¶ Diuers men / diuersly they sayden
The argument they casten vp and down
Many a subtell reason forthe they sayden
They speken of Magike / and abusioun
But finally / as in conclusioun
They can not seen in that non auauntage
Ne in non other way / saue in mariage.

¶ Than sawe they therin suche difficulte,
By way of reason / to speke al playne
Bicause that there was suche diuersite
Bitwene her bothe lawes / that they sayne
They trowe yͭ no christen prince wolde fayne
Wedden his childe vnder our lawes swete
That vs was tauȝt / by Mahounde our pphete

¶ And he answerde: rather than I lese
Custaunce / I wol be christen doutles
I mote ben hers / I may non other chese
I pray you holde your argumentes in pees
Saueth my lyfe / and be not recheles
To getten her / that hath my lyfe in cure
For in this wo / I may not long endure

¶ What nedeth greatter delatation
I say / by treatie and ambassadrye
And by the popes mediation
And al the chirche / and al the cheualry
That in distruction of Maumetry
And in encrease of Christes lawe dere
They ben accorded / as ye shal here.

¶ Howe that the Soudon and his baronage
And al his lieges / shulde ichristned be
And he shal han Custaunce in mariage
And certayne golde / I not what quantite
And her to fynde sufficient surete
The same accorde was sworne on either syde
Nowe faire Custaūce / almighty god yͤ gyde

¶ Nowe wolden som men waiten / as I gesse
That I shulde tellen al the purueyaunce
That the Emperour of his noblesse
Hath shapen for his daughter dame Custāce
Wel may men knowen / that so gret ordynāce
May no man tellen in a lytell clause
As was arayde for so highe a cause

Bisshoppes ben shapen with her for to wende
Lordes and ladies / and knightes of renowne
And other folke ynowe / this is the ende
And notified is throughout the towne
That euery wight / with great deuotioun
Shulde pray Christ / that he this mariage
Receyue in gree / and spede this voiage

¶ The day is come of her departyng
I say the woful day natural is come
That there may be no lengre tariyng
But forwarde they hem dresse al and some
Custaunce / that with sorowe is al ouercome
Ful pale arist / and dresseth her to wende
For wel she sey / there is non other ende

¶ Alas / what wondre is it though she wept?
That shal be sent to a straunge nation
Fro frendes / that so tenderly her kept
And to be bounden vnder subiection
Of one / she knoweth not his condition
Husbondes ben al good and han ben yore
That knowen wyues / I dare say no more

Father (she said) thy wretched childe Custāce
Thy yonge daughter / fostred vp so softe
And ye my mother / my soueraigne plesance
Ouer al thyng (out take Christ on lofte)
Custaunce your childe her cōmaundeth ofte
Vnto your grace: for I shal to Surrye
Ne shal I neuer more se you with eye

¶ Alas / vnto the Barbary nation
I must anon / sithen it is your wyl
But Christ that starfe for our redemption
So yeue me grace / his hestes to fulfyll
I wretched woman no force though I spyll
Women arn borne to thraldom and penaūce
And to ben vnder mannes gouernaunce

I trow at Troy / whan Thirus brake yͤ wal
Of Ilyon / ne whan brente was Thebes cyte
Ne Rome for the harme of Hanybal
That Romayns hath venquesshed tymes thre
Nas herde / suche tendre wepyng for pyte
As was in the chambre for her departyng
But forth she mote / wheder she wepe or syng.

O firste

The man of lawes tale.

¶ O first mouyng cruel firmament
With thy diurnal swegh/ that croudest aye
And hurtlest al fro Est to Occident
That naturally wolde holde another way
Thy croudyng set the heuen in suche array
At the begynnyng of this feirs vyage
That cruel Mars hath slayne this mariage

¶ O infortunate assendent tortuous
Of whiche the lorde is helpelesse fal/ alas
Out of his angle/into his derkest house
O Mars/ O occiser/as in this caas
O feble Mone/ vnhappy ben thy paas
Thou knittest þ there thou nart not receyued
Ther thou were wel/ fro thece art þu weyued

¶ Imprudent emperour of Rome/ alas
Was there no philosofer in thy towne?
Is no tyme bette than other in suche cas?
Of voiage/is there non electiowne?
Namely to folke of hye condicioun
Nat whan a rote is of a byrthe iknowe
Alas we ben to leude/ or to slowe

¶ To ship is brought this woful faire mayd
Solempnely/ with euery circumstaunce
Nowe Jesu Christ be with you al (she sayd)
Ther nys no more/ but farewel fair Custāce
She payneth her to make good countenance
And forthe I let her sayle in this manere
And tourne I wol agayne to my matere.

¶ Explicit prima pars: et sequitur pars secunda.

The mother of the Soudon/ wel of vices
Aspied hath her sonnes playne entent
Howe he wol lete his olde sacrifices
And right anon/she for her counsayle sent
And they ben comen/ to know what she ment
And whan assembled was this folke in fere
She sette her down/& said/ as ye shal here.

¶ Lordes (quod she) ye knowen euerichone
Howe that my sonne is in poynt to lete
The holy lawes of our Alkaron
yeuen by goddes messangere Machomete
But one auowe to grete god I hete
The lyfe shal rather out of my body stert
Or Machomettes lawe go out of my hert

What shulde vs tyden of this newe lawe
But thraldome to our bodies and penaunce
And afterwarde in hel to ben drawe
For we reneyed Mahounde our creaunce?
But lordes/ wol ye make assuraunce
As I shal say/ assentyng to my lore
And I shal make vs safe for euermore

They sworen/ and assenten euery man
To lyue with her and dye/ and by her stonde
And eueriche in the best wise that he can
To strengthen her/ shal his frendes fonde
And she hath this empryse take in honde
Whiche ye shal here/ that I shal deuise
And to hem al she spake in this wise.

We shul vs first fayne/christendom to take
Colde water shal not greue vs but a lyte
And I shal suche a reuel and a feest make
That as I trowe/ I shal the Soudon quite
For tho his wyfe be christened neuer so whyte
She shal haue nede to wasshe away the rede
Though she a fonte ful of water wt her lede

¶ O Soudonnesse/rote of iniquite
Virago thou Semyram the secounde
O serpent vnder femenynete
Lyke to the serpent depe in hell ybounde
O fayned woman/al that may confounde
Vertu and innocence/through thy malyce
Is bredde in the/a nest of euery vyce.

¶ O Sathan enuyous/ syn thylke day
That thou were chased from our herytage
Wel knewest thou to women the olde way
Thou madest Eue to bring vs in seruage
Thou wolte fordone this christen maryage
Thyn instrument/so welaway the whyle
Makest thou of womē/whā thou wolt begyle.
This

¶ This Soudonesse/whom I blame ⁊ wery
Let priuely her counsayle gon her way
What shulde I in this tale lenger tarye?
She rydeth to the Soudon on a day
And sayd him/that she wolde reneye her lay
And christendom of prestes hondes fonge
Repentyng her/she hethen was so longe

Besechyng him/ to done her that honour
That she might haue the cristen folke to feste
To plesen hem/I wol done my laboure
The Soudon sayth/I wol don at your heste
And knelyng/thanketh her of that requeste
So glad he was/ he nyst not what to say
She kyst her sonne/⁊ home she goth her way

¶ Aryued ben these christen folke to londe
In Surre/with a great solempne route
And hastely this Soudon sent his sonde
First to his mother/⁊ al the reygne aboute
And sayd/his wyfe was comen out of doute
And prayden hem for to ryden ayenst ẏ quene
The honoure of his reygne for to sustene

Great was the prese/⁊ ryche was the raye
Of Surreyens/ and Romayns ymette yfere
The mother of the Soudon/ryche and gay
Receyueth her with al glad chere
As any mother myght her doughter dere
Unto the next cite there besyde
A softe paas solempnely they ryde

¶ Nought trowe I/the triumphe of Iulyus
Of whiche that Lucan maketh suche a bost
Was royaller/ and more curious
Than was thassemblyng of this blissful host
But this Scorpion/ this wicked gost
The sodōnesse/ for al her flatteryng
Cast under al this/ful mortally to styng

The Soudon cometh himselfe sone after this
So ryally/that wonder is to tel
He welcometh her with moche ioye ⁊ blys
And thus in myrthe ⁊ ioy I let hem dwell
The fruyte of euery tale is for to tell
Whan tyme come/ men thought it for the best
That reuel stynte/and men gon to rest

¶ The tyme come/this olde Soudōnesse
Ordayned hath the feest/of whiche I tolde
And to the feest/christen folke hem dresse
In general/ bothe yonge and olde
There may men feest and ryalte beholde
And deyntes mo than I can deuyse
But al to dere they boughten it or they ryse

¶ O Soudon/wo ẏ euer thou art successour
To worldly blysse/ springed with bytternesse
The ende of ioye/of our worldly laboure
Wo occupyeth the ende of our gladnesse
Herken this counsayle/for thy sykernesse
Upon thy glad day haue thou in mynde
The unware wo or harm/ ẏ cometh behynde

For shortly for to tellen at a worde
The Soudon/ and the cristen euerychone
Ben al to hewe/ ⁊ stycked at the borde
But it were onely dame Custaunce alone
This olde Soudōnesse/cursed crone
Hath with her frendes don this cursed dede
For she her selfe wolde al the countre lede

Ne there was surreyen none ẏ was cōuerted
That of the counsayle of the Soudon wot
That he nas al to hewe/er he asterted
And Custaunce han they taken anon foteshot
And in a shyppe al sterneslesse (god wot)
They han her set/⁊ bydden her lerne to sayle
Out of Surrey ayenwarde to Itayle.

¶ A certayne tresour/that she thyder ladde
And sothe to sayne/vitayle great plente
They han her yeuen/⁊ clothes eke she had
And forthe she sayleth in the salte se
O my Custaunce/ful of benygnite
O emperours yonge doughter dere
He that is lorde of fortune/be thy stere.

She blesseth her/and with ful pytous voice
Unto the crosse of Christ/tho sayd she.
O clere/ o welful auter/ holy croice
Reed of the lambes blode/ ful of pyte
That wesshe ẏ worlde fro the olde iniquite
Me fro the fende/and fro his clawe kepe
That day that I shal drenchen in the depe

Victo-

The Man of Law's Tale (B 372–455; T. 4792–4875)

The man of lawes tale.

¶ Victorious tree/ protection of trewe
That onely worthy were for to bere
The kyng of heuyn/with his woundes newe
The white lambe/that hurt was with a spere
Flemere of feendes/ out of him and here
On whiche thy lymmes / faithfully extenden
Me kepe/& yeue me might my life to amenden

¶ yeres and dayes fleteth this creature
Thrughout the see of Grece/ vnto the strayte
Of Marocke/as it was her auenture
O/ many a sory mele may she bayte
After her dethe ful ofte may she wayte
Or that the wylde wawes wolde her dryue
Unto the place there she shulde aryue.

Men mighten asken/why she was not slayn
Eke at the feest/ who myght her body saue?
I answere to that demaunde agayn
Who saued Danyel in that horrible caue?
There euery wyght/ were he maister or knaue
Was with the lyon frette or he asterte
No wyght but god/that he bare in his herte.

¶ God lyst to shewe his wonderful myracle
In her/ for she shulde sene his mighty werkes
Christ that is to euery harme tryacle
By certayn meanes often/as knowen clerkes
Dothe thing for certayn ende/ ẏ full derke is
To mans wytte/that for our ygnoraunce
Ne con nat knowe his prudent puruey aunce

Nowe syth that she was not at ẏ feest yslawe
Who kepeth her fro the drenchyng in the see?
Who kept Jonas in the fysshes mawe
Tyl he was spouted out at Nenyue?
Wel may men knowe/it was no wight but he
That kept the people Ebrak from drenchyng
With drue fete/through the see passyng

Who hath the four spyrites of the tempeste
That power had/bothe to anoye londe & see
Bothe northe and southe/and also west & este
Anoyeth neyther see/ne londe/ne tre
Sothly the cōmaunder therof was he
That fro the tempest aye this woman kepte
As wel whan she woke as whan she slepte

Wher might this woman mete & drinke haue?
Thre yere and more/ how lasteth her vitayle?
Who fedde the Egypcian Marye in the caue
Or in deserte (none but Christ sans fayle)
Fyue thousāde folke it was as gret maruaile
With loues fyue and fysshes two to fede
God sent his foyson at her great nede.

She driueth forthe in to our Occian
Throughout the wylde see/tyl at the laste
Under an holde/that nempne I ne can
Fer in Northumberlonde/the wawe her caste
And in the sande her shyppe stycked so faste
That thence nolde it not of al a tyde
The wyl of Christ was ẏ she shuld ther byde

¶ The constable of the castel downe is fare
To seen this wrecke/& al the shyp he sought
And fonde this wery woman ful of care
He founde also the tresoure that she brought
In her langage/mercy she besought
The lyfe out of her body for to twyn
Her to delyuer of wo that she was in.

¶ A maner latyn corrupte was her speche
But algates therby was she vnderstonde
The constable/ whan hym lyst no lenger seche
This woful woman brought he to londe
She kneleth downe/& thanketh goddes sonde
But what she was/she wolde no man sey
For foule ne fayre/though she shulde dey

She sayd she was so mased in the see
That she foryate her mynde/by her trouthe
The constable of her hath so great pyte
And eke his wyfe/ that they wepen for routhe
She was so dyligent withouten slouthe
To serue & plese eueryche in that place
That al her louen/that loken in her face

The constable/& dame Hermegylde his wyfe
Were paynems/and that contre euery where
But Hermegylde loued her right as her lyfe
And Custaunce hath so long soiourned there
In orisons/ with many a bytter tere
Tyl Jesu hath conuerted through his grace
Dame Hermegylde/cōstablesse of that place.

In al

In al that londe durst no christen route
Al christen folke ben fledde from that coūtre
Through paynems/ that cōquered al about
The plages of the North/ by londe and see
To Wales fledde the christianyte
Of olde Bretons / dwellyng in that Ile
There was her refute/ for the meane whyle

But yet nas ther neuer cristen breton so exiled
That there nas some in her priuete
Honoured Christe/ & heathen folke begyled
And nye the castel suche there dwellen thre
That one of hem was blynde/ & myght not se
But it were with thylke eyen of his mynde
With whiche men seen/ after they ben blynde

¶ Bright was the sonne/ as in somers day
For whiche the constable/ and his wyfe also
And Custaunce/ han taken the right way
Towarde the see/ a furlong way or two
To playen/ and to romen to and fro
And in her walke/ thre blynde men they met
Croked and olde/ with eyen faste yshette

In ẏ name of Christ/ cryed this blynd breton
Dame Hermegylde/ yeue me syght agayne
This lady waxe a frayde of the soun
Leste that her husbonde/ shortly for to sayne
Wold her for Iesus Christes loue haue slayne
Tyl Custāce made her bolde/ & bad her werch
The wyl of Christ/ as doughter of his cherch

The constable woxe abasshed of that syght
And sayd: what amounteth al this fare?
Custaunce answerde: sir it is Christes might
That helpeth folke out of the fendes snare
And so ferforth she gan our lawe declare
That she the constable/ er that it was eue
Cōuerted hath/ & on Christ made him byleue

This cōstable was nothing lord of this place
Of whiche I speke/ ther he Custaunce fonde
But kept it strongly/ many a wynter space
Vnder Alla/ kyng of Northumberlonde
That was ful wyse/ & worthy of his honde
Agayne the Scottes/ as men may wel here
But turne I wol agayne to my matere

¶ Sathan/ that euer vs wayteth to begyle
Sawe of Custaunce al her perfectioun
And cast anon how he might quyte her wyle
And made a yong knight/ ẏ dwelt in the toun
Loue her so hotte/ of foule affectioun
That verily/ him thought ẏ he shulde spyll
But he of her ones might haue his wyll

He woeth her/ but it auayled nought
She wolde do no synne by no wey
And for dispyte/ he compassed in his thought
To maken her on shamfull dethe to dey
He wayteth whan the constable is awey
And priuely on a nyght he crepte
In to Hermegyldes chambre whyle she slepte

¶ Wery forwaked in her orisons
Slepeth Custaunce and Hermegylde also
This knight/ through Sathans temptacions
Al softely is to the bedde ygo
And cutte the throte of Hermegylde a two
And layde the blody knyfe by dame Custāce
And wēt his way/ ther god yeue him mischāce

Sone after cometh the cōstable home agayn
And eke Alla/ that kyng was of that londe
And sawe his wyfe dispytously islayne
For whiche he wept and wronge his honde
And in the bedde the blody knyfe he fonde
By dame Custāce/ alas what might she say?
For very wo/ her wytte was al away

To kyng Alla was tolde al this mischaunce
And eke the tyme/ & where/ and in what wyse
That in a shyppe was foūden this Custaūce
As here before ye han herde me deuyse
The kynges hert/ for pyte gan agryse
Whan he sawe so benygne a creature
Fal in disease and in misaduenture

For as ẏ lambe towarde his deth is brought
So stante this innocent byforen the kyng
This fals knight/ ẏ hath this treson wrought
Bereth her on hōde/ ẏ she hath don this thing
But nathelesse there was great mornyng
Amonge the people/ & sayd they can not gesse
That she had done so great a wyckednesse
G. For

For they han sene her euer so vertuouse
And louyng Hermegylde/right as her lyfe
Of this bare wytnesse euerychе in ye house
Saue he that Hermegylde slow wt his knyfe
This gentle kyng hath caught a gret motyfe
Of this wytnesse/& thought he wold enquere
Deper in this case/the trouthe to lere

¶Alas Custaũce/thou haste no champyon
Ne fyght canste thou not/so welaway
But he that starfte for our redemption
And bonde Sathan/& yet lyth there he lay
So be thy stronge champyon this daye
For but if Christ on the myracle kythe
Without gylte thou shalt ben slayne aswythe

She set her down on knees/& thus she saide
Immortal god/that sauedest Susanne
Fro false blame/and thou mercyful mayde
Marye I mene/doughter to seynt Anne
Byforne whose chylde angels syng Osanne
If I be gyltlesse of this felonye
My socoure be/or els shal I dye

¶Haue ye not sene somtyme a pale face
(Amonge a prees)of him that hath ben lad
Towarde his deth/ wher as him get no grace
And suche a colour in his face hath had
That mẽ might know his face ye was bystad
Amonges al the faces in that route
So standeth Custaunce/& loketh her aboute

¶O quenes/lyueng in prosperite
Duchesses/and ye ladyes euerychon
Haue some routhe on her aduersyte
An emperours doughter stante alone
She hath no wight/ to whõ to make her mone
O bloode royal/that stondeth in this drede
Ferre ben thy frendes at thy great nede.

¶This Alla kyng/ hath suche compassyoun
As gentle herte is ful of pyte
That from his eyen ran the water doun.
Nowe hastely do fette a boke(quod he)
And if this knyght wol swere/ howe that she
This woman slowe/yet wol we vs auyse
Whom that we wol shal ben our iustyse

¶A breton boke/ written with Euangeles
Was fette/ and theron he swore anone
She gilty was / and in the mean whiles
An honde him smote on the necke bone
That downe he fyll atones/ as a stone
And bothe his eyen brast out of his face
In sight of euery body in that place

¶A voice was herde/ in generall audience
That said:Thou hast disclandred giltles
The doughter of holy chirche / in hye presence
Thus hast thou don/and yet I holde my pees
Of this marueile / agast was all the prees
As dismayde folke/ they stoden euerichone
For drede of wreche/ saue Custance alone

Great was ye drede / and eke the repentaũce
Of hem that hadden wrought suspection
Upon this sely innocent Custaunce
And for this myracle, in conclusyon
And by Custaunces mediation
The kyng/ and many another in that place
Conuerted was/thanked by goddes grace

This false knight was slayn for his vntroth
By iugement of Alla hastely
And yet Custaunce/had of his dethe gret roth
And after this/ Jesus of his mercy
Made Alla wedden full solempnely
This holy mayde / that is so bright & shene
And thus hath christ made Custaũce a quene

But who was wofull/if I shulde not lye
Of this weddyng : but Donogelde & no mo
The kynges mother/full of tiranny
Her thought her cursed hert brast a two
She wolde not her sonne had do so
Her thought a dispite/ that he shulde take
So straunge a creature vnto his make.

Me lyst not of the chaffe ne of the stree
Make so longe a tale/as of the corne
What shulde I tell of the royalte
Of ye mariage/or whiche course goth beforne
Who bloweth in a trompe or in an horne
The frute of euery tale is for to say
They eten and drinken/ daunce and play

They

The Man of Law's Tale (B 624–707 ; T. 5044–5127)

They gon to bedde/ as it was skyll & ryght
For though that wyues ben ful holy thynges
They muste take in pacience anyght
Suche maner necessaryes/as ben plesynges
To folke that han wedded hem with rynges
And say a lytel her holynesse a syde
As for the tyme/it may none other betyde

On her he gatte a man chylde anon
And to a bysshoppe/and to his constable eke
He toke his wyfe to kepe/ whan he is gon
To Scotlondwarde/his fomen for to seke
Nowe fayre Custãce/ yͭ is so humble & meke
So longe is gone with childe tyl that styll
She halte her chambre/abyding Chustes wil

¶ The tyme is come/a man chylde she bare
Maurycius at fontstone they hym calle
This constable dothe forth come a messanger
And wrote to his kyng/that cleped was Alle
Howe that this blyssful tydyng is byfall
And other tydinges nedeful for to say
He taketh the letter/ & forthe he gothe his way

¶ This messanger to done his auauntage
Unto the kynges mother rydeth swythe
And salueth her ful fayre in his langage
Madame (quod he) ye may be glad & blythe
And thanketh god an hundred thousãde sythe
My lady quene hath chylde/ withouten doute
To ioye and blysse of al this reigne aboute

Lo here the letters sealed of this thyng
That I mote beare/in al the haste I may
Yeue ye wol ought unto your sonne yͤ kyng
I am your seruaunt bothe nyght and day
Donegylde answerde/as at this tyme nay
But here I wol al night thou take thy reste
To morowe wol I say the what my leste

This messãger dronke sadly both ale & wyne
And stolen were his letters priuely
Out of his boxe/ whyle he slept as a swyne
And counterfeted was ful subtelly
Another letter/ wrought full synfully
Unto the kyng dyrecte of this matere
I. to his constable/ as ye shal after here

The letter spake/the quene delyuered was
Of so horryble a fendlyche creature
That in the castel none so hardy was
That any whyle durst therin endure
The mother was an elfe by auenture
Icome/ by charmes or by sorcerye
And euery wyght hateth her companye.

Wo was this kyng/whan he yͤ letter had seyn
But to no wight he tolde his sorowes sore
But with his owne honde he wrote ageyn
Welcome the sonde of Christ for euermore
To me/ that am newe lerned in his lore
Lorde/ welcome be thy lust and thy plesaunce
My lust I put all in thyne ordinaunce

¶ Kepeth this childe/all be it foule or fayre
And eke my wife/ unto myn home cõmyng
Christ whan hym lyst/ may sende me an heire
More agreable than this/to my likyng
This letter he sealeth/ priuely wepyng
Whiche to the messangere was taken sone
And forth he gothe/there nys no more to done

¶ O messanger/ fulfylled of dronkennesse
Strõge is thy brethe/thy lymmes faltren aye
And thou bewrayest al secretnesse
Thy mynde is lorne/thou iangelest as a iaye
Thy face is turned in a newe araye
There dronkennesse reyneth in any route
There nys no cõnsayle hyd withouten doute

¶ O Donegild/ I ne haue non englisshe digne
Unto thy malyce/and thy tyrannye
And therfore to the fende I the resigne
Let him endyte of thy traytrye
Fye mannysshe fye: O nay by god I lye
Fye fendisshe spiryte/for I dare wel tell
Though thou here walke/thy spiryt is in hell

¶ This messãger cometh fro yͤ king agayne
And at the kynges mothers house he lyght
And she was of this messanger ful fayne
And plesed him in all that euer she myght
He dronke/and wel his gyrdel under pyght
He slepeth/and he snorteth in his gyse
Al nyght/tyl the sonne gan aryse

G.ii. Efte

Efte were his letters stolen euerychon
And counterfeted letters in this wyse:
The kynge cõmaundeth his constable anon
Vp payne of hongyng on an hye iewyse
That he ne shulde suffren in no wyse
Custaunce/ within his realme for to abyde
Thre dayes/ and a quarter of a tyde

But in the same shyppe/ as he her fonde
Her and her yonge sonne/ and al her gere
He shulde croude/ and put fro the londe
And charge her/ that she neuer eft come there
O Custaunce/ wel may thy goste haue fere
And slepyng in thy dreame/ ben in penaunce
Whan Donegylde/ cast al this ordynaunce

This messanger on ẏ morowe whã he woke
Vnto the castel halte the next way
And to the constable he the letter toke
And whan that he this pytous letter sey
Ful ofte he sayd (alas) and wela way
Lorde Christ (q̃d he) how may this world endure
So ful of synne is many a creature

O mighty god/ if that it be thy wyll
Syn thou art rightful iuge/ how may it be?
That thou wolte suffre innocence to spyll?
And wycked folke to reigne in prosperyte
O/ good Custaunce (alas) so wo is me
That I mote be thy tourmentour/ or els dey
On shames dethe/ there nys non other wey

¶ Wepen bothe yonge and olde in that place
Whan that the kyng this cursed letter sent
And Custaunce with a deedly pale face
The fourth day/ towarde her shippe she went
But nathelesse/ she taketh in good entent
The wyl of Christ/ ⁊ knelyng in the stronde
She sayd lorde/ aye welcome be thy sonde

He that me kepte fro that false blame
Whyles I was on the londe amonges you
He can me kepe fro harme/ ⁊ eke fro shame
In the salte see/ al though I se not howe
As stronge as euer he was/ he is nowe
In hym truste I/ and in his mother dere
That is to me/ my sayle and eke my stere

Her lytel chylde lay wepyng in her arme
And knelyng pitously/ to hym she sayde
Peace lytel sonne/ I wol do the none harme
With that her kercher of her heed she brayde
And ouer his lytel eyen she it layde
And in her arme/ she lulleth it ful fast
And in to heuen her eyen vp she caste.

¶ Mother (quod she) ⁊ mayde bright Marye
Sothe is/ that through womans eggement
Mankynde was lorne/ ⁊ dampned aye to dye
For whiche thy childe was on crosse yrent
Thy blyssful eyen sawe al his turment
Than is there no comparyson bytwene
Thy wo / and any wo that man may sustene

Thou se thy childe yslayne byfore thyn eyen
And yet nowe lyueth my lytel childe parfaye
Nowe lady bright/ to whom al woful cryen
Thou glorie of womanheed/ thou fayre may
Thou hauen of refute/ bright sterre of day
Rewe on my childe/ of thy gentylnesse
That rewest on euery ruful in distresse

O lytell childe (alas) what is thy gilte?
That neuer wroughtest synne/ as yet parde
Why woll thyn harde father haue the spilte?
O mercy: dere constable (quod she)
As let my lytell childe dwell here with the
And if thou darst not sauen hym fro blame
So kysse him ones/ in his fathers name

Therwith she loketh backwarde to the londe
And said: farwell husbonde routhlesse
And vp she rist, and walketh down ẏ stronde
Towarde the shippe/ her foloweth all ẏ prees
⁊ euer she prayeth her child to holden his pees
And taketh her leue/ and with an holy entent
She blesseth her/ and into the shippe she went

Vitayled was the shippe/ it is no drede
Habundantly/ for her full long space
And other necessaries that shulde nede
She had inowe/ heried be goddes grace
For wynde ⁊ wedder/ almighty god purchace
And bringe her home/ I can no better say
But in the see/ she driueth forthe her way

Alla

¶ Alla the kyng cometh home sone after this
Unto his castel/ of whiche I tolde
And asketh where his wyfe ⁊ his chylde is
The constable gan aboute his herte to colde
And playnly al the maner hun tolde
As ye han herde/ I can tel it no better
And shewth the kyng his seale and his letter

And sayd: lorde as ye cōmaunded me
Up payne of dethe/ so haue I done certayne
This messanger turmented was/ tyl he
Must beknowen/ and tel plat and playne
Fro night to night/ in what place he had layn
And thus by wytte and subtel enqueryng
ymaged was/ by whom this harm gan sprīg

¶ The honde was knowen/ ẏ the letter wrote
And al the venym of this cursed dede
But in what wyse/ certaynly I note
The effecte is this/ that Alla out of drede
His mother slow/ that may men playnly rede
For that she traytoure was to her alegaunce
Thus endeth olde Donegild with mischaūce

¶ The sorowe that this Alla nyght ⁊ day
Maketh for his childe/ and for his wyfe also
There is no tonge that it tel may
But nowe wol I to Custaunce go
That fleteth in the see/ in payne and wo
Fyue yere and more/ as lyked Christes sonde
Or that her shyppe aproched unto londe

¶ Under an hethen castel/ at the laste
Of whiche the name in my text I not fynde
Custaunce and eke her chylde the see up caste
Almighty god/ that saueth al mankynde
Haue on Custāce/ ⁊ on her child some mynde
That fallen is in hethen honde efte sone
In poynte to spyll/ as I shal tel you sone

Down fro ẏ castel cometh ther many a wight
To gauren on this shyppe/ and on Custaūce
But shortly fro the castel on a nyght
The lordes stewarde/ god yeue him mischaūce
A thefe/ that had reneyed our creaunce
Came into the shyp alone/ and sayd he sholde
Her lemman be/ whether she wolde or nolde

Wo was the wretched woman tho bygon
Her childe cryed/ and she cryed pitously
But blyssful Marye halpe her anon
For with her stroglyng/ wel and mightyly
The thefe fel ouer the borde/ al sodaynly
And in the see he drenched for vengaunce
And thus hath christ unwēmed kept Custāce

¶ O foule luste of luxure/ lo thyn ende
Nat onely that thou faynteſt mans mynde
But verily/ thou wolt his body shende
The ende of thy werke/ or of thy lustes blynd
Is cōplaynīng: how many on may mē fynd
That not for werke somtyme/ but for thētent
To don this synne/ ben eyther slayne or shent

How may this weke woman haue ẏ strēgth
Her to defende agaynst this renegate?
O Golyas/ unmesurable of length
Howe might Dauid make the so mate?
So yonge/ and of armure so desolate
Howe durst he loke on thy dredful face?
Wel may men sene/ it is but goddes grace.

¶ Who yaue Judith courage or hardynesse
To sleen him Holofernes in his tente
And to delyuer out of wretchydnesse
The people of god? I say/ for this entent
That right as god/ spyrite and vygore sente
To hem/ and saued hem out of mischaunce
So sent he might and vigore to Custaunce

Forth goth her ship thorowe ẏ narow mouth
Of Subalter and septe/ fletyng aye
Somtyme weste/ ⁊ somtyme northe ⁊ south
And somtyme este/ ful many a wery daye
Tyl Christes mother/ yblessed be she aye
Hath shapen/ through her endlesse goodnesse
To make an ende of al her heuynesse.

¶ Explicit secūnda pars/ et sequitur pars tertia.

The man of lawes tale.

¶ Now let vs stynte of Custãce but a throwe
And speke we of the Romayne emperoure
That out of Surrey hath by letters knowe
The slaughter of christen folke, & dishonour
Done to his doughter/ by a false traytour
I meane the cursed wicked Soudonnesse
That at the feest/let sleen bothe more & lesse

For whiche this Emperour hath sent anon
His senatour/with royal ordynaunce
And other lordes/god wote many one
On Surreyns to done hye vengeaunce
They brennen/ sleen/ & brigen hem to mischãce
Ful many a day: but shortly this is the ende
Homward to Rome/they shapen hem to wẽde

This senatour repayreth with victorye
To Rome warde/ saylyng ful royally
And met the shyp driuyng/as sayth the storye
In whiche Custaunce/ sate ful pitously
Nothyng knewe he what she was/ne why
She was in suche array/ne she nolde sey
Of her estate/though she shulde dey

He bringeth her to Rome/and to his wyfe
He yaue her/and her yonge sonne also
And with the senatour she ladde her lyfe
Thus can our lady bring out of wo
Woful Custaunce/ and many another mo
And longe tyme dwelled she in that place
In holy werkes euer/as was her grace.

The senatours wyfe her aunte was
But for al that/she knewe her neuer the more
I wol no lenger tarye in this caas
But to king Alla/the whiche I spake of yore
That for his wyfe wepeth/and syketh sore
I wol retourne/and let I wyl Custaunce
Vnder the senatours gouernaunce.

¶ Kyng Alla/which yͤ had his mother slayne
Vpon a day fel in suche repentaunce
That if I shortly tellen al shal/ & playne
To Rome he cometh/to receyue his penaũce
And putten him in the popes ordynaunce
In hye & in lowe/and Iesu christ besought
Foryeue his wicked werkes/ that he wrought

The fame anon through Rome town is born
Howe Alla kyng/shal come on pilgrymage
By herbegers that wenten hym byforne
For whiche the senatour/ as was vsage
Rode him agayne/and many of his lynage
As wel to shewen his hye magnifycence
As to done any kyng reuerence.

¶ Great chere dothe this noble senatour
To kyng Alla / and he to him also
Eueryche of hem dothe other great honour
And so vpfel/that on a day or two
This senatour is to kyng Alla go
To feest/ and shortly if I shal not lye
Custaunces sonne went in his companye

Som mẽ wold sayne/at yͤ request of Custãce
This senatour had ladde this childe to feest
I may not tellen euery circumstaunce
Be as be may/there was he at leste
But sothe it is/right at his mothers heste
Byforn Alla/ duryng the meate space
The childe stode/ lokyng in the kynges face

This Alla king/hath of this child gret wõder
And to the senatour he sayd anon
Whose is yͤ fayre childe/that stondeth yonder?
I not(quod he)by god and by saynt Iohn
A mother he hath/but father hath he non
That I of wote/but shortly in a stounde
He tolde Alla/howe the childe was founde

But god wote (quod this senatour also)
So vertuous a lyuer in my lyfe
Ne sawe I neuer/ as she/ne herde of mo
Of worldly woman/mayden/ ne of wyfe
I dare wel say/ she had leuer a knyfe
Through her brest/ than ben a woman wicke
There is no man couthe bring her to yͤ pricke

Nowe was the childe as lyke Custaunce
As possyble is/ a creature for to be
This Alla hath the face in remembraunce
Of Dame Custaunce/and theron mused he
Yeue that the childes mother were aught she
That is his wyfe/and priuely he syght
And spedde him fro the table/that he myght

Parfay

The Man of Law's Tale (B 953–1036; T. 5373–5456)

Parfay he thought/ ỹ fantome is in myn heed
I ought deme of skylful iugement
That in the salte see my wyfe is deed
And afterwarde he made his argument
What wot I/if Christ hath hyther sent
My wyfe by see: as wel as he her sente
To my countrey/ fro thens ỹ she was wente

And after anon/home with the senatour
Gothe Alla/for to se this wonder chaunce
This senatour dothe Alla great honour
And hastely he sent after Custaunce
But trusteth wel/her luste not to daunce
Whan she wyste wherfore was that sonde
Unneth upon her fete myght she stonde.

¶ Whan Alla sawe his wife/fayre he her gret
And wept/that it was routhe for to se
For at the first loke he on her set
He knewe wel verely/that it was she
And for sorowe/as dombe stante as a tre
So was her herte shet in distresse
Whan she remembreth his unkyndnesse

Twyse she swouned in his owne syght
He wepeth and him excuseth pitously
Nowe god (q̃d he) and his halowes bright
So wysly on my soule haue mercy
That of your harme/as gyltlesse am I
As is Maurys my sonne/so lyke your face
Els the fende me fetche out of this place.

¶ Long was the sobbyng/ & the bytter payne
Or that her woful herte myght cese
Great was the pyte to here hem complayne
Through whiche playntes gan her wo encrese
I praye you al my laboure to relese
I may not tel her wo/tyl to morowe
I am so wery to speke of her sorowe

But fynally/whan that the sothe is wyste
That Alla gyltlesse was of her wo
I trowe an hundred tymes ben they kyste
And suche a blysse is there bytwyxt hem two
That saue the ioye/that lasteth euermo
There is no lyke/that any creature
Hath seyn or shal/whyle ỹ worlde may dure

Tho prayed she her husbonde mekely
In relesyng of her pytous payne
That he wolde pray her father specially
That of his maiesty he wolde enclyne
To vouchesafe somday with him to dyne
She prayed him eke/he shulde by no way
Unto her father no worde of her to say

¶ Som men wolde say/ ỹ the child Mauryce
Dothe this message untyl this emperour
But as I gesse/Alla was not so nyce
To him that was of so souerayne honour
As he that is of christen folke the flour
Sent any chylde/but it is bette to deme
He went him selfe/and so it may wel seme

This emperour graunted gentelly
To come to dyner/as he him bysought
That al was redy he loked besyly
Upon this childe/& on his doughter thought
Alla gothe to his ynne/and as him ought
Arrayde for this feest in euery wyse
As ferforth as his connyng may suffyce

The morowe came/& Alla gan him dresse
And eke his wyfe/the emperour for to mete
And forth they ryde in ioye and in gladnesse
And whan she sawe her father in the strete
She lyght a downe and falleth him to fete
Father (q̃d she) your yonge chylde Custaũce
Is nowe ful clene out of your remembraũce

I am your doughter Custaunce (quod she)
That whylom ye han sent into Surrye
It am I father/ that in the salte see
Was put alone/ and dampned for to dye
Nowe good father/ I you mercy crye
Sende me no more in to hethennesse
But thanken my lorde here of his kyndnesse.

¶ Who can the pytous ioye tellen all
Bytwyxt hem thre: syn they ben thus ymette
But of my tale make an ende I shall
The day gothe faste/I wol no lenger lette
This glad folke to dyner ben sette
In ioye and blysse/at meate I let hem dwell
A thousande folde wel more than I can tell

This

The Squiers prologue.

This childe Maurys was sythen Emperour
Made by the pope/and lyued christenly
To Christes churche he dyd great honour
But I let al this story passen by
Of Custaunce is my tale specially
In olde Romayne iestes men may fynde
Maurys lyfe/I beare it not in mynde

This kyng Alla/ whan he his tyme sey
With this Custaunce/ his holy wyfe so swete
To Englonde ben they come the right wey
Where as they lyue in ioye and in quyete
But lytel whyle it lasteth I you hete
Ioye of this worlde/ for tyme wol not abyde
Fro day to night/ it chaungeth as the tyde

Who lyued euer in suche delyte a day
That he ne meued eyther in conscience
Or yre/or talent of some kyn affray
Enuye or pride/or passyon/or offence?
I ne say/ but for this ende/ and this sentence
That lytel whyle in ioye or in plesaunce
Lasteth the blysse of Alla with Custaunce

For deth/that taketh of hye & lowe his rente
Whan passed was a yere/ euyn as I gesse
Out of this worlde kyng Alla he hente
For whom Custance hath ful gret heuynesse
Nowe let vs prayen god his soule blesse
And dame Custaunce/ fynally to say
Towarde the towne of Rome gothe her way

To Rome is come this holy creature
And fyndeth her father hole and sounde
Nowe is she skaped al her auenture
And whan that she her father hath yfounde
Downe on her knees gothe she to grounde
Wepyng for tendernesse in herte blythe
She herieth god/an hundred thousande sythe

In vertue and holy almesdede
They lyuen al/and neuer a sonder wende
Tyl dethe departen hem/this lyfe they lede
And fareth nowe wel/my tale is at an ende
Nowe Iesu christ/ yͭ of his myght may sende
Ioye after wo/gouerne vs in his grace
And kepe vs al/that ben in this place.

¶ Thus endeth the man of lawes tale/and here foloweth the Squiers prologue.

Our hoste on his styropes stode anon
And said: good men herkeneth eueryrchon
This was a thrifty tale for the nones
Sir parysshe preest (qd he) for goddes bones
Tel vs a tale/as was thy forwarde yore
I se wel that ye lerned men in lore
Can moche good/ by goddes dignyte
The parson him answerde/benedicite
What eyleth the man/so synfully to swere?
¶ Our host answerd/ O Ienkyn/ be ye there
Now good men (qd our host) herkeneth to me
I smell a loller in the wynde (quod he)
Abydeth for goddes digne passyon
For we shal haue a predycation
This loller here/wol prechen vs somwhat.
¶ Nay by my fathers soule/ that shal he nat
Sayd the Squier/here shal he not preche
Here shal he no gospel glose ne teche
We leueth al in the great god (quod he)
He wolde sowen some diffyculte
Or sprenge cockel in our clene corne
And therfore hoste/I warne the byforne
My ioly body/shal a tale tell
And I shalryngen you so mery a bell
That I shal waken al this companye
But it shal not ben of philosofye
Ne phisyke/ne termes queynte of lawe
There is but lytel laten in my mawe.

¶ Here endeth the Squiers prologe/and herafter foloweth his tale.

A T Sarra/ in the londe of Tartary
There dwelt a kyng that warred Surry
Thrugh which ther died many a doughty mã
This noble kyng was called Cambuscan
Whiche in his tyme was of so-great renoun
That there nas no where/ in no regyoun
So excellent a lorde in al thyng
Hym lacked naught that longed to a kyng
As of the secte/ of whiche he was borne
He kept his lay/ to whiche he was sworne
And therto he was hardy/ wyse/ and ryche
And pytous and iuste alway lyche
Trewe of his worde/ benygne and honorable
Of his corage/ as any centre stable
yonge/ fresshe/ & stronge/ in armes desyrous
As any bacheler of al his hous
A fayre person he was/ and fortunate
And kept alway so royal astate
That there nas no where suche another man.
This noble king/ this tartre/ this Cãbuscan
Had two sonnes by Elfheta his wyfe
Of whiche the eldest hyght Algarsyfe
That other was cleped Camballo.
¶ A doughter had this worthy kyng also
That yongest was/ and hyght Canace
But for to tel you al her beaute
It lythe not in my tonge/ ne in my connyng
I dare not undertake so hye a thyng
Myn englysshe eke is unsuffycient
It muste ben a rethor excellent
That couthe his colours/ longyng for ye arte
If he shulde discryue here euery parte
I am none suche/ I mote speke as I can
And so byfel/ that this Cambuscan
Hath twenty wynter borne his dyademe
As he was wont/ fro yere to yere I deme
He let the feest of his natiuyte
Done cryen/ throughout Sarra his cyte
The laste ydus of Marche/ after the yere.
Phebus the sonne/ ful ioly was and clere
For he was nye his exaltation
In Martes face/ and in his mantion
In Aryes/ the collorike/ the hote sygne
Ful lusty was the wether and benygne
For whiche the foules/ ayenst the sonne shene
What for the season/ and the yonge grene
Ful loude songe her affections
Hem semed han getten hem protections
Ayen the swerde of wynter kene and colde.
¶ This Cãbuscan/ of which I haue you told
In royal vestementes/ sytte on his deys
With dyademe/ ful hye in his paleys
And helde his feest so royal and so ryche
That in this worlde nas there non it lyche
Of whiche/ if I shal tel of al the array
Than wolde it occupye a sõmers day
And eke it nedeth not to deuyse
At euery course/ the ordre of her seruyce
I wol not tel of her straunge sewes
Ne of her swannes/ ne of her heronsewes
Eke in that londe/ as tellen knightes olde
Ther is some meate/ that is ful dayntly holde
That in this londe men recche of it but small
There is no man that may reporten all.
I wyl not tarye you/ for it is prime
And for it is no fruyte/ but losse of tyme
Unto my first purpose I wol haue recourse.
¶ And so byfel that after the thirde course
Whyle that this king sytte thus in his noblay
Herkenyng his mynstralles her thynges play
Byforne him at his borde delyciously

In at

The Squire's Tale (F 9–79; T. 10323–10393)

In at the halle dore al sodaynly
There come a knyght on a stede of brasse
And in his honde a brode myrrour of glasse
Upon his thombe he had of golde a rynge
And by his syde a naked swerde hongyng
And up he rydeth to the hye borde
In al the halle ne was there spoke a worde
For marueyle of the knyght/ him to beholde
Ful besyly they wayten yonge and olde.
¶ This straūge knyght yͭ come thus sodenly
Al armed saue his heed/ ful royally
Salued kyng and quene/ and lordes all
By ordre/ as they sytten in the hall
With so hye reuerence and obeysaunce
As wel in speche as in countenaunce
That Gawayne with his olde curtesye
Though he come ayen out of fayrye
Ne coude him not amende of no worde
And after this/ before the hye borde
He with a manly voyce sayd his message
After the forme used in his langage
Without vyce of syllable or of letter
And for his tale shulde seme the better
Accordant to his wordes was his chere
As teacheth arte of speche hem that it lere
Al be that I can not sowne his style
Ne I ne can not clymben so hye a style
yet say I thus/ as to my comen entente
Thus moche amounteth al that euer he mente
If it so be/ that I haue it in my mynde.
¶ He sayd: The kyng of Araby and of ynde
My liege lorde/ on this solempne day
Salueth you/ as he best can and may
And sendeth you/ in honoure of your feest
By me that am redy at your heest
This stede of brasse/ that easyly and well
Can in the space of a day naturell
This is to say/ in four and twenty houres
Where so ye lyst/ in drought or in shoures
Beren your body in to euery place
Into whiche your herte wylleth to pace
Without wem of you/ through foule or fayre
Or if ye lyst to fleen in the eyre
As dothe an Egle/ whan him lyst to sore
This same stede shal beare you euermore
Withouten harme/ tyl ye ben there you leste
Though that ye slepen on his backe and reste
And turne agayn with the writhyng of a pyn
He that it wrought coude ful many a gyn
He wayted ful many a constellation
Or he had done this operatyon
And knew ful many a seale ⁊ many a bonde
¶ This myrrour eke yͭ I haue in myn honde
Hath suche a might / that men may in it se
Whan there shal fallen any aduersyte
Unto your reigne/ or to your selfe also
And openly se/ who is your frende and foe
And ouer al this/ if any lady bright
Hath set her herte on any maner wyght
If he be false/ she shal the treason se
His newe loue/ and al his subtelte
So openly/ that there shal nothyng hyde
Wherfore agayne this lusty sōmer tyde
This myrrour and this rynge/ that ye may se
He hath sent to my lady Canace
your excellent doughter that is here.
¶ The vertue of this rynge/ if ye wol here
Is this/ that if she lyst it for to were
Upon her thombe/ or in her purse it bere
There is no foule/ that fleeth under heuen
That she ne shal understonde his steuen
And knowe his meanyng openly and playne
And answere him in his langage agayne
And euery grasse that groweth upon rote
She shal wel knowe/ ⁊ whom it wol do bote
Al be his woundes neuer so depe and wyde.
¶ This naked swerde/ yͭ hangeth by my syde
Suche vertue hath/ yͭ what man so ye smyte
Throughout his armure it wol kerue ⁊ byte
Were it as thycke as a braunched oke
And what man that is woūded wͭ the stroke
Shal neuer be hole/ tyl that you lyst of grace
To stroken him with yͤ platte in thylke place
There he is hurte/ this is as moche to sayne
Ye mote with the platte swerde agayne
Stroken him in the wounde/ ⁊ it wol close
This is very sothe withouten glose
It fayleth not/ whyles it is in your holde.
⁊ whan this knight hath thus his tale tolde
He rydeth out of the halle/ and down he lyght
His stede/ whiche that shone as sonne bright
Stante in the courte styl as any stone
The knight is in to chambre ladde anone
He is unarmed/ and to the meate ysette

And

And al that harneys byforne him fette
This is to sayn/the swerde ꝛ eke the myrrour
Al borne was in to the hye tour
With certayne officers ordeyned therfore
And to Canace the rynge is bore
Solempnely/there she sate at the table
But sykerly without any fable
The horse of brasse/ that may not be remeued
It stant/ as it were to the grounde yglewed
There may no man out of the place it dryue
For none engyne/or wyndlas/or polyue
And cause why/for they can not the crafte
And therfore in the place they han it lafte
Tyl yͤ the knight hath taught hem yͤ manere
To voyden him/as ye shal after here.
¶ Great was yͤ prees/ that swarmed to ꝛ fro
To gauren on the horse/ that stondeth so
For it so hye was/ꝛ so brode and longe
So wel proporcyoned for to ben stronge
Ryght as it were a stede of Lumbardye
Therwith so horsly/and so quycke of eye
As it a gentle courser of Poyle were
For certes / fro his tayle to his ere
Nature ne arte coude him not amende
In no degre/as al the people wende
But euermore her moste wonder was
Howe that it couthe gon/and was of bras
It was of fayrie/as the people semed
Dyuers folke dyuersly they demed
As many heedes/as many wyttes there ben
They murmure/as dothe a swarme of been
And maden skylles after her fantesyes
Rehersyng of the olde poetryes
And sayden it was ylyke the Pegase
The horse that had wynges for to flee
Or els it was the grekes horse Synon
That brought Troye to distruction
As men in this olde bokes rede.
Myn hert (qd one) is euermore in drede
I trowe some men of armes ben therin
That shapen hem this cyte for to wyn
It were right good/ yͤ such thīges were know
An other rowned to his felawe lowe
And sayd he lyed/for it is rather ilyke
An apparence made by some magyke
As iogglours playen at these feestes grete
Of sondry thoughtes/thus they iangle ꝛ trete
As leude people demeth comenly
Of thynges that ben made more subtelly
Than they can in her leudenesse comprehende
They demen gladly to the badder ende.
And some of hem wondren on the myrrour
That borne was vp to the mayster toure
Howe men might in it suche thynges se.
And other answerde/certes it myght wel be
Naturally by composycions
Of angels and of slye reflections
And sayden/in Rome was suche on
They speken of Alocen and Vitilion
And Aristote/that writeth in her lyues
Of queynte myrrours/and of prospectiues
As knowen they that han her bokes herde.
And other folke han wondred on the swerde
That wolde perce through euery thyng
And fel in speche of Telophus the kyng
And of Achilles for his queynte spere
For he couthe with it heale and dere
Right in such wyse as mē may wͭ the swerde
Of which right now ye haue your seluē herde
They speken of sondry hardyng of metal
And speken of medycyns eke withal
And howe/and whan it shulde hardned be
Whiche is vnknowe algate to me.
¶ Tho speke they of Canaces rynge
And sayden al/that suche a wonder thyng
Of crafte of rynges herde they neuer non
Saue that Moyses/and kyng Salomon
Had a name of connyng of suche arte
Thus sayen the people/ꝛ drawen hem aparte
But natheless/some sayden that it was
Wonder to maken of ferne asshen/glas
And yet is glas not lyke asshen of ferne
But for they han knowen it so ferne
Therfore they sesen her ianglyng ꝛ her wōder
As sore wondren some on cause of thunder
On ebbe ꝛ fludde/on gossomer/and on myste
And on al thyng/tyl the cause is wyste.
Thus ianglen they/and demen and deuyse
Tyl that the kyng gan fro his borde aryse.
¶ Phebus hath lefte the angle merydional
And yet ascendyng was the beest royal
The gentle lyon with his Aldrian
Whan that this tartre kyng Cambuscan
Rose from his borde/there as he sate full hye
Byforne

The Squire's Tale (F 174–267; T. 10488–10581)

The Squyers tale.

Byforne him gothe the loude mynstralcye
Tyl he came to his chambre of paramentes
There as they sownen dyuers instrumentes
That is lyke an heuen for to here
Nowe dauncen lusty Venus children dere
For in the fysshe her lady sate ful hye
And loketh on hem with a frendly eye.
¶ This noble kyng is sette vpon his trone
This straunge knight is fet to hym ful sone
And in the daunce he gothe with Canace
Here is the reuel and the iolyte
That is not able a dull man to deuyse
He must han knowe loue and her seruyse
And ben a feestlyche man/ as fresshe as May
That shulde you deuyse suche array
¶ Who couthe tellen you the forme of daunces
So vncouth/ and so fresshe countynaunces:
Suche subtyl lokynges/ and dissymulynges
For drede of ialouse mens apperceyuynges
No man but Launcelot/ and he is deed
Therfore I passe ouer al this lustyheed
I say no more/ but in this iolynesse
I lete hem/ tyl men to supper dresse.
¶ The stewarde byddeth spyces for to hye
And eke the wyne/ in al this melodye
The vsshers and the squyers ben ygone
The spyces and the wyne is comen anone
They eten & dronken/ & whan this had an ende
Vnto the temple/ as reason was/ they wende
The seruyce is done/ they soupen al by day
What nedeth it to rehersen her array:
Eche man wot wel/ that at a kynges feest
Is plenty/ to the moste and to the leest
And deyntes mo/ than ben in my knowyng.
And after supper gothe this noble kyng
To seen this horse of brasse/ with al his route
Of lordes and of ladyes hym aboute
Such wõdrĩg ther was on this hors of bras
That sythen the great siege of Troye was
There as men wondred on an horse also
Ne was there suche a wondring/ as was tho
But fynally/ the kyng asketh the knyght
The vertue of this horse and the myght
And prayde him to tellen of his gouernaunce.
The horse anon gan to tryppe and daunce
Whan yͤ this knight layde honde on his rayne
And sayd/ sir there is no more to sayne
But whan you lyste to ryden any where
Ye mote tryll a pyn/ stante in his ere
Whiche I shal tel you bytwene vs two
ye mote nempne him to what place also
Or to what countre you lyst to ryde
And whan ye come there you lyste abyde
Bydde him discende/ and trylle a nother pyn
For therin lyeth the effecte of al the gyn
And he wol downe discende/ & don your wyll
And in that place he wol abyde styll
Though al the world had the cõtrary sworne
He shal not thens be ythrowe ne yborne
Or if you lyst bydde him thens gon
Tryl this pyn/ and he wol vanysshe anon
Out of the syght of euery maner wyght
And come ayen/ be it day or nyght
Whan that you lyst to clepen him agayne
In suche a gyse/ as I shal to you sayne
Bytwyxt you and me/ and that ful sone
Ryde whã you lyst/ ther nys no more to done
¶ Enfourmed whan yͤ king was of yͤ knight
And hath conceyued in his wytte aright
The maner and the forme of al this thyng
Ful glad and ful blythe/ the noble kyng
Repayreth to his reuel/ as byforne
The bridel is in to the toure yborne
And kept amonge his iewels lefe and dere
The horse vanysshed/ I not in what manere
Out of her syght/ ye get no more of me
But thus I lete in luste and iolyte
This Camüyscan/ his lordes festyng
Tyl wel nye the day began to spring.

¶ Explicit prima pars/ et sequitur pars secunda.

The norice of digestyon/ the slepe
Gan on hem wynke/ & bad hem take kepe
That myrth/ drinke/ & labour wol haue reste
And with a galpyng mouthe hem al he keste
And sayd/ it was tyme to lye adoun
For blode was in his domynacioun
Cheryssheth blode/ natures frende (qd̄ he)
They thanken him galpyng/ by two by thre
And euery wight gan drawen him to his reste
As slepe hem bade/ they toke it for the beste.
Her dremes shul not nowe ben itolde for me

Full

The Squire's Tale (F 268–357; T. 10582–10671)

Ful were her heedes of fumosyte
That causeth dremes/of which ther is no char
They slepen/tyl it was prime large (ge
The moste parte/but it were Canace
She was ful mesurable/as women be
For of her father had she take her leue
To gon to rest/sone after it was eue
Her lyst not appalled for to be
Nor on the morowe/vnfestlyche for to se
And slept her first slepe/and awoke
For suche a ioy she in her herte toke
Both of her queynt Rynge/& of her myrrour
That twenty tymes she chau̅ged her colour
And in her slepe/right for impressyon
Of her myrrour/she had a vysyon
Wherfore/or the sonne vp gan glide
She cleped her maistresses her besyde
And sayd/her luste for to aryse.
¶ These olde women/that ben gladly wyse
As is her maystresse/ answerde her anon
And said : madame/ whider wol ye gon
Thus erly? for folke ben al in reste.
¶ I wol (quod she aryse) for me leste
No lenger for to slepe/but walken aboute.
Her maystresse cleped women a great route
And vp they ryse/wel ten or twelue
Vp ryseth fresshe Canace her selue
As ioly and bright/as the yonge sonne
That in the Ram is four degrees vp ronne
No hygher was he/whan she redy was
And forthe she walketh an easye paas
Arrayed after the lusty season sote
Lightly for to playen/& to walken on fote
Nought but fyue or syxe of her meyne
And in a trenche/fer in the parke gothe she.
¶ The vapour/whiche yͤ fro the erthe glode
Maketh the sonne to seme ruddy and brode
But nathelesse/it was so fayre a syght
That it made al her hertes for to lyght
What for the ceason/ and for the morownyng
And for the foules that she herde synge
For right anon/she wyste what they ment
Right by her songe/ and knewe al her entent.
¶ The knotte why/that euery tale is tolde.
If it be taryed tyl luste be colde
Of hem that han it herkened after yore
The sauour passeth/euer lenger the more
For fulsomnesse of prolixite
And by the same reason thynketh me
I shulde vnto the same knot condiscende
And make of her walkyng sone an ende.
¶ Amydde a tre / for drye as whyt as chalke
As Canace was playeng in her walke
There sate a faucon ouer her heed ful hye
That with a pytous voyce gan to crye
That al the wodde resowned of her cry
And beaten had her selfe so pitously
With bothe her wynges/ tyl the reed blode
Ran endelonge the tre/there as she stode
And euer in one/she cryed and shright
And with her becke/her seluen so she pyght
That there nas Tygre/ne cruel beste
That dwelleth in wodde/eyther in foreste
That nolde han wept/if that they wepe coude
For sorowe of her/she shright alway so loude
For there nas neuer yet man on lyue
If that he couthe a faucon wel discryue
That herde of suche another of fayrenesse
As wel of plumage/as of gentylnesse
Of shappe/ of al that might irekened be
A faucon peregryn than semed she
Of ferrde londe/& euermore as she stoode
She swowned now & now/for lacke of blood
Tyl welny is she fall fro the tree.
¶ This fayre kynges doughter/this Canace
That on her fynger bare the queynte rynge
Through which she vnderstode wel euery thīg
That any foule may in his leden sayne
And coude answere him in his leden agayne
Hath vnderstande/what this faucon seyde
And welny for routhe almost she deyde
And to the tre she gothe ful hastely
And on this faucon loketh ful pitously
And helde her lappe abrode/for wel she wyste
The faucon muste fallen from the twyste
Whan yͤ she swowned neyt/for lacke of bloode
A longe whyle to wayten there she stoode
Tyl at the laste she spake in this manere
Vnto the hauke/as ye shalen after here.
¶ What is the cause/if it be for to tell
That ye ben in this furyal payne of hell?
Quod Canace/vnto this hauke aboue
Is this for sorowe of dethe/or losse of loue?
For as I trowe/these ben causes two

H. That

¶ That causen most a gentill hert wo
Of other harme it nedeth not to speke
For ye vpon your selfe you wreke
Whiche proueth well / that eyther ire or drede
Mote ben encheson of your cruell dede
Syn that I se none other wyght you chace
For the loue of god/so doth your selfe grace
Or what may be your helpe/for west or est
Ne sawe I neuer er now / no byrde ne beest
That farde with hym selue so pitously
Ye slee me with your sorowe verely
I haue of you so great compassioun
For goddes loue come fro the tre adowne
And as I am a kynges doughter trewe
If that I verely the causes knewe
Of your disease/if it lay in my myght
I wolde amende it/certes or it be nyght
As wisely helpe me great god of kynde
And herbes shall I right ynowe finde
To hele with your hurtes hastely
  Tho shright this faucon yet more spitously
Than euer she dyd/ & fell to grounde anone
And lyeth a swoune deed as is a stone
Tyll Canace hath in her lappe itake
Unto the tyme she gan of swoune awake
And after that she of swoune gan abreyde
Right in her haukes leden thus she saide
  That pite renneth soone in gentyll herte
(Felyng his semilitude in paynes smert)
Is proued al day/ as men may se
As well by werke as by authorite
For gentle hert kepeth gentilnesse
I se wel/ that ye haue of my distresse
Compassion/ my faire Canace
Of very womanly benignyte
That nature in your principles hath sette
But for non hope for to fare the bette
But for to obey vnto your hert free
And for to make other beware by me
As by the whelpe/ chastised is the Lion
Right for that cause/ and for that conclusion
While that I haue a leyser and a space
Myne harm I wol confessen or I pace
And euer while that one her sorowe tolde
That other wepte/ as she to water wolde
Tyl that the Faucon badde her to be styll
And with a sike/ thus she said her tyll.

¶ There I was bredde / alas that ilke day
And fostred in a roche of marble gray
So tenderly / that nothyng eyleth me
I ne wist not what was aduersite
Tyll I coude flye/ full hye vnder the skye
  There dwelte a Tercelet me fast by
That semed well of all gentilnesse
All were he ful of trayson and of falsnesse
It was so wrapped vnder humble chere
And vnder hewe of trouth / & in such manere
Under plesaunce/and vnder busy payne
That no wight coud haue wende he coud fayn
So depe in greyne he died his colours
Right as a serpent hideth him vnder flours
Tyll he may se his tyme for to bite
Right so/ this god of loues ipocrite
Dothe so his serymones and obeysaunce
With his dissimulyng/ & fayre assemblaunce
That sowneth vnto gentilnesse of loue
As in a tombe is all the faire aboue
And vnder the cors / suche as ye wote
Suche was this ipocrite colde and hote
And in this wise he serued his entent
That saue the fende/non wist what he ment
Tyll he so long had weped and complayned
And many a yere his seruyce to me fayned
Tyl that myn hert/ to pitous and to nyce
Al innocent of his cruel malyce
For ferde of his dethe/ as thought me
Upon his othes and his suretee
Graunted him loue/ vpon this condition
That euermore myn honour and my renoun
Were saued, bothe preuy and apert
This is to say/ that after his desert
I yaue him al myn hert and al my thought
God wote / and in other wise nought
And toke his hert in chaunge of myn for aye
But sothe is said/ gone sithen many a day
A trewe wight and a thefe thynketh not one
  And whan he sawe the thyng so fer igone
That I graunted him fully my loue
In suche a gise/as I haue said aboue
And yeuen him my trewe hert as fre
As he swore he yafe his hert to me
  Anon this tigre/ ful of doublenesse
Fyl on his knees with so deuout humblesse
With hye reuerence/ and eke by his chere

So ly[illegible]

The Squire's Tale (F 452–545 ; T. 10766–10859)

So lyke a gentyl louer/ as of manere
So rauysshed/ as it semed for ioye
That neuer Troylus/ ne Paris of Troy
Iason certes/ ne non other man
Syn Lameth was/ that alderfirst began
To louen two/ as writen folke beforne
Ne neuer sithen Adam was borne
Ne couthe man by twenty thousande parte
Counterfete the sophymes of his arte
Ne were worthy to vnbocle his galoche
Ther doublenesse or faynyng shulde aproche
Ne so couth thanke a wight/ as he dyd me
His maner was an heuen for to se
Tyl any woman/ were she neuer so wise
So paynteth he his chere poynt deuyse
As wel his wordes/ as his countenaunce
And I so loued hym for his obeysaunce
And for the trouthe that I demed in his hert
That if so were/ that any thyng him smert
Al were it neuer so lyte/ and I it wyst
Me thought I felte dethe at my herte twist
And shortly/ so ferforth this thyng went
That my wyl was his wylles instrument
That is to say/ my wyl obeyed his wyll
In al thyng/ as ferre as reason fyll
Kepyng the boundes of my worship euer
Ne neuer had I thyng so lefe ne so leuer
As him god wote/ ne neuer shal no mo
This last lenger than a yere or two
That I supposed of him nothyng but good.

But finally/ thus at the last it stode
That fortune wolde that he most twyn
Out of that place/ whiche that I was in
Where me was wo/ it is no question
I can not make of it discription
For o thyng dare I tell boldely
I knowe what the payne of dethe is therby
Suche harm I felte/ that he ne myght beleue
¶ So on a day of me he toke his leue
So sorowfully eke/ that I wende verely
That he had felte as moche harm as I
Whan that I herde him speke/ & saw his hewe
But natheles/ I thought he was so trewe
And eke that he repaire shulde agayne
Within a lytell while sothe to sayne
And reason wolde eke/ that he must go
For his honour/ as ofte happeth so
That I made vertue of necessite
And toke it well/ sithe it must nedes be
As I best might/ I hidde fro him my sorowe
And toke him by ye hond/ seit Iohn to borowe
And said thus: lo I am yours all
Beth suche as I haue ben to you and shall

What he answerde/ it nedeth not reherce
Who can sayn bet than he/ who can do wers?
Whan he hath al wel ysaid/ than hath he done
Therfore behoueth him a longe spone
That shal eten with a fende/ thus herde I say

So at the last he mote forth his way
And forthe he fleeth tyl he come there him lest
Whan it come him to purpose for to rest
I trowe he had thilke text in mynde
That al thyng repayring to his kynde
Gladeth hem selue/ thus sayn men as I gesse
Men louen of kynde newfanglenesse
As briddes don/ that men in cages fede
For thogh thou nyght & day take of hem hede
And strawe her cage faire and softe as sylke
And gyue hem sugre/ hony/ breed and mylke
yet right anon as his dore is vppe
He with his fete wolde sporne adown his cup
And to the wood he wolde/ and wormes eate
So newfangle ben they of her meate
And louen nouelries of proper kynde
No gentilnesse of blode may hem bynde
So ferde this Tercelet/ alas the day

Tho he were gentel borne/ fresshe and gaye
And goodly for to se/ and humble and free
He sawe vpon a tyme a kyte flee
And sodainly he loued this kyte so
That all his loue is clene fro me goo
And hath his trouthe falsed in this wyse
Thus hathe the kyte my loue in her seruice
And I am lorne without remedy.

And with ye worde this faucon gan to crye
And swouned ofte in Canaces barme
Great was ye sorowe for that haukes harme
That Canace/ and all her women made
They nyst howe they might her faucon glade
But Canace home bereth here in her lappe
And softely in plaisters gan her wrappe
There as she with her becke had hurt her selue

Nowe can not Canace but herbes delue
Out of the grounde and make salues newe

H.ii. That

Of herbes precious and fyne of hewe
To helen with the hauke fro day to nyght
She dothe her beſyneſſe/ and all her myght
And by her beddes heed ſhe made a mewe
And couered it with veluettes blewe
In ſygne of trouthe/ that is in women ſene
And all withouten ẏ Mewe is peynted grene
In whiche were peynted all theſe falſe foules
As ben theſe tydeſes/tercelettes/and owles
Ryght for diſpyte were peynted hem beſide
Pyes on hem for to crye and chyde
This leue I Canace her hauke keypnge
I wol nomore as nowe ſpeke of her rynge
Tyl it come efte to purpos for to ſayn
How that this faucon gate her loue agayn
Repentant/ as the ſtory telleth vs
By mediation of Camballus
The kynges ſonne/of whiche I of tolde
But henſforthe I wol my proces holde
To ſpeken of auentures/ and of batayls
That yet was neuer herd of ſo gret marueyle
First wol I tell you of Cambuſcan
That in his tyme many a cyte wan
Howe that he wan Theodora to his wife
And after wol I ſpeke of Algarſyſe
For whom ful ofte in great perill he was
Ne had he ben holpen by the horſe of bras
And after woll I ſpeke of Camballo
That fought in lyſtes with the brethern two
For Canace/ er that he myght her wyn
And there I left/I wol again begyn.

Explicit ſecunda pars.

Apollo whirleth vp his chare ſo hye
Tyll that the god Mercurius houſe he ſlye.

There can be founde no more of this
fore ſaid tale/ whiche hath ben
ſought ỉ dyuers places.

Here foloweth the wordes of the Mar-
chaunt to the Squyer/ and the
wordes of the Hoſt to the
Marchaunt.

In faith Squier/ thou haſt the wel iquyt
And gentelly/ I praiſe wel thy wyt
Qd the Marchant/ conſydring thyne youth
So felyngly thou ſpekeſt/ I the alouth
As to my dome/there is non that is here
Of eloquence/ that ſhalbe thy pere
Yf ẏ thou lyue/ god gyue ẏ right good chaũce
And in vertue ſende the perſeueraunce
For of thy ſpekyng I haue great deynte
I haue a ſonne/ and by the Trinite
I had leuer than twenty poundesworth londe
(Though it nowe were fallen in my honde)
He were a man of ſuche diſcreſſion
As that ye ben : fye on poſſeſſyon
But if a man be vertuous with all
I haue my ſonne ſnybbed/ and yet ſhall
For he to vertue lyſteth nat to entende
But for to play at diſe/ and to ſpende
And leſe all that he hath/ is his vſage
And he had leuer talke with a page
Than to cõmen with any gentyll wight
Where he myght lerne gentelneſſe aright
Strawe for your gẽtylneſſe (qd our hoſt)
What Marchaunt/pardy well thou woſt
That eche of you mote tellen at the leſt
A tale or two/ or breken your beheſt
That know I wel (qd the marchãt) certain
I pray you haue me nat in diſdayn
Though I to this man ſpeke a worde or two
Tel on thy tale withouten wordes mo
Gladly ſir hoſt (quod he) I wol obey
Unto your wyl/now herkeneth what I ſay
I wol you nat contray in no wiſe
As farre as my wittes may ſuffyſe
I pray to god that it may pleſen you
Than wotte I well/it is god ynowe.

Thus endeth the wordes of the hoſt
and the marchant/and here foloweth
the Marchauntes prologue.

Wepyng and waylyng/ care ⁊ other ſorowe
I haue ynowe/both euyn ⁊ eke a morowe

The Squire's Tale: Words of the Host: The Merchant's Prologue
(F 640–708, E 1213, 1214; T. 10954–11020, 9089, 9090)

The Marchauntes prologue Fo. xxxiii.

Quod the marchaunt/and so haue other mo
That wedded be/I trowe that it be so
For wel I wote it fareth so by me
I haue a wife/the worst that may be
For though the fende coupled to her were
She wolde him ouermatch I dare well swere
What shulde I reherce in speciall
Her high malyce ∻ she is a shrewe at all
  There is a longe and a large difference
Betwixt Grisyldes great pacience
And of my wife the passyng cruelte
Were I unbounde/ also mote I the
I wolde neuer efte come in the snare
We wedded men lyue in sorowe and care
Assay who so wol/and he shal fynde
That I say soth/ by saynt Thomas of Inde
As for the more parte/I say nat all
God shelde that it shulde so befall
  Ah good sir host/ I haue wedded be
These monethes two/and more nat parde
And yet I trowe he that all his lyfe
Hath wedded be/ though men him rife
In to the hert/ ne couthe in no manere
Tell so moche sorowe/as I nowe here
Coude tell/of my wyues cursednesse
  Now qd our host marchant/so god ye blesse
Syn ye be so moche knowe of that arte
Full hertely I pray you tell us parte
  Gladly quod he/but of myn owne sore
For sory hert I tell may no more.

¶ Here endeth the marchantes prologue/
and here foloweth his tale.

  Whilom there was dwelling in Lõbardy
A worthy knyght/ that borne was at Pauy
In whiche he lyued in great prosperite
And sixty yere a wifeles man was he
And folowed aye his bodely delyte
On women/there as was his appetyte
As don these foles that ben seculeres
And whan that he was past sixty yeres
Were it for holynesse or dotage
I can not sayn/ but suche a great corage
Had this knyght to ben a wedded man
That day and nyght he dothe al that he can
To espy/ where that he wedded myght be
Prayeng our lorde to graunten him that he
Mighten ones knowen of that blyssfull lyfe
That is bitwixt an husbande and his wyfe
H.iii. And

The Merchant's Prologue and Tale (E 1215–1260; T. 9091–9136)

And for to lyuen vnder that holy bonde
With which god first man and woman bonde
Non other lyfe (said he) is worthe a bean
For wedlocke is so easy and so clean
That in this worlde it is a paradise
Thus saith this olde knyght that is so wise.
 And certaynly/ as sothe as god is kyng
To take a wife/ it is a glorious thyng
And namely whan a man is olde and hore
Than is a wife the frute of his tresore
Than shulde he take a yonge wife and a faire
On whiche he myght engendren hym an heire
And lede his lyfe in ioye and in solace
Where as these bachelers syngen alas
Whan that they fynden any aduersyte
In loue/ whiche nys but childes vanyte
And trewly it sytte well to be so
That bachelers han ofte payne and wo
On brotell grounde they bylden brotelnesse
They finde freelte/ whā they wenen sekernesse
They lyue but as briddes or beestes
In lyberte/ and vnder nyce arestes
There as a wedded man in his estate
Lyueth a lyfe blissfully and ordynate
Vnder the yoke of mariage ybounde
Wel may his hert in ioye and blysse habounde
For who can be so buxome as a wife?
Who is so trewe and eke so tentife
To kepe him sicke and hole? as is his make
For well ne wo she nyll him nat forsake
She nys nat wery him to loue and serue
Though that he lye bedreed tyll he sterue
And yet some clerkes sayn/ that it is nat so
Of whiche Theophrast is one of tho
What force though Theophrast lyst to lye
 Ne take no wife (quod he) for husbondrye
As for to spare in housholde thy dispence
A trewe seruaunt dothe more dilygence
Thy good to kepe/ than thyn owne wife
For she wol clayme halfe parte all her lyfe
 And if that thou be sicke/ so god me saue
Thy very frendes or a trewe knaue
Wol kepe the better/ than she that wayteth aye
After thy good/ and hath don many a day
And if thou take a wife/ to the vntrewe
Ful ofte tyme it shal the sore rewe
This sentence/ and an hundred sithes worse
Writeth this man there/ god his bones curse
But take no kepe of suche vanyte
Defieth Theophrast/ and herkeneth me.
¶ A wife is goddes yefte verily
All other maner yeftes hardely
As landes/ rentes/ pasture/ or cōmune
Or mouables/ all ben yeftes of fortune
That passen/ as a shadowe on a wall
But drede nat/ if playnly speke I shall
A wife wol last and in thyn house endure
Wel lenger than the lyst parauenture
 Mariage is a ful great sacrament
He whiche hath no wife I holde him shent
He lyueth helples/ and al desolate
I speke of folke in seculer estate.
 And herkneth why/ I say nat this for nougt
A woman is for mannes helpe iwrougt
The hye god/ whan he had Adam maked
And sawe him alone bely naked
God of his great goodnesse said than
Lette vs maken an helpe to this man
Lyke to him selfe/ and than he made Eue
 Here may ye se/ and hereby may ye preue
That a wife is mannes helpe and conforte
His paradise terrestre and his disporte
So buxome and so vertuous is she
They must nedes lyue in vnyte
One flesshe they ben/ & two soules as I gesse
Nat but one hert in wele and in distresse
 A wife/ ah saynt Mary/ benedicite
Howe myght a man haue any aduersite
That hath a wife? certes I can nat say
The blysse that is betwixt hem twey
There may no tonge tellen or hert thynke
If he be poore/ she helpeth him to swynke
She kepeth his good/ and wasteth neuer a del
Al that her husbonde lust/ her lyketh wel
She saith nat ones nay/ whan he saith ye
Do this (saith he) al redy sir (saith he)
¶ O blyssful order of wedlocke precious
Thou arte so mery/ and eke so vertuous
And so cōmended/ and so approued eke
That euery man/ that halte him worth a leke
Vpon his bare knees ought all his lyfe
Thanken god/ that him hath sent a wife
Or pray to god him for to sende
A Wife/ to last vnto his lyues ende

For

The Merchant's Tale (E 1261–1354; T. 9137–9228)

For than his lyfe is sette in sekernesse
He may nat be disceyued / as I gesse
So that he werche after his wyues rede
Than may he boldely bearen vp his hede
They ben so trewe and also wise
For whiche / if thou wolt werchen as the wyse
Do alway so / as women wol the rede
 Lo howe that Jacob / as these clerkes rede
By good counsaile of his mother Rebecke
Bounde the kydde skyn about his necke
For whiche his fathers benyson he wan
 Lo Judith / as the storie tell can
By wise counsaile goddes people kept
And slewe him Holofernes while he slept
 Lo Abigail by counsaile / howe she
Saued her husbonde Naball / whan that he
Shulde haue be slayne. And loke Hester also
By good counsaile delyuered out of wo
The people of god / and made him Mardochee
Of Assuere enhaunsed for to be.
¶ There nys nothyng in gree superlatyfe
(As saith Senec) aboue an humble wife
Suffre thy wyues tonge / as Caton byt
She shall cōmaunde / and thou shalt suffre it
And yet she woll obey of curtesy.
 A wife is keper of thyn husbondrie
Well may the sicke man wayle and wepe
There as there nys no wife the house to kepe
I warne the / if wisely thou wylt werche
Loue wel thy wife / as Christ loueth his cherch
If thou loue thy selfe / thou louest thy wife
No man hateth his flesshe: but in his lyfe
He fostreth it / and therfore bydde I the
Cherisshe thy wife / or thou shalt neuer ithe
Husbōde and wife / what so men iape or play
Of worldely folke holde the seker way
They be so knyt / there may non harm betide
And namely vpon the wyues syde
 For which this January / of whiche I tolde
Consydred hath in his dayes olde
The lusty lyfe / the vertuous quiete
That is in mariage hony swete
And for his frendes on a day he sent
To tellen hem theffecte of his entent.
¶ With face sadde / his tale hath he hem tolde
He said frendes / I am hoore and olde
And almost (god wot) on the pyttes brinke
Vpon my soule somwhat must I thynke
I haue my body folyly dispended
Blessed be god / it shall ben amended
For I wolt ben certayne a wedded man
And that anon in al the hast I can
Vnto some mayde / faire and tender of age
I pray you shapeth for my mariage.
All sodainly / for I wol nat abyde
And I wol fonden to espye on my syde
To whom I may be wedded hastely
But for as moche as ye ben more than I
Ye shullen rather suche a thyng espyen
Than I / and there me lust best to alyen
 But one thyng warn I you my frēdes dere
I wol non olde wife haue in no manere
She shall nat passe fyftene yere certayn
Olde fisshe & yonge flesshe wol I haue fayn
Better is (q̄d he) a pyke than a pickerell
And better than olde befe is the tender veell
I wol no woman of thirty wynter age
It nys but beanstrawe and great forage
And eke these olde wedowes (god it wote)
They connen so moche crafte in Wades bote
So moche broken harme whan hem lyst
That with hem shulde I neuer lyue in rest
For sondrie scholes maketh subtel clerkes
A woman of many scholes halfe a clerke is
But certainly / a yonge thyng may men gye
Right as men may warm wax wt hādes ply
Wherfore I say you plainly in a clause
I nyl non olde wife haue for this cause
 For if so were that I had myschaunce
And in her couthe haue no plesaunce
Than shulde I lede my lyfe in auoutry
And so streight to the deuyll whan I dye
Ne children shulde I non vpon her geten
Yet had I leuer houndes had me eten
Than that myne heritage shulde fall
In straunge hondes: and thus I tell you all
I dote nat / I wotte the cause why
Men shulde wedden: and furthermore wot I
There speketh many a man of mariage
That wot no more of this than doth my page
For whiche causes men shulde take a wife
Yf he may nat lyuen chast his lyfe
Take him a wife with great deuotion
Bicause of lefull procreation
Of children / to the honour of god aboue
And

And nat onely for paramour or for loue
And for they shulden lechery eschewe
And yelde her dettes whan that it is dewe
Or for that eche man shulde helpen other
In myschefe/as a suster shulde the brother
And lyue in chastite full heuenly.
¶ But sirs (by your leaue that am nat I
For god be thanked/ I dare make auaunt
I fele my lymmes hole and sufficiaunt
To don all that a man belongeth to
I wotte my selue best what I may do
Though I be hore/I fare as dothe a tree
That blossometh er that frute iwoxe be
The blossomed tree is neither dry ne deed
I fele no where hore but on my heed
Myn hert and my lymmes been as grene
As laurell is through the yere to sene
And sithen that ye han herde all myn entent
I pray you to my wyll ye wol assent.
Dyuers men dyuersly him tolde
Of mariage/ many ensamples olde
Some blameth it/some praysseth it certayne
But at the last/ shortly for to sayne
(As al day falleth altercation
Betwixt frendes in disputation)
There fell a strife betwixt his brethern two
Of whiche that one was cleped Placebo
Justynus sothly called was that other
¶ Placebo said: O January brother
Full lytell nede han ye my lorde so dere
Counsaile ta axe of any that is here
But that ye ben so full of sapience
That you ne lyketh for your hye prudence
To wayne fro the worde of Salomon
This worde saithe he vnto euerichone
Worke al thyng by counsayle/ thus said he
And than shalt thou nat repent the
But tho that Salomon speke suche a worde
Myn owne dere brother and my lorde
So wisely god my soule bring to ease & rest
I holde your own counsayle for the best.
For brother myn/take of me this motyfe
I haue ben nowe a court man al my lyfe
And god wote / though I nowe vnworthy be
I haue stonden in full great degre
Abouen lordes in ful great estate
yet had I neuer with non of hem debate
I neuer hem contraried trewly
I wotte well that my lorde can more than I
That he saithe/I holde it ferme and stable
I say the same/or els thyng semblable
A ful great fole is any counsaylour
That serueth any lorde of hye honour
That dare presume/or ones thynke it
That his counsayle shulde passe his lordes wit
Nay/lordes be no foles be my fay
Ye haue your selfe spoken here to day
So hye sentence/so holy/and so well
That I consent/and conferme euery dell
Your wordes all/ and your opinyon
By god there nys no man in all this town
Ne in Itayle/coude bette haue sayd
Chust holdeth him of this full wel apayde
And trewly it is an hye corage
Of any man that is stopen in age
To taken a yong wyfe/ by my father kyn
Your hert hongeth on a ioly pyn
Doth nowe in this matere right as you lest
For finally I holde it for the best.
¶ Justynus that aye satte and herde
Right in this wise to Placebo he answerde
Nowe brother myne be pacyent I you pray
Sith ye haue said/ now herkneth what I say
¶ Senec among other wordes wyse
Saith/ that a man ought him wel auyse
To whom he yeueth his londe or his catell
And sithens I ought auyse me right well
To whom I gyue my good away fro me
Well moche more I ought auysed be
To whom I gyue my body : for alway
I warne you well it is no childes play
To take a wife without auysement
Men must enquere (this is myn assent)
Wheder she be sobre/ wise/or dronkelewe
Or proude/or other wayes a shrewe
A chider/ or a waster of thy good
Other riche or poore/or els a man is wood
Al be it so/that no man fynde shall
Non in this worlde/ that trotteth hole in all
Ne man/ne beest/suche as men can deuise
But natheles/it ought ynough suffise
With any wife/ if so were that she had
Mo good thewes/than her vices badde
And all this asketh layser to enquere

For

For god wotte I haue wept many a tere
Ful preuely/sithe I had a wife
Praise who so wol a wedded mannes lyfe
Certeyn I fynde in it but cost and care
And obseruaunces of all blysses bare
And yet god wote/my neighbours about
And namely of women many a rout
Sayn that I haue the most stedfast wyfe
And eke the mekest one that beareth lyfe
But I wot best/where wringeth me my sho
ye may for me/right as you lyst do
Auyse you/ ye ben a man of age
Howe that ye entren into mariage
And namely with a yonge wife and a faire
By him that made water/ erthe/ and ayre
The yongest man that is in all this rout
Is besy ynowe to bringe it about
To haue his wife alone/ trusteth me
Ye shall nat pleasen her yeres thre
This is to sayn/ to don her plesaunce
A wife asketh ful moche obseruaunce
I praye you that ye be nat yuell apayde.
Wel (qd̄ this January) ⁊ hast thou al said:
Strawe for thy Senec/ and for thy ꝓuerbes
I count it nat worth a pannyer ful of herbes
Of schole termes/wiser men than thou
As thou hast herde/ assenteth it right nowe
To my purpose Placebo/what say ye:
I say it is a cursed man (qd̄ he)
That letteth matrymony sekerly
And with that worde they risen sodainly
And ben assented fully/ that he shulde
Be wedded whan him lyst/ ⁊ where he wolde
Highe fantasy and curiousnesse
Fro day to day/gan in the soule empresse
Of January/about his mariage
Many faire shappe/and many faire visage
There passeth through his hert night by night
As who so toke a myrrour polysshed bright
And sette it in a comen market place
Than shulde he se many a figure pace
By his myrrour/and in the same wise
Gan January within his thought deuise
Of maydens/whiche that dwellen besyde
He wyst nat where he myght abyde
For if that one had beautie in her face
Another stont so in the peoples grace
For her sadnesse and her benignyte
That of the people grettest voice had she
And some were riche/ and had badde name
But natheles/ bitwyxt ernest and game
He at last apoynted him on one
And lete all other from his hert gone
And chese her of his owne authorite
For loue is blynde al day/and may nat se
And whan that he was in his bedde ybrought
He purtreyde in his hert and in his thought
Her fresshe beaute/ and her age tender
Her myddle small/ her armes long ⁊ slender
Her wise gouernaunce/and her gentylnesse
Her womanly bearyng/and her sadnesse
And whan that he was on her condiscended
Him thoght his choise myght nat ben amēded
For whan that he him selfe concluded had
Him thought eche other mannes wyt so bad
That impossyble it were to reply
Ayenst his choice/this was his fantasy
¶ His frendes sent he to/ at his instaunce
And prayeth hem to don him that plesaunce
That hastely they wolde to him come
He wolde abridgen her labour al and some
Nedeth no more for him to go ne ryde
He was apoynted there he wolde abyde
¶ Placebo came/and eke his frendes sone
And alderfirst he badde hem al abone
That non of hem non argumentes make
Ayenst his purpose that he hath itake
Whiche purpose was plesaũt to god (said he)
And very grounde of his prosperite.
He said there was a mayden in the town
Whiche of beautie hath great renown
Al were it so/she were of small degre
Suffiseth him her youthe and her beaute
Whiche mayde he said/ he wolde haue to wife
To leden in ease and in holynesse his lyfe
And thonketh god/ yͭ he might hauen her all
That no wight his blysse parten shall
And prayeth hem to labour in this nede
And shapeth that he fayle nat to spede
For than he said/ his spyrite was at ease
Than is (qd̄ he) nothyng may me displease
Saue o thynge pricketh in my conscience
The whiche I wol reherce in your presence.
¶ I haue (quod he) herde said full yore ago
There

The Marchauntes tale.

There may no man haue parfite blysses two
This is to say/in erthe and eke in heuyn
For though he kept him fro the synnes seuyn
And eke from euery braunche of thilke tre
yet is there so parfite prosperite
And so great ease and lust in mariage
That euer I am agast nowe in myn age
That I shal lede nowe so mery a lyfe
So delycate without wo or strife
That I shall haue myne heuen in erthe here
For sithen very heuen is bought so dere
With tribulation and great penaunce
Howe shulde I than lyuyng in such plesaũce
As all wedded men done with her wyues
Cõe to the blisse/ ther Christ eterne on lyue is
This is my drede/ and ye my brethern twey
Assoyleth me this question I you prey.
¶ Iustinus/ whiche that hated his foly
Answered anon right in his iapery
And for he wolde his long tale abrege
He wolde non authorite allege
But said: sir/ so there be non obstacle
Other than this/ god of his hye myracle
And of his mercy may so for you wirche
That er ye han your rightes of holychirche
Ye may repent of wedded mannes lyfe
In whiche ye sayn is neyther wo ne strife
And els god forbede/ but if he sent
A wedded man grace him to repent
Wel ofter/ rather than a syngle man
And therfore sir/ the best rede that I can
Dispeyreth you nat/ but haue in memory
Parauenture she may be your purgatory
She may by goddes meane and goddes whip
Than shal your soule vp to heuen skip
Swifter than dothe an arowe out of a bowe
I hope to god herafter ye shal knowe
That there nys non so great felycite
In mariage/ ne neuer non shal be
That you shal lette of your saluation
So that ye vse it as skyl is and reason
The lustes of your wife attemperatly
And that ye please her nat to amorously
And that ye kepe you eke fro other syn
My tale is don/ for my wytte is thyn
Beth nat agast herof my dere brother
But let vs wade fro this mater to another
The wife of Bathe/ if ye vnderstande
Of mariage/ whiche ye haue in hande
Declareth ful wel in a lytell space
Fareth nowe wel/ god haue you in his grace.
And with this worde/ Iustyne & his brother
Han take her leaue/ and eche of hem of other
For whan they sawe it must nedes be
They wrought so by wise and slye treate
That she this mayde whiche May hight
As hastely as euer that she myght
Shal wedded be to this Ianuary
I trowe it were to long to you to tary
yf I you tolde of euery escrite and bonde
By whiche she was feffed in his londe
Or for to herken of her riche array
But finally icomen is the day
That to chirche both ben they went
For to receyue the holy sacrament
Forth cometh ye prest/ wt stole about his neck
And badde her be lyke Sara and Rebecke
In wisedom aud trouth of mariage
And said his orisons/ as is the vsage
And crouched hem/ & bad god shuld hem bles
And made al seker ynowe with holynesse
Thus ben they wedded with solempnyte
And at feest sytteth he and she
With other worthy folke vpon the deyes
Al ful of ioy and blysse is the paleyes
And ful of instrumentes and of vitayle
The most deyntes of al Itaile
Beforn him stode instrumẽtes of such sown
That Orpheus/ ne of Thebes Amphion
Ne made neuer suche a melody.
¶ At euery cours came loude mynstralcy
That neuer Ioab tromped for to here
Neither Theodomas yet halfe so clere
At Thebes/ whan the cyte was in dout
Bacchus the wyne hem skynketh al about
And Venus laugheth on euery wight
For Ianuary was become her knyght
And wolde bothe assayen his corage
In lyberte/ and eke in mariage
And with her fire bronde in her honde about
Daunceth before the bride and al the rout
And certainly/ I dare wel sayn right this
Emenius that god of weddyng is
Saw neuer i his life/ so mery a wedded man
Holde

Holde thou thy peace thou poet Marcian
That writest vs that ilke weddyng mery
Of her philology and him Mercury
And of the songes that the Muses songe
To small is bothe thy penne & eke thy tonge
For to discryuen of this mariage
Whan tēder youth hath iwedded stouping age
There is suche myrth/ ẏ it may nat be written
Assayeth your selfe/ than may ye witten
If that I lacke or non in this matere
May that sytte/ with so benigne a chere
Her to beholde/ it semed fayrey
Quene Hester loked neuer with suche an eye
On Assuere/ so meke a loke hath she
I may you nat deuyse all her beaute
But thus moche of her beaute tel I may
That she was lyke ẏ bright morowe of May
Fulfylde of al beaute/ and of plesaunce
This January is rauysshed in a traunce
And at euery tyme he loked in her face
But in his hert/ he gan her to manace
That he ẏ night/ i his armes wold her streyn
Harder/ than euer Paris dyd Heleyn
But natheles/ yet had he great pite
That thilke night offende her most he
And thought alas/ O tender creature
Nowe wolde god ye myght wel endure
Al my corage/ it is so sharpe and kene
I am agast ye shal it nat sustene
But god forbede/ that I dyd al my might
Nowe wolde god that it were waye night
And that the night wolde last euer mo
I wolde that al these people were a go
And finally he dothe all his labour
As he best might/ sauyng his honour
To hast hem fro the meat in subtel wise
The tyme came/ that reason was to rise
And after that men daunceṇ/ & drinke fast
And spices all about the house they cast
And ful of ioye and blysse is euery man
Al but a squyer/ that hight Dampan
Whiche carfe before the knyght many a day
He was so rauisshed on his lady May
That for very payne he was ny wode
Almost he swelte/ and swouned there he stode
So sore hath Venus hurt him with her brāde
So fresshe she was/ and therto so lyrande
And to his bedde he went him hastely
No more of him at this tyme speke I
But there I let hym wepe ynowe and playne
Tyll the fressh May wol rewen on his payn.
O perilous fire/ ẏ in the bedstrawe bredeth
O famyler foe/ that his seruice bedeth
O seruaunt traytour/ false homely hewe
Lyke to the adder slye in bosome vntrewe
O January dronken in plesaunce
God shilde vs al frō your aquaintaunce
Of mariage/ se howe this Danuan
Thyne owne squiere and thy borne man
Entendeth to don the villany
God graunt the thyn homely foe to espye
For in this worlde nys wers pestilence
Than homely foe/ al day in thy presence
Parfourmed hath the son his arke dyurne
No lengre may the body of him soiourne
On orizont/ as in that latitude
Night with his mantel/ that is derke & rude
Gan for to sprede/ the hemysphery about
For whiche departed is the lusty rout
Fro January/ with thonke on euery syde
Home to her houses lustely they ryde
There as they don her thynges/ as hem lest
And whan they sawe her tyme to go to rest
Sone after this lusty January
Wol go to bedde/ he wolde no lenger tary
He drinketh ypocras/ clarrey/ and vernage
Of spices hote/ to encrease his corage
And many a lectuary had he ful fyne
Suche as the cursed monke dan Cōstantyne
Hath written in his boke of Coitu
To eten hem al he nolde nothyng eschewe
And thus to his preuy frendes said he
For goddes loue/ as sone as it may be
Let voyde all this house in curteys wise sone
Men drinken/ and the trauers drewe anon
So hasted January/ it must be done
The bride was brought to bed as styl as ston
And whan the bed was with ẏ preest iblessed
Out of the chābre hath euery wight hem dres-
And January hath fast in armes take (sed
His fresshe May/ his paradise/ his make
He lulleth her/ he kysseth her ful ofte
With thicke bristels of his berde vnsofte
Lyke ẏ skyn of houndfissh/ as sharp as brere
For

For he was shaue al newe in his manere
He rubbeth her vpon her tendre face
And said thus: Alas/ I mote trespace
To you my spouse/ and you greatly offende
Or tyme come/ that I wol down discende
  But natheles/ considreth this (q̄d he)
There nys no workman/ what so euer he be
That may bothe wirche wel and hastely
This wol be don at leyser parfitly
It is no force howe long that we play
In trewe wedlocke coupled be we tway
And blessed be the yoke that we been in
For in our actes we mowe do no syn
A man may do no synne with his wife
Ne hurt him selfe with his owne knyfe
For we haue leaue to play vs by the lawe
  Thus laboureth he/ tyll the day gan dawe
And than he taketh a soppe in fyne clarre
And vpright in his bedde than sytteth he
And after that he syngeth ful loude and clere
And kyst his wife/ and maketh wanton chere
He was al coltishe/ and ful of ragery
And ful of gergon/ as is a flecked pye
The slacke skynne about his necke shaketh
While that he sange/ so chaunteth he & craketh
But god wot what May thought in her herte
Whan she him sawe/ vp sytting in his sherte
In his night cappe/ with his necke lene
She prayseth not his playeng worth a bene
Than/ said he thus: my rest wol I take
Nowe day is come/ I may no lenger wake
And down he layde his heed/ & slept tyl prime
And afterwarde/ whan that he sawe his tyme
Vp riseth January/ but the fresshe May
Holdeth her chambre to the fourth day
As vsage is of wyues for the best
For euery labour somtyme mote haue rest
Or els longe may he not endure
This is to say/ no lyues creature
Be it fisshe or beest/ brydde or man
  Nowe wol I speke of woful Damian
That langureth for loue/ as ye shal here
Therfore I speke to him in this manere.
¶ I say/ O sely Damian/ alas
Answere to this demaunde/ as in this caas
Howe shalt thou to thy lady fresshe May
Tell thy wo? she wol alway say nay
Eke if thou speke/ she wol thy wo bewray
God be thyn helpe/ I can no better say
  This sicke Damian in Venus fyre
So brenneth/ that he dieth for desyre
For whiche he put his life in auenture
No lenger might he in this wise endure
But priuely a penner gan he borowe
And in a lettre wrote he al his sorowe
In maner of a complaynt or a lay
Vnto this faire and fresshe lady May
And in a purse of silke/ hongyng on his shert
He hath it put/ and layde it at his hert
¶ The mone at noon tyde that ilke day
(That January hath ywedded fresshe May)
Out of Taure was in the Canker gliden
So long hath May in her chambre bidden
As custome is/ vnto these nobles all
A bride shal nat eaten in the hall
Tyll dayes four/ or thre at the lest
Ipassed ben/ than let her gon to fest.
¶ The fourth day cōplete fro noon to noon
Whan that the hye masse was ydoon
  In hall satte this January and May
As fresshe as is the bright somers day
  And so befyl/ howe that this good man
Remembreth him vpon this Damian
And said: saynt Mary/ howe may this be
That Damian entendeth not to me?
Is he aye sicke: or howe may this betide?
  His squiers/ which that stoden him beside
Excused him/ bicause of his sickenesse
Whiche letted him to don his besynesse
Non other cause might make him tary
  That me forthinketh (q̄d this January)
He is a gentle squyere be my trouthe
If that he died/ it were harme and routhe
He is as wise/ discrete/ and secre
As any man that I wotte of his degre
And therto manly and seruysable
And for to be a thrifty man right able
But after meate/ as sone as euer I may
I wol my selfe viset him/ and eke May
To don him al the conforte that I can
And for that worde/ him blessed euery a man
That of his bounte and of his gentilnesse
He wolde so comforten in his distresse
His squier/ for it was a gentle dede

Dame

Dame (q̃d this January) take good hede
That after meate/ ye and your women all
(Whan ye haue ben in chãbre out of this hal)
That al ye gone to se this Dampan
Dothe him disporte/ he is a gentyll man
And telleth him that I wol him visite
Haue I nothyng but rested me a lyte
And spede you fast/ for I woll abyde
Tyll that ye slepe fast by my syde
And with that worde he gan to him call
A squyer/ that was Marshal of his hall
And tolde him certayn thynge that he wolde.
This fresh May hath streight her way ihold
With all her women/ vnto this Dampan
Downe by his beddes syde satte she than
Confortyng him as goodly as she may.
This Dampan/ whan that he his tyme say
In secrete wise/ his purse and eke his byll
(In whiche he had written al his wyll)
Hath put in to her honde withouten more
Saue that he sighed wonders depe and sore
And sothly/ to her right thus said he
Mercy/ and that ye discouer nat me
For I am deed/ if that this thyng be kydde
This purse hath she in her bosome hydde
And went her way/ ye gete no more of me
But vnto January icome is she
And on his beddes syde she sytte ful softe
He taketh her/ and kysseth her ful ofte
And layde him downe to slepe/ & that anon
She fayned her/ as that she must gon
There as ye wote/ that euery wight hath nede
And whan she of this byl hath taken hede
She rent it al to cloutes/ and at last
In to the preuy/ sothly she it cast.
Who studieth nowe but faire fresshe May?
And adown by January she lay
That slepte/ tyll the cough hath hym awaked
Anon he prayde her to stripe her all naked
He wolde of her (he said) haue some plesaũce
He said her clothes dyd him encombraunce
And she obeyeth be she lefe or lothe
But lest that precious folke be wᵗ me wrothe
Howe that he wrought/ I dare nat to you tell
Or wheder she thought it paradise or hell
But I lette hem worche in her wise
Tyl euynsong ryng/ that they must arise.

Were it by desteny or by auenture
Were it by influence/ or by nature
Or constellation that in suche estate
The heuen stode/ that tyme fortunate
(Was for to put a byll of Venus warkes)
For al thyng hath tyme/ as sayn clerkes
To any woman for to gete her loue
I can nat say/ but the great god aboue
That knoweth/ that non acte is causeles
He demeth all/ for I wol holde my pees.
But sothe is this/ howe ẏ this fresshe May
Hath take suche impression that day
Of pyte/ on this sicke Dampan
That fro her hert she dryue ne can
The remembraunce for to don him ease
Certain (thouȝt she) whom this thĩg displease
I recke nat/ for this I him assure
I loue him best of any creature
Though he no more had than his shert.
Lo pyte renneth soone in gentyll hert
Here may ye se/ howe excellent franchise
In women is/ whan they hem narowe auyse
Some tyrant is/ as there ben many one
That hath an hert as harde as any stone
Whiche wolde haue lete him sterue in ẏ place
Wel rather than haue graunted him her grace
And her reioysed in her cruell pride
And nat haue retched to been an homycide.
This gentyll May/ fulfylled of al pyte
Right so of her honde a lettre made she
In whiche she graunteth him her very grace
There lacketh nought/ but onely tyme & place
Where that she might to his lust suffise
For it shal be/ right as he wol deuyse
And whan she sawe her tyme vpon a day
To visite this Dampan goth this faire May
And subtelly this lettre down she thrist
Vnder his pyllowe/ rede it if him lyst
She taketh him by the hõde/ & herd him twist
So secretely/ that no wight of it wist
And badde him ben al hole/ & forth she went
To January/ whan that he for her sent.
Vp riseth Dampan the next morowe
All passed was his sickenesse and his sorowe
He kembeth him and proyneth him & piketh
And dothe all that his lady lust and lyketh
And eke to January he gothe as lowe

I   As euer

As euer dyd a dogge for the bowe
He is so plesaunt to euery man
For crafte is all/ who that it can
That euery wight is fayn to speken him gode
And fully in his ladies grace he stode
   Thus lette I Dampan about his nede
And in my tale/ forthe I woll procede.
¶ Some clerkes holden that felycite
Stont in delyte/ and therfore certayn he
This noble January with all his might
In honest wise, as longeth to a knyght
Shope him to lyue full delyciously
His housyng/ his array/ as honestly
To his degre/ was made as a kynges
Among other of his honest thynges
He had a garden walled all with stone
So faire a garden was there neuer none
For out of dout/ I verily suppose
That he that wrote the Romant of the Rose
Ne couth of it the beaute well deuyse
Ne Priapus/ ne myght nat suffise
Though he be god of gardens/ for to tell
The beaute of the garden/ and of the well
That stont vnder a laurer alway grene
Full ofte tyme kyng Pluto and his quene
Proserpina/ and all her fayrie
Disporten hem/ and maken melody
About that well/ and daunced as men tolde
   This noble knight/ this January the olde
Suche deynte hath/ in it to walke and play
That he woll suffre no wight to bere the kaye
Saue he him selfe/ for the small wicket
He bare alway of syluer a clycket
With whiche/ whan that him lyst vnshet
And whan that he wolde pay his wife her det
In somer season/ thider wolde he go
And May his wyfe/ & no wight but they two
And thinges which that were nat don a bedde
He in the garden ꝑfourmed hem and spedde
   And in this wise/ many a mery day
Lyued this January and this fresshe May
But worldly ioye may nat alway endure
To January/ ne to no lyueng creature.
¶ O sodayne hap/ O thou fortune vnstable
Lyke to the Scorpion disceyuable
That flatrest w^t thy heed whan y^u wolt stige
Thy tayle is dethe/ thrugh thyn enuenomyng
O brotell ioye/ O swete poyson queynt
O monster/ that so sodainly canst peynt
Thy giftes/ vnder the hewe of stedfastnesse
That thou disceyuest bothe more and lesse
Why hast thou January thus descreyued?
And haddest him for thy frende receyued
And now thou hast beraft him bothe his eyen
For sorowe of whiche desireth he to dyen
   Alas/ this noble January that is so fre
Amydde his lust and his prosperite
Is woxen blynde/ and all sodainly
His dethe therfore desireth he vtterly
And therwithall/ the fire of ielousy
(Lest that his wife shulde fall in some foly)
So brent his hert/ that he wolde fayne
That some man/ bothe hym & her had slayne
For neuer after his dethe/ ne in his lyfe
Ne wolde he that she were loue ne wife
But euer lyue a wydowe in clothes blake
Sole/ as the turtle dothe ẏ hath lost her make
But at the last/ after a month or tway
His sorowe gan to swage/ sothe to say
For whan he wyst it might non other be
He paciently toke his aduersyte
Saue out of dout may he nat forgone
That he nas ielous euer more in one
Whiche ielousy/ it was so outragious
That neyther in hall ne in non other hous
Ne in non other place neuer mo
He nolde suffre her/ neither ride ne go
But if that he had honde on her alway
For whiche full often wepeth fresshe May
That loueth Dampan so benignely
That she mote either dye sodainly
Or els she mote haue him at her lest
She wayteth whan her hert shulde to brest
   Vpon that other syde Dampan
Become is/ the sorowfullest man
That euer was/ for neither nyght ne day
Ne myght he speke a worde to fresshe May
As to his purpose of no suche matere
But if that January must it here
That had an honde vpon her euer mo
But natheles/ by writyng to and fro
And preuy signes/ wist he what she ment
And she knewe all the signes of his entent.
¶ O January/ what myght the it auayle?
Tho

Tho thou mightest se/ as fer as shippes sayle
For as good is a blynde man disceyued be
As to be disceyued/ whan that a man may se.
 Lo Argus/ whiche had an hundred eyen
For all that euer he couthe pore and pryen
yet was he blent/ and god wotte so ben mo
That wenen wisely that it is nat so
Passe ouer is an ease/ I say no more.
 This fressh May/ of which I spake of yore
In warme waye hath printed this clyket
That January bare of that small wicket
By whiche vnto his garden ofte he went
And Dampan that knewe her entent
The clyket counterfayted priuely
There nys no more to say/ but hastely
Some wonder by this clicket shal betyde
Whiche ye shull heren/ if ye woll abyde.
¶ O noble Ouide/ soth sayest thou god wote
What sleight is it/ though it be longe and hote
That he nyll fynde it out in some manere
By Pyramus and Thisbe/ maye men lere
Though they were kept ful long streit ouer al
They ben accorded/ rownyng through a wall
Ther nys no wight couth fynde such a sleight
But nowe to purpose/ er ye dayes eight
Were passed/ er the moneth of Iule befyll
That January hath caught so great a wyll
Through eggyng of his wife/ him for to play
In his garden/ & no wight but they tway
That in a morowe/ vnto this May said he
Rise vp my wife/ my loue/ my lady free
The turtell voice is herde my lady swete
The wynter is gon/ with all his raynes wete
Come forth nowe with thyn eyen columbyne
Nowe fayrer ben thy brestes than is wyne
The garden is enclosed all about
Come forthe my white spouse out of dout
Thou hast me wounded in my hert/ o/ wife
No spotte in the nas in all thy life
Come forth and lette vs taken our disport
I chese the for my wife and my confort
 Suche olde leude wordes vsed he
On Dampan a signe made she
That he shulde go before with his clicket
This Dampan hath opened this wicket
And in he stert/ and that in suche manere
That no wight might it se ne here
And styll he sate vnder a busshe anon.
 This January/ as blynde as is a ston
With May in his honde/ and no wight mo
In to his fresshe garden is he go
And clapte to the wicket sodainly.
 Nowe wife (q^d he) here nys but thou & I
That arte the creature that I best loue
For by that lorde that sytte vs all aboue
I had leuer dyen on a knyfe
Than the offende/ dere trewe wife
For goddes sake thynke howe I the chees
Nat for couetise/ ne other good doutlees
But onely for the loue I had to the
And though that I be olde and may nat se
Be to me trewe/ and I woll tell you why
Certes/ thre thynges shall ye wyn therby
 First loue of Christ/ & to your selfe honour
And all myn heritage/ town and toure
I gyue it you/ maketh charters as ye list
This shall be don to morowe er sonne ryst
So wisely god my soule bring to blysse
I pray you on couenaunt that ye me kysse
And though that I be ielous wite me nought
ye ben so depe enprinted in my thought
That whan I consyder your beaute
And therwithall/ the vnlikly elde of me
I may nat certes/ though I shulde dye
Forbere/ to ben out of your company
For very loue/ this is withouten dout
Now kysse me wife/ and lette vs rome about
 This fressh May/ whā she these wordꝫ herd
Benignely to January answerde
But first and forwarde she began to wepe
I haue (quod she) a soule for to kepe
As well as ye/ and also myn honour
And of wifehode thilke tender flour
Whiche that I haue ensured in your honde
Whan that the preest to you my body bonde
Wherfore I woll answere in this manere
By the leaue of you my lorde so dere
 I pray god that neuer dawe that day
That I ne sterue/ as foule as woman may
Yf euer I do to my kynne that shame
Or els that I empayre so my name
That I be falsse/ and if I do that lacke
Do stripe me/ and putte me in a sacke
And in the next ryuer do me drenche

I. ii. I am

The Merchant's Tale (E 2108–2201; T. 9982–10075)

I am a gentyll woman/ and no wenche
Why speke ye thus/ but men ben euer vntrew
And women haue reprofe of you/ aye newe
Ye can non other cōmunyng/ I leue
But speke to vs of vntrust and repreue
And with ẏ worde she sawe where Damian
Sate in the busshe/ and knele he began
And with her fynger signes made she
That Dampan shulde clymbe vp on a tre
That charged was with frute/ & vp he went
For verily he knewe all her entent
And euery signe that she couth make
Welbet than January her owne make
For in a letter she had tolde him all
Of this mater/ howe that he worch shall
And thus I lete him sytte in the pery
And January and May romyng full mery.
¶ Bright was the day/ & blewe ẏ fyrmamēt
Phebus of golde doun hath his stremes sente
To gladen euery flour with his warmnesse
He was that tyme in Gemyny/ as I gesse
But lytell fro his declynation
The causer of Iouis exaltation
And so befyll that bright morowe tyde
That in the garden/ on the farther syde
Pluto/ that is the kyng of Fayrye
And many a lady in his company
Folowyng his wife/ the quene Proserpyne
Eche after other right as a lyne
Whiles she gadred floures in a mede
In Claudian ye may the story rede
Howe in his grisely carte he her fette
This kyng of Fayry doun him sette
Vpon a benche of turues fresshe and grene
And right anon thus said he to his quene.
My wife (q̄d he) that may nat say nay
The experience so proueth it euery day
The treason/ which that women doth to man
Tenne hundred thousande tell I can
Notable/ of your vntrouth and brotelnesse
O Salomon/ richest of all richesse
Fulfylde of sapience/ and of worldly glory
Full worthy ben thy wordes in memory
To euery wight/ that wytte and reason can
Thus prayseth he the bounte of man
Among a thousande men yet fonde I one
But of all women fonde I neuer none
Thus saith the kyng/ ẏ knoweth yoʳ wicked-
And Iesus filius Sirach/ as I gesse (nesse
Ne speketh of you but selde reuerence
A wylde fire/ a corrupte pestilence
So fall vpon your bodies yet to nyght
Ne se ye nat this honorable knyght:
Bicause (alas) that he is blynde and olde
His owne man shall maken him cokolde
Lo where he sytte/ the lechour in the tre
Nowe woll I graunt of my maieste
Vnto this olde blynde worthy knyght
That he shall haue agayn his eye sight
Whan that his wyfe wolde don him villany
Than shall he knowe all her harlotry
Bothe in reprefe of her and other mo.
Ye shall (q̄d Proserpyne) and woll ye so:
Nowe be my mothers soule sir I swere
That I shall yeuen her sufficient answere
And all women after for her sake
That though they ben in any gylte itake
With face bolde/ they shullen hem selue excuse
And bere hem doun/ that wolde hem accuse
For lacke of answere/ non of hem shull dyen
All had he sey a thyng with bothe his eyen
Yet shulde we women so visage it hardely
And wepe and swere/ and chide subtelly
That ye shall ben as leude as gees
What recketh me of your auctoritees:
I wotte well this iewe/ this Salomon
Fonde of vs women foles many one
But though he ne fonde no good woman
Yet there hath ifonde many another man
Women full trewe/ full good/ & full vertuous
Witnesse of hem that dwell in Christes hous
With martyrdom/ they preued her constaunce
The Romain iestes eke make remēbraunce
Of many a very trewe wife also
But sir/ be nat wrothe that it be so
Though that he said he fonde no good womā
I pray you take the sentence of the man
He ment thus/ that in souerayn bounte
Nys non but god/ that sytteth in trynite.
Eye/ for very god that nys but one
What make ye so moche of Salomon:
What though he made a tēple goddes hous:
What though he were riche and glorious:
So made he a temple of false goddis
Howe

How might he don a thyng ỹ more forbode is
Parde as faire as ye his name enplaster
He was a lechour/ and an idolaster
And in his elde/ very god forsoke
And if that god nadde (as saith the boke)
Yspared him for his fathers sake/ he shulde
Haue lost his reigne soner than he wolde
I sette nat of all the villany
That ye of women write/ a butterflye
I am a woman/ nedes mote I speke
Or els swell/ tyll myn hert breke
For sithen he said/ that we ben iangleresses
As euer mote I hole broke my tresses
I shall nat spare for no curtesy
To speke hem harme/ that wolde vs villany.
Dame (qd this Pluto) be no lenger wroth
I gyue it vp: but sithe I swore myn othe
That I wolde graunt him his sight ayen
My worde shal stande/ ỹ warn I you certeyn
I am a kyng/ it sytte me nat to lye.
And I (qd she) a quene of Fayrie
Her answere she shall haue I vndertake
Lette vs no mo wordes herof make
Forsoth I woll no lenger you contrary.
Nowe lette vs turne agayn to January
That in the garden with this faire May
Syngeth merier than the poppyngay
You loue I best/ and shall/ and other non
So long about the aleyes is he gon
Tyll he was comen ayenst thilke pery
Where as this Damyan sitteth full mery
On hye/ among these fresshe leues grene.
This fresshe Maye/ that is so bright ꝛ shene
Gan for to sike/ and said: alas my syde
Nowe sir (qd she) for ought that may be tyde
I must haue of these peeres that I here se
Or I mote dye/ so sore longeth me
To eten of the small peres grene
Helpe for her loue that is heuyn quene
I tell you well a woman in my plyte
May haue to frute so great an appetyte
That she may dyen/ but she it haue.
Alas (qd he) that I ne had here a knaue
That couth clymbe/ alas/ alas (qd he)
For I am blynde. ye sir no force (qd she)
But wolde ye vouchsafe for goddes sake
The pery in your armes for to take
For well I wotte that ye mystrust me
Than shulde I clymbe well ynough (qd she)
So I my fote myght sette vpon your backe
Forsoth said he/ in me shall be no lacke
Might I you helpe with myn hert blode
He stoupeth doun/ ꝛ on his backe she stode
And caught her by a twist/ and vp she goth
Ladies I praye you be nat wroth
I can nat glose/ I am a rude man
And sodainly anon this Damyan
Gan pullen vp the smocke/ and in he thronge
A great tent/ a thrifty and a longe
She said it was the meryest fytte
That euer in her lyfe she was at yet
My lordes tent serueth me nothyng thus
It foldeth twifolde by swete Iesus
He may nat swyue worth a leke
And yet he is full gentyll and full meke
This is leuer to me than an euynsong
And whan that Pluto sawe this wronge
To January he gaue agayn his syght
And made him se aswell as euer he myght
And whan he had caught his sight agayn
Ne was there neuer man of thyng so fayn
But on his wife his thought was euer mo
Vp to the tree he cast his eyen two
And sawe how Damian his wife had dressed
In suche manere/ it may nat be expressed
But if I wolde speke vncurtesly
And vp he yaf a roryng and a crye
As dothe the mother whan the childe shall dye
Out helpe/ alas (harowe) he gan to crye
For sorowe almost he gan to dye
That his wife was swyued in the pery
O stronge lady hore what dost thou?
¶ And she answered: sir what ayleth you?
Haue patience and reason in your mynde
I haue you holpen of bothe your eyen blynde
Vp peryll of my soule/ I shall nat lyen
As me was taught to helpe with your eyen
Was nothyng bette for to make you se
Than strogle with a man vpon a tree
God wote I dyd it in full good entent
¶ Strogle (qd he) ye algate in it went
Styffe and rounde as any bell
It is no wonder though thy bely swell
The smocke on his brest lay so theche
And euer me though he poynted on the breche
God gyue you bothe on shames dethe to dyen

The Marchauntes tale.

He swyued the/ I sawe it with myne eyen
And els I be honged by the halse
Than is (qd she) my medicyn false
For certayn/ if that ye myght se
Ye wolde nat say theke wordes to me
Ye haue some glymsyng/ and no parfite syght
I se (qd he) as well as euer I myght
Thanked be god/ with both myne eyen two
And by my trouth me thought he dyd so
Ye mase ye mase/ good sir (qd she)
This thanke haue I for that I made you se
Alas (qd she) that euer I was so kynde
Now dame (qd he) let al passe out of mide
Come down my lefe/ and if I haue myssayde
God helpe me so/ as I am yuell apayde
But by my fathers soule/ I wende haue seyn
Howe that this Damyan had by the leyn
And that thy smocke had lyen vpon his brest
Ye sir (qd she) ye may wene as ye lest
But sir/ a man that waketh out of his slepe
He may nat sodainly well taken kepe
Vpon a thyng/ ne se it parfitely
Tyll that he be adawed verily
Right so a man that longe hath blynde be
Ne may nat sodainly so well yse
First whan the sight is newe comen a gayn
As he that hath a daye or two ysayn
Tyll that your sight istabled be a while
There may full many a sight you begyle
Beware I pray you/ for by heuen kyng
Full many a man weneth to se a thyng
And it is all another than it semeth
He that myscouceyueth ofte mysdemeth
And with that worde she lepe doun fro the tre
This January/ who is gladde but he:
He kyssseth her/ he clyppeth her full ofte
And on her wombe he stroketh her full softe
And to his paleys home he hath her ladde
Nowe good men I pray you/ beth ye all glad
Thus endeth here my tale of January
God blesse vs al/ and his mother Mary.

¶ Thus endeth the Marchantes tale and here foloweth the wife of Bathes prologue.

Experience/ though none authorite
Were i this world/ is right ynow for me
To speke of wo that is in maryage
For lordynges/ syth I twelue yere was of age
Thonked be god/ that is eterne on lyue
Husbondes at chirche dore haue I had fyue

The Merchant's Tale: The Wife of Bath's Prologue (E 2378–2418, D 1–6; T. 10252–10292, 5583–5588)

If I so ofte myght haue wedded be
And al were worthy men in her degre.
But me was tolde not longe ago iwys
That sythen Chust went neuer but onys
To weddyng/in the cane of Galilee
That by thilke ensample taught he me
That I ne shulde wedded be/but ones.
¶ Lo here/ which a sharpe worde for ỹ nones
Besyde a well/Jesu god and man
Spake in repreve of the Samaritan
Thou hast had fyue husbandes (qd̄ he)
And that ilke man that nowe hath the
Is not thyne husbonde: thus said he certayn
What he ment therby I can not sayn
But that I aske/ why the fyfte man
Was nat husbonde to the Samaritan
Howe many myght she haue in mariage?
yet herde I neuer tellen in myne age
Upon this nombre trewe diffynition
Men may deuyne/and glosen vp and doun
But well I wotte expresse without lye
God badde vs for to wexe and multiply
That gentyll text can I well understonde
Eke well I wotte (he said) myn husbonde
Shuld leaue father & mother/ and take to me
But of nombre no mention made he
Of bigamye or of octogamye
Why shull men speke of it villany?
Lo he the wise kyng Salomon
I trowe had wyues mo than one
As wolde god it lefull were to me
To be refresshed halfe so ofte as he
Which a gifte of god had he/ for all his wyuis
No man hath such/ ỹ in this worlde a lyue is
God wotte this noble kyng/as to my wytte
The first nyght had many a mery fytte
With eche of hem/so wel was him a lyue
Blessed be god/ I haue had fyue
Welcome the syxte whan euer he shal
For sothe I wol not kepe me chaste in al
Whan myn husbonde is fro the worlde ygon
Some crysten man shal wedde me anon
For than the apostel sayth/that I am fre
To wedde a goddeshalfe/ where it lyketh me
He sayth/that to be wedded is no synne
Better is to be wedded than to brinne

What recketh me though folke say villany
Of shrewde Lameth/and of his bigamy
¶ I wotte well Abraham was an holy man
And Jacob eke/ as fer as euer I here can
And eche of hem had wyues mo than two
And many another holy man also
Where can ye say in any maner age
That euer god defended mariage
By expresse wordes? I pray you tell me
Or where cōmaunded he virginyte?
I wotte as well as ye/ it is no drede
The Apostell/ whan he spake of maydenhede
He said/ therof precept had he none
Men may counsayle a woman to be one
But counsaylyng is no cōmaundement
He put it in our owne iugement
For had god cōmaunded maydenhede
Than had he dampned weddyng out of drede
And certes/if there were no sede ysowe
Virgynite than wherof shulde it growe?
Poule durste not comaunde at the leste
A thing/of which his mayster yafe none heste
The darte is set vp for virgynite
Catche who so may/ who renneth beste let se.
But this worde is not take of euery wyght
But there as god lyst yeue it of his myght
I wotte wel that the apostel was a mayde
But nathelesse/ though that he wrote & sayde
He wolde that euery wight were suche as he
Al nys but counsayle to virginite
And for to ben a wyfe he yaue me leue
Of indulgence/so it be not to repreue
To wedde me/if that my make dye
Without exception of bygamye
Al were it good no woman for to touche
He ment as in his bedde or in his couche
For peryl is/ bothe fyre and towe to assemble
ye knowe what this ensample may resemble
This is al and some/he helde virginite
More parfyte than weddyng in freelte.
¶ Freelte clepe I/but if that he and she
Wolde lede her lyfe al in chastyte
I graunt it wel/ I haue none enuye
Though maydenhede preferre bygamye
It lyketh hem to be clene in body and goste
Of myne estate I wol make no boste
For well ye knowe/ a lorde in his housholde
Hath

The wyfe of Bathes prologue.

Hath nat euery vessell all of golde
Some ben of tree/ and don her lorde seruyce
God clepeth folke to him in sondry wise
And euery che hath of god a proper gifte
Some this/some that/as him lyketh shifte
Virginyte is great perfection
And continence eke with deuocion
But Christ/that of perfection is well
Badde nat euery wight he shulde go sell
All that he had/and gyue it to the poore
And in suche wise folowe him and his fore
He spake to hem/that wolde lyue parfitly
And lordinges (by your leaue) that am nat I
I woll bestowe the floure of all myn age
In the actes and frute of mariage
  Tell me also/to what conclusyon
Were membres made of generation?
And of so parfite wise a wight iwrought
Trusteth well/ they were nat made for nouzt
Glose who so woll/ and saye vp and doun
That they were made for purgatioun
Of vryne/ and other thynges smale
And eke to knowe a female from a male
And for non other cause/ what say ye no?
The experience wotte wele it is nat so
So that the clerkes be nat with me wroth
I saye that they were maked for bothe
This is to sayn/ for office and for ease
Of engendrure/there we nat god displease
Why shulde men els in her bokes sette
That man shulde yelde to his wife her dette
  Now wherwith shuld he pay his payment?
If he ne vsed his sely instrument
Than were they made vpon a creature
To purge vryn/and eke for engendrure
  But I say nat/that euery wight is holde
That hath suche harnesse/as I to you tolde
To gon and vsen hem in engendrure
Than shulde men take of chastite no cure
  Christ was a mayde/and shapen as a man
And many a saynt/sithen the worlde began
Yet lyued they euer in parfyte chastite
I nyll enuy no virginyte
Lette hem with bredde of pure whete be fedde
And lette vs wyues eate barly bredde
And yet with barly bred/ Marke tell can
Our lorde Iesu refresshed many a man
In suche a state as god hath cleped vs
I woll perseuer/ I nam nat precious
In wifehode woll I vse myn instrument
As frely as my maker hath it sent
If I be daungerous/god gyue me sorowe
My husbōde shal it haue both euyn & morow
Whan that him lyst come forth & pay his det
An husbande woll I haue I woll nat let
Whiche shall be bothe my dettour & my thrall
And haue his tribulation with all
Vpon his flesshe/ while that I am his wife
I haue the power duryng all my lyfe
Vpon his proper body/and nat he
Right thus the apostle tolde to me
And badde our husbondes for to loue vs well
All this sentence me lyketh euery dell.
¶ Vp stert the Pardoner/and that anon
Nowe dame quod he/by god & by saynt Iohn
Ye ben a noble prechour in this caas
I was about to wedde a wife/ alas
What/shulde I bye it on my flesshe so dere?
Yet had I leuer wedde no wife to yere
  Abyde qd she/ my tale is nat begon
Nay/thou shalte drinke of another ton
Er that I go/ shall sauer worse than ale
And whan that I haue tolde forth my tale
Of tribulation that is in mariage
Of whiche I am expert in all myn age
This is to say/ my selfe hath ben the whippe
Than mayst thou chese whider thou wolt sip
Of thilke tonne/ that I shall sette a broche
Beware of it/ er thou to nere aproche
For I shall tell ensamples mo than ten
Who so woll nat beware by other men
By him shall other men corrected be
These same wordes writeth Ptholome
Rede in his almagest / and take it there.
  Dame I woll pray you/if your wyll were
Said this Pardoner/as ye began
Tell forth your tale/ spareth for no man
And teche vs yong men of your practike
  Gladly (qd she) if it may you lyke
But that I pray to all this company
Yf that I speke after my fantasy
As taketh nat a grefe of that I say
For myn entent is nat but to play
  Nowe sirs/than shall I tell forth my tale?
As euer

The Wife of Bath's Prologue (D 100–193; T. 5682–5775)

As euer mote I drinke wyne or ale
I shall say soth. tho husbondes that I had
Thre of hem were good/ and two were bad
The thre good men were riche and olde
Unnethes myght they the statute holde
In whiche they were bounden unto me
ye wotte well what I mean of this parde
As god me helpe/ I laugh whan I thynke
How pitously a night I made hem to swynke
But by my faye/ I tolde of it no store
They had me yeue her londe and her tresore
Me neded no lenger to do dilygence
To wynne her loue/ and do hem reuerence
They loued me so well by god aboue
That I ne tolde no deynte of her loue
A wise woman woll besy her euer in one
To gete her loue/ ther as she hath none
But sithen I had hem holy in myn honde
And that they had gyue me all her londe
What/ shulde I take kepe hem for to please?
But if it were for my profite and myn ease
I sette hem so a worke by my faye
That many a night they songen welaway
The bacon was nat fet for hem I trowe
That some men haue in Essexe at Donmowe
I gouerned hem so well after my lawe
That eche of hem full blysfull was & fawe
To bring me gay thinges fro the fayre
They were ful fayn whan I spake hem faire
For god it wotte/ I chidde hem spitously
Nowe herkeneth howe I bere me properly.
ye wise wyues that can understonde
Thus shull ye speke/ and bere hem on honde
For halfe so boldly there can no man
Swere and lye/ as a woman can
I saye nat this by wyues that ben wise
But if it be/ whan they hem mysse auyse
A wise wife shall/ if that she can her gode
Bere hem in honde the cowe is wode
And take wytnesse of her own mayde
Of her assent: but herkeneth howe I sayde.
¶ Sir olde keynarde/ is this thyn array
Why is myne neighbours wife so gay?
She is honoured ouerall where she goth
I sytte at home/ and haue no thrifty cloth
What dost thou at myn neighbours hous?
Is she so faire? art thou so amorous?
What rownest thou wt our mayd? benedicite
Sir olde lechour/ let thy iapes be
And if I haue a gossip or a frende
(Without gilte) thou chidest as a fende
If that I walke or play unto his house
Thou comest home as dronken as a mouse
And prechest on thy benche with yuell prefe
Thou sayst to me/ it is a great myschefe
To wedde a poore woman for costage
And if that she be riche of high parage
Than sayst thou/ it is a very tourmentry
To suffre her pride and her melancoly
And if that she be faire/ thou very knaue
Thou sayest that euery holour woll her haue
She may no while in chastite abyde
That is assayled on euery syde
Thou sayst som folke desyren us for richesse
Some for our shap/ & some for our fairnesse
And some/ for she can either syng or daunce
And some for gentylnesse or for dalyaunce
Some for her hondes and her armes smale
Thus gothe all to the deuyll by thy tale.
Thou sayst men may nat kepe a castel wal
It may so long assayled be ouer all
And if that she be foule/ thou sayest that she
Coueteth euery man that she may se
For as a spanyell/ she woll on hem lepe
Tyl that she fynde some man y wol her chepe
Ne non so gray gose goth there in the lake
(As sayst thou) woll ben without her make
And sayst/ it is a harde thyng for to welde
A wight/ that no man wolt his thonke helde.
Thus sayst thou lorel/ whan yu gost to bed
That no wiseman nedeth for to wedde
Ne no man that entendeth unto heuyn
With wylde thunder dent and fire leuyn
Mote thy wicked necke be to broke.
Thou sayst/ droppyng houses/ & eke smoke
And chidyng wyues/ maken men to flee
Out of her owne house/ ah/ benedicite
What ayleth suche an olde man for to chide?
Thou sayst/ we wyues woll our vices hide
Tyll we be fast/ and than we wol hem shewe
Well may this be a prouerbe of a shrewe.
Thou sayst/ y oxen/ horse/ asses/ & houndes
They ben assayde at dyuers stoundes
Basyns/ lauers/ er that men hem bye

Spones

The wyfe of Bathes prologue.

Spones/ stoles/ and all suche husbondry
And so be pottes/ clothes/ and arrayes
But folke of wyues maken non assayes
Tyll they ben wedded/ olde dottarde shrewe
And sayst/ how we wol than our vices shewe
Thou sayest also/ that it displeaseth me
But if that thou wylte preyse my beaute
And but thou pore alwaye on my face
And clepe me faire dame in euery place
And but thou make a feest on that ilke day
That I was borne/ & make me fresshe & gay
And but thou don to my norice honour
And to my chamberer within my bour
And to my fathers folke/ and his alyes
Thus sayest thou olde barell full of lyes.
And yet of our prentise Jenkyn
For his crispe heer/ shynyng as golde fyne
And for he squireth me bothe vp and down
Hast thou caught a false suspectioun
I wol him nat/ tho thou were deed to morow.
But tel me this/ why hidest thou w^t sorowe
The keyes of thy chest away fro me?
It is my good as well as thyn parde
What/ wenest thou make an ydiot of our dāe
Now by that lorde/ that called is saynt Jame
Thou shalt nat both though thou were wode
Be maister of my body and of my good
That one y^u shalte forgon maugre thyn eien
What helpeth it of me to enquere and spyen?
I trowe thou woldest locke me in thy chyst?
Thou shuldest saye: wife/ go where you lyst
Take your disporte/ I wol leue no tales
I knowe you for a trewe wife dame Ales
We loue no man/ that taketh kepe or charge
Where that we go/ we wol be at our large.
¶ Of all men yblessed mote he be
The wise astrologien dan Ptholome
That saithe this prouerbe in his almagest
Of all men his wisedom is the best
That recketh nat whō hath ye worlde in hōde.
By this prouerbe thou shalte vnderstonde
Haue thou ynowe/ what dare ye recke or care
Howe merely that other folke fare
For certes/ olde dottarde by your leue
Ye shall haue queynt ynowe at eue
He is to great a nygarde that woll werne
A man/ to lyght a candell at his lanterne
He shall haue neuer the lasse lyght parde
Haue thou ynowe/ thou darst nat playn the.
Thou sayest also/ that if we make vs gaye
With clothes/ or with precious array
That it is peryll of our chastite
And yet with sorowe/ thou must enforsen the
And say these wordes in the apostels name
In habite made with chastite and shame
Ye women shulde appareyle you (q^d he)
And nat in tressed heer/ and gay perre
As perll/ ne with golde/ ne clothes riche
After the text/ ne after thy rubriche
I nyll nat worche as moche as a gnatte.
¶ Thou sayest also/ I was lyke a catte
But who so wolde senge the cattes skynne
Than wolde the catte dwellen in his inne
And if the cattes skyn be slicke and gaye
She nyll nat dwell in house halfe a day
But forthe she woll or any day be dawed
To shewe her skyn/ and gon a catrewawed.
¶ Thus thou sayest/ if I be gay sir shrewe
I woll ren out/ my borell for to shewe
Sir olde fole/ what helpeth the to spyen
For though thou play Argus w^t his. C. eyen
To be my wardcors/ as he can best
In faithe he shall nat kepe me but me lest
Yet couth I make his berde/ so mote I the
¶ Thou sayest eke/ that there ben thĩges thre
The whiche troublen all this erthe
And that no wight may endure the ferth
O lefe sir shrewe/ Jesu shorte thy lyfe
Yet prechest thou/ & sayest: an hateful wife
Y reckened is/ for one of these myschaunces
Ben there non other resemblaunces?
That ye may lyken your parables to
But if a sely wife be one of tho.
Thou lykenest eke/ womens loue to hell
To barayn londe/ there water may nat dwell
Thou lykenest it also to wylde fyre
The more it brenneth/ the more it hath desyre
To consume any thyng that brent wolde be.
Thou sayest/ right as wormes shēden a tre
Right so a wife distroyeth her husbonde
This knowen they that ben to wyues bonde.
¶ Lordĩges/ right thus as ye haue vnderstōd
Bare I stiffely myn olde husbande on honde
That thus they sayden in her dronknesse
And

The Wife of Bath's Prologue (D 288–381; T. 5870–5963)

And all was false/but as I toke witnesse
Of Jenkyn/ and of my nece also
O lorde the payne I dyd hem/and the wo
Full gyltles by goddes swete pyne
For as an horse/ I couth bothe bite ⁊ whyne
I couth playn/ though I were in the gylte
Or els often tyme I had ben spylte
Who so first to myl cometh/ first grynt
I playned first/ and so was our warre istynt
They were ful glad to excusen hem blyue
Of thyng/that they a gylt neuer in her lyue
Of wenches wolde I bere hem on honde
whan yͭ for sicke/unnethes nught they stonde
Yet tickled I his hert / for that he
Wende I had of him so great cheerte
I swore/ that al my walkyng out by nyght
Was for to espy wenches/ that he dight
Under that colour had I moche myrthe
For all suche witte/is gyuen us in our birthe
Disceite/ wepyng/ spynnyng/ god hath gyue
To women/ kyndly while that they lyue
And thus of o thyng I may auaunt me
At thende I had the best in eche degre
By sleight or force/or by some maner thyng
As by contynuall murmure or grutchyng
Namely a bedde had they mischaunce
There wolde I chide/⁊ don hem no plesaunce
I wolde no lenger in the bedde abyde
(Yf I felte his arme ouer my syde)
Tyll he had made his raunsom unto me
Than wolde I suffre him do his nycete
And therfore/ euery man this tale I tell
wyne who so may/ all ben for to sell
with empty hondes men may no haukes lure
For wynnyng wolde I all his lust endure
And make me than a fayned appetite.
And yet in bacon had I neuer delyte
That maked me euer yͭ I wolde hem chide
For though the pope had sytten hem besyde
I wolde nat spare hem at her own borde
For be my trouth I quyt hem word for worde
As helpe me very god omnypotent
Tho I right nowe shulde make my testamēt
I ne owe hem a worde / but it is quytte
I brought it so about by my wytte
That they must gyue it up/as for the best
Or els had we neuer ben in rest

For though he loked as wode as a lyon
yet shulde he fayle of his conclusyon.
Than wolde I say/ good lefe take kepe
Howe mekely loketh wylken our shepe
Cõe nere my spouse/⁊ let me kysse your cheke
ye shulde be all pacient and meke
And haue a swete spiced conscience
Sithe ye so preche of Jobs pacyence
Suffreth alway/ sith ye so well can preche
And but if you do/ we shall you teche
That it is faire to haue a wife in pece
One of us two mote obeyen doutles
And sithe a man is more resonable
Than a woman is/ye must ben sufferable
What ayleth you to grutche thus and grone?
Is it for ye wolde haue my queynt alone?
Why take it all. lo/haue it euery dell
Peter I shrewe you/ but ye loue it well.
For if I wolde sell my belechose
I couth walke as fresshe as any rose
But I woll kepe it for your owne toth
ye be to blame by god/I say you soth
Suche maner wordes had we on honde
Nowe woll I speke of my fourth husbonde.
¶ My fourth husbonde was a reuelour
This is to say/he had a paramour
And I was yong and full of ragery
Stubburne and stronge/and ioly as a pye
Well coude I daunce to an harpe smale
And syng ywis/ as a nyghtingale
Whan I had drõken a draught of swete wyne
Metellus/ the foule churle the swyne
That with a staffe byrafte his wife her lyfe
For she drõke wyne:though I had be his wife
Ne shulde he nat haue daunted me fro drinke
And after wyne of Uenus must I thynke
For also seker/as colde engendreth hayle
A lycorus mouth must haue a lecherous taile
In women vynolent is no defence
This knowe lechours by experience.
But lorde Christ/ whan it remembreth me
Upon my youth/and my iolyte
It tickleth me about myn hert rote
Unto this day it dothe myn hert bote
That I haue had my worlde/as in my tyme
But age alas/ that all woll enuenyme
Hath me birafte my beaute/and my pith
Lette

Lette go farwell/the deuyll go therwith
The floure is gon, there nys no more to tell
The bran (as I best can) nowe mote I sell
But yet to be right mery wol I fonde
Nowe forth to tel of my fourth husbonde.
¶ I saye I had in hert great dispite
That he of any other had delyte
But he was quyt/by god and by saynt Ioce
I made him of the same wode a troce
Nat of my body in no foule manere
But certainly/ I made folke suche chere
That in his own grece I made him fry
For anger/ and for very ielousy
By god/ in erthe I was his purgatory
For whiche I hope his soule be in glory
For god it wotte/ he satte ful ofte and songe
Whan that his shoe ful bytterly him wronge
There was non/ saue god & he/ that wist
In many wise/howe sore that I him twist
He dyed whan I came fro Hierusalem
And lyeth in graue vnder the Rode beem
All nys his tombe so curious
As was the sepulture of him Darius
Whiche that Appelles wrought so subtelly
It is but wast to bury him preciously
Let him farwell/god gyue his soule good rest
He is nowe in his graue and in his chest.
¶ Nowe of my fyfth husbonde woll I tell
God lette neuer his soule come in hell
And yet was he to me the most shrewe
That fele I on my ribbes all by rewe
And euer shal/ vnto myn endyng day
But in our bedde he was so fresshe and gay
And therwithall/ he couth so well me glose
Whan that he wolde haue my bele chose
That though he had me bete on euery bone
He couthe wynne agen my loue anon
I trowe I loued him the better/ for that he
Was of his loue so daungerous to me
We women haue/if that I shall nat lye
In this matere/a queynt fantasy
Waite what thyng we may nat lightly haue
Therafter woll we al day crye and craue
Forbyd vs thyng/ and that desyren we
Prese on fast/ and than woll we flee
With daunger vttren we all our chaffare
Great prees at market maketh dere ware
And to great chepe is holde at to lytell price
This knoweth euery woman that is wise.
¶ My fyfth husbonde/god his soule blesse
Whiche I toke for loue and no richesse
He somtyme was a clerke of Oxenforde
And had lefte schole/ & went at home to borde
With my gossip/dwellyng in our town
God haue her soule / her name was Alysoun
She knewe my hert/ and eke my preuyte
Better than our parisshe preest so mote I the
To her bewrayed I my counsayle all
For had my husbonde pist agayn the wall
Or don a thing/ that shulde haue cost his lyfe
To her/ and to another worthy wife
And to my nece/ whiche that I loued well
I wolde haue tolde his counsaile euery dell
And so I dyd full often god it wote
That made his face full ofte reed and hote
For very shame/ and blamed him ofte/ for he
Had tolde to me so great a preuyte.
¶ And so befyll/ that ones in a lent
So ofte tyme I to my gossyp went
For euer yet I loued to go gaye
And for to walke in March/April/and Maye
Fro house to house/to harken sondry tales
That Ienkyn clerke/ & my gossyp dame Ales
And I my selfe/ in to the feldes went
My husbonde was at London all that lent
I had the better layser for to pley
And for to se/and eke for to be sey
Of lusty folke/ what wyst I where my grace
Was shapen for to ben/or in what place?
Therfore made I my visytations
To vigilies/ and to processyons
To preachyng eke/ and to pilgrymages
To playes of myracles/and to mariages
And weared on my gay skarlet gytes
These wormes/these moughtz/ ne these mytes
Vpon my parell frette hem neuer a dell
And wost thou why? for they were vsed well
Nowe woll I tell forthe what happed me
I say/ that in the feldes walked we
Tyll trewly we had suche dalyaunce
This clerke and I/that of my purueyaunce
I speke to him/ and said howe that he
Yf I were wedowe / shulde wedde me
For certainly/ I saye for no bobaunce

Yet

Yet was I neuer without purueyaunce
Of maryage/ne of other thynges eke
I holde a mouses wytte not worthe a leke
That hath but one hole to sterten to
And if that fayle/than is al ydo.
  I bare him on hande he had enchaunted me
My dame taught me forsothe that subtylte
And eke I said/ I mette of him al nyght
He wolde a slayne me/as I laye vpright
And al my bedde was ful of very blood
But yet I hope truely he shul do me good
For blode betokeneth golde/as I was taught
And al was fals/I dremed of him right nauzt
But as I folowed aye my dames lore
As wel of that/as of other thinges more.
  But nowe sir let me se/ what shal I sayne?
A ha/by god I haue my tale agayne
  Whan that my fourth husbãde was on bere
I wepte algate/and made sorie chere
As wyues moten/for it is vsage
And with my kerchefe couered my vysage
But for that I was purueyed of a make
I wepte but small/and that I vndertake
To church was my husbãde borne on morowe
With neyghbours/that for him made sorowe
And Janken our clerke was one of tho
As helpe me god/whan that I sawe him go
After the bere/me thought he had a payre
Of legges and of fete/ so clene and so fayre
That al my herte I yaue vnto his holde
He was I trowe/twenty wynter olde
And I was fourty/yf that I shal saye sothe
But yet I had alway a coltes tothe
Gaptothed I was/& that bycame me wele
I had the prynte of dame Venus seele
As helpe me god/I was a lusty one
And fayre/ riche/and yonge/ and wel bygone
And truely/as myn husbonde tolde me
I had the beste queynte that myght be
For certes I am al fully Venerian
In felyng/and my herte is Marcian
Venus me yaue my lust & my lycorousnesse
And Mars yaue me my sturdy hardynesse
Myn ascendent was Taure/& Mars therin
Alas alas/that euer loue was syn
I folowed aye myne inclynation
By vertue of my constellation
That made me I couthe not withdrawe
My chambre of Venus from a good felawe
Yet haue I Martes marke vpon my face
And also in a nother priuy place
For god so wysly be my saluation
I loued neuer by no discretion
But euer folowed myne appetyte
Al were he shorte/longe/ blacke/or whyte
I toke no kepe/so that he lyked me
Howe poore he was/ ne eke of what degre.
What shulde I say? but at the monthes ende
This ioly clerke Janken/that was so hende
Hath wedded me with great solempnyte
And to him yafe I al the londe and fee
That euer was yeuen me here byfore
But afterwarde repented me ful sore
He nolde suffre nothyng of my lyste
By god he smote me ones with his fyst
For that I rente out of his booke a lefe
That of that stroke/my eres wept defe
Stubborne I was/as is a lyonesse
And of my tonge a veray iangleresse
And walke I wolde/as I had done byforne
Fro house to house/although he had it sworne
For whiche ful ofte tyme wolde he preche
And me of olde Romayn iestes teche
  Howe he Sulpicius Gallus lefte his wyfe
And her forsoke terme of his lyfe
Not but for open heed he her sey
Lokyng out at his dore on a dey.
  A nother Romayn tolde he me by name
That for his wyfe was at a sõmer game
Without his wetyng/he forsoke her eke
  And than wolde he vpon his Byble seke
That ilke prouerbe of Ecclesiaste
Where he cõmaundeth/and forbyddeth faste
A mã shal not suffre his wife go royle aboute
  Than wolde he say right thus out of doute
¶ Who so buyldeth his house al of salowes
And pricketh his blynde horse ouer ẏ falowes
And suffreth his wyfe for to seche halowes
He is worthy to be honged on the galowes.
  But al for nought/I sette not an hawe
Of his prouerbes/ne of his olde sawe
Ne I wolde not of him corrected be
I hate him that my vices telleth me
And so do mo (god wotte) than I

k This

The wyfe of Bathes prologue.

This made him wood with me all vtterly
I nolde nat forbere hym in no caas
Now woll I say you soth by saint Thomas
Why that I rent out of his boke a lefe
For whiche he smote me/ that I was defe
He had a boke/ that gladly nyght and daye
For his disporte/ he wolde rede alway
He cleped it Valery/ and Theophrast
At whiche boke he lough alway ful fast
And eke ther was a clerke somtyme at Rome
A cardynall/that hight saynt Jerome
That made a boke ayenst Jouinian
In whiche boke there was eke Tertulyan
Crisyppus/ Trotula/ and Helowys
That was abbesse nat ferre fro Parys
And eke the parables of Salomon
Ouydes arte/and bokes many one
And all these were bounden in one volume
And euery nyght and day was his costume
(Whan he had leyser and vacatioun
From other worldly occupatioun)
To reden in this boke of wicked wyues
He knewe of hem mo legendes and lyues
Than ben of good women in the Byble
For trusteth well/it is an impossyble
That any clerke wolde speke good of wyues
But if it ben of holy sayntes lyues
Ne of non other woman neuer the mo
Who peynted the lyon. tell me who
By god/if women had writen stories
As clerkes han/ within her oratories (nesse
They wold haue written of men more wicked
Than all the marke of Adam may redresse
The children of Mercury and Venus
Ben in her workyng full contrarious
Mercury loueth wisedom and science
And Venus loueth riot and dispence
And for her dyuers disposition
Eche falleth in others exaltation
And thus god wotte/ Mercury is desolate
In Pisces/ where Venus is exaltate
And Venus falleth where Mercury is reysed
Therfore no woman of no clerke is preysed
The clerke whan he is olde/ & may nought do
Of Venus werkes/nat worth his olde shoe
Than sytte he down/ and write in his dotage
That women con nat kepe her mariage

But nowe to purpose/ why I tolde the
That I was beten for a boke parde
Vpon a nyght Jenken/that was our sire
Redde vpon his boke/ as he sate by the fyre
Of Eue first/that for her wickednesse
Was all mankynde brought to wretchednesse
For whiche þ Jesu christ him selfe was slayn
That bought vs with his hert blode agayn
Lo here expresse of women may ye fynde
That woman was the losse of all mankynde
Tho rad he me how Sãpson lost his heeres
Slepyng/ his leman cut hem with her sheres
Thorowe whiche treson lost he bothe his eyen
Tho rad he me/if that I shall nat lyen
Of Hercules/and of his Deianyre
That caused him to sette him selfe a fyre
Nothyng forgate he the care and the wo
That Socrates had with his wyues two
Howe that Xantippe cast pysse on his heed
This sely man satte styll/ as he were deed
He wyped his heed/no more durst he sayn
But er the thonder stynt there cometh rayn
Of Pasiphae/that was quene of Crete
For shrewdnesse him thought that tale swete
Fye/speke no more/it is a grisely thyng
Of her horrible lust and her lykyng
Of Clytemnestra for her lechery
That falsely made her husbande for to dye
He rad it with well good deuotion
He tolde me eke/for what occasyon
Amphiaraus at Thebes lost his lyfe
My husbonde had a legende of his lyfe
Eriphilem that for an ouche of golde
Hath preuily vnto the grekes tolde
Where that her husbonde hyd him in a place
For whiche he had at Thebes sory grace
Of Lyma tolde he me/and of Lucy
They both made her husbondes for to dye
That one for loue/that other was for hate
Lyma her husbonde on an euyn late
Enpoysoned had/for that she was his foe
Lucia lykerous loued her husbonde so
That for he shulde alway vpon her thynke
She gaue him suche a loue maner drynke
That he was deed/er it were morowe
And thus algates husbondes han sorowe
Than tolde he me/ howe one Latumeus
Cõplayned

Complayned to his felowe Arius
That in his garden growed suche a tree
On whiche (he said) that his wyues thre
Honged hem selfe for hertes dispitous
O lefe brother (qd this Arius)
Yeue me a plant of this blyssfull tree
And in my garden planted shall it be.
Of later date of wyues hath he redde
That some han slayn her husbondes in bedde
And let her lechour dight hem all the nyght
Whiles that the cors lay in flore vpright
And some had dryue nayles in her brayn
Whiles they slepe/ & thus they haue hem slayn
Some haue yeue hem poyson in her drinke
He spake more harme than hert may thynke
And therwithall he knewe mo prouerbes
Than in this worlde there groweth grasse or
Bette is (qd he) thyne habitation (herbes
Be with a lyon/ or a foule dragon
Than with a woman vsyng for to chyde
Bette is (qd he) high in the rofe to abyde
Than with an angrye wife down in an hous
They ben so wicked and so contrarious
They haten/that her husbondes louen aye
He said / a woman cast her shame away
Whan she cast of her smocke: and farther mo
A faire woman/but she be chast also
Is lyke a golde ryng on a sowes nose
Who coude wene/ or who coude suppose
The wo/that in myne hert was and pyne
And whan I sawe he wolde neuer fyne
To reden on this cursed boke all nyght
All sodainly thre leues haue I plyght
Out of his boke/right as he radde/and eke
I with my fyst so toke him on the cheke
That in the fire he fell backwarde a doun
And vp he stert/as dothe a wode lyoun
And with his fyst he smote me on myn heed
That in the flore I laye as I were deed
And whan he sey howe styll that I lay
He was a gast/and wolde haue fledde awaye
Tyl at the last out of my swoun I brayde
Oh/ hast thou slayn me false thefe I sayde
For my londe thus hast thou murdred me?
Er I be deed/yet woll I ones kysse the
And nere he cam/and kneled faire a doun
And said: dere suster/swete Alysoun
As helpe me god I shall the neuer smyte
That I haue don/it is thy selfe to wyte
Foryeue it me/and that I the beseke
And yet efte sones I hytte him on the cheke
And said: thefe/thus moche am I be wreke
Nowe woll I dye/I may no lenger speke.
But at the last/with mokell care and wo
We fell accorded within our seluen two
He yaf me all the bridell in myn honde
To haue the gouernaunce of house & londe
And of his tonge/ and of his honde also
And made him bren his boke anon tho
And whan I had goten vnto me
By maistry / all the soueraynte
Than he said: myne own trewe wife
Dothe as thou lyste/ the terme of all thy lyfe
Kepe thyne honour/ and eke myn estate
After that day we had neuer debate
God helpe me so/ I was to him as kynde
As any wife fro Denmarke vnto Inde
And also trewe/and so was he to me
I praye to god/ that sytte in maieste
So blysse his soule/for his mercy dere
Nowe woll I say my tale if ye woll here.
¶ The frere lough whan he had herd all this
Nowe dame (q he) so haue I ioye or blysse
This is a long preamble of a tale
And whan the Sompner herde þ frere gale
Lo (qd this sompner) by goddes armes two
A frere woll entermete him euermo
Lo good men/ a flye and eke a frere
Woll fall in euery disshe and eke matere
What spekest thou of preambulation?
what amble or trot/either peace or syt a doun
Thou lettest our disporte in this matere.
¶ ye wolt thou so þ Sōpner (qd the Frere)
Nowe by my faye I shall / er that I go
Tell of a Sompner/ suche a tale or two
That all the folke shull laugh in this place.
Nowe els frere I beshrewe thy face
(Quod this sompner) and I be shrewe me
But if I tell tales two or thre
Of freres/er I come to Sittyngburne
That shall make thyne hert for to murne
For well I wotte thy pacience is goon.
¶ Our Hoost cried peace/and that anoon
And said: Lette the woman tell her tale

ye faren as folke / that dronken ben of ale
Do dame/tel forthe your tale/& that is beste
Al redy sir (quod she) right as you leste
If I haue lycence of this worthy frere
yes dame/tel forthe your tale/I wol it here.

¶ Here endeth the wyfe of Bathes prologue / and here be- gynneth her tale.

In the olde dayes of kyng Artoure
(Of which ŷ Bretons speken great honour)
Al was this londe fulfylled of fairy
The Elfe quene/with her ioly company
Daunsed ful ofte in many a grene mede
This was the olde opinyon as I rede
I speke of many an hundred yere a go
But nowe can no man se none elfes mo
For nowe the great charyte and prayeres
Of lymytours and other holy freres
That serchen euery lande and euery streme
As thicke as motes in the sonne beme
Blissyng halles/chambres/kichẽs/& boures
Cyties/ borowes/ castelles/and hye toures
Thropes/ bernes/shepens/and deyries
This maketh/that there ben no fayries
For there as wonte to walke was an elfe
There walketh nowe the lymitour him selfe
In vndermeles/and in mornynges
And sayth his matyns / & his holy thynges
As he gothe in his lymitacioun
Women may go safely vp and doun
In euery busshe/and vnder euery tre
There nys none other incubus but he
And he ne wyl done hem no dishonour.
¶ And so fell it/that this kyng Artour
Had in his house a lusty bacheler
That on a day come ridyng fro the ryuer
And happed/that alone as he was borne
He sawe a mayde walkyng him byforne
Of whiche mayde anon/maugre her hede
(By very force) he berafte her maydenhede
For whiche oppression was suche clamour
And suche pursute vnto kyng Artour
That dampned was this knight to be deed
By course of lawe/& shulde haue lost his heed
Peraduenture suche was the statute tho
But that the quene/and other ladyes mo
So longe prayden the kyng of grace
Tyl he his lyfe graunted in that place
And yaue him to the quene/ al at her wyll
To chese where ŷ she wolde him saue or spyll
The quene thãketh ŷ king with al her myght
And after this/thus spake she to the knight
Whan she sey her tyme on a day.
¶ Thou standest yet (qđ she) in suche aray
That of thy lyfe yet haste thou no suerte
I grãute the thy lyfe/if that thou canst tel me
What thyng is it/that women moste desyren
Beware/ and kepe thy necke bone from yren
And if thou canste not tel it me anon
yet wol I yeue the leue for to gon
A twelue moneth and a day/to seke and lere
An answere suffycient in this matere
And suertie wol I haue/ er that thou passe
Thy body for to yelde in this place.
¶ Wo was the knight/& sorowfully he syketh
But what? he may not done al as him lyketh
And at laste he chese him for to wende
And come ayen/right at the yeres ende
With such answer/ as god wolde him puruay
And taketh his leue/ & wendeth forth his way
He seketh euery house and euery place
Where as he hopeth for to fynde grace
To lerne/what thyng women louen moost
But he ne couthe aryuen in no coost
Where as he might fynde in this matere
Two creatures acordyng yfere
Some sayd/women loued beste rychesse
Some sayd honour/some said iolynesse
Some sayd riche aray/some said lust a bedde
And ofte tyme to ben wydowe and wedde
Some said/ that our herte is moste y esed
Whan that we ben flatered and yplesed
He gothe ful nye the sothe/I wol not lye
A man shal wynne vs beste with flaterye
And with attendaunce/and with busynesse
Ben we lymed bothe more and lesse.
And some men sayn/howe ŷ we louen beste
For to ben fre/and do right as vs leste
And that no man repreue vs of our vyce
But say that we be wyse/& nothyng nyce
For trewly there nys none of vs all
If any wight wolle clawe vs on the gall
That

The Wife of Bath's Tale (D 852–940; T. 6434–6522)

That we nyll kyke/ for that he saith vs sothe
Assay/ and he shall fynde it/ that so dothe
For be we neuer so vicious within
We woll be holden wise and clene of syn.
And some men sayn/ ẏ great delite haue we
For to ben holde stable and eke secre
And in o purpose stedfastly to dwell
And nat bewray thyng that men vs tell
But that tale is nat worthe a rake stele
Parde we women con nothyng hele
Wytnesse of Midas/ woll ye here the tale:
¶ Ouyde/ among other thynges smale
Said/ Midas had vnder his long heeres
Growyng on his heed/ two asses eeres
The whiche vice he hidde/ as he best myght
Full subtelly from euery mannes syght
That saue his wife/ there wist of it no mo
He loued her most/ and trusted her allo
He prayde her/ that to no creature
She nolde tellen of his dissygure.
She swore him/ nat for al ẏ worlde to wyn
She nolde do that villany/ ne that syn
To maken her husbōde haue so foule a name
She nolde nat tell it for her own shame
But natheles/ her thought that she dyde
That she so long shulde a counsaile hyde
Her thought it swole so sore about her hert
That nedely some worde she most a stert
And sith she durst tellen it to no man
Down to a marris fast by she ran
Tyll she came there/ her hert was on a fyre
And as a byttour bumbeth in the myre
She layde her mouth vnto the water adown
Bewray me nat thou water with thy sown
Quod she/ to the I tell it/ and to no mo
My hubsonde hath long Asses eres two
Nowe is myn hert all hole/ nowe it is out
I myght no lenger kepe it out of dout.
¶ Here mowe ye se/ though we a tyme abyde
yet out it mote/ we can no counsayle hyde
The remenaunt of the tale/ if ye wyl here
Redeth Ouyde/ and there ye may it lere.
¶ This knight/ of whiche my tale is specially
Whan that he sawe/ he might not come therby
This is to say/ what women louen moste
Within his herte sorowfull was his goste
But home he gothe/ he myght not soiourne
The day was come/ he muste home returne
And in his way/ it happed hym to ryde
In al his care/ vnder a foreste syde
Where he sawe apon a daunce go
Of ladyes foure and twenty/ and yet mo
Toward the daūce he drowe him/ ⁊ that yerne
In hope that some wysdome shulde he lerne
But certaynly/ er that he came fully there
Vanisshed was the daūce/ he nyste not where
No creature sawe he that bare lyfe
Saue in ẏ grene/ he saw sytting an olde wife
A fouler wyght there may no man deuyse
Agayne the knight the olde wyfe gan aryse
And sayd: sir knight/ here forthe lyeth no way
Tel me what ye seken by your fay
Parauenture it may the better be
This olde folke conne moche thing (qd̄ she)
¶ My lefe mother (qd̄ this knyght) certayne
I nam but deed/ but if that I can sayne
What thing it is/ that women moste desyre
Coude ye me wisse/ I wold quite wel yor hire
Plight me thy trouth here ī my hōde (qd̄ she)
The next thing that I require the
Thou shalte it do/ if it be in thy myght
And I wol tel it you/ or it be nyght.
Haue here my trouth (qd̄ ẏ knight) I graūt
¶ Than quod she/ I may me wel auaunt
Thy lyfe is safe/ for I wol stonde therby
Vpon my lyfe/ the quene wyl say as I
Let se/ whiche is the proudest of hem all
That weareth on a kerchefe or a call
That dare say nay/ of that I shal you teche
Let vs go forthe without lenger speche.
Tho rowned she a pistel in his ere
And bade him to be glad/ and haue no fere.
¶ Whā they ben comen to ẏ court/ this knight
Sayd/ he had holde his day/ as he had hight
And redy was his answere/ as he sayde
Ful many a noble wyfe/ and many a mayde
And many a wydowe/ for that they be wyse
(The quene her selfe/ syttyng as a iustyse)
Assembled ben/ his answere for to here
And afterwarde this knight was bode apere.
To euery wyght cōmaunded was sylence
And that the knight shulde tel in audyence
What thing that worldly women loued best
This knyght ne stode not styl as doth a beste

K.iii. But

The wyfe of Bathes tale.

But to his question anon answerde
With manly voyce/ that al the courte it herde
My liege lady: generally/quod he
Women desyren to haue souerayntie
As well ouer her husbondes as her loue
And for to ben in maistrye hem aboue
This is your moste desyre/ though ye me kyll
Dothe as you lyste/ I am here at your wyll.
¶ In al the courte nas there wyfe ne mayde
Ne wydowe/ that contraryed/ that he sayde
But sayd/he was worthy han his lyfe.
And with ẏ worde/ vp sterte the olde wyfe
Whiche ẏ the knight fonde sytting on ẏ grene
Mercy (qd̄ she) my souerayne lady quene
Er that your courte departe do me right
I taught this answere vnto this knight
For whiche he plight me his trouthe there
The first thing I wolde of him requere
He wolde it do/if it lay in his myght
Before the courte than praye I the sir knyght
(Quod she)that thou me take vnto thy wyfe
For wel thou woste/that I haue kept thy lyfe
If I say false/saye nay vpon thy fay.
¶ This knight answerd / alas and welaway
I wote right well/ that suche was my beheste
For goddes loue chese a newe requeste
Take al my good/and let my body go.
Nay qd̄ she/than I shrewe vs bothe two
For though that I be foule/olde/and poore
I nolde for al the metall ne the ore
That vnder erthe is graue/or lythe aboue
But if I thy wyfe were and thy loue.
¶ My loue(quod he) nay my dampnation
Alas that any of my nacion
Shulde euer so foule disparaged be
But al for naught/the ende is this/that he
Cōstrayned was/ ẏ nedes must he her wedde
And taketh this olde wyfe/⁊ gothe to bedde.
¶ Nowe wolden some men say parauenture
That for my neglygence/I do no cure
To tellen you the ioye and the array
That at the feest was that ylke day.
To the whiche thing answere shortly I shal
I say there was no ioy ne feest at al
There nas but heuynesse and moche sorowe
For priuely he wedded her on a morowe
And al day after hydde him as an oule
So wo was him/his wyfe loked so foule.
Gret was ẏ sorow ẏ knight had i his thouȝt
Whan he was with his wife a bedde ibrought
He waloweth/and turneth to and fro.
¶ His olde wyfe lay smylyng euermo
And sayd: O dere husbonde/O benedicite
Fareth euery knight thus as ye?
Is this the lawe of kyng Artours house?
Is euery knyght of his loue so daungerouse?
I am your owne loue/and eke your wyfe
I am she/whiche that saued hath your lyfe
And certes yet dyd I neuer you vnryght
Why fare ye thus with me the first nyght
Ye faren lyke a man that had loste his wytte
Fy/what is my gilte? for goddes loue tel me it
And it shal be amended if I may.
¶ Amended (qd̄ this knyght) alas nay nay
That wol not ben amended neuer mo
Thou arte so lothly/and so olde also
And therto comen of so lowe a kynde
That litel wōder is though I walow ⁊ wynde
So wolde god(qd̄ he) myn herte wolde brest.
¶ Is this(qd̄ she)the cause of your vnrest?
Ye certaynly quod he/no wonder nys.
¶ Nowe sir(qd̄ she) I couthe amende al this
If that me lyst/er it were dayes thre
So wel ye myght beare you vnto me.
But for ye speke of suche gentylnesse
As is discended out of olde richesse
That therfore shullen ye be gentilmen
Suche errogaunce is not worthe an hen.
Lo who that is moste vertuous alway
Preuy and aperte/and moste entendeth aye
To do the gentill dedes/that he can
Take him for the greatest gentilman.
Christ wolde we claymed of him oͬ gētilnesse
Not of our elders/for our olde rychesse
For though they yeue vs al her herytage
For whiche we claymen to ben of hye parage
Yet may they not byquethe/for no thyng
To none of vs/her vertuous lyuing
That made hem gentilmen ycalled be
And badde vs folowen hem in suche degre.
¶ Wel can the wyse poete of Florence
That hight Daunte/speke in this sentence
Lo in suche maner ryme is Dauntes tale
Ful selde vp ryseth by his braunches smale
Prowesse

Prowesse of man: for god of his goodnesse
wol that we clayme of him our gentilnesse
For of our elders may we nothyng clayme
But tēporal thing/ yͤ mē may hurte ⁊ mayin
   Eke euery wight wote this as wel as I
If gentilnesse were planted naturally
Unto a certayne lynage downe the lyne
Preuy ⁊ aperte/than wolde they neuer fyne
To done of gentilnesse the fayre office
They might don no vilanye ne vice.
   Take fyre ⁊ beare it in to the derkest hous
Bytwixt this and the mounte Caucasus
And let men shytte the dores/and go thenne
yet wol the fyre as fayre lye and brenne
As twenty thousande men might it beholde
His office natural aye wol it holde
Up peryll of my lyfe/tyll that it dye.
¶ Here may ye se wel/ howe that gentrye
Is not annexed to possession
Sythen folke don not her operacion
Alway as dothe the fyre/lo in his kynde
For god it wotte/ men may ful often fynde
A lordes sonne done shame and vilanye
And he that wol haue pryse of his gentrye
For he was borne of a gentill house
And had his elders noble and vertuouse
And nyll him selfe don no gentill dedes
Ne folowe his gentil auncetre that deed is
He nys not gentil / be he duke or erle
Fye vilaynes/synful dedes maketh a cherle
For gentilnesse nys but the renomie
Of thyn auncesters/ for her high bountie
Whiche is a stronge thyng to thy persone
The gentilnesse cometh fro god alone
Than cometh our very gentilnesse of grace
It was nothyng byqueth vs with our place.
¶ Thynketh howe noble/as sayth Ualerius
Was thilke Tullius Hostilius
That out of pouertie rose to hye noblesse
Redeth Senek/and redeth eke Boece
There shal ye seen expresse/no drede is
That he is gentil/ that dothe gentil dedes
And therfore dere husbonde/ I thus conclude
Al were it that myn auncesters were rude
yet may that hye god/and so hope I
Graunt me grace to lyue vertuously
Than am I gentil / whan I begynne
To lyue vertuously/and leuen synne.
   And there as ye of pouertie me repreue
The hye god/on whom that we byleue
In wylfull pouerte chese to lede his lyfe
And certes euery man/mayde/ and wyfe
Maye vnderstonde/Iesu heuen kyng
Ne wolde not chese a viciouse kpuyng.
   Glad pouert is an honest thing certayne
This wol Seneke and other clerkes sayne
Who so wolde holde him payde of his pouerte
I.holde him ryche/al had he not a sherte
He that coueyteth is a ful poore wyght
For he wolde han/that is not in his myght
But he yͤ naught hath/ne coueyteth to haue
Is ryche/al though ye holde him but a knaue
Very pouert is synne properly
   Iuuenal sayth of pouert merily
The poore man/whan he gothe by the way
Byforne theues/he may synge and play
Pouert is hatefull good: and as I gesse
A ful great bringer out of busynesse
A great amender eke of sapience
To him that taketh it in pacience
Pouert is/al though it seme clenge
Possession/that no wyght wol chalenge.
Pouerte ful often/whan a man is lowe
Maketh his god and eke him selfe to knowe.
Pouert a spectacle is/as thynketh me
Through whiche one may his very frendes se
And therfore/syn that I you not greue
Of my pouert/no more me repreue.
¶ Nowe sir/ eke of elde ye repreued me
And certes sir/though none autorite
Were in no booke/ye gentils of honour
Sayne that men shuld an olde wight honour
And clepe hem father for her gentilnesse
And autours shal I fynde/as I gesse.
¶ Now there as ye sayn/ yͤ I am foule ⁊ olde
Than drede you not to ben a cokewolde
For fylthe/elthe/and foule/also mote I the
Ben great wardeyns vpon chastite
But natheles/syn I knowe your delyte
I shal fulfyl your worldly appetyte
   Chese now (q̄d she) one of these thīges twey
To haue me foule and olde/tyl that I dey
And be to you a trewe humble wyfe
And neuer you displease in al my lyfe

The Freres prologue.

Or els wol ye haue me yonge and fayre
And take your auenture of the repayre
That shal come to your house/bycause of me
Or in some other place/ may wel be :
Now chese your seluen/ whether ỳ you lyketh
¶ This knyght auyseth him/and sore syketh
But at the last/ he sayd in this manere:
My lady and my loue/and wyfe so dere
I put me in your wyse gouernaunce
Cheseth your selfe/ whiche maye be more ple=
And moste honour to you & me also (saunce
I do no force whether of the two
For as you lyketh/it suffyseth me.
Thā haue I gote of you ỳ maistry(q̄d she)
Syn I may chese/and gouerne as my leste
Ye certes wyfe(q̄d he) I holde it for the beste.
Kysse me(q̄d she) we be no lenger wrothe
For by my trouthe/I wol be to you bothe
This is to say/to be bothe fayre and good
I pray to god that I mote sterue wood
But I to you be also good and trewe
As euer was wyfe/sythen ỳ world was newe
And but I be to morowe as fayre to sene
As any lady/empresse/or quene
That is bytwene the Este & eke the weste
Dothe with my lyfe right as you leste
Cast vp the courteyn/and loke howe it is.
¶ And whan the knight sawe al this
That she so fayre was/and so yonge therto
For ioy he hente her in his armes two
His herte bathed in a bathe of blysse
A thousande tymes a rowe he gan her kysse
And she obeyed him in euery thyng
That mought done him plesure or lykyng
And thus they lyued vnto her lyues ende
In parfyte ioy : and Iesu Christ vs sende
Husbondes meke/ yonge/ and fresshe a bedde
And grace to ouerlyue hem that we wedde.
And eke I pray to god/to short her lyues
That wyl not be gouerned by her wyues
And olde/and angry nygardes of dispence
God sende hem soue a very pestylence.

¶ Here endeth the wyfe of Bathes tale/ and here begynneth the Freres prologue.

His worthy lymytour/this noble frere
¶ He made alway a maner louryng chere
Vpon the Sompner/but for honeste
No vilaynes worde as yet to him spake he
But at the last/ he sayd to the wyfe
Dame/ god yeue you right good lyfe
ye haue touched here/also mote I the
In schole mater/a ful great diffyculte
ye haue said moche thyng right wel I saye
But dame/here as we ryden by the waye
Vs nedeth not to speken but of game
And lete auctorites a goddes name
To prechyng/and to schole of clergy.
But if it lyke vnto this companye
I wol you of a Sompner tel a game
Parde ye may wel knowe by the name
That of a Sompner may no good be sayde
I pray/ that none of you be yuel apayde
A sompner is a renner vp and doun
With maūdementes/for fornycatioun
And is ybeate at euery townes ende.
Tho spake our host & said: sir ye shulde ben
And curteys/as a man of your estate (hende
In this companye we wol no debate
Telleth your tale/and let the Sompner be
Nay (q̄d the Sompner) let him say to me
What so him lyst : whan it cometh to my lote
By god I shal him quite euery grote
I shal him tell whiche a great honour
It is/to be a flateryng lymytour
And eke of many an other maner cryme
Whiche nedeth not to rehersen at this tyme
And his offyce I shal him tel iwys
Our hoste answerde:peace/no more of this
And afterwarde he sayd vnto the frere
Tel forthe your tale/myn owne maister dere.

¶ Here endeth the Freres prologue/and here after foloweth his tale.

The Wife of Bath's Tale: The Friar's Prologue (D 1223–1298; T. 6805–6882)

Hylom there was dwellyng in my coūtre
W An archedeken/a man of hye degre
That boldly dyd execution
In punisshyng of fornycation
Of witchcrafte/and eke of baudrie
Of defamacion/and aduoutrie
Of churche reues/and of testamentes.
Of contractes/and lacke of sacramentes
Of vsure/and of symonye also
But certes lechours dyd he moche wo
They shulden synge/if they weren hente
And smale tythers they were foule ishente
If any person wolde vpon hem playne
There might asterte hem no pecunyal payne
For smale tythes / and small offrynge
He made the people pitously to synge
For er the bisshop caught hem with his hoke
They were in the archedekens booke
And than had he (thorough his iurdiction)
Power to done on hem correction
He had a Sompner redy to his honde
A slyer boye was there none in Englonde
For subtelly he had his espiayle
That taught him where he might auayle.
He couthe spare of lechours one or two
To techen him to foure and twenty mo
For though this sōpner wode were as an hare
To tel his harlotrye I wol not spare
For we ben out of his correction
They haue of vs no iurdiction
Ne neuer shullen/terme of al her lyues.
¶ Peter so ben women of the stewes.
(Qd this Sompner) yput out of our cure.
Peace with mischaūce/& with misauenture
Sayd our hoste/and let him tell his tale
Nowe telleth forthe/& let the Sompner gale
Ne spareth not/ myn owne maister dere.
¶ This fals thefe/this Sōpner (qd the frere)
Had alway baudes redy to his honde
As any hauke to lure/in Englonde
That telleth him al the secre that they knewe
For her aquayntaūce was not come of newe
They weren his aprouers priuely
He toke him selfe a great profyte therby
His maister knewe not alwaye what he wan
Without maundement/a lewde man
He coude sōmon/on payne of christes curse
And they were glad to fyllen his purse
And made him great feestes at the nale
And right as Iudas had purses smale
And was a thefe: right suche a thefe was he
His maister had but halfe his deutie
He was (if I shal yeuen him his laude)
A thefe/a sompner/and eke a baude.
He had eke wenches of his retinue
That whether sir Roberde/or sir Hue
Or Iohan/or Rafe/or who so that it were
That lay by hem/they tolde it in his eere
Thus were the wenches and he of one assent
And he wolde fetche a fayned maundement
And sōmon hem to the chapitre bothe two
And pylle the man/and let the wenche go
Than wolde he say/frende I shal for thy sake
Do stryken the out of our letters blake
The dare no more as in this case trauayle
I am thy frende/ there I may the auayle
Certayne he knewe of bribries mo
Than possible is to tell in yeres two
For in this worlde nys dogge for the bowe
That can an hurte dere from an hole knowe
Bet than the Sompner knewe a slye lechour
Or auouter/or els any paramour
For that was the fruite of al his rente

Ther-

Therfore on it he sette all his entent.
And so befyll that ones on a day
This sompner waytynge euer on his pray
Rode for to sõmon an olde wedowe a ribybe
Faynyng a cause/ for he wolde haue a bribe
And happed that he sawe beforn him ride
A gay yoman vnder a forest syde
A bowe he bare/ and arowes bright & shene
He had vpon him a courtpye of grene
An hatte vpon his heed with strynges blake
Sir qd this sompner/ haile and well ytake
¶ Welcome qd he/ and euery good felawe
Whider ridest yͧ vnder this grenwode shawe
Said this yoman/ wolte thou ferre to day ?
This sompner him answerd/ and said: nay
Here fast by (qd he) is myn entent
To riden/ for to reysen vp a rent
That longeth to my lordes dewte.
Arte thou than a bayly ? ye (qd he)
He durst nat than/ for very fylth and shame
Say that he was a sompner/ for the name
Depardieux / qd this yoman/ lefe brother
Thou arte a bayly/ and I am another
I am vnknowen/ as in this countre
Of thyn acqueyntaunce I woll pray the
And eke of brotherhed/ if that thou list
I haue golde and syluer in my chist
Yf that ye happe to come in our shire
All shall be thyn/ right as thou wolt desyre
Grãtmercy ꝙ this sompner/ by my faithe
Euerich in other his trouthe laythe
For to be sworne brethern/ tyll they dey
And with that worde they riden forth her wey
This sõpner with ye/ was as full of iãgles
As full of venym/ as ben these wariangles
And euer enquyring vpon euery thyng
Brother qd he / where is your dwellyng
Another day/ if that I shulde you seche ?
This yoman him answerde in soft speche
Brother qd he/ ferre in the North countre
Where as I hope somtyme I shall the se
Or we departe/ I shall the so well wysse
That of myn house thou shalte neuer mysse.
Now brother qd this sompner/ I you pray
Teche me/ while we riden by the way
Sith that ye ben a baylye/ as am I
Some subtelte/ tell me faithfully
In myn offyce/ howe I may most wynne
And spareth nat for conscience ne for synne
But as my brother/ tell me howe don ye
Nowe by my trouth brother dere/ said he
As I shall tellen the a faithfull tale
My wages ben full straite and smale
My lorde is harde to me and daungerous
And myne office full laborous
And therfore/ by extorcion I leue
Forsothe all that men woll me yeue
Algate by sleight or by violence
From yere to yere/ I wyn all my dispence
I can no better tellen faithfully
Nowe certes qd this somynour/ so fare I
I spare nat to take god it wote
But if it be to heuy or to hote
That I may getten in counsayle priuely
No maner conscience of that haue I
Nere myn extorcion/ I myght nat lyuen
Of suche iapes woll I nat be shriuen
Stomake ne conscience knowe I non
I shrewe all these shrift fathers euerichon
Well be we met by god and swete saynt Iame
But lefe brother/ tell me thy name
Quod this sompner/ in this mean while
This yoman gan a lytell for to smyle
¶ Brother qd he / wolte thou that I the tell ?
I am a fende/ my dwellyng is in hell
And here I ride about my purchasyng
To wete where I may gete any thyng
My purchase is theffecte of all my rent
Loke howe thou ridest for the same entent
To wyn good/ thou reckest neuer howe
Right so fare I/ for ride woll I nowe
Vnto the worldes ende for a pray
Ah/ ꝙ this sompner/ benedicite/ what ye say
I wende ye were a yoman trewly
Ye haue a mannes shappe as well as I
Haue ye a fygure than determynate
In hell/ there ye ben in your estate ?
Nay certainly qd he/ there haue we non
But whan vs lyketh/ we can take vs one
Or els make you seme we ben shape
Somtyme lyke a man or lyke an ape
Or lyke an Angell can I ride or go
It is no wonder thyng though it be so
A lousy iuggler can disceyue the

And

And parde yet can I more crafte than he
 Why ꝙ the Somnour / ryde ye than or gon
In sondrie shappe / and nat alway in one?
 For we ꝙ he / woll vs suche forme make
As most able is our prayes for to take
 What maketh you to haue all this labour?
¶ Full many a cause lefe sir Somnour
Said this fende / but all thyng hath tyme
The day is short / and it is passed pryme
And yet ne gote I nothyng in this day
I woll entende to wynnyng / if that I may
And nat entende our wyttes to declare
For brother myne / thy wyttes ben all to bare
To vnderstāde al / though I wolde tel hem the
But for thou askest why laboren we
For somtyme be we goddes instrumentes
And meanes to don his cōmaundementes
What that him lust on his creatures
In dyuers arte and in dyuers fygures
Withouten him we haue no myght certayn
Yf that him lyst to stonden there agayn
And somtyme at our praye haue we leue
Onely the body / & nought the soule to greue
Wytnesse of Job / whom we deden wo
And somtyme haue we myght of bothe two
This is to sayn / of body and soule eke
And somtyme we ben suffred for to seke
Vpon a man / and don his soule vnrest
And nat his body / and all is for the best
Whan he withstandeth our temptation
It is a cause of his saluation
All be it that it was nat our entent
He shulde be safe / but that we wolde him hent
And somtyme be we seruauntes vnto man
As the archbisshoppe saynt Dunstan
And to the apostell eke seruaunt was I
 Yet tell me ꝙ this somnour faithfully
Make ye you newe bodies thus alway
Of elementes? the fende answered nay
Somtyme we fayn / and somtyme we arise
With deed bodies in sondrie wise
And speke as renably / faire and well
As the Phitonesse dyd to Samuel
And yet wolde some men say it was nat he
I do no force of your deuynite
But o thyng I warne the / I woll nat iape
Thou wolte algates wete howe we be shape
Thou shalt herafterwarde (my brother dere)
Come / where the nedeth nat of me to lere
For thou shalt by thyne own experience
Conne in the chare rede of this sentence
Bette than Vergyll / while he was on lyue
Or Daunt also. Now we lette vs ride blyue
For I woll holde company with the
Tyll it be so that thou forsake me
 Nay ꝙ this somnour / ẏ shall nat betide
I am a yoman knowen full wyde
My trouth woll I holde to ẏ / as in this caas
For though thou were the deuyll Sathanas
My trouth woll I holde to my brother
As I am sworne / and eche of vs to other
For to be trewe brother in this caas
And brother / we gon to our purchaas
Take thou thy parte / that men woll the yeue
And I shall myn / and thus shall we both leue
And if that any of vs haue more than other
Let him be trewe / & parte it with his brother
 I graunt qd the deuyll / by my fay
And wt that worde they riden forth her way
And right at thentryng of the townes ende
(To which the sōpner shope him for to wēde)
They sawe a carte / that charged was wt hay
Whiche that a carter droue forth on his way
Depe was the way / for whiche the carte stode
This carter smote / & stryued as he were wode
Heit scot heit brok / what spare ye for ẏ stones
The fende ꝙ he / you fetch both body & bones
As ferforth as euer ye were yfoled
So moche wo as I haue for you tholed
The deuyll haue all / both horse / carte / & hay
 Qd this sōpnour / here shal we haue a pray
And nere ẏ fende he drew / as nought ne were
Full preuily / and rowned in his ere
Herken brother herken / by thy faith
Herest thou what the carter saith?
Hent it anon / for he hath yeue it the
Both hay and carte / and eke his caples thre
 Nay qd the deuyll / god wotte neuer a dele
It is nat his entent trust me wele
Aske him thy selfe / if thou trowest nat me
Or els stynt a while and thou shalte se
 This carter thacked his horse on the croupe
And they begon to drawe and to stoupe
Heit nowe qd he / that Jesu christ you blesse
And

And al his hondy werke bothe more and lesse
That was wel yt wight myn own sparde boy
I pray god saue the and saynt Loye
Nowe is my carte out of the slowe parde.
Lo brother qd the fende/ what tolde I the
Here may ye seen myn owne dere brother
The carle spake o thige but he thouzt another
Lette vs go forthe about our viage
Here wyn we nothyng vpon cariage
Whan ẏ they comen somwhat out of ẏ town
This Sompner to his brother gan to rowne
Brother qd he/ here wonneth an olde rebecke
That had almost as lefe to lese her necke
As for to yeue a peny of her good
I wol haue. vii. d. tho that she were wood
Or I woll sompne her to our offyce
And yet god wotte of her knowe I no vice
But for thou canst nat/ as in this countre
Wynne thy cost/ take here ensample of me.
This Sõpner clappeth at ẏ wedowes gate
Come out he said/ thou olde veritrate
I trowe thou hast some frere or preest wt the
Who clappeth ther said this wife/ benedicite
God saue you sir/ what is your swete wyll
I haue qd he/ of sõmons of the here a byll
Vp payne of cursyng loke that thou be
To morowe before our Archdeacons kne
To answere to the court of certayn thynges
Nowe lorde qd she/ Jesu kyng of kynges
So wisely helpe me/ as I ne may
I haue ben sicke/ and that full many a day
I may nat go so ferre/ qd she/ ne ryde
But I be deed/ so pricketh it in my syde
May I nat aske a lybell sir Somnpnour
And answere there by my proctour
To suche thyng as men wolde apposen me:
Yes qd this Somnpnour/ paye anon let se
Twelue pens to me/ and I wyll the acquyte
I shall no profite haue therof but lyte
My maister hath the profite/ and nat I
Come of and lette me ryden hastely
Gyue me. vii. d. I may no lenger tary
Twelfpens qd she/ lady saynt Mary
So wisely helpe me out of care and synne
This wyde worlde though I shulde it wynne
Ne haue I nat. vii. d. within my holde
Ye knowe well/ that I am poore and olde
Kyth your almesse on me poore wretche
Nay than qd he/ the foule fende me fetche
Yf I the excuse/ though thou shuldest be spylt
Alas qd she/ god wotte yet haue I no gylt
¶ Paye me qd he/ or by swete saynt Anne
I woll bere away thy newe panne
For dette/ whiche thou owest me of olde
Whan thou madest thyne husbonde cokolde
I payde at home for thy correction
Thou lyest qd she/ by my sauation
Ne was I neuer er nowe/ wedowe ne wife
Somnpned vnto your court in all my lyfe
Ne neuer I nas but of my body trewe
Vnto the deuyll blacke and rough of hewe
Yeue I thy body and my panne also.
And whan the deuyll herde her curse so
Vpon her knees/ he said in this manere
Nowe Mably/ myn owne mother dere
Is this your wyll in ernest that ye sey:
The deuyll qd she/ fette him er he dey
And pan and all/ but he woll him repent.
Nay olde stotte/ that is nat myn entent
Qd this Somnpnour/ for to repent me
For any thyng that I haue had of the
I wolde I had thy smocke and euery clothe.
Nowe brother qd the deuyll/ be nat wrothe
Thy body and this pan is myne by right
Thou shalte with me to hell yet to nyght
Where thou shalte knowen of our preuyte
More than a maister of deuynite
And with ẏ worde the foule fende him hent
Body and soule/ he with the deuyll went
Where that Somnpnours haue their heritage
And god that made after his ymage
Mankynde/ saue and gyde vs all and some
And leue the somnpnour good man to become
Lordiges I coud haue told you/ ꝙ this frere
Had I had leyser/ of this Somnpnour here
After the text of Christ/ Poule/ and Johan
And of other doctours many one
Suche peynes/ as your hertes myght agrise
Albeit so/ that no tonge may it deuyse
Though ẏ I myght a thousande wynter tell
The peynes of that cursed house of hell
But for to kepe vs fro that cursed place
Wake/ and prayeth Jesu of his grace
So kepe vs from the temptour Sathanas
Herkneth

The Friar's Tale (D 1562–1655 ; T. 7144–7237)

Herkeneth this worde/beware as i this caas
The lyon sytteth in his awayte alway
To slee the innocent/if that he may
Disposeth aye your hertes to withstonde
The fende/ y^t you wolde make thral a bonde
He may not tempte you over your myght
For Christ wol be your champion a knyght
And prayeth/that this Sompner him repente
Of his misdede/er that the fende him hente.

¶ Here endeth the Freres tale/& begynneth the Sompners prologue.

This Sompner in his styropes hye stode
Upon this frere/ his herte was so wode
That lyke an aspen lefe he quoke for yre
Lordynges (qd he) but one thyng I desyre
I you beseche/ that of your curtesy
Sythens ye han herde this false frere lye
As suffreth me I may my tale tell
This frere bosteth that he knoweth hell
And god wote that is lytel wonder
Freres and fendes ben but lytel a sonder
For parde/ye han ofte tyme herde tell
Howe that a frere ravysshed was to hell
In spyrit ones by a visyoun
And as an angel ledde him up and doun
To shewe him the paynes that there were
In al the place sawe he not a frere
Of other folke he sawe ynowe in wo
Unto the aungel spake the frere tho
Nowe sir qd he/han freres suche a grace
That none of hem shal come in this place?
¶ Yes qd this aungel/ many a myllioun
And unto Sathanas ladde he him adoun
And nowe hath Sathanas suche a tayle
Broder than of a Caryke is the sayle
Holde up thy tayle thou Sathanas (qd he)
Shewe forthe thyn erse/let the frere se
Where is the neste of freres in this place
And er that halfe a forlonge way of space
(Right as bees swarmen out of an hyve)
Out of the dyvels erse they gan dryve
Twenty thousande freres on a route
And throughout hell swarmed al aboute
And comen ayen/ as faste as they myght go
And into his erse they crepten everychon
He clapte his tayle ayen/and lay styll.
¶ This frere/whan he loked had his fyll
Upon the turmentes of this sorye place
His spyrite god restored of his grace
Unto his body ayen/and he awoke
But natheles/yet for fere he quoke
So was the dyvels erse aye in his mynde
That is his heritage of very kynde
God save you al/ save this cursed frere
My prologue wol I ende in this manere.

¶ Here endeth the Sompners prologue/and foloweth his tale.

L ioii

The Friar's Tale: The Somnour's Prologue (D 1656–1708; T. 7238–7290)

Lordynges ther is in yorkshyre/as I gesse
A A marshy countrey called Holdernesse
In whiche there went a limytour aboute
To preach/ and eke to begge/ it is no doute
And so byfell that on a day this frere
Had preched in a church in his manere
And specially abouen euery thyng
Excited he the people in his prechyng
To trentals / and to yeuen for goddes sake
Wherwith men mighten holy houses make
There as diuyne seruyce is honoured
Not there as it is wasted and deuoured
Ne there it nedeth not for to be yeuen
As to possessioners that mowen els lyuen
Thonked be god/ in wele and haboundaunce
Trentals delyuereth (sayde he) fro penaunce
Her frendes soules/as wel olde as yonge
If that they be hastely ysonge
Not for to holde a preest ioly and gay
(He syngeth not but one messe a day)
Delyuereth out(q̄d he) anon the soules
Ful harde it is with flesshe hoke or wt oules
To ben yclawed/or to brenne or bake
Nowe spedeth you hastely for Christes sake.
And whan this frere had said al his entent
With qui cum patre/forthe his way he went
Whē folke ī church/had yeue hī what hem lest
He wente his way/no lenger wolde he rest
With scryppe & typped staffe/ytucked hye
In euery house he gan to pore and prie
And begged mele and chese/or els corne
His felowe had a staffe typped with horne
A payre of tables al of Iuory
And a poyntel polisshed fetously
And wrote alway the names as he stoode
Of al folke/ that yaue hem any goode
Askaunce as he wolde for hem prey
Yeue vs a busshel wheate/malte/or rey
A goddes kychel/or a tryppe of chese
Or els what ye lyst/I may not chese
A goddes halfpeny / or a masse peny
Or yeue vs of your brawne/if ye haue any
A dagon of your blanket/ leue dame
Our suster dere/ lo here I write your name
Bacon or befe/or suche thing as ye fynde
A sturdy harlot went hem ay behynde
That was her hostes man/ and bare a sacke
And that mē yaue hem/ layde it on his backe
And whan he was out at the dore anone
He planed away the names euerychone
That he byfore had written in his tables
He serued hem with nyfles and with fables.
¶ Nay there thou lyest Sōpner(q̄d the frere)
Peace(q̄d our host)for Christes mother dere
Tell forthe thy tale/and spare it not at all
So thriue I q̄d the Sompner/so I shall.
¶ So longe he went fro hous to house tyl he
Came to an house/ther as he was wont to be
Refresshed more than in an hundred placis
Sicke lay the good man/ whose the place is
Bedred vpon a couche lowe he lay
Deus hic (q̄d he) O Thomas frēde good day
Sayd this frere/ curtesly and softe
Thomas god yelde it you/ful ofte
Haue I vpon this benche faren ful wele
Here haue I eaten many a mery mele
And fro the benche he droue away the catte
And layde adowne his potent and his hatte
And eke his scryppe/& set him softe adowne
His felowe was go walked in to the towne
Forthe with his knaue/in to that hostelrye
Where as he shope him that ilke night to lye.
¶ O dere maister/quod this syke man
Howe haue ye faren sythen Marche began
I sawe you not this fourtenight and more.
¶ God wot(q̄d he) laboured haue I ful sore
And specially for thy saluacion
Haue I sayd many a preciouse orison
And for our other frendes/god hem blesse
I haue this day ben at your churche at messe
And sayd a sermon/ after my symple wytte
Not al after the text of holy writte
For it is harde to you/as I suppose
And therfore I wol teche you al the glose
Glosyng is a glorious thyng certayne
For letter sleeth/ as we clerkes sayne
There haue I hem taught to ben charitable
And spende her good there as it is resonable
And there I sawe our dame / a where is she?
¶ yonder in the yerde/I trowe she be
Sayd this man/and she wol come anon.
¶ Eye mayster welcom ye be by saynt Iohn
Sayd this wyfe/howe fare ye hertely?
¶ This frere aryseth vp ful curtesly

And

And her enbraseth in his armes narowe
And kysseth her swetely/ ⁊ cherketh as a spa-
Wͭ his lyppes/dame (qd he) right wele (rowe
As he that is your seruaunt euery dele
Thanked be god/ that you yaue soule ⁊ lyfe
yet sawe I not this day so fayre a wyfe
In al the churche/so god saue me
 Ye god amende al fautes sir (qd she)
Algates welcome ye be/ by my fay.
 Graũt mercy dame/ yͭ haue I foũde alway
But of your great goodnesse/by your leue
I wol pray you/that ye not you greue
I wol with Thomas speke a lytel throwe
These curates ben ful neglygent ⁊ slowe
To gropen tenderly a mannes conscience
In shrift/ ⁊ in prechyng is my diligence
And to studye on Peters wordes ⁊ Poules
I walke to fysshe christen mennes soules
To yelde Jesu Christ his propre rent
To sprede his wordes/is al myn entent.
¶ Nowe by your leue dere maister (qd she)
Chydeth him wel for seynt charyte
He is aye angry as a pysse myre
Though that he haue al that he can desyre
Though I him wry anight/ ⁊ make hi warm
And ouer him lay my legge or myn arme
He groneth lyke our bore yͭ lyeth in the stye
Other disporte of him right none haue I
I may not please him in no maner caas.
 O Thomas/ ie vous die/ Thomas Thomas
This maketh yͤ fende/ this must ben amẽded
Ire is a thyng that god hyghly defended
And therof wol I speke a worde or two.
¶ Nowe maister (qd the wyfe) er that I go
What wol ye dyne? I wol go ther aboute.
 Nowe dame (qd he) ie vous die sanz doute
Haue I not of a capon but the lyuer
And of your whyte breed/ but a shyuer
And after that a rosted pygges heed
(But I nolde not for me no beest were deed)
Than had I ynowe for my suffysaunce.
I am a man of lytel sustynaunce
My spyrite hath his fostryng in the byble
My body is aye so redy and so penyble
To wake/that my body is distroyde
I pray you dame/be ye nought anoyde
Though I so frendly you my coũsaile shewe
By god/ I nolde haue tolde it but a fewe.
¶ Nowe sir (qd she) but one worde er ye go
My childe is deed/ within these wekes two
Sone after that ye wente out of this toun
 His dethe sawe I by reuelacioun
Sayd this frere/ at home in our dortoure
I dare wel sayne/ er that halfe an houre
After his dethe/ I sawe him borne to blysse
In myn auisyon/ god me so wysse
So dyd our sexten/ and our fermerere
That han ben true freres this fyfty yere
They may nowe/ god be thanked of his lone
Maken her iubely/ and walken alone
And vp I arose/ and al our couente eke
With many a tere trylling on our cheke
Withouten noyse or clateryng of belles
Te deum was our songe/ and nothing elles
Saue that to Christ I sayde an orison
Thanking him of my reuelacion
For sir and dame/ trusteth me right well
Our orisons been more effectuell
And more we seen of Christes secret thynges
Than borel folke/ although they were kynges
We lyue in pouerte/ and in abstinence
And borel folke in rychesse and dispence
In meate ⁊ drinke/ and in her foule delyte
We han this worldly luste al in dispyte
Lazar and Diues/ lyueden diuersely
And diuers guerdons had they therby
Who so wol pray/ he muste faste ⁊ be clene
And fatte his soule/ ⁊ make his body lene
We fare as sayth the apostel/ clothe and foode
Suffiseth vs/ though they be not ful goode
The clennesse ⁊ the fastyng of vs freres
Maketh that Christ accepteth our prayeres.
¶ Lo Moyses/ fourty dayes ⁊ fourty nyght
Fasted/ er that the hye god of his myght
Spake with him in the mounte of Synay
With empty wombe/ fastyng many a day
Receyued he the lawe/ that was written
With goddes fynger/ and Hely wel ye witten
In mount Oreb/ er he had any speche
With the hygh god/ that is our soules leche
He fasted longe/ and was in contemplaunce.
¶ Aaron/ yͭ had the temple in gouernaunce
And eke the other preestes euerychone
Into the temple whan they shulde gone

The Somnour's Tale (D 1803–1896; T. 7385–7478)

The Sompners tale.

To prayen for the people/and done seruyce
They nolde drinke in no maner wyse
No drinke/ that dronke might hem make
But there in abstynence pray and wake
Lest that they deyden/take hede what I say
But they be sobre that for the people pray
Ware that I say/ no more for it suffyseth
Our lorde Jesu/as holy writte deuyseth
yaue vs ensample of fastyng and prayeres
Therfore we mendicantes/ we sely freres
Ben wedded to pouert and continence
To charite/humblenesse/and abstinence
To persecution for rightwysnesse
To wepyng/mysericorde/and clennesse
And therfore may ye se that our prayeres
(I speke of vs mendicant / we freres)
Ben to the hye god more acceptable
Than yours/ with your fest at your table.
¶ Fro Paradyse first/if I shal not lye
Was man out chased for his glotonye
And chaste was man in paradyse certayne
But herken now Thomas what I shal sayn
I haue no text therof/as I suppose
But I fynde it in maner of a glose
That specially our swete lorde Jesus
Spake this by freres/whan he sayd thus
Blessed be they that poore in spyrite ben
And so forthe al the gospel may ye seen
Whether it be lyker our perfection
Or hers that swymmen in possession
Fye on her pompe/ and on her glotonye
And in her leudenesse/ I hem defye
Me thynketh they ben lyke Jouinyan
Fatte as a whale/ and walkyng as a swan
As vinolent as botel in the spence
Her prayere is of ful lytell reuerence
Whā they for soules say ẏ psalme of Dauid
Lo bouffe they sayn (Cor meum eructauit)
Who foloweth Christes gospel and his lore
But we : that humble be/chaste/and poore
Werkers of goddes worde/& not auditours
Therefore ryght as an hauke at a lours
Up springeth in to the eyre/so prayeres
Of charitable and chaste busy freres
Maken her lours to goddes eeres two
Thomas Thomas/so mote I ryde or go
And by that lorde that cleped is seynt Yue
Ne yu our broder were/ yu shuldest not thriue
For in our chapitre pray we day and nyght
To Christ/that he the sende helth & myght
Thy body for to welden hastely.
¶ God wotte qd he/nothyng therof fele I
As helpe me Christ/ as in fewe yeres
Haue I spended vpon dyuers maner freres
Wel many a poūde/yet fare I neuer the bette
Certayne my good haue I almoste besette
Farwel my good/for it is almoste ago.
The frere answerd/o Thōms dost thou so :
What nedeth the dyuers freres seche :
What nedeth him that hath a parfyte leche
To sechen other leches in the toun :
your inconstaunce is your confusioun
Holde ye me than/or els our couent
To prayen for you insuffycient :
Thomas/that iape nys not worthe a myte
your maladye is for we haue to lyte
A/yeue that couent halfe a quarter otes
And yeue that couent foure & twenty grotes
And yeue that frere a penny / and let him go
Nay nay Thomas/ it may nothyng be so
What is a ferthyng worth parted in twelue :
Lo/ eche thyng that is oned in him selue
Is more stronge/than whan it is so skatered
Thomas/ of me thou shalte not ben islatered
Thou wolste haue al our labour for nought
The hye god that al this world hath wrought
Sayth / ẏ the workeman is worthy his hyre
Thomas/naught of your tresoure I desyre
As for my selfe/but that al our couent
To pray for you is aye so dyligent
And for to buylden Christes owne chyrche
Thomas/if ye wol lerne for to wyrche
Of buyldyng vp of chyrches may ye fynde
If it be good/ in Thomas lyfe of Inde.
ye lyggen here ful of angre and of yre
With which ẏ diuel setteth your herte on fyre
And chyden here this holy innocent
Your wyfe/that is so meke and pacient
And therfore trowe me Thomas if you leste
Ne chyde not with thy wyfe/as for the beste
And beare this worde away by thy faythe
Touching suche thyng/lo what ẏ wyse sayth
Within thy house be thou no lyon
To thy subiectes do thou none oppression
Ne

The Somnour's Tale (D 1897–1990 ; T. 7479–7572)

Ne make not thyn aquayntaunce to fle
 And yet Thomas/estsones charge I the
Beware of her that in thy bosome slepeth
Ware the of the serpent/ that so slyly crepeth
Vnder the grasse/and styngeth ful subtelly
Beware my sonne/and herken paciently
That twēty thousāde men han lost her lyues
For striuyng with her lemmans & her wyues
Nowe sens ye haue so holy and meke a wyfe
What nedeth you Thomas to make stryfe?
There nys iwysse no serpent so cruell
(Whan men treden on his taile)ne halfe so fel
As a woman is/ whā she hath caught an yre
Vengeaunce is than al her desyre.
¶ Ire is a synne/one of the greatest of seuen
Abhomynable vnto the hygh god of heuen
And to him selfe it is a distruction
This euery leude vicare and parson
Can say/howe yre engendreth homecyde
Ire is in sothe the executour of pride
 I coulde of yre say so moche sorowe
That my tale shulde laste tyl to morowe
And therfore I pray god bothe day & nyght
That to an yrous man he sende lytel myght
It is great harme/and eke great pyte
To set an yrouse man in hye degre.

 Whylom there was an yrous potestate
As saythe Seneke/that duryng his estate
Vpon a day out rydden knightes two
And as fortune wolde it shulde be so
That one of hem came home/ ye other nought
Anon the knight before the iuge is brought
That sayd thus:thou hast thy felowe slayne
For whiche I deme the to the deth certayne
And to another knyght cōmaunded he
Go lede him to the dethe I charge the
And hapned as they went by the wey
Towarde the place/there he shulde dey
The knight came/ which mē wēde had be dede
Than thought they it was the beste rede
To lede hem bothe to the iudge agayne
They sayden lorde/ the knight hath not slayn
His felowe/here he stante hole alyue.
 ye shullen be deed(qd he)so mote I thriue
That is to say/bothe one/two/and thre
And to the first knight/right thus spake he.
 I dampned the/thou muste algate be deed
And thou muste also lese nedes thyn heed
For thou arte cause why thy felawe deyth
And to the thirde knight/right thus he sayth
Thou haste not done that I cōmaunded the
And thus he dyd hem sleen al thre.

 Irouse Cambyses was eke dronkelewe
And aye delyted him to ben a shrewe
And so byfell/ a lorde of his meyne
That loued well vertuous moralyte
Sayd on a day bytwixt hem two right thus
A lorde is loste/if he be aught vycious
And dronkennesse eke is a foule recorde
Of any man/and namely of a lorde
There is many an eye and many an eere
Awayting on a lorde/he notte where
For goddes loue drinketh more temperatly
Wyne maketh a man to lese wretchedly
His mynde/ and his lymmes euerychone.
¶ The reuers shalte thou se(qd he)anone
And preue it by thyn owne experience
That wyne ne dothe to folke no suche offence
There nys no wyne byreueth me my might
Of honde/of foote/ne of myn eye syght
And for dispyte he dronke mochell more
An hundred tymes than he dyd before
And right anon/this cursed yrous wretche
Let this knightes sonne byforne him fetche
Cōmaūding him he shulde byforne him stōde
And sodainly he toke his bowe in honde
And vp the strynge he pulled to his eere
And with an arowe he slough the childe there
Nowe whether haue I a syker honde or none
Qd he? is al my might and mynde agone?
Hath wyne byreued me myn eyen syght?
¶ What shulde I tel the answer of the knight
His sonne was slayne/there is no more to say
Beware therfore/with lordes howe ye play
Synge Placebo/and I shal if I can
But if it be vnto a poore man
To a poore man/one shulde his vices tell
But not to a lorde/though he shuld go to hell.

 Lo yrous Cirus/ thilke Percien
Howe distroyedhe the ryuer of Gysen?
For that an horse of his was dreynt therin

The Somnpners tale.

When he went Babylone to wynne
He made that the ryuer was so small
That men might ryde and waden ouer all.
¶ Lo/ what said he/that so wel teche can
Ne be no felowe to none proue man
Ne with no wode man walke by the way
Leste thou repent/I wol no farther say.
¶ Now Thomas leue brother/leaue thyn yre
Thou shalte me fynde as iuste/as is a squyre
Holde not the dyuels knyfe aye in thyn herte
Thyn angre dothe the al to sore smerte
But shewe to me al thy confessyon.
¶ Nay (qd the sycke man) by saynt Symon
I haue be shriue this day of my curate
I haue tolde him al myn estate
It nedeth no more to speke of it/ saythe he
But if me lyst/of myn humilite.
yeue me thā of thy gold/to make our cloistre
Qd he/for many a muskle & many an oystre
Whan other men haue ben ful wel at ese
Hath ben our foode/our cloystre for to rese
And yet god wotte/vnneth the foundament
Parfourmed is/ne of our pauement
Is not a tyle yet within our wones
By god we owen fourty pounde for stones
Now helpe Thomas/for hym yͭ harowed hell
For els mote we our bokes selle
And if you lacke our predication
Than gothe this worlde al to distruction
For who so wol fro this worlde vs bereue
So god me saue/Thomas by your leue
He wolde byreue out of this worlde the sonne
For who can techen & worchen/as we conne
And that is not of lytel tyme (qd he)
But sythe Helye was/ or Helyse
Han freres ben/that fynde I of recorde
In charite/ ythonked be our lorde
Nowe Thomas/ for saynte charite
And downe anon he sytteth on his kne.
¶ This sicke man woxe nye woode for yre
He wolde the frere had ben a fyre
With his false dissymulacion
Suche thynges as ben in my possessyon
(Qd he) that may I yeue/and none other
Ye sayn me thus/howe yͭ I am your brother.
Ye certes (qd this frere) trusteth me wele
I toke our dame our letter and our sele.

¶ Nowe (qd he) wel/ & somwhat shal I yeue
Vnto your holy couent/while I lyue
And in thyn honde/ thou shalt it haue anone
On this condycion/and other none
That thou departe it so/ my leue brother
That euery frere/haue as moche as other
This shalte thou swere on thy professyon
Without fraude or cauelacion.
¶ I swere it (qd the frere) by my faythe
And therwithal his honde in his he laythe
Lo here my faythe/in me shal be no lacke.
¶ Than put thyn honde down by my backe
Sayd this man/and grope well behynde
Byneth my buttocke/ there thou shalte fynde
A thyng/that I haue hydde in priuyte
Ah/ thought the frere/that shal go with me
Adowne he shofth his honde to the clyfte
In hope to fynde there some good gyfte
And whan this sicke man felte this frere
Aboute his towel/gropyng here and there
Amyd his honde/he let the frere a farte
There nys no capell/drawyng in a carte
That might haue let a farte of suche a soun.
¶ The frere vp starte/as dothe a wode lyon
A false chorle (qd the frere) for goddes bones
This haste thou in dispyte do/ for the nones
Thou shalte abye this farte/if I may
His meyny/that herde of this affray
Came leapyng in/and chased out the frere
And forthe he gothe/with a ful angry chere
And fette his felowe/there as lay his store
He loked as he were a wylde bore
He grynted his tethe/so was he wrothe
A sturdye pace/downe to the courte he gothe
Wher as there woned a man of great honour
To whom that he was alway confessour
This worthy man/ was lorde of that vylage
This frere came/as he were in a rage
Where as this lorde sate eatyng at his borde
Vnnethes might the frere speke o worde
Tyll at the laste he sayd/god you se.
¶ This lorde gan loke/and sayd benedicite
What frere John/ what maner world is this
I se wel that somthyng is amys
ye loke as though yͤ wodde were ful of theuis
Syt downe/ & tel me what youe grefe is
And it shal be amended/if that I may.

I haue

¶ I haue (qd he) had a dispyte to day
God yelde it you/ adowne in your village
That in this worlde/is none so poore a page
That he nolde haue abhomynacioun
Of that I haue receyued in your toun
And yet me greueth nothyng so sore
As that the olde churle/ with lockes hore
Blasphemed hath our holy couent eke.
¶ Nowe maister (qd this lorde) I you beseke
No maister sir (qd he) but seruitour
Though I haue had in schole that honour
God lyketh not/ that men vs Raby calle
Neyther in market/ ne in your large halle.
No force (qd he) but tel me of your grefe.
¶ Sir (qd this frere) an odious mischefe
This day is betyd/ to myne ordre/ and to me
And so per consequens to eche degre
Of holy churche/ god amende it sone.
Sir (qd the lorde) ye wote what is to done
Distempre you not/ ye ben my confessour
Ye ben the salte of the erthe/ and the sauour
For goddes loue your pacience nowe holde
Telleth me your grefe: & he anon him tolde
As ye han herde byfore/ ye wotte wel what
The lady of the house/ aye styll satte
Tyl she had herde what the frere sayde.
Eye goddes mother (qd she) & blisful mayde
Is there nought els/ tel me faythfully
Madame (qd he) howe thynketh ye therby
Howe that me thynketh: so god me spede
I say a churle hath done a churles dede
What shulde I say/ god let him neuer the
His sicke heed is ful of vanyte
I holde him in a maner of frenesye.
Madame (qd he) by god I shal not lye
But I in any wyse may ben on him a wreke
I shal slaunder him ouer al/ where I speke
That false blasphemour/ that charged me
To parte it/ that might not departed be
To euery man ilyche/ with mischaunce.
The lorde sate styl/ as he were in a traunce
And in his herte he rolled vp and doun
Howe that this churle had ymagynacioun
To shewe suche a probleme to the frere
Neuer erst or nowe ne herde I suche a matere
I trowe the dyuell put it in his mynde
In al Arsmetrike/ there shal no man fynde
Byfore this day/ of suche a questyon
Who shulde make a demonstracion:
That euery man shulde haue ilyke his parte
Of a sowne or sauour of a farte
O nyce proude churle/ I shrewe thy face.
Lo sirs (qd the lorde) with harde grace
Who euer herde of suche a thyng or nowe:
To euery man ilyke/ tell me howe:
It is an impossible/ it may not be
Eye nyce churle/ god let him neuer the
The romblyng of a farte/ and euery soun
Nys but of eyre reuerberacioun
And euer it wasteth lytel and lytel away
There is no man can demen/ by my fay
If that it were departed equally
What: lo my churle: lo/ yet how shrewdly
Vnto my confessour to day he spake
I holde him certayne a demoniake.
Now eteth your meate/ & let ye churle go play
Let him go hongen him selfe a dyuel way.
Nowe stode the lordes squier at the borde
That carfe his meate/ & herd worde by worde
Of al thing/ of whiche I haue you sayde
My lorde (qd he) be not yuel apayde
I couthe tel for a gowne clothe
To you sir frere/ so that ye ben not wrothe
How that this farte shulde euyn ydeled be
Amonges your couent/ if it lyketh the.
Tel on (qd ye lorde) & thou shalt haue anon
A gowne clothe/ by god & by saynte John
My lorde (qd he) whan ye the weder is faire
Withouten wynde/ or perturbyng of ayre
Let bring a carte whele here in to this hall
But loke he haue his spokes all
Twelue spokes hath a carte whele cōmenly
And bring me than .xii. freres/ wote ye why:
For thyrtene is a couent as I gesse
Your confessour here/ for his worthynesse
Shal perfourme vp the nombre of his couēt
Thā shullen they knelen adown by one assēt
And to euery spokes ende/ in this manere
Full sadly lay his nose shal a frere
Your noble confessour there/ god him saue
Shal holde his nose vpright vnder the naue
Than shal this churle/ wt bely styffe & tought
As any tabour/ hyther ben ybrought
And set him on the whele/ right of this carte
Vpon

Vpon the naue/⁊ make him let a farte
And ye shullen se/by peryl of my lyfe
By prefe/whiche is demonstratyfe
That equally the sowne of it wyl wende
And eke the stynke/vnto the spokes ende
Saue that this worthy man your cõfessour
(Bycause he is a man of great honour)
Shal haue the first frutes/as reson is
The noble vsage of freres yet is this.
The worthest mā of hem shul first be serued
And certaynly/he hath it wel deserued
He hath to day taught vs so moche good
With preching in the pulpet there he stood
That I may vouchesafe/I say for me
He had the first smell of fartes thre
And so wolde al his brethern hardely
He bereth him so fayre and holily.
¶The lord/yͤ lady/⁊ eche man/saue the frere
Sayd that Iankyn spake in this matere
As wel as Euclide dyd or Ptholome
Touchyng the churles sayde subtilte
And hye wytte made him speke as he spake
He nys no foole/ne no demonyake
And Ianken hath ywonne a newe gowne
My tale is done/we ben almoste at towne.

¶Here endeth the Sompners tale/and here foloweth the clerke of Oxēfordes prologue.

Sir clerke of Oxforde/our hoste sayde
ye ryde as styl ⁊ coye/as dothe a mayde
Were newe spoused/syttyng at yͤ borde
This day ne herde I of your mouth a worde
I trowe that ye studye aboute some sophyme
But Salomon sayth/al thyng hath tyme
For goddes sake/bethe of better chere
It is no tyme nowe to studye here
Tel vs some mery tale by your fay
For what man is entred in to a play
He nedes mote vnto that play assent
But precheth not/as freres done in lent
To make vs for our olde synnes to wepe
Ne that thy tale make vs not to slepe.
Tel vs some mery thyng of auentures
your termes/your fygures/⁊ your coloures
kepe hem in store/tyl so be that ye endyte
Hyghe style/as whan men to kynges write
Speketh so playne at this tyme/I you pray
That we may vnderstonde what ye say.
¶This worthy clerke benygnly answerde
Hoste(q͞d he)I am vnder your yerde
ye haue of vs as nowe the gouernaunce
And therfore wol I do you obeysaunce
As farre as reason asketh hardely
I wol you tell a tale/whiche that I
Lerned at Padowe/of a worthy clerke
As preued is by his wordes and his werke
He is nowe deed/and nayled in his cheste
I pray to god sende his soule good reste.
Fraunces Petrarke/the laureat poete
Hyght this clerke/whose rhetorike swete
Enlumyned al Itayle of poetrye
As Liniane dyd of phylosophye
Or lawe/or other arte perticulere
But deth yͭ wol not suffre vs dwellen here
But as it were the twynklyng of an eye
Hem bothe hath slayne/and al we shal dye.
¶But for to tellen of this worthy man
That taught me this tale/as I first began
I say that he first with hye style endyteth
(Or he the body of his tale writeth)
A proheme/in whiche discriueth he
Piemount/and of Saluce the countre
And speketh of Apēnyne the hylles hye
That ben the boundes of west Lumbardye
And of mount Vesulus in speciall
Where as the Poo/out of a wel small
Taketh his first spring and his sours
That estwarde euer increseth in his cours
To Emelle warde/to Ferare/and to Venyse
The whiche a longe tyme were to deuyse
And truly/as to my iugement
Me thynketh it a thyng impartinent
Saue that hym lyste conuey his matere
But this is his tale as ye shullen here.

¶Here endeth the prologue of the clerke of Oxforde/and here foloweth his tale.

There

There is/ in the west syde of Itayle
Down at the rote of Vesulus ye colde
A lusty playne/ habundaunt of vitayle
wher many a town & tour thou maist behold
That fouded were/ in tyme of fathers olde
And many a nother delectable syght
And Saluces/ this noble countre hyght

A Markes whylom was in that londe
As were his worthy elders him byfore
And obeysaunt aye redy to his honde
Were al his lieges/ bothe lesse and more
Thus in delyte he lyued/ and hath done yore
Beloued & drad/ through fauour of fortune
Bothe of his lordes and of his cōmune

Therwith he was/ as to speke of lynage
The gentylest yborne of al Lomberdy
A fayre person/ & stronge/ and yong of age
And ful of honour and curtesye
Discrete ynowe/ his countre for to gye
Saue in some thynges he was to blame
And Walter was this yonge lordes name

I blame him thus/ that he consydred nought
In tyme cōmyng/ what him might betyde
But on his lust present was all his thought
And for to hauke and hunt on euerysyde
Wel ny all other cures lette he slyde
And eke he ne wolde/ that was worst of all
Wedde no wife/ for ought that myght befall

Onely that poynt his people bare so sore
That flockmele on a day to him they went
And one of hem/ that wisest was of lore
(Or els that the lorde wolde best assent
That he shulde tell him what his people mēt
Or els coude he shewe suche matere)
He to the Marques sayd / as ye shullen here.

¶ O noble Marques/ your humanyte
Assureth vs/ and yeueth vs hardynesse
As ofte tyme as is necessyte
That we may to you tell our heuynesse
Accepteth lorde of your gentylnesse
That we to you with pitous hert playne
And lette your eares nat my voice disdayne

All haue I nat to done in this matere
More than another hath in this place
yet for as moche/ as ye my lorde so dere
Haue alway shewed me fauour and grace
I dare

I dare the better aske of you a space
Of audience/to shewen our requeste
And ye my lorde to done right as you leste

For certes lorde:so wel vs lyketh you
And al your werkz/ & euer haue don/ that we
Ne coulde our owne selfe deuysen howe
We myght more lyuen in felycite
Saue one thing lorde/if it your wyll be
That for to be a wedded man/ you lest
Thā were your people in souerain hertes rest

Boweth your necke vnder the blyssful yoke
Of soueraynte/and not of seruyse
Whiche men clepen spousayle or wedloke
And thinketh lorde/amōg your thoughtes wise
Howe that our dayes passen in sundrie wyse
For though we slepe or wake/ ronne/ or ryde
Aye fleeth the tyme/it wol no man abyde

And though your grene youthe floure/as yet
In crepeth age alway as styll as stone
And dethe manaseth euery age/and smyte
In eche estate/for there escapeth none
And also certayn/ as we knowen echone
That we shul dye/& vncertayne we all
Ben of that day/that dethe shall on vs fall

Accepteth than of vs the trewe entent
That neuer yet refused your heste
And we wol al lorde/if ye wol assent
Chese you a wyfe in shorte tyme/ at the lest
Borne of the gentillest and of the meste
Of al this londe/so that it aught seme
Honour to god & you/as nere as we can deme

Delyuer vs out of al this busy drede
And take a wyfe/for hye goddes sake
For if it so befell/ as god forbede
That thorowe dethe/ your linage shuld slake
And that a straunge successour shulde take
your heritage/ O/ wo were vs on lyue
Wherfore we pray you hastely to wyue.

¶ Her meke prayere and her pytouse chere
Made the Markes for to haue pyte
Wol ye (qd he) myn owne people dere
To that I neuer erst thought/ constrayne me
I me reioyced of my lyberte
That selden tyme is founde in mariage
There I was free/ I mote ben in seruage

But natheles/I se your true entente
And trust vpon your wytte/ & haue done aye
Wherfore of my fre wyl I woll assente
To wedden me/as sone as euer I may
But there/as ye haue profred me to day
To chese me a wyfe/I you relese
That choyce/and pray you of that profer cese

For god it wote/that children ofte been
Vnlyke her worthy elders/ hem before
Bounte cometh all of god/ & nat of the streen
Of whiche they ben engendred and ibore
I trust in goddes bounte/and therfore
My mariage / myn estate/ and rest
I him be take/he may don as him lest

Lette me alone in chesyng of my wife
That charge vpon my backe I woll endure
But I you pray/ and charge vpon your lyfe
That what wife I take/ye me ensure
To worship her/whiles her lyfe may dure
In worde and werke/here/ and els where
As she an Emperours doughter were

And furthermore/ thus shall ye swere/ þ ye
Ayenst my choice shal neuer grutch ne stryue
For sithe I shall for go my lyberte
At your request/ as euer mote I thryue
There as myn hert is set / there woll I wyue
And but ye woll assent/ in suche manere
I pray you speketh no more in this matere

With herty wyll they sworen and assent
To all this thyng/ there said no wight nay
Besechyng him of grace er they went
That he wolde hem graunt a certayn day
Of his spousaile/ as soone as euer he may
For yet alway the people somwhat dredde
Lest this Marques wolde no wife wedde

He graunted hem a day/suche as him lest
On whiche he wolde be wedded sekerly

And

And said he dyd al this at her request
And they with humble entent ful buxomly
Knelyng vpon her knees ful reuerently
Him thonked al/and thus they han an ende
Of her entent/and home ayen they wende

And here vpon he toke his officers
Cōmaundyng for the feest to puruay
And to his priuy knightes and squiers
Suche charge yaue/as he lyst on hem lay
And they to his cōmaundement obey
And eche of hem dothe his dilygence
To done to the feest reuerence.

¶ Explisit pars prima/et
sequitur secunda.

Nought ferre fro thilke place honorable
Where as this Markes shope his mariage
There stode a thrope/of syght ful delectable
In whiche poore folke of that village
Hadden her beestes and herbygage
And of her labour toke her sustenaunce
After that the erthe yaue hem habundaunce

Amonge this poore folke/ther dwelled a man
Whiche that was holden poorest of hem all
But hye god somtyme sende can
His grace vnto a lytel oxe stall
Janicola/men of that thrope him call
A doughter had he/fayre ynoughe to syght
And Grisylde this yonge mayden hyght

But for to speke of vertuous beaute
Than was she one the fayrest vnder sonne
And full poorely yfostred was she
No lykerouse lust was in her herte ironne
Well ofter of the wel than of the tonne
She dronke/and for she wolde vertue plese
She knewe wel laboure/but not ydell ese

But thoughe this mayde were tender of age
Yet in the brest of her virginite
There was enclosed/ sadde and rype corage
And in great reuerence and charyte
Her olde poore father fostred she
A fewe shepe spynnyng on the felde she kept
She wolde not ben idell tyl she slept

And whā she homwarde came/ she wold brīg
Wortes and herbes/tymes ful ofte
Whiche she shradde ⁊ sethe for her lyuyng
And made her bedde ful harde/ ⁊ nothīg softe
And aye she kepte her fathers lyfe on lofte
With euery obeysaunce and dilygence
That chylde might do to the fathers reuerēce.

¶ Vpon Grisylde the poore creature
Wel ofte hath the Markes sette his eye
As he an huntyng rode parauenture
And whan it fel/that he might her aspye
He (not with wanton lokyng of folye)
His eyen caste vpon her/but in sadde wyse
Vpon her chere/he wolde him ofte auyse

Cōmending in his herte her womanhede
And eke her vertue/passyng euery wight
Of so yonge age/as wel in chere as in dede
For though the people haue no great insight
In vertue: he consydred full right
Her bounte/and disposed that he wolde
Her wedde/ if he euer wedde shulde.

The day of weddyng com/ but no wight can
Tel/ what woman it shulde be
For whiche maruaile/ wondred many a man
And sayden/whan they were in her priuete
Wol not our lorde yet leaue his vanyte
Wol he not wedde/alas alas the whyle
Why wol he thus him selfe and vs begyle

But nathelesse this Markes hath do make
Of gemmes/ set in golde and in asure
Broches and ringes/for Griseldes sake
And of her clothyng/toke he the mesure
Of a mayden lyke to her stature
And eke of other ornamentes all
That to suche a weddyng shulde fall

The tyme of vndren/in the same day
Approched/that the weddyng shulde be
And al the paleys put was in array
Bothe halle and chambre/eche in his degre
Houses of offyce stuffed with great plente
There mayste thou se of daynteous vitayle
That may be founde/as fer as lasteth Itayle
This

The clerke of Oxēfordes tale:

This royal Markes/rychely arayde
Lordes and ladyes in his companye
The whiche that to the feest were prayde
And of his retinue the bachelery
With many a sowne of sondrie melodye
Unto the village/ of which I tolde
In this aray/the right way hath holde.

¶ Grisylde (god wotte of this ful innocent
That for her was shape al this array)
To fetche water at a wel went
And cometh home as sone as euer she may
For wel she herde say/that ylke day
That the Markes shuld wedde/& if she might
She wolde fayne seen some of that syght

She thouȝt: I wold wt other maydens stōde
That ben my felowes in our dore and se
The Markes/and therto wol I fonde
To done at home/as sone as it may be
The labour/ whiche that longeth to me
And than may I at leyser it beholde
If she the way to the castell holde

And as she wolde ouer the dresshold gon
The Markes came/and gan her for to call
And she sette downe her water potte anon
Besyde the threshold of the oxe stall
And downe upon her knees she gan to fall
And with sadde countenaunce kneled styll
Tyl she had herde what was the lordes wyll.

This thoughtful Markes spake to ȳ mayde
Wel soberly/and said in this manere
Where is your father Gnisylde/ he sayd:
And she with reuerence and meke chere
Answerde/lorde he is al redy here
And in she gothe/without lenger lette
And to the Markes she her father fette

He by the honde than toke this oldeman
And sayd thus/whan he had him asyde
Ianycola/ I neyther may ne can
Lenger the plesaunce of myn herte hyde
If that thou vouche safe/what so euer betyde
Thy doughter wol I take/or that I wende
As for my wyfe/to my lyues ende

Thou louest me/I wotte wel certayne
And arte my faythful liege man ybore
And al that lyketh me/I dare wel sayne
It lyketh the/and specially therfore
Tel me that poynte/that I haue said before
If that thou wolt to this purpose drawe:
To take me for thy sonne in lawe

¶ This sodayne case/the man astoned so
That reed he weyt abasshed/& al quakyng
He stode/ ne unneth sayd he wordes mo
But onely thus (qd he) lorde my wyllyng
Is as ye wol/ ne ayenst your lyking
I wol nothing/ye be my lorde so dere
Right as you lyste/gouerne this matere

Than wol I thus (qd this Markes) sothly
That in thy chambre/I/you/and she
Haue a collation/and wost thou why:
For I wol aske her/if her wyl be
To be my wyfe/and rule her after me
And al this shal she done in thy presence
I wol not speke out of thyn audyence

And in the chambre/while they were about
The treties/whiche ye shal after here
The people came into the house without
And wondred hem/ in how honest manere
So tentifly she kept her father dere
But utterly Grisylde wonder myght
For neuer erste sawe she suche a syght

No wonder is though she be astoned
To se so great a gest come into that place
She was neuer to suche gestes woned
For whiche she loked with full pale face.
But shortly fro this mater for to pace
These weren the wordes ȳ the Markes sayde
To this benygne and very faythful mayde

¶ Grisylde he said/ ye shal wel understonde
It lyketh unto your father and me
That I you wedde/and eke it may so stonde
As I suppose/that ye wol that it so be
But these demaundes I aske first (qd he)
That sythen it shal be done in hasty wyse
Wol ye therto assent/or els you auyse

I say

I say thus/be ye redy with good herte
To al my luste/and that I frely may
As me best lyketh/ though ye laugh or smerte
And neuer ye to grutche/nyght ne day
Whan I say ye/that ye say not ones nay
Neyther i worde/ne by frowning coũtenaũce
Swere this/ & here I swere our aliaũce

¶ Wõdring vpon these wordes/ quakyng for
She sayd:lorde/indigne & vnworthy (drede
Am I/to thylke honour that ye me bede
But right as ye wol/ so wol I
And here I swere/ that neuer wyllyngly
In word/werke/ne thouȝt/I nyl you disobey
For to be deed/though me were loth to dey.

¶ This is ynough Grisylde myn (q̄d he)
And forthe he gothe with a sobre chere
Out at the dore/and after came she
And to the people/he said in this manere
This is my wyfe (q̄d he) that stondeth here
Honoureth her/ & loueth her/ I you pray
Who so me loueth/there nys no more to say

And for that no thyng of her olde gere
She shulde bring in to his house/he badde
That women shulde dispoylen her right there
Of whiche these ladyes were nothyng gladde
To handle her clothes/ in which she was clad
But natheless/this mayden bught of hewe
Fro foote to heed they clothed han al newe

Her heer han they kembed/ yͭ laye vntressed
Ful rudely/and with her fyngres smale
A crowne on her heed they han idressed
And set it ful of ouches great and smale
Of her array/ what shulde I make a tale?
Vnneth the people her knew for her fayrnesse
Whan she transfourmed was in such richesse

¶ This Markes hath her spoused wͭ a ringe
Bought for the same cause/& than her set
Vpon an horse snowe white/ wel amblynge
And to his paleys/or he lenger let
With ioyful people/that her ladde and met
Conueyed her/& thus the day they spende
In reuel/tyl the sonne gan discende

And shortly forthe this tale for to chace
I saye/ that to this newe Markesesse
God hath p̄sent suche fauour of his grace
That it semed not/as by her lyklynesse
That she was borne and fedde in rudenesse
As in a cote/or in an oxe stall
But nourisshed in an emperoures hall

To euery wyght/she woxen is so dere
And worshipful/ yͤ folke ther as she was bore
And fro her byrthe/knewe her yere by yere
Vnneth trowed they/but durst haue swore
That to Ianycola/ of whiche I spake before
She doughter nas/for as by coniecture
Hem thought she was a nother creature

For though that euer vertuous was she
She was encreased in suche excellence
Of thewes good/set in hye bounte
And so discrete/and fayre of eloquence
So benygne/and digne of reuerence
And coulde the peoples hertes so embrace
That eche her loued that loked in her face

Not onely of Saluce in the town
Publysshed was the bountie of her name
But eke besyde/in many a regioun
If one sayd wel/an other sayd the same
So spradde of her bountie the fame
That men & women/bothe yonge and olde
Gone to Saluces her to beholde.

¶ This Walter lowly/ and full royally
Wedded hath with fortunate honeste
In goddes peace: lyueth full easely
At whom/ & outwarde grace ynough had he
And for he sawe that vnder lowe degre
Was honest vertue hyd/the people him helde
A prudent man/and that is sene wel selde.

¶ Not onely this Grisylde/ through her wyt
Couthe al the feate of wyfely humblesse
But eke/whan the case required it.
The comen profyte coulde she redresse
There nas discorde/rancour/ne heuynesse
In al the londe/that she ne couthe apese
And bring hem all wisely in rest and ese

M Though

Though her husbonde absent were or none
If gentilmen/ or other of her contre
Were wrothe/she wolde bring hem at one
So wyse and rype wordes had she
And iugement of so great equite
That she fro heuen sent was/as men wende
People to saue/and euery wronge to amende.

¶ Not longe tyme after this Grisylde
Was wedded/she a doughter had ybore
Al had she leuer haue borne a man chylde
Glad was the Markes and his folke therfore
For though a mayde childe came al before
She may to a man childe attayne
By lykelyhode/sythens she is not barayne.

¶ Explicit pars secunda: Et incipit pars tercia.

There fel/ as it befalleth oft tymes mo
Whan yͭ this childe had sucked but a throwe
This Markes in his herte longed so
To tempte his wyfe/her sadnesse to knowe
That he ne myght out of his herte throwe
This marueylous desyre/ his wyfe to assaye
Nedelesse god wot/he thought her to affray

He had assayed her ynoughe before
And fonde her euer good/what nedeth it
Her for to tempte & alway more and more
Though some man praise it for a subtyl wyt
But as for me/I say ful yuel it syt
To assay a wyfe/ whan that it is no nede
And put her in anguysshe and in drede

For which this Markꝫ wrouȝt ī this manere
He came alone a night there as she lay
With sterne face/and right vgly chere
And sayd thus: Grisylde (q̄d he) that day
That I the toke out of thy poore aray
And put the in estate of hye noblesse
Thou hast not that forgoten/as I gesse

I say Grisylde/the present dignyte
In whiche I haue put the/as I trowe
Maketh not the foryetfull for to be
That I the toke in poore astate ful lowe
For any wele/thou must thy selfe knowe
Take hede of euery worde what I sey
There is no wight that hereth but we twey

Thou wottest thy self/ how yͭ thou came here
In to this house/it is not longe ago
And though to me thou be bothe lefe and dere
Vnto my gentyls thou art nothyng so
They say/to hem it is great shame and wo
For to ben subiette/and ben in seruage
To the/that borne arte in so small a village

And namely sythe thy doughter was ybore
These wordes haue they spoken doutles
But I desyre/as I haue done byfore
To lyue my lyfe with hem/in rest and pees
I may not in this case be recheles
I mote done with thy doughter/for the best
Not as I wolde/ but as my gentyls lest

And yet god wote/this is ful lothe to me
But nathelesse without thy wetyng
I wol naught do/but thus I wol (q̄d he)
That thou to me assent/as in this thyng
Shewe nowe thy paciēce/ in thy werkyng
That thou me hight and swore in our village
That day that maked was our mariage

¶ Whan she had herde al this/she not ameued
Neyther in worde/in chere/ ne in coūtenaunce
For as it semed/ she was not agreued
She sayd lorde/al lyeth in your plesaunce
My childe and I/ with hertely obeysaunce
Ben yours al/and ye may saue or spyll
With your owne/worketh your owne wyll

There may nothyng/so god my soule saue
Lyking to you/that may displese me
Ne I desyre nothyng for to haue
Ne drede for to lese/saue onely ye
This wyll is in my herte/and aye shal be
No length of tyme/or deth it may deface
Neyther change my corage into another place

Glad

¶ Glad was the Markes of her answering
But yet he fayned as he were not so
Al drery was his chere/and his lokyng
Whan that he shulde out of the chambre go
Sone after this/a forlonge way or two
He priuely had tolde al his entent
Unto a man/and to his wyfe him sent

In maner of a sergeant was this priuy man
The whiche he faythful ofte founde had
In thynges great/& eke suche folke wel can
Done execucyon of thynges badde
The lorde knewe wel/ he him loued & dradde
And whan this sergeant wyst his lordes wyl
In to the chambre he stalked him ful styll

¶ Madame he sayd/ye mote foryeue it me
Though I do thing/ which I am cōstrayned
ye be ful wyse/and full wel knowe ye
That lordes hestes may not be fayned
They may wel bewayled and complayned
But men muste nedes unto her luste obey
And so wol I/there nis no more to sey

This childe I am cōmaunded to take
And spake no more/but up the chylde he hent
Dispytously/and gan a chere to make
As though he wolde haue slayne it or he went
Grisylde must al suffre/ and consent
And as a lambe/she sytteth meke and styll
And let this cruel sergeaunt do his wyll.

¶ Suspecte was the fame of this man
Suspecte his face/suspecte his worde also
Suspecte the tyme in whiche he this began
Alas her doughter/that she loued so
She wende he wolde haue slayne it right tho
But nathelesse/she neyther wepte ne syked
Confirmyng her to that the Markes lyked

But at the laste to speke she began
And mekely she the sergeaunt prayde
(So as he was a worthy gentilman)
That she might kysse her childe er yͭ it deyde
And in her barme/this lytel childe she leyde
With ful sadde face/and gan the childe blysse
And lulled it/and after gan it kysse

And thus she sayd in her benygne voyce
Farwel my childe/ I shal the neuer se
But sythen I haue marked yͭ with the croyce
Of thilke father yblessed mote thou be
That for us dyed upon the rode tree
Thy soule lytel childe/I him betake
For this nyght shalte thou dyen for my sake

¶ I trowe that to a norice in this caas
It had ben harde/this routhe for to se
Wel might a mother than crye alas
But nathelesse/so sadde and stedfast was she
That she endured al her aduersyte
And to the sergeaunt mekely she sayde
Haue here ayen your lytel yonge mayde

And goth nowe (qd she) & doth my lordes hest
And o thyng wolde I pray you of your grace
But if my lorde forbyd it you at the leste
Buryeth this lytel body in some place
That no beestes ne byrdes it to race
But he no worde to that purpose wolde say
But toke the childe/ and went anon his way.

This sergeaunt came to the lorde agayne
And of Grisyldes wordes/ and of her chere
He tolde him worde by worde/ short & playne
And him presented with his doughter dere
Somwhat this lorde had routh i his manere
But nathelesse/his purpose helde he styll
As lordes done/whan they wol haue her wyll

And badde the sergeaunt that ful priuely
He shuld this childe wel soft wynde & wrappe
With al the circumstaunce tenderly
And cary it in a cofre/ or in a lappe
But on payne of his heed of to swappe
That no man shulde knowe of his entent
Ne whence he came/ne whyther he went

But at Boleyne/to his suster dere
That thilke tyme of Pauye was countesse
He shulde it take/and shewe her this matere
Besechyng her to done her busynesse
This childe to fostre in al gentylnesse
And whose chylde yͭ it was/he bade her hyde
From euery wyght/for ought yͭ might betyde

The Clerk's Tale (E 512–595; T. 8388–8471)

This sergeaūt goth/& hath fulfylled this thīg
But to this Markes nowe retourne we
For nowe gothe he ful ofte ymaginyng
If by his wyues chere/he myght se
Or by her wordes/ perceyue that she
Were chaunged/but he neuer coulde fynde
But euer in one ilyke sadde and kynde

As glad/as humble/as busy in seruyse
And eke in loue/as she was wont to be
Was she to him/in euery maner wyse
Ne of her doughter one worde spake she
None accident/ for none aduersyte
was sene in her/ne neuer her doughters name
Nempned she/for ernest ne for game.

¶ Explicit tertia pars: Et incipit pars quarta.

In this estate/ passed ben foure yere
Er she with child was/but as god wolde
A man childe she bare by this Waltere
Wel gracious/ and fayre to beholde
And whan folke it to the father tolde
Not onely he/but al the countre merye
Was for the childe/ & god they thonke & herye

Whan it was two yere olde/ & from the brest
Departed from his norice on a daye
This Markes caught yet another lest
To tempten his wyfe efte sones/ if he may
O nedelesse was she tempted/I dare wel saye
But wedded men ne conne no mesure
Whan they fynde a pacient creature.

¶ Wife (q̄d this Markes) ye haue herd or this
My people heuely beareth our mariage
And namely sythen my sonne borne is
Nowe is it worce than euer in our age
The murmure sleeth myn herte & my corage
For to myn eeres cometh the voyce so smerte
That it wel nye distroyed hath my herte

Nowe say they thus/whan Walter is agone
Than shal the bloode of Ianycola succede
And ben our lorde/for other haue we none
Suche wordes say my people/it is no drede
Wel ought I of suche murmure take hede
For certaynly I drede suche sentence
Though they not plainly speke ī myn audiēce

I wolde lyue in peace/if that I myght
Wherfore I am disposed vtterly
As I his suster serued by nyght
Right so I thynke to serue him priuely
Thus warne I you/that ye not sodaynly
Out of your selfe/for no wo shulde outraye
Bethe pacient/and therof I you praye.

¶ I haue (q̄d she) sayd/and euer shall
I wol ne nyl nothyng certayne
But as you lyst: Nought greueth me at all
Though yt my doughter & my sōne be slayne
At your cōmaundement: this is to sayne
I haue had no parte of children twayne
But first sycknesse/ & after wo and payne

Ye ben our lorde/dothe wt your owne thinge
Right as you lyste/ and asketh no rede of me
For as I lefte at home my clothyng
Whan I came first to you/right so (q̄d she)
Lefte I my wyll/and al my lyberte
And take your clothing: wherfore I you pray
Do your wyl/I wol to it obay

And certes/if I had prescience
Your wyll to knowe/er ye your luste me tolde
I wolde it done/without neglygence
But nowe I wote your lust/& what ye wolde
Al your plesaunce/ firme & stable I holde
For wyste I that my deth wolde don you ese
Gladly wolde I suffre it you to plese

Dethe may make no comparysoun
Vnto your loue: And whan this Markes say
The constaūce of his wyfe/he caste adoun
His eyen two: and wondred howe she may
In suche pacience/ suffreth al this array
And forthe he gothe/with drery countenaūce
But to his herte/it was ful great plesaunce

This

¶ This vgly sergeant/ in the same wyse
That he her doughter caught/ right so he
Or worse/ if he coulde werse deuyse
Hath hent her sonne/ ẏ was full of beaute
And euer in one/ so pacient was she
That she no chere made of heuynesse
But kyssed her childe/ & after gan him blesse

Saue this she prayde him/ if that he myght
Her lytell sonne he wolde in erthe graue
His tendre lymmes/ delycate to syght
Fro foules and fro beestes to saue
But she none answere of him might haue
He went his way/ as he nothing rought
But to Boloyne he tenderly it brought.

¶ This Markes wondred euer lenger ẏ more
Upon her pacience/ and if that he
Ne had sothely knowen ther before
That parfytely her children loued she
He wolde haue wende/ that for some subtelte
And of malyce/ or cruel corage
That she had suffred this with sadde vysage.

But he knewe wel/ ẏ next him selfe certayne
She loued her children best/ in euery wyse
But nowe of women wolde I aske fayne
If these assayes myght not suffyse
What coulde a sturdy husbonde more deuyse
To preue her wyfehode/ and her stedfastnesse
But he contynuyng euer in sturdynesse

But there be folke of suche condicion
That whan they han a certayne purpose take
They couth not stynte of her entencion
But as they were bounden to a stake
They wol not of that purpose slake
Right so this Markes/ hath fully purposed
To tempte his wyfe/ as he was first disposed

He wayteth/ if by wordes or countenaunce
She were to him chaunged of corage
But neuer coulde he fynde varyaunce
She was aye in one herte and vysage
And euer the further that she was in age
The more truer (if it were possyble)
She was to him in loue/ and more penyble

For whiche it semeth thus/ that of hem two
There nas but one wyll: for as Walter lest
The same luste was her plesaunce also
And god be thonked/ al fel for the beste
She shewed wel/ for no worldly vnreste
A wyfe/ as for her selfe/ nothing sholde
Wyllen in effecte/ but as her husbonde wolde.

¶ The sclaũder of Walter/ wõder wyde sprad
That of cruel herte/ ful wretchedly
(For he a poore woman wedded had)
Hath murdred bothe his children priuely.
Whiche murmure was amonge hem comenly
No wonder was: for to the peoples ere
Ther cãe no worde/ but ẏ they murdred were

For whiche/ there as his people ther before
Had loued him wel/ disclaũdred of his defame
Made hem/ that they hated him therfore
To ben a murtherer is an hatefull name
But nathelesse/ for ernest ne for game
He of his cruel purpose wolde not stent
To tempt his wyfe/ was al his entent.

¶ Whan ẏ his doughter. xii. yere was of age
He to the courte of Rome/ in subtel wyse
(Enfourmed of his wyl) sent his message
Cõmaundyng hem/ suche bylles to deuyse
As to his cruel purpose may suffyse
Howe that the pope/ for his peoples reste
Bade him wedde another/ if that him leste

I say he bade/ they shulde counterfete
The popes bulle/ makyng mencion
That he hath leue/ his first wyfe to lete
As by the popes dispensacion
To stynte rancoure and discencion
Betwyxt his people & him/ thus spake ẏ bull
The whiche they han publisshed at the full.

¶ The rude people/ as no wonder nys
Wenden ful well/ it had ben right so
But whan these tydinges come to Grisyldis
I deme/ that her herte was ful wo
But she was lyche sadde euermo
Disposed was this humble creature
The aduersyte of fortune to endure

Abydyng euer his luste and his plesaunce
To whom she was yeuen/ hert and all
As to her worldly suffysaunce
But certaynly/if I this storie tel shall
This Markes ywritten hath in speciall
A letter/in whiche he shewed his entent
And priuely/ he it to Boloyne sent

To the erle of Pauy/ whiche that had tho
Wedded his suster: he prayde specially
To bringen him ayen his children two
In honorable estate al openly
But one thyng he hiin prayde al vtterly (re
That he to no wight/ though men wold enque
Shulde tellen whose children they were

But say that the mayden shulde wedded be
Vnto the Markes of Saluce anon
And as the erle was prayde/so dyd he
For at a day ysette/he on his way is gone
Towarde Saluce/and lordes many one
In ryche aray/this mayden for to gyde
Her yonge brother rydyng by her syde

Araped was towarde her maryage
This mayden fresshe/ful of gemmes clere
And her brother/that seuen yere was of age
Araped was eke fresshely in his manere
And thus in great noblesse and glad chere
Towarde Saluce/ shapen her iournay
Fro day to day/ryding forthe her way.

Explicit quarta pars: Et sequitur pars quinta.

Amonge al this/after his wicked vsage
This Markes his wyfe yet to tempten more
(To the vtterest profe of her corage
Fully to haue experyence and lore
If that she were as stedfaste (as before)
He on a day in open audyence
Ful boystously hath sayd her this sentence.

Certes Grisyld/I had ynough of plesaūce
To han you to my wyfe/ for your goodnesse
And for your trouthe /and your obeysaunce
Not for your lynage/ne for your rychesse
But I nowe knowe in very sothfastnesse
That in great lordshyp/if I me wel auyse
There is great seruytude in sondrie wyse

I may not done/as euery ploughman may
My people me constrayneth for to take
Another wyfe/and cryen day by day
And eke the pope/this rancoure for to slake
Consenteth it/that dare I vndertake
And truely/thus moche I wol you say
My newe wyfe is comyng by the way

Be stronge of herte/& voyde anon her place
And thilke dowery that ye brought to me
Take it ayen/I graunte it of my grace
Retourneth to your fathers house (qd he)
No man may alway haue prosperite
With euen herte/I rede you to endure
The stroke of fortune/or of auenture.

And she ayen answerde in pacience:
My lorde (qd she) I wote and wyste alway
Howe that bytwyxt your magnifycence
And my pouert/no man can ne may
Maken no comparyson/it is no nay
I helde me neuer digne in no manere
To ben your wyfe/ne yet your chamberere

And in this house/there ye me lady made
(The hye god take I/as for my wytnesse
And al so wysely/ as he my soule glade)
I helde me neyther lady ne maystresse
But humble seruaunt to your worthynesse
And euer shal/ whyle my lyfe may endure
Abouen euery worldly creature

That ye so longe of your benygnite
Haue holde me in honour and nobley
(Where I was not worthy for to be)
That thonke I god & you/to whom I prey
So yelde it you/there is no more to sey
Vnto my father gladly wol I wende
And with him dwell to my lyues ende

There

There I was fostred of a childe ful small
Tyl I be deed/my lyfe there wol I lede
A wydowe clene in herte/ body and all
For sythen I yaue to you my maydenhede
And am your trewe wyfe/it is no drede
God shylde suche a lordes wyfe to take
Another man / to husbonde or to make

And of your newe wyfe/god of his grace
So graunt you welthe and high prosperite
For I wol gladly yeue her my place
In whiche I was blysful wonte to be
For sythen it lyketh you my lorde(qd she)
(That whylom weren al my hertes reste)
That I shal gon: I shal go whan you leste.

¶ But there as ye me profred suche dowayre
As I first brought/it is wel in my mynde
It were my wretched clothes/nothing fayre
The which to me now were ful harde to finde
Oh/good god: howe gētill and howe kynde :
ye semed by your speche and your vysage
The day that maked was our maryage :

But sothe is sayd/algate I fynde it trewe
For in effecte it is proued nowe on me
Loue is not olde/as whan it is newe
For certes lorde/for none aduersyte
To dyen in this case/it shal neuer be
That euer in worde or worke I shal repent
That I you yaue myn herte in good entent

My lorde ye wote/that in my fathers place
ye dyd me strype out of my poore wede
And richely ye cladde me of your grace
To you brought I naught els out of drede
But faythe/nakednesse/and maydenhede
But here ayen your clothyng I restore
And eke my weddyng ringe for euermore

The remenaunt of your iewels redy be
Within your chambre/dare I safely sayne
Naked out of my fathers house(qd she)
I came: and naked I mote turne agayne
Al your plesaunce wolde I folowe fayne
But yet I hope it be not your entent
That I smocklesse out of your paleys went

Ye coulde not do so dishonest a thyng
That ilke wombe/in which your children lay
Shulde before the people/ in my walking
Be sene al bare: wherfore I you pray
Let me not lyke a worme go by the way
Remembreth you myn owne lorde so dere
I was your wyfe/ though I vnworthy were

Wherfore in rewarde of my maydenhede
Whiche I to you brought/& not ayen bere
As vouchesafe to yeue me to my mede
But suche a smocke as I was wonte to were
That I therwith may wrie yͤ wombe of here
That was your wyfe: & here I take my leue
Of you/ myn owne lorde/lest I you greue

¶ The smock (qd he) yͭ thou hast on thy backe
Let it be styll/and bere it forthe with the
But wel vnneth that worde he spake
But went his way/for routhe and pyte
Before the folke her selfe strypeth she
And in her smocke/with foote & heed al bare
Towarde her fathers house forthe is she fare

The folke folowed wepyng in her wey
And fortune euer they cursed as they gone
But she fro wepyng kept her eyen drey
Ne in this tyme/worde spake she none
Her father/that this tydinges herde anone
Cursed the day and tyme/that nature
Shope him to ben a lyues creature

For out of doute/this olde poore man
Was euer suspecte of her maryage
For euer he demed/sythen it began
That whan the lorde ifylled had his corage
Him wolde thinke it was a disparage
To his estate/so lowe for to alyght
And voyden her/as sone as euer he might.

¶ Ayenst his doughter hastely gothe he
(For he by yͤ noyse of folke knew her cōmig)
And with her olde cote/as it might be
He couered her/ful sore wepyng
But on her body might he it not bring
For rude was the clothe/& she more of age
By dayes fele than was her mariage.

Thus

¶ Thus with her father/ for a certayne space
Dwelleth this floure of wysely pacience
That neuer by her wordes/ne by her face
Byfore the folke/ne eke in absence
Ne shewed she/that her was done offence
Ne of her hye estate no remembraunce
Ne had she/as by her countenaunce.

No wonder is/for in her great estate
Her goste was euer in playne humylite
No tender mouthe/ne herte delycate
Ne pompe/ne semblaunce of royalte
But ful of pacience and benygnyte
Discrete/and prideleffe / and aye honorable
And to her husbonde euer meke and stable.

¶ Men speke of Iob/ & most of his hūblesse
As clerkes (whan hem lyste) can wel endyte
Namely of men: but in sothfastnesse
Though clerkes prayse women but a lyte
There can no man in humblesse hem aquyte
As women can: ne be halfe so trewe
As women ben/but it befall of newe.

¶ Explicit quinta pars; et sequitur pars sexta.

Fro Boloyne is the erle of Pauy come
Of whiche the fame spronge to more & lesse
And to the peoples eeres/al and some
Was couthe eke/howe a newe Marquesesse
He with him brought/ i pompe & such richesse
That was neuer sene with mannes eye
So noble aray/ in west Lumbardye.

¶ The Markes/that shope & knewe al this
Er yͤ this erle was come/sent his message
To thylke poore and sely Grisyldis
And she with humble herte/& glad vysage
Not with swellyng herte in her corage
Came at his heste/& on her knees her sette
And reuerently and wysely she him grette.

¶ Grisylde (qd he) my wyll is vtterly
This mayde/that wedded shal be vnto me
Receyued be to morowe al so royally
As it is possyble in my house to be
And eke that euery wyght in his degre
Haue his estate in syttyng and seruyse
And also plesaunt/as ye can beste deuyse

I haue no woman suffycient certayne
The chambres for to araye in ordynaunce
After my luste: and therfore wolde I fayne
That thyn were al suche gouernaunce
Thou knowest eke of olde al my plesaunce
Though thyn aray be badde/& yuel besey
Do thou thy deuer at the leste wey.

¶ Not onely lorde that I am glad (qd she)
To done your luste/but I desyre also
you for to please/and serue in my degre
Withouten faynyng/and shal euer mo
Ne neuer for no wele/ne for no wo
Ne shal the goste within my herte stent
To loue you beste/ withal my trewe entent

And with yͤ worde/she gan the house to dyght
And tables to sette/and beddes to make
And payned her to done al that she myght
Prayeng the chamberers for goddes sake
To hasten hem/ and faste swepe and shake
And she the moste seruysable of hem all
Hath euery chambre arayed/and his hall.

¶ Abouten vndren gan this erle alyght
That wt hi brought these noble children twey
For whiche the people ranne to se that syght
Of her araye/so rychely besey
And than at erste amonges hem they sey
That Walter was no foole/ though hym leste
To chaunge his wife: for it was for the beste

For she is fayrer/as they demen all
Than is Grisylde/and more tender of age
And fayrer frute bytwene hem shal fall
And more plesaunce/for her hye lynage
Her brother eke/so fayre was of his age
That him to seen yͤ people had caught plesaūce
Cōmendyng nowe the Markes gouernaūce.

¶ O sterne people/ vnsad and vntrewe
Aye vndiscrete/and chaungyng as a fane

Dely-

Delyting euer in rumer that is newe
For lyke the moone euer waye ye & wane
Euer ful of clappyng/dere ynough a iane
your dome is false/your cōstaunce euel preueth
A ful great foole is he that on you leueth

Thus sayden sadde folke in that cyte
Whan that the people gased vp and doun
For they were gladde/right with the nouelte
To haue a newe lady of her toun
No more of this make I nowe mencioun
But to Grisylde ayen wol I me dresse
And tellen her constaunce/and her busynesse.

¶ Wel busy was Grisylde on euery thyng
That to the feest was appertinent
Right naught was she abasshed of her clothing
Though they were rude/& somwhat to rent
But with glad chere/to the yate is went
With other folke/ to greten the Marquesesse
And after dothe she forthe her busynesse .

With right glad chere/ the gestes she receyueth
And buxomly/eueryche in his degre
That no man defaute there persevueth
But euer they wondren/ what she might be
That in so poore aray was for to se
And coulde suche honour/ and reuerence
And worthyly they praysen her prudence

In al the meane whyle she ne stente
This mayden and eke her brother to cōmende
With al her herte/and benygne entente
So wel/ that no man coude her prise amende
But at the laste/ whan these lordes wende
To sytten adowne to meate/he gan to call
Grisylde/as she was busy in the hall.

Grisylde(qd he) as it were in his play
Howe lyketh the my wyfe/and her beaute
Right wel my lorde(qd she)for in good fay
A fayrer sawe I neuer none than she
I pray to god so yeue you prosperite
And so hope I/that he wol to you sende
Plesaunce ynough/vnto your lyues ende.

¶ But one thyng I beseche/ and warne also
That ye pricke with no turmentyng
This tender mayden/as ye han do mo
For she is fostred in her norisshyng
More tenderly/in my supposyng
She coulde not aduersyte endure
As coulde a poore fostred creature

And whan this Walter sawe her pacience
Her glad chere/and no malyce at all
And he so ofte hath done her offence
And she aye constante/and stable as a wall
Contynuyng euer her innocence ouer all
This sturdy Markes/gan his herte dresse
To rewe vpon her wyfely stedfastnesse.

¶ This is ynough/Grisylde myne(qd he)
Be no more agaste/ne yuel apayde
I haue thy faythe/and thy benygnite
As wel as euer woman was assayde
In great estate/or poorely arrayde
Nowe knowe I dere wyfe thy stedfastnesse
And her in armes toke/and gan to kesse.

And she for wonder/toke therof no kepe
She herde not what thing he to her sayde
She fared as she had sterte out of her slepe
Tyl she out of her masednesse abrayde
Grisylde (qd he) by god that for vs deyde
Thou arte my wyfe/and none other I haue
Ne neuer had/as god my soule saue

This is thy doughter/which yu hast supposed
To ben my wyfe/and none other feythfully
And this shal bē myn heyr/as I haue disposed
Thou bare hem in thy body trewly
At Boloyne haue I kepte hem pryuely
Take hem ayen/for now mayst thou not say
That thou hast lorne any of thy childrē tway

And folke/that other wyse han sayd of me
I warne hem wel/ that I haue done this dede
For no malyce/ne for no cruelte
But for to assay in the thy womanhede
And not for to slee my children/god forbede
But for to kepen hem priuely and styll
Tyl I thy purpose knewe/& all thy wyll

¶ Whā she this herde/a swoune down she fal-
For pytous ioy/& after her swounyng (leth
She

She bothe her yonge children to her calleth
And in her armes/ pitously wepyng
Enbraced hem bothe/tenderly kyssyng
Ful lyke a mother/with her salte teeres
She bathed bothe her vysage and her heeres.

¶ O whiche a pytous thing it was to se
Her swounyng/⁊ her pytous voyce to here
Graũt mercy lorde/god thõke it you (qd̃ she)
That ye haue saued me my children dere
Nowe recke I neuer to be deed right here
Sythen I stõde in your loue/⁊ in your grace
No force of dethe/ne whan my spyrite pace.

¶ O tendre/ O dere/ O yonge children myne
Your woful mother wende stedfastly
That cruell houndes/or some foule vermyne
Had eten you/ but god of his mercy
And your benygne father/so tenderly
Hath done you kepe: and in that same stoũde
Al sodaynly she swapte downe to the groũde

And in her swounyng/so sadly holdeth she
Her children two/ whan she gan hem enbrace
That with great sleyght and diffyculte
The children from her armes they gan to race
O many a tere/on many a pytouse face
Downe ran/of hem that stoden there besyde
Unneth aboute her myght no man abyde.

¶ Walter her gladdeth/ ⁊ her sorowe slaketh
She ryseth vp al abasshed from her traunce
And euery wight her ioy and feest maketh
Tyl she hath caught ayen her countynaunce
Walter her dothe so faythfully plesaunce
That it was deyntie to seen the chere
Betwixt hem two/whan they were met yfere.

¶ These ladyes/whan they her tyme sey
Han taken her/and into chambre gon
And stryppen her out of her rude array
And in a clothe of golde/that bright shone
With a crowne of many a ryche stone
Upon her heed/they her in to hall brought
And there she was honoured as she ought.

Thus hath this pytous day a blissfull ende
For euery man and woman dothe his might
This day in myrthe and reuel to dispende
Tyl on the welken shone the sterres bright
For more solempne/in euery mannes syght
This feest was/and greater of costage
Than was the reuel of her mariage.

¶ Well many a yere/in hye prosperite
Lyuen these two/ in concorde and in rest
And richely his doughter maryed he
Unto a lorde/ one of the worthyest
Of al Itayle/and than in peace and rest
His wyues father in his courte he kepte
Tyl that his soule out of his body crepte

¶ His sonne succedeth in his heritage
In rest and peace/ after his fathers day
And fortunate was eke in mariage
Al put he not his wyfe in great assay
This worlde is not so stronge/ it is no nay
As it hath ben in olde tymes yore
And herkeneth what thautour sayth therfore.

This story is sayd/not for ye wyues sholde
Folowen Grisylde/as in humylite
For it were importable/ tho they wolde
But that euery wight in his degre
Shulde be constante/ in al aduersyte
As was Grisilde/wherfore Petrarke writeth
This storye/whiche with hye style he endyteth

For sythe a woman was so pacient
Unto a mortall man/wel more we ought
Receyue al in gree that god vs sent
For great skyll he preueth that he wrought
But he ne tempteth no man that he bought
As sayth saynt Iame/ if ye his pystel rede
He preueth folke but a day/it is no drede

And suffreth vs as for our exercyse
With sharpe scourges of aduersyte
Wel ofte to be beaten/in sondrie wyse
Not for to knowe our wyll/for certes he
Or we were borne/ knewe al our frelte
And for our best/is al his gouernaunce
Let vs lyue than in vertuous suffraunce

But one worde herkeneth lordynges or ye go
It were ful harde to fynde nowe a dayes
Gri-

In al a countre Grisyldes thre or two
For if they were put to suche assayes
The golde of hem hath so bad a layes
With brasse / for thoughe it be fayre at eye
It wolde rather braste a two than plye

For which here / for the wyves love of Bathe
Whose lyfe and secte / mighty god mayntene
In hygh maistry / or els were it skathe
I wyl with lusty herte / fresshe and grene
Saye you a songe / to glade you I wene
And let us stynte of ernest matere
Herkeneth my songe / yͭ sayth in this manere.

Lenvoye de Chaucer a les maris de nostre temps.

Grisylde is deed / and eke her pacience
And bothe at ones buryed in Itayle
For whiche I crye in open audyence
No wedded man be so hardy to assayle
His wyves pacience / in truste to fynde
Grisyldes / for in certayne he shal fayle.

O noble wyves / ful of hye prudence
Let no humylite your tonge nayle
Ne let no clerke have cause ne dilygence
To write of you a storie of suche mervayle
As of Grisylde / pacient and kynde
Lest Chechyface swalowe you in her entrayle

Foloweth Ecco / that holdeth no sylence
But ever answereth at the countre tayle
Bethe not adassed for your innocence
But sharpely taketh on you the governayle
Enprynteth wel this lesson in your mynde
For cōmen profyte / sythnesse it may avayle

Ne dredeth hem not / doth hem no reverence
For though thyn husbāde armed be in mayle
The arrowes of thy crabbed eloquence
Shal perce his brest / and eke his adventayle
In ielousye eke / loke thou him bynde
And yͭ shal make him couche as doth a quaile

If thou be fayre / there folke ben in presence
Shewe thou thy visage / and thyn apparayle
If thou be foule / be fre of thy dispence
To get the frendes aye do thy travayle
Be aye of chere / as light as lefe on lynde
And let him care / wepe / wringe / and wayle.

Ye archwyves / stōdeth aye at your defence
Sythe ye be stronge / as is a great camayle
Ne suffreth not / that men do you offence
And ye sklendre wyves / feble as in batayle
Beth egre as any tygre is in Inde
Aye clappeth as a myll / I you counsayle.

Here endeth yͤ clerkes tale of Oxforde / and here foloweth the wordes of our hoste.

This worthy clerk / whā ended was his tale
Our hoste sayd and swore by cockes bones
Me were lever than a barell of ale
My wyfe at home had herde this legēde ones
This is a gentle tale for the nones
As to my purpose / wyste ye my wyll
But thing that wol not be / let it be styll.

Here endeth the wordes of our hoste and here foloweth the Frankeleyns prologue.

These olde gentyll britons in her dayes
Of dyvers avētures maden layes
Rymed first in her mother tonge
Whiche layes / with her instrumētes they song
Or els reden hem for her plesaunce
And one of hem have I in remembraunce
Whiche I shall say / as wyllyng as I can
But sirs / bicause I am a borell man
At my begynnyng first I you beseche
Have me excused of my rude speche
I lerned never rhetorike certayne
Thing that I speke / mote be bare and playne
I slepte never on the mounte of Pernaso
Ne lerned never Marcus Tullius Cicero
Coloures ne knowe I none / withouten drede
But suche coloures as growen in the mede
Or els suche as men dyen or paynte
Coloures of rhetorike / ben to me quaynte
My spyrite feleth not of suche matere
This is my tale / if ye wol it here.

Here endeth the Frankeleyns prologue.

In

The Clerk's Tale: The Franklin's Prologue (E 1165–1212: F 709–728; T. 9041–9088: 11021–11040)

The frankeleyns tale.

Here begynneth the Frankeleyns tale.

In Armorike/that called is Britayne
There was a knight/ỷ loued & dyd his payne
To serue ladies in his beste wyse
And many a labour/& many a great emprise
He for his lady wrought/er she were wonne
For she was one the fayrest vnder sonne
And eke therto cōmen of hye kynrede
That wel vnneth durst this knyght for drede
Tel her his wo/his payne/and his distresse
But at the laste/she of her worthynesse
And namely for his meke obeysaunce
Hath suche a pyte caught of his penaunce
That priuely she fyll of his acorde
To take him for her husbonde & her lorde
Of such lordship/as mē haue ouer her wyues
And for to lede in the more blysse her lyues
Of his fre wyl/ he swore her as a knyght
That neuer in al his lyfe/day ne nyght
Ne shulde he take vpon him no maistrye
Agayne her wyl/ ne kythe her ielousye
But her obey/and folowe her wyl in all
As any louer to his lady shall
Saue that the name of soueraynte
That wolde he haue/for shame of his degre.
She thonked him/& with ful great humblesse
She sayd: sir/ sythe of your gentylnesse
ye profred me to haue so large a rayne
Ne wolde god neuer bytwyxt vs twayne
As in my gylte/ were eyther werre or stryfe
Sir/I wol be your trewe humble wyfe
Haue here my trouthe/ tyl that my hert breste
Thus ben they bothe in quiete and in reste.
¶ For one thyng sirs/ safely dare I seyne
That frendes/eueryche other must obeyne
If they wol longe holden companye
Loue wol not be constrayned by maistry
Whan maistrye cometh/ the god of loue anon
Beateth his wynges/and farewel he is gon
Loue is a thing / as any spyrite free
Women of kynde desyren lyberte
And not to be constrayned as a thrall
And so done men/if I sothe say shall
Loke who that moste pacient is in loue
He is at his auauntage al aboue
Pacience is an hye vertue certayne
For it venquissheth/as these clerkes sayne
Thynges that rygour shal neuer attayne
For euery worde mē may not chyde or playne
Lerneth to suffre/or els so mote I gone
ye shall it lerne/ whether ye wol or none
For in this world certayne no wyght ther is
That

That he ne doth or saith somtyme a mys
Ire/ sickenesse/ or constellation
Wyne/ wo/ or chaungyng of complection
Causeth full ofte to don a mysse or speken
On every wrong/ a man may not be wreken
After the tyme/ must be temperaunce
To every wight that can of governaunce
And therfore/ hath this worthy wise knyght
To lyue in ease / suffraunce her hight
And she to him full wisely gan swere
That never shulde there be defaut in here
  Here may men se/ humble and wise accorde
Thus hath she take her servant ⁊ her lorde
Servaunt in loue/ and lorde in mariage
Than was he bothe in lordship and seruage
Seruage : nay/ but in lordship aboue
Sithen he hath bothe his lady and his loue
His lady certes/ and his wife also
The whiche that lawe of loue accordeth to
And whan he was in this prosperite
Home with his wife he goth/ in to his countre
Nat fer fro Dēmarke/ ther his dwelling was
Where as he lyueth in ioye and in solas
  Who coude tell/ but he had wedded be
The ioye/ the ease/ and the prosperite
That is betwixt an husbande ⁊ his wife :
Evermore lasted this blyssfull lyfe
Tyll that this knyght/ of which I speke thus
That of Caere Juda/ was cleped Aruerragus
Shope him to dwell/ a yere or twayne
In Englande/ that cleped was Britayne
To seken in armes worship and honour
For all his lust he sette in suche labour
And dwelt there two yere/ the boke saith thus
¶ Nowe woll I stynt of this Aruerragus
And speke I woll of Dorigen his wife
That loueth her husbonde as her hertes lyfe
For his absence/ wepeth she and syketh
As don these noble wyues whan hem lyketh
She mourneth/ wayleth/ fasteth/ ⁊ playneth
Desire of his presence/ her so constrayneth
That all this wyde worlde set she at nought
  Her frendes/ whiche knewe her heuy thouȝt
Comforten her/ in all that ever they may
They prechen her/ and tellen her night ⁊ day
That causeles she slewe her selfe/ alas
And every comfort possyble in this caas
They don to her/ with all her busynesse
And al for to maken her leue her heuynesse.
¶ By processe/ as ye knowen everychone
Men mowen so longe grauen in a stone
Tyl some fygure therin printed be
So longe han they comforted her/ tyll she
Receyued hath by hope and by reson
The enpryntyng of her consolacion
Through which her great sorow gan aswage
She may not alway induren suche a rage
And eke Aruyragus in al this care
Hath sent his letters home of his welfare
And that he wol come hastely agayne
Or els had this sorowe her herte slayne.
  Her frendes sawe her sorowe gan to slake
And prayden her on knees/ for goddes sake
To come and romen in her companye
Away to driuen her derke fantasye
And fynally she graunted that requeste
For wel she sawe it was for the beste.
¶ Nowe stode her castel faste by the see
And ofte with her frendes walked she
Her to disporte on the bankes hey
Where as she may shyppes and barges sey
Saylyng her course/ where hem lyst go
But yet was that a parcel of her wo
For to her selfe ful ofte alas sayd she
Is there no shyppe/ of so many as I se
Wol bring home my lorde : thā were my herte
Warisshed of these bytter paynes smerte.
¶ Another tyme/ wolde she sytte and thynke
And caste her eyen downwarde fro the brinke
But whan she sawe the gryssly rockes blake
For very feare/ so wolde her herte quake
That on her fete she myght not her sustene
Than wolde she sytte adowne vpon the grene
And pitously in to the see beholde
And say right thus/ with sorouful sykes colde
¶ Eterne god/ that through thy purueyaunce
Ledest this worlde/ by certayne governaunce
In ydle as mē sayn/ doste thou nothing make
But lorde/ these grissly fendely rockes blake
That semen rather a foule confusyon
Of werke/ than a fayre creacion
Of suche a parfyte god/ wyse and ful stable
why haue ye wrouȝt this werke vnresonable :
For by this werke/ northe/ south/ west/ ne este
There nys fostred/ man/ byrde/ ne beste
It dothe no good/ but anoyeth

The Franklin's Tale (F 780–875; T. 11092–11187)

Se ye not lorde / howe mãkinde it distropeth
An hũdred thousande bodyes of mankynde
Haue rockes islayn / al be they not in mynde
Syn mãkind is so fayre a p̃te of thy werke
That thou it madest like thyn owne werke
Than semed it ye had a great cherte
Towarde mãkynde / but how thã may it be
That ye suche menes maken it to distroyen?
Which menes don no good / but euer anoyen.
¶ I wote wel clerkes wol sayne as hem lest
By argumentes / that al is for the best
Though I ne can not the causes wel knowe
But thilke god / yͭ made the wynde to blowe
As kepe my lorde / this is my conclusyon
To clerkes lete I al this disputacion
And wolde god that all these rockes blake
Were sonken in to hell for his sake.
These rockes slee myn hert for feare
Thus wolde she say wͭ many a pitous teare
Her frendes sawe it was for her no disport
To romen by the see / but discomfort
And shapen hem to playen somwhere elles
They leden her by ryuers and by welles
And eke in other places delytables
They daunceen and they playen at the tables
So on a day / right in the morowe tyde
Unto a gardayne / that was there besyde
In whiche that they had made her ordynaũce
Of vitayles / and other purueyaunce
They gon and playen hem al the longe day
And this was in the syxte morowe of May
Which May hath painted wͭ his soft shoures
This gardayne ful of leues and of floures
And crafte of mannes honde so curiously
Arayed had this garden truely
That neuer nas there garden of suche prise
But if it were the very paradyse
The odour of floures / and the fresshe syght
Wolde haue made any herte lyght
That euer was borne / but if to gret sicknesse
Or to great sorowe helde it in distresse
So was it ful of beautie / with plesaunce.
And after dyner gonne they daunce
And synge also / saue Dorigene alone
That yet unto her selfe made her mone
For she ne sey him on the daunce go
That was her husbonde / and her loue also
But nathelesse / she muste her tyme abyde
And with good hope / let her sorowe slyde.
¶ Upon this daunce / amonge other men
Daunced a squier before Dorigen
That fressher was / and iolyer of aray
As to my dome / than is the monthe of May
He syngeth & daunseth / passyng euery man
That is or was / sythen the worlde began
And therwithal / & men shulde him discryue
One of the beste faryng men on lyue
Yonge / stronge / vertuouse / riche / and wyse
And wel beloued / and holden of great prise
And shortly / if I the sothe tel shall
Unwetyng of this dorigene at all
This lusty squier / seruaunt to Venus
Whiche ycleped was Aurelyus
Had loued her beste of any creature
Two yere and more / as was his auenture
But neuer durst he tell her his greuaunce
Withouten cuppe he dronke al his penaunce
He was dispayred / nothyng durst he say
Saue in his songes / somwhat wold he wray
His wo / as in generall complaynyng
He sayd he loued / and was beloued nothyng
Of whiche matere made he many layes
Songes / complayntes / roundels / virelayes
Howe that he durste not his sorowe tell
But languysshe / as dothe a fury in hell
And dye he muste (he sayd) as dyd Ecco
For Narcissus / that durst not tell his wo.
¶ In other maner than ye herde me say
Ne durste not he to her his wo bewray
Saue peraduenture somtyme at daunces
There yonge folke kepen her obseruaunces
It may wel be / he loked on her face
In suche a wyse / as men that asken grace
But nothyng wyste she of his entent
Nathelesse it happed / er they thence went
Bycause that he was her neyghbour
And was a man of worshyp and honour
And had knowen him of tymes yore
They fel in speche / and so forthe more & more
Unto his purpose than drowe Aurelyus
And whan he sawe his tyme he sayd thus.
¶ Madame (q̃d he) by god yͭ this world made
So that I wyste / yͭ I might your hert glade
I wolde that day / that your Arueragus
Went ouer the see / that I Aurelyus
Had went ther yͭ I shuld neuer come agayne
For

The Franklin's Tale (F 876–971 ; T. 11188–11283)

For wel I wote my seruyce is in vayne
My guerdon nys but brestyng of myn herte
Madame rueth vpon my paynes smerte
For with one worde ye may me slee or saue
Here at your foote god wold ẏ I were graue
I ne haue as nowe no leyser more to sey
Haue mercy swete/or ye wol do me dey.
¶ She gan to loke vpon Aurelyus
Is this your wyll (q̄d she) and say ye thus?
Neuer erste (q̄d she) ne wyst I what ye mente
But nowe I knowe Aurelyus your entente
By thilke god/that yaue me soule and lyfe
Ne shal I neuer be vntrewe wyfe
In worde ne in werke/as ferre as I haue wyt
I wol ben his to whom I am knyt
Take this for a fynal answere of me
But after this in play thus sayd she.
¶ Aurelyus (q̄d she) by god aboue
Yet wol I graunte you to ben your loue
(Sythen I se you so pitously complayne)
Loke what day that endelonge Britayne
Ye remeue al the rockes/stone by stone
That they ne let shyppe ne bote to gone
I say whā ye haue made these costes so clene
Of rockes/that there nys no stone ysene
Than wol I loue you best of any man
Here haue my trouth/in al that euer I can.
Is there none other grace in you (q̄d he?)
¶ No by that lorde (q̄d she) that maked me
For wel I wote that it shal neuer betyde
Let suche folye out of your herte glyde
What deyntie shulde a man haue in his lyfe
For to go loue a nother mannes wyfe?
That hath her body whan so that him lyketh
¶ Aurelius ful ofte sore syketh
Wo was Aurely/whan he this herde
And with a sorouful chere he thus answerde.
¶ Madame (q̄d he) this were impossyble
Than mote I dye on sodayne deth horryble
And with that worde he turned him anone.
¶ Tho come her other frendes euerichone
And in the aleyes romeden vp and doun
And nothing wyste of this conclusyoun
But sodaynly began to reuel newe
Tyl that the bright sonne loste his hewe
For the orizont hath refte the sonne his lyght
This is as moche to say/as it was nyght
And home they gon in ioy and in solas
Saue onely wretched Aurelyus/alas
He to his house is gone with sorowfull harte
He sayd he myght not from his dethe astarte
Him semed/that he felte his herte colde
Vp to heuen his hondes gan he holde
And on his knees bare/he set him adoun
And in his rauyng sayd this orisoun
For very wo out of his wytte he brayde
He ne wyst what he spake/but thus he sayde
With pytous hert hath his cōplaynt begonne
Vnto the goddes/and firste vnto the sonne
He sayd: God Apollo and gouernour
Of euery plante/herbe/tree/and flour
That yeuest after thy declynacion
To eke of hem his tyme and ceson
As thyn herberowe chaungeth lowe ⁊ hye
Lorde Phebus/caste thy merciable eye
On wretched Aurelyus/whiche am but lorne
Lo lorde/my lady hath my dethe isworne
Without gylte/but thy benignyte
Vpon my deedly herte haue some pyte
For wel I wote lorde Phebus/if ye leste
Ye may me helpe saue my lady beste
Nowe vouche ye saue/that I you deuyse
Howe that I may be holpen ⁊ in what wyse.
¶ Your blisful suster Lucina the shene
That of the see is goddesse and quene
Though Neptunus hath deite in the see
Yet emperesse abouen him is she
Ye knowen wel lorde/right as her desyre
Is to be quickened and lyghted of your fyre
For whiche that she foloweth you ful besily
Right so the see desyreth naturally
To folowen her that is goddesse
Bothe of the see/and ryuers more and lesse
Wherfore lorde Phebus/this is my request
Do this myracle/or do myn herte brest
That nowe next at this opposycion
Whiche in signe shal be the lyon
As prayeth her so great a floode to bring
That fyue fadome at the leste/it ouer spring
The hyest rocke in Armorike Britayne
And let this floode dure yeres twayne
Than certes to my lady may I say
Holdeth your heste/the rockes ben away
This thyng may ye lightly done for me
Pray her to gon no faster course than ye
I say thus/prayeth your suster that she go

N.ii. No

The Frankeleyns tale.

No faster course than ye in yeres two
Than shal she be at the ful alway
And sprynge floode lastyng bothe night & day
And but she vouchsafe in suche manere
To graunte me my soueraygne lady dere
Pray her to synken euery rocke adoun.
In to her owne derke regyoun
Vnder the grounde/ there Pluto dwelleth in
Or neuermore shal I my lady wyn
Thy tẽple in Delphos/ wol I barefote seke
O lorde Phebus/ se the teres on my cheke
And on my payne haue some compassyoun
And with that worde/ in swoune he fel adoun
And longe tyme he lay in a traunce.
His brother/ whiche þ knew of his penaũce
Vp caught him/ and to bed him brought
Dispeyred in this turment and this thought
Lette I this woful creature lye
Chese he whether he wol lyue or dye
¶ Aruyragus with heale and great honour
(As he that was of chyualry the floure)
Is comen home/ and other worthy men
O blissful arte thou nowe Dorigen
That haste thy lusty husbonde in thyn armes
That fressh knight/ þ worthy man of armes
That loueth the/ as his own hertes lyfe
Nothyng lyst him to be ymaginatyfe
If any wight had spoken (while he was out)
To her of loue/ therof had he no dout
He entendeth nat to suche matere
But daũceth/ iusteth/ & maketh her gode chere
And thus in ioye & blysse I let hem dwell
And of wofull Aurelyus woll I tell.
¶ In langour and in tourment dispitous
Two yere and more/ laye wretched Aurelyus
Er any fote on erthe he myght gone
Ne comforte in this tyme had he none
Saue of his brother/ whiche was a clerke
He knewe of all this wo & all this werke
For to non other creature certayn
Of this mater/ durst he no worde sayn
Vnder his brest he bare it more secre
Than euer dyd Pamphilus for Galathe
His brest was hole without for to seen
But in his hert aye/ was the arowe keen
And well ye knowen that of a sursanure
In surgery/ is perlous the cure
But men might touch the arow or cõe therby
His brother wepeth and wayleth priuely
Tyl at the laste him fel in remembraunce
That while he was at Orlyaũce in Fraunce
(As these clerkes yonge that ben lykerouse)
To reden artes they ben curyouse
Seken in euery halke and in euery herne
Pertyculer science for to lerne
He him remembred that vpon a dey
At Orlyaunce in studye a booke he sey
Of magyke naturell/ whiche his felawe
That was in that tyme a bacheler of lawe
Al were he there to lerne another crafte
Had priuely vpon his deyke ylafte
Whiche booke spake of mochel operacions
Touching the foure and twenty mansyons
That longen to the moone/ and suche folye
As in our dayes is not worthe a flye
For holy churche faythe in our byleue
Ne suffreth none illusyon vs to greue
And whan this boke was in his remẽbraũce
Anon for ioye his herte gan daunce
And to him selue he sayd priuely
My brother shal be warissħed sykerly
For I am syker that there be sciences
By whiche men maken dyuers aparences
Suche as these subtel tregetoures play
For ofte at feestes haue I wel herde say
That tragetors/ within an hall large
Haue made come in water and a barge
And in the hall rowen vp and doun
Somtyme hath semed a grym lyoun
And somtyme floures spring as in a merde
Somtyme a vyne/ and grapes whyte & reede
Somtyme a castel of lyme and stone
And whan him lyked/ voyden hem anone
Thus semed it to euery mannes syght.
¶ Nowe than conclude I thus/ if þ I myght
At Orlyaunce some olde felowe fynde
That had this moones mansyons in mynde
Or other magyke naturell aboue
He shulde wel make my brother haue his loue
For with an apparaunce a clerke may make
To mannes syght/ that al the rockes blake
Of Britayne/ were voyded euerychone
And shyppes by the brinke to comen & gone
And in suche forme enduren a yere or two
Than were my brother warisshed of his wo
Than must she nedes holde her beheste

The Franklin's Tale (F 1068–1163; T. 11380–11475)

Or els he shal shame her at the feste.
¶ What shulde I make a lenger tale of this
Unto his brothers bedde he comen is
And suche comforte he yaue him for to gone
To Orlyaunce/ that he up sterte anone
And on his way than is he forthe yfare
In hope to ben lessed of his care.
¶ Whan they were comen almoste to yͤ cyte
(But if it were a two forlonge or thre)
A yonge clerke romyng by him selfe they met
Whiche that in latyn thriftely hem gret
And afterwarde he sayd a wonder thyng
I knowe the cause of your cōmyng
And er they farther any foote wente
He tolde hem al that was in her entente.
¶ This Breton clerke asked him of felowes
The whiche he had knowen in olde dayes
He answerde him/ that they deed were
For whiche he wepte ofte ful many a tere.
¶ Downe of his horse Aurelius light anon
And with this magycien forthe is he gon
Home to his house/ and made him wel at ese
Hem lacked no vitayle that hem might p̄lese
So wel araped an house as there was one
Aurelyus in his lyfe sawe neuer none.
¶ He shewed him/ or he went to suppere
Forestes and parkes/ ful of wylde dere
He sawe there hertes/ with her hornes hye
The greatest that euer were sene with eye
He se of hem an hundred slayne with hoūdes
And some of arowes bled wt bytter woūdes
He sawe/ whan voyded were the wylde dere
These fauconers/ upon a fayre ryuere
That with the haukes han the heron slayne.
Tho sawe he knightes iustyng in a playn
And after this he dyd him suche plesaunce
That he him shewed his lady in a daunce
On whiche him selfe dau̅ced as him thought
And whā this maister/ yͭ this magike wrouȝt
Sawe it was tyme/ he clapped his hōdes to
And farwel our reuel/ al was ago
And remeued neuer out of his house
Whyle they sawe al this syght meruaylouse
But in his studye there his bokes be
They saten styl/ no wight but they thre.
¶ To him this maister called his squier
And sayd him thus/ is redy our supper
Almost an hour it is/ I undertake
Sythen I you bade our supper redy make
Whan that these worthy men went with me
Into my studye/ there as my bokes be
¶ Sir (qd the squier) whan it lyketh you
It is al redy/ though ye wol right nowe.
¶ Go we suppe than (qd he) for the best
These amerous folke sōtyme mote haue rest
And after supper fell they in trete
What sōme shuld this maisters guerdon be
To remeue al the rockes of Britayne
And eke from Girōde to the mouth of sayne.
¶ He made it strāge/ & swore so god him saue
Lasse thā a thousāde poūde wold he not haue
Ne gladly for that sōme nolde he it don.
¶ Aurelyus with blyssful herte anon
Answerde thus: Fye on a thousande poūde
This wyde worlde/ which men say is rounde
I wolde it yeue/ if I were lorde of it
This bargayne is ful driue/ for we be knyt
Ye shal be payde truely by my trouthe
But loke nowe for no neglygence or slouthe
Ye taryen us here no lenger than to morowe
Nay (qd this clerke) here my trouth to borow
¶ To bedde is gon Aurelius whan him leste
And wel nye almight he had his reste
What for his labour/ and his hope of blysse
His woful herte of penaunce had a lysse.
¶ Upon the morowe whan that it was day
To Britayne toke they the right way
Aurelius/ and this magicyen him besyde
And ben discended there they wolde abyde
And this was/ as the boke dothe remembre
In the colde frosty seson of Decembre.
¶ Phebus wayed olde/ & hewed lyke laton
That afore in his hote declynacion
Shone as yͤ brēnyng gold wt stremes bright
But nowe in Capricorne adowne he lyght
Where as he shone ful pale/ I dare wel sayne
The bytter froste/ with the sledder rayne
Distroyed hath the grene in euery yerde
Ianus syt by the fyre with double berde
And drinketh of his bugle horne the wyne
Bifore him stont braune of the tusked swyne
And nowel cryeth euery lusty man.
¶ Aurelyus/ in al that euer he can
Dothe to this maister chere and reuerence
And prayeth him to don his dyligence
To bringen him out of his paynes smerte

N.iii. Or

The Franklin's Tale (F 1164–1259; T. 11476–11571)

Or with a swerde that he wolde slyt his herte.
  This clerke suche routhe hath on this man
That nyght & day he spedeth him that he can
To wayte a tyme of his conclusyon
This is to say/ to make illusyon
Or suche an apparence or iogelrye
I ne can no termes of astrologye
That she and euery wight shulde wene & say
That of Britayne the rockes were away
Or els they were sonken vnder the grounde
Tyl at the laste he hath his tyme yfounde
To make his iapes and his wretchydnesse
Of suche superstycious cursydnesse
His tolletan tables he forthe brought
Ful wel corrected/him lacked nought
Neyther his collecte/ne his expans yeres
Ne his rootes/ne his other geres
As ben his centrys/and his argumentes
And his proporcionell conuenyences
For his equacions in euery thyng
And by his eyght speres in his werkyng
He knew ful wel howe far alnath was shoue
Fro the heed of thylke fyxe Aries aboue
That in the nynthe spere consydred is
Ful subtelly he had calked al this
And whan he had founde his first mansyon
He knewe the remenaunt by proporcion
And knewe the rysing of the moone wele
And in suche face/the terme and euery dele
And knewe also his other obseruaunces
For suche illusyons and suche mischaunces
As hethen folke vsed in thilke dayes
For whiche ne maked he no lenger delayes
But through his magike/for a weke or tway
It semed that al the rockes were away.
¶ Aurelyus/whiche that dispayred is
Whether he shal haue his loue/or fare amys
Awayteth night and day on this myracle
And whan he knewe there was non obstacle
But yͤ voyded were these rockes euerychon
Downe to the maisters fete he fel anon
And sayd/I woful wretche Aurelius
Thanke you lorde and lady myn Venus
That me hath holpen fro my cares colde
And to yͤ temple his way forthe hath he holde
Where as he knewe he shulde his lady se
And whan he sawe his tyme/ anon right he
With dredfull herte/& with humble chere
Salued hath his souerayne lady dere.
¶ My rightful lady (qd this woful man)
Whom I serue and loue/as I best can
And lothest were of al this worlde displese
Nere it that I for you haue suche disese
That I muste dye here at your fete anon
Nought wold I tel you how wo me is begon
But certes eyther muste I dye or playne
ye slee me gyltlesse for very payne
But of my dethe/though ye haue no routhe
Auysen you/er that ye breken your trouthe
Repenteth you/for that ylke god aboue
For ye slee me/ bycause that I you loue
For madame/ wel ye wote that ye haue hight
Not that I chalenge any thyng of right
Of you my souerayn lady/but of your grace
But in a garden yonde in suche a place
ye wotte right wel what ye heyght me
And in myn honde your trouth plyght ye
To loue me best/ god wotte ye sayd so :
Al be it I am vnworthy therto
Madame I speke it for the honour of you
More than for to saue myn hertes lyfe nowe
I haue done right as ye cōmaunded me
And if ye vouchesafe/ye may go se
Doth as you list/haueth your heste in mynde
For quicke or deed/right ther ye shal me fynde
In you lythe al to do me lyue or deye
But wel I wote the rockes ben aweye
  He toke his leue/and she astonyed stode
In al her face there nas a droppe of bloode
She wende neuer han come in suche a trappe
¶ Alas (qd she) that euer this shulde happe
For wende I neuer by possibylite
That such a mister or meruayle might be
It is ayenst the processe of nature
And home she gothe a sorouful creature
For very feare vnnethes may she go
She wepeth and wayleth a day or two
And swouneth/that it was routhe to se
But why it was to no wight tolde she
For out of towne was gon Arueragus
But to her selfe she spake/and sayd thus
In her complaynt/as ye shal after here
With face pale/& with sorouful chere.
¶ Alas (qd she) on the fortune I playne
That vnware hast wrapped me ī thy chayne
Fro whiche to escape/ wot I no socoure
Saue

Haue onely dethe/or els dishonoure
One of these two behoueth me to chese
But nathelesse/yet had I leuer to lese
My lyfe/than of my body to haue a shame
Or knowe my selfe false/or lese my name
And with my dethe/I may be quyt iwys
Hath there not many a wyfe er this
And many a mayde/islayne her selfe alas
Rather than with her body done trespas
And certes lo/these stories beren wytnesse
Whan thurty tyrantes/ful of cursydnesse
Had slayne Phidon/ in Athenes at the feest
They cōmaunded his doughters to areste
And bringen hem byforne hem in dispyte
Al naked/to fulfyl her foule delyte
And in her fathers bloode/he dyd hem daūce
Vpon the pauement/god yeue him mischaūce
For which these woful maydens ful of drede
Rather than they wolde lesen her maydenhede
They priuely ben sterte in to a well
And drenched hem selfe/as bokes tell.
¶ They of Messene let enquire and seke
Of Lacidomony fifty maydens eke
On whiche they wolde haue don her lechery
But there was none of al that company
That she nas slayne: and with a glad entent
Chese rather for to dyen/than for to assent
To ben oppressed of her maydenhede
Why shulde I than to dye ben in drede?
¶ Lo eke the tyraunt Aristoclides
That loued a mayde/ yͭ hight Symphalydes
Whan that her father slayne was on a nyght
Vnto Dyanes temple gothe she anon right
And hente the ymage/with her armes two
Fro whiche image wolde she neuer go
No wight might fro it her hondes race
Tyl she was slayne/right in the selfe place.
¶ Now sythnes yͤ maidens had suche dispyte
To ben defouled with mannes foule delyte
Wel ought a wyfe rather her selfe slee
Than be defouled/as thynketh me.
¶ What shal I say of Hasdruballes wyfe?
That at Cartage byrafte her selfe her lyfe
For whā she sawe yͤ romanes wan the town
She toke her children al/and lepte adown
Into the fyre/and chese rather to dye
Than any roman dyd her villanye.
¶ Hath not Lucrece islayne her selfe/ alas
At Rome/there she oppressed was
Of Tarquyne/for her thought it was shame
To lyue/whan that she had lost her name.
¶ The eyght maydens of Melesye also
Han slayn hem selue for very drede and wo
Rather than folke of Gaule shuld hē oppresse
Mo than a thousande stories/as I gesse
Couthe I nowe tel/as touchyng this matere.
¶ Whan Abradas was slayn/his wife so dere
Her selfe slowe/and let her bloode to glyde
In Abradas woundes/brode and wyde
And said/my body at the leste way
There shal no wight defoule if I may.
¶ What shulde I mo ensamples herof sayn?
Sythens that so many han hem selfe slayne
Wel rather than they wolde defouled be
I wol conclude that it is best for me
Wel rather slee my selfe in some manere
As dyd Demotions doughter dere
Bycause that she nolde not defouled be.
¶ O Sedasus/it is ful great pyte
To reden howe thy doughters dyden/alas?
That slowen hem selfe for such a maner caas
As great a pyte was it or wel more
The Theban mayden/that for Nichanore
For one of Macedone had her oppressed
With her dethe her maydenhede she redressed.
¶ What shal I sayne of Nycerates wyfe
That for suche case birafte her selfe her lyfe?
¶ Howe trewe was eke to Alcibyades
His loue/that for to dyen rather chees
Than for to suffren his body vnburyed be.
¶ Lo whiche a wyfe was Alceste (qd she)
What sayth Homere of good Penelope?
Al Grece knoweth of her chastyte.
¶ Parde of Laodomia is written thus
That whā at Troy was slayn Protheselaus
No lenger nolde she lyue after his day.
¶ The same of noble Portia tel I may
Withouten Brutus couthe she not lyue
To whom she had al her herte igyue.
¶ The parfyte wyfehode of Artemisy
Honoured is/throughout al Barbary
¶ Oh Thenta quene/ thy wifely chastyte
To al wyues may a myrrour be.
The same thing I saye of Bilia
Of Rodogone/and eke Valeria.
¶ Thus playned Dorigene a day or twey
Purpos.

Purpoſyng euer that ſhe wolde dey
But natheleſſe vpon the thirde nyght
Home came Arueragus/the worthy knight
And aſked her why ſhe wepte ſo ſore
And ſhe gan wepen euer lenger the more
¶ Alas (qđ ſhe) that euer was I borne
Thus haue I ſaid (qđ ſhe) thus haue I sworn
And tolde him al/ as ye haue herde before
It nedeth not to reherce it no more.
¶ This huſbōde wt glad chere in ſōdrie wyſe
Anſwerde and ſayd/as I ſhal you deuyſe
Is there aught els Dorigene but this.
¶ Nay nay (qđ ſhe) god helpe me ſo as wys
This is to moche/and it were goddes wyll.
¶ Ye wyſe (qđ he) let ſlepe that is ſtyll
It may be wel yet parauenture to day
ye ſhal your trouthe holde by my fay
For god ſo wyſly haue mercy on me
I had wel leuer ſtycked for to be
For very loue/whiche that I to you haue
But if ye ſhulde your trouthe ſaue
Trouth is the hyeſt thing that men may kepe
But with that worde he braſt anon to wepe
And said/I you forbyd on payne of dethe
That neuer whiles you laſteth lyfe or brethe
To no wight tel of this miſauenture
As I may beſte I wol my wo endure
Ne make no countenaunce of heuyneſſe
That folke of you may deme harme ne geſſe
And forthe he cleped a ſquier and a mayde
Gothe forthe anon with Dorigene he ſayde
And bringeth her in ſuche a place anone
They toke her leue/ & on her way they gone
But they ne wyſte why ſhe thyder went
She nolde no wight tel her entent.
¶ This ſquier/whiche that hyght Aurelyus
On Dorigen/ whiche that was ſo amerous
Of auenture happed her to mete
Amydde the towne/ right in the hye ſtrete
As ſhe wolde haue gon the way forthe right
Towarde the garden/there as ſhe had hyght
And he was to the gardenwarde alſo
For wel he ſpyed whan ſhe wolde go
Out of her houſe/to any maner place
But thus they met of auenture or of grace
And he ſalueth her with glad entent
And aſked of her whyder that ſhe went.
¶ And ſhe anſwerde halfe as ſhe were madde
Vnto the garden as my huſbonde badde
My trouthe for to holde/ alas alas.
  Aurelyus gan wondren of this caas
And in his herte had great compaſſyon
Of her chere/and of her lamentacion
And of Arupragus the worthy knyght
That bade her holde al that ſhe had hyght
So loth he was ỹ ſhe ſhuld breke her trouthe
And in his herte he caught of it great routhe
Conſydring the beſte on euery ſyde
That fro his luſte were him better abyde
Than do ſo hye a churliſſhe wretchydneſſe
Ayenſt fraunchiſe/ & ayenſt al gentilneſſe
For whiche in fewe wordes said he thus
  Madame/ſaythe to your lorde Aruiragus
That ſythen I ſe this great gentilneſſe
Of him/ and eke I ſe wel your diſtreſſe
That ye to me thus ſhuld holde your trouthe
Certes me thynketh it were great routhe
I haue wel leuer euer to ſuffre wo
Than departe the loue bytwixt you two
I you releſe madame into your honde
Quyte euery ſurement and euery bonde
That ye haue made to me/as here byforne
Sythens thilke tyme that ye were borne
My trouth I plight/I ſhal you neuer repreue
Of no beheſte/and here I take my leue
As of the treweſt and the beſte wyfe
That euer yet I knewe in al my lyfe
But euery wight beware of her byheſte
On Dorigene remembreth at the leſte
Thus can a ſquyer done a gentill dede
As wel as can a knight/withouten drede.
¶ She thonked him vpon her knees al bare
And home vnto her huſbonde is ſhe fare
And tolde him al/as ye han herde me ſayde
And be ye ſyker/he was ſo wel apayde
That it were impoſſyble me to wrte
  What ſhulde I lenger of this caſe endyte?
Arueragus/ and Dorigen his wyfe
In ſouerayne blyſſe leden forthe her lyfe
Neuer after was there anger hem bytwene
He cheriſſhed her/as though ſhe were a quene
And ſhe was to him trewe for euermore
Of theſe two folkes ye get of me nomore.
  Aurelyus/that his coſte hath al forlorne
Curſeth the tyme that euer he was borne
Alas (qđ he) alas that euer I beheyght
Of

Of pured golde a thousande pōde of weight
Unto this phylosopher/ howe shal I do?
I se no more/ but that I am fordo
Myn herytage mote I nedes sell
And ben a begger/ here may I no lēger dwell
And shame al my kynrede in this place
But I of him may get better grace
But nathelesse I wol of him assay
At certayne dayes/ yere by yere to pay
And thonke him of his great curtesye
My trouthe wol I kepe/ I wol not lye.
¶ With herte sore/ he gothe unto his cofer
And brought golde unto this phylosopher
The value of fyve hundred ponde as I gesse
And him beseecheth of his gentilnesse
To graunt him dayes of the remenaunt
And sayd: mayster I dare wel make avaunt
I fayled never of my trouthe as yet
For syckerly my dette shal be quyt
Towardes you/ howe that ever I fare
To gon a beggyng in my kyrtel bare
But wolde ye vouchesafe upon suerte
Two yere or thre for to respyte me
Than were I wel/ for els mot I sell
Myn herytage/ there is no more to tell.
¶ This phylosopher soberly answerde
And sayd thus/ whan he this worde herde
Have I not holde covenaunt unto the?
Yes certes/ wel and truely (qd̄ he)
¶ Haste thou not had thy lady as the lyketh?
No no (qd̄ he) and sorily he syketh
¶ What was the cause/ tel me if yͭ thou can?
Aurelyus anon his tale began
And tolde him al as ye han herde byfore
It nedeth not to reherce it any more.
He sayd Arveragus of gentilnesse
Had lever dye in sorowe and in distresse
Than his wyfe were of her trouthe fals
The sorowe of Dorigene he tolde him als
Howe lothe she was to ben a wycked wyfe
And that she had lever have loste her lyfe
And yͭ her trouth she swore through innocēce
She never erste herde speke of apparence
That made me have of her so great pyte
And right as frely as he sent her to me
As frely sent I her to him agayne
This is al & some/ there nys no more to sayn.
The philosopher answerde/ leve brother
Everiche of you dyd gentilly to other
Thou arte a squier/ and he is a knyght
But god forbyd/ for his blissful myght
But if a clerke coulde done a gentill dede
As wel as any of you/ it is do drede.
Sir I relese the thy thousande pounde
As nowe thou were crope out of the groūde
Ne never er nowe haddest thou knowen me
For sir/ I wol not taken a peny of the
For al my crafte/ ne nought for my travayle
Thou haste ipayed right wel for my vitayle
It is ynough/ and farwel & have good day
And toke his horse/ & rode forthe on his way.
¶ Lordynges this question wold I aske now
Whiche was the moste fre/ as thynketh you?
Nowe telleth me/ er that I ferther wende
I can no more/ my tale is at an ende.

¶ Here endeth the Frankelcyns tale/ and begynneth the seconde nonnes prologue.

The mynistre and the norice unto vyces
Whiche yͭ men clepen in englisshe idlenesse
That is porter of the yate of delyces
To eschue/ & by her contrarye her oppresse
That is to sayne/ by lefull besynesse
Wel ought we to don our entent
Leste that the fende through idlenesse us hent

For he that with his thousande cordes slye
Continuelly us wayteth to be clappe
Whan he may man in ydlenesse espye
He can so lightly catche him in his trappe
Tyl that a man be hente/ right by the lappe
He nys not ware the fende hath him in honde
Wel ought us werche/ & ydlenesse withstōde

And though men dredden never for to dye
Yet se men wel by reson doutles
That ydlenesse is rote of slogardye
Of which there cometh never no good encres
And sithnes that slouthe holdeth hem in a lees
Only to slepe/ and for to eate and drinke
And to devouren al that other swynke

And for to put us from suche ydelnesse
That cause is of so great confusyon
I have

The Franklin's Tale: The Second Nun's Prologue (F 1560–1624: G 1–23; T. 11864–11928: 15469–15491)

The seconde nonnes prologue.

I haue here done my faythful besynesse
After the legende in translacion
Right of thy glorious lyfe and passion
Thou wt thy garlōde/wrought wt rose & lely
The mene I/mayde and marter seynt Cecely

And thou that arte floure of virgins all
Of whom that Bernarde lyst so wel to write
To the at my begynnyng first I call
Thou comforte of vs wretches/ do me endyte
Thy maydēs deth/ ẏ wan thorow her merite
The eternal lyfe/ and of the fende victorie
As men may after rede in her storie

Thou maydē & mother/doughter of thy sōne
Thou well of mercy/synful soules cure
In whom that god of boūte chese for to wōne
Thou humble and hye ouer euery creature
Thou noblest/so farre ouer nature
That no disdayne the maker had of kynde
His sōne in bloode & flesshe to clothe & wynde

Whiche in the cloystre of thy blissful sydis
Toke mannes shappe/ the eterne loue & pees
That of the true compas/lorde & gyde is
Whom heuen/erthe/ and see/withouten les
Aye heryen/and thou virgyne wemles
Bare of thy body/& dweldest mayden pure
The creatour of euery creature

Assembled is in the magnifycence
With mercy/goodnesse/and with suche pyte
That thou arte the sonne of excellence
Not onely that helpest hem that prayen the
But often tyme of thy benignyte
Full frely/ or that men thyn helpe beseche
Thou goest beforne/ and arte her lyues leche

Now helpe thou blissful / & meke fayre mayde
Me flemed wretche/in this deserte of gall
Thinke on the woman of Canane / that sayd
That whelpes eaten some of ẏ crōmes small
That from her lordes table ben ifall
And though ẏ I vnworthy doughter of Eue
Be synful/yet accepteth my beleue

And for that fayth is deed withouten werkis
So for to werche/yeue me wytte and space
That I be quyt from ẏ place ẏ most derke is
O thou that arte so fayre and ful of grace
Be myn aduocate in that hye place
There as without ende is songe Osanna
Thou Christes mother/ & doughter of Anna

And of thy light/my soule in prison lyght
That troubled is by the contagyon
Of my body/ and also by the wyght
Of erthly luste/and also false affection
O hauen/ O refute/ O saluacion
Of hem that ben in sorowe and distresse
Nowe helpe/for to my werke I wol me dresse

¶ yet I pray you that reden that I write
Foryeueth me/that I do no dyligence
This ilke storie subtelly to endyte
For bothe haue I the wordes & the sentence
Of him that at the payntes reuerence
The storie wrote/and folowen her legende
And pray you that ye wol my werke amende

¶ First wol I you the name of seynt Cecily
Expowne/as men may in her storie se
It is to saye in englisshe/heuens lylly
For pure chastnesse of virgynite
Or for she wytnesse had of honeste
And grene of conscience/and of good fame
The sote sauoure lylye was her name

Or Cecily is to say/ the way to blynde
For she ensample was by good techyng
Or els Cecily/as I written fynde
Is ioyned by a maner conioynyng
Of heuen and Lya/ in her fyguring
The heuen is set for thought of holynesse
And lya/for her lastyng besynesse

Cecily may eke be sayd in this manere
Wantyng of blyndnesse/for her great lyght
Of sapience/ and for her thewes clere
Or els Lo/ this maydens name bright
Of heuen & Leos cometh/ of whiche by right
Men might the heuen of people her call
Ensample of good and wyse werkes all

For Leos people/ in Englisshe is to say
And right as men may in the heuen se

The

The Second Nun's Prologue (G 24–107 ; T. 15492–15575)

The sonne/and moone/& sterres euery way
Right so men gostly/in this mayden fre
Sawen of faythe/the great magnanymite
And eke the clerenesse hole of sapience
And sondrie werkes/bright of excellence

And right so as these philosophers write
That heuen is swyfte/rounde/& eke brennyng
Right so was fayre Cecily the whyte
Ful swyfte and besy in euery good workyng
And rounde and hole in good perseueryng
And brennyng euer in charyte ful bright
Nowe haue I declared you what she hyght.

¶ Here endeth the seconde nonnes pro-
logue/and begynneth her tale.

This mayde bright Cecile/as her lyfe sayth
Was comen of Romayns/& of noble kynde
And so forthe fostred vp in the fayth
Of Christ/& bare his gospel in her mynde
She neuer cessed/as I written fynde
Of her prayere/and god to loue and drede
Besechyng him to kepe her maydenhede

And whan this mayde shulde vnto a man
I wedded be/that was ful yonge of age
Whiche that ycleped was Valeryan
And daye was come of her maryage
She ful deuoute and humble in her corage
Vnder her robe of golde/ỹ sate ful fayre
Had next her fleshe yclad her in an heyre

And whyles that the organs made melodye
To god alone thus in herte songe she
O lorde/my soule and eke my body gye
Vnwemmed/lest I confounded be
And for his loue that dyed vpon a tre
Euery seconde or thirde day she faste
Aye byddyng in her orisons ful faste.

¶ The night came/& to bedde must she gone
With her husbonde/as often is the manere
And priuely she sayd vnto him anon
O swete and wel byloued spouse dere
There is a counsayle/and ye wol it here
Whiche that right fayne I wold to you sayne
So that ye me ensure/it not to bewrayne.

¶ Valeryan gan faste vnto her swere
That for no case/ne thyng that myght be
He shulde neuer to none bewrayen here
And than at erste/thus to him sayd she
I haue

The Second Nun's Prologue and Tale (G 108–151 ; T. 15576–15619)

The seconde nonnes tale.

I haue an angell/ whiche that loueth me
That wt gret loue/ where so I wake or slepe
Is redy aye/ my body for to kepe

And if that he may felen out of drede
That ye me touche or loue in vylonye
He right anon wyl slee you with the dede
And in your youthe thus shall ye dye
And if that ye in clene loue me gye
He wol you loue as me/ for your clennesse
And shewe you of his ioye and brightnesse.

¶ This Valeryan/ corrected as god wolde
Answerde ayen/ if I shal trust the
Let me that aungell se/ and him beholde
And if that it a very aungell be
Than wol I done as thou haste prayde me
And if thou loue another man forsothe
Right wt this sworde thā wol I sle you bothe

¶ Cecyle answerde anon in this wyse
If that ye luste/ that angell shul ye se
So that ye trowe on Christ and you baptyse
Gothe forthe to Via apia (qd she)
That from this town ne stant but myles thre
And to the poore folke that there dwell
Say hem right thus/ as I shal you tell

Tell hem that I Cecyle/ you to hem sende
To shewen you the good Urban the olde
For secret nedes/ and for good entent
And whan that ye saynte Urban han beholde
Tell him the wordes/ that I to you tolde
And whan that he hath purged you fro synne
Than shal ye se that aungel er ye twynne.

¶ Valeryan is to that place ygon
And right as him was taught by his lernyng
He founde this holy Urban anon
Amonge these sayntes buryals loutyng
And he anon/ without taryeng
Dyd his message/ and whan he had it tolde
Urban for ioy/ gan his hondes vp holde

The teres from his eyen let he fall
Almighty god/ O Iesu christ (qd he)
Sower of chaste counsayle/ hierde of vs all
The frute of thilke sede of chastyte
That thou haste sowe in Cecile/ take to the
Lo lyke a besy bee/ withouten gyle
The serueth aye thyn owne thrall Cecile

For thilke spouse/ that she toke but newe
Ful lyke a fierse lyon/ she sendeth here
As meke as any lambe was to ewe
And with that worde/ anon there gan apere
An olde man/ cladde in whyte clothes clere
That had a boke with letters of golde in hōde
And gan byforne Valeryan for to stonde.

¶ Valeryan as deed fel downe for drede
Whan he this olde man sawe standyng so
Whiche forth with anon he herde him rede
O lorde/ O faythe/ O god withouten mo
Of christendom/ and father of al also
Abouen al/ and ouer al euery where
These wordes al with golde written were

Whan this was radde/ thā sayd this olde man
Leuest thou this thyng or none/ say ye or nay
I leue al this thyng (qd Valeryan)
Vnder the heuen no wight ne thynke may
Sother thyng than this/ I dare wel say
Tho vanysshed the olde man/ he nyst where
And pope Urban him christened right there.

¶ Valeryan gothe home/ & fyndeth Cecilye
Within his chambre/ with an aungel stonde
This aungel had of rose and of lyllye
Crownes two/ the whiche he bare in honde
And first to Cecyle/ as I vnderstonde
He yaue that one/ and after gan he take
That other to Valeryan her make

With body clene/ & with vnwemmed thought
Kepeth aye wel these crownes (qd he)
From paradyse to you I haue hem brought
Ne neuer more shullen they rotten be
Ne lese her swete sauour/ trusteth me
Ne neuer wight shal sene hem with eye
But he be chaste/ and hate vilonye

And thou Valeryan/ for thou so sone
Assenteddest to good counsayle also
Say what yu lyst/ & thou shalt haue thy bone
I haue a brother (qd Valeryan tho)

That

The Second Nun's Tale (G 152–235; T. 15620–15703)

That in this worlde I loue no man so
I pray you that my brother may haue grace
To knowe the trouthe/as I do in this place.

The angel answerd/god lyketh your request
And bothe with the palme of martirdome
Shal ye come vnto the blissful feest
And with yͤ worde Tyburce his brother come
And whan that he the sauoure vndernome
Whiche that the roses and the lylyes caste
Within his herte he gan to wonder faste

And sayd: I wonder this tyme of the yere
Whence that this sote sauoure cometh so
Of roses and lylies/that I smell here
For though I had hem in myn hondes two
The sauour myght in me no deper go
The swete smel/ that in myn herte I fynde
Hath chaunged me al in another kynde.

¶ Valeryan sayd/two crownes haue we
Snowe whyte ꝛ rose reed/that shyneth clere
Whiche that thyn eyen han no might to se
And as thou smellest hem thrugh my prayere
So shalt thou seen hem my leue brother dere
If it so be that thou wylte without slouthe
Byleue a right/and knowe the very trouthe

¶ Tyburce answerde/ sayest thou this to me
In sothnesse/ or in dreme herken I this ?
In dremes (qd Valeryan) han we be
Vnto this tyme/brother myn iwys
But nowe at erst/ our dwellyng in trouth is
How wost thou (qd Tyburce) ꝛ in what wise
Quod Valeryan/that I shal the deuyse.

The angel of god hath me yͤ trouth itaught
Whiche thou shalt seen/ꝛ thou wylte reney
The ydols/ and be clene/and els naught
And of the myracles of these crownes twey
Saynt Ambrose in his preface luste to sey
Solempnly this noble doctour dere
Cōmendeth it/and sayth in this manere.

¶ The palme of martirdom for to receyue
Seynt Cecyle/fulfylled of goddes yefte
The worlde ꝛ eke her chambre gan she weyue
Witnesse Tyburce/and Cecyles shrifte
To whiche god of his bounte wolde shyfte
Crownes two/of floures wel smellyng
And made the angel hem tho crownes bring

The mayde hath brought hem to blisse aboue
The world hath wist what it is worth certayn
Deuocion and chastyte wel for to loue
Tho shewed him Cecile al open and playne
That al ydolles ben but thynges in vayne
For they ben dombe/ꝛ therto they ben defe
And charged him his ydoles for to lefe

Who that troweth not this/a beest he is
(Qd this Tyburce) if that I shal not lye
She kyssed his brest whan she herde this
And was ful glad he couthe trouth espye
This day take I the for myn allye
Sayd this blissful mayden fayre and dere
For after that she sayd as ye may here.

¶ Lo right so as the loue of Christ (qd she)
Made me thy brothers wyfe/right in yͤ wyse
Anon for myn alye here take I the
Sythens that thou wolte thyn ydoles dispyse
Go with thy brother nowe/ꝛ the baptyse
And make the clene/so yͭ thou mayst beholde
The angels face/of whiche thy brother tolde.

Tiburce answerde/and said: brother dere
First tel me whyther I shal/ꝛ to what man
To whom he sayd/come forth wͭ good chere
I wol the lede vnto the pope Vrban
To Vrban brother myn Valeryan
(Qd this Tiburce) wylt thou me thyder lede ?
Me thynketh that it were a wonder dede

Ne menest thou not Vrban (qd he tho)
That is so ofte dampned to be deed
And wonneth in halkes to and fro
And dare not ones put forthe his heed
Men shulde him brenne in a fyre so reed
If he were foūde/and men might him spye
And we also/that bere him companye

And whyles we seken thilke diuinite
That is yhidde in heuen priuely
Algate ybrent in this worlde shulde we be
To whom Cecile answerde boldely

O.   Men

The seconde nonnes tale.

Men might drede wel and skylfully
This lyfe to lese/ myn owne dere brother
If this were lyuing only and non other

But there is better lyuyng in other place
That neuer shal be loste/ ne drede the nought
Which goddes sone vs told through his grace
That fathers sonne hath al thing wrought
And al y wrought is with a skylful thought
The goste that from the father gan procede
Hath souled hym without any drede

By worde and by myracle/ so goddes sonne
Whan he was in this worlde/declared here
That there is other lyfe there men may wone
To whom answerde Tiburce: O suster dere
Ne saydest thou right nowe in this manere
There nas but one god lorde in sothfastnesse
And now of thre how may thou bere witnesse

¶ That shal I tel (qd she) or that I go
Right as a man hath sapyences thre
Memoyre/engyne/and intellecte also
So in suche beyng of diuinite
Thre persons may there right wel be
Tho gan she there ful besily him preche
Of Christes sonne/and of his paynes teche

And many poyntes of his passyon
How goddes sone i this world was withholde
To do mankynde playne remissyon
That was bounde in synnes & cares colde
Al these thynges she vnto Tiburce tolde
And after this Tiburce in good entent
With Valeryan to pope Vrban went

That thonked god/& with glad hert & lyght
He christned him/ and made him in that place
Perfyte in his lernyng goddes knyght
And after this Tiburce gate suche grace
That euery day he sawe in tyme and space
The aungel of god/and euery maner boone
That he god asked/ it was sped ful soone

¶ It were ful harde by order for to sayne
Howe many wonders Jesu for him wrought
But at the laste/ to tel shorte and playne
The sergeaũt of the towne hem sought

And hem byfore Almache the preuost brought
Whiche hem aposed/ & knewe al her entent
And to the ymage of Jupiter hem sente

And sayd/ who so wol do no sacrifyce
Swappe of his heed/ this is my sentence here
Anon these martyrs/that I you deuyse
One Maximus that was an officere
Of the prefectes/ and his councelere
Hem hent/ & whan he forth the sayntes ladde
Him selfe he wept for pyte that he had

Whan Maximus had herde this sayntes lore
He gate hem of the turmentours leue
And had hem to his house withouten more
And with her preching/er that it were eue
They gonne from the turmentour reue
And from Maximus/ & from his folke echon
The false faythe/ to trowen in god alone

¶ Cecile came/ whan it was woxen nyght
With preestes/that hem christened al in fere
And afterward/whan day was woxen light
Cecile hem sayd with a sober chere
Nowe Christes owne knightes leue & dere
Casteth al away the werkes of derknesse
And armeth you in armoure of brightnesse

Ye han for sothe ydone a great batayle
Your cours is don/your fayth hath you cõser=(ued
Gothe to the crowne of lyfe y may not fayle
The rightful iuge/whiche ye han serued
Shal yeue it you as ye it deserued
And whan this thing was sayd / as I deuyse
Men ladde hem forth to done the sacrifyse

But whan they were vnto the place ibrought
To tel shortly the conclusyoun
They nolde ensence ne sacrifyce right nought
But on her knees/they saten hem adoun
With humble herte and sadde deuocioun
And losten bothe her heedes in the place
Her soules went to the kyng of grace.

¶ This Maximus/ y sawe this thing betyde
With pytouse teres tolde it anon right
That he her soules sawe to heuen glyde
With aungels ful of clerenesse and of lyght
And

And with his worde cōuerted many a wyght
For whiche Almachius dyd him so to bete
With whyppes of leede/tyl he his life gan lete

Cecile him toke/and buryed him anone
By Tyburce and Valeryan sothly
Within her buryeng place vnder a stone
And after this Almachius hastely
Bad his mynisters fetchen openly
Cecily/ so that she might in his presence
Do sacrifyce/and Iuppyter encence

But they conuerted at her wyse lore
Wepten ful sore/and yaue ful credence
Vnto her worde/ and cryden more and more
Christ goddes sonne/without difference
Is very god/this is all our sentence
That hath a seruaunt so good him to serue
Thus wt o voice we trowe though we sterue

¶ Almachius/that herde al this doyng
Bad fetche Cecily/ that he might her se
And alderfirst this was his askyng
What maner woman arte thou (qd he:)
I am a gentylwoman borne (quod she)
I aske of the (quod he) though it the greue
Of thy relygion and of thy byleue:

¶ Ye haue bygon your question folishly
(Qd she) that wolde two answers conclude
In one demaunde/ye asken leudly
Almachius answerde to that symilitude
Of whence cōmeth thyn answere so rude
Of whēce (qd she) whan yt she was frayned
Of conscience/ and of good fayth vnfayned.

¶ Almachius sayd/ ne takest thou none hede
Of my power: and she him answerde thys
Your myght (qd she) ful lytell is to drede
For euery mortal mannes power nys
But lyke a bladder full of wynde iwys
For with a nedels poynte / whan it is yblowe
May al the boste of it be layde ful lowe

Ful wrongfully beganste thou (qd he)
And yet in wronge is thy perceueraunce
Woste thou not howe our mighty princes fre
Haue thus cōmaunded & made ordynaunce:
That euery christen wight shal haue penaūce
But if that he his cristendome withsey
And gon al quite/if he wol it reney.

¶ Your princes erren/as your nobles dothe
Quod tho Cecile/in a wode sentence
Ye make vs gilty/and it is not sothe
For ye that knowen wel our innocence
For as moche as we done a reuerence
To Christe/and for we bere a cristen name
Ye put on vs a cryme and eke a blame

But we that knowen thilke name so
For vertuous/we may it not withsey.
Almachius answerd/ chese one of these two
Do sacrifyce/or christendom reney
That thou mowe scapen by that wey
At whiche worde the holy blisful mayde
Gan for to laught/& to the iuge she sayde.

¶ O iugge confused in thy nycete
Wolte thou that I reneye innocence
To make me a wycked wight (qd she)
Lo he dissymuleth here in audience
He stareth and wodeth in his aduertence
To whom Almachius sayd: O sely wretche
Thou wost not how far my my3t may stretch

Hath not our mighty princes yeuen
To me/bothe power and eke auctorite
To make folke to dyen or to lyuen:
Why spekest thou so proudly than to me:
I ne speke it not but stedfastly (qd she)
Not proudly/for I say as for my syde
I hate deedly thilke vyce of pride

And if thou drede not a sothe for to here
Than wol I shewen al openly by right
That thou haste made a ful great lesyng here
Thou sayste thy princes han yeue the might
Bothe to slee and eke to quicke a wight
Thou ne mayest but only lyfe byreue
Thou haste non other power ne leue

But thou mayst say/ thy prīces han ye maked
Mynistre of dethe/ for if thou speke of mo
Thou lyest/for thy power is ful naked
Do way thy boldnesse/sayd Almachius tho

O.ii. And

And do sacrifyce to our goddes er thou go
I recke not what wronge thou me proffer
For I can suffre/as can a philosopher

But thilke wronges may I not endure
That thou spekest of our goddes here (qd he)
Cecile answerde/ O nyce creature
Thou saydest no worde sythens yu spakest to
That I ne knewe therwith thy nycete (me
And that thou were in euery maner wyse
A leude officer/and a vayne iustyce

The lacketh nothyng to thyn vtter eyen
That thou nart blynd/ for thing y we seen al
That is a stone/that men wel may asppen
That ilke stone/a god thou wolte it call
I rede the let thyn honde vpon it fall
And taste it wel/& stone thou shalte it fynde
Sens that thou seest not wt thyn eyen blynde

It is a shame that the people shall
So scorne the/and laugh at thy folye
For comenly men wotte it wel ouer all
That mighty god is in his heuens hye
And these ymages/wel mayste thou aspye
To the ne to hem selfe may they not profyte
For in her effecte/they be not worthe a myte

¶ Thus and suche other wordes sayd she
And he woxe wrothe/& bad she shulde be lede
Home to her house/and in her house (qd he)
Brenne her in a bathe/with flames rede
And as he bade/ right so was done the dede
For in a bathe they gan her faste shetten
And night & day great fyre vnder they beten

Al the longe night/and eke the day also
For al the fyre/and eke the bathes hete
She sate al colde/and felte of it no wo
It made her not a droppe for to swete
But in that bathe her lyfe she mote lete
For Almachie/with a ful wicked entent
To sleen her in the bathe/ his sonde sente

Thre strokes in the necke he smote her tho
The turmentour/but for namaner chaunce
He might not smyte al her necke a two
And for there was that tyme an ordynaunce
That no mā shuld do no person such penaunce
The fourth stroke to smyte/softe or sore
This turmentour durste smyte no more

But halfe deed/with her necke ycoruen there
He lefte her lye/ and on his way he went
The christen folke that aboute her were
With shetes home ful fayre her hente
Thre dayes lyued she in this turmente
And neuer cesed she the faythe to teche
That she had fostred hem/she gan to preche

And hem she yaue her mouables & her thyng
And to the pope Urban betoke hem tho
And sayd/ I asked this of the heuen kyng
To haue respyte thre dayes and no mo
To recōmaunde to you/er that I go
These soules/and that I might so werche
Here of myn house perpetuellyche a cherche

Saynt Urban/with his dekens priuely
The body fette/and buryed it by night
Amonge his other ayntes honestly
Her house the churche of saynt Cecile hyght
Saynte Urban halowed it/as he wel might
In whiche vnto this day/in noble wyse
Men don to Christ & to his payntes seruyce.

¶ Here endeth the seconde nonnes tale/ and here begynneth the prologue of the chanons yoman.

W Han ended was the lyfe of saynt Cecyle
Er we fully had ryden fyue myle
At Boughton vnder the blee/vs gan a take
A man/that clothed was in clothes blake
And vnder that he had a whyte surplyse
His hakeney/that was al pomely gryse
So swette/that it wonder was to se
It semed that he had pricked myles thre
The horse eke that his yoman rode vpon
So swette/that vnneth might he gon
Aboute the paytrell stode the fome ful hye
He was of fome as flecked as a pye
A male twy folde on his croper lay
It semed that he carped lytel aray
Al lyght for sōmer rode this worthy man
And in my herte wondren I began
What that he was/ tyll I vnderstode

Howe

What that he was/ tyll that I understode
Howe that his cloke was sewed to his hode
For which/ whan I had longe auysed me
I demyd him some chanon for to be
His hatte hynge at his backe by a lace
For he had rydden more than trot or pace
He rode aye prikyng as he were wode
A clote lefe he had layde under his hode
For swette/ and for to kepe his heed fro hete
But it was ioye for to se him swete
His forheed dropped/as a styllatorie
Were ful of plantayne or of peritorie
And whan he was come/he gan crye
God saue (quod he) this ioly companye
Faste haue I pricked (qd he) for your sake
Bycause that I wolde you ouertake
To ryden in this mery company.
¶ His yoman was eke ful of curtesye
And sayd syrs/nowe in the morowe tyde
Out of your hostery I sawe you ryde
And warned here my lorde and souerayne
Whiche that to ryden with you is ful fayne
For his disporte/he loueth dalyaunce.
Frende for thy warnīg god yeue ȳ good chāce
Than sayd our host/ certayne it wolde seme
Thy lorde were wyse/& so I may wel deme
He is ful ioconde also dare I say
Can he ought tell a mery tale or tway
With whiche he glade may this companye.
¶ Who sir my lorde? ye without lye
He can of myrthe and eke of iolyte
Not but ynough also sir trusteth me
And ye him knewe also wel as do I
Ye wolde wonder howe wel and thriftely
He couthe werke/and that in sondrie wyse
He hath taken on him many a great emprise
Whiche were ful harde/for any that is here
To bring aboute/but they of him it lere
As homely as he rydeth amonge you
If ye him knewe/it wold ben for your prowe
Ye nolde not forgon his aquayntaunce
For mochel good I dare say in balaunce
Al that I haue in my possession
He is a man of hye discression
I warne you wel he is a passing wyse man.
¶ Wel (qd our hoste) I pray the tel me than
Is he a clerke or non? tel what he is.
¶ A clerke/nay he is greter thā a clerke iwys
Sayd the yoman/and in wordes fewe
Hoste of his crafte somwhat wol I shewe
I say my lorde can suche a subtelte
But al his crafte ye may not wete of me
And somwhat helpe I yet to his worchyng
That al the grounde that we be on rydyng
Tyl we come to Caunterbury towne
He coulde all clene turne up and downe
And paue it al of syluer and of golde.
¶ And whan this yoman had thus ytolde
Unto our hoste: he sayd benedicite
This thyng is wonder meruaylous to me
Sens that thy lorde is of so hye prudence
(Bicause of which/men shulde him reuerēce)
That of his worshyp recketh he so lyte
His ouerest sloppe is not worthe a myte
As in effecte to him/so mote I go
It is al baudy and to tore also
Why is thy lorde so slotlyche I the pray
And is of power better clothes to bey?
If that his dede acorde with thy speche
Tel me that/and that I the beseche.
¶ Why (qd this yeman) wherto aske ye me?
God helpe me so/for he shal neuer ythe
But I wol not auowe that I saye
And therfore kepe it secret I you praye
He is to wyse in fay/as I beleue
That is ouerdone nyl not preue
And right as clerkes sayne/ it is a vyce
Wherfore I holde him in that/lewde & nyce
For whan a man hath ouer great a wytte
Ful ofte it happeth him to misusen it
So dothe my lorde/and that me greueth sore
God amende it/I can say you no more.
¶ Therof no force good yeman (qd our host)
Sens of the connyng of thy lorde thou wost
Tel howe he dothe/I pray the hertely
Sens that he is so crafty and so sly
Where dwellen ye/if it to tell be?
¶ In the subbarbes of a towne (qd he)
Lurkyng in hernes and in lanes blynde
Where these robbers/and theues by kynde
Holden her priuy fearful resydence
As they that dare not shewen her presence
So fare we/if that I shal say the sothe.
¶ Yet (qd our hoste) let me talke tothe
Why arte thou so discoloured in thy face?
¶ Peter (qd he) god yeue it harde grace

O.iii. I am

The Canon's Yeoman's Prologue (G 570–665; T. 16038–16133)

The prologue of the chanons yeman:

I am so vsed in the hotte fyre to blowe
That it hath chaunged my colour as I trowe
I am not wonte in no myrrour to prie
But swynke sore/ and lerne to multiplye
We blondren euer/ and pooren in the fyre
And for al that/ we faylen of our desyre
For euer we lacken our conclusyon
To moche folke we do illusyon
And borowe golde/ be it a pounde or two
Or ten or twelue/ or many sommes mo
And make hem wene at the leste way
That of a pounde we coulde make tway
yet is it false/ and aye han we good hope
It for to done/ and after it we grope
But that science is so ferre vs byforne
We mowe not/ al though we had it sworne
It ouertake/ it slytte away so faste
It wol vs make beggers at the laste.
¶ Whiles this yeman was thus i his talkyng
This chanon drewe him nere/ & herde al thing
Whiche this yeman spake/ for suspection
Of mennes speche euer had this chanon
For Cato sayth/ he that giltye is
Demeth al thyng be spoke of him iwys
Bycause of that/ he gan so nyghe to drawe
To his yeman/ to herken al his sawe
And thus he sayd vnto his yeman tho
Holde nowe thy peace/ & speke no wordes mo
For if thou do/ thou shalte it sore abye
Thou slaundrest me here in this companye
And eke discouerest that thou shuldest hyde.
¶ ye (qd our host) tel on what so euer betyde
Of al his thretyng/ recke the not a myte.
¶ In fayth (qd he) no more do I but lyte
And whan this chanon sawe it wolde not be
But his yeman wolde tel his priuyte
He fledde away for very sorowe and shame.
¶ A (qd the yeman) here shal ryse a game
Al that I can/ anon wol I you tell
Sens he is gon/ the foule fende him quell
For neuer here after wol I with him mete
For peny ne for pounde/ I you behete
He that me brought first vnto that game
Er that he dye/ sorowe haue he and shame
For it is ernest to me by my faythe
That fele I wel/ what so any man saythe
And yet for al my smerte and al my grefe
For al my sorowe/ laboure and mischefe
I couthe neuer leaue it in no wyse
Nowe wolde god my wytte might suffyse
To tellen al that longeth to that arte
But nathelesse/ yet wol I tell you a parte
Sens that my lorde is gon/ I wol not spare
Suche thyng as I knowe I wol declare.

¶ Here endeth the prologue of the chanons yoman/ and here foloweth his tale.

K iij

The Canon's Yeoman's Prologue (G 666–719; T. 16134–16187)

WIth this chanon I dwelte seuen yere
And of his science am I neuer the nere
Al that I had/I haue loste therby
And god wotte/so hath many mo than I
There I was wonte to be right fresshe & gay
Of clothyng/and eke of other good aray
Nowe may I weare an hose vpon myn heed
And wher my coloure was both fresshe & reed
Nowe it is wanne/and of a leeden hewe
Who so it vseth/sore shal him rewe
And of my swynke/yet blered is myn eye
Lo whiche auauntage it is to multiplye
That slyding science hath me made so bare
That I haue no good/where that euer I fare
And yet I am endetted so therby
Of golde/that I haue borowed trewly
That whyle I lyue/I shal it quyte neuer
Let euery man beware by me euer
What maner man that casteth him therto
If he contynue/I holde his thrifte ydo
So helpe me god/therby shal he neuer wyn
But empte his purse/& make his wyttes thyn
And whan he/thorowe his madnesse & folye
Hath loste his owne good/through ieopardye
Than he exciteth other men therto
To lese her good/as him selfe hath do
For vnto shrewes/ioye it is and ese
To haue her felawes in payne and disese
For thus was I ones lerned of a clerke
Of that no charge/I wol speke of our werke
¶ Whan we be there/ as we shal exercyse
Our eluisshe crafte/we semen wonder wyse
Our termes ben so clergiall and so quaynte
I blowe the fyre/tyl myn herte faynte.
¶ What shulde I tel eche proporcion
Of thynges/ whiche we werchen vpon:
As on fyue or syxe vnces/ may wel be
Of syluer/or of some other quantyte
And besye me to tellen you the names
Of orpyment/brent bones/yron squames
That into poudre grounden ben ful small
And in an erthen potte/howe put is all
And salte yput in/and also papere
Byfore these poudres that I speke of here
And wel ycouered/with a lampe of glas
And of moche other thing that there was
And of the pottes and glas engluting
That of the ayre might passe out no thing
And of the esy fyre and smerte also
Whiche that was made/and of the care & wo
That we had in our maters sublimyng
And in amalgamyng/and calsenyng
Of quicksyluer/icleped Mercurye crude
For al our sleyght/we conne not conclude
Our orpyment/ and sublimed Mercury
Our grounde lytarge eke on the porphirye
Of eche of these/ vnces a certayne
Not helpeth vs/ our laboure is in vayne
Ne eke our spyrites assencioun
Ne yet our maters/ that lyen al fyxe adoun
Mowe in our werkyng nothing auayle
For loste is al our laboure & our trauayle
And al the coste/a twenty dyuel way
Is loste also/ whiche we vpon it lay.
¶ There is also ful many a nother thyng
That is to our crafte apertaynyng
Though I by ordre hem ne reherce can
Bycause that I am a leude man
Yet wol I tellen hem/ as they come to mynde
Though I ne can sette hem in her kynde
As bole armonyake/verdegrece/boras
And sondrie vessels made of erthe and glas
Our vrinals/ and our discensories
Vyols/ crosselettes/and sublimatories
Concurbytes/and alembykes eke
And other suche/dere ynough a leke
It nedeth not to reherce hem all
Waters rubyfyeng/and boles gall
Arsneke/ sal armonyake/and brimstone
And herbes coulde I tel eke many one
As Egrimonye/valeryan/ and lunarye
And other suche/if that me lyste to tarye
Our lampes brennyng bothe night and day
To bringen about our crafte/if that we may
Our fournyce eke of calcinacion
And of waters albifycacion
Vnslecked lyme/chalke/and gleyre of an eye
Poudres dyuers/asshes/donge/pysse/& cley
Sered pokettes/salt peter/and vitriole
And dyuers fyres/made of wodde and cole
Sal tartre/alcaly/and sal preparate
And combust maters/ and coagulate
Cley made wt horse dōge/ mans heere/& oyle
Of tartre alym/glas/berme/worte/& argoile
Resalgor/and other maters enbybyng
And eke of our maters encorporing

And

The tale of the chanons yoman.

And of our syluer citrynacion
Our sementyng/ and eke fermentacion
Our Ingottes testes / and many mo
I wol you tel as was me taught also
The foure spyrites/and the bodyes seuen
By order/as ofte I herde my lorde nemene.
¶ The first spyrite quicke syluer cleped is
The seconde orpyment/the thirde iwys
Sal armonyake/ the fourthe brimstone
¶ The bodyes seuen eke/so here hem anone
Soll golde is/and Luna syluer we threpe
Mars yron/Mercurye quicksyluer we clepe
Saturnus lede/and Jupiter is tynne
And Venus coper/by my father kynne.
¶ This cursed crafte/who so wol exercyse
He shal no good haue that may him suffyse
For al the good he spendeth theraboute
He lese shal/ therof haue I no doute
Who so that lysten to vtter his folye
Let him come forthe & lerne to multiplye
And euery man that hath aught in his cofer.
Let him apere/and wexe a philosopher
Askaunce that crafte is so light for to lere
Nay nay god wot/al be he monke or frere
Preest or chanon/or any other wight
Though he sytte at his boke both day & night
In lernyng of this eluysshe nyce lore
Al is in vayne/and parde moche more
Is to lere a leude man this subtelte
Fye speke not therof/it wol not be
Al coulde he letterure/or coulde he none
As in effecte/he shal fynde it al one
For bothe two/by my saluacion
Concluden in multiplycacion
Ilyche wel/ whan they haue al ydo
This is to sayne/they faylen bothe two.
¶ yet forgate I moche rehersayle
Of waters corosyfe/and of lymayle
And of bodyes mollifycacion
And also of her induracion
Oyles/ablucions/ metall fusyble
To tellen you al/ wolde passe any byble
That o where is/wherfore as for the beste
Of al these names nowe wol I reste
For as I trowe/ I haue you tolde ynowe
To reyse a fende/al loke he neuer so rowe.
¶ A nay let be the phylosophers stone
Alixer cleped / we seken faste echeone
For had we him/ than were we syker ynowe
But vnto god of heuen I make auowe
For al our crafte/whan that we han al ydo
And al our sleyght/ he wol not come vs to
He hath made vs spende moche goode
For sorow of which/ almost we waxen wode
But that good hope crepeth in our herte
Supposyng euer/ though we sore smerte
To ben releued by him afterwarde
Supposyng and hope is sharpe and harde
I warne you wel it is to syken euer
That future temps hath made men disceuer
In trust therof/al that euer they had
yet of that arte/they coulde not waxe sad
For vnto him it is a bytter swete
So semeth it/for ne had they but a shete
Whiche yͭ they might wrappen hem in anight
And a bratte to walken in a day lyght
They wolden hem sel/& spēde it on this crafte
They conne not stynte/tyl no thyng be lafte
And euer more/ where that euer they gon
Men may hem ken by smell of brimstone
For al the worlde they stynken as a gote
Her sauour is so rammysshe and so hote
That though a man a myle from hem be
The sauour wol enfecte him trusteth me
Lo/ thus by smellyng/ & by threde bare aray
If that men lyst/this folke knowe they may
And if a man wol aske hem priuely
Why they be clothed so vnthriftely
Right anon they wol rowne in his ere
And sayne/if that they aspyed were
Men wolde hem slee/bycause of her science
Lo thus these folke bytrapen innocence
Passe ouer this/I go my tale vnto.
¶ Er that the potte be on the fyre ydo
Of metalles/with a certayne quantyte
My lorde hem tempreth/& no man but he
Nowe he is gon/I dare say boldely
For as men sayne/ he can done craftely
Algate I wotte wel he hath suche a name
And yet ful ofte he renneth in the blame
And wotte ye howe/ ful ofte it happeth so
The potte tobreketh/and farwel al is go
These metalles ben of so great violence
Our walles may not make hem resystence
But if they were wrought of lyme and stone
They percen so/& through the wall they gone
And some of hem synken in to the grounde
Thus haue we loste by tymes many a pounde

The Canon's Yeoman's Tale (G 816–913; T. 16284–16381)

And some are scatered all the floore aboute
Some lepen into the rofe withouten doute
Tho ŷ the fende not in our syght him shewe
I trowe that he with vs be/that ilke shrewe
In hell where that he is lorde and syre
Ne is there no more wo/ne angre ne yre
Whan that our potte is broke/as I haue sayd
Euery man chyte/& holte him yuel apayde
Some sayd it was longe of the fyre makyng
Some sayd nay/it was on the blowyng
Than was I ferde/for that was myn offyce
¶Strawe (qd the thirde) ye ben leude & nyce
It was not tempred as it ought to be.
¶Nay(qd the fourthe)stynte & herken me
Bycause our fyre was not made of beche
That is the cause/and none other so theche
I can not tel wheron it is alonge
But wel I wotte great stryfe is vs amonge.
What(qd my lord)ther nys no more to done
Of these peryles I wol be ware efte sone
I am right syker/that the potte was crased
Be as be maye/be ye not amased
As vsage is/let swepe the floore as swythe
Plucke vp your herte/& be glad and blythe.
The mullocke on an heape yswepte was
And on the floore caste a canuas
And al this mullocke in a syue ythrowe
And systed and yplucked many a throwe.
¶Parde (qd one) somwhat of our metall
Yet is there here/thoughe we haue not all
And tho this thyng mishapped hath as nowe
Another tyme it may ben wel ynowe
We mote put our good in aueuture
A marchaunt parde/may not aye endure
Trusteth me wel in his prosperyte
Somtyme his good is drowned in the see
And somtyme it cometh safe vnto the londe
Peace(qd my lord)the next tyme I wol fonde
To bring our crafte al in an other plyte
And but I do syr/let me haue the wyte
There was defaute in somwhat wel I wote
¶An other sayd/the fyre was ouer hote
But be it hote or colde/I dare say this
That we concluden euer more amys
We faylen of that whiche we wolde haue
And in our madnesse euer more we raue
And whan we be togyther euerychon
Euery man semeth as wyse as Salomon
But al thing/whiche that shyneth as ŷ golde
Is not golde/as I haue herde tolde
Ne euery appell that is fayre at eye
Nys not good/what so men clappe or crye.
¶Right so it fareth amonge vs
He that semeth the wysest by Jesus
Is moste foole/whan it cometh to the prese
And he that semeth truest is a thefe
That shal ye know/er that I from you wede
By that I of my tale haue made an ende.
¶There was a chanon of relygyoun
Amonges vs/wolde enfecte al a toun
Though it as great were as Nynyue
Rome/Alysaundre/Troye/and other thre
His sleyght and his infynyte falsnesse
There couthe no man writen as I gesse
Though that he myght lyue a thousande yere
In al this worlde of falsnesse nys his pere
For in his termes he wol him so wynde
And speke his wordes in so slye a kynde
Whan he comen shal with any wight
That he wol make him dote anon right
But it a fende be as him selfe is
Ful many a man hath he begyled er this
And mo wol/if that he may lyue a whyle
And yet men ryden & gone ful many a myle
Him for to seke/and haue aquayntaunce
Not knowyng of his false gouernaunce
And if ye luste to gyue me audyence
I wol it tellen here in your presence.
¶But worshypful chanons relygyouse
Ne demeth not that I sclaunder your house
Al though my tale of a chanon be
Of euery ordre some shrewe is parde
And god forbyd that al a companye
Shulde rue a syngler mannes folye
To slaunder you is not myn entente
But to correcte that mysse is mente
This tale was not onely tolde for you
But eke for other mo/ ye wot wel howe
That amonge Chrystes apostels twelue
There was no traytour but Iudas him selue
Than why shulde the remenante haue blame
That gyltlesse were/by you I say the same
Saue onely this/if ye wol herken me
If any Iudas in your couent be
Remeueth him betyme/I you rede
If shame or losse may causen any drede
And

And be nothyng displesed I you pray
But in this case herkeneth what I say.

In London was a preest annuellere
That therin had dwelte many a yere
Whiche was so plesaunt and so seruysable
Unto the wife / where he was at table
That she wolde suffre him nothyng to paye
For borde ne clothyng / went he neuer so gay
And spendyng syluer had he right ynowe
Therof no force / I woll procede as nowe
And tell forthe my tale of the chanon
That brought this preest to confusyon.
¶ This false chanon came upon a daye
Unto this preestes chambre / where he laye
Besechyng him to lene him a certayn
Of golde / and he wolde quyte him ayen
Leneth me a marke (qd he) but dayes thre
And at my day I woll quyte it the
And if it so be / that thou fynde me false
Another daye hange me by the halse
This preest toke him a marke / & that swith
And this chanon him thanked ofte syth
And toke his leaue / and went forth his wey
And at thirde day brought his money
And to this preest he toke this golde ayen
Wherof this preest was gladde and fayn
¶ Certes (qd he) nothyng anoyeth me
To lene a man a noble / two or thre
Or what thyng were in my possessyon
Whan he so trewe is of condicion
That in no wise he breke wol his day
To suche a man I can neuer say nay.
What qd this chanon / shulde I be untrewe
Nay / that were thyng fallen of newe
Trouthe is a thyng that I woll euer kepe
Unto the day / in whiche I shal crepe
Into my graue / or els god forbede
Beleueth this as syker as your crede
God thanke I / and in good tyme be it sayde
That there nas neuer man yet yuel apayde
For golde ne syluer that he to me lent
Ne neuer falshede in myn herte I ment.
And sir (qd he) nowe of my priuete
Sens ye so goodlyche haue ben to me
And kythe to me so great gentilnesse
Somwhat to quyte with your kyndenesse
I wol you shewe / if ye wol it lere
(I shal it shewe to you anon right here)
Howe I can werche in philosophye
Taketh good hede / ye shal it se with your eye
That I wol done a maistrye or I go.
¶ Ye sir (qd the preest) and wol ye so
Marye therof I pray you hertely.
¶ At your comaundement sir truely
(Qd the chanon) and els god forbede
Lo howe this thefe couthe his seruyce bede
Ful sothe it is that suche profered seruyse
Stynketh / as wytnesseth the olde wyse
And that ful sone I wol it uerifye
In this chanon / rote of al trecherye
That euermore delyte hath and gladnesse
Suche fendely thoughtes in his hert empresse
How chrystes people he may to mischefe bring
God kepe us from his false dissymulyng.
¶ What wyst this preest wt whom y he delte
Ne of his harme comyng nothyng he felte
O sely preest / O sely innocente
With couetyse anon thou shalte be blente
O graceelesse / full blynde is thy concepte
Nothyng arte thou ware of his discepte
Whiche that this foxe hath shapen to the
His wylye wrenches thou mayste not fle
Wherfore to go to the conclusyon
That referreth to thy confusyon
Unhappy man / anon I wol me hye
To tell thyn unwytte ne thy folye
And eke the falsnesse of that other wretche
As ferforthe as my connyng wol stretche.
¶ This chanon was my lorde ye wolde wene
Syr host in faythe / and by the heuen quene
It was another chanon / and not he:
That can an hundred folde more subtelte
He hath betrayed folke many a tyme
Of his falsnesse it doleth me to ryme
Euer whan I speke of his falshede
For shame of him / my chekes wayen rede
Algates they begynnen for to glowe
For rednesse haue I non / right wel I knowe
In my uisage / for fumes dyuerce
Of metals / whiche ye haue herde me reherce
Consumed and wasted hath my rednesse
Nowe take hede of this chanons cursydnesse.
Syr (qd he) to the preest / let your man gon
For quicksyluer / that we it had anon
And let him bringe unces two or thre

And

And whan he cõmeth/ as faste shul ye se
A wonder thing/ whiche ye sawe neuer er this
  Sir (qd̄ the preest) it shal be done iwys
He badde his seruaunt fetch him this thyng
And he al redy was at his byddyng
And went him forth/ and came anon agayne
With this quicksyluer/ shortly for to sayne
And toke these vnses thre to the chanoun
And he hem layde wel and fayre adoun
And bade the seruaunt coles for to bring
That he anon might go to his werkyng.
¶ The coles right anon were yfet
And this chanon toke out a crosselet
Of his bosome/ and shewed it to the preest
This instrument (qd̄ he) whiche yͭ thou seest
Take in thy honde/ and put thy selfe therin
Of this quicksyluer an vnce and begyn
In the name of Christ to weye a philosopher
There be ful fewe/ whiche I wolde it profer
To shewe hem this moche of my science
For here shul ye se by experience
That this quicksyluer I wol mortifye
Right in your syght anon withouten lye
And make it as good syluer and as fyne
As there is any in your purse or myne
Or els where/ and make it malliable
And els holde me false and vnstable
Amonges folke euer to appere.
¶ I haue a poudre/ that coste me dere
Shal make al good/ for it is cause of all
My connyng/ whiche I you shewe shall
Voydeth your man/ and let him be therout
And shette the dore/ whyles we ben aboute
Our priuetie/ that no man vs espye
Whyles that we werken in our philosophye.
Al as he bade/ fulfylled was in dede
This ylke seruaunt anon out yede
And his maister shette the dore anon
And to her labour spedily they gon
  This preest at this cursed chanons byddyng
Vpon the fyre anon set this thyng
And blewe the fyre/ & besyed him ful faste
And this chanon into this croslet caste
A pouder/ I not wherof it was
ymade/ eyther of chalke/ erthe/ or glasse
Or somwhat els/ was not worthe a flye
To blynde with this preest/ & badde him hye
These coles for to couchen al aboue
The crosselet/ for in token that I the loue
(Quod this chanon) thyn hondes two
Shal werke al thyng that here shal be do.
  Graũt mercy (qd̄ the preest) & was ful glad
And couched coles/ as the chanon bad
And whyle he besy was/ this fendely wretche
This false chanon/ the foule fende him fetche
Out of his bosome toke a bechen cole
In whiche ful subtelly was made an hole
And therin was put of syluer lymayle
An vnce/ and stopped was without fayle
The hole with waxe/ to kepe the lymayle in
  And vnderstandeth that this false gyn
Was nat made there/ but it was made byfore
And other thinges that I shal you tel more
Herafter/ whiche that he with him brought
Er he came there/ to begyle him he thought
And so he dyd/ er they wente a twynne
Tyl he had turned him/ coulde he not blynne
It dulleth me/ whan that I of him speke
On his falshede/ fayne wolde I me wreke
If I wyste howe/ but he is here and there
He is so variaunt/ he bydeth no where.
¶ But taketh hede syrs nowe for goddes loue
He toke his cole/ of whiche I spake aboue
And in his honde he bare it priuely
And whyles the preest couched besily
The coles/ as I tolde you er this
This chanon sayd/ frende ye done amys
This is not couched as it ought to be
But sone I shal amende it (quod he)
Nowe let me medle therwith but a whyle
For of you haue I pyte by saynt Gyle
Ye ben right hotte/ I se wel howe ye swete
Haue here a clothe and wype away the wete
And whyle the preest him wyped hace
This chanon toke the cole/ I shrewe his face
And layde it abouen apon the mydwarde
Of the croslet/ and blewe wel afterwarde
Tyl that the coles gonne faste brenne.
¶ Nowe yeue vs drinke/ qd̄ this chanon then
As swythe al shal be wel I vndertake
Sytte we downe/ and let vs mery make
And whan this chanons bechen cole
Was brent al/ the lymayle out of the hole
Into the crosselet anon fell adoun
And so it muste nedes by resoun
Sens it so euen aboue couched was

But

But therof wyste the preest nothyng/ alas
He demed al the coles lyche goode
For of the sleyght/nothing he vnderstode.
And whan this alkamistre sawe his tyme
Ryseth vp sir preest (qd he) & stondeth by me
And for I wot wel yngot haue I none
Goth walketh forthe/ & bringe a chalke stone
For I wol make it of the same shappe
That an yngot is/if I may haue happe
And bring eke with you a bolle or a panne
Ful of water/and ye shal se thanne
Howe that our besynesse shal happe & preue
And yet for ye shal haue no misbyleue
Ne wronge concepte of me in your absence
I wol not ben out of your presence
But go with you/& come with you agayne
The chambre dore/ shortly to sayne
They opened and shette/& went forth her wey
And forthe with hem they caryed the key
And comen ayen withouten any delay
What shulde I tarye al the longe day
He toke the chalke/and shope it in the wyse
Of an yngot/as I shal you deuyse.
I saye he toke out of his owne sleue
A teyne of syluer/yuel mote he cheue
Whiche that was but an vnce of weyght
And taketh hede nowe of his cursed sleyght
He shope his yngot/in lenght and in brede
Of the teyne/withouten any drede
So slily that the preest it not aspyde
And in his sleue agayne he gan it hyde
And from the fyre toke vp his matere
And in to the yngot it put with mery chere
And into the water vessel he it caste
Whan that him lyst/ & bade the preest as faste
Loke what ther is/put in thyn honde & grope
Thou shalte fynde there syluer as I hope
What dyuel of hell shulde it els be
Shauynge of syluer/syluer is parde.
He put in his honde/and toke vp a teyne
Of syluer fyne/and glad in euery vayne
Was this preest/whan he sawe it was so
Goddes blessyng and his mothers also
And al hallowes/haue ye sir chanon
Sayd this preest/and I her malyson
But and ye vouchsafe to teche me
This noble craft and this subtelte
I wol be yours/in al that euer I may
Qd the Chanon/ yet woll I make assay
The seconde tyme/that ye mowe take hede
And ben expert of this/and in your nede
A nother day assay in myn absence
This disciplyne/ and this crafty science
Lette take another ounce (qd he) tho
Of quicke syluer/ withouten wordes mo
And don therwith/as I haue don er this
With that other/whiche that nowe syluer is.
¶ This preest him besyeth in all that he can
To don as this Chanon/this cursed man
Cõmaunded him/ and fast blewe the fyre
For to come to the effecte of his desyre
And this chanon/ right in the mean whyle
All redy was/this preest eft to begyle
And for a countynaunce in his honde bare
An holowe sticke/take kepe and beware
In thende of whiche an vnce and no more
Of syluer lymaile putte was all before
Was in his cole/ and stopped with weye wele
For to kepen in his lymaile euery dele
And whiles this preest was in his besynesse
This chanon with his sticke gan him dresse
To him anon/ and his pouder cast in
As he dyd erst/the deuyll out of his skyn
Him torne/I praye to god for his falshede
For he was euer false in thought and dede
And with his stycke/ aboue the crosselette
That was ordayned with that false iette
He styreth the coles/tyl al relent gan
The waxe agayne the fyre/as euery man
But he a fole be/ wot wel it mote nede
And al that in the hole was/out yede
And into the crosselet hastely it fell
The preest supposed nothyng but well
But besyed him faste/& was wonder fayne
Supposyng nought but trouth/ soth to sayn
He was so glad/that I can not expresse
In no manere his mirthe and his gladnesse
And to the chanon he profered efte sone
Body and good: ye(qd the chanon) anone
Tho I be poore/crafty thou shalt me fynde
I warne the yet is there more behynde
Is there any coper here within sayd he?
Ye sir(qd the preest) I trowe there be.
Els go bye some/and that aswythe?
Nowe good syr go forthe thy way & hythe.
¶ He went his way/& with the coper he came
And

The Canon's Yeoman's Tale (G 1201–1296 ; T. 16669–16764)

And this Chanon in his honde it name
And of that coper wayed out but an vnce
Al to symple is my tonge to pronounce
As to mynistre of my wytte the doublenesse
Of this chanon/rote of al cursydnesse
He semed frendly/to hem yͤ knew him nought
But he was fendly/bothe in werke & thought
It weryeth me to tel of his falsenesse
And nathelesse/ yet wol I it expresse
To the entent that men may beware therby
And for none other cause truely.
¶ He put this vnce of coper into the crosselet
And on the fyre as swythe he hath it sette
And cast in pouder/ & made the preest to blow
And in his workyng for to stoupe lowe
As he dyd erste/and al nas but a iape
Right as him lyste/ the preest he made his ape
And afterwarde in the yngot he it caste
And in the panne put it at the laste
Of water/and in he put his owne honde
And in his sleue/ as ye byforehonde
Herde me tel/ he had a syluer teyne
He slily toke it out/ this cursed heyne
Vnwetyng this preest of his false crafte
And in the pannes botome he hath it lafte
And in the water rombleth to and fro
And wonder priuely toke vp also
The coper teyne/not knowyng this preest
And hydde it/and hent him by the brest
And to him spake/& thus sayd in his game
Stoupeth adowne/by god ye be to blame
Helpeth me nowe/ as I dyd you whylere
Put in your honde/ and loketh what is there.
¶ This preest toke vp this syluer teyne anon
And than sayd the chanon/let vs gon
With these thre teynes/which we han wrought
To some goldsmyth/ and wete if it be ought
For by my faythe/I nolde for my hoode
But if it were syluer fyne and goode
And that as swythe proued shal be.
¶ Vnto the goldsmyth/with these teynes thre
They went/and put them in assaye
To fyre and hāmer/ might no man say nay
But they were as them ought for to be.
¶ This sotted preest/who was gladder thā he
Was neuer byrde gladder ayenst the day
Ne nightyngale/ayenst the seson of May
Was neuer none/that lyste better to synge
Ne lady lustier in carollyng
And for to speke of loue and womanhede
Ne knyght in armes/ to don a hardy dede
To stonden in grace of his lady dere
Than had this preest/this crafte to lere
And to the chanon/thus he spake/and said
For the loue of god/ that for vs all deyd
And as I may deserue it vnto you
What shall this receit cost/telleth me nowe?
¶ By our lady (qd this chanon) it is dere
I warne you wel/ saue I and a frere
In Englande/there can no man it make.
No force (qd he) nowe sir for goddes sake
What shal I pay/ tel me I you pray.
Iwys (qd he) it is ful dere I say
Syr at one worde/if that ye lyst it haue
Ye shal paye fourty pounde/so god me saue
And nere the frendshyp that ye dyd er this
To me/ye shulde pay more iwys.
¶ This preest the sōme of fourty poūde anon
Of nobles fette/ and tolde hem euerychon
To this chanon/for this ilke recepte
Al his worchyng was fraude and discepte.
Sir preest he said/I kepe for to haue no loos
Of my crafte/ for I wolde it were kept cloos
And as ye loue me/kepeth it secre
For and men knowe al my subtelte
By god men wolde haue so great enuye
To me/bycause of my philosophye
I shulde be deed/there were non other way
¶ God it forbyd (qd the preest) what ye say
Yet had I leuer spende al the good
Whiche that I haue/and els waxe I wood
Than that ye shulde fallen in suche mischefe
For your good wyl haue ye right good prefe
(Qd the chanon) and farwel graunt mercy
He went his way/& neuer the preest him sey
After that day: & whan that this preest sholde
Maken assay/at suche tyme as he wolde
Of this recepte/farwel it nolde not be
Lo thus beiaped and begyled was he
Thus maketh he his introduction
To bring folke to her distruction.
Consydereth sirs/howe in eche estate
Betwyxt men and golde is debate
So ferforthe/that vnnethes there is none
This moultiplyeng blyndeth so many one
That in good fayth/I trowe that it be

P The

The tale of the chanons yeman:

The grettest cause of suche scarsyte
These phylosophers speken so mistyly
In this crafte/ that men can not come therby
For any wytte that men haue nowe a dayes
They may wel chattre & iangle as do ỷ iayes
And in her termes/ set her luste and payne
But to her purpose shul they neuer attayne
A man may lightly lerne/ if he haue ought
To multiplye/ and bring his good to nought
Lo/ suche a lucre is in this lusty game
A mans myrthe it wol turne al to grame
And empten also great and heuy purses
And maken folke to purchase curses
Of hem that han also her good ylente
O fye for shame/ they that han be brente
Alas/ can not they flye the fyres hete
Ye that it vsen/ I rede that ye it lete
Lest ỷ ye lesen al/ for better than neuer is late
Neuer to thriue/ were to longe a date
Though ỷ ye prolle aye/ ye shal it neuer fynde
Ye ben as bolde as is bayarde the blynde
That blondereth forth/ & peril casteth he none
He is as bolde to renne ayenst a stone
As for to go besyde in the way
So faren ye/ that multiplyen I say
If that your eyen can not sene a right
Loketh that your mynde lacke not his syght
For though ye loke neuer so brode & stare
Ye shal not wynne a myte in that chaffare
But waste al that ye may rape and renne
Withdrawe the fyre/ lest it to faste brenne
Medleth with that arte no more I mene
For if ye done/ your thrifte is gon ful clene
And right as swythe I wol you tellen here
What ỷ the philosophers sayn in this matere.
¶ Lo thus sayth Arnolde of the newe toun
As his rosarye maketh mencioun
He sayth right thus/ withouten any lye
There may no man Mercurye mortifye
But if it be with his brothers knowleging
Lo howe that he/ whiche first said this thyng
Of philosophers father was/ Hermes
He sayth howe the dragon doutles
Ne dyeth not/ but if he be slayne
With his brother: And this is for to sayne
By the dragon Mercurye/ and none other
He vnderstode ỷ brimstone was his brother
That out of Sol and Luna were ydrawe
And therfore sayd he/ take hede to my sawe
Let no man besye him this arte for to seche
But he that the entencion and speche
Of philosophers vnderstonde can
And if he do/ he is a lewde man
For this science/ and this connyng (qđ he)
Is of the secre of the secres parde.
¶ Also there was a disciple of Plato
That on a tyme sayd his maister to
As his boke Senior wol bere wytnesse
And this was his demaunde in soth fastnesse
Tell me the name of the priuy stone.
¶ And Plato answerde vnto him anone
Take the stone that Titanos men name.
¶ Which is ỷ (qđ he) Magnatia is the same
Sayd Plato: ye sir and is it thus:
This is ignotum per ignotius
What is magnatia/ good sir I you pray.
¶ It is a water that is made I say
Of elementes foure (quod Plato)
¶ Tel me the roche good sir (qđ he tho)
Of that water/ if it be your wyll.
Nay nay (qđ Plato) certayne that I nyll
The philosophers were ysworne echone
That they shulde discouer it vnto none
Ne in no boke it write in no manere
For vnto Christ it is so lefe and dere
That he wol not that it discouered be
But where it lyketh to his deite
Man to enspyre and eke for to defende
Whan that him lyketh/ lo this is his ende.
¶ Than cõclude I thus/ sens ỷ god of heuen
Ne wyl not that the philosophers nemen
Howe that a man shal come vnto this stone
I rede as for the beste/ let it gone
For who so maketh god his aduersarye
As for to werche any thing in contrarye
Vnto his wyll/ certes neuer shal he thriue
Though that he multeplye terme of his lyue
And there a poynte/ for ended is my tale
God sende euery true man bote of his bale.

¶ Here endeth the tale of the chanons yeman/ and here foloweth the doctour of phisykes prologue.

Whan

WHan this yeman his tale ended had
Of this false chanon/ which was so bad
Our hoste gan say/ truely and certayne
This preest was begyled/ sothe for to sayne
He wenyng for to be a phylosopher
Tyl he right no golde lefte in his cofer
And sothly this preest had alther iape
This cursed chanon put in his hoode an ape
But al this passe I ouer as now
Sir doctour of Phisyke/ yet I pray you
Tel vs a tale of some honest matere
It shal be done/ if that ye wol it here
Sayd this doctour/ and his tale bygan anon
Now good men (qd he) herkeneth euerychon.

¶ Here endeth the doctour of physikes prologue/ and here begynneth his tale.

THere was/ as telleth vs Tytus Liuius
A knyght/ that cleped was Virginius
Fulfylled of honour and of worthynesse
And stronge of frendes/ and of rychesse.
A doughter he had by his wyfe
And neuer had he mo in al his lyfe
Fayre was this mayde in excellent beaute
Abouen euery wight that man may se
For nature hath/ with souerayne dilygence
Formed her in so great excellence
As though she wolde say/ lo I nature
Thus can I forme and paynte a creature
Whan that me lyste/ who can me counterfete
Pygmaliõ not/ though he alway forge ⁊ bete
Or graue or paynte/ for I dare wel sayne
Appelles/ or zeusis/ shulde werche in vayne
To graue or paynte/ or forge or bete
If they presumed me to counterfete
For he that is the fourmer principall
Hath made me his vycar generall
To fourme and paynte erthely creaturis
Right as me lyste/ for al thyng in my cure is
Vnder the moone/ that may wane and waxe
And for my werke/ nothyng wol I axe
My lorde and I ben fully of a corde
I made her to the worshyp of my lorde
So do I al myn other creatures
Of what coloure they be/ or of what fygures
Thus semeth me that nature wolde say.
This mayde was of age twelue yere ⁊ tway
In whiche that nature hath suche delyte
For right as she can paynte a lilye whyte
And rody as rose/ right with suche paynture
She paynted hath this noble creature
Er she was borne/ vpon her lymmes fre
Were als bright as suche colours shulde be

P.ii. And

The Doctor's Prologue and Tale (C 1–36; T. 11929–11970)

The doctour of phisykes tale.

And Phebus died had her tresses grete
Lyke to the stremes of his burned hete
And if that excellent were her beaute
A thousande folde more vertuous was she
In her ne lacketh no conditioun
That is to preyse/ as by discretioun
As wel in body as in gost/ chaste was she
For whiche she floured in virginite
With al humylyte and abstynence
With al attemperaunce/ and pacience
With mesure eke/ and beryng of array
Discrete she was in answeryng alway
Tho she were wyse as Pallas / dare I sayn
(Her facounde eke/ ful womanly and playn)
No counterfayted termes had she
To seme wyse : but after her degree
She spake/ and al her wordes more & lesse
Sownyng in vertue and in gentylnesse
Shamfast she was/ in maydes shamfastnesse
Constant in hert/ and ever in busynesse
To dryve her out of all slogardry
Bacchus had of her mouthe no maistry
For wyne and youth done Venus encrece
As men in fyre wol casten oyle or grece
And of her owne vertue unconstrayned
She hath ful ofte her sicke fayned
For that she wolde flye the company
Where lykely was to treten of foly
As is at feestes/ at revels/ and at daunces
That ben occasyons of dalyaunces
Suche thinges maken children for to be
To sone rype and bolde/ as men may se
Whiche is ful perillous/ and hath ben yore
For al to sone may she lerne lore
Of boldnesse/ whan she is a wyfe.
And ye maistresses in your olde lyfe
That lordes doughters han in governaunce
Ne taketh of my wordes no displesaunce
Thynke that ye ben set in governynges
Of lordes doughters/ onely for two thynges
Eyther for ye han kepte your honeste
Eyther ye han fall in freelte
And knowen wel ynough the olde daunce
And conne forsake fully mischaunce
For evermore/ therfore for Christes sake
Kepeth wel tho that ye undertake.
A theef of venyson that hath forlafte
His lykerousnesse/ and al his theves crafte
Can kepe a forest best of any man
Nowe kepeth hem wel/ for & ye wol ye can
Loketh wel/ to no vice that ye assent
Lest ye be dampned for your yvel entent
For who so dothe/ a traytour is certayn
And taketh kepe of that I shal you sayn
Of al treyson soverayne pestilence
Is/ whan a wight betrayeth innocence
Ye fathers/ and eke ye mothers also
Though ye han children/ be it one or mo
Yours is the charge of al her sufferaunce
Whiles they ben in your governaunce
Beth ware/ that by ensample of your lyveng
Either by your neglygence in chastisynge
That they ne perisshe: for I dare wel say
If that they don/ ye shal ful sore obey
Under a sheperde softe and neglygent
The wolf hath many a shepe & lambe to rent
Suffyseth one ensample nowe as here
For I mote turne ayen to my matere.
This mayde/ of which I tel my tale expresse
She kepte her selve/ she neded no maistresse
For in her lyveng maydens myght rede
As in a boke/ every good worke and dede
That longeth to a mayde vertuous
She was so prudent and so bountuous
For whiche out spronge on every syde
Bothe of her beaute and of her bounte wyde
That thorowe the londe they preysed her echon
That loved vertue/ save envy alone
That sorye is of other mennes wele
And gladde is of her sorowe/ and unhele
The doctour maketh this discriptioun
This mayde went on a day into the toun
Towarde the temple/ with her mother dere
As is of yonge maydens the manere.
Nowe was there a Justice in the toun
That governour was of that regioun
And so befyl/ this Justice his eyen cast
Upon this mayde/ avisyng her ful fast
As she came forby/ there as the Juge stode
Anon his hert chaungeth and his mode
So was he caught with beaute of this mayd
And to him selfe ful prively he sayd
This mayde shal be myne for any man
Anon the fende in to his hert ran
And taught him sodainly/ by what sleight
The mayde to his purpose wynne he myght
For

For certes/by no force/ ne by no mede
Him thought he was not able for to spede
For she was stronge of frendes/and eke she
Confirmed was in suche soueraynė beaute
That wel he wyste he might her neuer wynne
As for to make her with her body synne
For whiche with great deliberatioun
He sent after a clyent in to the toun
The whiche he knewe ful subtyl & full bolde
This iuge vnto this clyent his tale hath tolde
In secrete wyse/and made him to ensure
He shulde tell it vnto no creature
And if he dyd/he shulde lese his hede
Whan assented was this cursed rede
Glad was the iuge/and made good chere
And yaue him gyftest precious and dere.
¶ Whan shapen was al this conspyracie
Fro poynt to poynt/howe that his lecherie
Parfourmed shulde be ful subtelly
As ye shullen after here openly
Home gothe this clyent/ yͭ hyght Claudius
This false iuge/ that hyght Appius
So was his name/for it is no fable
But knowen for an historial thing notable
The sentence of it sothe is out of doute
This false iuge gothe nowe faste aboute
To hasten his delyte/ al that he may
And so byfell/that sone after on a day
This false iuge/ as telleth vs the storie
As he was wonte/ sate in his consystorie
And yaue his domes vpon sondrie caas
This false clyent came forth a ful gret paas
And sayd lorde/if it be your wyll
As dothe me right vpon this pytous byll
In whiche I playne vpon Virginius
And if he wol say it is not thus
I wol proue it/and fynde good wytnesse
That sothe is that my byll wol expresse.
¶ The iuge answerde/of this in his absence
I may not yeue diffynite sentence
Let do him call/and I wol gladly here
Thou shalte haue right/and no wronge here.
¶ Virginius came to wete the iuges wyll
And right anon was radde this cursed byll
The sentence of it/ was as ye shal here.
¶ To you my lorde Appius so dere
Sheweth your poore seruaunt Claudius
Howe that a knight called Virginius
Ayenst the lawe/and ayenst al equite
Holdeth expresse ayenst the wyl of me
My seruant / which that is my thrale by right
Which from myn hous was stolen on a night
Whyles she was ful yonge/I wol it preue
By wytnesse lorde/so that ye you not greue
She is not his doughter/what so he say
Wherfore my lorde iustyce I you pray
Yelde me my thrall/if it be your wyll
Lo this was al the sentence of that byll.
¶ Virginius gan vpon the clyent beholde
But hastely/er he his tale tolde
He wolde haue defended it/as shulde a knight
And by witnesse of many a trewe wight
That al was false/that sayd his aduersary
This cursed iuge wolde no lenger tary
Ne here a worde more of Virginius
But yaue his iugement/and sayd thus.
¶ I deme anon this clyent his seruaunt haue
Thou shalte no lenger her in thyn house saue
Go bring her forthe/& put her in our warde
This client shal haue his thral/thus I award
¶ And whan this worthy knight Virginius
Through the assent of the iuge Appius
Muste by force his dere doughter yeuen
Vnto the iuge/in lechery to lyuen
He gothe him home/& set him in his hall
And lete anon his dere doughter call
And with face deed as asshen colde
Vpon her humble face he gan beholde
With fathers pyte/ stickyng through his herte
Al wolde he not from his purpose conuerte.
¶ Doughter (qd he) Virginia by thy name
There ben two wayes/eyther dethe or shame
That thou muste suffre/ alas yͭ I was borne
For neuer thou deseruedest wherforne
To dyen/with a sworde or with a knyfe
Oh dere doughter/comforte of my lyfe
Whiche I haue fostred vp with suche plesaũce
That thou ne were out of my remembraũce
O doughter/whiche that arte my laste wo
And in my lyfe my laste ioye also
O iemme of chastyte/in pacience
Take thou thy dethe/this is my sentence
For loue/ and not for hate thou muste be deed
My pitous honde mote smyte of thyn heed
Alas that euer Appius the sey
Thus hath he falsly iuged the to day

The Doctor's Tale (C 133–228; T. 12067–12162)

And tolde her al the case/as ye before
Han herde/it nedeth not to tell it more.
¶ O mercy dere father (qd this mayde)
And with that worde/bothe her armes layde
Aboute his necke/as she was wonte to do
The teeres braste out of her eyen two
And sayd/ O good father shal I dye
Is there no grace ? is there no remedye ?
¶ No certes dere doughter myn (qd he)
Than yeue me leaue father myn (qd she)
My dethe to complayne a lytel space
For parde/Jepte yaue his doughter grace
For to complayne/er he her slough/ alas
And god it wote/nothing was her trespas
But that she ranne her father first to se
To welcome him/ with great solempnyte
And with that worde she fel a swoune anon
And after/ whan her swounyng was gon
She ryseth vp/and to her father sayde
Blissed be god that I shal dye a mayde
Yeue me my dethe/er that I haue a shame
Doth wt your child your wil a goddes name
And with that worde/she prayeth him ful ofte
That with his swerde he shuld smyte her softe
And with that worde/a swoune down she fell
Her father/with sorowfull herte and fell
Her heed of smote/and by the toppe it hente
And to the iuge he it yaue in presente
As he sate in dome in consistorie
Whan the iuge it sawe/as sayth the storie
He bade take him/ and honge him also faste
But right anon al the people in thrast
To saue the knight/for routhe and for pyte
For knowen was the iuges iniquite
The people anon had suspecte in this thyng
By maner of this clyentes chalengyng
That it was by the assent of Appius
They wyste wel that he was lecherous
For whiche vnto Appius they gon
And kesten him in prison right anon
Where as he slowe him selfe/ and Claudius
That seruaunt was vnto this Appius
Was demed for to be honged vpon a tre
But Virginius/of his great pyte
So prayed for him/ that he was exiled
And els certes he had ben begyled
The remenaunt were honged/more and lesse
That consented were to this cursydnesse.

¶ Here may men se how syn hath his meryte
Beware/for no mā wote how god wol smyte
In no degre/ne in no maner wyse
The worme of conscience wol aryse
Of wicked lyfe/ though it so priuy be
That no man wote of it but god and he
Whether he be leude man or lered
He not howe sone he may ben afered
Therfore I rede you this counsayle take
Forsake synne/ or synne you forsake.

¶ Here endeth the doctour of phisykes tale/ and foloweth the wordes of the hoste.

Our hoste gan swere/as he were woode
Harowe (qd he) by nayles and by bloode
This was a false thefe/& a cursed iustice
As shamful dethe/ as herte may deuyse
Come to the iustice and her aduocas
Algate this sely mayden is slayne/ alas
Alas to dere abought she her beaute
Wherfore I say/ that al men may se
That yeftes of fortune/or of nature
Ben cause of dethe of many a creature
Her beaute was her dethe/ I dare wel sayne
Alas so pitously as she was slayne
But herof wol I not procede as nowe
Men haue ful ofte more harme than prowe
But truely myn owne maister dere
This is a pytous tale for to here
But nathelesse/ passe ouer is no force
I pray to god to saue thy gentil cors
And thy vrinalles/and thy iordanes
Thyn ypocras/and eke thy galyanes
And euery boxe ful of letuarye
God blesse hem and our lady saynt Marye
So mote I the/ thou arte a propre man
And lyke a prelate/by saynt Runyan
Saue that I can not speke wel in terme
But wel I wote/thou dost myn hert to yerne
That I haue almost ycaught a cardyacle
By corpus domini/ but I haue tryacle
Or els a draught of moyste corny ale
Or but I here anon a nother mery tale
My herte is loste/for pyte of this mayde
Thou belamy/thou Iohan pardoner he sayd
Tell vs some mery tale/ or iape/ right anon.

¶ H

The Doctor's Tale: Words of the Host (C 229–319; T. 12163–12253)

It shal be don (qd he) by saynt Runyon
But first (qd he) here at this ale stake
I wol bothe drinke/ and eate of a cake
But right anon/ these gentels gon to crye
Nay/ let him tel vs of no rebaudrye
Tel vs some moral thing/ that we mowe lere
Some wytte/ and than wol we gladly here
I graunt (qd he) iwys/ but I mote thinke
On some honest thing/ whiles yͭ I drinke.

¶ Here endeth the wordes of the host/ and here foloweth the prologue of the Pardoner.

Lordynges (qd he) in chyrch whan I prech
I payne me to haue an hauteyn speche
And ryng it out/ as rounde as dothe a bel
For I can al be roote/ that I tel
My teme is alwaye/ and euer was
(Radix omnium malorum est cupiditas)
First I pronounce fro whens I come
And than my bylles I shewe al and some
Our liege lorde seale on my patent
That shewe I fyrst/ my body to warent
That no man be so bolde/ preest ne clerke
Me to distourbe/ of Christes holy werke
And after that/ tel I forthe my tales
Bulles of Popes/ and of Cardynales
Of Patriarkes/ and of Bysshopes I shewe
And in latyn I speke wordes a fewe
To sauer with my predication
And for to steere men to deuotion
Than shewe I forth my long chrystal stones
ycrammed ful of cloutes and of bones
Relykes they ben/ as wene they echone
Than haue I in laton a sholderbone
Whiche that was of an holy iewes shepe.
Good men saye I/ take of my wordes kepe
If that this bone be wasshen in any wel
If cowe or calfe/ shepe/ or oxe swel
That any worme hath eten/ or hem stonge
Take water of this wel/ and wasshe his tong
And it is hole anon: and farthermore
Of pockes/ and of scabbes/ and euery sore
Shal shepe be hole/ that of this wel
Drinketh a draught/ take kepe of that I tel.
¶ If the good man that the beestes oweth
Wol euery day/ er the cocke croweth
Fastyng drinke of this wel a draught
As thilke holy iewe our elders taught
His beestes and his store shal multiplye
And sirs/ also it healeth ielousye
For though a man be fal in ielous rage
Let make with this water his potage
And neuer shal he more his wyfe mistryst
Though he in sothe the defaute by her wyst
Al had she take preestes two or thre.
¶ Here is a myttayne eke/ that ye may se
He that his honde wol put in this mittayne
He shal haue moultiplyeng of his grayne
Whan he hath sowen/ be it whete or otes
So that he offer good pens or grotes.
And men & women/ o thyng I warne you
If any wight ben in this churche nowe
That hath done synne horrible/ that he
Dare not for shame of it shriuen be
Or any woman/ be she yonge or olde
That hath made her husbonde cokewolde
Suche folke shul haue no powre ne no grace
To offre to my relykes in this place
And who so fyndeth him out of suche blame
Cometh vp and offre in goddes name
And I assoyle him by the auctorite
Suche as by bulle was graunted to me.
¶ By this gaude haue I wonne euery yere
An hundred marke/ sythen I was pardonere
I stonde lyke a clerke in my pulpet
And the lewde people byn downe yset
I preche so as ye haue lered here before
And tel an hundred iapes more
Than payne I me to stretche forthe my necke
And este and west/ vpon the people I becke
As dothe a doue/ syttyng vpon a berne
My hondes and my tonge gon ful yerne
That it is ioy to se my besynesse
Of auarice/ and of suche cursydnesse
Al my prechyng is for to maken hem fre
To yeuen her pens/ and namely vnto me
For myn entent is not but for to wynne
And nothing for correction of synne
I recke neuer/ whan that they ben beryed
Though her soules gon a blackburyed
For certes many a predycation
Cometh oft tyme of yuel entencion.
¶ Some for plesaunce of folke/ & for flatery
To ben auaunced by hipocrysy
And

The Pardoners prologue.

And some for veyne glorie/and some for hate
For whan I dare not other wayes debate
Than wol I styng hem with my tōge smerte
In prechyng/so that he shal not asterte
To ben diffamed falsly/if that he
Hath trespased to my bretherne or to me
For though I tell not his propre name
Men shal wel knowe that it is the same
By signes/or by other circumstaunces
Thus quyte I folke/ ẏ dothe vs displesaūces
Thus put I out my venym vnder hewe
Of holynesse/to semen holy and trewe
But shortly myn entent I wol deuyse
I preche of nothyng but of coueytyse
Therfore my teme is yet/and euer was
Radix omnium malorum est cupiditas.
¶ Thus can I preache ayenst the same vyce
Whiche that I vse/and that is auaryce
But though my selfe be gilty in that synne
Yet can I maken other folke to twynne
From auarice/and sore hem to repent
But that is not my principall entent
I preche nothyng but for coueytyse
Of this matere/it ought ynough suffyse.
Than tel I hem ensamples many one
Of olde stories/longe tyme agone
For leude people louen tales olde
Whiche thinges they can wel reporte & holde
What trowe ye? whiles that I may preche
And wynne golde and syluer for to teche
That I wol lyue in pouert wilfully?
Nay nay/I thought it neuer trewly
For I wol preche and begge in sondrie londes
I wol not do no labour with myn hondes
Ne make baskettes/and lyue therby
Bycause I wol not begge idelly
I wol none of the apostels counterfete
I wol haue money/mault/ chese/ & whete
Al were it yeuen of the poorest page
Or of the poorest wydowe in a village
Though her children shuld sterue for fampne
Nay/I wol drinke the lycoure of the wyne
And haue a ioly wenche in euery toun
But herkeneth lordynges my conclusyoun.
Your lyking is that I shulde tel a tale
Nowe I haue dronken a draught of corny ale
By god I hope I shal tel you a thyng
That shal by reson ben at your lyking
For though my selfe be a ful vycious man
A morall tale yet I you tel can
Whiche I am wonte to preche/for to wynne
Now holdeth yo[r] peace/my tale I wol begyn.

¶ Here endeth the Pardoners prologue/and here folowe with his tale.

The Pardoner's Prologue (C 411–462; T. 12845–12396)

IN Flaunders whilom ther was a cōpany
Of yonge folke/ that haunted foly
As hasarde/ ryotte/ Stewes/ & tauernes
Where as with harpes/ lutes/ and geternes
They daunced & playen at dyce night & day
And eten also/ ouer that her might may
Through whiche they don the dyuel sacrifyce
Within the dyuels temple/ in cursed wyse
By superfluite abhomynable
Her othes ben so great and so dampnable
That it is grisly for to here hem swere
Our blissed lordes body they al to tere
Hem thought Iewes rent him not ynough
And eche of hem at others synne lough.
And right anon comen in tombesteres
Fetys and smale and yonge froytereres
Syngers with harpes/ baudes/ and waferers
Whiche that ben verely the diuels offycers
To kyndlen and blowe the fyre of lechery
That is anexed vnto glotony
The holy writte take I to my wytnesse
That lechery is in wyne and dronkenesse.
¶ Lo howe that dronken Lothe vnkyndly
Lay by his doughters two vnwetyngly
So dronke he was/ he nyst what he wrought
And therfore sore repent him ought
Herodes/ who so wol the stories seche
There may ye lerne/ & by ensample teche
Whan he of wyne was replete at his feste
Right at his owne table/ yaue his heste
To sleen Iohan the Baptiste ful giltlesse
Seneke sayth eke good wordes doutlesse
He sayth he can no difference fynde
Betwixt a man that is out of his mynde
And a man that is dronkelewe
But woodnesse that is fallen in a shrewe
Perseuereth lenger than dothe dronkenesse
O gloteny/ ful of cursydnesse
O cause first of our confusyon
O orygenal of our dampnacion
Tyl Christ had bouzt vs wt his blode agayn
Lo howe dere/ shortly for to sayn
Bought was first this cursed vilanye
Corrupt was al this worlde through glotony
Adam our forn father/ and his wyfe also
Fro Paradyce/ to labour and to wo
Were driuen for that vyce/ it is no drede
For whyles that Adam fasted/ as I rede
He was in paradyce/ and whan that he
Ete of the frute/ defended on the tre
Anon he was out caste to wo and payne
O glotenye/ on the wel ought vs to playne.
¶ Oh/ wyste a man howe many maladyes
Foloweth of excesse and of glotenyes
He wolde ben the more mesurable
Of his dyete/ syttyng at his table
Alas the shorte throte/ the tender mouthe
Maketh that este/ & west/ northe/ and southe
In erthe/ in eyre/ in water/ men to swynke
To getten a gloton dayntye mete and drinke
Of this mater/ o Poule wel canste thou trete
Meate vnto wombe/ & wombe eke vnto mete
Shal god distroy bothe as Poule sayth
Alas/ a foule thing it is by my fayth
To say this worde/ and fouler is the dede
Whan men so drinketh of the whyte and rede
That of his throte he maketh his priue
Through thilke cursed superfluite.
¶ The apostle sayth/ weping ful pitously
There walken many/ of whiche tolde haue I
I say it nowe weping with pitous voyce
There ben enemyes of Christes croyse
Of whiche the ende is deth/ wombe is her god
O bely/ O wombe/ O stynkyng cod
Fulfylled of donge and of corrupcioun
At eyther ende of the foule is the soun
Howe great coste and laboure is to fynde
These cokes: how they stāpe/ strayn/ & grinde
And turne substaunce in to accident
To fulfyl al thy lykerous talent
Out of the harde bones knocken they
The mary/ for they caste it not awey
That may go through the gullet safe & sote
Of spycerie/ of leues/ barke/ and rote
Shal ben his sauce ymade by delyte
To maken him haue a newer apetyte
But certes he that haunteth suche delytes
Is deed/ whiles that he lyueth in the vyces
¶ A lecherouse thing is wyne and dronkenesse
It is ful of stryuing and of wretchydnesse
Oh dronken man/ disfygured is thy face
Sower is thy brethe/ foule art thou to enbrace
And through thy drōken nose sowneth ẏ soun
As tho thou saydest aye/ Sampson Sāpson
And yet god wote Sāpson drōke neuer wyne
Thou fallest/ as it were a sticked swyne
Thy

The Pardoner's Tale (C 463–556; T. 12397–12490)

Thy tonge is lost / and al thyn honeste cure
For dronkennesse is very sepulture
Of mannes wytte / and his discretion
In whom that drinke hath dompnation
He can no counsaile kepe / it is no drede
Nowe kepe you fro the white and fro ẏ rede
Namely fro the white wyne of Lepe
That is to sel in Fisshe strete and in Chepe
This wyne of Spayne crepeth subtelly
In other wynes growyng fast by
Of whiche riseth suche fumosyte
That whan a man hath drõk draughtes thre
And weneth that he be at home in Chepe
He is in Spayne / right at the towne of Lepe
Nought at Rochel / ne at Burdeaux toun
And than wol he say / Sampsoun Sãpsoun
But herkneth lordiges o worde / I you pray
That al the soueraygne actes / dare I say
Of victories in the olde Testament
That thorowe very god / that is omnypotent
Were don in abstynence and in prayere
Loketh the Byble / and there ye mowe it lere.
Loketh Attyla / the great conquerour
Deyd in his slepe / with shame and dishonour
Bledyng aye at his nose in dronknesse
A capitayne shulde lyue in sobernesse.
And ouer al this / auyse you right well
What was cõmaunded vnto Lamuel:
Nat Samuel: but Lamuel saye I
Redeth the Byble / and fyndeth it expresly
Of wyne yeuyng to hem that haue iustyce
No more of this / for it may ynough suffyce.

And nowe that I haue spoke of glotonye
Nowe wol I defende you hasardrie
Hasarde is very mother of lesynges
And of discepte / and cursed forswerynges
Blasphemé of christ / mãslauzter / ⁊ wast also
Of batayle ofte tyme / and of other mo
It is reprefe / and contrarye to honour
For to be holden a cõmen hasardour
And euer the hyer that he is of estate
The more he is holden desolate
If that a prince vse hasardrie
In al gouernaunce and policie
He is as by comen oppinyon
Holde the lesse in reputacion. (dour
¶ Stylbon / ẏ was holde a wyse ambassa-
Was sent in to Corinthe wt ful great honour
Fro Calydone / to maken hem alyaunce
And whan he came / happed this chaunce
That al the greatest that were of ẏ londe
Playeng at hasarde he hem fonde
For whiche / as sone as it might be
He stale him home ayen to his countre
And sayd / there wol I not lese my name
I nyll not take on me so great defame
For to alye you to none hasardours
Sendeth other wyser enbassadours
For by my trouthe / me were leuer dye
Than I shulde you to hasardours alye
For ye that ben so gloriouse in honours
Shal not alye you with hasardours
As by my wyl / ne by my tretie
This wyse philosopher / thus sayd he.
¶ Loke eke howe to kyng Demetrius
The kyng of Parthes / as the boke sayth vs
Sent him a payre of dyce of golde in scorne
For he had vsed hasardrie there byforne
For whiche he helde his glorie ⁊ his renoun
At no value or reputacioun
Lordes might fynde other maner play
Honest ynough to driue the day away.

Nowe wol I speke of othes false ⁊ great
A worde or two / as other bokes entreat
Great sweryng is thing abhomynable
And false swering is yet more reprouable
The hye god forbade sweryng at all
Wytnesse of Matheu / but in speciall
Of swering / sayth the holy Ieromye
Thou shalte swere sothe thyn othes / ⁊ not lye
And swere in dome and eke in rightwysnesse
But ydle swering is a cursydnesse.
¶ Beholde and se that in the first table
Of hye goddes hestes honorable
Howe that the seconde heste of him is this
Take not my name in ydelnesse amys
Lo / he rather forbyddeth suche swering
Than homicide / or any other cursed thing
I say as thus / by order it stondeth
This knoweth they ẏ his hestes vnderstõdeth
Howe that the seconde heste of god is that
And further more / I wol the tell al plat
That vengeaũce shal not parte fro his hous
That of his othes is to outragyous

By

The Pardoner's Tale (C 557–650; T. 12491–12584)

By goddes preciouse herte/and his nayles
And by the blode of Christ / that is in Hayles
Seuen is my chaunce/and thyn fyue & thre
By goddes armes/if thou falsly play me
This daggar shal thorowe thyn herte go
This frute cometh of thilke bones two
Forswering/ire/falsnesse/and homicyde
Now for the loue of Christ/that for vs dyde
Leaueth your othes/bothe great and smale
For I shal tel you a meruaylous tale.
¶ These ryottours thre/of whiche I tell
Longe erste or prime ronge any bell
Were set hem in a tauerne to drinke
And as they sate/they herde a bell clynke
Byforne a cors/ỷ was carved to his graue
That one of hem gan call to his knaue
Go bette (quod he) and aske redyly
What cors is this/that passeth forthe by
And loke that thou reporte his name wele.
¶ Sir (qd he) it nedeth neuer a dele
It was me tolde er ye came here two houres
He was parde an olde felowe of yours
Al sodainly was he slayne to night
For dronke as he sate on his benche vpright
There came a priuy thefe/men clepen dethe
That in this countray al the people slethe
And with his speare he smote his herte a two
And went his way/withouten wordes mo
He hath a thousande slayne/ this pestilence
And maister/er ye come in his presence
Me thynketh that it were necessarye
For to beware of suche an aduersarye
Bethe redy for to meten him euer more
Thus taught me my dame/ I say no more.
¶ By saynt Mary/ sayd this tauernere
The childe sayth sothe/for he hath this yere
Hence ouer a myle/ slayne in a great village
Bothe man and woman/childe and page
I trowe his habytacion be there
To ben auysed/great wysdome it were
Er that he dyd a man dishonour.
¶ ye goddes armes (qd this ryottour)
Is it suche perill with him for to mete?
I shal him seche by style and eke by strete
I make a vowe/by goddes digne bones
Herkeneth felowes/we thre ben al ones
Let eche of vs holde vp his honde to other
And eche of vs become others brother
And we wol slee this false traytour dethe
He shal be slayne/ that so many slethe
By goddes dignite/ er that it be night
¶ To gyder han these thre her trouthes plight
To lyue and dye eche of hem with other
As though he were his owne brother
And vp they sterten al dronken in this rage
And forthe they gone/towarde that village
Of whiche the tauerner hath spoke before
And many a grisly othe han they swore
And Christes blessed body they to rent
Dethe shal be deed/and we may him hent.
¶ Whan they han gone not fully a myle
Right as they wolde haue troden ouer a style
An olde poore man with hem mette
This olde man ful mekely hem grette
And sayd/nowe lordynges god you se.
¶ The proudest of these ryottours thre
Answerde ayen/what chorle with harde grace
Why art thou al forwrapped saue thy face?
Why lyuest thou so longe in so great age?
¶ This olde man gan loken in his visage
And sayd thus: for I can not fynde
A man/though I walked into Inde
Neyther in cyte/ ne in no village
That wol chaunge his youthe for myn age
And therfore mote I haue myn age styll
As longe tyme as it is goddes wyll.
Ne dethe alas/nyl not haue my lyfe
Thus walke I lyke a restlesse caitYfe
And on the groũd/ which is my mothers gate
I knocke with my staffe erlyche and late
And say/ leue mother let me in
Lo howe I vanisshe/flesshe/bloode/& skyn
Alas/whan shall my bones ben at reste
Mother with you wolde I chaũge my cheste
That in my chamber longe tyme hath be
Ye for an heren cloute to wrappe in me
But yet to me she wol not done that grace
For whiche ful welked is my face
But sirs/ to you it is no curtesye
To speken vnto an olde man villanye
But he trespace in worde eyther in dede
In holy writte/ye may your selfe wel rede
Ayenst an olde man/hore vpon his heede
ye shulde aryse/therfore I you rede
Ne doth vnto an olde man no harme as now
No more than ye wolde a man dyd you

In

The Pardoner's Tale (C 651–746; T. 12585–12680)

In age/if that ye may so longe abyde
And god be with you/whether ye go or ryde
I mote go thyder as I haue to go
¶ Nay olde chorle/by god thou shalt not so
Sayd these other hasardours anon
Thou partest not so lightly by saynt Iohn
Thou spakest right now of thilke trayter deth
That in this countre al our frendes sleth
Haue here my trouthe thou arte his espye
Tel where he is/ or els thou shalt dye
By god and by the holy sacrament
For sothely thou arte of his assent
To slee vs yonge folke/thou false thefe.
¶ Nowe sirs/if it be to you so lefe
To fynde dethe/turne vp this croked way
For in that groue I lefte him by my fay
Vnder a tree/and there he wol abyde
Ne for your boste he nyll him nothyng hyde
Se ye yõder oke/right there ye shal him fynde
God saue you/ that bought ayen mankynde
And you amende/thus sayd this olde man.
¶ Than euerych of these ryottours ran
Tyl they came to the tree/ & there they founde
Floreynes of golde fyne/ycoyned rounde
Wel nye a seuen busshels/as hem thought
No lenger than after dethe they sought
But eche of hem so glad was of that syght
For that the floreyns so fayre ben and bright
That downe they sytte/ by the precious horde
The worst of hem spake the first worde.
¶ Brethern (qd he) take kepe what I say
My wytte is great/ though I borde and play
This tresure hath fortune to vs yeuen
In myrthe and iolyte our lyfe to lyuen
And lightly as it cõmeth/ so wol we spende
Hey/ goddes precious herte : who wende
To day/that we shulde haue so fayr a grace ?
But might this golde be caryed fro this place
Home to my house/ or els to yours
(For wel I wote that al this golde is ours)
Than were we in hye felycite
But trewly by day it may not be
Men wolde say/ that we were theues stronge
And for our owne tresoure don vs honge
This tresour muste ycaried be by night
As wisly and as slily as it might
Wherfore I rede/let loke amonge vs all
To drawe/& let se where the cutte wol fall
He that hath ye shortest cutte/ with hert blythe
Shal renne to towne/and that ful swyth :
To bring vs breed & drinke ful priuely
And two of vs shal kepe ful subtelly
This tresour wel/and if he wol not tarye
Whan it is nyght/we wol this tresour cary.
By one assent/where as vs lyste best
That one of hem brought grasse in his fest
And bad hẽ draw/& loke on whom it wold fal
And it fell on the yongest of hem all
And forthe towarde the towne he went anone
And also sone as he was gone
That one of hem spake vnto that other
Thou wost wel/thou arte my sworne brother
Thy profyte wol I tel the right anone
Thou woste well that our felowe is gone
And here is golde/and that ful great plente
That shal departed be amonge vs thre
But nathelesse/if that I can shape it so
That it departed were amonge vs two
Had I not done a frendly turne to the
That other answerd/I not how yt might be
I wolde wel that the golde were ours two
What shulde we do/ that it might be so ?
¶ Shal it be cõusayle (said the first shrewe)
And I shal tel the in wordes fewe
What we wol done/and bring it wel aboute.
¶ I graunt (qd that other) out of doute
That by my trouth/I wol the not bewrayne
¶ Now (qd he) thou wost wel we ben twayne
And twayne of vs shal stronger be than one
Loke whan he is sette/ and than anone
Aryse/as though thou woldest wt him play
And I shal ryuen him through ye sydes tway
Whyles yt thou strugglest with him as i game
And with thy dagger/loke thou do the same
And than shal al the golde departed be
My dere frende/betwyxt the and me
Than may we bothe our lustes fulfyll
And play at dyce/right at our owne wyll
And thus accorded ben these shrewes tway
To slee the thirde/ as ye herde me say.
This yongest/ whiche yt went to the towne
Ful often in his herte he rolled vp and downe
The beautie of these floreyns fayre & bright
O lorde (qd he) if so were that I might
Haue al this tresour to my selfe alone
There nys no man/that lyueth vnder trone
Of

Of god/ that shulde lyue so mery as I
And at the laste the fende our enemy
Put in his thought/that he shulde poyson bey
With whiche he might sleen his felowes twey
For why/the fende fonde him in suche lyuing
That he had leue to sorowe him to bring
For this was vtterly his entente
To sleen hem bothe /and neuer to repente.
¶ And forth he gothe/ no lenger wold he tary
In to the towne/ vnto a potecary
And prayde him that he wol him sell
Some poyson/ that he might his rattes quell
And eke there was a polkat in his hawe
That as he sayd/his capons had yslawe
And said/ he wolde wreken him if yͤ he might
Of vermyn/ that distroyed hem by night.
¶ The potycary answerde/thou shalt haue
A thynge/as wisly god my soule saue
In al this worlde there nys no creature
That eeteth or drinketh of this confecture
Not but the mountenaūce of a corne of whete
That he ne shal his lyfe anon forlete
Ye sterue he shal/ and that in lesse whyle
Thā thou woldest gon a pace/not but a myle
This poyson is so harde and so violent.
¶ This cursed man hath in his honde hent
This poyson in a boxe/and sythe he rā
In to the next strete vnto a man
And borowed him large botels thre
And in the two/the poyson poured he
The thirde he kept clene for his drinke
For al the night he shope him for to swynke
In caryeng of the golde out of that place
And whan this riottour/with sorie grace
Had fylde with him his great bottels thre
To his felowes ayen repayred he.
¶ What nedeth it therof to sermon more:
For right as they had caste his dethe before
Right so they han him slayne/& that anone
And whan this was done/than spake yͤ one
Nowe let vs syt and drinke/ & make vs mery
And afterwarde we wolne his body bury
And after that it happed hem par caas
The one toke the botel/therin the poyson was
And dronke / and yaue his felowe drinke also
Through which anon they steruen both two.
¶ But certes I suppose that Auicenne
Wrote neuer in no cannon/ne in no fenne
More wonder sorowes of enpoysonnyng
Than had these wretches two in her endyng
Thus ended ben these homicides two
And eke the false enpoysonner also.
O cursed synne/ful of al cursydnesse
O traytours homicide / O wickydnesse
O glotenye/ luxure/and hasardye
Thou blasphemour of Christ with vilanye
And othes great/of vsage and of pride
Alas mankynde/howe may it betyde
That to thy creatoure/which yͤ the wrought
And with his precious bloode the bought
Thou arte so false and so vnkynde / alas:
Now good mē/god foryeue you yoʳ trespas
And ware you fro the synne of auaryce
Myn holy pardon/may you al waryshe
So that ye offre nobles or starlynges
Other els syluer spones/broches/or rynges
Boweth your heed vnder this bulle
Cometh vp ye wyues / & offreth of your woll
Your names here I entre in my rolle anon
In to the blisse of heuen shul ye al gon
I you assoyle by myn high powere
Ye that offren/as clene and eke clere
As ye were borne. Lo sirs/ thus I preche
And Iesu Christ/ that is our soules leche
So graunt you his pardon to receyue
For that is best/ I wol you not disceyue
But sirs/one worde foryate I in my tale
I haue relykes/ and pardon in my male
As fayre as any man in Englonde
Whiche were yeuen me by the popes honde
If any of you wol of deuocion
Offren/and haue myn absolucion
Cometh forthe anon/ and kneleth here adoun
That ye may haue parte of my pardoun
Or els taketh pardon as ye wende
Al newe and fresshe/ at euery townes ende
So that ye offren alway newe and newe
Nobles or pens/whiche ben good and trewe
It is great honour to euerych that is here
That ye may haue a sufficient pardonere
To assoyle you/in countre there ye ryde
For auentures/whiche that may betyde
For peraunenture there may fall one or two
Downe of her horse/& breke her necke a two
Loke whiche suertie it is to you all
That I am in your felowshyp yfall

Q That

That maye assoyle you bothe more and lasse
Whan that the soule shal fro the body passe
I rede that our hoste shal begynne
For he is moste enuelopte of synne
Cometh forthe sir hoste/ and offre first anon
And thou shalte kysse the relykes eueryehon
ye for a grote/ vnbokyll anon thy purse.
¶ Nay nay (qd he) than haue I christes curse
Let be (qd he) it shal not be so theriche
Thou woldest make me kysse thyn old breche
And swere it were a relyke of a seynt
Though it were with thy foũdement depeynt
But by the crosse/ which seynt Helayne fonde
I wolde I had thy coylons in myn honde
In stede of relykes / or of sanctuarye
Let cutte hem of/ I wol helpe the hem to cary
They shul be shryned in an hogges torde
This pardoner answerde not a worde
So wrothe he was/ he wolde no worde say.
¶ Now (qd our hoste) I wol no lenger play
With the/ ne with non other angry man.
¶ But right anon the worthy knight began
Whan that he sawe that al the people loughe
Nomore of this/ for it is right ynoughe
Sir pardoner/ be mery and glad of chere
And ye sir hoste / that ben to me so dere
I praye you that ye kysse the pardoner
And pardoner/ I pray the drawe the ner
And as we dyd/ let vs laughe and play
Anon they kyssed/ and ryden forthe her way.

¶ Here endeth the Pardoners tale/ & here begynneth the Shipmãs prologue.

Nowe frendes sayd our hoste so dere
Howe lyketh you by Iohan the pardonere :
He hath vnbokeled wel the male
He hath vs tolde right a thrifty tale
As touchyng of his mysgouernaunce
I pray to god yeue him good chaunce
As ye han herde/ of these ryottours thre
Nowe gentill mariner/ hertely I pray the
Tel vs a good tale/ and that right anon
It shal be done/ by god & by saynt Iohn
Sayd this maryner/ as wel as euer I can
And right anon his tale he thus began.

¶ Here endeth the Shypmans prologue/ and here folowеth his tale.

¶ A mar

A marchāt/ whilom dwelled at salt Denise
That rich was/ for which men held him wise
A wife he had/ of excellent beaute
And compynable/ and reuelous was she
Whiche is a thyng that causeth more dispence
Than worthe is al the chere and reuerence
That men hem done/ at feestes and at daūces
Suche salutations and countynaunces
Passeth/ as dothe the shadowe on a wal
But wo is him that paye mote for al
The sely husbonde algate he mote paye
He mote vs bothe cloth and eke arraye
Al for his owne worshippe/ richely
In whiche array we dauncen iolyly
And if that he may nat/ parauenture
Or els lust no suche spence endure
But thynketh/ that it is wast and lost
Than mote another paye for our coste
And lende vs golde/ and that is perilous
This noble Marchant helde a noble hous
For whiche he had al day great repayre/
For his largesse/ and for his wyfe was fayre
That wonder is: but herkeneth to my tale
Amonge all his gestes great and smale.
There was a monke/ a fayre man & a bolde
I trowe thurty wynter he was olde
That euer in one/ was drawyng to that place
This yonge monke/ ꝥ so fayre was of face
Aquaynted was with this good man
Sythens that he first knowlege began
That in his house/ as famylier was he
As it is possyble any frende to be
And for as moche/ as this good man
And eke this monke/ of whiche I began
Were bothe two borne in one village
The monke him claymed/ as for cosynage
And he agayne sayd not ones nay
But was as glad therof/ as foule of day
For to his herte it was a great plesaunce
Thus ben they knytte with eterne alyaunce
And eche of hem gan other for to ensure
Of brotherheed/ whyles her lyfe may dure.
¶ Fre was daun Iohan/ & namely of dispēce
As in that house/ and ful of dyligence
To do plesaunce / and eke great costage
He forgate not to yeue the leste page
In al that house/ but after her degre
He yaue the lorde/ and sythen his meyne
Whan ꝥ he came/ some maner honest thyng
For whiche they were as glad of his cōmyng
As foule is fayne/ whan the sonne vp ryseth
No more herof as nowe/ for it suffyseth.
¶ But so byfell/ this marchaunt on a day
Shope him to make redy his aray
Towarde the towne of Bruges for to fare
To bye there a porcion of ware
For whiche he hath sent to Parys anon
A messanger/ and prayde hath dan Ihon
That he shuld come to saint Denys to playne
With him/ and with his wyfe/ a day or twayn
Or he to Bruges went/ in al wyse.
¶ This noble monke/ of which I you deuyse
Hath of his abbot/ as him lyst lycence
Bycause he was a man of hye prudence
And eke an officer/ out for to ryde
To seen her graunges/ and her bernes wyde
And vnto saynt Denys he cometh anon.
Who was so welcome/ as my lord dan Ihon
Our dere cosyn/ ful of curtesye
With him he brought a iubbe of maluesye
And eke a nother ful of fyne vernage
And volatily/ as was aye his vsage
And thus I let hem bothe eate/ drinke/ & play
This marchant & this monke/ a day or tway.
¶ The thirde day this marchaunt vp ryseth
And on his nede sadly him auyseth
And vp in to his countyng house gothe he
To reken with him selfe/ as wel may be
Of thilke yere/ howe it with him stoode
And howe he spended had his goode
And if that he encresed were or none
His bokes and his bagges many one
He layth afore him/ on his counter borde
Ful ryche was his tresour and his horde
For whiche ful faste his counter dore he shet
And eke he nolde no man shulde him let
Of his accomptes/ for the mene tyme
And thus he sate tyl it was passed prime.
Dan Iohan was rysen in ꝥ morow also
And in the garden walked two and fro
And hath his thynges sayd ful curtesly.
¶ This good wyfe come walkyng priuely
In to the garden/ there he walked softe
And him salueth/ as she hath done ful ofte
A mayden childe came in her companye
Whiche as her luste/ she may gouerne & gye

D.ii. For

For yet vnder the yerde was the mayde.
¶ O dere cosyn dan Johan/she sayde
What eyleth you so rathe to a ryse?
¶ Nece (qd he) it ought ynough suffise
Fyue houres for to slepen on a nyght
But it were for an olde palled wyght
As ben these olde wedded men/ that lye & dare
As in a forme sytteth a wery hare
Al forstraught/ with hoũdes gret & smale
But dere nece / why loke ye so pale?
I trowe certes/that our good man
Hath you laboured/sythe this night began
That you were nede to resten hastely
And with that worde/ he lough ful merily
And with his owne thought he woxe al reed.
 This fayre wyfe/gan to shake her heed
And sayd thus/ye god wote al (qd she)
Nay cosyn myn/it stondeth not so with me
For by that god that yaue me soule and lyfe
In al the realme of Fraũce/ is there no wyfe
That lesse luste hath to that sory play
For I may syngen alas/ and welaway
That I was borne/ but to no wight (qd she)
Dare I not tel/howe it stonte with me
Wherfore I thinke out of this world to wende
Or els of my selfe sone to make an ende
So ful I am of drede and eke of care.
¶ This mõke began vpon this wyfe to stare
And sayd alas/nay nece god forbede
That ye for any sorowe/ or for any drede
For do your selfe/ but telleth me your grefe
Perauenture I may in your mischefe
Counsayle or helpe/& therfore telleth me
Al your anoye/for it shal secre be
For on my porthose I make an othe
That neuer in my lyfe/for lefe ne lothe
Ne shal I not of no counsayle you bewray.
 The same ayen to you (qd she) I say
By god and by this porthose/I you swere
Though men wolde me al in to peces tere
Ne shal I neuer/for to go to hell
Bewray o worde / of thing that ye me tell
Not for no cosynage/ne for alyaunce
But verily for loue and affyaunce
Thus ben they sworne/and here vpon kyste
And ilke of hem tolde other what hem lyste.
¶ Cosyn (quod she) if I had a space
As I haue none/and namely in this place
Than wolde I tel a legende of my lyfe
That I suffred haue/sythe I was a wyfe
With myn husbonde/though he be your cosyn
 Nay (qd this mõke) by god & seynt Martyn
He nys no more cosyn vnto me
Than is this lefe/that hongeth on the tre
I clepe him so/by saynte Denys of Fraunce
To haue the more cause of aquayntaunce
Of you/whom I haue loued specially
Abouen al other women sykerly
This swere I you on my professyoun
Telleth your grefe/leste he come adoun
And hasteth you/and goth your way anon.
 My dere loue (qd she) O my dan John
Ful lefe me were this counsayle to hyde
But out it mote/it may no lenger abyde.
 My husbonde is to me the worste man
That euer was/sythe the worlde began
But sythen I am a wyfe/it sytte not to me
To tellen no wight of our priuyte
Neyther in bedde/ne in none other place
God shylde I shulde tel it for his grace
A wyfe ne shulde not say of her husbonde
But al honoure/ as I can vnderstonde
Saue vnto you/ thus moche tel I shall
As helpe me god/he is nought worthe at all
In no degre/the value of a flye
But yet me greueth moste his nygardye
And wel ye wote/ that women naturally
Desyren thinges syxe/ as wel as I
They wolden that her husbondes shulde be
Hardy/and wyse/riche/and therto fre
And buxom to his wyfe/and fresshe a bedde
But by that ilke lorde that for vs bledde
For his honoure/ my selfe to arraye
A sonday next/I mote nedes paye
An hundred frankes/or els am I lorne
yet were me leuer that I were vnborne
Than me were done a slaunder or a vilanye
And if myn husbonde eke might it aspye
I nere but loste/ and therfore I you prey
Lene me this sõme/or els mote I dey
Dan John I say/ lene me this hũdred frãkes
Parde I wol not fayle you my thankes
If that ye lyste to do that I you pray
For at a certayne day I wol you pay
And to done you what plesaunce & seruyce
That I may don/right as ye lyste deuyse.

And

The Shipman's Tale (B 1287–1382; T. 13027–13122)

And but I do/ god take on me vengeaunce
As foule as euer had Genilon of Fraunce.
¶ This gentil mōke answerd in this manere
Nowe truly myn owne lady dere
I haue (q̄d he) on you so great routhe
That I you swere/and plight my trouthe
That whā your husbōde is to Flaūders ifare
I wol delyuer you out of al this care
I wol bringe you an hundred frankes
And with that he caught her by the flankes
And her enbraced harde/and kyssed her ofte
Gothe nowe your way (q̄d he) al styl & softe
And let vs dyne as sone as euer ye may
For by my kalender it is prime of the day
Gothe nowe/ & beth as true as I shal be.
Nowe els god forbyd sir sayd she
And forthe she gothe/as ioly as a pye
And bade the cokes that they shulde hem hye
So that men might dyne/and that anone
Vp to her husbonde is this wyfe gone
And knocked at his counter dore boldely.
Qui est la (q̄d he) Peter it am I
(Quod she) howe longe wol ye fast?
Howe longe tyme wol ye recken and caste
Your somes/your bokes/& your thynges?
The dyuel haue parte of al such reckenynges
Ye haue ynough (q̄d she) of goddes sonde
Come down to day/& let your bagges stonde
Ne be ye not ashamed/that dan Iohn
Shal fastyng al this longe day gon?
What let vs go here masse and go dyne.
¶ Wyfe (q̄d this mā) lytel canst thou diuyne
The curyous besynesse that we haue
For of chapmen/so god me saue
And by that lorde that called is seynt Iue
Scarsly amonge twenty/ twelue shal thriue
Contynuelly/lastyng vnto their age
We may wel make chere & good vysage
And driue forthe the worlde/as it may be
And kepe our estate in priuyte
Tyl we be deed/ or els that we play
A pylgrimage/or gone out of the way
And therfore haue I great necessyte
Vpon this queynte worlde to auyse me
For euermore we mote stonde in drede
Of happe and fortune/ in our chapmanhede
To Flaūders wol I gone to morow at day
And come ayene as sone as euer I may
For whiche my dere wyfe/I the beseke
As be to euery wight buxom and meke
And for to kepe our good be curyouse
And honestly gouerne wel our house
Thou haste ynough/in euery maner wyse
That to a thrifty huswyfe may suffyse
The lacketh none array/ne no vitayle
Of syluer in thy purse thou mayst not fayle
And with ẏ worde/his counter dore he shette
And down he gothe/no lenger wolde he lette
And hastely a masse was there isayde
And spedely the tables were layde
And to dyner faste they hem spedde
And richly the chapman this monke fedde.
And after dyner/dan Iohan soberly
This chapman toke a parte al priuely
And sayd him thus/cosyn it stondeth so
That wel I se/to Bruges ye wol go
God and saynt Austen spede you and gyde
I pray you cosyn/wysely that ye ryde
Gouerneth you also wel of your dyete
Al temperatly/and namely in this hete
Betwyxt vs two nedeth no straunge fare
Farwel cosyn/god shylde you fro care
If any thing there be by day or by night
And it lye in my power or in my might
That ye me wol cōmaunde in any wyse
It shal be done/right as ye wol deuyse
O thing or that ye go/ if that it may be
I wolde pray you for to lene me
An hundred frankes/ for a weke or twey
For certayne beestes/ that I mote nedes bey
To store with a place that is ours
God helpe me so/ I wolde it were yours
I shal not fayle surely at my day
Not for a thousande frankes/a myle way
But let this thing be secret/I you pray
For yet this night these beestes mote I bey
And fare nowe wele/myn owne cosyn dere
Graunt mercy of your coste and your chere.
¶ This noble marchaunt/gentilly anon
Answerde and sayd/O cosyn dan Iohn
Nowe sikerly/this is a smal request
My golde is yours/whan that you leste
And not only my golde/but my chaffare
Take what ye lyste/god shilde that ye spare
But one thing is/ye knowe it wel ynough
Of chapmen/that her money is her plough

The Shipman's Tale (B 1383–1478; T. 13123–13218)

Ye may creaunce/ whyle we haue a name
But goldlesse for to be it is a shame
Paye it ayen/ whan it lythe at your ese
After my might/ fayne wolde I you plese.
¶ These hundred frankes/ set he forthe anon
And priuely he toke hem to dan John
No wight of this worlde/ wyste of this lone
Sauyng this marchaũt/ & dan Johan alone
They drinke & speke/ & rome a while and pley
Tyl that dan Johan rydeth to his abbey.
¶ The morow came/ & forth ryd this marchãt
To Flaũders warde/ his prẽtes brought him
Tyl he came to Bruges/ wel & merily (auãt
Nowe gothe this marchaunt/ wel and besily
About his nedes/ & byeth/ and creaunseth
He neyther playeth at the dyce ne daunseth
But as a marchaunt/ shortly to tell
He ledde his lyfe/ and there I let him dwell.
¶ The sonday next/ ẏ this marchãt was gon
To saynt Denys is comen dan John
With crowne & berde al fresshe & newe ishaue
In al this house/ there nas so lytel a knaue
Ne no wight els/ but he was ful fayne
For ẏ my lorde dan John was comen agayn
And shortly to the poynte for to gon
The his fayre wyfe acordeth with dan John
That for these hũdred frãkes he shuld al night
Haue her in his armes/ bolte vpright
And this acorde parformed was in dede
In myrthe al nyght a besy lyfe they lede
Tyl it was day/ ẏ dan Johan yede his way
And bade the meyne farwel & haue good day
For none of hem/ ne no wyght in the toun
Had of dan Johan any suspection
And forthe he rydeth/ home to his abbey
Or where him lyste/ no more of him I sey.
¶ This marchaunt/ whan ended was ẏ faire
To sainte Denis he gan for to repaire
And with his wife he maketh feest & chere
And telleth her that the chaffare is so dere
That nedes muste he make a cheuesaunce
For he was bounden in a reconusaunce
To pay twenty thousande shildes anon
For whiche this marchaunt is to Paris gon
To borowe of certayne frendes that he had
A certayne frankes/ & some with him he lad
And whan he was comen in to the toun
For chierte and great affection
Unto dan Johan he first gothe him to pley
Nought for to borowe of him no money
But for to wete and se of his welfare
And for to tellen him of his chaffare.
As frendes done/ whan they ben mette in fere
Dan Johan him maketh feest & mery chere
And he him tolde ayen ful specially
Howe he had bought/ ful wel and graciously
Thonked be god/ al hole his marchaundise
Saue that he muste/ in al maner wise
Maken a cheuesaunce/ as for his beste
And than shulde he be in ioye and reste
Dan John answerd/ certes I am right fayn
That ye in heale be comen home agayne
And if I were riche/ as haue I blisse
Of twẽty thousãde shildes shuld ye not misse
For ye so kyndely/ this other day
Lent me golde/ and as I can and may
I thonke you/ by god and by saynt Jame
But nathelesse/ I toke it vnto our dame
Your wife at home/ the same golde agayne
Upon your benche/ she wote it wel certayne
By certayne tokens/ that I can her tell
Nowe by your leue/ I may no lenger dwell
Our abbot wol out of this towne anon
And in his companye I mote gon
Grete wel our dame/ myn owne nece swete
And farwele dere cosyn/ tyll we mete.
¶ This marchant that was ful ware & wyse
Creaunced hath/ and eke payde in Parys
To certayne lombardes/ redy in her hondes
This sõme of golde/ & gate of hem the bondes
And home he gothe/ as mery as a popyngay
For wel he knewe he stode in suche aray
That nedes muste he wyn by that viage
A thousande frankes/ aboue al his costage.
¶ His wife ful redy met him at the gate
As she was wonte/ of olde vsage algate
And al that night in mirthe they be sette
For he was ryche/ and clerely out of dette
Whã it was day/ this marchant gan embrace
His wyfe al newe/ & kyssed her in her face
And vp he gothe/ & made it wonder tough
No more (qd she) by god ye haue ynough
And wantonly ayen with him she playde
Tyl at the laste this marchant thus saide.
By god (qd he) I am a lytel wrothe
With you my wife/ al though it be me lothe

And

The Shipman's Tale (B 1479–1574; T. 13219–13314)

And wot ye why? by god as I gesse
For ye haue made a maner of straungenesse
Betwyxt me and my cosyn dan John
Ye shulde haue warned me/ or I had gon
That he had you an hundred frankes payde
By redy token/ & helde him yuel apayde
For that I to him spake of cheuesaunce
He semed so/ as by his countenaunce
But nathelesse/ by god our heuen kyng
I thought not to aske of him nothing
I pray the wife/ ne do no more so
Tell me alway er that I fro the go
If any dettour/ hath in myn absence
Ypayde the/ leste through thy neglygence
I might him aske a thing that he hath payde.
¶ This wyfe was not a ferde ne affrayde
But boldely she said/ and that anon
Mary I defye that false monke dan John
I kepe not of his tokens neuer a dele
He toke me certayne golde/ I wot it wele
What yuel thedom on his monkes snoute
For god it wote/ I wende without doute
That he had yeue it me/ bycause of you
To don therwith myn honoure & my prow
For cosynage/ and eke for belle chere
That he hath had ful often tymes here
But sythe I se it stonte in suche disioynte
I wol answere you shortly to the poynte.
Ye haue mo slacker dettours than am I
For I wol pay you wel and redily
Fro day to day/ and if so be I fayle
I am your wyfe/ score it on my tayle
Or els I shal pay it as sone as euer I may
For by my trouth/ I haue on myn aray
And not in waste/ bestowed it euery dele
And for I haue bestowed it so wele
To your honour/ for goddes sake I say
As be not wrothe/ but let vs laughe & play
Ye shal my ioly body haue to wedde
By god I nyl not pay you but a bedde
Foryeue it me/ myn owne spouse dere
Turneth hitherwarde/ and make better chere.
¶ This marchant sawe ther was no remedye
And for to chide/ it was but a folye
Sithen that the thing may not amended be
Nowe wife he said/ and I foryeue it the
But in thy life/ be no more so large
Kepe bet my good/ this yeue I the in charge
Thus endeth nowe my tale/ & god vs sende
Talinge inough/ vnto our lyues ende.

¶ Here endeth the Shypmans tale/ and foloweth the wordes of our hoste.

Wel said by corpus domini (qd our host)
Nowe longe mote thou sayle by the coste
Thou gentil maister/ gentil marinere
God gyue yͤ mōke a thousāde last quad yere
A ha felowes/ beware of suche a iape
The monke put in the marchātes hode an ape
And in his wyues eke/ by saynt Austyn
Draweth no monkes more in to your inne
But nowe passe ouer/ & let vs seke aboute
Who shal tel nowe first of al this route
An other tale/ and with that worde he sayde
As curtesly/ as it had ben a mayde.
My lady prioresse/ by your leue
So that I wiste yͭ I shulde you not greue
I wol deme/ that ye tellen sholde
A tale next/ if so be that ye wolde
Nowe wol ye vouchsafe/ my lady dere
Gladly (qd she) and said in this manere.

¶ Here endeth the wordes of our hoste/ & here begynneth the Prioresses prologue.

Domine dñs noster: quã admirabile est nomen tuũ in vniuersa terra.

Lorde our lord/ thy name how meruailous
Is in this wyde worlde ispradde (qd she)
For not only thy laude precious
Parfourmed is/ by men of dignyte
But by the mouth of children thy bounte
Parfourmed is/ for on the breest soukyng
Somtyme shewen they thyn hering

Wherfore in laude/ as I can best and may
Of the and of the white lilly floure
Whiche that the bare/ & is a mayde alway
To tellen a storie/ I wol do my laboure
Nought that I may encrese her honoure
For she her selfe is honour and rote
Of bountie/ next her sonne of soules bote

O mo-

The Priorestes tale.

Mother mayden / O mayden & mother fre
O busshe vnbrent / brennyng in Moyses sight
That rauisshedest downe fro the deyte
Through thyn hūblesse / the gost ỹ in the light
Of whose vertue / whan he in thyn hert pight
Conceyued was the fathers sapyence
Helpe me to tell it in thy presence

Lady thy bounte / and thy magnifycence
Thy vertue and thy great humilyte
There may no tonge expresse / in no science
For somtyme lady / er men pray to the
Thou goest before / of thy benignyte
And gettest vs the light / through thy prayere
To gyden vs vnto thy sonne so dere

My connyng is to weake / O blissfull quene
For to declare thy high worthynesse
That I ne may the weyght sustene
But as a child of twelue monthe olde or lesse
That can vnnethes any worde expresse
Right so fare I / and therfore I you pray
Gydeth my songe / that I shal of you say.

¶ Here endeth ỹ Priorestes prologue / and here foloweth her tale.

T Here was in Asye / in a great cyte
Amonges christen folke a iewrye
Sustayned by a lorde of that countre
For foule vsure / and lucre of villany
Hateful to Christ / and to his company
And through the strete men might ride & wēde
For it was free / and open at euery ende

A lytel schole of christen folke there stode
Down at the farther ende / in which ther were
Children an hepe / comen of christen blode
That lerned in that schole / yere by yere
Suche manere doctryne / as men vsen here
This is to say / to synge and to rede
As smale children don in her childhede

Amōges these children was a wedowes son
A lytel clergion / that. vii. yere was of age
That day by day to schole was his won
And also eke / where he sey the ymage
Of Christes mother / had he in vsage
As him was taught / to knele a down and say
An Aue maria / as he goth by the way

Thus hath this wedow / her litel child itaught
Our blyssed lady / Christes mother dere
To worship aye / and he forgate it naught
For the sely childe / wolde al day soone lere
But aye / whan I remēbre me on this matere
Saynt Nicholas stōdeth euer in my presence
For he so yonge to Christ dyd reuerence

This

This lytel childe his lytel boke lernyng
As he sate in the schole at his prymere
He (Alma redemptoris mater) herde syng
As children lered her antiphonere
And as he durst/ he drewe aye nere and nere
And herkened to the wordes and the note
Tyl he the first verse couth al by rote

Nought wist he what this latyn was to say
For he so yonge and tender was of age
But on a day his felowe gan he pray
To expowne him the song/ in his langage
Or tellen him why this songe was in vsage
This prayde he him to constre and declare
Ful ofte tyme/ vpon his knees bare

His felowe/ whiche that elder was than he
Answerd him thus/ this song I haue herd say
Was made of our blessed lady free
Her to salewe/ and eke her for to prey
To ben our helpe & socoure whan we dey
I can no more expowne in this mater
I lerne songe/ I can but small grãmer

¶ And is this songe ꝑmade in reuerence
Of Christes mother/ sayd this innocent :
Nowe certes I wol done my dilygence
To conne it al er Christmasse be went
Though that I for my primer shal be shent
And shulde be beten thrise in an houre
I wol it conne/ our lady to honoure

His felawe taught him homwarde priuely
Fro day to day/ tyl he couthe it by rote
And than he songe it wel and boldely
Fro worde to worde/ acordyng to the note
Twyse a day it passeth through his throte
To scholewarde/ & homeward whan he went
On Christes mother set was al his entent

As I haue sayd throughout the iewerye
This lytel childe as he came to and fro
Ful merily than wolde he synge and crye
O Alma redemptoris mater/ euer mo
The swetnesse hath his herte persed so
Of Christes mother/ that to her to pray
He can not stynte of syngyng by the way.

¶ Our first foe/ the serpent Sathanas
That hath in iewes herte his waspes neste
Vp swale and sayd/ O ebrake people alas
Is this a thyng to you that is honest
That suche a boy shal walke as him leste
In your dispyte/ and syngen of suche sentẽce
Whiche is ayenst your lawes reuerence.

¶ From thence forth/ the iewes han conspyred
This innocent out of this worlde to chase
An homicide therto han they hyred
That in an aley/ had a priuy place
And as the childe gan forby to pace
This cursed iewe him hent/ and helde faste
And cutte his throte/ & in a pytte him caste

I say that in a wardrope they him threwe
Where that the iewes purged her entrayle
O cursed folke/ of herawdes al newe
What may your yuel entent you auayle
Murther wol out/ certes it wol not fayle
And namely ther ẏ honour of god shal sprede
The bloode out cryeth on your cursed dede

¶ O Mater/ sowned vnto virginite
Now maist thou synge folowyng euer in on
The whyte lambe celestyal (qd he)
Of whiche the great euangelyst saynt John
In Pathmos wrote/ whiche sayth ẏ they gon
Before this lambe/ & synge a songe al newe
That neuer flesshly women they ne knewe.

¶ This poore wydowe/ awayteth al ẏ night
After her lytel childe/ and he came nought
For whiche as sone as it was day light
With face pale/ for drede and besy thought
She hath at schole/ & els where him sought
Tyl fynally/ she gan so farre aspye
That he was laste seyne in the iewrye

With mothers pyte/ in her breste enclosed
She goth as she were halfe out af her mynde
To euery place/ where she hath supposed
By lyklyhede her childe for to fynde
And euer on Christes mother/ meke & kynde
She cryed/ and at last thus she wrought
Amonge the cursed iewes she him sought
She

The Prioress's Tale (B 1706–1789; T. 13446–13529)

The Prioresses tale.

She freyneth and she prayeth pitously
To euery iewe that dwelleth in thilke place
To tellen her/ if her childe went there by
They sayd nay/ but Iesu of his grace
Yaue in her thought/ within a lytel space
That in that place/ after her sonne she cryde
There he was cast/ in a pytte besyde.

¶ O great god/ that perfourmyst thy laude
By mouthe of innocence/ lo here thy might
This iemme of chastyte/ this Emeraude
And eke of martyrdome the rubye bright
There he with throte yeorue lay vpright
He (Alma redemptoris) gan to synge
So loude that al the place gan to ringe.

¶ The christen folke/ yͤ through yͤ strete went
In comen/ for to wonder on this thyng
And hastely they for the prouoste sent
He came anon/ without taryeng
And heryeth Christ/ that is of heuen kyng
And eke his mother/ honour of mankynde
And after that/ the iewes let he bynde.

This childe with pytous lamentation
Was vp taken/ syngyng his songe alway
And with honoure/ and great processyon
They caryen him to the nexte abbey
His mother swounyng by the bere lay
Vnneth might the people that were there
This newe Rachel bringe fro his bere

¶ With turment & with shamful deth ilke one
This prouoste dothe these iewes for to sterue
That of this murder wyste/ & that anone
He nolde no suche cursydnesse obserue
Yuel shal he haue/ that yuell wol deserue
Therfore with wylde horse he dyd hem drawe
And afterwarde he honge hem by the lawe

¶ Vpon his bere aye/ lythe this innocent
Beforne the chefe aulter/ whiles yͤ masse laste
And after that/ the abbot with his couent
Hem spedde/ for to burye him als faste
And whan they holy water on him caste
Yet spake yͤ child/ whã spreint was holy water
And songe/ O Alma redemptoris mater.

This abbot/ whiche that was an holy man
As monkes ben/ or els ought to be
This yonge childe to couer he began
And sayd: O dere childe/ I haylse the
By vertue of the holy trinyte
Tel me what is thy cause for to synge
Sythens thy throte is cutte to my semyng.

¶ My throte is cutte/ vnto my necke bone
Sayd this childe/ as by way of kynde
I shulde haue deyde/ ye longe tyme agone
But Iesu Christ/ as ye in bokes fynde
Wol that his glorie laste and be in mynde
And for the worshyp of his mother dere
Yet may I synge (O Alma) loude and clere

This well of mercy / Christes mother swete
I loued alway/ as after my connyng
And whan that I my lyfe shulde forlete
To me she came/ and bade me for to synge
This antem verily in my deyeng
As ye han herde/ & whan that I had songe
Me thought she laide a grayne vpon my tõge

Wherfore I synge/ and synge mote certayne
In honoure of the blissful mayden fre
Tyl fro my tonge/ of taken is the grayne
And after that/ thus she sayd to me
My lytel childe/ nowe wol I fetche the
Whan that the grayne is fro thy tonge ytake
Be not agaste/ I wol the not forsake.

¶ This holy monke/ this abbot him mene I
His tong out caught/ & toke a way the grayne
And he yaue vp the goste ful softly
And whan this abbot had this wonder seyne
His salte teeres stryked downe as rayne
And grosse he fel al platte to the grounde
And styl he lay/ as he had ben ybounde

The couent lay eke vpon the pament
Weppyng and heryeng Christes mother dere
And after that they rysen/ & forthe ben went
And toke a way this martyr fro the bere
And in a tombe of marble stones clere
Enclosen they his lytel body swete
There he is nowe/ god leue vs for to mete.
O yonge

The Prioress's Tale (B 1790–1873; T. 13530–13613)

O yonge Hewe of Lyncoln slayne also
With cursed iewes/ as it is notable
For it is but a lytel whyle ago
Pray eke for vs/ we synful folke vnstable
That of his mercy/god be mercyable
On vs/ his great mercy multiply
For the reuerence of his mother Mary.

Here endeth the Priorelle tale. And here folowe the wordes of the Host to Chaucer.

Whan said was this myracle/ euery man
As sobre was/as wonder was to se
Tyl that our hoste to iapen began
And than at erste/ he loked vpon me
And sayd thus: what man arte thou (quod he)
Thou lokest/as thou woldest fynde an hare
For euer vpon the grounde I se the stare

Aproche nere/ and loke vp merily
Now ware you sirs/ & let this mā haue place
He in the waste is shapen as wel as I
This were a popet in armes to enbrace
For any woman/ small and fayre of face
He semeth eluysshe by his countenaunce
For vnto no wight dothe he dālyaunce

Say now sōwhat/sithēs other folke han said
Tel vs a tale of myrthe/and that anon
Hoste (quod he) ne be not yuel apayde
For other tale certes can I none
But of a ryme/ I lerned yore agone
Ye that is good (quod he) we shullen it here
Som dayntе thing/ me thinketh by thy chere.

Here endeth the wordes of the Host and here foloweth the ryme of sir Thopas.

Listeneth lordynges in good intent
And I wol tell verament
Of myrthe and of solas
Al of a knight was fayre and gent
In batayle and in turnament
His name was sir Thopas.
Iborne he was in ferre countre
In Flaunders/ al beyonde the see
At Poperyng in the place.
His father was a man ful fre
And a lorde he was of that countre
As it was goddes grace.
Sir Thopas was a doughty swayne
Whyte was his face as payne mayne
His lyppes reed as rose
His rudde is lyke scarlet in grayne
And I you tel in good certayne
He had a semely nose.
His heer/ his berde was lyke safroun
That to his gyrdell raught adoun
His shone of cordewane.
Of Bruges were his hosen broun
His robe was of chekelatoun
That coste many a iane.
He couthe hunte at the wylde dere
And ryde an haukyng forby the ryuere
With grey goshauke on honde
Therto he was a good archere
Of wrastlyng was there none his pere
There any Ram shulde stonde.
Ful many a mayde bright in boure
They mourne for him paramoure
Whan hem were bet to slepe.
But he was chaste/ and no lechoure
And swete as is the bramble floure
That beareth the reed hype.
And so byfell vpon a day
Forsothe/as I you tel may
Sir Thopas wolde out ryde
He worthe vpon his stede gray
And in his honde a launce gay
A longe sworde by his syde.
He pricketh thorowe a fayre foreste
Therin was many a wylde beest
Ye bothe bucke and hare.
And as he pricketh northe and este
I tel you/him had almeste
Betydde a sore care.
There springen herbes great and smale
The lycores and the setuale
And many a clowe gelofer
And nutmygges/to put in ale
Whether it be newe or stale
Or for to lye in cofer.
The byrdes syngen/ it is no nay
The sperhauke and the poppyngay
That ioy it was to here.

The

The ryme of syr Thopas.

The throstell eke made his lay
The wodcocke vpon the spray
She song ful loude and clere.
¶ Sir Thopas fyl in loue longyng
And whan he herde the throstel syng
He pricked as he were wode
His faire stede in his prickyng
So swette/ that men might him wring
His sydes were al blode.
¶ Sir Thopas eke so wery was
For prickyng on the softe gras
So fiers was his corage
That doun he layde him in that place
To maken his stede some solace
And gaue him good forage.
¶ Oh/ saynt Mary/ benedicite
What ayleth this loue at me
To blynde me so sore:
Me dremed al this nyght parde
An elfe quene shal my lemman be
And slepe vnder my gore.
¶ An Elfe quene wol I loue ywis
For in this worlde no woman is
Worthy to be my make in towne
Al other women I forsake
And to an Elfe quene I me betake
By dale and eke by downe.
¶ In to his sadel he clombe anone
And pricketh ouer style and stone
An Elfe quene for to espye
Tyl he so longe hath ridden and gon
That he fonde in a priue wone
The countre of Fayrie. So wylde
For in that countre nas there non
Neither wyfe ne childe
Tyl him there came a great Giaunt
His name was called sir Olyphaunt
A perylous man of dede.
He said childe/ by Termagaunt
But if thou pricke out of my haunt
Anon ysle thy steed with mace
Or euer I go out of this place
¶ Here is the quene of Fayry
With harpe and pipe/ and symphony
Dwellyng in this place.
The childe said/ als so mote I the
To morowe wol I meten the
Whan I haue myne armure.
And yet I hope par ma faye
That thou shalte with this launce gay
Abyen it ful sore: Through thy mawe
Shal I perce/ if I maye
Or it be fully prime of the daye
For here thou shalt be slawe.
Sir Thopas drowe abacke ful faste
This gyaunt at him stones caste
Out of a fell staffe slynge
But fayre escaped sir Thopace
And al was through goddes grace
And thorowe his fayre berynge.
¶ yet lystneth lordynges to my tale
Meryer than the nightyngale
For nowe I wol ye rowne
Howe sir Thopas/ with sydes smale
Prickyng ouer downe and dale
Is comen ayen to towne.
His mery men comaunded he
To maken him bothe game and gle
For nedes muste he fyght
With a gyaunt/ with heedes thre
For paramoures and iolyte
Of one that shone full bright.
Do come he sayd my mynstrales
And gestours/ for to tellen vs tales
Anon in myn armyng
Of romaunces that ben royals
Of popes and of cardynals
And eke of loue longyng.
They fette him first the swete wyne
And meede eke in a mazelyne
And royal spycerye
Of gynger breed that was ful fyne
Of lycores and eke comyne
With sugre that is trye.
He dyd nexte his whyte lere
Of clothe of lake fyne and clere
A breche and eke a sherte.
And next his sherte an hakcton
And ouer that an haberion
For percyng of his herte.
And ouer that a fyne hauberke
Was al ywrought of Iewes werke
Full stronge it was of plate
And ouer that his cote armoure
As whyte as is the lyly floure
In whiche he wolde debate.

His

The Ryme of Sir Thopas (B 1959–2058; T. 13699–13797)

His shylde was al of golde so reed
And therin was a bores heed
A carbocle by his syde.
And there he swore on ale and breed
Howe that the gyaunt shulde be deed
Betyde what betyde.
His iambeux were of cure buly
His swordes shethe of yuore
His helme of laton bright
His sadel was of ruel bone
His bridel as the sonne shone
Or as the moone light
His spere was of fyne syprees
That byddeth warre/ & nothing pees
The heed ful sharpe ygrounde
His stede was al dappel gray
He gothe an aumble by the way
Ful softely and rounde in londe.
¶ Lo lordes myn/ here is a fyt
If ye wol any more of it
To tellen it wol I fonde.
N Owe holde your mouthe for charite
Bothe knyght and lady fre
And herkeneth to my spell
Of batayle and of chevalrye
And of ladyes love drery
Anon I wol you tel.
Men speken of Romaunces of pris
Of Hornechilde/ and of Ipotys
Of Bevys/ and of sir Gye
Of sir Lybeaux/ and Playndamoure
But sir Thopas/ he bereth the floure
Of ryal chevalrye.
His good stede he bestrode
And forthe upon his way glode
As sparke out of the bronde.
Upon his creste he bare a toure
And therin stycked a lilly floure
God shylde his cors fro shonde
And for he was a knight auentrouse
He nolde slepen in none house
But lygge in his hood.
His bright helme was his wanger
And by hym fedde his destrer
Of herbes fyne and good
Him selfe dronke water of the wel
As dyd the knight sir Persyvel
So worthy under wede.

¶ Here endeth the ryme of sir Thopas/ and begynneth ẏ wordes of our host.

No more of this for goddes dignyte
(Qd our hoste) for thou makest me
So wery of thy very leudenesse
That also wysly god my soule blesse
Myn eeres aken of thy drafty speche
Nowe suche a ryme/ the dyvel I beteche
This may wel be cleped ryme dogrel (qd he)
Why so (qd I) why wolte thou let me
More of my tale/ than any other man
Sens that it is the beste ryme I can
By god (qd he) playnly at o worde
Thy drafty rymyng is not worthe a torde
Thou doest nought els but spendest tyme
Sir at one worde/ thou shalt no lenger ryme
Let se whether thou canste tel aught in geste
Or tel in prose somwhat at the leste
In which ther may be some myrth or doctrine
Gladly (qd I) by goddes swete pyne
I wol you tel a lytel thing in prose
That ought lyke you/ as I suppose
Or els ye be certes to daungerous
It is a morall tale vertuous
Al be it tolde somtyme in sondrie wyse
Of sondrie folke/ as I shal you devyse
As thus/ ye wote that every evangelyst
That telleth us the payne of Iesu Christ
Ne sayth not al thyng as his felawe dothe
But nathelesse her sentence is al sothe
And al acorden in her sentence
Al be there in her tellyng difference
For some of hem sayne more/ & some lesse
Whan they his pytouse passyon expresse
I meane of Marke/ Mathew/ Luke/ & Iohn
But doutlesse her sentence is al on
Therfore lordynges/ I you beseche
If that ye thynke I varye in my speche
As thus/ though I tel somwhat more
Of proverbes/ than ye han herde byfore
Comprehended in this lytel treatyse here
To enforcen with the effect of my matere
And though I not the same wordes say
As ye han herde/ yet to al you I pray
Blameth me not/ for in my sentence
Shul ye not fynde mochel difference
Fro the sentence of this tretes lyte

R After

After the whiche/this mery tale I write
And therfore herkeneth/what I shal say
And let me tell my tale I you pray.

¶ Here endeth the wordes of our hoste/ and here begynneth Chaucers tale of Melibeus

A Yonge man called Mellibeus/ mighty & ryche/ begate vpon his wife that called was Prudence/a doughter whiche that called was Sophye. ¶ Vpon a daye byfell that he for his disporte is went into the feldes him to playe: His wyfe and eke his doughter hath he lefte within his house/ of whiche the dores were fast ishette. Foure of his olde foos han it aspide/ and setten ladders to the walles of his house/and by ẏ wyndowes ben entred/ and bete his wyfe/ and wouded his doughter with fyue mortall woundes/ in fyue sondrie places: That is to say/in her fete/in her hondes/in her eeres/ in her nose/& in her mouthe/ and leften her for deed/and wenten her waye.

Whan Melibeus retourned was in to his house/and se al this mischefe/he like a madde man rentyng his clothes/ gan to wepe & crye.

Prudence his wyfe/as ferforth as she durste besought him of his weppynge for to stynte: But not for thy he gan to wepe and crye euer lenger the more. ¶ This noble wife Prudēce remembred her vpon the sentence of Ouyde/ in his boke that cleped is the remedye of loue/ where as he saythe/ he is a foole that distourbeth the mother to wepe in ẏ deth of her childe tyl she haue wepte her fyll/ as for a certayne tyme: and than shal a man done his dilygēce with amyable wordes to recomforte and pray her of her weppynge for to stynte. For whiche reson this noble wyfe Prudence/ suffred her husbonde to wepe and crye/ as for a certayne space: and whan she sawe her tyme/ she said him in this wyse. Alas my lorde (qd she) why make ye your selfe for to be lyke a foole? forsothe it apperteyneth not vnto a wyse man to maken suche a sorowe. your doughter wt the grace of god/ shal warisshe & escape. And al were it so that she right nowe were deed/ye ne ought not as for her dethe your selfe distroye. Senek sayth/ ẏ wise mā shal not take to gret discomforte for the dethe of his children/ but certes he shuld suffre it in paciēce/as wel as he abydeth the dethe of his owne proper person.

¶ This Mellebeus answerde anon and said: What man (qd he) shuld of his weping stynt that hath so great a cause for to wepe? Jesus him selfe our lorde/ wepte for the dethe of Lazarus his frende. Prudence answerd/ certes wel I wote a temperate weppyng is nothyng defended to him ẏ sorouful is/ amonge folke in sorow/but it is rather grāted him to wepe. The apostel Poule vnto ẏ Romans writeth/ men shuld reioyce wt hem that maketh ioye/& wepe with such folke as wepen. But though a temperate weping be grāted/certes outrageous weppyng is defēded. Mesure of weping shulde be cōsydred after ẏ lore that techeth vs Senek. Whan ẏ thy frende is deed (qd he) let not thyn eyen to moist ben of teeres/ne to moche drie: although teeres comen to thyn eyen/ let hem not fall. And whan thou haste forgon thy frende/do diligēce to gette a nother frende: and this is more wisdom than for to wepe for thy frēde whiche thou hast lorne/ for therin is no bote. And therfore if ye gouerne you by sapiēce/put away sorowe out of your herte. Remēbreth you that Jesus Sirake sayth/a man that is ioyous and glad in herte/ it him conserueth flourisshyng in his age: But sothely a sorouful hert maketh his bones drie. He sayth eke thus/that sorowe in herte sleeth ful many a man. Salomon sayth/ ẏ right as moughthes in the shepes fleyse anoyeth the clothes/ and the smale wormes the tree/ right so anoyeth sorowe ẏ hert of man/ wherfore vs ought as wel in the dethe of our children/ as in the losse of our temporal goodes/haue pacience.

Remembre you vpon pacient Jobe/ whan he had loste his children and his temporal substāūce/ and in his body endured and receyued ful many a greuous trybulacion/ yet sayd he thus: Our lorde it sent to me/ our lorde hath byrafte it me/right so as our lorde wold/right so it be done/iblessed be the name of our lorde.

To these forsaid thinges Melibeus vnto his wife Prudēce answerd: Al thy wordes (qd he) ben

ben true/ ⁊ therto profytable/ but truely myn herte is troubled wt this sorowe so greuously/ that I not what to do. Let cal (qd̄ Prudence) your true frēdes al ⁊ thy lynage/ which yͭ ben wyse/ ⁊ telleth to hem your case/ and herkeneth what they say in counsayling/ ⁊ gouerne you after her sentēce. Salomon sayth/ werke al thy thinges by counsaile/ ⁊ thou shalte neuer rue. Than by counsaile of his wyfe Prudēce/ this Melibeus let cause a great congrygacion of people/ as surgyens/ physicions/ olde folke and yonge/ ⁊ some of his olde enemyes reconciled (as by her semblant) to his loue and to his grace: And therwithal there came some of his neyghbours/ that dyd him reuerence more for drede thā for loue/ as it happeth oft. There comen also ful many subtyl flaterers/ ⁊ wise aduocates lerned in the lawe. And whan these folke togyders assembled were/ this Melibeus in sorouful wise shewed hem his case/ and by the maner of his speche/ it semed yͭ in herte he bare a cruel yre/ redy to don vengeance vpon his foos/ ⁊ sodainly he desyred yͭ werre shulde begyn/ but nathelesse yet asked he counsayle vpon this mater. A surgyen by lycence and assent of suche as were wyse vp rose/ ⁊ vnto Melibeus said as ye shal here.

¶ Sir (qd̄ he) as to vs surgiens apertayneth that we do to euery wight the beste yͭ we can/ where as we ben withholden/ ⁊ to our pacient that we don no damage: Wherfore it happeth many tyme ⁊ ofte/ that whan two men haue eueriche wounded other/ one surgyen healeth hem both/ wherfore vnto our arte it is not pertinēt to norisshe werre/ ne parties to supporte. But certes as to yͭ warisshing of your doughter/ al be it so that perilously she be wounded/ we shal do so tētyfe besynesse fro day to night that with yͭ grace of god she shal ben hole and sounde/ as sone as is possible. Almost right in the same wyse the physiciens answerd/ saue that they sayden a fewe wordes more: That right as maladies ben by her cōtraries cured/ right so shal man warisshe werre by peace. His neighbours ful of enuye/ his fayned frēdes that semed reconciled/ and his flatterers/ maden semblaūce of wepyng/ ⁊ enpayred and agrutched moche of this mater/ in praysinge greatly Melibe of might/ of power/ of richesse and of frendes/ dispysing the power of his aduersaries: and said vtterly/ yͭ he anon shulde wreken him on his foos/ and begyn werre.

Vp rose than an aduocat that was wyse/ by leue ⁊ by counsayle of other yͭ were wyse/ and said: The nede for the whiche we ben assēbled in this place/ is ful heuy thing/ ⁊ a gret mater bycause of the wronge and of the wickydnesse that hath be don/ and eke by reson of gret damages that in tyme cōmynge ben possible to fallen for the same/ ⁊ eke by reson of the great richesse ⁊ power of the parties bothe/ for the whiche resons it were a ful great peryll to erren in this mater. Wherfore Melibeus this is our sentence/ we coūsaile you abouen al thīg/ that right anon thou do thy dylygence in keping of thy propre person/ in such a wyse that thou ne want none espye ne watche/ thy body for to saue: And after that we coūsaile that in thyn house thou set suffycient garryson/ so as they may as wel thy body as thy hous defēde: But certes to mouen werre/ or to don sodainly vengeance/ we may not deme in so lytel tyme that it were profytable/ wherfore we aske leyser ⁊ space to haue deliberacion in this case to deme/ for the cōmen prouerbe sayth thus: He that sone demeth sone shal repēt. And eke men sayne/ thilke iuge is wyse that sone vnderstondeth a mater/ ⁊ iugeth by leyser: For al be it tarieng be noyful/ algate it is not to be reproued in yeuynge of iugement/ ne in vengeaunce taking/ whan it is suffycient ⁊ resonable. And yͭ shewed our lorde Jesu Christ by ensample/ for whan yͭ woman was taken in auoutry ⁊ was brought ī his presēs to knowen what shuld be don of her person/ al be it yͭ he wyst wel him selfe what he wold answere/ yet ne wolde he not answere sodenly/ but he wold haue deliberacion/ ⁊ in the grounde he wrote twyse/ ⁊ by this cause we asken deliberacion: and we shal than by the grace of god counsayle you yͭ thing that shal be profytable.

Vp sterte than the yonge folke at ones/ ⁊ the most part of yͭ cōpany haue skorned this olde wise mā/ ⁊ begon to make noise ⁊ said. Right so as whyles yͭ yron is hote men shuld smyte/ right so men shulde wreken her wrōges while

The Tale of Melibeus (B 2191–2225; T. §§ 7–12)

that they ben fresshe & newe/ and with loude voice they cryed/ werre werre. Up rose tho one of the olde wise/ & with his honde made coūtenaunce ỹ they shulde holden hem styl & yeuen hym audyence. Lordynges (qd̄ he) ther is ful many a man that cryeth werre werre/ ỹ wote ful lyte what werre amoūteth. Werre at his begynnyng hath so great an entryng and so large/ that euery wight may entre whan hym lyketh/ & lightly fynde werre: but certes what ende therof shal fal/ it is not lightly to know. Whan that werre is ones bygon / there is ful many a childe unborne of his mother/ ỹ shal sterue yonge bicause of thilke werre/ other els lyue in sorowe/ or dye in wretchydnesse: And therfore or ỹ any werre be bygon/ men muste haue great counsayle & good delyberacion. And whan this olde man wende to enforcen his tale by reson / wel nye al at ones bygon for to ryse for to breken his tale/ & bydden hym ful ofte his wordes for to abregge: For certes he that precheth to hem that list not to here his wordes/ his sermon hem anoyeth. For Jesus Syrake sayth/ ỹ wepyng in musyke is a noyous thing. This is as moche to say/ as moche auayleth it to speke byforne folke to whiche his speche anoyeth/ as it is for to syngen byforne hem that wepe. And whan this wyse man sawe ỹ him wanted audiēce/ al shamfast he set him adown ayen. For Salomon saith. There as thou mayste not haue audyence/ enforce ỹ not to speke. I se wel (qd̄ this wyse man) that the cōmen prouerbe is soth/ ỹ good counsayle wanteth/ whan it is moste nede.

Yet had this Melibeus in his coūsayle many folke/ that priuely in his eere coūsailed hym certayne thinges / & counsayled hym the contrary in general audience. Whan Melibeus had herde that the greatest parte of his counsaile were accorded that he shuld make werre/ anon he cōsented to her counsayling/ & fully affirmed her sentence. Than dame Prudēce/ whan ỹ she sawe her husbōde shope hym for to awreke hym on his enemies/ & to begyn werre: she in ful hūble wise/ whan she sawe her tyme said to him these wordz. My lord (qd̄ she) I you beseche as hertely as I dare or can/ ne haste you not to faste/ and for al guerdons yeue me audiēce. For Peter Alphōs saith. Who so doth to the good or harme/ haste the not to quite it/ for in this wyse thy frende wol abyde/ and thyn enemy shal the lenger lyue in drede. The prouerbe sayth/ he hasteth wel ỹ wisely can abyde: And in wicked haste is no profyte.

This Melibe answerd to his wife Prudēce: I purpose not (qd̄ he) to werke by thy counsaile/ for many causes & resons/ for certes euery wight wolde holde me than a fole. This is to say/ if I for thy counsayling wolde chaūge thinges that ben ordayned and affirmed by so many wise. Secondly/ I say that al women ben wicked/ & none good of hem al. For of a thousande men saith Salomon/ I fonde one good man: but certes of al women founde I neuer non. And also certes/ if I gouerned me by thy coūsayle/ it shuld seme that I had yeue the ouer me ỹ maistry: & god forbyd that it so were. For Jesus Syrake saith/ that if ỹ wife haue maystrye/ she is contraryous to her husbōde. And Salomon sayth. Neuer in thy lyfe to thy wyfe/ ne to thy childe/ ne to thy frēde/ ne yeue no power ouer thy self/ for better it were that thy children aske of thy thinges that hem nedeth / than thy selfe to be in the handes of thy children. And also if I wol werche by thy counsaile/ certes my coūsayle must be somtyme secre tyl it were tyme that it must be knowen: and this ne may not be/ if I shuld be coūsayled by the. Whā dame Prudēce ful debonairly and with gret pacience/ had herde al that her husbōd liked for to say/ than asked she of hym lycence for to speke/ & sayd in this wyse. My lorde (qd̄ she) as to your first reson / it maye lightly ben answerd. For I say that it is no folye to chaūge counsayle/ whan the thing is chaunged/ or els whan ỹ thing semeth otherwise thā it semed afore. And more ouer I say/ though that ye haue sworne & behyght to performe your emprise / and by iuste cause ye do it not: men shuld not say therfore ye were a lyer & forsworn. For ỹ boke saith/ that ỹ wise man maketh no lesynge/ whan he turneth his corage for ỹ better. And al be it that your emprise be establisshed & ordeyned by gret moultytude of folke/ yet dare you not acomplisshe thilke ordynaūce but you lyketh: for ỹ trouth of of thinges and the profyte ben rather foũden in fewe folke that ben wyse and ful of reson/ than by great multitude of folke/ there euery man cryeth and clattereth what him lyketh: sothly suche multitude is not honest. And as to the seconde reson/ where as ye saye/that all women ben wicked: saue your grace. Certes ye dispyse al women in this wyse/ and he that al dispyseth/as sayth the boke/al displeaseth. And Senecke sayth/ that who so wol haue sapience/ shal no man dispraysе/ but he shal gladly teche the science that he can/ without presumpcion or pride: and suche thinges as he nought ne can/he shal not ben a shamed to lerne hem/ and to enquire of lesse folke than him selfe. And yͭ there hath ben many a good woman/may lightly be proued: For certes sir our lorde Jesu Christ nolde neuer han discended to be borne of a woman/if al women had be wicked. And after that/for the great boũte that is i women/our lorde Jesu Christ/whan he was rysen fro dethe to lyfe/ apered rather to a woman than to his apostels. And though that Salomon sayde/ he founde neuer women good/it foloweth not therfore that al women be wicked: for though that he ne founde no good woman/ certes many an other man hath founde many a woman ful good and trewe. Or els parauenture the entent of Salomon was this/ that in souerayne bountie he founde no woman/this is to say: that there is no wight that hath parfyte bountie saue god alone/ as he him selfe recordeth in his euangelie. For there nys no creature so good that him ne wanteth somwhat of the perfection of god that is his maker. Your thirde reson is this/ ye say that if that ye gouerne you by my counsayle/it shulde seme that ye had yeue me the maistry and the lordshyp of your person. Sir saue your grace it is not so/for if so were that no man shulde be counsayled but onely of hem that han lordship and maistrye of his person/ men nolde not be counsayled so ofte. For sothly thilke man that asketh coũsayle of a purpose/yet hath he fre wyl whether he wol do after that coũsayle or non. And as to your fourthe reson/ there as ye sayne that the ianglerye of women can hyde thinges that they wot not/as who saith/that a woman can not hyde that she wote. Sir/these wordes ben vnderstonde of women that ben ianglers & wicked/of whiche women men sayne yͭ thre thinges driuen a man out of his house/ that is to say/ smoke/ droppynge of rayne/ and wicked wyues. And of such women Salomon saith/ that a man were better dwell in deserte/ than with a woman yͭ is riottous. And sir by your leaue it am not I/for ye haue ful ofte assayde my great sylence and my great pacience/ and eke howe wel that I can hyde & heale thinges that men oughten secretly to hyden. And sothly as to your fyfte reson/where as ye say that in wicked counsayle women venquisshe men: God wote that thilke reson stante here in no stede: for vnderstondeth/ nowe ye asken counsayle for to do wickednesse: And if ye wolde werken wickydnesse/ and your wyfe restrayneth thilke wicked purpose/ & ouercome you by reson and by good counsayle/ certes your wife ought rather to be praysed than blamed. Thus shulde ye vnderstonde the philosopher that sayth/ in wicked coũsayle women venquisshe her husbondes. And ther as ye blame al women and her resons/ I shal shewe you by many ensamples that many women haue be ful good/and yet ben/ & her counsaile holsom and profitable. Eke some men han said that the counsayle of women is eyther to dere/ or to lytel worthe. But al be it so that ful many women be badde/ & her counsaile vile and nought worthe/ yet han men foũde ful many a good woman/& ful discrete & wyse in counsayling. Lo Jacob through the counsaile of his mother Rebecke/ wan yͤ benyson of his father/ & the lordship of al his brethern. Judeth trough her good counsayle/delyuered yͤ cite of Bethulie/ in whiche she dwelt/ out of yͤ honde of Holofern yͭ had it al beseged/ & wolde haue distroyed it. Abigayle delyuered Naball her husbõd fro Dauid yͤ king/ yͭ wold haue slayn him/ & apeased the yre of the king by her wytte and by her good coũsel. Hester by her coũsell enhaũsed greatly the people of god in yͤ reigne of Assuerus the kyng. And the same bountie in good coũsayling of many a good woman may mẽ rede & tel. And furthermore whã that our lorde had created Adam oure former fa- ther/he said in this wyse: It is not good to be a man alone: make we an helper to him selfe semblable. Here maye ye se that if that wo- men were not good/⁊ her counsaile good and profytable/ our lorde god of heuen ne wolde neyther han wrought hem/ ne called hem the helper of man/ but rather confusion to man.

And there sayd a clerke ones in two verses. What is better than golde? Jasper. What is better than Jasper? wysdome. And what is better than wysdom? woman. And what is better than a good woman? ỷ is a good man. And what is better thã a good man? nothĩg. And sir/by many other reasons may ye sene/ that many women ben good/and eke her coũ- sayle good and profytable. And therfore sir/ if that ye wol truste to my counsayle/ I shal restore you your doughter hole and sounde/ and eke that I wol do you so moche/ that ye shal haue honoure in this case.

Whan Melybe had herde the wordes of his wyfe prudence/ he said thus. I se wel that the wordes of Salomon be soth. For he saith/the wordes that be spoken discretly by ordynaũce ben honycombes/ for they yeuen swetnesse to the soule/ and holsomnesse to the body. And wyfe by cause of thy swete wordes/ and eke for I haue proued and assayed thy great sa- pyence and thy great trouthe: I wol gouerne me by thy counsayle in al thing.

¶ Now sir (qd dame Prudence) and sythens that ye vouchsafe to be gouerned by my coun sayle/ I wol enforme you howe that ye shal gouerne your selfe in chosyng of your coun- saylours. Ye shal first in al your werke meke ly besechynge to the hye god that he wolde be your counsaylour/ and shapeth you to suche entent that he yeue you counsayle ⁊ comforte/ as taught Thobye his sonne. At al tymes thou shalte blisse god/ and praye him to dresse thy wayes/ and loke eke that thy counsayles ben in him euer more. Saynt James sayth/ if any man of you haue nede of sapience/aske it of god. And afterwarde/ than shullen ye take counsayle in your selfe/ ⁊ examyne well your owne thoughtes/ of suche thynges as you thynketh that ben beste for your profyte.

And than shal ye driue fro your hert thynges that be contraryous to good coũsayle: that is to saye/ ire/ couetyse/ and hastynesse.

¶ First he that asketh counsaile of him selfe/ certes he must be withouten yre and wrath in him selfe/for many causes. The first is this: He that hath great ire and wrathe in him selfe he weneth alway that he may do thynge that he may not do. And secondly/he that is yrous and wrothful/ he may not wel deme: And he that may not wel deme/may not wel coũsell. The thirde is this/he that is irous and wroth/ as sayth Senecke/ may not speke but blame- ful thinges/ and with thilke vycious wordes he styreth other folke to angre ⁊ to yre. And eke sir ye muste driue couetyse out of your herte. For the apostell saythe/that couetyse is the rote of al harmes. And trusteth right well that a couetous mã ne can not deme ne thinke but onely to fulfyll the ende of his couetyse: and certes that ne may neuer be acõplisshed/ for euermore/ the more haboundaunce that he hath of richesses/ the more he desyreth. And sir/ ye muste also driue out of your herte hasty- nesse: For certes ye may not deme for the best a sodayne thought that falleth in your herte/ but ye muste auyse you on it ful ofte: For as ye haue herde here byfore/ the comen prouerbe is this. He that sone demeth/ sone repenteth.

Sir/ ye ne be not alway ĩ lyke disposycion/ for certes some thing that semeth somtyme to you that is good for to do/an other tyme it se- meth to you the contrarye.

And whan ye han taken counsayle in your selfe/⁊ han demed by good delyberacion suche thynge as you semeth beste/ than rede I you that ye kepe it secrete. Bewraye ye not your counsayle to no person/but if so be ỷ ye wene sikerly that through your bewrayeng/ your condycion shal be to you the more profytable. For Jhesus Sirake saythe: neyther to thy foe ne to thy frende discouer not thy secret/ ne thy folye: for they wol yeue you audyence and lo- kyng/and supportacion in your presence/and scorne you in yor abscẽce. A nother clerke saith/ that scarsly shall you fynde any person that may kepe counsaile secretly. The bõke sayth/ while ỷ thou kepest thy coũsayle in thyn hert/

thou

thou kepest it in thy prison: and whan thou bewrayest thy counsayle to any wight/ he holdeth the in his snare. And therfore you is better to hyde your counsayle in your herte/ than to pray him to whom ye haue bewrayed your counsaile/ that he wol kepe it close styll. For Seneca sayth: If so be that thou mayst not thyn owne counsayle hyde/ howe darste thou pray any other wight thy counsayle secrete to kepe. But nathelesse if thou wene sikerly that the bewrayeng of thy counsayle to a person wol make thy condycion stonde in the better plight/ than shalte thou tel him thy cou̅sayle in this wyse. First thou shalte make no semblante whether the were lever peace or warre/ or this or that/ ne shewe him not thy wyll ne thyn entent: for truste wel that comenly these cou̅saylours ben flatterers/ namely the counsaylers of great lordes/ for they enforce hem alwaye rather to speke plesaunt wordes/ enclynyng to the lordes luste/ than wordes that ben trewe or profytable/ and therfore men say that the riche man hath selde good counsayle/ but if he haue it of him selfe. And after that thou shalt consyder thy frendes and thyn enemyes. And as touchynge thy frendes/ thou shalt consyder whiche of hem ben most faythful and moste wyse/ and eldest/ and most approued in counsailynge: and of hem shalte thou aske thy cou̅sayle/ as the case requireth.

I say/ that first ye shal cal to your cou̅saile your frendes that ben trewe. For Salomon saythe: that right as the herte of a man delyteth in sauoure that is sote/ right so the counsayle of trewe frendes yeueth swetnesse to the soule. And he saythe also/ there may nothyng be lykened to the true frende: For certes golde ne syluer be not so moche worthe as the good wyl of a trewe frende. And also he sayth that a trewe frende is a stronge defe̅ce/ who so that it fyndeth hath a great tresure. Than shal ye also consyder if that your true frendes be discrete and wise: for the boke saith/ aske alway thy counsayle of them that ben wyse. And by this same reason shal ye cal to your cou̅saile your frendes that ben of age/ suche as seme and ben experte in many thinges/ and ben approued in counsayling. For the boke sayth/ that in olde men is sapie̅ce/ and in longe tyme the prudence. And Tullius saythe/ that great thinges ben not aye accomplisshed by stre̅gth ne by delyuernesse of body/ but by counsaile/ by auctorite of persones/ and by science: the whiche thre thynges ne ben not feoble by age/ but certes they enforce & encreace day by day. and than shal ye kepe this for a general rule. First shal ye call to your counsayle a fewe of your fre̅des that ben especial. For Salomon saith/ many frendes haue thou/ but amonge a thousa̅de chose the one to be thy cou̅sailour: for al be it so that thou first ne tel thy counsayle but to a fewe/ thou mayste afterwarde tel it to mo folke if it be nede. But loke alway that thy counsaylers haue those condycions that I haue sayd before/ that is to saye/ that they be trewe/ wise/ & of olde experience. And werke not alway in euery nede by one counsayler alone: for somtyme behoueth it to be counsayled by many. For Salomon sayth/ saluacion of thinges is where as there be many counsaylers.

¶ Nowe haue I tolde you of whiche folke ye shal be cou̅sailed: Nowe wol I tel you which counsayle ye ought to eschue. Firste ye shal eschue the counsaylinge of fooles. Salomon saythe/ take no cou̅sayle of a foole/ for he wol counsayle but after his owne lust and his affection. The boke saith/ that the propertie of a foole is this: He troweth lightly harme of euery man/ and lightly troweth al bountie in him selfe. Thou shalt eschue the counsayling of al flatterers/ whiche as enforcen hem rather to prayse your persone by flattery/ than for to tel you the sothfastnesse of thynges. Wherfore/ Tullius saith/ amonge al the pestilence that ben in frendship/ the greatest is flaterye. And therfore it is more nede yͭ thou eschue & drede flaterers/ tha̅ any other people. The boke sayth/ thou shalt rather flee fro the swete wordes of flatering and praysing/ than fro the egre wordes of thy frendes that sayth the sothes. Salomon saithe/ that the wordes of a flaterer is a snare to catche innoce̅ce. He saithe also/ he that speketh to his frende wordes of flatery & of plesaunce/ he setteth a nette before his fete to catche him. And therfore Tulli-

Tullius saith. Enclyne not thyn eeres to flaterers/ ne take no counsaile of flaterers. And Caton sayth. Auyse the wel/ and eschue the wordes of swetnesse & of plesaunce. And eke thou shalt eschue the cou͂saylyng of thyn olde enemyes that ben reconciled. The boke saith/ that no wight retourneth safely in to yͤ grace of his olde enemy. And Esope saith/ ne trust not to hem/ to whiche thou hast somtyme had werre or enemyte/ ne tel hem not thy cou͂saile. And Seneke telleth the cause why it may not be/ for he saith/ there as great fyre hath longe tyme endured/ that there dwelleth some vapoure of hete. And therfore saith Salomon/ in thyn olde foe truste thou neuer. For sikerly though thy enemy be reco͂ciled/ and make the signe of humilite/ & lout to the with his heed/ truste him neuer: for certes he maketh thilke fayned humilite more for his profyte than for any humilite/ or for any loue of thy person/ bycause yͤ he demeth to haue victorie ouer thy persone by suche fayned countynaunce/ the whiche victorie he might not haue by strife or werre. And Petrus Alphons saith/ make no felowship with thyn olde enemies/ for if thou do hem boutie/ they wollen peruerte it to wickednesse. And eke thou must eschue the counsayling of hem that ben thy seruauntes/ and beren the gret reuerence: for parauenture they sayen it more for drede than for loue. And therfore sayth a philosopher in this wise. There is no wight parfetly true to him that he dredeth. And Tullius sayth/ there is no might so great of any emperour that longe may endure/ but he haue loue of the people and drede. Ye shal eschue also the counsayling of folke that ben dronkelewe/ for they ne can no counsaile hyde. For Salom̃. saith/ there nis no priuite ther as reigneth dronkenesse. Ye shal haue also in suspecte the counsayling of suche folke as counsayle you one thing priuely/ and cou͂saile you the contrary openly. For Cassidorie sayth/ that it is a maner sleight to hynder his enemy whan he sheweth to done a thing openly/ and werketh priuely the contrarye. Thou shalte haue also in suspecte the counsayling of wicked folke/ that be alway ful of fraude. And Dauid sayth/ that blissful is the man yͤ hath not folowed the counsailinge of shrewes.

Thou shalte also eschue the counsailinge of yonge folke/ for her counsayling is not rype/ as Salomon sayth.

¶ Nowe sir/ sythens I haue shewed you of suche folke as ye shal be counsailed of/ and so lowe it: nowe wol I teche you howe ye shall examyne your counsaile. After the doctrine of Tullius/ in examenyng of your counsaylours/ ye shall consyder many thynges.

First thou shalt consyder thilke thynge that thou purposest/ and vpon that thynge yͤ thou wolte haue cou͂saile/ that very trouthe be said and co͂serued/ this is to say/ tel truely thy tale: for he that sayth false/ may not wel be counsayled in that case/ of whiche he lyeth. After this thou shalte consyder the thynges that acorden to that thou purposest for to do by thy cou͂saylours/ if reason accorde therto/ and eke if thy might maye attayne therto: and if the more parte and the better parte of your counsaylours accorden therto or no. Than shalte thou consyder what thyng shal folowe of her counsaylinge: As hate/ peace/ werre/ grace/ profyte/ or damage/ and meny other thinges: and in al thinges thou shalte chose the beste/ and weyue al other thiges. Than shalt thou consyder of what rote is engendred the mater of thy counsayle/ and what fruite it may conceyue and engender. Thou shalt eke co͂syder al thy causes/ from whence they be spronge. And whan thou haste examyned thy cou͂saile/ as I haue sayd/ and whiche partye is the better and more profytable/ and haste approued it by many wyse folke & olde/ than thou shalt consider/ if thou maist performe it/ and make of it a good ende. For certes reson wol not that any man shal begyn a thinge/ but if he might performe it as him ought: ne no wight shulde take vpon him so heuy a charge/ but that he might beare it. For the prouerbe saith/ he that to moche enbraceth distrayneth lytell. And Caton sayth/ assay to do suche thinges as thou haste power to done/ lest the charge oppresse the to sore/ that the behoueth weyue thyng that thou haste begonne. And if so be that thou be in dout/ whether thou maist perfourme a thinge or none/ chose rather for to

suffer

The Tale of Melibeus (B 2370–2406; T. §§ 23, 24)

suffre than to begynne. And Peter Alphons sayth/ if thou haste might to do a thynge/of whiche thou muste repente/ it is better holde thy tonge styll than for to speke. Than maist thou vnderstonde by stronger resons/ that if thou haste power to perfourme a werke/of whiche thou shalt repente the/ than is it better thou suffre than begyn. Well sayne they that defenden euery wyght to assaye a thinge of which he is in doute whether he may perfourme it or none. And after whan ye haue examined your counsayle (as I haue sayde before) and knowe wel/ that ye maye performe your emprise: conferme it than sadly tyl it be at an ende. ¶Nowe it is reason and tyme that I shewe you/whan and wherfore that ye maye chaunge your counsayle/ withouten repro[...]e. Sothly a man may chaunge his purpose and his counsayle/ if the cause ceaseth/ or whan a newe case betydeth. For the lawe sayth/that vpon thinges that newly betydeth/ behoueth newe counsayle. And Senek sayth/if thy counsaile is come to the eeres of thyn enemyes/ chaunge thy counsayle. Thou mayste also chaunge thy counsayle/if so be thou fynde that by errour or by any other cause/harme or damage may betyde. Also if thy counsayle be dishonest / other els come of dishonest cause / chaunge thy counsayle. For the lawe sayth/ that al behestes that be dishonest/ne ben of no value: And eke/ if so be that it be vnpossyble or may not gladly be parformed or kepte.

And take this for a general rule/ that euery counsayle that is enfourmed so strongly/that it may not be chaunged for no condycion that may betyde/I say ẏ ilke counsayle is wicked.

Melibeus/ whan he had herde the doctryne of his wyfe dame Prudence/ answerde in this wyse. Dame (quod he) as yet vnto this tyme ye han wel taught me/as in gouernayle howe I shal gouerne me in the chosynge and in the withholdynge of my counsayle: but nowe wolde I fayne that ye wolde condiscende in especial/howe ẏ ye semeth by our counsaylours that we haue chose in this present nede.

¶My lorde (quod she) I beseche you in all humblesse/that ye wol not wylfully replye agaynst my resons/ne distemper your hert though I speke thing that you displese/ for god wote as in myn entent/ I speke it as for your beste and for your honoure and profyte eke/ and sothly I hope that your benignyte wol take it in pacience. And trusteth me wel that your counsaile in this case ne shulde not (as to speke properly) be called a counsayling/ But a mocion or a mouyng of folye / in whiche counsayle ye haue erred in many a sondrie wyse.

First ye haue erred in ẏ assemblyng of your counsaylours: For first ye shulde haue cleped a fewe folke to your counsayle/ and after ye might haue shewed it to mo/ if it had be nede. But ye haue cleped to your counsayle a great multytude of people/ ful chargeous and full noyous for to here. Also ye haue erred/ for there as ye shulde haue onely cleped to your counsayle your trewe frendes/olde and wise/ ye haue cleped straunge folke/ yonge folke/ false flatterers/ and enemyes reconcyled/and folke that done you reuerēce withouten loue. And eke ye haue erred / for ye haue brought with you to your counsaile ire/ couetyse/ and hastynesse/ the whiche thre thynges ben contrary to euery good counsayle/ honest & profytable/ the whiche thre thinges ye haue not distroyed neyther in your selfe ne in your counsaylours/as ye ought. ye haue erred also for ye haue shewed to your counsaylours your talent and your affections to make werre anon/ and for to do vengeaunce/ & they haue espyde by your wordes/to what thyng ye ben enclyned: and therfore haue they rather counsayled you to your talente/ than to your profyte. ye han erred eke / for it semeth that you suffyseth to haue be counsayled by these counsaylours onely/and with lytel auysement/ where as in so hye and in so great a nede/ it had ben necessary mo counsaylours/ and more delyberacion to performe your emprise. ye han erred also/for ye haue not examyned your counsayle in the forsayd maters/ne in dewe maner as the case requireth. ye haue erred also / for ye made no diuision bytwene your true frendes & your fayned counsaylours: ne ye haue not knowen the wyl of your trewe counsaylours & frendes/ olde/ and wyse/ but ye haue caste

caste al her wordes in an hochepot/ & enclyned
your herte to the more parte and to the gretter
nombre of fooles than of wyse men. And ther
fore ẏ coūsaylinges that ben at cōgregacions
and multitudes of folke/ there as men take
more regarde to the nomber than to the sapi-
ence of persons/ ye sene wel/ that in such coun
saylinges/ fooles han the maistrye. Melibe
answerde and sayd ayen: I graunt well that
I haue erred/ but there as thou hast tolde me
here byforne/ that he nys not to blame that
chaungeth his counsayle in certayne case/ and
for certayne and iuste cause/ I am all redy
to chaunge my counsaylours right as thou
woldest deuyse. The prouerbe saythe/ for to
done synne is mānisshe/ but certes for to per-
seuer longe in synne/ is werke of the dyuell.

To this sentēce answereth anon dame Pru-
dence & said: Examyneth (qd she) wel your
counsayle/ and let vs se whiche of hem hath
spoke moste resonably/ and taught you beste
counsayle. And for as moche as the examina
cion is necessarye/ lette vs begyn at surgens
and physiciens/ that first spake of this mater.
I say that physiciens and surgiens haue said
you in your coūsayle discretly/ as hem ought:
and in her speche sayd ful wisely/ that to the
offyce of hem apertayneth to done to euery
wight honoure and profyte/ and no wight to
anoye/ and after her crafte tó don great dyli-
gence vnto the cure of hem/ whiche they haue
in her gouernaūce. And sir/ right as they haue
answerde wisely and discretly/ right so rede I
that they ben hyely and souerainly guerdoned
for her noble speche/ & eke for they shul more
done their ententife besynesse in the curacion
of your doughter: for al be it so they ben your
frēdes/ therfore shullen ye not suffre/ that they
serue you for naught/ but ye ought therafter
guerdon hem/ and pay hem her largesse. And
as touching the preposicion/ whiche the physi-
ciens entreteden in this case/ this is to sayne/
that in maladies is/ that cōtrarie is warisshed
by an other contrarie: I wolde fayne knowe
howe ye vnderstonde thilke texte/ and what is
your sentence. Certes (qd Melibeus) I vn-
derstonde it in this wise. Right as they han do
me a cōtrarie/ so shulde I done hem an other/
for right as they han venged hem vpon me/
and done me wronge/ right so woll I venge
me vpon hem/ and don hem wronge/ and than
haue I cured one contrarie by an other.

Lo/ lo (qd dame Prudence) howe lightly is
euery man enclyned to his owne desyre & his
owne plesaunce. Certes (qd she) the wordes
of the physiciens ne shuld not ben vnderstōde
in that wise/ for certes wickydnesse is not con-
trarie to wickydnesse/ ne vengeaunce is not
contrarie to vengeaūce/ ne wronge to wrōge/
but euery of hem encreseth & engendreth other.
But certes the wordes of the phisiciens shulde
be vnderstonde in this wyse/ for good & wic-
kydnesse ben two contraryes: and peace and
werre/ vengeāce & suffraūce/ discorde & acorde/
and many other thinges: But certes wickyd-
nesse shalbe warisshed with goodnes/ discorde
by acorde/ werre by peace/ & so forthe in other
thinges. And therto acordeth saynt Poule the
apostel in many places: He sayth/ ne yeld not
harme for harme/ ne wicked speche for wicked
speche/ but do wel to hem ẏ don to ẏ harme/ &
blesse them that sayth the harme. And in ma-
ny other places he amonissheth peace & acorde.

But nowe wol I speke of the coūsayle/ whi-
che was yeue vnto you by men of lawe/ and
the wyse folke and olde folke/ that sayden al
by one acorde as ye herde byforne/ that ouer
al thinges ye shal done your besynesse & dyli-
gence to kepe your person/ and to warnstore
your house: And they saide also/ that in this
case ye ought to werchen ful wisely and with
great delyberacion. And sir/ as to the firste
poynte/ that toucheth the kepyng of your per-
son: ye shal vnderstōde that he ẏ hath werre/
shal euer deuoutely & mekely prayen/ byforn
al thinges/ that Iesu Christ of his mercy wol
haue him in his protection/ and to be his soue-
rayne helper at his nede: For certes in this
worlde there nys no wight that may be coun-
sayled and ykepte suffyciently without the ke-
pynge of our lorde Iesu Christ. To this sen-
tence acordeth the prophete Dauid that sayth:
If god ne kept the cyte/ in ydel waketh he that
it kepeth. Nowe sir/ than shulde he cōmytte
the kepyng of your person to your true fren-
des/ that ben approued and yknowe/ and of
hem

hem shul ye aske helpe/ your person to kepe. For Caton saith: If thou haue nede of helpe/ aske it of thy frendes/ for there nys none so good a physicien as thy true frende. And after this than shal ye kepe you fro al straunge folke/ & fro lyers/ and haue alway in suspecte her companye. For Peter Alphons sayth. Ne take no company by yͤ way of no straūge man/ But if so be that thou haste knowen him of lenger tyme: And if so be that he fall in to thy companye/ parauenture withouten thyn assent & good wyl/ enquire than as subtelly as thou canst of his conuersacion/ and of his lyfe byforne/ and fayne thy way/ sayeng thou woldest go thyder as thou wolte not go/ and if he beare a spere/ holde the on the right syde of him/ and if he beare a swerde/ holde the on the lefte syde of him. And than shal ye kepe you wisely from al maner of suche people as I haue sayd you here byfore/ and hem and her counsayle eschue. And after this than shal ye kepe you/ in suche maner/ that for any presumpsion of your bodely strength/ that ye dispyse not ne acounte not the might of your aduersary so lyte/ that ye lete the kepyng of your person for your presumpcion/ for euery wyse mā dredeth his enemy. And Salomon saith: A very foole is he that of al hath drede: But certes he that thorowe hardynesse of his herte/ and through the hardynesse of him selfe/ hath to great presumpcion/ him shal yuel betyde. Than shal ye euermore encountrewayte enbusshementes/ and al espyaile. For Seneke sayth: The wyse man that dredeth harmes/ escheweth harmes: He ne falleth in to no perylles/ that peryll escheweth. And al be it so that thou seme/ that thou be in secret place/ yet shalte thou alway don dylygence in kepyng of thy person/ this is to say/ ne be not neglygent to kepe thyn owne person/ not onely for thy greatest enemy/ But also for thy leste enemy. Seneke saith/ a man that is wel aduysed/ he dredeth his leste enemye. Ouyde sayth/ that the lytel wesell wol slee the great bulle & the wylde herte. And the prouerbe sayth/ that a lytel thorne wol greue a kyng ful sore/ and a lytel hounde wol holde the wylde bore. But nathelesse I say not thou shalt be so cowarde/ that thou doute where as is no drede. The boke sayth/ that some men haue great luste to disceyue/ But yet they drede to be disceyued. And kepe the fro the companye of skorners: for the boke sayth/ with skorners ne make no company/ but flye her wordes as venym.

¶ Nowe as to the seconde poynte/ where as your wyse counsaylours counsayled you to warnestore your house with great dilygence/ I wolde fayne knowe howe ye vnderstonde thilke wordes/ and what is your sentence.

Melibeus answerde and sayd/ certes I vnderstonde it in this wyse/ that I shall warnestore myn house with toures/ suche as haue castels and other maner edyfices/ and armure and artheries/ bitwene which thinges I may my person and my house so kepe and defende/ that myn enemyes shullen be in drede myn house to aproche. To this sentence answerde anon Prudence. Warnisshyng (qd she) of hye toures & of hye edyfices/ is with great costages and with great trauayle/ and whan that they ben accōplisshed/ yet ben they not worthe a strawe/ but if they ben defended with trewe frendes/ that ben olde and wyse. And vnderstondeth wel/ that the greatest and the strōgest garnyson that ryche men maye haue/ as well to kepen her ꝑsone as her goodes is/ that they be byloued with her subiectes/ and with her neyghbours. For thus sayth Tullius/ that there is a maner garryson/ that no man may venquisshe ne discomfyte/ and that is a lorde to be byloued of his cytezyns/ & of his people.

¶ Nowe sir/ as to the thirde poynte/ where as your olde and wyse cōusaylours sayd/ that ye ought not sodainly ne hastely procede in this nede/ but that ye oughten puruayen and apparayle you in this case/ with great dylygēce and delyberacion. Verily I trowe that they sayde right trewly & right sothe. For Tullius saith: In euery dede or thou begyn it/ apparayle the with great dylygence. Than say I/ in vengeaunce takynge/ in werre/ in batayle/ and in warnestoring/ or thou begyn I rede that thou apparayle the therto/ and do it with great delyberacion. For Tullius sayth: The longe apparelyng to fore the batayle/ maketh shorte victorie. And Cassidorus sayth: The garryson

The Tale of Melibeus (B 2496–2537; T. §§ 31–35)

ryson is stronger/ whan it is longe tyme avysed. But nowe let vs speke of the counsayle that was acorded by your neyghbours/ suche as don you reuerence withouten loue/ your olde enemyes reconciled/ your flatterers/ that counsayled you certayne thinges priuely/ and openly coūsayled you yͤ contrarye. The yong folke also/ that counsayled you to venge you/ and to make werre anon. Certes sir/ as I haue sayde byfore/ ye haue greatly erred to clepe suche maner of folke to your counsayle/ whiche counsaylours ben ynoughe reproued by the resons aforsayd. But nathelesse let vs nowe discende to the special. ye shul first procede after the doctryne of Tullius. Certes the trouthe of this mater or of this counsayle/ nedeth not dyligently to enquire/ for it is wel wyste/ whiche they ben that han done you this trespas and vilanye/ and howe many trespasours/ and in what maner they haue done al this wronge to you/ and al this vilanye. And after this/ than shul ye examyne the seconde cōdicion/ whiche Tullius addeth ī this mater. For Tullius putteth a thinge/ whiche that he clepeth consentyng: this is to saye/ who ben they/ and whiche ben they/ and howe many/ that cōsenten to thy counsayle in thy wylfulnesse/ to done hasty vengeaunce. And let vs consyder also who ben they/ and howe many they ben that consented to your aduersaries. As to the first poynt/ it is wel knowen which folke they be/ that cōsented to your hasty wylfulnesse. For trewly al tho that coūsayle you to maken sodayne werre/ ne be not your frendes. Let se nowe whiche ben they that ye holden so greatly your frēdes/ as to your person: For al be it so that ye be mighty & riche/ certes ye ben but a lone: for trewly ye ne haue no childe but a doughter/ ne ye haue no bretheren ne cosyns germayns/ ne none other nye kynrede/ wherfore your enemyes shulde stynte to plede with you/ ne to distroye your person.

Ye knowe also that your rychesse mot be dispended in dyuers parties. And whan yͭ euery wight hath his parte/ they wollen take but lytel regarde to venge your dethe. But thyn enemyes ben thre/ & they haue many bretheren/ children/ cosyns/ & other nye kynred: & though so were/ that thou haddest slayne of hem two or thre/ yet dwelleth ther ynowe to auenge her dethe/ and to sle thy person. And though so be that your kynrede be more stedfaste and syker than the kyn of your aduersaryes/ yet neuer the lesse your kynrede is but after kynrede/ for they ben but lytel sybbe to you/ and the kynne of your enemyes ben nye sybbe to hem. And certes as in that/ her condycion is better than is yours. Than let vs consyder also of the counsaylinge of hem that counsayled you to take sodayne vengeaunce/ whether it acorde to reson or non: And certes ye know wel nay/ for as by right and reson/ there may no man take vengeaūce of no wight/ but the iuge that hath iurisdiction of it/ whan it is graunted him to take vengeaunce hastely or attemperatly/ as the lawe requireth. And yet more ouer of thilke worde that Tullius clepeth cōsentyng/ thou shalte consent/ if that thy might and thy power may consente and suffyse to thy wylfulnesse/ and to thy counsaylours: And certes thou mayste well saye naye/ for sykerly as for to speke properly/ we may do no thing but suche thing as we maye done rightfully: and certes righfully ye may take no vengeaunce/ as of your owne propre auctorite. Than may ye se that your power ne consenteth not ne accordeth not with your wylfulnesse. Nowe let vs examyne the thirde point/ that Tullius clepeth consequence. Thou shalt vnderstōde that the vengeaunce that thou purposest for to take is consequent/ and therof foloweth an other vengeaūce/ peryl/ and werre/ and other damages withouten nombre/ of whiche we be not ware/ as at this tyme. And as touching the fourthe poynte/ yͭ Tullius clepeth engendring/ thou shalte consyder/ that this wronge/ whiche that is done to the/ is engendred of the hate of thyn enemyes/ and of the vengeaunce takyng vpon hem/ that wolde engender another vengeaunce/ and mochel sorowe & wastyng of rychesse/ as I sayd ere. Nowe sir/ as touchyng the fyfte poynte/ that Tully clepeth causes/ whiche is the laste poynte/ thou shalte vnderstonde/ that the wronge that thou haste receyued/ hath certayne causes/ whiche that clerkes callen ouen/ and efficien/

and

The Tale of Melibeus (B 2538–2584; T. §§ 36, 37)

and causa longinqua/and causa propinqua/ that is to saye / the ferre cause / and the nyghe cause. The ferre cause is almighty god/ that is cause of al thynges. The nere cause is the thre enemyes. The cause accidental was hate. The cause material/ben the fyue woundes of thy doughter. The cause formal/is the maner of their werkynge that brought ladders/ and clambe in at thy wyndowes. The cause final was for to sle thy doughter/ it letted not in as moche as in them was. But for to speke of the ferre cause/ as to what ende they shulde come/or fynally what shal betyde of them in this case/ ne canne I not deme/but by coniectyng and supposing: for we shal suppose that they shal come to a wicked ende/ bycause that the boke of decrees sayth. Selde or with great payne/ ben causes brought to a good ende/ whan they ben badly begonne.

Nowe sir/if men wolde aske me why that god suffred men to do you this villany. Truly I can not wel answere/as for no sothfastnesse. For the Apostel saithe/ that the scyences and the iugementes of our lorde god almighty ben ful depe/ there may no man comprehende ne sertche hem. Nathelesse by certayne presumpcions & coniectynges/ I holde and byleue/ that god whiche that is ful of iustyce & of rightwisnesse/ hath suffred this betyde/ by iuste cause resonable. ¶ Thy name is Melybee/ this is to saye/ a man that drinketh hony. Thou haste dronke so moche hony of swete temporel rychesses/and delytes of honours of this worlde/ that thou arte dronke/ and haste forgoten Jesu Christ thy creatour: Thou ne haste not done to him suche honour and reuerence as the ought/ ne thou ne haste not taken kepe to the wordes of Ouide/ that sayth. Under the hony of the goodes of thy body/is hyd the venym that sleeth thy soule.

And Salomon sayth: If it so be that thou hast founde hony/ ete of the same hony/ that that suffyseth: For if so be that thou ete of the same hony out of mesure/ thou shalte spewe/ and also be nedy and poore. And parauenture almighty god Jesu Christ/ hath yͭ in dispyte/ and hath turned away fro the his face/ and his eeres of myserycorde and mercy. And also he hath suffred & gyue lycēce/ yͭ thou thus shuldest be punisshed & chastised/in the maner that thou haste trespased and offended. Thou hast done synne agaynst our lorde Christ/ for certes the thre enemyes of mankynde/ that is to saye: the flesshe/ the fende/ and the worlde/ thou haste suffred hem entre in to thyne herte wylfully/ by the wyndowes of thy body/and hast not defended thy selfe suffyciētly agaynst their assautes & their temptaciōs/ so that they haue wouded thy soule in fyue places/ this is to say: The deedly synnes/ that ben entred in to thy hert by thy fyue wyttes. And in yͤ same maner our lorde Christ hath wolde and suffred that thy thre enemyes ben entred in to thy house by the wyndowes/ and haue wounded thy doughter in the forsayd maner.

Truely (qd Melibee) I se wel that ye enforce you moche by wordes to ouercome me / in suche maner that I shal not venge me on myn enemyes/ shewyng me the peryles & the yuels that might fal of this vengeaunce/but who so wolde consyder in al vengeaūces/ the perils and yuels that might sue of vengeaūce takyng/a man wolde neuer take vengeaūce/ and that were harme: For by the vengeaūce takyng/ben the wicked men disceuered fro the good men. And they that haue wyl to do wickednesse/restrayn their wicked purpose/whan they se the punisshyng & chastysing of the trespasours: And yet say I more/ that right as a synguler person synneth in takynge vengeaunce of a nother man/ right so synneth the iuge/if he do no vengeaunce of hem that haue deserued. For Senec sayth thus: That maister he sayth is good/ yͭ preueth shrewes. And as Cassiodor saith: A man dredeth to do outrages/whan he wote and knoweth/ that it displeseth to the iuges and souerayne. And an other sayth: The iuge that dredeth to do right maketh men shrewes. And saynt Poule the apostle sayth in his epistle/whan he writeth unto the Romayns/ that the iuges beare not the speere without cause/ but they beare it to punissh the shrewes & misdoers/and for to defende the good men. ¶ If ye wol than take vengeaunce of your enemyes/ye shul returne and haue your recourse to the iuge that hath

S the

the iurisdyction vpon hem / and he shall punysshe hem/ as the lawe asketh & requireth.

A ha/sayd Melibee/this vengeaunce lyketh me no thyng/ I bethynke me nowe/ and take hede how that fortune hath nourisshed me fro my childhode/and hath holpe me to passe many a stronge paas: Nowe I wol assaye her/ trowing with goddes helpe/that she shal helpe me my shame for to auenge.

TRuely sayd Prudẽce/ if ye wol werke by my coũsayle/ye shal not assay fortune by no waye: ne ye shal not lene or bowe vnto her/after the worde of Senek. For thinges that ben folisshly done/ and that ben done in hope of fortune/ shal neuer come to good ende. And as the same Seneke saythe: The more clere and the more shynyng that fortune is/ the more brytel and the soner broke she is. Trusteth not in her/ for she is not stedfast ne stable. For whan thou trowest to be moste sure & stedfast of her helpe/ she wol fayle and disceyue the. And where as ye say/ yt fortune hath nourisshed you fro your childhod/ I say yt in so moche ye shal the lesse trust in her/ & in her wytte. For Seneke saythe: What man that is nourisshed by fortune/she maketh him a great foole. Nowe than syth ye desyre and aske vengeaunce/ and the vengeaunce that is done after the lawe/and before the iuge/ne lyketh you not/ and the vengeaũce that is done in hope of fortune is perylous & vncertayne/ than haue ye none other remedye / but for to haue your recourse vnto the souerayne iuge/ that vengeth al vilanyes and wronges. And he shal venge you/ after that him selfe witnesseth/ where as he sayth: Leaue the vengeaunce to me/and I shal do it.

¶ Melibe answerde/if I ne venge me of the vilany that men haue don to me/ I sõmon or warn hem/that haue don to me that villany/ and al other/ to do me an other villanye. For it is written: If thou take no vengeaunce of an olde vilany/thou sõmonest thyn aduersaryes to do the a newe vilany: And also for my suffraũce men wolde do me so moche vilany/ that I might neither bere it ne sustayn it/ & so shulde I be put & holden ouer lowe. For men sayn/in mykel suffring shal many thyngz fal vnto the/whiche thou shalt not mowe suffre.

¶ Certes (qd Prudence) I graũt you/that ouer moche suffraũce is not good/ but yet ne foloweth it not therof/ yt euery person/to whõ men do vilanye/shulde take of it vengeaũce: for that appertayneth and longeth al only to iuges/for they shulde venge the vilanyes and iniuryes: And therfore those two auctorites that ye haue said afore/ ben onely vnderstõde in the iuges: For whã they suffre ouer moche the wronges & vilanyes to be done/ without punisshment/they sõmon not a man al onely for to do newe wrõges/but they cõmaunde it. Also a wyse man sayth/that the iuge that correcteth not the synner/ cõmaundeth & byddeth him do synne. And the iuges and souerayns/ might in their londe so moche suffre of ye shrewes & misdoers/that they shulde by suche suffraunce/ by processe of tyme/ wexe of suche power & might/ that they shulde put out the iuges and the soueraynes from their places/ and at laste/ make hem lese her lordshyppes.

But let vs nowe suppose/ yt ye haue leue to venge you: I say ye be not of might & power as nowe to venge you/ for if ye wol make cõparison vnto the might of your aduersaryes/ ye shulde fynde in many thynges that I haue shewed you er this/ that their cõdycion is better than yours/ and therfore saye I/ that it is good as nowe/that ye suffre and be pacyent.

Ferthermore/ ye knowe wel that after the comen sawe/it is a wodnesse/a man to stryue with a stronger or a more mighty man than he is him selfe/ and for to stryue with a man of euen strength/that is to say/with as strõge a man as he is/ it is peryll: and for to stryue with a weker man/ it is foly. & therfore shuld a man flye stryuĩg as mikel as he might. For Salomon saythe: It is a great worshyp to a man to kepe him fro noyse & stryfe: and if it so befal & happe that a man of greater might and strength than thou arte/do the greuaũce: studye & besye the rather to styl the same greuaunce/ than for to venge the. For Seneke saythe/that he putteth him in great peryl/that striueth wt a greater man thã he is him selfe. And Caton saith/if a man of higher astate or degre

degre/or more mighty than thou/do the anoye or greuaũce/suffre him: for he that ones hath greued the/may an other tyme releue the and helpe the. Yet sette I case ye haue lycence for to venge you. I saye that there ben full many thinges/that shal restrayne you of vengeaunce taking/and make you for to enclyne to suffre/ and for to haue paciẽce in the wronges that haue ben done to you. First & formest if ye wol consyder the fautes that ben in your owne person/for whiche fautes god hath suffred you haue this trybulaciõ/as I haue said to you here before. For the poete saythe/ that we ought paciẽtly take the trybulacions that come to vs/ whan that we thynke & consyder that we haue deserued to haue thẽ. And saynt Gregorie sayth/ that whan a man cõsydereth wel the nombre of his defautes & of his synnes/ the paynes and the trybulacions that he suffreth/ seme the lesse vnto him. And in as moche as him thynketh his synnes more heuy and greuous/ in so moche semeth his payne the lighter & the esyer vnto him. Also ye owe to enclyne and bowe your herte to take the pacience of our lorde Iesu Christ/as saith saynt Peter in his epystles. Iesu Christ he saythe hath suffred for vs/ & yeuen ensample to euery man to folowe and sewe him/for he dyd neuer synne/ ne neuer came there a villaynous worde out of his mouthe. Whan men cursed him/ he cursed hem not. And whan men bete him/he manaced hem not. Also the great pacience/ whiche saintes ỹ ben in paradyse haue had in trybulacion ỹ they haue suffred/ without her deserte or gylt/ought moche styre you to pacience. Fertheremore/ye shul enforce you to haue pacience/consydring that the trybulacions of this worlde but lytel whyle endure/ and sone passed ben and gon/and the ioy that a man seketh to haue by pacience in trybulacions is perdurable/after that ỹ apostle sayth in his epystle. The ioye of god he saythe/ is perdurable/that is to say/euerlastyng. Also troweth and byleueth stedfastly that he is not wel nourysshed and wel taught/that can not haue pacyence/ or wol not receyue pacience. For Salomon saythe/ that the doctryne and the wytte of a man is knowen by pacyence. And in an other place he sayth/ that he that is pacyent/gouerneth him by great prudence.

And the same Sacomon saythe. The angry and wrathful man maketh noyses/ and the pacient man attempreth and stylleth hem. He saythe also/it is more worthe to be pacient than to be right stronge. And he that maye haue the lordshyp of his owne herte is more to prayse/ than he that by his force or strength taketh great cyties. And therfore sayth saint Iame in his epystle/ that pacyence is a great vertue of perfectyon.

Certes (qd Melibee) I graũt you dãe Prudence/that pacience is a great vertue of perfection/but euery mã may not haue the perfection that ye seke/ ne I am not of the nombre of right perfyte men. For myn herte may neuer be in peace/ vnto the tyme it be auenged. And al be it so that it was great peryll to myn enemyes to do me a villanye/ in takyng vengeaũce vpon me/ yet toke they no hede of the perylL/ but fulfylled her wycked wyl and her corage: And therfore me thynketh men ought not repreue me/though I put me in a lytel peryll/for to auẽge me/& though I do a great excesse/ that is to saye: that I venge one outrage by an other.

¶ Ah (qd dame) Prudence/ye say your wyl as you lyketh: But in no case of the worlde a man shulde not do outrage ne excesse for to venge him. For Cassiodor saith/ that as yuel dothe he that vengeth him by outrage/ as he that dothe the outrage. And therfore ye shall venge you after the order of right/ that is to say/by the lawe/and not by excesse ne by outrage. And also if you wol venge you of ỹ outrage of your aduersaries in other maner than right cõmaundeth/ ye synne. And therfore saythe Seneke: that a man shal neuer venge shreudnesse by shreudnesse. And if ye say that right asketh to defende violence by violence/ and fightyng by fightyng: certes ye say soth/ whan the defence is done without interual/ or without taryeng or delay/ for to defende him/ and not for to venge him. And it behoueth that a man put suche attemperaũce in his defence/ that men haue no cause ne mater to repreue

S.ii.

preue him that defendeth him of outrage and excesse/ for els were it agayne reason. Parde ye knowe wel/ ẏ ye make no defence as now/ for to defende you/ but for to venge you: and so sheweth it that ye haue no wyl to do your dede attemperatly/ and therfore me thynketh that pacience is good. For Salomon sayth/ that he ẏ is not pacient shal haue gret harme.

CErtes said Melibee I grauñt you / that whan a man is impacient and wrothe of that that toucheth him not/ and that appertayneth not vnto him/ though it harme him it is no wonder. For the lawe sayth/ that he is coulpable/ that entremeteth or meteth with suche thynges as apertayneth not vnto him. And Salom. saith/ that he that entremetleth of the noise or strife of another man/ is like to him that taketh a straũge hoũde by the eeres: For right as he/ that taketh a straunge hoũde by the eeres/ is other while bytten by ẏ hoũde/ right so in the same wyse it is reason that he haue harme that by his impacience medleth him of the noyse of an other man/ where as it appertayneth not vnto him. But ye knowe wel that this dede/ that is to say my grefe and my disese/ toucheth me right nygh. And therfore though I be wrothe and impacient/ it is no meruayle: and sauynge your grace I can not se that it might greatly harm me/ though I toke vengeaunce/ for I am rycher & more mighty thã myn enemyes be: And wel know ye that by money and by hauyng great possessyons/ ben al thynges of this worlde gouerned. And Salomon sayth/ al these thynges obey to money.

Whan Prudence had herde her husbonde auaunt him of his rychesse and his moneye/ dispraysing the power of his aduersaries/ she spake and sayd in this wyse. Certes dere sir/ I graunt you that ye be ryche and mighty/ and that the richesse is good to hem that haue wel goten hem / and that well can vse hem. For right as the body of a man may not lyue without the soule/ no more may it lyue without the temporel goodes/ and by richesse may a man get him great frendes. And therfore sayth Pamphillus: If a nerthes doughter he sayth be riche/ she may chese of a thousande men/ whiche she wol take to her husbonde: for of a thousande/ one wol not forsake her ne refuse her. And this Pamphillus saythe also: If thou be right happy/ that is to say/ if thou be ryche/ thou shalt fynde a great nombre of felowes & frendes. And if thy fortune chauge/ farwel frendshyp & felowshyp/ for thou shalt be alone without any companye/ but if it be the companye of poore folke. And yet sayth this Pamphilus more ouer/ that they that ben bonde and thral of lynage/ shal be made worthy and noble by the rychesses. And right so as by the richesses there come many goodnesses/ right so by pouertie come there many harmes and yueles/ for great pouertie constrayneth a man to do many yuels. And therfore calleth Cassiodor pouertie ẏ mother of ruyne/ that is to say/ the mother of ouerthrowyng or of fallyng downe. And therfore sayth Peter Alfonce: One of the greatest aduersyties of this worlde is whan a fre man by kynde or of byrthe/ is cõstrayned by pouerty to ete the almesse of his enemye. And the same sayth Innocent/ in one of his bokes: He sayth/ that sorowfull and mishappy is the condycion of a poore begger/ for if he aske not his meate/ he dyeth for hunger/ and if he aske/ he dyeth for shame: and algates necessite cõstrayneth him to aske. And therfore sayth Salomon/ that better is to dye/ than for to haue such pouerte. And as the same Salomon sayth: Better it is to dye of bytter dethe/ than for to lyue in suche wyse. By these resons that I haue sayd vnto you/ & by many other resons that I coulde say/ I graunt you that rychesses ben good/ to hem that getten hem wel/ and to hem that wel vsen tho richesses: And therfore wol I shewe you howe ye shal behaue you in gatheryng of richesses/ & in what maner ye shullen vse hem.

First ye shal get hem without great desyre/ by good leyser/ sokyngly and not ouer hastely/ for a man that is to desyring to gette richesse/ habandoneth him first to theft and to al other yuels. And therfore sayth Salomon: He that hasteth him to besily to weye riche/ he shal be non innocent. He sayth also/ that the richesse that hastely cometh to a man/ sone and lightly gothe

gothe & passeth from a man/ But that richesse
that cometh lytel & lytel/ weyeth alwaye and
multiplyeth. And sir/ ye shal gette richesse by
your wytte and by your trauaile/ vnto your
profyte/ and that without wronge or harme
doynge to any other persone. For the lawe
sayth/ there maketh no man him selfe riche/
if he do harme to an other wight/ this is to
say: that nature defendeth and forbyddeth by
right/ that no man make him selfe riche vnto
the harme of a nother person. And Tullius
sayth/that no sorowe ne no drede of dethe/ne
nothyng ỹ may fal vnto a man/is so moche
ayenst nature/as a man to encreace his own
profyte/to the harme of an other man. And
though the great and mightye men gette ry-
chesses more lightly than thou/yet shalt thou
not be idel ne slowe to do thy profyte/for thou
shalt in al wise flye idlenesse. For Salomon
sayth/ that idelnesse techeth a man to do ma-
ny yuels. And the same Salomon saith/that
he that trauayleth and besyeth him to tylthe
his londe/ shal eete breed: but he that is idell
and casteth him to no besynesse ne occupaci-
on/ shal fal in to pouerte & dye for hunger.
And he that is idel & slowe/ can neuer fynde
couenable tyme for to do his profyte. For
there is a versifyer sayth/ that the ydel man
excuseth him in wynter/by cause of the great
colde/and in sōmer bycause of the heete. For
these causes saythe Caton/ waketh and en-
clyne you not ouer moch for to slepe/ for ouer
moche reste nourissheth and causeth many
vyces. And therfore saythe saint Jerom/do
some good dedes/that the dyuel whiche is our
enemy/ne fynde you not vnoccupped/ for the
dyuel ne taketh not lightly vnto his werking
such as he fyndeth occupped in good werkes.
Than thus/in gettyng richesses ye must flye
idelnesse. And afterwarde ye shul vse the ri-
chesses / which ye haue gote by your wyt and
by your trauayle/ in suche maner/that men
holde you not to scarce ne to sparyng/ne fole
large/that is to say/ouer large a spender: For
right as men blame an auaricyous man by
cause of his scarcite & chyncherye/ in the same
wise is he to blame that spēdeth ouer largely.
And therfore saith Caton: Vse (saith he) the
richesses that thou hast goten in such maner/
that men may haue no mater ne cause to cal
the nother wretche ne chynche: For it is great
shame to a man to haue a poore herte and a
riche purse. He saythe also/ the goodes that
thou haste gote/vse them by mesure/that is to
say/spende mesurably/ for they that folisshly
waste and dispēde the goodes that they haue/
whan they haue no more propre of her owne/
than they shape hem to take the goodes of an
other man. I say than that ye shal flye aua-
rice/vsyng your richesse in suche maner/ that
men saye not that your richesses ben buryed/
but that ye haue hem in your might & in your
weldyng. For a wyse man repreueth the aua
ricyous man/ and saythe thus in this verses
two. Wherto & why burieth a man his goo-
des by his great auaryce / and knoweth well
that nedes he must dye/for dethe is the ende of
euery man/ as in this presente lyfe ÷ And for
what cause or encheson ioyneth he hym/ or
knytteth he him so faste vnto his goodes/that
al his wyttes mowe not disceuer him/ ne de-
parte him fro his goodes/ and knoweth wel/
or ought to knowe/ ỹ whan he is deed/he shal
no thing beare with him out of this worlde.
And therfore saythe saynt Augustyn/that the
auaricyous man is lykened vnto hell/ that
the more it swaloweth/ the more desyre it hath
to swalowe and deuoure. And as wel as ye
wolde eschue to be called an auarycious man
or chynche / as well shulde ye kepe and go-
uerne you in suche a wyse/ that men cal you
not foole large. Therfore saythe Tullius/
The goodes of thyne house ne shulde not be
hydde ne kepte so close / but that they myght
be opened by pyte and debonayrte/ that is to
say/ to yeue hem parte that haue great nede.
Ne thy goodes shulde not be so open/ to be eue
ry mans goodes. Afterwarde in gettyng of
your richesses and in vsynge hem/ ye shal al-
way haue thre thynges in your herte / that is
to say/our lorde god/ cōscience/ & good name.
First ye shal haue god in your herte/ and for
no richesse ye shulde do any thing/which may
in any maner displese god your creatour and
maker. For after the worde of Salomon/ it
is better to haue a lytel good with the loue of

S.iii. god

god/ than to haue moche good and tresoure/ and lese the loue of his lorde god. And the prophete saythe/that better it is to be a good man/ and haue lytel good & tresour/ than to be holden a shrewe/ and haue great rychesse. And yet I say ferthermore/that ye shulde alway do your besynesse to get you richesses/ so that ye get hem with good conscience. And the apostle sayth/that there nys thing in this worlde/ of whiche we shulde haue so great ioy/as whan our conscience bereth vs good wytnesse. And the wise man saith: ẏ the substaunce of a man is ful good/whan synne is not in mans conscience. Afterwarde in gettyng of your richesses and in vsyng of hem/ ye muste haue great besynesse & great dyligence/that your good name be alwaye kept and conserued. For Salomon saythe/ that better it is/& more it auayleth a man to haue a good name/ than for to haue many richesses: And therfore he saythe in an other place. Do great dilygence saythe Salomon/ in kepyng of thy frendes and of thy good name/ for it shal leger abyde with the than any tresour/ be it neuer so precious. And certes he shulde not be called a great gentylman/ that after god & good conscience/ al thynges lefte/ ne dothe his dyligence & besynesse to kepe his good name. And Cassyodor saythe/ that it is a syne of a gentyl herte/ whan a man loueth and desyreth to haue a good name. And therfore sayth saynt Augustyn/that there ben two thynges that ben right necessarye & also nedeful: and that is good conscience/ & good lose/ that is to saye: good conscience to thyn owne person inwarde/and good lose for thy neyghbour outwarde. And he that trusteth him so moche in his good conscience/ that he displyseth & setteth at nought his good name or loose/ and recketh not though he kepe not his good name/ nys but a cruel churle.

Sir/nowe haue I shewed you howe ye shuld do in gettyng richesses/ & howe ye shulde vse hem: and I se wel that for ẏ trust that ye haue in your richesses/ye wol moue werre and batayle. I counsaile you that ye begyn no werre in trust of your richesses/ for they ne suffyse not werres to maintayne. And therfore sayth a philosopher: That man that desyreth and wolde algates haue werre/ shal neuer haue suffisaunce: for the richer that he is/the greater dispences must he make/ if he wol haue worshyp & victorie. And Salomon saith/that the greater richesses that a man hath/ ẏ more dispendours he hath. And therfore sir/ al be it so that for your riches ye may haue moch folke/ yet behoueth it not/ ne it is not good to begyn werre/ where as ye may in other maner haue peace/ vnto your worshyp & profyte: For the victorie of batayls ẏ ben in this worlde/lythe not in great nombre or multytude of people/ ne in the vertue of man/but it lyth in the wyl and in the honde of our lorde god almighty. And therfore Iudas Machabeus/ which was goddes knight/ whan he shulde fight ayenst his aduersary/that had a greater nombre and a greater multytude of folke/ & stronger than was his people of Machabee/ yet he recomforted his lytel company/ and said right in this wyse: Al so lightly said he/may our lorde god almighty yeue victorie to a fewe folke/ as to many folke/ for the victorie of a batayle cometh not by the great nombre of people/ but it cometh from our lorde god of heuen. And dere sir/ for as moche as there is no man certayne/if it be worthy ẏ god yeue him victorie or not/after that Salomon sayth/ therfore euery man shuld gretly drede werres to begyn: and bycause that in batayles fal many peryls/and happeth other whyle/that as sone is the great man slayne as the lytel man. And as it is written in the seconde boke of kynges: The dedes of batayles ben auenturous & nothing certayne/ for as lightly is one hurt with a speere as an other: And for ther is great peryl in werre/ therfore shulde a man flye and eschue werre in as moche as a mā may goodly. For Salomon saythe/ he that loueth peryll/shal fal in peryll.

After that dame Prudence had spoken in this maner/ Melibe answerde and said. I se wel dame Prudēce/ that by your fayre wordes and your resons that ye haue shewed me/ that ẏ werre lyketh you nothyng/ but I haue not yet herde your counsaile howe I shal do in this nede.

Certes

Certes (said she) I cou͞saile you that ye acorde with your aduersaries/ & that ye haue peace with hem. For saynt James saithe in his Epistell: that by concorde & peace small riches weye great: and by debate & dyscorde riches decay. And ye knowe wel/ that one of the greatest & most soueraine thynge yͭ is in this worlde/ is vnite and peace. And therfore saith our lord Jesu Christ to his apostels/ i this wise: wel happy ben they/ that loue and purchace peace/ for they be called yͤ childre of god. Ah/ said Melibe/ nowe se I wel/ that ye loue nat myn honoure ne my worshippe. ye knowe wel that myn aduersaris haue begon this debate & brige by their outrage. And ye se wel yͭ they ne require ne pray me of peace/ ne they aske nat to be reconsiled. Wol ye thā that I go meke me/ & obey me to hem/ & crye hem mercy? Forsoth that were nat my worship. For right as men say/ ouer great hu͞blenesse engendreth dispraysing / so fareth it by to great humylite or mekenesse.

Than began dame Prudēce to make semblant of wrath/ & said: Certes sir/ saue your grace. I loue your honour & profite as I do myn owne/ & euer haue do: ye ne none other neuer se the cōtrary. And yet/ if I had said/ that ye shulde haue purchased peace & recōsilyation/ I ne had moche mistake me/ ne said amysse. For the wise man saith: the discension begynneth by another man / & the reconsilyng begynneth by thy selfe. And the pphet saith: flye shrewdnesse/ and do goodnesse/ seke peace & folowe it/ in asmoche as in the is. Yet say I nat/ that ye shulde rather pursue to your aduersaris for peace/ than they shulde to you: For I knowe wel that ye ben so harde herted/ that ye wol do nothyng for me. And Salo. saith: He that hath ouer harde an hert/ he at last shal myshappe or misbetyde.

Whan Melibee had herde dame Prudence make sēblaunt of wrath/ he said in this wise. Dame I praye you/ that ye be nat displeased of thyng that I say/ for ye knowe wel that I am angry & wroth/ and that is no wonder: & they that ben wroth / wot not wel what they do/ ne what they saye. Therfore the prophete saith: that troubled eyen haue no clere sight. But say and counsaile me as you lyketh/ for I am redy to do right as ye wol desire: And if ye repreue me of my folye/ I am the more holden to loue and prayse you. For Salomon saith/ that he that repreueth him that doth foly/ he shal fynde greater grace than he that disceyueth him by swete wordes.

Than saide dame Prudence/ I make no semblaunt of wrath ne of anger/ but for your great profyte/ for Salomon saith: He is more worth/ that repreueth or chydeth a fole for his folye/ shewyng him semblau͞t of wrathe/ than he that supporteth him and praiseth him in his misdoyng/ and laugheth at his folye. And this same Salomon saithe afterwarde: That by yͤ sorouful visage of a man/ that is to say/ by the sorie & heuy countenau͞ce of a man/ the fole correcteth and amendeth him selfe.

Than said Melibe/ I shal not conne answere vnto so many faire reasons as ye put to me and shewe: say shortly your wyl & your counsaile/ and I am al redy to performe and fulfyl it. ¶ Than dame Prudence discouered al her wyl vnto him and said. I counsaile you (said she) aboue al thynges/ that ye make peace bytwene god and you/ and be reconsyled vnto him and to his grace/ for as I haue saide you here before/ god hath suffred you to haue this tribulacion & disese for your synnes: and if ye do as I saye you/ god wol sende your aduersaries vnto you/ and make hem fall at your fete/ redy to do your wyl and your cōmaundement. For Salomon saith/ Whan the condycion of man is plesaunt and lyking to god/ he chaungeth the hertes of the mans aduersaries/ and constraineth hem to beseche him of peace & of grace. And I praye you let me speke with your aduersaries priuely/ for they shal not knowe that it be of your wyl or your assent: And than whan I know their will and their entent/ I maye counsaile you the more surely.

Dame saide Melibe/ dothe your will and your liking/ for I put me holy in your disposycion and ordynaunce.

Than dame Prudence/ whan she sawe the good wyll of her husbonde/ delybered & toke aduyse aduise in her selfe/ thynkyng howe she might bring this nede vnto a good conclusyon and to a good ende: And whan she saw her tyme/ she sente for these aduersaries to come vnto her in a priue place. And shewed wisely vnto hem the great goodes that come of peace/ & the great harmes & perils that ben in werre/ and said to hem in a goodly maner: howe yͭ hem ought haue great repentaunce of the iniury and wrong/ that they had done to Melibeus her lorde/ & vnto her & to her doughter.

And whan they herde yͤ goodly wordes of dame Prudence/ they were so supprised & rauysshed/ and had so gret ioye of her/ that wōder was to tel. ¶ Ah/ lady (said they) ye haue shewed vnto vs the blessyng of swetnesse after the sayeng of Dauid the pphete/ For yͤ reconsylyng which we be nat worthy to haue in no manere. But we ought require it with great cōtrition and humilite/ that ye of your goodnesse haue presented vnto vs. Nowe se we wel/ that the science and connyng of Salomon is ful trewe/ for he saith: That swete wordes multiply & encreace frendes/ and maketh shrewes to be debonaire and meke.

Certes (said they) we put our dede and all our mater & cause/ al holy in your good wyl/ and been redy to obey at the cōmaundement of our lorde Melibeus. And therfore dere & benigne lady: we praye and beseche you/ as mekely as we can and may/ that it lyke vnto your great goodnesse/ to fulfyl in dede/ your goodly wordes. For we cōsider and knowe/ that we haue offended and greued our lorde Melibeus out of measure: so forsorth/ yͭ we be nat of power to make him amendes. And therfore we oblige and bynde vs and our frēdes/ for to do al at his wyll and cōmaundement: but parauenture he hath suche heuynesse/ and suche wrathe to vs warde/ bicause of our offence/ that he wol enioyn vs suche a payne/ as we mowe nat beare ne sustayne. And therfore noble lady/ we besech your womanly pite/ to take suche aduysement in this nede/ that we ne our frendes be nat disherited ne distroyed/ through our foly.

Certes (said Prudēce) It is an harde thīge and right perilous/ that a man put him al vtterly in arbytration & iugement/ and in the might and power of his enemy: For Salo. saith: leueth me/ & yeueth credence to yͭ I shal say: Ne yeueth neuer yͤ power ne gouernāce of thy goodes/ to thy son/ to thy wyfe/ to thy frende/ ne to thy brother: ne yeue thou neuer might ne mastry ouer thy body while thou liuest. Now/ sith he defendeth yͭ a man shulde nat yeue to his brother ne to his frende/ the might of his body. By a strōger reason he defēdeth & forbedeth a man to yeue him selfe to his enemy. And nathelesse I coūsaile you yͭ ye mystrust nat my lorde: for I wot wel and knowe verily/ that he is debonair & meke/ large/ curteis/ and nothing desirous ne couitous of goodes ne riches. For there is nothyng in this worlde yͭ he desireth/ saue onely worship and honour. Ferthermore I knowe/ and am right sure/ yͭ he shal nothyng do in this nede/ without my counsaile: and I shal so worke in this case/ that by the grace of our lorde god/ ye shalbe reconsyled vnto vs.

Than said they with one voyce/ worshypful lady we put vs and our goodes al fully in your wyl and disposycion/ & ben redy to come/ what day that it lyketh vnto your noblesse to lymyte vs or assyne vs for to make our oblygacion & bonde as stronge as it lyketh vnto your goodnes/ that we mowe fulfyl the wyl of you & of my lorde Melibe.

Whan dame Prudēce had herd the answere of these men/ she bad hem go ayen priuely/ & she returned to her lorde Melibe/ & tolde him how she foūde his aduersaries ful repentaūt/ knowlegyng ful lowly her synnes & trespas/ and how they were redy to suffre al payne/ requiryng & prayeng him of mercy and pyte.

Than said Melibe/ he is wel worthy to haue pardon & foryeuenesse of his synne/ that excuseth not his synne/ but knowlegeth and repenteth him/ askyng indulgēce. For Seneke saith/ there is the remission and foryeuenesse/ where as the confessyon is: for confession is neyghbour to innocence. And therfore I assent and confirme me to haue peace/ but it is good that we do nought without the assente and wyl of our frendes.

Than was Prudēce right gladde and ioyful

full/ and saide: Certes sir / ye haue well and goodly answered: for right as by the counsaile/assent/and helpe of your frendes/ye haue be steered to venge you and make werre: Right so/ without her counsaile shall ye not accorde you/ ne haue peace with your aduersaries. For the sawe saithe: There is nothĩg so good/ by waye of kynde/ as a thynge to be vnwounde by hym that it was yvounde.

Than dame Prudence/ without delay or tarieng/ sent anon her messanger for her kynsfolke and her olde frendes / whiche that were trewe and wise: and tolde hem by order/ ĩ the presence of Melibe/al yͤ mater/as it is aboue expressed and declared. And prayed hem that they wolde saye their aduyse and counsayle/ what best were to do in this nede. And whan Melibeus frendes had taken her aduyse and delyberation of the forsaid mater/ & had examyned it by great busynesse and dilygence. They yaue ful coũsaile for to haue peace and rest/ & that Melibee shulde receyue with good hert his aduersaris/ to foryeuenesse & mercy.

And whan dame Prudence had herde thassent of her lorde Melibee/and the counsaile of his frendes accorde with her wyl and her entencion/she was wõderly gladde in her hert/ and said. There is an olde prouerbe (sayde she) That the goodnesse that thou mayst do this day/do it/and abide it nat/ne delay it nat tyl the next day. And therfore I counsaile/ that ye sende your messengers/such as be discrete and wise/vnto your aduersaries: tellĩg hem on your behalfe/ that if they wol treat of peace and accorde / that they shape hem without delay or taryeng/ to come vnto vs: whiche thing performed was in dede. And whan these trespasours/ and repentyng folke of her folyes/that is to say / the aduersaries of Melibeus/had herde what these messangers said vnto hem/they were right gladde and ioyful. and answered ful mekely and benignely/yelding grace and thankes to her lorde Melibee/ and to al his company: and shope hem without delay to go with the messangers / and obeyed to the cõmaundement of her lorde Melibeus. And right anon they toke her way to the courte of Melibe/and toke with hem some of their true frendes/to make faythe for hem/ and for to be her borowes: And whan they were comen to the presence of Melibee/he said to hem these wordes. It stondeth thus/ saide Melibee/and sothe it is/that causelesse & without skyll and reson/ye haue done great iniuries and wronges to me and my wyfe Prudẽce/and to my doughter also/for ye haue entred in to my house by violence/and haue don suche outrage/ that al men knowe wel that ye haue deserued dethe. And therfore woll I knowe and wete of you/whether ye woll put the punisshynge and the chastysing & the vengeaunce of this outrage/in the wyl of me and of my wife/ or ye wol not.

Than the wysest of hem thre answerd for hem al/and said. Sir (said he) we know wel that we ben vnworthy to come to the courte of so great a lorde and so worthy as ye be/ for we haue so gretly mistaken vs/ and haue offended and agylted in suche wise again your high lordeshyp/ that truely we haue deserued the dethe/but yet for the great goodnesse & debonairte/that al the world witnesseth of your person/we submytte vs to the excellence and benignyte of your gracious lordshyp/ & ben redy to obey to al your cõmaundementes/beseching you/ that of your merciable pyte ye wol consyder our great repentaunce/ & lowe submissyon/& graunt vs foryeuenesse of our outragyous trespace and offence: For wel we knowe/ that your lyberall grace and mercy stretcheth ferther in to the goodnesse/than don our outragious gyltes and trespaces in to the wickednesse. Al be it yͭ cursedly & dampnably we haue agylted against your high lordshyp.

Than Melibee tooke hem vp fro the grounde ful benignly/ and receyued her obligacions and her bondes by her othes vpon her pledges and borowes/ and assyned hem a certayn day to returne vnto his courte/ for to receyue and accept the sentence and iugement yͭ Melibeus wolde cõmaunde to be don on hem/by the causes aforsaid/which thynges ordayned/euery man returned to his house.

And whan dame Prudẽce sawe her tyme/ she fayned & asked her lorde Melibe/what vẽgeaũce he thought to take on his aduersaries.

To

The tale of Chaucer.

To whiche Melibe answered / & said: Certes (said he). I thynke and purpose me fully to disherit them of al that euer they haue / and for to putte them in exile for euer.

Certes said dame Prudẽce / this were a cruell sentence / and moche ayenst reason. For ye be riche ynough / and haue no nede of other mennes riches. And ye might lyghtly in this wyse gete you a couetous name / whiche is a vicious thyng / and ought be eschewed of euery good man. For after yͭ sayeng of the apostel. Couetise is rote of al harmes. And therfore it were better to you to lese so moch good of your owne / than for to take of their good in this maner. For better it is to lese good with worship / than to wyn good with vilanye and shame. And euery man ought to do his dilygence and his busynesse / to gete him a good name. And yet shall he not onely busy him in kepyng his good name / but he shal also enforce him alwaye to do some thynge / by whiche he may renewe his good name. For it is written / that the olde good lose of a man or good name / is soone gone and past / whan it is not renewed. And as touchynge / that ye say that ye wol exile your aduersaries: that thynketh me moche ayenst reason / and out of measure / consydring the power that they haue yeue you vpon them selfe. And it is written: yͭ he is worthy to lese his pryuilege / that mysuseth the might and power that is gyuen him. And I sette case / ye might enioyne hem that payne by right & lawe / whiche I trowe ye may nat do: I say / ye might not put it to execution / for parauenture than it were lyke to tourne to the werre / as it was before. And therfore if ye wol that men do you obeisaũce / ye muste demean you more curteisly / that is to say: ye must yeue more easy sentences and iugement. For it is written: he that most curteisly cõmaundeth / to him men moost obey. And therfore I praye you / that in this necessite and in this nede / ye caste you to ouercome your hert. For as Senec saith: he that ouercometh his hert / ouercometh twise. And Tully saith: there is nothyng so cõmendable in a great lorde / as whan he is debonaire & meke / and apeseth him lightly. And I pray you that ye wol nowe forbere to do vengeaunce / in suche a maner / that your good name maye be kepte and conserued / and that men may haue cause & mater to prayse you of pyte & mercy: and yͭ ye haue no cause to repent you of thĩge that is done. For Senecke saith: he ouercometh in an yuell manere / that repenteth hym of his victorie. Wherfore I pray you / let mercy be in your hert / to theffecte and entent / that god almightye haue mercy vpon you in his last iugement. For saint James saith in his Epistell: iugement without mercy shal be do to him / that hath no mercy of another wight.

Whan Melibee had herde the great skylles and reasons of dame Prudẽce / and her wise informations and techynges / his hert gan enclyne to the wyll of his wife: consydringe her trewe entent / confirmed him anon and assented fully to worke after her counsaile: & thanked god / of whom procedeth al goodnesse and vertue / that him had sent a wife of so great discretion. And whan the day came that his aduersaries shulde appere in his presence / he spake to hem goodly / and said in this wyse.

Al be it so / that of your pride and high presumption and foly / and of your negligence & vnconnyng / ye haue misborne you / and trespaced vnto me / yet for as mikell as I se and beholde your great humilyte / and that ye be sory and repẽtaunt of your giltes / it cõstrayneth me to do you grace & mercy: Wherfore I receyue you to my grace / and forgiue you holy al the offences / iniuries / and wronges / that ye haue don ayenst me and myne / to theffecte and ende / that god of his endlesse mercy wol at the tyme of our dyeng forgyue vs our giltes / that we haue trespaced to him in this wreched worlde. For doutlesse if we be sory and repentaunt for the synnes and gyltes / whiche we haue trespaced in yͭ sight of our lorde god: he is so fre and so merciable / that he woll forgyue vs our giltes / and bring vs to the blisse that neuer shal haue ende. A M E N.

¶ Here endeth the tale of Chaucer and here foloweth the Monkes prologue.

The Tale of Melibeus (B 3024–3078; T. §§ 76–78)

W Han ended was the tale of Melibee
And of Prudence / and her benignyte
Our Host said / as I am faithful man
And by the precious corps Maduan
I had leuer than a barel of ale
That Good lefe my wife had herde this tale
For she nothyng is of suche pacience
As was this Melibeus wife Prudence
By goddes bones / whan I bete my knaues
She bringeth me the great clubbed staues
And crieth / slee the dogges euerichone
And breke bothe backe and euery bone
And if that any neighbour of myne
Wol not in churche to my wife enclyne
Or be so hardy / to her to trespace
Whan she cometh hom / she rampeth i my face
And crieth false cowarde wreke thy wife
By corpus domini / I wol haue thy knyfe
And thou shalt haue my distaffe / & go spynne
Fro day tyl nyght / she wol thus begynne.
¶ Alas she saith / that euer she was shape
To wedde a mylksop / a cowarde ape
That wol be ouerlede with euery wight
Thou darst not stonde by thy wyues right
This is my lyfe / but if that I wolde fight
And out at dore / anon I mote me dight
And els I am lost / but if that I
Be lyke a wylde lyon / fole hardy
I wot wel she wol do me slee some day
Some neighbour / and than go my way
For I am perlous with knyfe in honde
Al be it that I dare not her withstonde
For she is bigge in armes be my faithe
That shal he fynde / that her mysdooth or saith
But lette vs passe away from this matere.
¶ My lorde he said / Sir monke: be mery of chere
For ye shal tel vs a tale trewly
Lo Rochester stondeth here fast by
Ride forth myn own lorde / breke not our game
But by my trouthe I knowe not your name
Wheder I shal cal you my lorde dan Jhon
Or dan Thomas / dan Robert / or dan Albon
Or of what house be ye / by your father kyn
I vowe to god / thou hast a ful faire chyn
It is a gentyl pasture there thou gost
Thou arte not lyke a pynaunt or a ghost
Vpon my faithe thou arte some officere
Some worthy Seyten / or some Celerere
For by my fathers soule / as to my dome
Thou arte a mayster / whan thou art at home
No poore cloysterer / ne no poore nouyse
But a gouernoure ware and wise
And therwith of brawne and of bones
A wel faryng person for the nones
I pray to god yeue him confusyon
That first the brought in to religyon
Thou woldest be a trede foule a right
Haddest thou as gret leue / as thou hast might
To perfourme al thy lust in engendrure
Thou haddest begoten many a creature
Alas / why werest thou so wyde a cope
God yeue me sorowe / and I were pope
Not only thou / but euery mighty man
Though he were shore highe vpon his pan
Shulde haue a wyfe / for al this world is lorn
Religyon hath take vp al the corne
Of tredyng / and borel men ben shrimpes
Of feble trees there cometh wretched ympes
This maketh that our heires be so slender
And feble / that they may not wel engender
This maketh that our wyues wol assay
Religyous folke / for they may better pay
Of Venus paymentes / than mowe we
God wote no lussheburghs paye ye
But be not wroth my lorde / though I play
Ful ofte in game a sothe haue I herde say.
This worthy monke toke al in pacience
And sayd / I wol do my dilygence
As ferre as sowneth in to honeste
To tel you a tale / ye two or thre
And if ye lyst to herken hytherwarde
I wol you sayne / the lyfe of saynt Edwarde
Or els tragedyes first I wol tell
Of whiche I haue an hundred in my cell.
Tragedy is to tel a certayne story
As olde bokes maken memory
Of hem that stode in great prosperyte
And be fallen out of hye degre
In to mysery / and ended wretchedly
And they ben versifyed comenly
Of syxe fete / whiche men call exametron
In prose eke ben endyted many on
And in metre / many a sondrie wyse
Lo / this ought ynough to suffyse
Nowe herkeneth / if you lyste for to here
But first I beseche you in this matere
Though

The Monk's Prologue (B 3079–3174 ; T. 13895–13990)

Though I be order tel nat these thynges
Be it of Popes/ Emperours/ or kynges
After her ages/ as men written fynde
But tellen hem/ some before & some behynde
As it cometh nowe to my remembraunce
Haue me excused of myne ignoraunce.

¶ Here endeth the Monkes pro-
logue/ and here begyn-
neth his tale.

I Wyl bewayle/ in maner of tragedy
The harm of hem yͭ stoden in hye degre
And fyll/ so that there nas no remedy
To bringe hem out of her aduersyte
For certayn / whan that fortune lyst to flye
There may no man of her yͭ course withholde
Lette no man trust on blynde prosperite
Bethware by this ensample yonge & olde

¶ Lucifer.

¶ At Lucifer/ though he an angel were
And nat a man / at him wyl I begynne
For though fortune may nat angel dere
From hye degre/ yet fel he for his synne
Doun in to hel/ where he is yet inne
O Lucifer/ brightest of angels al
Now art thou Sathanas/ yͭ maist nat twyn
Out of mysery/ in whiche thou arte fal

¶ Adam.

¶ Lo Adam/ in the felde of Damascene
With goddes owne fynger wrought was he
And not begoten of mannes sperm vnclene
And welte al paradise sauyng o tree
Neuer worldly man had so hye degre
As Adam/ tyl he for mysgouernaunce
Was dryuen out of his high prosperite
To labour and to hel/ and to myschaunce.

¶ Sampson.

¶ Lo Sampson/ whiche yͭ was annunciate
By the angel/ longe or his natiuite
And was to god almighty consecrate
And stode in nobles/ while he myght se
Was neuer such another/ as was he
To speke of strength/ and therto hardynesse
But to his wyues tolde he his secre
Through whiche he slough him for wretched- (nesse

Sampson/ this noble & mighty champion
Without wepen/ saue his hondes twey
He slough and al to rent the lyon
Towarde his weddyng/ walkyng by the wey
His falsse wyfe coulde him so plese & pray
Tyl she his counsayle knewe/ & she vntrewe
Vnto his foes/ his counsayle gan bewray
And hym forsoke/ and toke another newe

An hundred foxes toke Sampson for yre
And al her tayles he togyther bonde
And set the foxes tayles al on fyre
For he in euery tayle hath put a bronde
And they brent al the cornes in that londe
And her olyues/ and her vynes eke
A thousāde men eke he slough with his honde
And had no wepen/ but an asse cheke

Whan they were slayne/ so thrifted him that he
Was wel nye lorne/ for whiche he gan to prey
That god wolde of his payne/ haue some pyte
And sende him drinke/ or els mote he dey
And of this asse cheke/ that was so drey
Out of a wange tothe/ sprange anon a well
Of whiche he dronke ynough/ shortly to sey
Thus halpe him god/ as Judicum can tell

By very force/ at Gasa on a nyght
Maugre the Philystens of that cite
The gates of the towne/ he hath vp plyght
And on his backe/ ycaried hem hath he
High on an hyll/ where as men myght hem se
O noble mighty Sampson/ lefe and dere
Had thou nat tolde to women thy secre
In al this worlde ne had be thy pere

This Sāpson neither syder drāke ne wyne
Ne on his heed cam rasour none ne shere
By precepte of the messangere diuyne
For al his strength/ in his heeres were
And fully twenty yere by yere
Of Israel/ he had the gouernaunce
But after soon shal he wepe many a tere
For women shal bringe him to myschaunce

Vnto his lemman Dalyda he tolde
That in his heeres/ al his strength lay
And falsely to his foes she him solde

And

And slepyng in her barme upon a day
She made to clyppe or shere his heeres away
And made his fomen al his crafte espyen
And whan that they hun fonde in suche aray
They bounde hun faste/ and put out his eyen

But er his heeres were clypped or ishaue
There was no bonde that might hun bynde
But nowe is he put in prison in a caue
Where as they made him at the querne grynde
O noble Sãpson/ strongest of mankynde
O whylom iuge in glorie and rychesse
Now mayste thou wepe wt thyn eyen blynde
Sith thou art frõ wele fal ĩ to wretchydnesse

The ende of this caytife was/ as I shal sey
His fomen made a feest upon a daye
And made hun/ as their foole byfore hem pley
And this was in a temple of great araye
But at last he made a foule afray
For he two pyllers shoke/ & made hem fall
And downe fel the temple al/ and there it lay
And sloughe him selfe/ and eke his fomen all

This is to say/ the princes everychone
And eke thre thousãde bodyes were ther slayn
With fallyng of the great temple of stone
Of Sampson wol I no more sayne
Beth ware by this ensample olde and playne
That no men tel her counsaile to her wyues
Of such thing as they wold haue secret sayne
If that it touche her lymmes or her lyues.

¶ Herrules.

Of Hercules/ the soueraygne cõquerour
Syngen his werkȝ/ laude/ & hye renoun
For in his tyme/ of strength he bare the floure
He slough and rafte the skyn of the lyoun
And of the Centaurs/ layde the boste adoun
He Harpias slewe/ the cruel byrdes fell
He the golden appels rafte fro the dragon
He drewe out Cerberus/ the hounde of hell

He slewe the cruel tyraunt Busirus
And made his horse to frete him flessh & bone
He slough the very serpent venemous
Of Achelous two hornes/ brake he that one
And he slewe Cacus/ in a caue of stone
He slough the gyaunt Antaeus the stronge
He slough the grisly bore/ and that anon
And bare his heed upon his spere longe

Was neuer wight/ sythe the worlde began
That slough so many monsters/ as dyd he
Through the wyde worlde/ his name ran
What for his strenght and his bounte
And every realme went he for to se
He was so stronge/ ỹ no man might him let
And at bothe worldes endes/ he Trophe
In stede of boũdes/ of brasse a pyllour set.

¶ A lemman had this noble champyon
That hight Deianire/ as fresshe as May
And as clerkes make mencion
She hath him sent a shyrte fresshe and gay
Alas this shirte/ alas and wel awaye
Enuenomed was subtelly with all
That er he had weared it halfe a daye
It made his flesshe al fro his bones fall.

But nathelesse/ some clerkes her excusen
By one that hight Nessus/ that it maked
Be as be may/ I wol her not accusen
But on his body/ the shyrte he ware al naked
Tyl the flesshe was with the venym slaked
And whan he sawe none other remedye
In hote coles/ he hath him selfe iraked
For with no venym dayned he to dye

Thus sterfe this worthy mighty Hercules
Lo/ who may truste in fortune any throwe
For him that foloweth al this worlde of prees
Or he be ware/ is ofte layde ful lowe
Ful wyse is he/ that him selfe can knowe
Beware/ for whan that fortune lyst to glose
Than wayteth she/ her man downe to throwe
By suche a waye/ as he wolde leste suppose.

¶ Nabugodonosor.

The mighty trone/ the precious tresore
The glorious septre/ & royal maieste
That had the kyng Nabugodonosore
With tonge unneth may discryued be.
He twyse wanne Hierusalem/ that cyte
The vessel of the temple he with him lad
At Babilon was his soueraygne se
In whiche his glorie and his delyte he had.

T The

The fayrest children of the blode royall
Of Hierusalem/he dyd do gelde anone
And made eche of hem to ben his thrall
Amonge all other Danyell was one
That was the wysest of euerychone
For he the dremes of the kyng expowned
Where as in Caldee clerkes were there none
That wyst to what fyne his dreme sowned

This proude kyng let make a statu of golde
Sixty cubites longe/ and seuen in brede
To whiche ymage/bothe yonge and olde
Cōmaunded he to loute/and haue in drede
Or in a furneys/ful of flames rede
He shulde be deed/that wolde not obey
But neuer wolde assent to that dede
Danyel/ ne his yonge felowes twey

¶ This kyng of kinges/proude and elate
Wende god/ that sytteth in maieste
Ne might him not bereue of his estate
But sodainly he loste his dignyte
And lyke a beest/him semed for to be
And ete hey as an oxe/and lay therout
In rayn/ with wylde beests walked he
Tyl a certayne tyme was come aboute

And lyke an Egles fethers were his heeres
And his nayles lyke byrdes clawes were
God relesed him at certayne yeres
And yaue him wytte/& than with many a tere
He thonked god/and all his lyfe in fere
Was he/ to do a mysse/or more trespace
And er that he layde was on his bere
He knewe ꝧ god was ful of might & grace.

¶ Balthaser.

HIs sonne/whiche ꝧ hight Balthasare
That helde ꝧ reign after his faders day
He by his father coulde not beware
For proude he was of herte/ and of aray
And eke an ydolaster was he aye
His hygh estate/assured him in pride
But fortune caste him downe/ & there he laye
And sodainly his reigne gan deuyde

A feest he made/vnto his lordes all
Vpon a tyme/ he made hem blythe be
And than his officers gan he call
Gothe bringe forthe the vessels (q̄d he)
Whiche that my father/in his prosperyte
Out of the temple of Hierusalem byrafte
And to our goddes thonken we
Of honour/ that our elders with vs lafte

His wyfe/his lordes/and his concubynes
Aye dronken/whyles her appetytes laste
Out of this noble vessels/ sondrie wynes
And on a wall/this kyng his eyen caste
And sawe an hōde armelesse/ that wrote faste
For feare of whiche he quoke/ & syghed sore
This honde ꝧ Balthasar made so sore agaste
Wrote (Mane techel phares) and no more

¶ In al that londe/magycien was ther none
That coude expowne what this letter ment
But Danyel expowned it anone
And said/kyng/god thy father sent
Glorie and honour/reigne/tresour/& rent
And he was proude/& nothing god he drad
And therfore great wrathe god vpon him sent
And him byrafte the reigne that he had

He was out caste of mannes companye
With asses was his habytacion
And ete hey as a beest/in wete and drie
Tyl that he knewe/by grace and by reson
That god of heuen hath domynacion
Ouer euery reigne/and euery creature
And than had god of him compassyon
And him restored his reigne and his fygure.

¶ Eke thou ꝧ arte his sonne/ art proude also
And knowest al these thynges priuely
And arte rebel to god/ and his foe
Thou dranke eke of his vessels boldly
Thy wyfe eke/and thy wenches synfully
Dronke of the same vessels sondrie wynis
And heryed false goddes cursedly
Therfore to the shapen great payne is

This honde was sent fro god/ ꝧ on the wall
Wrote (Mane techel phares) truste me
Thy reigne is done/thou wotest not all
Deuyded is thy realme/and it shal be
To Medes and to Perciens (quod he)
And that same night/the kyng was slawe
And

And Darius occupyed his dignyte
Though he therto had neyther right ne lawe

Lordynges/ here ensample mowe ye take
Howe that in lordshyp is no sykernesse
For whan that fortune wol a man forsake
She beryth away his reigne/ and his richesse
And eke his frendes/bothe more and lesse
And what man hath frendes/through fortune
Myshap wol make him enemyes I gesse
This prouerbe is ful sothe/ and ful comune.

¶ zenobia.

Z Enobia of Palmerye quene
(As writeth percyens of her noblesse)
So worthy was in armes/and so kene
That no wight passed her in hardynesse
Ne in lynage/ne in none other gentylnesse
Of kynges blode of Perce she is discended
I say that she had not moste fayrnesse
But of her shap she might not be amended

From her childhode I fynde that she fledde
Offyce of woman/and to woode she went
And many a wylde hertes blode she shedde
With arowes brode/that she to hem sent
She was so swyfte/that she anon hem hent
And whan that she was elder/she wolde kyll
Lyons/ libardes/and beeres al to rent
And in her armes welde hem at her wyll

She durst wylde beestes dennes seke
And renne in the mounteyns al the nyght
And slepe vnder a busshe/& she coulde eke
Wrastell by very force/and by very might
With any yonge man/were he neuer so wight
There might no thing in her armes stonde
She kepte her maydenhede from euery wight
To no man dayned she to be bonde

But at laste/ her frendes hath her maryed
To Odenat/a prince of that countre
Al were it so/that she hem longe taryed
And ye shal vnderstonde/howe that he
Had suche fantasyes as had she
But nathelesse/whan they were knyt in fere
They lyued in ioye and in felycite
For eche of hem had other lefe and dere

Saue one thyng/she wolde neuer assent
By no way/that he shulde by her lye
But ones/for it was her playne entent
To haue a childe/the worlde to multiplye
And also sone as she might aspye
That she was not with childe with that dede
Than wolde she suffre him do his fantasye
Efte sones/and not but ones out of drede

And if she were with childe at that caste
Nomore shulde he play that game
Tyl fully fourty dayes were paste
Than wolde she ones suffre him the same
Al were this Odenat wylde or tame
He gate no more of her/for thus she sayde
It was to wyues lechery and shame
In other case/if men with hem playde

¶ Two sonnes by this Odenat had she
The whiche she kept in vertue and letture
But nowe vnto our tale turne we
I say that so worshypful a creature
And wyse therwith/and large with mesure
So penyble in werre/and curteys eke
Ne more laboure might in werre endure
Was non/though al this world me wold seke

Her ryche araye/ne myght not be tolde
As wel in vessel as in her clothyng
She was al cladde in perry and in golde
And eke she lefte not for none huntyng
To haue of sondrie tonges folke knowyng
Whan that she leyser had for to entende
To lerne bokes was al her lykyng
Howe she in vertue her lyfe might dispende

And shortly of this storie for to treate
As doughty was her husbonde as she
So that they conquered many reignes great
In the Orient/ with many a fayre cyte
Appertaynaunt vnto the maieste
Of Rome/& with strength helde them faste
Ne neuer might her foe men do her flee
Al the whyle that Odenates dayes laste

Her batayles/who so lyste hem for to rede
Agayne Sapor the kyng/and other mo
And howe al this proces fyll in dede

T.ii. Thy

Why she cōquered / & what tytle she had therto
And after of her mischefe and of her wo
Howe that she was besieged / and ytake
Let him to my mayster Petrarke go
That writeth ynough of this / I vndertake

¶ Whan Odenat was deed / she mightyly
The realmes helde / & with her owne honde
Agaynst her foos she fought truely
That ther was no prince ne king / in al ẏ londe
But were glad / if they that grace fonde
That she ne shulde vpon his londe werrey
With her they made alyaunce by bonde
To be in peace / and let hem ryde and pley

The emperour of Rome Claudius
Ne him before / the romayne Galyen
Ne durste neuer be so coragyous
Ne none Armen / ne none Egypcien
Ne Surrien / ne none Arabyen
Within the felde / that durst with her fyght
Leste ẏ she wolde hem with her hondes sleen
Or with her meyne / put hem to flyght

In kynges habyte went her sonnes two
As the heires of her realmes all
And Hermanno and Titamallo
Her names were / as perciens hem call
But aye fortune / hath in her hony gall
This mighty quene / may no whyle endure
Fortune out of her reigne made her to fall
To wretchydnesse / and to mysauenture.

¶ Aurelian / whan that the gouernaunce
Of Rome came in his hondes twey
He shope vpon this quene to do vengeaunce
And with his legions / he toke his wey
Towarde zenobia / and shortly for to say
He made her flye / and at laste her hent
And fettered her / and eke her chyldren tway
And wan the londe / & home to Rome he went

Amonge other thynges that he wan
Her chare / that of gold was wrought & pierre
This great Romayn / this Aurelian
Hath with him ladde / that for men shulde se
Before his trymphe walked she
With golden chaynes on her necke hongyng
Crowned she was / as after her degre
And ful of pierre charged her clothyng

¶ Alas fortune / she that whylom was
Dredeful to kynges / and to emperoures
Nowe gaureth al the people on her / alas
And she that helmed was in starke stoures
And wan by force townes stronge / & toures
Shal on her heed nowe were autrempte
And she that bare the septre ful of floures
Shal beare a distaffe / her coste for to quyte.

¶ Nero.

Al though that Nero were as vycious
As any fende / ẏ lyth ful lowe adoun
Yet he / as telleth vs Suetonius
Al this worlde had in subiection
Bothe este / and west / and Septentryon
Of rubyes / saphers / and of perles whyte
Were al his clothes broudred vp and doun
For he in gemmes greatly gan delyte

More delycate / more pompous of aray
More proude / was neuer Emperour / than he
That ilke clothe that he had weared o day
After that tyme / he wolde it neuer se
Nettes of golde threde had he great plente
To fysshe in Tiber / whan him lyst to play
His lustes were as lawe / in his degre
For fortune as his frende wolde him obay

He Rome brente for his delycacye
The Senatours he slewe vpon a day
To here howe her wyues wolde wepe & crye
And sloughe his brother / & by his syster laye
His mother made he in a pytouse aray
For he her wombe let slytte / to beholde
Where he conceyued was / so welaway
That he so lytel of his mother tolde

No teeres out of his eyen / for that sighe
Ne came / but said / a fayre woman was she
Great wonder is / that he coude or myght
Be domysman / of her deed beaute
The wyne to bring him / cōmaunded he
And dranke anon / non other wo he made
Whan might is ioyned vnto cruelte
Alas / to depe wyl the venyme wade

In

In youthe a mayster had this emperour
To teche him lettrure/and curtesye
For of moralyte he was the floure
As in his tyme/ but if his bokes lye
And whyles his maister had of him maistrye
He made him so connyng and so souple
That longe tyme it was or tyrannye
Or any vyce/ durste in him uncouple

Senec his mayster was/of whiche I deuyse
Bycause Nero had of him suche drede
For he for his vyces wolde him chastyse
Discretly as by worde/ and not by dede
Sir he wolde say/an emperour mote nede
Be vertuouse/and hate tyrannye
For whiche he made him in a bathe to blede
On bothe his armes/tyl he must dye

This Nero had eke of a customaunce
In youthe/ayenst his mayster to ryse
Which afterwarde/him though gret greuaunce
Bycause he ofte wolde him chastyse
Therfore he made him dye in this wyse
To chose in a bathe to dye in this manere
Rather than to haue a nother turmentyse
And thus hath Nero slayne his mayster dere

¶ Nowe fel it so/that fortune lyste no longer
The hygh pride of Nero to cherysshe
For tho he were stronge/yet was she stronger
She thought thus/ by god I am to nyce
To set a man/that is fulfylled of vyce
In hye degre/ and an emperour him call
By god out of his sete I wol him tryce
Whan he leste weneth/ sonest shal he fall

The people rose vpon him on a nyght
For his defaute/and whan he it aspyed
Out of his dores anon he hath him dyght
Alone/and there he wende haue ben alyed
He knocked faste/ & aye the more he cryed
The faster shette they the dores all
Tho wyste he wel/he had him selfe begyled
And went his way/ no lenger durste he call

The people cryed & rombled vp and doun
That with his eeres he herde howe they sayde
Where is this false tyraunt/this Neroun
For feare ful nere out of his wytte he brayde
And to his goddes/ right pitously he prayde
For socoure/but it might not betyde
For drede of this/him thought that he deyde
And ranne in to a gardeyn/ him to hyde

And in this gardayne/founde he chorles twey
Syttyng by a fyre great and reed
And to the chorles two he gan to prey
To slee him/ and to gyrde of his heed
That to his body/whan he were deed
Were no dispyte done/for his diffame
Him selfe he slough/he coulde no better rede
Of whiche fortune lough and had game.

¶ Holofernes.

Was neuer capitayne vnder a kyng
That reignes mo/ put in subiectyoun
Ne stronger was in felde/of al thyng
As in his tyme/ne greater of renoun
Ne more pompous in hygh presumpcioun
Than Holopherne/ whiche fortune aye kyste
And so lycorously ladde him vp and doun
Tyl that he deed was er that he wyste

Not only that this worlde had of him awe
For lesyng of rychesse and lyberte
But he made euery man reneye his lawe
Nabugodonosor was lorde/sayd he
None other god shulde honoured be
Ayenst his hest/there dare no wight trespace
Saue in Bethulia/a stronge cyte
Where Eliachym was preest of that place

¶ But take kepe of the dethe of Holopherne
Amyd his host/he dronke laye al nyght
Within his tent/large as is a berne
And yet for al his pompe/ & al his might
Judith/a woman/as he lay vpright
Sleppyng/his heed of smote/ and fro his tente
Ful priuely she stale/from euery wight
And with his heed/vnto her towne she wente.

¶ Antiochus.

WHat nedeth it of kyng Antiochus
To tel his hygh and royall maieste
His great pride/ his werke venemus
For suche an other man nas neuer as he
Redeth what that he was in Machabe

T.iii. And

And redeth the proude wordes that he sayd
And why he fyl from his prosperyte
And in an hyll/ howe wretchedly he deyde

Fortune him had enhaunsed so in pride
That verily he wende he might attayne
Unto the sterres/ upon euery syde
And in a balaunce/ to wey eche mountayne
And al the floodes of the see restrayne
And goddes people had he moste in hate
Hem wolde he slee/ in turment and in payne
Wenyng that god ne might his pride abate

And for that Nychanore and Tymothe
By iewes were venquisshed mightyly
Unto the iewes suche an hate had he
That he bad greythe his chare ful hastely
And swore and sayd/ ful dispytously
Unto Hierusalem he wolde eftsone
To wreke his yre on it ful cruelly
But of his purpose was he let ful sone

God for his manace him sore smote
With inuysible wounde/ aye incurable
That in his guttes carfe so and bote
That his paynes were importable
And certainly the wreche was resonable
For many a mannes guttes dyd he payne
But from his purpose/ cursed & dampnable
For al his smerte/ he nolde him not restrayne

But bade anon/ aparayle his hoste
And sodainly/ or he than was ware
God daunted al his pride/ & al his boste
For he so sore fel out of his chare
That al his lymmes and his skyn to tare
So that he ne myght go ne ryde
But in a chayre/ men aboute him bare
Al forbrused bothe backe and syde

The wreche of god him smote so cruelly
That in his body wicked wormes crept
And therwith al he stanke so horribly
That none of al his meyne/ that him kept
Whether that he woke or els slept
Ne myght not of him the stynke endure
And in his mischefe he wayled & eke wept
And knewe god/ lorde of euery creature

To al his hoste/ and to him selfe also
Ful lothsom was the stynke of his carayne
No man might him beare to ne fro
And in his stynke/ & in his horryble payne
He sterfe ful wretchedly on a mountayne
Thus hath this robbour/ and this homycide
That many a man made to wepe and playne
Suche guerdon/ as belongeth to pride.

¶ Alexander.

The story of Alexander is so cōmune
That euery wight/ ÿ hath discretioun
Hath herde somwhat or al/ of his fortune
This wyde worlde/ as in conclusyoun
He wanne by strength/ and for his renoun
They were glad for peace unto him sende
The pride of man/ and boste he layde adoun
Where so he came/ unto the worldes ende

Comparyson might yet neuer be maked
Betwixt him/ and an other conqueroure
For al this world/ for drede of hī hath quaked
He was of knyghthod/ & of fredome floure
Fortune him made the heyre of high honoure
Saue wyne & women/ nothīg might aswage
His hygh entent in armes and laboure
So was he ful of louyng corage

What price were it to him/ though I you tolde
Of Darius/ & of a hundred thousande mo
Of princes/ erles/ and knyghtes bolde
Whiche he conquered/ and brought to wo
I say as ferre as a man may ryde or go
The world was his/ what shuld I more deuise
For though I wrote and tolde you euer mo
Of his knighthode/ it might not suffyse

Twelue yere he reigned/ as I rede i Machabe
Philyppes sonne of Macedone he was
That first was kyng of Grece/ that countre
O worthy gentyll Alexander/ alas
That euer shulde the fal suche a caas
Enpoysonned of thy folke thou were
Thy syce/ fortune hath turned in to an ace
And yet for the ne wept she neuer a tere

Who shal yeue men teeres to complayne
The dethe of gentilnesse/ and of fraunchise
That al the worlde welded in his demayne
And

And yet him thought it myght not suffyse
So ful was his corage of hygh empryse
Alas/who shal me helpe to endyte
False fortune/and poyson to dispyse ⁊
The whiche of al this wo I wyte.

¶ Julius Cesar.

BY wisdom/manhode/⁊ hygh laboure
From humble bed to royal maieste
Up rose he/ Julius the conqueroure
That al the occident/by londe and see
Wan by strength of honde/or els by trete
And unto Rome made hem tributary
And sythe of Rome/ emperour was he
Tyl that fortune wext his adversary

O mighty Cesar/that in Thessaly
Ayenst Pompei/father thyn in lawe
That of the Orient had the chyvalry
As ferre as that the day begynneth to dawe
Them through knighthode hast take ⁊ slawe
Save fewe folke/yͤ with Pompeius fledde
Through which thou puttest al yͤ oriẽt in awe
Thanke fortune/ that so wel the spedde

¶ But nowe a lytel whyle I wol bewayle
This Pompei/ this noble governour
Of Rome/whiche that fledde at this batayle
I say one of his men/a false traytour
His heed of smote/to wynne him favour
Of Julius/and to him the heed brought
Alas Pompei/ of the orient conquerour
That fortune unto suche a fyne the wrought

¶ To Rome agayne repayreth Julius
With his tryumphe lauriate ful hye
But on a tyme Brutus Cassius
That ever had of his hye estate envye
Ful prively had made conspyracye
Ayenst this Julius/in subtel wyse
And cast the place/ in whiche he shulde dye
With bodkyns/as I shal you devyse

This Julius unto the capitol went
Upon a day/as he was wonte to gone
And in the capitol/anon him hent
This false Brutus/ and his other fone
And stycked him with bodkyns anone
With many a wounde/ ⁊ thus they let him lye
But never grutched he at no stroke but one
Or els at two/but if his story lye

So manly was this Julius of herte
And so wel loved estately honeste
That tho his deedly woũdes so sore smerte
His mantel over his hyppes caste he
For no man shulde se his privyte
And as he lay in dyeng on a traunce
And wyste verily that dye shulde he
Of honesty yet had he remembraunce

¶ Lucan to the this storie I recomende
And to Sueton/ and Valery also
That of this storie writen worde and ende
Howe that these conquerours two
Fortune was first a frende/ ⁊ sythe a foe
No man truste upon her favour longe
But have her in awayte for evermo
Wytnesse on al the conquerours stronge.

¶ Cresus.

The ryche Cresus/whylom kyng of Lyde
Of whiche Cresus/Cirus sore him drad
yet was he caught amydde al his pride
And to brenne/men to the fyre him lad
But such a rayne down frõ yͤ firmamẽt shad
That queynt the fyre/⁊ made him to scape
But to beware yet no grace he had
Tyl fortune on the galowes made him gape

Whan he escaped was/he coulde not stent
For to begyn a newe werre agayne
He wende wel/for that fortune him sent
Suche happe/ yͭ he escaped through the rayne
That of his foes he might not be slayne
And eke a sweven upon a nyght he mette
Of whiche he was so proude/⁊ eke so fayne
That in vengeaunce he al his herte sette

Upon a tree he was/as him thought
There Jupiter him wisshe/ both backe ⁊ syde
And Phebus eke a fayre towel him brought
To drie him with/⁊ therwith wext his pride
And to his doughter/that stode him besyde
Whiche yͭ he knewe in hye sentence habounde
He bade her tell what it signyfyed
And she his dreme right thus dyd expounde
The

The tree (qđ she) the galous is to mene
And Iupiter betokeneth snowe and rayne
And Phebus/ with his towell so clene
Betokeneth the sonne beames/ sothe to sayne
Thou shalte honged be/ father certayne
Rayne shal the wasshe/ & sonne shal the drie
Thus she warned him full plat & full playne
His doughter/ that called was Phanye

And honged was Cresus the proude kyng
His royal trone might him not auayle
Tragedye is none other maner thynges
Ne can in syngyng crye ne bewayle
But for that fortune alday wol assayle
with vnware stroke/ the reignes ẏ ben proude
For whā men trusteth her/ than wol she fayle
And couer her bright face with a cloude.

Peter of Spayne.

O noble/ o worthy Petro/ glory of Spayne
Whom fortune helde so hygh in maieste
Wel ought men thy pytous dethe complayne
Out of thy londe/ thy brother made the fle
And after at a siege by subtelte
Thou were betrayed/ & ladde vnto his tente
Where as he with his owne honde slewe the
Succedyng in thy reigne and in thy rente

The felde of snowe/ wᵗ thegle of black therin
Caught with the lymrod/ coloured as ẏ glede
He brewe this cursydnesse/ & al this synne
The wycked neste was werker of this dede
Not Charles/ Oliuer/ that toke aye hede
Of trouthe and honoure/ but of Armorike
Genilon Oliuer/ corrupt for mede
Brought this worthy kyng in suche a brike.

Petro king of Cypre.

O Worthy Petro/ kyng of Cypre also
That Alisaundre wan by high maistry
Ful many an hethen wroughtest thou wo
Of whiche thyn owne lieges had enuy
And for no thyng/ but for thy chyualrye
They in thy bed han slayn the by the morowe
Thus can fortune her whele gouerne & gye
And out of ioye bring men to sorowe

Barnabo Viconte.

Of Millan great Barnabo Vicounte.
God of delyte/ & scourge of Lūbardye
Why shulde I not thyn infortune accounte
Sens in astate thou clomben were so hye
Thy brothers sōne/ that was thy double alye
For he thy neuewe was/ and sonne in lawe
Within his prison made the to dye
But why ne how not I/ ẏ thou were slawe.

Hugelyne of Pyse.

Of the erle Hugelyne of Pyse the lāgour
There may no tonge tel for pyte
But lytel out of Pyse stonte a toure
In whiche toure in prison put was he
And with him ben his lytel children thre
The eldest scarsly fyue yere of age
Alas fortune/ it was a great crueltie
Suche byrdes for to put in suche a cage

Dampned was he to dye in that prison
For Roger/ whiche that bysshop was of Pyse
Had on him made a false suggestyon
Through whiche ẏ people gan vpon him ryse
And put him in prison/ in suche a wyse
As ye haue herde/ and meate & drinke he had
So small/ that vnnethe it may suffyse
And therwithal it was ful poore and bad

And on a day befel/ that in that houre
Whā that his meate wont was to be brought
The gayler shette the doores of the toure
He herde it wel/ but he spake right nought
And in his herte anon there fyl a thought
That they for hunger wolde do him dyen
Alas (qđ he) alas that I was wrought
Therwith the teeres fyl fro his eyen

His yonge sonne/ that thre yere was of age
Vnto him sayd/ father father why do ye wepe
Whan wyl the gaylour bring our potage
Is there no morsel breed that ye do kepe
I am so hungry/ that I may not slepe
Nowe wolde god that I might slepe euer
Than shulde not hunger in my wombe crepe
There nys nothing but breed ẏ me were leuer

Thus day by day/ this childe began to crye
Tyl in his fathers arme adowne it laye
And sayd/ farwel father I mote dye
And kyste his father/ and deyde the same day
And whan the woful father dyd it sey

For

For wo/ his armes two he gan to byte
And said alas/ fortune and welaway
Thy false whele/ my wo al may it wyte

His children wende/ that it for hunger was
That he his armes gnewe/ and not for wo
And said: father/ do nat so (alas)
But rather eate the flesshe vpon vs two
Our flessh yu yaue vs/ take our flessh vs fro
And eate ynough/ right thus they to him said
And after that with in a day or two
They layde hem in his lappe adoun/ & deyde

Thus ended is this mighty erle of Pise
Him selfe dispeyred eke/ for hungre starfe
From high estate fortune away him carfe
Of this Tragedy/ it ought ynough suffyse
Who so wol here it in a longer wise
Redeth the great poete of Itayle
That hyght Dante/ for he can it al deuyse
Fro poynt to point/ not a worde wol he fayle.

¶ Here endeth the Monkes tale.

¶ Here stynteth the knyght the monke of his tale/ and here foloweth the prologue of the Nō-nes preest.

Ho (qd ye knight) good sir nomore of this
That ye haue sayd/ is right ynough ywys
And mokel more/ for lytel heuynesse
Is right ynough to moche folke/ I gesse
I saye for me/ it is a great disease
Where as men haue be in welth and ease
To here of her sodayne fal/ alas
And the contrary is ioye and solas
As whan a man hath ben in pore estate
And clymbeth vp/ and weyxeth fortunate
And there abideth in prosperite
Suche thynges is gladsome/ as thynketh me
And of suche thyng were good for to tell.
Ye (qd our Host) by saynt Poules bell
ye say right sothe/ this Monke clappeth loude
He spake/ how fortune couered with a cloude
I wote not what/ and also of a Tragedy
Right nowe ye herde/ and perdy no remedy
It is for to bewaylen/ ne complayne
That that is done/ and als it is a payne
As ye haue sayd/ to here of heuynesse
Sir mōke no more of this/ so god you blesse
your tale anoyeth al this company.
Suche talkyng is not worth a butterfly
For therin is there no disporte ne game
Therfore sir monke/ dan Piers by your name
I pray you hertely/ tel vs somwhat elles
For sykerly/ nere clynkyng of your belles
That on your bridell honge/ on euery syde
By heuen kyng/ that for vs al dyde
I shulde er this han fal downe for slepe
Al though the slough had ben neuer so depe
Than had your tale al be tolde in vayne
For certainly/ as that these clerkes sayne
Where as a man may haue none audyence
Nought helpeth it to tel his sentence
And wel I wote/ the substaunce is in me
If any thing/ shal wel reported be
Sir/ saye somwhat of huntyng I you pray
Nay (qd this mōke) I haue no lust to play
Nowe let an other tel/ as I haue tolde.
¶ Thā spake our host/ wt rude speche & bolde
And said/ vnto the nonnes preest anon
Come nere thou prest/ cōe hider thou sir John
Tel vs such a thing/ as may our hertes glade
Be blythe/ though thou ryde vpon a iade
What though thy horse be bothe foule & lene
If he wol serue the/ recke not a bene
Loke that thy herte be mery euer mo
¶ yes sir (qd he) yes host/ so mote I go
But I be mery/ iwys I wol be blamed
And Right anon/ his tale he hath atamed
And thus he sayd/ vnto vs euerychon
This swete preest/ this goodly man sir John.

¶ Here endeth the prologue of the nonnes preest/ and here foloweth his tale.

The tale of the nonnes preest.

A Poore wydowe/som dele ystept in age
was whilom dwelling i a pore cotage
Besyde a groue/ stondyng in a dale
This wydowe/ of whiche I tel you my tale
Sens the day that she was laste a wyfe
In pacience/ledde a ful symple lyfe
For lytel was her catel and her rent
By husbondrie/ of suche as god her sent
She fonde her selfe/ & eke her doughters two
Thre large sowes had she/and no mo
Thre kyne/ & eke a shepe that hyght Mall
Wel sooty was her boure/and eke her hall
In whiche she ete many a slender mele
Of poynant sauce/ ne knewe she neuer a dele
Ne deynty morcel passed through her throte
Her dyet was accordaunt to her cote
Replection ne made her neuer syke
A temperate dyete was her phisyke
And exercyse/and hertes suffysaunce
The goute let her nothing for to daunce
Ne apoplexie shent not her heed
No wyne ne dranke she/ whyte ne reed
Her borde was most serued wt whyte & blacke
Milke & broun breed/ i which she fōde no lack
Seynde bakon/ & somtyme an eye or twey
For she was as it were a maner dey.
A yerde she had/ enclosed al aboute
With styckes/ and drie dytched without
In whiche she had a cocke hyght Chaūteclere
In al the londe/ of crowyng nas his pere
His voyce was meryer than the mery orgon
On masse dayes/that in the churches gon
Wel sykerer was his crowyng in his loge
Than is a clocke/ or in an abbey an orloge
By nature he knewe eche assentioun
Of the equinoctiall in the toun
For whan degrees.xv. were assended
Than crewe he/ that it might not be amended
His combe was redder than the fyne corall
And batelled/ as it had be a castel wall
His byll was blacke/ as any gete it shone
Lyke asure were his legges and his tone
His nayles whyter than the lylly floure
And lyke the burned golde was his coloure.
This gentill cocke/had in gouernaunce
Seuen hennes/to done his plesaunce
Whiche were his systers/ and his paramours
And wonder lyke to him/as of colours
Of whiche the fayrest hewed in the throte
Was called fayre damosel Pertelote
He sethered her an hundred tymes a daye
And she him pleaseth/ al that euer she maye
Curteys she was/ discrete/ and debonayre
And compenable/and bare her selfe so fayre
Sens the tyme that she was seuenyght olde
That truly she/she hath the herte in holde
Of Chaunteclere/ lokyng in euery lyth
He loueth her so/ that wel was him therwith
But suche a ioye it was to here hem synge
Whan the bright sonne gan to springe
In swete acorde/ my lefe is ferre in londe
For that tyme/as I haue vnderstonde
Beestes and byrdes coulde speke and synge
And it so fyll/ that in the dawnyng
As Chaunteclere/ amonge his wyues all
Sate on his perche/that was in the hall
And next him sate his fayre Pertelote
This Chaūteclere gan to grone in his throte
As a man in his dreme is drenched sore
And whan y Pertelot thus herde him rore
She was agaste/ and sayd herte dere
What ayleth you to grone in this manere
ye be a very sleper/ fye for shame.
And he answerde thus/by god madame
I pray you/that ye take it not in grefe
By god I mette/ I was in suche mischefe
Right nowe/that yet myn hert is sore a fryght
Nowe god (qd he) my sweuen reche a ryght
And kepe my body out of foule prisoun
Me mette/that I romed vp and doun
Within our yerde/where I sawe a beest
Was lyke an hoūde/ & wold haue made arest
Vpon my body/and wolde haue had me deed
His colour was betwyxt yelowe and reed
And typped was his tayle/ & bothe his eeres
With black/ vnlike the remenant of his heeres
His snowte small/with glowyng eyen twey
Yet for his loke/almoste for feare I dey
This causeth me my gronyng doutlesse.
Away (qd she) fye for shame hertlesse
Alas (qd she) for by god aboue
Nowe haue ye loste my herte/ & al my loue
I can not loue a cowarde by my faythe
For certes/ what so any woman sayth
We al desyre/if that it myght be
To haue husbondes/hardy/ wyse/and fre.

And

And secrete/and no nygarde/ne no fole
Ne him that is agaste of euery tole
Ne none auauntour/by that god aboue
Howe durst ye say for shame/vnto your loue
That any sweuen might make you a ferde ?
Haue ye no mannes herte/and haue a berde ?
Alas/and con ye be a ferde of sweuenis ?
Nothing but vanyte god wotte in sweuen is
Sweuens ben engendred of replections
And of fume/ and of complections
Whan humours ben to habūdant in a wight
Certes this dreme/ which ye haue met to night
I tel you trouthe/ ye may trust me
Cometh of superfluyte/& reed colour parde
Whiche cause folke to drede in her dremes
Of arowes/ and of fyre with reed lemes
Of reed beestes/that wol hem byte
Of conteke/and of waspes great and lyte
Right as the humour of melancolye
Causeth many a man in slepe to crye
For fere of great bulles/and beres blake
Or els that blacke dyuels wol hem take
Of other humours coulde I tel also
That worke a man in slepe moche wo
But I wol passe/ as lightly as I can.
Lo Caton/whiche that was so wyse a man
Sayd he not thus/do no force of dremes
Nowe sir(q̄d she) whan we flye fro yͤ bemes
For goddes loue/ as taketh some laxatyfe
Vp peryl of my soule/ and of my lyfe
I counsayle you the beste/ I wol not lye
That bothe of colour/ and of melancolye
Ye purge you/and for ye shul not tary
Though in this towne/be none apotecary
I shal my selfe two herbes teche you
That shal be for your heale/ & for your prow
And in our yerde/tho herbes shal I fynde
The whiche haue of her properte by kynde
To purge you byneth / and eke aboue
Foryete not this/for goddes owne loue
Ye be right colerike of complection
Where the sonne is in his ascention
Ne fynde you not replete of humours hote
For if ye do/I dare wel say a grote
That ye shal haue a feuer terciane
Or els an ague/that may be your bane
A day or two/ ye shal haue digestyues
Of wormes/or ye take your laxatyues
Of laurell/centorie/and of femetere
Or els of elder beryes/ that growe there
Of catapuce/ or of gaytres beries
Of herbe yue/growyng i our yerde yͤ mery is
Plucke hem vp as they growe/& eate hem in
Be mery husbonde/for your father kyn
Dredeth no dreme/I can say you no more.
¶ Madame (q̄d he) gramercy of your lore
But nathelesse/as touchyng dan Catoun
That of wisdom hath so great renoun
Though he bade no dremes for to drede
By god/men may in olde bokes rede
Of many a man/more of auctorite
Than euer Caton was/so mote I the
That al the reuers sayth of his sentence
And haue wel founde by experyence
That dremes ben signyfycations
As wel of ioye/as of trybulations
That folke endure/in this lyfe present
There nedeth to make of this none argument
The very prefe sheweth it in dede
One of the greatest auctours that men rede
Saythe thus/ yͤ whilom two felowes went
On pylgrimage/in ful good entent
And happed so/they come in to a toun
Where as there was suche congregation
Of people/and eke of strayte herbygage
That they ne fonde/ as moche as a cotage
In whiche they bothe might loged be
Wherfore they mote of necessyte
As for that nyght/departe company
And eche of hem gothe to his hostelry
And toke his lodgyng/as it wolde fall
That one of hem/was lodged in a stall
Farre in a yerde/with oxen of the plough
That other man was lodged wel ynough
As was his auenture/or his fortune
That vs gouerneth al/as in commune
And so befell / longe or it were day
This man mette in his bedde/ there as he lay
Howe that his felowe gan vpon him call
And sayd (alas) for in an oxes stall
This nyght shal I be murdred/there I lye
Nowe helpe me dere brother or I dye
In al haste/come to me (he said)
This man out of his slepe for feere abrayde
But whan he was waked of his slepe
He turned him/and toke of this no kepe
Him

The tale of the nonnes preest.

Him thought his dreme was but a vanyte
Thus twyse in his slepe dremed he
  And at the thirde tyme/ yet his felawe
Cam as him thouȝt/ & sayd I now am slawe
Beholde my blody woundes/ depe & wyde
A ryse vp erly/ in the morowe tyde
And at the west gate of the towne (qd he)
A carte ful of donge/ there shalte thou se
In whiche my body is hydde ful priuely
Do thou that carte areste boldly
My golde caused my dethe/sothe to sayne
And tolde him euery poynt how he was slayn
With a ful pytous face/pale of hewe
And trust wel his dreme/he foũde right trewe
For on the morowe/as sone as it was day
To his felowes inne/he toke the waye
And whan that he came to the oxes stall
After his felowe/ he began to call.
  The hosteler answerde him anon
And said/sir your felowe is gon
As sone as it was day/he went out of yͤ toun
  This man gan fall in suspectioun
Remembring of his dremes that he mette
And forthe he gothe/no lenger wolde he lette
Vnto the westgate of the towne/and fonde
A donge carte/ as it were to donge londe
That was araped in the same wyse
As ye haue herde the deed man deuyse
And with hardy herte/he gan to crye
Vengeaunce and iustyce of this felonye
My felowe murdred is this same night
And in this carte he lythe/gapyng vpright
I crye out on the mynisters (quod he)
That shulde kepe and rule this cyte
Harowe alas/here lythe my felowe slayne
  What shulde I more of this tale sayne?
The people out starte/& cast yͤ carte to groũde
And in the myddell of the donge they founde
The deed man/that murdred was al newe.
¶ O blysful god/that arte so good & trewe
Lo/ howe thou bewrayest murdre alway
Murdre wol out/that se we day by day
Murdre is so wlatsome and abhomynable
To god/that so iuste is and resonable
That he ne wol it suffre heled to be
Though it abyde a yere/two/or thre
Murdre wol out/this is my conclusyoun.
  And right anon/the mynisters of the town
Haue hente the carter/ and sore him pyned
And eke the hosteler so sore engyned
That they beknewe her wickednesse anone
And were honged by the necke bone
  Here may ye se/ that dremes ben to drede.
¶ And certes/ in the same lefe I rede
Right in the next chapiter after this
I gabbe not/ so haue I ioye and blys
  Two men wolde haue passed ouer the se
For certayne causes/in to a ferre countre
If the wynde ne had be contrarye
That made hem in a cyte to tarye
That stode ful mery vpon an hauen syde
But on a daye/ ayenst an euen tyde
The wynde gan chaunge/& blewe as hem lest
Joly and glad/they went to rest
And caste hem ful erly for to sayle
But herken/to one man fyl a great meruayle
  To one of hem/ in slepyng as he lay
He met a wonders dreme/agayn the day
Him thought a man stode by his beddes syde
And him cõmaunded/that he shulde abyde
And sayd him thus/if thou to morowe wende
Thou shalte be dreynt/my tale is at an ende.
¶ He woke/& tolde his felowe what he mette
And prayed him his voyage for to lette
As for that day/he prayed him for to abyde.
  His felowe/ that lay by his beddes syde
Gan for to laugh/ and scorned him ful faste
No dreme (qd he) may so my herte agaste
That I wol let for to do my thynges
I set not a strawe for thy dremynges
For sweuens ben but vanytees and iapes
Men meten alday of owles and of apes
And eke of many a mase ther withall
And dremen of thing that neuer was/ ne shal
But sythe I se that thou wolte here abyde
And thus slouthe wylfully thy tyde
God wote it rueth me/and haue good day
And thus he toke his leue/ and went his way
  But er he had halfe his course sayled
I not why/ne what mischaunce it ayled
But casuelly the shyppes botome to rent
And shyp and men/ vnder the water went
In syght of other shyppes besyde
That with hem sayled at the same tyde
  And therfore fayre Pertelot so dere
By suche ensamples olde/mayste thou lere
That

The Nun's Priest's Tale (B 4201–4296; T. 15017–15112)

That no man shulde be to rechelesse
Of dremes / for I say the doutlesse
That many a dreme ful sore is for to drede
  Lo in the lyfe of saynt Kenelm we rede
That was Kenelphus sonne / the noble kyng
Of Mercenrike / howe Kenelm mette a thyng
A lytel er he were murdred on a day
His murder in his vision he say
His norice him expowned it euery dele
His sweuen / and badde him kepe him wele
Fro trayson / but he was but seuen yere olde
And therfore lytel tale he therof tolde
Of any dreme / so holy was his hert
By god / I had rather than my shert
That ye had herde his legende / as haue I
  Dame Pertelot / I say to you trewly
Macrobius / that writeth the auision
In Affrike / of the worthy Scipion
Affyrmeth dremes / and saith that they been
Warnyng of thynges / that we after seen
  And farthermore I pray you loketh wel
In the olde Testament / of Danyel
Yf he helde dremes for vanyte
  Rede eke of Joseph / and there shal ye se
Wonders ben somtyme / but I say nat al
Warnyng of thynges / that after shal fal.
¶ Lo of Egipt the kyng / that hight Pharao
His baker / and his butteler also
Wheder they felte non effecte in dremes:
Who so wol seke actes of sondrie remes
May rede of dremes a wonder thyng
  Lo Cresus / whiche was of Lyde kyng
Mette he not that he / satte vpon a tree
Whiche signified he shulde honged be
  Lo Adromeda / that was Hectors wife
That day that Hector shulde lese his lyfe
She dremed in the same night beforne
Howe the lyfe of Hector shulde be lorne
Yf that day he went vnto bataile
She warned him / but it might nat auaile
He wente for to fyght neuertheless
But he was slayne anon of Achilles
But that tale is to long to tel
And eke it is nigh day I may nat dwel
  Shortely I say / as for conclusion
That I shal haue of this auision
Aduersite: and I say farthermore
That I ne tel of laxatyues no store
For they ben venemous / I wote it wele
I hem defye / I loue hem neuer a dele
  But let vs speke of myrthe / ⁊ stynte al this
Madame Pertelot / so haue I blys
Of one thing god hath me sent large grace
For whan I se the beautie of your face
Ye be so scarlet reed aboute your eyen
It maketh al my drede for to dyen
For also syker / as In principio
Mulier est hominis confusio.
¶ Madame / the sentence of this latyn is
Woman is mannes ioye and his blys
For whan I fele on night your softe syde
Al be it that I may not on you ryde
For that our perche is made so narowe alas
I am so ful of ioye and of solas
That I defye bothe sweuen and dreme
And with yͤ worde he flewe down fro yͤ beme
For it was day / and eke the hennes all
And with a chucke / he gan hem for to call
For he had founde a corne lay in the yerde
Royal he was / and no more aferde
He fedderd Pertelot twenty tyme
And tradde her eke as oft / er it was prime
He loketh as he were a grymme lyoun
And on his toes he romed vp and doun
Him deyned not to set his fete to the grounde
And chucked / whan he had a corne ifounde
And to him than ran his wyues all
  As royal as a prince in his hall
Leaue I this Chaunteclere / in his pasture
And after wol I tell of his auenture.
¶ Whan yͤ monthe / in whiche yͤ worlde began
That hight Marche / yͤ god first made man
Was complete / and passed were also
Sythe Marche began / twenty dayes ⁊ two
Befyl that Chauntecler / in al his pride
His seuen wyues walkyng him besyde
Caste vp his eyen to the bright sonne
That in the signe of Taurus was ironne
Fourty degrees ⁊ one / and somwhat more
He knewe by kynde / and by none other lore
That it was prime / ⁊ crew wt a blissful steuen
The sonne he sayd is clombe vp to the heuen
Fourty degrees ⁊ one / ⁊ somwhat more iwys
Madame Pertelot / my worldes blysse
Herken howe this blisful byrdes synge
And se the fresshe floures howe they springe

D. Ful

The tale of the nonnes preest.

Ful is myne hert of reuel/ and solas
But sodainly him fel a sorouful caas
For euer the later ende of ioye is wo
God wote/ worldly ioye is soone ago
And if a rethore coude faire endite
He in a cronycle myght sauely write
As for a souerayne notabilyte
  Nowe euery wise man herken to me
This storie is al so trewe I vndertake
As is the boke of Launcelot du Lake
That women holde in ful great reuerence
Nowe wol I turne ayen to my sentence.
¶ A col foxe (ful of sleight and iniquite)
That in the groue had wonned yeres thre
By hygh ymagynacion aforne caste
The same nyght/ through the hedge braste
In to the yerde/ there Chauntecleere the fayre
Was wonte and eke his wyues to repayre
And in a bedde of wortes styll he lay
Tyl it was passed vndren of the day
Waytyng his tyme/ on Chauntecleere to fall
As gladly done these homycides all
That in a wayte lye to murdre men
  O false murdrer/ ruckyng in thy den
O newe Scariot/ and newe Genylon
False dissymuler/ O greke Synon
That broughtest Troy vtterly to sorowe
O Chauntecler/ acursed be the morowe
That thou in thy yerde flewe from ye bemes
Thou were ful wel warned by thy dremes
That ilke day was peryllous to the
But what ye god afore wote/ must nedes be
After the opynion of certayne clerkes
Witnesse of him/ that any clerke is
That in schole is great altercation
In this mater/ and great disputacion
And hath ben/ of an hundred thousande men
But I ne can not boulte it to the bren
As can the holy doctour saynt Austyn
Or Boece/ or the bysshop Bradwardyn
Whether that goddes worthy forewetyng
Strayneth me nedely to do a thyng
(Nedely clepe I symple necessyte)
Or if the fre choyce be graunted me
To do that same thyng/ or do it nought
Though god forwote it/ or it was wrought
Or if his wetyng strayneth neuer a dele
But by necessyte condycionele

  I wol not haue to done of suche matere
My tale is of a cocke/ as ye shal here
That toke his coũsayle of his wife wt sorowe
To walke in the yerde vpon the morowe
That he had met the dreme/ as I you tolde
Womens counsayles ben ful ofte colde
Womens counsayle brought vs first to wo
And made Adam fro paradise to go
There as he was ful mery/ and wele at ease
But for I not/ whom I myght displease
If I counsaile of women wolde blame
Passe ouer/ I said it in my game (re
Redeth authors/ wher they trete of such mate
And what they say of women/ ye mowe here
These ben the cockes wordes/ and not myne
I can of women no harme deuyne.
¶ Faire in the sonde/ to bathe her merily
Lieth Pertelot/ and al her susters by
Ayenst the sonne/ and Chauntecleere so free
Songe merier/ than the Mermayde in the see
For Phisiologus saithe vtterly
Howe that they syngen wel and merily
  And so befyl/ as he cast his eye
Among the wortes on a butterflye
He was ware of this foxe that laye ful lowe
Nothyng than lyst him for to crowe
But cried cocke cocke/ and vp he stert
As one that was affrayde in his hert
For naturally/ beestes desyreth to flye
Fro her contrary/ if he may it se
Tho he neuer erst had seen it with his eye.
This Chauntecleere/ whan he gan him espye
He wolde haue fledde/ but the foxe anone
Said gentyl sir/ alas: what wol ye done?
Be ye afrayde of me/ that am your frende?
  Nowe certes: I were worse than a fende
Yf I to you wolde harme/ or villany
I am not come your counsaile to espye
But trewly the cause of my cõmyng
Was onely to here howe ye syng
For sothly ye haue as mery a steuen
As any angel hath/ that is in heuen
Therwith ye haue of musyke more felyng
Than had Boece/ or any that can syng
My lorde your father/ god his soule blesse
And eke your mother/ of her gentylnesse
Haue in my house ben/ to my great ease
And certes sir/ ful fayne wolde I you please.
But

But for men speken of syngyng / I wol sey
So mote I broken wel myn eyen twey
Saue you / ne herde I neuer man so synge
As dyd your father in the mornynge
Certes it was of herte / al that he songe
And for to make his voyce more stronge
He wolde so payne him / ẏ with both his eyen
He muste wynke / so loude he muste crye
And stonden on his typtoes ther withall
And stretche forthe his necke / longe and small
And eke he was of suche discrecion
That there was no man in no regyon
That him in songe or wysdom myght passe
I haue wel redde dan Burnell the asse
Amonge his verses / how ẏ there was a cocke
For that a preestes sonne yaue him a knocke
Upon his legges / whyle he was yonge & nyce
He made him for to lese his benefyce
But certayne there is no comparyson
Betwyxt the wysdom and discrecion
Of your father / and of his subtylte
Nowe syngeth sir / for saynte charyte
Let se / can ye your father counterfete.
¶ This Chaūteclere his wynges gan to bete
As a man that coulde not his treson aspye
So was he rauysshed with his flaterye
Alas ye lordes / many a false flaterour
Is in your courte / & many a false lesyngour
That please you wel more / by my faythe
Than he that sothfastnesse vnto you saythe
Redeth Ecclesiast of flaterye
Beware ye lordes of her trecherye.
¶ This Chaūteclere stode hye vpon his toos
Stretchyng his necke / & helde his eyen cloos
And gan to crowe loude for the nones
And dan Russell the foxe starte vp at ones
And by the gorget hent Chaunteclere
And on his backe towarde ẏ woode him bere
For yet was there no man that him sued
O destyne / that mayste not be eschued
Alas that Chaunteclere flewe fro the bemes
Alas his wyfe raught not of dremes
And on a friday fyll al this mischaunce
O Venus that arte goddesse of plesaunce
Sithnes ẏ thy seruaūt was this Chaūteclere
And in thy seruyce dyd al his powere
More for delyte / than the worlde to multiplye
Why woldest ẏu suffre him on thy day to dye?
¶ O Gaulfryde / dere mayster souerayne
That whā ẏ worthy king Richard was slayn
With shot / complaynedest his dethe so sore
Why ne had I nowe thy science and thy lore
The friday for to chyde / as dyd ye
For on a friday / shortly slayne was he
Thā wold I shew you how ẏ I coude playn
For Chaunteclers drede / and for his payne.
¶ Certes suche crye / ne lamentacion
Nas neuer of ladyes made / whan that Ilion
Was won / & Pirrus with his bright swerde
Whan he hent king Priam by the berde
And slough him (as saythe Eneidos)
As made al the hennes in the cloos
Whan they had lost of Cauteclere the syght
But souerayneley dame Pertelot shright
Wel louder than dyd Hasdruballes wyfe
Whan that her husbonde had loste his lyfe
And that the Romayns had brent Cartage
She was so ful of turment and of rage
That wylfully in to the fyre she sterte
And brent herselfe / with a stedfaste herte.
¶ O woful hennes / right so cryed ye
As whan that Nero brent the cyte
Of Rome / cryed the senatours wyues
For that her husbondes shulde lese her lyues
Withouten gylte Nero hath hem slayne
Nowe wol I turne to my tale agayne.
¶ The sely wydowe / & her doughters two
Herde the hennes crye and make wo
And out at the dore sterte they anon
And sawe the foxe towarde the wodde gon
And bare vpon his backe the cocke away
And cryed out harowe and wel away
A ha the foxe / and after him they ran
And eke with staues / many a nother man
Ran Coll our dogge / Talbot / & eke garlonde
And Malkyn / with her distaffe in her honde
Ran cowe & calfe / and eke the very hogges
For they so sore a ferde were of the dogges
And shoutyng of men / and of women eke
They ran so / her herte thought to breke
They yellen as fendes do in hell
The duckes cryed / as men wolde hem quell
The geese for feare flewe ouer the trees
Out of the hyues came the swarme of bees
So hydous was the noyse / a benedicite
Certes Iacke Strawe / ne his meyne

V.ii. Ne

Ne made neuer shoutes halfe so shrill
Whan that they wolde any flemmyng kyll.
As that day was made vpon the foxe
Of brasse they blewe the trompes & of boxe
Of horne & bone/I which they blew & pouped
And therwith they shriked and shouted
It semed/as though heuen shulde fall
Nowe good men I pray you herken all.
  Lo howe fortune turneth sodainly
The hope and the pride of her enemy
This cocke that lay vpon the foxes bake
In al his drede/vnto the foxe he spake
And said/sir: if I were as ye
yet shulde I say/ as wyse god helpe me
Turneth ayen/ye proude churles all
A very pestylence vpon you fall
Nowe am I come vnto this woodes syde
Maugre your heed/ the cocke shal here abyde
I wol hym ete in faythe/and that anone
¶ The foxe answerd/in fayth it shal be done
And as he spake the worde/al sodainly
This cocke brake from his mouthe deliuerly
And hygh vpon a tree he flewe anon
And whan the foxe sawe that he was gon
  Alas (qd he) o Chaunteclere alas
I haue (qd he) do to you trespas
In as moche as I made you aferde
Whã I you hent/& brought out of your yerde
But sir/ I dyd it not in no wicked entent
Come downe/ & I shal tel you what I ment
I shal you say sothe/ god helpe me so.
¶ Nay than (qd he) I shrewe vs bothe two
And first I shrew my self/ both blode & bones
If thou begyle me ofter than ones
Thou shalte no more with thy flaterye
Do me synge with a wynkyng eye
For he that wynketh/ whan he shulde se
Al wylfully/god let him neuer thee.
  Nay (qd ẏ foxe) but god yeue him mischãce
That is so indiscrete of gouernance
That iangleth/ whan that he shulde haue pees.
¶ Lo/ suche it is for to be recheles
And neglygent/and truste on flaterye
But ye that holde this tale a lye
As of a foxe/of a cocke/and of a hen
Taketh the moralyte good men
For saynt Poule sayth/al that writen is
To our doctryne it is written iwys
Taketh the fruite/and let the chaffe be styll
  Nowe good god / if that it be thy wyll
As sayth my lorde/ so make vs al good men
And bringe vs to thy hygh blysse. Amen.

¶ Here endeth the tale of the nonnes preest/ and here foloweth the Mancyples prologue.

  Sir nonnes preest/our hoste sayd anone
yblessed be thy breche and euery stone
This was a mery tale of Chaunteclere
But by my trouthe/if thou were seculer
Thou woldest be a tredfoule a ryght
For if thou haue corage/as thou hast myght
The were nede of hennes/as I wene
ye more than seuen tymes seuentene
Se whiche brawnes hath this gentil preest
So great a necke/and suche a large breest
He loketh as a sperhauke with his eyen
Hym nedeth not his colours for to dyen
With brasyl/ ne with grayne of Portyngale
  But sir/fayre fall you for your tale
And after that/he with ful mery chere
Sayd to a nother man/ as ye shal here.
¶ Wote ye not where stondeth a lytel towne
Whiche that is called Bob vp and downe
Vnder the blee/in Caunterbury way
There gan our hoste to iape and to play
And said/ sirs: what ? dunne is in the myre
Is there no man/for prayer ne for hyre
That wol awake our felowe behynde
A thefe him myght ful lightly robbe & bynde
Se howe he nappeth/se for cockes bones
Howe he wol fal from his horse atones
Is that a coke of London/with mischaunce
Do him comforte/he knoweth his penaunce
For he shal tel a tale by my fey
Al though it be not worthe a botel of hey
Awake thou coke (qd he) god yeue the sorowe
What eyleth the to slepe by the morowe
Hast thou had fleen al night/or art thou dronke
Or hast thou al night with som queen iswonke
So that thou mayste not holde vp thyn heed.
  This coke that was ful pale/& nothing reed
Said/ sir host: so god my soule blesse
There

There is fal on me great heuynesse
But I not why/ me were leuer to slepe
Than the best gallon of wyne in chepe
¶ Wel (qd the Manciple) if it may do ese
To the sir coke/ and to no wight displese
Whiche that here ryde in this companye
And that our hoste wyl of his curtesye
I wol as nowe excuse the of thy tale
For in good faythe thy visage is ful pale
Thyn eyen dase/ sothely as me thynketh
And wel I wote/ thy breth ful sowre stynketh
That sheweth wel thou arte not wel disposed
Of me certayne thou shalt not be glosed
  Se howe he galpeth/ lo this dronken wight
As though he wolde vs swalowe anon right
Holde close thy mouthe/ by thy father kyn
The dyuel of hell set his fote therin
Thy cursed brethe wyl enfecte vs all
Fye stynking swyne/ fye foule mote the befal
Taketh hede sirs of this lusty man
Nowe swete sir/ wol ye iuste at the van
Therto me thynketh ye be wel shape
I trowe that ye haue dronken wyne ape
And that is whan men play at strawe.
  And wt his speche the coke weyed al wrawe
And on the manciple he gan to nodde faste
For lacke of speche: & down his horse him cast
Where as he lay/ tyl that men him vp toke
This was a fayre cheuesaunce of a coke
Alas that he ne had holde him by his ladyll
And er that he ayen were in the sadyll
There was a great shouyng to and fro
To lyfte him vp/ and moche care and wo
So vnweldy was this sely palled goste
And to the Manciple than spake our host.
¶ Bycause that drinke hath domynation
Vpon this man/ by my saluation
I trowe leudely wol he tel his tale
For were it wyne/ or olde moysty ale
That he hath dronke/ he speketh so in the nose
And snyueleth fast/ and eke hath the pose
  He also hath to do more than ynough
To kepe him on his caple out of the slough
And if he fal from his caple efte sone
Than shal we al haue ynough to done
In lyftyng vp his dronken corce
Tel on thy tale/ of him make I no force
  But yet Manciple/ in fayth thou art to nyce
Thus openly to repreue him of his vyce
An other day he wol parauenture
Reclayme the/ and bring the to lure
I mene he speke wyl of smale thynges
And for to pynche at thy reckenynges
That were not honest/ if it came to prefe.
¶ No (qd the mãciple) yt were a gret mischefe
So myght he lumge me in to the snare
Yet had I leuer paye for the mare
Which he rydeth on/ thã he shuld wt me stryue
I wol not wrathe him/ so mote I thriue
That I spake/ I sayd it but in bourde
And wote ye what/ I haue here in my gourde
A draught of wyne/ ye of a rype grape
And right anon ye shal se a good iape
This coke shal drinke therof/ if I maye
Vp payne of my lyfe he wol not say naye
  And certainly/ to tellen as it was
Of this vessell the coke dranke faste/ alas
What nedeth it/ he dranke ynough beforne
And whan he had pouped in his horne
To the Manciple he toke the gourde agayne
And of the drinke the coke was ful fayne
And thonked him/ in suche wyse as he coude
  Than gan our host to laugh wonder loude
And sayd: I se wel it is necessary
Wher that we gon/ good drike with vs to cary
For that wyl turne rancoure and disese
To accorde & loue/ and many a worde to pese
  O Bacchus/ yblessed be thy holy name
That so canste turne ernest in to game
Worshyp and thonke be to thy deite
Of that mater ye get no more of me.
Tel on thy tale thou Mãciple/ I the pray
  Wel sir (qd he) herkeneth what I say.

¶ Here endeth the Manciples prologue/ and here foloweth his tale.

D.iii.

The Manciples tale.

Whan Phebus dwelled here in erth adoun
As olde bokes make mencioun
He was the moste lusty bacheler
Of al the worlde/ and eke the best archer
He slough Pheton the serpent/ as he lay
Slepyng ayenst the sonne vpon a day
And many a nother noble worthy dede
He with his bowe wrought/ as mē mowe rede
Play he coulde on euery mynstralcye
And synge/ that it was a melodye
To here of his clere voyce the soun
Certes the kyng of Thebes/ Amphion
That with his songe/ walled the cyte
Coude neuer synge halfe so wel as he
Therto he was the semelyst man
That is or was/ sythe the worlde began
What nedeth it his feture to discryue ∸
For in this worlde nas none so fayre a lyue
He was therwith fulfylled of gentylnesse
Of honoure/ and of perfyte worthynesse
This Phebus/ yͭ was floure of bachelerye
As wel in fredome/ as in chyualrye
For his disporte/ in signe eke of victory
Of Pheton/ so as telleth vs the story
Was wonte to beare in his honde a bowe
Now had this Phebus in his house a crowe
Within a cage ifostred many a daye
And taught it speche/ as men teche a iaye
Whyte was this crowe/ as is a whyte swan
And countrefete the speche of euery man
He coulde/ whan he shulde tel a tale
There was in al this worlde no nyghtyngale
Ne coulde/ by an hundred thousande dele
Synge so wonderly mery and wele
Nowe had this Phebus in his house a wyfe
Whiche that he loued more than his lyfe
And nyght and day/ dyd euer his dilygence
Her for to plese/ and do her reuerence
Saue onely/ if I the sothe shal sayne
Jelous he was/ ⁊ wolde haue kept her fayne
For him were lothe/ iaped for to be
And so is euery wight/ in suche degre
But al for naught/ for it auayleth nought
A good wyfe/ that is clene of werke ⁊ thought
Shulde not be kept in none awayte certayne
And trewly the labour is in vayne
To kepe a shrewe/ for it wol not be
This holde I for a very nycete
To spyll laboure/ for to kepe wyues
Thus writen olde clerkes in her lyues
But nowe to purpose/ as I first began
This worthy Phebus/ dothe al that he can
To plese her/ wenyng through suche plesaūce
And for his manhode/ ⁊ for his gouernaunce
That

The Manciple's Tale (H 105–158; T. 17054–17107)

That no man shulde put him from her grace
But god it wote/there may no man embrace
As to distrayne a thyng/whiche that nature
Hath naturally set in a creature
Take any byrde/and put him in a cage
And do al thyn entent/and thy corage
To foster it tenderly with meate and drinke
Of al dayntiees that thou canste bethynke
And kepe it also clenly as thou may
Al though the cage of golde be neuer so gay
yet had this byrde/ by twenty thousande folde
Leuer in a forest/that is wyde and colde
Go ete wormes/and suche wretchydnesse
For euer this birde wyl do his besynesse
To escape out of his cage/whan he maye
His lyberte the birde desyreth aye.
Let take a catte/ & foster her with mylke
And tender flesshe/& make her couche of sylke
And let her se a mouse go by the wall
Anon she weyueth flesshe/& couche/and all
And euery deyntie/that is in that house
Suche appetyte hath she to ete the mouse
Lo here hath luste his domynacion
And appetyte flemeth discrecion.
A she wolfe/ hath also a vylanous kynde
The leudest wolfe that she may fynde
Or leste of reputacion/that wol she take
In tyme whan her luste to haue a make
Al these ensamples speke I by these men
That ben vntrue/ & no thyng by women
For men haue euer a lycorouse appetyte
On lower thyng/ to perfourme her delyte
Than on her wyues/be they neuer so fayre
Ne neuer so trewe/ ne so debonayre
Flesshe is so newfangel/with mischaunce
That we ne conne in no thyng haue plesaunce
That souneth vnto vertue/any whyle.
¶ This Phebus/whiche thought no gyle
Disceyued was/for al his iolyte
For vnder him an other had she
A man of lytell reputation
Nought worthe to Phebus/in comparyson
The more harme is/it happeth ofte so
Of whiche there cometh moche harme & wo
And so befel/ whan Phebus was absent
His wyfe anon hath for her lemman sent
Her lemman/certes that is a knauyssh speche
Foryeue it me/and that I you beseche.
¶ The wyse Plato sayth/as ye mowe rede
The worde must nedes acorde with the dede
If men shulde tel proprely a thyng
The worde muste cosyn be to the werkyng
I am a boystouse man/right thus say I
There is but lytel difference truely
Betwyxt a wyfe/that is of hye degre
If of her body dishonest she be
And a poore wenche/other than this
If it so be they werke bothe amys
But for the gentyl is in estate aboue
She shal be called his lady and his loue
And for that tother is a poore woman
She shal be called his wenche/or his lemman
And god it wote/myn owne dere brother
Men lay as lowe that one as that other
Right so betwyxt a tytlelesse tyraunt
And an outlawe/or a thefe erraunt
The same I say/there is no dyfference
To Alysaunder was tolde this sentence
That for the tyraunt is of greater might
By force of meyne/to slee downe right
And brenne house & home/and make al playn
Lo therfore is he called a capitayne
And for the outlawe hath but small meyne
And may not do so great an harm/as he
Ne bringe a countrey to so great mischefe
Men callen him an outlawe or a thefe.
¶ But for I am a man not textuele
I wol not tel of textes neuer a dele
I wol go to my tale/as I began.
Whan Phebus wyfe had sent for her lemman
Anon they wrought al their luste volage
This whyte crowe/ that henge aye in the cage
Behelde their werke/and sayd neuer a worde
And whan hom was come Phebus ye lorde
This crowe songe/cuckowe/cuckow/cuckow
What birde (qd Phebus) what syngest thou:
Ne were thou not wont so merily to synge
That to my herte it was a reioysyng
To here thy voyce/ alas/ what songe is this:
¶ By god (qd he) I synge not amys
Phebus (qd he) for al thy worthynesse
For al thy beaute/and thy gentylnesse
For al thy songe/ and thy mynstralsye
For al thy wayting/blered is thyn eye
With one of lytel reputacyon
Not worthe to the in comparyson

The

The mountenaũce of a gnat/ so mote I thriue
For on thy bed/thy wyfe I sawe hym swyue
What wol ye more? ỷ crowe anon him tolde
By sadde tokens/and by wordes bolde
Howe that his wyfe had done her lechery
Him to great shame/and to great vyllany
And tolde him eft/ he sawe it with his eyen
¶ This Phebus gan awayward for to wryen
Him though his woful herte braste a two
His bowe he bent/and set therin a flo
And in his yre he hath his wyfe slayne
This is the effecte/ there is no more to sayne
For sorowe wherof/he brake his mynstralsye
Bothe harpe and lute/ getern/ and sautrye
And eke he brake his arowes/ and his bowe
And after that/thus spake he to the crowe.
¶ Traytour (qd he) with tonge of scorpion
Thou haste me brought to my confusyon
Alas that I was wrought/ why nere I deed?
O dere wyfe/o gemme/o lustyheed
That were to me so sadde/ & eke so trewe
Nowe lyest thou deed/ with face pale of hewe
Ful gyltlesse/that durst I swere iwys
O rakell honde/to do so foule amys
O troubled wytte/ o yre retchelesse
That vnauysed smytest gyltlesse
O wantrust/ ful of false suspection
Where was thy wytte and thy discretion
Oh/ euery man beware of rekylnesse
Ne trowe no thyng/ without strong wytnesse
Smyte not to sone/ or thou wete why
And be auysed wel and sykerly
Or ye do any execution
Vpon your yre/ for suspection
Alas/ a thousande folke hath rekell yre
Fully fordone/ & brought hem in the myre
Alas for sorowe I wol my selfe sle
And to the crowe/ o false thefe sayd he
I wol quite anon thy false tale
Thou songe whylom/lyke a nyghtyngale
Nowe shalt thou false thefe/thy songe forgon
And eke thy whyte fethers euerychon
Ne neuer in al thy lyfe shalte thou speke
Thus shul men on a traytour be awreke
Thou & thyn offspring euer shal be blake
Ne neuer swete noyse shal ye make
But euer cryen ayenst tempest and rayne
In token/that through the my wyfe is slayne
And to the crowe he sterte/and that anon
And pulled of his whyte fethers euerychon
And made him blacke/ & reft him al his songe
And eke his speche/ & out at dore him slonge
Vnto the dyuel/ whiche I him betake
And for this cause ben al crowes blake.
¶ Lordinges/by this ensãple I wol you pray
Beware/and take kepe what I say
Ne telleth neuer no man in your lyfe
Howe that an other man hath dight his wyfe
He wol you hate mortally certayne
Dan Salomon/as wyse clerkes sayne
Techeth a man to kepe his tonge well
But as I sayd/I am not textuell
But nathelesse/thus taught me my dame
My sonne thinke on ỷ crowe a goddes name
My sõne kepe wel thy tonge/ & kepe thy frende
A wycked tonge is worse than a fende
My sonne/ from a fende men may hem blesse
My sonne/god of his endelesse goodnesse
Walled a tonge with tethe/and lyppes eke
For man shulde him auyse what he speke
My sonne/ ful ofte for to mykel speche
Hath many a man be spylte/as clerkes teche
But for lytel speche/spoken auysedly
Is no man shente/to speke generally
My sonne/thy tonge shuldest thou restrayne
At al tymes/but whan thou doest thy payne
To speke of god/in honoure and prayere
The first vertue sonne/if thou wolt lere
Is to restrayne/and kepe wel thy tonge
Thus lerne children/ whan they be yonge
My sonne/of mykel spekyng vnauysed
(There lasse spekyng had ynough suffysed)
Cometh mykel harme/ thus was me taught
In moche speche/synne wanteth naught
Woste thou wherfore a rakell tonge serueth
Right as a sworde forcutteth and forkerueth
An arme on two/my dere sonne right so
A tonge cutteth frendshyp al a to
A iangler is to god abhomynable
Rede Salomon/so wyse and honourable
Rede Dauid in his psalmes/ rede Senecke
My sonne speke not/ ne with thy heed becke.
Dissymule as thou were deefe/ if ỷ thou here
The ianglour speketh of perlous matere.
The flemyng sayth/lerne if that thou leste
That lytel ianglyng causeth moche reste
My

My sõne/ if thou no wicked worde hast sayde
The dare not drede for to be bewrayde
But he that hath missayd/ I dare wel sayne
He may by no way clepe his worde agayne
Thyng that is sayd/ is sayd/ & forthe it gothe
Though him repent/ or him be neuer so lothe
He is thral to him/ to whom he hath sayde
A tale/ for whiche he is nowe yuel apayde
My sonne beware/ & be none auctour newe
Of tidynges/ whether they be false or trewe
Where so thou come/ amonge hye or lowe
Kepe wel thy tonge/ & thynke on the crowe.

¶ Here endeth the Manciples tale/ and here begynneth the Persons prologue.

BY that ŷ Manciple had his tale ended
The sõne fro ŷ southe syde is discẽded
So lowe/ that it was not to my syght
Degrees of fyue and twenty on hyght
Ten at clocke it was/ so as I gesse
For eleuen fote/ a lytel more or lesse
My shadowe was at that tyme/ as there
Of suche fete as my length parted were
In syxe fete equally of proportion
Therwith the moones exaltation
I mene Libra/ alway gan ascende
As we were entryng at the thropes ende
For whiche our hoste/ as he was wont to gye
Aye in this case/ this ioly companye
Sayd in this wyse/ lordynges euerychon
Nowe lacketh vs no tale more than one
Fulfylled is my sentence and my decre
Who wol nowe tel a tale let se
Almoste fulfylled is myn ordynaunce
I pray to god so yeue him right good chaũce
That telleth this tale to vs lustely
Sir preest (qd he) arte thou a vicary
Or arte thou a person/ say sothe by thy fay
Be what thou be/ breke thou not our play
For euery man saue thou/ hath tolde his tale
Vnbokell/ & shewe vs what is in thy male
For trewly me thynketh by thy chere
Thou shuldest knyt vp wel a great matere
Tel vs a fable anon/ for kockes bones
¶ This person him answerde al atones
Thou gettest fable none tolde of me
For Poule/ that writeth to Tymothe
Repreueth hem that wayuen sothfastnesse
And tellen fables/ and suche wretchydnesse
Why shulde I sowe draffe out of my fyste
Whã I may sowe whete/ if that me lyst
For whiche I saye/ if that ye lyst to here
Moralyte/ and of vertuous matere
And than/ if ye wol yeue me audience
I wolde ful fayne at Christes reuerence
Done you plesaunce leful/ as I can
But trusteth wel/ I am a sotherne man
I can not ieste/ rum/ ram/ ruf/ by letter
And god wote/ ryme holde I but lytel better
And therfore if ye lyst/ I wol not glose
I wol you tel a lytel tale in prose
To knyt vp al this feest/ and make an ende
And Iesu for his grace/ wyt me sende
To shewe you the way/ in this voyage
Of thilke perfyte glorious pylgrimage
That hyght Hierusalem celestyall
And if ye vouchsaue/ anon I shall
Begyn vpon my tale/ for whiche I pray
Tel your aduyse/ I can no better say
But nathelesse this medytation
I put it aye/ vnder the correction
Of clerkes/ for I am not textuell
I take but the sentence/ trusteth well
Therfore I make protestation
That I wol stonde to correction.
¶ Vpon this worde/ we haue assented sone
For as it semed/ it was for to done
To ende in some vertuous sentence
And for to yeue him space and audyence
And bade our hoste he shulde to him say
That al we/ to tell his tale him pray
Our hoste had the wordes for vs all
Sir preest (qd he) now fayre mote you befall
Sayth what ye lyste/ & we shal gladly here
And with that worde he sayd in this manere
Telleth (qd he) your medytacioun
But hasteth you/ the sonne wol adoun
Beth fructuous/ and that in lytel space
And to do wel/ god sende you his grace.

¶ Here endeth the Persons prologue/ and herafter foloweth his tale.

The Persons tale.

¶ Jeremi. vi. State super vias/ et videte/ et introgate de semitis antiquis/ que sit via bona/ et ambulate in ea: et inuenietis refrigerium animabus vestris.

Our swete lorde god of heuen/ that no man wol perissh/ but wol that we tourne all to the knowlege of him/ and to the blyssful lyfe that is perdurable/ amonessheth vs by the prophete Jeremye/ that sayth in this wyse. Stondeth vpon the wayes and seeth/ and asketh of olde pathes: that is to say/ of olde sentẽces/ whiche is the good waye/ and walketh in that waye/ and ye shal fynde refresshynge for your soules. &c. Many ben the wayes espyrituels that lede folke to our lorde Jesu Christ/ and to the reigne of glorie: Of whiche wayes there is a ful noble way/ & ful couenable/ whiche may not fayle to man ne to woman/ that through synne hath misgone fro the right way of Hierusalem celestyall: and this way is called penitence/ of whiche man shulde gladly herken and enquire with al his herte/ to wete what is penitence/ and whiche is called penitence/ and howe many maners ben of actions or werkynges of penitence/ and howe many speces there ben of penitence/ and whiche thynges apertayne and behoue to penitence/ and whiche thynges distourbe penitence.

Saynt Ambrose sayth/ that penitence is the playnynge of man for the gylte that he hath done/ and no more to do any thing for whiche hym ought to playne. And some doctours sayth/ Penitence is the waymentyng of man that soroweth for his synne/ and payneth him selfe/ for he hath misdon. Penitence with certayne circumstaunces/ is very repentaunce of a man that holte hym selfe in sorowe/ & other payne for his gyltes: and for he shal be very penytent/ he shal first bewayle synnes that he hath done/ and stedfastly purpose in his herte to haue shrifte of mouthe/ & to do satisfaction/ and neuer to do thynge/ for whiche him ought more bewayle or complayne/ and contynewe in good workes: or els his repentaunce maye not auayle. For as saynt Isoder sayth. He is a iaper and a lyer/ and no very repẽtaunt/ that estsone doth thyng/ for whiche him ought repent. Weppynge and not for to stynte to do synne/ may not auayle: But nathelesse men shal hope that at euery tyme that mã falleth/ be it neuer so ofte/ that he may aryse through penaunce/ if he haue grace: but certayne it is great doute/ for as saithe saynt Gregorye. Unnethes ariseth he out of syn/ that is charged

The Parson's Tale (I 75–91; T. §§ 1, 2)

ged with the charge of yuel vsage. And therfore repentaunt folke/ that stynt for to synne/ and leue synne or synne leue thē/ holy churche holdeth them syker of their saluacion. and he that synneth/ and verily repenteth him in his laste ende: holy churche yet hopeth his saluacion/ by ŷ gret mercy of our lorde Jesu christ/ for his repentaunce: but take the syker way.

¶ And nowe syth I haue declared you/ what thyng is Penitēce/ nowe ye shal vnderstonde/ that there ben thre actions of penitence. The first is/ that a man be baptysed after that he hath synned. Saynt Austyn sayth/ but he be penytent for his olde synful lyfe/ he maye not begyn the newe clene lyfe: For certes if he be baptysed without penitēce of his olde gylt/ he retayneth ŷ marke of baptym/ but not the grace ne the remissyon of his synnes/ tyll he haue very repentaunce. An other defaute is this/ that men do deedly synne after that they haue receyued baptisme. The thirde defaute is this/ that men fal in venyall synnes after her baptisme/ fro day to day. Therof sayth saynt Augustyn/ that penitence of good and humble folke/ is the penitence of euery daye.

The speces of penytence ben thre: That one of hem is solempne: an other is cōmune/ and the thirde is priuy. That penaūce that is solempne is in two maners: As to be put out of holy churche in lent/ for slaughter of chyldren/ and suche maner thynge. An other is whan a man hath synned openly/ of whiche synne the fame is openly spoken in the countrey: and than holy churche by iugement/ distrayneth him for to do open penaunce.

Cōmen penaunce is/ that preestes enioyne men in certayne case: as for to go perauēture naked in pylgrymage/ or barefote. Priuy penaunce is that/ that men do al daye for priuy synnes/ of whiche we shriue vs priuely/ and receyue priuy penaunce. ¶ Nowe shalt thou vnderstond/ what is behoueful and necessary to very perfyte penytence: and this stonte on thre thynges. Contrycion of herte/ cōfession of mouthe/ ⁊ satisfaction. For whiche sayth saynt Johan Chrisostom. Penitence distrayneth a man to accept benignely euery payne/ that him is enioyned/ with contrycion of hert/ and shrifte of mouthe/ with satisfaction: and in werkyng of al maner humylite. And this is fruteful penitence ayenst thre thynges/ in whiche we wrathe our lorde Jesu Christ: this is to say/ By delyte in thynkynge/ by retchelesnesse in spekyng/ ⁊ by wicked synful werkyng. And ayenst these wycked gyltes is penitence/ that may be lykened vnto a tree.

The rote of this tree is contrycion/ that hydeth him in the herte of him that is very repentaunt/ right as the roote of a tree hydeth him in the erthe. Of this rote of cōtrycion springeth a stalke/ that bereth braunches and leues of confessyon/ and frute of satisfaction. For whiche Christ saith in his gospel. Doth digne fruite of penitēce/ for by this fruite men may knowe the tre/ and not by the rote that is hyd in the herte of man/ ne by the braunches/ ne the leues of cōfessyon. And therfore our lorde Jesu Christ sayth thus: By the fruite of hem shal ye knowe hem. Of this rote also springeth a sede of grace/ the whiche sede is mother of al sykernesse/ and this sede is eigre ⁊ hote. The grace of this sede spri̅geth of god/ through remembraunce on the daye of dome/ and on the paynes of hell. Of this mater sayth Salomon/ that in the drede of god/ man forleteth his synne. The heate of this sede is the loue of god/ and ŷ desyring of the ioye perdurable: This hete draweth the herte of man to god/ and doth him hate his synne: For sothly there is no thyng that sauoureth so wel to a childe/ as the mylke of his nouryce/ ne nothyng is to him more abhomynable than ŷ mylke/ whan it is medled with other meate. Right so the synful man that loueth his synne/ him semeth that it is to him most swete of any thyng/ but fro that tyme he loueth sadly our lorde Jesu Christ/ and desyreth the lyfe perdurable/ there is to him no thyng more abhomynable: For sothly the lawe of god is the loue of god. For whiche Dauid the prophete sayth: I haue loued thy lawe/ ⁊ hated wickydnesse: He that loueth god/ kepeth his lawe and his worde.

¶ This tree sawe the prophete Danyel in spiryte/ on the vysyon of Nabugodonosor/ whan he counsayled him to do penitence. Penaūce is the tree of lyfe/ to hem that it receyue/ and he that

that holdeth him in very penitence is blessed/ after the sentence of Salomon. In this penytence or contrycion/ man shal vnderstonde foure thynges/ that is to say: What is contrycion/ and whiche ben the causes that moue a man to contrycion/ and howe he shulde be contryte/ and what contrycion auayleth to the soule. Than is it thus/ that contrycion is the very sorowe/ that a man receyueth in his hert for his synnes/ with sadde purpose to shuue him/ and to do penaunce/ and neuer more to do synne: And this sorow shal be in this maner/ as sayth sayute Bernarde: It shal be heuy and greuouse/ and ful sharpe and poynaunt in herte. ¶ First/ for a man hath agilted his lorde and his creatoure/ and more sharpe and poynaunt/ for he hath agilted his father celestyal: And yet more sharpe & poynaunt/ for he hath wrathed and agilted him that bought him/ that with his preciouse bloode hath delyuered vs fro the bondes of synne/ and fro the cruelte of the dyuel/ & fro the paynes of hell.

The causes that ought moue a man to contrycion ben syxe. First a man shal remembre him of his synnes/ but loke that that remembraunce ne be to him no delyte/ by no waye/ but great shame and sorowe for his synnes. For Iob saith/ synful men done workes worthy of confessyon. And therfore sayth Ezechiel: I wol remembre me al the yeres of my lyfe/ in the bytternesse of my herte. And god sayth in the Apocalipse: Remembre ye from whence that ye ben fall/ for before that tyme that ye synned/ ye were chyldren of god/ and lymmes of the reigne of god: But for your synne ye ben wexen thrall and foule/ & membres of the fende: hate of angels/ slaunder of holy churche/ and foode of the false serpent/ perpetual matere of the fyre of hell: And yet more foule and abhomynable/ for ye trespace so ofte tymes/ as doth an hounde yͭ returneth ayen to eete his own spewyng: & yet be ye fouler/ for your long cōtynuyng in synne/ & your synful vsage/ for whiche ye be roted in your synne/ as a beest in his donge. Suche maner of thoughtes make a man to haue shame of his synne/ and no delyte. As god sayth/ by the prophete Ezechiel: ye shal remembre you of your wayes/ & they shul displese you sothly. Synnes ben the wayes that lede folke to hell.

The seconde cause that ought make a man to haue disdayne of syn is this/ that as sayth saynt Peter: Who so doth syn/ is thrall of synne/ and synne putteth a man in great thraldome. And therfore sayth the prophete Ezechiel: I went sorouful/ in disdayne of my selfe. Certes wel ought a man haue disdayne of synne/ and withdrawe him fro that thraldom and vilonye. And lo what sayth Senecke in this mater/ he sayth thus: Thoughe I wyste/ that neyther god ne man shulde neuer knowe it/ yet wolde I haue disdayne for to do synne. And the same Senecke also sayth: I am borne to greatter thynge/ than to be thral to my body/ or for to make of my body a thral. Ne a fouler thral maye no man ne woman make of his body/ than for to yeue his body to synne/ al were it the foulest churle/ or the foulest woman that lyueth/ and leste of value/ yet is he than more foule/ and more in seruytude. Euer fro the hygher degre that man falleth/ the more is he thrall/ and more to god and to the worlde vyle and abhomynable. O good god/ wel ought man haue great disdayne of synne/ syth yͭ through synne/ there he was free he is made bonde. And therfore sayth saynt Austyn: If thou hast disdayne of thy seruaunt/ if he offende or synne/ haue thou than disdayne that thou thy selfe shuldest do synne. Take rewarde of thyn owne valewe/ that thou ne be to foule to thy selfe. Alas wel ought they than haue disdayne to be seruauntes and thralles to synne/ and sore to be ashamed of them selfe/ that god of his endelesse goodnesse hath sette in hyghe astate/ or yeue hem wytte/ strenght of body/ heale/ beutie/ or prosperyte/ and bought hem fro the dethe with his herte blode/ that they so vnkyndly/ agaynst his gentylnesse/ quite him so vilaynously/ to slaughter of her owne soules. O good god/ ye women yͭ ben of great beautie/ remembreth you on the prouerbe of Salomon. He sayth he lykeneth a fayre woman/ that is a foole of her body/ to a rynge of golde yͭ were worne on the groyne of a sowe: For

For right as a sowe wroteth in euery ordure/ so wroteth she her beaute in stynking ordure of synne.

The thirde cause yͤ ought meue a man to contrycion/ is drede of the daye of dome/ ⁊ of the horrible paynes of hell. For as saynt Ierom sayth: At euery tyme that me remembreth of the daye of dome/ I quake: For whan I ete and drinke/ or what so that I do/ euer semeth me that yͤ trompe sowneth in myn ere: Ryseth ye vp that ben deed/ and cometh to the iugemēt. O good god/ moche ought a man to drede such a iugemēt/ ther as we shal be al/ as saint Poule sayth/ before the sete of our lorde Iesu Christ/ where as he shal make a general congregation/ where as no man may be absent/ for certes there auayleth non essoyne ne excusation/ and not only that our defautes shal be iuged/ but also that al our werkes shal openly be knowen. And as saith saint Bernarde/ there ne shal no pledyng auayle/ ne no sleight: We shal yeue rekenyng of euery idell worde. There shal we haue a iuge that may not be disceyued ne corrupte/ and why? For certes/ al our thoughtes ben discouered/ as to him/ ne for prayer ne for mede/ he shal not be corrupte. And therfore sayth Salomon: The wrathe of god ne wol not spare no wight/ for prayere ne for yefte. And therfore at the daye of dome/ there is no hope to escape. Wherfore/ as saith saynt Anselm: ful great anguisshe shal yͤ synful folke haue at that tyme: There shal the feirs and wrothe iuge sytte aboue/ and vnder him the horrible pytte of hell open/ to distroy him that muste beknowe his synnes/ whiche synnes openly ben shewed before god and before euery creature: And on the left side/ mo dyuels than any herte may thynke/ for to hale ⁊ drawe the synful soules to the payne of hell/ and within the hertes of folke shal be the byting cōscience/ and without forthe shal be the worlde al brēnyng: whyther shal than the wretched synful man flye to hyde him? Certes he may not hyde him/ he must come forth and shewe him. For certes/ as saith saint Ierom/ the erth shal cast him out of it ⁊ the see also/ ⁊ the ayre that shal be ful of thonder clappes ⁊ lightnynges.

Now sothly/ who so wel remembreth him of these thinges: I gesse/ that his synne shal not turne him in delyte/ but to great sorowe/ for drede of the payne of hell. And therfore saith Iob to god: suffre lorde/ that I may a whyle bewayle ⁊ wepe/ er I go without returnynge to the derke londe/ couered with the derknesse of dethe/ to the londe of misese ⁊ of derknesse/ where as is yͤ shadowe of deth/ where as there is none ordre or ordynaunce/ but ferefull drede that euer shal laste. Lo/ here may ye se/ that Iobe prayed respyte a whyle/ to bewepe and wayle his trespace: for sothly one day of respite is better than al yͤ tresour of this world. And for as moche as a man may acquite him selfe before god by penitence in this worlde/ and not by tresour/ therfore shulde he pray to god to yeue him respit a while/ to bewepe and wayle his trespace: For certes/ al the sorowe that a man might make fro the begynnyng of the worlde/ nys but a lytel thing/ at regarde of the sorowe of hell. The cause why that Iobe calleth hell the londe of derknesse/ vnderstondeth that he calleth it londe or erth/ for it is stable and neuer shal fayle/ ⁊ derke: for he that is in hell hath defaute of syght material/ for certes the derke light that shal come out of the fyre that euer shal brēne/ shal turne him al to payne that is in hell/ for it sheweth him to the horryble dyuels that him turmenteth/ couered with the derknesse of dethe/ that is to say/ that he that is in hell/ shal haue defaute of the syght of god: for certes the syght of god is the lyfe perdurable. The derknesse of dethe/ ben yͤ synnes that the wretched man hath done/ whiche that distourbe him to se the face of god/ right as the derke cloude betwyxt vs ⁊ the sonne. Londe of misese/ bicause that there ben thre maner of defautes/ ayenst thre thynges that folke of this worlde haue in this present lyfe/ that is to say: honours/ delyces/ and rychesse. Ayenst honour haue they in hell/ shame and confusyon: For wel ye wote/ that men call honour the reuerence that man dothe to man/ but in hell is non honour ne reuerēce/ For certes/ no more reuerēce shal be do ther to a king/ than to a knaue. For whiche god saith by the prophete Ieremy: Those folke that me

X dispyse

dispyse/ shal be in dispyte. Honoure is also called gret lordship: there shal no wight serue other/ but of harme & turment. Honoure is also called great dignyte & hyghnesse/ but in hell shal they be al fortroden of dyuels. As god saythe: the horryble dyuels shal go and come vpon the heedes of dampned folke: and this is/ for as moch as the higher yͭ they were in this present lyfe/ the more shal they be abated & defoyled in hell. Ayenst the richesse of this worlde shal they haue misese of pouerte/ that shal be in foure thinges: In defaute of tresoure. Of whiche Dauid sayth: The riche folke that enbrace & knyt al her herte to tresour of this worlde/ shal slepe in the sleppyng of dethe/ and nothyng ne shul they fynde in her hondes of al her tresour. And more ouer the misese of hell shal be in defaute of meete and drinke. For god sayth thus by Moyses: They shal be wasted with honger/ & the byrdes of hell shal deuour hem/ with bytter deth/ and the gall of the dragon shal be her drinke/ and the venym of the dragon her morsels. Also her misease shal be in defaute of clothīg/ for they shal be naked in body/ as of clothing/ saue the fyre in whiche they brenne/ and other fylthes: & naked shal they be of soule/ of al maner vertues/ which yͭ is the clothing of the soule. Where ben than the gay robes/ the soft shetes/ & the smal shertes? Lo/ what saith god of hem by the prophete Isaye/ that vnder hem shal be strewed moughtes/ & her couertures shal be of wormes of hell? Also her misease shal be in defaute of frēdes/ for he is not poore that hath good frendes/ but there is no frēde/ for neyther god ne no creature shal be frende to hem/ & eche of hem shal hate other wͭ deedly hate: The sonnes & the doughters shal rebell ayenst father & mother/ & kynred ayenst kynred/ chyde & dispyse eche other/ bothe day and night/ as god sayth by the prophete Michias: And the louynge children yͭ whylom loued so flesshly eche other/ wold eche of hem eete other if they myght. For howe shulde they loue togyther in the paynes of hell/ whan they hated eche other in yͤ prosperite of this life? for trust wel/ her flesshly loue was deedly hate. As sayth the prophete Dauid: Who so yͭ loueth wickednesse/ he hateth his soule/ & who so hateth his owne soule/ certes he may loue none other wight in no maner: And therfore in hel is no solace ne no frendshyp/ but euer yͤ more kynredes that ben in hel/ the more cursynges/ the more chydinges/ and the more deedly hate there is amonge hem. Also they shal haue defaute of al maner delyces/ for certes delyces ben after the appetytes of yͤ fyue wyttes: as syght/ heryng/ smellyng/ sauouring/ and touchynge. But in hell her syght shal be ful of derknesse & of smoke/ and therfore ful of teares/ and her herynge ful of waylyng & gryntyng of tethe: As sayth Iesu Christ. Her nosethrilles shal be ful of stynking. And/ as saith Isaye the prophete: Her sauourynge shal be ful of bytter gall/ and as touchyng of al her bodyes/ ycouered with fyre that neuer shall quenche/ & with wormes that neuer shal dye. As god sayth by the mouthe of Isaye: and for as moch as they shal not wene that they may dye for payne/ and by dethe flye fro payn/ that may they vnderstonde in the wordes of Iob/ that sayth: There is the shadowe of dethe. Certes a shadowe hath yͤ lykenesse of the thīg of whiche it is shadowed/ but shadowe is not the same thyng of which it is shadowed: right so fareth the payne of hell/ it is lyke dethe/ for the horryble anguissh. And why? For it payneth hem euer as though they shuld dye anon/ but certes they shal not dye. For as saith saint Greg. to wretched captifes shal be deth wͭ out deth/ & ende wͭ out ende/ & defaut wͭ out faylīg/ for her deth shal alwey liue/ & her end shal euermore begyn/ & her defaute shal not fayle.

And therfore sayth saint Iohan the Euangelyst/ they shal folowe dethe & they shal not fynde him/ and they shal desyre to dye/ & dethe shal flye fro hem. And also Iob sayth/ that in hel is no ordre of rule. And al be it so/ that god hath create al thyng in right order/ & nothyng without order/ but al thynges ben ordred & nombred/ yet nathelesse they that ben dampned ben nothyng in order/ ne holde non order/ for the erthe ne shal bere hem no fruite. For/ as the prophete Dauid sayth: God shal distroye the fruite of the erthe/ as for hem/ ne water/ ne shal yeue hem no moysture/ ne the

eyre

fyre no refresshyng/ ne fyre no lyght. For as sayth saynt Basilie: The brenyng of the fyre of this worlde shal god yeue in hell to hem that ben dāpned/ but the light ⁊ the clerenesse shal be yeue in heuen to his chyldren: right as good men yeue flesshe to her children/ ⁊ bones to her houndes. And for they shal haue none hope to escape/ sayth saynt Iob at laste/ that there shal errour and grisly drede dwell without ende. Horrour is alwaye drede that is to come/ and this drede shal alway dwell in the hertes of hem that be dampned. And therfore haue they loste al her hope for seuen causes. First for god that is her iuge shal be without mercy to hem/ and they may not plese him ne none of his payntes/ ne they may not yeue no thyng for her raunsom/ ne they shal haue no voyce to speke to him/ ne they may not fle fro payne/ ne they haue no goodnesse in hem that they maye shewe to delyuer hem fro payne. And therfore saythe Salomon: The wicked man dyeth/ and whan he is deed/ he shal haue no hope to escape fro payne. Who so than wolde wel vnderstond the paynes/ ⁊ bethinke him wel that he hath deserued those paynes for his synnes/ certes he shulde haue more talent to syghe and wepe/ than for to synge and playe. For as saythe Salomon/ who so that had the science to knowe the paynes that ben ordayned for synne/ he wolde make sorowe. That science/ as sayth saynt Austyn/ maketh a man to weyment in his herte.

The fourthe poynt that ought make a man haue contrycion/ is the sorouful remembraunce of the good that he hath lefte to do here in erthe/ and also the good that he hath loste. Sothly the good werkes yͭ he hath lefte/ eyther they be the good werkes that he wrought er he fyll in deedly synne/ or els the good werkes that he wrought whyle he lay in synne. Sothly the good werkes that he dyd before that he fell in synne ben al mortyfied/ astoned/ and dul by ofte synnyng. The werkes that he dyd whyle he lay in synne be deed/ as to the lyfe perdurable in heuen: than the good werkes yͭ ben mortifyed by oft synnig/ which he dyd beyng in charite/ may not quick ayen without very penytēce. And of it saythe god by yͤ mouthe of Ezechiel: If the rightful man returne ayen fro his rightwysnesse ⁊ do wickednesse/ shal he lyue? nay: for al yͤ good werkes that he hath do/ ne shal neuer be in remembraūce/ for he shal dye in his synne. And vpon yͭ chapitre sayth saynt Gregorie thus/ that we shal vnderstonde this principally: If that we don deedly syn/ it is for nought than to reherce or drawe in to memorie yͤ good werkes that we haue wrought before: for certes in the werkig of deedly synne/ ther is no trust to no good werke that we haue done before: that is to say/ as for to haue therby the lyfe perdurable in heuen. But nathelesse the good werkes quicken and come agayne/ and helpe and auayle to haue yͤ life perdurable in heuen whā we haue cōtrycion: But sothly the good werkes that men don whyle they be in deedly synne/ for as moch as they were don in deedly syn/ they may neuer quicke: for certes/ thyng that neuer had lyfe/ maye neuer quicke: And nathelesse al be it that they auayle not to haue the lyfe perdurable/ yet auaile they to abredge of the payne of hel/ or els to get temporel rychesses/ or els yͭ god wol the rather enlumyne or light the herte of the synful man to haue repentaūce/ ⁊ eke they auayle for to vse a man to do good werkes/ that yͤ fende haue the lesse power of his soule. And thus yͤ curteys lorde Iesu Christ ne wol yͭ no good werke be loste/ for in somwhat it shal auayle. But for as moche as the good werkes that mē don while they ben in good lyfe/ ben al amortised by syn folowyng: ⁊ also syth that al the good werkes that mē don whyle they be in deedly synne ben vtterly deed/ as for to haue yͤ lyfe perdurable/ Wel maye that man that no good werke ne dothe/ synge that new fresshe songe (Iay tout pardu mon temps/ et mon labure) For certes synne byreueth a man bothe goodnesse of nature/ ⁊ also the goodnesse of grace. For sothly the grace of the holy goost fareth like fyre that maye not be ydell/ for fyre fayleth anon as it forleteth his werking: and right so grace fayleth anon as it forleteth his werkyng. Than leseth the synful man the goodnesse of glory/ that only is behyght to good men that labour and werke. Wel may he be sory than yͭ oweth

X.ii. al his

al his lyfe to god/ as longe as he hath lyued/ and also as longe as he shal lyue/ ŷ no goodnesse ne hath to paye with his dette to god/ to whom he oweth al his lyfe: for truste wel he shal yeue accomptes/as sayth saynt Bernarde of al ŷ goodes that haue ben yeue him in this present lyfe/ and how he hath hem dispended/ in so moch that there shal not perissh an heere of his heed/ ne a moment of an houre/ne shal not perysshe of his tyme/that he ne shal yeue of it a rekenyng.

The fyfth thynge that ought to moue a man to contricion / is remembraunce of the passion that our lorde Iesu Christ suffred for our synnes. For as sayth saynt Bernarde/whyle that I lyue I shal haue remembraunce of the trauayles that our lorde Iesu Christ suffred in prechynge/ his werynesse in trauaylyng/his temptacions whan he fasted/ his longe wakynges whan he prayed/ his teeres whan that he wepte for pyte of good people/the wo/ the shame/and the fylth that men sayd to him: of the foule spyttyng that men spyt in his face/ of ŷ buffettes that men yaue him: of the foule mowes and of the reproues that men said to him: of the nayles/with whiche he was nayled to the crosse/ and of al the remenaunt of his passyon that he suffred for my synnes/ & no thyng for his gylte. And ye shal vnderstonde/that in mans synne is euery maner ordre or ordynaunce turned vp so downe. For it is sothe/ that god/ reason/ sensualyte/ and the body of man/ben ordayned that eche of these foure thynges shulde haue lordshyp ouer that other: as thus. God shuld haue lordshyp ouer reson/and reson ouer sensualyte/and sensualyte ouer the body of man. But sothly whan man synneth/ al this ordre or ordynaũce is turned vp so down. And therfore thã/ for as moch as reson of man ne wol not be subiect ne obeysaunt to god/that is his lorde by right/therfore leseth it ŷ lordshyp that it shulde haue ouer sensualyte/ and also ouer the body of man. And why: for sensualyte rebelleth than ayenst reson: and by that way leseth reson the lordshyp ouer sensualyte & ouer the body: For right as reson is rebell to god/ right so is bothe sensualyte rebel to reson & to the body also: And certes this disordynaũce & this rebellion our lorde Iesu Christ bought vpon his precious body ful dere: & herkeneth in what wyse. For as moche than as reson is rebel to god/ therfore is man worthy to haue sorow & to be deed. This suffred our lord Iesu Christ for man/ after that he had be betrayed of his discyple/ & distrayned & bounde/ so that his blode brast out at euery nayle of his hondes/as sayth saynt Austyn. And ferthermore/ for as moche as reson of man wol not daũte sensualyte/whan it may/therfore is man worthy to haue shame: & this suffred our lord Iesu Christ for man/whan they spyt in his visage. And ferthermore/for as moch thã as the caytyfe body of man is rebel bothe to reson & to sensualyte/ therfore it is worthy dethe/ & this suffred our lorde Iesu Christ vpon the crosse/ where as there was no parte of his body free without great payne & bytter passyon: and al this suffred our lorde Iesu Christ that neuer forfayted. And therfore resonably may be said of Iesu in this maner: To moche am I payned for thinges that I neuer deserued/and to moch defouled for shame that man is worthy to haue: And therfore may ŷ synful man wel say/as sayth saynt Bernarde. Acursed be the bytternesse of my synne/for whiche ther must be suffred so moche bytternes. For certes after the diuers discordãce of our wickidnesse/ was the passyon of Iesu christ ordayned in dyuers thynges: as thus. Certes synful mans soule is betrayed of the dyuel by couetyse of temporel prosperite/ & scorned by disceyte whan that he cheseth flesshly delyces/and yet it is turmẽted by impaciẽce of aduersite/ & bespet by seruage & subiection of synne/ & at the laste it is slayne fynally. For this disordinaũce of synful man was Iesu Christ first betrayed/ & after ŷ was he boũde/that came for to vnbynde vs of synne & of payne. Than was he bescorned/ ŷ only shuld haue be honoured in al thinges. Than was his visage ŷ ought be desyred to be sene of al mankynde/ in whiche visage angels desyre to loke/ vilaynsly be spet. Than was he scourged that nothing had trespased/ and fynally than was he crucifyed & slayne. Than was acõplisshed the wordes of Isaye:

He

He was woũded for our misdedes / & defoyled for our felonyes. Nowe syth that Jesu Christ toke on him the payn of al our wickydnesses / moche ought synful man wepe and bewayle / that for his synnes goddes sõne of heuen shuld al this payne endure.

The syxte thyng yͤ shulde meue a man to contricion / is the hope of thre thynges / that is to say: foryeuenesse of synne / and the yeft of grace for to do well / & the glorie of heuen / with whiche god shal rewarde man for his good dedes: And for as moche as Jesu Cryst yeueth vs these yeftes of his largenesse and of his souerayn boũtie / therfore is he called (Jesus Nazarenus rex Judeorum) Jesus is to say / sauyour or saluacion / on whom men shal hope to haue foryeuenesse of synnes / whiche that is properly saluacion of synnes. And therfore said the angel to Joseph / thou shalte call his name Jesus / that shal saue his people of her synnes. And herof sayth saynt Peter: There is none other name vnder heuen that is yeue to any man / by whiche a man may be saued / but only Jesus. Nazarenus is as moche for to saye / as flourisshyng / in whiche a man shal hope that he that yeueth him remissyon of synnes / shal yeue him also grace wel for to do. I was at the dore of thyn hert sayth Jesus / & called for to enter: he that openeth to me shal haue foryeuenesse of synne. I wol entre in to him by my grace / & suppe with him by the good werkes yͭ he shal do / whiche werkes ben the fode of the soule / & he shal suppe with me / by yͤ great ioy that I shal yeue him. Thus shal man hope for his werkes of penaũce / that god shal yeue him his reigne / as he behyght him in the gospel. Nowe shal a man vnderstonde in whiche maner shal be his contrycion: I say that it shal be vnyuersal and total / this is to say: a man shal be very repẽtaunt for al his synnes that he hath done in delyte of his thought / for it is right perillous. For there ben two maner of consentynges / that one of hem is called consentyng of affection / whan a man is moued to do synne / and than delyteth him longe for to thynke on that synne / and his reson apperceyueth it wel that it is synne ayenst the lawe of god / and yet his reason restrayneth not his foule delyte or talent / though he se wel apertly that it is ayenst the reuerence of god / al though his reson ne consent not to do that synne in dede / yet saye some doctours that suche delyte that dwelleth longe is ful perylous / al be it neuer so lytel. And also a man shulde sorowe / namely for al that euer he hath desyred ayenst the lawe of god / with perfyte cõsentyng of his reson / for therof is no doute that it is deedly synne in cõsentyng: for certes there is no deedly synne but that it is first in mans thought / and after that in his delyte / and so forthe in to consentyng and in to dede. Wherfore I say yͭ many men ne repent hem neuer of suche thoughtes and delytes / ne neuer shriue hem of it / but only of the dede of great synnes outwarde: wherfore I say that suche wicked delytes ben subtyll begylers of hem that shal be dampned. More ouer / man ought to sorowe for his wicked wordes as wel as for his wicked dedes: for certes the repentaũce of a synguler synne / and not repentaunt of al his other synnes / or els repent him of al his other synnes / and not of a synguler synne / may not auayle: For certes god almighty is al good / and therfore eyther he foryeueth al / or els right nought. And therfore saythe saynt Augustyn: I wote certainly that god is enemy to euery synner: and howe than he that obserueth one synne / shal he haue foryeuenesse of those other synnes? Naye. And more ouer contrycion shulde be wonder sorouful and anguisshous / & therfore yeueth him god plainly his mercy: And therfore whan my soule was anguisshed and sorouful within me / than had I remẽbraunce of god / that my prayer myght come to him. Ferthermore / contrycion must be contynuell / and that man haue stedfast purpose to shriue him and to amende him of his lyfe. For sothly whyle contrycion lasteth / man maye euer hope to haue foryeuenes. And of this cometh hate of synne / that distroyeth bothe synne in him selfe / and also in other folke at his power. For whiche saythe Dauid: They that loue god hate wickydnesse: For to loue god is for to loue that he loueth / and hate that he hateth. The laste thyng that men shal vnder-

X.iiii. stonde

stonde is this / Wherfore auayleth cōtrycion. I say yͤ contrycion somtyme delyuereth man fro synne: Of which Dauid sayth / I say said Dauid / I purposed fermely to shriue me / and thou lorde relesydedest my synne. And right so as contrycion auayleth not without sad purpose of shrifte if man haue oportunyte / right so lytel worthe is shrifte or satysfaction without contrycion. And more ouer contrycion distroyeth the prison of hell / ⁊ maketh weake and feble al the strēgthes of the dyuels / and restoreth the yeftes of the holy goost and of al good vertues / and it clenseth yͤ soule of synne and delyuereth it fro the payne of hell / ⁊ fro the company of the dyuel / and fro the seruage of synne / and restoreth it to al goodes spirituels / and to the company and comunyon of holy churche. Ferthermore it maketh him that whylom was sonne of yre / to be the sonne of grace: And al these thīges ben proued by holy writte. And therfore he that wolde set his entent to these thinges he were ful wyse / for truly he ne shulde haue than in al his lyfe corage to synne / but yeue his herte and body to serue Christ / and therof do him homage. For truly our lorde hath spared vs so mekely in our folyes / that if he ne had pyte of mannes soule / a sory songe might we al synge.

¶ Explicit prima pars penitentie: et incipit pars secunda.

The seconde parte of penytence is confessyon / that is signe of contrycion. Now shul ye vnderstonde what is cōfession / and if it ought nedes be done or no / ⁊ whiche thynges be couenable to very cōfessyon. First shalt thou vnderstonde / yͭ confessyon is very shewyng of synnes to the preest: this is to say very / for he must confesse him of al the condycions that belonge to his synne / as ferforth as he can: al must be sayd / and nothyng excused ne hyd / and not auaunt the of thy good werkes. Also it is necessarye to vnderstonde whence that synnes spring / ⁊ howe they entre / and whiche they ben. Of the springynge of synnes sayth the saynt Poule in this wyse: that right as by one man synne entred firste in to this worlde / and through synne deth / right so the dethe entreth in to al men that synne / and this man was Adam / by whom synne entred in to this worlde / whan he brake the cōmaundement of god. And therfore he that first was so myghty yͭ he ne shulde haue dyed / becam so that he muste nedes dye whether he wolde or no / ⁊ al his progenye in this worlde yͭ in the said man synned. Loke that in the state of innocence / whan Adam ⁊ Eue were naked in paradyse / ⁊ shamed not therof / howe the serpēt wilyest of al other beestes that god made / sayd to the woman: Why cōmaūded god you that ye shuld not ete of euery tre ī paradyse? The woman answerd: Of the fruite said she of the trees of paradyse we fede vs / but of the fruite of the myddle tree of paradyse god forbode vs to ete and touche / leste we shulde dye. The serpent said to the woman: Nay nay / ye shal not dye of dethe / for sothe god wote that what day that ye ete therof your eyen shal open / ⁊ ye shal be as goddes knowyng good ⁊ harme. The woman than sawe that the tree was good to fedynge / ⁊ fayre to the eyen / ⁊ delectable to syght / she toke of the fruite of the tre and ete / ⁊ yaue to her husbonde / and he ete / and anon the eyen of hem bothe opened: And whan that they knewe that they were naked / they sowed of fygge leues ī maner of breches to hyde her membres. There maye ye se that deedly synne hath first suggestion of the fende as sheweth here by yͤ adder / ⁊ afterwarde the delyte of the flesshe / as sheweth by Eue / ⁊ after that consentyng of reson / as sheweth here by Adam. For trust wel though so it were that the fende tempted Eue / that is to say yͤ flesshe / and the flesshe had delyte in the beutie of the fruite defended / yet certes tyl that reson / that is to say Adam / consented to the etyng of the fruite / yet stode he in the state of innocēce. Of the said Adam toke we the sayd orignal syn / for of him flesshly discended be we al / and engendred of vyle and corrupte matere: And whan the soule is put in our bodyes / right anon is contracte orignal synne / and that that was erst but onely payne of concupiscēce is af-is afterwarde bothe payne and synne/ & therfore we ben al borne sonnes of wrathe and of dampnation perdurable/ if it nere baptym yͭ we receyue/ whiche benymmeth vs the coulpe but forsothe the pyne dwelleth with vs as to temptation/ which pyne hight Concupiscẽce. This cõcupiscence whan it is wrongfully disposed or ordayned in man/ it maketh him coueyte by couetise of flesshe flesshely synne by sight of his eyen/ as to erthly thynges/ & also couetise of highnesse by pride of herte.

Nowe as to speke of the firste couetise that is concupiscence/ after the lawe of our membres that were laufully made/ and by rightful iugement of god/ I saye/ for asmoche as man is nat obeyssant to god that is his lorde/ therfore is the flesshe to hĩ disobeysant thrugh concupiscence/ whiche is called nourisshynge of synne/ and occasion of synne. Therfore al the while that a man hath within him yͤ pyne of cõcupiscence/ it is impossyble but he be tẽpted somtyme and moued in his flesshe to syn. And this thyng maye nat fayle as long as he lyueth. It maye wel wexe feble by vertue of bapteme and by the grace of god through penitence/ but fully ne shal it neuer quench that he ne shal sõtyme be moued in him self/ but if he were al refrayned by sickenesse or by malyce of sorcery or colde drinkes. For so/ what saith saynt Poule: the flesshe coueteth ayenst the spirite/ and the spirite ayenst the flesshe: they ben so contrary & so stryuen/ that a man maye nat alway do as he wolde. The same saynt Poule/ after his great penaunce/ in water and in londe: in water by nyght & by day/ in great peryl and in great pyne. In londe famyne and thurst/ colde and clothlesse/ & ones stoned almost to dethe. Yet (sayd he) alas/ I caytife man/ who shal delyuer me fro the prisone of my caytife body? And saynt Jerom/ whan he longe tyme had dwelled in deserte/ where as he hadde no company but of wylde beestes/ where as he had no meate but herbes and water to drinke/ ne no bedde but the naked erthe/ wherfore his flesshe was blacke as an Ethiopien for hete/ and nye distroyed for colde. Yet (said he) that the brennynge of lechery boyled in al his body. Wherfore I wot well that they be disceyued that saye/ they be nat tempted in her bodies. Wytnesse saint James that saith/ that euery wight is tempted in his owne cõscience/ that is to say: yͭ eche of vs hath mater & occasion to be tẽpted of the nourisshyng of syn that is in his body. And therfore saith saint John theuangelyst: if we say that we ben without syn we disceyue our self/ and truthe is nat in vs. Now shal ye vnderstõde how syn wexeth & encreseth ĩ man. The first thyng is the same nourisshyng of syn/ of which I spake before/ the flesshly cõcupiscence/ and after that cometh suggestion of yͤ deuyl/ this is to say the deuyls belous/ with which he bloweth in man the fire of cõcupiscence/ and after that a man bethinketh him wheder he wol do or no/ that thyng to whiche he is tempted. And than if a man withstõde & weyue yͤ first entisyng of his flesshe & of the fende/ than it is no syn/ & if so be he do nat/ thã feleth he anon a flame of delyte/ & than it is good to beware and kepe him wel/ or els he wol fal anon to cõsentyng of syn/ & than wol he do it/ if he may haue tyme & place. And of this mater saithe Moises by the deuyl/ in this maner: the fende saithe/ I wol chace & pursue man by wicked suggestion/ & I wol take him by mouing and steryng of syn/ and I wol departe my prise of my praye by delyberation/ & my luste shalbe accõplysshed in delyte/ I wol drawe my swerde in cõsentyng. For certes/ right as a swerde depteth a thynge in two peces/ right so cõsentyng depteth god fro man/ & than woll I slee him with my honde in dede of syn: thus saith the fende. For certes/ than is a man al deed in soule/ & thus is syn accõplysshed with tẽptation/ by delyte & consẽtyng: & than is the syn actuel. Forsoth syn is in two maners/ either it is venyal or deedly synne. Sothly whan man loueth any creature more thã Jesu christ our creatour/ than it is deedly synne/ & venyall synne it is/ if man loue Jesu Christ lesse than him ought. Forsoth the dede of this venyal synne is ful perillous/ for it mynissheth the loue that man shulde haue to god more & more. And therfore if a man charge him selfe with many suche venyal synnes: certes but if so be that he sõtyme discharge hym of hem by shrifte/

shrifte. They maye ful lightly mynysshe in
hym al the loue that he hath to Iesu Chrust/ &
in this wise skippeth venial syn ito dedly sin.
For certes/ the more that a man chargeth his
soule with venyal synnes/ the more he is en-
clyned to fall in to deedly synne. And ther-
fore lette vs nat be neglygent to charge vs
of venyal synnes. For the prouerbe saith/ yͭ
many smal make a great. Herken this en-
sample. A great wawe of the see cometh sō-
tyme with so great a violence/ that it drow-
neth the shippe. And the same harme dothe
somtyme the smal dropes of water that en-
treth through a lytel creueys/ in to yͤ tymbre
and in to the botome of the shippe/ if men be
so neglygent that they discharge hem not by
tymes. And therfore al though there be a dif-
ferēce betwyxt these two causes of drownyng/
algates the shyppe is drowned. Right so fa-
reth it somtyme of deedly synne and of anoy-
ous venyal synnes/ whan they multiplie in
man so greatly/ that those worldly thynges
that he loueth/ through whiche he synneth ve-
nyally/ is as great in his herte as the loue of
god/ or more: and therfore the loue of euery
thyng that is not beset in god/ ne done princi-
pally for goddes sake/ al though that a man
loue it lesse than god/ yet is it venyall synne/
and deedly synne whan the loue of ony thyng
weyeth in yͤ hert of man/ as moche as the loue
of god or more. Deedly synne as sayth saynt
Austyn/ is whan a man turneth his herte fro
god/ whiche yͭ is very souerayne bountie that
may not chaunge/ & yeueth his herte to thyng
that may chaunge & flytte: and certes that is
euery thīg saue god of heuen. For soth is that
if a man yeue his loue/ whiche that he oweth
to god with all his hert/ vnto a creature/ cer-
tes as moche of loue as he yeueth to that same
creature/ so moche he byreueth fro god/ & ther-
fore dothe he synne: For he that is dettour to
god ne yeldeth not to god al his dette/ that is to
say/ al the loue of his hert. Nowe sythe man
vnderstōdeth generally which is venyal syn/
than it is couenable to tel specially of synne/
whiche that many a man perauēture demeth
hem no synnes/ & shriueth him not of the same
thynges/ & yet nathelesse they be synnes sothly
as these clerkes write/ this is to say: At euery
tyme yͭ man eeteth or drynketh more than suf-
fyseth to yͤ sustenaūce of his body/ in certayne
he doth synne: and also whan he speketh more
than it nedeth/ it is synne. Also whan he her-
keneth not benignly the cōplaynt of yͤ poore:
Also whan he is in heele of body and wol not
faste whan other folke faste/ without cause re-
sonable: also whan he slepeth more than ne-
deth/ or whan he cometh perchaūce to late to
churche/ or to other werkes of charite: Also
whan he vseth his wife without souerayn de-
syre of engēdrure to the honour of god/ or for
the entēt to yelde to his wyfe dette of his body.
Also whan he wol not visyte the syke or the
prisoner/ if he maye. Also if he loue, wyfe or
childe or other worldly thing more than reson
requireth. Also if he flatter or blandyse more
than him ought for any necessyte. Also if he
mynissh or withdrawe yͤ almesse of the poore.
Also if he aparayle his meete more delyciously
than nede is/ or eete to hastely by likorousnes.
Also if he talke vanytees at churche or at god-
des seruyce/ or that he be a talker of ydle wor-
des of folye or vilany/ for he shal yelde acōp-
tes of it at the day of dome. Also whan he be-
highteth or assureth to do thinges that he may
not performe. Also whan that he by lightnesse
or foly missayeth or scorneth his neyghbour.
Also whan he hath any wicked suspection of
thing that he ne wote of sothfastnesse. These
thinges & mo without nombre be synnes/ as
sayth saynt Austyn. Nowe shal men vnder-
stonde/ that al be it so yͭ non erthly man may
eschue al venyal synnes/ yet may he refrayne
him by the brennyng loue that he hath to our
lorde Iesu Christ/ and by prayers and confes-
syon and other good werkes/ so that it shal be
but lytel grefe. For as sayth saint Augustyn/
If a man loue god in such maner/ that al that
euer he dothe is the loue of god/ or for the loue
of god verily/ for he brenneth in the loue of
god: loke howe moche that one droppe of wa-
ter/ whiche dothe fall in to a great fourneys
full of fyre annoyeth or greueth the brēnīg
of the fyre: in lyke maner anoyeth or greueth
a venyal synne vnto that mā whiche is sted-
faste and perfyte in the loue of our sauyour
Iesu

Iesu Christ. Ferthermore men may also restrayne and put away venyal synne/ by commenyng and receyuyng worthely the body of our sauyour Iesu Chist. Also by takyng of holy water/ by almesse dede/ by general confession of Confiteor at masse/ and at Complyn/ and by blessynges of Bisshopes & preestes/ and by other good workes.

¶ De septem peccatis mortalibus/ et de eorum dependentiis circumstātiis/ et speciebus.

NOwe it is expedyent to tell/ whiche been the seuen deedly synnes/ ẏ is to saye/ chefetayns of synnes. Al they renne in o lees/ but in dyuers maners.

Nowe ben they called seuen Lence/ for as moche as they be chefe/ and spring of al other synnes. Of the rote of these seuen synnes/ than is Pride the general rote of al harmes. For of this rote springeth certayn brāches: as Ire/ Enuy/ Accidie or slouth/ Auarice or couetise/ to cōmen vnderstondynge glotonye and lecherye: And eche of these chefe synnes haue her brāches and twigges/ as it shalbe declared in her chapiters folowynge. And though so be/ ẏ no man can vtterly tel the nōbre of twigges/ and of the harmes that come of pride/ Yet wol I shewe aparte of hem/ as ye shal vnderstonde. There is Inobedience/ auauntyng/ ipocrisy/ dispite/ errogance/ impedence/ swellyng of hert/ insolence/ elation/ impacience/ stryfe/ contumacy/ presumption/ irreuerence/ pertinacy/ veyne glory/ and many other twigges ẏ I can nat declare. Inobedience is he that disobeyeth for dispyte the cōmaūdementes of god/ to his soueraynes/ and to his gostly father. Auaunter is he that bosteth of the harme or of the boūte that he hath done. Ipocryte is he that hideth to shewe him suche as he is/ and sheweth him to seme suche as he is nat. Dispitous is he that hath disdayne of his neighbour/ that is to say/ of his euyn christen/ or hath dispyte to do that hym ought to do. Erroganee is he that thynketh that he hath those boūties in him that he hath nat/ or weneth that he shulde haue hem by his desertes/ or els that he demeth he is that he is nat. Impedente is he/ that for his pride hath no shame of his pride ne synne. Swellynge of hert/ is whan man reioyseth him of harme that he hath done. Insolence is he that dispiseth in his iugement al other folke/ as in regarde of his value/ of his cōnyng/ of his spekyng/ and of his beryng. Elation is whan he ne maye neyther suffre to haue maister ne felowe. Impaciente is he that wol nat be taught ne rebuked of his vyce/ and by stryfe denyeth trouthe wittyngly/ and defendeth his foly. Contumyae is he that through his indignation is ayenst euery auctorite or power of hem that ben his soueraynes. Presūption is whan a man vndertaketh an emprise that him ought nat do or els that he maye nat do/ and this is called surquidie. Irreuerence is/ whan manne dothe nat honour there as him ought to do/ and loke to be reuerenced. Pertinacy is whan men defende her foly/ & trust to moche on her owne wytte. Vaynglory is for to haue pompe and delyte in his temporel hynesse/ and glorye him in worldly estates. Ianglynge is whan men speke to moche before folke and clappeth as a myll/ and take no kepe what they saye. And yet is there a preuy spice of pride/ that wayteth firste to be salewed or he wol salue/ al be he lesse worthy than that other is. and also he wayteth or desyreth to sytte/ or els to go aboue hym in the way/ or kysse paye/ to be encensed/ or go to offryng before his neighbour/ and such semblable thinges ayenst his duetie parauēture/ but that he hath his hert and his entent/ in suche a proude desyre/ to be magnified and honoured before the people. Nowe been there two maner of prides. One of hem is within the herte of a man/ and that other is without. Of whiche forsaid thynges sothly and mo than I haue sayd apertayne to pride/ that is in the herte of man/ & other spices of pride ben without/ but natheles/ that one of these spices of pride is signe of that other/ right as the gay leuesel at the tauerne/ is signe of the wyne that is in the celer. And this is in many thynges: as in speche & cōtenaunce/ & outragious aray of

clothyng

clothyng: For certes/if ther had be no synne in clothyng/ Christ wolde nat so soone haue noted and spoken of the clothyng of yͤ riche men in the gospel. And as saint Greg. saith that precious clothynge is coulpable/ for the derthe of it and for his softnesse/ and for his straungenesse and disguisynge: and for the superfluyte/ or for the inordynate scantnesse of it. Alas: may nat a mã se as ĩ our dayes the synful costlewe array of clothynge/ and namely in to moche superfluyte/ or els in to disordynate scantnesse. As to the firste syn in superfluyte of clothynge/ suche that maketh it so dere to the harme of the people/ nat onely the coste of enbroudyng/the disguysed endentyng/or barryng/ oundyng/ palynge/ wyndyng/ or bendyng/ and semblable waste of clothe in vanytee/ But there is also yͤ costlewe furryng in her gownes/so moche pounsynge of chesel to make hooles/ somoch daggyng of sheres forthe/with the superfluite in length of yͤ foresaid gownes/ trapsing in the donge and in the myre/ on horse and also on fote/ as wel of man as of woman. That al that traylyng is verily as in effecte wasted/ consumed thredebare and rotten with donge/ rather than it is yeue to the poore/to great dõmage of the foresaid poore folke/ and that in sondrie wise/ this is to say: that the more the clothe is wasted/ the more muste it cost to the poore people for the scarsenesse. And moreouer/if so be that they wolde yeue suche pounsed and dagged clothynge to the poore people/it is nat cõuenient to were for her astate/ ne sufficient to her necessyte/ to kepe hem fro the distemperaunce of the fyrmament.

Upon that other syde/to speke of the horrible disordynate scantnesse of clothynge/ as been these cutted sloppes or hanselynes/ yͭ through her shortnesse couer nat the shameful mẽbres of man/to wicked entent. Alas/some of hem shewe the bosse of her shap/ and the horrible swole membres that semeth lyke the malady of Hernia/ in the wrappynge of her hosen/ & also the buttockes of hem fare as it were the hinder pte of a she ape in the ful of the mone. And moreouer the wretched swollen mẽbres that they shewe through disguysing/ in departyng of her hosen/ in white & reed semeth that halfe her shameful preuy mẽbres were flayn And if so be that they departe her hosen in other colours/as is white and blewe/ or white and blacke/or blacke and reed/ and so forthe: Than semeth it as by variaunce of colour yͭ the halfe parte of her preuy membres/ben corrupte by the fire of saynt Anthony/ or by canker/or other suche myschaũce. Of the hynder parte of her buttockes it is ful horryble for to se/for certes in that partie of her body there as they purge her stynkĩg ordure/that foule partie shewe they to the people proudly in dispyte of honestie/ whiche honestie that Iesu Christ and his frendes obserued to shewe in her lyfe.

Now as to the outragious array of women/ god wote that though the visages of some of hem seme ful chaste & debonayre/ yet notifye in her araye or atyre/ lycorousnesse & pride: I say not yͭ honeste ĩ clothing of mã or woman is vncouenable/ but certes the superfluyte of disordynate quãtite of clothing is reprouable. Also the synne of ornement or of aparayle is in thynges that appertayne to rydinge/ as in company/ delycate horses that ben holden for delyte/that ben so fayre/ fatte/ & costlewe/and also in many a nyce knaue/that is sustayned bycause of hem/in curious harneys/as in sadels/ cropers/peytrels/ & bridels couered with precious clothyng/ & riche barres of plates of golde & of syluer. For whiche god saith by zacharie the prophete/ I wol confounde the ryders of suche horses. These folke take lytel regarde of the ridyng of goddes sõne of heuen/ and of his harneis whan he rode vpon yͤ asse/ and had non other harneys but the poore clothes of his disciples/ ne we rede not that euer he rode on other beest. I speke this for the syn of superfluite/and not for resonable honesty/ whan reson it requireth. And more ouer/certes pride is greatly notifyed in holdynge of great meyny/ whan they ben of lytel profyte or of right no profyt/and namely whan that meyne is felonous & dãmageous to the people by hardynesse of high lordshyp/or by way of offyces. For certes suche lordes sell than her lordshyppe to the dyuell of hell/ whan they sustayne the wickydnesse of her meyne.

Or

Or els/ whan these folke of lowe degree: as those that kepe hostelries/ sustayne thefte of her hostelers/ and that is in many maner of disceites: those maner of folke ben the flyes that folowe the hony/ or els the houndes that folowe the carayn. Suche forsaid folke strāgel spiritually her lordships: For suche/ thus saith Dauid the prophet. Wicked deth might come on those lordshippes/ and god yeue that they might discende in to hell/ all downe/ all downe: For in her houses ben iniquities and shrewdnesse/ and nat god of heuen. And certes/ tyl they don amendement/ right as god yaue his blessyng to Pharao by the seruyce of Jacob/ and to Laban by the seruice of Joseph: Right so god wol yeue his curse to suche lordshippes/ as sustayn ȳ wickednesse of her seruauntes/ but they come to amēdement. Pride of the table appereth also ful ofte: for certes/ riche men ben called to festes/ ⁊ poore folke ben put away and rebuked. And also in excesse of dyuers meates and drinkes/ and namely suche maner bake meates and disshmetes brennyng of wylde fyre: peynted and castelled with paper and semblable waste/ so that it is abusyon to thynke. And also in to great preciousnesse of vessel ⁊ curiosite of minstralcy/ by whiche a man is stered more to delytes of lechery/ if so be that he sette his herte the lesse vpon our lorde Jesu Christ/ certainly it is a synne. And certenly the delytes mi3t be so great in this case/ ȳ a man might lightlye fal by hem in to a deedly synne. The especes that sourde of pride/ sothly whā they sourde of malyce ymagyned/ auysed/ ⁊ forecast/ or els of vsage ben deedly syn/ it is no dout. And whan they sourde by freelte vnauysed sodenly/ and sodenly withdrawe ayen/ all be they greuous synnes/ I gesse that they be nat deedly. Nowe might men aske/ wherof that pride sourdeth and springeth. I say that somtyme it sprīgeth of the goodes of nature/ somtyme of the goodes of fortune/ and somtyme of the goodes of grace. Certes the goodes of nature stondeth onely in goodes of body/ or good3 of the soule. Certes goodes of body bē heel of body/ strength/ delyuernesse/ beautie/ gentry/ franchise. Goodes of nature of the soule/ ben good wt sharpe vnderstōding/ subtel engin/ vertu naturel/ good memory. Goodes of fortune/ be riches/ hye degrees of lordships/ praysinges of the people. Goodes of grace: ben science/ power to suffre spirituel trauayle/ benigne/ vertuous contēplation/ vndstōdyng of tēptation/ ⁊ semblable thyng3: of whiche forsaid goodes: certes it is a ful great foly/ a man to haue pride in any of hem al. Nowe/ as for to speke of goodes of nature/ god wot/ ȳ somtyme we haue hem in nature/ asmoch to our domage as to our ꝑfite. As to speke of heel of body/ truly it passeth ful lightly/ ⁊ also it is ful oft occasion of sickenesse of the soule: for god wot ȳ flessh is a great enemy to the soule: ⁊ therfore ȳ more ȳ the body is hole/ the more be we in peril to fal. Also for to haue pride in his strength of body/ it is an hye foly: for certes the flesshe coueteth ayenst the spirit: ⁊ the more strong ȳ the flesshe is/ ȳ sorer may the soule be. And ouer al this strēgth of body ⁊ worldly hardinesse/ causeth ful ofte many man to peril ⁊ myschaūce. ⁊ also to haue pride of his gentry/ is ri3t great foly: for oftyme ȳ gentry of the body/ taketh awey the gentry of the soule: ⁊ also we ben al of o father and mother: ⁊ al we been of o nature/ rotten ⁊ corrupt/ bothe riche ⁊ poore. Forsoth o maner gentry is for to praise/ that apparelleth mannes courage. Wytte/ vertue/ ⁊ moralyte/ maketh hym Christes childe. For truste wel/ that ouer what man that syn hath maystry/ he is a very churle to synne.

Nowe ben there general signes of gentylnesse: as eschewyng of vyce ⁊ ribaudry/ and seruage of synne: in worde/ in werke/ and cōtynuaunce and vsyng of vertue/ curtesy/ and clennesse/ and to be lyberall: that is to saye/ large by measure: for that that passeth measure/ is folye and syn: Another is to remēbre him of bounte/ that he of other folke hath receyued: Another is to be benygne to his good subiectes. Wherfore saith Senecke: there is nothyng more couenable to a man of hyghe astate/ than debonairte and pyte. And therfore these flyes that men cal bees/ whan they make her kynge/ they chese one that hath no pricke/ wherwith he maye stynge.

Ano-

Another is/ man to haue a noble hert and a dilygent/ to attayne to the high vertuous thynges. Nowe certes/ a man to haue pride in the goodes of grace/is also an outragius foly: for those giftes of grace that shulde haue tourned hym to goodnesse / and to medicyn/ tourneth him to venym and confusion/ as saith saynt Grego. Certes also/ who so hath pride in the goodesse of fortune / he is a ful great fole: For sōtyme is a man a great lorde by the morne/that is a captife & a wretche or it be night: and somtyme the riches of a man is cause of his deth. Somtyme the delyces of a man/ is cause of greuous malady through whiche he dieth. Certes/ the cōmendation of the people is/ somtyme ful false & brotel for to trust. This day they prayse/ to morowe they blame. God wot/ desire to haue cōmēdation of ẏ people/ hath caused deth to many a busy man. Nowe sith that so is/ that ye haue vnderstonde what is pride/ and whiche be the speces of it/and whens it sourdeth and springeth: nowe ye shal vnderstōde whiche is the remedy ayenst it. Humilyte or mekenesse is the remedy ayenst pride/ that is a vertue/ through whiche a man hathe very knowlege of him selfe/ & holdeth of him selfe nor price ne deyntie/ as in regarde of his desertes/considring euer his freelte. Now ben there thre maner of humilites: As humilyte in herte / another humilite is in mouth / and the thirde is in workes. The humilite in hert is in four maners: That one is/whan a mā holdeth him self as nought worth before god of heuen. The seconde is/whan he dispiseth non other man. The third is/ whan he ne recketh nat/ though men hold him nought worthe. And the fourth is/whan he is nat sory of his humiliation. Also the humilite of mouth is in foure thynges. In a temperate speche/ in humilite of speche/and whan he confesseth with his owne mouth/ that he is such as him thynketh/ that he is in his herte: Another is/ whan he praiseth the bounte of another man and nothynge therof mynissheth. Humilite also in werke/ is in four maners. The first is/whan he putteth other men before him/the secōde is to chese the lowest place ouer al/ the thirde is/ gladly to assent to good counsaile/ the fourth is/ to stonde gladly to the awarde of his soueraynes/ or of him that is in hier degre: Certain this is gret werke of humilite.

De Inuidia.

After Pride woll I speke of the foule synne of Enuy / whiche that is after the worde of ẏ philosofer/sorowe of other mēnes prosperite. And after the worde of saynt Augustin: it is sorowe of other mēnes wele/ and the ioye of other mennes harm. This foule synne is platly agaynst the Holygost: al be it so/that euery synne is ayenst the holy gost: yet natheles/ for asmoch as bounte aptayneth proprely to the holigost: and enuy cometh proprely of malyce/therfore it is proprely ayenst the bounte of the holigost. Now hath malyce two speces/that is to saye/ hardinesse of herte in wickednesse / or els the flesshe of a man is so blynde/ that he consydreth nat that he is in syn/or recketh nat that he is in synne/ whiche is the hardynesse of the deuyll. That other spece of Enuy is/whan that a man denyeth trouth/whan he knoweth ẏ it is trouth and also whan he repēteth the grace that god hath yeue to his neighbour: & al this is by enuy. Certes/than is enuy the worst synne that is/for sothly al other synnes be somtyme onely ayenst o special vertue: but certes/enuy is ayenst al vertues and al goodnesse. For it is sory ayenst al the bounteis of her neighbour/ and in this maner/ it is dyuers from al other synnes. Alas: for there ne is any synne that it ne hath some delyte in it selfe/saue only Enuye/ that euer hath in it selfe anguysshe & sorowe. The speces of Enuy ben these: there is first sorowe of other mens goodnesse and of her prosperyte/ and prosperyte is kyndely mater of ioy: Than is Enuye a synne ayenst kynde. The seconde spece of Enuye/is ioye of other mens harme/ & that is proprely lyke to the dyuel / that euer reioyseth him of mannes harme. Of these two speces cometh backbyting/ and this synne of backbytyng or detracting hath certayne speces/as thus: Some mā praiseth his neighbour by a wicked entēt/ for

for he maketh alway a wicked knot at the last ende: alway he maketh a but at the laste ende that is digne of more blame/ than is worth al the praysing. The seconde spece is/ that if a man be good/ or doth or sayth a thyng to good entent/ the backbyter wol turne al that goodnesse vp so downe/ to his shreude entent. The thirde is to amynisshe the boūtie of his neyghbour. The fourthe spece of backbytynge is this/ yͭ if men speke goodnesse of a man/ than wol the backbyter saye: Parfay suche a man is yet better than he/ ĩ dispraysing of him that men prayse. The fyfthe spece is this/ for to consent gladly and herke gladly to the harme that men speke of other folke: This synne is ful great/ & aye encreseth after the wicked entent of yͤ backbyter. After bacbityng cometh grutchyng or murmuration/ and somtyme it springeth of impacience ayenst god/ and somtyme ayenst man. Ayenst god it is whan a man grutcheth ayenst payne of hel/ or ayenst pouertie/ or losse of catell/ or ayenst rayne or tempest/ or els grutcheth yͭ shrewes haue prosperite/ or els for that good men haue aduersyte: & al these thynges shulde men suffre paciently/ for they come by the rightful iugemēt and ordynaunce of god. Somtyme cometh grutchyng of auarice/ as Iudas grutched ayenst Maudeleyn/ whan she anoynted the heed of our lorde Iesu Christe/ with her precious oyntment. This maner murmuryng is suche as whan man grutcheth of goodnesse yͭ hym selfe doth/ or that other folke done of her owne catell. Somtyme cometh murmure of pride/ as whan Symon yͤ Pharisee grutched ayenst Maudeleyn/ whan she aproched to Iesu christ and wept at his fete for her synnes. And somtyme it sourdeth of enuye/ whan men discouer a mans harme that was priuy/ or bereth him on honde thyng that is false. Murmure also is ofte amonge seruaūtes that grutche whan her soueraynes bydde hem do leful thynges/ and for as moche as they dare not opēly withsay the cōmaundement of her soueraynes/ yet wol they say harme and grutche & murmure priuely for very dispyte: whiche wordes they call the dyuels pater noster/ though so be that the dyuel had neuer pater noster/ but yͭ leude folke yeueth it such a name. Somtyme it cometh of yre or priuy hate/ that norissheth rancour in yͤ herte/ as afterwarde I shal declare. Than cometh also bytternesse of herte/ thorowe which bytternesse euery good dede of his neyghbour semeth to hym bytter & vnsauery. Than cometh discorde that vnbyndeth al maner of frendshyp. Than cometh scornyng of his neyghbour/ al do he neuer so wel. Than cometh accusyng/ as whan man seketh occasyon to anoye his neyghbour/ whiche is lyke the crafte of the dyuel/ that wayteth bothe day and night to accuse vs al. Than cometh malignyte/ throughe whiche a man anoyeth his neyghbour priuely if he may: and if he maye not/ algate his wicked wyl shal not let as for to brenne his house priuely/ or enpoyson or sle his beestes/ and semblable thynges. Nowe wol I speke of the remedye ayenst this foule synne of enuye. First is the loue of god principally/ and louyng of his neyghbour as him selfe: for sothly that one ne may not be without that other. And trust wel that in the name of thy neyghbour thou shalt vnderstonde the name of thy brother/ for certes al we haue one father flesshly and one mother/ that is to saye Adam & Eue/ and also one father spyrituel/ that is god of heuen. Thy neyghbour art thou boūde for to loue/ and wyl him al goodnesse/ and therfore saythe god: Loue thy neyghbour as thy selfe/ that is to say/ to saluation bothe of lyfe and soule. And more ouer thou shalte loue him in worde & in benigne admoneshing and chastysyng/ and comfort him in his noyaunces/ & pray for him with al thy herte. And in dede thou shalt loue him in suche wyse that thou shalte do to him in charyte/ as thou woldest that it were done to thyn own person: and therfore thou ne shalte do hym no domage in wicked worde/ ne harme in his body ne in his catel/ ne in his soule by entysing of wicked ensample. Thou shalte not desyre his wyfe ne none of his thinges. Vnderstonde also that in the name of neyghbour is comprehended his enemy: Certes man shal loue his enemye by the cōmaundemēt of god: & sothly thy frende thou shalte loue in god. I saye thyn enemye shalte thou loue for goddes sake/ by his com-

Y maun-

maundement/ for if it were reason that man shulde hate his enemy/ forsothe god nolde not receyue vs to his loue that ben his enemyes. Ayenst thre maner of wronges ẏ his enemye dothe to him/he shal do thre thynges/as thus: ayenst hate and rancoure of hert/ he shal loue him in hert: Ayenst chyding ⁊ wicked wordes/ he shal praye for his enemye: Ayenst wicked dedes/he shal do him boūtie. For Christ saith: Loue your enemyes/ and praye for hem that speke you harme/ and for hem that chace and pursue you: and do bountie to hem that hate you. Lo/thus cōmaundeth vs our lorde Jesu Christ to do to our enemyes: Forsothe nature driueth vs to loue our frēdes/and parfay our enemyes haue more nede of loue thā our frendes/ ⁊ they that more nede haue/ certes to hem shal men do goodnesse. And certes in that dede haue we remembraunce of the loue of Jesu Christ that dyed for his enemyes: And in as moche as that loue is more greuous to perfourme/ so moche is the more gret the meryte/ and therfore the louynge of our enemye hath confounded the dyuels venyme: For right as the dyuel is confounded by humylite/right so is he wounded to the deth by the loue of our enemy/certes than is loue the medicyn that casteth out the venym of enuye fro mans herte. The spyces of this place shal be more largely declared in her chappyters folowyng.

De Ira.

After Enuye wol I discryue the synne of Ire/ for sothly who so hath enuye vpon his neyghbour/ anon he wol comenly fynde hym a mater of wrathe in worde or in dede/ayenst him to whom he hath enuye: And as wel cometh ire of pride as of enuy/for sothly he ẏ is proude or enuyons is lightly wroth. This syn of yre/ after the discryuyng of saint Austyn is wicked wyl to be auēged by worde or by dede. Ire after the phylosopher/ is the feruent bloode of man yquicked in his herte/ through which he wolde harme to him that he hateth: for certes the herte of man by eschaufing ⁊ mouyng of his bloode/ weyeth so troubled/that it is out of al maner of iugement of reason. But ye shal vnderstonde that Ire is in two maners/that one of hem is good/ and that other is wicked. The good yre is by ielousye of goodnes/through which a mā is wroth with wickednesse/ ⁊ ayenst wickednesse. And therfore sayth a wyseman/that ire is bet than playe. This ire is with debonairte/ and it is wrothe without bytternesse/not wrothe ayenst the man/ but wrothe with the misdede of the man: As sayth the prophete Dauid: Irascimini/et nolite peccare. Nowe vnderstōde that wicked ire is in two maners/ that is to saye/ sodayne ire or hasty ire without auysement ⁊ consentyng of reson: The meanynge and the sence of this is/that the reson of a man ne consent not to that sodayne ire/ and than it is venyall. Another ire is ful wicked/that cometh of felonye of herte/auysed ⁊ caste before/with wicked wyl to do vengeaunce/ and therto his reson cōsenteth: and sothly this is deedly syn. This ire is so displesaunt to god/ that it troubleth his house/and chaseth the holy goost out of mans soule/ and wasteth ⁊ distroyeth that lykenesse of god/that is to say/the vertue that is in mans soule/ and putteth in him the lykenesse of the dyuel/ and taketh the man fro god that is his rightful lorde. This is a ful great plesaunce to the dyuel/ for it is the dyuels fornayes that is eschaufed with the fyre of hell: For certes right so as fyre is more mighty to distroy erthly thynges than any other elemēt/ right so ire is mighty to distroye al spyrituell thynges. Loke howe that fyre of smale coles that ben almoste deed vnder asshen/ wol reuyue or quicke ayen whan they ben touched wt brimstone/right so ire wol euermore quick ayen whan it is touched by the pride that is couered in mans herte. For certes fyre ne may not come out of nothyng/ but if it were firste in ẏ same thing naturally: as fyre is drawen out of flyntes with stele. And right so as pride is many tymes mater of ire/ right so is rancour norice and keper of ire. There is a maner tree/as saithe saynt Isodore/ that whan a man maketh fyre of the sayde tree/ and couer the coles of it with asshen/ sothly the fyre of it wol laste a yere or more: And right so fareth it of rancour whan it is ones conceyued in the

hertes

hertes of some men / certes it woll laste perauenture from one Eester day vntyll an other Ester day or more. But certes that same man is ful ferre from the mercy of god al ŷ while.

In this forsayd dyuels fourneys there forge thre shrewes: Prude that aye bloweth and encreaceth the fyre by chydyng and wicked wordes: Than stondeth enuye and holdeth hotte yron in the fyre vpon the herte of man with a payre of longe tonges of longe rancour. And than stondeth the synne of cõtumelie or stryfe and cheste / and battereth and forgeth by vylaynous repreuynges. Certes this cursed syn anoyeth bothe to the man hym selfe and also his neyghboure / For sothely almoste al the harme or damage that any man dothe to his neyghbour cõmeth of wrathe: for certes outragyous wrathe dothe al that euer the foule fende wylleth or cõmaundeth hym / for he ne spareth neyther our lorde Jesu Christ / neither his swete mother. And in his outragious angre and yre / alas alas / ful many and dyuers at that tyme / feleth in his herte ful wyckedly bothe of Christ and also of al his halowes: Is not this a cursed vyce? yes certes. Alas it taketh fro man his wytte and his reason / and all his debonayre lyfe spirituel that shulde kepe his soule. Certes it withdraweth also goddes dewe lordshyp / ⁊ that is mans soule / and the loue of his neyghbours. It stryueth also al daye ayenst trouthe / it reueth hym the quyete of his herte / and subuerteth his soule.

Of yre cometh these stynkyng engendrures. First hate / ŷ is olde wrath / Discorde / through whiche a man forsaketh his olde frende that he hath loued ful longe. And than cometh werre and euery maner of wrõge that a man dothe to his neyghboure in body or in catell. Of this cursed synne of yre cometh also manslaughter. And vnderstonde wel that homicide / that is manslaughter is in dyuers wyse:

Some manere of homycide is spirituell / and some is bodily. Spirituel manslaughter is in. vi. thynges. Firste by hate as sayth saynt Johan: He that hateth his brother / is an homicide. Homicide is also by backbiting / of whiche backbytyng sayth Salomon / that they haue two swerdes / with whiche they slee her neyghbours: For sothly as wicked is to take fro him his good name as his lyfe. Homicide is also in yeuynge of wicked counsell by fraude / as for to yeue counsayle to areyse wrongful customes / and talages. Of whiche sayth Salomon: A lyon rorynge and a beere hongry / be lyke to the cruell lordes in with holdyng or abredgyng of the shepe or the hyre of the wages of seruauntes / or elles in vsurye / or in withdrawynge of the almesse of poore folke. For whiche the wyse man sayth / Fedeth hym that almoste dyeth for honger / for sothely but if ye fede him ye slee hym. And al these ben deedly synnes. Bodyly manslaughter is whan thou sleest hym with thy tonge: An other maner is / whan thou commaundest to slee a man / or els yeuest counsayle to slee a man. Manslaughter in dede is in foure maners. That one is by lawe / right as a Justyce dampneth him that is coulpable to the dethe: But let the Justyce be ware that he do it rightfully / and that he do it not for despyte to spyll bloode / but for kepynge of rightwysnesse. An other homicide is done for necessyte / as whan a man sleeth an other in his defence / and that he ne maye none other wyse escape without slaughter of his aduersarye / he dothe synne / and he shal beare penaunce as for deedly synne. Also if a man by case or aduenture shote an arowe or caste a stone / with which he sleeth a man / he is an homicide. Also if a woman by neglygẽce ouerlyeth her childe in her sleppynge / it is homicide ⁊ deedly synne. Also whan man distourbleth concepcion of a chylde / and maketh a woman eyther bareyne by drinkynge of venemous herbes / thorough whiche she may not cõceyue / or sleeth a chylde by drinkes / or els putteth certayne materyall thynges in her secree places to slee the chylde / or els doth vnkyndly synne / by whiche a man or a woman shedeth her nature in maner or in a place there as a chylde maye not be conceyued. Or els if so be that a woman hath conceyued / and hurteth her selfe / and by that misshappe the chylde is slayne / yet it is homicide. What say we of those women that murderen her children for bycause of eschewynge of worldly shame? Certes it is an horryble

Y.ii. ho-

homicide. Homicide is also if a man approche to a woman by desyre of lecherye/ thorough whiche ẏ childe is perisshed/ or els smyteth a woman wetyngly/ through whiche she leseth her chylde: Al these ben homicides and horrible deedly synnes. Yet come there of ire mo synnes/ as well in worde as in thought/ and dede: As he that arretteth upon god/ or blameth god of the thyng of whiche he is him selfe gylty/ or dispyseth god and al his halowes/ as done the cursed hasardours in dyuers coūtreys: This cursed synne done they/ whan they fele in her herte ful wickedly of god and of his halowes. Also whan they trete unreuerētly the sacrament of the auter/ that synne is so great that unneth it may be releaced/ but that the mercy of god passeth al his werkes/ it is so great and he so benygne. Than cometh of ire an atterly angre/ whan a man is sharply amonested in his shrifte to leaue his synne: Than wol he be angry/ and answere hokerly and angerly/ or defende or excuse his synne by unstedfastnesse of his flesshe/ or els he dyd it for to holde companye with his felowes/ or els he sayth the fende entyced him/ or els he dothe it for his youthe/ or els his complexcion is so coragious that he may not forbeare/ or els it is his destenye he sayth unto a certayne age/ or els he sayth it cometh him of gentylnesse of his auncesters/ and semblable thynges. Al these maner of folke so wrappe hem in her synnes/ that they ne wol not delyuer hemselfe: For sothly no wyght that excuseth him selfe wylfully of his synne/ may not be delyuered of his synne tyl that he mekely beknoweth his synne. After this than cometh swearynge/ that is expresse ayenst the cōmaundement of god/ and this befalleth often of angre and of ire. God sayth/ Thou shalte not take the name of thy lorde god in veyne or in ydel. Also our lorde Jesu Christ sayth by the worde of saynte Mathewe: Ne wyl ye not swere in al maner/ neyther by heuen/ for it is goddes trone/ ne by erthe/ for it is the benche of his fete/ ne by Hierusalem/ for it is the cyte of a great kynge/ ne by thyn heed/ for thou mayste not make an heere neyther whyte ne blacke: but saye by your worde/ ye ye/ naye naye: and what that is more/ it is of yuel. Thus sayth Christ. For Christes sake sweare not so synfully in dismembringe of Christ: By soule/ herte/ bones/ and body. For certes it semeth that ye thynke that the cursed iewes ne dismembred not ynoughe the precyous persone of Christ/ but ye dismembre him more. And if so be that the lawe compel you to swere/ than ruleth you after the lawe of god in your sweryng/ as sayth Jeremie .iiii. cap. Thou shalte kepe thre condycions/ thou shalt sweare in trouthe/ in dome and in rightwysenesse/ this is to saye/ thou shalte sweare sothe/ For euery lesynge is ayenst Christ/ for Christ is very trouthe. And thynke wel this that euery great swearer not compelled lawfully to swere/ the plage shal not departe fro his house/ whyle he useth suche unleful swearynge. Thou shalte swere also in dome/ whan thou arte constreyned by thy domes man to wytnesse trouthe: Also thou shalte not sweare for enuye/ neyther for fauour/ neyther for mede or rewarde/ but onely for rightwysnesse and for declarynge of it to the honour and worshyppe of god/ and to the aydynge and helpe of thyn euyn christen. And therfore euery man that taketh goddes name in ydell/ or falsely sweareth with his mouthe/ or els taketh on hym the name of Christ to be called a christen man/ and lyueth ayenst Christes lyuynge and his techynge/ al they take goddes name in ydell. Loke also what sayth saynt Peter/ Actuum iiii. capitu. Non est aliud nomen sub celo. &c. There is none other name sayth saynt Peter under heuen yeue to men/ in whiche they may be saued/ that is to say/ but the name of Jesu Christ. Take hede eke howe precious is the name of Jesu Christ/ as sayth saynte Poule/ ad Philipenses .ii. In nomine Jesu. &c. That in the name of Jesu euery kne of heuenly creatures/ erthly/ and of hell shulde bowe/ for it is so hye and so worshypfull/ that the cursed fende in hell shulde tremble to here it named. Than semeth it that men that sweare so horribly by his blessed name/ that they dispyse it more boldely than the cursed iewes/ or els the dyuel that trēbleth whan he hereth his name.

Nowe certes sythe that swearynge/ but if it

be

be lawfully done/ is so hyely defended: moche more is forsweryng falsely/ and yet nedelesse.

What say we also of hem that delyte hem in swearyng/ and holde it a genterye or a manly dede to sweare great othes? And what of hem that of very usage ne cease not to sweare gret othes/ al be the cause not worthe a strawe? Certes this is horrible synne. Swearyng sodeinly is also a great syn. But let us go now to that horryble synne swearynge of adiuracion & cōiuracion/ as done these false enchantours or nigramācers ī basyns ful of water/ or in a bright swerde/ in a cercle/ in a fyre/ or in the sholderbone of a shepe? I can not saye but that they done cursedly and dampnably ayenst Christ/ & al the faythe of holy churche.

What saye we of hem that byleue on Deuinales/ as by flyght or by noyse of byrdes or of beestes/ or by sorte/ by Geomancie/ by dremes/ by chirkyng of dores or crakyng of houses/ by gnawyng of rattes/ and suche maner wretchydnesse? Certes al these thynges ben defended by god and holy churche/ for whiche they ben acursed tyl they come to amendemēt that on suche fylthe sette her byleue. Charmes for woundes or maladye of men or of beestes/ if they take any effecte/ it may be parauenture that god suffreth it/ for folke shulde yeue the more faythe & reuerence to his name.

Nowe wol I speke of leasynges whiche generally is false signyfyaunce of worde in entent to disceyue his euen christen. Some leasyng/ is of whiche there cometh none auauntage to no wight/ and some leasynge turneth to the profyte or ease of o man/ and to the damage of a nother man. A nother leasynge is for to saue his lyfe or his catel/ whiche cometh of delyte for to lye/ in whiche delyte they woll forge a longe tale/ & peynt it with al circumstaunces/ where al the tale of the grounde is false. Some leasyng cometh for he wol susteyne his wordes: Some leasynge cometh of retchelesnesse without auysement/ and semblable thynges. Lette us nowe touche the vyce of flaterye/ whiche ne cometh not gladly but for drede/ or for couetyse. Flaterye is generally wrongful praysyng. Flaterers ben the dyuels nouryces/ that norisshe his chyldren with mylke of losyngerye: Forsoth Salomon sayth that flatery is worse than detraction/ for somtyme detraction maketh an hauteyne man be the more humble/ for he dredeth detraction/ but certes flatery maketh a man tenhaunce his hert and his coūtenaunce. Flaterers be the dyuels enchaūtours/ for they make a man to wene hym selfe be lyke/ that he is not lyke. Those be lyke to Iudas that betray a man to sel hī to his enemy. Flatterers ben the dyuels chapleyns that euer syng Placebo. I reken flaterye in the vyces of yre: for ofte tyme if a man be wrothe with a nother/ than woll he flatter some wight to susteyne him in his quarell. Speke we nowe of suche cursyng as cometh of irous herte. Malyson generally may be sayd euery maner power of harme: Suche cursynge bereueth man fro the reigne of god/ as sayth saynt Poule. And oft tyme suche cursynge wrongfully returneth ayen to hym that curseth/ as byrde that turneth ayen to his owne neste. And ouer al thyng men ought eschewe to curse her children and yeue to the dyuel her engendrure as ferre forthe as in hem is: certes it is great peryl and great synne. Lette us than speke of chydyng and reproche/ whiche ben full great woundes in mans herte/ for they unsowe the semes of frendshyp in mans herte: for certes unneth maye a man playnly be accorded with him/ that him openly hath reuyled and repreued/ and disclaundred: This is a ful gastly synne as Christ sayth in the gospel. And take hede nowe that he that repreueth his neyghbourre/ eyther he repreueth hym by some harme of payne that he hath upon his body/ as mesell/ croked/ harlot/ or by some synne that he dothe. Nowe if he repreue him by harme of payne/ than turneth the reprefe to Iesu Christ: For payne is sende by the rightwyse sonde of god/ and by his suffraunce/ be it meselry/ meyme/ or maladye: And if he repreue him uncharytably of synne/ as thou holour/ thou dronkelewe harlot/ and so forthe. Than pertayneth that to the reioysynge of the dyuell/ whiche euer hath ioy that men done synne. And certes chydyng may not come but of vylaynous herte/ for after the haboundaunce of the herte

Y.iii. speketh

speketh the mouthe ful ofte. And ye shal understonde/ that loke by any waye whan any man shal chastyse or correcte another/ that he beware from chidyng or repreuyng: for truely but he beware/ he maye ful lightly quicken the fyre of angre and of wrathe/ whiche he shulde quenche: And peraventure sleeth him whiche he myght chastyse with benignyte. For as sayth Salomon: The amiable tonge is the tree of lyfe/ that is to saye/ of lyfe spirytuel. And sothly a dissolute tonge sleeth the spyrites of hym that repreueth/ and also of him whiche is repreued. Lo/ what sayth saint Augustyn: There is nothynge so lyke the dyuels childe/ as he whiche ofte chydeth.
A seruaunt of god behoueth not to chide. And though that chydynge be a vylaynous thyng betwyxt al maner folke/ yet it is certes most uncouenable bytwene a man and his wyfe/ for there is neuer reste. And therfore saythe Salomon: An house that is uncouered and droppyng and a chyding wyfe/ ben a lyke.

A man whiche is in a droppynge house in many places/ thoughe he eschewe the droppynge in o place/ it droppeth on him in another place: So fareth it by a chydynge wyfe/ if she chyde hym in one place she wol chyde him in a nother: And therfore better ⁊ greatly more plesaunt is a morsel or lytell gobet of breed with ioye/ than an house fylled full of delyces with chydynge and guerryng / saythe Salomon. Saynt Poule saythe: O ye women/ beth ye subgette to your husbondes / as you behoueth and ought in god: And ye men loueth your wyues/ ad Colonicenses.iii.

Afterwarde speke we of scornynge whiche is a wicked synne/ and namely whan he scorneth a man for his good werkes: For certes suche scorners fare lyke the foule tode/ that maye not endure to smell the swete sauour of the vyne whan it flourysshethe. These scorners ben partyng felowes with the dyuel/ for they haue ioye whan the dyuel wynneth/ and sorowe if he leseth. They ben aduersaryes of Jesu Christ/ for they hate that he loueth/ that is to saye/ saluation of soule.

Speke we nowe of wicked counsayle/ the whiche is a traytour/ for he disceyueth hym that trusteth in him: Ut Achitofel ad Salomonem. But nathelesse/ yet is his wycked counsayle first ayenst him selfe/ for as saythe the wyse man: euery false lyuynge hath this propertie in him selfe/ that he that woll anoye a nother man/ he anoyeth firste him selfe. And men shal understonde/ that man shall not take his counsayle of false folke/ ne of angrye folke/ or greuous folke/ ne of folke that loue specially to moche worldly folke/ namely in counsaylynge of soules.

Nowe cometh the synne of hem that sowe and make discorde amonge folke/ whiche is a synne that Christ hateth utterly/ and no wonder is: for he deyde for to make concorde. And more shame do they to Christ than dyd they that him crucifyed: For god loueth better that frendshyp be amonges folke than he dyd his owne body/ whiche that he gaue for unyte. Therfore ben they lykened to the dyuel that euer be aboute to make discorde. Nowe cometh the synne of double tonge/ such as speke fayre before folke/ and wickedly behynde/ or els they make semblaunt as though they spake of good entencion/ or els in game and playe/ and yet they speke of wicked entent.

Nowe cometh bewrayenge of counsayle/ throughe whiche a man is diffamed: Certes unneth maye he restore the domage. Nowe cometh menace/ that is an open folye/ for he that ofte menaceth/ he thretteth more than he may performe ful ofte tyme. Nowe cometh ydell wordes/ that is without profyte of hym that speketh the wordes/ ⁊ also of him that herkeneth the wordes: Or els ydel wordes ben those that ben nedelesse or without entent of naturel profyte. And al be it that ydel wordes be somtyme venyal syn/ yet shulde men doute hem/ for we shal yeue rekenynge of hem before god. Nowe cometh iangelyng that may not be without synne. And as saythe Salomon: it is a signe of apert folye. And therfore a philosopher sayd whan men asked him howe that he shulde please the people/ he answerde: Do many good werkes ⁊ speke fewe iangles. After this cometh the synne of iaperies/ that ben the dyuels apes/ for they make folke to laughe at her iaperye/ as folke do at at the gawdes of an ape: Whiche iapes defendeth saynte Poule. Loke howe that vertuous wordes and holy cõforte hem that trauayle in the seruyce of Christ. Right so comforteth the villanous wordes and knackes of iapers hem/ that trauayle in the seruyce of the deuyll. These been the synnes of the tonge/ that come of yre and of other synnes.

¶ The remedy ayenst Ire.

The remedy ayenst Ire/ is a vertue ye men cal Mansuetude/ that is Debonairte/ and also another vertue that men clepe Pacience or sufferaunce. Debonairte withdraweth and refreyneth the steerynges and mouynges of mannes corage in herte/ in suche maner that they ne skyppe nat out by angre ne yre. Sufferaunce suffreth swetely al the anoyaunces & wronges that men done to man outwarde. Saynt Jerome saith this of debonairte/ that it dothe no harm to no wight/ ne saith: ne for no harme that men do ne saye/ he ne chafeth ayenst reason. This vertue somtyme cometh of nature: for as saith ye philosopher/ A man is a quicke thyng by nature/ debonaire & tretable to goodnesse: but whan debonairte is enformed of grace/ than it is the more worth.

Pacience is another remedy ayenst ire/ and is a vertue that suffreth swetely euery mannes goodnesse/ and is nat wroth for no harm that is done to hym. The philosopher saithe/ that pacience is the vertue that suffreth debonairly al the outrages of aduersyte/ & euery wicked worde. This vertue maketh a man lyke to god/ and maketh hym goddes owne childe: as saith Christ. This vertue disconfyteth thyne enemy. And therfore saith the wise man: If thou wolde venquesshe thyn enemy lerne to suffre. And thou shalte vnderstonde that a man suffreth four maner of greuaunces in outwarde thynges/ ayenst the whiche four he must haue four maner of paciences.

The firste greuaunce is of wicked wordes/ whiche suffred Jesu Christ without grutchĩg ful paciently/ whan the iewes dispysed hym ful ofte. Suffre thou therfore paciently/ for the Wyse man saithe: If thou stryue with a foole/ though the foole be wroth or though he laugh/ alwaye thou shalt haue no rest. That other greuaunce outwarde is to haue domage of thy catell: There ayenst suffred Christ ful paciently/ whan he was dispoyled of al that he had in this lyfe/ and that was but his clothes. The thirde greuaunce is a man to haue harme in his body: That suffred Christ full paciently in al his passyon. The fourth greuaunce is in outragyous laboure in werkes: wherfore I saye/ that folke that make her seruauntes to trauayle to greuouslye or out of tyme/ as in holy dayes/ sothly they do great synne. Here ayenst suffred Christ ful pacyently/ and taught vs pacyence/ whan he bare vpon his blessed shulders ye crosse/ vpon whiche he shuld suffre dispytous dethe. Here may men lerne to be pacient/ for certes not onely christen be pacyent for loue of Jesu Christ/ and for rewarde of the blessed lyfe that is perdurable/ but certes the olde paynems that neuer were christened/ cõmended and vsed the vertue of pacience. A philosopher vpon a tyme that wold haue beate his discyple for his great trespace/ for which he was moued/ and brought a rodde to beate the childe/ and whan this chylde sawe the rodde/ he sayd to his mayster: What thynke ye to do? I woll beate the sayd the mayster for thy correction: Forsothe sayd the childe/ ye ought first correct your selfe that haue loste al your pacience for the offẽce of a childe. Forsothe sayd the mayster al wepyng/ thou sayest sothe: Haue thou the rodde my dere childe/ and correcte me for myn impaciẽce. Of pacience cometh obediẽce/ thrugh whiche a man is obediẽt to Christ & to al hem to whiche he ought be obedient in Christ. And vnderstonde wel ye obedience is perfyte whan that a man dothe gladly & hastely with good hert entierly/ al that he shulde do. Obedyence generally is to performe the doctryne of god and of his soueraignes/ to whiche him ought to be obeysaunt in al rightwisnesse.

¶ De Accidia.

Fter the synnes of Enuy & yre/ now wol I speke of the synne of Accidie: for enuy blyndeth the hert of a man/ & yre troubleth a man and accidie maketh hĩ heuy/ thoughtful & pẽsyf. Enuy & ire makẽ bitternesse ĩ hert/ which bitternesse is moder of accidie/ & taketh fro hĩ the

the loue of al goodnesse/than is accidie the an
guysshe of trouble of hert. And saynt Augu
styn saith: It is anoye of goodnesse & anoye
of harme. Certes this is a dampnable syn/
for it dothe wronge to Iesu Christ/in as mo-
che as it venometh the seruice that men ought
do to Christ/as saithe Salomon: but accidie
dothe no suche dilygence. He dothe al thynge
with anoye and with wrawnesse/ slacknesse/
and excusation: With ydelnesse and vnlust.
For whiche the boke sayth: A cursed be he
that dothe the seruyce of god neglygently.
Than is accidie enemy to euery estate of mā.
For certes thestate of man is in thre maners.
Either it is in the estate of Innocency / as
was the estate of Adam before that he fyl in
to synne/ in which estate he was holde to wor
ke/ as in praysyng & laudyng god. Another
estate is the estate of synful men: in whiche
estate men ben holden to labour in prayeng
to god for amendement of her synnes/ & that
he wol graunt hem to ryse out of her synnes.
Another estate is the state of grace/ in whi-
che state he is holden to workes of penytence:
and certes to al these thinges is accidie cōtra-
ry/ for he loueth no busynesse at al. Now cer
tes/this foule synne accidie is also a ful grete
enemy to the lyfelode of y body/for it ne hath
no purueyance ayenst tēporel necessite/ for it
forsloweth/forslogeth/and distroyeth al goo-
des tēporel by rechelesnesse. The .iiii. thynge
is/ y accidie is lyke hem that ben in the payne
of hel/ bicause of her slouthe & heuynesse: for
they that be dāpned ben so bounde/ that they
may neither wel do ne thynke. Of accidie co
meth first y a man is anoyed & encombred to
do any goodnesse/ & maketh that god hath ab
homination of suche accidie / as saithe saynt
John. Nowe cometh slouth that wol nat suf
fer no hardnesse ne penaūce: for sothly slouth
is so tender & so delycate; as saith Salomon/
that he wol suffre no hardnesse ne penaūce/ &
therfore he marreth al y he doth. Ayenst this
rotten syn of accidie & slouth/ shulde men ex-
ercise hem selfe & vse hem to do good workes:
and manly & vertuously catche corage to do/
thynkyng that our lorde Iesu Christ quyteth
euery good dede/ be it neuer so lyte. Usage of
labour is a great thynge. For it maketh; as
saithe saynt Bernarde/ the labourer to haue
stronge armes and harde senewes: & slouthe
maketh heuy/ feble/ and tender. Than co-
meth drede to begyn to worke any good wor-
kes. For certes he that enclyneth to synne/
hym thynketh it is so great an emprise for to
vndertake the workes of goodnesse / and ca-
steth in his herte/ that the circumstaunces of
goodnesse ben so greuous and weightye for
to suffre/ that he dare nat vndtake to do wor
kes of goodnesse/ as saith saynt Gregorye.
Nowe cometh wanhope/that is dispeyre of
the mercy of god/ that cometh somtyme of to
moche outragious sorowe/ and somtyme of
to moche drede/ ymaginynge y he hath do so
moche synne/that it wol nat aueyle hym/ tho
he wolde repent hym and forsake synne: tho-
rough whiche dispeyre or drede/ he abandon-
neth al his herte to euery manere synne / as
saithe saynt Augustyne. Whiche dampna-
ble synne/if it contynewe vnto his ende/ it is
called synnynge in the Holygoost.
This horryble synne is so peryllous / that
he that is dispeyred there nys no felony ne no
syn that he douteth for to do / as shewed well
by Iudas. Certes aboue al synnes than is
this synne most displesant to Christ & moost
aduersarye. Sothly he that dispeyreth hym
is lyke to the cowarde champyon recreaunt/
that flyeth without nede. Alas alas/nedeles
is he recreaunt/and nedelesse dispayred. Cer-
tes the mercy of god is euer redy to the peny-
tente person/and is aboue al his werkes.
Alas canne not a man bethynke hym on the
gospell of saynt Luke. xv. Where as Christ
saythe/ that as well shal there be ioye in he-
uen vpon a synful man that dothe penytēce/
as vpon four score & nynetene rightful men
that nede no penytence. Loke ferther in the
same gospel the ioy and the feest of the good
man that had loste his sonne/whan his sonne
with repentaunce was retourned to his fa-
ther. Can they not remembre hem also /
that (as sayth saynt Luke) Capi. xxv.
Howe that the thefe that was hanged besyde
Iesu Christe / sayde: Lorde remembre me/
whan thou commest in to thy reigne.

For

Forsothe said Christ/ I saye to the: To daye shalte thou be with me in paradise. Certes/ there is nō so horryble synne of man/ that ne may in his lyfe be distroyed by penytēce/ thorough vertue of the passyon and of the dethe of Christ. Alas what nede men than to be dispayred/ sythe that his mercy is so redy and large? Aske and haue. Than cometh sompnolence/ that is sluggy slombring/ whiche maketh a man heuy and dull in body & in soule/ and this synne cometh of slouthe: And certes the tyme that by waye of reason man shulde not slepe/ is by the morowe/ but if there were cause reasonable. For sothely the morowe tyde is most couenable a man to say his prayers/ and for to thanke god/ & to honour god/ and to yeue almesse to the poore/ that cometh firste in the name of Jesu Christ. Lo/ what sayth Salomon? who so wol by the morowe awake to seke me/ he shal fynde me. Than cometh neglygence or retchelesnesse/ that recketh of nothyng. And though that ignoraunce be mother of al harmes/ certes neglygence is the norice. Neglygence ne dothe no force whan he shal do a thynge/ whether he do it well or euyll. The remedye of these two synnes is/ as saythe the wyse man: That he that dredeth god spareth not to do that he ought to do/ and he that loueth god he wol do dylygēce to plese god by his werkes/ and abandone hym selfe with al his myght wel for to do. Than cometh ydelnesse/ that is the yate of al harmes. An ydel man is lyke to a place yͭ hath no walles/ yͤ dyuel may entre on euery syde/ or shote at him that is discouert/ by temptacion on euery syde. This ydelnesse is the thorruke of al wycked and vilayne thoughtes/ and of all ordure. Certes the heuen is yeue to hem that wyll laboure/ and not to ydell folke. Also Dauid saythe/ that they ne be not in the labour of men/ ne they shal not be whypped with men/ that is to say in purgatorye. Certes than semeth it they shal be turmented with the dyuels in hell/ but if they do penaunce.

Than cometh the synne that men call Tarditas/ as whan a man is so latered/ or taryenge or he wol tourne to god: and certes that is a great foly. He is lyke hym that falleth in the dyche/ and wol not aryse. And this vyce cometh of false hope/ that he thynketh he shal lyue longe/ but that hope fayleth ful ofte.

Than cometh lachesse/ that is he that whan he begynneth any good worke/ anon he wol leaue and stynte it/ as done they that haue any person to gouerne/ and ne take of hym no more hede/ anon as they fynde any contrary or any anoye. These ben the newe sheperdes/ that lete their shepe wittyngly go renne to the wolfe that is in the breres/ or do nat force of her owne gouernaunce. Of this cometh pouerte and distruction bothe of spirituell and temporell thynges. Than cometh a maner coldnesse that freseth the hert of man. Than cometh vndeuotion/ through whiche a man is so blont/ and as saith saynt Bernard/ hath suche langour in his soule/ yͭ he may neyther rede ne synge in holy churche/ ne here ne thinke of no deuocyon/ ne trauayle with his hondes i no good worke/ that it nys to him vnsauery and al apalled. Than wexeth he slowe and slombry and soone wol be wrothe/ and soone is enclyned to hate and enuy. Than cometh the synne of worldly sorowe/ suche as is called Tristitia/ that sleeth a man/ as sayth saint Poule. For certes suche sorowe worketh the dethe of the soule and body also/ for therof cometh that a man is anoyed of his owne lyfe. Wherfore suche sorowe shorteth full ofte the lyfe of man/ er that his tyme is come by way of kynde.

Remedium contra peccatum Accidie.

Ayenst this horrible synne of Accidie/ and the braunches of the same/ there is a vertue that is called Fortitudo or strength that is an affection/ throughe whiche a man dispyseth anoyous thynges: This vertue is so mighty and so rygorous/ that it dare withstonde mightily/ and wisely kepe him selfe fro peryls that ben wicked/ and wrastell ayenst thassautes of yͤ dyuel/ for it enhaūceth & enforceth yͤ soule/ right as accidie abateth & maketh it feble: for this fortitude may endure by lōge suffraunce the trauayles that ben couenable.

This

This vertue hath many speces / yͤ first is cal-
led Magnanimite / that is to say / gret corage.
For certes there behoueth great corage ayenst
accidie / lest that it ne swalowe yͤ soule by the
synne of sorowe / or distroye it by wanhope.
Certes this vertue maketh folke vndertake
harde and greuous thynges by her owne wyl
wisely and resonably. And for as moche as
the deuyl fighteth ayenst a man more by sub-
tylte & sleight than by strength / therfore shall
a man withstõde hym by wytte / reason / and
discretion. Than are there the vtues of faithe
and hope in god and in his payntes / to eschue
and accomplisshe the good workes / in yͤ whi-
che he purposeth fermely to contynue. Than
cometh suretie or sikernesse / and that is whan
a man ne douteth no traueyle in tyme cõmyn
ge / of the good workes that he hath begonne.
Than cometh Magnifycence / that is to saye /
whan a man dothe and pformeth great wor-
kes of goodnesse that he hath begon / and that
is thende why that men shulde do good wor-
kes. For in the accomplysshing of good wor-
kes / lyeth the great guerdon. Than is there
Constance / that is stablenesse of corage / and
this shulde be in hert by stedfast faith / and in
mouthe / in beryng / in chere / and in dede. Also
there ben mo special remedies ayenst accidie /
in dyuers workes: as in consyderation of the
paynes of hel / the ioyes of heuen / and in trust
of the grace of the holygoost / that wyl yeue
him myght to performe his good entent.

De Auaricia.

After Accidie wol I speke of Auaryce /
and of coueitise. Of whiche syn saint
Poule saith: the rote of al harmes is couetise /
ad Timoth. vi. For sothly whan the hert of
man is confounded in it selfe & troubled / and
that the soule hath lost the cõfort of god / than
seketh he an ydel solace of worldly thynges.
Auarice / after the discription of saynt Augu-
styn / is a lycorousnesse in hert to haue erthly
thynges. Some other folke saye / that aua-
rice is for to purchace many erthely thynges /
and nothynge to yeue to hem that haue nede.
And vnderstonde that auarice stondeth nat
onely in londe ne catel / but somtyme in sciẽce
and glorye / & in euery maner of outragious
thynges is auarice. And couetise is this.
Couetise is for to coueit suche thinges yͤ thou
hast nat. And auarice is to with holde & kepe
suche thynges as thou haste without right.
Sothly this auarice is a synne that is ful dã-
pnable / for al holy writ curseth it / & speketh a
yenst yͤ vice / for it dothe wrong to Iesu christ:
for it taketh fro him the loue that men to him
owe / and tourneth it backewarde ayenst all
reason / and maketh that the auaricious man
hath more hoope in his cattell / than in Iesu
Christe / and dothe more obseruaunce in ke-
pyng of his treasour / than he dothe in the ser-
uyce of Iesu Christ. And therfore sayth saît
Poule: ad Ephesios quinto: That an auari-
cious man is the thraldome of idolatrye.
What difference is there betwixt an ydolaster
and an auaricyous man? But that an ydo-
laster parauenture ne hath nat but a maw-
met or two / & the auaricious man hath ma-
ny. For certes euery floreyn in his coffre / is
his maumet. And certes the syn of maume-
try is the first that god defended / as in the. x.
cõmaundement it beareth wytnesse / in Exo-
di. capi. xx. Thou shalte haue no false god-
des before me / ne thou shalte make to the no
graue thynge. Thus is an auaricious man /
that loueth his treasour before god / an idola-
ster / And through this cursed synne of aua-
ryce and Couetyse / cometh these harde lord-
shippes / through whiche they ben streyned by
tyllages / customes / and cariages / more than
her duety or reason is / or elles take they of
her bondmen amerciamentes / whiche might
more resonably be called extortiõs than mer-
ciamẽtes. Of whiche amerciamentes or raũ
somynge of bondmen / some lordes stewar-
des saye that it is rightful / for as moche as a
churle hath no temporell thynge / that it ne is
his lordes / as they say. But certes these lord
shippes do wrong / that bereue their bondmen
thynges that they neuer yaue hem. Augusti-
nus de Ciuitate dei. Libro. ix. Sothe is / that
the condition of thraldom / and the first cause
of thraldome was for synne.
Thus may ye se / that thoffence deserued thral
dome / but nat nature. Wherfore these lordes
ne

ne shulde not moche glorifye hem in her lordeshyps / sythe that they by naturall condycion ben not lordes ouer thralles / but for that thraldom came firste by the deserte of synne. And moreouer there as the lawe saythe / that temporell goodes of bonde folke ben the goodes of her lorde: ye / that is for to vnderstonde / the goodes of the emperour / to defende hem in her right / but not to robbe hem ne reue hem. Therfore saythe Seneca: thy prudence shulde lyue benignly with the thralles. Those that thou callest thy thralles / ben goddes people: and for humble people ben Christes frendes / they ben cōtuberniall with the lordes. Thinke also that of suche sede as chorles springe / of such sede spring lordes: as wel may the chorle be saued as the lorde. The same dethe that taketh the chorle / suche dethe taketh the lorde. Wherfore I rede do right so with the chorle as thou woldest that thy lorde dyd with ye if thou were in his plyght. Euery synful man is a chorle to syn: I rede the lorde certes / that thou werke in suche wise with thy chorles / that they rather loue the than drede the. I wote well that there is degree aboue degree / as reson is / and skyll is that men do her deuoyre there as it is due: But certes extortions and dispyte of your vnderlynges is dampnable. And ferdermore vnderstonde wel / that these conquerours or tyrauntes make ful ofte thralles of hem that ben borne of as royal bloode as ben they that hem conquere. This name of thraldom was neuer erst knowe / tyl that Noe said that his sonne Canam shulde be thral to his bretherne for his synne. What say we than of hem that pyll and do extorcions to holy churche: Certes the swerde that men yeue first to a knight / whan he is newe dubbed / signyfyeth that he shulde defende holy churche / and not robbe and pyl it / and who so dothe he is traytour to Christ. And as saythe saynt Austyn / they ben the dyuels woulues that strangle the shepe of Iesu Christ / & done worse than woulues / for sothly whan the woulfe hath ful his wombe / he stynteth to strāgle shepe: But sothly the pyllours and distroyers of holy churche goodes ne do not so / for they ne stynte neuer to pyll. Nowe as I haue sayde / sythe so is that synne was first cause of thraldom / than is it thus / that at the tyme that al this worlde was in synne / than was al this worlde in thraldom and in subiection / but certes sythe the tyme of grace came / god ordayned ye some folke shuld be more hye in estate and in degre / and some folke more lowe / and that eche shulde be serued in his astate. And therfore in some countreys there they be thralles / whan they haue turned hem to the faythe / they make her thralles free out of thraldom: and therfore certes the lorde oweth to his man that ye man oweth to the lorde. The pope calleth him selfe seruaunt of the seruaūtes of god / but for as the estate of holy churche ne might not haue ben / ne the comen profyte might not haue be kept / ne peace ne rest in erthe / but if god had ordayned that some man had hyer degree / and some men lower: Therfore was soueraynte ordayned to kepe / mayntayne / and defende her vnderlynges and her subiectes in reason / as ferforthe as it lyeth in her power / and not to distroy ne confounde hem. Wherfore I say / that those lordes that ben lyke wolues that deuour the possessyons or the catell of poore folkes wrongfully / without mercy or mesure / they shal receyue by ye same mesure that they haue mesured to poore folke / the mesure of Iesu Christ but it be amended. Nowe cometh disceyte betwyxt marchaunt & marchaunt. And thou shalt vnderstonde that marchaundyse is in two maners / that one is bodily / and that other is goostly: that one is honest and leful / and that other is dishonest and vnleful.

The bodily marchaundyse that is leful & honest is this: that there as god hath ordayned that a reigne or a countraye is suffysaunt to him selfe / than it is honeste and lefull that of haboundaunce of this countrey / menne helpe an other countrey that is nedy: And therfore there muste be marchauntes to bring fro one countrey to that other her marchaundyse.

That other marchaundyse that men haunten with fraude / and trecherye / and disceyte / with leasynges and false othes / is right cursed and dampnable. Espyrituel marchaundyse is properly Symonye / that is ententyfe desyre to bye thynge any espyrituell / that

is a

is thynge whiche apertayneth to the sayntuarye of god/ and to cure of the soule. This desyre if so be that a man do his dilygēce to perfourme it/ al be it that his desyre ne take non effecte/ yet it is to him a deedly synne/ and if he be ordred/ he is irreguler. Certes symony is called of Symon Magus/ that wolde haue bought for temporel catell the yeste that god had yeue by the holy goost to saint Peter and to the apostels: And therfore vnderstōde that he that selleth and he that byeth thyngz espyrituels/ ben called Symonyakes/ be it by catel/ be it by procuryng or by flesshly prayer of his frendes/ flesshly frendes or espirituel frendes: flesshly in two maners/ as by kynred or other frendes: Sothly if they praye for him that is not worthy and able/ it is symonye if he take the benefice/ and if he be worthy and able ther is none. That other maner is whan man or woman prayeth for folke to auaūce hem only for wicked flesshly affection/ whiche they haue vnto the persons/ and that is foule symonye. But certes in seruyce/ for whiche men yeuen thinges espirytuel vnto her seruaūtes/ it must be vnderstonde that the seruyce muste be honest/ or els not/ & also that it be without bargeyning/ and that the person be able. For as sayth the saynt Damasen: Al the synnes of the worlde at regarde of this synne/ are as thyng of naught/ for it is ẏ greatest synne that may be after the synne of Lucifer & of Antichrist: For by this synne god forleseth ẏ churche and the soule whiche he bought with his precious bloode/ by hem that yeue churches to hem that ben not worthy/ for they put in theues hondes that steale the soules of Jesu Christ/ & distroy his patrimony. By suche vnworthy preestes and curates haue lewde men lesse reuerence of the sacramētes of holy churche/ and suche yeuers of churches put ẏ children of Christ out/ and put ī the churche the dyuels own sonnes: they sell the soules that lambes shulde kepe to the wolfe whiche strangleth hem: and therfore shal they neuer haue parte of the pasture of lambes/ that is the blysse of heuen. Nowe cometh hasardrie with his apertenauntes/ as tables and raffles/ of whiche cometh discepte/ false othes/ chydynges/ & al raunysse/ blasphemynges/ and renyenges of god/ and hate of his neyghbours/ waste of goodes/ myspendyng of tyme/ and somtyme manslaughter. Certes hasardours ne mowe not be without great synne. Of Auarice cometh also lesynges/ theft/ false wytnesse/ and false othes: and ye shal vnderstonde that these be great synnes/ and expresse ayenst the cōmaundementes of god/ as I haue sayde. False wytnesse is in worde/ and also in dede: In worde as for to byreue thy neyghbours good name by thy false wytnesse/ or byreue him his catel or his herytage/ by thy false wytnessing/ whan thou for yre or for mede/ or for enuye/ bearest false wytnesse/ or accusest him/ or excuseth thy selfe falsly. Ware ye questmongers and notaries: Certes for false wytnessynge was Susan in ful great sorowe & payn/ and many another mo. The syn of thefte is also expresse ayenst goddes hest/ & in two maners/ corporel & spūel/ the tēporel theft is: As for to take thy neybours catell ayenst his wyl/ be it by force or by sleight/ be it by mette or by mesure: by stealynge also of false eudytementes vpon him/ and in borowyng of thy neyghbours catell/ in entent neuer to pay it ayen/ & semblable thinges. Espyrituel thefte is sacrylege/ that is to say/ hurtyng of holy thynges sacred to Christ in two maners/ by reson of the holy place/ as churches or churche yerdes: For whiche euery vilaynous synne that men don in suche places may be called sacrilege/ or euery violence in the semblable places. Also they that withdrawe falsely the rightes that longe to holy churche and plesyng. And generally sacrilege is to reue holy thing fro holy place/ or vnholy thinge out of holy place/ or holy thinge out of vnholy place.

Releuatio contra peccatum Auaricie.

Nowe shal ye vnderstonde/ that releuing of auarice is misericorde and pyte largely taken. And men might aske why that misericorde and pyte are releuyng of auarice: Certes the auaricious man sheweth no pyte ne miserycorde to the nedeful man/

man. For he despyteth hym in the keppynge of his treasure/ and nat in the rescuyng ne releuynge of his euyn christen. And therfore speke I firste of mysericorde. Than is mysericorde (as saithe the Philosopher) A vertue/ by whiche the corage of man is stered/ by the mysease of hym that is myseased. Vpon whiche misericorde foloweth pite/ in performyng and fulfyllyng of charitable workes of mercy/ helpeth and comforteth him that is myseased. And certes these thynges moue and stere a man to mesericorde of Iesu Christ/ that he yaue him selfe for our offence/ & suffred dethe for mysericorde/and forgaue vs our original synnes/and therby released vs fro the paynes of hell/and mynisshed the paynes of purgatorie by penitens/ and yeueth grace wel to do/ and at laste the blysse of heuen. The speces of misekicorde ben for to lene/ and also for to yeue: for to foryeue and releace/ & for to haue pyte in herte and compassyon/of the mischefe of his euen christen/ and also to chastyse there as nede is. Another maner of remedy ayenst auarice/is resonable largesse: but sothly here behoueth the consyderacion of ẏ grace of Iesu Christ/and of the temporel goodes/ and also of the goodes perdurable ẏ Iesu Christ yafe to vs/and to haue remembraunce of the dethe whiche he shal receyue/he knoweth not whan where/ne howe: and also that he shal forgo al that he hath/ saue onely that whiche he hath expended in good werkes.

But for as moche as some folke been vnmesurable/ menne ought for to auoyde and eschue folysshe largesse/the whiche some people call waste.

Certes he that is foole large/yeueth not his catell/ but he leseth his catell:

Sothly what thynge that he yeueth for veyngloryе/ as to mynstrels and to folke to beare his renome in the worlde/he hath synne therof and none almesse: Certes he leseth foule his good ẏ he ne seketh with the yeste of his good nothing but synne. He is lyke to an horse that seketh rather to drinke drouy or troubled water than for to drinke water of the clere welle. To hem appertaynen the sayd cursynge/ that Christ shal yeue at the daye of dome/ to hem that shal be dampned.

¶ Sequitur de Gula.

After Auarice cometh Glotenу/ which is expresse ayenst the cōmaundement of god. Gloteny is vnmesurable appetyte to eete or to drinke/or els to do ynough to the vnmesurable appetyte and disordeyned couetyse to eate or to drynke. This synne corrupteth al this worlde/ as is wel shewed in the synne of Adam & of Eue. Loke also what saythe saynt Poule of glotenye. Many (saythe he) gone/of whiche I haue often said to you/ and nowe I say it weppynge/ that ben the enemyes of the crosse of Christ/ of whiche the ende is dethe/ and of whiche her wombe is her god and her glory/in confusyon of hem that so deuour erthly thynges. He that is vsed to this synne of glotenye/ he ne maye no synne withstonde/ he must be in seruage of al vyces/ for it is the dyuels hourde/ there he hydeth and resteth hym. This synne hath many speces: The firste is dronkenesse that is the horryble sepulture of mans reson: and therfore whan a man is dronke he hath loste his reson: And this is dedly synne. But sothly whan that a man is not wonte to stronge drinke/and parauenture ne knoweth not the strength of the drinke/or hath feblesse in his heed/or hath trauayled/through whiche he drinketh the more/ al be he sodaynly caught with drinke/it is no dedly synne/ but venyal. The seconde spece of glotenye is/that the spyrite of a man weyeth all troubled/ for dronkennesse byreueth him the discretion of his wytte.

The thirde maner spece of glotonye is whan a man deuoureth his meate/ & hath not rightful maner of eetyng. The fourth is whan through the great abundaūce of his meete/the humours in his body ben distempred. The fyfth is foryetfulnesse by to moche drinkyng/ for whiche somtyme a man forgetteth er the mornyng what he dyd on the euenyng before.

In other maner ben distyncte the speces of glotenye after saynt Gregorie. The first is

3 for

for to eate before tyme to eate. The seconde is whan a man gyueth hym to delycate meate or drinke. The thirde is whan men take to moche ouer measure. The fourthe is curiosyte/ with great entent to make and apparayle his meate. The fyfthe is for to eate to gredely.

These ben ye fyue fyngers of the dyuels honde/ by whiche he draweth folke to synne.

The remedy ayenst Glotony.

Ayenst glotony the remedy is abstynence/ as saithe Galyene: but that I holde nat meritorious/ if he do it for the heale of his body. Saynt Augustyne woll that abstynence be done for vertue/ and with pacience. Abstynence (saithe he) is lytel worthe/ but if a man haue good wyl therto/ and but if he be enforced by pacience and charyte/ and that men do it for goddes sake/ & in hope to haue the blysse of heuen. The felowes of abstynence be attemperaunce/ that holdeth the meane in all thynges. Also shame that escheweth al dishonestie. Suffisaunce that seketh no riche meates ne drinkes/ ne dothe nat force of outragious apparaylyng of meate. Measure also/ that restreyneth by reason/ the vnmesurable appetyte of eatyng. Sobernesse also/ that restrayneth the outrage of drinke. Sparynge also/ that restrayneth the delycate ease to sytte longe at meate/ wherfore some folke stonden of her owne wyl whan they eete/ bycause they wol eate at lasse leysar.

De Luxuria.

After Glotonye cometh Lecherye/ for these two synnes been so nye cosyns/ that ofte tyme they woll nat departe. God wote this synne is ful displesaunt to god/ for he said hym selfe: do no lechery. And therfore he putteth great paynes ayenst this synne. For in the olde lawe/ if a woman thrall were take in this synne/ she shulde be beate with starres to dethe. And if she were a gentylwoman she shulde be slayne with stones. And if she were a bysshops doughter/ she shulde be brent by goddes cōmaundement. Moreouer by the syn of lechery/ god drowned al the worlde and after that he brent fyue cytees with thunder and lightnyng/ and sanke hem in to hel.

Nowe lette vs speke than of the sayd stynkyng synne of lechery/ that men cal auowtrye of wedded folke/ that is to saye/ if that one of hem be wedded or els bothe.

Saynt Iohan saythe/ that auoutrers shalbe in hell in a stacke brennynge of fyre and of brimstone for the stenche of her ordure: Certes the brekynge of this sacrament is an horryble thyng: It was made of god hym selfe in paradyse/ and confermed by Iesu Christ/ as wytnesseth saynt Mathewe in the gospell: A man shal leaue father and mother & take hym to his wyfe/ and they shalbe two in one flesshe.

This sacrament betokeneth the knyttynge togyther of Christe and holy churche. And not onely that god forbade auoutrye in dede/ but also he cōmaunded that thou shuldest not coueyte thy neyghbours wyfe. In this heste saythe saynt Augustyn is forboden al maner coueytyse to do lecherye. Lo/ what sayth saynt Mathewe in the gospell/ that who so seeth a woman to coueytyse of his luste/ he hath done lecherye with her in his herte. Here may ye se that not onely the dede of this synne is forboden/ but also the desyre to that synne. This cursed synne anoyeth greuouslye hem that it haunte: and first to her soule/ for he oblygeth it to synne and to payne of dethe/ whiche is perdurable. Vnto the body anoyeth it greuously also/ for it dryeth hym and wasteth/ and shenteth hym/ and of his bloode he maketh sacryfyce to the fende of hell: It wasteth his catell and his substaunce. And certes if it be a foule thynge a man to waste his catell on women: yet it is a fouler thynge whan that for suche ordure women dispende vpon men her catell and her substaunce. This synne as saythe the Prophete/ taketh from man and woman her good fame and her honour/ and it is full delectable and pleasaunt to the dyuell. For therby wynneth he the more parte of this wretched worlde. And right as a marchaunt delyteth hym moste in that chaffare whiche he hath moste auauntage and profyte of/ ryght so delyteth the fende in this ordure.

This

This is that other honde of the dyuell/ with fyue fyngers/ to catche the people to his vylanye. The first is the folysshe lokynge of the folysshe woman and of the folisshe man/ that sleeth right as ȳ Basilycok or cokatrice sleeth folke by venym of his syght: for the couetyse of the eyen foloweth the couetyse of the herte. The secōde fyngre is the vilaynous touching in wicked maner. And therfore sayth Salomon: that who so toucheth and handleth a woman/ he fareth as that man that handleth the scorpyon/ whiche styngeth and sodaynly sleeth through his enuenymyng/ or as who so that toucheth warme pytche blemyssheth his fyngers. The thirde is foule wordes/ whiche fareth lyke fyre/ whiche right anon brenneth the herte. The fourth fynger is the kyssyng: And truely he were a great foole that wolde kysse the mouthe of a brennyng ouen or of a forneys. And more fooles ben they that kysse in vilanye/ for that mouthe is the mouthe of hel/ and namely these olde dotardes holours/ whiche wol kysse and flycker/ and besy hem selfe thoughe they maye naught do. Certes they ben lyke to houdes: For an hounde whan he cometh nygh to the rosere/ or by other benches/ though so be that he maye not pysse/ yet wol he heue vp his legge and make a countenaunce to pysse. And for that many man weneth that he maye not synne for no lycorousnesse that he dothe with his wyfe. Truely that oppinyon is false: God wote a man maye slee him selfe with his owne knyfe/ and make hym selfe dronke of his owne tonne. Certes be it wyfe/ be it chylde or any worldly thing/ that he loueth before god/ it is his maumet/ and he is an ydolaster. A man shulde loue his wyfe by discrecyon/ paciently and attemperatly/ and than is she as though it were his suster. The fyfthe fyngre of the dyuels honde is the stynking dede of lecherye. Truely the fyue fyngers of glotonye the dyuel putteth in to the wombe of a man: And with his fyue fyngers of lecherye he gryppeth hym by the reynes/ for to throwe hun in to the furneys of helle/ there as they shall haue the fyre and the wormes that euer shal laste/ and wepyng and waylynge/ and sharpe hungre & thurste/ grymnesse of dyuels/ whiche shal al to trede hem withouten ende. Of lecherye as I sayd sourdeth and springeth dyuers speces: As fornicacyon/ that is bytwene man and woman whiche be not maryed/ and is deedly synne/ and ayenst nature: Al that is enemye and distruction to nature is ayenst nature. Parfay the reason of a man telleth him wel also that it is deedly synne/ for as moch as god forbade lecherye. And saynte Poule yeueth hem the reigne that nys dewe to no wight but to hem that done deedly synne. Another synne of lechery is to byreue a maydes maydenhede/ for he that so dothe/ certes he casteth a mayden out of the hyest degre that is in this presente lyfe/ and bpreueth her that precious frute that the boke calleth the hundred frutes/ I ne can saye it none other wyse in Englysshe/ but in latyn it hyght (Centesimus fructus) Certes he that so dothe is cause of many damages and vilanyes/ mo than any man can reken: right as he is cause of many domages somtyme that beestes do in the felde/ that breke the hedge or the closure/ through whiche he distroyeth that maye not be restored: For certes no more maye maydenhede be restored than an arme that is smytte fro the body maye retourne ayen and wexe: She maye haue mercy/ this wote I wel/ if that she haue wyll to do penitence/ but neuer shal it be that she nas corrupte. And al be it so that I haue spoke somwhat of auoutry/ also it is good to shewe the peryles that longe to auoutrye/ for to eschewe that foule synne. Auoutrye in latyn is for to saye/ approchyng of an other mannes bedde/ throughe whiche those that somtyme were one flesshe/ abandone her bodyes to other persones. Of this synne as sayth the wyse man folowe many harmes: Firste breakyng of faythe/ and certes in faythe is the keye of christendome: and whan that faythe is broke and loste/ sothly christendom stont veyne and without fruite. This synne is also thefte/ for thefte generally is to reue a wyght his thynge ayenst his wyll. Certes this is the foulest thefte that may be/ whan that a woman stealeth her body fro her husbonde and yeueth it to her holour to defoyle her/ and stealeth her soule fro Christ/ and yeueth it to the dyuell: This is a fouler thefte than for to breake a churche and steale away the chalyce/ for these auouterers breke the temple of god spyrituelly/ and steale the vessell of grace/ that is the body and the soule: For whiche Christ shall distroye hem/ as sayth saynt Poule. Sothly of this thefte doubted greatly Joseph/ whan that his lordes wyfe prayed him of vylanye/ whan he sayde: Lo my lady howe my lorde hath take to me vnder my warde/ al that he hath in this worlde/ ne nothynge of his thynges is out of my power/ but onely ye that be his wyfe: and howe shulde I than do this wickednesse and synne so horrible ayēst god/ and ayenst my lorde/ god it forbede. Alas/ al to lytel is suche trouthe nowe founde. The thirde harme is the fylth/ through whiche they breake the cōmaundement of god/and defoyle the auter of matrimonye/ that is Christ. For certes in so moche as the sacrament of maryage is so noble and so digne/ so moche is it greater synne for to breake it: For god made mariage in paradyse in the estate of innocencie/ to multyplye mankynde in the seruyce of god/ and therfore is the brekynge therof the more greuous/ of whiche brekyng come false heyres ofte tyme/ that wrōgfully occupye folkes herytages/ and therfore wol Christ put hem out of the reigne of heuen/ that is herytage to good folke. Of this brekyng cometh also ofte tyme that folke vnware wedde or synne with her owne kynrede: and namely these harlottes that haunte bordels of these foule women/ that maye be lykened to a commune gonge/ where as men pourge her ordure. What saye we also of putours/ that lyue by the horryble synne of putrie/ and constreyne women to yeue to hem a certayne rent of her bodily puterie/ ye somtyme of his own wyfe or his childe/ as done these baudes: Certes these ben cursed synnes. Vnderstōde also that auoutrye is sette gladly in the ten commaundementes bytwene theft & manslaughter/ for it is the greatest thefte that maye be/ for it is thefte of body and of soule/ and it is lyke to homicide for it kerueth a two & breketh a two hem that first were made of one flesshe. And therfore by ẏ olde lawe of god they shuld be slayne/ but nathelesse by the lawe of Jesu Christ/ that is lawe of pyte/ whan he sayd to the woman that was foūde in auoutrye/ and shulde haue be slayne with stones after the wyl of the iewes/ as was her lawe: Go said Jesu Christ/ and haue no more wyll to do synne. Sothly the vengeaunce of auoutrye is awarded to the paynes of hell/ but if so be that it be distourbed by penitence. Yet ben there mo speces of this cursed synne/ as whan that one of hem is relygyous or els bothe/ or of folke that ben entred in to ordre/ as subdeaken/ deaken/ or preest/ or hospitaliers. And euer the hyer that he is in ordre/ the greater is the synne. The thynges that greatly agredge her synne is the brekyng of her auowe of chastyte whan they receyued the order. And moreouer sothe is that holy order is chefe of al the tresorie of god and his especial signe & marke of chastyte/ to shewe that they ben ioyned to chastyte/ whiche is the most precious lyfe that is: and these ordred folke ben specially tytled to god and of the specyal meyne of god/ for whiche whan they done deedly synne they ben the traytours of god & of his people/ for they lyue of the people. Preestes ben aungels as by the dignyte of her misterye/ but forsothe saynt Poule sayth that Sathanas transfourmeth hym in an aungell of lyght. Sothly the preest that haunteth deedly synne he maye be lykened to the aungell of derknesse/ transfourmed in the angell of lyght/ he semeth angel of lyght/ but forsoth he is angell of derkenesse. Suche preestes be the sonnes of Hely/ as sheweth in the booke of kynges/ that they were the sonnes of Belial/ that is the dyuel. Beliall is to saye without iuge/ and so fare they/ hem thynketh they be free and haue no iuge/ no more than hath a free bulle that taketh whiche cowe that him lyketh in the towne. So fare they by women/ for right as one fre bulle is ynoughe for al a towne/ right so is a wicked preest corrupcion ynough for al a parysshe/

rysshe/or for al a countre: These preestes/as sayth the boke/ne can not mynystre the mysterye of preesthode to the people/ ne they knowe not god/ they ne helde hem not apayed/ as sayth the boke/ of sodden flesshe that was to hem offred/ but they toke by force the flesshe that was rawe. Certes/ so these shrewes ne helde hem not apayed of rosted & sodde flesshe/ with whiche the people fedde hem in great reuerence/ but they woll haue rawe flesshe of folkes wyues and her doughters/ and certes these women that cōsent to her harlotrye don great wronge to Christ and to holy churche/ al halowes/and al soules/ for they bireue al these hem that shulde worshyp Christ & holy churche / and praye for christen soules/ and therfore haue suche preestes and her lemmans also that consent to her lechery/ the cursynge of al the courte christien/ tyl they come to amendement. The thirde spece of auoutrye is somtyme betwyxt a man and his wyfe/ and that is whan they take no regarde in her assemblynge/but onely to her flesshly delyte/ as sayth saynt Jerome/and ne reken of nothyng but that they ben assembled bycause they ben maryed/ al is good ynough/ as they thynke: But in suche folke hath the dyuel power/ as sayd the angel Raphael to Thobie/for in her assemblyng they put Jesu Christ out of her herte/ and yeue hem selfe to al ordure. The fourthe spece is the assemble of hem that ben of one affynyte/or els of hem/ with whiche her fathers or her kynred haue dealed in the synne of lecherye: This synne maketh hem lyke to houndes/ that take no kepe to kynrede. And certes parētele is in two maners/ eyther goostly or flesshly: goostly as for to deale with his godsyb/ for right so as he that engendreth a childe is his flesshly father/right so is his god father his father espyrituel: for whiche a woman may in no lesse synne assemble with her godsyb/than with her owne flesshely brother. The fyfth spece is that abhomynable synne/ of whiche abhomynable syn no man vnneth ought speke ne write/ natheless it is openly rehersed in holy writ. This cursed synne done men & women in dyuers entent and in dyuers maner: But though that holy writte speke of horryble synne/certes holy writ may not be defoyled/ no more than the sonne that shyneth on the donghyll. An other synne aperteyneth to lechery that cometh slepyng/and this synne cometh often to hem that ben maydens/ and also to hem that be corrupt/ and this syn men call Polucion/ that cometh of thre maners: Somtyme of languisshyng of body/ for the humours ben to ranke and habundāt in the body of man/ somtyme of infyrmyte/ for feblenesse of the vertue retētyfe/as phisyke maketh mencion: Somtyme for surfet of meate and drinke/& somtyme of vilaynous thoughtes that ben enclosed in mannes mynde whan he gothe to slepe/ whiche may not be without synne/ for whiche men must kepe hem wysely/ or els may men synne ful greuously.

Remedium contra peccatum luxurie.

Nowe cometh the remedy ayenst lecherye/ and that is generally chastyte and continence that restrayne al disordynate meuynges that come of flesshely talentes. And euer the gretter meryte shal he haue that moste restreyneth the wicked chaufynges of the ordour of this synne/ and this is in two maners: That is to saye/chastyte in maryage/and chastyte in wydowhede. Nowe shalt thou vnderstonde that matrimony is leful assemblyng of man and woman that receyuen by vertue of this sacrament/the bonde through whiche they may not be departed in al her lyfe/ that is to say/while that they lyue both. This/as saith the boke/is a ful great sacrament/god made it as I haue sayd in paradyse/ & wolde hym selfe be borne in maryage: & for to halowe mariage he was at a weddyng/ where as he turned water in to wyne/ whiche was the firste myracle that he wrought in erthe before his discyples. Trewe effecte of maryage clenseth fornycation and replenissheth holy churche of good lynage/for that is the ende of mariage/& chaungeth dedely synne in to venial synne/bytwene hem that ben wedded/ and maketh the hertes as one of hem that ben wedded / as wel as the bodies.

Very mariage was establysshed by god / er that synne began / whan naturall lawe was in his ryght poynt in Paradise. And it was ordayned that oo man shulde haue but o woman / and o woman but o man / as saith sait Augustyne / by many reasons.

First for mariage is figured betwixt Crist and holy churche.

Another is for a man is heed of a woman / alwaye by ordynaunce it shulde be so. For if a woman hadde mo men than one / than shulde she haue mo heedes than one / and that were a right horryble thynge before god / and also a woman myght nat please so many fol ke atones: and also there shulde neuer be rest ne quiete amonge hem / for eche of hem wolde aske her owne right. And farthermore / no man shulde knowe his owne engendrure / ne who shuld haue his heritage / and the woman shulde be the lesse beloued.

Nowe cometh how that a man shulde bere him with his wyfe / and namely in two thynges: that is to saye / in sufferaunce and reuerence / as shewed Christe whan he first made woman. For he ne made her of the heed of Adam / for she shulde nat claym to great lordshippe / for there as the woman hath the maistrye / she maketh to moche baryaunce / there nede no mo ensamples of this / the experiēce al day / ought ynough suffice.

Also certes / god ne made nat woman of the foote of Adame / for she shulde nat be holde to lowe / for she can nat paciently suffre: but god made woman of the rybbe of Adam / for woman shulde be felowe vnto man.

Man shulde beare him to his wyfe in faith / in trouth / and in loue (as saith saint Poule) that a man shulde loue his wyfe / as Christ loueth holy churche / that loued it so wel that he dyed for it: so shulde a man for his wyfe / if it were nede. ¶ Nowe howe that a woman shulde be subiecte to her husbōde: that telleth saynt Peter / first in obedience. And also as saith the Decree: A woman that is a wife / as long as she is a wyfe / she hath none auctorite to swere ne beare wytnesse / without leaue of her husbonde ỷ is her lorde / alwaye he shulde be so by reason. She shulde also serue him in al honeste / and be attemperate of her array.

I wol wel that they shulde set her entent to please her husbondes / but nat by queintise of her aray. Saint Jerom saith: wyues that be apparelled in sylke & p̄cious purple / ne mowe nat clothe hem in Jesu christ. Saint Gregori saith also: that no wight seketh p̄cious aray / but onely for vaynglorye to be honoured the more of the people. It is a great foly a woman to haue great array outwarde / & in her selfe be foule inwarde. A wyfe shulde also be mesurable in lokyng / in bearyng / & in laughyng / and discrete in al her wordes & her dedes / and aboue al worldely thynges she shuld loue her husbonde with al her herte / and to him be true of her body: So shulde an husbonde be to his wyfe: For sythe that al the body is the husbondes / so shulde her herte be / or els there is betwyxte hem two / as in that no perfyte mariage. Than shal men vnderstonde that for thre thynges a man & his wyfe flesshely may assēble. The first is for thētent of engēdrure of children to the seruyce of god / for certes that is the cause fynal of matrimonye. Another cause is to yelde eche of hem to other the dettes of her bodyes / for neyther of hem hath power ouer her owne bodies. The thirde is for to eschue lechery & vilanye. The fourth is forsothe deedly synne. As to the first is merytorie: the seconde also / for as sayth the decre / ỷ she hath meryte of chastyte that yeldeth to her husbōde the dette of her body / ye though it be ayenst her lykyng & the luste of her herte. The thirde maner is venyall synne / and truely scarsly may any of these be without venial synne for the corrupcion & for the delyte. The fourthe maner is for to vnderstōde / if they assemble only for amorous loue / & for none of the forsayde causes / but for to accomplysshe the brennyng delyte / they recke not how oft / sothly it is deedly syn: and that with sorowe some folke wol payne hem more to do thā to her appetyte suffyseth. ¶ The seconde maner of chastyte is for to be a clene wydowe & eschewe the enbrasynges of a man / and desyre the enbrasyng of

Jesu

Jesu Christ: These ben those that haue ben wyues/ and haue forgote her husbondes/ and also women that haue done lecherye/ & ben receyued by penitence. And certes if that a wyfe coulde kepe her al chaste by lycence of her husbõde/ so that she yeue neuer none occasion that he offende/ it were to her a great merite. This maner of woman that obserueth chastyte in clothyng and in countenaunce/ abstynent in eatyng and drinkyng/ in spekynge & in dede/ she is the vessel or the boxe of the blessed Maudelayne that fulfylleth holy churche of good odoure. The thirde maner of chastyte is virgynyte/ and it behoueth that she be holy in herte/ and clene of body/ than is she spouse of Jesu Christ/ and she is the lyfe of aungels: she is the praysynge of this worlde/ and she is as these martyrs in regaly: She hath in her that tonge may not tell ne herte thynke. Virgynyte bare our lorde Jesu Christ/ and virgyn was him selfe.

¶ Another remedy ayenst lecherye is specially to withdrawe suche thynges as yeue occasyon to that vylanye: as ease/ eatynge/ and drinkynge: For certes whan the potte boylleth strongly/ the best remedy is to withdrawe the fyre. Sleppynge longe in great quyete is also a great nouryce to lecherye.

¶ Another remedy ayenst lechery is that a man or a woman eschewe the companye of hem by whiche he douteth to be tempted: For al be it so that the dede is withstonde/ yet is there great temptacyon. Sothely a whyte walle/ all thoughe it ne brenne not fully by stickynge of the candell/ yet is the wall blacke of the flame. Full ofte tyme I rede that no man truste in his owne perfection/ but he be stronger than Sampson/ or holyer than Danyel/ or wyser than Salomon.

Nowe after that I haue declared you as I canne/ the seuyn deedly synnes/ and some of her braunches/ with her remedies. Sothly if I coude/ I wolde tel you the tenne cõmaundementes/ but so hye doctryne I putte to dyuines. Nathelesse I hope to god they ben touched in this treatyse eche of hem.

¶ Sequitur secunda pars penitentie.

Now for asmoch as the secõde parte of penytence stont in confession of mouth/ as I began in the first cha. I say saint Austen saith: Synne is euery worde & euery dede/ and al that men conuecte ayenst ẏ law of Jesu crist/ and this is for to synne in hert/ in mouth/ and in dede/ by the fyue wyttes/ whiche ben sight/ herynge/ smellyng/ tastyng or sauour/ and felynge. Nowe is it good to vnderstonde/ that that agredgeth moche euery syn. Thou shalt consider what thou arte that doste the synne/ wheder thou be male or female/ yong or olde/ gentyl or thral/ free or seruaunt/ hole or sicke/ wedded or syngle/ ordred or vnordred/ wyse or fole/ clerke or seculer/ if she be of thy kynrede bodily or gostly/ or no/ if any of thy kynrede haue synned with her or no/ & many mo thynges. Another circumstaunce is this/ whoder it be done in fornycation or in auoutry or no/ in maner of homycede or no/ horryble great synnes or smal/ and howe long thou haste cõtynued in synne. The thirde circumstaunce is the place there thou haste done synne/ wheder in other mennes houses or in thyne owne/ in felde/ in churche or in churchyarde/ in churche dedicate or no. For if the churche be halowed and manne or woman spyl his kynde within that place by waye of synne or wycked temptation/ the churche is enterdited/ and the preest that dyd suche a vyllany/ the terme of al his lyfe he shulde no more synge masse. and if he dyd/ he shulde do deedly syn at euery tyme that he so songe masse. The fourth circumstaunce is/ by whiche medyatours or by whiche messangers/ or for enticement/ or for consentement to beare company with felowshippe. For many a wretche for to beare cõpany/ wol go to the dyuell of hell. Wherfore they that egge or consent to the synne/ ben parteners of the synne/ and of the temptation of the synner. The fyfth circumstaunce is how many tymes that he hath synned/ if it be in his mynde/ & howe ofte he hath fallen. For he that ofte falleth in syn/ he dispyseth the mercy of god and encreseth his syn/ and is vnkynde to Christ.

to Chrifte / and he weyeth the more feble to withstonde synne / and synneth the more lightly and the later ryseth / and is more slowe to shryue him / and namely to him that is his cōfessour. For whiche that folke whan they fal ayen to her olde folyes / either they leaue their olde confessour / or els they departe her shrifte in dyuers partes. But sothly suche departed shrifte deserueth no mercy of god for her synnes. The sixte cyrcumstaunce is / why that a man synneth as by temptation: and if hym selfe procure that temptation / or by the exciting of other folke / or if he synne with a woman by force or by her assent / or if ye woman maugre her heed haue be a forced or none. This shal she tel / wheder it were for couetyse or pouerte / or if it were by her procurement or no / and suche other thynges. The seuenth circumstaunce is / in what maner he hath do his synne / or howe that she hath suffred that folke haue do to her. And the same shal the man tel playnly with al the cyrcumstaunces. & wheder he hath synned with cōmen bordel womā or none / or done his synne in holy tymes or none / in fastynge tyme or none / or before his shrift or after his later shrifte / and hath parauenture broke therby his penaunce enioyned / by whose helpe or whose counsaile / by sorcery or crafte / al must be tolde / & al these thynges after as they be gret or smale / and grudge the cōscience of man or woman. And eke ye preest that is thy iuge / maye the better be auysed of his iugement in yeueng of penaunce / & that is after thy contrition. For vnderstonde wel that after tyme that a man hath defoyled his baptyme by synne / if he wol cōe to saluation there is non other way but by penaūce / shrift / and satisfactyon / and namely by the two / if there be a confessour to whom he may shryue him / and the thirde if he haue lyfe to performe it. Than shal a man loke and consyder / that if he wol make a trewe and a profitable confession / there muste be four condytions.

First it must be in sorousulnesse of hert / as saith the kyng Ezechiel to god / I wol remembre me al the yeres of my lyfe in bytternesse of my herte. This condytion of bytternesse hath fyue signes. The first is / that cōfession muste be shamefast / nat for to couer ne hyde her synne / for he hath offended his lorde god and defoyled his soule. And herof saith saīt Augustyn: The hert traueyleth for shame of his synne / & for he hath great shamefastnesse he is worthy to haue great mercy of god / whiche was the confession of the Publycan / that wolde nat heaue vp his eyen to heuen for he had offended god of heuen: for whiche shamfastnesse he had anon the mercy of god. And therof saith saynt Augusten: that suche shāeful folke be next foryeuenesse and mercy.

Another signe is humilyte in confession / of whiche saith saynt Peter: Humbleth you vnder the might of god: the honde of god is strōge in confession / for therby god foryeueth the thy synnes / for he alone hath the power. And this humilyte shal be in herte / & in outwarde signes: For right as he hath humilyte to god in his hert / right so shulde he humble his body outwarde to the preest / that sytteth in goddes stede. For whiche in no maner / sithe that Christ is souerayne / and the preest mean and mediatour betwixt Christ and ye synner / and the synner is laste by waye of reason. Than shulde nat the synner sytte as hye as his confessour but knele before him or at his fete / but if sickenesse cause it: For he shal nat take hede who sytteth there / but in whose place he sytteth. A man that hath trespassed to a lorde / and cometh to aske mercy and make his acorde / & sytteth him downe by him / men wolde holde hym outragious and nat worthy so soone for to haue remissyon of his trespace.

The thirde signe is / howe thy shrifte shulde be ful of teares if thou maye / & if thou may nat wepe with thy bodily eyen / than wepe in thyne herte / whiche was the confession of saīt Peter. For after that he hadde forsake Iesu Christ / he went out and wepte ful bitterly.

The fourthe signe is / that thou ne lette nat for shame to shewe thy cōfession: Suche was the confession of Magdaleyn / that ne spared for no shame of hem that were at the feest / to go to our lorde Iesu christ & beknowe to him her synnes. The fyfth signe is / that a man

or a

or a woman be obeysaunt to receyue the penaunce that hem is enioyned. For certes Jesu Christ/ for the offences of man was obedient to dethe. The seconde condition of very confession is/ that it be hastely done. For certes/ if a man had a deedly wounde/ euer the lenger that he taryeth to heale hym self/ the more wolde it corrupt and haste hym to his dethe/ & also the woūde wolde be the worse for to hele. And right so fareth synne/ that longe tyme is in a man vnshewed. Certes a man ought hastely shewe his synnes for many causes/ as for drede of dethe/ that cometh ofte sodaynly/ and no certayne what tyme it shall be/ ne in what place/ and also the drenchynge of o syn draweth in another: and also the lenger that he tarieth the farther he is fro Christ. And if he abyde to his laste daye/ scarcely maye he shryue hym or remembre hym of his synnes/ or repent for ÿ greuous malady of his dethe. And for asmoche as he ne hath in his lyfe herkened Jesu Christe whan he hath spoken/ he shal crye to Jesu Christ at his laste day/ and scarcely wol he herken hym. And vnderstōde that this condition must haue four thynges.

Thy shrifte must be prouyded before and auysed/ for wicked haste dothe no profyte/ if a man shriue hym of his synnes: be it of Pride/ or enuy/ and so forthe with the speces and cyrcumstaunces of synne. And that he haue cōprehended in his mynde the nombre & greatnesse of his synnes/ and howe longe he hath lyen in synne. And also that he hath be contrite for his synnes/ and in stedfaste purpose (by ÿ grace of god) neuer ayen to fal to syn. And also that he drede and counterwaite him selfe that he flye the occasion of synne/ to whiche he is enclyned. Also thou shalte shriue the of al thy synnes to o man/ and nat parte to o man and parte to another/ That is to vnderstonde/ in entent to departe thy confession for shame or drede/ for it is but stranglyng of thy soule. For certes Jesu Christe is entierly al good/ in him nys none imperfection/ & therfore either he foryeueth al perfitely/ or els neuer a deale. I saye nat that if thou be assigned to thy penytencer for certayne syn that thou arte boūde to shewe hym al ÿ remenaunt of thy synnes/ of whiche thou hast be shryuen of thy curate/ but if it lyke to the of thy humilyte/ this is no parte of thy shrifte. Ne I saye nat there as I speke of diuysion of cōfession/ that if thou haue lycence to shryue the to a discrete and an honest preest where the lyketh/ & by lycence of thy curate/ that thou ne mayest wel shryue the to hym of al thy synnes/ Lette no synne be vntolde as ferre as thou hast remembraunce. And whan thou shalte be shreuen to thy curat/ tel him al thy synnes ÿ thou hast do sithe thou were last shryuen. This is no wicked entent of diuisyon of shrifte.

Also the very shrifte asketh certayne conditions. First that thou shryue the by thy free wyl/ nat constrayned for shame of folke/ sickenesse/ ne suche other thynges. For it is reason/ that he ÿ trespaceth by his free wyl/ that by his free wyl he confesse his trespace/ and that none other man tel his syn but hymself/ ne he shal nat nay ne deny his syn/ ne wrathe him ayenst the preest for amonesshing him to leaue his synne. The seconde condytion is/ that thy shrifte be lowful/ that is to saye/ that thou shriuest the. And also the preest that hereth thy cōfession be verily in the fayth of holy churche/ and that a man ne be not dispeyred of the mercy of Jesu christ/ as Cayin or Judas. And also a man must accuse him selfe of his own trespace & not another/ but he shal blame and wyte him selfe & his owne malyce of his synne/ & none other: But nathelesse/ if that another man be occasion or entycer of his syn/ or the estate of a person be suche by whiche his synne is agredged/ or els ÿ he may not plainly shriue him but he tell the person with whiche he hath synned/ than may he tel/ so that his entent ne be not to backbyte the person/ but only to declare his confessyon. Thou ne shalt not also make no leasynges in thy confession for humylyte/ parauenture to say that thou haste cōmysed and done suche synnes as of whiche that thou ne were neuer gyltye. For saynt Augustyn sayth/ if that thou bycause of thyn humylite makest lesinges on thy selfe/ though thou were not in synne before/ yet arte thou

than

than in synne through thy leasynge. Thou must also shewe thy synne by thyne owne ꝓper mouth/ but thou be dombe and nat by no letter: For thou that hast done the syn/ shalte haue the shame therfore. Thou shalt nat eke paynt thy confessyon by fayre subtell wordes/ to couer the more thy synne: for than begylest thou thy selfe and nat the preest/ thou must tel it playne/ be it neuer so foule ne horryble. Thou shalte also shriue the to a preest/ that is discrete to counsaile the/ and also thou shalte nat shriue the for vayngloryl/ ne for ypocrisy/ ne for no cause but onely for the loue & feare of Jesu Christ/ and heale of thy soule. Thou shalte nat also ren to the preest sodaynly to tel him lightly thy synne/ as who saithe/ to tel a iape or a tale/ but auisedly and with good deuotion: And generally shriue the ofte if thou ofte fal ofte arise by confession. And though thou shriue the ofter than ones of the synne whiche thou hast be shriuen of/ it is the more merite. And as saith saynt Augustyne/ thou shalte haue yͤ more lightly foryeuenesse and grace of god/ bothe of synne & payne. And certes ones a yere at leest/ it is lauful to be housled/ for surely ones a yere al thynges renouellen. ¶ Nowe haue I tolde you of very confession/ that is the .ii. pte of penytence.

¶ Explicit secũda pars penitentie: Et sequitur tertia pars.

The thirde parte of penytence is satysfaction/ and that stont most generally in almesse dede and bodily payne. Nowe ben there thre maner of almesse. Contrition of hert/ where a man offreth hym selfe to god.

Another is/ to haue pytie of defaute of his neighboure. And the thirde is in gyueng of good counsayle/ goostly and bodily where as men haue nede/ and namely in sustenaunce of mans fode. And take kepe yͭ a man hath nede of these thingꝫ generally/ he hath nede of fode of clothyng/ and of herborowe: He hath nede of charitable counsaile/ visityng in prison/ in sickenesse/ and sepulture of his body. And if thou mayst nat visite the nedeful in thy persone/ visite hem with thy message & yeftes.

These been generally the almesse & workes of charite/ of hem that haue temporal richesse or discretion in counsaylyng. Of these workes shalte thou here at the daye of dome.

These almesses shalt thou do of thyn owne proper thynges/ and hastely & priuely if thou mayst: But natheless/ if thou mayst nat do it priuely/ thou shalte nat forbeare to do almesse though men se it/ so that it be nat do for thanke of the worlde/ but onely for thanke of Jesu christ. For as witnesseth saynt Mathue Cap. v. A cyte maye nat be hydde that is set on a mountayne/ ne men lyght nat a lantern to putte it vnder a bussel/ but sette it vpon a candelsticke to yeue light to men in the house.

Right so shul your lyght/ light before men/ that they may se your good workes/ and glorifye our father that is in heuen.

Nowe as to speke of bodily payne/ it stonte in prayers/ wakyng/ fastynge/ vertuous techyng of orisons. And ye shal vnderstonde/ that orisons or prayers/ is to saye/ a pytous wyl of herte/ that setteth it in god/ and expresseth by worde outwarde to remeue harmes/ & to haue thinges spirituel and durable/ & somtyme temporal thynges. Of whiche orisons certes in the orison of the Pater noster: hath Jesu Christ enclosed moost thynges. Certes it is priuileged of thre thynges in his dignyte/ for which it is more digne than any other prayer/ for that Jesu christ him selfe made it/ and it is shorte/ for it shulde be lerned yͤ more lightly/ and to holde it the more easy in hert/ & help him selfe the ofter with that orison: And for a man shulde be the lesse wery to saye it/ & nat excuse him to lerne it/ it is so shorte and easy: and for it cõprehendeth in it selfe al good prayers. The exposition of this holy prayer that is so excellent and digne/ I referre to the maisters of theology/ saue thus moche wol I say that whan thou prayest/ that god shulde foryeue the thyne offẽces/ as thou foryeuest hem that haue offended the: Be wele ware that thou be nat out of charite. This holy orison amynissheth also venyal synne/ and therfore it appertayneth specially to penytence.

This

This prayer must be trewly said and in parfyte faith/ and that men pray to god ordinatlye/ discretely/ and deuoutly/ and alwaye a man shal put his wyl to be subiecte to ẏ wyl of god. This orison must also be sayd with great humblesse and full pure and honestly/ and nat to the anoyaunce of any man or woman/ It muste also be contynewed with the workes of charite. It auayleth also ayenst the vyces of the soule: For as saith saynt Jerome: By fastyng ben saued the vices of the flesshe/ and by prayer the vices of the soule.

After this thou shalte vnderstonde/ that bodily prayer stont in wakyng. For Jesu christ saithe: Wake ye and praye/ that ye ne entre in to wicked temptation. Ye shul vnderstonde also/ that fastynge stont in thre thynges: In forberyng of bodily meate and drinke/ in forberyng of worldly iolyte/ and in forberynge of deedly syn: this is to saye/ that a man shal kepe him fro deedly synne with al his myght.

And thou shalte vnderstonde also/ that god ordayned fastynge/ and to fastynge parteyneth four thynges. Largenesse to poore folke Gladnesse of hert spirituel: nat to be angrye ne anoyed/ ne grutche for he fasteth/ and also resonable hour to eate by measure/ that is to saye/ a man shal nat eate in vntyme/ ne sytte the lenger at the table for he fasteth.

Than shalte thou vnderstonde/ that bodily payne stonte in disciplyne or techyng by worde or writynge/ or by ensample. Also in wearyng of heer or stamyn/ or of habergeons on her naked flesshe for Christes sake/ and that suche maner penaunces/ ne make nat thyne herte bytter or angrye/ ne anoyed of thy selfe/ for better is to cast awaye thyne heer/ than to cast awaye the swetnesse of Jesu Christ. And therfore saithe saynt Poule: Clothe you/ as they that ben chosen of god in hert/ of myséricorde/ debonairte/ sufferaunce/ and suche maner of clothyng/ of whiche Jesu christ is more pleased/ than with heeres or habergeons.

Than is disciplyne also in knockyng of thy brest/ in scourgyng with roddes/ in knelyng/ in tribulation/ in suffrynge paciently wrōges that ben do to the/ & also in pacient suffrynge of sickenesse/ or lesynge of worldly goodes or catel/ or wyfe/ chylde/ or other frendes.

Than shalt thou vnderstonde whiche thynges distourbe penaunce/ and that is in foure maners/ drede/ shame/ hope/ and wāhope/ that is disperation. And for to speke first of drede for whiche he weneth that he maye suffre no penaunce. There ayenst is remedye for to thynke that bodily penaunce is but shorte and lytel/ at regarde of the payne of hell that is so cruell & so longe/ that it lasteth without ende.

Nowe ayenst the shame that a man hath to shriue him/ and namely these ypocrytes that wolde be holde so perfyte/ that they haue no nede to shriue hem. Ayenst that shame shulde a man thynke that by way of reason that he that hath not be a shamed to do foule thynges/ certes him ought not be a shamed for to do fayre thynges/ and that is confessyons.
A man shulde also thynke that god seeth and knoweth all his thoughtes and all his werkes: To him maye nothynge be hydde ne couered. Men shulde also remembre hem of the shame that is to come at the daye of dome to hem that ben not penytent & shriuen in this presente lyfe: For al the creatures in erth and in hell shal se apertly/ al ẏ they hydde in this worlde. Nowe for to speke of the hope of hem that ben so neglygente & slowe to shriue hem: that stondeth in two maners. That one is/ that he hopeth for to lyue longe/ and for to purchace moche rychesse for his delyte/ and than he wol shriue him: And as he sayth/ him semeth than tymely ynough to come to shrifte.

Another is of surquidrie that he hath in christes mercy. Ayenst the firste vyce he shall thynke that our lyfe is in no sykernesse/ and also that all the rychesses in this worlde ben in auenture/ and passe as a shadowe on the wall. And as saythe saynt Gregorie/ that it apperteyneth to the great righwysenesse of god/ that neuer shall the payne stynte of hem that neuer wolde withdrawe hem fro synne her thankes/ but euer contynued in synne: for that perpetual wyl to do syn/ shall they haue perpetuall payne. Wanhope is in two maners. The first wāhope is in ẏ mercy of god.

That

What other is that they thynke that they ne might not longe perseuer in goodnesse. The first wanhope cometh of that he demeth that he hath synned so greatly and so ofte/ and so longe lyen in synne that he shal not be saued. Certes ayenst that cursed wanhope shulde he thinke that the passion of Iesu Christ is more stronge for to Vnbynde than synne is stronge for to bynde. Ayenst the seconde wanhope he shal thynke that as often as he falleth he may ryse agayne by penytence: and though he neuer so longe hath lyen in synne/ the mercy of Christ is alway redy to receyue him to mercy. Ayenst the wanhope that he demeth he shulde not longe perseuer in goodnes/ he shal thynke that the feblenesse of the dyuel may nothynge do but if men wol suffre him/ and also he shal haue strength of the helpe of Iesu Christ and of al holy churche/ and the protection of angels if hym lyste.

Than shall men Vnderstonde what is the frupte of penaunce/ and after the wordes of Iesu Christe/ it is endlesse blysse of heuen. There ioye hath neuer ende/ no contrarite of wo ne greuaunce: ther al harmes ben passed of this presente lyfe/ there as is the sykernesse fro the payne of hel/ there as is the blysful cōpany that reioyce hem euermo/ eueriche of others ioye: there as the body of man/ that sōtyme was foule and darke/ is more clere than the sonne: there as yͤ body that somtyme was sicke/ freyle/ and feble/ and mortal/ is immortal/ and so stronge & hole/ that there ne maye nothyng appeyre it: there as is neyther hunger/ thurst/ ne colde/ but euery soule replenysshed with the sight of the perfyte knowyng of god. This blysful reigne may men purchace by pouerte espirituel/ and the glorie by lownesse/ the plente of ioye by hunger and thurst/ and the rest by trauayle/ and the lyfe by dethe and mortifycation of synne: to which lyfe he Vs bringe/ that bought Vs with his precious blode. A M E N.

Here endeth the Persones tale.

Thus endeth the boke of Caunterbury tales. And herafter foloweth the Romaunt of the Rose.

The Romaunt of the Rose.

Many men sayn yͭ in sweueniges
Ther nys but fables ⁊ lesynges
But mē may some sweuen sene
Whiche hardely yͭ false ne bene
But afterwarde ben apparaūt
This maye I drawe to warraunt
An authour/ that hight Macrobes
That halte nat dremes false ne lees
But vndothe vs the auysioun
That whilom mette kyng Cipioun
And who so saith/ or weneth it be
A iape/ or els nycete
To wene that dremes after fal
Lette who so lyste a fole me cal
For this trowe I/ and say for me
That dremes signifiaunce be
Of good and harme to many wightes
That dremen in her slepe a nyghtes
Ful many thynges couertly
That fallen after al openly
Within my twenty yere of age
Whan that loue taketh his corage
Of yonge folke/ I went soone
To bedde/ as I was wonte to done
And faste I slepte/ and in slepyng
Me mette suche a sweuenyng
That lyked me wonders wele
But in that sweuen is neuer a dele
That it nys afterwarde befal
Right as this dreme wol tel vs al.
Nowe this dreme wol I ryme a right
To make your hertes gaye and lyght
For loue it prayeth/ and also
Cōmaundeth me that it be so
And if there any aske me
Whether that it be/ he or she
Howe this booke/ whiche is here
Shal hatte/ that I rede you here
It is the Romance of the Rose
In whiche al the arte of loue I close.
¶ The mater fayre is of to make
God graunt me in gree that she it take
For whom that it begonnen is
And that is she/ that hath ywis
So mokel prise/ and therto she
So worthy is beloued to be
That she well ought of prise and right
Be cleped Rose of euery wight
That it was May me thought tho
It is fyue yere or more ago
That it was May/ thus dremed me
In tyme of loue and iolyte
That al thyng gynneth waxen gay
For there is neyther buske nor hay
In May/ that it nyl shrouded bene
And it with newe leues wrene
These woddes eke recoueren grene
That drye in wynter ben to sene
And the erthe wexeth proude withall
For swote dewes that on it fall
And the poore estate forgette
In whiche that wynter had it sette
And than becometh the grounde so proude
That it wol haue a newe shroude
And maketh so queynt his robe and fayre
That it had hewes an hundred payre
Of grasse and floures/ ynde and Pers
And many hewes ful dyuers
That is the robe I mene ywys
Through whiche the grounde to praysen is
The byrdes that han left her songe
Whyle they han suffred colde ful stronge
In wethers grylle/ and derke to sight
Ben in Maye/ for the sonne bright
So gladde/ that they shewe in syngyng
That in her herte is suche lykyng
That they mote syngen and ben lyght
Than dothe the nightyngale her myght
To maken noyse/ and syngen blythe
Than is blyssful many a sythe
The chelaundre/ and the poppyngay
Than yonge folke entenden aye
For to ben gaye and amorous
The tyme is than so sauorous
Harde is his herte that loueth nought
In May/ whan al this myrthe is wrought
Whan he may on these braunches here
The smale byrdes syngen clere
Her blyssful swete songe pytous
And in this seson delytous
Whan loue affirmeth al thyng
Me thought one night/ in my slepyng
Right in my bedde/ ful redyly
That it was by the morowe erly
And vp I rose/ and gan me clothe
Anon I wysshe myn hondes bothe

Aa.ii. A syl-

Romaunt of the Rose: 1–96

The Romaunce of the Rose.

A syluer nedyl forthe I drowe
Out of an aguyler queynt ynowe
And gan this nedyl threde anone
For out of towne me lyste to gone
The sowne of briddes for to here
That on these buskes syngen clere
That in the swete season that lefe is
With a threde bastyng my sleuys.
Alone I wente in my playeng
The smal foules songe herkenyng
That payned hem ful many a payre
To synge on bowes blossomed fayre
Iolyfe and gaye/ ful of gladnesse
Towarde a Ryuer gan I me dresse
That I herde renne faste by
For fayrer playeng none saugh I
Than playen me by that ryuere
For from an hyl that stode there nere
Come downe the streme full styffe and bolde
Clere was the water/ and as colde
As any welle is/ sothe to sayne
And somdele lasse it was than Sayne
But it was strayter/ wele away
And neuer saugh I er that daye
The water that so wele lyked me
And wonder gladde was I to se
That lusty place/ and that ryuere
And with that water that ran so clere
My face I wysshe / tho sawe I wele
The botome ypaued everydele
With grauel/ ful of stones shene
The medowes softe/ sote/ and grene
Beet right on the water syde
Ful clere was than the morowe tyde
And ful attempre out of drede
Tho gan I walken thorowe the Mede
Downwarde aye/ in my playeng
The ryuers syde coostyng
And whan I had a whyle ygone
I sawe a Garden right anone
Ful longe and brode/ and everydele
Enclosed was/ and walled wele
With hye walles enbatayled
Portrayed without/ and wel entayled
With many riche portreytures
And bothe the ymages and peyntures
Gan I beholde besely
And I wol tel you redely
Of thilke ymages the semblaunce
As ferre as I haue remembraunce.
¶ A mydde sawe I Hate stonde
That for her wrathe and yre/ and onde
Semed to be a mynoresse
An angry wight a chideresse
And ful of gyle/ and fel corage
By semblaunt was that ylke ymage
And she was nothyng wele arayde
But lyke a wode woman afrayde
yfrounced foule was her visage
And grynnyng for dispitous rage
Her nose snorted vp for tene
Ful hydous was she for to sene
Ful foule and rusty was she this
Her heed ywrithen was ywis
Ful grymly with a great towayle.
¶ An ymage of another entayle
A lyfte halfe was her fast by
Her name aboue her heed sawe I
And she was called Felony
¶ Another ymage that Vyllany
ycleped was/ sawe I and fonde
Vpon the wall on her right honde
Vyllany was lyke somdele
That other ymage/ and trusteth wele
She semed a wicked creature
By countenaunce in portreyture
She semed be ful dispytous
And eke ful proude/ and outragious
Wel coude he paynt I vndertake
That suche an ymage coude make
Ful foule and chorlych semed she
And eke villeynous for to be
And lytel coulde of norture
To worshippe any creature.
¶ And nexte was paynted Couetyse
That eggeth folke in many a gyse
To take and yeue right nought agayne
And gret tresours vp to layne
And that is she/ that for vsure
Leneth to many a creature
The lasse for the more wynnyng
So couetous is her brennyng
And that is she for pennes feele
That techeth for to robbe and steele
These theues/ and these smale harlotes
And that is routhe/ for by her throtes

Ful

Ful many one hongeth at the last
She maketh folke compasse and cast
To taken other folkes thynge
Through robbery/ or myscoueytyng
And that is she that maketh trechours
And she maketh false pledours
That with her termes and her domes
Done maydens/ children/ and eke gromes
Her heritage to forgo
Ful croked were her hondes two
For couetyse is euer wode
To gryppen other folkes goode
Couetyse/ for her wynnyng
Ful lefe hath other mennes thyng
¶ Another ymage sette saugh I
Nexte Couetyse fast by
And she was cleped Auarice
Ful foule in payntyng was that vice
Ful sadde and caytife was she eke
And also grene as any leke
So yuel hewed was her coloure
Her semed to haue lyued in langour
She was lyke thyng for hunger deed
That ladde her lyfe onely by breed
Kneden with eysel stronge and egre
And therto she was leane and megre
And she was cladde ful poorely
Al in an olde torne courtpy
As she were al with dogges torne
And bothe behynde and eke beforne
Clouted was she beggarly
A mantel honge her fast by
Vpon a benche weyke and smal
A burnette cote honge there with al
Furred with no menyuere
But with a furre rough of heere
Of lambe skynnes heuy and blake
It was ful olde I vnder take
For Auarice to clothe her wele
Ne hasteth her neuer a dele
For certainly it were her lothe
To wearen ofte that ilke clothe
And if it were forweared/ she
Wolde haue ful great nycete
Of clothyng/ er she bought her newe
Al were it badde of wol and hewe
This Auarice helde in her hande
A purse that honge by a bande
And that she hydde and bonde so stronge
Menne must abyde wonder longe
Out of the purse er there come ought
For that ne cometh in her thought
It was not certayne her entent
That fro that purse a peny went
And by that ymage nygh ynough
Was paynted Enuy/ that neuer lough
Nor neuer wel in her herte ferde
But if she eyther sawe or herde
Some great mischaunce/ or great disese
Nothyng may so moche her plese
As mischefe and misauenture
Or whan she seeth discomfyture
Vpon any worthy man fall
Than lyketh her wel withall
She is ful glad in her corage
If she se any great lynage
Be brought to naught/ in shamful wyse
And if a man in honour ryse
Or by his wytte/ or by his prowesse
Of that hath she great heuynesse
For trusteth wel she gothe nye wood
Whan any chaunce happeth good
Enuye is of suche crueltе
That fayth ne trouthe holdeth she
To frende ne felawe/ badde or good
Ne she hath kynne none of her blood
That she nys ful her enemy
She nolde/ I dare sayne hardely
Her owne father fared wele
And sore abyeth she euery dele
Her malyce/ and her male talent
For she is in so great turment
And hate suche/ whan folke dothe good
That nygh she melteth for pure wood
Her herte kerueth and so breketh
That god the people wel awreketh
Enuye iwys shal neuer let
Some blame vpon the folke to set
I trowe that if Enuye iwys
Knewe the best man that is
On this syde or beyonde the see
yet somwhat lacken him wolde she
And if he were so hende and wyse
That she ne might al abate his prise
yet wolde she blame his worthynesse
Or by her wordes make it lesse

A a.iii. I sawe

I sawe Enuye in that payntyng
Had a wonderful lokyng
For she ne loked but awrie
Or ouertwharte/ al baggyngly
And she had a foule vsage
She might loke in no vysage
Of man ne woman/ forthe right playne
But shette her one eye for disdayne
So for enuye brenned she
Whan she might any man se
That fayre/ or worthye were/ or wyse
Or els stode in folkes prise
¶ Sorowe was paynted next Enuye
Vpon that wal of masonrye
But wel was sene in her colour
That she had lyued in langour
Her semed to haue the iaundice
Not halfe so pale was Auaryce
Ne nothyng lyke of leanesse
For sorowe/thought/and great distresse
That she had suffred day and nyght
Made her yelowe/ and nothyng bright
Ful fade/pale/and megre also
Was neuer wight yet halfe so wo
As that her semed for to be
Nor so fulfylled with yre/as she
I trowe that no wight might her plese
Nor do that thyng that might her ese
Nor she ne wolde her sorowe slake
Nor comforte none vnto her take
So depe was her wo begonne
And eke her herte in angre ronne
A sorouful thyng wel semed she
Nor she had nothyng slowe be
For to cratchen al her face
And for to rent in many place
Her clothes/and for to teare her swyre
As she that was fulfylled of yre
And al to torne lay eke her heere
Aboute her shulders/here and there
As she that had it al to rent
For angre and for male talent
And eke I tel you certaynly
Howe that she wept ful tenderly
In worlde nys wyght so harde of herte
That had sene her sorowes smerte
That nolde haue had of her pyte
So wo begone a thyng was she

She al to dassht her selfe for wo
And smote togyder her hondes two
To sorowe was she ful ententyfe
That woful rechelesse caytyfe
Her rought lytel of playeng
Or of clyppyng or kissyng
For who so sorouful is in herte
Him luste not to play ne sterte
Ne for to dauncen/ne to synge
Ne may his herte in temper bringe
To make ioye on euen or morowe
For ioy is contrarie vnto sorowe.
¶ Elde was paynted after this
That shorter was a foote iwys
Than she was wonte in her yonghede
Vnneth her selfe she might fede
So feble and eke so olde was she
That faded was al her beaute
Ful salowe was waxen her colour
Her heed for hore was whyte as flour
Iwys great qualme ne were it none
Ne synne/al though her lyfe were gone
Al woxen was her body vnwelde
And drie and dwyned al for elde
A foule forwelked thyng was she
That whylom rounde and softe had be
Her eeres shoken faste withall
As from her heed they wolde fall
Her face frounced and forpyned
And bothe her hondes lorne fordwyned
So olde she was/that she ne went
A foote/but it were by potent
The tyme that passeth nyght and daye
And restlesse trauayleth aye
And steleth from vs so priuely
That to vs semeth sykerly
That it in one poynt dwelleth euer
And certes it ne resteth neuer
But gothe so faste/and passeth aye
That there nys man that thynke may
What tyme that nowe present is
Asketh at these clerkes this
For men thynke it redily
Thre tymes ben passed by
The tyme that may not soiourne
But gothe/and may neuer retourne
As water that downe renneth aye
But neuer droppe retourne maye

There

There may nothyng as tyme endure
Metal/nor erthly creature
For al thing it frette and shal
The tyme eke that chaungeth al
And al dothe waye/and fostred be
And al thyng distroyeth he
The tyme that eldeth our auncestours
And eldeth kynges and emperours
And that us al shal overcomen
Er that dethe us shal have nomen
The tyme that hath al in welde
To elden folke had made her elde
So inly/that to my wetyng
She might helpe her selfe nothyng
But turned ayen unto childhede
She had nothyng her selfe to lede
Ne wytte ne pythe in her holde
More than a chylde of two yere olde
But nathelesse I trowe that she
Was fayre somtyme/and fresshe to se
Whan she was in her rightful age
But she was paste al that passage
And was a doted thyng becomen
A furred cappe on had she nomen
Wel had she clad her selfe and warme;
For colde might els done her harme
These olde folke have alway colde
Her kynde is suche/whan they ben olde.
¶ Another thyng was don there write
That semed lyke an Ipocryte
And it was cleped Pope Holy
That ilke is she/that prively
Ne spareth never a wicked dede
Whan men of her taken none hede
And maketh her outwarde precious
With pale vysage and pytous
And semeth a symple creature
But there nys no misaventure
That she ne thynketh in her corage
Ful lyke to her was thilke ymage
That maked was lyke her semblaunce
She was ful symple of countenaunce
And she was clothed and eke shod
As she were for the love of god
Yolden to relygion
Suche semed her devocion
A psauter helde she faste in honde
And besyly she gan to fonde
To make many a faynte prayere
To god/ and to his sayntes dere
Ne she was gaye/ fresshe/ ne iolyfe
But semed to be ful ententyfe
To good werkes/and to fayre
And therto she had on an hayre
Ne certes she was fatte nothyng
But semed wery for fastyng
Of colour pale and dede was she
From her the gates aye werned be
Of paradyse/that blysful place
For suche folke maken leane her grace
As Christ sayth in his Euangyle
To gette hem prise in towne a whyle
And for a lytel glory veigne
They lesen god and eke his reigne.
¶ And alderlast of everychone
Was paynted Povert al alone
That not a peny had in holde
Al though she her clothes solde
And though she shulde an honged be
For naked as a worme was she
And if the wether stormy were
For colde she shulde have dyed there
She ne had on but a strayte olde sacke
And many a cloute on it there stacke
This was her cote/ and her mantele
No more was there never a dele
To clothe her with/I undertake
Great leyser had she to quake
And she was put/that I of talke
Ferre fro these other/up in an halke
There lurked/ and there coured she
For poore thyng where so it be
Is shamfaste/and dispysed aye
Acursed may wel be that daye
That poore man conceyved is
For god wote al to selde iwys
Is any poore man wel ycedde
Or wel arayed or ycledde
Or wel beloved/in suche wyse
In honour/ that he may aryse.
¶ Al these thinges wel avysed
As I have you er this devysed
With golde and asure over all
Depaynted were upon the wall
Square was the wall/and hygh somdele
Enclosed/ and ybarred wele

In

In stede of hegge/ was that gardyn
Come neuer shepherde therin
In to that gardyn/ wel wrought
Who so that me coulde haue brought
By ladders/ or els by degre
It wolde wel haue lyked me
For suche solace/ suche ioy/ and pley
I trowe that neuer man ne sey
As was in that place delycious
The gardyn was not daungerous
To herberowe byrdes many one
So ryche a yere was neuer none
Of byrdes songe/ and braunches grene
Therin were byrdes mo I wene
Than ben in al the realme of Fraunce
Ful blyssful was the accordaunce
Of swete pytous songe they made
For al this worlde it ought glade
 And I my selfe so mery ferde
Whan I her blyssful songes herde
That for an hundred poūde wolde I
If that the passage openly
Had be vnto me free
That I nolde entren for to se
Thassemble/ god kepe it fro care
Of byrdes/ whiche therin ware
That songen through her mery throtes
Daunces of loue/ and mery notes.

Whan I thus herde foules synge
I fel faste in a waymentyng
By whiche arte/ or by what engyn
I might come in to that gardyn
But way I couthe fynde none
In to that gardyn for to gone
Ne nought wyst I if that there were
Eyther hole or place where
By whiche I might haue entre
Ne there was none to teche me
For I was al a lone I wys
For wo and anguisshe of this
Tyl at laste bethought I me
That by no way ne might it be
That there nas ladder ne way to pace
Or hole/ in to so fayre a place
Tho gan I go a ful great paas
Enuyron/ euen in compas
The closyng of the square wall
Tyl that I founde a wycket small
So shette/ that I ne might in gone
And other entre was there none.

Vpon this dore I gan to smyte
That was fetys/ and so lyte
For other way coulde I not seke
Ful longe I shoke/ and knocked eke
And stode ful longe al herkenyng
If that I herde any wight comyng
Tyl that the dore of thylke entre
A mayden curteys opened me
Her heere was as yelowe of hewe
As any basen scoured newe
Her flesshe tender as is a chyke
With bent browes/ smothe and slyke
And by mesure large were
The openyng of her eyen clere
Her nose of good proporcion
Her eyen gray/ as is a faucon
With swete brethe/ and wel sauoured
Her face whyte/ and wel coloured
With lytel mouthe and rounde to se
A cloue chynne eke had she
Her necke was of good fasshyon
In length and gretnesse by reson
Without bleyne/ scabbe/ or royne
Fro Hierusalem vnto Burgoyne
There nys a fayrer necke iwys
To fele howe smothe and softe it is
Her throte also whyte of hewe
As snowe on braunche snowed newe
Of body ful wel wrought was she
Men neden not in no countre
A fayrer body for to seke
And of fyne Orfrays had she eke
A chapelet/ so semely on
Ne wered neuer mayde vpon
And fayre aboue that chapelet
A rose garlande had she set
She had a gay mirrour
And with a ryche golde tressour
Her heed was tressed queyntly
Her sleues sewed fetously
And for to kepe her hondes fayre
Of gloues whyte she had a payre
And she had on a cote of grene
Of clouthe of Gaunt/ withouten wene

Well

Romaunt of the Rose: 481–574

Wel semed by her apparayle
She was not wonte to great trauayle
For whan she kempt was fetously
And wel araped and richely
Than had she done al her iournee
For mery and wel begon was she
  She ladde a lusty lyfe in May
She had no thought/ by night ne day
Of nothyng/ but if it were onely
To grayth her wele and vncouthly.

  Whan that this dore had opened me
This May/ semely for to se
I thonked her as I best myght
And asked her howe that she hyght
And what she was/ I asked eke
And she to me was nought vnmeke
Ne of her answere daungerous
But fayre answerde/ and sayd thus
  Lo sir/ my name is Idelnesse
So clepe men me/ more and lesse
Ful mighty and ful ryche am I
And that of one thyng namely
For I entende to nothyng
But to my ioye/ and my playeng
And for to kembe and tresse me
Aquaynted am I and priue
With Myrthe/ lorde of this gardyne
That fro the lande of Alexandrine
Made the trees hyther be fette
That in this garden ben ysette
And whan the trees were woxen on hyght
This wall/ that stante here in thy syght
Dyd Myrthe enclosen al aboute
And these ymages al without
He dyd hem bothe entayle and peynte
That neyther ben iolyfe ne queynte
But they ben ful of sorowe and wo
As thou haste sene a whyle ago.

AND ofte tyme him to solace
Sir Myrthe cometh in to this place
And eke with him cometh his meyne
That lyuen in luste and iolyte
And nowe is Myrthe therin/ to here
The byrdes howe they syngen clere
The mauys and the nyghtyngale
And other ioly byrdes smale
And thus he walketh to solace
Hym and his folke/ for swetter place
To playen in/ he may not fynde
Al though he sought one in tyl Inde
The alther fayrest folke to se
That in this worlde may founde be
Hath Myrthe with him in his route
That folowen him alwayes aboute.

  Whan Idelnesse had tolde al this
And I had herkened wel ywys
Than sayd I to dame Idelnesse
Nowe also wisly god me blesse
Sythe Myrthe/ that is so fayre and fre
Is in this yerde/ with his meyne
Fro thylke assemble/ if I may
Shal no man werne me to day
That I this nyght ne mote it se
For wel wene I there with him be
A fayre and ioly companye
Fulfylled of al curtesye
And forthe without wordes mo
In at the wicket went I tho
That Ydelnesse had opened me
In to that garden fayre to se.

  And whan I was in ywys
Myn herte was ful glad of this
For wel wende I ful sykerly
Haue ben in paradyse erthly
So fayre it was/ that trusteth well
It semed a place espyrituell
For certes as at my deuyse
There is no place in paradyse
So good in for to dwell or be
As in that garden thought me
For there was many a byrde syngyng
Throughout the yerde al thringyng
In many places were nightyngales
Alpes/ fynches/ and wodwales
That in her swete songe delyten
In thilke places as they habyten
  There might men se many flockes
Of turtles and lauerockes
Chalaundres fele sawe I there
That wery nighe forsongen were
And thrustels/ teryns/ and mauise
That songen for to wynne hem prise

And

And eke to surmount in her songe
That other byrdes hem amonge
By note made fayre seruyse
These byrdes/that I you deuyse
They songe her songe/as fayre and well
As angels don espirituell
And trusteth me/ whan I hem herde
Ful lusty and wel I ferde.
For neuer yet suche melodye
Was herde/of man that might dye
Suche swete songe was hem amonge
That me thought it no byrdes songe
But it was wonder lyke to be
Songe of Meremaydens of the see
That for her syngyng is so clere
Though we mermaydens clepe hem here
In englisshe/ as is our vsaunce
Men clepe hem Sereyns in Fraunce.

Ententyfe weren for to synge
These byrdes/that not vnkonnyng
Were of her crafte/ and aprentyse
But of songe subtyl and wyse
And certes/ whan I herde her songe
And sawe the grene place amonge
In herte I wext so wonder gay
That I was neuer erst/ er that day
So iolyfe/nor so wel bygo
Ne mery in herte/as I was tho
And than wyste I/ and sawe ful wel
That ydelnesse me serued wel
That me put in suche iolyte
Her frende wel ought I for to be
Sythe she the dore of that gardyn
Had opened/and me lette in.

From hence forthe/ howe that I wrought
I shall you telle/ as me thought
First wherof Myrthe serued there
And eke what folke there with him were
Without fable I wol discryue
And of that garden eke as blyue
I wol you tellen after this
The fayre fasshyon al iwys
That wel wrought was for the nones
I may not tel you al atones
But as I may and can/I shal
By ordre tellen you it al

Ful fayre seruyce/and eke ful swete
These byrdes maden as they sete
Layes of loue/ful wel sownyng
They songen in her iargonyng
Some hye/ and some eke lowe songe
Vpon the braunches grene isprонge
The swetnesse of her melodye
Made al myn herte in reuelrye
And whan that I had herde I trowe
These byrdes syngyng on a rowe
Than might I not withholde me
That I ne went in for to se
Sir Myrthe/for my desyring
Was him to sene ouer al thyng
His countenaunce and his manere
That syght was to me ful dere.

Tho went I forthe on my right honde
Downe by a lytel pathe I fonde
Of myntes ful/ and fenell grene
And faste by without wene
Syr Myrthe I founde/ and right anon
Vnto sir Myrthe gan I gon
There as he was him to solace
And with him/ in that lusty place
So fayre folke and so fresshe had he
That whan I sawe/I wondred me
Fro whence suche folke might come
So fayre they weren al and some
For they were lyke/ as to my syght
To angels/ that been fethered bryght.
These folke/ of whiche I tel you so
Vpon a karole wenten tho
A lady karoled hem/that hyght
Gladnesse/ blysful and lyght
Wel coulde she synge and lustely
None halfe so wel and semely
And couthe make in songe suche refraynyng
It sate her wonder wel to synge
Her voyce ful clere was and ful swete
She was not rude ne vnmete
But couthe ynough of suche doyng
As longeth vnto karollyng
For she was wonte in euery place
To syngen first/folke to solace
For syngyng moste she gaue her to
No crafte had she so lefe to do.

Tho

Tho mightest thou karolles sene
And folke daunce and mery bene
And made many a fayre tournyng
Upon the grene grasse spryngyng
There mightest thou se these flutours
Mynstrales and eke iogelours
That wel to synge dyd her payne
Some songe songes of Lorayne
For in Loreyne her notes be
Ful swetter than in this countre
There was many a tymbestere
And saylours/ that I dare wele swere
Couthe her crafte ful parfetly
The tymbres up ful subtelly
They caste/ and hente ful ofte
Upon a fynger fayre and softe
That they fayled neuer mo
Ful fetys damosels two
Right yonge/ and ful of semelyhede
In kyrtels/ and none other wede
And fayre tressed euery tresse
Had Myrthe done for his noblesse
Amydde the carole for to daunce
But herof lyeth no remembraunce
Howe that they daunsed queyntly
That one wolde come al priuely
Agayne that other/ and whan they were
To gyther almoste/ they threwe yfere
Her mouthes so/ that through her play
It semed as they kyste alway
To dauncen wel couthe they the gyse
What shulde I more to you deuyse
Ne bode I neuer thence go
Whyles that I sawe hem daunce so
Upon the karoll wonder faste
I gan beholde/ tyl at laste
A lady gan me for to espye
And she was cleped Curtesye
The worshypful/ the debonayre
I pray to god euer fall her fayre
Ful curtesly she called me
What do ye there Beau sire (qd she)
Come/ and if it lyke you
To dauncen/ daunseth with us now
And I without taryeng
Went in to the karollyng
I was abasshed neuer a dele
But it to me lyked right wele
That Curtesy me cleped so
And bade me on the daunce go
For if I had durste certayne
I wolde haue karoled right fayne
As man that was to daunce right blythe
Than gan I loken ofte sythe
The shap/ the bodyes/ and the cheres
The countenaunce and the maneres
Of al the folke that daunsed there
And I shal tel what they were.

Ful fayre was Myrthe/ ful longe & hygh
A fayrer man I neuer sygh
As rounde as appel was his face
Ful roddy and whyte in euery place
Fetys he was and wel besey
With metely mouthe/ and eyen grey
His nose by mesure wrought ful right
Crypse was his heere/ and eke ful bright
His shuldres of a large brede
And smallysshe in the gyrdelstede
He semed lyke a purtreyture
So noble he was of his stature
So fayre/ so ioly/ and so fetyse
With lymmes wrought at poynt deuyse
Delyuer/ smerte/ and of great myght
Ne sawe thou neuer man so lyght
Of berde unneth had he nothyng
For it was in the first spryng
Ful yonge he was/ and mery of thought
And in samette/ with byrdes wrought
And with golde beten ful fetously
His body was clad ful richly
Wrought was his robe in straunge gyse
And al to slyttered for queyntyse
In many a place/ lowe and hye
And shode he was with great maystrye
With shone decoped/ and with lace
By drury/ and by solace
His leefe a rosen chapelet
Had made/ and on his heed it set
And wete ye who was his lefe
Dame Gladnesse there was him so lefe
That syngeth so wel with glad corage
That from she was twelue yere of age
She of her loue graunt him made
Sir Myrthe her by the fynger hade
Daunsyng/ and she him also

Great

Great loue was atwyxt hem two
Bothe were they fayre and bright of hewe
She semed lyke a rose newe
Of colours/ and her flesshe so tendre
That with a brere smale and tendre
Men might it cleue/ I dare wel sey
Her forheed frounceles al pley
Bent were her browes two
Her eyen gray/ and glad also
That laugheden aye in her semblaunt
First or the mouthe by couenaunt
I wot not what of her nose I shal discryue
So fayre hath no woman alyue
Her heere was yelowe/ and clere shynyng
I wot no lady so lykyng
  Of Orfrayes fresshe/ was her garlande
I whiche sene haue a thousande
Sawe neuer iwys no garlande yet
So wel wrought of sylke as it
And in an ouergylte samyte
Cladde she was/ by great delyte
Of whiche her leefe a robe werde
The meryer she in her herte ferde
  And next her went/ on her other syde
The god of loue/ that can deuyde
Loue/ and as him lyketh it be
But he can cherles daunten/ he:
And maken folkes pride fallen
And he can wel these lordes thrallen
And ladyes put at lowe degre
Whan he may hem to proude se.

  This god of loue of his fasciouu
Was lyke no knaue/ ne quystroun
His beutie greatly was to prise
But of his robe to deuyse
I drede encombred for to be
For not ycladde in sylke was he
But al in floures and flourettes
Ypaynted al with amorettes
And with losenges and scochons
With byrdes/ lyberdes/ and lyons
And other beestes wrought ful wele
His garnement was euerydele
Ypurtrayed and ywrought with floures
By dyuers medelyng of colours
Floures there were of many gyse
Yset by compace in a syse
There lacked no floure to my dome
Ne not so moche as floure of brome
Ne vyolet/ ne eke perwynke
Ne floure non/ that men can on thynke
And many a rose lefe ful longe
Was entermedled there amonge
And also on his heed was set
Of roses reed a chapelet
  But nightyngales a ful great route
That flyen ouer his heed aboute
The leaues felden as they flyen
And he was al with byrdes wryen
With popingay/ with nightyngale
With chalaundre/ and with wodewale
With fynche/ with larke/ ⁊ with archangell
He semed as he were an angell
That downe were comen fro heuen clere
  Loue had with him a bachelere
That he made alwayes with him be
Swete Lokyng/ cleped was he
This bacheler stode beholdyng
The daunce/ and in his honde holdyng
Turke bowes two/ ful wel deuysed had he
That one of hem was of a tree
That beareth a fruite of sauoure wicke
Ful croked was that foule stycke
And knotty here and there also
And blacke as bery/ or any slo
  That other bowe was of a plante
Without wemme/ I dare warante
Ful euen and by proporcioun
Trectes ⁊ longe/ of ful good facyoun
And it was paynted wel and twhitten
And ouer al diapred and written
With ladyes and with bacheleres
Ful lyghtsome and glad of cheres
  These bowes two helde Swete Lokyng
That semed lyke no gadlyng
And ten brode arowes helde he there
Of whiche fyue in his righthonde were
But they were shauen wel and dyght
Nocked/ and fethered aryght
And al they were with golde begon
And stronge poynted euerychon
And sharpe for to keruen wele
But yron was there none ne stele
For al was golde/ men might se
Out take the fethers and the tree.

The

The swyftest of these arowes fyue
Out of a bowe for to driue
And best fethered for to flye
And fayrest eke/was cleped Beautie
That other arowe/that hurteth lesse
Was cleped (as I trowe) Symplesse
The thyrde cleped was Fraunchyse
That fethered was in noble wyse
With valour and with curtesye
The fourthe was cleped companye
That heuy for to shoten is
But who so shoteth right iwys
May therwith don great harme and wo
The fyfte of these/and laste also
Fayre Semblaunt men that arowe call
The leest greuous of hem all
yet can it make a full great wounde
But he may hope his sores sounde
That hurte is with that arowe iwys
His wo the bette bestowed is
For he may soner haue gladnesse
His langour ought be the lesse.

Fiue arowes were of other gyse
That ben ful foule to deuyse
For shafte and ende/sothe for to tell
Were also blacke as fende in hell
The first of hem is called Pride
That other arowe next hym besyde
It was cleped Vylanye
That arowe was/as with felonye
Enuenymed/and with spytous blame
The thirde of hem was cleped Shame
The fourthe Wanhope cleped is
The fyfte the Newe thought iwys.

These arowes that I speke of here
Were al fyue on one manere
And al were they resemblable
To hem was wel syttyng and able
The foule croked bowe hydous
That knotty was/and al roynous
That bowe semed wel to shete
These arowes fyue/that ben vnmete
And contrarye to that other fyue
But though I tell not as blyue
Of her power/ne of her myght
Herafter shal I tellen right
The sothe/and eke sygnyfyaunce
As ferre as I haue remembraunce
Al shal be sayd I vndertake
Er of this booke an ende I make.

Nowe come I to my tale agayne
But alderfirst/I wol you sayne
The fasshyon and the countenaunces
Of al the folke that on the daunce is
The god of Loue iolyfe and lyght
Ladde on his honde a lady bright
Of hygh prise/and of great degre
This lady called was Beaute
And an arowe/ of whiche I tolde
Ful wel thewed was she holde
Ne she was derke ne browne/ but bright
And clere as the moone lyght
Agayne whom al the sterres semen
But smale candels/as we demen
Her flesshe was tendre as dewe of floure
Her chere was symple as byrde in boure
As whyte as lylye or rose in ryse
Her face gentyl and tretyse
Fetys she was/ and smale to se
No wyntred browes had she
Ne popped her/for it neded nought
To wyndre her/or to paynte her ought
Her tresses yelowe/and longe straughten
Vnto her heles downe they raughten
Her nose/her mouthe/& eye and cheke
Wel wrought/and al the remenaunt eke
A ful great sauour and a swote
Me thought in myn herte rote
As helpe me god/whan I remembre
Of the fasshyon of euery membre
In worlde is none so fayre a wight
For yonge she was/and hewed bright
Sore plesaunt/and fetys with all
Gent/ and in her myddell small
Besyde Beaute yede Rychesse
And hyght lady of great noblesse
And great of price in euery place
But who so durste to her trespace
Or tyl her folke/in werke or dede
He were ful hardy out of drede
For bothe she helpe and hyndre may
And that is not of yesterday
That ryche folke haue ful great myght

B.b. To

To helpe/ and eke to greue a wight
 The best and greattest of valour
Dydden Richesse ful great honour
And besy weren her to serue
For that they wolde her loue deserue
They cleped her Lady great and smal
This wyde worlde her dredeth al
This worlde is al in her daungere
Her courte hath many a losengere
And many a traytour enuyous
That ben ful besy and curious
For to dispreyse/ and to blame
That best deseruen loue and name
To forne the folke hem to begylen
These losyngeours hem preyse and smylen
 And thus the worlde with worde anoynten
But afterwarde they prill and poynten
The folke/ right to the bare bone
Behynde her backe whan they ben gone
And foule abaten folkes prise
Ful many a worthy man and wyse
Han hyndred/ and ydon to dye
These losyngeours with her flatery
And maketh folke ful straunge be
There as hem ought ben pryue
Wel yuel mote they thryue and thee
And yuel aryued mote they be
These losengeours ful of enuy
No good man loueth her company.

 Rychesse a robe of purple on hadde
Ne trowe nat that I lye or madde
For in this worlde is none it lyche
Ne by a thousande dele so riche
Ne none so fayre/ for it ful wele
With Orfreys leyde was euerydele
And purtrayde in the rybanynges
Of dukes stories/ and of kynges
And with a bende of golde tassyled
And knoppes fyne of golde amyled
About her necke of gentyl entayle
Was shette the riche Cheuesayle
In whiche there was ful great plente
Of stones clere/ and fayre to se.
 ¶ Richesse a gyrdel had vpon
The bokell of it was of a ston
Of vertue great/ and mokel of myght
For who so bare the stone so bright
Of venym durst him nothyng dout
Whyle he the stone had hym about
That stone was greatly for to loue
And tyl a riche mannes behoue
Worthe al the golde in Rome/ and Fryse
The Mourdant wrought in noble gyse
Was of a stone ful precious
That was so fyne and vertuous
That whole a man it couthe make
Of palsye/ and of tothe ake
And yet the stone had suche a grace
That he was seker in euery place
Al thylke day not blynde to bene
That fastyng might that stone sene
The barres were of golde ful fyne
Vpon a tyssue of Satyne
Ful heuy/great/and nothyng lyght
In eueryche was a besaunt wyght
 Vpon the tresses of rychesse
Was set a cercle for noblesse
Of brende golde/that ful lyght shone
So fayre trowe I was neuer none
But he were konnyng for the nones
That coulde deuyse al the stones
That in that cercle shewen clere
It is a wonder thyng to here
For no man coulde preyse or gesse
Of hem the value or richesse
Rubyes there were/ Saphirs/ Ragounces
And Emeraudes/more than two ounces
But al before ful subtelly
A fyne Charboncle sette sawe I
The stone so clere was and so bright
That al so sone as it was nyght
Men myght sene to go for nede
A myle or two/in length and brede
Suche lyght sprange out of the stone
That Richesse wonder bright shone
Bothe her heed/and al her face
And eke aboute her al the place
 Dame Rychesse on her honde gan lede
A yonge man ful of semelyhede
That she best loued of any thyng
His luste was moche in housholdyng
In clothyng was he ful fetyse
And loued wel to haue horse of prise
He wende to haue reproued be
Of thefte or murdre/if that he

Had

Had in his stable an hackenay
And therfore he desyred aye
To ben aqueynted with Richesse
For al his purpose/as I gesse
Was for to make great dispence
Withouten warnyng or defence
And Richesse myght it wele sustene
And her dispences wele mayntene
And hym alway suche plentie sende
Of golde and syluer for to spende
Without lackynge or daungere
As it were pourde in a garnere.

And after on the daunce went
Largesse/ that sette al her entent
For to ben honorable and free
Of Alexanders kynne was she
Her most ioye was ywis
Whan that she yafe/ and said: haue this
Nat Auarice the foule captife
Was halfe to grype so ententyfe
As Largesse is/ to yeue and spende
And god alwaye ynowe her sende
So that the more she yaue awaye
The more ywis she had alwaye
Great loos hath Largesse/ and great prise
For bothe wyse folke and unwyse
Were wholy to her bandon brought
So wel with yeftes hath she wrought
And if she had an enemy
I trowe that she couthe craftely
Make hym ful soone her frende to be
So large of yeftes/and wyse was she
Therfore she stode in loue and grace
Of riche and poore in euery place
A ful great foole is he ywis
That bothe riche and poore/and nygarde is
A lorde may haue no maner vyce
That greueth more than auarice
For nygarde neuer with strength of hande
May wynne hym great lordship or lande
For frendes al to fewe hath he
To done his wyl performed be
And who so wol haue frendes here
He maye nat holde his treasour dere
For by ensample tel I this
Right as an adamant ywis
Can drawen to hym subtelly
The yron/that is layde therby
So draweth folkes hertes iwys
Syluer and golde that yeuen is
Largesse had on a robe fresshe
Of riche purpure Sarlynysshe
Wel fourmed was her face and clere
And opened had she her colere
For she right there had in present
Unto a lady made present
Of a golde broche/ful wel wrought
And certes it missate her nought
For through her smocke wrought with sylke
The flesshe was sene as whyte as mylke
Largesse/ that worthy was and wyse
Helde by the honde a knyght of prise
Was sybbe to Arthour of Breteigne
And that was he that bare the enseigne
Of worshyp/and the Gouffaucoun
And yet he is of suche renoun
That men of hym say fayre thynges
Before barons/erles/and kynges
This knyght was comen al newly
Fro tourneyeng faste by
There had he done great chyualrie
Through his vertue and his maystrie
And for the loue of his lemman
He caste downe many a doughty man
And nexte hym daunced dame Fraunchise
Arayed in ful noble gyse
She nas nat browne ne dunne of hewe
But white as snowe yfallen newe
Her nose was wrought at poynt deuyse
For it was gentyl and tretyse
With eyen glade/ and browes bent
Her heer downe to her heles went
And she was symple as downe on tree
Ful debonayre of hert was she
She durst neither saye ne do
But that/that hyr longeth to
And if a man were in distresse
And for her loue in heuynesse
Her herte wolde haue ful great pyte
She was so amyable and free
For were a man for her bestadde
She wolde ben right sore a dradde
That she dyd ouer great outrage
But she hym holpe his harme taswage
Her thought it al a vylanye

B.b.ii. And

And she had on a sukkeny
That nat of hempe heerdes was
So fayre was none in al Arras
Lorde it was ryddeled fetysly
There nas nat a poynt trewly
That it nas in his right assyse
Ful wel yclothed was Fraunchise
For there nys no clothe sytteth bette
On damosel/ than dothe rokette
A woman wel more fetyse is
In rokette/ than in cote ywis
The white rokette ryddeled fayre
Betokeneth that ful debonayre
And swete was she that it bere
By her daunced a Bachelere
I can nat tellen you what he hyght
But fayre he was and of good hyght
Al had he ben/ I saye no more
The lordes sonne of Wyndesore.
¶ And next that daunced Curtesy
That preysed was of lowe and hye
For neither proude ne fole was she
She for to daunce called me
I praye god gyue her good grace
For whan I come first in to the place
She nas nat nyce/ ne outrageous
But wyse and ware/ and vertuous
Of fayre speche/ and fayre answere
Was neuer wight myssayde of here
She bare no rancour to no wyght
Clere browne she was/ and therto bright
Of face and body auenaunt
I wotte no lady so plesaunt
She were worthy for to bene
An emperesse or crowned quene.
And by her went a knyght dauncyng
That worthy was and wel spekyng
And ful wel conde he done honour
The knyght was fayre and styffe in stour
And in armure a semely man
And wel beloued of his leman.
¶ Fayre Idelnesse than saugh I
That alwaye was me fast by
Of her haue I without fayle
Tolde you the shappe and appareyle
For (as I sayd) Lo/ that was she
That dyd to me so great bounte
She the gate of that gardyn
Undyd/ and let me passen in
And after daunced as I gesse
And she fulfylled of lustynesse
That nas not yet .xii. yere of age
With herte wylde/ and thought volage
Nyce she was/ but she ne mente
None harme ne sleight in her entente
But onely lust and iolyte
For yonge folke/ wel weten ye
Haue lytel thought/ but on her play
Her lemman was besyde alway
In suche a gyse that he her kyste
At al tymes that him lyste
That al the daunce myght it se
They make no force of preuyte
For who so spake of hem yuel or wele
They were a shamed neuer a dele
But men myght sene hem kysse there
As it two yonge dowues were
For yonge was thylke bachelere
Of beaute wot I non his pere
And he was right of suche an age
As Youthe his lefe/ and suche corage
The lusty folke that daunced there
And also other that with hem were
That weren al of her meyne
Ful hende folke/ wyse/ and free
And folke of fayre porte truely
There were al comenly
Whan I had sene the countenaunces
Of hem that ladden thus these daunces
Than had I wyl to gon and se
The gardyn that so lyked me
And loken on these fayre Laurelles
On Pyne trees/ Cedres/ and Olmetres
The daunces than ended were
For many of hem that daunced there
Were with her loues went away
Under the trees to haue her play.

A Lorde they lyued lustely
A great foole were he sykerly
That nolde his thankes suche lyfe lede
For this dare I sayne out of drede
That who so myght so wel fare
For better lyfe durst him not care
For there nys so good paradyse
As to haue a loue at his deuyse

Out

Out of that place went I tho
And in that gardyn gan I go
Playeng a songe ful merily
The god of Loue ful hastely
Vnto him Swete Lokyng clepte
No lenger wolde he that she kept
His bowe of golde/that shone so bright
He had hym bent anon right
And he ful sone sette an ende
And at a brayde he gan it bende
And toke him of his arowes fyue
Ful sharpe and redy for to driue
Nowe god that sytteth in maieste
Fro dedly woundes he kepe me
If so be that he had me shete
For if I with his arowe mete
It had me greued sore ywis
But I that nothyng wyste of this
Went vp and downe/ful many a way
And he me folowed faste alway
But no where wolde I rest me
Tyll I had in al the gardyn be.

The gardyn was by mesuryng
Right euen and square in compasyng
It as longe was as it was large
Of fruite had euery tree his charge
But it were any hydous tree
Of whiche there were two or thre
There were/and that wote I ful wele
Of Pome garnettes a ful great dele
That is a fruite ful welle to lyke
Namely to folke whan they ben syke
And trees there were/great foyson
That baren nuttes in her season
Suche as men notemygges call
That swote of sauour ben withall
And Almandres great plente
Fygges/and many a date tre
There weren/ if men had nede
Through the gardyn/in lenght and brede
There was eke weyyng many a spyce
As clowe gylofre/and lycorice
Gyngere/and greyn de Parys
Canell/ and setewale of pris
And many a spyce delytable
To eeten whan men ryse fro table
And many homely trees ther were
That peches/ coynes/and apples bere
Medlers/plommes/peeres/chesteyns
Cheryse/ of whiche many one fayne is
Notes/aleys/and bolas
That for to sene it was solas
With many hygh laurer/and pyne
Was renged clene al that gardyne
With Cipres/and with Oliueris
Of whiche that nygh no plenty here is
There were Elmes great and stronge
Maples/asshe/oke/aspe/planes longe
Fyne ewe/popler/and lyndes fayre
And other trees ful many a payre
What shulde I tel you more of it?
There were so many trees yet
That I shulde al encombred be
Er I had rekened euery tree
These trees were sette that I deuyse
One from another in assyse
Fyue fadome or syxe/ I trowe so
But they were hye and great also
And for to kepe out wel the sonne
The croppes were so thicke yronne
And euery braunche in other knytte
And ful of grene leues sytte
That sonne myght there none discende
Lest the tender grasses shende
There myght men Does and Roes y se
And of squyrels ful great plente
From bowe to bowe alwaye lepynge
Connes there were also playenge
That comyn out of her clapers
Of sondrie colours and maners
And maden many a tourneyeng
Vpon the fresshe grasse spryngyng
In places sawe I welles there
In whiche there no frogges were
And fayre in shadowe was euery wel
But I ne can the nombre tel
Of stremys smal that by deuyse
Myrthe had done come through condyse
Of whiche the water in rennyng
Gan make a noyse ful lykyng
About the brinkes of these welles
And by the stremes ouer al elles
Sprange vp the grasse/as thicke yset
And softe as any veluet
On whiche men myght his leman ley

As on a fetherbed to slepe
For the erthe was ful softe and swete
Through moisture of the wel wete
Spronge vp the sote grene gras
As fayre/ as thicke/ as myster was
But moche amended it the place
That therthe was of suche a grace
That it of floures hath plente
That bothe in somer and wynter be
  There sprange the vyolet al newe
And fresshe peruynke riche of hewe
And floures yelowe/ white/ and rede
Suche plente grewe there neuer in mede
Ful gaye was al the grounde and queynt
And poudred/ as men had it peynt
With many a fresshe and sondre floure
That casten vp ful good sauour
  I wol nat longe holde you in fable
Of al this garden delectable
I mote my tonge stynten nede
For I ne maye withouten drede
Naught tellen you the beaute al
Ne halfe the bounte there with al
  I went on right honde and on lefte
About the place/ it was nat lefte
Tyl I had al the garden bene
In the esters that men myght sene
  And thus whyle I wente in my playe
The god of loue me folowed aye
Right as an hunter can abyde
The beest/ tyl he seeth his tyde
To shoten at goodnesse to the dere
Whan that hym nedeth go no nere
  And so befyl/ I rested me
Besydes a wel vnder a tree
Whiche tree in Fraunce men cal a Pyne
But sithe the tyme of kyng Peppyne
Ne grewe there tree in mannes syght
So fayre/ ne so wel woxe in hight
In al that yarde so high was none
And springyng in a marble stone
Had nature set/ the sothe to tel
Vnder that pyne tree a wel
And on the border al without
Was written in the stone about
Letters smal/ that sayden thus
Here starfe the fayre Narcisus.
  Narcisus was a bachelere
That loue had caught in his dangere
And in his nette gan hym so strayne
And dyd him so to wepe and playne
That nede him must his lyfe forgo
For a fayre lady that hight Echo
Him loued ouer any creature
And gan for hym suche payne endure
That on a tyme she him tolde
That if he her louen nolde
That her behoued nedes dye
There laye none other remedy
  But nathelesse for his beaute
So fers and daungerous was he
That he nolde graunten her askyng
For wepyng/ ne for fayre prayeng
  And whan she herde hym werne her so
She had in hert so great wo
And toke it in so great dispyte
That she without more respyte
Was deed anon: but ere she deyde
Ful pitously to god she prayde
That proude herted Narcisus
That was in loue so daungerous
Might on a day ben hampred so
For loue/ and ben so hote for wo
That neuer he myght to ioye attayne
Than shulde he fele in euery vayne
What sorowe trewe louers maken
That ben so vilaynously forsaken.

This prayer was but resonable
  Therfore god helde it ferme & stable
For Narcisus shortly to tel
By auenture came to that wel
To rest him in the shadowyng
A day/ whan he come from huntyng
  This Narcisus had suffred paynes
For rennyng al day in the playnes
And was for thurst in great distresse
Of herte/ and of his werynesse
That had his brethe almost benomen
Whan he was to that wel ycomen
That shadowed was with braunches grene
He thought of thilke water shene
To drinke/ and fresshe hym wele withal
And downe on knees he gan to fal
And forthe his necke and heed out straught
To drynke of that wel a draught

And

And in the water anon was sene
His nose/his mouthe/his eyen shene
And he therof was al abassshed
His owne shadowe had hym betrassshed
For wel wende he the forme se
Of a chylde of great beaute
Wel couthe loue him wreke tho
Of daunger and of pride also
That Narcisus somtyme hun bere
He quytte him wel his guerdon there
For he mused so in the well
That shortely the sothe to tell
He loued his owne shadowe so
That at laste he starfe for wo
For whan he sawe that he his wyll
Might in no maner way fulfyll
And that he was so faste caught
That he him couthe comforte naught
He loste his wytte/right in that place
And deyde within a lytell space
And thus his waryson he toke
For the lady that he forsoke
Ladyes I praye ensample taketh
Ye that ayenst your loue mistaketh
For if her dethe be you to wyte
God can ful wel your whyle quyte.

Whan that this lettre/of whiche I tell
Had taught me that it was the welle
Of Narcisus in his beaute
I gan anon withdrawe me
Whan it fell in my remembraunce
That him betyd suche mischaunce
But at the laste than thought I
That scathlesse/ful sykerly
I myght vnto the welle go
Wherof shulde I abasshen so
Vnto the welle than went I me
And downe I louted for to se
The clere water in the stone
And eke the grauel/whiche that shone
Downe in the botome/as syluer fyne
For of the welle/this is the fyne
In worlde is none so clere of hewe
The water is euer fresshe and newe
That welmeth vp/with wawes bright
The mountenaunce of two fynger hight
Aboute it is grasse springyng
For moyste so thycke and wel lykyng
That it ne may in wynter dye
No more than may the see be drye.
Downe at the botome set sawe I
Two cristall stones crafte ly
In thilke fresshe and fayre well
But o thyng sothly dare I tell
That ye wol holde a great meruayle
Whan it is tolde/withouten fayle
For whan the sonne clere in syght
Caste in that welle his bemes bright
And that the heete discended is
Than taketh the cristall stone ywis
Agayne the sonne an hundred hewes
Blewe/yelowe/and reed that fressh & newe is
yet hath the meruaylous cristall
Suche strength/that the place ouer all
Both foule and tree/and leues grene
And all the yerde in it is sene
And for to don you to vnderstonde
To make ensample wol I fonde
Right as a myrrour openly
Sheweth al thyng that stondeth therby
As wel the colour/as the fygure
Withouten any couerture
Right so the cristall stone shynyng
Withouten any discevuyng
The entrees of the yerde accuseth
To him that in the water museth
For euer in whiche halfe that ye be
ye may wel halfe the gardyne se
And if he turne/he may right wele
Sene the remenaunt euery dele
For there is none so lytel thyng
So hydde ne closed with shyttyng
That it ne is sene/as though it were
Paynted in the cristall there
This is the myrrour perillus
In whiche the proude Narcisus
Sey al his fayre face bright
That made hym sithe to lye vpright
For who so loke in that myrrour
There maye nothyng ben his socour
That he ne shal there se somthyng
That shal hym lede in to laughyng.
Ful many a worthy man hath it
yblent/for folke of greatest wyt
Ben soone caught here and wayted

With

Withouten respyte ben they bayted
Here cometh to folke of newe rage
Here chaungeth many wight corage
Here sythe no rede ne wytte therto
For Venus sonne/dan Cupido
Hath sowen there of loue the sede
That helpe ne sythe there none/ne rede
So cercleth it the welle aboute
His gynnes hath he set withoute
Right for to catche in his panters
These damosels and bachelers
Loue wyl none other byrde catche
Though he set eyther nette or latche
And for the sede that here was sowen
This welle is cleped/as wel is knowen
The welle of Loue/ of very right
Of whiche there hath ful many a wight
Spoken in bokes dyuersely
But they shul neuer so verily
Discripcion of the welle here
Ne eke the sothe of this matere
As ye shul/whan I haue vndo
The crafte that her belongeth to.

Al way me lyked for to dwell
To sene the christall in the well
That shewed me ful openly
A thousande thynges faste by
But I may say in sory houre
Stode I to loken or to powre
For sythen I sore syghed
That Myrrour hath me nowe entriked
But had I first knowen in my wyt
The vertue and strengthes of it
I nolde not haue mused there
Me had bette ben els where
For in the snare I fell anone
That had bytresshed many one
In thylke Myrrour sawe I tho
Amonge a thousande thynges mo
A Roser charged ful of rosis
That with an hedge aboute enclosis
Tho had I suche luste and enuye
That for Parys ne for Pauye
Nolde I haue lefte to gone and se
There greatest heape of roses be
Whan I was with this rage hente
That caught hath many a man and shente

Towarde the Roser gan I go
And whan I was not ferre therfro
The sauour of the roses swote
Me smote right to the herte rote
As I had al enbaumed me
And if I ne had endouted me
To haue ben hated or assayled
My thankes wol I not haue fayled
To pull a rose of al that route
To bere in myn honde aboute
And smellen to it where I went
But euer I dredde me to repent
And leste it greued or forthought
The lorde that thilke gardyn wrought
Of roses there were great wone
So fayre wure neuer in Rone
Of knoppes close/some sawe I there
And some wel better woxen were
And some there ben of other moyson.
That drowe nygh to her season
And spedde hem faste for to sprede
I loue wel suche roses rede
For brode roses/and open also
Ben passed in a day or two
But knoppes wyl fresshe be
Two dayes at leest/or els thre
The knoppes greatly lyked me
For fayrer may there no man se
Who so myght haue one of all
It ought hym ben ful lefe withall
Might I garlonde of hem geten
For no richesse I wolde it leten
Amonges the knoppes I chese one
So fayre/that of the remenaunt none
Ne preyse I halfe so wel as it
Whan I auyse in my wyt
For it so wel was enlumyned
With colour reed/as wel fyned
As nature couthe it make fayre
And it hath leaues wel foure payre
That kynde hath set through his knowyng
Aboute the redde roses sprungyng
The stalke was as rysshe right
And theron stode the knoppe vpright
That it ne bowed vpon no syde
The swote smell spronge so wyde
That it dyed al. the place aboute
Whan I had smelled the sauour swote

No

No wyl had I fro thence yet go
But somdele nere it went I tho
To take it/but myn honde for drede
Ne durste I to the Rose bede
For thystels sharpe of many maners
Netles/thornes/and hoked breres
For moche they distourbled me
For sore I dradde to harmed be.

The god of Loue/ with bowe bent
That al day set had his talent
To pursue and to spyen me
Was stondyng by a fygge tree
And whan he sawe howe that I
Had chosen so ententifly
The bothum more vnto my paye
Than any other that I say
He toke an arowe/ful sharply whette
And in his bowe whan it was sette
He streight vp to his eere drough
The stronge bowe/that was so tough
And shotte at me so wonder smerte
That through myn eye vnto myn herte
The takel smote/and depe it wente
And therwithal suche colde me hente
That vnder clothes warme and softe
Sythen that day I haue chyuered ofte
Whan I was hurte thus in stounde
I fell downe platte vnto the grounde
Myn herte fayled/ and faynted aye
And longe tyme in swoune I laye
But whan I came out of swounyng
And had wytte/and my felyng
I was al mate/ and wende ful wele
Of bloode haue lorne a ful great dele
But certes the arowe that in me stoode
Of me ne drewe no droppe of bloode
For why/I founde my woundes al drey
Than toke I with myn hondes twey
The arowe/and ful faste it out plyght
And in the pullyng sore I syght
So at the laste the shafte of tree
I drough out/with the fethers thre
But yet the hoked heed ywis
The whiche Beaute called is
Gan so depe in myn herte pace
That I it myght not arace
But in myn hert styl it stoode
Al bledde I not a droppe of bloode
I was bothe anguysshous and trouble
For the peryll that I sawe double
I nyste what to say or do
Ne get a leche my woundes to
For neyther through grasse ne rote
Ne had I helpe of hope ne bote
But to the bothum euer mo
Myn herte drewe/for al my wo
My thought was in none other thyng
For had it ben in my kepyng
It wolde haue brought my lyfe agayne
For certes euenly/I dare wel sayne
The sight onely/and the sauoure
Alegged moche of my langoure
Than gan I for to drawe me
Towarde the bothom fayre to se
And Loue had get him in his throwe
Another arowe in to his bowe
And for to shote gan hym dresse
The arowes name was Symplesse
And whan that Loue gan nygh me nere
He drowe it vp withouten were
And shotte at me with al his myght
So that this arowe anon right
Throughout eygh as it was founde
In to myn herte hath made a wounde
Than I anon dyd al my crafte
For to drawen out the shafte
And therwithal I syghed efte
But in myn herte the heed was lefte
Whiche aye encresed my desyre
Vnto the bothom drowe I nere
And euermo that me was wo
The more desyre had I to go
Vnto the Roser/where that grewe
The fresshe bothom/so bright of hewe
Better me were to haue letten be
But it behoued nede me
To don right as myn herte badde
For euer the body muste be ladde
After the herte/in wele and wo
Of force togyder they muste go
But neuer this archer wolde fyne
To shote at me with al his pyne
And for to make me to him mete
The thirde arowe he gan to shete
Whan best his tyme he myght espye

The

The whiche was named Curtesye
In to myn herte it dyd auale
A swoune I fel/ bothe deed and pale
Longe tyme I lay/and styred nought
Tyl I abrayde out of my thought
And faste than I auysed me
To drawe out the shafte of tree
But euer the heed was lefte behynde
For aught I couthe pull or wynde
So sore it stycked whan I was hytte
That by no crafte I myght it flytte
But anguysshous and ful of thought
I felte suche wo/my wounde aye wrought
That somoned me alway to go
Towarde the Rose/ that plesed me so
But I ne durste in no manere
Bycause the archer was so nere
For euermore gladly as I rede
Brent chylde of fyre hath moche drede
And certes yet for al my peyne
Though that I sygh/yet arowes reyne
And grounde quarels/sharpe of steele
Ne for no payne that I might fele
yet might I not my selfe with holde
The fayre Roser to beholde
For Loue me yaue suche hardyment
For to fulfyll his cōmaundement
Vpon my fete I rose vp than
Feble/as a forwounded man
And forthe to gon might I sette
And for the archer nolde I lette
Towarde the Roser faste I drowe
But thornes sharpe/mo than ynowe
There were/and also thystels thicke
And breres brimme for to pricke
That I ne myght get grace
The roughe thornes for to pace
To sene the Roses fresshe of hewe
I muste abyde/though it me rewe
The hedge aboute so thycke was
That closed the Roses in compas
But o thyng lyked me right wele
I was so nyghe/I myght fele
Of the bothom the swote odoure
And also se the fresshe coloure
And that right greatly lyked me
That I so nere might it se
Suche ioye anon therof had I
That I forgate my maladye
To sene I had suche delyte
Of sorowe and angre I was al quyte
And of my woundes that I had thore
For no thyng lyken me myght more
Than dwellen by the Roser aye
And thence neuer to passe awaye
But whan a whyle I had be thare
The god of Loue/ whiche al to share
Myn herte with his arowes kene
Casteth him to yeue me woundes grene
He shotte at me ful hastely
An arowe named Company
The whiche takell is ful able
To make these ladyes merciable
Than I anon gan chaungen hewe
For greuaunce of my wounde newe
That I agayne fel in swounyng
And syghed sore/in complaynyng
Sore I complayned that my sore
On me gan greuen more and more
I had non hope of allegeaunce
So nygh I drowe to dysperaunce
I rought of dethe/ne of lyfe
Whether that loue wolde me drife
If me a martyr wolde he make
I myght his power not forsake
And whyle for anger thus I woke
The god of Loue an arowe toke
Ful sharpe it was and pugnaunt
And it was called Fayre semblaunt
The whiche in no wyse wol consent
That any louer hym repente
To serue his loue/with herte and all
For any peryll that may befall
But though this arowe was kene grounde
As any rasour that is founde
To cutte and kerue at the poynte
The god of Loue it had anoynt
With a precious oyntment
Somdele to yeue alegement
Vpon the woundes that he hade
Through the body in my herte made
To helpe her sores/and to cure
And that they may the bette endure
But yet this arowe/without more
Made in myn herte a large sore
That in ful great payne I abode

But aye the oyntement went abrode
Throughout my woundes large & wyde
It spredde aboute in euery syde
Thorough whose vertue/and whose myght
Myn herte ioyful was and lyght
I had ben deed and al to shent
But for the precious oyntment
The shafte I drowe out of the arowe
Rokyng for wo right wonder narowe
But the heed/whiche made me smerte
Lefte behynde in myn herte
With other foure/I dare wel say
That neuer wol be take away
But the oyntment halpe me wele
And yet suche sorowe dyd I fele
That al day I chaunged hewe
Of my woundes fresshe and newe
As men might se in my vysage
The arowes were so ful of rage
So varyaunt of diuersyte
That men in eueryche might se
Bothe great anoye/and eke swetnesse
And ioye meynt with bytternesse
Nowe were they easy/nowe were they wood
In hem I felte bothe harme and good
Nowe sore without aleggement
Nowe softyng with oyntment
It softned here/and pricketh there
Thus ease and anger togyther were.

THe god of Loue delyuerly
Come lepande to me hastely
And sayd to me in great iape
Yelde the/for thou may not escape
May no defence auayle the here
Therfore I rede make no daungere
If thou wolte yelde the hastely
Thou shalt rather haue mercy
He is a foole in sykernesse
That with daunger or stoutnesse
Rebelleth/there that he shulde plese
In suche folye is lytel ese
Be meke/where thou muste nedes bowe
To stryue ayen is nought thy prowe
Come atones/and haue ydo
For I wol that it be so
Than yelde the here debonairly
And I answered ful humbly
Gladly sir/at your byddyng
I wol me yelde in al thyng
To your seruyce I wol me take
For god defende that I shulde make
Ayen your byddyng resystence
I wol not don so great offence
For if I dyd/it were no skyll
Ye may do with me what ye wyll
Saue or spyll/and also slo
Fro you in no wyse may I go
My lyfe/my dethe/is in your honde
I may not laste out of your bonde
Playne at your lyste I yelde me
Hopyng in herte/that somtyme ye
Comforte and ese shul me sende
Or els shortly/this is the ende
Withouten helthe/I mote aye dure
But if ye take me to your cure
Comforte or helthe/howe shulde I haue
Sythe ye me hurte/but ye me saue
The helthe of loue mote be founde
Where as they token first her wounde
And if ye lyst of me to make
Your prysoner/I wol it take
Of herte and wyll fully at gre
Holy and playne I yelde me
Without feynyng or feyntyse
To be gouerned by your emprise
Of you I here so moche prise
I wol ben hole at your deuyce
For to fulfyll your lykyng
And repente for nothyng
Hopyng to haue yet in some tyde
Mercy/of that I abyde
And with that couenaunt yelde I me
Anon downe knelyng vpon my kne
Proferyng for to kysse his fete
But for nothyng he wolde me lete.

And sayd/I loue the bothe and prise
Sens that thyn answer dothe me ese
For thou answered so curtesly
For nowe I wote wel vtterly
That thou arte gentyl by thy speche
For though a man ferre wolde seche
He shulde not fynden in certayne
No suche answere of no vilayne
For suche a worde ne myght nought

Isse

Isse out of a vylaynes thought
Thou shalt not lesen of thy speche
For thy helpyng wol I eche
And eke encresen that I maye
But first I wol that thou obaye
Fully for thyn auauntage
Anon to do me here homage
And sythe kysse thou shalte my mouthe
Whiche to no vilayne was neuer couthe
For to aproche it/ne for to touche
For sauf of cherles I ne vouche
That they shal neuer neigh it nere
For curteys/and of fayre manere
Wel taught/and ful of gentylnysse
He muste ben/that shal me kysse
And also of ful hygh fraunchyse
That shal atteyne to that emprise
And first of o thyng warne I the
That payne and great aduersyte
He mote endure/and eke trauayle
That shal me serue/without fayle
But there agaynst the to comforte
And with thy seruyce to disporte
Thou mayst ful glad and ioyful be
So good a mayster to haue as me
And lorde of so hygh renoun
I beare of loue the Gonfenoun
Of Curtesy the banere
For I am of the selfe manere
Gentyll/curteys/meke/and fre
That who euer ententyfe be
Me to honoure/doute/and serue
And also that he hym obserue
Fro trespace and fro vilanye
And hym gouerne in curtesye
With wyll and with entencion
For whan he first in my prison
Is caught/than muste he vtterly
Fro thence forthe ful besyly
Caste hym gentyll for to be
If he desyre helpe of me
Anon without more delay
Withouten daunger or affray
I become his man anone
And gaue hym thankes many a one
And kneled downe with hondes ioynt
And made it in my porte ful queynt
The ioye went to my hert rote
Whan I had kyssed his mouthe so swote
I had suche myrthe and suche lykyng
It cured me of languysshyng
He asked of me than hostages
I haue he sayd taken fele homages
Of one and other/where I haue bene
Distreyned ofte/withouten wene
These felons ful of falsyte
Haue many sythes begyled me
And through her falshede her luste acheued
Wherof I repent/and am agreued
And I hem get in my daungere
Her falshede shul they bye ful dere
But for I loue the/I say the playne
I wol of the be more certayne
For the so sore I wol nowe bynde
That thou away ne shalt not wynde
For to denyen the couenaunt
Or done that is not auenaunt
That thou were false/it were great ruthe
Sythe thou semest so ful of truthe
Sir/if the lyst to vnderstande
I meruayle the askyng this demaunde
For why or wherfore shulde ye
Hostages or borowes aske of me
Or any other sykernesse
Sythe ye wot in sothfastnesse
That ye me haue surprised so
And hole myne herte taken me fro
That it wol do for me nothyng
But if it be at your byddyng
Myn herte is yours/and myn right nought
As it behoueth/in dede and thought
Redy in al to worche your wyll
Whether so turne to good or yll
So sore it lusteth you to plese
No man therof may you disese
Ye haue theron sette suche iustyse
That it is werreyed in many wyse
And if ye doute it nolde obey
Ye may therof do make a key
And holde it with you for hostage
Nowe certes this is none outrage
(Quod loue) and fully I acorde
For of the body he is ful lorde
That hath the herte in his tresore
Outrage it were to asken more.

¶ Than

Than of his aumener he drough
A lytel key fetise ynough
Whiche was of golde polysshed clere
And sayd to me/ with this key here
Thyne herte to me nowe wol I shette
For al my iowel loke and knette
I bynde under this lytel key
That no wight maye cary awey
This key is ful of great poste
With whiche anon he touched me
Under the syde ful softely
That he myne herte sodainly
Without anoye hadde speered
That yet right nought it hath me deered
Whan he hadde done his wyl al out
And I had putte hym out of dout
Sir I sayd: I haue right great wyl
your luste and pleasure to fulfyl
Loke ye my seruyce take at gree
By thilke faythe ye owe to me
I saye nought for recreaundyse
For I nought doute of your seruyce
But the seruaunt traueyleth in vayne
That for to seruen dothe his payne
Unto that lorde/ whiche in no wyse
Conne hym no thanke for his seruyce.
Loue sayde/ dismay the nought
Syth thou for socour hast me sought
In thanke thy seruyce wol I take
And highe of degree I wol the make
If wyckednesse ne hynder the
But (as I hoope) it shal nought be
To worshyppe no wight by auenture
Maye come/ but if he payne endure
Abyde and suffre thy distresse
That hurteth nowe/ it shal be lesse
I wotte my selfe what maye the saue
What medicyne thou woldest haue
And if thy trouthe to me thou kepe
I shal unto thyne helpyng eke
To cure thy woundes and make hem clene
Where so they be olde or grene
Thou shalte be holpen at wordes fewe
For certainly thou shalte wel shewe
Where that thou seruest with good wyl
For to accomplysshen and fulfyl
My comaundementes daye and nyght
Whiche I to louers yeue of right.

Ah sir/ for goddes loue (sayd I)
Er ye passe hens ententyfely
Your comaundementes to me ye say
And I shal kepe hem if I may
For hem to kepen is al my thought
And if so be I wote hem nought
Than maye I unwyttingly
Wherfore I praye you entierly
With al myne herte/ me to lere
That I trespace in no manere
The god of Loue than charged me
Anon/ as ye shal here and se
Worde by worde/ by right empryse
So as the Romaunt shal deuyse
The maister leseth his tyme to lere
Whan the disciple wol nat here
It is but vayne on hym to swynke
That on his lernynge wol nat thynke
Who so luste loue/ lette him entende
For nowe the Romance begynneth to amende
Nowe is good to here in faye
If any be that canne it saye
And poynt it as the reason is
Sette for other gate ywis
It shal nat wel in al thyng
Be brought to good understondyng
For a reder that poynteth yl
A good sentence maye ofte spyl
The boke is good at the endyng
Made of newe and lusty thyng
For who so wol the endyng here
The craste of loue he shal nowe lere
If that he wol so longe abyde
Tyl I this Romance maye unhyde
And undo the signyfiaunce
Of this dreme in to Romaunce
The sothfastnesse that nowe is hydde
Without couerture shal be kydde
Whan I undone haue this dremyng
Wherin no worde is of leasyng.

Villany at the begynnyng
I wol saye loue ouer al thyng
Thou leaue/ if thou wolte be
False/ and trespace ayenst me
I curse and blame generally
Al hem that louen villany
For villany maketh villayne

L.c. And

And by his dedes a chorle is seyne
  These vilayns arne without pyte
Frendshyp/loue/and al bounte
I nyl receyue vnto my seruyce
Hem that ben vilayns of emprise
  But vnderstonde in thyn entent
That this is not myn entendement
To clepe no wight in no ages
Onely gentyl for his lynages
But who so is vertuous
And in his porte not outragyous
Whan suche one thou seest the beforne
Though he be not gentyl borne
Thou mayste wel seyne this is in sothe
That he is gentyl/by cause he dothe
As longeth to a gentylman
Of hem none other deme I can
For certaynly withouten drede
A chorle is demed by his dede
Of hye or lowe/as ye may se
Or of what kynrede that he be
Ne say nought for none yuel wyll
Thyng that is to holden styll
It is no worshyp to missey
Thou mayste ensample take of Key
That was somtyme for missayeng
Hated bothe of olde and yonge
As ferre as Gaweyn the worthy
Was praysed for his curtesye
Kaye was hated/for he was fell
Of worde dispytous and cruell
Wherfore be wyse and aqueyntable
Goodly of worde/and resonable
Bothe to lesse and eke to mare
And whan thou comest there men are
Loke that thou haue in custome aye
First to salue hem if thou may
And if it fall that of hem some
Salue the first/be not dōme
But quyte hem curtesly anon
Without abydyng/er they gon
  For nothyng eke thy tonge applye
To speke wordes of rybaudye
To vilayne speche/in no degre
Late neuer thy lyppe vnbounden be
For I nought holde him in good faythe
Curteys that foule wordes saythe
And al women serue and preyse
And to thy power her honour reyse
And if that any missayere
Dispyse women/that thou mayste here
Blame him/and bydde him holde him styll
And sette thy might/ and al thy wyll
Women and ladyes for to plese
And to do thyng that may hem ese
That they euer speke good of the
For so thou mayste best praysed be
  Loke fro pride thou kepe the wele
For thou mayste bothe parceyue and fele
That pride is bothe foly and synne
And he that pride hath him within
Ne may his herte in no wyse
Meken ne souplen to seruyce
For pride is founde in euery parte
Contrarye vnto loues arte
And he that loueth trewly
Shulde him conteyne iolyly
Without pride in sondrie wyse
And him disgysen in queyntyse
For queynte aray/without drede
Is nothyng proude/who taketh hede
For fresshe aray/as men may se
Without pride may ofte be
  Mayntayne thy selfe after thy rent
Of robe and eke of garnement
For many sythe fayre clothyng
A man amendeth in moche thyng
  And loke alwaye that they be shape
What garnement that thou shalte make
Of him that can best do
With al that parteyneth therto
Poyntes and sleues be wel syttande
Right and streight on the hande
Of shone and bootes/newe and fayre
Loke at the leest thou haue a payre
And that they sytte so fetously
That these rude may vtterly
Merueyle/ sythe that they sytte so playne
Howe they come an or of agayne
Weare strayte gloues with aumere
Of sylke/and alway with good chere
Thou yeue/if thou haue rychesse
And if thou haue naught spende the lesse
Alway be mery/ if thou may
But waste not thy good alway
Haue hatte of floures/ as fresshe as May

Cha

Chapelet of Roses of Whitsonday
For suche araye ne costneth but lyte
Thyne hondes wasshe/ thy tethe make white
And lette no fylthe vpon the be
Thy nayles blacke/ if thou mayst se
Voyde it away delyuerly
And kembe thyne heed right iolyly
Farce nat thy visage in no wyse
For that of loue is nat themprise
For loue dothe haten/ as I fynde
A beaute that cometh nat of kynde
Alway in hert I rede the
Gladde and mery for to be
And be as ioyful as thou canne
Loue hath no ioye of sorouful manne
That yuel is ful of curtesy
That knoweth in his malady
For euer of loue the sicknesse
Is meynte with swete and bytternesse
The sore of loue is meruaylous
For nowe the louer ioyous
Nowe can he playne/ nowe can he grone
Nowe can he syngen/ nowe maken mone
To day he playneth for heuynesse
To morowe he playneth for iolynesse
The lyfe of loue is ful contrarye
Whiche stoundemeale can ofte varye
But if thou canste myrthes make
That men in gre wol gladly take
Do it goodly/ I cōmaunde the
For men shulde where so euer they be
Do thynge that hem syttyng is
For therof cometh good loos and pris
Wherof that thou be vertuous
Ne be not straunge ne daungerous
For if that thou good ryder be
Pricke gladly that men may se
In armes also if thou conne
Pursue tyl thou a name hast wonne
And if thy voyce be fayre and clere
Thou shalt maken no great daungere
Whan to synge they goodly pray
It is thy worshyp for to obey
Also to you it longeth aye
To harpe and gyterne/ daunce and playe
For if he can wel fote and daunce
It may him greatly do auaunce
Amonge eke for thy lady sake
Songes and complayntes that thou make
For that wol meuen in her herte
Whan they reden of thy smerte
Loke that no man for scarce the holde
For that may greue the manyfolde
Reson wol that a louer be
In his yeftes more large and fre
Than chorles that ben not of louyng
For who therof can any thyng
He shal be lefe aye for to yeue
In loues lore who so wolde leue
For he that through a sodayne syght
Or for a kyssyng anon ryght
Yaue hole his herte/ in wyl and thought
And to hym selfe kepeth right nought
After this swyfte/ it is good reson
He yeue his good in abandon.

NOwe wol I shortly here reherce
Of that I haue sayd in verce
Al the sentence by and by
In wordes fewe compendously
That thou the better mayste on hem thynke
Whether so it be thou wake or wynke
For the wordes lytel greue
A man to kepe/ whan it is breue
Who so with loue wol gon or ryde
He mote be curteyes/ and voyde of pride
Mery/ and ful of iolyte
And of largesse alosed be.

First I ioyne the here in penaunce
That euer without repentaunce
Thou set thy thought in thy louyng
To laste without repentyng
And thinke vpon thy myrthes swete
That shal folowe after whan ye mete.

And for thou trewe to loue shalt be
I wyl/ and cōmaunde the
That in one place thou set al hole
Thyn herte/ without halfen dole
For trecherye and sykernesse
For I loued neuer doublenesse
To many his herte that wol departe
Eueryche shal haue but lytel parte
But of him drede I me right nought
That in one place setteth his thought

C.c. ii. Ther.

Therfore in o place it sette
And sette it neuer thens flette
For if thou yeuest it in lenyng
I holde it but a wretched thyng
Therfore yeue it hole and quyte
And thou shalte haue the more meryte
If it be lent/ than after soone
The bounte and the thanke is done
But in Loue/ free yeuen thyng
Requyreth a great guerdonyng
Yeue it in yefte al quyte fully
And make thy gifte debonairly
For men that yefte holde more dere
That yeuen is with gladsome chere
That gifte nought to praysen is
That man yeueth maugre his
Whan thou hast yeuen thyne hert (as I
haue sayde) the here openly
Than auentures shul the fal
Whiche harde and heuy ben with al
For ofte whan thou bethynkest the
Of thy louyng/ where so thou be
Fro folke thou must departe in hye
That none perceyue thy malady
But hyde thyne harme thou must alone
And go forthe sole/ and make thy mone
Thou shalte no whyle be in o state
But whylom colde and whilom hate
Nowe reed as Rose/ nowe yelowe and fade
Suche sorowe I trowe thou neuer hade
Cotidien/ ne quarteyne
It is nat so ful of peyne
For often tymes it shal fal
In loue/ among thy paynes al
That thou thy selfe al holy
Foryeten shalte so vtterly
That many tymes thou shalte be
Styl as an ymage of tree
Domme as a stone/ without steryng
Of fote or honde/ without spekyng
Than soone after al thy payne
To memorye shalte thou come agayne
A man abasshed wonder sore
And after syghen more and more
For wytte thou wele withouten wene
In suche astate ful ofte haue bene
That haue the yuel of loue assayde
Wherthrough thou arte so dismayde.

After a thought shal take the so
That thy loue is to ferre the fro
Thou shalte saye (god) what may this be
That I ne maye my lady se?
Myne herte alone is to her go
And I abyde al sole in wo
Departed fro myne owne thought
And with myne eyen se right nought
Alas myne eyen sene I ne may
My careful hert to conuay
Myne hertes gyde / but they be
I prayse nothyng what euer they se
Shul they abyde than/ nay
But gone and visyten without delay
That myne herte desyreth so
For certainly/ but if they go
A foole my selfe I maye wel holde
Whan I ne se what myne hert wolde
Wherfore I wol gone her to sene
Or eased shal I neuer bene
But I haue some tokenyng
Than gost thou forthe without dwellyng
But ofte thou faylest of thy desyre
Er thou mayst come her any nere
And wastest in vayne thy passage
Than fallest thou in a newe rage
For want of syght/ thou gynnest murne
And hom warde pensyfe thou dost returne
In great myschefe than shalte thou be
For than agayne shal come to the
Sighes and playntes with newe wo
That no itchyng pricketh so
Who wote it nought/ he maye go lere
Of hem that byen loue so dere
No thynge thyne herte appesen maye
That ofte thou wolte gone and assaye
If thou mayst sene by auenture
Thy lyues ioye/ thyne hertes cure
So that by grace/ if thou myght
Attayne of her to haue a syght
Than shalte thou done none other dede
But with that syght thyne eyen fede
That fayre fresshe whan thou mayst se
Thyne hert shal so rauysshed be
That neuer thou woldest thy thankes lete
Ne remoue/ for to se that swete
The more thou seest in sothfastnesse
The more thou coyptest of that swetnesse

The

The more thyn herte brenneth in fyre
The more thyn herte is in desyre
For who consydreth euery dele
It may be lykened wonder wele
The payne of loue vnto a fere
For euermore thou neyghest nere
Thought/or who so that it be
For very sothe I tel it the
The hotter euer shal thou brenne
As experyence shal the kenne
Where so comest in any coste
Who is next fyre he brenneth moste
And yet forsothe for al thyn hete
Though thou for loue swelte and swete
Ne for no thyng thou felen may
Thou shalt not wyllen to passe away
And though thou go/yet muste the nede
Thynke al day on her fayre hede
Whom thou behelde with so good wyll
And holde thy selfe begyled yll
That thou ne haddest none hardyment
To shewe her aught of thyn entent
Thyn herte ful sore thou wolte dispyse
And eke repreue of cowardyse
That thou so dull in euery thyng
Were dome for drede/without spekyng
Thou shalt eke thynke thou dyddest folye
That thou were her so faste bye
And durste not auntre the to say
Some thyng/er thou came away
For thou haddest no more wonne
To speke of her whan thou begonne
But yet she wolde for thy sake
In armes goodly the haue take
It shulde haue be more worthe to the
Than of tresour great plente
Thus shalte thou morne and eke cõplayne
And get encheson to gon agayne
Vnto thy walke/or to thy place
Where thou behelde her fleshly face
And neuer for false suspection
Thou woldest fynde occasyon
For to gone vnto her house
So arte thou than desyrouse
A syght of her for to haue
If thou thyn honour myghtest saue
Or any erande mightest make
Thyder/for thy loues sake
Ful fayne thou woldest/but for drede
Thou goest not/lest that men take hede
Wherfore I rede in thy goynge
And also in thyn agayne cõmynge
Thou be wel ware that men ne wyt
Feyne the other cause than it
To go that waye/or faste bye
To heale wel is no folye
And if so be it happe the
That thou thy loue there mayste se
In syker wyse thou her salewe
Wherwith thy coloure wol transmewe
And eke thy bloode shal al to quake
Thy hewe eke chaungen for her sake
But worde and wytte/with chere ful pale
Shul wante for to tel thy tale
And if thou mayste so ferforthe wynne
That thou reson durste begynne
And woldest sayne thre thynges or mo
Thou shalte ful scarsly sayne the two
Though thou bethynke the neuer so wele
Thou shalt foryete yet somdele.

BVt if thou deale with trecherye
For false louers mowe al folye
Sayne what hem luste withouten drede
They be so double in her falshede
For they in herte can thynke o thynge
And sayne another in her spekynge
And whan thy speche is ended all
Right thus to the it shal befall
If any worde than come to mynde
That thou to saye haste lefte behynde
Than thou shalt brenne in great martyre
For thou shalt brenne as any fyre
This is the stryfe and eke the affraye
And the batell that lasteth aye
This bargayne ende may neuer take
But if that she thy peace wyl make
And whan the nyght is comen anon
A thousande angres shal come vpon
To bedde as faste thou wolte the dyght
Where thou shalt haue but smal delyght
For whan thou wenest for to slepe
So ful of payne shalt thou crepe
Sterte in thy bedde aboute ful wyde
And turne ful ofte on euery syde
Nowe downwarde groffe/& nowe vpright

And wasowe in wo the longe nyght
Thyn armes shalt thou sprede a brede
As man in werre were forwerede
Than shal the come a remembraunce
Of her shappe and her semblaunce
Wherto none other may be pere
And wete thou wel without were
That the shal se somtyme that nyght
That thou haste her/that is so bright
Naked bytwene thyn armes there
Al sothfastnesse as though it were
Thou shalte make castels than in Spayne
And dreme of ioy/al but in vayne
And the delyten of right nought
Whyle thou so slombrest in that thought
That is so swete and delytable
The whiche in sothe nys but a fable
For it ne shal no whyle laste
Than shalte thou syghe and wepe faste
And say dere god/what thyng is this
My dreme is turned al amys
Whiche was ful swete and apparent
But nowe I wake it is al shent
Nowe yede this mery thought away
Twenty tymes vpon a day
I wolde this thought wolde come agayne
For it alegeth wel my payne
It maketh me ful of ioyfull thought
It sleeth me that it lasteth nought
Ah lorde/ why nyl ye me socoure?
The ioye I trowe that I langoure
The dethe I wolde me shulde slo
Whyle I lye in her armes two
Myn harme is harde withouten wene
My great vnease ful ofte I mene.

But wolde Loue do so I might
Haue fully ioye of her so bright
My payne were quytte me rychely
Alas to great a thyng aske I
It is but foly/and wronge wenyng
To aske so outragyous a thyng
And who so asketh folily
He mote be warned hastely
And I ne wote what I may say
I am so ferre out of the way
For I wolde haue ful great lykyng
And ful great ioy of lasse thyng
For wolde she of her gentylnesse
Withouten more/ me ones kesse
It were to me a great guerdon
Relece of al my passyon
But it is harde to come therto
Al is but foly that I do
So hygh I haue myn herte sette
Where I may no comforte gette
I wote not where I say wel or nought
But this I wote wel in my thought
That it were better of her alone
For to stynte my wo and mone
A loke on her I caste goodly
That for to haue al vtterly
Of an other al hole the play
Ah lorde where I shal byde the day
That euer she shal my lady be
He is ful cured/that may her se
A god/ whan shal the dawnyng spring?
To lyggen thus is an angry thyng
I haue no ioy thus here to lye
Whan that my loue is not me bye
A man to lyen hath great disese
Whiche may not slepe/ne rest in ese
I wolde it dawed/and were nowe day
And that the nyght were went away
For were it day/I wolde vp ryse
Ah slowe sonne/shewe thyn enprise
Spede the to sprede thy beemes bright
And chace the derknesse of the nyght
To put away the stoundes stronge
Whiche in me lasten al to longe

The nyght shalt thou contynue so
Without rest/in payne and wo
If euer thou knewe of loue distresse
Thou shal mowe lerne in that sicknesse
And thus enduryng shalt thou lye
And ryse on morowe vp erly
Out of thy bedde/and harneys the
Er euer dawnyng thou mayst se
Al priuely than shalt thou gone
What whyder it be thy selfe alone
For reyne/or hayle/for snowe/for slete
Thyder she dwelleth/ that is so swete
The whiche may fall a slepe be
And thynketh but lytel vpon the
Than shalt thou go/ful foule aferde
Loke if the gate be vnsperde

And

And wayle without in wo and payne
Ful yuel a colde in wynde and rayne
Than shalt thou go the dore before
If thou mayste fynde any shore
Or hole/or refte/what euer it were
Than shalte thou stoupe/and lay to eere
If they within a slepe be
I mene al saue thy lady free
Whom wakyng if thou mayst aspye
Go put thy selfe in iupardye
To aske grace/and the bymene
That she may wete without wene
That thou nyght no rest haste had
So sore for her thou were bestad
 Women wel ought pyte to take
Of hem that sorowen for her sake
And loke for loue of that relyke
That thou thynke none other lyke
For whan thou haste so great annoy
Shal kysse the er thou go awey
And holde that in ful great deynte
And for that no man shal the se
Before the house/ne in the way
Loke thou begon agayne er day
Suche comyng/ and suche goyng
Suche heuynesse/and suche wakyng
Maketh louers withouten any wene
Under her clothes pale and lene
For Loue leueth colour ne cleernesse
Who loueth trewe hath no fatnesse
Thou shalte wel by thy selfe se
That thou must nedes assayed be
For men that shape hem other way
Falsely her ladyes for to betray
It is no wonder though they be fatte
With false othes her loues they gatte
For ofte I se suche losengeours
Fatter than Abottes or priours
 Yet with o thynge I the charge
That is to saye/ that thou be large
Unto the mayde/ that her dothe serue
So best her thanke thou shalt deserue
Yeue her yeftes/and get her grace
For so thou may thanke purchace
That she the worthy holde and fre
Thy lady/and al that may the se
Also her seruauntes worshyp aye
And please as muche as thou may
Great good through hem may come to the
Bycause with her they ben priue
They shal her tel howe they the fande
Curteys and wyse/and wel doande
And she shal preyse wel the more
Loke out of londe thou be not fore
And if suche cause thou haue/that the
Behoueth to gone out of countre
Leaue hole thyn herte in hostage
Tyl thou agayne make thy passage
Thynke longe to se the swete thyng
That hath thyn herte in her kepyng
 Nowe haue I tolde the/in what wise
A louer shal do me seruyce
Do it than/if thou wolte haue
The mede/ that thou after craue.

When Loue al this had boden me
I sayd him/sir howe may it be
That louers may in suche manere
Endure the payn ye haue said here
I meruayle me wonder faste
Howe any man may lyue or laste
In suche payne/and suche brennyng
In sorowe and thought/and suche sighyng
Aye unreleued wo to make
Whether so it be they slepe or wake
In suche anoy contynuelly
As helpe me god this meruayle I
Howe man/but he were made of stele
Might lyue a monthe/suche paynes to fele.

The god of loue than sayd me
Frende/by the faythe I owe to the
May no man haue good/ but he it bye
A man loueth more tenderlye
The thyng/ that he hath bought most dere
For wete thou wel without were
In thanke that thynge is taken more
For whiche a man hath suffred sore
Certes no wo ne may attayne
Unto the sore of loues payne
None yuel therto ne may amounte
No more than a man counte
The droppes that of the water be
For drie as wel the great see
Thou myghtest/as the harmes tell
Of hem that with Loue dwell

In

In seruyce/ for peyne hem sleeth
And that eche man wolde flye the dethe
And trowe they shulde neuer escape
Nere that hoope couth hem make
Gladde as man in prison sete
And maye nat getten for to ete
But barlye breed/ and water pure
And lyeth in vermyn and in ordure
With al this yet caune he lyue
Good hope suche comforte hath hym yeue
Whiche maketh wene that he shal be
Delyuered and come to lyberte
In fortune is ful trust
Though he lye in strawe or dust
In hoope is al his sustaynyng
And so for louers in her wenyng
Whiche loue hath shytte in his prisoun
Good hope is her saluatioun
Good hope (howe sore that they smerte)
yeueth hem bothe wyl and herte
To profer her body to martyre
For Hope so sore dothe hem desyre
To suffre eche harm that men deuyse
For ioye that afterwarde shal aryse.

Hope in desyre catche victorie
In hoope of loue is al the glorie
For hoope is al that loue maye yeue
Nere hoope/ there shulde no lenger lyue
Blessed be hoope/ whiche with desyre
Auaunceth louers in suche manyre
Good hope is curteyse for to please
To kepe louers from al disease
Hoope kepeth his londe/and wol abyde
For any peryll that maye betyde
For hoope to louers/ as most chese
Dothe hem endure al myschefe
Hoope is her helpe whan myster is
And I shal yeue the eke ywis
Thre other thynges/ that great solace
Dothe to hem that be in my lace
The first good that maye be founde
To hem that in my lace be bounde
Is Swete thought/ for to recorde
Thyng wherwith thou canst accorde
Best in thyne herte/ where she be
Thynkyng in absence is good to the
Whan any louer dothe complayne
And lyueth in distresse/ and in payne
Than Swete thought shal come as blyue
Awaye his angre for to dryue
It maketh louers to haue remembraunce
Of comforte/ and of highe plesaunce
That Hoope hath hight hym for to wynne
For thought anone than shal begynne
As ferre god wotte / as he can fynde
To make a myrrour of his mynde
For to beholde he wol nat lette
Her persone he shal afore hym sette
Her laughyng eyen persaunt and clere
Her shappe/ her forme/ her goodly chere
Her mouthe/ that is so gratious
So swete/ and eke so sauerous
Of al her feyters he shal take hede
His eyen with al her lymmes fede.

Thus Swete thynkyng shal aswage
The payne of louers/ and her rage
Thy ioye shal double without gesse
Whan thou thynkest on her semelynesse
Or of her laughyng/ or of her chere
That to the made thy lady dere
This comforte wol I that thou take.
And if the nexte thou wolte forsake
Whiche is nat lesse sauerous
Thou shuldest nat ben to daungerous.
The seconde shal be Swete speche
That hath to many one be leche
To bringe hem out of wo and were
And helpe many a bachelere
And many a lady sent socour
That haue loued paramour
Through spekyng/ whan they might here
Of her louers to hem so dere
To me it voydeth al her smerte
The whiche is closed in her herte
In herte it maketh hem glad and lyght
Speche whan they mowe haue syght
And therfore nowe it cometh to mynde
In olde dawes as I fynde
That clerkes writen that her knewe
There was a lady fresshe of hewe
Whiche of her loue made a songe
On him for to remembre amonge
In whiche she sayd/ whan that I here
Speken of him that is so dere

To

To me it voydeth al smerte
Iwys he sytteth so nere myn herte
To speke of him at eue or morowe
It cureth me of al my sorowe
To me is none so hygh plesaunce
As of his person dalyaunce
She wyste ful wel that Swete spekyng
Comforteth in ful moche thyng
Her loue she had ful wel assayde
Of him she was ful wel apayde
To speke of him her ioye was set
Therfore I rede the that thou get
A felowe that can wel concele
And kepe thy counsayle/and wel hele
To whom go shewe holly thyn herte
Bothe wel and wo/ioye and smerte
To gette comforte to him thou go
And priuely bytwene you two
Ye shal speke of that goodly thyng
That hath thyn herte in her kepyng
Of her beaute and her semblaunce
And of her goodly countenaunce
Of al thy state/thou shalt him say
And aske him counsayle howe thou may
Do any thyng that may her plese
For it to the shal do great ese
That he may wete thou truste him so
Bothe of thy wele and of thy wo
And if his herte to loue be sette
His companye is moche the bette
For Reson wol he shewe to the
Al vtterly his priuyte
And what she is he loueth so
To the playnly he shal vndo
Without drede of any shame
Bothe tel her renome and her name
Than shal he forther ferre and nere
And namely to thy lady dere
In syker wyse/ ye euery other
Shal helpen as his owne brother
In trouthe without doublenesse
And kepen close in sykernesse
For it is noble thyng in fay
To haue a man thou darste say
Thy priue counsayle euery dele
For that wol comforte the right wele
And thou shalt holde the wel apayed
Whan suche a frende thou haste assayed.

The thirde good of great comforte
That yeueth to louers moste disporte
Cometh of syght and beholdyng
That cleped is Swete lokyng
The whiche may none ese do
Whan thou arte ferre thy lady fro
Wherfore thou prese alway to be
In place/ where thou mayst her se
For it is thyng moste amerous
Moste delytable and fauerous
For to aswage a mannes sorowe
To sene his lady by the morowe
For it is a ful noble thyng
Whan thyn eyen haue metyng
With that relyke precious
Wherof they be so desyrous
But al day after sothe it is
They haue no drede to faren amys
They dreden neyther wynde ne rayne
Ne non other maner payne
For whan thyn eyen were thus in blysse
Yet of her curtesye ywysse
Alone they can not haue her ioye
But to the herte they conuoye
Parte of her blysse to him thou sende
Of al this harme to make an ende
The eye is a good messangere
Whiche can to the herte in suche manere
Tydynges sende/that hath sene
To voyde him of his paynes clene
Wherof the herte reioyseth so
That a great partye of his wo
Is voyded/and put away to flyght
Right as the derknesse of the nyght
Is chased with clerenesse of the moone
Right so is al his wo ful soone
Deuoyded clene/whan that the syght
Beholden may that fresshe wyght
That the herte desyreth so
That al his derknesse is ago
For than the herte is al at ese
Whan they sene that may hem plese
Nowe haue I declared the al out
Of that thou were in drede and doute
For I haue tolde the faythfully
What the may curen vtterly
And al louers that wol be
Faythful/and ful of stabylite

Good

Good hope alwaye kepe by thy syde
And swete thought make eke abyde
Swete Lokynge and swete Speche
Of al thyne harmes they shal be leche
Of euery thou shalte haue great plesaunce
If thou canst byde in sufferaunce
And serue wel without fayntise
Thou shalte be quyte of thyne emprise
With more guerdoun/ if that thou lyue
But al this tyme this I the yeue.

The god of Loue whan al the day
Had tauzt me/ as ye haue herd say
And enformed compendously
He vanysshed awaye al sodainly
And I alone lefte al soole
So ful of complaynt and of doole
For I sawe no man there me by
My woundes me greued wonderly
Me for to curen nothyng I knewe
Saue the bothom bright of hewe
Wheron was sette hooly my thought
Of other comforte knewe I nought
But it were through the god of Loue
I knewe nat els to my behoue
That myght me ease or conforte gete
But if he wolde hym entermete
The roser was withouten dout
Closed with an hedge without
As ye to forne haue herde me sayne
And fast I besyed and wolde fayne
Haue passed the haye/ if I myght
Haue getten in by any sleyght
Vnto the bothom so fayre to se
But euer I dradde blamed to be
If men wolde haue suspectioun
That I wolde of ententioun
Haue stole the Roses/ that there were
Therfore to entre I was in fere
But at the laste/ as I bethought
Wheder I shulde passe or nought
I sawe come with a gladde chere
To me/ a lusty bachelere
Of good stature and of good height
And Bialacoil forsoth he height
Sonne he was to Curtesy
And he me graunted ful gladly
The passage of the vtter hay
And sayd/ sir: howe that ye may
Passe/ if your wyl be
The fresshe Roser for to se
And ye the swete sauour fele
Your warrans may right wele
So thou the kepe fro folye
Shal no man do the vylanye
If I may helpe you in ought
I shal not fayne/ dredeth nought
For I am bounde to your seruyse
Fully deuoyde of feyntyse
Than vnto Bialacoyl sayd I
I thanke you sir ful hertely
And your beheste take at gre
That ye so goodly profer me
To you it cometh of great fraunchyse
That ye me profer your seruyse
Than after ful delyuerly
Through the breres anon went I
Wherof encombred was the haye
I was wel plesed/ the sothe to saye
To se the bothom/ fayre and swote
So fresshe spronge out of the rote.

And Bialacoyle me serued wele
Whan I so nyghe me might fele
Of the bothom the swete odour
And so lusty hewed of colour
But than a chorle/ foule him betyde
Besyde the roses gan him hyde
To kepe the roses of that Rosere
Of whom the name was Daungere
This chorle was hyd there in the greues
Couered with grasse and with leues
To spye and take whom that he fonde
Vnto that Roser put an honde
He was not soole/ for there was mo
For with him were other two
Of wicked maners/ and yuel fame
That one was cleped by his name
Wicked tonge/ god yeue him sorowe
For neyther at eue ne at morowe
He can of no man good speke
On many a iuste man dothe he wreke
There was a woman eke that hyght
Shame/ that who can reken ryght
Trespace was her fathers name
Her mother Reson/ and thus was shame
Brought

Brought of these ylke two
And yet had Trespasse neuer ado
With Reason/ ne neuer ley her by
He was so hydous and so vgly
I meane this/ that Trespasse hight
But Reason conceyueth of a sight
Shame of that I spake aforne
And whan that Shame was thus borne
It was ordayned/ that Chastite
Shulde of the Roser lady be
Whiche of the bothoms more and lae
With sondrie folke assayled was
That she ne wyste what to do
For Venus her assayleth so
That nyght and day from her she stal
Bothoms and Roses ouer al
To Reason than prayeth Chastyte
Whom Venus hath flemed ouer the see
That she her doughter wolde her lene
To kepe the Roser fresshe and grene
Anone Reason to Chastyte
Is fully assented/ that it be
And graunted her/ at her request
That Shame/ bycause she is honest
Shal keper of the Roser be
And thus to kepe it/ there were thre
That none shulde hardy be ne bolde
(Were he yonge or were he olde)
Agayne her wyl awaye to bere
Bothoms ne roses/ that there were
I hadde wel spedde/ had I nat bene
Awayted with these thre and sene
For Bialacoil/ that was so fayre
So gratious and debonayre
Quytte hym to me ful curtesly
And me to please badde that I
Shulde drawe me to the bothom nere
Prese in to touche the rosere
Whiche bare the roses/ he yafe me leue
This graunt ne myght but lytel greue
And for he sawe it lyked me
Right nygh the bothom pulled he
A leafe al grene/ and yaue me that
The whiche ful nyghe the bothom sat
I made of that leafe ful queynt
And whan I felte I was aqueynt
With Bialacoil/ and so pryue
I wende all at my wyl hadde be

Than wext I hardy for to tel
To Bialocoil howe me befel
Of Loue/ that toke and wounded me
And sayd/ Sir so mote I the
I maye no ioye haue in no wyse
Vpon no syde/ but it ryse
For sithe (if I shal nat feyne)
In herte I haue had so great peyne
So great anoye and suche affraye
That I ne wotte what I shal saye
I drede your wrathe to deserue
Leuer me were/ that knyues kerue
My body shulde in peces smal
Than in any wyse it shulde fal
That ye wrathed shulde ben with me
Saye boldely thy wyl (quod he)
I nyl be wrothe if that I maye
For nought that thou shalte to me saye.

Than sayd I sir/ not you displease
To knowen of my great vnese
In whiche only Loue hath me brought
For paynes great/ disese/ and thought
Fro day to day he dothe me drie
Supposeth not sir/ that I lye
In me fyue woundes dyd he make
The sore of whiche shal neuer slake
But ye the bothom graunt me
Whiche is moste passaunt of beaute
My lyfe/ my dethe/ and my martyre
And tresour/ that I most desyre
Than Bialacoil affrayde all
Sayd sir/ it may not fall
That ye desyre it may not aryse
What wolde ye shende me in this wyse?
A mokel foole than I were
If I suffred you away to bere
The fresshe bothom/ so fayre of syght
For it were neyther skyl ne right
Of the Roser ye broke the rynde
Or take the rose aforne his kynde
Ye are not curteys to aske it
Let it style on the Roser syt
And lette it growe tyl it amended be
And parfetly come to beaute
I nolde not that it pulled were
Fro the Roser that it bere
To me it is so lefe and dere

With

With that anon sterte out Daungere
Out of the place where he was hydde
His malyce in his chere was kydde
Ful great he was and blacke of hewe
Sturdy and hydous/ who so him knewe
Lyke sharpe urchons his heer was growe
His eyes reed sparclyng as the fyre glowe
His nose frounced ful kyrked stode
He come cryande as he were woode
And sayd/ Bialacoyl tel me why
Thou bryngest hyder so boldely
Him that so nyghe the Rosere
Thou worchest in a wronge manere
He thynketh to dishonour the
Thou arte wel worthy to haue maugre
To lette hym of the rosere wytte
Who serueth a felonne is yuel quytte
Thou woldest haue done great bounte
And he with shame wolde quyte the
Flye hence felowe/ I rede the go
It wanteth lytel he wol the slo
For Bialacoyl ne knewe the nought
Whan the to serue he sette his thought
For thou wolte shame him/ if thou myght
Bothe agayne reason and right
I wol no more in the affye
That comest so slyghly for tespy
For it proueth wonder wele
Thy sleight and trayson euery dele
I durst no more make there abode
For the chorle/ he was so wode
So ganne he thrette and manace
And through the haye he dyd me chace
For feare of him I trymbled and quoke
So chorlisshly his heed he shoke
And sayd/ if efte he myght me take
I shulde nat from his hondes scape
Than Bialacoil is fledde and mate
And I al soole disconsolate.
Was lefte alone in payne and thought
For shame to dethe I was nygh brought
Than thought I on my highe foly
Howe that my body utterly
Was yeue to payne and to martyre
And therto hadde I so great yre
That I ne durst the hayes passe
There was no hoope/ there was no grace
I trowe neuer man wyste of payne
But he were laced in loues chayne
Ne no man/ and sothe it is
But if he loue/ what anger is
Loue holdeth his heest to me right wele
Whan payne (he sayd) I shulde fele
No herte maye thynke/ ne tonge sayne
A quarter of my wo and payne
I myght nat with the angre last
Myne herte in poynt was for to brast
Whan I thought on the rose/ that so
Was through Daunger caste me fro
A longe whyle stoode I in that state
Tyl that me sawe so madde and mate
The lady of the highe warde
Whiche from her towre loked thiderwarde.

Reason men clepe that lady
Whiche from her toure delyuerly
Come downe to me without more
But she was neyther yonge ne hore
Ne hygh ne lowe/ ne fatte ne lene
But best/ as it were in a mene
Her eyen two were clere and lyght
As any candell/ that brenneth bright
And on her heed she had a crowne
Her semed wel an hygh person
For rounde enuyron her crownet
Was ful of ryche stones fret
Her goodly semblant by deuyse
I trowe was made in paradyse
For nature had neuer suche a grace
To forge a werke of suche compace
For certeyne/ but if the letter lye
God him selfe/ that is so hye
Made her after his ymage
And yafe her sythe suche auauntage
That she hath might and seignorie
To kepe men from al folye
Who so wol trowe her lore
Ne may offenden neuermore.

And whyle I stode thus derke and pale
Reson began to me her tale
She sayde/ Al hayle my swete frende
Foly and childhode wol the shende
Whiche the haue put in great affray
Thou haste bought dere the tyme of May
That made thyn herte mery to be

In

In yuel tyme thou wentest to se
The gardyn/ wherof ydelnesse
Bare the keye and was maistresse
Whan thou yedest in the daunce
With her and had aqueyntaunce
Her aqueyntaunce is perylous
First softe/ and after noyous
She hath trasshed without wene
The god of Loue hadde the nat sene
Ne had Idelnesse the conueyde
In the verger/ where Myrthe him pleyde
If folly haue supprised the
Do so that it recouered be
And be welware to take no more
Counsayle/ that greueth after sore
He is wyse/ that wol hym selfe chastyse
And though a yonge man in any wyse
Trespasse amonge/ and do folly
Lette hym nat tary/ but hastely
Lette hym amende what so be mys
And eke I counsayle the ywis
The god of Loue holly foryete
That hath the in suche payne sette
And the in herte tourmented so
I can nat sene howe thou maist go
Other wayes to garysoun
For Daunger/ that is so feloun
Felly purposeth the to werrey
Whiche is ful cruel the sothe to sey.

AND yet of Dangere cometh no blame
In rewarde of my doughter Shame
Whiche hath the Roses in her warde
As she that maye be no musarde
And wicked tonge is with these two
That suffreth no man thyder go
For er a thynge be do he shal
Where that he cometh ouer al
In fourty places/ if it be sought
Say thyng that neuer was don ne wrought
So moche trayson is in his male
Of falsnesse for to sayne a tale
Thou delest with angry folke ywis
Wherfore to the better is
From these folke awaye to fare
For they wol make the lyue in care
This is the yuel that loue they cal
Wherin there is but foly al
For loue is folly euery dell
Who loueth/ in no wyse maye do wel
Ne sette his thought on no good werke
His schole he leseth/ if he be a clerke
Or other crafte eke/ if that he be
He shal nat thryue therin/ for he
In loue shal haue more passyoun
Than Monke/ hermyte/ or chanoun
This payne is herde out of measure
The ioye maye eke no whyle endure
And in the possessyoun
Is moche trybulatioun
The ioye it is so shorte lastynge
And but in happe is the gettyng
For I se there many in trauayle
That at laste foule fayle
I was nothyng thy counsayler
Whan thou were made the homager
Of god of Loue to hastely
There was no wysdom but foly
Thyn herte was ioly/ but not sage
Whan thou were brought in suche a rage
To yelde the so redily
And to Loue of his great maystry.

I Rede the loue away to driue
That maketh the retche not of thy lyue
The foly more fro day to day
Shal growe/ but thou it put away
Take with thy tethe the bridel faste
To daunte thyn herte/ and eke the caste
If that thou mayst to get the defence
For to redresse thy first offence
Who so his herte alway wol leue
Shal fynde amonge that shal him greue.

Whan I her herde thus me chastyse
I answerde in ful angry wyse
I prayde her cesse of her speche
Eyther to chastyse me or teche
To bydde me my thought refreyne
Whiche Loue hath caught in his demeyne
What wene ye Loue wol consente
(That me assayleth with bowe bente)
To drawe myn herte out of his honde
Whiche is so quickly in his bonde
That ye counsayle may neuer be
For whan he first arested me

D. d. He

He toke myne herte so sore him tyll
That it is nothyng at my wyll
He thought it so hym for to obey
That he it sparred with a key
I pray you let me be al styll
For ye may wel/if that ye wyll
Your wordes waste in ydelnesse
For utterly/withouten gesse
Al that ye sayne is but in vayne
Me were lever dye in the payne
Than Love to mewarde shulde arette
Falshede or treson on me sette
I wol me get prys or blame
And love trewe to save my name
Who that me chastyseth/I him hate
With that worde Reson went her gate
Whan she sawe for no sermonyng
She myght me fro my foly bring
Than dismayed I lefte al soole
Forwery/ forwandred as a foole
For I ne knewe no cherysaunce
Than fel in to my remembraunce
Howe Love bade me to purvey
A felowe/to whom I might sey
My counsell and my privyte
For that shulde moche avayle me
With that bethought I me/ that I
Had a felowe fast by
Trewe and syker/ curteys/ and hende
And he was called by name a frende
A trewer felowe was no where non
In haste to him I went anon
And to him al my wo I tolde
Fro him right nought I wolde withholde
I tolde him al without were
And made my compleynt on Daungere
Howe for to se he was hydous
And to mewarde contraryous
The whiche through his cruelte
Was in poynte to have meymed me
With Bialacoil whan he me sey
Within the gardyn walke and pley
Fro me he made him for to go
And I belefte alone in wo
I durste no lenger with him speke
For Daunger sayd he wolde be wreke
Whan that he sawe howe I wente
The fresshe bothom for to hente
If I were hardy to come nere
Bytwene the hay and the Rosere.

This frende whan he wyst of my thought
He discomforted me right nought
But sayd felowe/be not so madde
Ne so abasshed nor bestadde
My selfe I knowe ful wel Daungere
And howe he is fiers of chere
At prime temps/love to manace
Ful ofte I have ben in his case
A felon first though that he be
After thou shalt him souple se
Of longe passed I knewe him wele
Ungoodly first though men him fele
He wol meke after in his berynge
Ben/ for servyce and obeyssynge
I shal the tel what thou shalt do
Mekely I rede thou go him to
Of herte pray him specially
Of thy trespace to have mercy
And hote him wel here to plese
That thou shalte never more him displese
Who can best serve of flatery
Shal plese Daunger moste utterly.

My frende hath sayd to me so wele
That he me eased hath somdele
And eke alegged of my turment
For through him had I hardement
Agayne to Daunger for to go
To preve if I might meke him so.

TO Daunger came I al ashamed
The whiche aforne me had blamed
Desyring for to pese my wo
But over hedge durste I not go
For he forbode me the passage
I founde him cruel in his rage
And in his honde a great burdown
To him I kneled lowe adown
Ful meke of porte/and symple of chere
And sayd sir/I am comen here
Onely to aske of you mercy
That greveth me ful greatly
That ever my lyfe I wrathed you
But for to amenden I am come now
With al my might/bothe loude and styll

To

To done right at your owne wyl
For Loue made me for to do
That I haue trespassed hiderto
Fro whom I ne maye withdrawe myne hert
yet shal I neuer for ioye ne smert
(What so befal good or il)
Offende more agayne your wyl
Leuer I haue endure disease
Than do that shulde you displease.

I You requyre/ and praye that ye
Of me haue mercy and pyte
To stynt your yre/ that greueth so
That I wol swere for euer mo
To be redressed at your lykyng
yf I trespasse in any thyng
Saue that (I praye the) graunt me
A thynge/ that maye nat warned be
That I maye loue al onely
None other thynge of you aske I
I shal done al wel ywis
yf of your grace ye graunt me this
And ye maye nat letten me
For wel wote ye/ that loue is free
And I shal louen suche that I wyl
Who euer lyke it wel or yl
And yet ne wolde I for al Fraunce
Do thynge to do you displesaunce.

Than Daungere fyl in his entent
For to foryeue his male talent
But al his wrathe yet at last
He hath released/ I prayde so fast
Shortely (he sayd) thy request
Is nat to mokel dishonest
Ne I wol nat werne it the
For yet nothynge engreueth me
For though thou loue thus euermore
To me is neither softe ne sore
Loue where that the lyst/ what retcheth me
So ferre fro my Roses be
Trust nat on me for none assaye
In any tyme to passe the haye
Thus hath he graunted my prayere
Than went I forthe withouten were
Unto my frende/ and tolde hym al
Whiche was right ioyful of my tale
(He sayd) nowe gothe wel thyne affayre
He shal to the be debonayre
Though he aforne was dispitous
He shal herafter be gratious
If he were touched on some good veyne
He shulde yet rewen on thy peyne
Suffre I rede/ and no boost make
Tyl thou at good mes mayst hym take
By sufferaunce/ and wordes softe
A man maye ouercome ofte
Hym/ that aforne he had in drede
In bokes sothely as I rede
Thus hath my frende with great comfort
Auaunced me with high disporte
Whiche wolde me good/ as moche as I
And than anone ful sodainly
I toke my leaue/ and streight I went
Unto the haye/ for great talent
I hadde to sene the freshe bothom
Wherin laye my saluatioun
And Daungere toke kepe/ if that I
Kepe hym couenaunt trewly
So sore I dradde his manasyng
I durste nat breke his byddyng
For lest that I were of hym shent
I brake nat his cōmaundement
For to purchase his good wyl
It was for to come there tyl
His mercy was to ferre behynde
I kepte/ for I ne myght it fynde
I complayned and syghed sore
And languysshed euermore
For I durst nat ouer go
Unto the Rose I loued so
Throughout my demyng utterly
That he had knowlege certainly
Than Loue me ladde in suche a wyse
That in me there was no feyntise
Falsheed/ ne no trechery
And yet he ful of villany
Of disdayne/ and cruelte
On me ne wolde haue pyte
His cruel wyl for to refrayne
Tho I wepte alwaye/ and me complayne
And whyle I was in this tourment
Were come of grace/ by god sent
Fraunchise/ and with her Pyte
Fulfylde the bothom of bounte
They go to Daungere anon ryght

D.d.ii. To

To forther me with al her myght
And helpe in worde and in dede
For wel they sawe that it was nede
First of her grace dame Fraunchise
Hath taken of this emprise
She sayd/ Daungere great wronge ye do
To worche this man so moche wo
Or pynen him so angerly
It is to you great villany
I canne nat se/ why ne how
That he hath trespassed agayne you
Saue that he loueth/ wherfore ye shulde
The more in cherete of him holde
The force of loue maketh hym do this
Who wolde him blame he dyd amys
He leseth more than ye maye do
His payne is harde/ ye maye se so
And Loue in no wyse wolde consent
That ye haue power to repent
For though that quicke ye wolde him slo
Fro loue his herte may nat go
Nowe swete sir/ it is your ease
Him for to angre or disease
Alas/ what maye it you auaunce
To done to him so great greuaunce
What worshippe is it agayne him take
Or on your man a werre make
Sithe he so lowly euery wyse
Is redy/ as ye luste deuyse
If Loue haue caught him in his lace
You for to bey in euery caas
And ben your subiecte at your wyl
Shulde ye therfore wylken him yl
Ye shulde him spare more al out
Than him that is bothe proude and stout
Curtesy wol that ye socure
Hem/ that ben meke vnder your cure
His hert is harde that wol nat meke
Whan men of mekenesse him beseke.

THis is certayne/ sayd Pyte
We se ofte that humylyte
Bothe yre/ and also felony
Venquyssheth/ and also melancoly
To stonde forthe in suche duresse
This cruelte and wickednesse
Wherfore I pray you sir Daungere
For to mayntene no lenger here
Suche cruel werre agayne your man
As holly yours as euer he can
Nor that ye worchen no more wo
Vpon this captife/ that languyssheth so
Whiche wol no more to you trespace
But put him holly in your grace
His offence ne was but lyte
The god of Loue it was to wyte
That he your thrall so greatly is
And if ye harme him ye done amys
For he hath had ful harde penaunce
Syth that ye refte him thaqueyntaunce
Of Bialacoil/ his moste ioye
Whiche al his paynes might acoye
He was before anoyed sore
But than ye doubled him wel more
For he of blysse hath ben ful bare
Sythe Bialacoil was fro hym fare
Loue hath to hym great distresse
He hath no nede of more duresse
Voydeth from him your yre I rede
Ye may not wynnen in this dede
Maketh Bialacoil repayre agayne
And haueth pyte vpon his payne
For Fraunchyse wol/ and I Pyte
That mercyful to him ye be
And sythe that she and I accorde
Haue vpon him misericorde
For I you pray/ and eke moneste
Nought to refusen our requeste
For he is harde/ and fel of thought
That for vs two wol do right nought
Daunger ne might no more endure
He meked him vnto mesure.

I wol in no wyse/ sayth Daungere
Deny/ that ye haue asked here
It were to great vncurtesye
I wol ye haue the companye
Of Bialacoil/ as ye deuyse
I wol him let in no wyse
To Bialacoil than went in hye
Fraunchise/ and sayd ful curtesly
Ye haue to longe be deignous
Vnto this louer/ and daungerous
Fro him to withdrawe your presence
Whiche hath do to him great offence
That ye not wolde vpon him se

Wher-

Wherfore a sorouful man is he
Shape ye to paye him/and to please
Of my loue if ye wol haue ease
Fulfyl his wyl / sithe that ye knowe
Daunger is daunted and brought lowe.
Through helpe of me and of Pyte
you dare no more aferde be
I shal do right as ye wyl
Saith Bialacoil/for it is skyl
Sithe Daunger wol that it so be
Than Fraunchise hath him sent to me.

Byalacoil at the begynnyng
Salued me in his cōmyng
No straungenesse was in him sene
No more than he ne had wrathed bene
As fayre semblaunt than shewed he me
And goodly/ as aforne dyd he
And vp the honde without dout
Within the haye right al about
He ladde me with right good chere
Al enuyron the vergere
That Daunger hadde me chased fro
Nowe haue I leaue ouer al to go
Nowe am I raysed at my deuyse
Fro hel vnto paradyse
Thus Bialacoil of gentylnesse
With al his payne and besynesse
Hath shewed me onely of grace
The estres of the swote place
I sawe the Rose whan I was nygh
Was greatter woxen/ and more high
Fresshe/ roddy/ and fayre of hewe
Of coloure euer yliche newe
And whan I hadde it longe sene
I sawe that through the leues grene
The Rose spredde to spaunysshinge
To sene it was a goodly thynge
But it ne was so sprede on brede
That men within myght knowe the sede
For it couert was and close
Bothe with the leues and with the rose
The stalke was euen and grene vpright
It was theron a goodly syght
And wel the better without wene
For the seed was nat sene
Ful fayre it sprad de the god of blesse
For suche another/ as I gesse
Aforne ne was ne more vermayle
I was abawed for maruayle
For euer the fayrer that it was
The more I am bounden in loues laas
Longe I abode there sothe to saye
Tyl Bialacoil I ganne to praye
Whan that I sawe him in no wyse
To me warnen his seruyce
That he me wolde graunt a thynge
Whiche to remembre is wel syttynge
This is to sayne/ that of his grace
He wolde me yeue leysar and space
To me that was so desyrous
To haue a kyssynge precious
Of the goodly fresshe Rose
That so swetely smelleth in my nose
For if it you displeased nought
I wolde gladly/ as I haue sought
Haue a cosse therof freely
Of your yefte/ for certainly
I wol none haue/ but by your leue
So lothe me were you for to greue

He sayd/ frende so god me spede
Of Chastite I haue suche drede
Thou shuldest nat warned be for me
But I dare nat for Chastyte
Agayne her dare I nat mysdo
For alwaye byddeth she me so
To yeue no louer leaue to kysse
For who therto maye wynnen ywisse
He of the surplus of the praye
My lyse in hoope to gette some daye
For who so kyssynge maye attayne
Of loues payne hath (sothe to sayne)
The best and most auenaunt
And ernest of the remenaunt.

Of his answere I sighed sore
I durst assaye him tho no more
I hadde suche drede to greue him aye
A man shulde nat to moche assaye
To chase his frende out of measure
Nor putte his lyfe in auenture
For no man at the first stroke
Ne maye nat fel downe an oke
Nor of the reysyns haue the wyne
Tyl grapes be rype and wel afyne
D. d. iii. Bi

Be sore empressed/ I you ensure
And drawen out of the pressure
But I forpeyned wonder stronge
Though that I abode right longe
After the kysse/ in payne and wo
Sithe I to kysse desyred so
Tyl that rennynge on my distresse
There come Venus the goddesse
(Whiche aye werreyeth Chastite)
Came of her grace to socour me
Whose myght is knowe ferre and wyde
For she is mother of Cupyde.

The god of Loue/ blynde as stone
That helpeth louers many one
This lady brought in her right honde
Of brennynge fyre a blasyng bronde
Wherof the flame and hote fyre
Hath many a lady in desyre
Of Loue brought/ and sore hette
And in her seruyce her hert is sette
This lady was of good entayle
Right wonderful of apparayle
By her atyre so bright and shene
Men myght perceyue wel and sene
She was nat of Relygioun
Nor I nyl make mencioun
Nor of robe/ nor of tresour
Of broche/ neither of her riche attour
Ne of her gyrdel about her syde
For that I nyl nat longe abyde
But knoweth wel/ that certainly
She was arraped richely
Deuoyde of pride certayne she was
To Bialacoil she went a paas
And to hym shortely in a clause
She sayd/ sir: what is the cause
Ye ben of porte so daungerous
Vnto this louer/ and daynous
To graunt him nothyng but a kysse
To warne it him ye done amysse
Sithe wel ye wotte/ howe that he
Is loues seruaunt/ as ye maye se
And hath beaute/ wherthrough is
Worthy of loue to haue the blys
Howe he is semely beholde and se
Howe he is fayre/ howe he is free
Howe he is swote/ and debonayre
Of age yonge/ lusty/ and fayre
There is no lady so hawtayne
Duchesse/ countesse/ ne chastelayne
That I nolde holde her vngoodly
For to refuse him vtterly
His brethe is also good and swete
And eke his lyppes roddy and mete
Onely to playne/ and to kysse
Graunt him a kysse of gentylnysse
His teth arne also white and clene
Me thynketh wronge withouten wene
If ye nowe warne him/ trusteth me
To graunt that a kysse haue he
The lasse ye helpe him that ye haste
And the more tyme shul ye waste
Whan the flame of the very bronde
That Venus brought in her right honde
Hadde Bialacoil with his hete smete
Anone he badde me withouten lete
Graunt to me the rose kysse
Than of my payne I ganne to lysse
And to the rose anone went I
And kyssed it ful faithfully
There nede no man aske/ if I was blythe
Whan the sauour softe and lythe
Stroke to myne hert without more
And me alegged of my sore
So was I ful of ioye and blysse
It is fayre suche a floure to kysse
It was so swote and sauerous
I myght nat be so anguysshous
That I mote gladde and ioly be
Whan that I remembre me
Yet euer amonge sothly to sayne
I suffre noye and moche payne.

The see may neuer be so styl
That with a lytel wynde at wyl
Ouer whelme and tourne also
As it were woode in wawes go
After the calme the trouble sonne
Mote folowe/ and chaunge as the moone
Right so fareth Loue/ that selde in one
Holdeth his ancre/ for right anone
Whan they in ease wene best to lyue
They ben with tempest al fordryue
Who serueth Loue/ canne tel of wo
The stoundmele ioye mote ouergo

Nowe

Nowe he hurteth/and nowe he cureth
For selde in o poynte loue endureth.

Nowe is it right me to procede
Howe Shame gan medle and take hede
Through whom fel angres I haue hade
And howe the stronge wall was made
And the castell of brede and length
That god of Loue wan with his strength
Al this in Romance wyll I sette
And for no thyng ne wyll I lette
So that it lykyng to her be
That is the flour of beaute
For she may best my labour quyte
That I for her loue shal endyte
Wicked tonge that the coupne
Of euery louer can deuyne
Worste/and addeth more somdele
(For wicked tonge sayth neuer wele)
To mewarde bare he right great hate
Espyeng me erly and late
Tyl he hath sene the great chere
Of Bialacoil and me yfere
He might not his tonge withstonde
Worse to reporte than he fonde
He was so ful of cursed rage
It satte hym wele of his lynage
For hym an Irisshe woman bare
His tonge was fyled sharpe and square
Poignaunt and right keruyng
And wonder bytter in spekyng
For whan that he me gan espye
He swore (affirmyng sykerly)
Bytwene Bialacoil and me
Was yuel aquayntaunce and priue
He spake therof so folilye
That he awaked Ielousye
Whiche al afrayde in his risyng
Whan that he herde ianglyng
He ran anon as he were wode
To Bialacoil there that he stode
Whiche had leuer in this caas
Haue ben at Reynes or Amyas
For foote hote in his felonye
To hym thus sayd Ielousye
Why haste thou ben so neglygent
To kepen/whan I was absent
This verger here left in thy warde:
To me thou haddest no regarde
To truste (to thy confusyon)
Hym thus/ to whom suspection
I haue right great/ for it is nede
It is wel shewed by the dede
Great faute in the nowe haue I founde
By god anone thou shalte be bounde
And faste loken in a toure
Without refuyte or socoure.

HOr shame to longe hath be the fro
Ouer soone she was ago
Whan yu hast lost bothe drede & fere
It semed wel she was nat here
She was besy in no wyse
To kepe the and chastice
And for to helpen Chastite
To kepe the Roser/as thynketh me
For than this boye knaue so boldly
Ne shulde nat haue be hardy
In this verge hadde suche game
Whiche nowe me tourneth to great shame.

BIalacoil nyst what to saye
Ful fayne he wolde haue fledde away
For feare haue hydde/ nere that he
Al sodainly toke him with me
And whan I sawe he had so
This Ielousye take vs two
I was astoned/and knewe no rede
But fledde away for very drede.

Than Shame came forthe ful symply
She wende haue trespaced ful greatly
Humble of her porte/and made it symple
Wearyng a vayle in stede of wymple
As nonnes done in her abbey
By cause her herte was in affray
She gan to speke within a throwe
To Ielousye/ right wonder lowe
First of his grace she besought
And sayd sir/ne leueth nought
Wicked tonge/that false espye
Whiche is so glad to fayne and lye
He hath you made/through flateryng
On Bialacoil a false leasyng
His falsnesse is not nowe a newe
It is to longe that he hym knewe

This

This is not the first daye
For wicked tonge hath custome aye
Yonge folkes to bewrye
And false lesynges on hem lye.

Yet neverthelesse I se amonge
That the loigne it is so longe
Of Bialacoil/ hertes to lure
In loves servyce for to endure
Drawyng suche folke him to
That he hath nothyng with to do
But in sothnesse I trowe nought
That Bialacoil had ever in thought
To do trespace or vilanye
But for his mother Curtesye
Hath taught him ever to be
Good of aqueyntaunce and prive
For he loveth none hevynesse
But myrthe and play/and al gladnesse
He hateth al trechours
Soleyne folke and envyous
For ye weten howe that he
Wol ever glad and ioyful be
Honestly with folke to pley
I have be neglygent in good fey
To chastyse him/therfore nowe I
Of herte I crye you here mercy
That I have ben so recheles
To tamen hym withouten lees
Of my foly I me repente
Nowe wol I hole set myn entente
To kepe bothe lowe and styll
Bialacoil to do your wyll

Shame Shame (sayd Jelousy)
To be bytrasshed great drede have I
Lecherye hath clombe so hye
That almoste blered is myn eye
No wonder is/if that drede have I
Over al reigneth lechery
Whose myght groweth nyght and dey
Bothe in cloystre and in abbey
Chastyte is werreyed over all
Therfore I wol with syker wall
Close bothe roses and rosere
I have to long in this manere
Lefte hem unclosed wylfully
Wherfore I am right inwardly
Sorouful/ and repente me
But nowe they shal no lenger be
Unclosed/ and yet I drede sore
I shal repent ferthermore
For the game gothe al amys
Counsayle I must newe iwys
I have to longe trusted the
But nowe it shal no lenger be
For he may best in every coste
Disceyve/that men trusten moste
I se wel that I am nyghe shent
But if I sette my ful entent
Remedye to purvey
Wherfore close I shal the wey
Fro hem that wol the rose espye
And come to wayte me vilonye
For in good faythe and in trouthe
I wol not let for no slouthe
To lyve the more in sykernesse
Do make anon a fortresse
Than close the roses of good favour
In myddes shal I make a tour
To put Bialacoil in prison
For ever I drede me of treson
I trowe I shal hym kepe so
That he shal have no might to go
Aboute to make companye
To hem that thynke of vilanye
Ne to no suche as hath ben here
Aforne/ and founde in him good chere
Whiche han assayled him to shende
And with her trowandyse to blende
A foole is eyth to begyle
But may I lyve a lytel while
He shal forthynke his fayre semblaunt.

And with that worde came Drede avaunt
Whiche was abasshed/and in great fere
Whan he wyste Jelousye was there
He was for drede in suche affray
That not a worde durste he saye
But quakyng stode ful styl alone
(Tyl Jelousye his way was gone)
Save Shame/that him not forsoke
Bothe Drede and she ful sore quoke
That at laste Drede abrayde
And to his cosyn Shame sayde

Shame (he sayd) in sothfastnesse
To me it is great hevynesse

That

That the noyse so ferre is go
And the sclaunder of vs two
But sythe that it is befall
We may it not agayne call
Whan ones spronge is a fame
For many a yere withouten blame
We haue ben/ and many a day
For many an Aprill/ and many a May
We han passed/ not shamed
Tyl Jelousye hath vs blamed
Of mystrust and suspection
Causelesse/ without encheson
So we to Daunger hastely
And let vs shewe hym openly
That he hath not a right wrought
Whan that he set not his thought
To kepe better the purprise
In his doyng he is not wyse
He hath to vs do great wronge
That hath suffred nowe so longe
Bialacoil to haue his wyll
Al his lustes to fulfyll
He muste amende it vtterly
Or els shal he vilaynously
Exyled be out of this londe
For he the werre may not withstonde
Of Jelousye/ nor the grefe
Sythe Bialacoil is at mischefe.

TO Daunger Shame & Drede anon
The right way ben gon
The chorle they founde hem aforne
Lyggyng vnder an hawethorne
Vnder his hed no pylowe was
But in the stede a trusse of gras
He slombred/ and a nappe he toke
Tyl Shame pitously him shoke
And great manace on him gan make
Why slepest thou/ whan thou shulde wake
(Quod Shame) thou doest vs vilanye
Who trusteth the/ he dothe folye
To kepe roses or bothoms
Whan they ben fayre in her sesons
Thou arte woxe to famyliere
Where thou shulde be straunge of chere
Stoute of thy porte/ redy to greue
Thou doest great folye for to leue
Bialacoil here inne to call
The yonder man/ to shenden vs all
Though that thou slepe/ we may here
Of Jelousye great noyse here
Arte thou nowe late/ ryse vp an hye
And stoppe sone and delyuerly
Al the gappes of the hay
Do no fauour/ I the pray
It falleth nothyng to thy name (blame
To make fayre semblant/ where thou mayste

IF Bialacoil be swete and free
Dogged and fel thou shuldest be
Frowarde and outragyous iwys
A chorle chaungeth that curteys is
This haue I herde ofte in sayeng
That man may for no dauntyng
Make a sperhauke of a bosarde
Al men wol holde the for musarde
That debonayre haue founden the
It sytteth the nought curteys to be
To do men plesaunce or seruyse
In the it is recreaundyse
Let thy werkes ferre and nere
Be lyke thy name/ whiche is Daungere
Than al abawed in shewyng
Anon spake Drede/ right thus sayeng
And said/ Daunger I drede me
That thou ne wolte besy be
To kepe that thou haste to kepe
Whan thou shuldest wake/ thou art a slepe
Thou shalte be greued certainly
If the aspye Jelousye
Or if he fynde the in blame
He hath to day assayled Shame
And chased away/ with great manace
Bialacoil out of this place
And swereth shortly that he shall
Enclose him in a sturdy wall
And al is for thy wickydnesse
For that the fayleth straungenesse
Thyn herte I trowe be fayled all
Thou shalte repent in speciall
If Jelousye the sothe knewe
Thou shalte forthynke/ and sore rewe.

With that the chorle his clubbe gan shake
Frownyng his eyen gan to make
And hydous chere/ as man in rage

For

For yre he brent in his visage
Whan that he herde him blamed so
He said/ out of my wytte I go
To be discomfyte I haue great wronge
Certes I haue nowe lyued to longe
Sithe I maye nat this closer kepe
Al quycke I wolde be doluen depe
If any man shal more repayre
In to this gardyn for foule or fayre
Myne herte for yre gothe a fere
That I lette any entre here
I haue do folly nowe I se
But nowe it shal amended be
Who setteth fote here any more
Truly he shal repent it sore
For no man more in to this place
Of me to entre shal haue grace
Leuer I had with swerdes twayne
Throughout myn herte/in euery vayne
Perced to be/with many a wounde
Than slouthe shulde in me be founde
From hensforthe by nyght or day
I shal defende it if I may
Withouten any exception
Of eche maner condycion
And if I it any man graunte
Holdeth me for recreaunte.

THan Daunger on his fete gan stonde
And hente a burdon in his honde
Wrothe in his ire ne lefte he nought
But through the verger he hath sought
If he myght fynde hole or trace
Where through that me mote forthe by pace
Or any gappe/he dyd it close
That no man might touche a rose
Of the Roser all aboute
He shytteth euery man without
Thus day by day Daunger is wers
More wonderfull and more dyuers
And feller eke/ than euer he was
For hym ful ofte I synge alas
For I ne may nought/through his yre
Recouer that I moste desyre
Myn herte alas/wol brest a two
For Bialacoil I wrathed so
For certaynly in euery membre
I quake/ whan I me remembre
Of the bothom/ whiche I wolde
Ful ofte a day sene and beholde
And whan I thynke vpon the kysse
And howe moche ioye and blysse
I had through the sauour swete
For wante of it I grone and grete
Me thynketh I fele yet in my nose
The swete sauour of the rose
And nowe I wote that I mote go
So ferre the fresshe floures fro
To me ful welcome were the dethe
Absence therof (alas) me sleethe
For whylom with this rose/ alas
I touched nose/ mouthe/ and face
But nowe the dethe I must abyde
But Loue consent another tyde
That ones I touche may and kysse
I trowe my payne shal neuer lysse
Theron is al my couetyse
Whiche brent myn herte in many wyse
Nowe shal repayre agayne syghyng
Longe watche on nyghtes/ and no slepyng
Thought in wysshyng/ turment/ and wo
With many a turnyng to and fro
That halfe my payne I can not tell
For I am fallen in to hell
From paradyse and welthe/ the more
My turment greueth more/ and more
Anoyeth nowe the bytternesse
That I toforne haue felte swetnesse
And wicked tonge/ through his falshede
Causeth al my wo and drede
On me he leyeth a pytous charge
Bycause his tonge was to large.

Nowe it is tyme shortly that I
Tell you somthyng of Ielousy
That was in great suspection
Aboute him lefte he no mason
That stone coulde laye/ ne querrour
He hyred hem to make a tour
And first the roses for to kepe
Aboute hem made he a diche depe
Right wonder large/ and also brode
Upon the whiche also stode
Of squared stone/ a sturdy wall
Whiche on a cragge was founded all
And right great thicknesse eke it bare
Aboute

About it was founded square
An hundred fadome on euery syde
It was al lyche longe and wyde
Lest any tyme it were assayled
Ful wel about it was batayled
And rounde enuyron eke were sette
Ful many a riche and fayre tourette
At euery corner of this wall
Was sette a toure ful principall
And eueriche hadde without fable
A portcolyse defensable
To kepe of enemyes/ and to greue
That there her force wolde preue
And eke amydde this purprise
Was made a toure of great maistryse
A fayrer saugh no man with syght
Large and wyde/ and of great myght
They dradde none assaut
Of gynne/gonne/nor skaffaut
The temprure of the mortere
Was made of lycour wonder dere
Of quicke lyme persaunt and egre
The whiche was tempred with vynegre
The stone was harde of adamant
wherof they made the foundemant
The toure was rounde made in compas
In al this worlde no richer was
Ne better ordayned there withal
About the toure was made a wal
So that betwixt that and the toure
Roses were sette of swete sauour
With many roses that they bere
And eke within the castel were
Springoldes/gonnes/ bowes/ and archers
And eke about at corners
Men seyne ouer the wal stonde
Great engyns/who were nerehonde
And in the kernels here and there
Of arblasters great plentie were
None armure myght her strok withstonde
It were foly to preace to honde
Without the dytche were lystes made
With wal batayled large and brade
For men and horse shulde not attayne
To nyghe the dyche ouer the playne
Thus Jelousye hath enuyron
Sette aboute his garnyson
With walles rounde/and dyche depe
Onely the Roser for to kepe
And Daunger erly and late
The keyes kepte of the vtter gate
The whiche openeth towarde the eest
And he had with him at leest
Thurty seruauntes echone by name
That other gate kept Shame
Whiche opened/as it was couthe
Towarde the parte of the southe
Sergeauntes assigned were her to
Ful many/her wyl for to do
Than Drede had in her baillye
The kepyng of the conestablerye
Towarde the northe I vnderstonde
That opened vpon the lyfte honde
The whiche for nothyng may be sure
But if she do besy cure
Erly on morowe/and also late
Strongly to shette and barre the gate
Of euery thyng that she may se
Drede is a ferde/where so she be
For with a puffe of lytel wynde
Drede is astonyed in her mynde
Therfore for stealyng of the rose
I rede her not the yate vnclose
A foules flyght wol make her fle
And eke a shadowe if she it se.

Than Wicked tonge ful of enuye
With soudyours of Normandye
As he that causeth al the bate
Was keper of the fourthe gate
And also to the tother thre
He went ful ofte for to se
Whan his lotte was to wake a nyght
His instrumentes wolde he dyght
For to blowe and make sowne
Ofter than he hath enchesoun
And walken ofte vpon the wall
Corners and wickettes ouer all
Ful narowe serchen and espye
Though he naught fonde/ yet wolde he lye
Discordaunt euer fro armony
And distoned from melodye
Controue he wolde/and foule fayle
With hornepypes of Cornewayle
In floytes made he discordaunce
And in his musyke with mischaunce

He

He wolde seyne with notes newe
That he fonde no woman trewe
Ne that he sawe neuer in his lyfe
Unto her husbonde a trewe wyfe
Ne none so ful of honeste
That she nyl laughe and mery be
Whan that she hereth or may espye
A man speken of lecherye
Eueryche of hem hath some vyce
One is dishonest/another is nyce
If one be ful of vilanye
Another hath a lykerous eye
If one be ful of wantonnesse
Another is a chyderesse.

Thus wicked tonge/god yeue him shame
Can put hem euerychone in blame
Without deserte and causelesse
He lyeth/though they ben gyltlesse
I haue pyte to sene the sorowe
That walketh bothe eue and morowe
To innocentes dothe suche greuaunce
I pray god yeue him yuel chaunce
That he euer so besye is
Of any woman to seyne amys
Eke Ielousye/ god confounde
That hath made a toure so rounde
And made aboute a garyson
To sette Bealacoil in prison
The whiche is shette there in the tour
Ful longe to holde there soiour
There for to lyue in penaunce
And for to do him more greuaunce
Whiche hath ordayned Ielousye
An olde vecke for to espye
The maner of his gouernaunce
The whiche dyuel in her enfaunce
Had lerned of loues arte
And of his pleys toke her parte
She was expert in his seruyse
She knewe eche wrenche and euery gyse
Of Loue/and euery wyle
It was harde her to begyle
Of Bealacoil she toke aye hede
That euer he lyueth in wo and drede
He kepte him koye/and eke priue
Leest in him she had se
Any foly countenaunce
For she knewe al the olde daunce
And after this whan Ielousye
Had Bealacoil in his baillie
And shette him vp that was so fre
For sure of him he wolde be
He trusteth sore in his castell
The stronge werke him lyketh well
He dradde not that no glotons
Shulde steale his roses or bothoms
The roses weren assured all
Defenced with the stronge wall
Nowe Ielousye ful wel may be
Of drede deuoyde in lyberte
Whether that he slepe or wake
For of his roses may none be take.

But I (alas) nowe morne shal
Bycause I was without the wal
Ful moche doole and mone I made
Who had wyste what wo I hade
I trowe he wolde haue had pyte
Loue to dere had solde me
The good that of his loue had I
I wente aboute it al queyntly
But nowe through doublyng of my payne
I se he wolde it sell agayne
And me a newe bargayne lere
The whiche al out the more is dere
For the solace that I haue lorne
Than I had it neuer aforne
Certayne I am ful lyke in dede
To him that caste in erthe his sede
And hath ioye of the newe spring
Whan it greneth in the gynnyng
And is also fayre and freshe of floure
Lusty to sene/swote of odoure
But er he it in shetes shere
May fall a wether that shal it dere
And make it to fade and fall
The stalke/ the greyne/ and floures all
That to the tyllers is fordone
The hope that he had to sone
I drede certayne that so fare I
For hope and trauayle lykerly
Ben me byrafte al with a storme
The floure nyl seden of my corne
For Loue hath so auaunced me
Whan I began my puuyte

To

To Bailacoil al for to tel
Whom I ne founde frowarde ne fel
But toke agree al hole my play
But loue is of so harde assaye
That al atones he reued me
Whan I wente best abouen to haue be
It is of loue/as of fortune
That chaungeth ofte/and nyl contune
Whiche whilom wol on folke smyle
And glombe on hem another whyle
Nowe frende nowe foe shalte her fele
For a twynclynge tourneth her whele
  She canne writhe her heed awaye
This is the concourse of her playe
She canne areyse that doth mourne
And whirle adowne and ouertourne
Who sytteth hyghest/ but as her lust
A foole is he that wol her trust
For it is I that am come downe
Through charge and reuolutioun
Sithe Bialacoil mote fro me twynne
Shette in the prison yonde withinne
His absence at myne herte I fele
For al my ioye and al myne hele
Was in hym/ and in the Rose
That but you wol/ whiche hym dothe close
Openne/ that I maye hym se
Loue wol nat that I cured be
Of the paynes that I endure
Nor of my cruel auenture.

Ah/ Bialacoil myne owne dere
Though thou be nowe a prisonere
Kepe at leest thyne herte to me
And suffre nat that it daunted be
Ne lette nat Ielousy in his rage
Putten thyne herte in no seruage
Al though he chastice the without
And make thy body vnto hym stout
Haue herte as harde as diamaunt
Stedfast/and naught plyaunt
In prison though thy body be
At large kepe thyne herte free
A trewe herte wol nat plye
For no manace that it maye drye
If Ielousye dothe the payne
Quyte him his while thus agayne
To venge the at leest in thought
If other waye thou mayst nought
And in this wyse subtelly
Worche/ and wynne the maistry
But yet I am in great affraye
Lest thou do nat/ as I saye
I drede thou canst me great maugre
That thou enprisoned arte for me
But that nat for my trespas
For through me neuer discouered was
Yet thynge / that ought be secree
Wel more annoye is in me
Than is in the of this myschaunce
For I endure more harde penaunce
Than any canne sayne or thynke
That for the sorowe almost I synke
Whan I remembre me of my wo
Ful nyghe out of my wytte I go.
  Inwarde myne herte I fele blede
For comfortlesse the dethe I drede
Owe I nat wel to haue dystresse
Whan false/ through her wickednesse
And traytours/ that arne enuyous
To noyen me/ be so coragious
  Ah/ Bialacoile ful wel I se
That they hem shape to disceyue the
To make the buxome to her lawe
And with her corde the to drawe
Where so hem lust/ right at her wyl
I drede they haue the brought there tyl
Without comforte/thought me slethe
This game wol bringe me to my dethe
For if your good wyl I lese
I mote be deed I maye nat chese
And if that thou foryete me
Myne hert shal neuer in lykynge be
Nor elswhere fynde solace
If I be putte out of your grace
As it shal neuer ben I hoope
Than shulde I fal in wanhope
  Alas/in wanhope: naye parde
For I wol neuer dispeyred be
If hope me fayle/ than am I
Vngratious and vnworthy
In hoope I wol conforted be
For Loue/ whan he betaught her me
Sayd/ that hoope where so I go
Shulde aye be relees to my wo
  But what and she my bales bete

And be to me curteis and swete
She is in nothynge ful certayne
Louers she putte in ful great payne
And maketh hem with wo to dele
Her fayre behest discepueth fele
For she wol behote sykerly
And faylen after utterly
  Ah/ that is a ful noyous thyng
For many a louer in louyng
Hangeth upon her/ and trusteth fast
Whiche lese her traueyle at the last
  Of thyng to cōmen she wotte right nought
Therfore if it be wisely sought
Her counsayle foly is to take
For many tymes/ whan she wol make
A ful good sylogisme/ I drede
That afterwarde there shal in dede
Folowe an yuel conclusyoun
This putte me in confusyoun
For many tymes I haue it sene
That many haue begyled bene
For truste that they haue sette in hoope
Whiche fel hem afterwarde a slope.

But nathelesse yet gladly she wolde
That he that wol him with her holde
Hadde al tymes her purpose clere
Without discepte or any were
That she desyreth sykerly
Whan I her blamed I dyd foly
But what auayleth her good wyl
Whan she ne maye staunche my stounde yl
That helpeth lytel that she maye do
Outtake beheest unto my wo
And heest certayne in no wyse
Without yefte is nat to preyse.

  Whan heest and dede a sondre vary
They done a great contrary
Thus am I possed up and downe
With doole/ thought/ and confusyoune
Of my disease there is no nombre
Daungere and Shame me encombre
Drede also/ and Jelousye
And Wicked Tonge ful of enuye
Of whiche the sharpe and cruel Ire
Ful ofte me putte in great martyre
They haue my ioye fully lette
Sithe Bialacoil they haue beshette
Fro me in prison wickedly
Whome I loue so entierly
That it wol my bane be
But I the sooner maye him se
  And yet more ouer worste of al
There is sette to kepe/ foule her befal
A rympled vecke ferre ronne in rage
Frownyng and yelowe in her visage
Whiche in awayte lyeth day and nyght
That none of hem may haue a syght.

Nowe mote my sorowe enforced be
Ful sothe it is that Loue yafe me
Thre wonder yeftes of his grace
Whiche I haue lorne nowe in this place
Sithe they ne maye without drede
Helpen but lytel who taketh hede
For here aueyleth no Swete thought
And swete Speche helpeth right nought
  The thirde was called Swete Lokyng
That nowe is lorne without lesyng.

  Yeftes were fayre/ but nat for thy
They helpe me but symply
But Bialacoil loosed be
To gone at large/ and to be free
For him my lyfe lyeth al in dout
But if he come the rather out
  Alas I trowe it wol nat bene
For howe shulde I euermore him sene:
He maye nat out/ and that is wronge
Bycause the Toure is so stronge
Howe shulde he out/ or by whose prowesse
Of so stronge a forteresse:
  By me certayne it nyl be do
God wotte I haue no wytte therto
But wel I wotte I was in rage
Whan I to Loue dydde homage
Who was in cause (in sothfastnesse)
But her selfe dame Idelnesse:
Whiche me conueyde through fayre prayere
To entre in to that fayre vergere
She was to blame me to leue
The whiche nowe dothe me sore greue
A fooles worde is nought to trowe
Ne worthe an apple for to lowe
Menne shulde him snybbe bitterly

At

At prime temps of his foly
I was a foole/and she me leued
Through whom I am right nought releued
She accomplysshed al my wyll
That nowe me greueth wonder yll.

Reason me sayde what shulde fall
A foole my selfe I may wel call
That loue asyde I had nat layde
And trowed that dame Reson sayde
Reson had bothe skyll and ryght
Whan she me blamed/with al her myght
To medle of loue/that hath me shent
But certayne nowe I wol repent.

And shulde I repent? nay parde
A false traytour/than shulde I be
The dyuels engyns wolde me take
If I my lorde wolde forsake
Or Bialacoil falsly betraye
Shulde I at mischefe hate him? naye
Sythe he nowe for his curtesye
Is in prison of Ielousye
Curtesye certayne dyd he me
So moche/that it may not yolden be
Whan he the hay passen me lete
To kysse the Rose/fayre and swete
Shulde I therfore conne him maugre
Nay certaynly/it shal not be
For Loue shal neuer yeue good wyll
Here of me/through worde or wyll
Offence or complaynt more or lesse
Neyther of Hope nor Idelnesse
For certes it were wronge that I
Hated hem for her curtesye.
There is not els/but suffre and thynke
And waken whan I shulde wynke
Abyde in hope/tyl Loue through chaunce
Sende me socour or allegeaunce
Expectant aye tyl I may mete
To getten mercy of that swete.

Whylom I thynke howe Loue to me
Sayd he wolde take at gre
My seruyce/if vnpacience
Caused me to done offence
He sayd/in thanke I shal it take
And hygh mayster eke the make
If wickednesse ne reue it the
But sone I trowe that shal not be
These were his wordes by and by
It semed he loued me trewly
Nowe is there not but serue him wele
If that I thynke his thanke to fele
My good myn harme/lythe hole in me
In loue may no defaute be
For trewe loue ne fayled neuer man
Sothly the faute mote nedes than
As god forbyd/be founde in me
And howe it cometh/I can not se
Nowe let it gone as it may go
Whether Loue wol socoure me or slo
He may do hole on me his wyll
I am so sore bounde hym tyll
From his seruyce I may not flene
For lyfe and dethe withouten wene
Is in his hande/I may not chese
He may me do bothe wynne and lese
And sythe so sore he dothe me greue
Yet if my luste he wolde acheue
To Bialacoil goodly to be
I yeue no force what fel on me
For though I dye/as I mote nede
I pray Loue of his goodlyhede
To Bialacoil do gentylnesse
For whom I lyue in suche distresse
That I mote dyen for penaunce
But first/without repentaunce
I wol me confesse in god entent
And make in haste my testament
As louers done that felen smerte
To Bialacoil leaue I myn herte
Al hole/without departyng
Or doublenesse of repentyng.

Cõment Raison vient a Lamant.

Thus as I made my passage
In compleynt/and in cruel rage
And I not where to fynde a leche
That couthe vnto myn helpyng eche
Sodainly agayne comen doun
Out of her tour I sawe Reasoun
Discrete and wyse/and ful plesaunt
And of her porte ful auenaunt
The right way she toke to me
Which stode in great perplexite

E.e.ii. That

That was posshed in euery syde
That I nyst where I myght abyde
Tyl she demurely sadde of chere
Sayd to me as she came nere
Myne owne frende/ arte thou greued?
Howe is this quarel yet atcheued
Of loues syde? anone tel me
Hast thou nat yet of loue thy fyl?
Arte thou nat wery of thy seruyce?
That the hath in suche wyse?
What ioye haste thou in thy louyng?
Is it swete or bytter thyng
Canst thou yet chese/ lette me se
What best thy socour myght be.

Thou seruest a ful noble lorde
That maketh the thral for thy rewarde
Whiche aye reneweth thy tourment
With foly so he hath the blent
Thou fel in myschefe thylke daye
Whan thou dyddest/ the sothe to saye
Obeysaunce/ and eke homage
Thou wroughtest nothyng as the sage
Whan thou became his liege man
Thou dyddest a great foly than
Thou wystest nat what fel therto
With what lorde thou haddest to do
If thou haddest him wel knowe
Thou haddest nought be brought so lowe
For if thou wystest what it were
Thou noldest serue him halfe a yere
Nat a weke/ nor halfe a daye
Ne yet an hour without delaye
Ne neuer I loued paramours
His lordshyppe is so ful of shours
knowest him ought?
Lamaunt. Ye dame parde
Raysoun. Nay nay Lamaunt. yes I
Raysoun. Wherfore lette se
Lamaunt. Of that he sayd I shulde be
Gladde to haue suche lorde (as he)
And maister of suche seignorie
Raysoun. knowest him no more?
Lamaunt. Naye certes I
Saue that he yafe me rules there
And went his waye/ I nyst where
And I abode bounde in balaunce
Lo/ there a noble conysaunce.

Raysoun.

BVt I wol that thou knowe him nowe
Begynnynge and ende/ sithe that thou
Arte so anguysshous and mate
Dissygured out of astate
There maye no wretche haue more of wo
Ne caytife none enduren so
It were to euery manne syttyng
Of his lorde haue knowlegyng
For if thou knewe him out of dout
Lightly thou shuldest escapen out
Of thy prysone that marreth the
Lamaunt. Ye dame sithe my lorde is he
And I his manne made with myne honde
I wolde ryght fayne vnderstonde
To knowe of what kynde he be
If any wolde enforme me.

Raysoun.

I Wolde (sayd Reason) the lere
Sithe thou to ferne hast suche desyre
And shewe the withouten fable
A thynge that is nat demonstrable
Thou shalte withouten science
And knowe withouten experience
The thyng that may nat knowen be
Ne wyst ne shewed in no degree
Thou mayst the sothe of it nat wrytten
Though in the it were written
Thou shalte nat knowe therof more
Whyle thou arte ruled by his lore
But vnto him that loue wol flye
The knotte maye vnclosed be
Whiche hath to the/ as it is founde
So longe to knytte and nat vnbounde
Nowe sette wel thyne ententioun
To here of Loue discriptioun.

LOue it is an hateful pees
A free acquytaunce without relees
And through the frette ful of falshede
A sikernesse al sette in drede
In herte is a dispeyryng hoope
And ful of hoope it is wanhoope
Wyse woodnesse/ and woyde Reasoun
A swete peryl in to drowne
An heuy burthen lyght to beare
A wicked wawe awaye to weare
It is Carybdes perilous
Disagreable and gratious

It is descordaunce that can accorde
And accordaunce to discorde
It is connynge without science
Wysedom without sapyence
Wytte without discretioun
Hauoyre without possessyoun
It is lyke hele and hole sickenesse
A truste drowned and dronknesse
And helthe ful of maladye
And charyte ful of enuye
And angre ful of habundaunce
And a gredy suffysaunce
Delyte right ful of heuynesse
And dreryed ful of gladnesse
Bytter swetnesse and swete errour
Right yuel sauoured good sauour
Sen that pardone hath withinne
And pardone spotted without synne
A payne also it is ioyous
And felonye ryght pytous
Also playe that selde is stable
And stedfast right meuable
A strength weyked to stonde upright
And feblenesse ful of myght
Wytte unauysed/ sage folye
And ioye ful of tourmentrye
A laughter it is weppynge aye
Rest that trauayleth nyght and daye
Also a swete helle it is
And a sorouful paradys
A plesaunt gayle and easy prisoun
And ful of frost somer seasoun
Pryme temps ful of frostes whyte
And Maye deuoyde of al delyte
With seer braunches blossoms ungrene
And newe frute fylled with wynter tene
It is a slowe maye nat forbeare
Ragges rybaned with golde to weare
For al so wel wol loue be sette
Under ragges as riche rochette
And eke as wel by amorettes
In mournyng blacke/ as bright burnettes
For none is of so mokel prise
Ne no manne founden so wyse
Ne none so highe is of parage
Ne no manne founde of wytte so sage
No manne so hardy ne so wighte
Ne no manne of so mokel myght
None so fulfylled of bounte
That he with loue maye daunted be
Al the worlde holdeth this waye
Loue maketh al to gone myswaye
But it be they of yuel lyfe
Whome Genius cursed man and wyfe
That wrongly werke agayne nature
None suche I loue/ ne haue no cure
Of suche as loues seruauntes bene
And wol nat by my counsayle flene
For I ne preyse that louynge
Wherthrough men at the laste endynge
Shal cal hem wretches ful of wo
Loue greueth hem and shendeth so
But if thou wolte wel loue eschewe
For to escape out of his mewe
And make al hoole thy sorowe to slake
No better counsayle mayst thou take
Than thynke to fleen wel ywis
Maye nought helpe els/ for wytte thou this
If thou flye it/ it shal flye the
Folowe it/ and folowen shal it the.

¶ Lamaunt.

Whan I hadde herde al Reason sayne
Whiche had spilte her speche in vayne
Dame (sayd I) I dare wel saye
Of this auaunt me wel I maye
That from your schole so deuiaunt
I am/ that neuer the more auaunt
Right nought am I through your doctryne
I dulle under your disciplyne
I wotte no more than wyste euer
To me so contrary and so fer
Is euery thynge that ye me lere
And yet I canne it al by partuere
Myne herte foryeteth therof right nought
It is so written in my thought
And depe greuen it is so tender
That al myne herte I can it render
And rede it ouer communely
But to my selfe lewdest am I.

But sithe ye Loue discryuen so
And lacke and preise it bothe two
Defyneth it in to this letter
That I maye thynke on it the better
For I herde neuer diffyned here
And wylfully I wolde it lere

E.e.iii. If

If loue be serched wel and sought
It is a sickenesse of the thought
Annexed and knedde betwixt twayne
With male and female with o chayne
So frely that byndeth/ that they nyl twynne
Whether so therof they lese or wynne
The rote springeth through hoote brennynge
In to disordynate desyringe
For to kyssen and enbrace
And at her luste them to solace
Of other thynge loue retcheth nought
But setteth her herte and al her thought
More for delectatioun
Than any procreatioun
Of other frute by engendrure
Whiche loue to god is nat pleasure
For of her body fruyte to gette
They yeue no force/ they are so sette
Upon delyte to playe in fere
And some haue also this manere
To faynen hem for loue seke
Suche loue I preyse nat at a leke
For paramours they do but fayne
To loue trewly they disdayne
They falsen ladyes traytoursly
And swerne hem othes utterly
With many a leasyng/ and many a fable
And al they fynden disceyuable
And whan they han her luste getten
The hoote ernes they al forgetten
Women the harme byen ful sore
But menne this thynken euermore
That lasse harme is/ so mote I thee
Disceyue them/ than disceyued be
And namely where they ne maye
Fynde none other meane waye
For I wotte wel in sothfastnesse
That what dothe nowe his besynesse
With any woman for to dele
For any luste that he maye fele
But if it be for engendrure
He dothe trespasse I you ensure
For he shulde setten al his wyl
To getten a lykely thynge hym tyl
And to sustayne/ if he myght
And kepe forthe by kyndes ryght
His owne lykenesse and semblable
For bycause al is corrumpable
And fayle shulde successyoun
Ne were their generatioun
Our sectes sterne for to saue
Whan father or mother arne in graue
Her chyldren shulde/ whan they ben dede
Ful dilygent bene in her stede
To use that warke on suche a wyse
That one may through another ryse
Therfore sette kynde therin delyte
For men therin shulde hem delyte
And of that dede be nat erke
But ofte sythes haunt that werke
For none wolde drawe therof a draught
Ne were delyte / whiche hath him caught
This had subtyl dame Nature
For none gothe right I the ensure
Ne hath entent hoole ne parfyte
For her desyre is for delyte
The whiche fortened crease/ and eke
The playe of loue/ for ofte seke
And thral hem selfe they be so nyce
Un to the prynce of euery vyce
For of eche synne it is the rote
Unlefull luste/ though it be sote
And of al yuel the racyne
As Tullyus canne determyne
Whiche in his tyme was ful sage
In a booke he made of age
Where that more he prayseth elde
Though he be croked and unwelde
And more of cōmendatioun
Than youthe in his discriptioun
For youthe sette bothe man and wyfe
In al parel of soule and lyfe
And parel is/ but men haue grace
The parel of youthe for to pace
Without any dethe or distresse
It is so ful of wyldnesse
So ofte it dothe shame or domage
To him or to his lynage
It ledeth man/ nowe up nowe downe
In mokel dissolutioun
And maketh him loue yuel company
And lede his lyfe disrulyly
And halte hym payde with none estate
Within hym selfe is suche debate
He chaungeth purpose and entent
And yalte in to some couent

To

To lyuen after her emprise
And leseth fredom and fraunchyse
That nature in him had sette
The whiche agayne he may not gette
If he there make his mansyon
For to abyde professyon
Though for a tyme his herte absente
It may not fayle/he shal repente
And eke abyde thilke day
To leaue his abyte/and gon his way
And leseth his worshyp and his name
And dare not come agayne for shame
But al his lyfe he dothe so mourne
Bycause he dare nat home retourne
Fredom of kynde so loste hath he
That neuer may recured be
But that if god him graunte grace
That he may/ er he hence pace
Conteyne vnder obedyence
Through the vertue of pacience
For youthe set man in al folye
In vnthrifte and in rybaudrie
In lechery/and in outrage
So ofte it chaungeth of corage
Youthe gynneth ofte suche bargayne
That may not ende without payne
In great parell is set youth hede
Delyte so dothe his bridell lede
Delyte this hangeth/drede the nought
Bothe mans body and his thought
Onely through youthes chambere
That to done yuell is customere
And of naught els taketh hede
But onely folkes for to lede
In to disporte and wyldenesse
So is frowarde from sadnesse
But elde draweth hem therfro
Who wote it not/he may wel go
And mo of hem/that nowe arne olde
That whylom youthe had in holde
Whiche yet remembreth of tender age
Howe it hem brought in many a rage
And many a foly therin wrought
But nowe that elde hath him through sought
They repent hem of her folye
That youthe hem put in ieopardye
In parell and in moche wo
And made hem ofte amysse to do
And sewen yuell companye
Ryot and auoutrye.

But elde gan agayne restrayne
From suche foly/and restrayne
And set men by her ordynaunce
In good rule and in gouernaunce
But yuel she spendeth her seruyse
For no man wol her loue neyther preyse
She is hated/this wote I wele
Her acqueyntaunce wolde no man fele
Ne han of elde companye
Men hate to be of her alye
For no man wolde becomen olde
Ne dye/ whan he is yonge and bolde
And elde merueyleth right greatly
Whan they remembre hem inwardly
Of many a perillous emprise
Whiche that they wrought in sondrie wyse
Howe euer they might without blame
Escape away without shame
In youthe without domage
Or reprefe of her lynage
Losse of membre/shedyng of blood
Parell of dethe/or losse of good
Woste thou not where youthe abyt
That men so preysen in her wyt?
With Delyte she halte soiour
For bothe they dwellen in o tour
As longe as youthe is in season
They dwellen in one mansyon
Delyte of youthe wol haue seruyce
To do what so he wol deuyse
And youthe is redy euermore
For to obeye for smerte of soore
Vnto Delyte/ and him to yeue
Her seruyce/ whyle that she may lyue.

Where elde abytte/I wol the tel
Shortly/ and no while dwel
For thyder behoueth the to go
If dethe in youthe the nat slo
Of this iourney thou mayst nat fayle
With her labour and trauayle
Lodged ben with sorowe and wo
That neuer out of her courte go
Payne and dystresse/syckenesse/and yre
And melancoly that angry syre

Ben

Bene of her paleys senatours
Gronyng and grutchyng/ her herbegeours
The daye and nyght her to tourment
With cruel dethe they her present
And tellen her erlyche and late
That dethe stondeth armed at her gate
Than brynge they to her remembraunce
The foly dedes of her enfaunce
Whiche causen her to mourne in wo
That youthe hath her begyled so
Whiche sodainly awaye is hasted
She weped the tyme that she hath wasted
Complaynynge of the preterytte
And the present/ that nat abytte
And of her olde vanyte
That but aforne her she maye se
In the future some socoure
To leggen her of her doloure
To graunt her tyme of repentaunce
For her synnes to do penaunce
And at the laste so her gouerne
To wynne the ioye that is eterne
Fro whiche go backwarde youthe he made
In vanyte to drowne and wade
For present tyme abydeth nought
It is more swyfte than any thought
So lytel whyle it dothe endure
That there nys compte ne measure
But howe that euer the game go
Who lyst to loue ioye and myrthe also
Of loue/ be it he or she
Hye or lowe who it be
In fruyte they shulde hem delyte
Her parte they maye nat els quyte
To saue hem selfe in honeste
And yet ful many one I se
Of women/ sothly for to sayne
That desyre/ and wolde fayne
The playe of loue/they be so wylde
And nat coueyte to go with chylde
And if with chylde they be perchaunce
They wol it holde a great myschaunce
But what so euer wo they fele
They wol nat playne/ but concele
But if it be any foole or nyce
In whome that shame hath no iustyce
For to delyte echone they drawe
That haunt this worke bothe hye and lawe
Saue suche that arne worthe right nought
That for money wal be bought
Suche loue I preyse in no wyse
Whan it is gouen for couetyse
I preyse no woman/ though so be woode
That yeueth her selfe for any goode
For lytel shulde a man telle
Of her/that wel her body selle
Be she mayde/ be she wyfe
That quycke wol selle her by her lyfe
Howe fayre chere that euer she make
He is a wretche I undertake
That loued suche one/ for swete or soure
Though she hym called her paramoure
And laugheth on him/and maketh him feest
For certainly no suche beest
To be loued is nat worthy
Or beare the name of Drury
None shulde her please/ but he were woode
That wol dispoyle him of his goode
Yet nathelesse I wol nat saye
That she for solace and for playe
Maye a iewel or other thynge
Take of her loues free yeuynge
But that she aske it in no wyse
For drede of shame/ or couetyse
And she of hers maye him certayne
Without sclaunder yeuen agayne
And ioyne her hertes togyder so
In loue/ and take and yeue also
Trowe nat that I wol hem twynne
Whan in her loue there is no synne
I wol that they togyder go
And done al that they hanne ado
As curteys shulde and debonayre
And in her loue beren hem fayre
Without vyce/ bothe he and she
So that alwaye in honeste
Fro folly loue to kepe hem clere
That brenneth hertes with his fere
And that her loue in any wyse
Be deuoyde of couetyse
Good loue shulde engendred be
Of trewe hert/ iuste/and secree
And nat of suche as sette her thought
To haue her luste/ and els nought
So are they caught in loues lace
Trewly for bodily solace

Flesshly

Flesshely delyte is so present
With the/that set al thyn entent
Without more/what shulde I glose
For to get and haue the Rose
Whiche maketh the so mate and wood
That thou desyrest none other good
But thou arte not an ynche the nerre
But euer abydest in sorowe and werre
As in thy face it is sene
It maketh the bothe pale and lene
Thy might/ thy vertue gothe away
A sory gest in good fay
Thou herborest in thyn inne
The god of Loue whan thou let inne
Wherfore I rede thou shette him oute
Or he shal greue the out of doute
For to thy profyte it wol turne
If he no more with the soiourne
In great mischefe and sorowe sonken
Ben hertes/that of loue arne dronken
As thou perauenture knowen shall
Whan thou hast lost the tyme all
And spent thy thought in ydlenesse
In waste/and woful lustynesse
If thou mayst lyue the tyme to se
Of loue for to delyuered be
Thy tyme thou shalte bewepe sore
The whiche neuer thou mayst restore
For tyme loste/as men may se
For nothyng may recouered be
And if thou scape/yet at laste
Fro loue that hath the so faste
Knytte and bounden in his lace
Certayne I holde it but a grace
For many one as it is seyne
Haue loste/and spent also in veyne
In his seruyce without socour
Body and soule/good/ and treasour
Wytte/ and strength/and eke rychesse
Of whiche they had neuer redresse.

¶ Lamant.

THus taught ⁊ preched hath Reason
But Loue spylte her sermon
That was so imped in my thought
That her doctryne I set at nought
And yet ne sayd she neuer a dele
That I ne vnderstode it wele
Worde by worde the mater all
But vnto Loue I was so thrall
Whiche calleth ouer al his praye
He chaseth so my thought aye
And holdeth myne herte vnder his sele
As trusty and trewe as any stele
So that no deuocion
Ne had I in the sermon
Of dame Reason/ ne of her rede
It toke no soiour in myn heede
For al yede out at one ere
That in that other she dyd lere
Fully on me she lost her lore
Her speche me greued wonder sore.

THat vnto her for ire I sayde
For anger/as I dyd abrayde
Dame/and is it your wyl algate
That I not loue/but that I hate
Al men/as ye me teche
For if I do after your speche
Sythe that ye seyne loue is not good
Than must I nedes say with mode
If I it leue/in hatred aye
Lyuen/and voyde loue awaye
From me a synful wretche
Hated of al that tetche
I may not go none other gate
For eyther muste I loue or hate
And if I hate men of newe
More than loue/it wol me rewe
As by your prechyng semeth me
For Loue nothyng ne prayseth the
Ye yeue good counsayle sykerly
That precheth me al day/ that I
Shulde not loues lore alowe
He were a foole wolde you not trowe
In speche also ye han me taught
Another loue that knowen is naught
Whiche I haue herde you not repreue
To loue eche other by your leue
If ye wolde diffyne it me
I wolde gladly here to se
At the lest if I may lere
Of sondrie loues the manere.

¶ Raison.

CErtes frende/a foole arte thou
Whan that thou nothyng wolte alow
That I for thy profyte saye
Yet wol I saye the more in faye

For

For I am redy at the leest
To accomplysshe thy request
But I not where it wol aueyle
In vayne parauenture I shale traueyle
Loue there is in sondrye wyse
As I shal the here deuyse
For some loue leful is and goode
I meane nat that whiche maketh the woode
And bringeth the in many a fytte
And rauyssheth fro the al thy wytte
It is so merueylous and queynt
With suche loue be no more aqueynt.

Cōment Raison diffinist Amistie.

Loue of frendshippe also there is
Whiche maketh no man done amys
Of wyl knytte betwixte two
That wol nat breke for wele ne wo
Whiche longe is lykely to contune
Whan wyl and goodes ben in cōmune
Grounded by goddes ordynaunce
Hoole without discordaunce
With hem holdynge cōmunte
Of al her good in charyte
That there be none exceptioun
Through chaungynge of ententioun
That eche helpe other at her nede
And wisely hele bothe worde and dede
Trewe of meanyng/ deuoyde of slouthe
For wytte is nought without trouthe
So that the tone dare al his thought
Sayne to his frende/ and spare nought
As to him selfe without dredynge
To be discouered by wreying
For gladde is that coniunctioun
Whan there is none suspectioun
Whome they wolde proue
That trewe and parfyte weren in loue
For no man maye be amyable
But if he be so ferme and stable
That fortune chaunge him nat ne blynde
But that his frende al waye him fynde
Bothe poore and ryche in o state
For if his frende through any gate
Wol complayne of his pouerte
He shulde nat byde so longe/ tyl he
Of his helpynge him requyre
For good dede done through prayere
Is solde and bought to dere ywis
To hert that of great valure is
For herte fulfylled of gentylnesse
Canne yuel demeane his distresse
And man that worthy is of name
To askenne often hath great shame
A good manne brenneth in his thought
For shame whan he asketh ought
He hath great thought/ and dredeth aye
For his disease whan he shal praye
His frende/ lest that he warned be
Tyl that he preue his stabilyte
But whan that he hath founden one
That trusty is and trewe as stone
And assayed him at al
And founde him stedfast as a wal
And of his frendshippe be certayne
He shal him shewe/ bothe ioye and payne
And al that dare thynke or saye
Without shame/ as he wel maye
For howe shulde he a shamed be
Of suche one as I tolde the
For whan he wotte his secree thought
The thirde shal knowe therof right nought
For twey in nombre it bette than thre
In euery counsayle and secree
Repreue he dredeth neuer a dele
Who that besette his wordes wele
For euery wyse manne out of drede
Canne kepe his tonge tyl he se nede
And fooles canne nat holde her tonge
A fooles belle is soone ronge
Yet shal a trewe frende do more
To helpe his felowe of his sore
And socour him whan he hath nede
In al that he maye done in dede
And gladder that he him pleaseth
Than his felowe that he easeth
And if he do nat his request
He shal as moche him molest
As his felowe/ for that he
Maye nat fulfyl his volunte
Fully/ as he hath requyred
If bothe the hertes loue hath fyred
Joye and wo they shal departe
And take euenly eche his parte
Halfe his anoye he shal haue aye
And comforte what that he maye

And

And of this blysse parte shal he
If loue wol departed be.

And whylom of this vnyte
Spake Tullius in a dyte
And shulde maken his request
Vnto his frende/that is honest
And he goodly shulde it fulfyll
But it the more were out of skyll
And other wyse not graunte therto
Except only in causes two
If men his frende to dethe wolde driue
Let him be besy to saue his lyue
Also if men wollen him assayle
Of his worshyp to make him fayle
And hyndren him of his renoun
Let him with ful entencioun
His deuer done in eche degre
That his frende ne shamed be
In this two case with his might
Takyng no kepe to skyll nor right
As ferre as loue may him excuse
This ought no man to refuse
This loue that I haue tolde to the
Is no thyng contrarye to me
This wol I that thou folowe wele
And leaue the tother euery dele
This loue to vertue al entendeth
The tother fooles blent and shendeth.

Another loue also there is
That is contrarye vnto this
Whiche desyre is so constrayned
That is but wyl fayned
Away fro trouthe it dothe so varye
That to good loue it is contrarye
For it maymeth in many wyse
Syke hertes with couetyse
Al in wynnyng and in profyte
Suche loue setteth his delyte
This loue so hangeth in balaunce
That if it lese his hope parchaunce
Of lucre/that he is set vpon
It wol fayle/and quenche anon
For no man may be amorous
Ne in his lyuyng vertuous
But he loue more in moode
Men for hem selfe/ than for her goode
For loue that profyte dothe abyde
Is false/and bydeth not in no tyde
Loue cometh of dame Fortune
That lytel whyle wol contune
For it shal chaungen wonder soone
And take eclyps right as the moone
Whan he is from vs lette
Through erthe/that betwixt is sette
The sonne and her/ as it may fall
Be it in partie/or in all
The shadowe maketh her bemes merke
And her hornes to shewe derke
That parte/where she hath loste her lyght
Of Phebus fully/and the syght
Tyl whan the shadowe is ouerpaste
She is enlumyned ageyn as faste
Through the brightnesse of the sonne bemes
That yeueth to her agayne her lemes
That loue is right of suche nature
Nowe is fayre/and nowe obscure
Nowe bright/nowe clipsy of manere
And whilom dymme/& whylom clere
As soone as pouerte gynneth take
With mantel and wedes blake
Hydeth of loue the light away
That in to nyght it turneth day
It may not se richesse shyne
Tyl the blacke shadowes fyne
For whan rychesse shyneth bright
Loue recouereth ayen his lyght
And whan it fayleth/he wol flyt
And as she greueth/so greueth it
Of this loue here what I saye
The ryche men are loued aye
And namely tho that sparande bene
That wol not wasshe her hertes clene
Of the fylthe/nor of the vyce
Of gredy brennyng auaryce
The ryche man ful fonde is ywis
That weneth that he loued is
If that his herte it vnderstode
It is not he/ it is his good
He may wel weten in his thought
His good is loued/and he right nought
For if he be a nygarde eke
Men wol nat set by him a leke
But haten him/ this is the sothe
Lo what profyte his catel dothe

Of

Of euery man that may him se
It getteth him nought but enmyte
But he amende hym selfe of that vyce
And knowe him selfe/he is not wyse
Certes he shulde aye frendly be
To get hym loue also ben fre
Or els he is not wyse ne sage
No more than is a gote ramage
That he not loueth/ his dede proueth
Whan he his richesse so wel loueth
That he wol hyde it aye and spare
His poore frendes sene forfare
To kepen aye his purpose
Tyl for drede his eyen close
And tyl a wicked dethe him take
Hym had leuer a sondre shake
And let al his lymmes a sondre ryue
Than leaue his richesse in his lyue
He thynketh to parte it with no man
Certayne no loue is in him than
Howe shulde loue within hym be
Whan in his herte is no pyte
That he trespaseth wel I wate
For eche man knoweth his estate
For wel him ought to be reproued
That loueth nought/ne is not loued
But sithe we arne to fortune comen
And hath our sermon of her nomen
A wonder wyll I tel the nowe
Thou herdest neuer suche one I trowe
I not where thou me leuen shall
Though sothfastnesse it be all
As it is written/and is sothe
That vnto men more profyte dothe
The frowarde fortune and contraire
Than the swote and debonaire
And if the thynke it is doutable
It is through argument prouable
For the debonayre and softe
Falseth and begyleth ofte
For lyche a mother she can cherishe
And mylken as dothe a norice
And of her good to him deles
And yeueth him parte of her iowelles
With great rychesse and dignite
And hem she hoteth stabylite
In a state that is not stable
But chaungyng aye and variable
And fedeth him with glorie veyne
And worldly blysse noncertayne
Whan she him setteth on her whele
Than wene they to be right wele
And in so stable state withall
That neuer they wene for to fall
And whan they sette so hygh be
They wene to haue in certeynte
Of hertly frendes to great nombre
That nothyng might her state encombre
They truste hem so on euery syde
Wenyng with hym they wolde abyde
In euery parel and mischaunce
Without chaunge or variaunce
Bothe of catel and of good
And also for to spende her blood
And al her membres for to spyll
Onely to fulfyll her wyll
They maken it hole in many wyse
And hoten hem her ful seruyse
Howe sore that it do hem smerte
Into her very naked sherte
Herte and al so hole they yeue
For the tyme that they may lyue
So that with her flaterye
They maken fooles glorifye
Of her wordes spekyng
And han chere of a reioysyng
And trowe hem as the Euangyle
And it is al falshede and gyle
As they shal afterwarde se
Whan they arne fall in pouerte
And ben of good and catell bare
Than shul they sene who frendes ware
For of an hundred certaynly
Nor of a thousande ful scarsly
Ne shal they fynde vnnethes one
Whan pouerte is comen vpon
For thus Fortune that I of tell
With men whan her lust to dwell
Maketh hem to lese her conysaunce
And norissheth hem in ignoraunce.

But frowarde fortune and peruerse
Whan high estates she dothe reuerse
And maketh hem to tomble downe
Of her whele with sodayne tourne
And from her rychesse dothe hem flye

And

And plongeth hem in pouerte
As a stepmother enuyous
And layeth a playstre dolorous
Vnto her hertes wounded egre
Whiche is not tempred with vynegre
But with pouerte and indygence
For to shewe by experience
That she is Fortune verilye
In whom no man shulde affye
Nor in her yeftes haue fyaunce
She is so ful of varyaunce
  Thus can she maken hye and lowe
Whan they from rychesse arne throwe
Fully to knowen without were
Frende of affecte/and frende of chere
And whiche in loue weren trewe and stable
And whiche also weren varyable
After fortune her goddesse
In pouerte/ either in rychesse
For al that yeueth here out of drede
Vnhappe bereueth it in dede
For in fortune lette not one
Of frendes/whan fortune is gone
I meane tho frendes that wol fle
Anon as entreth pouerte
And yet they wol not leaue hem so
But in eche place where they go
They cal hem wretche/scorne/ and blame
And of her misshappe hem diffame
And namely suche as in rychesse
Pretendeth moste of stablenesse
Whan that they sawe him set on lofte
And weren of him socoured ofte
And most yholpe in al her nede
But nowe they take no maner hede
But leyne in voyce of flaterye
That nowe appereth her folye
Ouer al where so they fare
And synge/ go farewel feldefare
  Al suche frendes I beshrewe
For of trewe there be to fewe
But sothfaste frendes/ what so betyde
In euery fortune wollen abyde
They han her hertes in suche noblesse
That they nyl loue for no rychesse
Nor for that fortune may hem sende
They wollen hem socour and defende
And chaunge for softe ne for sore
For who is frende loueth euermore
Though men drawe swerde his frende to slo
He may not hewe her loue a two
But in case that I shal say
For pride and ire lese it he may
And for reproue by nycete
And discoueryng of priuyte
With tonge woundyng/ as felon
Through venemous detraction
  Frende in this case wol gon his way
For nothyng greue him more ne may
And for nought els wol he fle
If that he loue in stabylite
And certayne he is wel begone
Amonge a thousande that fyndeth one
For there may be no rychesse
Ayenst frendshyp of worthynesse
For it ne may so hygh attayne
As may the valoure/sothe to sayne
Of him that loueth trewe and well
Frendshyp is more than is catell
For frende in courte aye better is
Than peny in purse certis
And fortune misshappyng
Whan vpon men she is fallyng
Through misturnyng of her chaunce
And caste hem out of balaunce
  She maketh through her aduersyte
Men ful clerely for to se
Hym that is frende in existence
From hym that is by apparence
For in fortune maketh anone
To knowe thy frendes fro thy fone
By experyence right as it is
The whiche is more to prayse ywis
Than in moche rychesse and tresour
For more depe profyte and valour
Pouertie/and suche aduersyte
Before/than dothe prosperyte
For that one yeueth conysaunce
And the tother ignoraunce.

  And thus in pouerte is in dede
Trouthe declared fro falshede
For faynte frendes it wol declare
And trewe also/what way they fare
For whan he was in his rychesse
These frendes ful of doublenesse

F. s.   Offred

Offred him in many wyse
Herte and body/ and seruyce
What wolde he thã haue you to haue bought
To knowen openly her thought
That he nowe hath so clerely sene
The false begyled he shulde haue bene
And he hadde than parceyued it
But Richesse nolde nat sette him wytte
Wel more auauntage dothe him than
Sithe that it maketh him a wyse man
The great myschefe that he parceyueth
Than dothe Richesse that him disceyueth
Richesse riche ne maketh nought
Him that on treasour sette his thought
For richesse stonte in suffysaunce
And nothynge in habundaunce
For suffysaunce al onely
Maketh menne to lyue richely.

HOr he that hath mytches tweyne
Ne value in his demayne
Lyueth more at ease/ & more is riche
Than dothe he that is chiche
And in his berne hath sothe to sayne
An hundred mauys of whete grayne
Though he be chapman or marchaunt
And haue of golde many besaunt
For in the gettyng he hath suche wo
And in the kepyng drede also
And sette euermore his besynesse
For to encrease/ and nat to lesse
For to augment and multiplye
And though on heapes that lye him by
Yet neuer shal make his richesse
Asseth vnto his gredynesse
But the poore that retcheth nought
Saue of his lyuelode in his thought
Whiche that he getteth with his traueyle
He dredeth naught that it shal feyle
Though he haue lytel worldes goode
Meate and drynke/ and easy foode
Upon his traueyle and lyuyng
And also suffysaunt clothyng
Or if in sickenesse that he fal
And lothe meate and drynke withal
Though he haue nat his meate to bye
He shal bethynke him hastely
To putte him out of al daungerr
That he of meate hath no myskere
Or that he maye with lytel eke
Befounden/ whyle that he is seke
Or that men shul hym berne in haste
To lyue tyl his syckenesse be paste
To some Maysondewe besyde
He caste nought what shal him betyde
He thynketh nought that euer he shal
In to any syckenesse fal.

ANd though it fal/ as it maye be
That al be tyme spare shal he
As mokel as shal to hym suffyce
Whyle he is sycke in any wyse
He dothe for that he wol be
Content with his pouerte
Without nede of any manne
So moche in lytel haue he canne
He is apayde with his fortune
And for he nyl be importune
Unto no wyght/ ne onerous
Nor of her goodesse coueytous
Therfore he spareth/ it maye wel bene
His poore estate for to sustene.

OR if hym luste nat for to spare
But suffreth forthe/ as nat ne ware
At laste it hapneth/ as it maye
Right vnto his laste daye
And take the worlde as it wolde be
For euer in herte thynketh he
The sooner that dethe hym slo
To paradyse the sooner go
He shal/ there for to lyue in blysse
Where that he shal no good mysse
Thyder he hoopeth god shal him sende
After his wretched lyues ende
Pythagoras him selfe reherses
In a booke that the golden verses
Is cleped/ for the nobilyte
Of the honorable dyte
Than whan thou gost thy body fro
Free in the heyre thou shalte vp go
And leauen al humanyte
And purely lyue in deite
He is a foole withouten were
That troweth haue his countrey here
In erthe is nat our countre

Thal

That may these clerkes seyne and se
In Boece of consolation
Where it is maked mention
Of our countre playne at the eye
By techyng of phylosophye
Where leude men might lere wyt
Who so that wolde translaten it
If he be suche that can wel lyue
After his rent/may him yeue
And not desyreth more to haue
Than may fro pouerte him saue
A wyse man sayd/as we may sene
Is no man wretched/but he it wene
Be he kyng/knyght/or rybaude
And many a rybaude is mery and baude
That swynketh/& bereth bothe day & nyght
Many a burthen of great myght
The whiche dothe him lasse offence
For he suffreth in pacience
They laugh and daunce/ tryppe and synge
And lay nought vp for her lyuyng
But in the tauerne al dispendeth
The wynnyng that god hem sendeth
Than gothe he fardels for to bere
With as good chere as he dyd ere
To swynke and trauayle he not faynteth
For to robben he disdayneth
But right anon/after his swynke
He gothe to tauerne for to drinke
Al these are ryche in habundaunce
That can thus haue suffysaunce
Wel more than can an vsurere
As god wel knoweth/without were
For an vsurer/so god me se
Shal neuer for rychesse ryche be
But euermore poore and indygent
Scarce and gredy in his entent.

For sothe it is/whom it displese
There may no marchaunt lyue at ese
His herte in suche a where is set
That it quycke brenneth to get
Ne neuer shal/though he hath geten
Though he haue golde in garners yeten
For to be nedy he dredeth sore
Wherfore to getten more and more
He set his herte and his desyre
So hote he brenneth in the fyre
Of couetyse/that maketh him wood
To purchare other mennes good
He vnderfongeth a great payne
That vndertaketh to drinke vp Sayne
For the more he drinketh aye
The more he leaueth/the sothe to saye
Thus is thurst of false gettyng
That laste euer in coueyting
And the anguysshe and distresse
With the fyre of gredynesse
She fyghteth with hym aye/and stryueth
That his herte a sonder ryueth
Suche gredynesse him assayleth
That whan he moste hath/moste he fayleth
Physiciens/ and aduocates
Gone right by the same yates
They sell her science for wynnyng
And haunte her crafte for great gettyng
Her wynnyng is of suche swetnesse
That if a man fall in sickenesse
They are ful glad/for her encrese
For by her wyll/without lese
Eueryche man shulde be seke
And though they dye/they set not a leke
After whan they the golde haue take
Ful lytel care for hem they make
They wolde that fourty were sicke at ones
Ye two hundred/in flesshe and bones
And yet two thousande/as I gesse
For to encresen her rychesse
They wol not worchen in no wyse
But for lucre and couetyse
For physicke gynneth first by (phy)
The phisycien also sothely
And sythen it gothe fro fye to fye
To truste on hem it is folye
For they nyl in no maner gre
Do right nought for charyte
Eke in the same secte are sette
Al tho that prechen for to gette
Worshyps/honour/and rychesse
Her hertes arne in great distresse
That folke lyue not holily
But abouen al specially
Suche as prechen veynglorie
And towarde god haue no memorie
But forthe as ypocrites trace
And to her soules dethe purchace

And outwarde shewyng holynesse
Though they be ful of cursednesse
Nat lyche to the apostels twelue
They disceyue other and hem selue
Begyled is the gyler than
For preachyng of a cursed man
Though to other maye profyte
Hym selfe it aueyleth nat a myte
For ofte good predicatioun
Cometh of yuel entencioun
To hym nat vayleth his prechyng
Al helpe he other with his teachyng
For where they good ensample take
There is he with vaynglorie shake
But lette vs leuen these prechours
And speke of hem that in her tours
Heape vp her golde/ and faste shette
And sore theron her herte sette
They neyther loue god ne drede
They kepe more than it is nede
And in her bagges sore it bynde
Out of the sonne/ and of the wynde
They putte vp more than nede ware
Whan they seue poore folke forfare
For hungre dye/ and for colde quake
God can wel vengeaunce therof take
The great mischeues hem assayleth
And thus in gadring aye trauayleth
With moche payne they wynne rychesse
And drede hem holdeth in distresse
To kepe that they gather faste
With sorowe they leaue it at the laste
With sorowe they bothe dye and lyue
That vnto rychesse her hertes yeue
And in defaute of loue it is
As it sheweth ful wel ywis
For if these gredy/ the sothe to sayne
Loueden/ and were loued agayne
And good loue reigned ouer all
Suche wickednesse ne shulde fall
But he shulde yeue/ that moste good had
To hem that weren in nede bestad
And lyue without false vsure
For charyte/ ful clene and pure
If they hem yeue to goodnesse
Defendyng hem from ydelnesse
In al this worlde than poore none
We shulde fynde I trowe not one
But chaunged is this worlde vnstable
For loue is ouer al vendable
We se that no man loueth nowe
But for wynnyng and for prowe
And loue is thralled in seruage
Whan it is solde for auauntage
Yet women wol her bodyes sell
Suche soules gothe to the dyuel of hell.

When Loue had tolde hem his entent
The baronage to counsayle went
In many sentences they fyll
And dyuersly they sayde her wyll
But after discorde they accorded
And her acorde to Loue recorded
Sir sayden they/ we ben alone
By euen accorde of euerychone
Out take Rychesse al onely
That sworne hath ful hauteynly
That she the castell nyl not assayle
Ne smyte a stroke in this batayle
With darte ne mace/ speare/ ne knyfe
For man that speketh/ or bereth the lyfe
And blameth your empryse ywis
And from our hoste departed is
At leest way/ as in this plyte
So hath she this man in dispyte
For she sayth he ne loued her neuer
And therfore she wol hate hym euer
For he wol gather no tresore
He hath her wrathe for euermore
He agylte her neuer in other caas
Lo here al holy his trespas
She sayth wel/ that this other day
He asked her leaue to gone the way
That is cleped to moche yeuyng
And spake ful fayre in his prayeng
But whan he prayed her/ poore was he
Therfore she warned hym the entre
Ne yet is he not thriuen so
That he hath getten a peny or two
That quytely is his owne in holde
Thus hath Rychesse vs all tolde
And whan Rychesse vs this recorded
Withouten her we ben accorded.

And we fynde in our accordaunce
That False Semblant and Abstynaunce
With

With al the folke of her batayle
Shul at the hynder gate assayle
That Wicked Tonge hath in kepyng
With his Normans ful of ianglyng
And with hem Curtesy and Largesse
That shul shewe her hardynesse
To the olde wyfe that kepte so harde
Fayre Welcomyng within her warde
Than shal Delyte and Wel Helyng
Fonde/ Shame adowne to bryng
With al her hoost early and late
They shul assaylen that ylke gate
Agaynst Drede shal Hardynesse
Assayle/ and also Sykernesse
With al the folke of her leadyng
That neuer wyst what was fleyng.

FRaunchise shal fyght and eke Pyte
With Daungere ful of crueltе
Thus is your hoost ordayned wele
Downe shal the Castel euery dele
If eueryche do his entent
So that Venus be present
Your mother ful of vessellage
That canne ynough of suche vsage
Withouten her maye no wight spede
This werke/ neither for worde ne dede
Therfore is good ye for her sende
For through her maye this worke amende.

LOrdynges/ my mother the goddesse
That is my lady/ and my maistresse
Nys nat al at my wyllyng:
Ne dothe nat al my desyringe.
yet canne she somtyme done labour
Whan that her luste in my socour
As my nede is for to atcheue
But nowe I thynke her nat to greue
My mother is she/ and of childe hede
I bothe worshippe her/ and eke drede
For who that dredeth sire ne dame
Shal it abye in body or name
And natheles/ yet conne we
Sende after her if nede be
And were she nygh she comen wolde
I trowe that nothynge myght her holde

My mother is of great prowesse
She hath tane many a fortresse
That coste hath many a pounde er this
There I nas not present ywis
And yet men sayd it was my dede
But I come neuer in that stede
Ne me ne lyketh so mote I the
That suche toures ben take with me
For why: Me thynketh that in no wyse
It maye be cleped but marchaundyse.

GO bye a courser blacke or white
And paye therfore/ than arte thou quite
The marchaunt oweth the right nought
Ne thou him whan thou it bought
I wol nat selling clepe yeuyng
For selling asketh no guerdonyng
Here lythe no thanke/ ne no meryte
That one gothe from that other al quyte
But this sellyng is nat semblable
For whan his horse is in the stable
He maye it selle agayne parde
And wynnen on it/ suche happe maye be
Al maye the manne nat lese ywis
For at the leest the skynne is his
Or els/ if it so betyde
That he wol kepe his horse to ryde
Yet is he lorde aye of his horse
But thylke chaffare is welle worse
There Venus entremeteth ought
For who so suche chaffare hath bought
He shal nat worchyn so wysely
That he ne shal lese al vtterly
Bothe his money/ and his chaffare
But the seller of the ware
The prise and profyte haue shal
Certayne the byer shal lese al
For he ne canne so dere it bye
To haue lordshippe/ and ful maistry
Ne haue power to make lettyng
Neyther for yefte ne for preachyng
That of his chaffare maugre his
Another shal haue as moche ywis
If he wol yeue as moche as he
Of what countrey so that he be
Or for right nought so happe maye
If he canne flatter her to her paye
Bene than suche marchauntes wyse:
No/ but fooles in euery wyse
Whan they bye suche thynge wylfully

F. f. iii. There

There as they lese her good folysy
But nathelesse/ this dare I saye
My mother is nat wonte to paye
For she is neither so foole ne nyce
To entremete her of suche vyce
But truste wel/ he shal paye al
That repent of his bargayne shal
Whan pouerte putte him in distresse
Al were he scholer to Rychesse
That is for me in great yernyng
Whan she assenteth to my wylyng.

BUt my mother saynt Venus
And by her father Saturnus
That her engendred by his lyfe
But nat vpon his wedded wyfe
yet wol I more vnto you swere
To make this thyng the surere
Nowe by that faithe/ and that beaute
That I owe to al my bretherne free
Of whiche there nys wight vnder heuyn
That canne her fathers names neuyn
So dyuers and so many there be
That with my mother haue be pryue
yet wolde I swere for sickernesse
The Pole of helle to my wytnesse
Nowe drynke I nat this yere clarre
If that I lye/ or forsworne be
For of the goddes the vsage is
That who so him forswereth amys
Shal that yere drynke no clarre
Nowe haue I sworne ynough parde
If I forswere me than am I lorne
But I wol neuer be forsworne
Sithe Rychesse hath me fayled here
She shal abye that trespas ful dere
Atte leest waye but her arme
With swerde/ or sparth/ or gysarme
For certes sythe she loueth nat me
Fro thylke tyme that she maye se
The castel and the toure to shake
In sorye tyme she shal a wake
If I maye gryppe a ryche manne
I shal so pulle him/ if I canne
That he shal in a fewe stoundes
Lese al his markes/ and his poundes
I shal him make his pens out slynge
But they in his garner sprynge
Our maydens shal eke plucke him so
That him shal neden fethers mo
And make him selle his londe to spende
But he the bette conne him defende.

POore men han made her lorde of me
Al though they nat so myghtye be
That they maye fede me in delyte
I wol nat haue hem in dispyte
No good man hateth hem/ as I gesse
For chynche and feloun is richesse
That so canne chase hem and dispyse
And hem defoule in sondrye wyse
They louen ful bette/ so god me spede
Than dothe the riche chynchy grede
And bene (in good faythe) more stable
And trewer/ and more seruyable
And therfore it suffyseth me
Her good herte/ and her beaute
They han on me sette al her thought
And therfore I foryet hem nought
I wol hem bringe in great noblesse
If that I were god of Rychesse
As I am god of Loue sothely
Suche routhe vpon her playnt haue I
Therfore I muste his socour be
That payneth him to seruen me
For if he deyde for loue of this
Than semeth in me no loue there is

Sir sayde they/ sothe is euerydele
That ye reherce/ and we wote wele
Thylke othe to holde is resonable
For it is good and couenable
That ye on riche men han sworne
For sir/ this wote we wel beforne
If riche men done you homage
That is as fooles done outrage
But ye shul nat forsworne be
Ne lette therfore to drynke clarre
Or pyment maked fresshe and newe
Ladyes shul hem suche pepyr brewe
If that they fal in to her laas
That they for wo mowe sayne alas
Ladyes shullen euer so curteis be
That they shal quyte your othe al free
Ne seketh neuer other vicayre
For they shal speke with hem so fayre

That

That ye shal holde ye payde ful wele.
Though ye you medle neuer a dele
Late ladyes worche with her thynges
They shal hem tel so fele tydinges
And moue hem eke so many requestes
By flatery/ that not honest is
And therto yeue hem suche thankynges
What with kyssyng/and with talkynges
That certes if they trowed be
Shal neuer leaue hem londe ne fee
That it nyll as the moeble fare
Of whiche they first delyuered are
Nowe may ye tell vs al your wyll
And we your hestes shal fulfyll.

BVt False semblant dare not for drede
Of you sir/medle hym of this dede
For he saythe/that ye ben his fo
He not/ if ye wol worche hym wo
Wherfore we praye you al beausire
That ye forgyue hym nowe your ire
And that he may dwell as your man
With Abstynence his dere lemman
This our acorde and our wyll nowe
Parfey sayd Loue/ I graunt it you
I wol wel holde hym for my man
Nowe let hym come/and he forthe ran
False semblant (qd Loue) in this wyse
I take the here to my seruyce
That thou our frendes helpe alway
And hyndreth hem neyther nyght ne day
But do thy myght hem to releue
And eke our enemyes that thou greue
Thyne be this might/ I graunt it the
My kyng of harlotes shalte thou be
We wol that thou haue suche honour
Certayne thou arte a false traytour
And eke a thefe/sythe thou were borne
A thousande tymes thou arte forsworne
But nathelesse in our heryng
To put our folke out of doutyng
I bydde the teche hem/ wost thou howe?
By some general signe nowe
In what place thou shalt founden be
If that men had myster of the
And howe men shal the best espye
For the to knowe is great maistrye
Tel in what place is thyn hauntyng

Sir I haue ful dyuers wonnyng.
That I kepe not rehersed be
So that ye wolde respyten me
For if that I tell you the sothe
I may haue harme and shame bothe
If that my felowes wysten it
My tales shulden me be quyt
For certayne they wolde hate me
If euer I knewe her cruelte
For they wolde ouer al holde hem styll
Of trouthe/that is agayne her wyll
Suche tales kepen they not here
I myght eftsone bye it ful dere
If I sayd of hem any thyng
That aught displeaseth to her heryng
For what worde that hem pricke or byteth
In that worde none of hem delyteth
Al were it gospel the euangyle
That wolde reproue hem of her gyle
For they are cruell and hautayne
And this thyng wote I wel certayne
If I speke aught to payre her loos
Your courte shal not so wel be cloos
That they ne shal wyte it at last
Of good men am I nought agast
For they wol taken on hem nothyng
Whan that they knowe al my meanyng
But he that wol it on hym take
He wol him selfe suspecious make
That he his lyfe let couertly
In gyle and in Ipocrisy
That me engendred and yaue fostryng
They made a ful good engendring
(Quod Loue) for who so sothly tell
They engendred the dyuel of hell.

But nedely/howe so euer it be
(Quod Loue) I wyl and charge the
To tell anon thy wonnyng places
Heryng eche wight that in this place is
And what lyfe that thou lyuest also
Hyde it no lenger nowe/ wherto?
Thou must discouer al thy wurchyng
Howe thou seruest/and of what thyng
Though that thou shuldest for thy sothe sawe
Ben alto beaten and to drawe
And yet arte thou not wont parde
But nathelesse/though thou beten be

Thou

Thou shalt not be the first that so
Hath for sothsawe suffred wo.

Sir/ sythe that it may lyken you
Though that I shulde be slayne right nowe
I shal done your cōmaundement
For therto haue I great talent.

Withouten wordes mo/ right than
False Semblant his sermon began
And sayd hem thus in audyence
Barons/ take hede of my sentence
That wight that lyste to haue knowyng
Of False semblant/ ful of flateryng
He must in worldly folke hym seke
And certes in the cloysters eke
I won no where/ but in hem twey
But not lyke euen/ sothe to say
Shortly I wol herberowe me
There I hope best to hulstred be
And certainly/ sykerest hydyng
Is underneth humblest clothyng
Relygious folke ben ful couerte
Seculer folke ben more apperte
But nathelesse/ I wol not blame
Relygyous folke/ ne hem diffame
In what habyte that euer they go
Relygyon humble/ and trewe also
Wol I not blame/ ne dispyse
But I nyl loue it in no wyse
I meane of false relygious
That stoute ben/ and malycious
That wollen in an habyte go
And setten not her herte therto.

Relygious folke ben al pytous
Thou shalt not seue one dispytous
They louen no pride/ ne no stryfe
But humbly they wol lede her lyfe
With whiche folke wol I neuer be
And if I dwell/ I fayne me
I may wel in her habyt go
But me were leuer my necke a two
Than lette a purpose that I take
What couenaunt that euer I make
I dwell with hem that proude be
And ful of wyles and subtelte
That worshyp of this worlde coueyten
And great nede connen expleyten
And gon and gadren great pytaunces
And purchace hem the acqueyntaunces
Of men that mighty lyfe may leden
And fayne hem poore/ and hem selfe feden
With good morsels delycious
And drinken good wyne precyous
And preche vs pouert and distresse
And fysshen hem selfe great rychesse
With wyly nettes/ that they caste
It wol come foule out at the laste
They ben fro clene relygion went
They make the worlde an argument
That hath a foule conclusyon
I haue a robe of relygyon
Than am I al relygyous
This argument is al roignous
It is not worthe a croked brere
Habyt ne maketh neyther monke ne frere
But clene lyfe and deuocion
Maketh good men of relygyon
Nathelesse/ there can none answere
Howe hygh that euer his heed he shere
With rasour whetted neuer so kene
That gyle in braunches cutte thurtene
There can no wight distyncte it so
That he dare say a worde therto.
But what herberowe that euer I take
Or what semblant that euer I make
I meane but gyle/ and folowe that
For right no more than gybbe our cat
(That awayteth myce & rattes to kyllen)
Ne entende I but to begylen
Ne no wight may/ by my clothyng
Wete with what folke is my dwellyng
Ne by my wordes yet parde
So softe and so plesaunt they be
Beholde the dedes that I do
But thou be blynde thou oughtest so
For varye her wordes fro her dede
They thynke on gyle without drede
What maner clothyng that they were
Or what estate that euer they bere
Lered or lewde/ lorde or lady
Knyght/ squyer/ burgeys/ or bayly.

Right thus whyle False semblāt sermoneth
Eftsones Loue him aresoneth
And

And brake his tale in his speakyng
As though he had him tolde leasyng
And sayd: What dyuel is that I here?
What folke haste thou us nempned here?
Maye men fynde relygioun
In worldly habytatioun?
  Ye sir/ it foloweth nat that they
Shulde lede a wicked lyfe parfey
Ne nat therfore her soules lese
That hem to worldly clothes chese
For certes it were great pyte
Menne maye in seculer clothes se
Florisshen hooly relygioun
Ful many a saynt in felde and towne
With many a virgyn glorious
Deuoute/ and ful relygious
Han dyed/ that cōmen clothe aye beren
yet sayntes neuerthelesse they weren
I coude recken you many a ten
Ye/ welnygh al these holy women
That menne in churches herry and seke
Bothe maydens/ and these wyues eke
That baren ful many a fayre chylde here
Weared alwaye clothes seculere
And in the same dyden they
That sayntes weren/ and ben alwaye.
  ¶ The. xi. thousande maydens dere
That beren in heuen her cierges clere
Of whiche men rede in churche and syng
Were take in seculer clothyng
Whan they receyued martyrdome
And wonnen heuen unto her home
Good herte maketh the good thought
The clothynge yeueth ne reueth nought
The good thought and the worchyng
That maketh the relygion flouryng
There lyeth the good relygioun
After the right ententioun.

  Who so tooke a wethers skynne
And wrapped a gredy wolfe therinne
For he shulde go with lambes white
Wenest thou nat he wolde hem byte?
Yes: Neuerthelesse/ as he were wode
He wolde hem wirry/ and drinke the blode
And wel the rather hem disceyue
For sithe they coude nat perceyue
His tregette/ and his cruelte
They wolde him folowe al tho he flye.
If there be wolues of suche hewe
Amonges these apostles newe
Thou holy churche thou mayste be wayled
Sythe that thy cyte is assayled
Through knyghtes of thyn owne table
God wot thy lordshyp is doutable
If they enforce it to wyn
That shulde defende it fro within
Who myght defence ayenst hem make
Without stroke it mote be take
Of trepeget or mangonel
Without displayeng of pensel
And if god nyl done it socour
But let renne in this colour
Thou must thy heestes letten be
Than is there nought/ but yelde the
Or yeue hem trybute doutles
And holde it of hem to haue pees
But greater harme betyde the
That they al maister of it be
Wel conne they scorne the withall
By day stuffen they the wall
And al the nyght they mynen there
Nay/ thou planten muste els where
Thyn ympes/ if thou wolt fruite haue
Abyde not there thy selfe to saue.

But nowe peace/ here I turne agayne
I wol no more of this thyng sayne
If I may passen me hereby
I might maken you wery
But I wol heten you alway
To helpe your frendes what I may
So they wollen my company
For they be shent al utterly
But if so fall/ that I be
Ofte with hem/ and they with me
And eke my lemman mote they serue
Or they shul not my loue deserue
Forsothe I am a false traytour
God iuged me for a thefe trechour
Forsworne I am/ but wel nygh none
Wote of my gyle/ tyl it be done.

  Through me hath many one deth receyued
That my treget neuer aperceyued
And yet receyueth/ and shal receyue

That

That my falsnesse shal neuer apercepue
But who so dothe/ if he wyse be
Him is ryght good be ware of me
But so slyghe is the apercepuynge
That al to late cometh knowynge
For Protheus that coude him chaunge
In euery shappe/ homely and straunge
Coude neuer suche gyle ne treasoune
As I/ for I come neuer in towne
There as I myght knowen be
Though men me bothe myght here and se
Ful wel I canne my clothes chaunge
Take one/and make another straunge
Nowe am I knyght/ nowe chastelayne
Nowe prelate/ and nowe chapelayne
Nowe preest/nowe clerke/and nowe fostere
Nowe am I maister/ nowe scholere
Nowe monke/nowe chanon/nowe bayly
What euer myster manne am I.
  Nowe am I prince/ nowe am I page
And canne by herte euery langage
Somtyme am I hoore and olde
  Nowe am I yonge/ stoute/ and bolde
Nowe am I Robert/ nowe Robyn
Nowe Frere mynor/ nowe Jacobyn
And with me foloweth my loteby
To done me solace and company
That hight dame Abstynence/ and raigned
In many a queynt arraye fayned
Ryght as it cometh to her lykyng
I fulfyl al her desyringe.
  Somtyme a womans clothe take I
Nowe am I a mayde/ nowe lady
  Somtyme I am relygious
Nowe lyke an anker in an hous
  Somtyme am I prioresse
And nowe a nonne/ and nowe abbesse
And go through al regiouns
Sekynge al relygiouns
  But to what order that I am sworne
I take the strawe and beate the corne
To iolye folke I enhabyte
I aske no more but her habite
  What wol ye more in euery wyse
Ryght as me lyste I me disgyse?
  Wel canne I beare me vnder wede
Vnlyke is my worde to my dede
Thus make I in to my trappes fal
The people/ through my priuyleges al
That bene in christendome a lyue
  I maye assoyle/ and I maye shryue
That no prelate maye lette me
Al folke/ where euer they founde be
I not no prelate may done so
But it the Pope be/ and no mo
That made thilke establisshyng
Nowe is not this a propre thyng?
But were my sleightes apercepued
As I was wonte/and woste thou whye?
For I dyd hem a tregetry
But therof yeue I a lytel tale
I haue the syluer and the male
So haue I preched and eke shriuen
So haue I take/so haue I yeuen
Through her foly/husbonde and wyfe
That I lede right a ioly lyfe
Through symplesse of the prelacye
They knowe not al my tregettrye.

BVt for as moche as man and wyfe
Shulde shewe her parisshe preest her lyfe
Ones a yere/as sayth the boke
Er any wight his housel toke
Than haue I priuyleges large
That may of moche thyng discharge
For he may say right thus parde
  Sir preest/in shrifte I tel it the
That he to whom that I am shriuen
Hath me assoyled/and me yeuen
Penaunce sothlye for my syn
Whiche that I fonde me gilty in
Ne I ne haue neuer entencion
To make double confession
Ne reherce efte my shrift to the
O shrift is right ynough to me
This ought the suffyse wele
Ne be not rebell neuer a dele
For certes/though thou haddest it sworne
I wote no preest ne prelate borne
That may to shrift efte me constrayne
And if they done I wol me playne
For I wote where to playne wele
Thou shalt not streyne me a dele
Ne enforce me/ne not me trouble
To make my confessyon double
Ne I haue none affection

To

To haue double absolution
The first is right ynough to me
This latter assoylng quyte I the
I am vnbounde/what mayst thou fynde
More of my synnes me to vnbynde
For he that might hath in his honde
Of al my synnes me vnbonde
And if thou wolte me thus constrayne
That me mote nedes on the playne
There shal no iuge imperyall
Ne bysshop/ne offyciall
Done iugement on me/for I
Shal gone and playne me openly
Vnto my shriftfather newe
That hyght Frere wolfe vntrewe
And he shal chuse him for me
For I trowe he can hamper the
But lorde he wolde be wrothe withall
If men him wolde Frere wolfe call
For he wolde haue no pacience
But done al cruell vengience
He wolde his myght done at the leest
Nothyng spare for goddes heest
And god so wyse be my socour
But thou yeue me my sauyour
At Ester/whan it lyketh me
Without preasyng more on the
I wol forthe/and to him gone
And he shal housell me anon
For I am out of thy grutchyng
I kepe not deale with the nothyng
Thus may he shriue him/that forsaketh
His parysshe preest/and to me taketh
And if the preest wol him refuse
I am ful redy him to accuse
And him punisshe and hamper so
That he his churche shal forgo.

But who so hath in his felyng
The consequence of suche shriuyng
Shal sene/that preest may neuer haue might
To knowe the conscience aright
Of him/that is vnder his cure
And this is ayenst holy scripture
That byddeth euery heerd honest
Haue very knowyng of his beest
But poore folke that gon by strete
That haue no golde/ne somes grete
Hem wolde I set to her prelates
Or let her preestes knowe her states
For to me right nought yeue they
And why it is/for they ne may
They ben so bare/ I take no kepe
But I wol haue the fatte shepe
Let parisshe preestes haue the lene
I yeue not of her harme a bene
And if that prelates grutche it
That oughten woth be in her wyt
To lese her fatte beestes so
I shal yeue hem a stroke or two
That they shal lesen with force
Ye/ bothe her mytre and her croce
Thus iape I hem/ and haue do longe
My priuileges ben so stronge.

False Semblant wolde haue stynted here
But Loue ne made him no suche chere
That he was wery of his sawe
But for to make him glad and fawe
He said/ Tel on more specially
Howe that thou seruest vntruely
Tel forthe/ and shame the neuer a dele
For as thyn habyt sheweth wele
Thou seruest an holy heremyte
Sothe is/ but I am but an ypocryte
Thou gost and prechest pouerte?
Ye sir/ but rychesse hath poste
Thou prechest abstynence also?
Sir/ I wol fyllen so mote I go
My paunche/of good meate and wyne
As shulde a maister of diuyne
For howe that I me poore fayne
Yet al poore folke I disdayne.

I Loue better the acqueyntaunce
Ten tymes of the kyng of Fraunce
Than of a poore man of mylde mode
Though that his soule be also good
For whan I se beggers quakyng
Naked on myxins al stynkyng
For hongre crye/and eke for care
I entremet not of her fare
They ben so poore/and ful of pyne
They might not ones yeue me a dyne
For they haue nothyng but her lyfe
What shulde he yeue that licketh his knyfe?
It is

It is but folly to entremete
To seke in houndes nest fatte mete
Lette beare hem to the spyttle anone
But for me/ comforte gette they none
But a riche sicke vsurere
Wolde I visyte and drawe nere
Him wol I comforte and rehete
For I hoope of his golde to gete
And if that wicked dethe him haue
I wol go with him to his graue
And if there any reproue me
Why that I lette the poore be
Wost thou howe I not ascape
I saye and swere him ful rape
That riche menne han more tetches
Of synne/ than han poore wretches
And hanne of counsayle more myster
And therfore I wolde drawe hem ner
But as great hurte/ it maye so be
Hath a soule in right great pouerte
As soule in great richesse forsothe
Al be it that they hurten bothe
For richesse and mendicitees
Bene cleped two extremytees
The meane is cleped Suffysaunce
There lyeth of vertue the aboundaunce
For Salomon ful wel I wote
In his Parables vs wrote
As it is knowe of many a wight
In his thrittene chapiter right
God thou me kepe for thy poste
Fro richesse and mendycite
For if a riche manne him dresse
To thynke to moche on richesse
His herte on that so ferre is sette
That he his creatour dothe foryette
And him that beggeth wol aye greue
Howe shulde I by his worde him leue
Vnneth that he nys a mycher
Forsworne/ or els goddes lyer
Thus saithe Salomon sawes
Ne we fynde written in no lawes
And namely in our christen laye
Who so saithe ye/ I dare say naye
That Christ/ ne his apostels dere
While that they walked in erthe here
Were neuer seen her bred beggyng
For they nolden beggen for nothyng
And right thus were men wont to teche
And in this wyse wolde it preche
The maisters of dyuinyte
Somtyme in Parys the cyte.

And if men wolde there gayne appose
The naked texte and lette the glose
It myght soone assoyled be
For menne maye wel the sothe se
That pardie they myght aske a thynge
Plainly forthe without beggynge
For they weren goddes heerdes dere
And cure of soules hadden here
They nolde nothyng begge her foode
For after Christ was done on rodde
With their proper hondes they wrought
And with trauayle/ and els nought
They wonnen al her sustenaunce
And lyueden forthe in her penaunce
And the remenaunt yaf awaye
To other poore folkes alwaye
They neither bylden towre ne halle
But they in houses smal with alle
A mighty man that canne and maye
Shulde with his honde and body alwaye
Wynne him his foode in laboring
If he ne haue rent or suche a thyng
Al though he be relygious
And goo to seruen curyous
Thus mote he done/ or do trespas
But if it be in certayne caas
That I can reherce/ if myster be
Right wel/ whan the tyme I se.

Seke the boke of saynt Austyne
Be it in paper or perchmyne
There as he writte of these worchynges
Thou shalt sene that none excusynges
A parfyte man ne shulde seke
By wordes/ ne by dedes eke
Al though he be religyous
And god to seruen curyous
That he ne shal/ so mote I go
With propre hondes/ and body also
Get his fode in laboring
If he ne haue proprete of thyng
Yet shulde he sell al his substaunce
And with his swynke haue sustenaunce

If he

If he be parfyte in bounte
Thus han the bookes tolde me
For he that wol gone ydelly
And vseth it aye besyly
To haunten other mennes table
He is a trechour ful of fable
Ne he ne may by good reason
Excuse him by his orison
For men behoueth in some gyse
Men sometyme in goddes seruyse
To gone and purchasen her nede
Men mote eaten/ that is no drede
And slepe/ and eke do other thyng
So longe may they leaue prayeng
So may they eke her prayer blynne
Whyle that they werke her meate to wynne
Seynt Austyn wol therto accorde
In thilke boke that I recorde
Justinian eke/ that made lawes
Hath thus forboden by olde sawes.

No man/ vp payne to be deed
Mighty of body/ to begge his breed
If he may swynke it for to gete
Men shulde him rather mayme or bete
Or done of him aperte iustyce
Than suffren him in suche malyce
They done not wel so mote I go
That taken suche almesse so
But if they haue some priuilege
That of the payne hem wol alege
But howe that is/ can I not se
But if the prince disceyued be
Ne I ne wene not sykerly
That they may haue it rightfully
But I wol not determyne
Of princes power/ ne defyne
Ne by my worde comprehende iwys
If it so ferre may stretche in this
I wol not entremete a dele
But I trowe that the boke sayth wele
Who that taketh almesses/ that be
Dewe to folke that men may se
Lame/ feble/ wery/ and bare
Poore/ or in suche maner care
That conne wynne hem neuer mo
For they haue no power therto
He eateth his owne dampnyng
But if he lye/ that made al thyng
And if ye suche a truaunt fynde
Chastyse him wel/ if ye be kynde
But they wolde hate you parcaas
If ye fyllen in her laas
They wolde eftsones do you scathe
If that they might/ late or rathe
For they be not ful pacient
That han the worlde thus foule blent
And weteth wel/ that god bad
The good man sell al that he had
And folowe him/ and to poore it yeue
He wolde not therfore that he lyue
To seruen him in mendience
For it was neuer his sentence
But he bad werken/ whan that nede is
And folowe him in good dedes
Saynt Poule/ that loued al holy churche
He bade the apostels for to wurche
And wynnen her lyuelode in that wyse
And hem defended truandyse
And sayd/ werketh with your honden
Thus shulde the thyng be vnderstonden
He nolde iwys haue byd hem beggyng
Ne sellen gospel/ ne prechyng
Lest they berafte/ with her askyng
Folke of her catel or of her thyng
For in this worlde is many a man
That yeueth his good/ for he ne can
Werne it for shame/ or els he
Wolde of the asker delyuered be
And for he him encombreth so
He yeueth him good to late him go
But it can him no thyng profyte
They lese the yefte and the meryte
The good folke that Poule to preched
Profred him ofte/ whan he hem teched
Some of her good in charyte
But therfore right nothyng toke he
But of his hondewerke wolde he gete
Clothes to wryne him/ and his mete.

Tell me than howe a man may lyuen
That al his good to poore hath yeuen
And wol but onely bydde his bedes
And neuer with hondes labour his nedes
Maye he do so? Ye sir: And howe?
Sir/ I wol gladly tell you

Seynt Austen sayth/a man may be
In houses that han properte
As templers/and hospytelers
And as these chanons regulers
Or whyte monkes/or these blake
I wol no mo ensamples make
And take therof his susteynyng
For therin lythe no beggyng
But other wayes not ywis
Yet Austyn gabbeth not of this
And yet ful many a monke laboureth
That god in holy churche honoureth
For whan her swynkyng is agon
They rede and synge in churche anon.

And for there hath ben great discorde
As many a wight may beare recorde
Upon the estate of mendicience
I wol shortly in your presence
Tel howe a man may begge at nede
That hath not wherwith him to fede
Maugre his felowes iangelynges
For sothfastnesse wol none hydynges
And yet parcase I may abey
That I to you sothly thus sey.

LO here the case especial
If a man be so bestyal
That he of no crafte hath science
And nought desyreth ignorence
Than may he go a beggyng yerne
Tyl he some maner crafte can lerne
Through whiche without truandyng
He may in trouthe haue his lyuyng
Or if he may done no labour
For elde/or sicknesse/or langour
Or for his tendre age also
Than may he yet a beggyng go
Or if he haue perauenture
Through usage of his noriture
Lyued ouer delyciously
Than oughten good folke comenly
Han of his mischefe some pyte
And suffren him also/ that he
May gon aboute and begge his breed
That he be not for honger deed
Or if he haue of crafte connyng
And strength also/ and desyring
To worchen/as he had what
But he fynde neyther this ne that
Than may he begge tyl that he
Haue geten his necessyte
Or if his wynnyng be so lyte
That his labour wol not acquyte
Suffyciantly al his lyuyng
yet may he go his breed beggyng
Fro doore to doore/he may go trace
Tyl he the remenant may purchace
Or if a man wolde undertake
Any emprise for to make
In the rescous of our lay
And it defenden/ as he may
Be it with armes/or lettrure
Or other couenable cure
If it be so he poore be
Than may he begge/tyll that he
May fynde in trouthe for to swynke
And get him clothe/meate/and drinke
Swynke he with his hondes corporell
And not with hondes espyrituell.
IN al this case/and in semblables
If that there ben mo resonables
He may begge/as I tell you here
And els not/in no manere
As Willyam Seynt Amour wolde preche
And ofte wolde dispute and teche
Of this mater al openly
At Parys ful solempnly
And also god my soule blesse
As he had in this stedfastnesse
The accorde of the Uniuersite
And of the people/as semeth me.

No good man ought it to refuse
Ne ought him therof to excuse
Be wrothe or blythe/ who so be
For I wol speke/and tell it the
Al shulde I dye/and be put doun
As was seynt Poule in derke prisoun
Or be exiled in this caas
With wronge/as mayster William was
That my mother Hypocrise
Banysshed for her great enuye.

My mother flemed him Seynt Amour
This noble dyd suche labour

To

To susteyne euer the loyaste
That he to moche agylte me
He made a boke/and let it write
Wherin his lyfe he dyd al write
And wolde yche reneyed begging
And lyued by my traueylyng
If I ne had rent ne other good
What weneth he that I were wood?
For labour might me neuer plese
I haue more wyl to ben at ese
And haue wel leuer/sothe to say
Before the people pattre and pray
And wrie me in my foyerie
Under a cope of papelardie.

(Of Loue) what dyuel is this that I here
What wordes tellest thou me here
What sir Falsnesse that apert is
Than dredest thou not god? No certis
For selde in great thyng shal he spede
In this worlde/that god wol drede
For folke that hem to vertue yeuen
And truely on her owne lyuen
And hem in goodnesse aye contene
On hem is lytel thrifte ysene
Suche folke drinken great misese
That lyfe may me neuer plese
But se what golde han usurers
And syluer eke in garners
Taylagiers/and these monyours
Baylisses/bedels/prouost/countours
These lyuen wel nygh by raupne
The smale people hem mote enclyne
And they as wolues wol hem eten
Upon the poore folke they geten
Ful moche of that they spende or kepe
Nys none of hem that he nyl strepe
And wrine hem selfe wel at full
Without scaldyng/they hem pull
The stronge the feble ouergothe
But I that weare my symple clothe
Robbe bothe robbyng and robbours
And gyle gyling/and gylours
By my treget/I gather and threst
The great tresour in to my cheste
That lyeth with me so faste bounde
Myn hygh paleys do I founde
And my delytes I fulfyll
With wyne at feestes/at my wyll
And tables ful of entremees
I wol no lyfe/but ease and pees
And wynne golde to spende also
For whan the great bagge is go
It cometh right with my iapes
Make I not wel tomble myn apes
To wynnen is alway myn entent
My purchace is better than my rent
For though I shulde beten be
Ouer al I entremet me
Without me may no wight dure
I walke soules for to cure
Of al the worlde cure haue I
In brede and length boldly
I wol bothe preche/and eke counsaylen
With hondes wyl I not trauaylen
For of the Pope I haue the bull
I ne holde not my wyttes dull
I wol not stynten in my lyue
These Emperours for to shriue
Of kynges/dukes/and lordes grete
But poore folke al quyte I lete
I loue no suche shriuyng parde
But it for other cause be
I recke not of poore men
Her astate is not worthe an hen
Where fyndest thou a swynker of labour
Haue me unto his confessour?
But Empresses/and duchesses
These quenes/and eke countesses
These abbesses/and eke bygyns
These great ladyes palasyns
These iolye knyghtes/and baylives
These nonnes/and these burgeys wyues
That ryche ben/and eke plesyng
And these maydens welfaryng
Where so they clad or naked be
Uncounsayled gothe there none fro me
And for her soules sauete
Al lorde and lady/and her meyne
I aske/whan they hem to me shriue
The proprete of al her lyue
And make hem trowe/bothe moste and leest
Her parysshe preest nys but a beest
Ayens me and my company
That shrewes ben/as great (as I)
For whiche I wol not hyde in holde

G.g.ii. No

No pryuite that me is tolde
That I by worde or signe ywis
Ne wol make hem knowe what it is
And they wollen also tellen me
They hele fro me no pryuite
And for to make you hem parceyuen
That vsen folke thus to disceyuen
I wol you sayne withouten drede
What menne maye in the Gospel rede
Of saynt Mathue the gospelere
That sayth/ as I shal you saye here.

Vpon the chayre of Moyses
Thus it is glosed doutlees
(That is the olde Testament
For therby is the chayre ment)
Sytte Scribes and Pharysen
That is to sayne/ the cursed men
Whiche that we hypocrites call
Dothe that they preche I rede you all
But dothe nat as they done a dele
That bene nat wery to saye wele
But to do wel/ no wyl haue they
And they wolde bynde on folke alwaye
That bene to begyled able
Burdons that ben inportable
On folkes shulders thynges they couchen
That they nyl with her fyngers touchen
And why wol they nat touche it why?
For hem ne lyste nat sykerly
For sadde burdons that men taken
Make folkes shulders aken
And if they do ought that good be
That is for folke it shulde se
Her burdons larger maken they
And make her hemmes wyde alwaye
And louen seates at the table
The fyrste/ and most honorable
And for to haue the firste chayres
In synagogges/ to hem ful dere is
And wyllen that folke hem loute and grete
Whan that they passen through the strete
And wollen be cleped maister also
But they ne shulde nat wyllen so
The gospel is there agaynst I gesse
That sheweth wel her wickednesse.

Nother custome vse we
Of hem that wol ayenst vs be
We hate him deedly euerychone
And we wol werrey him/ as one
Hym that one hateth/ hate we al
And coniecte/ howe to done him fal
And if we sene him wynne honour
Rychesse or preyse/ through his valour
Prouende/ rente/ or dignyte
Ful faste ywis compassen we
By what ladder he is clomben so
And for to maken him downe to go
With traryson we wol hym defame
And done him lese his good name
Thus from his ladder we him take
And thus his frendes foes we make
But worde ne wete shal he noon
Tyl al his frendes bene his foon
For if we dyd it openly
We myght haue blame redily
For hadde he wyste of our malyce
He hadde him kepte/ but he were nyce.

Another is this/ that if so fall
That there be one amonge vs all
That dothe a good tourne/ out of drede
We sayne it is our alder dede
Ye sykerly/ though he it sayned
Or that him lyste/ or that him dayned
A manne through him auaunced be
Therof al parceners be we
And tellen folke/ where so we go
That manne through vs is sprongen so
And for to haue of menne preysyng
We purchace through our flatterynge
Of riche menne of great poste
Letters/ to wytnesse our bounte
So that manne weneth that maye vs se
That al vertue in vs be
And alwaye poore we vs sayne
But howe so that we begge or playne
We bene the folke without leasyng
That al thynge haue without hauyng
Thus be we dradde of the people ywis
And gladly my purpose is this.
¶ I deale with no wight/ but he
Haue golde and treasour great plente
Her acqueyntaunce wel loue I
This is moche my desyre shortely
I entremete me of brocages

I make

I make peace/ and mariages
I am gladly executour
And many tymes a procuratour
I am somtyme messagere
That falleth nat to my mystere
And many tymes I make enqueste
For me that offyce is nat honest
To deale with other mennes thynge
That is to me a great lykynge
And if that ye haue ought to do
In place that I repeyre to
I shal it speden through my wyt
As soone as ye haue tolde me it
So that ye serue me to paye
My seruyce shal be yours alwaye
But who so wol chastyce me
Anone my loue loste hath he
For I loue no manne in no gyse
That wol me repreue/ or chastice
But I wolde al folke vndertake
And of no wight no teachynge take
For I that other folke chastye
Wol nat be taught fro my folye.

I Loue none Hermytage more
Al desertes/ and holtes hoore
And great woodes euerychone
I lette hem to the Baptyst Iohn
I queth him quyte and him relesse
Of Egipte al the wyldernesse
To ferre were al my mansyons
Fro al cytees and good towns
My paleys and myne house make I
There menne maye renne in openly
And saye that I the worlde forsake
But al amydde I bylde/ and make
My house / and swymme and playe therinne
Bette than a fysshe dothe with his fynne.

Of Antechristes menne am I
Of whiche that Christ sayth openly
They haue habyte of holynesse
And lyuen in suche wickednesse
To the coppe/ if him talent toke
Of the Euangelystes booke
There myght he se by great traysoun
Ful many false comparysoun
As moche as through his great myght
Be it of heate or of lyghte
The sonne surmounteth the moone
That troubler is/ and chaungeth soone
And the natte kyrnel the shelle
I skorne nat that I you telle
Right so withouten any gyle
Surmounteth this noble Euangyle
The worde of any Euangelyst
And to her tytell they token Christ
And many suche comparysoun
Of whiche I make no mencioun
Myght menne in that booke fynde
Who so coude of hem haue mynde.

The vnyuersyte that tho was a slepe
Gan for to brayde / and taken kepe
And at the noyse/ the heed vp cast
Ne neuer sythen slepte it fast
But vp it sterte/ and armes tooke
Ayenst this false horryble booke
Al redy batayle for to make
And to the Iuge the booke they take
But they that broughten the boke there
Hent it anone awaye for fere
They nolde shewe it no more a dele
But than it kepte/ and kepen wele
Tyll suche a tyme that they maye se
That they so stronge woxen be
That no wight maye hem wel withstonde
For by that boke they durst nat stonde
Awaye they gonne it for to bere
For they ne durste nat answere
By exposytioun no gloose
To that that clerkes wol appose
Ayenst the cursednesse ywis
That in that booke written is
Nowe wotte I nat/ ne I can nat se
What maner ende that there shal be
Of al this that they hyde
But yet algate they shal abyde
Tyl that they maye it bette defende
This trowe I best wol be her ende.

Thus Antechrist abyden we
For we bene al of his meyne
And what manne that wol nat be so
Right soone he shal his lyfe for go
Outwarde Lamben semen we

G.g.iii. Full

Ful of goodnesse and of pyte
And inwarde we withouten fable
Bene gredy Wolues ravysable
 We envyroun bothe londe and see
With al the worlde werryen we
We wol ordayne of al thynge
Of folkes good/ and her lyvyng.

 If there be castell or cytee
Wherin that any bougerons be
Al though that they of Mylayne were
For therof bene they blamed there
 Or of a wyght out of measure
Wolde leane her golde/ and take usure
For that he is so coveytous
Or if he be to Lecherous
Or these that haunten Simonye
Or Provost ful of trechery
Or Prelate lyveng iolyly
Or preest that halte his queyn him by
Or olde hoores hostylers
Or other baudes or bordellers
Or els blamed of any vyce
Of whiche men shulden done iustyce
 By al the sayntes that we prey
But they defende them with lamprey
With luce/ with elys/ with samons
With tendre gees/ and with Capons
With tartes/ or with chesses fatte
With deyntie flaunes/ brode and flatte
With caleweys/ or with pullayle
With conynges/ or with fyne vitayle
That we under our clothes wyde
Maken through our golet glyde
Or but he wol do come in haste
Roe venyson bake in paste
Whether so that he loure or groyne
He shal have of a corde a loygne
With whiche men shal him bynde and lede
To brenne him for his synful dede
That men shul here him crye and rore
A myle way aboute and more
Or els he shal in prison dye
But if he wol his frendshyp bye
Or smerten that/ that he hath do
More than his gylte amounteth to
 But and he couthe/ through his sleight
Do maken up a tourr of heyght
Nought rought I/ wheder of stone or tre
Or erth=/ or turves though it be
Though it were of no vounde stone
Wrought with squyre and scantilone
So that the tour were stuffed well
With al rychesse temporell
 And than that he wolde up dresse
Engyns/ bothe more and lesse
To caste at us by every syde
To bere his good name wyde
 Suche sleightes I shal you neven
Barels of wyne/ by syxe or seven
Or golde in sackes great plente
He shulde soone delyvered be
And if he have no suche pytences
Let him study in equipolences
And lette lyes/ and fallaces
If that he wolde deserve our graces
Or we shal beare him suche wytnesse
Of synne/ and of his wretchydnesse
And done his lose so wyde renne
That al quicke we shulde him brenne
Or els yeve him suche penaunce
That is wel worse than the pytaunce.

 For thou shalte never for nothyng
Con knowen a right by her clothyng
The traitours ful of trecherye
But thou her werkes can aspye
 And ne had the good kepyng be
Whylom of the universyte
That kepeth the key of cristendome
We had ben turmented al and some
 Suche ben the stynkyng prophetis
Nys none of hem/ that good prophete is
For they through wicked entencion
The yere of the incarnacion
A thousande/ and two hundred yere
Fyve and fyfty/ ferther ne nere
Broughten a boke/ with sory grace
To yeven ensample in cōmune place
That sayd thus/ though it were fable
This is the Gospel perdurable
That fro the holy goost is sent
Wel were it worthe to ben brent
Entytled was in suche manere
This boke/ of whiche I tell here
 There nas no wight in al Parys

Before

Beforne our Lady at parvys
That they ne myght the booke by
The sentence pleased hem wel trewly.
  But I wol stynte of this matere
For it is wonder longe to here
But hadde that ylke boke endured
Of better estate I were ensured
And frendes have I yet parde
That han me set in great degre.

Of al this worlde is Emperour
Gyle my father/the trechour
And Empresse my mother is
Maugre the holy goste iwys
Our mighty lynage/and our route
Reigneth in every reigne aboute
And wel is worthy we mynistres be
For al this worlde governe we
And can the folke so wel disceyve
That none our gyle can perceyve
And though they done/they dare not say
The sothe dare no wight bewray
  But he in Christes wrathe him ledeth
That more than Christ my bretherne dredeth
He nys no ful good champion
That dredeth suche similacion
Nor that for payne wol refusen
Vs to correcte and accusen
  He wol not entremete by right
Ne have god in his eye sight
And therfore god shal him punyce
But me ne recketh of no vyce
Sythen men vs loven comunably
And holden vs for so worthy
That we may folke repreve echone
And we nyll have reprefe of none
Whom shulden folke worshyppen so
But vs that stynten never mo
To patren/whyle that folke may vs se
Though it not so behynde hem be.

And where is more woode folye
Than to enhaunce chivalrye
And love noble men and gay
That joly clothes weren alway
If they be suche folke as they semen
So clene/ as men her clothes demen
And that her wordes folowe her dede
It is great pyte out of drede
For they wol be none hypocritis
Of hem me thynketh great spyte is
I canne nat love hem on no syde
  But beggers with these hoodes wyde
With sleighe and pale faces leane
And graye clothes nat ful cleane
But fretted ful of tatarwagges
And highe shoes knopped with dagges
That frouncen lyke a quayle pype
Or bootes rivelyng as a gype
  To suche folke/ as I you devyse
Shulde princes and these lordes wyse
Take al her londes and her thynges
Bothe warre and peace in governynges
To suche folke shulde a prince hym yeve
That wolde his lyfe in honour lyve.

  And if they be nat as they seme
That serven thus the worlde to queme
There wolde I dwelle to disceyve
The folke/ for they shal nat parceyve
  But I ne speke in no suche wyse
That men shulde humble habytte dispyse
So that no pride there vnder be
No manne shulde hate/ as thynketh me
The poore man in suche clothynge
But god ne preyseth him nothynge
That saith he hath the worlde forsake
And hath to worldly glorie hym take
And wol of suche delyces vse
Who maye that begger wel excuse?
  That papelarde/ that him yeldeth so
And wol to worldly ease go
And saith that he the worlde hath lefte
And gredily it gryppeth efte
He is the hounde/ shame is to sayne
That to his castynge gothe agayne.

But vnto you dare I nat lye
But myght I felen or espye
That ye parceyved it nothynge
Ye shulde have a starke leasynge
Right in your honde thus to begynne
I nolde it lette for no synne
  The god loughe at the wonder tho
And every wyght ganne laughe also
And sayd: Lo here a manne aright
For to be trusty to every wight.

False

FAlse semblant (q Loue) say to me
Sythe I thus haue auaunced the
That in my courte is thy dwellyng
And of rybaudes shalt be my kyng
Wolt thou wel holden my forwardes?
ye sir/ from hence forwardes
We wol a people upon him areyse
And through our gyle/ done him seise
And him on sharpe speares ryue
Or other wayes bringe him fro lyue
But if that he wol folowe ywis
That in our booke written is.

THus moche wol our booke signifye
That whyle Peter hath maistrye
May neuer Iohan shewe wel his might
Nowe haue I you declared right
The meanyng of the barke and rynde
That maketh the entencions blynde
But nowe at erst I wol begyn
To expowne you the pythe within
And the seculers comprehende
That Christes lawe wol defende
And shulde it kepen and mayntenen
Ayenst hem that al sustenen
And falsly to the people techen
That Iohan betoketh hem to prechen
That there nys lawe couenable
But thilke gospel perdurable
That fro the holy goste was sent
To turne folke that ben miswent.

The strength of Iohan they understonde
The grace in whiche they say they stonde
That dothe the synful folke converte
And hem to Iesu christ reuerte
Ful many an other horriblete
May men in that booke se
That ben cōmaunded doutelesse
Ayenst the lawe of Rome expresse
And al with Antechrist they holden
As men may in the boke beholden
And than cōmaunden they to sleen
Al tho that with Peter been
But they shal neuer haue that myght
And god to forne/ for stryfe to fyght
That they ne shal ynough fynde
That Peters lawe shal haue in mynde
And euer holde/ and so mayntene
That at the laste it shal be sene
That they shal al come therto
For aught that they can speke or do
And thilke lawe shal not stonde
That they by Iohan haue understonde
But maugre hem/ it shal adoun
And ben brought to confusyoun
Had neuer your father here beforne
Seruaunt so trewe/ sythe he was borne
That is ayenst al nature
Sir/ put you in that auenture
For though ye borowes take of me
The sykerer shal ye neuer be
For hostages/ ne sykernesse
Or chartres/ for to beare wytnesse
I take your selfe to recorde here
That men ne may/ in no manere
Teren the wolfe out of his hyde
Tyl he be slayne/ backe and syde
Though men him beate and al defyle
What wene ye that I wol begyle?
For I am clothed mekely
There under is al my trechery
Myn herte chaungeth neuer the mo
For none habyt/ in whiche I go
Though I haue chere of symplenesse
I am not wery of shrewdnesse
My lemman/ strayned Abstenaunce
Hath myster of my puruey aunce
She had ful longe ago be dede
Nere my counsayle and my rede
Let her alone/ and you and me
And Loue answerde/ I truste the
Without borowe/ for I wol none
And False semblant the these anone
Right in that ilke same place
That had of treson al his face
Right blacke within/ and whyte without
Thankyng him/ gan on his knees loute.

Than was there nought/ but euery man
Nowe to assaute/ that saylen can
(Quod Loue) and that ful hardely
Than armed they hem comenly
Of suche armour/ as to hem fell
Whan they were armed/ fiers and fell
They went hem forthe al in a route

And

And set the castel al aboute
They wyl not away for no drede
Tyl it so be that they ben dede
Or tyl they haue the castel take
And four batels they gan make
And parted hem in four anon
And toke her way/ and forthe they gone
The foure gates for to assayle
Of whiche the kepers wol not fayle
For they ben neyther sicke ne dede
But hardy folke/and stronge in dede.

Nowe wol I sayne the countenaunce
Of False semblant/ and Abstynaunce
That ben to wicked tonge went
But first they helde her parlyment
Whether it to done were
To maken hem be knowen there
Or els walken forthe disgysed
But at the laste they deuysed
That they wolde gone in tappynage
As it were in a pilgrymage
Lyke good and holy folke unfeyned
And dame Abstynence streyned
Toke on a robe of Camelyne
And gan her gratche as a Bygyne
A large couerchiefe of threde
She wrapped al aboute her hede
But she forgate not her psaltere
A payre of beedes eke she bere
Upon a lace/al of whyte threde
On whiche that she her beades bede
But she ne bought hem neuer a dele
For they were gyuen her/I wote wele
God wote of a ful holy frere
That sayd he was her father dere
To whom she had ofter went
Than any frere of his couent
And he visyted her also
And many a sermon sayd her to
He nolde let for man on lyue
That he ne wolde her ofte shriue
And with so great deuocion
They made her confession
That they had oft for the nones
Two heedes in one hoode at ones
Of fayre shappe/ I deuysed her the
But pale of face somtyme was she
That false traytouresse untrewe
Was lyke that salowe horse of hewe
That in the Apocalips is shewed
That signifyeth to folke beshrewed
That ben al ful of trecherye
And pale/through hypocrisye
For on that horse no colour is
But onely deed and pale ywis
Of suche a colour enlangoured
Was Abstynence iwys coloured
Of her estate she her repented
As her visage represented
She had a burdowne al of thefte
That Gyle had yeue her of his yefte
And a skryppe of faynte distresse
That ful was of elengenesse
And forthe she walked sobrely
And False semblant saynt/ie vous die
And as it were for suche mistere
Done on the cope of a frere
With chere symple/and ful pytous
His lokyng was not disdeynous
Ne proude/ but meke and ful pesyble
About his necke he bare a Byble
And squierly/ forthe gan he gon
And for to rest his lymmes upon
He had of treason a potent
As he were feble/ his way he went
But in his sleue he gan to thring
A rasour sharpe/ and wel bytyng
That was forged in a forge
Whiche that men clepen Coupe gorge
So longe forthe her waye they nomen
Tyl they to Wicked Tonge comen
That at his gate was syttyng
And sawe folke in the way passyng
The pilgrymes sawe he faste by
That beren hem ful mekely
And humbly they with him mette
Dame Abstynence first him grette
And sythe him False semblant salued
And he hem/but he not remeued
For he ne dredde hem not a dele
For whan he sawe her faces wele
Alway in herte/ him thought so
He shulde knowe hem bothe two
For wel he knewe dame Abstynaunce
But he ne knewe not Constreynaunce

He

He knewe nat that she was constrayned
Ne of her theues lyfe fayned
But wende she come of wyl al free
But she come in another degree
And if of good wyl she beganne
That wyl was fayled her thanne.

And False Sēblant had he sayne alse
But he knewe nat that he was false
yet false was he/ but his falsnesse
Ne coude he nat espye/ nor gesse
For Semblant was so slye wrought
That Falsenesse he ne espyed nought
But haddest thou knowen hym beforne
Thou woldest on a boke haue sworne
Whan thou him saugh in thylke araye
That he/ that whilome was so gaye
And of the daunce Joly Robyn
Was tho become a Jacobyn
But sothely what so menne hym cal
Frere prechours bene good menne al
Her order wickedly they beren
Suche mynstrelles/ if they weren
So bene Augustyns/ and Cordylers
And Carmes/ and eke Sacked freers
And al freres shodde and bare
Though some of hem ben great and square
Ful hooly men/ as I hem deme
Eueryche of hem wolde good man seme
But shalte thou neuer of apparence
Sene conclude good consequence
In none argument ywis
If existens al fayled is
For menne maye fynde alwaye sopheme
The consequence to enueneme
Who so that hath hadde the subtelte
The double sentence for to se.

Whan the pylgrymes cōmen were
To Wicked Tonge that dwelled there
Her harneys nygh hem was algate
By Wicked tonge adowne they sate
That badde hem nere him for to come
And of tidynges telle him some
And sayd hem: What case maketh you
To come in to this place nowe.

Sir sayd Strayned Abstynaunce
We for to drye our penaunce
With hertes pytous and deuoute
Are cōmen/ as pylgrimes gon aboute
Wel nyght on fote alway we go
Ful doughty ben our heeles two
And thus bothe we ben sent
Throughout this worlde that is miswent
To yeue ensample/ and preche also
To fysshen synful menne we go
For other fysshynge/ ne fysshe we
And sir/ for that charyte
As we be wonte/ herborowe we craue
Your lyfe to amende Christ it saue
And so it shulde you nat displease
We wolden/ if it were your ease
A shorte sermon vnto you sayne
And Wicked Tonge answered agayne
The house (quod he) suche (as ye se)
Shal nat be warned you for me
Say what you lyst/ and I wol here
Graunt mercy swete sir dere.

(Quod alderfirst) dame Abstynence
And thus began she her sentence
Sir/ the firste vertue certayne
The greatest/ and moste soueraygne
That may be founde in any man
For hauynge/ or for wytte he can
That is his tonge to refrayne
Therto ought euery wight him payne
For it is better styll be
Than for to speken harme parde
And he that herkeneth it gladly
He is no good man sykerly
And sir/ abouen al other synne
In that arte thou moste gilty inne
Thou spake a iape/ not longe a go
And sir/ that was right yuel do
Of a yonge man/ that here repayred
And neuer yet this place apayred
Thou saydest he awayted nothyng
But to disceyue Fayre welcomyng
Ye sayd nothyng sothe of that
But sir/ ye lye/ I tel you plat
He ne cometh no more/ ne gothe parde
I trowe ye shal him neuer se
Fayre Welcomyng in prison is
That ofte hath played with you er this
The fayrest games that he coude

Without

Without fysthe styl or soude
Nowe dare she nat her selfe solace
ye han also the manne do chace
That he dare neyther come ne go
What meueth you to hate him so:
But properly your wicked thought
That many a false leasyng hath thought
That meueth your foole eloquence
That iangleth euer in audyence
And on the folke areyseth blame
And dothe hem dishonour and shame
For thynge that maye haue no preuyng
But lykelynesse/ and contryuyng.

For I dare sayne/ that Reason demeth
It is nat al sothe thynge that semeth
And it is synne to controue
Thynge that is to reproue
This wote ye wele/ and sir: therfore
ye arne to blame the more
And nathelesse/ he recketh lyte
He yeueth nat nowe therof a myte
For if he thought harme parfaye
He wolde come and gone al daye
He coude him selfe nat abstene
Nowe cometh he nat/ and that is sene
For he ne taketh of it no cure
But if it be through auenture
And lasse than other folke algate
And thou her watchest at the gate
With speare in thyne arest alwaye
There muse musarde al the daye
Thou wakest night and day for thought
Iwis thy traueyle is for nought
And Ielousye withouten fayle
Shal neuer quyte the thy traueyle
And skathe is/ that Fayre Welcomyng
Without any trespassyng
Shal wrongfully in prison be
There wepeth and languyssheth he
And though thou neuer yet ywis
Agyltest manne no more but this
Take nat a grefe it were worthy
To putte the out of this bayly
And afterwarde in prison lye
And fettre the tyl that thou dye
For thou shalte for this synne dwelle
Right in the dyuels arse of helle
But if that thou repent the
Mafaye/ thou lyest falsely (qd he)
What/ welcome with myschaunce nowe
Haue I therfore herbered you
To saye me shame/ and eke reproue
With sorye happe to your behoue
Am I to day your herbegere
Go herber you elswhere/ than here
That han a lyer called me
Two tregetours arte thou and he
That in myn house/do me this shame
And for my sothe sawe ye me blame
Is this the sermon that ye make:
To al the dyuels I me take
Or els god thou me confounde
But er men dydden this castel founde
It passeth not ten dayes or twelue
But it was tolde right to my selue
And as they sayd/ right so tolde I
He kyste the Rose pryuely
Thus sayd I nowe/ and haue sayd yore
I not where he dyd any more
Why shulde men say me suche a thyng
If it had ben gabbyng
Right so sayd I/ and wol saye yet
I trowe I lyed not of it
And with my bemes I wol blowe
To al neyghbours arowe
Howe he hath bothe comen and gone
Tho spake False semblant right anone
Al is not gospel out of doute
That men sayne in the towne aboute
Lay no deefe eere to my spekyng
I swere you sir/it is gabbyng
I trowe ye wote wel certaynly
That no man loueth him tenderly
That sayth him harme/if he wote it
Al be he neuer so poore of wyt
And sothe is also sykerly.
This knowe ye sir/ as wel as I
That louers gladly wol visyten
The places there her loues habyten
This man you loueth/ and eke honoureth
This man to serue you laboureth
And clepeth you his frende so dere
And this man maketh you good chere
And euery where that you meteth
He you saleweth/ and he you greteth

He

He preseth nat so ofte/that ye
Ought of his comyng encombred be
There presen other folke on you
Ful ofter than he dothe nowe
And if his herte him strayned so
Unto the Rose for to go
Ye shulde hym sene so ofte nede
That ye shulde take him with the dede
He coude his comynge nat forbeare
Though he hym thursled with a speare
It nere nat than/ as it is nowe
But trusteth wel/ I swere it you
That it is clene out of his thought
Sir/ certes he ne thynketh it nought
No more ne dothe Fayre Welcomyng
That sore abyeth al this thyng
And if they were of one assent
Ful soone were the Rose hent
The maugre youres wolde be
And sir/ of o thyng herkeneth me
Sith ye this man/that loueth you
Han sayd suche harme/ and shame nowe
Wytteth wel/ if he gessed it
Ye maye wel demen in your wyt
He nolde nothynge loue you so
Ne callen you his frende also
But nyght and daye he wol wake
The castel to distroye and take
If it were sothe/ as ye deuyse
Or some manne in some maner wyse
Might it warne him euerydele
Or by him selfe parceyue wele
For sithe he myght nat come and gone
As he was whylome wonte to done
He myght it soone wyte and se
But nowe al other wyse wote he
Than haue we sir al utterly
Deserued helle/ and iolyly
The dethe of helle doutlesse
That thrallen folke so gyltlesse.

False Semblant so proueth this thyng
That he canne none answeryng
And seeth alwaye/ suche apparaunce
That nygh he fel in repentaunce
And sayd him/ sir: It maye wel be
Semblant/ a good manne semen ye
And Abstynence/ ful wyse ye seme
Of o talent you bothe I deme
What counsayle wol ye to me yeuen:
Right here anon thou shalt be shriuen
And say thy synne/ without more
Of this shalte thou repent sore
For I am preest/ and haue poste
To shriue folke of most dignyte
That ben as wyde as worlde may dure
Of al this worlde I haue the cure
And that had neuer yet persoun
Ne vycarie of no maner toun
And god wotte I haue of the
A thousande tymes more pyte
Than hath thy preest parochial
Though he thy frende be special
I haue auauntage in o wyse
That your prelates ben not so wyse
Ne halfe so lettred (as am I)
I am lycenced boldely
In diuynite for to rede
And to confessen out of drede
If ye wol you nowe confesse
And leaue your synnes more and lesse
Without abode/ knele downe anon
And you shal haue absolucion.

¶ Finis.

¶ Here endeth the Romaunt of the Rose: And here foloweth the boke of Troylous and Creseyde.

Troylus and Creseyde.

The double sorow of Troilus to tellen
That was kig Priamꝰ son of Troy
In louyng/ howe his auentures fellen
From wo to wele/ and after out of ioye
My purpose is/ er that I parte froye
Thou Thesiphone/ thou helpe me for tendite
These woful verses/ that wepen as I write

To the I clepe/ thou goddesse of tourment
Thou cruel furye/ sorowynge euer in payne
Helpe me that am the sorouful instrument
That helpeth louers/ as I can complayne
For wel sytte it/ the sothe for to sayne
A woful wight to haue a drery fere
And to a sorouful tale a sorye chere

For I that god of loues seruauntes serue
Ne dare to loue/ for myne vnlykelynesse
Prayen for spede/ al shulde I therfore sterue
So farre am I fro his helpe in derkenesse
But nathelesse/ if this maye done gladnesse
To any louer/ and his cause auayle
Haue he my thāke/ and myne be the trauayle

But ye louers that bathen in gladnesse
If any drope of pyte in you be
Remembreth you of passed heuynesse
That ye haue felte/ and on the aduersyte
Of other folke/ and thynketh howe that ye
Han felte/ that loue durste you displease
Or ye hanne won him with to great an ease

And prayeth for hem that ben in the cace
Of Troylus/ as ye maye after here
That he hem brynge in heuen to solace
And eke for me prayeth to god so dere
That I haue myght to shew in some manere
Suche payne and wo/ as loues folke endure
In Troylus vnsely auenture

And byddeth eke for hem that ben dispeyred
In loue/ that neuer wyl recouerd be
And eke for hem that falsely ben apeyred
Through wicked tonges/ be it he or she
Thus byddeth god for his benignyte
So grāūt hem soon out of this worlde to pa
That ben dispayred out of loues grace (ce

And byddeth eke for hem that ben at ease
That god hem graunt aye good p̄seueraunce
And sende hem grace her loues for to please
That it to loue be worshippe and plesaunce
For so hoope I my selfe best to auaunce
To praye for hem/ that loues seruauntes be
And write her wo/ and lyue in charite

And for to haue of hem compassyoun
As though I were her owne brother dere
Nowe herkeneth with a good entencioun
For nowe wyl I go streight to my matere
In whiche ye maye the double sorowes here
Of Troylus/ in louynge of Creseyde
And howe she forsoke him er that she deyde.

It is wel wist/ how yͤ grekes strōge
In armes wᵗ a thousāde shippes went
To Troye wardes/ and the cyte longe
Besiegeden nyghe ten yeres er they stent
And in dyuers wyse/ and one entent
The rauysshyng to wreke of quene Heleyne
By Parys don/ they wroughten al her peyne

Nowe fel it so/ that in yͤ towne there was
Dwellyng a lorde of great auctorite
A great diuyne/ that cleped was Calcas
That in that science so experte was/ that he
Knewe wel/ that Troye shulde distroyed be
By answere of his god/ that hight thus
Dan Phebus/ or Apollo Delphicus

So whan this Calcas knew by calculyng
And eke by the answere of this god Apollo
That grekes shulde suche a people bryng
Thorowe whiche that Troye must be fordo
He caste anone out of the towne to go
For wel he wyst by lorte/ that Troye sholde
Distroyed be/ ye wolde who so nolde

Wherfore to departen softely
Toke purpose ful this forknowyng wyse
And to the grekes host ful priuely
He stale anone/ and they in curteis wyse
Dyd hym bothe worshippe and seruyce
In trust that he hath connyng hem to rede
In euery peryll/ whiche that was to drede

H.h.ii. Great

Great rumour rose/whan it was first espied
In al the towne/ and openly was spoken
That Calcas traytour fledde was and alyed
To hem of Grece/ & cast was to be wroken
On him/ that falsly hath his faith broken
And sayd : he and al his kynne atones
Were worthy to be brent bothe fel and bones

Nowe had Calcas lefte in this myschaunce
Unwyst of this false and wicked dede
A doughter/ whiche was in great penaunce
And of her lyfe she was ful sore in drede
And wyst neuer what best was to rede
And as a wydowe was she/ and al alone
And nyst to whom she might make her mone

Cresyde was this ladyes name aright
As to my dome/ in al Troyes cyte
Most fayrest lady/ fer passyng euery wight
So angelyke shone her natyfe beaute
That no mortal thynge semed she
And therwith was she so parfyte a creature
As she had be made in scornyng of nature

This lady/that al daye herde at eare
Her fathers shame falshed/and traysoun
(Ful nygh out of her wyt for sorowe & feare
In wydowes habite large of samyte browne)
Before Hector on knees she fyl adowne
His mercy badde/ her selfe excusyng
With pytous voice/ and tenderly wepyng

Nowe was this Hector pytous of nature
And sawe/that she was sorouful begone
And that she was so fayre a creature
Of his goodnesse he gladed her anone
And sayd : lette your fathers trayson gone
Forth with myschaunce/ & ye your selfe in ioye
Dwelleth with us/ while you lyst in Troye

And al ye honour/that men may do you haue
As ferforth as though your father dwelt here
Ye shul haue/ and your body shul men saue
As fer as I maye ought enquyre and here
And she him thanked with ful humble chere
And ofter wolde and it had ben his wyl
Toke her leaue/went home and helde her styl

And in her house she abode with suche meyne
As tyl her honour nede was to holde
And whyle she was dwellyng in that cyte
She kept her estate/& of yonge and olde
Ful wel beloued/and wel men of her tolde
But whether that she children had or none
I rede it nat/therfore I let it gone

¶ The thynges fellen as they don of werre
Betwyxen hem of Troye and grekes ofte
For som day boughten they of Troye it derre
And efte the grekes founden nothyng softe
The folke of Troye : & thus Fortune a lofte
And under efte gan hem to whelmen bothe
After her course/aye while ye they were wroth

But howe this towne came to distruction
Ne falleth not to purpose me to tell
For it were a longe digressyon
Fro my mater/and you to longe to dwell
But the Troyan iestes/as they fell
In Omer/or in Dares/or in Dyte
Who so that can/may reden hem as they write

But though ye grekes hem of Troye shetten
And her cyte besieged al aboute
Her olde usages nolde they not letten
As to honouren her goddes ful deuoute
But aldermost in honour out of doute
They had a relyke hyght Palladion
That was her trust abouen euerychon

And so befyl/ whan comen was the tyme
Of April/ whan clothed is the mede
With newe grene/ of lusty veer the pryme
And swete smellyng floures white and rede
In sondrye wyse shewed as I rede
The folke of Troye/ their obseruaunces olde
Palladions feest went for to holde

Unto the temple in al their best wyse
Generally there went many a wight
To herken of Palladions seruyce
And namely many a lusty knyght
And many a lady fressh/ and mayden bright
Ful wele arayed bothe most and leest
Bothe for the season and the hye feest

Among

Among these other folke was Creseyda
In wydo wes habite blacke: but natheles
Right as our first letter is nowe an A
In beaute first / so stoode she makeles
Her goodly lokynge gladed al the prees
Nas neuer sene thyng to be praysed derre
Nor vnder cloude blake so bright a sterre

As was Creseyde / they sayden euerychone
That her behelde in her blacke wede
And yet she stoode ful lowe and styl alone
Behynde other folke in lytel brede
And nye the doore vnder shames drede
Symple of atyre / and debonayre of chere
With ful assured lokynge and manere

This Troylus / as he was wont to gyde
His yonge knyghtes / ladde hem vp & downe
In thylke large temple on euery syde
Beholdyng aye the ladyes of the towne
Nowe here nowe there / for no deuociowne
Had he to none / to reuen him his rest
But gan to prayse and lacke whom him lest

And in his walke ful fast he gan to wayten
If knyght or squyer of his company
Gan for to syke / or lette his eyen bayten
On any woman / that he coude espye
He wolde smyle / and holde it a folye
And saye hem thus: O lorde she slepeth softe
For loue of the / whan thou turnest ful ofte

I haue herde tel pardieux of your lyuyng
Ye louers / and eke your leude obseruaunces
And whiche a labour folke haue in winnyng
Of loue / and in kepyng suche doutaunces
And whan your praye is lost / wo & penaunces
O / very fooles / blynde and nyce be ye
There is nat one can ware by another be

And with yͤ worde he gan cast vp the browe
Ascaunces lo / is this nat wel yspoken
At whiche the god of Loue gan loken rowe
Right for dispite / and shope him to be wroken
He kydde anone his bowe was nat broken
For sodainly he hytte him at the ful
And yet as proude a pecocke gan he pul

O blynde worlde / o blynde entencioun
Howe often falleth al theffecte contrayre
Of surquedrie and foule presumpcioun
For caught is proude / & caught is debonaire
This Troylus is clomben on the stayre
And lytel weneth / that he mote discenden
But al day fayleth that fooles wenden

As proude bayarde begynneth for to skyppe
Out of the waye / so pricketh him his corne
Tyl he a lasshe haue of the longe whyppe
Than thinketh he / though I praūce al beforne
First in the trayse / ful fatte & newe yshorne
Yet am I but an horse / and horses lawe
I must endure / and with my feeres drawe

So fared it by this fiers and proude knyght
Though he a worthy kynges sonne were
And wende nothyng had had suche myght
Ayenst his wyl / that shulde his hert stere
Yet with a loke his hert woxe on fyre
That he yͤ nowe was most in pride aboue
Woxe sodainly most subiecte vnto loue

For thy ensample taketh of this man
Ye wyse / proude / and worthy folkes all
To skornen loue / whiche that so sone can
The fredom of your hertes to him thrall
For euer it was / and euer it be shal
That loue is he that althyng may bynde
For no man may fordo the lawe of kynde

That this be sothe / hath preued and dothe yet
For this (trowe I) ye knowe al & some
Men reden nat that folke han greater wyt
Than they / yͭ han ben most with loue ynome
And strengest folke ben therwith ouercome
The worthyest and greatest of degre
This was and is / and yet men shal it se

And truelyche that lyste wel to be so
For alderwysest han therwith ben plesed
And they that han ben aldermoste in wo
With loue / han ben comforted most and esed
And ofte it hath the cruell herte apesed
And worthy folke made worthyer of name
And causeth moste to dreden vyce and shame

H. h. iii. Nowe

Nowe sythe it may nat goodly be withstonde
And is a thyng so vertuous in kynde
Refuseth nought to loue/for to ben bonde
Sythe as him seluen lyst he may you bynde
The yerde is bet that bowen wol & wynde
Than that that brest/and therfore I you rede
Nowe foloweth him/that so wel can you lede

But for to tellen forthe in speciall
As of this kynges sonne/ of whiche I tolde
And leuen other thyng collaterall
Of him thynke I/my tale forthe to holde
Bothe of his ioye/ and of his cares colde
And his werke/as touchyng this matere
For I it gan/I wol therto refere

Within the tēple he went him forthe playeng
This Troylus/of euery wight aboute
On this lady/ and nowe on that lokyng
Where so she were of towne/ or of without
And vpon case byfel/that through a route
His eye perced/and so depe it went
Tyl on Creseyde it smote/and there it stent

And sodaynly for wonder wext astoned
And gan her bet beholde in thrifty wyse
O very god thouzt he/ wher hast thou woned
That arte so fayre/and goodly to deuyse
Therwith his herte gan to sprede and ryse
And softe syghed/leste men might him here
And caught ayen his first playeng chere

She nas nat with the moste of her stature
But al her lymmes so wel answeryng
Weren to womanhode/that creature
Was neuer lasse mannysshe in semyng
And eke the pure wyse of her meanyng
Shewed wel/ that men might in her gesse
Honour/estate/and womanly noblesse

Tho Troylus/ right wonder wel with all
Gan for to lyke her meanyng and her chere
Whiche somdele deignous was/for she let fall
Her loke alyte a syde/in suche manere
Ascaunces/what may I not stonden here
And after that/her lokyng gan she lyght
That neuer thought him sene so good a syght

And of her loke in him there gan to quicken
So great desyre/and suche affection
That in his hertes bottom gan to stycken
Of her his fyxe/and depe impressyon
And though he erste had pored vp and down
Than was he glad his hornes in to shrinke
Vnnethes wyste he howe to loke or wynke

Lo/he that lete him seluen so connyng
And scorned hem that loues paynes dryen
Was ful vnware that loue had his dwellyng
Within the subtyll stremes of her eyen
That sodainly him thought he felte dyen
Right with her loke/ the spyrite in his herte
Blessed be loue/that thus can folke conuerte

She this in blacke/lykyng to Troylus
Ouer al thyng he stode for to beholde
But his desyre/ne wherfore he stode thus
He neyther chere made/ne worde tolde
But from a ferre/ his maner for to holde
On other thyng somtyme his loke he caste
And efte on her/ whyle that the seruyce laste

And after this/nat fullyche al a whaped
Out of the temple al eselyche he wente
Repentyng him that he had euer iaped
Of loues folke/leste fully the discente
Of scorne fyl on him selfe/but what he mente
Leste it were wyste on any maner syde
His wo he gan dissymulen and hyde

Whan he was fro this temple thus departed
He streyght anon vnto his palayes turneth
Right with her loke/ through shotten & darted
Al fayneth he in luste that he soiourneth
And al his chere & speche also he bourneth
And aye of loues seruauntes euery whyle
Him selfe to wrie/at hem he gan to smyle

And sayd lorde/so they lyue al in lust
Ye louers/for the connyngest of you
That serueth moste ententiflyche and best
Him tyte as often harme therof as prowe
Your hyre is quyt ayen/ye god wot howe
Nat wele for wele/but scorne for good seruise
In faythe your order is ruled in good wyse

In

In no certayne ben your obseruaunces
But it a fely fewe poyntes be
Ne nothyng asketh so great attẽdaunces
As dothe your laye/ and that knowe al ye
But that is nat the worste/ as mote I the
But tolde I you the worste poynt/ I leue
Al said I sothe/ ye wolden at me greue

But take this/ that ye louers ofte eschewe
Or els done of good entention
Ful ofte thy lady wol it mysse constrewe
And deme it harme in her opynion
And yet if she for other encheson
Be wroth/ thã shalt thou haue a groin anone
Lorde/ wel is him that maye ben of you one

But for al this/ whan that he seeth his tyme
He helde his pees/ non other bote him gayned
For loue began his fethers so to lyme
That wel vnneth vnto his folke he fayned
That other besy nedes him distrayned
So wo was him/ that what to done he nyst
But bad his folke to gon where as hem lyst

And whan that he in chambre was alone
He downe on his beddes fete him sette.
And first he gan to syke/ and efte to grone
And thought aye on her so withoten lette
That as he satte and woke/ his spyrite mette
That he her saugh/ and temple/ & al the wyse
Right of her loke/ and gan it newe auyse

Thus gan he make a myrrour of his mynde
In whiche he saugh al holy her fygure
And that he wel coude in his herte fynde
It was to him a right good auenture
To loue suche one/ and if he dyd his cure
To seruen her/ yet myght he fal in grace
Or els/ for one of her seruauntes pace

Imaginyng/ that traueyle nor grame
Ne myght/ for so goodly one be lorne
As she/ ne him for his desyre no shame
Al were it wyst/ but in prise and vp borne
Of al louers/ wel more than beforne
This argumented he/ in his gynnyng
Ful vnauysed of his wo cõmyng

Thus toke he purpose loues crafte to sewe
And thought he wolde worken priuely
First to hyde his desyre in mewe
From euery wight yborne/ al outerly
But he might aught recouered ben therby
Remembryng him/ that loue to wyde yblowe
Yelte bytter fruite/ though swete sede be sowe

And ouer al this/ ful mokel more he thought
What for to speke/ and what to holden inne
And what to arten/ her to loue he sought
And on a songe anonright to begynne
And gan loude on his sorowe for to wynne
For with good hope/ he gan fully assente
Creseyde for to loue/ and nought repente

And of his songe not onely his sentence
As writte myn auctour called Lollius
But playnly saue our tonges difference
I dare wel say/ in al that Troylus
Sayd in his songe/ lo euery worde right thus
As I shal sayne/ and who so lyste it here
Lo next this verse/ he may it fynde here.

¶ The song of Troylus.

¶ If no loue is/ o god what fele I so
And if loue is/ what thyng and whiche is he
If loue be good/ from whence cometh my wo
If it be wycke/ a wonder thynketh me
Whan euery turment and aduersyte
That cometh of him/ may to me sauory thinke
For aye thurste I the more that yche it drinke

And if that at myn owne lust I brenne
From whẽce cometh my waylig & my pleynte
If harme agree me/ wherto playn I thenne
I not/ ne why/ vnwery that I feynte
O quicke dethe/ o swete harme so queynte
Howe may of the in me/ be suche quantyte
But if that I consente that it so be

And if that I consente/ I wrongfully
Complayne ywis/ thus possed to and fro
Al stereless within a bote am I
Amydde the see/ atwixen wyndes two
That in contrarye stonden euer mo
Alas/ what is this wonder maladye?
For heate of colde/ for colde of heate I dye

And

And to the god of loue thus sayd he
With pytous voyce/O lorde nowe yours is
My spyrite/whiche that ought youres be
You thonke I lorde/yͭ han me brought to this
But whether goddesse or woman ywis
She be/I not whiche/that ye do me serue
But as her man I wol aye lyue and sterue.

ye stonden in her eyen mightyly
As in a place to your vertue digne
Wherfore lorde/if my seruyce or I
May lyken you/so beth to me benigne
For myn estate royal here I resigne
In to her honde/and with ful humble chere
Become her man/as to my lady dere

In him ne deigned sparen blood royall
The fyre of loue/wherfro god me blesse
Ne him forbare in no degre for all
His vertue/or his excellent prowesse
But helde him as his thrall lowe in distresse
And brende him so in sondrie wyse aye newe
That sixty tymes a day he lost his hewe

So mochel day fro day his owne thought
For luste to her/gan quicken and encrease
That euery che other charge he set at nought
For thy ful ofte/ his hotte fyre to cease
To sene her goodly loke he gan to prease
For therby to ben eased wel he wende
And aye the nere he was/ the more he brende

For aye the nere the fyre the hotter is
This (trowe I) knoweth al this companye
But were he ferre or nere/I dare say this
By nyght or day/ for wisdom or folye
His herte/whiche that is his brestes eye
Was aye on her/ that fayrer was to sene
Than euer was Heleyne/or Polixene

Eke of the day there passed not an houre
That to him selfe a thousande tyme he seyde
God goodly/to whom I serue and laboure
As I best can/nowe wolde god Creseyde
ye wolden on me rewe/er that I deyde
My dere herte alas/myn heele and hewe
And lyfe is loste/but ye wol on me rewe

Al other dredes weren from him fledde
Bothe of thassiege/and his sauacion
Ne in desyre non other fownes bredde
But argumentes to his conclusyon
That she on him wolde han compassyon
And he to ben her man/whyle he may dure
Lo here his lyfe/and from his dethe his cure

The sharpe shoures fell of armes preue
That Hector or his other brethrene dydden
Ne made him only therfore ones meue
And yet was he/where so men went or rydden
Foũde one the beste/ and lengest tyme abyden
There peryll was/and dyd eke suche trauayle
In armes/that to thynke it was meruayle

But for none hate he to the grekes had
Ne also for the rescous of the toun
Ne made him thus in armes for to mad
But onely so/for this conclusyoun
To lyken her the bette for his renoun
Fro day to day in armes so he spedde
That the Grekes as the dethe him dredde

And fro this forth tho refte him loue his slepe
And made his meate his foe/ & eke his sorowe
Gan multiplye/that who so toke kepe
It shewed in his hewe bothe eue and morowe
Therfore a tytle he gan him for to borowe
Of other sicknesse/leste men of him wende
That the hotte fyre of loue him brende

And sayd he had a feuer/and fared amys
But were it certayne I can nat say
If that his lady vnderstode nat this
Or fayned her she nyste/one of the twey
But wel rede I/that by no maner wey
Ne semed it/that she on him rought
Or of his payne/what so euer he thought

But than felte this Troylus suche wo
That he was wel nigh wode/for aye his drede
Was this/that she some wight loued so
That neuer of him she wolde han taken hede
For whiche him thought he felte his hert blede
Ne of his wo ne durst he nought begynne
To tellen her/for al this worlde to wynne

But

But whan he had a space from his care
Thus to him selfe ful ofte he gan to playne
He sayd/ o foole nowe arte thou in the snare
That whylom iapedest at loues payne
Now art yͧ hent/now gnaw thyn own chayn
Thou were aye woned eche louer reprehende
Of thing fro whiche thou canst ẏ not defende

What wol nowe euery louer sayne of the
If this be wyst ? but euer in thyn absence
Laughen in scorne/and sayne lo there goth he
That is the man of great sappence
That helde vs louers leste in reuerence
Now thanked be god/he may gon in ẏ daũce
Of hem that loue lyste febly auaunce

But o thou woful Troylus/ god wolde
Sythe thou must louen/through thy destyne
That thou beset were on suche one/ ẏ sholde
Knowe al thy wo/al lacked her pyte
But also colde in loue towardes the
Thy lady is/as froste in wynter moone
And thou fordo/as snowe in fyre is soone

God wolde I were aryued in the porte
Of dethe/to whiche my sorowe wol me lede
Ah lorde / to me it were a great comforte
Than were I quyt of languyssyng in drede
For be my hyd sorowe yblowe in brede
I shal bejaped ben a thousande tyme
More than ẏ foole/ of whose folye men ryme

But nowe helpe god/ and ye swete/for whom
I playne/ycaught ye neuer wight so faste
O mercy dere herte/and helpe me from
The deth/for I/whyle that my lyfe may laste
More than my selfe wol loue you to my laste
And with some frendly loke gladeth me swete
Though neuer more thyng ye me byhete

¶ These wordes/and ful many an other mo
He spake/and called euer in his compleynte
Her name/for to tellen her his wo
Tyl nyghe that he in salte teeres dreynte
Al was for naught/ she herde not his pleynte
And whan that he bethought on that folye
A thousande folde his wo gan multiplye

Bewaylyng in his chambre thus alone
A frende of his/ that called was Pandare
Came ones in vnware/and herde hym grone
And sawe his frende in suche distresse ⁊ care
Alas (quod he) who causeth al this fare ?
O mercy god/what vnhap may this mene ?
Han nowe thus sone grekes made you lene ?

Or haste thou some remorce of conscience ?
And arte nowe fall in some deuocioun
And waylest for thy synne and thyn offence
And hast for ferde caught a contricioun
God saue hem/ that besieged han our toun
That so can lay our iolyte on presse
And bringe our lusty folke to holynesse

These wordes sayd he for the nones all
That wͭ such thĩg he mizt him angry maken
And with his anger don his sorowe fal
As for a tyme/and his corage awaken
But wel wyste he/as ferre as tonges spaken
There nas a man of gretter hardynesse
Than he/ne more desyred worthynesse

¶ What cas (qđ Troylus) or what auenture
Hath gyded the to sene me languyssyng
That am refuse of euery creature ?
But for the loue of god/at my prayeng
Go hence away/for certes my deyeng
Wol the disese/and I mote nedes dey
Therfore go way/there nys no more to sey

But if thou wene I be thus sycke for drede
It is nat so/and therfore scorne nought
There is an other thyng I take of hede
Wel more thã aught ẏ grekes han yet wrouzt
Which cause is of my deth for sorow ⁊ thought
But though that I nowe tell it the nẽ leste
Be thou not wrothe/I hyde it for the beste

This Pãdare/ẏ nygh malte for wo ⁊ routhe
Ful often sayd alas/what may this be
Nowe frende (qđ he) if euer loue or trouthe
Hath ben er this betwyxen the and me
Ne do thou neuer suche a cruelte
To hyden fro thy frende so great a care
Woste thou nat wel that I am Pandare ?

I wol

I wol parten with the al thy payne
If it so be I do the no comforte
As it is frendes right/sothe for to sayne
To enterparten wo/as glad disporte
I haue and shal/for trewe or false reporte
In wronge and right yloued the al my lyue
Hyde nat thy wo fro me/but tel it blyue

Than gan this sorouful Troylus to syke
And said him thus / God leue it be my best
To tellen the/for sythe it may the lyke
Yet wol I tel it/though my herte brest
And wel wote I/ thou mayste do me no rest
But leste thou deme I truste nat to the
Nowe herke frende/for thus it stant with me

Loue/ ayenst the whiche who so defendeth
Him seluen moste/him alder leest auayleth
With dispeyre so sorousfully me offendeth
That streight vnto the dethe myn hert sayleth
Therto desyre/so brennyngly me assayleth
That to ben slayne it were a greater ioye
To me/than kyng of Grece be and of Troye

Suffyseth this/my ful frende Pandare
That I haue said/for now wost thou my wo
And for the loue of god my colde care
So hyde it wel/I tolde it neuer to mo
For harmes mighten folowen mo than two
If it were wyst/but be thou in gladnesse
And let me sterue vnknowe of my distresse

Howe hast thou thus vnkyndly a longe
Hyd this fro me/ thou fole? (qđ Pandarus)
Parauenture thou mayst after such one lōge
That myn auyse anon may helpen vs
This were a wonder thing (qđ Troylus)
Thou couldest neuer in loue thy selfen wysse
Howe dyuel mayst thou brīgen me to blysse?

Tye Troylus/nowe herke (quod Pandare)
Though I be nyce/it happeth often so
That one that ayes dothe ful yuell fare
By good cōsaile can kepe his frende therfro
I haue my selfe seyne a blynde man go
There as he fell/that coude loken wyde
A foole may eke a wyse man ofte gyde

A whetstone is no keruyng instrument
But yet it maketh sharpe keruyng tolis
And ther thou wost ẏ I haue aught miswent
Eschue thou ẏ/for suche thing to schole is
Thus often wyse men ben ware by foolis
If thou so do/thy wyt is wel bywared
By his contrarye is euery thyng declared

For how myȝt euer swetnesse haue be knowe
To hym / that neuer tasted bytternesse?
Ne no man wote what gladnesse is I trowe
That neuer was in sorowe/or some distresse
Eke white by blacke/by shā eke worthinesse
Eche set by other/more for other semeth
As men may sene/and so the wyse it demeth

Sythe thus of two contraryes is o lore
I that haue in loue so ofte assayed
Greuaunces/ ought connen wel the more
Counsaylen the/of that thou arte dismayed
And eke the ne ought nat ben yuel apayed
Though I desyre with the for to bere
Thyn heuy charge/it shal the lasse dere

I wote wel that it fared thus by me
As to thy brother Parys/an hierdesse
Whiche that cleped was Oenone
Wrote in a complaynte of her heuynesse
Ye sawe the letter that she wrote/ I gesse
Nay neuer yet iwys (quod Troylus)
Nowe (qđ Pandare) herkeneth it was thus

Phebus/that first fonde arte of medicyne
(Quod she) and coude in euery wightes care
Remedy and rede/ by herbes he knewe fyne
yet to him selfe his connyng was ful bare
For loue had him so bounden in a snare
Al for the doughter of the kyng Admete
That al his craft ne coude his sorowe bete

Right so fare I/vnhappy for me
I loue one best/and that me smerteth sore
And yet parauenture can I reden the
And nat my selfe/repreue me no more
I haue no cause I wot wel for to soore
As dothe an hauke/that lysteth for to play
But to thyn helpe/yet somwhat can I say

And

And of o thyng/ right syker mayst thou be
That certayne/ for to dyen in the payne
That I shal neuer mo discouer the
Ne by my trouthe/ I kepe not restreyne
The fro thy loue/ al though it were Heleyne
That is thy brothers wyfe/ if yche it wyste
Be what she be/ and loue her as the lyst

Therfore/ as frendfullyche in me assure
And tel me platte/ what is thyn encheson
And fynall cause of wo/ that ye endure
For douteth nothyng/ myn entencion
Nas nat to you of reprehensyon
To speke as nowe/ for no wight may byreue
A man to loue/ tyl that him lyst to leue

And weteth wel/ that bothe two ben vyces
Mystrusten al/ or elles al leue
But wel I wot/ the meane of it no vyce is
As for to trusten some wight is a preue
Of trouth/ and for thy wolde I fayne remeue
Thy wronge cõceyte/ & do the som wight trust
Thy wo to tell/ and tell me if the lust

The wyse eke sayth/ wo him that is alone
For and he fall/ he hath none helpe to ryse
And sythe thou haste a felowe/ tell thy mone
For this nys nought certayne the next wyse
To wynnen loue/ as techen vs the wyse
To walowe and wepe/ as Niobe the quene
Whose teeres yet in marble ben ysene

Let be thy weppyng/ and thy drerynesse
And let vs lyssen wo/ with other speche
So may thy woful tyme seme lesse
Delyte naught in wo/ thy wo to seche
As don these fooles/ that her sorowes eche
With sorowe/ whan they han misauẽture
And lusten nought to sechen other cure

Men sayne to wretche is consolacion
To haue another felawe in his payne
That ought wel ben our opinyon
For bothe thou and I of loue playne
So ful of sorowe am I/ sothe to sayne
That certainly/ no more harde grace
May syt on me/ for why there is no space

If god wol/ thou art nought agast of me
Leste I wolde of thy lady the begyle
Thou wost thy selfe/ whom that I loue parde
As I best can/ gon sythen longe whyle
And sythen thou wost/ I do it for no wyle
And sythe I am he/ that thou trusteth moste
Tel me somwhat/ sens al my wo thou woste.

¶ Yet Troylus/ for al this no worde sayde
But longe he lay styll/ as he deed were
And after this/ with sykyng he abrayde
And to Pandarus voyce he lente his eere
And vp his eyen caste he/ and than in fere
Was Pandarus/ leste that in frenseye
He shulde fall/ or els sone deye

And sayd awake/ ful wonderlyche & sharpe
What slombrest thou/ as in a lytargye ∴
Or arte thou lyke an asse to the harpe
That hereth soun/ whan men ẏ stringes ply ∴
But in his mynde/ of that no melodye
May synke him to gladen/ for that he
So dull is/ in his bestyalite

And with this/ Pandare of his wordes stent
But Troylus to him no thyng answerde
For why/ to tel was nought his entent
Neuer to no man/ for whom that he so ferde
For it is sayd/ men maken ofte a yerde
With whiche the maker is him selfe ybeten
In sondrie maner/ as these wyse treten

And namelyche in his counsayle tellyng
That toucheth loue/ that ought ben secre
For of him selfe it wol ynough out spring
But if that it the bet gouerned be
Eke somtyme it is crafte to seme flee
For thyng/ whiche in effecte men hunten faste
Al this gan Troylus in his herte caste

But nathelesse/ whan he had herde him crye
A wake he gan/ and syke wonder sore
And sayd frende/ though that I styll lye
I nam nat deefe/ nowe peace & crye no more
For I haue herde thy wordes/ and thy lore
But suffre me my fortune to bewaylen
For thy prouerbes may nought me auaylen

Nor

Nor other cure canst thou none for me
Eke I nyl not ben cured/ I wol dey
What knowe I of the quene Niobe:
Let be thyn olde ensamples/ I the prey
No frende (qd̄ Pandarus) therfore I sey
Suche is delyte of fooles to bewepe
Her wo/ but seken boote they ne kepe

Nowe knowe I that reson in the fayleth
But tel me/ if I wyste what she were
For whom that the al misauẽture ayleth
Durste thou that I tolde it in her eere
Thy wo/ sith thou darst not thy selfe for feere
And her besought/ on the to han some routhe
Why nay (qd̄ he) by god and by my trouthe

What/ not as besily (quod Pandarus)
As though myn owne lyfe lay in this nede
Why no parde sir (quod this Troylus)
And why: for that thou shuldest neuer spede
Woste thou that wel: ye that is out of drede
(Quod Troylus) for al that euer ye conne
She wol to no suche wretche as I be wonne

(Quod Pandarus) alas what may this be
That thou dispayred arte/ thus causelesse
What/ lyueth nat thy lady/ benedicite
Howe wost thou so/ that thou arte gracelesse
Suche yuel is not alwaye botelesse
Why put nat impossible thus thy cure
Sythe thyng to come is ofte in auenture

I graunt wel that thou endurest wo
As sharpe as dothe he Tesiphus in hell
Whose stomake foules tyren euer mo
That hyghten Bultures / as bokes tell
But I may not endure that thou dwell
In so vnskylful an opinyon
That of thy wo nys no curacion

But ones nyll thou/ for thy cowarde herte
And for thyn ire/ and folysshe wylfulnesse
For wantrust tellen of thy sorowes smerte
Ne to thyn owne helpe/ do besynesse
As moche as speke a worde/ ye more or lesse
But lyest as he that of lyfe nothyng retche
What woman coude loue suche a wretche

What may she demen other of thy dethe
If thou thus dye/ and she not why it is
But that for feare/ is yolden vp thy brethe
For grekes han besieged vs ywis
Lorde which a thãke shalt yͧ haue thã of this
Thus wol she sayne/ & al the towne atones
The wretche is deed/ the dyuel haue his bones

Thou mayst alone here wepe/ crye/ & knele
But loue a woman that she wote it nought
And she wol quite it that thou shalte nat fele
Unknowe vnkyst/ and lost that is vnsought
What many a man hath loue ful dere abou3t
Twenty wynter that his lady ne wyste
That neuer yet his ladys mouth he kyste

What/ shuld he therfore fallen in dispayre:
Or be recreaunt for his owne tene
Or slayne him selfe/ al be his lady fayre
Nay nay: but euer in one be fressh & grene
To serue and loue/ his dere hertes quene
And thynke it is a guerdone her to serue
A thousande parte more / than he can deserue

And of that worde toke hede Troylus
And thought anone/ what folye he was in
And howe that sothe him sayde Pandarus
That for to sleen him selfe/ might he nat wyn
But bothe done vnmanhode and a syn
And of his dethe his lady nought to wyte
For of his wo/ god wote she knewe ful lyte

And with yͭ thought/ he gan ful sore syke
And said/ Alas: what is me best to do
To whom Pandare sayd/ if the lyke
The best is/ that thou tel me thy wo
And haue my trouth/ but if thou fynde it so
I be thy bote/ or it be ful longe
To peces do me drawe/ and sythen honge

Ye/ so sayst thou (qd̄ Troylus) alas:
But god wote it is naught the rather so
Ful harde it were to helpen in this caas
For wel fynde I/ that fortune is my foe
Ne al the men that ryde conne or go
May of her cruel whele the harme withstonde
For as her lyst/ she playeth with fre & bonde

Quod

(Qđ Pandarus) than blamest thou fortune
For thou arte wroth/ ye nowe at erst I se
Wost thou nat wel that fortune is cōmune
To euery maner wight/ in some degree
And yet thou hast this comforte/ so perde
That as her ioyes moten ouergone
So mote her sorowes passen euerichone

For if her whele stynt/ any thyng to tourne
Than cesseth she fortune anone to be
Now sith her whele by no way may soiourne
What woste thou if her mutabylite
Right as thy seluen lust wol don by the
Or that she be nought ferre fro thyn helpyng
Parauenture thou haste cause for to synge

And therfore woste thou what/ I the beseche
Let be thy wo/ and turnyng to the grounde
For who so lyst haue healyng of his leche
To him byhoueth first vnwrie his wounde
To Cerberus in hell aye be I bounde
Were it for my suster al thy sorowe
By my wyl she shulde be thyn to morowe

Loke vp I say/ and tel me what she is
Anon/ that I may gon aboute thy nede
Knowe ych her aught/ for my loue tel me this
Than wolde I hope rather for to spede
  Tho gan the veyne of Troylus to blede
For he was hyt/ and woxe al reed for shame
A ha (qđ Pandare) here begynneth game

And with that worde/ he gan him for to shake
And sayd theef/ thou shalte her name tell
But tho gan sely Troylus for to quake
As though men shulde han had him in to hell
And sayd alas/ of al my wo the well
Than is my swete foe called Creseyde
And wel nigh with ẏ worde for feare he deyde

  And whan ẏ Pādare herde her name neuen
Lorde he was glad/ and sayd/ frende so dere
Nowe fare a right/ for Ioues name in heuen
Loue hath beset the wel/ be of good chere
For of good name/ & wysdom/ and manere
She hath ynough/ and eke of gentylnesse
If she be fayre/ thou woste thy selfe I gesse

Ne neuer sey a more bounteous
Of her estate/ ne a gladder: ne of speche
A frendlyer/ ne more gracious
For to do wel/ ne lasse had nede to seche
What for to don/ and al this bet to eche
In honour/ to as ferre as she may stretche
A kynges herte semeth by hers a wretche

And for thy loke of good comforte thou be
For certainly the first poynt is this
Of noble corage/ and wele ordayne the
A man to haue peace with him selfe ywis
So oughtest thou/ for nought but good it is
To louen wel/ and in a worthy place
The ought nat clepe it happe/ but grace

And also thynke/ and therwith glade the
That sithe thy lady vertuous is al
So foloweth it/ that there is some pyte
Amonges al these other in general
And for they se that thou in special
Require nought/ that is ayen her name
For vertue stretcheth nat him selfe to shame

But wel is me/ that euer I was borne
That thou beset arte in so good a place
For by my trouth i loue I durst haue sworne
The shulde neuer haue tydde so faire a grace
And wost yͧ why? for yͧ were wōt to chace
At loue in scorne/ and for despite hem cal
Saynt Idiote/ lorde of these foles al

Howe often hast thou made thy nyce iapes
And said/ that loues seruauntes euerichone
Of nycete/ ben very goddes apes
And some wolde monch her meate alone
Lyggynge a bedde/ & make hem for to grone
And some thou saydest had a blaūche feuere
And praydest god/ they shulde neuer keuere

And some of hem/ toke on hem for the colde
More than ynough/ so saydest thou ful ofte
And some han fayned ofte tyme and tolde
Howe that they waken/ whan they slepe softe
And thus they wolde haue set hem self a lofte
And nathelesse were vnder at the last
Thus saydest thou/ and iapedest ful fast

I.i. Yet

Yet sadyest thou/ that for the more parte
These louers wolde speke in general
And thoughten it was a syker arte
For faylyng for to assayen oueral
Nowe maye I iape of the/ if that I shal
But natheles/ though that I shulde dey
Thou arte none of tho/ I dare wel sey

Nowe bete thy brest/ and say to god of Loue
Thy grace lorde/ for nowe I me repent
Yf I myspake/ for nowe my selfe I loue
Thus saye with al thyne hert/ in good entent
(Quod Troylus) ah lorde/ I me consent
And pray to the/ my iapes thou foryeue
And I shal neuer more whyle I lyue

Thou sayst wel (q̃d Pādare) & nowe I hope
That thou the goddes wrath hast al apesed
And sythe thou haste wepten many a drope
And said such thīg/ wherwith thy god is plesed
Nowe wolde neuer god/ but thou were eased
And thynke wel she/ of whom ryst al thy wo
Here after may thy comforte ben also

For thylke groūde/ ẏ beareth the wedes wicke
Beareth eke these holsome herbes/ as ful ofte
Next the foule nettle/ rough and thicke
The rose wexeth/ soote/ smoth/ and softe
And next the valey is the hyll a lofte
And next the derke night the glade morowe
And also ioye is next the fyne of sorowe

Nowe loke that attempre be thy bridel
And for the beste aye suffre to the tyde
Or els al our labour is on ydel
He hasteth wel/ that wysely can abyde
Be dyligent and trewe/ and aye wel hyde
Be lusty/ free/ perseuer in thy seruyse
And al is wel/ if thou werke in this wyse

But he that departed is in euery place
Is nowhere hole/ as writen clerkes wyse
What wonder is/ if suche one haue no grace
Eke wost thou how it fareth of some seruyse
As plante a tree or herbe/ in sondrie wyse
And on the morowe pull it vp as blyue
No wonder is/ though it may neuer thriue

And sythe that god of loue hath the bestowed
In place digne vnto thy worthynesse
Stonde fast/ for to good porte hast þu rowed
And of thy selfe/ for any heuynesse
Hope alway wel/ for but if drerynesse
Or ouerhaste our bothe labour shende
I hope of this to maken a good ende

And wost thou why/ I am the lasse afered
Of this mater/ with my nece trete
For this haue I herde saye of wyse lered
Was neuer man or woman yet begete
That was vnapte to suffre loues hete
Celestyal/ or els loue of kynde
For thy some grace I hope in her to fynde

And for to speke of her in special
Her beaute to bethynken/ and her youthe
It syt her nought/ to ben celestyal
As yet/ though that her lyst bothe and kouthe
And trewly it syt her wel right nouthe
A worthy knyght to louen and cheryce
And but she do/ I holde it for a vyce

Wherfore I am/ and wol ben aye redy
To payne me to do you this seruyce
For bothe you to please/ this hoope I
Here after/ for ye ben bothe wyse
And conne it counsayle kepe in suche a wyse
That no man shal the wyser of it be
And so we maye ben gladed al thre

And by my trouth I haue right nowe of the
A good conceit/ in my wytte as I gesse
And what it is/ I wol nowe that thou se
I thynke that sithe Loue of his goodnesse
Hath the conuerted out of wickednesse
That thou shalte ben the best post I leue
Of al his lay/ and most his foes greue

Ensample why/ se nowe these great clerkes
That erren aldermost ayen a lawe
And ben conuerted from her wicked werkes
Thrugh grace of god/ ẏ lest hem to wt drawe
Than arne they folke ẏ han most god in awe
And strengest faythed ben I vnderstonde
And conne an errour alderbest withstonde

Whan

Whan Troylus had herde Pandare assented
To ben his helpe/in louyng of Creseyde
Wext of his wo/as who sayth untormēted
But hotter wext his loue/and than he sayde
With sobre chere/as though his herte playde
Nowe blisful Uenus helpe/ er that I sterue
Of the Pandare/I mowe some thāke deserue

But dere frende/howe shal my wo be lesse
Tyl this be done/and good eke tel me this
Howe wylt thou sayne of me and my distresse
Leste she be wrothe/this drede I moste ywis
Or wol not heren al/howe it is
Al this drede I/and eke for the manere
Of the her eme/she nyl no suche thyng here

(Qd̄ Pandarus) thou haste a ful gret care
Leste the chorle may fall out of the moone
Why lorde: I hate of the the nyce fare
Why/ entremete of that thou haste to doone
For goddes loue/ I bydde the aboone
So let me alone/and it shal be thy beste
Why frende (qd̄ he) thā done right as the leste

But herke Pandare o worde/for I nolde
That thou in me wendest so great folye
That to my lady I desyren shulde
That toucheth harme/ or any vylanye
For dredelesse me were leuer dye
Than she of me aught els understood
But that/that might sownen in to good

Tho lough this Pandarus/& anon answerde
And I thy borowe/fye no wight dothe but so
I raught nat though she stode and herde
Howe that thou sayest/ but farwel I wol go
A dieu/be glad/god spede us bothe two
yeue me this labour/and this busynesse
And of my spede/be thyn al the swetnesse

Tho Troylus gan downe on knees to fall
And Pandare in his armes hente faste
And sayd/nowe fye on the grekes all
yet parde/god shal helpen at laste
And dredelesse/if that my lyfe may laste
And god to forne/to some of hem shal smerte
And yet me athinketh yͭ this auaunt masterte

Nowe Pandare/I can no more say
Thou wise/thou wost/thou maist/thou art al
My lyfe my dethe/hole in thyn honde I say
Helpe me nowe (qd̄ he) Yes by my trouthe I shal
God yelde the frende/& this in special
(Quod Troylus) that thou me recōmaunde
To her that maye me to the dethe cōmaunde

This Pandarus tho/desyrous to serue
His ful frende/he sayd in this manere
Farwel/& thynke I wol the thanke deserue
Haue here my trouth/& that thou shalt here
And went his way/ thinkyng on this matere
And howe he best might besechen her of grace
And fynde a tyme therto/and a place

For euery wight that hath a house to founde
He renneth nat the werke for to begynne
With rakel honde/ but he wol byde a stounde
And sende his hertes lyne out fro withyn
Aldertirst his purpose for to wynne
Al this Pandare in his herte thought
And cast his werke/ful wysely er he wrought

But Troylus lay tho no lenger downe
But anon up on his stede baye
And in the felde he played the lyoun
Wo was that greke/ yͭ with him met that daye
And in the towne/his maner tho forthe aye
So goodly was/and gat him so in grace
That eche him loued/that loked in his face

For he bycame the frendlyest wight
The gentylest/ and eke the moste fre
The thriftyest/and one the beste knight
That in his tyme was/or might be
Deed were his iapes and his crueltie
His hygh porte/and his maner straunge
And eche of hem/gan for a vertue chaunge

Nowe let us stynte of Troylus a stounde
That fareth lyke a man/that hurte is sore
And is somdele of akyng of his wounde
ylessed wel/but heled no dele more
And as an easy pacient the lore
Abyte/of him that gothe aboute his cure
And thus he driueth forthe his auenture

Explicit liber primus. I.i.ii.

The seconde boke of Troylus.

OUt of these blacke wawes for to sayle
O wynde/ the weder gynneth clere
For in this see/ the bote hath suche trauayle
Of my connyng/ that vnneth I it stere
This see clepe I the tempestous matere
Of dispayre/ that Troylus was in
But nowe of hope the kalendes begyn

O lady myn that called arte Cleo
Thou be my spede fro this forthe/ & my muse
To ryme wel this boke tyl I haue do
Me nedeth here none other arte to vse
For why/ to euery louer I me excuse
That of no sentement I this endyte
But out of latyn/ in my tonge it write

Wherfore I nyl haue neyther thãke ne blame
Of al this worke/ but pray you mekely
Disblameth me/ if any worde be lame
For as myn auctour sayd/ so say I
Eke though I spake of loue vnfelyngly
No wonder is/ for it no thyng of newe is
A blynde man can not iugen wel in hewis

I knowe that in forme of speche is chaunge
Within a thousande yere/ and wordes tho
That hadden prise/ now wõder nyce & strãge
Thynketh hem/ and yet they spake hem so
And spedde as wel in loue/ as men nowe do
Eke for to wynnen loue/ in sondrie ages
In sondrie londes/ sondrie ben vsages

And for thy/ if it happe in any wyse
That here be any louer in this place
That herkeneth/ as the storie wol deuyse
Howe Troylus came to his ladyes grace
And thinketh/ so nolde I nat loue purchace
Or wondreth on his speche or his doyng
I not/ but it is to me no wondring

For euery wight/ whiche that to Rome went
Halte nat o pathe/ ne alway o manere
Eke in some londe were al the gamen shent
If that men farde in loue/ as men don here
As thus/ in open doyng or in chere
In vysityng/ in forme/ or sayd our sawes
For thy men sayne/ eche coũtre hath his lawes

Eke scarsely ben there in this place thre
That haue in loue sayd lyke/ and done in al
For to this purpose this maye lyken the
And the right nought/ yet al is done or shal
Eke some men graue in tre/ some i stone wal
As it betyde/ but sithe I haue begonne
Myne authour shal I folowe/ as I konne.

¶ Explicit Prohemium.

IN May yͭ mother is of monthes glade
That fresh flours/ blewe/ white/ & rede
Ben quicke ayen/ that wynter deed made
And ful of baume is fletyng euery mede
Whan Phebus doth her bright beames sprede
Right in the white Bole/ it so betydde
As I shal synge/ on Mayes day the thridde

That Pandarus for al his wyse speche
Felte eke his parte of loues shottes kene
That coude he neuer so wel of louyng preche
It made his hewe a daye ful ofte grene
So shope it/ that him fyl that day a tene
In loue/ for whiche in wo to bedde he went
And made er it were daye ful many a went

The swalowe Proigne/ with a sorouful lay
Whan morowe com/ gan make her waymen- (tig
Why she forshapen was/ and euery lay
Pandare a bedde/ halfe in a slomberyng
Tyl she so nighe him made her waymẽtyng
Howe Thereus gan forthe her suster take
That with the noyse of her he gan awake

And to call/ and dresse him vp to ryse
Remembring him/ his arande was to done
From Troylus/ and eke his great empryse
And cast/ & knewe in good plyte was yͤ mone
To done voyage/ and toke his way ful soone
Vnto his neces paleys/ there besyde
Nowe Ianus god of entre/ thou him gyde

Whan he was come Into his neces place
Where is my lady/ to her folke (quod he)
And they him tolde/ and in forthe he gan pace
And founde two other ladyes syt and she
Within a paued parlour/ and they thre
Herden a mayden hem reden the geste
Of the siege of Thebes/ whyle hem leste.

Quod

(Quod Pandarus) madame god you se
With your boke/ and al the companye
Eyghe vncle myn/ welcome iwys (quod she)
And vp she rose/and by the honde in hye
She toke him fast/ and sayd/ this night thrye
To good mote it turne/of you I mette
And with ye worde/she down on beche him set

Ye nece/ye shul faren wel the bet
If god wol al this yere (quod Pandarus)
But I am sory that I haue you let
To herken of your boke ye praysen thus
For goddes loue what sayth it/tel it vs
Is it of loue/or some good ye me lere
Vncle (quod she) your maystresse is nat here

With that they gonnen laugh/& tho she seyde
This romaunce is of Thebes/that we rede
And we haue herde how ye king Layus deyde
Through Edippus his sonne/& al the dede
And here we stynten/at these letters rede
Howe the byshop/as the boke can tell
Amphiorax/fyll through the grounde to hell

(Quod Pandarus) al this know I my selue
And al thassiege of Thebes/and the care
For herof ben there maked bokes twelue
But let be this/and tell me howe ye fare
Do way your barbe/& shewe your face bare
Do way your booke/ryse vp & let vs daunce
And let vs done to May some obseruaunce

Eyghe/ god forbyd (quod she) be ye mad
Is that a wydowes lyfe/so god you saue
By god ye maken me right sore adrad
ye ben so wylde/it semeth as ye raue
It sate me wel bet aye in a caue
To byde/and rede on holy payntes lyues
Let maydens gon to daunce/& yonge wyues

As euer thriue I (quod this Pandarus)
Yet coulde I tel a thing/to don you play
Nowe vncle dere (quod she) tel it vs
For goddes loue/is than thassiege awey
I am of grekes ferde/so that I deye
Nay nay (qd he) as euer mote I thriue
It is a thyng wel bet than suche fyue

Ye holy god (quod she) what thing is that
What bet than suche fyue? eyghe nay ywis
For al this worlde/ne can I reden what
It shulde ben/some iape I trowe it is
And but your seluen tell vs what it is
My wyt is for to arede it al to lene
As helpe me god/I not what that ye meene

And I your borowe/ne neuer shal (qd he)
This thing be tolde to you/as mote I thriue
And why vncle myn/why so (quod she)
By god (qd he) that wol I tel as blyue
For prouder woman is there none on lyue
And ye it wyste/in al the towne of Troye
I iape nat/so euer haue I ioye

Tho gan she wondren more than before
A thousande folde/& downe her eyen caste
For neuer sythe the tyme that she was bore
To knowen thyng/desyred she so faste
And with a syke/she sayd him at the laste
Nowe vncle myne/I nyl you nat displese
Nor asken more/that may do you disese

So after this/ with many wordes glade
And frendly tales/and with mery chere
Of this & that they speke/and gonnen wade
In many an vnkouth glad & depe matere
As frendes done/whan they bethe yfere
Tyl she gan asken him howe Hector ferde
That was the townes wall/& grekes yerde

Ful wel I thanke it god/ sayd Pandarus
Saue in his arme he hath a lytel wounde
And eke his fresshe brother Troylus
The wyse worthy Hector the seconde
In whom that euery vertue lyst habounde
As al trouthe/and al gentylnesse
Wysdom/honour/fredom/and worthynesse

In good faythe eme (qd she) that lyketh me
They faren wel/god saue hem bothe two
For trewlyche/I holde it great deynte
A kynges sonne in armes wel to do
And be of good condicions therto
For great power/and moral vertue here
Is selde ysene in one persone yfere

I.i. iii. In

The seconde boke of Troylus.

In good faythe that is sothe (qd Pandarus)
But by my trouth/ the kyng hath sõnes twey
That is to meane/ Hector and Troylus
That certaynly though that I shulde dey
They ben as voyde of vyces/ dare I sey
As any men that lyuen vnder sonne
Her might is wyde yknowe/ & what they cõne

Of Hector nedeth it no more for to tell
In al this worlde/ there nys a bettre knyght
Than he that is of worthynesse the well
And he wel more vertue hath than might
This knoweth many a wise & worthy knight
The same prise of Troylus I sey
God helpe me so/ I knowe nat suche twey

By god (quod she) of Hector that is sothe
Of Troylus the same thyng trowe I
For dredelesse/ men telleth that he dothe
In armes day by day/ so worthely
And beareth him here at home so gentilly
To euery wight/ that al prise hath he
Of hem that me were leuest praysed be

Ye say right sothe iwys (quod Pandarus)
For yesterday/ who so had with him ben
Might haue wondred vpon Troylus
For neuer yet so thicke a swarme of been
Ne flewe/ as grekes fro him gonne fleen
And through the felde in euery wightes eere
There was no crye/ but Troylus is there

Nowe here/ now there/ he hunted hem so faste
There nas but grekes bloode/ and Troylus
Nowe him he hurte/ and him al down he caste
Aye where he went it was arayed thus
He was her dethe/ and shelde & lyfe for vs
That as yͭ day/ there durst him non withstõde
Whyle that he helde his blody swerde in honde

Therto he is the frendlyest man
Of great estate/ that euer I sawe my lyue
And where him lyst/ best felowshyp can
To suche as him thynketh able for to thriue
And with that worde/ tho Pãdarus as blyue
He toke his leaue/ and sayd I wol gon hen
Nay/ blame haue I vncle (quod she then)

What eyleth you to be thus wery soone
And namelyche of women/ wol ye so ?
Nay sytteth downe/ by god I haue to doone
With you/ to speke of wysdome er ye go
And euery wight that was aboute hem tho
That herde that/ gan ferre away to stonde
Whyle they two had al that hem lyst in honde

Whan yͭ her tale al brought was to an ende
Of her estate/ and of her gouernaunce
(Quod Pandarus) nowe tyme is yͭ I wende
But yet I say/ aryseth let vs daunce
And caste your wydowes habyt to mischaũce
What lyst you thus your selfe to dissfygure
Sythe you is tydde so glad an auenture

But wel bethought/ for loue of god (qd she)
Shal I nat weten what ye meane of this
No/ this thyng asketh leyser tho (quod he)
And eke me wolde moche greue ywis
If I it tolde/ and ye it toke amys
Yet were it bet my tonge to holde styll
Than say a sothe/ yͭ were ayenst your wyll

For nece/ by the goddesse Mynerue
And Iupyter/ that maketh the thonder rynge
And the blyssful Venus/ that I serue
Ye ben the woman in this worlde lyuyng
Withouten paramours/ to my wetyng
That I best loue/ and lothest am to greue
And that ye weten wel your selfe I leue

Iwis myn vncle (quod she) graunt mercy
Your frendshyp haue I founden euer yet
I am to no man holden trewly
So moche as you/ and haue so lytel quyt
And with the grace of god/ emforth my wyt
As in my gylte/ I shal you neuer offende
And if I haue er this I wol amende

But for the loue of god/ I you beseche
As ye be he/ that I loue moste and tryste
Let be to me your fremed maner speche
And say to me your nece/ what you lyste
And with that worde/ her vncle anon her kyst
And sayd/ gladly my leue nece dere
Take it for good/ that I shal say you here

With

With that she gan her eyen downe to caste
And Pandarus to coughe gan a lyte
And sayd: Nece alwaye lo/to the laste
Howe so it be/ that some men hem delyte
With subtel arte her tales for tendyte
yet for al that in her entencioun
Her tale is al for some conclusyoun

And sithe thende is euery tales strength
And this mater is so behouely
What shulde I paynt/ or drawen it on length
To you that ben my frende so faithfully
And with that worde he gan right inwardly
Beholden her/ and loken in her face
And sayd/ on suche a myrrour good grace

Than thought he thus/ if I my tale endyte
Aught harde/or make a processe any whyle
She shal no sauour haue therin but lyte
And trowe I wolde her in my wyl begyle
For tendre wyttes wenen al be wyle
Where as they can nat playnlych vnderstonde
For thy her wyt to seruen wol I fonde

And loked on her in a besy wyse
And she was ware that he behelde her so
Ah lorde (qd she) so faste ye me auyse
Sawe ye me neuer er nowe/ what say ye no?
Yes yes (quod he) and bet wol er I go
But by my trouthe I thought nowe/if ye
Be fortunate/for nowe men shal it se

For euery wight/some goodly auenture
Somtyme is shape/if he it can receyuen
But if he nyl take of it no cure
Whan that it cometh/but wylfully it weyuen
Lo/neyther case nor fortune him deceyuen
But right his owne slouth & wretchydnesse
And suche a wight is for to blame I gesse

Good auenture/ O belle nece haue ye
Ful lightly founden/and ye conne it take
And for the loue of god/and eke of me
Catche it anon/leste auenture slake
What shulde I lenger processe of it make
Yeue me your honde for in this worlde is non
If that you lyst a wight so wel begon

And sythe I speke of good entencioun
As I to you haue tolde wel here beforne
And loue as wel your honour and renoun
As any creature in al the worlde yborne
By al the othes that I haue you sworne
And ye be wrothe therfore/or wene I lye
Ne shal I neuer sene you efte with eye

Bethe nat agaste/ne quaketh nat/ wherto
Ne chaungeth nat for feare so your hewe
For hardely the worste of this is do
And though my tale as nowe be to you newe
Yet trust alway/ye shal me fynde trewe
And were it thyng yͭ me thought vnsyttyng
To you wolde I no suche tales bring

Nowe my good eme/for goddes loue I pray
(Quod she) come of and tel me what it is
For bothe I am agaste what ye wol say
And eke me longeth it to wete ywis
For whether it be wel/or be amys
Say on/let me nat in this feare dwell
So wol I done/nowe herkeneth I shal tell

Nowe nece myne/the kynges dere sonne
The good wyse worthy/fresshe and free
Whiche alway for to done wel is his wonne
The noble Troylus so loueth the
That but ye helpe it wol his bane be
Lo here is al/ what shulde I more sey
Doth what you lyst/to make him lyue or dey

But if ye let him dye/I wol steruen
Haue here my trouthe/nece I nyl nat lyen
Al shulde I with this knyfe my throte keruen
With that the teeres burste out of his eyen
And sayd/if that ye done vs bothe dyen
Thus giltlesse/than haue ye fysshed fayre
What mende ye/though yͭ we bothe apayre

Alas/he whiche that is my lorde so dere
That trewe man/that noble gentyl knyght
That naught desyreth/but your frendly chere
I se him dyen/there he gothe vpright
And hasteth him/with al his full might
For to ben slayne/if his fortune assente
Alas that god you suche a beaute sente

If it

If it be so that ye so cruel be
That of his dethe you lysteth nought to retch
That is so trewe and worthy/ as we se
No more than of a iaper or a wretch
If ye be suche/ your beaute may nat stretch
To make amendes of so cruel a dede
Auysement is good before the nede

Wo worthe the fayre Gēme vertulesse
Wo worthe that herbe also that dothe no bote
Wo worthe the beaute that is routhlesse
Wo worth that wight that trede eche vnd fote.
And ye that ben of beaute croppe and rote
If therwithal in you ne be no routhe
Than is harme ye lyuen by my trouthe

And also thynke wel/ that this is no gaude
For me were leuer/ thou/ I/ and he
Were honged/ than I shulde ben his baude
As highe as men myght on vs al yse
I am thyne Eme/ the shame were to me
As wel as the/ if that I shulde assent
Through myne abet/ ẏ he thyn honour shent

Now vnderstonde/ for I you naught requere
To bynde you to hym/ through no beheste
Saue onely that ye make him better chere
Than ye han done er this/ and more feste
So that his lyfe be saued at the leste
This al and some/ ⁊ playnly our intente
God helpe me so/ I neuer other mente

Lo/ this request is nought but skyl iwys
Ne doute of reson parde is there none
I set the worste/ that ye dreden this
Men wolde wondre to sene him come ⁊ gone
Therayenst answere I thus anone
That euery wight/ but he be foole of kynde
Wol deme it loue of frendshyp in his mynde

What/ who wol demen though he se a man
To temple gon/ that he the ymages eeteth
Thynke eke/ howe wel and wisely that he can
Gouerne him selfe/ ẏ he nothing foryeteth
That wher he cometh/ he pris ⁊ thōke hī geteth
And eke therto he shal come here so selde
What force were it/ though al ẏ town behelde

Suche loue of frendes reigneth al this town
And wrie you in that mantel euermo
And god so wys be my sauacion
As I haue sayd/ your best is to do so
But good nece/ alway to stynte his wo
So let your daunger/ sugred ben alyte
That of his dethe/ ye be nat al to wyte

¶ Cresyde/ whiche ẏ herde him in this wyse
Thought/ I shal felen what he meaneth ywis
Nowe eme (qd̄ she) what wolde ye deuyse?
What is your rede/ I shulde done of this?
That is wel sayd qd̄ he/ certayne best is
That ye him loue ayen for his louyng
As loue for loue/ is skylful guerdonyng

Thynke eke howe elde wasteth euery houre
In eche of you/ a parte of beaute
And therfore/ er that age the deuoure
Go loue/ for olde there wol no wight of the
Let this prouerbe/ afore vnto you be
To late yware/ qd̄ beaute/ whan it paste
And elde daunteth daunger/ at the laste

The kynges foole is wont to crye loude
Whan ẏ him thinketh a woman bereth her hye
So longe mote ye lyue/ and al proude
Tyl crowes fete growe vnder your eye
And sende you than a myrrour in to prie
In whiche that ye may se your face a morowe
Nece/ I bydde wysshe you nomore sorowe

With this he stynte/ and cast downe the heed
And she began to brest awepe anon
And said/ alas for wo/ why nere I deed
For of this worlde/ the faythe is al agone
Alas/ what shulden straunge to me done
Whan he that for my beste frende I wende
Rate me to laue/ and shulde it me defende

Alas/ I wolde haue trusted douteles
That if that I/ through my disauenture
Had loued eyther him/ or Achilles
Hector/ or any maner creature
Ye nolde haue had no mercy ne mesure
On me/ but alway had me in repreue
This false worlde alas/ who may it leue

What

What? is this al the ioye and al the feest?
Is this your rede? is this my blyssful cage?
Is this the very mede of your beheest?
Is al this paynted processe sayd (alas)
Right for this fyne/O lady myn Pallas
Thou in this dredeful case for me puruey
For so astonyed am I/that I dey

With that she gan ful sorowfully to syke
Ne may it be no bet (quod Pandarus)
By god I shal no more come here this weke
And god to forne/that am mistrusted thus
I se wel nowe/ye setten lyght of vs
Or of our dethe alas/I woful wretche
Might he yet lyue/of me were nought to retch

O cruell god/o dispytous Marte
O furies thre of hell/on you I crye
So let me neuer out of this house departe
If that I mente harme or villanye
But sythe I se my lorde mote nedes dye
And I with him/here I me shriue and sey
That wickedly ye done vs bothe dey.

But sythe it lyketh you/that I be deed
By Neptunus that god is of the see
Fro this forthe shal I neuer eten breed
Tyl I myn owne herte bloode may see
For certayne I wol dye as sone as he
And vp he sterte/and on his way he raught
Tyll she agayne him by the lappe caught

Creseyde/whiche ẏ wel nygh starfe for feare
So as she was the feerfullest wight
That might be/and herde eke with her eere
And sawe the sorouful ernest of the knyght
And in his prayer sawe eke none vnryght
And for the harme eke that might fall more
She gan to rewe/& dredde her wonder sore

And thought thus/vnhappes fallen thicke
Alday for loue/and in suche maner caas
As men ben cruel in hem selfe and wicke
And if this man slee here him selfe/alas
In my presence/it nyl be no solas
What men wolde of it deme/I can nat say
It nedeth me ful slyghly for to play

And with a sorowfull sygh/she sayd thrie
Ah lorde/what me is tydde a sory chaunce
For myn estate lyeth in a ieopardye
And eke myn emes lyfe lythe in balaunce
But nathelesse/with goddes gouernaunce
I shal so done/myn honour shal I kepe
And eke his lyfe/and stynte for to wepe

Of harmes two/the lesse is for to chese
Yet had I leuer maken him good chere
In honour/than myn emes lyfe to lese
Ye sayne ye nothyng els me requere?
No wys (qd̄ he) myn owne nece dere:
Nowe wel (qd̄ she) & I wol done my payne
I shal myn herte ayen my lust constrayne

But ẏ I nyl nat holden him in honde
Ne loue a man/that can I naught ne may
Ayenst my wyl/but els wol I fonde
Myn honour saue/plesen him fro day to day
Therto nolde I nat ones haue sayd nay
But that I dredde/as in my fantasye
But cesse cause/aye cesseth maladye

But here I make a protestacion
That in this processe if ye deper go
That certaynly/for no sauacion
Of you/though that ye steruen bothe two
Though al the worlde on o day be my fo
Ne shal I neuer on him haue other routhe
I graunte wel (qd̄ Pandare) by my trouthe

But may I trust wel to you (quod he)
That of this thyng that ye han hight me here
Ye wol it holde truely vnto me
Ye doutlesse (qd̄ she) myn vncle dere
Ne that I shal haue cause in this matere
(Quod he) to playne/or ofter you to preche
Why no parde/what nedeth more speche

Tho fyll they in other tales glade
Tyl at the laste/o good eme (quod she tho)
For loue of god whiche that vs bothe made
Tel me howe first ye wysten of his wo
Wot none of it but ye/he sayd no
Can he wel speke of loue (qd̄ she) I prey
Tel me/for I the bet me shal puruey

Tho

Tho Pandarus a lyte gan to smyle
And sayd: By my trouth I shal nowe tel
This other day / nat gone ful longe whyle
Within the paleys gardyn by a wel
Ganne he and I / wel halfe a day to dwel
Right for to speken of an ordynaunce
Howe we the Grekes myghten disauaunce

Soone after that we gone for to lepe
And casten with our dartes to and fro
Tyl at the last / he sayd / he wolde slepe
And on the grasse adowne / he layde him tho
And I after gan to romen / to and fro
Tyl that I herde / as I walked alone
Howe he began / ful wofully to grone

Tho gan I stalke him softely behynde
And sekerly the sothe for to sayne
As I can clepe ayen nowe to my mynde
Right thus to Loue / he gan him for to playne
He sayd: Lorde / haue routh vpon my payne
Al haue I ben rebel in myne entent
Nowe (Mea culpa) lorde I me repent

O god / that at thy disposytioun
Ledest the fyne / by iuste purueyaunce
Of euery wight / my lowe confessioun
Accepte in gree / and sende me suche penaunce
As lyketh the / but from disesperaunce
That maye my goost departe alway fro the
Thou be my shylde / for thy benignyte

For certes lorde / so soore hath she me woũded
That stode in blacke / with lokyng of her eyen
That to myne hertes botome it is yfounded
Through which I wot / ẏ I mote nedes dyen
This is ẏ worst / I dare me nought bewreyen
And wel the hooter ben the gledes rede
That men hem wryen with asshen pale ⁊ deed

With that he smote his heed adowne anone
And gan to muttre / I nat what trewly
And I with that gan styl awaye to gone
And lete therof / as nothyng wyst had I
And come agayne anon and stoode him by
And sayd awake / ye slepen al to longe
It semeth nought that loue doth you wronge

That slepen so / that no man may you wake
Who sey euer er this so dul a man
Ye frende (quod he) do ye your heedes ake
For loue / and lette me lyuen as I can
But lorde that he for wo was pale and wan
Yet made he tho as fresshe a countenaunce
As though he shulde haue led the newe dãce

This passed forth / tyl nowe this other day
It fel that I come romyng al alone
In to his chambre / ⁊ founde howe ẏ he lay
Vpon his bedde: but man so sore grone
Ne herde I neuer / and what was his moone
Ne wyst I nought / for as I was cõmyng
Al sodaynly / he lefte his complaynyng

Of whiche I toke somwhat suspectioun
And nere I come / and founde hym wepe sore
And god so wyse be my sauatioun
As neuer of thyng had I no routh more
For neyther with engyn / ne with no loore
Vnnethes myght I fro the dethe him kepe
That yet fele I myne herte for hym wepe

And god wote neuer sithe that I was borne
Was I so besy no man for to preche
Ne neuer was to wight so depe sworne
Er he me tolde / who myght ben his leche
But nowe to you rehersen al his speche
Or al his woful wordes for to sowne
Ne byd me nought / but ye wol se me swoun

But for to saue his lyfe / and els nought
And to non harme of you / thus am I driuen
And for ẏ loue of god that vs hath wrought
Suche chere him doth / that he ⁊ I may lyuen
Now haue I platte to you myne hert shriuen
And sithe ye wote that myne entent is clene
Take hede therof / for none yuel I mene

And right good thrifte / I pray to god haue ye
That han suche one ycaught withouten nette
And be ye wyse / as ye be fayre to se
Wel in the rynge / than is the Ruby sette
There were neuer two so wel ymette
Whan ye ben his al hole / as he is your
There mighty god yet grãt vs se ẏ hour

Nay

Nay therof spake I nat : A ha (quod she)
As helpe me god/ ye shenden euery dele
A mercy dere nece/ anon (quod he.)
What so I spake/ I ment nought but wele
By Mars the god/ that helmed is of stele
Now bethe not wroth/ my blode/ my nece dere
  Nowe wel (quod she) foryeuen be it here

With this he toke his leaue/ and home he went
ye lorde howe he was glad/ and wel bygon
Creseyde arose/ no lenger she ne stent
But straight in to her closet wente anon
And set her downe/ as styll as any stone
And euery worde gan vp ⁊ downe to wynde
That he had sayd/ as it came her to mynde

And woxe somdele astoned in her thought
Right for the newe case/ but whan that she
Was ful auysed/ tho founde she right nought
Of peryll/ why that she ought aferde be
For man may loue of possibylite
A woman so/ his herte may tobreste
And she nat loue ayen/ but if her leste

But as she sate alone/ and thought thus
Thascrye arose at scarmoche al without
And men cryed in the strete/ se Troylus
Hath right now put to flyght the grekes route
With that gonne al her meyne for to shoute
A/ go we se/ cast vp the yates wyde
For through this strete he mot to Paleys ryde

For other way is fro the yates none
Of Dardanus there open is the cheyne
With that come he/ and al his folke anone
An easy pace rydyng/ in routes tweyne
Right as his happy day was sothe to seyne
For whiche men sayth may nat distourbed be
That shal betyde of necessyte

This Troylus sate on his baye stede
Al armed saue his heed/ ful rychely
And wounded was his horse/ ⁊ gan to blede
On whiche he rode a pace ful softely
But suche a knyghtly syght trewly
As was on him/ was nat withouten fayle
To loke on Mars/ that god is of batayle

So lyke a man of armes/ and a knyght
He was to sene/ fulfylled of hygh prowesse
For bothe he had a body/ and myght
To don that thyng/ as wel as hardynesse
And eke to sene him in his geare dresse
So fresshe/ so yonge/ so weldy semed he
It was an heuen vpon him for to se

His helme to hewen was in twenty places
That by a tyssue honge/ his backe behynde
His sheld to dassHed with swerdes ⁊ wt maces
In whiche men might many an arowe fynde
That thyrled had horne/ nerfe/ and rynde
And aye the people cryed/ here cometh our ioy
And next his brother/ holder vp of Troye

For whiche he wext a lytel reed for shame
Whan he so herde the people vpon him cryen
That to beholde/ it was a noble game
Howe sobrelyche he caste adowne his eyen
Creseyde anon gan al his chere espyen
And let it so softe in her herte synke
That to her selfe she sayd/ who yaue me drike

For al her owne thought/ she woxe al reed
Remembring her right thus/ lo this is he
Which that myn vncle swereth he mot be deed
But I on him haue mercy and pyte
And with that thought for pure ashamed she
Gan in her heed to pull/ and that as faste
Whyle he and al the people forthby paste

And gan to caste/ and rollen vp and down
Within her thought his excellent prowesse
And his estate/ and also his renoun
His wytte/ his shap/ and eke his gentylesse
But moste her fauour was/ for his distresse
Was al for her/ and thought it were a routhe
To sleen suche one/ if that he ment trouthe

¶ Nowe might some enuyous iangle thus
This was a sodayne loue/ howe might it be
That she so lightly loued Troylus
Right for the first syght : ye parde :
Nowe who so sayd so/ mote he neuer the
For euery thyng/ a gynnyng hath it nede
Er al be wrought/ withouten any drede

For

For I saye nat/ that she so sodainly
Yafe him her loue/ but that she gan enclyne
To lyken him tho/ and I haue tolde you why
And after that/ his manhode and his pyne
Made that loue within her gan to myne
For whiche by processe/ and by good seruyce
He wanne her loue/ and in no sodayne wyse

And also blyssful Venus wel arayed
Satte in her seuenth house of heuen tho
Disposed wele/ and with aspectes payed
To helpe sely Troylus of his wo
And sothe to sayne/ she nas nat al a foe
To Troylus/ in his natiuyte
God wote/ that wele the sooner sped he

Nowe lette vs stynt of Troylus a throwe
That rydeth forthe/ and lette vs turne fast
Vnto Creseyde/ that heng her heed ful lowe
There as she sate alone/ and gan to cast
Wheron she wolde apoynt her at the last
If it so were/ her Eme ne wolde cesse
For Troylus/ vpon her for to presse

And lorde so she gan in her thought argue
In this mater/ of whiche I haue you tolde
And what to don best were/ and what eschue
That plyted she ful ofte in many folde
Now was her hert warme/ now was it colde
And what she thought/ so what shal I write
As myne authour lysteth for tendyte

She thought first/ that Troylus persone
She knewe by syght/ and eke his gentylnesse
And thus she sayd/ al were it nought to done
To graunt him loue/ yet for his worthynesse
It were honour with play/ & with gladnesse
In honeste/ with suche a lorde to deale
For myne estate/ and also for his heale

Eke wel wot I/ my kynges sonne is he
And sithe he hath to se me suche delyte
Yf I wolde vtterlyche his syght flye
Peraunter he myght haue me in dispite
Through which I mizt stonde in worse plyte
Nowe were I wyse/ me hate to purchace
Without nede/ there I may stonde in grace

In euery thyng/ I wote there lyth measure
For though a man forbydde dronkenesse
He nought forbyddeth that euery creature
Be drynkelesse for alwaye as I gesse
Eke sithe I wot for me is his distresse
I ne ought nat for that thyng him dispise
Sithe it is so/ he meaneth in good wyse

And eke I knowe/ of longe tyme agone
His thewes good/ and that he nys nat nyce
No vauntour sayne men/ certayne he is non
To wyse is he/ to done so great a vyce
Ne als I nyl him neuer so cherice
That he shal make auaunt by iust cause
He shal me neuer bynde in suche a clause

Nowe sette I case/ the hardest is ywis
Men myght demen that he loueth me
What dishonour were it vnto me this?
Maye iche him lette of that/ why nay parde?
I knowe also/ and alwaye here and se
Men louen women al this towne about
Be they the werse? why nay without dout?

I thynke eke howe/ he worthy is to haue
Of al this noble towne the thriftyest
That woman is/ if she her honour saue
For out and out he is the worthyest
Saue onely Hector/ whiche that is the best
And yet his lyfe lythe al nowe in my cure
But suche is loue/ and eke myne auenture

Ne me to loue/ a wonder is it nought
For wel wot I my selfe/ so god me spede
Al wol I that none wyst of this thought
I am one the fayrest out of drede
And goodlyest/ who so that taketh hede
And so men sayne in al the towne of Troye
What wonder is: though he of me haue ioye

I am myne owne woman wel at ese
I thanke it god/ as after myne estate
Right yonge/ and stonde vnteyd in lusty lese
Withouten ielousye/ and suche debate
Shal no husbonde sayne to me checke mate
For either they ben ful of ialousye
Or maisterful/ or louen nouelry

What

What shal I done? to what fyne lyue I thus?
Shal I nat loue / in case if that me leste ?
What pardieux I am nat religyus
And though that I myn herte set at reste
Upon this knyght / that is the worthyest
And kepe alway myn honour / and my name
By al right it may do me no shame

But right as whan the sonne shyneth bright
In Marche / that chaungeth oft tyme his face
And that a cloude is put with wynde to flight
Whiche ouersprat the sonne / as for a space
A cloudy thought gan through her soule pace
That ouerspradde her bright thoughtes all
So that for feare almost she gan to fall

That thought was this: Alas sythe I am fre
Shulde I nowe loue / and put in ieopardye
My sykernesse / and thrallen lyberte
Alas / howe durste I thynken that folye?
May I not wel in other folke aspye
Her dredeful ioy / her constreynt / & her payne
Ther loueth non / þ she ne hath way to playne

For loue is yet the moste stormy lyfe
Right of him selfe / that euer was begonne
For euer some mystrust / or nyce stryfe
There is in loue / some cloude ouer the sonne
Therto we wretched women nothyng conne
Whan vs is wo / but wepe and syt and thynke
Our wreche is this / our owne wo to drinke

Also wicked tonges ben so prest
To speke vs harme / eke men ben so vntrewe
That right anon as cessed is her lest
So cesseth loue / and forthe to loue a newe
But harme ydo is done / who so it rewe
For though these mē for loue hem first to rēde
Ful sharpe begynnyng breketh ofte at ende

Howe ofte tyme may men rede and sene
The treson / that to women hath be do ?
To what fyne is suche loue / I can nat sene
Or where becometh it / whan it is go
There is no wyght that wote / I trowe so
Where it becometh / lo / no wight on it sporneth
That erst was nothyng / in to naught turneth

Howe besy (if I loue) eke muste I be
To plesen hem / that iangle of loue / & demen
And coyen hem / that they say no harme of me
For though there be no cause / yet hem semen
Al be for harme / that folke her frēdes quemen
And who may stoppen euery wicked tonge?
Or sowne of belles / whyle þ they ben ronge?

And after that her thought gan for to clere
And sayd / he which that nothing vndertaketh
Nothyng acheueth / be him lothe or dere
And with an other thought her herte quaketh
Than slepeth hope / and after drede awaketh
Now hote now colde / but thus betwixen twey
She ryste her vp / & went her for to pley

Adowne the stayre / anonright tho she wente
In to her gardyn / with her neces thre
And vp & downe / they maden many a wente
Flexippe and she / Tarbe / and Antigone
To playen / that it ioy was to se
And other of her women a great route
Her folowed in the gardyn al aboute

This yerde was large / & rayled al the aleyes
And shadowed wel / wt blosomy bowes grene
And benched newe / and sonded al the wayes
In which she walketh arme in arme betwene
Tyl at the laste Antigone the shene
Gan on a troyan songe to syngen clere
That it an heuen was / her voyce to here

She said: O Loue / to whom I haue / & shal
Ben humble subiect / trewe in myn entent
As I best can / to you lorde yeue yche al
For euer more myn hertes lust to rent
For neuer yet thy grace no wight sent
So blysful cause as me / my lyfe to lede
In al ioye and suretie / out of drede

The blysful god / hath me so wel beset
In loue iwys / that al that bereth lyfe
Ymagynen ne coulde howe to be bet
For lorde withouten ielousye or stryfe
I loue one / whiche that most is ententyfe
To seruen wel / vnweryly or vnfayned
That euer was / & leste with harme distayned

K.k. As he

The seconde boke of Troylus.

As he that is the wel of worthynesse
Of trouthe grounde/myrrour of goodlyheed
Of wytte Apollo/ stone of sykernesse
Of vertue rote/of luste fynder and heed
Through whiche is al sorowe fro me deed
Iwys I loue him best/so dothe he me
Nowe good thrift haue he/ where soeuer he be

Whom shulde I thanken but you god of loue
Of al this blysse/in whiche to bathe I gynne
And thanked be ye lorde/for that I loue
This is the right lyfe that I am inne
To flemen al maner vyce and synne
This doth me so to vertue for to entende
That day by day I in my wyll amende

And who that sayth yͭ for to loue is vyce
Or thraldom/though he fele in it distresse
He eyther is enuyous/or right nyce
Or is vnmyghty for his shrewdnesse
To louen/for suche maner folke I gesse
Diffamen loue/as nothyng of him knowe
They speken/but they bente neuer his bowe

What is the sonne worse of kynde right ?
Though yͭ a man/for feblenesse of his eyen
May nat endure on it to se for bright
Or loue the worse/that wretches on it cryen
No wele is worthe/ that may no sorowe dryen
And for thy/who that hath an heed of verre
Fro caste of stones ware him in the werre

But I with al myn herte and al my might
As I haue sayd/wol loue vnto my laste
My dere herte/and al myn owne knyght
In whiche myn herte growen is so faste
And his in me/that it shal euer laste
Al dredde I first loue him to begyn
Nowe wot I wel there is no peryll in

And of her songe right with yͭ worde she stent
And therwithal/nowe nece (qđ Creseyde)
Who made this songe/now with so good entēt
Antygone answerde anon/and sayde
Madame iwys the goodlyest mayde
Of great estate in al the towne of Troye
And led her lyfe in moste honour and ioye

Forsothe so semeth it by her songe
Quod tho Creseyde/ and gan therwᵗ to syke
And sayd : Lorde/is there suche blysse amōge
These louers/ as they can fayre endite
Ye wysse quod fresshe Antigone the white
For al the folke that haue or ben on lyue
Ne conne wel the blysse of loue discryue

But wene ye that euery wretche wote
The parfite blysse of loue/ why nay ywis
They wenen al be loue/ if one be hote
Do way do waye/ they wote nothynge of this
Menne mote asken of payntes/ if it is
Ought faire in heuen/ & why? for they can tel
And aske fendes/ if it be foule in hel

Creseyde vnto yͭ purpose naught answerde
But sayd/ iwys it wol be nyght as faste
But euery worde/whiche that she of her herde
She gan to printen in her herte faste
And aye gan loue her lasse for to agaste
Than it dyd erst/and synken in her herte
That she waye somwhat able to conuerte

The dayes honour/and the heuens eye
The nyghtes foe/ al this clepe I the sonne
Gan westren faste/& downwarde for to wrie
As he that had his dayes course yronne
And white thinges woxen dymme and donne
For lacke of light/and sterres for to apere
That she and al her folke in went yfere

So whan it lyked her to gon to reste
And voyded weren they that voyden ought
She sayd/ that to slepen wel her leste
Her women sone tyl her bed her brought
Whā al was husshe/than lay she styl & thought
Of al this thyng the maner and the wyse
Reherce it nedeth nat/for ye ben wyse

A nyghtyngale vpon a Cedre grene
Vnder the chambre wall/there as she lay
Ful loude songe ayen the moone shene
Parauenture in his byrdes wyse a lay
Of loue/that made her herte fresshe & gay
That herkened she so longe in good entente
Tyl at the laste the deed slepe her hente

And

And as she slept/anon right tho her mette
Howe that an Egle fethered whyte as bone
Vnder her brest his longe clawes sette
And out her herte he rent/and that anone
And dyd his herte in to her brest to gone
Of which she naught agrose/ne nothĩg smert
And forthe he flyeth/with herte lefte for herte

¶ Nowe let her slepe/& we our tales holde
Of Troylus/that is to paleys rydden
Fro the scarmyshe of whiche I tolde
And in his chambre sate/and hath abydden
Tyl two or thre of his messangers yeden
For Pandarus/and soughten him ful faste
Tyl they him foũde/& brought him at the last

This Pandarus came leapyng in at ones
And sayd thus/ who hath ben wel ybete
To day with swerdes/& slonge stones
But Troylus / that hath caught him an hete
And gan to iape/& sayd/lorde ye sweete
But ryse and let vs soupe/& go to reste
And he answerde him/do we as the leste

With al the haste goodly as they myght
They spedde hem fro the souper/and to bedde
And euery wight out at the dore him dyght
And whyder him lyst/vpon his way him sped
But Troylus thought that his herte bledde
For wo/tyl that he herde some tydynge
And sayd frende/shal I nowe wepe or synge

(Quod Pandarus) be styll & let me slepe
And do on thyn hoode/thy nedes spedde be
And chese if thou wolt synge/daunce/or lepe
At shorte wordes thou shalte trowe me
Sir/ my nece wol don wel by the
And loue the beste/by god & by my trouthe
But lacke of pursute make it in thy slouthe

For thus ferforthe I haue thy werke begon
Fro day to day/tyl this day by the morowe
Her loue of frendshyp haue I to the won
And therfore hath she layd her faith to borow
Algate a foote is hamesed of thy sorowe
What shulde I lenger sermon of it holde
As ye haue herde before/al he him tolde

But right as floures through ẏ cold of night
Iclosed/ stoupen in her stalkes lowe
Redressen hem ayen the sonne bright
And spreden in her kynde course by rowe
Right so gan tho his eyen vp to throwe
This Troylus/and sayd: O Venus dere
Thy might thy grace/yheryed be it here

And to Pandarus he helde vp both his hõdes
And sayd/lorde al thyn be that I haue
For I am hole/and brosten ben my bondes
A thousande Troyes/ who so that me yaue
Eche after other/god so wys me saue
Ne myght me so gladen/ so myn herte
It spredeth so for ioye it wol to sterte

But lorde how shal I don? how shal I lyuen
Whan shal I next my dere herte se?
Howe shal this longe tyme away be driuen?
Tyl that thou be ayen at her fro me
Thou mayst answere/abyde abyde: but he
That hangeth by the necke/sothe to sayne
In great disease abydeth for the payne

Al easily nowe/for the loue of Marte
(Qđ Pandarus) for euery thing hath tyme
So longe abyde/tyl that the nyght departe
For al so syker as thou lyest here by me
And god to forne/ I wol be there at prime
And for thy werke somwhat/as I shal saye
Or on some other wyght this charge laye

For parde god wot/I haue euer yet
Ben redy the to serue/and this nyght
Haue I nat fayned/but emforthe my wyt
Done al thy lust/and shal with al my might
Do nowe as I shal sayne/and fare aright
And if thou nylte/wyte al thy selfe thy care
On me is naught alonge thyn yuel fare

I wote wel that thou wyser arte than I
A thousande folde: but if I were as thou
God helpe me so/as I wolde vtterly
Right of myn owne honde write her nowe
A letter/in whiche I wolde her tellen howe
I farde amysse/and her beseche of routhe
Nowe helpe thy selfe/ & leaue it for no slouthe

K.k.ii. And

And I my selfe shal therwith to her gon
And whan thou woste ẏ I am with her there
Worthe thou vp on a courser right anon
ye hardely/right in thy beste gere
And ryde forth by ẏ place/as naught ne were
And thou shalt fynde vs (if I may) syttyng
At some wyndowe/in to the strete lokyng

And if the lyst/than mayst thou vs salue
And vpon me make thou thy countenaunce
But by thy lyfe beware/and faste eschue
To taryen ought/god shyld vs fro mischaūce
Ryde forthe thy way & holde thy gouernaūce
And we shal speke of the somwhat I trowe
Whan thou arte gon/to do thyn eeres glowe

Touchyng thy lettre thou art wyse ynough
I wot thou nyste it deignelyche endyte
As make it with these argumentes tough
Ne scryuenyshe or craftely thou it write
Beblotte it with thy teeres eke alyte
And if thou write a goodly worde al softe
Though it be good/reherce it nat to ofte

For though the beste harpour vpon lyue
Wolde on the beste sowned ioly harpe
That euer was/with al his fyngers fyue
Touche aye o strynge/or aye o warble harpe
Were his nayles poynted neuer so sharpe
It shulde make euery wight to dull
To here his glee/& of his strokes full

Ne iombre eke no discordant thing yfere
As thus/to vsen termes of physyke
In loues termes holde of thy matere
The forme alway/and do that it be lyke
For if a peyntour wolde paynte a pyke
With asses fete/and heded as an ape
It cordeth nat/so were it but a iape

This counsayle lyked wel vnto Troylus
But as a dredeful louer/he sayd this
Alas my dere brother Pandarus
I am ashamed for to write iwys
Leste of myn innocence I sayd amys
Or that she nolde it for dispyte receyue
Than were I deed/ther might it nothīg weyue

To that Pandare answerde/if the lest
Do that I say/and let me therwith gon
For by ẏ that lorde that formed eest and west
I hope of it to bring answere anon
Right of her honde/& if that thou nylt non
Let be/and sory mote he ben his lyue
Ayenst thy lust/that helpeth the to thriue

(Quod Troylus) depardieux yche assente
Sythe that the lyst/I wol aryse and write
And blyssful god pray yche with good entente
The vyage and the lettre I shal endyte
So spede it/and thou Mynerua the whyte
Yeue thou me wyt/my lettre to deuyse
And set him down/& wrote right in this wyse

First he gan her his right lady call
His hertes lyfe/his lust/his sorowes leche
His blysse/and eke these other termes all
That in suche case ye louers al seche
And in ful humble wyse/as in his speche
He gan him recōmaunde vnto her grace
To tell al howe/it asketh mokel space

And after this ful lowly he her prayde
To be nought wrothe/though he of his folye
So hardy was to her to write/and sayde
That loue it made/or els muste he dye
And pitously gan mercy for to crye
And after that he sayd/and lyed ful loude
Him selfe was lytel worthe/& lasse he coude

And that she wolde haue his cōnyng excused
That lytel was/and eke he dredde her so
And his vnworthynesse aye he acused
And after that than gan he tel his wo
But that was endelesse withouten ho
And said/he wolde in trouth alway him holde
And redde it ouer/and gan the lettre folde

And with his salte teeres gan he bathe
The ruby in his signet/and it sette
Vpon the wexe deliuerlyche and rathe
Therwith a thousande tymes/er he lette
He kyste tho the lettre that he shette
And sayd/lettre a blyssful destyne
The shapen is/my lady shal the se

This

This Pandare toke the letter/& that be tyme
A morowe/ and to his neces paleys sterte
And fast he swore/that it was passed prime
And gan to iape/ and sayd : ywis myne herte
So fresshe it is/ although it sore smerte
I maye nat slepe neuer a Mayes morowe
I haue a iolye wo/ a lusty sorowe

Creseyde/ whan that she her [illegible] herde
With dredeful herte/ and desyrous to here
The cause of his comynge/ thus answerde
Nowe by your faithe myn vncle (q she) dere
What maner wyndes gydeth you nowe here
Tel vs your iolye wo/and your penaunce
Howe ferforth be ye putte in loues daunce

By god (qd he) I hope alwaye behynde
And to laughe/ it thought her hert brest
(Quod Pãdarus) loke alway that ye fynde
Game in myn hood/ but herkneth if you lest
Ther is right nowe cõe in to the towne a gest
A greke espye/ and telleth newe thynges
For whiche I come to tel you newe tidynges

In to the gardyn go we/ and ye shal here
Al preuely of this a longe sermoun
With that they wenten arme in arme yfere
In to the gardyn fro the chambre doun
And whan he was so farre / that yͭ soun
Of that he spake/ no man heren myght
He sayd her thus/ and out the letter plyght

Lo/ he that is al hooly yours free
Him recõmaundeth lowly to your grace
And sente you this letter here by me
Auyseth you on it/ whan ye han space
And of some goodly answere you purchace
Or helpe me god so/ playnly for to sayne
He may nat longe lyuen for his payne

Ful dredefully tho gan she stonde styl
And toke it nat/but al her humble chere
Gan for to chaunge/and sayd scripte nor byl
For loue of god/that toucheth suche matere
Ne bringe me none/and also vncle dere
To myne estate haue more regarde I pray
Than to his lust/ what shulde I more say

And loketh nowe if this be resonable
And letteth nat for fauour ne for slouthe
To sayne a sothe/nowe is it couenable
To myn estate/by god and by my trouthe
To take it/or to haue of him routhe
In harmyng of my selfe/or in repreue
Beare it ayen/for him that ye on leue

This Pandarus gan on her for to stare
And sayd/nowe is this the grettest wonder
That euer I sawe/let be this nyce fare
To dethe mote I smytten be with thonder
If for the cytie/whiche that stondeth yonder
Wolde I a lettre vnto you bring or take
To harm of you: what lyst you thus it make

But thus ye faren wel nyghe al and some
That he that moste desyreth you to serue
Of him ye retche lest/ where he become
And whether that he lyue/ or els sterue
But for al that/that euer I may deserue
Refuse it nat (qd he) and hente her faste
And in her bosome the lettre downe he thraste

And sayd her/nowe caste it away anon
That folke may sene/& gauren on vs twey
(Quod she) I can abyde tyl they be gon
And gan to smyle/& sayd him/ eme I pray
Suche answere as you lyst your selfe puruey
For trewly I wol no lettre write
No than wol I (quod he) so ye endyte

Therwith she lough/ and sayd go we dyne
And he gan at him selfe iape faste
And sayd nece/I haue so great a pyne
For loue/ that eueryche other day I faste
And gan his beste iapes forthe to caste
And made her so to laugh at his folye
That she for laughter wende for to dye

And whan that she was comen in to the hall
Nowe eme (qd she) we wol go dyne anon
And gan some of her women to her call
And streyght in to her chambre gan she gone
But of her besynesses this was one
Amonges other thynges/ out of drede
Ful priuely this lettre for to rede

R.R. iii.　　Auysed

Auysed worde by worde in euery lyne
And foũde no lacke/ she thought he coude his
And vp it put & went her in to dyne (goode
And Pandarus/that in a stodye stoode
Er he was ware/she toke hym by the hoode
And sayd/ye were caught er that ye wyste
I vouchesafe (qd he) do what you lyste

Tho wysshen they/and set hem downe & ete
And after noone ful slyghly Pandarus
Gan drawe him to ye wyndowe nye the strete
And sayd nece/who hath araped thus
The yonder house/that stante aforyene vs
Whiche house (qd she) and gan for to beholde
And knewe it wel/& whose it was hym tolde

And fellen forthe in speche of thynges smale
And saten in the wyndowe bothe twey
Whan Pandarus sawe tyme vnto his tale
And sawe wel that her folke were al away
Nowe nece myn tel on (quod he) I pray
Howe lyketh you the lettre that ye wote
Can he theron/for by my trouthe I not

Therwith al rosy hewed tho woxe she
And gan to hym/and sayd/so I trowe
Aquyte hym wel for goddes loue (qd he)
My selfe to medes wol the lettre sowe
And helde his hondes vp/and sate on knowe
Nowe good nece/be it neuer so lyte
Yeue me the labour/ it to sowe and plyte

ye/ for I can so writen (quod she) tho
And eke I not what I shulde to hym say
Nay nece (qd Pandare) say nat so
yet at the leste/thonketh hym I pray
Of his good wyl: O/doth hym nat to dey
Nowe for the loue of me my nece dere
Refuseth nat at this tyme my prayere

Depardieux (qd she) god leue al be wele
God helpe me so/this is the first lettre
That euer I wrote/ye al or any dele
And in to a closet for to auyse her bettre
She went alone/& gan her herte vnfettre
Out of disdaynes prison/but a lyte
And set her downe/& gan a lettre write

Of whiche to tell in shorte is myn entent
Theffecte/as ferre as I can vnderstonde
She thonked hym/of al that he wel ment
Towardes her/ but holden hym in honde
She nolde nat ne make her seluen bonde
In loue/but as his suster hym to plese
She wolde aye fayne/ to done his herte an ese

She shette it/and to Pandare in to gon
There as he sate/ and loked in to strete
And downe she sette her by hym on a stone
Of iaspre/vpon a quysshen of golde ybete
And sayd/ As wisely helpe me god the grete
I neuer dyd a thyng with more payne
Than write this/to whiche ye me constrayne

And toke it hym: He thonked her/and sayde
God wote of thing ful often lothe begonne
Cometh ende good: and nece myne Creseyde
That ye to hym of harde nowe ben ywonne
Ought he be glad/ by god & yonder sonne
For why/ men sayth impressions lyght
Ful lightly ben aye redy to the flyght

But ye han played the tyraunt al to longe
And harde was it your herte for to graue
Nowe stynte/that ye no lenger on it honge
Al wolden ye the forme of daunger saue
But hasteth you to done hym ioye haue
For trusteth wel/to longe ydone hardnesse
Causeth dispyte ful often for distresse

And right as they declared this matere
Lo Troylus/right at the stretes ende
Came rydyng with his tenthe sõme ysere
Al softely/and thyderwarde gan bende
There as thy sate/as was his way to wende
To paleys warde/and Pandare him aspyde
And sayd/ nece ysee who cometh here ryde

O/ flye nat in/ he seethe vs I suppose
Leste he may thynken that ye him eschue
Nay nay (qd she) & woxe as redde as rose
With that he gan her humbly salue
With dredful chere/and ofte his hewes mue
And vp his loke debonairly he caste
And becked on Pandare/& forthe by paste

God

God wot if he sate on his horse aright
Or goodly was besene that ylke day
God wote wher he were lyke a mãly knyght
What shulde I dretche/or tell of his aray
Creseyde/whiche that al these thynges sey
To tell in shorte/her lyked al yfere
His person/ his aray/ his loke/ his chere

His goodly maner/and his gentyllesse
So wel/that neuer sythe that she was borne
Ne had she suche routhe of his distresse
And howe so/ she hath harde ben here beforne
To god hope I/she hath now caught a thorne
She shal nat pull it out this next wyke
God sende mo suche thornes on to pyke

Pandare/whiche that stode her faste by
Felte yron hotte/and he began to smyte
And sayde/nece I pray you hertely
Tell me that I shal asken you alyte
A woman ỹ were of his dethe to wyte
Withouten his gylt/but for her lacke of routh
Were it wel done (q̃d she) nay by my trouthe

God helpe me so (q̃d he) ye say me sothe
Ye felen wel your selfe that I naught lye
Lo/ yonde he rydeth (q̃d she) ye so he dothe
Wel q̃d Pandare/as I haue tolde you thrie
Let be your nyce shame/and your folye
And speke with him/in easyng of his herte
Let nycete nat do you bothe smerte

But theron was to heauen and to done
Consydryng althyng/ it may nat be
And why? for shame/ & it were eke to sone
To graunten him so great a lyberte
For playnly her entent/as (sayd she)
Was for to loue him vnwyst/ if she might
And guerdon him with nothĩg but with sight

But Pandare thought/ it shal nat be so
If that I may/this nyce opinyon
Shal nat ben holden fully yeres two
What shulde I make of this a longe sermon?
He muste assent on that conclusyon
As for the tyme/and whan that it was eue
And al was wel/he rose and toke his leue

And on his way faste homwarde he spedde
And right for ioy he felte his herte daunce
And Troylus he founde alone abedde
That lay/as don these louers in a traunce
Betwixen hope and derke disesperaunce
But Pandare/right at his in comynge
He song/ as who sayth/lo/ somwhat I bring

And sayd/who is in his bedde so sone
yburyed thus? it am I frende (quod he)
Who Troylus? nay/ helpe me so the moone
(Quod Pandarus) thou shalt vp ryse and se
A charme that was sent right nowe to the
The whiche can healen the of thyn accesse
If thou do forthwith al thy besynesse

ye through the myght of god (q̃d Troylus)
And Pandarus gan him the lettre take
And sayd/parde god hath holpen vs
Haue here a lyght/ and loke on al these blake
But ofte gan the herte glade and quake
Of Troylus/whyle he it gan to rede
So as the wordes yaue him hope or drede

But fynally he toke al for the beste
That she him wrote/ for somwhat he behelde
On whiche he thought he myght his hert reste
Al couered she the wordes vnder shelde
Thus to the more worthy parte he helde
That what for hope/& Pandarus beheste
His great wo foryede he at the leste

But as we maye al day our seluen se
Through wood or cole the more fyre
Right so encrease of hoope/of what it be
Therwith ful ofte encreaseth eke desyre
Or as an oke cometh of a lytel spyre
So through this letter/whiche ỹ she him sent
Encreasen gan desyre of whiche he brent

Wherfore I saye alway/that day and nyght
This Troylus gan to desyren/ more
Than he dyd erst thrugh hope/& dyd his myght
To pressen on/as by Pandarus lore
And written to her of his sorowes sore
Fro day to day/ he lete it nought refreyde
That by Pãdare he somwhat wrote or seyde
And

And dyd also his other obseruaunces
That tyl a louer longeth in this caas
And after that his dyce turned on chaunces
So was he eyther glad/ or sayd alas
And helde after his gestes aye his paas
And after suche answers/ as he hadde
So were his dayes sory eyther gladde

But to Pandare alway was his recours
And pitously gan aye on him to playne
And him besought of rede/ and some socours
And Pandarus/ that sawe his wode payne
Weyt wel nygh deed for routhe/ sothe to sayne
And besyly with al his herte caste
Some of his wo to sleen/ and that as faste

And sayd/ Lorde & frende/ and brother dere
God wote that thy disease dothe me wo
But wylt thou stynten al this woful chere
And by my trouthe/ er it be dayes two
And god toforne/ yet shal I shape it so
That thou shalt come in to a certayne place
Ther as yͧ maist thy selfe prayen her of grace

And certaynly I not if thou it woste
But they that ben experte in loue/ it say
It is one of the thynges fortheretħ moste
A man to haue a leyser for to pray
And syker place/ his wo for to bewray
For in good hert it mote some routh impresse
To here and se the gyltlesse in distresse

Parauenture thinkest thou/ though it be so
That kynde wolde her don for to begynne
To haue a maner routhe vpon my wo
Sayth daunger nay/ thou shalt me neuer wyn
So ruleth her hertes goste within
That though she bende/ yet she stonte on rote
What in effecte is this vnto my bote

Thynke here ayen/ whan that the sturdy oke
On whiche men hacketh ofte for the nones
Receyued hath the happy fallyng stroke
The great sweyght dothe it come al at ones
As done these rockes/ or these mylne stones
For swyfter course cometh thig yͭ is of wight
Whan it discendeth/ than don thynges lyght

But rede that boweth downe for euery blaste
Ful lightly cesse wynde/ it wol aryse
But so nyl nat an oke/ whan it is caste
It nedeth me nought longe the forbyse
Men shal reioysen of a great emprise
Atcheued wel/ and stant withouten dout
Al haue men ben the lenger there about

But Troylus/ nowe tel me if the lest
A thyng/ whiche that I shal asken the
Whiche is thy brother/ that thou louest best?
As in thy very hertes preuyte
Iwis my brother Deiphebus/ tho (qd̄ he)
Nowe (qd̄ Pandare) er houres twise twelue
He shal the ease/ vnwyst of it him selue

Nowe lette me alone/ and worken as I may
(Quod he) and to Deiphebus went he tho
Whiche had his lorde/ & great frende ben aye
Saue Troylus no man he loued so
To tel in shorte/ without wordes mo
(Quod Pandarus) I pray you that ye be
Frende to a cause/ whiche that toucheth me

Yes parde (qd̄ Deiphebus) wel thou woste
Al that euer I may/ and god to fore
Al nere it but for the man I loue moste
My brother Troylus/ but say wherfore
It is/ for syth the day that I was bore
I nas/ ne neuer mo to ben I thynke
Ayenst a thyng that might the forthynke

Pandare gan him thanke/ and to him seyde
Lo sir/ I haue a lady in this towne
That is my nece/ and called is Creseyde
Whiche some men wolde done oppressyoun
And wrongfully haue her possessyoun
Wherfore I of your lordshyp you beseche
To ben our frende/ withouten more speche

Deiphebus him answerde: O/ is nat this
That thou spekest of to me thus straungely
Creseyde my frende? He sayd him yes
Than nedeth (qd̄ Deiphebus) hardely
No more of this to speke/ for trusteth wel yͭ I
Wol be her champion with spore and yerde
I ne rought nat/ though al her foes it herde

But

But tel me howe/ for thou woste this matere
I myght best auaylen/ nowe let se
(Quod Pandarus) if ye my lorde so dere
Wolden as nowe do this honour to me
To prayen her to morowe/ so that she
Came vnto you/ her playntes to deuyse
Her aduersaryes wolde of it agryse

And if I more durst pray as nowe
And chargen you to haue so great trauayle
To haue some of your brethern here with you
That myghten to her cause bet auayle
Than wote I wel she myght neuer fayle
For to ben holpen/ what at your instaunce
What with her other frendes gouernaunce

Deiphebus/ whiche that comen was of kynde
To al honour and bounte to consente
Answerde/ it shal be done: And I can fynde
yet greater helpe to this in myne entent
What woldest thou sayn/ if for Helenye I sent
To speke of this/ I trowe it be the beste
For she may leden Parys as her leste

Of Hector/ which that is my lorde my brother
It nedeth nat to praye him frende to be
For I haue herde hym/ o tyme and eke other
Speken of Creseyde suche honour/ that he
May sayne no bet/ suche hap to hym hath she
It nedeth nat his helpes more craue
He shal be suche/ right as we wol him haue

Speke thou thy selfe also to Troylus
On my behalfe/ and pray him with vs dyne
Sir/ al this shal be done (quod Pandarus)
And toke his leaue/ and neuer gan to fyne
But to his neces house as streight as lyne
He came/ and founde her fro the meate aryse
And set him downe/ & spake right in this wyse

He sayd/ O very god/ so haue I ronne
Lo nece myn/ se ye nat howe I swete
I not where ye the more thanke me conne
Be ye nat ware howe false Poliphete
Is nowe aboute eftsones for to plete
And bringe on you aduocacies newe?
I/ no (quod she) and chaunged al her hewe

What is he more aboute me to dretche
And done me wronge/ what shal I don/ alas
yet of him selfe nothyng wolde I retche
Nere it for Antenor and Eneas
That ben his frendes in suche maner caas
But for the loue of god/ myn vncle dere
No force of that/ let him haue al yfere

Withouten that/ I haue ynough for vs
Nay (qd̄ Pandare) it shal nothyng be so
For I haue ben right nowe at Deiphebus
At Hector/ and myn other lordes mo
And shortly maked eche of hem his foe
That by my thrifte/ he shal it neuer wynne
For aught he can/ whan so that he begynne

And as they casten what was best to done
Deiphebus/ of his owne curtesye
Came her to pray/ in his propre persone
To holde him on the morowe companye
At dyner/ whiche she nolde nat denye
But goodly gan to his prayere obey
He thonked her/ and went vpon his wey

Whan this was done/ this Pandare anon
To tel in shorte/ & forthe he gan to wende
To Troylus/ as styll as any stone
And al this thyng he tolde him worde & ende
And howe that he Deiphebus gan to blende
And sayd him/ nowe is tyme if yͭ ye conne
To beare the wel to morowe/ & al is wonne

Now speke/ now pray/ now pitously cōplayn
Let nat for nyce shame/ drede/ or slouthe
Somtyme a man mote tel his owne payne
Beleue it/ and she wol haue on the routhe
Thou shalt ben saued by thy faythe in trouth
But wel wote I/ thou nowe arte in a drede
And what it is/ I say that I can arede

Thou thinkest now/ howe shuld I don al this
For by my cheres mosten folke aspye
That for her loue is/ that I fare amys
Yet had I leuer vnwyst for sorowe dye
Nowe thynke nat so/ for thou doest gret folye
For I right nowe haue founden a manere
Of sleight/ for to keueren al thy chere

Thou

Thou shalte gon ouernyght / & that blyue
Unto Deiphebus house / as the to play
Thy maladye away the bet to driue
For whiche thou semest sycke soth for to say
Sone after that / in thy bedde the lay
And say thou mayste no lenger vp endure
And lye right there / and byde thyn auenture

Say that thy feuer is wonte the for to take
The same tyme / and laste tyl a morowe
And let se nowe how wel thou canste it make
For parde sicke is he that is in sorowe
Go nowe farwel / and Uenus here to borowe
I hope and thou this purpose holde ferme
Thy grace she shal fully there conferme

(Quod Troylus) ywis thou nedelesse
Counsaylest me / that sicklyche I me fayne
For I am sicke in ernest doutelesse
So that wel nyghe I sterue for the payne
(Qđ Pandarus) thou shalt the better playne
And haste the lasse nede to counterfete
For him demeth men hote / ỷ seeth hem swete

Lo / holde the at thy tryste close / and I
Shal wel the deere vnto thy bowe driue
Therwith he toke his leaue al softely
And Troylus to paleys went blyue
So glad ne was he neuer in al his lyue
And to Pandarus rede gan al assent
And to Deiphebus house at night he went

What nedeth it you to tellen al the chere
That Deiphebus vnto his brother made
Or his axis / or his sicklyche manere
How men gonne him with clothes for to lade
Whã he was layde / & how mẽ wold him glade
But al for naught / he helde forth aye the wise
That ye han herde Pandare er this deuyse

But certayne is / er Troylus him leyde
Deiphebus had prayde him ouernyght
To ben a frende / and helpyng to Creseyde
God wote that he graunted anon right
To ben her ful frende with al his might
But suche a nede was it to pray him thenne
As for to bydde a woode man to renne

The morowe came / & neyghen gan the tyme
Of meastyde / that the fayre quene Heleyne
Shope her to ben an houre after the prime
With Deiphebus / to whom she nolde fayne
But as his suster / homely sothe to sayne
She came to dyner / in her playne entente
But god & Pandare wyst al what this mente

Came eke Creseyde al innocent of this
Antygone her nece / and Tarbe also
But flye we nowe prolixite best is
For loue of god / and let vs faste go
Right to theffecte / withouten tales mo
Why al this folke assembled in this place
And let vs of her saluynges pace

Great honour dyd hem Deiphebus certayne
And fedde hem wel / with al that might lyke
But euermo alas / was his refrayne
My good brother Troylus the syke
Lyth e yet / and therwithal he gan to syke
And after that he payned him to glade
Hem as he might / and chere good he made

Complayned eke Heleyne of his sicknesse
So faythfully that it pyte was to here
And euery wight gan waxen for axes
A leche anon / and sayde in this manere
Men curen folke / this charme I wol the lere
But there sate one / al lyste her nat to teche
That thought / yet best coulde I ben his leche

After complaynt him gonnen they to preyse
As folke don yet whan sõe wight hath begon
To preyse a man / and with prise him reyse
A thousande folde yet higher than the son
He is / he can / that fewe lordes kon
And Pandarus of that they wolde afferme
He nought forgate her praysyng to conferme

Herde al this thyng Creseyde wel ynough
And euery worde gan ne for to notifye
For whiche with sobre chere her herte lough
For who is that ne wolde her glorifye
To mowen suche a knyght done lyue or dye
But al passe I / lest ye to longe dwel
But for o fyne is al that euer I tel

The

The tyme came fro dyner for to ryse
And as hem ought/arysen everychone
And gonne a whyle of this and that devyse
But Pandarus brake al this speche anon
And sayd to Deiphebus/wol ye gon
If your wyll be/as I you prayde
To speken of the nedes of Creseyde

Heleyne/whiche that by the honde her helde
Toke first the tale and sayd/go we blyve
And goodly on Creseyde she behelde
And sayd/ Ioves let him never thrive
That doth you harme/& reve him sone of lyve
And yeve me sorowe/but he shal it rue
If that I may/ and al folke be true

Tel thou thy neces case (quod Deiphebus)
To Pandarus/for thou canste best it tell
My lordes and my ladyes/it stante thus
What shulde I lenger (qd he) do you dwell
He ronge hem out a proces lyke a bell
Upon her foe/that hyght Poliphete
So heynous/that men might on it spete

Answerde of this eche worse of hem thā other
And Poliphete they gonnen thus to waryen
An honged be suche one/were he my brother
And so he shal/for it ne may nought varyen
What shulde I lenger in this tale taryen
Playnlyche al at ones they her hyghten
To ben her frēde/in al that ever they mighten

Spake than Heleyne/and sayd Pandarus
Wote aught my lord my brother of this mater
I meane Hector/or wote it Troylus
He sayd ye/but wol ye me nowe here
Me thynketh thus/syth that Troylus is here
It were good/if that ye wolde assent
She tolde him her selfe al this er she went

For he wol have the more her grefe at herte
Bycause so/that she a lady is
And by your wyl/ I wol but in right sterte
And do you wete/and that anon ywis
If that he slepe/or wol aught here of this
And in he lepte/and sayd him in his eere
God have thy soule/brought have I thy bere

To smylen of this gan tho Troylus
And Pandarus without rekenyng
Out went anon to Heleyne and Deiphebus
And sayd hem/so there be no taryeng
Ne more prease/he wol wel that ye bring
Creseyde my lady/that is here
And as he may enduren/ he wol her here

But wel ye wote/the chambre is but lyte
And fewe folke may lightly make it warme
Nowe loketh ye/for I wol have no wyte
To bring in prease/that might don him harm
Or him deseasen/for my better arme
Yet were it bet she bydde tyll efte soonis
Nowe loke ye that knowen what to done is

I say for me best is/as I can knowe
That no wight in ne wende/but ye twey
But it were I/for I can in a throwe
Reherce her case/unlyke that she can sey
And after this she may ones him prey
To ben good lorde in shorte/& take her leve
This may nat mokel of his ese him reve

And eke for she is straunge/he wol forbere
His ease/whiche that him dare nat for you
Eke other thyng that toucheth nat to her
He wol it tell/I wote it wel right nowe
That secrete is/and for the townes prowe
And they that knewe nothyng of his entent
Without more/to Troylus in they went

Heleyne in al her goodly softe wyse
Gan him salue/and womanly to play
And sayd iwys/ye mote algate aryse
Nowe fayre brother be al hole I pray
And gan her arme right over his sholder lay
And him with al her wyt to recomforte
As she best coulde/she gan him to disporte

So after this (qd she) we you beseke
My dere brother Deiphebus and I
For love of god/and so dothe Pandare eke
To ben good lorde & frende right hertely
Unto Creseyde/whiche that certaynly
Receyveth wronge/as wote wel here Pādare
That can her case wel bet than I declare

This

This Pandarus gan newe his tonge affyle
And al her case reherce/and that anon
Whan it was sayd/sone after in a whyle
(Quod Troylus) as sone as I may gone
I wol right fayne/with al my might ben one
Haue god my trouthe/her cause to sustene
Now good thrift haue ye (qd Heleyn yͤ quene)

(Quod Pandarus) and it your wyl be
That she may take her leaue/er that she go
O/ els god forbyd it (tho quod he)
If that she vouchsafe for to do so
And with that worde (qd Troylus) ye two
Deiphebus/and my suster lefe and dere
To you haue I to speke of a matere

To ben auysed by your rede the better
And founde (as hap was) at his beddes heed
The coppye of a tretyse/and a lettre
That Hector had him sent/to asken reed
If suche a man was worthy to ben deed
Wote I naught who/but in a grisly wyse
He prayde hem anon on it auyse

Deiphebus gan this lettre for to vnfolde
In ernest great/ so dyd Heleyne the quene
And romyng outwarde/fast it gonne beholde
Downwarde a steyre/in to an herber grene
This ylke thyng redden hem bytwene
And largely the mountenaūce of an houre
They gonne on it to reden and to pore

Nowe let hem rede/and turne we anon
To Pandarus/that gan ful softe prie
That al was wel/and out he gan to gon
In to the great chambre/and that in hye
And sayd/ god saue al this companye
Come nece myn/my lady quene Heleyne
Abydeth you/and eke my lordes tweyne

Ryse/take with you your nece Antigone
Or whom you lyste/or no force hardely
The lasse prease the bet/come forthe with me
And loke that ye thonken humbly
Hem al thre/and whan ye may goodly
Your tyme yse/taketh of hem your leue
Leste we to longe his restes him byreue

Al innocent of Pandarus entente
(Quod tho Creseyde) go we vncle dere
And arme in arme/inwarde wt him she went
Auysyng wel her wordes and her chere
And Pandarus/in ernestful manere
Sayd/al folke for goddes loue I praye
Stynteth right here/and softely you playe

Auyseth you what folke ben here within
And in what plyte one is/god him amende
And inwarde thus ful softely begyn
Nece I coniure/and highly you defende
On his halfe/ whiche that soule vs al sende
And in the vertue of corownes twayne
Slee nat this man/yͭ hath for you this payne

Fye on the dyuel/ thynke whiche one he is
And in what plyte he lythe/come of anon
Thynke al suche taryed tyde but lost it nys
That wol ye bothe sayne/whan ye ben one
Secondly/there yet deuyneth none
Vpon you two/come of nowe if ye conne
Whyle folke is blent/ lo/al the tyme is wonne

In tyteryng and pursute/and delayes
The folke deuyne/at waggyng of a stree
And though ye wolde han after mery dayes
Than dare ye nat/and why? for she and she
Spake suche a worde/thus loked he and he
Leste tyme be loste/I dare not with you dele
Come of therfore/and bryngeth him to hele

But nowe to you/ye louers that ben here
Was Troylus nat in a cankedorte
That lay/& might the whisprynge of hem here
And thought o lord/right now renneth my sort
Fully to dye/ or haue anon comforte
And was the first tyme he shulde her pray
Of loue/ O mighty god what shal he say.

Explicit liber secundus.

O Blyssful light/ of whiche yͤ bemes clere
Adorneth al the thirde heuen fayre
O sonnes lefe/o Ioues doughter dere
Plesaunce of loue/ o goodly debonayre
In gentyl hertes aye redy to repayre
O very cause of heale and of gladnesse
Yheryed be thy might and thy goodnesse

In

In heuen and hell/ in erthe/ and salte see
Is felte thy might/if that I wel discerne
As man/beest/fysshe/herbe/ and grene tree
The fele in tymes with vapour eterne
God loueth/and to loue wol naught werne
And in this worlde no lyues creature
Withouten loue is worth/ or may endure

Ye Joues first/to thylke affectes glade
Through whiche that thynges lyuen al/ & be
Comenden/and amorous hem made
On mortal thyng/and as you lyst aye ye
yeue hem in loue/ ease/ or aduersyte
And in a thousande formes down him sente
For loue in erthe/& whom you lyst he hente

Ye feirs Mars apeasen of his ire
And as you lyst/ye maken hertes digne
Algates hem that ye wol set a fyre
They dreden shame/and vyces they resigne
Ye don hem curteys be/fresshe/and benigne
And hye or lowe/after a wight entendeth
The ioyes that he hath/ your might it sendeth

Ye holden reigne and house in vnyte
Ye sothfast cause of frendshyp ben also
ye knowen al thilke couered qualyte
Of thinges/ whiche that folke wondren so
Whan they can nat construe howe it may go
She loueth him/or why he loueth here
As why this fysshe & nat that cometh to were

ye folke a lawe haue set in vniuerse
And this knowe I by hem that louers be
That who so stryueth with you hath ŷ werse
Nowe lady bright/for thy benignyte
At reuerence of hem that seruen the
Whose clerke I am/so techeth me deuyse
Some ioye of that is felt in thy seruyce

ye/ in my naked herte sentement
In hylde/and do me shewe of thy swetnesse
Caliope/thy voyce be nowe present
For nowe is nede/seest thou nat my distresse
Howe I mote tel anonright the gladnesse
Of Troylus/to Venus heryinge
To whiche who nede hath/ god him bring.

¶ Incipit liber Tertius.

Lay al this meane whyle Troylus
Recordyng his lesson in this manere
Mafey thought he/ thus wol I say and thus
Thus wol I playne vnto my lady dere
That worde is good/& this shal be my chere
This nyl I nat foryeten in no wyse
God leue him werken as he can deuyse

And lorde so that his herte gan to quappe
Heryng her come/and shorte for to syke
And Pandarus that ledde her by the lappe
Came nere/and gan in at the curteyn pyke
And sayd/god do bote on al syke
Se who is here/you comen to visyte
Lo/here is she that is your dethe to wyte

Therwith it semed as he wepte almoste
A/ a/ (quod Troylus) so routhfully
Where me be wo/o mighty god thou woste
Who is al there/ I se nat trewly
Sir (quod Creseyde) it is Pandare and I
ye/ swete herte alas/I may nat ryse
To knele/and do you honour in some wyse

And dressed him vpwarde/and she right tho
Gan bothe her hondes softe vpon him ley
O for the loue of god/do ye nat so
To me (quod she) ey what is this to sey
Sir/ comen am I to you for causes twey
First you to thonke/and of your lordshyp eke
Contynuaunce I wolde you beseke

This Troylus that herde his lady pray
Of lordship/him woxe neither quicke ne deed
Ne myght o worde for shame to it say
Al though men shulden smyten of his heed
But lorde so he woxe sodaynlyche reed
And sir/his lesson that he wende conne
To prayen her/ is through his wyt yronne

Creseyde al this aspyed wel ynough
For she was wyse/& loued him neuer the lasse
Al were he in al aperte/or made it tough
Or was to bolde/to synge a foole a masse
But whan his shame gan somwhat to passe
His resons/as I may my rymes holde
I wol you tel/as techen bokes olde

The thirde boke of Troylus.

In chaunged voyce/right for his very drede
Whiche voyce eke quoke/& therto his manere
Goodly abasshte/ and nowe his hewes rede
Nowe pale/vnto Creseyde his lady dere
With loke downe cast/& humble yolden chere
Lo/ the alderfirst worde that him aster
Was twyse/ mercy/ mercy swete hertete

And stynte a whyle/& whã he might out brig
The next worde was/god wote for I haue
As faythfully as I haue had konnyng
Ben yours al/god so my soule saue
And shal/tyl that I woful wight be graue
And though I dare ne can vnto you playne
Iwys I suffre nat the lasse payne

Thus moche as nowe/ah/womanlyche wyfe
I may out bring/and if this you displese
That shal I wreke vpon myn owne lyfe
Right sone I trowe/ and do your herte an ese
If with my dethe/your herte may apese
But sens that ye han herde me somwhat sey
Nowe retche I neuer howe sone ẏ I dey

Therwith his manly sorowe to beholde
It myght haue made an hert of stone to rewe
And Pandare wept as he to water wolde
And poked euer his nece newe and newe
And sayd/wo begon ben hertes trewe
For loue of god/make of this thyng an ende
Or slee vs bothe at ones/er that ye wende

I/ what (qd she) by god and by my trouthe
I not nat what ye wylne that I sey
Ey/what (qd he) that ye haue on him routhe
For goddes loue/ and dothe him nat to dey
Nowe than thus (qd she) I wolde him prey
To tell me the fyne of his entente
yet wyste I neuer wel what that he mente

What that I meane/O swete herte dere
(Quod Troylus) o goodly fresshe free
That with the stremes of your eyen clere
ye walden somtyme frendly on me se
And than agreen that I may ben he
Withouten braunche of vyce/on any wyse
In trouthe alway/to do you my seruyse

As to my lady right/and chefe resorte
With al my wytte and al my dylygence
And to haue right as you lyste comforte
Vnder your yerde egall to myn offence
As dethe/if that I breake your defence
And that ye deigne me so moche honour
Me to cõmaunden aught in any hour

And I to ben your very humble trewe
Secrete/and in my paynes pacient
And euer to desyren fresshly newe
To seruen/and to ben aye ylike dilygent
And with good herte/al holy your talent
Receyuen wel/howe sore that me smerte
Lo/this meane I/ myn owne swete herte

(Quod Pandarus) lo here an harde requeste
And reasonable/a lady for to werne
Nowe nece myn/by Natall Ioues feest
Were I a god/ye shulde sterue as yerne
That heren wel this man wol nothyng yerne
But your honour/& sene him almost sterue
And ben so lothe to suffre him you to serue

With that she gan her eyen on him caste
Ful easely/and ful debonairly
Auysyng her/and hyed nat to faste
With neuer a worde/but sayd him softely
Myn honour safe/ I wol wel trewly
And in suche forme/as I can nowe deuyse
Receyuen him fully to my seruyce

Besechyng him for goddes loue/ that he
Wolde in honour of trouthe and gentyllesse
As I wel meane/ eke meanen wel to me
And myn honour/with wyt and besynesse
Aye kepe/and if I may done him gladnesse
From hence forthe/iwys I nyl nat fayne
Nowe bethe al hole/no lenger ye ne playne

But nathelesse/this warne I you (qd she)
A kynges sonne although ye be ywis
Ye shal no more haue souerayntee
Of me in loue/than right in that case is
Ne nyl forbeare if that ye done amys
To wrathe you/and whyle that ye me serue
Cherysshen you/right after that ye deserue

And

And shortly dere herte/and al my knyght
Beth glad/and draweth you to lustynesse
And I shal trewly/with al my ful might
your bytter turnen al to swetenesse
If I be she/that may do you gladnesse
For euery wo ye shal recouer a blysse
And him in armes toke/and gan him kysse

Fyl Pandarus on knees/and vp his eyen
To heuen threwe/and helde his hondes hye
Immortal god (qd he) that mayst nat dyen
Cupide I meane/of this mayste glorifye
And Venus/ thou mayste maken melodye
Withouten honde/me semeth that in towne
For this myracle yche here eche bell sowne

But ho/ no more nowe of this matere
For why : this folke wol comen vp anon
That haue the lettre redde/lo I hem here
But I coniure the Creseyde/ and one
And two/thou Troylus whā thou maist gon
That at myn house ye ben at my warnyng
For I ful wel shal shapen your cōmyng

And easeth there your hertes right ynough
And let se whiche of you shal beare the belle
To speke of loue aryght/& therwith he lough
For there haue I a leyser for to telle
(Quod Troylus) howe longe shal I dwelle
Er this be done: qd he/ whan thou maist ryse
This thyng shal be right as you list deuyse

With that Heleyne/and also Deiphebus
Tho comen vpward/right at the stayres ende
And lorde so tho gan gronen Troylus
His brother and his suster for to blende
(Qd Pandarus) it tyme is that we wende
Take nece myn your leaue at al thre
And let hem speake/& cometh forthe with me

She toke her leaue at hem ful thriftely
As she wel coulde: & they her reuerence
Vnto the ful dydden hardely
And wonder wel speaken in her absence
Of her/ in praysyng of her excellence
Her gouernaunce/her wyt/and her manere
Comendeden/that it ioye was to here

Nowe let her wende vnto her owne place
And turne we to Troylus agayne
That gan ful lightly of the lettre pace
That Deiphebus had in the gardyn seyne
And of Heleyne and him he wolde feyne
Delyuered ben/and sayd that him leste
To slepe/and after tales haue a reste

Heleyne him kyste/and toke her leue blyue
Deiphebus eke/and home wente euery wight
And Pandarus/as faste as he may driue
To Troylus tho came/as lyne ryght
And on a paillet/al that gladde nyght
By Troylus he lay/ with mery chere
To tale/& wel was hem they were yfere

Whan euery wight was voyded/but they two
And al the dores weren faste yshette
To tel in shorte/without wordes mo
This Pandarus/without any lette
Vp rose/and on his beddes syde him sette
And gan to speken in a sobre wyse
To Troylus/as I shal you deuyse

Myn alderleuest lorde/and brother dere
God wot & thou/that it sate me so sore
Whan I the sawe so languysshyng to here
For loue of which thy wo woxe alway more
That I with al my might/and al my lore
Haue euer sythen done my besynesse
To bringe the to ioye out of distresse

And haue it brought to such plyte as y^u woste
So y^t through me thou stondest now in way
To faren wel/I say it for no boste
And woste thou why/but shame it is to say
For the haue I begon a gamen play
Whiche that I neuer done shal efte for other
Al tho he were a thousāde folde my brother

That is to say/for the am I becomen
Betwyxen game and ernest/suche a mene
As maken women vnto men to comen
Al say I nat/ thou woste wel what I mene
For the haue I my nece/of vyces clene
So fully made thy gentyllesse tryst
That al shal ben/ right as thy selfe lyste

L.l. ii. But

But god/ that al wotteth take I to wytnesse
That neuer I this for couetyse wrought
But onely for to abredge that distresse
For whiche wel nye thou dydest/ as me thouzt
But good brother/do nowe as the ought
For goddes loue/and kepe her out of blame
Sens thou arte wyse/& saue alway her name

For wel thou woste/the name as yet of her
Amōges ẏ people/as (who saith) halowed is
For that man is vnbore I dare wel swere
That euer wyste that she dyd amys
But wo is me/that I that cause al this
May thynken that she is my nece dere
And I her eme/and traytour eke yfere

And were it wyste that I through myn engyn
Had in myn nece yput this fantasye
To done thy lust/ and holly to be thyn
Why? al the worlde wolde vpon it crye
And say/that I the worste trecherye
Dyd in this case/that euer was begonne
And she fordone/ & thou right naught ywōne

Wherfore er I wol ferther gone or paas
Yet efte I the beseche/and fully say
That priuyte go with vs in this caas
That is to sayne/that thou vs neuer wray
And be nat wrothe/though I the ofte pray
To holden secre suche an hygh matere
For skylful is (thou woste wel) my prayere

And thynke/what wo there hath betyd er this
For makyng of auauntes/as men rede
And what myschaunce in this worlde yet is
Fro day to day/right for that wicked dede
For whiche these wyse clerkes that ben dede
Haue euer this prouerbed to vs yonge
That the first vertue is to kepe the tonge

And nere it that I wylne as nowe abredge
Diffusyon of speche/ I coulde almost
A thousande olde stories the aledge
Of women loste/through false & fooles bost
Prouerbes canste thy selfe ynowe/ & woste
Ayenst that vyce for to ben a blabbe
Al sayd men sothe/as often as they gabbe

O tonge alas/so often here beforne
Haste thou made many a lady bright of hewe
Sayd/ welaway the day that I was borne
And many a maydens sorowe for to newe
And for the more parte al is vntrewe
That men of yelpe/& it were brought to preue
Of kynde/none auauntour is to leue

Auauntour and a lyer/al is one
As thus. I pose a woman graunt me
Her loue/and sayth that other wol she none
And I am sworne to holden it secre
And after I tel it two or thre
Iwys I am auauntour at the leest
And lyer eke/for I breke my behest

Nowe loke than/if they be nat to blame
Such maner folke/what shal I clepe hē what
That hem auaunte of women/and by name
That yet behyght hem neuer this ne that
Ne knowe hem more than myn olde hat
No wonder is/so god me sende heele
Though women dreden with vs men to deele

I say nat this for no mistrust of you
Ne for no wyse men/but for fooles nyce
And for the harme that in the worlde is nowe
As wel for folye ofte/as for malyce
For wel wote I/ in wyse folke that vyce
No woman dredeth/ if she be wel auysed
For wyse ben by fooles harme chastysed

But nowe to purpose/leue brother dere
Haue al this thing that I haue said in mynde
And kepe the close/and be nowe of good chere
For al thy dayes thou shalt me trewe fynde
I shal thy processe set in suche a kynde
And god toforne/that it shal the suffyse
For it shal be/right as thou wolte deuyse

For wel I wote/thou meanest wel parde
Therfore I dare this fully vndertake
Thou woste eke/ what thy lady graunted the
And day is set the chartres to make
Haue now good nyght/I may no leger wake
And byd for me/syth thou arte nowe in blysse
That god the sende dethe/or soone lysse

Who might tellen halfe the ioye or feest
Whiche that the soule of Troylus tho felte
Heryng theffect of Pandarus beheest
His olde wo/that made his herte swelte
Gan tho for ioye wasten/ and to melt
And al the rychesse of his syghes sore
At ones fledde/he felte of hem no more

But right so as these holtes/and these hayis
That han in wynter deed ben and drie
Reuisten hem in grene/whan that May is
Whan euery lusty lysteth to play
Right in that selfe wyse/sothe to say
Woxe sodaynly his herte ful of ioye
That gladder was there neuer man in Troye

And gan his loke on Pandarus vp caste
Ful soberly/and frendly on to se
And sayd/frende/ in Apryl the laste
As wel thou woste/if it remembre the
Howe nyghe the dethe for wo thou founde me
And howe thou dyddest al thy besynesse
To knowe of me the cause of my distresse

Thou woste howe longe I it forbare to say
To the/ that arte the man that I best tryst
And peryll none was it to the to bewray
That wyst I wel: but tel me if the lyste
Sythe I so lothe was/that thy selfe it wyste
Howe durste I mo tellen of this matere:
That quake nowe/ & no wight may vs here

But nathelesse/by that god I the swere
That as him lyst may al this world gouerne
And if I lye/ Achylles with his spere
Myn herte cleaue/al were my lyfe eterne
As I am mortal/ if I late or yerne
Wolde it bewray/ or durst/ or shulde conne
For al the good that god made vnder sonne

That rather dye I wolde/and determyne
As thynketh me nowe/stocked in pryson
In wretchydnesse/in fylthe/and in vermyne
Captyfe to cruell kyng Agamenon
And this in al the temples of this towne
Vpon the goddes al/I wol the swere
To morowe day/if that the lyketh here

And that thou haste so moche ydon for me
That I ne may it neuer more deserue
This knowe I wel/al might I nowe for the
A thousande tymes on a morowe sterue
I can no more/but that I wol the serue
Right as thy slaue/whyther so thou wende
For euer more/vnto my lyues ende

But here with al myn herte I the beseche
That neuer in me thou deme suche folye
As I shal sayne/me thought by thy speche
That this whiche thou me doest for companye
I shulde wene it were a baudrye
I am nat woode/al if I leude be
It is nat so/that wot I wel parde

But he that gothe for golde/or for rychesse
On suche messages/ call him what ye lyste
And this that thou doest/cal it gentylnesse
Compassyon/and felawshyp/and tryst
Departe it so/for wyde where is wyste
Howe that there is dyuersyte requires
Betwixen thynges lyke/ as I haue lered

And that thou knowe I thinke nat ne wene
That this seruyce a shame be or iape
I haue my fayre suster Polixene
Cassandre/Helayne/or any of the frape
Be she neuer so fayre/or wel yshape
Tel me/ whiche thou wyste of euerychone
To haue for thyne/and let me than alone

But syth that thou haste done me this seruyce
My lyfe to saue/and for non hope of mede
So for the loue of god/this great emprise
Parfourme it out/nowe is the moste nede
For hygh and lowe/withouten any drede
I wol alway thyn hestes al kepe
Haue nowe good nyght/& let vs bothe slepe

Thus helde hem eche of other wel apayde
That al the worlde ne might it bet amende
And on the morowe whan they were arayde
Eche to his owne nedes gan entende
But Troylus/though as the fyre he brende
For sharpe desyre of hope/and of plesaunce
He nat forgate his good gouernaunce

L.l.iii. But

The thirde boke of Troylus.

But in him selfe/ with mãhode gan restreyne
Eche rakel dede/and eche unbridled chere
That al that lyuen sothe to sayne
Ne shulde haue wyst/by worde or by manere
What that he mente/as touchyng this matere
From euery wight/as ferre as is the cloude
He was so wyse/and wel dissymulen coulde

And al the whyle whiche that I nowe deuyse
This was his lyfe/with al his ful myght
By day he was in Martes hygh seruyce
That is to sayne/in armes as a knyght
And for the more parte the longe nyght
He lay and thought howe that he might serue
His lady best/her thanke for to deserue

Nyl I nat sweare/al though he lay softe
That in his thought he nas somwhat disesed
Ne that he turned on his pillowes ofte
And wolde of that him missed haue ben eased
But in suche case/men be nat alway pleased
For naught I wot/no more than was he
That can I deme of possibylyte

But certayne is/to purpose for to go
That in this whyle/as written is in geste
He sawe his lady somtyme/and also
She with him spake/ whan yt she durst a leste
And by her bothe auyse/as was the beste
Apoynteden ful warely in this nede
So as they durste/howe they wolde procede

But it was spoken in so shorte a wyse
In suche awayte alway/and in suche fere
Leste any wight deuynen or deuyse
Wolde of hem two/or to it lay an eere
That al this worlde so lefe to hem ne were
As that Cupide wolde hem grace sende
To maken of her speche right an ende

But thylke lytel that they spake or wrought
His wyse goste toke aye/ of al suche hede
It semed her he wyste what she thought
Withouten worde/so that it was no nede
To bydde him aught to don/or aught forbede
For whiche she thought yt loue/al come it late
Of al ioye/ had opened her the yate

And shortly of this processe for to pace
So wel his werke and wordes he besette
That he so ful stode in his ladys grace
Twenty thousande tymes er she lette
She thonked god she euer with him mette
So coulde he him gouerne in suche seruyce
That al the worlde ne might it bet deuyse

For she founde him so discrete in all
So secrete/ and of suche obeysaunce
That wel she felte he was to her a wall
Of steele/and shelde of euery displesaunce
That to ben in his good gouernaunce
So wyse he was/she was nomore afered
I meane as ferre as ought ben requyred

And Pandarus to quicke alway the fyre
Was euer ylyke prest and dyligent
To ease his frende was set al his desyre
He shoue aye on/ he to and fro was sent
He letters bare whan Troylus was absent
That neuer man/as in his frendes nede
Ne bare him bet than he/withouten drede

But now parauẽture som mã wayten wolde
That euery worde or sonde/loke or chere
Of Troylus/that I reherceu shulde
In al this whyle/unto his lady dere
I trowe it were a longe thyng for to here
Or of what wight yt stante in suche disioynte
His wordes al/or euery loke to poynte

For sothe I haue nat herde it done er this
In storie none/ne no man here I wene
And though I wolde/I coulde nat ywis
For there was some epystel hem betwene
That wold (as saith myn auctour) wel cõtene
Nye halfe this boke/of which hĩ lyst nat write
Howe shulde I than a lyne of it endyte

But to the great effecte/than say I thus
That stondyng in concorde and in quyete
This ylke two/Creseyde and Troylus
As I haue tolde/and in this tyme swete
Saue onely often might they nat mete
Ne leyser haue/her speches to fulfell
That it befyl/ right as I shal you tell

That

That Pandarus/that euer dyd his myght
Right for the fyne that I shal speke of here
As for to bringen to his house some nyght
His fayre nece/and Troylus ysere
Where as at leyser al this hygh matere
Touchyng her loue/were at ye ful vp bounde
Had out of doute a tyme to it founde

For he with great delyberation
Had euery thyng that therto might auayle
Forne caste/and put in execution
And neyther lefte for coste ne for trauayle
Come if hem lyste/ hem shulde nothyng fayle
And for to ben in aught aspyed there
That wyste he wel an impossyble were

Dredelesse it clere was in the wynde
Of euery pye/and euery let game
Nowe al is wel/for al the worlde is blynde
In this mater/bothe fremed and tame
This tymber is al redy vp to frame
Vs lacketh naught/ but that we weten wolde
A certayne houre/ in whiche she comen shulde

And Troylus/that al this purueyaunce
Knewe at the full/and wayted on it aye
And here vpon eke made great ordynaunce
And founde his cause/& therwith his aray
If that he were myssed nyght or day
There whyle he was aboute this seruyce
That he was gone to done his sacrifyce

And muste at suche a temple alone wake
Answered of Apollo for to be
And first to sene the holy laurer quake
Er that Apollo spake out of the tree
To tell him next whan grekes shulde flye
And for thy let him no man/god forbede
But pray Apollo helpe in this nede

Nowe is there lytel more for to done
But Pandare vp/and shortly for to sayne
Right sone vpon the chaūgyng of the moone
Whan lightlesse is ye worlde a night or twayne
And that the welken shope him for to rayne
He streyght a morowe vnto his nece wente
Ye haue wel herde the fyne of his entente

Whan he was comen/he gan anon to playe
As he was wonte/and of him selfe to iape
And fynally he swore/and gan her say
By this and that/she shulde him nat escape
No lenger done him after her to cape
But certainly/she muste by her leue
Come soupen in his house with him at eue

At whiche she lough/& gan her first excuse
And sayd: it rayneth: lo/ howe shulde I gone
Let be (qd he) ne stonde nat thus to muse
This mote be done/ ye shal come there anone
So at the laste/ herof they fell at one
Or els faste he swore her in her eere
He nolde neuer comen there she were

Sone after this/she to him gan rowne
And asked him if Troylus were there
He swore her nay/for he was out of towne
And sayd/ nece: I pose that he were there
You durste neuer haue the more feere
For rather than men might him there aspye
Me were leuer a thousandefolde to dye

Naught lyst myn auctour fully to declare
What that she thought/ whan he sayd so
That Troylus was out of towne ysare
And if he sayd therof sothe or no
But that withouten awayte with him to go
She graunted him/sythe he her that besought
And as his nece obeyed as her ought

But natheless/yet gan she hym beseche
(Al though with him to gone it was no feere)
For to beware of gosysshe peoples speche
That dremen thynges/ which that neuer were
And wel auyse him whom he brought there
And sayd him eme/sens I muste on you tryst
Loke al be wel/and do nowe as you lyst

He swore her this/by stockes and by stones
And by the goddes that in heuen dwell
Or els were him leauer soule and bones
With Pluto kyng/ as depe ben in hell
As Tantalus/what shulde I more tell
Whan al was wel/he rose and toke his leue
And she to souper came whan it was eue

With

With a certayne of her owne men
And with her fayre nece Antigone
And other of her women nyne or ten
But who was glad nowe/who as trowe ye?
But Troylus/that stode and myght it se
Throughout a lytel wyndowe in a stewe
There he beshet/sith mydnyght was in mewe

Unwyst of euery wight/but of Pandare
But to the poynt/nowe whan ŷ she was cõe
With al ioye/and al frendes fare
Her eme anone in armes hath her nome
And than to the supper al and some
Whan tyme was/ful softe they hem sette
God wote there was no deynte ferre to fette

And after supper gonnen they to ryse
At ease wel/with hert fresshe and glade
And wel was him that coude best deuyse
To lyken her/or that her laughen made
He songe/she playde/he tolde a tale of Wade
But at the laste/as euery thyng hath ende
She toke her leaue/and nedes wolde wende

But o fortune/executrice of wyerdes
O influentes of these heuens hye
Sothe is/that under god ye ben our hierdes
Though to us beestes/ben the causes wrie
This mene I now/for she gan homward hye
But execute was al besyde her leue
At the goddes wyl/for whiche she muste bleue

The bente moone with her hornes pale
Saturnus and Ioue/in Cãcro ioyned were
That suche a rayne from heuen gan auale
That euery maner woman that was there
Had of that smoky rayne a very feere
At whiche Pandare tho lough/& sayd thenne
Nowe were it tyme a lady to gon henne

But good nece/if I might euer please
you any thyng/than pray I you (quod he)
To don myn herte as nowe so great an ease
As for to dwell here al this nyght with me
For why? this is your owne house parde
For by my trouthe/I say it nat in game
To wende as nowe/it were to me a shame

Creseyde/whiche that coude as moche good
As halfe a worlde/toke hede of his prayere
And sens it rayned/and al was in a flode
She thouzt/as good chepe may I dwell here
And graunt it gladly with a frendes chere
And haue a thonke/as grutche & than abyde
For home to gone it may nat wel betyde

I wol (qd she) myn uncle liefe and dere
Sens that you lyst/it skyll is to be so
I am right glad with you to dwellen here
I sayd but agame I wolde go
Iwys graunt mercy nece (quod he) tho
Were it a game or no/sothe to tell
Nowe am I glad/sens that you lyste to dwell

Thus al is wel/but tho began aright
The newe ioye/and al the feest agayne
But pandarus/if goodly had he myght
He wolde haue hyed her to bedde fayne
And sayd/lorde this is an huge rayne
This were a wether for to slepen in
And that I rede us soone to begyn

And nece/wote ye where I wol you lay?
For that we shul nat syggen ferre a sonder
And for ye neyther shullen/dare I say
Here noyse of rayne/ne of thonder
By god right in my closet yonder
And I wol in that utter house alone
Ben wardayne of your women eueryechone

And in this myddel chambre that ye se
Shal your women slepen/wel and softe
And there I sayd/shal your seluen be
And if ye syggen wel to nyght/come ofte
And careth nat what wether is a lofte
The wyne anon/and whan so you leste
So we to slepe/I trowe it be the beste

There nys no more/but here after sone
They voyde/dronke/& trauers drawe anon
Gan euery wight that had naught to done
More in the place/out of the chambre gon
And euermore so sternelyche it rone
And blewe therwith so wonderlyche loude
That wel nyghe no man heren other coulde

Tho

Tho Pandarus her eme/right as him ought
With women/ suche as were her most aboute
Ful glad vnto her beddes syde her brought
And toke his leaue/and gan ful lowe loute
And sayd/here at this closet dore without
Right ouertwharte your women lyggen all
That whom you lyst of hem/ye may sone cal

So whan that she was in the closet layde
And al her women forthe by ordynaunce
A bedde weren/there as I haue sayde
There nas no more to skippen nor to praunce
But boden go to bedde with mischaunce
If any wyght sterynge were any where
And let hem slepen/that a bedde were

But Pandarus/ y^t wel couthe eche adele
The olde daunce/and euery poynte therin
Whan that he sawe that al thyng was wele
He thought he wolde vpon his werke begyn
And gan the stewe dore al softe vnpyn
As styll as stone/without lenger lette
By Troylus adownright he hym sette

And shortly to the poynte right for to gon
Of al this werke he tolde hym worde ⁊ ende
And sayd/make the redy right anon
For thou shalt in to heuen blysse wende
Nowe blyssful Venus/ thou me grace sende
(Quod Troylus) for neuer yet no dede
Had I er nowe/ ne halfendele the drede

(Quod Pandarus) ne drede the neuer adele
For it shal be right as thou wolte desyre
So thriue I/this nyght shal I make it wele
Or casten al the gruell in the fyre
yet blissful Venus/this night thou me enspyre
(Quod Troylus) as wys as I the serue
And euer bet and bet shal tyl I sterue

And if I had/O Venus ful of myrthe
Aspectes badde of Mars/or of Saturne
Or thou combuste/ or let were in my byrthe
Thy father pray/ al thylke harme disturne
Of grace/and that I glad ayen may turne
For loue of hym thou louedest in the shawe
I meane Adon/that with ye bore was slawe

Ioue eke/for the loue of fayre Europe
The which in forme of a bulle away thou fet
Now helpe/O Mars/thou w^t thy blody cope
For loue of Cipria/thou me naught ne let
O Phebus/thike whā Daphne her seluen shet
Vnder the barke/and Laurer woxe for drede
Yet for her loue/o helpe nowe at this nede

Mercurye/for the loue of her eke
For which Pallas was w^t Aglauros wrothe
Nowe helpe/and eke Dyane I the beseke
That this vyage be nat to the lothe
O fatall sustren/ whiche or any clothe
Me shapen was/ my destyne me sponne
So helpeth to this werke that is begon

(Qd̄ Pandarus) thou wretched mouces herte
Arte thou agast so that she wol the byte
Why/do on this furred cloke vpon thy sherte
And folowe me/ for I wol haue the wyte
But byde/and let me gon before alyte
And with that he gan vndone a trappe
And Troylus he brought in by the lappe

The sterne wynde so loude gan to route
That no wight other noyse nught here
And they that layen at the dore without
Ful sykerly they slepten al yfere
And Pandarus/with ful sobre chere
Gothe to the dore anon withouten lette
There as they laye/and softely it shette

And as he came ayenwarde priuely
His nece awoke/⁊ asketh/ who gothe there?
My dere nece (qd̄ he) it am I
Ne wondreth nat/ne haue of it no fere
And nere he came/and sayd her in her ere
No worde for loue of god I you beseche
Let no wight aryse/⁊ heren of our speche

What/ whiche way be ye comen? benedycite/
(Quod she) and howe vnwyst of hem all
Here at this secret trappe dore (qd̄ he)
(Quod tho Cresepde) let me some wight call
Eygh/ god forbyd that it shulde so fall
(Qd̄ Pandarus) that ye suche foly wrought
They might demen thīg they neuer er thought

It is

It is nat good a slepyng hounde to wake
Ne yeue a wight a cause for to deuyne
your women slepen al/I Vndertake
So that for hem the house men might myne
And slepen wollen tyl the sonne shyne
And whan my tale is brought to an ende
Unwyst right as I came/so wol I wende

Nowe nece myne/ ye shul wel Vnderstonde
(Quod he) so as ye women demen all
That for to holde in loue a man in honde
And him her lefe and dere herte call
And maken him an howue aboue a call
I meane/as loue an other in this mene whise
She dothe her selfe a shame/and him a gyle

Nowe wherby that I tell you al this
ye wote your selfe/as wel as any wight
Howe that your loue al fully graunted is
To Troylus/the worthyest wight
One of the worlde/and therto trouth yplight
That but it were on him alonge/ye nolde
Him neuer falsen/whyle ye lyuen sholde

Nowe stonte it thus/that syth I fro you went
This Troylus/right platly for to seyne
Is through a gutter by a priuy went
In to my chambre come in al this reyne
Unwyste of euery maner wight certeyne
Saue of my selfe/as wisely haue I ioye
And by the faythe I owe Priam of Troye

And he is come in suche payne and distresse
That but he be al fully woode by this
He sodaynly mote fall in to woodnesse
But if god helpe: and cause why is this
He saythe him tolde is of a frende of his
How ỹ ye shulde louen one/ that hight Horast
For sorow of which this night shal be his last

Creseyde/ whiche that al this wonder herde
Gan sodainly aboute her herte colde
And with a syghe she sorowfully answerde
Alas/I wende who so tales tolde
My dere herte wolde me nat holde
So lightly fausse/alas conceytes wronge
What harme they don: for now lyue I to longe

Horaste alas/and falsen Troylus
I knowe him nat/god helpe me so (qd she)
Alas/what wicked spyrite tolde him thus
Nowe certes eme/to morowe and I him se
I shal therof as full excusen me
As euer dyd woman/if him lyke
And with that worde she gan ful sore syke

O god (quod she) so worldly selynesse
Whiche clerkes callen false selycite
ymedled is with many a bytternesse
Ful anguysshous/ than is god wot (qd she)
Condycion of Veyne prosperyte
For eyther ioyes comen nat yfere
Or els no wight hath hem alway here

O brotyl wele of mannes ioye Vnstable
with what wight so thou be/or how thou play
Either he wot/ that thou ioye arte muable
Or wote it nat/ it mote ben one of tway
Nowe if he wote it nat/howe may he say
That he hath Very ioye and selynesse
That is of ignoraunce aye in derkenesse

Nowe if he wote that ioy is transytorie
As euery ioye of worldly thing mote flye
Than euery tyme/he that hath in memory
The drede of lesyng/ maketh him/that he
May in no parfyte sykernesse be
And if to lese his ioye/he set a myte
Than semeth it/that ioye is worthe ful lyte

Wherfore I wol diffyne in this matere
That trewly for aught I can espye
There is no Very wele in this worlde here
But o thou wicked serpent Ialousye
Thou misbyleued/and enuyous folye
Why haste thou Troylus made to me Vntryst
That neuer yet agylte/ that I wyste

(Quod Pandarus) thus fallen is this caas
Why Vncle myn (qd she) who tolde him this
Why dothe my dere herte thus/ alas:
ye wote/ ye nece myn (quod he) what is
I hope al shal be wel/that is amys
For ye may quenche al this/if that you leste
And dothe right so/I holde it for the beste

So

So shal I do to morowe/ ywis (quod she)
And god to forne/ so that it shal suffyse
To morowe alas/ that were fayre (q̄d he)
Nay nay/ it may nat stonden in this wyse
For nece myne/ this writen clerkes wyse
That peryl is with dretchyng in drawe
Nay/ suche abodes be nat worthe an hawe

Nece/ al thyng hath tyme I dare auowe
For whan a chambre a fyre is/ or an hal
Wel more nede is/ it sodaynly rescowe
Than to disputen and aske amonges al
Howe the candel in the strawe is fal
Ah benedicite/ for al among that fare
The harme is done/ and farwel feldefare

And nece myne/ ne take it nat a grefe
If that ye suffre him al nyght in this wo
God helpe me so/ ye had him neuer lefe
That dare I sayne/ nowe there is but we two
But wel I wote that ye wol nat so do
Ye ben to wyse to done so great foly
To putte his lyfe al nyght in ieopardy

Had I him neuer lefe : by god I wene
Ye had neuer thyng so lefe (quod she)
Nowe by my thrifte (quod he) yͭ shal be sene
For sithe ye make this ensample of me
If iche al nyght wolde him in sorowe se
For al the treasour in the towne of Troy
I bydde god/ I neuer mote haue ioye

Nowe loke than/ if ye that ben his loue
Shulde putte his lyfe al nyght in ieopardy
For thyng of nought/ now by yͤ god aboue
Nat onely this delay cometh of foly
But of malyce/ if that I shulde nat lye
What/ platly and ye suffre him in dystresse
Ye neyther bounte done ne gentylesse

(Quod tho Creseyde) wol ye done o thyng
And ye therwith shal stynte al his disease
Haue here and bere him this blewe ryng
For there is nothyng might him better plese
Saue I my selfe/ ne more his herte apese
And say my dere herte/ that his sorowe
Is causelesse/ that shal he sene to morowe

A rynge (q̄d he) ye haselwodes shaken
Ye nece myne/ yͤ rynge must haue a stone
That might deed men alyue maken
And suche a rynge trowe I that ye haue none
Discrecion out of your heed is gone
That fele I nowe (q̄d he) and that is routhe
O tyme ylost/ wel mayst thou cursen slouthe

Wote ye nat well that noble & hye corage
Ne sorowethe nat/ ne stynteth eke for lyte
But if a fole were in a ialous rage
I nolde setten at his sorowe a myte
But telle him with a fewe wordes whyte
An other day/ whan that I might him fynde
But this thyng stant al in another kynde

This is so gentyl and so tendre of herte
That with his deth he wol his sorowes wreke
For trust wel/ howe sore that him smerte
He wol to you no ialous wordes speke
And for thy nece/ er that his herte breke
So speke your selfe to him of this matere
For with a worde ye may his herte stere

Nowe haue I tolde what peryll he is in
And his comyng vnwyst is to euery wight
Ne parde harme may there be none/ ne syn
I wol my selfe be with you al this nyght
Ye knowe eke howe it is your owne knyght
And that by right/ ye muste vpon him tryste
And I al prest to fetche him whan you lyste

This accident so pytous was to here
And eke so lyke a sothe/ at prime face
And Troylus her knyght/ to her so dere
His priue cōmyng/ and the syker place
That though she dyd him as than a grace
Consydred al thynges as they stoode
No wonder is/ sens he dyd al for goode

Creseyde answerde/ as wisely god at reste
My soule brynge/ as me is for him wo
And eme iwys/ fayne wolde I done the beste
If that I a grace had for to do so
But whether that ye dwell/ or for him go
I am/ tyl god me bettre mynde sende
At Dulcarnon/ right at my wyttes ende

Quod

(Quod Pandarus) ye nece wol ye here
Dulcarnon is called flemyng of wretches
It semeth harde/ for wretches wol naught lere
For very slouthe/ or other wylful tetches
This is said by hem/ yͭ be nat worthe two fet-
But ye ben wyse/ & that ye han on honde (ches
Nys neyther harde/ ne skylful to withstonde

Than eme (qd she) dothe here of as you lyst
But er he come/ I wol vp first aryse
And for the loue of god/ sens al my tryst
Is on you two/ and ye bethe bothe wyse
So werketh nowe/ in so discrete a wyse
That I honour may haue/ and he plesaunce
For I am here/ al in your gouernaunce

That is wel sayd (qd he) my nece dere
There good thrifte on that wyse gentyl herte
But lyggeth styll/ & taketh him right here
It nedeth nat no ferther for him sterte
And eche of you easeth other sorowes smerte
For loue of god/ and Venus I the herye
For sone hope I/ that we shal ben merye

This Troylus ful sone on knees him sette
Ful sobrely/ right by her beddes heed
And in his beste wyse his lady grette
But lorde so she wore sodaynlyche reed
Ne though men shulde smyten of her heed
She coulde nat o worde aright out bringe
So sodaynly for his sodayne comynge

But Pandarus/ that so wel coulde fele
In euery thyng/ to play anon began
And sayd/ nece/ se howe this lorde can knele
Nowe for your trouthe/ se this gentyl man
And with that worde/ he for a quysshen ran
And sayd/ kneleth nowe whyle yͭ you leste
There god your hertes bring sone at reste

Can I naught sayn/ for she bad him nat ryse
If sorowe it put out of her remembraunce
Or els that she toke it in the wyse
Of duetie/ as for his obseruaunce
But wel fynde I/ she dyd him this plesaunce
That she him kyst/ al though she syked sore
And bade him sytte adowne withouten more

(Quod Pandarus) nowe wol ye wel begyn
Nowe dothe him sytte/ good nece dere
Vpon your beddes syde/ al there within
That eche of you the bet may other here
And with that worde he drewe him to the fiere
And toke a lyght/ & fonde his countenaunce
As for to loke vpon an olde romaunce

Creseyde that was Troylus lady right
And clere stode in a grounde of sykernesse
Al thought she her seruaunt & her knyght
Ne shulde non vntrouthe in her gesse
That nathelesse/ consydred his distresse
And that loue is in cause of suche folye
Thus to him spake she of his ialousye

Lo herte myne/ as wolde the excellence
Of loue/ ayenst the whiche that no man may
Ne ought eke goodly maken resystence
And eke vpcause I felte wel and saye
your great trouthe and seruyce euery day
And yͭ your hert al myne was/ sothe to sayne
This droue me for to rewe vpon your payne

And your goodnes haue I foūden alway yet
Of whiche my dere hert/ and al my knyght
I thanke it you/ as ferre as I haue wyt
Al can I nat as moche as it were right
And I emforth my cōnyng and my myght
Haue/ and aye shal/ howe sore that me smert
Ben to you trewe and hole with al myn hert

And dredelesse that shal be founden at preue
But herte myne/ what al this is to sayne
Shal wel be tolde/ so yͭ ye nought you greue
Though I to you right on yoͬ selfe cōplayne
For there with meane I finally payne
That halte your hert and myne in heuynesse
Fully to slayne/ and euery wronge redresse

My good myne/ not I/ for why ne howe
That ielousy alas/ that wicked wyuere
Thus causelesse is cropen in to you
The harme of which I wolde fayne delyuere
Alas/ that he al hole or of him slyuere
Shulde haue his refute in so digne a place
That Ioue/ him soone out of your hert race

But

But o thou/o auctour of nature
Is this an honour to thy dignyte
That folke vngylty suffre here iniure
And who that gylty is/al quyte gothe he
O were it lefull for to playne of the
That vndeserued suffrest ialousye
O/that I wolde vpon the playne and crye

Eke al my wo is this/that folke nowe vsen
To sayne right thus: ye/ialousye is loue
And wolde a busshell of venym al excusen
For that a grayne of loue is on it shoue
But that wote hygh Ioue that sytte aboue
If it be lyker loue/ hate/ or grame
And after that it ought beare his name

But certayne is/some maner ialousye
Is excusable/more than some iwys
As whan cause is/and some suche fantasye
With pyte so wel expressed is
That it vnneth dothe or saythe amys
But goodly drinketh vp al his distresse
And that excuse I for the gentillesse

And some so ful of furye is/ and dispyte
That it surmounteth his repressyon
But herte myne/ye be nat in that plyte
That thonke I god/ for whiche your passyon
I wol nat call it but illusyon
Of habundaunce of loue/and besy cure
That dothe your herte this disese endure

Of whiche I am sory/ but nat wrothe
But for my deuoire and your hertes reste
Where so you lyst/by ordal or by othe
By sorte/or in what wyse so you leste
For loue of god/let preue it for the beste
And if that I be gilty/do me dey
Alas/ what might I more done or sey

With that a fewe bright teeres newe
Out of her eyen fell/ and thus she seyde
Now god yͧ woste/ in thou3t ne dede vntrew
To Troylus was neuer yet Creseyde
With that her heed downe in the bed she leyde
And with the shete it wrighe/& syghed sore
And held her peace/nat a word spake she more

But nowe helpe god/to quenche al this sorow
So hope I that he shal/for he best may
For I haue sene of a ful misty morowe
Folowen ful ofte a mery somers day
And after wynter foloweth grene May
Men sene alday/and reden eke in stories
That after sharpe shoures ben victories

This Troylus/whan he her wordes herde
Haue ye no care/him lyste nat to slepe
For it thought him no strokes of a yerde
To here or se Creseyde his lady wepe
But wel he felte aboute his herte crepe
For euery teare whiche that Creseyde asterte
The crampe of deth/to strayne him by yͤ herte

And in his mynde he gan the tyme acurse
That he came there/and that he was borne
For nowe is wicke turned in to worse
And al that labour he hath done beforne
He wende it loste/ he thought he nas but lorne
O Pandarus thought he/alas thy wyse
Serueth of naught/so wela way the whyle

And ther withal he hynge adowne his heed
And fell on knees/and sorowfully he syght
What might he sayne? he felte he nas but deed
For wrothe was she yͭ shuld his sorowes light
But nathelesse/whan that he speken might
Than said he thus/god wot that of this game
Whan al is wyste/than am I nat to blame

Therwith the sorowe of his herte shette
That from his eyen fyl there nat a teere
And euery spirit his vygour in knette
So they astouped or oppressed were
The felyng of sorowe/or of his feere
Or of aught els/fledde were out of towne
Adowne he fyl al sodaynly in swoune

This was no lytel sorowe for to se
But al was hushte/& Pandare vp as faste
O nece peace/or we be loste (quod he)
Bethe nat agaste/but certayne at laste
For this or that/he in to bedde him caste
And sayd/ O thefe/ is this a mannes herte
And of he rente al to his bare sherte

M.iii. And

And sayd nece/but ye helpe vs nowe
Alas/your owne Troylus is lorne
Iwys so wolde I/and I wyste howe
Ful fayne (qd she) alas that I was borne
ye nece/wol ye pullen out the thorne
That stycketh in his herte (quod Pandare)
Say al foryeue/and stynte is al this fare

ye that to me (qd she) ful leuer were
Than al the good the sonne aboute gothe
And there withal she swore him in his eere
Iwys my dere herte I am nat wrothe
Haue here my trouthe/& many an other othe
Nowe speke to me/for it am I Creseyde
But al for naught/yet might he nat abreyde

Therwith his pouce/& paumes of his hondes
They gan to frote/& wete his temples twayne
And to delyuer him fro bytter bondes
She ofte him kyste/and shortly for to sayne
Hym to rewaken she dyd al her payne
And at the laste he gan his brethe to drawe
And of his swough sone after that adawe

And gan bet mynde/and reason to him take
But wonder sore he was abasshed ywis
And with a syghe whan he gan bet awake
He sayd/O mercy god/what thyng is this?
Why do ye with your seluen thus amys?
(Quod tho Creseyde) is this a mans game
What Troylus/wol ye do thus for shame?

And therwithal her arme ouer him she layde
And al foryaue/and ofte tyme him keste
He thonked her/and to her spake and sayde
As fyll to purpose/for his hertes reste
And she to that answerde him as her leste
And with her goodly wordes him disporte
She gan/and ofte his sorowes to comforte

(Quod Pandarus) for aught I can aspyen
This lyght nor I ne seruen here of naught
Lyght is nat good for sycke folkes eyen
But for the loue of god/sens ye ben brought
In thus good plyte/let now non heuy thought
Ben hangyng in the hertes of you twey
And bare the candell to the chymeney

Soone after this/ though it no nede were
Whan she suche othes as her lyst deuyse
Had of him take/her thought tho no fere
Ne cause eke none/to byd him thence ryse
yet lesse thyng than othes may suffyse
In many a case/for euery wight I gesse
That loueth wel/ meaneth but gentylesse

But in effecte she wolde wete anon
Of what man/and eke where/and why
He ialous was/sens there was cause non
And eke the signe that he toke it by
She bade him that to tell her besily
Or els certayne she bare him on honde
That this was done of malyce her to fonde

Withouten more/shortly for to sayne
He muste obey vnto his ladyes hest
And for the lasse harme he muste fayne
He sayd her/whan she was at suche a fest
She might on him haue loked at the lest
Not I nat what/al dere ynough a rysshe
As he that nedes muste a cause fysshe

And she answerde/ swete/ al were it so
What harme was yͭ/ sens I none yuel meane
For by that god that bought vs bothe two
In al thyng is myne entent cleene
Suche argumentes ne be nat worthe a beene
Wol ye the chyldysshe ialous countrefete
Nowe were it worthy that ye were ybete

Tho Troylus gan sorowfully to syke
Leste she be wroth/him thought his hert deyde
And sayd/alas/vpon my sorowes syke
Haue mercy swete herte myne Creseyde
And if that in tho wordes that I seyde
Be any wronge/ I wol no more trespace
Doth what you lyst/I am al in your grace

And she answerde/of gylte mysericorde
That is to sayne/ that I foryeue al this
And euermore on this nyght you recorde
And bethe wel ware ye do nomore amys
Nay dere herte myn (qd he) ywis
And now (qd she) that I haue you do smerte
Foryeue it me/myn owne swete herte

This

This Troylus with blysse of that supprised
Put al in goddes hande/as he that mente
Nothyng but wel/and sodainly avysed
He her in armes faste to him hente
And Pandarus/with a ful good entente
Layde him to slepe/and sayd/if ye be wyse
Sweveneth nat nowe/leste more folke aryse

What might or may the sely larke say
Whan that yͤ sperhauke hath him in his fote &
I can no more/but of these ylke tway
To whom this tale sugre be or soote
Though I tarye a yere/ somtyme I mote
After myn auctour tellen her gladnesse
As wel as I haue tolde her hevynesse

Creseyde/ whiche that felte her thus ytake
(As writen clerkes in her bokes olde)
Right as an aspen leefe she gan to quake
Whan she him felte her in his armes folde
But Troylus al hole of cares colde
Gan thanken tho the blysful goddes seven
Through sondrie paynes to bring folke to heven

This Troylus in armes gan her strayne
And sayd swete/as ever mote I gone
Nowe be ye caught/here is but we twayne
Nowe yeldeth you/for other boote is none
To that Creseyde answerde thus anone
Ne had I er nowe/my swete herte dere
Ben yolde iwys/I were nowe nat here

O/sothe is sayd/that healed for to be
As of a fever/or other great sicknesse
Men muste drinken/as we ofte se
Ful bytter drinke/and for to haue gladnesse
Men drinken ofte payne/and great distresse
I meane it here by/as for this aventure
That through a payn hath founden al his cure

And nowe swetnesse semeth more swete
That bytternesse assayed was byforne
For out of wo in blysse nowe they flete
Non suche they felten sens they were borne
Nowe is this bet/than bothe two be lorne
For love of god/take every woman hede
To werken thus/if it come to the nede

Creseyde al quyte from every drede and tene
As she that iuste cause had him to tryste
Made him suche feest/it ioye was to sene
Whan she his trouthe & clene entent wyste
And as aboute a tree with many a twyste
Bytrent and writhe the swete wodbynde
Gan eche of hem in armes other wynde

And as the newe abasshed nightyngale
That stynteth first/whan she begynneth syng
Whan that she hereth any heerdes tale
Or in the hedges any wight steryng
And after syker dothe her voyce out rynge
Right so Creseyde/whan her drede stente
Opened her herte/& tolde him her entent

And right as he that seeth his dethe yshapen
And dyen mote/in aught that he may gesse
And sodainly rescous dothe him escapen
And from his dethe is brought in sykernesse
For al this worlde/in suche present gladnesse
Was Troylus/and hath his lady swete
With worse happe god let us never mete

Her armes small/ her streyght backe & softe
Her sydes longe/ fleshly/smothe/and white
He gan to stroke/& good thrifte bade ful ofte
Her snowysse throte/ her brestes rounde & lyte
Thus in this heven he gan him to delyte
And therwithal a thousande tymes her kyste
That what to done for ioye unneth he wyste

Than sayd he thus/O love/o charyte
Thy mother eke/Citheria the swete
That after thy selfe/next heryed be she
Venus I meane/ the wel willy planete
And next that/ Imeneus I the grete
For never man was to you goddes holde
As I/ whiche ye haue brought fro cares colde

Benigne love/thou holy bonde of thynges
Who so wol grace/& lyste the nat honouren
Lo/his desyre wol flye withouten wyngen
For noldest thou of bountie hem socouren
That serven best/and moste alway labouren
yet were al loste/that dare I wel sayne certes
But if thy grace passed our desertes

And for thou me that lest thõke coude deserue
Of hem that nombred ben vnto thy grace
Hast holpen/ there I lykely was to sterue
And me bestowed in so highe a place
That thylke boundes may no blysse pace
I can no more/ but laude and reuerence
Be to thy bounte and thyne excellence

And therwithal Creseyde anon he kyst
Of whiche certayne she felte no disease
And thus sayd he/ nowe wolde god I wyst
Myne herte swete/ howe I you myght please
What man (qd he) was euer thus at ease
As I: on whiche the fayrest/and the best
That euer I sey/ deyneth her to rest

Here may men sene that mercy passeth right
The experience of that is felte in me
That am vnworthy to so swete a wight
But hert myne/ of your benygnite
So thynke/ that though I vnworthy be
yet mote I nede amenden in some wyse
Right through the vertue of your hye seruyce

And for the loue of god my lady dere
Sith he hath wrouzt me for I shal you serue
As thus I meane: Wol ye be my steere
To do me lyue/ if that you lyst/ or sterue
So teacheth me/ howe that I may deserue
Your thonke/ so yͭ I through myn ignoraũce
Ne do nothyng that you be displesaunce

For certes fresshe womanlyche wyfe
This dare I say/ that trouthe and dyligence
That shal ye fynden in me al my lyfe
Ne I wol nat certayne breken your defence
And if I do/ present or in absence
For loue of god/let slee me with the dede
If that it lyke vnto your womanhede

Iwys(qd she) myn owne hertes lust
My grounde of ease/and al myn herte dere
Graunt mercy/ for on that is al my trust
But let vs fall away fro this matere
For it suffyseth/this that sayd is here
And at o worde/withouten repentaunce
Welcome my knight/my peace/my suffysaũce

Of her delyte or ioyes/one of the leste
Were impossyble to my wyt to say
But iugeth ye/that haue ben at the feest
Of suche gladnesse/if that hem lyst play
I can no more/but thus these ylke tway
That nyght/betwixen drede and sykernesse
Felten in loue the great worthynesse

O blysful nyght/of hem so longe ysought
Howe blythe vnto hem bothe two thou were:
Why ne had I such feest wᵗ my soule ybouzt:
ye/ or the leste ioye that was there
Away thou foule daunger and thou feere
And let hem in this heuen blysse dwell
That is so hygh/that al ne can I tell

But sothe is/though I can nat tellen all
As can myn auctour of his excellence
yet haue I sayd/and god toforne shall
In euery thyng al holy his sentence
And if that I/at loues reuerence
Haue any worde in eched for the beste
Dothe therwithal right as your seluen leste

For my wordes here/ and euery parte
I speke hem al vnder correction
Of you that felyng haue in loues arte
And put it al in your discretion
To encreate or make dimynution
Of my langage/and that I you beseche
But nowe to purpose of my rather speche

These ylke two that bethe in armes laste
So lothe to hem a sonder gon it were
That eche from other wenden ben byraste
Or els lo/this was her moste feere
That al this thyng but nyce dreames were
For whiche ful oft eche of hem sayd/o swete
Clyppe I you thus/or els do I it mete

And lorde so he gan goodly on her se
That neuer his loke ne bleynte from her face
And sayd/o dere herte may it be
That it be sothe/that ye ben in this place
ye herte myne/ god thanke I of his grace
(Qd tho Creseyde) & therwithal hym kyste
That where her spyrite was/ for ioy she nyste

This Troylus ful ofte her eyen two
Gan for to kysse/and sayd: O eyen clere
It weren ye that wrought me suche wo
Ye humble nettes of my lady dere
Though there be mercy wrytten in your chere
God wote the texte ful harde is for to fynde
Howe coude ye/ withouten bonde me bynde

Therwith he gan her faste in armes take
And wel an hundred tymes gan he syke
Nat suche sorowfull syghes as men make
For wo/or els whan that folke be syke
But easy syghes/suche as ben to lyke
That shewed his affection withinne
Of suche syghes coulde he nat blynne

Sone after this/they spake of sondrie thinges
As fyl to purpose of this auenture
And playeng/entrechaungeden her rynges
Of whiche I can nat tellen no scripture
But wel I wot/a broche of golde and asure
In whiche a rubye set was lyke an herte
Creseyde him yaue/& stacke it on his sherte

Lorde trowe ye that a coueytous wretche
That blameth loue/and halte of it dispyte
That of tho pens that he can muckle & ketche
Was euer yet yeue to him suche delyte
As is in loue/in o poynt in some plyte
Nay doutlesse/for also god me saue
So parfyte ioye may no nygarde haue

They wol say yes/but lorde so they lye
Tho besy wretches ful of wo and drede
That callen loue a woodnesse of folye
But it shal fall hem/as I shal you rede
They shal forgon the whyte & eke the reede
And lyue in wo/ther god yeue hem mischaunce
And euery louer in his trouthe auaunce

As wolde god tho wretches/ that dispyse
Seruyce of loue/had eares also longe
As had Mida/ful of couetyse
And therto dronken had as hotte & stronge
As Cresus dyd/for his affectes wronge
To teachen hem/ that they ben in the vyce
And louers nat/al though they holde hem nice

These ylke two/of whom ȳ I you say
Whan that her hertes wel assured were
Tho gonnen they to speke and to play
And eke rehercen howe/whan/and where
They knewe first/ & euery wo or feere
That passed was/but al suche heuynesse
I thonke it god/was turned to gladnesse

And euer more/whan that hem fyl to speke
Of any thing of suche a tyme agon
With kyssyng al that tale shulde breke
And fallen in to a newe ioye anone
And dyden al her might/ sens they were one
For to recoueren blysse/and ben at eyse
And paysed wo with ioye countrepeyse

Reason wol nat that I speke of slepe
For it acordeth nat to my matere
God wote they toke of it ful lytell kepe
But leste this nyght that was to hem so dere
Ne shulde in vayne escape in no manere
It was byset in ioye and besynesse
Of al that sowneth in to gentylnesse

But whan the cocke/cōmune astrologer
Gan on his breste to beate/and after crowe
And Lucifer/the dayes messanger
Gan for to ryse/and out her beames throwe
And eestwarde rose/ to him ȳ coulde it knowe
Fortuna maior/that anon Creseyde
With herte sore/to Troylus thus seyde

Myne hertes lyfe/my trust/al my plesaunce
That I was borne alas / that me is wo
That day of vs mote make disceueraunce
For tyme it is to ryse/and hence go
Or els I am loste for euer mo
O nyght alas/why nylt thou ouer vs houe
As longe as whan Alcmena lay by Ioue

O blacke nyght/as folke in bokes rede
That shapen arte by god/this worlde to hyde
At certayne tymes/with thy derke wede
That vnder that men might in reste abyde
Wel oughten beestes to playn/& folke to chyde
That ther as day with labour wolde vs brest
That thou thus flyest/& deynest vs nat rest

M.m.iii. Thou

Thou doest alas/ to shortely thyne offyce
Tho rakle nyght/ there god maker of kynde
The for thyne haste/ and thyne unkynde vice
So faste aye to our himyspery bynde
That nevermore under ye groud thou wynde
For nowe for thou so hyest out of Troye
Haue I forgone thus hastely my ioye

This Troylus/ that with tho wordes felte
As thought him tho/ for pytous distresse
The bloody teares from his herte melte
As he that yet never suche heuynesse
Assayed had/ out of so great gladnesse
Gan therwithal Creseyde his lady dere
In armes strayne/ & holde in louely manere

O cruel day/ accuser of the ioye
That night & loue haue stole/ & faste ywrien
Acursed be thy comyng in to Troye
For every bore hath one of thy bright eyen
Envyous day/ what lyst the so to spyen
What hast thou lost/ why sekest thou this place
There god thy light so quenche for his grace

Alas/ what haue these louers the agylt?
Dispytous day/ thyn be the payne of hell
For many a louer haste thou slayne/ & wylt
Thy poringe in wol nowhere let hem dwell
What profrest thou thy light here for to sell?
Go sell it hem that smale seales graue
We wol the nat/ us nedeth no day haue

And eke the sonne Tytan gan he chyde
And sayd/ O foole/ wel may men the dispyse
That haste al night the dawnyng by thy syde
And suffrest her so soone up fro the ryse
For to disease us louers in this wyse
What holde your bed/ ther thou & thy morowe
I bydde god so yeue you bothe sorowe

Therwith ful sore he syghed/ & thus he seyde
My lady right/ and of my wele or wo
The well and roote/ o goodly myn Creseyde
And shal I ryse alas/ and shal I so?
Nowe fele I that myn herte mote a two
And howe shulde I my lyfe an houre saue
Sens that with you is al the lyfe I haue?

What shal I done? for certes I not howe
Ne whan alas/ I shal the tyme se
That in this plyte I may ben efte with you
And of my lyfe god wote howe shal that be
Sens that desyre right nowe so byteth me
That I am deed anon/ but I retourne
Howe shulde I long alas/ fro you soiourne?

But nathelesse/ myn owne lady bright
Were it so that I wyste utterly
That your humble seruaunt/ & your knyght
Were in your herte yset so fermely
As ye in myn/ the whiche trewly
Me leauer were than these worldes twayne
Yet shulde I bet enduren al my payne

To that Creseyde answerde right anon
And with a syghe she sayd/ O herte dere
The game ywys so ferforthe nowe is gon
That first shal Phebus fallen fro the sphere
And every the Egle ben the douues fere
And every rocke out of his place sterte
Er Troylus go out of Creseydes herte

Ye ben so depe within myn herte graue
That tho I wolde it turne out of my thought
As wisely very god my soule saue
To dyen in the payne/ I coulde nought
And for ye loue of god/ that us hath wrought
Let in your brayne none other fantasye
So crepe/ that it cause me to dye

And that ye me wolde haue as fast in mynde
As I haue you/ that wolde I you beseche
And if I wyste sothly that to fynde
God might nat a poynte my ioyes eche
But herte myn/ withouten more speche
Bethe to me trewe/ or els were it routhe
For I am thyn/ by god and by my trouthe

Beth glad for thy/ and lyue in sykernesse
Thus sayd I never er this/ ne shal to mo
And if to you it were a great gladnesse
To turne ayen sone after that ye go
As fayne wolde I as ye/ it were so
As wisely god myn herte bring to reste
And hym in armes toke/ and ofte keste

Ayenst

Ayenst his wyll/ sythe it mote nedes be
This Troylus vp rose/and faste him cledde
And in his armes toke his lady free
An hũdred tymes/and on his way him spedde
And with suche wordes/ as his hert bledde
He sayd: farewel my dere herte swete
That god vs graunt sounde & sone to mete

To whiche no worde for sorowe she answerde
So sore gan his partyng her distrayne
And Troylus vnto his paleys ferde
As wo bygon as she was/ sothe to sayne
So harde him wrõge of sharpe desire yͤ payn
For to ben efte there he was in plesaunce
That it may neuer out of his remembraunce

Retourned to his royal paleys sone
He softe vnto his bedde gan for to slynke
To slepe longe/as he was wonte to done
But al for nauzt/ he may wel lygge & wynke
But slepe may there non in his herte synke
Thinkĩg how she/ for whom desyre him brẽde
A thousãde folde was worth more thã he wẽd

And in his thought/gan vp & down to wynde
Her wordes al/and euery countenaunce
And fermely impressen in his mynde
The leste poynte/ that to him was plesaunce
And veryly of thylke remembraunce
Desyre al newe him brende/and lust to brede
Gan more than erst/& yet toke he none hede

Cresseyde also/right in the same wyse
Of Troylus gan in her herte shette
His worthynesse/his lust/ his dedes wyse
His gentylnesse/and howe she with him mette
Thonkyng loue/he so wel her bysette
Desyring ofte to haue her herte dere
In suche a place as she durst make him chere

Pandare a morowe/ whiche that cõmen was
Vnto his nece/and gan her fayre grete
And sayd/ Al this nyght so rayned it alas
That al my drede is/that ye nece swete
Haue lytel leyser had to slepe and mete
Al this night (qd̃ he) hath rayn so do me wake
That some of vs I trowe her heedes ake

And nere he came & sayd/ howe stante it nõwe
This mery morowe/nece howe can ye fare
Creseyde answerde/neuer the bet for you
Foxe that ye ben/god yeue your herte care
God helpe me so/ye caused al this fare
Trowe I (qd̃ she) for al your wordes whyte
O who so seeth you/knoweth you ful lyte

With that she gan her face for to wrie
With the shete/and woxe for shame al reed
And Pandarus gan vnder for to prie
And sayd nece/if that I shal ben deed
Haue here a sworde/and smyteth of my heed
With that his arme/al sodaynly he thruste
Vnder her necke/and at the laste her kyste

I passe al yͤ/ whiche chargeth naught to say
What/ god foryaue his dethe/and she also
Foryaue: and with her vncle gan to play
For other cause was there none than so
But of this thyng right to theffecte to go
Whan tyme was/ home to her house she went
And Pandare hath fully his entent

Nowe tourne we ayen to Troylus
That restlesse ful longe a bedde lay
And priuely sente after Pandarus
To him to come in al the hast he may
He come anone/ nat ones sayde he nay
And Troylus ful soberly he grette
And downe vpon the beddes syde him sette

This Troylus with al thaffectioun
Of frendly loue/ that hert maye deuyse
To Pandarus on knees fyl adowne
And er that he wolde of the place aryse
He gan him thanken on his best wyse
An hundred tyme he gan the tyme blesse
That he was borne/ to bring him to distresse

He sayd/ O frende of frendes/the alderbest
That euer was/ the sothe for to tel
Thou hast in heuen ibrought my soule at rest
Fro Phlegeton the fyrie flode of hel
That though I might a thousande tymes sel
Vpon a day my lyfe in thy seruyse
It myght nat a mote in that suffyse

The

The sonne/ whiche that al the worlde may se
Sawe neuer yet my lyfe/that dare I sey
So ioly/ fayre/ and goodly/ as is she
Whose I am al/ and shal tyl that I dey
And that I thus am hers/ dare I sey
That thanked be the hygh worthynesse
Of loue/and eke thy kynde besynesse

Thus haste thou me no lytel thyng iyeue
For why to the obliged be for aye
My lyfe/ & why? for through thyn helpe I lyue
Or els deed had I ben ago many a day
  And with that worde down in his bed he lay
And Pandarus ful soberly hym herde
Tyl al was sayd / and than he hym answerde

  My dere frende/ if I haue done for the
In any case/god wote it is me lefe
And am as glad as man may of it be
God helpe me so/but take nowe nat agrefe
That I shal sayne/beware of this myschefe
That there as nowe brought art to thy blysse
That thou thy selfe/ne cause it nat to mysse

For of fortunes sharpe aduersyte
The worste kynde of infortune is this
A man to haue ben in prosperyte
And it remembre/ whan it passed is
Thou art wyse ynough/ for thy do nat amys
Be nat to rakell/though thou sytte warme
For if thou be/certayne it wol the harme

Thou art at ese/and holde the wel therin
For also sure as redde is euery fyre
As great a crafte is to kepe wel as wynne
Brydle alway wel thy speche and thy desyre
For worldly ioye holdeth nat but by a wyre
That preueth wel/it brest alday so ofte
For thy nede is to werken with it softe

(Quod Troylus) I hope/and god to forne
My dere frende/that I shal so me beere
That in my gylte there shal no thing ben lorn
Ne I nyl nat rakle/as for to greuen here
It nedeth nat this mater ofte tere
For wystest thou myn herte wel Pandare
God wote of this thou woldest lyte care

Tho gan he tel him of his glad night
And wherof first his herte dradde/ and howe
And sayd frende/as I am trewe knyght
And by that fayth I owe to god and you
I had it neuer halfe so hote as nowe
And aye the more that desyre me byteth
To loue her best/the more it me delyteth

I not my selfe nat wisely/ what it is
But nowe I fele a newe qualyte
ye al another than I dyd er this
  Pandare answerde and sayd thus/that he
That ones may in heuen blysse be
He feleth other wayes dare I say
Than thilke tyme he first herde of it say

This is a worde for al/ that Troylus
Was neuer ful to speke of this matere
And for to praysen vnto Pandarus
The bounte of his right lady dere
And Pandarus to thanke / and maken chere
This tale was aye span newe to begynne
Tyl that the nyght departed hem a twynne

Soone after this/ for that fortune it wolde
Icomen was the blyssful tyme swete
That Troylus was warned/that he sholde
There he was erst/ Creseyde his lady mete
For whiche he felte his hert in ioye flete
And faithfully gan al the goddes hery
And lette se nowe/ if that he can be mery

And holden was the forme/ and al the gyse
Of her cōmynge/ and of his also
As it was erst/ whiche nedeth naught deuyse
But playnly to theffecte right for to go
In ioye and suretee Pandarus hem two
Abedde brought/ whan hem bothe lest
And thus they ben in quiete and in rest

Naught nedeth it to you/ sithe they ben mette
To aske at me/if that they blythe were
For if it erst was wel/tho was it bette
A thousande folde/this nedeth nat enquere
A go was euery sorowe and euery fere
And bothe ywis they had/ and so they wende
As moche ioye as herte maye comprehende

This

This nys no lytel thyng of for to sey
This passeth euery wyt for to deuyse
For eche of hem gan others luste obey
Felycite/ whiche that these clerkes wyse
Cōmenden so/ ne may nat here suffyse
This ioye may nat ywritten be with ynke
This passeth al that herte may bethynke

But cruel day/ so welaway the stounde
Gan for to aproche/ as they by signes knewe
For whiche hem thought felen dethes wounde
So wo was hem/ that chaungen gan her hewe
And day they gonnen to dispyse al newe
Callyng it traytour/ envyous and worse
And bytterly the dayes lyght they corse

(Quod Troylus) alas/ nowe am I ware
That Pyrous/ and tho swyfte stedes thre
Whiche that drawen forthe the sonnes chare
Han gon some bypathe in dispyte of me
And maketh it so sone day to be
And for the sonne him hasteth thus to ryse
Ne shal I neuer don him sacrifyse

But nedes day departe hem muste sone
And whan her speche don was/ & her chere
They twyn anon/ as they were wont to done
And setten tyme of metyng efte yfere
And many a night they wrouzt in this maner
And thus fortune a tyme ladde in ioye
Creseyde/ and eke this kynges sone of Troye

In suffysaunce/ in blysse/ & in syngynges
This Troylus gan al his lyfe to lede
He spendeth/ iusteth/ & maketh feestynges
He yeueth frely ofte/ and chaungeth wede
He helde aboute him alway out of drede
A worlde of folke/ as come him wel of kynde
The fresshest/ and the best he coulde fynde

That suche a voyce was of him/ & a steuen
Throughout ye world/ of honour and largesse
That it vp ronge vnto the yate of heuen
And as in loue he was in suche gladnesse
That in his herte he demed/ as I gesse
That there nys louer in this worlde at ease
So wel as he/ and thus gan loue him please

The goodlyhede or beaute/ whiche yt kynde
In any other lady had ysette
Can nat the mountenance of a gnat vnbynde
Aboute his herte/ of al Creseydes nette
He was so narowe ymasked/ and yknette
That is vndon on any maner syde
That nyl nat ben/ for aught that may betyde

And by the honde ful ofte he wolde take
This Pandarus/ and in to gardyn lede
And suche a feest/ and suche a processe make
Hym of Creseyde/ and of her womanhede
And of her beaute/ that withouten drede
It was an heuen his wordes for to here
And than he wolde synge in this manere

Loue/ that of erthe & see hath gouernaunce
Loue/ that his heestes hath in heuen hye
Loue/ that with an holsome alyaunce
Halte people ioyned/ as him lyst hem gye
Loue/ that knytteth lawe and company
And couples dothe in vertue for to dwel
Bynde this accorde/ that I haue tolde/ and tel

That yt the worlde wt faith/ which yt is stable
Dyuerseth so his stoundes accordynge
That elementes that beth so discordable
Holden a bonde/ perpetually duryng
That Phebus mote his rosy day forth bryng
And yt the mone hath lordship ouer ye nightes
Al this dothe Loue/ aye heried be his mightes

That/ that the see/ that gredy is to flowen
Constrayneth to a certayne ende so
His floodes/ that so fersly they ne growen
To drenchen erthe and al/ for euer mo
And if that Loue aught lette his brydel go
Al that nowe loueth a sonder shulde lepe
And loste were al/ yt Loue halte nowe to hepe

So wolde to god/ that authour is of kynde
That with his bonde/ Loue of his vertue lyst
To serchen hertes al/ and faste bynde
That frō his bonde no wight ye wey out wist
And hertes colde hem/ wolde I that hem twist
To make hem loue/ & that hem lyst aye rewe
On hertes sore/ and kepe hem that ben trewe

In

In al nedes for the townes werre
He was/and aye the first in armes dight
And certainly/but if that bookes erre
Saue Hector/moste ydradde of any wight
And this encrease of hardynesse and might
Come him of loue/ his ladyes thanke to wyn
That altered his spyrite so within

In tyme of truce on haukyng wolde he ryde
Or els hunte bore/ beare/or lyoun
The small beestes let he gon besyde
And whan ŷ he come rydyng in to the towne
Ful ofte his lady from her wyndowe downe
As fresshe as faucon/comen out of mue
Ful redy was him goodly to salue

And moste of loue ⁊ vertue was his speche
And in dispyte had al wretchydnesse
And douteless no nede was him beseche
To honouren hem/ that had worthynesse
And easen hem/that weren in distresse
And glad was he/if any wight wel ferde
That louer was/ whan he it wyste or herde

For sothe to sayne/he loste helde euery wight
But if he were in loues hygh seruyce
I meane folke that ought it ben of right
And ouer al this/so wel coulde he deuyse
Of sentement/and in so vncouthe wyse
Al his array/that euery louer thought
That al was wel/what so he said or wrought

And though that he be come of bloode royall
Him lyst of pride/at no wight for to chace
Benygne he was to eche in generall
For whiche he gate him thanke in euery place
Thus wolde loue/yheryed be his grace
That pride and yre/enuye/and auaryce
He gan to flye/and euery other vyce

Thou lady bright/the doughter of Diane
Thy blynde ⁊ wynged sonne eke dan Cupide
Ye sustren nyne eke/that by Helycone
In hyll Pernaso/lysten for to abyde
That ye thus ferre han deyned me to gyde
I can no more/but sens that ye wol wende
Ye heryed ben for aye withouten ende

Through you haue I sayd fully in my songe
Theffecte and ioye of Troylus seruyce
Al be that there was some disease amonge
As myn auctour lysteth to deuyse
My thirde boke nowe ende I in this wyse
And Troylus in luste and in quiete
Is with Creseyde/his owne herte swete

¶ Explicit liber Tertius.

But al to lytel/weleaway the whyle
Lasteth such ioye/ythonked be fortune
That semeth trewest/whan she wol begyle
And can to fooles so her songe entune
That she hem hent/that blet traitour cōmune
And whan a wight is from her whele ythrowe
Than laugheth she/⁊ maketh him the mowe

From Troylus she gan her bright face
Away to writhe/and toke of him non hede
And caste him clene out of his ladyes grace
And on her whele she set vp Diomede
For which myn hert right now gynneth blede
And nowe my pen alas/ with whiche I write
Quaketh for drede/of that I muste endyte

For howe Creseyde Troylus forsoke
Or at the leste/howe that she was vnkynde
Mote hence forthe/ben mater of my boke
As writen folke/through which it is in mynde
Alas that they shulde euer cause fynde
To speke her harme/⁊ if they on her lye
Iwys hem selfe shulde haue the vilanye

O ye Herynes nyghtes doughters thre
That endelesse complayne euer in payne
Megera/ Allecto/ and eke Tesiphone
Thou cruel Mars eke/father of Quiryne
This ylke fourth boke helpe me to fyne
So that the loos/ and loue/ and lyfe yfere
Of Troylus be fully shewed here.

¶ Incipit liber Quartus.

Lyggyng in host/ as I haue said er this
The grekes strōge/aboute Troy toun
Byfel/that whan that Phebus shynyng is
Vpon the brest of Hercules lyon
That Hector/with many a bolde baron
Caste on a day with grekes for to fyght
As he was wont/to greue hem what he might

Not

Not I howe longe or shorte it was bytwene
This purpose/ & that day they fyghten mente
But on a day wel armed bright and shene
Hector and many a worthy knyght out wente
With speare in honde/ and bygge bowes bente
And in the berde withouten lenger lette
Her fomen in the felde anon hem mette

The longe day with speares sharpe ygroũde
With arowes/ dartes/ swerdes/ & maces fell
They fyght/ & bringen horse & man to groũde
And with her axes out the braynes quell
But in the laste shoure/ sothe to tell
The folke of Troye hem seluen so missedden
That with ye worse at night hom they fledden

At whiche day was taken Anthenor
Maugre Polymydas/ or Monesteo
Xantyppe/ Sarpedon/ Palestynor
Polyte/ or eke the Troyan dan Rupheo
And other lasse folke/ as Phebuseo
So that for harme ye day the folke of Troye
Dredden to lese a great parte of her ioye

Of Priamus was yeue/ at grekes requeste
A tyme of truce/ and tho they gonnen trete
Her prisoners to chaungen moste and leste
And for the surplus yeuen sõmes grete
This thyng anon was couthe in euery strete
Bothe in thassege/ in towne/ and euery where
And with the first it came to Calkas eere

Whan Calkas knew this tretyse shulde holde
In consystorie amonge the grekes sone
He gan in thring/ forthe with lordes olde
And set him there as he was wonte to done
And with a chaunged face/ hem bade a bone
For loue of god/ to done that reuerence
To stynten noyse/ & yeue him audyence

Than sayd he thus/ lo lordes myne I was
Troyan/ as it is knowen out of drede
And if that you remembre/ I am Calkas
That alderfirst yaue comforte to your nede
And tolde wel howe that ye shulde spede
For dredelesse through you shal in a stounde
Ben Troy ybrent/ & beaten down to grounde

And in what forme/ or in what maner wyse
This towne to shende/ & al your luste to acheue
Ye haue er this wel herde me deuyse
This knowe ye my lordes/ as I leue
And for the grekes weren me so leue
I came my selfe in my propre persone
To teche in this/ how you was best to done

Hauyng unto my treasour/ ne my rent
Right no regarde/ in respecte of your ease
Thus al my good I lefte/ and to you went
Wenyng in this you lordes for to please
But al that losse ne dothe me no disease
I vouchsafe/ as wisely haue I ioye
For you to lese/ al that I haue in Troye

Saue of a doughter that I lefte/ alas ?
Slepyng at home/ whan out of Troy I stert
O sterne/ o cruel father that I was
How myght I haue in that so harde an hert ?
Alas that I ne had brought her in my shert
For sorow of which I wol nat liue to morow
But if ye lordes rewe upon my sorowe

For bycause that I sawe no tyme er nowe
Her to delyuer/ iche holden haue my pees
But nowe or neuer/ if that it lyke you
I may her haue right soone doutlees
O helpe and grace/ among al this prees
Rewe on this olde caytife in dystresse
Sith I through you haue al this heuynesse

Ye haue nowe caught/ and fettred in prison
Troyans ynowe/ and if your wylles be
My chylde with one maye haue redemption
Nowe for the loue of god/ and of bounte
One of so fele alas/ so yeue him me
What nede were it this prayer for to werne
Sith ye shul haue/ both folke & town as yern

On peryl of my lyfe I shal nat lye
Apollo hath me tolde ful faithfully
I haue eke founde it by astronomy
By sorte/ and by augury trewly
And dare wel saye the tyme is fast by
That fyre & flambe on al ye town shal sprede
And thus shal Troy turne to asshen dede

For

For certayne Phebus/ and Neptunus bothe
That makeden the walles of the toun
Ben with the folke of Troye alway so wroth
That they wol bring it to confusyoun
Right in despyte of kyng Lamedoun
By cause he nolde payen hem her hyre
The towne of Troye shal ben set on fyre

Tellyng his tale alway this olde grey
Humble in his speche and lokyng eke
The salte teeres from his eyen twey
Ful faste ronnen downe by eyther cheke
So longe he gan of socoure hem beseke
That for to heale him of his sorowes sore
They gaue him Antenor/ withouten more

But who was glad ynough/ but Calcas tho
And of this thyng ful sone his nedes leyde
On hem that shulden for the tretyse go
And hem for Antenor ful ofte preyde
To bringen home kyng Thoas/ & Creseyde
And whan Priam his safegarde sente
Thembassadours to Troy streight they wẽt

The cause I tolde of her cõmyng/ the olde
Priam the kyng/ ful sone in generall
Let here vpon his parlyment holde
Of whiche theffecte reherten you I shal
Thembassadours ben answerde for fynall
The eschaunge of prisoners/ and al this nede
Hem lyketh wel/ and forthe in they procede

This Troylus was present in the place
Whan asked was for Antenor Creseyde
For whiche ful sone chaungen gan his face
As he that with tho wordes wel nyghe deyde
But nathelesse he no worde to it seyde
Leste men shulde his affection espye
With mannes herte/ he gan his sorowes drie

And ful of anguysshe and of grisly drede
Abode/ what other lordes wolde to it sey
And if they wolde graunt/ as god forbede
Theschaũge of her/ thã thouȝt he thĩges twey
First/ howe to saue her honour/ & what wey
He might best theschaunge of her withstonde
Ful faste he caste howe al this might stonde

Loue him made al prest to done her byde
And rather dyen/ than she shulde go
But Reason sayde him on that other syde
Withouten assent of her/ do nat so
Leste for thy werke she wolde be thy foe
And sayn/ that through thy medlĩg is yblowe
Your bother loue/ there it was erst vnknowe

For whiche he gan delyberen for the best
And though the lordes wolde that she went
He wolde lete hem graunt what hem lest
And tel his lady first what that they ment
And whan that she had sayd him her entent
Therafter wolde he worken also blyue
Tho al the worlde ayen it wolde stryue

Hector whiche that wel the grekes herde
For Antenor/ howe they wolde haue Creseyde
Gan it withstonde/ and soberly answerde
Sirs/ she nys no prisoner (he seyde)
I not on you who that this charge leyde
But on my parte/ ye may eftsones hem tel
We vsen here/ no women for to sel

The noyse of people vp sterte than atones
As brymme as blase of strawe yset on fyre
For in fortune it wolde for the nones
They shulden her confusyon desyre
Hector (qd they) what gost may you enspyre
This woman thus to shilde/ and done vs lese
Dan Antenor/ a wronge waye nowe ye chese

That is so wyse/ and eke so bolde baroun
And we haue nede to folke/ as men may se
He is one the grettest of this towne
O Hector/ lette thy fantasies be
O kyng Priam (qd they) thus segge we
That al our voice is to forgone Creseyde
And to delyuer Antenore they preyde

O Iuuenal lorde/ trewe is thy sentence
That lytel wenen folke what is to yerne
That they ne fynden in her desyre offence
For cloude of errour lete hem discerne
What best is/ and lo/ here ensample as yerne
These folke desyren nowe delyueraunce
Of Antenore that brought hem to mischaũce

For

For he was after traytour to the toun
Of Troye alas/they quytte him out to rathe
O nyce worlde/lo thy discrecion
Creseyde/whiche that neuer dyd hem scathe
Shal nowe no lenger in her blysse bathe
But Antenor/he shal come home to towne
And she shal out/ thus sayd heere and howne

For whiche delybered was by parlyment
For Antenor to yelden out Cresyde
And it pronounced by the presydent
Though that Hector nay ful ofte prayde
And fynally/what wight that it withsayde
It was for naught/it muste ben/ and sholde
For substaunce of the parlyment it wolde

Departed out of parlyment echone
This Troylus/without wordes mo
Unto his chambre spedde him faste alone
But if it were a man of his or two
The whiche he bade out faste for to go
Bycause he wolde slepen/as he sayde
And hastely vpon his bedde him layde

And as in wynter leaues ben byrafte
Eche after other tyl trees be bare
So that there nys but barke & braunche ylafte
Lythe Troylus/byrafte of eche welfare
Ybounden in the blacke barke of care
Disposed woode out of his wytte to breyde
So sore him sate the chaungyng of Creseyde

He ryst him vp/and euery doore he shette
And wyndowe eke/& tho this sorouful man
Upon his beddes syde downe him sette
Ful lyke a deed ymage/pale and wan
And in his breste the heaped wo began
Out burste/and he to worken in this wyse
In his woodnesse/as I shal you deuyse

Right as the wylde bulle begynneth springe
Nowe here nowe there/ydarted to the herte
And of his dethe roreth/in complaynyng
Right so gan he aboute the chambre sterte
Smytyng his brest/aye with his fystes smert
His heed to the wall/his body to the grounde
Ful ofte he swapte him seluen to confounde

His eyen two for pyte of his herte
Out stremeden as swyfte as welles twey
The highe sobbes of his sorowes smerte
His speche him refte/ vnnethes myght he sey
O dethe alas/ why nylte thou do me dey?
Acursed be that daye whiche that nature
Shope me to ben a lyues creature

But after whan the fury and al the rage
Whiche that his hert twyste/and fast threst
By length of tyme somwhat gan aswage
Upon his bedde he layde him downe to rest
But tho began his teares more out to brest
That wonder is the body maye suffyse
To halfe this wo/whiche that I you deuyse

Than sayd he thus: Fortune alas the whyle
What haue I done? what haue I yͭ agylte?
Howe myghtest thou for routhe me begyle?
Is there no grace? and shal I thus be spylt?
Shal thus Creseyde awaye for yͭ thou wylte
Alas: howe mightest thou in thyn herte fynde
To ben to me thus cruell and vnkynde?

Haue I the nat honoured al my lyue?
As thou wel wotest/aboue the goddes all
Why wylte thou me fro ioye thus depriue
O Troylus/what may men nowe the call
But wretche of wretches/out of honour fall
In to misery/in whiche I wol bewayle
Creseyde alas/tyll that the brethe me fayle

Alas Fortune/if that my lyfe in ioye
Displeased had vnto thy foule enuye
Why ne haddest thou my father king of Troy
Berafte the lyfe/or done my brethern dye
Or slayne my selfe/ yͭ thus complayne & crye
I combre worlde/ that may of nothyng serue
But euer dye/and neuer fully sterue

If that Creseyde alone were me lafte
Naught raught I whyder thou woldest me
And her alas/thā hast thou me byraft (stere
But euermore/ lo this is thy manere
To reue a wight/that moste is to him dere
To preue in that thy gierful violence
Thus am I loste/there helpeth no defence

N.ii. O very

O Very lorde/ O loue/ o god alas
That knowest best myn hert/& al my thought
What shal my sorouful lyfe done in this caas
If I forgo that I so dere haue bought
Sens ye Cresyde & me haue fully brought
In to your grace/and both our hertes sealed
Howe may ye suffre alas it be repealed

What I may done I shal/whyle I may dure
On lyue/ in turment and in cruel payne
This infortune/or this disauenture
Alone as I was borne I wol complayne
Ne neuer wol I sene it shyne or rayne
But ende I wol as Edippe in derknesse
My sorouful lyfe/and dyen in distresse

O wery goste/that errest to and fro
Why nylt thou flyen out of the wofullest
Body: that euer might on grounde go
O soule/ lurkyng in this woful neste
Flye forthout myn herte/ and let it breste
And folowe alway Cresyde thy lady dere
Thy right place is nowe no lenger here

O woful eyen two/sens your disporte
Was al to sene Cresydes eyen bright
What shal ye done/but for my discomforte
Stöden for naught/& wepen out your syght
Sens she is queynt/yͭ wont was you to light
In veyne from this forth haue I eyen twey
Iformed/sens your vertue is awey

O my Cresyde/ O lady souerayne
Of this woful soule that thus cryeth
Who shal nowe yeuen comforte to thy payne
Alas no wight;but whan myn herte dyeth
My spryrite/which that so vnto you hyeth
Receyue in gree/for that shal aye you serue
For thy no force is/ though the body sterue

O ye louers/that hygh vpon the whele
Ben sette of Fortune/in good auenture
God lene that ye fynden aye loue of stele
And longe mote your lyfe in ioye endure
But whan ye comen by my sepulture
Remembreth that your felowe resteth there
For I loued eke/though I vnworthy were

O olde vnhollsome and mislyued man
Calkas I meane/alas what eyled the
To ben a greke: sens thou art borne Troyan
O Calkas/whiche that wolte my bane be
In cursed tyme waste thou borne for me
As wolde blyssful Ioue for his ioye
That I the had where I wolde in Troye

A thousande syghes hotter than the glede
Out of his brest/eche after other went
Medled with playnte newe/his wo to fede
For whiche his woful teeres neuer stente
And shortly so his sorowes him to rente
And woxe so mate/that ioye or penaunce
He feleth none/ but lyeth in a traunce

Pandare/whiche that in the parlyment
Had herde what euery lorde & burgeys seyde
And howe ful graunted was by one assent
For Antenor/ to yelden out Cresyde
Gan wel nygh wode out of his wyt to breyde
So that for wo he nyste what he mente
But in a race to Troylus he wente

A certayne knyght/that for the tyme kepte
The chambre doore/vndyd it hym anon
And Pandare that ful tenderly wepte
In to the derke chambre as styll as stone
Towarde the bedde gan softely:to gone
So confuse/that he nyste what to say
For very wo/his wytte was nyghe away

And with chere and lokyng al to torne
For sorowe of this/& with his armes folden
He stode this woful Troylus beforne
And on his pytous face he gan beholden.
But so ofte gan his herte colden
Seyng his frende in wo/ whose heuynesse
His herte slough/ as thought him for distresse

This woful wight/this Troylus that felte
His frende Pandare ycomen him to se
Gan as the snowe ayenst the sonne melte
For whiche this woful Pandare/of pyte
Gan for to wepe/as tenderly as he
And specheless thus ben these ylke twey
That neyther might for sorowe o worde sey

But

But at the laste/this woful Troylus
Nygh deed for smert/ gan bresten out to rore
And with a sorouful noyse he sayd thus
Amonges his sobbes and his syghes sore
Lo Pandare I am deed/ withouten more
Haste thou nat herde at parlyment he seyde
For Antenor howe loste is my Creseyde

This Pandare ful deed and pale of hewe
Ful pitoussly answerde/and sayd yes
As wisely were it false as it is trewe
That I haue herde/ and wote al howe it is
O mercy god/who wolde haue trowed this
Who wolde haue wende/ ye in so lytel a throwe
Fortune our ioye wolde haue ouerthrowe

For in this worlde there is no creature
As to my dome/that euer sawe ruyne
Straūger than this/through case or auēture
But who may al eschue or al deuyne
Suche is this worlde/for thy I thus defyne
Ne trust no wight to fynde in Fortune
Aye proprete/her yeftes ben cōmune

But tel me this/why thou art nowe so mad
To sorowen thus/ why lyst thou in this wyse
Sens thy desyre al holly haste thou had
So that by right/it ought ynough suffyse
But I that neuer felte in my seruyce
A frendly chere or lokyng of an eye
Let me thus wepe and waylen tyl I dye

And ouer al this/ as thou wel woste thy selue
This towne is full of ladyes al aboute
And to my dome/fayrer than suche twelue
As euer she was/shal I fynden in some route
Ye one or twey/ withouten any doute
For thy be glad myn owne dere brother
If she be loste/ we shal recouer an other

What god forbyd alway that eche plesaunce
In o thyng were/and in non other wight
If one can synge/another can wel daunce
If this be goodly/she is glad and light
And this is fayre/and that can good aright
Eche for his vertue holden is for dere
Bothe heroner and faucon for ryuere

And eke as writ zansis/that was ful wyse
The newe loue out chaseth ofte the olde
And vpon newe case lythe newe auyse
Thynke eke thy selfe to sauen art thou holde
Suche fyre by processe/shal of kynde colde
For sens it is but casuel plesaunce
Some case shal put it out of remembraunce

For also sure as day cometh after nyght
The newe loue/labour/or other wo
Or els selde seynge of a wight
Done olde affections al ouer go
And for thy parte/thou shalte haue one of tho
To abredge with thy bytter paynes smerte
Absence of her/ shal driue her out of herte

These wordes sayd he for the nones all
To helpe his frende/ lefte he for sorowe deyde
For doutelesse to don his wo to fall
He raught not what vnthrift that he seyde
But Troylus that nygh for sorowe deyde
Toke lytel hede/of al that euer he mente
One eere it herde/at the other out it went

But at the laste he answerde/ & sayd frende
This lechcrafte/or healed thus to be
Were wel syttyng/if that I were a fende
To trayen a wight/that trewe is vnto me
I pray god let this counsayle neuer ythe
But do me rather sterue anon right here
Er I thus done/as thou me woldest lere

She that I serue ywis/ what so thou seye
To whom myn herte enhabyt is by right
Shal haue me holly hers tyll that I deye
For Pandarus/ sens I haue trouth her hight
I wol nat ben vntrewe for no wight
But as her man I wol aye lyue and sterue
And neuer none other creature serue

And ther thou sayest thou shalt as fayre fynde
As she/let be/ make no comparyson
To creature yformed here by kynde
O leue Pandare/ in conclusyon
I wol nat ben of thyn opinyon
Touchyng al this/ for whiche I the beseche
So hold thy peace/thou sleest me wt thy spech

Thou byddest me I shulde loue another
Al fresshly newe/and let Creseyde go
It lythe nat in my power leue brother
And though I might/ yet wol I nat do so
But canste thou playen raket to and fro
Nettle in docke out/now this nowe ye Pãdare
Nowe foule fall her for thy wo that care

Thou farest eke by me Pandarus
As he/that whan a wight is wo bygon
He cometh to him a pace/and saith right thus
Thynke nat on smerte/& thou shalt fele none
Thou mayste me first transmewen in a stone
And reue me my passyons all
Or thou so lighly do my wo to fall

The dethe may wel out of my brest departe
The lyfe so longe may this sorowe myne
But fro my soule shal Creseydes darte
Out neuermore/but down with Proserpyne
Whan I am deed/I wol wonne in pyne
And there I wol eternally complayne
My wo/& howe that twynned be we twayne

Thou haste here made an argument for fyne
Howe that it shulde lasse payne be
Creseyde to forgon/for she was myne
And lyued in ease and in felycite
Why gabbest thou/that saydest vnto me;
That him is worse that is fro wele ythrowe
Than he had erst none of that wele knowe

But tel me nowe/sens ye the thynketh so light
To chaungen so in loue aye to and fro
Why haste thou nat done besily thy might
To chaungen her/that dothe the al thy wo?
Why nylste thou let her fro thyn herte go?
Why nylste thou loue another lady swete
That may thyn herte setten in quyete?

If thou haste had in loue aye yet mischaunce
And canste it nat out of thyn herte driue
I that lyued in lust and in plesaunce
With her/as moche as creature on lyue
Howe shulde I that foryet/and that so blyue
O where hast thou ben hyd so longe in mewe
That canste so wel and formelyche argewe

Nay god wote/naught worthe is al thy rede
For whiche/for what that euer may befall
Withouten wordes mo I wol ben deed
O dethe/that ender arte of sorowes all
Come nowe/sens I so ofte after the call
For sely is that dethe/ sothe for to sayne
That ofte ycleped/ cometh and endeth payne

Wel wote I/whyle my lyfe was in quiete
Er thou me slewe/I wolde haue yeuen hyre
But nowe thy cõmyng is to me so swete
That in this worlde/I nothyng so desyre
O dethe/sens with this sorowe I am a fyre
Thou eyther do me anon in teeres drenche
Or with thy colde stroke myn herte quenche

Sens that thou sleest so fele in sondrie wyse
Ayenst her wyll/vnprayed day and nyght
Do me at my request this seruyce
Delyuer nowe the worlde/ so doste thou right
Of me that am the wofullest wight
That euer was/for tyme is that I sterue
Sens I this world of right naught do I serue

This Troylus in teeres gan distyll
As lycoure out of allambyke ful faste
And Pandarus gan holde his tonge styll
And to the grounde his eyen downe he caste
But nathelesse/thus thought he at laste
What parde/rather than my felawe dey
Yet shal I somwhat more vnto him sey

And sayd frende/sens thou hast suche distresse
And sens the lyst myne argumentes blame
Why nylst thy seluen helpe don redresse
And with thy manhode letten al this game
Go rauisshe her/ne canst thou nat for shame?
And eyther let her out of towne fare
Or holde her styll/and leaue thy nyce fare

Arte thou in Troye/ and haste non hardymẽt
To take a wight/whiche that loueth the
And wolde her seluen ben of thyn assent
Nowe is nat this a nyce vanyte
Ryse vp anon/and let this wepyng be
And sythe thou arte a man/for in this hour
I wol ben deed/or she shal ben our

To

To this answerde hym Troylus ful softe
And sayd/twys my leue brother dere
Al this haue I my selfe yet thought ful ofte
And more thyng than thou deuysest here
But why this thīg is laft/ thou shalt wel here
And whan thou haste me yeuen audyence
Therafter mayst thou tell al thy sentence

First syn yu wost this toun hath al this werre
For rauysshyng of women so by might
It shulde nat ben suffred me to erre
As it stonte nowe/ne done so great vnright
I shulde haue also blame of euery wight
My fathers graunt if that I so withstode
Sens she is chaunged for the townes gode

I haue eke thought/so it were her assent
To aske her at my father of his grace
Than thynke I/this were her accusement
Sens wel I wot I may her nat purchace
For sens my father in so hygh a place
As parlyment/hath her eschaunge enseled
He nyll for me his lettre be repealed

Yet drede I moste her herte to perturbe
With vyolence/if I do suche a game
For if I wolde it openly disturbe
It muste be disclaundre to her name
And me were leuer dye than her diffame
As nolde god/ but I shulde haue
Her honour/ leuer than my lyfe to saue

Thus am I loste/for aught that I can se
For certayne is that I am her knight
I muste her honour leuer haue than me
In euery case/as louer ought of right
Thus am I with desyre and reason twyght
Desyre for to distourben her me redeth
And Reason nyl nat/ so myn herte dredeth

Thus wepyng/that he coulde neuer cease
He sayd alas/howe shal I wretche fare
For wel fele I alway my loue encrease
And hope is lasse and lasse Pandare
Encreasen eke the causes of my care
So welaway/why nyl myn herte breste
For as in loue there is but lytel reste

Pandare answerde/frende thou mayst for me
Done as the lyst/but had I it so hote
And thyn estate/she shulde go with me
Tho al this town cryed on this thing by note
I nolde set at al that noyse a grote
For whā men haue cryed than wol they roun
Eke wonder last but.ix.dayes neuer in toun

Deuyne nat in reason aye so depe
Ne curtesly/but helpe thy selfe anone
Bet is that other than thy seluen wepe
And namely sens ye two ben al one
Ryse vp/for by myn heed she shal nat gone
And rather be in blame a lytel yfounde
Thā sterue here as a gnat withouten woūde

It is no shame vnto you ne no vyce
Her to with holden/that ye loueth moste
Parauenture she might holde the for nyce
To letten her go thus vnto the grekes hoste
Thynke eke fortune/ as wel thy seluen woste
Helpeth hardy man vnto his emprise
And weyueth wretches/for her cowardyse

And though thy lady wolde alyte her greue
Thou shalt thy selfe thy peace herafter make
But as to me certayne I can nat leue
That she wolde it as nowe for yuel take
Why shulde than for feare thyn herte quake
Thynke howe Paris hath/that is thy brother
A loue/and why shalt thou nat haue another

And Troylus/o thyng I dare the swere
That if Creseyde / whiche that is thy lefe
Nowe loueth the/as wel as thou doest here
God helpe me so/she nyl nat take a grefe
Though thou do boote anon in this myschefe
And if she wylneth fro the for to passe
Than is she false/so loue her wel the lasse

For thy take herte/ ⁊ thynke right as a knight
Through loue is broken alday euery lawe
Kythe nowe somwhat thy corage ⁊ thy might
Haue mercy on thy selfe for any awe
Let nat this wretched wo thyn herte gnawe
But manly set the worlde on syxe ⁊ seuen
And if thou dye a marter go to heuen

N.n.iii. I wol

I wol my selfe ben with the at this dede
Though I and al my kyn vpon a stounde
Shulde in a strete/as dogges lyggen dede
Through gyrte with many a bloody wounde
In euery case I wol a frende be founde
And if the lysteth here steruen as a wretche
A dieu/ the dyuel spede him that retche

This Troylus gan with tho wordes quicken
And sayd frende/graunt mercy/ I assent
But certainly thou mayste nat so me pricken
Ne payne none ne may me so turment
That for no case/it is nat myn entent
At shorte wordes/though I dyen sholde
To rauysshen her/but if her selfe it wolde

Why/so meane I (qd̄ Pandarus) al this day
But tel me than/haste thou her wel assayde
That sorowest thus? & he answerde him nay
Wherof art thou (qd̄ Pādare) than dismayde
That noste nat that she wol ben yuel apayde
To rauisshen her/sens thou hast nat ben ther
But if that Ioue tolde it in thyn eere

For thy ryse vp as naught ne were anon
And wasshe thy face/ & to the kyng thou wēde
Or he may wondren whyder thou arte gon
Thou must with wisdom/ him & other blende
Or vpon case he may after the sende
Or thou beware/ and shortly brother dere
Be glad/ & let me werke in this matere

For I shal shape it so/that sykerly
Thou shalt this night sōtyme in som manere
Come speken with thy lady priuely
And by her wordes eke/as by her chere
Thou shalte ful sone apercey̆ue & wel here
Of her entent/and in this case the beste
And fare nowe wel/ for in this poynt I reste

¶ The swyfte fame/ which that false thynges
Equall reporteth lyke the thynges trewe
Was throughout Troy ifled/ wᵗ prest wynges
Fro man to man/and made his tale al newe
Howe Calcas doughter with her bright hewe
At parlyment without wordes more
Igraunted was/in chaunge of Antenore

The whiche tale anon right as Creseyde
Had herde/she whiche ẏ of her father rought
(As in this case) right nauȝt/ne whā he deyde
Ful besily to Iupiter besought
Yeue hem mischaunce/that this tretys brought
But shortly leste these tales sothe were
She durste at no wyght asken it for feere

As she that had her herte and al her mynde
On Troylus yset so wonder faste
That al this world ne muȝt her loue vnbynde
Ne Troylus out of her herte caste
She wolde ben his/ whyle ẏ her lyfe may last
And she thus brenneth bothe in loue & drede
So that she nyste what was best to rede

But as men sene in towne/and al aboute
That women vsen her frendes to visyte
So to Creseyde of women came a route
For pytous ioye/and wenden her delyte
And with her tales dere ynough a myte
These women/ whiche that in the cyte dwell
They set hem downe/ and sayd as I shal tell

(Quod first that one) I am glad trewly
Bycause of you/that shal your father se
Another sayd/ ywis so am nat I
For al to lytel hath she with vs be
(Quod tho the thirde) I hope iwys that she
Shal bringen vs the peace on euery syde
That whan she gothe/almighty god her gyde

Tho wordes and tho womannysshe thynges
She herde hem right as though she thēce were
For god it wote/her herte on other thyng is
Although the body sate amonge hem there
Her aduertence is alway els where
For Troylus ful faste her soule sought
Withouten worde/ on him alway she thought

These women that thus wenden her to plese
Aboute naught gonne al her tales spende
Suche vanyte ne can done her none ese
As she that al this meane whyle brende
Of other passyon than they wende
So that she felte almoste her herte dye
For wo/and wery of that companye

For

For whiche might she no lenger restrayne
Her teeres/they gan so vp to well
That gaue signes of her bytter payne
In whiche her spyrit was/and muste dwell
Remembryng her from heuen vnto which hell
She fallen was/sens she forgo the syght
Of Troylus/and sorousully she syght

And thylke fooles/syttyng her aboute
Wende that she wept and syghed sore
Bycause that she shulde out of the route
Departen/and neuer play with hem more
And they that had knowen her of yore
Se her so wepe/⁊ thought it was kyndnesse
And eche of hem wepte eke for her distresse

And besily they gonnen her to comforten
One thig god wote/on whiche she lytel thouȝt
And with her tales wenden her disporten
And to be glad they ofte her besought
But suche an ease therwith they her wrought
Right as a man is eased for to fele
For ache of heed/to clawen him on his hele

But after al this nyce vanyte
They toke her leue / and home they wenten al
Creseyde full of sorowfull pyte
In to her chambre vp went out of the hall
And on her bedde she gan for deed to fall.
In purpose neuer thence for to ryse
And thus she wrought/as I shal you deuyse

Her ownded heer/ẏ sonnysshe was of hewe
She rent/and eke her fyngers longe ⁊ smale
She wronge ful ofte/⁊ bade god on her rewe
And with the dethe to do bote on her bale
Her hewe whylom bright/that tho was pale
Bare wytnesse of her wo/and her constreynte
And thus she spake/sobbyng in her cōpleynte

¶ Alas (quod she) out of this regyoun
I woful wretche and infortuned wight
And borne in cursed constellacioun
Mote gone/and thus departen fro my knight
Wo worthe alas/that ilke dayes lyght
On which I sawe him first with eyen twayn
That causeth me/ and I him al this payne

Therwith the teeres from her eyen two
Downe fell/ as shoure in Aprill swythe
Her whyte brest she bette/and for the wo
After the dethe she cryed a thousande sythe
Sens he that wonte her wo was for to lythe
She mote forgon/for whiche disauenture
She helde her selfe a forlost creature

She sayd/ howe shal he done and I also
Howe shulde I lyue/if ẏ I from him twynne
O dere herte eke that I loue so
Who shal that sorowe sleen/ that ye ben inne?
O Calkas father/thyn be al this synne
O mother myn/that cleaped were Argyue
Wo worth that day/that thou me bare on lyue

To what fyne shulde I lyue ⁊ sorowen thus?
Howe shulde a fysshe withouten water dure?
What is Creseyde worthe from Troylus?
Howe shulde a plante or lyues creature?
Lyue withouten his kynde norture?
For whiche ful ofte/a by worde here I sey
That rotelesse mote grene sone dey

I shal don thus/sens neyther sworde ne darte
Dare I none handle/for the crueltе
That ylke day that I fro you departe
If sorowe of that nyl nat my bane be
Than shal no meate ne drinke come in me
Tyl I my soule out of my breste vnshethe
And thus my seluen wol I don to dethe

And Troylus/my clothes euerychone
Shul blacke ben/in tokenyng herte swete
That I am as out of this worlde agone
That wonte was you to set in quyete
And of myn ordre aye/tyl dethe me mete
The obseruaunce euer in your absence
Shal sorowe ben/complaynt/⁊ abstynence

Myn herte/and eke the woful goste therin
Byquethe I with your spyrite to complayne
Eternally/for they shal neuer twyn
For though in erthe twynned be we twayne
Yet in the felde of pyte/out of payne
That hight Elisos/shal we ben ylere
As Orpheus and Erudice his fere

Thus

The fourthe boke of Troylus.

Thus herte myn/for Antenor alas
I sone shal be chaunged/as I wene
But howe shul ye done in this sorouful caas
Howe shal your tendre herte this sustene
But herte myn/foryet this sorowe and tene
And me also/for sothly for to sey
So ye wel fare/I retche nat to dey

How we might it euer redde ben or ysonge
The playnt that she made in her distresse
I not/but as for me my lytel tonge
If I discryuen wolde her heuynesse
It shulde make her sorowe seme lesse
Than that it was/ and childysshly deface
Her hye complaynte/ and therfore I it pace

Pandare/whiche that sent from Troylus
Was vnto Creseyde/as ye haue herde deuyse
That for the beste it was acorded thus
And he ful glad to don him that seruyse
Vnto Creseyde in a ful secrete wyse
There as she lay/in turment and in rage
Came her to tell al holy his message

And fonde that she her seluen gan to trete
Ful pytously/for with her salte teeres
Her brest and face ybathed was ful wete
Her mighty tresses of her sonnysshe heeres
Vnbroyden/hangen al aboute her eeres
Whiche yaue him very signe of matiere
Of dethe/ whiche that her herte gan desyre

Whan she him sawe/ she gan for sorowe anon
Her tery face/atwyyte her armes hyde
For whiche this Pandare is so wo bygon
That in the house he might vnneth abyde
As he that felte sorowe on euery syde
For if Creseyde had erste complayned sore
Tho gan she playne a thousande tymes more

And in her aspre playnte/thus she seyde
Pandare/first of ioyes mo than two
Was cause/causyng vnto me Creseyde
That nowe transmued ben in cruell wo
Whether shal I say to you welcome or no?
That alderfirst me brought vnto seruyse
Of loue alas/that endeth in suche wyse

Endeth than loue in wo? ye or men lyeth
And al worldly blysse/as thynketh me
The ende of blysse aye sorowe it occupyeth
And who troweth nat that it so be
Let him vpon me woful wretche se
That my selfe hate/and aye my byrthe curse
Felyng alway/fro wicke I go to worse

Who so me seeth/ he seeth sorowe al atonis
Payne/turment/playnte/ wo/and distresse
Out of my woful body harme there none is
As langour/anguysshe/cruel bytternesse
Annoye/smert/ drede/furye/and eke sycknesse
I trowe ywis from heuen teeres rayne
For pyte of my aspre and cruel payne

And thou my suster/ful of discomforte
(Quod Pādarus) what thinkest thou to do?
Why nē haste thou to thy seluen some resport?
Why wylt thou thus thy selfe alas for do?
Leaue al this werke/and take nowe hede to
That I shal sayne/& herken of good entente
This message/ ẏ by me Troylus you sente

Turned her tho Creseyde/a wo makyng
So great/that it a dethe was for to se
Alas (q̄d she) what wordes may ye bring
What wol my dere herte sayne to me
Whiche that I drede neuer more to se
Wol he haue playnte or teeres er I wende
I haue ynough/if he therafter sende

She was right suche to sene in her vysage
As is that wight that men on bere bynde
Her face lyke of paradys the ymage
Was al ychaunged in another kynde
The play ẏ laughter/mē were wont to fynde
On her/and eke her ioyes euerychone
Ben fledde/and thus lythe Creseyde alone

Aboute her eyen two/a purpre ryng
Bytrent/in sothfast tokenyng of her payne
That to beholde it was a deedly thyng
For whiche Pandare might nat restrayne
The teeres from his eyen for to rayne
But nathelesse as he best might he seyde
From Troylus these wordes to Creseyde

Lo nece/

Lo nece/I trowe ye han herde al howe
The kyng with other lordes for the beste
Hath made eschaunge of Antenor and you
That cause is of this sorowe & this unreste
But howe this case dothe Troylus moleste
This may none erthly mannes tonge say
For very wo/his wytte is al away

For whiche we haue so sorowed/ he and I
That in to lytel/it had us bothe slawe
But through my counsayle this day fynally
He somwhat is fro weppyng withdrawe
And semeth me that he desyreth fawe
With you to ben al nyght for to deuyse
Remedy of this/if there were any wyse

This shorte & playne/ theffecte of my message
As ferforthe as my wytte can comprehende
For ye that ben of turment in suche rage
May to no longe prologe as nowe entende
And herupon ye may answere him sende
And for the loue of god my nece dere
So leaue this wo or Troylus be here

Great is my wo (qđ she) and syghed sore
As she that feleth deedly sharpe distresse
But yet to me his sorowe is mokell more
That loue him bet than he him selfe I gesse
Alas/for me hath he suche heuynesse
Can he for me so pitously complayne
Iwys this sorowe doubleth al my payne

Greuous to me god wot is for to twynne
(Quod she) but yet it harder is to me
To sene that sorowe/whiche that he is inne
For wel wote I/it wol my bane be
And dye I wol in certayne tho (quod she)
But byd him come/ er deth yͭ thus me threteth
Driue out yͤ goost/ whiche in myn hert beteth

These wordes sayd/she on her armes two
Fyll gruffe/and gan to wepen pitously
(Quod Pandarus) alas why do ye so
Sens ye wel wote the tyme is faste by
That he shal come/ aryse up hastely
That he you nat bywopen thus ne fynde
But ye wol haue him wode out of his mynde

For wyste he that ye farde in this manere
He wolde him selfe slee: and if I wende
To haue this fare/he shulde nat come here
For al the good that Priam may dispende
For to what fyne he wolde anon pretende
That knowe I wel/and for thy yet I sey
So leaue this sorowe/or playnly he wol dey

And shapeth you his sorowe for to abredge
And nat encrease/ lefe nece swete
Bethe rather to him cause of plat than edge
And with some wysdom/ye his sorowes bete
What helpeth it to wepen ful a strete
Or though ye bothe in salte teeres dreynte
Bet is a tyme of cure aye than of pleynte

I meane thus/whan I him hyther bringe
Sens ye be wyse/ and bothe of one assent
So shapeth howe to distourbe your goynge
Or come ayen sone after ye be went
Women ben wyse/in shorte auysement
And let sene howe your wyt shal auayle
And what yͭ I may helpe/it shal nat fayle

Go (quod Creseyde) and uncle trewly
I shal done al my might me to restrayne
From weppyng in his syght/and besily
Him for to glad/I shal done al my payne
And in my herte seken euery vayne
If to this sore there may ben founden salue
It shal nat lacke certayne on myn halue

Gothe Pandarus/and Troylus he sought
Tyl in a temple he founde him al alone
As he that of his lyfe no lenger rought
But to the pytouse goddes eueryechone
Ful tendrely he prayed/and made his mone
To done him sone out of this worlde to pace
For wel he thought ther was non other grace

And shortly al the sothe for to seye
He was so fallen in dispayre that day
That utterly he shope him for to deye
For right thus was his argument alway
He sayd he nas but lorne wel away
For al that cometh/cometh by necessyte
Thus to ben lorne it is my destyne

For

For certainly this wote I wel he sayde
That foresyght of diuyne purueyaunce
Had sene alway me to forgon Creseyde
Sens god seeth euery thyng out of doutaũce
And hem disposeth through his ordynaunce
In his merytes sothly for to be
As they shul comen by predestyne

But nathelesse alas/whom shal I leue.
For there ben great clerkes many one
That destyne/through argumentes preue
And some sayne that nedely there is none
But that free choyce is yeuen us euerychone
O welaway/so slygh arne clerkes olde
That I not whose opinyon I may holde

For some men sayne/ yͭ god seeth al byforne
Ne god may nat disceyued ben parde
Tha mote it fallen/though men had it sworn
That purueyaunce hath sene beforne to be
Wherfore I say/that from eterne if he
Hath wyst beforn our thouzt eke as our dede
We haue no free choyce/ as these clerkes rede

For other thought/nor other dede also
Might neuer ben/but suche as purueyaunce
Whiche may nat ben disceyued neuer mo
Hath feled byforne/withouten ignoraunce
For if there might ben a uaryaunce
To writhen out fro goddes purueyeng
There nere no prescience of thyng cõmyng

But it were rather an opinyon
Uncertayne/and no stedfast foreseyng
And certes that were an abusyon
That god shuld haue no parfyte clere wetyng
More than we men/ yͭ haue doutous wenyng
But suche an errour upon god to gesse
Were false and foule/and wicked cursednesse.

Eke this is an opinyon of some
That haue her toppe ful high ⁊ smothe yshore
They sayne right thus/ yͭ thing is nat to come
For that the prescience hath sene before
That it shal cõme/but they sayne yͭ therfore
That it shal come/therfore the purueyaunce
Wote it beforne withouten ignoraunce

And in this maner this necessyte
Retourneth in his parte contrary agayne
For nedefully behoueth it nat to be
That thilke thynges fallen in certayne
That bẽ purueyed/but nedefully as they sayn
Behoueth it that thynges whiche that fall
That they in certayne ben puruayed all

I meane as though I laboured me in this
To enquire which thĩge cause of which thĩg be
As whether that the prescience of god is
The certayne cause of the necessyte
Of thynges that to comen be parde
Or if necessyte of thyng comyng
Be cause certayne of the purueyeng

But nowe ne enforce I me nat in shewyng
How the ordre of yͤ causes stãt/but wel wot I
That it behoueth that the befallyng
Of thinges wyste before certainly
Be necessarye/al seme it nat therby
That prescience put fallyng necessayre
To thyng to come/al fall it foule or fayre

For if there syt a man yonde on a see
That by necessyte behoueth it
That certes thyn opinyon sothe be
That wenest or coniectest that he syt
And further ouer/nowe ayenwarde yet
Lo/ right so is it on the parte contrarye
As thus/nowe herken for I wol nat tarye

I say that if the opinyon of the
Be sothe for that he syt/than say I this
That he mote sytten by necessyte
And thus necessyte in eyther is
For in him nede of syttyng is ywis
And in the nede of sothe/and thus forsothe
There mote necessyte ben in you bothe

But thou maist sayne yͭ man syt nat therfore
That thyn opinyon of his syttyng sothe is
But rather for the man sate there before
Therfore is thyn opinyon sothe ywis
And I say/ though the cause of sothe of this
Cometh of his syttyng/yet necessyte
Is entrechaunged/bothe in him and in the
Thus

Thus in the same wyse out of doutaunce
I may wel maken/as it semeth me
My resonyng of goddes puruepaunce
And of the thynges that to comen be
By whiche reson men may wel yse
That thylke thynges that in erthe fall
That by necessyte they comen all

For al thoughe that forthing shal come ywis
Therfore is it purueyed certainly
Nat that it cometh for it purueyed is
Yet nathelesse behoueth it nedefully
That thyng to come be purueyed trewly
Or els thynges that purueyed be
That they betyden by necessyte

And this suffyseth right ynough certayne
For to distroye our free choyce euerydell
But nowe is this abusyon to sayne
That fallyng of the thynges temporell
Is cause of the goddes prescience eternell
Nowe trewly that is a false sentence
That thing to come shulde cause his prescĩece

What might I wene & I had such a thought?
But that god purueyeth thing that is to come
For that it is to come/and els nought
So might I wene that thinges al and some
That whylom ben byfall and ouercome
Ben cause of thylke souerayne puruepaunce
That forwote al/withouten ignoraunce

And ouer al this/yet say I more therto
That right as whan I wote there is a thyng
Iwis that thyng mote nedefully be so
Eke right so/whan I wote a thyng comyng
So mote it come/and thus the befallyng
Of thynges that ben wyst before the tyde
They mowe nat ben eschewed on no syde

Than sayd he thus/almighty Ioue in trone
That wottest of al this thyng ỹ sothfastnesse
Rewe on my sorowe/ and do me dyen sone
Or bringe Creseyde & me fro this distresse
And whyle he was in al this heuynesse
Disputyng with him selfe in this matere
Came Pandare in/& sayd as ye may here

O mighty god (qd Pandarus) in trone
Eygh/ who sawe euer a wyse man faren so?
Why Troylus/what thynkest thou to done?
Haste thou suche luste to ben thyn owne foe?
What parde/yet is nat Creseyde ago
Why lyst the so thy selfe fordon for drede
That in thyn heed/ thyn eyen semen dede?

Haste thou nat lyued many a yere beforne
Withouten her? and farde ful wel atease
Arte thou for her and for none other borne
Hath kynde the wrought al only her to please
Let be and thinke right thus in thy disease
That in the dyce/right as there fallen chaũces
Right so in loue there come & gon plesaunces

And yet this is a wonder most of al
Why thou thus sorowest sithe yu wost nat yet
Touchyng her goyng/howe that it shal fal
Ne if she can her selfe distourben it
Thou hast nat yet assayed al her wyt
A man maye al betyme his necke bede
Whan it shal of/ and sorowen at the nede

For thy take hede of al that I shal say
I haue with her yspoke and longe ybe
So as accorded was betwyxe vs twey
And euermo me thynketh thus/that she
Hath somwhat in her hertes puuyte
Wherwith she can/ if I shal aright rede
Distourbe al this/of which thou arte in drede

For whiche my counsayle is/whan it is night
Thou to her go/ and make of this an ende
And blyssful Iuno/through her great myght
Shal as (I hope) her grace vnto vs sende
Myne herte seith certayne she shal nat wende
And for thy put/thyne hert a whyle in rest
And holde thy purpose/for it is the best

This Troylus answerde/and syghed sore
Thou sayest right wel/and I wyl do right so
And what him lyste/he sayd vnto him more
And whan that it was tyme for to go
Full priuely him selfe withouten mo
Vnto her came/as he was wonte to done
And howe they wrought/ I shal you tell sone

Sothe

Sothe is/that whan they ganne first to mete
So gan the payne her hertes for to twyste
That neyther of hem other might grete
But hem in armes toke/and after kyste
The lasse woful of hem bothe nyste
Wher y he was/ne might o worde out bringe
As I sayd erste/for wo and for sobbyng

The woful teeres that they leten fall
As bytter weren out of teeres kynde
For payne/as is ligne/aloes/or gall
So bytter teeres wept nat as I fynde
The woful Myrra/through the barke & rynde
That in this worlde ther nys so harde an hert
That nolde haue rewed on her paynes smerte

But whan her woful wery gostes twayne
Retourned ben/there as hem ought to dwell
And that somwhat to weaken gan the payne
By length of playnte/& ebben gan the well
Of her teeres/and the herte vnswell
Wt broken voice/al horse for shright Creseyde
To Troylus these ylke wordes sayde

O Ioue I dye/and mercy the beseche
Helpe Troylus: & therwithal her face
Vpon his brest she layde/and loste speche
Her woful spyrit from his propre place
Right with the worde/ away in poynt to pace
And thus she lyth/with hewes pale and grene
That whylom fresshe and fayrest was to sene

This Troylus that on her gan beholde
Clepyng her name/ and she lay as for deed
Withouten answere/& felte her lymmes colde
Her eyen throwen vpwarde to her heed
This sorouful man/can nowe non other rede
But ofte tyme her colde mouthe he kyste
Where him was wo/god & him selfe it wyste

He ryseth him vp/& longe streight he her leyde
For signe of lyfe/for aught he can or may
Can he none fynde/in nothyng of Creseyde
For whiche his songe ful ofte is welaway
But whan he sawe that specheless she lay
With sorouful voyce/& herte of blysse al bare
He sayd/ howe she was fro this worlde yfare

So after that he longe had her complayned
His hondes wronge/& sayd that was to sey
And with his teeres salte her brest berayned
He gan tho teeres wypen of ful drye
And pitously gan for the soule preye
And sayd/ lorde that set arte in thy trone
Rewe eke on me/ for I shal folowe her sone

She colde was/and without sentement
For aught he wote/for brethe felte he none
And this was him a preignant argument
That she was forth out of this worlde agone
And whan he sawe there was non other wone
He gan her lymmes dresse/in suche manere
As men don hem that shal ben layde on bere

And after this/ with sterne and cruel hert
His swerde anon out of his sheth he twight
Him selfe to sleen/ howe sore that him smerte
So that his soule/ her soule folowen myght
There as the dome of Mynos wolde it dyght
Sith loue and cruel fortune it ne wolde
That in this worlde he lenger lyuen sholde

Than sayd he thus/fulfylde of high disdayne
O cruel Ioue/ and thou Fortune aduerse
This al and some/that falsely haue ye slayne
Creseyde/ and sith ye may do me no werse
Fye on your myght and workes so dyuerse
Thus cowardly ye shul me neuer wynne
There shal no dethe me fro my lady twynne

For I this worlde/sith ye haue slayn her thus
Wol lete/ and folowe her spyrite lowe or hye
Shal neuer louer sayne that Troylus
Dare nat for feare with his lady dye
For certayne I wol beare her company
But sithe ye wol nat suffre vs lyuen here
Yet suffreth that our soules ben yfere

And thou cyte/ in whiche I lyue in wo
And thou Priam/ and brethren al yfere
And thou my Mother/farwel for I go
And Attropose make redy thou my bere
And thou Creseyde/ o swete herte dere
Receyue nowe my spirite/ wolde he sey
With swerde at herte/ al redy for to dey

But

But as god wolde/of swough she abrayde
And gan to syghe/and Troylus she cryde
And he answerde/lady myn Cresejde
Lyue ye yet: and let his sworde downe glyde
ye hert myn/ that thanked be Cupyde
(Qd she) and therwithal she sore syght
And he began to glad her as he myght

Toke her in armes two and kyste her ofte
And her to glad/he dyd al his entent
For whiche her goost/that flykered aye a lofte
In to her woful herte ayen it went
But at the laste/as that her eye glent
Asyde/ anon she gan his sworde aspye
As it lay bare/and gan for feare crye

And asked him/ why he had it out drawe
And Troylus anon the cause her tolde
And how him selfe therwt he wold haue slaw
For whiche Creseyde vpon him gan beholde
And gan him in her armes faste folde
And sayd/o mercy god/lo whiche a dede
Alas/howe nyghe we weren bothe deede

Than if I nadde spoken/as grace was
Ye wold haue slayne your selfe anon (qd she)
ye douteless: and she answerde alas
For by that ylke lorde that made me
I nolde a forlonge way on lyue haue be
After your dethe/ to haue ben crowned queue
Of al ỹ londe the sonne on shyneth shene

But with this selue swerde/whiche ỹ here is
My selfe I wolde haue slayne (qd she) tho
But ho/for we haue right ynough of this
And let vs ryse & strayte to bedde go
And there let vs speken of our wo
For by that morter/whiche that I se brenne
knowe I ful wel/ that day is nat ferre henne

Whan they were in her bedde in armes folde
Naught was it lyke tho nyghtes here beforne
For pitously eche other gan beholde
As they that hadden al her blysse ylorne
Bewayling aye the day that they were borne
Tyl at the last/this sorouful wight Creseyde
To Troylus these ylke wordes seyde

Lo herte myn/ wel wote ye this (quod she)
That if a wight alway his wo complayne
And seketh nat howe holpen for to be
It nys but folye/and encreace of payne
And sens that here assembled be we twayne
To fynde bote of wo that we ben in
It were tyme al soone to begyn

I am a woman/as ful wel ye wotte
And as I am auysed sodainly
So wol I tel you/whyle it is hotte
Me thynketh thus/that neyther ye nor I
Ought halfe this wo to maken skylfully
For there is arte ynough for to redresse
That yet is mysse/and sleen this heuynesse

Sothe is/the wo the whiche we ben inne
For aught I wote/ for nothyng els is
But for the cause that we shulde twynne
Consydred al/ there nys no more amys
And what is than a remedye vnto this:
But that we shape vs sone for to mete
This al and some/my dere herte swete

Nowe that I shal wel bringen it aboute
To come ayen/sone after that I go
Therof am I no maner thyng in doute
For dredelesse/within a weke or two
I shal ben here/and that it may be so
By al right/ and in wordes fewe
I shal you wel an heape of wayes shewe

For whiche I wol nat make longe sermon
For tyme yloste may nat recouered be
But I wol go to my conclusyon
And to the beste/in aught that I can se
And for the loue of god foryeue it me
If I speake aught ayenst your hertes reste
For trewly I speke it for the beste

Makyng alway a protestacion
That now these wordes whiche I shal say
Nys but to shewen you my mocion
To fynde vnto our helpe the beste way
And taketh it none otherwyse I pray
For in effecte/what so ye me cõmaunde
That wol I don/for that is no demaunde

O.o. Nowe

Now herkeneth this/ ye haue wel Vnderstõde
My goyng graunted is by parlyment
So ferforth yͭ it maye nat ben withstonde
For al this worlde/as by my iugement
And sithe there helpeth non auysement
To letten it/ lette it passe out of mynde
And lette vs shape a better waye to fynde

The sothe is/ the twynnynge of vs twayne
Wol vs disease/ and cruelly anoye
But him behoueth somtyme haue a payne
That serueth loue/ if that he wol haue ioye
And sith I shal no farther out of Troye
Than I maye ryde ayen on halfe a morowe
It ought lasse causen vs for to sorowe

So as I shal nat so ben hyd in mewe
That day by day/myn owne herte dere
Sens wel ye wote that it is nowe a trewe
Ye shal ful wel al myn estate here
And er that truce is done/I shal ben here
Than haue ye bothe Antenor ywonne
And me also/bethe glad nowe if ye conne

And thinke right thus/Creseyde is now agon
But what/she shal come hastely ayen
And whan alas ÷ by god/ so right anon
Er dayes ten/this dare I safely sayne
And than at erste/shal we be so fayne
So as we shal togythers euer dwell
That al this worlde ne myght our blysse tell

I se that ofte tyme/there as we ben nowe
That for the beste/our counsayle for to hyde
Ye speke nat with me/ nor I with you
In fourtenyght/ne se you go ne ryde
May ye nat ten dayes than abyde
For myn honour/in suche auenture
Iwys ye nowe els lyte endure ÷

Ye knowe eke howe that al my kyn is here
But if that only it my father be
And eke myn other thynges al yfere
And namely my dere herte ye
Whom that I nolde leauen for to se
For al this worlde/as wyde as it hath space
Or els se I neuer Ioues face

Why trowe ye my father in this wyse
Coueyteth so to se me/but for drede
Leste in this towne that folkes me dispyse
Bycause of him/for his vnhappy dede
What wote my father what lyfe that I lede
For if he wyste in Troye howe wel I fare
Vs neded for my wendyng nat to care

Ye/ that euery daye eke more and more
Men treate of peace/and it supposed is
That men the quene Heleyne shal restore
And grekes vs restore that is mys
So though there nere comforte none but this
That men purposen peace on euery syde
Ye may the better at ease of herte abyde

For if that it be peace/myn herte dere
The nature of the peace mote nedes driue
That men muste entrecomune yfere
And to and fro eke ryde and gone as blyue
Al day as thicke as been flyen from an hyue
And euery wyght haue lyberte to bleue
Where as him lyste/ the bet withouten leue

And though so be yͭ peace there may be none
Yet hyther/though there neuer peace ne were
I muste come/for whyder shulde I gone
Or howe mischaunce shulde I dwell there
Amonge tho men of armes euer in feere
For whiche/ as wisly god my soule rede
I can nat sene wherof ye shulde drede

Haue here another way/ if it so be
That al this thyng ne may you nat suffyse
My father as ye knowen wel pardé
Is olde/and eke ful of couetyse
And I right nowe haue founden al the gyse
Withouten nette/wherwith I shal him hente
And herkeneth nowe/if that ye wol assent

Lo Troylus/ men sayne that ful harde it is
The wolfe ful/ and the wedder hole to haue
This is to sayne/that men ful ofte ywis
Mote spenden parte/ the remenant for to saue
For aye with golde/ men may the herte graue
Of him that set is vpon couetyse
And howe I meane/I shal it you deuyse

The

The mouable / which that I haue in this toun
Unto my father shal I take / and saye
That right for trust / and for saluation
It sent is / from a frende of his or twaye
The whiche frendes feruently him praye
To sende after more / and that in hye
Whyle that this town stant thus in ieopardye

And that shal be of golde an huge quantyte
Thus shal I sayne / but leste folke it aspyde
This may be sent by no wight but by me
I shal eke shewen him / if peace betyde
What frendes that I haue on euery syde
Towarde the courte / to done the wrathe pace
Of Priamus / and do him stonde in grace

So what for o thyng and for other swete
I shal him so enchaunten with my sawes
That right in heuen his soule is / shal he mete
For al Apollo / or his clerkes lawes
Or calculyng / auayleth nat thre hawes
Desyre of golde shal so his soule blende
That as me lyst / I shal wel make an ende

And if he wolde aught by his sorte it preue
If that I lye / in certayne I shal fonde
Distourben him / and plucke by the sleue
Makyng his sorte / and bearen him on honde
He hath nat wel the goddes understonde
For goddes speke in amphibologies
And for o sothe / they tellen twenty lyes

Eke drede fonde first goddes / I suppose
Thus shal I sayne / & that his cowarde herte
Made him amysse the goddes text to glose
Whan he for ferde out of Delphos sterte
And but I make him sone to conuerte
And done my rede / within a day or twaye
I wol to you oblige me to deye

And trewly / as written wel I fynde
That al this thyng was sayd of good entente
And that her herte trewe was and kynde
Towardes him / and spake right as she mente
And þ she starfe for wo nigh whan she wente
And was in purpose euer to be trewe
Thus writen they / that of her werkes knewe

This Troylus / with herte and eares sprad
Herde al this thyng deuysed to and fro
And verily it semed that he had
The selue wytte / but yet to let her go
His herte misyaue him euer mo
But fynally he gan his herte wreste
To trusten her / and toke it for the beste

For whiche the great furye of his penaunce
Was queynt wt hope / & therwith hem bytwene
Began for ioye the amerous daunce
And as the byrdes / whan the sonne is shene
Delyten in her songe / in leues grene
Right so the wordes / that they spake yfere
Delyten hem / and made her hertes clere

But nathelesse / the wendyng of Creseyde
For al this worlde may nat out of his mynde
For whiche ful ofte he pytously her preyde
That of her heste he might her trewe fynde
And sayd her / certes if ye be kynde
And but ye come at day set in Troye
Ne shal I neuer haue heale / honour / ne ioye

For al so sothe as sonne vpryst a morowe
And god so wisely thou me woful wretche
To reste bring / out of this cruel sorowe
I wol my seluen slee / if that ye dretche
But of my dethe though lytel be to retche
Yet er that ye me causen so to smerte
Dwell rather here myn owne swete herte

For trewly myn owne lady dere
The sleyghtes yet / that I haue herde you stere
Ful shaply ben to fallen al yfere
For thus men sayth / that one thinketh þ bere
But al another thynketh the ledere
Your sire is wyse / and sayd is out of drede
Men may the wyse out renne / & nat out rede

It is ful harde to halten vn espyed
Before a creppel / for he can the crafte
Your father is in sleyght as Argus eyed
For al be it that his mouable is him byrafte
His olde sleyght is yet so with him lafte
Ye shal nat blende him for your womanhede
Ne fayne aright / and that is al my drede

O.o.ii. I not

I not if peace shal euermo betyde
But peace or no/ for ernest ne for game
I wotte sith Calcas on the grekes syde
Hath ones ben/ and lost so foule his name
He dare no more come here agayne for shame
For whiche that we/ for ought I can espy
To trusten on/ nys but a fantasy

Ye shal eke seen your father shal you glose
To ben a wyfe/ and as he can wel preche
He shal some greke so preyse and wel alose
That rauysshen he shal you with his speche
Or do you done by force/as he shal teche
And Troylus on whom ye nyl haue routhe
Shal causelesse so steruen in his trouthe

And ouer al this your father shal dispyse
Vs al/and sayne this cyte nys but lorne
And that thassege neuer shal aryse
For why the grekes haue it al sworne
Tyl we ben slayne/ & down our walles torne
And thus he shal you with his wordes feere
That aye drede I/that ye wol bleuen there

Ye shal eke sene so many a lusty knyght
Amonge the grekes ful of worthynesse
And eche of hem/ with herte/wytte/ & myght
To pleasen you/done al his besynesse
That ye shul dullen of the rudenesse
Of sely Troyans/but if routhe
Remorde you/or vertue of your trouthe

And this to me so greuous is to thynke
That fro my brest it wol my soule rende
Ne dredlesse/in me there may nat synke
O good opinyon/if that ye wende
For why/your fathers sleight wol vs shende
And if ye gone/as I haue tolde you yore
So thynke I nam but deed/withouten more

For which with humble/trewe/& pitous herte
A thousande tymes mercy I you pray
So reweth on myn aspre paynes smerte
And dothe somwhat/as that I shal you say
And let vs steale away bytwixt vs tway
And thinke yͭ foly is/ whan a man may chese
For accident/ his substaunce for to lese

I meane thus/that sens we mowe or day
Wel steale away/and ben to gyther so
What wyt were it to putten in assay
(In case ye shulden to your father go)
If that ye mighten come ayen or no
Thus meane I/that were a great folye
To put that sykernesse in ieopardye

And vulgarly to speken of substaunce
Of treasour may we bothe with vs lede
Ynough to lyue in honour and plesaunce
Tyl vnto tyme that we shal ben dede
And thus we may eschewen al this drede
For euery other way ye can recorde
Myn herte ywis may therwith nat acorde

And hardely ne dredeth no pouerte
For I haue kyn and frendes els where
That though we comen in our bare sherte
Vs shulde neyther lacke golde ne geere
But ben honoured whyle we dwelten there
And go we anon/for as in myn entent
This is the beste/if that ye wol assent

Creseyde with a syghe/right in this wyse
Answerde: ywis my dere herte trewe
We may wel steale away/as ye deuyse
And fynden suche vnthrifty wayes newe
But afterwarde ful sore it wol vs rewe
And helpe me god so at my moste nede
As causelesse ye suffren al this drede

For thylke day that I for cherisshyng
Or drede of father/or for any other wight
Or for estate/delyte/or for weddyng
Be false to you/my Troylus my knight
Saturnus doughter Juno/throgh her might
As woode as Achamante do me dwell
Eternally with Stix in the pyt of hel

And this/ on euery god celestyal
I sweare it you/and eke on eche goddesse
On euery nymphe/ and deite infernall
On Satiry and Fauny more and lesse
That halue goddes ben of wyldernesse
And Attropos my threde of lyfe to breste
If I be false/ nowe trowe me if you leste

And

And thou Synoys/ that as an arowe clere
Through Troy rẽnest/ ay downward to yͤ see
Be wytnesse of this worde/ that sayd is here
That ylke day that I vntrewe be
To Troylus/ myn owne herte fre
That thou returne backwarde to thy well
And I with body and soule synke to hell

But that ye speke away thus for to go
And leten al your frendes/ god forbede
For any woman that ye shulden so
And namely sens Troy hath now suche nede
Of helpe/ and eke of o thyng taketh hede
If this were wyste/ my lyfe laye in balaunce
And yoʳ honour/ god shilde vs fro mischaũce

And if so be that peace herafter be take
As al day happeth after angre game
Why lorde the sorowe ⁊ wo ye wolden make
That ye ne durst come ayen for shame
And er that ye ieoparden so your name
Beth nat to hasty in this hotte fare
For hasty man ne wanteth neuer care

What trowe ye the people eke al aboute
Wolde of it say? it is ful lyght to arede
They wolden say/ and swere it out of doute
That loue ne draue you nat to done this dede
But luste volupTuous/ and cowarde drede
Thus were al loste ywis myn herte dere
Your honour/ whiche that nowe shyneth clere

And also thynketh on myn honeste
That floureth yet/ how foule I shuld it shēde
And with what fylthe it spotted shulde be
If in this forme I shulde with you wende
Ne though I lyued vnto the worldes ende
My name shulde I neuer ayenwarde wynne
Thus were I lost/ and yͭ were routh ⁊ synne

And forthy/ slee with reason al this hete
Men sayne the suffraunt ouercometh parde
Eke who so wol haue lefe/ he lefe mote lete
Thus maketh vertue of necessyte
By pacience/ and thynke that lorde is he
Of fortune aye/ that naught wol of her retche
And she ne daunteth no wight but a wretche.

And trusteth this/ that certes herte swete
Or Phebus suster/ Lucina the shene
The Lyon passe/ out of this Ariete
I wol ben here/ withouten any wene
I meane/ as helpe me Juno heuens quene
The tenthe day/ but if that dethe me assayle
I wol you sene/ withouten any fayle

And nowe so this be sothe (quod Troylus)
I shal wel suffre vnto the tenthe day
Sens that I se that nede it mote ben thus
But for the loue of god/ if it be may
So let vs stealen priuely away
For euer in one/ as for to lyue in reste
Myn herte saythe that it wol be the beste

O mercy god/ what lyfe is this (qd̄ she)
Alas/ ye slee me thus for very tene
I se wel nowe that ye mystrusten me
For by your wordes it is wel ysene
Nowe for the loue of Scythia the shene
Mistrust me nat thus causelesse for routhe
Sens to be true/ I haue you plight my trouth

And thynketh wel/ that somtyme it is wyt
To spende a tyme/ a tyme for to wynne
Ne parde lorne am I nat fro you yet
Though that we ben a day or two a twynne
Driue out tho fantasyes you withinne
And trusteth me/ and leaueth eke your sorowe
Or here my trouth/ I wol nat lyue tyl morow

For if ye wyste howe sore it dothe me smerte
Ye wolde cesse of this/ for god thou woste
The pure spyrit wepeth in myn herte
To sene you wepen/ whiche that I loue moste
And that I mote gone vnto the grekes hoste
Ye/ nere it that I wyste a remedye
To come ayen/ right here I wolde dye

But certes I am nat so nyce a wight
That I ne can ymagynen a way
To come ayen that day that I haue hyght
For who may holden a thing that wol away
My father naught/ for al his queynte play
And by my thrift/ my wendyng out of Troye
Another day shal turne vs al to ioye

O.o.iii. For

For thy with al myne herte I you beseke
If that you lyste done aught for my prayere
And for the loue whiche that I loue you eke
That er that I departe fro you here
That of so good a comforte and a chere
I maye you sene/ that ye may bring at rest
Myne herte/ whiche is at poynt to brest

And ouer al this I pray you (q̄d she) tho
Myne owne hertes sothfaste suffysaunce
Sithe I am thyne al hole withouten mo
That whyle that I am absent/no plesaunce
Of other/ do me fro your remembraunce
For I am euer agast/ for why men rede
That loue is thyng aye ful of besy drede.

For in this worlde there lyueth lady none
If that ye were untrewe/ as god defende
That so betrayed were/ or wo begone
As I/that al trouthe in you entende
And doutlesse/ if that iche other wende
I nere but deed/ and er ye cause fynde
For goddes loue/so beth me naught unkynde

To this answered Troylus/and seyde
Now god/to whom there nys no cause ywrie
Me glade/ as wys I neuer unto Creseyde
Sithe thylke day I sawe her first with eye
Was false/ ne neuer shal tyl that I dye
At shorte wordes/ wel ye may me leue
I can no more/ it shal be founde at preue

Graunt mercy good hert myne ywis (q̄d she)
And blysful Venus lette me neuer sterue
Er I may stonde of plesaunce in degre
To quyte hym wel/ that so wel can deserue
And whyle that god my wyt wyl me conserue
I shal so done/so trewe I haue you founde
That aye honour to me warde shal rebounde

For trusteth wel/that your estate royal
Ne veyne delyte/nor onely worthynesse
Of you in werre or turnay marcial
Ne pompe/array/nobley/or eke rychesse
Ne made me to rewe on your distresse
But moral vertue/grounded upon trouthe
That was yͤ cause I first had on you routhe

Eke gentyl herte/and manhede that ye had
And that ye had (as me thought) in dispyte
Euery thyng that sowned in to bad
As rudenesse/and peoplysshe appetyte
And that your reason brydled your delyte
This made abouen euery creature
That I was yours/ and shal whyle I may dure

And this may length of yeres nat fordo
Ne remuable fortune deface
But Iupiter/that of his might may do
The sorouful to be glad/so yeue us grace
Er nyghtes ten/to meten in this place
So that it may your herte and myn suffyse
And fareth nowe wel/for tyme is that ye ryse

And after that they longe ypleyned had
And ofte ykyst/and strayte in armes folde
The day gan ryse/ and Troylus hym clad
And rufully his lady gan beholde
As he that felte dethes cares colde
And to her grace he gan hym recõmaunde
Where he was wo/ this holde I no demaunde

For mannes heed ymagynen ne can
Ne entendement consyder/ ne tonge tel
The cruel paynes of this sorouful man
That passen euery turment downe in hell
For whan he sawe that she ne myght dwell
Whiche that his soule out of his herte rente
Withouten more/out of the chambre he went.

¶ Explicit li. iiii. Et incipit li. v.

Aprochen gan the fatal destyne
That Ioues hath in disposytioun
And to you angry Parcas sustren thre
Cõmytteth to done execution
For whiche Creseyde muste out of the toun
And Troylus shal dwell forthe in pyne
Tyl Lachesis his threde no lenger twyne

The golde tressed Phebus hygh on lofte
Thryse had al with his beames clere
The snowes molte/and zephirus as ofte
Ybrought ayen the tendre leaues grene
Sens that the sonne of Ecuba the quene
Began to loue her first/for whom his sorowe
Was al/that she departe shulde a morowe

Ful

Ful redy was at prime Diomede
Creseyde unto the grekes hoste to leed
For sorowe of whiche/she felte her herte blede
As she that nyste what was best to reed
And trewly/as men in bokes reed
Men wyste never woman have the care
Ne was so lothe out of a towne to fare

This Troylus withouten rede or lore
As man that hath his joyes eke forlore
Was waytyng on his lady ever more
As she that was sothfast croppe and more
Of al his lust or joyes here tofore
But Troylus nowe farwel al thy joye
For shalt thou never sene her efte in Troye

Sothe is/that whyle he bode in this manere
He gan his wo ful manly for to hyde
That wel unneth it sene was in his chere
But at the yate there she shulde out ryde
With certayne folke he hoved her to abyde
So wo bygon/al wolde he nat him playne
That on his horse unneth he sate for payne

For ire he quoke/so gan his herte gnawe
Whan Diomede on horse gan him dyght
And sayd unto him selfe this lyke sawe
Alas (quod he) thus foule a wretchydnesse
Why suffre I it? why nyl I it redresse?
Were it nat bet atones for to dye
Than evermore in langour thus to crye?

Why nyl I make at ones ryche and poore
To have ynough to done er that she go?
Why nyl I bringe al Troye upon a roore?
Why nyl I sleen this Diomede also?
Why nyl I rather with a man or two
Steale her away? why wol I this endure?
Why nyl I helpen to myn owne cure?

But why he nolde done so fel a dede
That shal I sayne/& why him lyste it spare
He had in herte alway a maner drede
Leste that Creseyde/in rumour of this fare
Shuld have ben slayn/so this was al his care
And els certayne/as I sayd yore
He had it done/withouten wordes more

Creseyde whan she redy was to ryde
Ful sorowfully she syghed/and sayd alas
But forthe she mote/for aught ye may betyde
And forthe she rydeth ful sorowfully a paas
There is none other remedye in this caas
What wonder is/though that her sore smerte
Whan she forgothe her owne swete herte.

This Troylus in gyse of curtesye
With hauke on honde/& with an huge route
Of knyghtes/rode and dyd her companye
Passyng al the valey/ferre without
And ferther wolde have rydden out of doute
Ful fayne/and wo was him to gon so sone
But turne he muste/and it was eke to done

And right with that was Antenor ycome
Out of the grekes hoste/and every wight
Was of him glad/& sayd he was welcome
And Troylus/al nere his herte lyght
He payned him/with al his full myght
Him to withholde of wepyng at leste
And Antenor he kyste/and made feste

And therwithal he muste his leave take
And caste his eye upon her pytously
And nere he rode/his cause for to make
To take her by the honde al soberly
And lorde so she gan wepen tenderly
And he ful softe and slyghly gan her sey
Nowe holde your day/and do me nat to dey

With that his courser turned he aboute
With face pale/ and unto Diomede
No worde he spake/ne none of al his route
Of whiche the sonne of Tideus toke hede
As he that kouthe more than the crede
In suche a crafte/and by the rayne her hente
And Troylus to Troye/homwardes wente

This Diomede/that ladde her by the bridell
Whan that he sawe the folke of Troye away
Thought/al my labour shal nat ben on ydell
If that I may/for somwhat shal I say
For at the worste/it shorte may our way
I have herde say eke/tymes twyse twelve
He is a foole that wol foryete him selve

But

But nathelesse/this thought he wel ynough
That certainly I am aboute naught
If that I speke of loue/or make it tought
For doutelesse/if she haue in her thought
Him that I gesse/he may nat ben ybrought
So sone away/but I shal fynde a meane
That she nat yet wete shal what I meane

This Diomede/as he that coulde his gode
Whā this was don/ gan fallen forth in speche
Of this and that/and aske why she stode
In suche disease/ and gan her eke beseche
That if that he encreasen might or eche
With any thyng her ease/ that she sholde
Cōmaunde it him/and sayd he don it wolde

For trewly he swore her as a knyght
That ther nas thīg/ wᵗ which he mizt her plese
That he nolde don his payne/ & al his might
To don it/for to don her herte an ese
And prayde her she wolde her sorowe apese
And sayd/ ywis we grekes can haue ioye
To honouren you/as wel as folke of Troye

He sayd eke thus/I wot you thinketh straūge
No wonder is/for it is to you newe
Thacqueyntaunce of these troyans to chaūge
For folke of Grece/that ye neuer knewe
But wolde neuer god/but if as trewe
A greke ye shulde amonge vs al fynde
As any troyan is/and eke as kynde

And by cause I swore you right nowe
To ben your frende/and helply to my might
And for that more acqueyntaunce eke of you
Haue I had/than another straunger wyght
So fro this forthe/I pray you day & nyght
Cōmaundeth me/howe sore that me smerte
To done/al that may lyke vnto your herte

And that ye me wolde/ as your brother treate
And taketh nat my frendshyp in dispyte
And though your sorowes ben for thīges gret
Not I nat why/but out of more respyte
Myn herte hath for to amende it great delyte
And if I may your harmes nat redresse
I am right sory for your heuynesse

For though ye troyās/with vs grekes wrothe
Haue many a day ben:alway yet parde
O god of loue/in sothe we seruen bothe
And for the loue of god my lady free
Whom so ye hate/as bethe nat wroth with me
For trewly there can no wight you serue
That halfe so lothe your wrath wolde deserue

And nere it that we ben so nere the tent
Of Calcas/ whiche that sene vs bothe may
I wolde of this you tel al myne entent
But this ensealed tyl another day
Yeue me your honde/ I am and shal be aye
God helpe me so/ whyle yͭ my lyfe may dure
Your owne/ abouen euery creature

Thus said I neuer er nowe to woman borne
For god myne herte as wisely glade so
I loued neuer woman here beforne
As paramours/ ne neuer shal no mo
And for the loue of god be nat my foe
Al can I nat to you my lady dere
Complayne aright/ for I am yet to lere

And wōdreth nought myne owne lady bright
Though yͭ I speke of loue to you thus blyue
For I haue herde or this of many a wight
Hath loued thynge he neuer sawe his lyue
Eke I am nat of power for to stryue
Ayenst the god of Loue/but him obey
I wol alwaye/ and mercy I you prey

There beth so worthy knyghtes in this place
And ye so fayre/ that eueriche of hem al
Wol payne him to stonden in your grace
But myght me so fayre a grace fal
That ye me for your seruaunt wolde cal
So lowly/ne so trewly you serue
Nyl none of hem/ as I shal tyl I sterue

Creseyde vnto that purpose lyte answerde
As she that was with sorowe oppressed so
That in effecte she naught his tales herde
But here & there/ nowe here a worde or two
Her thought her sorouful herte brast a two
For whan she gan her father ferre espye
Wel nyghe downe of her horse she gan to sye

But

But nathelesse she thonketh Diomede
Of al his trauayle and his good chere
And that him lyste his frendeshyp to her bede
And she accepteth it in good manere
And wol do fayne that is him lefe and dere
And trusten him she wolde/ and wel she might
As sayd she/ and from her horse she alyght

Her father hath her in his armes nōme
And twēty tymes he kyste his doughter swete
And sayd: o dere doughter myn welcome
She said eke/ she was fayne with him to mete
And stode forthe muet/ mylde/ and mansuete
But here I leaue her with her father dwell
And forthe I wol of Troylus you tell

To Troye is come this woful Troylus
In sorowe abouen al sorowes smerte
With felon loke/ and face dispytous
Tho sodainly downe from his horse he sterte
And through his paleys with a swolne herte
To chambre he went/ of nothyng toke he hede
Ne none to him dare speke o worde for drede

And there his sorowes that he spared had
He yaue an issue large/ and dethe he cryde
And in his throwes/ frenetyke and mad
He curseth Juno/ Apollo/ and eke Cupide
He curseth Bachus/ Ceres/ and Cipride
His byrthe/ him selfe/ his fate/ and eke nature
And saue his lady/ euery creature

To bed he gothe/ and wepleth there ⁊ turneth
In furye/ as dothe he Ixion in hell
And in this wyse he nygh tyl day soiourneth
But tho began his herte alyte vnswell
Through teeres/ whiche that gōnen vp to well
And pitously he cryed vpon Creseyde
And to him selfe right thus he spake ⁊ seyde

Where is myn owne lady lefe and dere?
Where is her whyte brest/ where is it where?
Where ben her armes/ and her eyen clere
That yesterday this tyme with me were?
Nowe may I wepe alone many a teere
And graspe aboute I may/ but in this place
Saue a pylowe/ I fynde naught to embrace

How shal I don whan shal she come agayn?
I not alas/ why lette I her go?
As wolde god I had as tho be slayn
O herte myn Creseyde/ O swete fo
O lady myn/ that I loue and no mo
To whom for euer more myn herte I dowe
Se howe I dye/ ye nyl me nat rescowe

Who seeth you nowe/ my right lode sterre?
Who sytteth right nowe in your presence?
Who can comforten nowe your hertes werre
Nowe I am gon/ whom yeue ye audyence?
Who speketh for me right now in your absēce
Alas no wight/ and that is al my care
For wel wote I/ as yuel as I ye fare

Howe shulde I thus ten dayes ful endure
Whan I the first nyght haue al this tene
Howe shal she eke sorouful creature
For tendernesse/ howe shal she this susteine
Suche wo for me/ o pytous/ pale/ ⁊ grene
Shal ben your fresshe womanly face
For langour er ye turne vnto this place

And whan he fyl in any slombrynges
Anon begynne he shulde for to grone
And dreamen of the dredfullest thynges
That might ben/ as mete he were alone
In place horryble/ makyng aye his mone
Or meten that he was amonges all
His enemyes/ and in her hondes fall

And therwithal his body shulde sterte
And with the sterte al sodainly awake
And suche a tremour fele aboute his herte
That of the feare his body shulde quake
And therwithal he shulde a noyse make
And seme as though he shulde fall depe
From hygh alofte/ and than he wolde wepe

And rewen on him selfe so pitously
That wonder was to here his fantasye
Another tyme he shulde mightely
Comforte him selfe/ and sayne it was folye
So causelesse/ suche drede for to drie
And efte begyn his aspre sorowes newe
That euery man might on his paynes rewe

Who

Who coulde tel al/or fully discryue
His wo/his playnt/his langour/& his pyne
Nat al the men that han or ben on lyue
Thou reder mayste thy selfe ful wel deuyne
That suche a wo my wyt can nat desyne
On ydel for to write it shulde I swynke
Whan that my wyt is wery it to thynke

On heuen yet the sterres weren sene
Although ful pale ywoxen was the moone
And whyten gan the orizonte shene
Al eestwarde/as it is wonte to doone
And Phebus with his rosy carte soone
Gan after that to dresse him vp to fare
Whan Troylus hath sent after Pandare

This Pandare/that of al the day beforne
Ne might hym comen this Troylus to se
Al though he on his heed it had sworne
For with the kyng Priam alday was he
So that it lay nat in his lyberte
Nowhere to gon/but on the morowe he went
To Troylus/whan that he for him sent

For in his herte he coulde wel deuyne
That Troylus al night for sorowe woke
And that he wolde tel him of his pyne
This knewe he wel ynough without boke
For whiche to chambre streight yͭ way he toke
And Troylus tho soberly he grette
And on the bed ful sone he gan hym sette

My Pandarus (qd Troylus) the sorowe
Whiche that I drie/I may nat longe endure
I trowe I shal nat lyuen tyl to morowe
For whiche I wolde alwayes on auenture
To the deuysen of my sepulture
The forme/and of my mouable thou dispone
Right as the semeth best is for to done

But of the fyre and flambe funerall
In whiche my body brennen shal to glede
And of the feest and playes palestrall
At my vigyle/I pray the take good hede
That that be wel/and offre Mars my stede
My sworde/myn helme/& leue brother dere
My shelde to Pallas yeue/that shyneth clere

The poudre/i which min hert ibrēde shal turn
That pray I the thou take/and it conserue
In a vessell that men clepeth an vrne
Of golde/and to my lady that I serue
For loue of whome thus pytously I sterue
So yeue it her/and do me this plesaunce
To prayen her to kepe it for a remembraunce

For wel I fele by my malady
And by my dreames/nowe and yore ago
Al certainly/that I mote nedes dye
The oule eke/whiche that hyght Ascaphylo
Hath after me shright al these nightes two
And god Mercury/now of me woful wretche
The soule gyde/and whan the lyst it fetche

Pandare answerde/and sayd Troylus
My dere frende/as I haue tolde the yore
That it is folye for to sorowen thus
And causelesse/for whiche I can no more
But who so wol nat trowen rede ne lore
I can nat sene in him no remedye
But let him worchen with his fantasye

But Troylus I pray the tel me nowe
If that thou trowe er this that any wight
Hath loued paramours as wel as thou
Ye god wot/and fro many a worthy knyght
Hath his lady gon a fourtenyght
And he nat yet made halfe endele the fare
What nede is the to maken al this care?

Sens day by day thou mayste thy seluen se
That from his loue/or els from his wyfe
A man mote twynnen of necessyte
Ye/though he loue her as his owne lyfe
Yet nyl he with him selfe thus maken stryfe
For wel thou woste my leue brother dere
That alway frendes may nat ben yfere

Howe don this folke/yͭ sene her loues wedded
By frendes might/as it betydeth ful ofte
And sene hem in her spouses bed ybedded
God wote they take it wisely fayre and softe
For why/good hope halt vp her herte a lofte
And for they can a tyme of sorowe endure
As tyme hem hurteth/a tyme dothe hem cure

So

So shuldest thou endure/and letten slyde
The tyme/and fonde to ben glad and lyght
Ten dayes nys nat so longe to abyde
And sens she to comen the hath behyght
She nyl her heste breken for no wyght
For drede the nat/that she nyl fynde way
To come ayen/my lyfe that durst I lay

Thy sweuenes eke/and al suche fantasye
Driue out/and let hem faren to mischaunce
For they procede of thy melancolye
That dothe the fele in slepe al this penaunce
A strawe for al swenenes signyfiaunce
God helpe me so/I counte hem nat a beene
Ther wot no man aright what dremes meene

For preestes of the temple tellen this
That dreames ben the reuelations
Of goddes/and als wel they tell ywis
That they ben infernales illusyons
And leches sayne/that of complections
Proceden they of faste/or glotonye
Who wot in sothe thus what they signyfye

Eke other sayne/that through impressyons
As if a wight hath faste a thyng in mynde
That therof cometh suche auysions
And other sayne/as they in bokes fynde
That after tymes of the yere by kynde
Men dreame/& that theffect gothe by ye moone
But leue no dreame/for it is nat to doone

Wel worthe of dremes aye these olde wyues
And trewly eke/augurye of these foules
For feare of which/men wenen lese her lyues
As rauens qualm/or schrichyng of these oules
To trowen on it/bothe false and foule is
Alas alas/that so noble a creature
As is a man/shulde drede suche ordure

For whiche with al myn herte I the beseche
Vnto thy selfe/that al this thou foryeue
And ryse nowe vp/withouten more speche
And let vs cast howe forth may best be driuen
The tyme/& eke howe fresshly we may lyuen
Whan she cometh/the which shal be right sone
God helpe me so/the beste is thus to done

Ryse/let vs speke of lusty lyfe in Troye
That we haue lad/and forthe the tyme driue
And eke of tyme comyng vs reioye
That bringen shal our blysse nowe so blyue
And langour of these twyse dayes fyue
We shal therwith so foryet or oppresse
That wel vnneth it don shal vs duresse

This towne is ful of lordes al aboute
And truce lasten al this meane whyle
Go we playen vs in some lusty route
To Sarpedon/nat hence but a myle
And thus thou shalte the tyme wel begyle
And driue it forth/vnto that blyssful morowe
That thou her se/that cause is of thy sorowe

Nowe ryse my dere brother Troylus
For certes it non honour is to the
To wepe/and in thy bedde to rouken thus
For trewly of o thyng trust to me
If thou thus lygge/a day/two or thre
The folke wol wene/that thou for cowardyse
The faynest sycke/& that thou darste nat ryse

This Troylus answerde: o brother dere
This knowen folke that haue ysuffred payne
That though he wepe/& make sorouful chere
That feleth harme and smert in euery vayne
No wonder is/and though I euer playne
Or alway wepe/I am nothyng to blame
Sens ye I haue lost/the cause of al my game

But sens of fyne force I mote aryse
I shal aryse/as sone as euer I may
And god/to whom myn herte I sacrifyse
So sende vs hastely the tenthe day
For was there neuer foule so fayne of May
As I shal ben/whan that she cometh in Troy
That cause is of my turment and my ioy

But whyder is thy rede (quod Troylus)
That we may play vs best in al this toun
By god my counsayle is (quod Pandarus)
To ryde and play vs with kyng Sarpedoun
So longe of this they speken vp and doun
Tyl Troylus gan at the laste assente
To ryse/& forthe to Sarpedon they wente
This

This Sarpedon/as he that honourable
Was euer his lyue/and ful of hye prowesse
With al that might yserued ben on table
That deyntie was/al coste it great rychesse
He fedde hem day by day/that suche noblesse
As sayden bothe the moste and eke the leest
Was neuer er that day wyste at any feest

Nor in this worlde there is none instrument
Delycious/through wynde or touche on corde
As ferre as any wight hath euer ywent
That tonge tell/or herte may recorde
But at that feest/it nas wel herde recorde
Ne of ladyes eke so fayre a companye
On daunce er tho/was neuer ysene with eye

But what auayleth this to Troylus
That for his sorowe/nothyng of it rought
But euer in one/as herte pytous
Ful besily Creseyde his lady sought
On her was euer al that his herte thought
Nowe this nowe that/so faste ymagynyng
That glad iwys can hym no festyng

These ladyes eke/that at this feest ben
Sens that he sawe his lady was awey
It was his sorowe vpon hem for to seen
Or for to here on instrumentes pley
For she that of his herte hath the key
Was absent/lo this was his fantasye
That no wight shulde maken melodye

Nor there nas houre in al the day or nyght
Whan he was ther as no man might hym here
That he ne sayd/o louesom lady bright
Howe haue ye faren sens that ye were there
Welcome ywis myn owne lady dere
But welaway/al this nas but a mase
Fortune his houe/entended bet to glase

The letters eke/that she of olde tyme
Had him ysent/he wolde alone rede
An hundred sythe/atwyxt noone and prime
Refyguryng her shappe/& her womanhede
Within his herte/and euery worde and dede
That passed was/& thus he droue to an ende
The fourthe day/and sayd he wol wende

And sayd leue brother Pandarus
Intendest thou that we shal here bleue
Tyl Sarpedon wol forthe conueyen vs
Yet were it fayrer that we toke our leue
For goddes loue/let vs nowe sone at eue
Our leaue take/and homwarde let vs turne
For trewly I nyl nat thus soiourne

Pandare answerde/be we comen hyther
To fetchen fyre/and rennen home agayne
God helpe me so/I can nat tellen whyther
We might gone/if I shal sothly sayne
There any wight is of vs more fayne
Than Sarpedon/and if we hence hye
Thus sodainly/I holde it vilanye

Whan that we sayden we wolde bleue
With him a weke/and nowe thus sodainly
The fourthe day/to take of hym our leue
He wolde wondren on it trewly
Let vs holden forthe our purpose fermely
And sens that ye behyghten him to abyde
Holde forwarde nowe/& after let vs ryde

This Pandarus/with al pyne and wo
Made him to dwell/and at the wekes ende
Of Sarpedon they toke her leaue tho
And on her way they spedden hem to wende
(Quod Troylus) nowe lorde me grace sende
That I may fynde at myn home cõmyng
Creseyde comen/and therwith gan he synge

Ye haselwode thought this Pandare
And to him selfe ful softely he seyde
God wote refroyden may this hotte fare
Er Calkas sende Troylus Creseyde
But nathelesse he iaped thus and seyde
And swore ywis/his herte him wel behight
She wolde come/as sone as euer she might

Whan they vnto the palayes were ycomen
Of Troylus/they downe of horse alyght
And to yͤ chambre/her way haue they nomen
And vnto tyme that it gan to nyght
They speken of Creseyde the lady bright
And after this/whan hem bothe leste
They spedde hem fro the supper vnto reste

On

On morowe/ as sone as day began to clere
This Troylus gan of his slepe to abreyde
And to Pandarus/ his owne brother dere
For loue of god/ ful pitously he seyde
As go we sene the paleys of Creseyde
For sens we yet may haue no more feest
So let vs sene her paleys at the leest

And therwithal his meyne for to blende
A cause he fonde in towne for to go
And to Creseydes house they gan wende
But lorde this sely Troylus was wo
Hym thought his sorouful herte braste a two
For whan he sawe her doores sperred all
Wel nygh for sorowe adowne he gan to fal

Therwith whan he was ware/ a gan beholde
Howe shet was euery wyndowe of the place
As frost him thought his herte gan to colde
For whiche with chaunged dedly pale face
Withouten worde/ he forthe by gan to pace
And as god wolde/ he gan so faste ryde
That no wight of his countenaunce aspyde

Than sayd he thus: o paleys desolate
O house of houses/ whylom best yhight
O paleys empty and disconsolate
O thou lanterne/ of which queynt is the light
O paleys/ whylom day that nowe arte night
Wel oughtest thou to fall/ and I to dye
Sens she is went/ that wonte was vs to gye

O paleys/ whylom crowne of houses all
Enlumyned with sonne of al blysse
O rynge/ of whiche the rubie is out fall
O cause of wo/ that cause haste ben of blysse
Yet sens I may no bet/ fayne wolde I kysse
Thy colde doores/ durste I for this route
And farwel shryne/ of whiche the saynt is out

Therwith he caste on Pandarus his eye
With chaunged face/ and pytous to beholde
And whan he might his tyme aright aspye
Aye as he rode/ to Pandarus he tolde
His newe sorowe/ and eke his ioyes olde
So pitously/ and with so deed an hewe
That euery wight/ might on his sorowe rewe

Fro thence forthe he rydeth vp and downe
And euery thyng came him to remembraunce
As he rode forthe by the places of the towne
In whiche he whylom had al his plesaunce
Lo/ yonder sawe I myn owne lady daunce
And in that temple with her eyen clere
Me caught first my right lady dere

And yonder haue I herde ful lustely
My dere herte laugh/ and yonder play
Sawe I her ones eke ful blyssfully
And yonder ones to me gan she say
Nowe good swete/ loue me wel I pray
And yonde so goodly gan she me beholde
That to the dethe myn herte is to her holde

And at the corner in the yonder house
Herde I myn alderleuest lady dere
So womanly/ with voyce melodyouse
Syngen so wel/ so goodly and so clere
That in my soule yet me thynketh I here
The blyssful sowne/ and in that yonder place
My lady first me toke vnto her grace

Than thought he thus/ o blyssful lorde Cupide
Whan I the processe haue in memorie
Howe thou me haste weryed on euery syde
Men might a boke make of it lyke a storie
What nede is the to seke on me victorie
Sens I am thyn/ and holy at thy wyll
What ioye hast thou thyn owne folke to spyll

Wel haste thou lorde ywroke on me thyn yre
Thou mighty god/ and dredeful for to greue
Nowe mercy lorde/ thou woste wel I desyre
Thy grace moste/ of al lustes leue
And lyue and dye I wol in thy beleue
For whiche I ne aske in guerdon but a boone
That thou Creseyde ayen me sende soone

Distrayne her herte as faste to returne
As thou doest myn to longen her to se
Than wote I wel that she nyl nat soiourne
Nowe blyssful lorde/ so cruell thou ne be
Vnto the bloode of Troye/ I pray the
As Juno was vnto the bloode Thebane
For which ye folke of Thebes caught her bane

P.p. And

And after this he to the yates wente
There as Creseyde out rode/ a ful good paas
And vp & downe there made he many a wēte
And to him selfe ful ofte he sayd alas
Fro hence rode my blysse and my solas
As wolde blyssful god nowe for his ioye
I might her sene ayen come to Troye

And to the yonder hyll I gan her gyde
Alas/ and there I toke of her my leue
And yonde I sawe her to her father ryde
For sorowe of whiche myn herte shal to cleue
And hyther home I come whan it was eue
And here I dwell/ out caste from al ioye
And shal/ tyl I may sene her efte in Troye

And of him selfe ymagyned he ofte
To ben defayted/ pale/ and woxen lesse
Than he was wonte/ & that men sayden softe
What may it be? who can the sothe gesse
Why Troylus hath al this heuynesse
And al this nas but his melancolye
That he had of him selfe suche fantasye

Another tyme ymagynen he wolde
That euery wight that went by the wey
Had of him routhe/ & that they sayne sholde
I am right sory/ Troylus wol dey
And thus he droue a day yet forthe or tweye
As ye haue herde/ suche lyfe gan he lede
As he that stode bytwixen hope and drede

For whiche hym lyked in his songes shewe
Thencheson of his wo/ as he best might
And made a songe/ of wordes but a fewe
Somwhat his woful herte for to lyght
And whan he was from euery mannes sight
With softe voyce/ he of his lady dere
That absent was/ gan synge as ye may here

O sterre/ of whiche I lost haue al the lyght
With herte sore/ wel ought I to bewayle
That euer derke in turment/ nyght by nyght
Towarde my deth/ with wynde I stere & sayle
For whiche the tenthe nyght/ if that I fayle
The gydyng of thy beames bright an houre
My shyp and me Carybdes wol deuoure

This songe whan he thus songen had soone
He fyl ayen in to his syghes olde
And euery nyght/ as was his wonte to doone
He stode the bright moone to beholde
And al his sorowe he to the moone tolde
And sayd/ ywis whan thou arte horned newe
I shal be glad/ if al the worlde be trewe

I sawe thyn hornes olde eke by the morowe
Whan hence rode my right lady dere
That cause is of my turment and my sorowe
For whiche/ o bright Lucyna the clere
For loue of god ren faste aboute thy spere
For whan thyn hornes newe gynnen sprynge
Than shal she come yͭ may my blysse brynge

The day is more/ and lenger euery nyght
Than they ben wonte to be/ him thought tho
And that the sonne went his course vnright
By lenger way than it was wonte to go
And sayd/ ywis I drede me euer mo
The Sonnes sonne Pheton be on lyue
And that his fathers carte amysse he driue

Vpon the walles faste eke wolde he walke
And on the grekes hoste he wolde se
And to him selfe right thus he wolde talke
Lo/ yonder is myn owne lady free
Or els yonder/ there the tentes be
And thence cometh this ayre that is so soote
That in my soule I fele it dothe me boote

And hardly this wynde that more and more
Thus stoundmele encreaseth in my face
Is of my ladyes depe syghes sore
I preue it thus/ for in none other space
Of al this towne/ saue only in this place
Fele I no wynde/ that sowneth so lyke payne
It sayth alas/ why twynned be we twayne

This longe tyme he driueth forthe right thus
Tyl fully passed was the nynthe nyght
And aye besyde him was this Pandarus
That besyly dyd al his full myght
Him to comforte/ and make his herte lyght
Yeuyng him hope alway the tenthe morowe
That she shal comen/ & stynten al his sorowe

Vpon

Upon that other syde eke was Cresepde
With women fewe/ amonge the grekes strõge
For whiche ful ofte a day/ alas she seyde
That I was borne/ wel may myn hert longe
After my dethe/ for nowe lyue I to longe
Alas/ and I ne may it nat amende
For nowe is worse than euer yet I wende

My father nyl for nothyng do me grace
To gone ayen/ for aught I can him queme
And if so be/ that I my terme pace
My Troylus shal in his herte deme
That I am false/ & so it may wel seme
Thus shal I haue unthonke on euery syde
That I was borne so wel a way the tyde

And if that I me put in ieopardye
To steale away by night/ and it befall
That I be caught/ I shal be holde a spye
Or els lo/ this drede I moste of all
If in the hondes of some wretche I fall
I nam but loste/ al be myn herte trewe
Nowe mighty god/ thou on my sorowe rewe

Ful pale I woxen was her bright face
Her lymmes leane/ as she that al the day
Stode whan she durst/ & loked on the place
There she was borne/ and dwelt had aye
And al the nyght wepyng alas she lay
And thus dispayred out of al cure
She ladde her lyfe/ this woful creature

Ful ofte a day she syghed eke for distresse
And in her selfe she went aye purtrayeng
Of Troylus the great worthynesse
And al his goodly wordes recordyng
Sens first that day her loue began to spring
And thus she sette her woful herte a fyre
Through remembraũce of that she gan desyre

In al this worlde there nys so cruel herte
That her had herde complaynen in her sorow
That nolde haue wepten for her paynes smert
So tenderly she wepte/ bothe eue & morowe
Her neded no teeres for to borowe
And this was yet the worste of al her payne
Ther was no wi3t/ to whom she durst playne

Ful rewfully she loked upon Troye
Beheloe the toures hygh/ and eke the hallis
Alas (quod she) the plesaunce and the ioye
The whiche that nowe al turned in to gall is
Haue I had ofte/ within yonder wallis
O Troylus/ what doest thou nowe she seyde
Lord whether thou yet thynke upon Creseyde

Alas/ that I ne had ytrowed on your lore
And went with you/ as ye me redde er this
Than had I nowe nat syghed halfe so sore
Who might haue sayd/ that I had done amys
To steale away with suche one as he is
But al to late cometh the lectuary
Whan men the corse unto the graue carye

To late is nowe to speke of that matere
Prudence alas/ one of thyn eyen thre
Me lacked alway/ er that I came here
For on tyme passed wel remembred me
And present tyme eke coulde I wel se
But future tyme/ er I was in the snare
Coulde I nat sene/ that causeth now my care

But nathelesse/ betyde what betyde
I shal to morowe at nyght/ by est or west
Out of this host steale/ on some syde
And gone with Troylus/ where as him lest
This purpose wol I holde/ and this is þ best
No force of wicked tonges iangllerye
For euer on loue/ haue wretches had enuy

For who so wol of euery worde take hede
Or rulen him by euery wyghtes wyt
Ne shal he neuer thriuen out of drede
For that that some men blamen euer yet
Lo/ other maner folke comenden it
And as for me/ for al suche barpaunce
Felycite clepe I my suffysaunce

For whiche/ without any wordes mo
To Troy I wol/ as for conclusyoun
But god it wot/ er fully monthes two
She was ful ferre fro that entencioun
For bothe Troylus and Troye toun
Shal knotlesse throughout her herte slyde
For she wol take a purpose for to abyde

P.p.ii. This

This Diomede/ of whom you tel I gan
Gothe nowe within him selfe aye arguyng
With al the sleight and al that euer he can
Howe he maye best with shortest taryeng
In to his nette Creseydes herte bryng
To this entente he couthe neuer fyne
To fysshen her/ he sayde out hoke and lyne

But nathelesse/ wel in his herte he thought
That she nas nat without a loue in Troye
For neuer sithen he her thens brought
Ne couthe he sene her laugh/ or maken ioye
He nyst howe best her herte for tacoye
But for tassey/ he sayde naught it ne greueth
For he that naught assayeth nauȝt atcheueth

Yet sayd he to him selfe vpon a nyght
Nowe am I nat a fole/ that wote wel howe
Her wo is/ for loue of another wyght
And her vpon to gon assaye her nowe
I maye wel wete/ it nyl nat ben my prowe
For wyse folke in bookes it expresse
Men shal nat wowe a wight in heuynesse

But who so myght wynnen suche a floure
Fro him/ for whõ she mourneth night & daye
He myght sayne he were a conquerour
And right anone/ as he that bolde was aye
Thought in his hert/ happe howe happe may
Al shulde I dye/ I wol her hert seche
I shal no more lesen but my speche

This Diomede/ as bookes vs declare
Was in his nedes prest and coragious
With sterne voice/ & mighty lymmes square
Hardy/ testyfe/ stronge/ and cheualrous
Of dedes lyke his father Tydeus
And some men sayne/ he was of tonge large
And heire he was/ of Calcidony and Arge

Creseyde meane was of her stature
Therto of shappe/ of face/ and eke of chere
There myght ben no fayrer creature
And ofte tyme this was her manere
To gone ytressed with her heeres clere
Downe by her colere/ at her backe behynde
Which with a threde of golde she wolde bynde

And saue her browes ioyneden yfere
There nas no lacke/ in aught I can espyen
But for to speken of her eyen clere
Lo/ trewly they written that her seyen
That paradys stode formed in her eyen
And with her ryche beaute euer more
Stroue loue in her/ ay which of hẽ was more

She sobre was eke/ symple/ and wyse withal
The beste ynorisshed eke that might be
And goodly of her speche in general
Charytable/ estately/ lusty/ and fre
Ne neuer more ne lacked her pyte
Tendre herted/ slydyng of corage
But trewly I can nat tell her age

And Troylus wel woxen was in hyght
And complete formed by proporcioun
So wel/ that kynde it naught amẽden myght
Yonge/ fresshe/ stronge/ and hardy as lyoun
Trewe as stele/ in eche condycioun
One of the beste entetched creature
That is or shal/ whyle ẏ the worlde may dure

And certainly/ in story as I it fonde
That Troylus was neuer vnto no wight
As in his tyme/ in no degre seconde
In daryng do/ that longeth to a knyght
Al might a gyaunt passen him of myght
His herte aye with the first and with the beste
Stode peregal to dare done what him leste

But for to tellen forthe of Diomede
It fyl/ that after on the tenthe day
Sens that Creseyde out of the cyte yede
This Diomede/ as fressh as braũche in May
Came to the tente there as Calkas lay
And fayned him with Calkas haue to doone
But what he mente/ I shal you tellen soone

Creseyde at shorte wordes for to tell
Welcomed him/ & downe him by her sette
And he was ethe ynough to maken dwell
And after this/ withouten longe lette
The spyces and the wyne men forth hem fette
And forthe they speke of this and that yfere
As frendes done/ of whiche some shal ye here

He

He gan first fallen of the werre in speche
Betwyxen hem and the folke of Troye toun
And of thassiege he gan eke her beseche
To tellen him what was her opinyoun
Fro that demaunde he so discendeth doun
To asken her/if that her straunge thought
The grekes gyse/ ꝛ werkes that they wrought

And why her father taryeth so longe
To wedden her vnto some worthy wight
Creseyde that was in her paynes stronge
For loue of Troylus her owne knyght
So ferforthe as she connyng had or might
Answerde him tho/but as of his entente
It semed nat she wyste what he mente

But nathelesse this ylke Diomede
Gan on him selfe assure/ꝛ thus he seyde
If I aright haue taken on you hede
Me thynketh thus/o lady myn Creseyde
That sens I first honde on your bridel leyde
Whan ye out came of Troye by the morowe
Ne might I neuer sene you but in sorowe

I can nat sayne what may the cause be
But if for loue of some troyan it were
The whiche right sore wolde athynken me
That ye for any wight that dwelleth there
Shulden spyll a quarter of a teere
Or pitously your seluen so begyle
For dredelesse it is nat worthe the whyle

The folke of Troye/as who sayth al ꝛ some
In prison ben/as ye your seluen se
Fro thence shal nat one on lyue come
For al the golde atwyxen sonne and see
Trusteth wel/and vnderstondeth me
There shal nat one to mercy gone on lyue
Al were he lorde of worldes twyse fyue

Suche wreche on hem for fetching of Heleyne
There shal be take/er that we hence wende
That Maunes/ which ye goddes ben of peyne
Shal ben agast that grekes wol hem shende
And men shal drede vnto the worldes ende
From hence forthe/to rauysshen any quene
So cruel shal our wreche on hem be sene

And but if Calkas lede be with ambages
That is to sayne/ with double wordes slye
Such as men clepen a worde wt two visages
Ye shal wel knowen that I nat ne lye
And al this thyng right sene it with your eye
And that anon/ ye nyl nat trowe howe soone
Nowe taketh hede/for it is for to doone

What wene ye your wyse father wolde
Haue yeuen Antenor for you anon
If he ne wyste that the cyte shulde
Distroyed ben: why nay so mote I gone
He knewe ful wel there shal nat scapen one
That Troyan is/and for the great feere
He durste nat that ye dwelte lenger there

What wol ye more/ o louesom lady dere
Let Troye and troyans fro your herte pace
Driue out ye bytter hope/ ꝛ make good chere
And clepe ayen the beautie of your face
That ye with salte teeres so deface
For Troye is brought in suche a ieopardye
That it to saue is nowe no remedye

And thynketh wel/ye shal in grekes fynde
A more parfyte loue/er it be nyght
Than any troyan is/and more kynde
And bet to seruen you wol don his might
And if ye vouchsafe my lady bright
I wol ben he/to seruen you my selue
Ye leauer than be lorde of Greces twelue

And with that worde he gan to waxen reed
And in his speche/ a lytel whise he quoke
And caste asyde a lytel with his heed
And stynte a whyle/ and afterwarde he woke
And sobrely on her he threwe his loke
And sayd I am/al be it to you no ioye
As gentyl a man/as any wight in Troye

For if my father Tydeus/he seyde
Ilyued had/I had ben er this
Of Calcidony and Arge a kyng Creseyde
And so hope I that I shal be ywis
But he was slayne alas/the more harme is
Vnhappely at Thebes al to rathe
Polymyte/and many a man to scathe

But herte myne/ sithe that I am your man
And ben the first/ of whom I seche grace
To serue you as hertely as I can
And euer shal whyle I to lyue haue space
So that/ er I departe out of this place
Ye wol me graunt that I maye to morowe
At better layser tel you of my sorowe

What shulde I tel his wordes that he seyde
He spake ynough for o day at the mest
It preueth wel he spake so/ that Creseyde
Graunted on the morowe at his request
For to speke with him at the leest
So that he nolde speke of suche matere
And thus she to him sayd/ as ye mowe here

As she that had her herte on Troylus
So fast/ that there may it none arace
And straungely she spake/ and sayd thus
O Diomede/ I loue that ylke place
There I was borne/ and Ioues for thy grace
Delyuer it soone of al that dothe it care
God for thy myght so leue it wel to fare

That grekes wold her wrath on Troy wreke
If that they myght I knowe it wel ywis
But it shal naught befallen as ye speke
And god to forne/ and farther ouer this
I wote my father wyse and redy is
And that he me hath bought/ as ye me tolde
So dere I am the more vnto him holde

That grekes ben of high conditioun
I wotte eke wel/ but certayne men shal fynde
As worthy folke within Troy toun
As connyng/ as parfyte/ and as kynde
As ben betwyxt Orcades and Inde
And that ye coude wel your lady serue
I trowe eke wel/ her thonke for to deserue

But as to speke of loue/ ywis she seyde
I had a lorde/ to whom I wedded was
The whose myn herte was al tyl he deyde
And other loue/ as helpe me nowe Pallas
There in myn herte nys/ ne neuer was
And that ye ben of noble and hygh kynrede
I haue wel herde it tellen out of drede

And that dothe me to haue so great a wonder
That ye wol scornen any woman so
Eke god wote/ loue and I ben fer asonder
I am disposed bet so mote I go
Vnto my dethe playne and make wo
What I shal after done/ I can nat say
But trewly as yet me lyst nat play

Myn herte is nowe in trybulatioun
And ye in armes besy day by day
Herafter whan ye wonnen haue the toun
Perauenture than/ so it happen may
That whan I se that I neuer ere say
Than wol I werke that I neuer ere wrought
This worde to you ynough suffysen ought

To morowe eke wol I speken with you fayne
So that ye touchen naught of this matere
And whan you lyst/ ye may come here agayn
And er ye gon/ thus moche I say you here
As helpe me Pallas/ with her heeres clere
If that I shulde of any greke haue routhe
It shulde be your seluen by my trouthe

I say nat therfore that I wol you loue
Ne say nat nay/ but in conclusyoun
I meane wel by god that syt aboue
And therwithal she caste her eyen doun
And gan to sigh & said/ Troilus & Troy toun
Yet bydde I god/ in quyete and in reste
I may you sene/ or do myn herte breste

But in effecte/ and shortly for to saye
This Diomede al fresshly newe agayne
Gan preasen on/ and faste her mercy praye
And after this the sothe for to sayne
Her gloue he toke/ of whiche he was ful fayne
And fynally/ whan it was woxen eue
And al was wel/ he rose and toke his leue

The bright Venus folowed and aye taught
The way there brode Phebus downe alight
And Cythera her chare horse ouer raught
To whirle out of the lyon/ if she might
And Signifer his candels sheweth bright
Whan that Creseyde vnto her bedde wente
Within her fathers fayre bright tente

Retur

Retournyng in her soule aye vp and downe
The wordes of this sodayne Diomede
His great estate/and peryl of the towne
And that she was alone/and had nede
Of frendes helpe/and thus began to brede
The cause why/the sothe for to tell
She toke fully purpose for to dwell

The morowe came/ and goostly for to speke
This Diomede is come vnto Creseyde
And shortly/leste that ye my tale breke
So wel he for him selfe spake and seyde
That al her syghes sore/downe he leyde
And fynally/the sothe for to sayne
He lefte her the great of al her payne

And after this/the storye telleth vs
That she him yaue the fayre baye stede
The whiche she ones wan of Troylus
And eke a broche (and that was lytel nede)
That Troylus was/she yaue this Diomede
And eke the bet from sorowe him to rescue
She made him weare a pencell of her sleue

I fynde eke in stories els where
Whan through the body hurte was Diomede
Of Troylus/tho wepte she many a teere
Whan that she sawe his wyde woundes blede
And that she toke to kepen him good hede
And for to healen him of his smerte
Men sayne/I not/ that she yaue him her herte

But trewly the storie telleth vs
There made neuer woman more wo
Than she/ whan that she falsed Troylus
She sayd alas/for nowe is clene ago
My name in trouthe of loue for euermo
For I haue falsed one the gentyllest
That euer was/ and one the worthyest

Alas/ of me vnto the worldes ende
Shal neyther ben ywritten nor ysonge
No good worde/for these bokes wol me shēde
Irolled shal I ben on many a tonge
Throughout ẏ worlde/my bell shal be ronge
And women moste wol hate me of all
Alas/ that suche a caas me shulde fal

They wol sayne/in as moche as in me is
I haue hem done dishonour welaway
Al be I nat the first that dyd amys
What helpeth that/to don my blame away
But sens I se there is no better way
And that to late is nowe for me to rewe
To Diomede I wol algate be trewe

But Troylus/ sens I no better may
And sens that thus departen ye and I
Yet pray I god so yeue you right good day
As for the gentyllest knyght trewly
That euer I sawe/to seruen faythfully
And best can aye his ladyes honour kepe
And with that worde she braste anon to wepe

And certes you ne haten shal I neuer
And frendes loue/that shal ye haue of me
And my good worde/al shulde I lyuen euer
And trewly I wolde right sorie be
For to sene you in aduersyte
And gyltlesse I wote wel I you leue
And al shal passe/and thus take I my leue

But trewly howe longe it was bytwene
That she forsoke him for this Diomede
There is none auctour telleth it I wene
Take euery man nowe to his bokes hede
He shal no terme fynden/out of drede
For though that he began to wowe her soone
Er he her wan/yet was there more to done

Ne me ne lyste this sely woman chyde
Ferther than the storie wol deuyse
Her name alas/is publysshed so wyde
That for her gylte it ought ynough suffyse
And if I might excuse her in any wyse
For she so sory was for her vntrouthe
Iwys I wolde excuse her yet for routhe

This Troylus/ as I before haue tolde
Thus driueth forth/as wel as he hath myght
But ofte was his herte hote and colde
And namely that ylke nynthe nyght
Whiche on the morowe she had him behyght
To come ayen/god wote ful lytel reste
Had he that nyght/nothyng to slepe him leste

The

The laurer crowned Phebus/ with his heate
Gan in his course aye vpwarde as he wente
To warmen of the eest see the waues weate
And Lyrees doughter songe/ with fressh entēt
Whan Troylus his Pandare after sente
And on the walles of the towne they pleyde
To loke/ if they can sene aught of Creseyde

Tyl it was noone/they stoden for to se
Who that there came/and euery maner wight
That came fro ferre/they sayden it was she
Tyl that they coulden knowen him aright
Nowe was his herte dull/nowe was it lyght
And thus beiaped stoden for to stare
Aboute naught/this Troylus ⁊ Pandare

To Pandarus/this Troylus tho seyde
For aught I wotte/before noone sykerly
In to this towne ne cometh nat here Creseyde
She hath ynough to done hardely
To wynnen from her father/so trowe I
Her olde father wol yet make her dyne
Er that she go/ god yeue his herte pyne

Pandarus answerd/it may wel ben certayne
And for thy let vs dyne/I the beseche
And after noone thā mayst thou come agayn
And whom they go/without more speche
And comen ayen/but longe may they seche
Er that they fynde that they after gape
Fortune hem bothe thynketh for to iape

(Quod Troylus) I se wel nowe that she
Is taryed with her olde father so
That er she come it wol nygh euen be
Come forthe/I wol vnto the yate go
These porters ben vnkonnyng euermo
And I wol done hem holden vp the yate
As naught ne were/al though she come late

The day gothe faste/⁊ after that came eue
And yet came nat to Troylus Creseyde
He loketh forthe by hedge/by tree/by greue
And ferre his heed ouer the wall he leyde
And at the laste he turned him/and seyde
By god I wote her meanyng nowe Pandare
Almoste ywis al newe was my care

Nowe doutelesse this lady can her goode
I wote she cometh rydyng priuely
I cōmende her wysdom by myn hoode
She wol nat maken people nycely
Gaure on her whan ẏ she cometh/ but softly
By nyght in to the town she thynketh ryde
And dere brother/ thynke nat longe to aūyde

We haue naught els for to don ywis
And Pandarus/nowe wylte thou trowen me
Haue here my trouthe I se her/ yonde she is
Heaue vp thyn eyen man/mayste thou nat se
Pandare answerde/nay so mote I the
Al wrōg by god/what sayst y^{u} mā wher art ?
That I se yonde/nys but a farre carte

Alas/thou sayest right sothe (qd Troylus)
But hardely it is nat al for nought
That in myn herte I nowe reioyce thus
It is ayenst some good/I haue a thought
Not I nat howe/but sens y^{t} I was wrought
Ne felte I suche a comfort dare I say
She cometh to night/my lyfe that durst I say

Pandarus answerde/it may be wel ynough
And helde with him/of al that euer he sayde
But in his herte he thought/and softe lough
And to him selfe ful soberly he sayde
From haselwodde/there ioly Robyn pleyde
Shal come al that thou abydest here
ye/ farwel al the snowe of ferne yere

The wardeyn of the yates gan to call
The folke/ which that without the yates were
And bade hem driuen in her beestes all
Or al the night they muste bleuen there
And ferre within the nyght/ with many a tere
This Troylus gan homwarde for to ryde
For wel he seeth it helpeth nat to a byde

But nathelesse he gladded him in this
He thought he misacounted had his day
And sayd/I vnderstonde haue al amys
For thylke night I laste Creseyde sey
She sayd I shal ben here/if that I may
Er that the moone/o dere herte swete
The Lyon passe/out of this Aryete

For

For whiche she may yet holde al her byheste
And on the morowe/ vnto the yate he wente
And vp and downe/ by west ⁊ eke by este
Vpon the walles made he many a wente
But al for naught/ his hope alway him blent
For whiche at nyght/ in sorowe ⁊ syghes sore
He wente him home/ withouten any more

This hope al clene out of his herte fledde
He ne hath wheron nowe lenger for to honge
But for yͤ payne him thought his herte bledde
So were his throwes sharpe/ ⁊ wonder strōg
For whan he sawe that she abode so longe
He nyste what he iudgen of it myght
Sens she hath broken that she him behyght

The thirde/ forthe/ fyfte/ and syxte day
After tho dayes ten/ of whiche I tolde
Betwyxen hope and drede his herte lay
Yet somwhat trustyng on her hestes olde
But whan he sawe she nolde her terme holde
He can nowe sene none other remedye
But for to shape him sone for to dye

Therwith the wicked spiryt/ god vs blesse
Whiche that men clepen woode ialousye
Gan in him crepe/ in al this heuynesse
For whiche bycause he wolde sone dye
He ne ete ne dronke for his melancolye
And eke from euery companye he fledde
This was the lyfe that al this tyme he ledde

He so defayte was/ that no maner man
Vnneth him myght knowen there he wente
So was he leane/ and therto pale and wan
And feble/ that he walketh by potente
And with his ire he thus him selfe shente
But who so asked him wherof him smerte
He sayd/ his harme was al aboute his herte

Priam ful ofte/ and eke his mother dere
His bretherne ⁊ his sustren gan him frayne
Why he so sorouful was in al his chere
And what thyng was yͤ cause of al his payne
But al for naught/ he nolde his cause playne
But sayd/ he felte a greuous maladye
Aboute his herte/ and fayne he wolde dye

So on a day he layde him downe to slepe
And so byfell that in slepe him thought
That in a forest faste he walked to wepe
For loue of her/ yͭ him these paynes wrought
And vp and downe/ as he that forest sought
He mette he sawe a bore/ with tuskes greate
That slept ayenst the bright sonnes heate

And by this bore/ faste in her armes folde
Lay kyssyng aye his lady bright Creseyde
For sorowe of whiche/ whan he it gan beholde
And for dispyte/ out of his slepe he breyde
And loude he cryed on Pandarus/ and seyde
O Pandarus/ nowe knowe I croppe ⁊ roote
I nam but deed/ there nys non other boote

My lady bright Creseyde hath me betrayde
In whom I trusted moste of any wight
She els where hath nowe her herte apayde
The blyssful goddes/ through her great might
Haue in my dreame yshewed it ful right
Thus in my dreme/ Creseyde haue I beholde
And al this thyng to Pandarus he tolde

O my Creseyde alas/ what subtylte?
What newe lust? what beaute? what science?
What wrathe of iuste cause haue ye to me?
What gylte of me? what fel experyence
Hath me rafte alas? thyn aduertence
O trust/ o faythe/ o depe assuraunce
Who hath me rafte Creseyde/ al my plesaūce

Alas/ why let I you from hence go?
For whiche wel nygh out of my wyt I breyde
Who shal nowe trowe on any othes mo?
God wote I wende/ o lady bright Creseyde
That euery worde was gospel that ye seyde
But who may bet begyle/ if him lyste
Than he on whom men wenen best to tryste

What shal I done/ my Pandarus alas?
I fele nowe so sharpe a newe payne
Sens that there is no remedye in this caas
That bet were it/ I with myn hondes twayne
My seluen slowe/ than alway thus to playne
For through yͤ deth my wo shuld haue an ende
Ther euery day with lyfe my selfe I shende

Pandare

Pandare answerde & sayd/ alas the whyle
That I was borne/haue I nat sayd er this
That dreames many a maner man begyle
And why? for folke expounden hem amys
Howe darste thou sayne that false thy lady is
For any dreame/right for thyn owne drede
Let be this thought/thou canst no dremes rede

Parauenture there thou dreamest of this bore
It may so be that it may signifye
Her father/whiche that olde is and eke hore
Ayen the sonne lythe on poynte to dye
And she for sorowe gynneth wepe and crye
And kysseth him/there he lythe on the groũde
Thus shuldest thou thy dreme ariȝt expoũde

Howe might I than done (quod Troylus)
To knowe of this/ye were it neuer so lyte
Now sayest thou wisely (qd this Pandarus)
My rede is this/sens thou canst wel endyte
That hastely a letter thou her write
Through which thou shalt wel bringen about
To knowe a sothe/of that thou arte in doute

And se nowe why? for this I dare wel sayne
That if so is/ that she vntrewe be
I can nat trowen that she wol write agayne
And if she write/thou shalt ful sone yse
As whether she hath any lyberte
To come ayen/or els in some clause
If she be let/she wol assigne a cause

Thou hast nat written to her sens yͭ she went
Nor she to the/and this I durste say
There may suche cause ben in her entente
That hardely thou woste thy seluen say
That her abode the best is for you tway
Nowe write her than/& thou shalt fele sone
A sothe of al/ there is no more to done

Acorded ben to this conclusyoun
And that anon/these ylke lordes two
And hastely sate Troylus adoun
And rolleth in his herte to and fro
Howe he may best discryuen her his wo
And to Creseyde his owne lady dere
He wrote right thus/ & sayd as ye may here.

¶ The copy of the letter.

Right fressh flour/whose I haue ben & shal
Withouten parte of els where seruyce
With herte/body/lyfe/lust/thought/and al
I woful wight/in euery humble wyse
That tonge can tell/or herte may deuyse
As ofte as mater occupyeth place
Me recõmaunde vnto your noble grace

Lyketh it you to weten swete herte
As ye wel knowe/howe longe tyme agon
That ye me left in aspre paynes smerte
Whan that ye went/of whiche yet bote non
Haue I non had/but euer worse bygon
Fro day to day am I/and so mote dwell
Whyle it you lyst/of wele and wo my well

For whiche to you/with dredeful herte trewe
I write/as he that sorowe driueth to write
My wo/that euery houre encreaseth newe
Complaynyng as I dare/ or can endyte
And that defaced is/that may ye wyte
The teares/ which that from myn eyen rayne
That wolden speke/ if yͭ they durste & playne

You first beseche I/ that your eyen clere
To loke on this defouled ye nat holde
And ouer al this/that ye my lady dere
Wol vouchesafe this letter to beholde
And by the cause eke of my cares colde
That sleeth my wyt/ if aught amys me sterte
Foryeue it me/myn owne swete herte

If any seruaunt durst or ought of right
Upon his lady pitously complayne
Than wene I that I ought be that wight
Cõsydred this/ that ye these monthes twayne
Haue taryed/there ye sayden sothe to sayne
But ten dayes ye nolde in hoste soiourne
But in two monthes/yet ye nat retourne

But for as moche/as me mote nedes lyke
Al that you lyst/I dare nat playne more
But humbly/with sorouful syghes syke
You write I myn vnresty sorowes sore
Fro day to day/desyring euer more
To knowen fully/if your wyl it were
Howe ye haue fared and don while ye be there

The

Whose welfare and heale eke god encrease
In honour suche/ that vpwarde in degree
It growe alwaye/ so that it neuer cease
Right as your herte aye can my lady free
Deuyse/ I pray to god so mote it be
And graunt it that ye soone vpon me rewe
As wisely as in al I am to you trewe

And if you lyketh knowen of the fare
Of me/ whose wo ther may no wyzt discryue
I can no more/ but chest of euery care
At wrytyng of this letter I was on lyue
Al redy out my woful gost to dryue
Whiche I delay/ and holde him yet in honde
Vpon the syght of mater of your sonde

Myne eyen two in vayne/ with whiche I se
Of sorouful teares salte arn woxen welles
My songe in playnt of myne aduersyte
My good in harm/ myn ease eke woxen hel is
My ioye in wo/ I can sey nowe nought elles
But turned is/ for whiche my lyfe I wary
Euery ioye or ease in his contrary

Which with your comyng home ayen to Troy
Ye may redresse/ and more a thousande sythe
Than euer I had encressen in me ioy
For was there neuer herte yet so blythe
To haue his lyfe/ as I shal ben as swythe
As I you se/ and though no maner routhe
Can meuen you/ yet thynketh on your trouth

And if so be my gylte hath dethe deserued
Or if you lyst no more vpon me se
In guerdon yet of that I haue you serued
Beseche I you/ myn owne lady fre
That hervpon ye wolden write me
For loue of god/ my right lode sterre
That deth may make an ende of al my werre

If other cause aught doth you for to dwell
That with your letter ye may me recomforte
For though to me your absence is an hell
With pacience I wol my wo comforte
And with your lettre of hope I wol disporte
Nowe writeth swete/ & let me thus nat playne
With hope or dethe/ delyuereth me fro payne

Iwys myn owne dere herte trewe
I wote that whan ye next vpon me se
So loste haue I myn heale/ & eke myn hewe
Creseyde shal nat conne knowen me
Iwys myn hertes day/ my lady fre
So thursteth aye myn herte to beholde
Your beaute/ that vnneth my lyfe I holde

I say no more/ al haue I for to sey
To you wel more than I tell may
But whether that ye do me lyue or dey
Yet pray I god/ so yeue you right good day
And fareth wel goodly fayre fresshe may
As ye that lyfe or dethe me may comaunde
And to your trouthe aye I me recomaunde

With heale suche/ that but ye yeuen me
The same heale/ I shal non heale haue
In you lythe/ whan you lyst that it so be
The day in whiche me clothen shal my graue
And in you my lyfe/ in you might for to saue
Me fro disease of al paynes smerte
And fare nowe wel myn owne swete herte.

Le vostre T.

This lettre forthe was sent vnto Creseyde
Of whiche her answere in effecte was this
Ful pitously she wrote ayen/ and seyde
That also sone as she myght ywis
She wolde come/ & mende al that was amys
And fynally she wrote and sayd then
She wolde come/ ye/ but she nyste when

But in her letter made she suche feestes
That wonder was/ & swore she loued him best
Of whiche he founde but botomlesse byhestes
But Troylus thou mayst nowe est & west
Pype in an Iuy lefe if that the lest (chaunce
Thus gothe ye worlde/ god shylde vs fro mis-
And euery wight that meneth trouth auaunce

Encreasen gan the wo fro day to nyght
Of Troylus/ for taryeng of Creseyde
And lessen gan his hope and eke his myght
For which al downe he in his bedde him leyde
He ne ete/ dronke/ ne slept/ ne worde seyde
Imagynyng aye that she was vnkynde
For which wel nigh he wext out of his minde

This

This dreme/of which I tolde haue eke beforn
May neuer come out of his remembraunce
He thought aye wel/he had his lady lorne
And that Ioues/ of his purueyaunce
Hym shewed had in slepe the signyfiaunce
Of her vntrouth/and his disauenture
And that the bore was shewed him in fygure

For whiche he for Sybille his suster sente
That called was Cassandre eke al aboute
And al his dreame he tolde her er he stente
And her besought assoylen him the doute
Of the stronge bore/with tuskes stoute
And fynally/ within a lytel stounde
Cassandre him gan thus his dreame expoūde

She gan first smyle/and sayd o brother dere
If thou a sothe of this desyrest to knowe
Thou muste a fewe of olde stories here
To purpose howe that fortune ouerthrowe
Hath lordes olde/through which wᵗin a throw
Thou shalt this bore knowe/⁊ of what kynde
He comen is/as men in bookes fynde

Diane/whiche that wrothe was and in yre
For grekes wolde done her sacrifyce
Ne encens vpon her auter sette on fyre
She for that grekes gonne her so dispyse
Wrake her in a wonder cruel wyse
For with a bore/as great as oxe in stall
She made vp frete her corne and vynes all

To slee the bore was al the countrey reysed
Amonge whiche there came this bore to se
A mayde/one of this worlde the best ypraysed
And Meleager/lorde of that countre
He loued so this fresshe mayden fre
That with his manhode/er he wolde stente
This bore he slough/and her the heed he sente

Of whiche/as olde bokes tellen vs
There rose a conteke and a great enuye
And of this lorde discended Tideus
By lyne/or els olde bokes lye
But howe this Meleager gan to dye
Through his mother/wol I you nat tell
For al to longe it were for to dwell

She tolde eke howe Tideus/er she stente
Vnto the stronge cyte of Thebes
(To claymen kyngdom of the cyte) went
For his felawe dan Polimites
Of whiche the brother dan Ethiocles
Ful wrongfully of Thebes helde the strength
This tolde she by processe al by length

She tolde eke howe Hemonydes asterte
Whan Tydeus slough fyfty knightes stoute
She tolde eke al the prophesies by herte
And howe that seuen kynges with her route
Besiegeden the cyte al aboute
And of the holy serpent/and the well
And of the furyes al she gan him tell

Associat ꝓfugum/Tydeus prio Polimidem
Tidea legatum docet insidiasqȝ secundis
Tertius Hermodien canit et vates latitantes
Mors furie Leuine quito narrant et angues
Quartus habet reges ineuntes prelia septem
Archymon bustum/ sexto ludiqȝ leguntur
Dat Graios Thebes vatē septimus vmbris
Octauo cecidit Tideus spes vita pelagis
Ipomedon nono moritur/cum Parthonepeo
Fulmine ꝑcusso/ decimo Canapus superatur
Vndecimo sese perimunt ꝑ vulnera fratres
Arguiam flentem/narrat duodecimus ⁊ ignem.

Of Archimories buryeng/ and the playes
And how Amphiorax fyl through the groūde
Howe Tideus was slayne/lorde of Argeyes
And howe Hyppomedon in a lytel stounde
Was dreynte/ and deed Parthonepe of woūde
And also howe Campaneus the proude
With thōder dynte was slayne/ ẏ cryed loude

He gan eke tel him howe that eyther brother
Ethiocles and Polimites also
At a scarmysshe/ eche of hem slough other
And of Argyues wepyng and her mo
And howe ẏ town was brent she tolde eke tho
And tho discended downe from iestes olde
To Diomede/and thus she spake and tolde

This ylke bore betokeneth Diomede
Tideus sonne/that downe descended is
Fro

Fro Meleager / that made the bore to blede
And thy lady / where so she be ywis
This Diomede her herte hath / and she his
Wepe if thou wolte or leave / for out of doute
This Diomede is in / and thou arte oute

Thou sayest nat soth (qd he) thou sorceresse
With al thy false goste of prophecie
Thou wenest ben a great deuyneresse
Nowe seest thou nat this foole of fantasye
Paynen her on ladyes for to lye
Away (quod he) there Joues yeue the sorowe
Thou shalt be fals parauenture yet to morowe

As wel thou mightest lyen on good Alceste
That was of creatures (but men lye)
That euer weren / kyndest and the beste
For whan her husbonde was in ieopardye
To dye him selfe / but if she wolde dye
She chese for him to dye / and gon to hell
And starfe anon / as us the bokes tell

Cassandre gothe / and he with cruell herte
Foryate his wo / for angre of her speche
And from his bedde al sodainly he sterte
As though al hole him had ymade a leche
And day by day he gan enquire and seche
A sothe of this / with al his ful cure
And thus he driueth forthe his auenture

Fortune / whiche that permutacion
Of thynges hath / as it is her cōmytted
Through pururyaunce and disposycion
Of hygh Joue / as reignes shal ben flytted
Fro folke i folke / or whā they shal ben smytted
Gan pull away the fethers bright of Troye
Fro day to day / tyl they ben bare of ioye

Amonge al this / the fyne of the ieoperdy
Of Hector gan approchen wonder blyue
The fate wolde his soule shulde unbodye
And shapen had a meane it out to driue
Ayenst whiche fate him helpeth nat to stryue
But on a day to fyghten gan he wende
At whiche alas / he caught his lyues ende

For whiche me thynketh euery maner wight
That haunteth armes / ought to bewayle
The dethe of him that was so noble a knyght
For as he drough a kyng by thauentayle
Unware of this / Achilles through the mayle
And through the body gan him for to ryue
And thus the worthy knight was refte of lyue

For whom as olde bookes tellen us
Was made such wo / that tonge it may nat tell
And namely the sorowe of Troylus
That next him was of worthynesse the well
And in this wo gan Troylus to dwell
That what for sorowe / loue / and for unreste
Ful ofte a day he bade his herte breste

But nathelesse / though he gan him dispayre
And dredde aye that his lady was untrewe
Yet aye on her his herte gan repayre
And as these louers done / he sought aye newe
To get ayen Creseyde bright of hewe
And in his herte he wente her excusyng
That Calkas caused al her taryeng

And ofte tyme he was in purpose greate
Him seluen lyke a pilgrym to disgyse
To sene her / but he may nat countrefeate
To ben unknowen of folke that weren wyse
Ne fynde excuse aright that may suffyse
If he amonge the grekes knowen were
For whiche he wept ful ofte many a tere

To her he wrote yet ofte tyme al newe
Ful pitously / he lefte it nat for slouthe
Besechyng her / sens that he was trewe
That she wol come ayen / & holde her trouthe
For whiche Creseyde upon a day for routhe
I take it so / touchyng al this matere
Wrote him ayen / and sayd as ye may here

¶ Cupides sonne / ensample of goodlyhede
O swerde of knyghthode / sours of gētylnesse
Howe might a wight in turment and in drede
And healelesse you sende / as yet gladnesse
I hertlesse / I sicke / I in distresse
Sens ye with me / nor I with you may deale
You neyther sende I herte may nor heale

Your letters ful the paper al ypleynted
Conceyued hath myn hertes pyte
I haue eke sene with teres al depaynted

Q.q. your

Your letter/and howe that ye requiren me
To come ayen/whiche yet ne may nat be
But why/leste that this lettre founden were
No mencion ne make I nowe for fere

Greuous to me (god wote) is your vnrest
your haste/and that the goddes ordynaunce
It semeth nat ye take it for the beste
Nor other thyng nys in your remembraunce
As thynketh me/but onely your plesaunce
But bethe nat wrothe/ and that I you beseche
For that I tary is al for wicked speche

For I haue herde wel more than I wende
Touchyng vs two/ how thinges haue ystõde
Whiche I shal with dissymulyng amende
And bethe nat wroth/I haue eke vnderstonde
Howe ye ne do but holden me in honde
But nowe no force/I can nat in you gesse
But al trouthe and al gentylnesse

Come I wol/but yet in suche disioynte
I stonde as now/that what yere/ or what day
That this shal be/that can I nat apoynte
But in effecte I pray you as I may
Of your good worde/& of your frendshyp ay
For trewly whyle that my lyfe may dure
As for a frende ye may in me assure

yet praye I you on yuel ye ne take
That it is shorte/whiche that I to you write
I dare nat there I am wel letters make
Ne neuer yet ne coulde I wel endyte
Eke great effecte men write in place lyte
Thentent is al/and nat the letters space
And fareth wel/god haue you in his grace.

La vostre C.

This Troylus thought this letter al straũge
Whan he it sawe/and sorowfully he syght
Him thought it lyke a kalendes of eschaunge
But fynally he ful ne trowen might
That she ne wolde him holden that she hyght
For with ful yuel wyll lyst him to leue
That loueth wel i such case though him greue

But nathelesse/men sayne that at the laste
For any thing/ men shal the sothe see
And suche a case betydde/and that as faste
That Troylus wel vnderstode that she
Nas nat so kynde/ as that her ought be
And fynally he wote nowe out of doute
That al is lost/ that he hath ben aboute

Stode on a day in his melancolye
This Troylus/and in suspectioun
Of her/ for whom he wende to dye
And so befyll/that throughout Troye toun
As was the gyse/ybore was vp and doun
A maner cote armure/as sayth the storie
Beforne Deiphebe/in signe of his victorie

The whiche cote/as telleth Lollius
Deiphebe it had rente fro Diomede
The same day/ and whan this Troylus
It sawe/he gan to taken of it hede
Auysyng of the length and of the brede
And al the werke/but as he gan beholde
Ful sodainly his herte gan to colde

As he that on the coler fonde within
A broche/ that he Creseyde yaue at morowe
That she from Troye muste nedes twyn
In remembraunce of him/ and of his sorowe
And she him layde ayen her faythe to borowe
To kepe it aye/but nowe ful wel he wyste
His lady nas no lenger on to tryste

He gothe him home/and gan ful sone sende
For Pandarus/and al this newe chaunce
And of this broche he tolde him worde & ende
Complaynyng of her hertes varyaunce
His longe loue/ his trouth/ and his penaunce
And after dethe/without wordes more
Ful faste he cryed/his reste him to restore

Than spake he thus/ O lady myn Creseyde
Where is your fayth / & where is your behest?
Wher is yo[r] loue/wher is your trouth he seyde
Of Diomede haue ye nowe al this feest?
Alas/I wolde haue trowed at the leest
That sens ye nolde in trouthe to me stonde
That ye thus nolde haue holden me in honde

Who shal nowe trowen on any othes mo?
Alas I neuer wolde haue wende er this
That ye Creseyde coulde haue chaunged so
Ne but I had agylte/and done amys

So cruel wende I nat your herte ywis
To slee me thus/alas your name of trouthe
Is nowe fordone/and that is al my routhe

Was there none other broche you lyst lete
To feste with your newe loue (quod he)
But thylke broche that I with teeres wete
You yaue/as for a remembraunce of me
None other cause alas/ ne had ye
But for dispyte/and eke for that ye mente
Al vtterly to shewen your entente

Through which I se/ y^t clene out of yor mynde
Ye haue me caste/and I ne can nor may
For al this worlde/ within myn herte fynde
To vnlouen you a quarter of a day
In cursed tyme I borne was weleaway
That you that done me al this wo endure
Yet loue I best of any creature

Nowe god (q^d he) me sende yet the grace
That I may meten with this Diomede
And trewly/if I haue might and space
Yet shal I make I hope his sydes blede
Nowe god (q^d he) that oughtest taken hede
To forthren trouthe/ and wronges to punyce
Why nylt thou don a vengeaunce of this vyce

O Pandarus/that in dremes for to tryste
Me blamed haste/& wonte arte ofte vpbreyde
Now mayste thou sene thy selfe/if that ye lyste
Howe trewe is nowe thy nece bright Creseyde
In sondry formes (god it wote) he seyde
The goddes shewen bothe ioye and tene
In slepe/and by my dreame it is nowe sene

And certainly/withouten more speche
From hence forthe/as ferforthe as I may
Myn owne dethe in armes wol I seche
I retche nat howe soone be the day
But trewly Creseyde/swete may
Whom I haue with al my might yserued
That ye thus done/I haue it nat deserued

This Pandarus/that al these thynges herde
And wyste wel he sayd a sothe of this
He nat a worde ayen to him answerde
For sory of his frendes sorowe he is
And shamed for his nece hath done amys
And stante astonyed of these causes tway
As styll as stone/ o worde ne coulde he say

But at the laste thus he spake/and seyde
My brother dere/I may do the no more
What shulde I sayne/I hate ywis Creseyde
And god it wote I wol hate her euermore
And that thou me besoughtest don of yore
Hauyng vnto myn honour ne my reste
Right no regarde/I dyd al that the leste

If I dyd aught/ that might lyken the
It is me lefe/and of this treason nowe
God wote that it a sorowe is to me
And dredelesse/for hertes ease of you
Right fayne I wold amende it/ wyst I howe
And fro this worlde/almighty god I pray
Delyuer her soone/I can no more say

Great was the sorowe & playnte of Troylus
But forthe her course fortune aye gan holde
Creseyde loueth the sonne of Tydeus
And Troylus mote wepe in cares colde
Suche is this worlde/who so it can beholde
In eche estate is lytel hertes reste
God leue vs to take it for the beste

In many cruell batayle out of drede
Of Troylus/this ylke noble knyght
(As men may in these olde bokes rede)
Was sene his knyghthod/& his great myght
And dredelesse his yre day and nyght
Ful cruelly the grekes aye abought
(And alway moste this Diomede) he sought

And ofte tyme (I fynde) that they mette
With bloody strokes/and with wordes greate
Assayeng howe her speares weren whette
And god it wote/with many a cruell heate
Gan Troylus vpon his helme to beate
But nathelesse/fortune it naught ne wolde
Of outher hande that eyther dyen shulde

And if I had ytaken for to write
The armes of this ylke worthy man
Than wolde I of his batayles endyte
And for that I to writen first began
Of his loue/I haue sayd as I can
His worthy dedes/who so lyste hem here
Rede Dares/he can tel hem al yfere

A. q. u. Let.

Besechyng every lady bright of hewe
And every gentyl woman/what she be
Al be it that Cresevde was untrewe
That for that gylte ye be nat wrothe with me
Ye may her gylt in other bokes se
And gladder I wol write/ if you lest
Penelopes trouthe/and good Alceste

Ne I say nat this al only for these men
But moste for women that betrayed be
Through fals folke/god yeve hē sorow amen
That with her great wyt and subtylte
Betrayen you/ and this meveth me
To speke/and in effecte you al I pray
Bethe ware of men/& herkeneth what I say

¶ Go lytel booke/go my lytel tregedye
There god thy maker yet er that I dye
So sende me might to make some comedye
But lytel boke/make thou none envye
But subiecte ben unto al poesye
And kysse the steppes/ wher as thou seest pace
Of Vergyl/Ovyde/Homer/Lucan/& Stace

And for there is so great dyversyte
In englysshe/and in writyng of our tonge
So pray I to god/that none miswrite the
Ne the mysse metre/for defaute of tonge
And redde where so thou be/or els songe
That thou be understonde/god I beseche
But yet to purpose of my rather speche

The wrathe/as I began you for to sey
Of Troylus/the grekes boughten dere
For thousandes his hondes maden dey
As he that was withouten any pere
Save in his tyme Hector as I can here
But welaway/save onely goddes wyll
Dispytously him slough the feirse Achyl

And whan that he was slayne in this manere
His lyght goste/ful blissfully is went
Up to the holownesse of the seventhe spere
In his place letyng everyche element
And there he sawe/ with ful avysement
The erratyke sterres/herkenyng armonye
With sownes ful of hevenysse melodye

And downe from thence/faste he gan avyse
This lytel spotte of erthe/ that with the see
Enbraced is/and fully gan dispyse
This wretched worlde/and helde al vanyte
To respecte of the playne felycite
That is in heven above/ and at the laste
Ther he was slayne/his loking down he caste

And in him selfe he lough/right at the wo
Of hem that wepten for his dethe so faste
And dampned al our werkes ȳ foloweth so
The blynde luste/ whiche that may nat laste
And shulden al our herte on heven caste
And forthe he went/shortly for to tell
There as Mercurie sorted him to dwell

Suche fyne hath lo / this Troylus for love
Suche fyne hath al his great worthynesse
Suche fyne hath his estate royal above
Such fyne his lust/such fyn hath his noblesse
Suche fyne hath false worldes brotelnesse
And thus began his lovyng of Creseyde
As I have tolde/and in this wyse he deyde

O yonge fresshe folkes/he or she
In whiche ȳ love up groweth with your age
Repayreth home from worldly vanyte
And of your hertes/up casteth the visage
To thylke god/that after his ymage
You made/and thynketh al nys but a fayre
This worlde ȳ passeth sone/ as floures fayre

And loveth him/the whiche that right for love
Upon a crosse our soules for to bey
First starfe & rose/and syt in heven above
For he nyl falsen no wight dare I sey
That wol his herte al holy on him ley
And sens he best to love is/and moste meke
What nedeth fayned loves for to seke

Lo here of paynems cursed olde rytes
Lo here what al her goddes may avayle
Lo here this wretched worldes appetytes
Lo here the fyne and guerdon for travayle
Of Iove/ Apollo/of Mars/ & suche rascayle
Lo here the forme of olde clerkes speche
In poetrye/if ye her bokes seche

O moral

O moral Gower / this boke I directe
To the / and to the Philosophical Strode
To vouchsafe there nede is to correcte
Of your benignytees and zeles goode
And to ŷ sothfast Christ that starfe on roode
With al myne herte / of mercy euer I pray
And to the lorde aright / thus I speke and say

Thou one / two / and thre / eterne on lyue
That raignest aye in thre / two / and one
Uncircumscript / and al mayst circumscryue
Us from visyble and inuysible fone
Defende / and to thy mercy euerichone
So make vs Jesus to thy mercy digne
For loue of mayde / and mother thyn benigne.

¶ Thus endeth the fyfth and laste booke of Troylus: and here foloweth the pyteful and dolorous testament of fayre Creseyde.

The testament of Creseyde

A Doly season tyl a careful dyte
Shulde corresponde / & be equiuolent
Ryȝt so it was whã I began to write
This tragedy / the weder right feruent
Whan Aries in myddes of the lent
Showres of hayle can fro the northe discẽde
That scantly fro the colde I myȝt me defende

yet neuertheles within myne orature
I stode / whan Tytan had his beames bright
Withdrawen downe / and scyled vnder cure
And fayre Uenus the beautie of the nyght
Upraysed / and sette vnto the west ful right
Her golden face in opposytiowne
Of god Phebus directe discendyng downe

Thrughout ŷ glasse her bemes brast so fayre
That I myght se on euery syde me by
The northern wynde had purifyed the ayre
And shedde his mysty cloudes fro the skye
The frost fresed / the blastes bytterly
Fro poole Artike come whiskyng loude & shyl
And caused me remoue ayenst my wyl

For I trusted that Uenus loues quene
To whom somtyme I hyght obedience
My faded herte of loue she wolde make grene
And therupon with humble reuerence
I thought to pray her hye magnifycence
But for great colde as than I letted was
And in my chambre to the fyre can pas

Though loue be hote / yet in a man of age
It kyndleth nat so soone as in youthheed
Of whom the blode is flowyng in a rage
And in the olde / the corage dul and deed
Of whiche the fyre outwarde is best remeed
To helpe by phisyke wher that nature fayled
I am experte / for bothe I haue assayled

I made the fyre and beaked me about
Than toke I drinke my spirites to conforte
And armed me wel fro the colde therout
To cutte the wynter nyght and make it shorte
I toke a queare / and lefte al other sporte
Written by worthy Chaucer glorious
Of fayre Creseyde / and lusty Troylus

And there I founde after that Dyomede
Receyued had that lady bright of hewe
Howe Troylus nere out of his wytte abrede
And wepte sore / with visage pale of hewe
For whiche wanhope his teares gan renewe
Whyle esperous reioysed hym agayne
Thus while in ioye he lyued & while in payne

Of her behest he had great comfortyng
Trustyng to Troy ŷ she wolde make retoure
Whiche he desyred most of al erthly thyng
For why she was his onely paramour
But whan he sawe passed bothe day & hour
Of her gayncome / in sorowe can oppresse
His woful herte / in care and heuynesse

Q.q.iii. Of

Of his distresse me nedeth nat reherse
For worthy Chaucer in that same boke
In goodly termes/ and in ioly verse
Compyled hath his cares who wyl loke
To breke my slepe another queare I toke
In whiche I founde the fatal desteny
Of fayre Creseyde/ whiche ended wretchedly

Who wot if al that Chaucer wrate was trewe
Nor I wotte nat if this narration
Be authorysed/ or forged of the newe
Of some poete by his inuention
Made to reporte the lamentation
And woful ende of this lusty Creseyde
And what distresse she was in or she deyde

Whan Diomede had al his appetyte
And more fulfylled of this fayre lady
Vpon another sette was al his delyte
And sende to her a lybel repudy
And her excluded fro his company
Than desolate she walked vp and downe
As some men sayne/ in the courte as cōmune

O fayre Creseyde/ the floure and a per se
Of Troy & Grece/ how were thou fortunate
To chaunge in fylthe al thy femynite
And be with fleshly luste so maculate
And go among the grekes early and late
So gyglotlyke/ takyng thy foule plesaunce
I haue pyte the shulde fal suche myschaunce

Yet neuerthelesse/ what euer men deme or say
In scornful langage of thy brutelnesse
I shal excuse/ as ferforth as I may
Thy womanhed/ thy wisedom and fairnesse
The whiche fortune hath put to such dystresse
As her pleased/ & nothyng through the gylte
Of the/ through wicked langage to be spylte

This fayre lady on this wyse destytute
Of al comforte and consolation
Right priuely without felowship or refute
Dissheuelde/ passed out of the town
A myle or two vnto a mansyoun
Bylded ful gay/ where her father Calcas
Whiche than amōg the grekes dwellyng was

Whan he her sawe/ the cause he can enquyre
Of her cōmyng/ she said sighyng ful sore
Fro Diomede had goten his desyre
He woxe wery and wolde of me no more
Mō Calcas doughter/ wepe thou nat therfore
Parauenture al cometh for the best
Welcome to me thou arte ful dere a gest

This olde Calcas/ after the lawe was tho
Was keper of the temple as a preest
In whiche Venus and her sonne Cupido
Were honoured/ and his chambre was nest
To whiche Creseyde with bale enewed ī brest
Vsed to passe/ her prayers for to say
Whyle at the laste vpon a solempne day

As custome was/ the people ferre and nere
Before the noone/ vnto the temple went
With sacrifyce/ deuout in their manere
But styl Creseyde heuy in her entent
In to the churche wolde nat her selfe present
For gyueng of the people any demyng
Of her expulse fro Diomede the kyng

But passed in to a secrete oratore
Where she myght wepe her woful desteny
Behynde her backe/ she closed fast the dore
And on her knees bare fel downe in hye
Vpon Venus and Cupyde angerly
She cryed out/ and sayd in this wyse
Alas that euer I made you sacrifyce

Ye gaue me ones a diuyne responsayle
That I shulde be the flour of loue in Troy
Nowe am I made an vnworthy outwayle
And al in care translated is my ioye
Who shal me gyde? who shal me nowe cōuoy
Sithe I fro Diomede/ and noble Troylus
Am clene excluded/ as abiecte odyous

O false Cupyde/ none is to wyte but thou
And thy mother of loue/ that blynde goddace
Ye caused me vnderstande alway and trowe
The seede of loue was sowen on my face
And ay grewe grene through yor souple grace
But now alas/ that seede with frost is slayne
And I fro louers lefte and al forlayne

Whan

The testament of Creseyde.

Whan this was sayd/ downe in an extasy
Rauysshed in spirte/ in a dreame she fel
And by apparaunce herde where she dyd lye
Cuppyde the kynge tynkyng a syluer bel
Whiche men myght here fro heuen in to hel
At whose sounde before Cuppyde aperes
The seuen planets discendyng fro their speres

Whiche hath power of al thyng generable
To rule and stere by their great influence
Weder and wynde/ and course variable
And first of al Saturne gaue his sentence
Whiche gaue to Cupide lytel reuerence
But as a boystous churle in his manere
Come crabbedly with austryne loke & chere

His face frounsed/ his lere was lyke the leed
His teth chattred/ and sheuered with the chyn
His eyen drouped hole sonken in his heed
Out at his nose the myldrop fast gan ryn
With lyppes blo/ and chekes leane and thyn
The yse yckels yt fro his heer downe honge
Was wonder great/ and as a speare as longe

Attour his belte his lyarte lockes lay
Feltred vnfayre/ ouerfret with frostes hoore
His garment and his gate ful gay of gray
His wyddred wede fro hi the wynde out wore
A boustous bowe within his honde he bor
Vnder his gyrdel a fasshe of felone flayns
Fedded with yse/ and heeded with holstayns

Than Jupiter right fayre and amyable
God of the sterres in the fyrmament
And nource to al thynge generable
Fro his father Saturne farre different
With burly face/ and browes bright & brent
Vpon his heed a garlonde wonders gay
Of floures fayre/ as it had ben in May

His voice was clere/ as christal was his eyen
As golden wyer so glyttryng was his heare
His garment and his gyte ful gay of grene
With golden lystes gylte on euery geare
A burly brande aboute his myddle he beare
In his right hande he had a grounden spere
Of his father/ the wrathe fro vs to bere

Nexte after him came Mars the god of yre
Of stryfe/ debate/ and al discentioun
To chide and fyght/ as feirse as any fyre
In harde harnesse hewmonde and habergioun
And on his haunch a rousty fel fauchoun
And in his hande he had a rousty sworde
Writhyng his face/ with many angry worde

Shakyng his brande/ before Cupide he come
With reed visage/ & grisely glowyng eyen
And at his mouthe a blubber stode of fome
Lyke to a boore/ whettyng his tuskes keyn
Right tulsure lyke/ but temperaunce in tene
An horne blewe with many boustous bragge
Which al this worlde wt warre hath made to
(wagge

Than faire Phebus/ lanterne & lãpe of light
Of man & beest/ bothe frute and florisshyng
Tender nource/ and banysshet of nyght
And of the worlde/ causyng by his mouyng
And influence/ lyfe in al erthly thyng
Without comforte of whom of force to nouzt
Must go dye/ that al this worlde hath wrouzt

As kyng royal/ he rode vpon a chare
The whiche Phiton somtyme gyded vnright
The brightnesse of his face whan it was bare
None myght beholde/ for persyng of his sight
This golden carte with firy beames bright
Foure yoked stedes ful different of hewe
But bayte or tyring through the speres drewe

The first was sorde/ wt mane as reed as rose
Called Eoye in to the orient
The seconde stede to name/ hight Ethiose
Whitely and pale/ and somdele ascendent
The thirde Perose/ right hote and eke feruent
The fourth was blacke/ called Philologee
Whiche rolleth Phebus downe in to the see

Venus was there present/ that goddes gay
Her sonnes quarel to defende and make
His owne complaynt/ cladde in a nyce aray
The one halfe grene/ thother halfe sable blake
White heer as golde/ kembet and shed a bake
But in her face semed great variaunce
Whyle parfite truth/ and whiles inconstaunce

Q.q.iiii. Vnder

The testament of Creseyde.

Under smylyng she was dissymulate
Prouocatyue with blynkes amorous
And sodaynly chaunged and alterate
Angry/ as any serpent venomous
Right pungitype with wordes odious
Thus variaunt she was who lyste take kepe
With one eye laugh/ and with the other wepe

In tokenyng that al fleshly paramour
Whiche Venus hath in rule and gouernaunce
Is somtyme swete/ somtyme bytter & sour
Right vnstable and ful of variaunce
Mynged with careful ioye and false plesaūce
Nowe hote now colde/now blyth/ now ful of
Now grene as lefe/ now wyddred & ago (wo

With boke in hande/than come Mercurious
Right eloquent and ful of rethorye
With polyte termes and delycious
With penne and ynke to reporte al redy
Settyng songes/ and syngyng merely
His hode was reed heled attour his crowne
Lyke tyl a poete of the olde fashyowne

Boyes he bare with fyne electuares
And sugred syropes for digestion
Spyces belongyng to the potiquares
With many holsome swete confectioun
Docter in phisyke cledde in a scarlet gown
And furred wele as suche one ought to be
Honest and good/ and nat a worde couth lye

Neyte after him come lady Synthia
The laste of al/ and swiftest in her spere
Of colour blake/ busked with hornes twa
And in the nyght she lysteth best tapere
Hawe as the leed/ of colour nothyng clere
For al the lyght she boroweth at her brother
Tytan/ for of her selfe she hath none other

Her gyte was gray and ful of spottes blake
And on her brest a chorle paynted ful euen
Bearyng a busshe of thornes on his bake
Which for his theft mizt clyme no ner ẏ heuen
Thus whan they gadred were ẏ goddes seuen
Mercurius they chosed with one assent
To be forespeker in the parlyment

Who had ben there and lykyng for to here
His faconde tonge/ and termes exquisyte
Of rethorike the practyke he might lere
In brefe sermon/ a preignant sentence write
Before Cupide valyng his cappe a lyte
Sper is the cause of that vacatioun
And he anon shewde his ententioun

Lo qd Cupide/ who wol blaspheme ẏ name
Of his owne god/ eyther in worde or dede
To al goddes he dothe bothe losse and shame
And shulde haue bytter paynes to his mede
I saye this by yonder wretche Creseyde
The which thrugh me was sōtyme flour of lo
Me & my mother she stately can reproue (ue

Sayeng of her great infelycite
I was the cause/ and my mother Venus
She called a blynde goddes and myght nat se
With sclaunder and defame iniurious
Thus her lyueng vnclene and lecherous
She wolde retorte in me and my mother
To whom I shewde my grace aboue al other

And sithe ye are al seuen deefycate
Participant of diuyne sapyence
This great iniure done to our hye estate
Me thike wt payne we shulde make recōpence
Was neuer to goddes done suche violence
As wel for you as for my selfe I say
Therfore go helpe to reuenge I you pray

Mercurius to Cupide gaue answere
And sayd/ sir kyng: my counsayle is that ye
Referre you to the hyest planet here
And take to him the lowest of degree
The payne of Creseyde for to modifye
As god Saturne with him take Synthia
I am content (qd he) to take they twa

Than thus proceded Saturne & the Moone
Whan they the mater ripely had degest
For the despite to Cupide that she had done
And to Venus open and manyfest
In al her lyfe with payne to be opprest
And tourment sore/ with sickenesse incurable
And to al louers be abhomynable

This

The testament of Creseyde.

This doleful sentēce Saturne toke on hande
And passed downe wher careful Creseyd lay
And on her heed he layde a frosty wande
Than laufully on this wyse can he say
Thy great fairnesse/ and al thy beauty gay
Thy wanton blode/ and eke thy golden heere
Here I exclude fro the for euermeere

I chaunge thy myrthe in to melancoly
Whiche is the mother of al pensyuenesse
Thy moyster and thy hete/ in to colde ⁊ dry
Thyne insolence/ thy play/ ⁊ thy wantōnesse
To great disease/ thy pompe and thy richesse
In to mortal nede and great penurite
Thou suffre shalte / and as a begger dye

O crewel Saturne/frowarde and angry
Harde is thy dome/ and to malycious
Of faire Creseyde/ why haste thou no mercy
Whiche was so swete/ gentyl/ and amorous
Withdrawe thy sentence and be gracious
As ỹ were neuer/so sheweth through thy dede
A wrekeful sentence gyuen on Creseyde

Than Synthia / whan Saturne past away
Out of her seate/ discended downe belyue
And reed a byl on Creseyde where she lay
Contaynyng this sentence diffynityue
Fro heale of body here I the depryue
And to thy syckenesse shalbe no recure
But in dolour thy dayes to endure

Thy christal eyen menged with blode I make
Thy voice so clere vnplesaunt heer and hace
Thy lusty lere ouerspred with spottes blake
And lumpes hawe appering in thy face
Where thou comest eche man shal flye ỹ place
Thus shalte ỹ go beggyng fro house to hous
With cuppe and clapper lyke a lazarous

This dooly dreame/ this vgly visyoun
Brought tyl an ende/ Creseyd fro it awoke
And al that courte and conuocatioun
Vanysshed away / than rose she vp and toke
A polysshed glasse/ ⁊ her shadowe couth loke
And whan she sawe her visage so deformate
If she in hert were wo/ I ne wyte god wate

Weppyng ful sore/ lo what it is (quod she)
With frowarde langage to moue ⁊ stere
Our crabbed goddes/ and so is sene on me
My blasphemyng now haue I bouzt ful dere
Al erthly ioye and myrthe I sette arere
Alas this day/ alas this woful tyde
Whan I began with my goddes to chyde

Be this was sayd/ a childe came fro the hal
To warne Creseyde the supper was redy
First knocked at the dore/ and efte couth cal
Madame/ your father byddeth you cōe in hye
He hath merueyle so long on groufe ye lye
And sayth your bedes bethe to longe somdele
The goddes wote al your entente ful wele

Quod she fayre chylde/ go to my father dere
And pray him come to speke with me anone
And so he dyd/ and sayd daughter what chere
Alas (quod she) father/ my myrthe is gone
Howe so (quod he) and she can al expone
As I haue tolde / the vengeaunce ⁊ the wrake
For her trespas/ Cupide on her couth take

He loked on her vgly lepers face
The whiche before was white as lely flour
Wringyng his handes/ oftymes sayd alace
That he had lyued to se that woful hour
For he knewe wel that there was no socour
To her syckenesse/ and that doubled his payne
Thus was ther care ynow betwyn hē twayne

Whan they togider mourned had ful lang
Quod Creseyde/ father I wolde nat be kende
Therfore in secrete wyse ye lette me gange
To yon hospital at the townes ende
And thider some meate for charite me sende
To lyue vpon/ for al myrthe in this erthe
Is fro me gone/ suche is my wicked werthe

Whan in a mantel / and a beuer hat
With cuppe and clapper wonder priuely
He opened a secrete gate and out therat
Conueyed her/ that no man shulde espy
There to a vyllage halfe a myle therby
Delyuered her in at the spyttel house
And dayly sende her parte of his almous

Some

The testament of Creseyde.

So knewe her wel & some had no knowlege
Of her / bicause she was so deformate
With byles blake ouerspred in her visage
And her fayre colour faded and alterate
yet they presumed for her hye regrate
And styl mournyng she was of noble kynne
With better wyl there they toke her inne

The day passed / and Phebus went to rest
The cloudes blake ouerheled al the skye
God wote if Creseyde were a sorouful gest
Seyng that vncouth fare and herborye
But meate or drinke she dressed her to lye
In a derke corner of the house alone
And on this wyse wepīg she made her mone

¶ Here foloweth the complaynt
of Creseyde.

O Soppe of sorowe sonken in to care
O caytife Creseyde nowe & euermare
Gone is thy ioye and al thy myrth in erthe
Of al blythnesse now arte thou blake & bare
There is no salue maye helpe thy sare
Fel is thy fortune / wicked is thy werthe
Thy blysse is banysshed and thy bale vnberd
Vnder the great god if I grauen ware
Wher men of Grece ne yet of Troy mizt herd

Where is thy chambre wantonly be sene
With burly bedde and bankers brouded bene
Spyces and wyne to thy colatioun
The cuppes al of golde and syluer shene
Thy swete meates serued in plates clene
With sauery sauce of a good facioun
Thy gay garmētes with many goodly goun
Thy plesaunt lawne pynned wt golden pene
Al is arere thy great royal renoun

Where is thy gardeyn with thy greces gay
And fresshe floures / whiche the quene Floray
Had paynted plesauntly in euery pane
Where thou were wonte ful merily in May
To walke / and take the dewe be it was day
And here the merle and maulyse many one
With ladies fayre in carollyng to gone
And se the royal renkes in their ray

This leper loge take for thy goodly bour
And for thy bedde / take nowe a bonch of stro
For wayled wyne and meates thou had tho
Take moulded breed / pirate / and syder sour
But cuppe and clapper nowe is al ago

My clere voice and my courtly carollyng
Is ranke as roke / ful hidous heer and hace
Deformed is the fygure of my face
To loke on it no pleople hath lykyng
Solped in syght / I say with sore sighyng
Lyeng among the leper folke alas.

O ladies fayre of Troy and Grece attende
My freyle fortune / myne infelycite
My great myschefe which no man can amēde
And in your mynde a myrrour make of me
As I am nowe parauenture that ye
For al your myght may cōe to the same ende
Or els worse if any worse may be
Beware therfore approches nere your ende

Nought is your fairnesse but a fadyng flour
Nouzt is your famous laude & hye honour
But wynde inflate in other mennes eares
your rosyng reed to rotyng shal retour
Example make of me in your memore
Whiche of such thīges / woful wytnesse beares
Al welth in erthe / as wynde away it weares
Beware therfore approcheth nere your hour

Thus chidyng with her drery destenye
Weppyng / she woke the nyght fro ende to ende
But al in vayne her dole / her careful cry
Might nat remedy / ne yet her mournīg mēde
A leper lady rose and to her wende
And sayd / why spurnes thou agayne the wal
To slee thy selfe / and mende nothyng at al

Sithe that thy weppyng but doubleth thy wo
I counsayle the make vertue of a nede
Go lerne to clappe thy clapper to and fro
And lerne after the lawe of lepers lede
Ther was no bote but forth with thā she yede
Fro place to place / while colde & hunger sore
Compelled her to be a ranke beggore

That-

The testament of Creseyde.

That same tyme of Troy the garnysoun
Whiche had the cheiftayne worthy Troylus
Through ieopdy of warre had stryken down
Knyghtes of Grece in nombre marueylous
With great tryumphe/ and laude victorious
Agayne to Troy right royally they rode
The way where Creseyde with the leper stode

Seyng that company come al with o steuyn
They gaue a crye / & shoke cuppes good spede
Worthy lordes/ for goddes loue of heuyn
To vs leper/ parte of your almesse dede
Than to her crye noble Troylus toke hede
Hauyng pyte / nere by the place gan pas
Wher Creseyde sat/nat wetyng what she was

Than vpon him she kest vp bothe her eyen
And with a blynke it come in tyl his thought
That he somtyme her face before had seyn
But she was i suche plyte he knewe her nouȝt
Yet than her loke in to his mynde he brought
The swete vysage/ and amorous blenkyng
Of fayre Creseyde/ sōtyme his owne derlyng

No wonder was/ suppose in mynde that he
Toke her fygure so soone/ and lo nowe why
The ydol of a thyng in case may be
So depe enprynted in the fantasy
That it deludeth the wyttes outwardly
And so appereth in forme and lyke estate
With in the mynde/ as it was fygurate

A sparke of loue than tyl his hert couth spr[illegible]g
And kyndeled his body in a fyre
With hote feuer/ in swette/ and trymblyng
Him toke/ whyle he was redy to expyre
To beare his shylde his brest begon to tyre
Within a whyle he chaunged many a hewe
And neuertheles nat one another knewe

For knightly pyte and memoriel
Of fayre Creseyde/ a gyrdel gan he take
A purse of golde/ and many a gay iewel
And in the skyrte of Creseyde down can shake
Than rode a way/ and nat a worde he spake
Pensyfe in herte whyle he came to the towne
And for great care oftsyth almost fel downe

The leper folke to Creseyde than couth drawe
To se the equal dystrybutioun
Of ye almous/ but whan the golde they sawe
Eche one to other priuely can rown
And sayd/ yon lorde hath more affectioun
Howe euer it be/ vnto yon lazarous
Than to vs al/ we knowe by his almous

What lorde is yon (qd she) haue ye no fele
That dothe to vs so great humanyte
Yes quod a leper man/ I knowe him wele
Sir Troylus it is/ a knyght gentyl and free
Whan Creseyde vnderstode that it was he
Styffer than stele there sterte a bytter stoūde
Thrughout her hert/ & fyl down to the groūde

Whan she ouercōe with syghyng sore & sadde
With many a careful crye and colde atone
Nowe is my brest with stormy stoūdes stadde
Wrapped in wo wretch ful wyl of one
Than fel in swoun ful ofte or she wolde fone
And euer in her swounyng cryed she thus
O false Creseyde/ & trewe knyght Troylus

Thy loue/ thy laude/ and al thy gentylnesse
I compted smal in my prosperite
So effated I was in wantonnesse
And clambe vpon the fyckel whele so hye
Al faythe and loue I promytted to the
Was in thy selfe fekel and furious
O false Creseyde/ & trewe knight Troylus

For loue of me thou keple countenaunce
Honest and chaste in conuersatioun
Of al women protectour and defence
Thou were/ and helped their opynioun
My mynde on flesshly foule affectioun
Was enclyned to lustes lecherous
Fye false Creseyde/ o trewe knyght Troylus

Louers beware/ and take good hede about
Whom that ye loue/ for whan ye suffre payne
I lette you wytte theris right fewe thrughout
Whō ye may trust to haue trewe loue agayne
Proue whan ye wol your labour is i vayne
Therfore I rede ye take them as ye fynde
For they are sadde as wedercocke in wynde

Bycause

Bycause I knowe the great unstablenesse
Brittel as glasse/ unto my selfe I say
Trustyng in other as great brutelnesse
As inconstaunt/ and as untrewe of faye
Though some be true/ I wot rizt fewe ar they
Who fyndeth truthe/ lette him his lady ruse
None but my selfe as nowe I wol accuse

Whan this was sayd/ with pay she sat down
And in this maner made her testament
Here I bequeth my corse and caryoun
With wormes and with toodes to be rent
My cuppe/ my clapper/ and myne ornament
And al my golde/ these leper folke shal haue
Whan I am deed/ to bury me in graue

This royal ryng sette with this Ruby reed
Whiche Troylus in dowry to me sende
To him agayne I leaue it whan I am deed
To make my careful dethe unto him kende
Thus I conclude shortely and make an ende
My spirite I leaue to Diane wher she dwelles
To walke with her in waste wodes ⁊ welles

O Diomede thou hast both broche ⁊ belte
Whiche Troylus gaue me in tokenyng
Of his trewe loue/ ⁊ with ẏ worde she swelte
And soone a leper man toke of the ryng
Than buryed her withouten taryeng
To Troylus forth with the rynge he bare
And of Creseyde the dethe he can declare

Whan he had herde her great infyrmite
Her legacy/ and lamentatioun
And howe she ended in suche pouerte
He swelte for wo and fel downe in a swoun
For sorowe his herte to brast was boun
Sigheng ful sadly sayde I can no more
She was untrewe/ and wo is me therfore

Sõe sayth he made a tombe of marble gray
And wrote her name and superscriptioun
And layde it on her graue where as she lay
In golden letters/ cõtaynyng this reasoun
Lo fayre ladyes / Creseyde of Troy the town
.Somtyme compted the flour of woman heed
Under this stone/ late leper lyeth deed

Nowe worthy women in this balade shorte
Made for your worshyp and instruction
Of charyte I monysshe and exhorte
Myngle nat your loue with false disception
Beare in your mynde this sore conclusyon
Of fayre Creseyde/ as I haue sayd before
Sithe she is deed/ I speke of her no more.

¶ Thus endeth the pyteful and dolorous testament of fayre Creseyde: and here foloweth the legende of good women.

The legende of good women.

A Thousãde tymes I haue herd: mẽ tel
That there is ioy ĩ heuen ⁊ payn ĩ hel
And I accorde it wele that it is so
But nathelesse yet wotte I wele also
That there nys non dwellyng in this countre
That eyther hath in heuen or in hel ybe
Ne maye of it none other wayes wytten
But as he herde sayd/ or founde it wrytten
For by assaye there may no man it preue
But god forbede/ but men shulde leue
Wel more thyng than they han sene with eye
Men shal nat wenen euery thyng a lye
But if him selfe it seeth/ or els it dothe
For god wote thyng is neuer the lesse sothe
Though euery wight ne may it nat ysee
Bernarde the Monke ne saugh al parde
Than mote we to bookes that we fynde
(Through whiche ẏ olde thynges ben ĩ mynde
And to the doctryne of these olde wyse)
Yeue credence/ in euery skylful wyse
That tellen of these olde appreued stories
Of holynesse/ of reignes/ of vyctories
Of loue/ of hate/ and other sondrye thynges
Of whiche I may nat make rehersynges
And if that olde bookes were away
Ylorne were of remembraunce the kay
Wel ought vs than/ honouren and beleue
These bokes/ there we han non other preue
And as for me/ though ẏ I can but lyte
On bookes for to rede I me delyte
And to hem yeue I faithe and ful credence
And in myne herte haue hem in reuerence
So hertely/ that there is game none
That fro my bookes maketh me to gone
But it be seldome on the holyday
Saue certaynly/ whan ẏ the month of May
Is comen/ and that I here the foules synge
And that the floures gynnen for to sprynge
Farwel my booke/ and my deuotioun
Nowe haue I than eke this condytioun
That of al the floures in the meede
Than loue I most these floures whyte ⁊ reed
Such ẏ men callen Dayesies in our toun
To hem haue I so great affectioun
As I sayd erst/ whan comen is the May
That in my bedde there daweth me no day
That I nam vp/ and walkyng in the meede
To seen this flour ayenst the sonne sprede
Whan it vp ryseth early by the morowe
That blyssful syght softneth al my sorowe
So gladde am I/ whan that I haue presence
Of it/ to done it al reuerence
As she that is of al floures floure
Fulfylled of al vertue and honoure
And euer ylyke fayre/ and fresshe of hewe
And euer I loue it/ and euer ylyke newe
And euer shal/ tyl that myne herte dye
Al swere I nat of this/ I wol nat lye
There loued no wight hotter in his lyue
And whan that it is eue I renne blythe
Assoone as euer the sonne gynneth west
To sene this flour/ howe it wol go to rest
For feare of nyght/ so hateth she derknesse
Her chere is playnly spred in the brightnesse
Of the sonne/ for there it wol vnclose
Alas that I ne had Englyssh/ ryme/ or prose
Suffysaunt/ this floure to preyse aright
But helpeth ye/ that han connyng and might
Ye louers that can make of sentement
In this case ought ye be dilygent
To forthren me somwhat in my labour
Whether ye ben with the lefe or with the flour
For wel I wote/ that ye han here beforne
Of makyng/ ropen/ and lad away the corne
And I come after/ glenyng here and there
And am ful gladde/ if I may fynde an ere
Of any goodly worde that ye han lefte
And though it happen me to rehersen efte
That ye han in your fresshe songes sayde
Forbereth me/ and beth nat yuel apayde
Sithe that ye se/ I do it in the honour
Of Loue: and eke in seruyce of the flour
Whom that I serue/ as I haue wyt or might
She is the clerenesse and the very lyght
That in this derke worlde me wynt ⁊ ledeth
The hert/ within my sorouful brest you dre-
And loueth so sore/ ẏ ye ben verily (deth
The maistres of my wytte/ and nothyng I
My worde/ my workes/ is knyt so in yo͛ bõde
That as an harpe obeyeth to the honde
And maketh it sowne after his fyngeryng
Right so mowe ye out of myne herte bring
Such voice/ right as you lyst/ to laugh or pay-
Be ye my gyde/ and lady soueraygne (ne
As to myn erthly god/ to you I call
Bothe in this werke/ and my sorowes al

But

But wherfore that I spake to yeue credence
To olde stories/and done hem reuerence
And that men musten more thyng byleue
Than men may sene at eye/or els preue
That shal I seyne/whan that I se my tyme
I may nat al atones speke in ryme
My besy goost/that thursteth alway newe
To sene this flour so yonge/so fressh of hewe
Constrayned me/with so gredy desyre
That in myn herte I fele yet the fyre
That made me to ryse er it were day
And this was nowe the first morowe of May
With dredeful hert/and glad deuocion
For to ben at the resurrection
Of this floure/whan that it shulde vnclose
Agayne the sonne/that rose as reed as rose
That in the brest was of the beest that day
That Angenores doughter ladde away
And downe on knees anon right I me sette
And as I coulde/this fresshe floure I grette
Knelyng alway/tyl it vnclosed was
Upon the smal/softe/swete gras
That was with floures swete embrouded all
Of suche swetnesse/and suche odour ouer all
That for to speke of gome/herbe/or tre
Comparyson may none ymaked be
For it surmounteth playnly al odoures
And of ryche beautie al floures
Forgotten had the erthe his poore estate
Of wynter/that hym naked made and mate
And with his sworde of colde so sore greued
Nowe hath the atempre sonne al that releued
That naked was/and clad it newe agayne
The smal foules/of the ceason fayne
That of the panter and the nette ben scaped
Upon the fouler/that hem made awhaped
In wynter/and distroyed had her brood
In his despyte hem thought it dyd hem good
To synge of hym/and in her songe dispyse
The foule chorle/that for his couetyse
Had hem betrayed/with his sophistrye
This was her songe: The fouler we defye
And al his crafte/and some songen clere
Layes of loue/that ioye it was to here
In worshippyng and praysing of her make
And for the newe blysful somers sake
Upon the braunches ful of blosmes softe
In her despyte/they turned hem ful ofte
And fo..gen/blyssed be saynt Valentyne
For on his day I chese you to be myne
Withouten repentyng/myn herte swete
And therwithal her beckes gonnen mete
yeldyng honour/and humble obeysaunce
To loue/and dydden her other obseruaunce
That longeth vnto loue/and to nature
Constrewe that as you lyst/I do no cure
And tho that had done vnkyndenesse
As dothe the Tydife/for newe fangelnesse
Besought mercy of her trespasyng
And humbly songe her repentyng
And sworen on the blosmes to be trewe
So that her makes wolde vpon hem rewe
And at the laste maden her acorde
Al founde they Daunger for the tyme a lorde
Yet Pyte/through his stronge gentyl might
Forgaue/and made mercy passen right
Through innocence/and ruled curtesye
But I ne cleape it nat innocence folye
Ne false pyte/for vertue is the meane
As Etycke sayth/in suche maner I meane
And thus these foules/voyde of al malyce
Acorded to loue/and laften vyce
Of hate/and songe all of one acorde
Welcome somer/our gouernour and lorde
And zephirus/and Flora gentelly
yaue to the floures softe and tenderly
Her swote brethe/and made hem for to sprede
As god and goddesse of the floury mede
In whiche me thought I might day by day
Dwellen alway/the ioly monthe of May
Withouten slepe/withouten meate or drinke
Adowne ful softly I gan to synke
And leanyng on my elbowe and my syde
The longe day I shope me for to abyde
For nothyng els/and I shal nat lye
But for to loke vpon the deysye
That wel by reason men it call may
The dayesy/or els the eye of the day
The emprice/and floure of floures all
I pray to god that fayre mote she fall
And al that louen floures/for her sake
But nathelesse/ne wene nat that I make
In praysing of the floure agayne the leefe
Nomore than of the corne agayne the sheefe
For as to me nys leuer none ne lother
I nam with holden yet with neuer nother
Ne

Ne I not who serueth leefe/ ne who the floure
Wel brouken they her seruyce or laboure
For this thyng is al of another tonne
Of olde stoue/er suche thyng was begonne
Whan that the sõne/out of the south gan west
And that this flour gan close/⁊ gan to rest
For derknes of the night/ the which she dredde
Home to myn house/ful swyftly I me spedde
To gon to reste/and erly for to ryse
To sene this flour to sprede/as I deuyse
And in a lytel herber that I haue
That benched was on turues fresshe ygraue
I bade men shulde me my couche make
For deyntie of the newe sõmers sake
I bade hem strawen floures on my bedde
Whan I was layde/and had myn eyen hedde
I fel a slepe/and slepte an houre or two
Me mette howe I lay in the medowe tho
To sene this floure/that I loue so and drede
And from a ferre came walkyng in the mede
The god of Loue/ and in his hande a quene
And she was cladde in royal habyte grene
A fret of golde she had next her heere
And vpon that a whyte crowne she beere
With flourouns smal/ and I shal nat lye
For al the worlde right as a dayesye
Ycorowned is/with whyte leaues lyte
So were the flourouns of her corowne whyte
For of o perle fyne orientall
Her whyte corowne was ymaked all
For which the white corowne/aboue the grene
Made her lyke a dayesye for to seme
Consydred eke her fret of golde aboue
Iclothed was this mighty god of Loue
In sylke embrouded/ful of grene greues
In whiche a fret of reed rose leues
The fresshest sens the world was first begõne
His gylte heere was corowned with a sonne
In stede of golde/ for heuynesse and weight
Therwith me thought his face shone so bright
That wel vnnethes might I him beholde
And ĩ his hãde/me thought I sawe him holde
Two firy dartes/as the gledes rede
And angelyke his wynges sawe I sprede
And al be that men sayne/that blynde is he
Algate me thought that he might se
For sternely on me he gan beholde
So that his lokyng dothe myn herte colde
And by the hande he helde this noble quene
Crowned with whyte/ and clothed al in grene
So womanly/so benigne/and so meke
That in this world/though that mẽ wold seke
Halfe her beautie shulde they nat fynde
In creature that formed is by kynde
And therfore may I sayne/as thynketh me
This songe/in prayssing of this lady fre.

Hyde Absolon thy gylte tresses clere
Hester lay thou thy mekenesse al adoun
Hyde Ionathas al thy frendely manere
Penelopee/ and Marcia Catoun
Make of your wyfehode no comparysoun
Hyde ye your beauties/ Isoude ⁊ Heleyne
My lady cometh/ that al this may distayne

Thy fayre body/let it nat apere
Lauyne/ and thou Lucrece of Rome toun
And Polixene/that boughten loue so dere
And Cleopatras/ with al thy passyoun
Hyde ye your trouthe of loue/⁊ your renoun
And thou Tisbe/that hast of loue suche payne
My lady cometh/that al this may distayne

Hero/ Dido /Laodomia/ al yfere
And Phillis/ hangyng for the Demophoun
And Canace/espyed by thy chere
Hipsyphile betrayed with Iasoun
Maketh of your trouth neyther boste ne soun
Nor Hypermistre/ or Ariadne/ ye twayne
My lady cometh/that al this may distayne

¶ This balade may ful wel ysongen be
As I haue sayd erst/by my lady fre
For certainly/al these mowe nat suffyse
To apperen with my lady in no wyse
For as the sonne wol the fyre distayne
So passeth al my lady soueraygne
That is so good/so fayre/so debonayre
I pray to god that euer fall her fayre
For nad comforte ben of her presence
I had ben deed/withouten any defence
For drede of Loues wordes/ and his chere
As whan tyme is/herafter ye shal here
Behynde this god of Loue vpon the grene
I sawe comyng of ladyes nynetene
In royal habyt/a ful easy pace

And

And after hem came of women suche a trace
That sens that god Adam had made of erthe
The thirde parte of mankynde/or the ferthe
Ne wende I nat by possibylyte
Had euer in this wyde worlde ybe
And trewe of loue/these women were echon
Now whether was that a wõder thing or non
That right anon/as that they gonne espye
This floure/whiche that I clepe the dayesye
Ful sodainly they stynten al at ones
And knesed downe/as it were for the nones
And songen with o voyce/heale and honour
To trouthe of womanhede/and to this flour
That beareth our alder prise in fyguryng
Her whyte corowne beareth the wytnessyng
And with that worde/acompas enuyroun
They sytten hem ful softely adown
First sate the god of loue/and sythe his quene
With the whyte corowne/clad al in grene
And sythen al the remenaunt/by and by
As they were of estate/ful curtesly
Ne nat a worde was spoken in the place
The mountenaũce of a furlong way of space
I knelyng by this floure/in good entente
Abode to knowen what this people mente
As styll as any stone/tyl at the laste
This god of loue/on me his eyen caste
And sayd/who kneleth there: and I answerde
Unto his askyng/whan that I it herde
And sayd/sir it am I/and come him nere
And salued him. (q̃d he) what dorst thou here
So nygh myn owne floure/so boldely
It were better worthy trewly
A worme to nighen nere my floure than thou
And why sir (q̃d I) and it lyke you?
For thou (q̃d he) arte therto nothyng able
It is my relyke/digne and delytable
And thou my foe/and al my folke werreyest
And of myn olde seruauntes thou missayest
And hyndrest hem/with thy translacion
And lettest folke from her deuocion
To serue me/and holdest it folye
To serue loue/thou mayest it nat denye
For in playne text/withouten nede of glose
Thou hast translated the Romaũt of ye Rose
That is an heresye ayenst my lawe
And makest wyse folke fro me withdrawe
And of Criseyde/thou hast sayd as the lyste
That maketh men to women lesse tryste
That ben as trewe as euer was any stele
Of thyn answere auyse the right wele
For though thou reneyed haste my lay
As other wretches haue done many a day
By seynt Venus/that my mother is
If that thou lyue/thou shalt repenten this
So cruelly/that it shal wel be sene
Tho spake this lady/clothed al in grene
And sayd/god right of your curtesye
Ye mote herken if he can replye
Agaynst al this/that ye haue to him meued
A god ne shulde nat be thus agreued
But of his deite he shal be stable
And therto gracious and mercyable
And if ye nere a god/that knowen al
Than might it be/as I you tellen shal
This man to you may falsely ben accused
That as by right/him ought ben excused
For in your court is many a losengeour
And many a queynt toteler accusour
That tabouren in your eares many a soun
Right after her ymaginatioun
To haue your dalyaunce/and for enuy
These ben the causes/and I shal nat lye
Enuy is lauender of the courte alway
For she ne parteth neyther nyght ne day
Out of the house of Cesar/thus saith Dant
Who so that gothe al gate she wol nat want
And eke peraunter for this man is nyce
He myght done it/gessyng no malyce
But for he vseth thynges for to make
Him recketh nought of what mater he take
Or him was boden make thylke twey
Of some persone/and durst it nat withsey
Or him repenteth vtterly of this
He ne hath nat done so greuously amys
To translaten that olde clerkes writen
As though that he of malyce wolde endyten
Dispyte of loue/and had him self it wrought
This shuld a rizt wise lorde haue ĩ his thought
And nat be lyke tyrauntes of Lombardy
That han no rewarde but at tyranny
For he that kynge or lorde is naturel
Him ought nat be tyraunt ne cruel
As is a fermour/to done the harme he can
He must thynke it is his liege man
And is his tresour/and his golde in cofer
This

This is the sentence of the phylosophre
A kyng to kepe his lieges in iustyce
Withouten doute that is his offyce
Al wol he kepe his lordes in her degre
As it is right and skyl/ that they be
Enhaunsed and honoured/and moste dere
For they ben halfe goddes/ in this worlde here
Yet mote he done bothe right to poore & ryche
Al be that her estate be nat bothe lyche
And haue of poore folke compassyon
For so/the gentyl kynde of the lyon
For whan a flye offendeth him or byteth
He with his tayle awaye the flye smyteth
Al easely/for of his gentrye
Him deyneth nat to wreke him on a flye
As dothe a curre/or els another beest
In noble corage ought ben areest
And weyen euery thyng by equite
And euer haue regarde vnto his owne degree
For sir/it is no maistrye for a lorde
To dampne a mā/ without answere of worde
And for a lorde/that is ful foule to vse
And it so be/he may him nat excuse
But asketh mercy with a dredeful herte
And profereth him/right in his bare sherte
To ben right at your owne iugement
Than ought a god by shorte auysement
Consydre his owne honour/and his trespace
For sythe no cause of dethe lyeth in this cace
You ought to ben the lightlyer mercyable
Leteth your ire/ and bethe somwhat tretable
The man hath serued you of his connynges
And forthred wel your lawe in his makynges
Al be it that he can nat wel endyte
Yet hath he made leude folke delyte
To serue you/in preysing of your name
He made the boke/ ẏ hight the house of Fame
And eke the dethe of Blaunche the duchesse
And the Parlyment of Foules/ as I gesse
And al the loue of Palamon and Arcyte
Of Thebes/though the storie is knowen lyte
And many an hymne/for your holydaies
That hyghten balades/roundels/virelayes
And for to speke of other holynesse
He hath in prose translated Boece
And made the lyfe also of saynt Cecyle
He made also/gone is a great whyle
Origenes vpon the Maudeleyne
Him ought nowe to haue the lesse payne
He hath made many a ley/ and many a thinge
Nowe as ye be a god/ and eke a kyng
I your Alceste/ whylom quene of Trace
I aske you this man right of your grace
That ye him neuer hurte in al his lyue
And he shal swearen to you/and that blyue
He shal neuer more agylten in this wyse
But shal maken as ye wol deuyse
Of women trewe in louyng al her lyfe
Where so ye wol/of mayden or of wyfe
And forthren you/as moche as he misseyde
Or in the Rose/or els in Creseyde
The god of Loue answerde her thus anon
Madame (quod he) it is so longe agon
That I you knewe/ so charitable and trewe
That neuer yet/sens the worlde was newe
To me ne founde I better none than ye
If that I wol saue my degree
I may nor wol nat werne your request
Al lyth in you/ dothe with him as you lest
I al foryeue withouten lenger space
For who so yeueth a yefte or dothe a grace
Do it be tyme/ his thanke shal be the more
And demeth ye what he shal do therfore
Go thanke nowe my lady here (q̄d he)
I rose/ and downe I sette me on my kne
And sayd thus: Madame/ the god aboue
Foryelde you that the god of Loue
Haue maked me his wrathe to foryeue
And grace so longe for to lyue
That I may knowe sothly what ye be
That haue me holpen/and put in this degre
But trewly I wende/ as in this caas
Nought haue agylte/ ne done to loue trespas
For why/ a trewe man withouten drede
Hath nat to parten with a theues dede
Ne a trewe louer ought me nat to blame
Though that I speke a false louer sōe shame
They ought rather with me for to holde
For that I of Creseyde wrote or tolde
Or of the Rose/ what so myne authour ment
Al gate god wotte it was myne entent
To forthren trouth in loue/ and it cheryce
And to ben ware fro falsnesse and fro vyce
By whiche ensample/this was my menyng
And she answerd/ let be thyne arguyng
For loue ne wol nat countrepleted be

In

In right ne wronge/and lerne that of me
Thou haste thy grace/ & holde the right therto
Now wol I sayn what penaunce thou shalt do
For thy trespace/ understonde it here
  Thou shalt while yͤ thou lyuest yere by yere
The moste partie of thy tyme spende
In makyng of a glorious legende
Of good women/maydens/and wyues
That weren trewe in louyng al her lyues
And tell of false men that hem betrayen
That al her lyfe ne do nat but assayen
Howe many women they may done a shame
For in your worlde that is now holde a game
And though the lyke nat a louer be
Speke wel of loue/ this penaunce yeue I the
And to the god of loue I shal so praye
That he shal charge his seruauntes by any way
To fortheren the/and wel thy labour quyte
Go nowe thy way/this penaunce is but lyte
And whan this boke is made/ yeue it yͤ quene
On my behalfe/at Eltham/or at Shene
The god of loue gan smyle/and than he sayde
Wost thou (qd he) wher this be wyfe or mayde
Or quene/ or countesse/ or of what degre
That hath so lytel penaunce yeuen the
That haste deserued sore for to smerte
But pyte renneth sone in gentyl herte
That mayst thou sene/she kytheth what she is
  And I answerde/ nay sir so haue I blys
No more/but that I se wel she is good
  That is a trewe tale by myn hoode
(Qd Loue) and thou knowest wel parde
If it be so that thou auyse the
Haste thou nat in a booke in thy cheste
The great goodnesse of the quene Alceste
That turned was in to a dayesye
She that for her husbonde chese to dye
And eke to gone to hell/rather than he
And Hercules rescued her parde
And brought her out of hell agayne to blys
  And I answerde agayne/and sayd yes
Nowe knowe I her/& is this good Alceste
The dayesye/and myn owne hertes reste
Nowe fele I wel the goodnesse of this wyfe
That bothe after her dethe/and in her lyfe
Her great bountie doubleth her renoun
Wel hath she quyt me myn affectioun
That I haue to her floure the dayesye
No wonder is though Ioue her stellyfye
As telleth Agaton/ for her great goodnesse
Her whyte corowne beareth of it wytnesse
For also many vertues had she
As smal flourouns in her corowne be
In remembraunce of her/and in honour
Crbylla made the dayesy and the flour
Icrowned al with white/ as men may se
And Mars yaue to her a corowne reed parde
In stede of Rubies set amonge the white
Therwith this quene woyereo for shame a lyte
Whan she was praysed so in her presence
Than sayd Loue/ a ful great neglygence
Was it to the/ that ylke tyme thou made
(Hyde Absolon thy tresses) in balade
That thou forgete her in thy songe to sette
Sithe that thou arte so greatly in her dette
And wost wel that kalender is she
To any woman/ that wol louer be
For she taught al the crafte of trewe louyng
And namely of wyfehode the lyuyng
And al the boundes that she ought kepe
Thy lytel wytte was thylke tyme a slepe
But nowe I charge the upon thy lyfe
That in thy Legende thou make of this wyfe
Whan thou haste other smale ymade before
And fare nowe wel/ I charge the no more
But er I go/ thus moche I wol the tel
Ne shal no trewe louer come in hel
  These other ladyes syttynge here a rowe
Ben in my balade/ if thou const hem knowe
And in thy bokes/ al thou shalt hem fynde
Haue hem nowe in thy legende al in mynde
I meane of hem that ben in thy knowyng
For here ben twenty thousande mo syttyng
Than thou knowest/good women all
And trewe of loue/ for aught that may befall
Make the metres of hem as the lest
I mote gon home/the sonne draweth west
To paradys/ with al this companye
And serue alway the fresshe dayesye
At Cleopatras I wol that thou begynne
And so forthe/ & my loue so shalt thou wynne
For let se nowe what man that louer be
Wol done so stronge a payne for loue as she
I wote wel that thou mayste nat al it ryme
That suche louers dyd in her tyme
It were to longe to reden and to here

Suffy.

Suffyseth me thou make in this manere
That thou reherce of al her lyfe the great
After these olde authours lysten for to treate
For who so shal so many a storye tel
Sey shortely or he shal to longe dwel
And with that worde my bokes gan I take
And right thus on my legende gan I make.

¶ Thus endeth the Prologue.

¶ Here begynneth the legende of Cleopatras quene of Egypt.

After the dethe of Ptholome the kyng
That al Egipt had in his gouernyng
Reigned his quene Cleopataras
Tyl on a tyme befel there suche a caas
That out of Rome was sent a senatour
For to conqueren realmes and honour
Unto the towne of Rome/ as was usaunce
To haue the worlde at her obeysaunce
And sothe to say/ Antonius was his name
So fyl it/ as fortune him ought a shame
Whan he was fallen in prosperyte
Rebel unto the towne of Rome is he
And ouer al this/ the suster of Cesare
He lefte her falsly/ er that she was ware
And wolde algates han another wyfe
For whiche he toke with Rome & Cesar stryfe
Nathelesse/ for sothe this ylke senatour
Was a ful worthy gentyl werryour
And of his dethe it was ful great domage
But loue had brought this mā in such a rage
And him so narowe bounden in his laas
And al for the loue of Cleopataras
That al the worlde he sette at no value
Him thought ther was nothyng to him so due
As Cleopatras/ for to loue and serue
Him thought that in armes for to sterue
In the defence of her/ and of her right
This noble quene/ eke loued so this knyght
Through his deserte/ and for his chyualrye
As certainly/ but if that bookes lye
He was of person/ and of gentylnesse
And of discretion/ and of hardynesse
Worthy to any wight that lyuen may
And she was fayre/ as is the rose in May
And for to maken shorte is the beste
She waxe his wyfe/ and had him as her leste
The weddyng and the feest to deuyse
To me that haue ytake suche emprise
And so many a storye for to make
It were to longe/ leste that I shulde slake
Of thyng that beareth more effecte & charge
For men may ouerlade a shyp or barge
And for thy/ to effecte than wol I skyppe
And al the remenaunt/ I wol let it slyppe
Octauian/ that woode was of this dede
Shope him an hooste on Antony to lede
Al utterly/ for his distruction
With stoute romaynes/ cruel as lyon
To shyp they went/ & thus I let hem sayle
Antonius was ware/ and wol nat fayle
To meten with these romaynes/ if he may
Toke eke his rede/ and bothe upon a day
His wyfe and he/ and al his hoste forth wente
To shyp anon/ no lenger they ne stente
And in the see it happed hem to mete
Up gothe the trumpe/ & for to shoute & shete
And paynen hem to sette on with the sonne
With grisly sowne/ out gothe the great gonne
And hertely they hurtlen in al at ones
And fro the toppe/ down cometh yͤ gret stones
In gothe the grapenel so ful of crokes
Amonge the ropes ran the sheryng hokes
In with the polaxe preaseth he and he
Behynde the maste/ begynneth he to flye
And out agayne/ and dryueth him ouer borde
He stycketh him upon his speares orde
He rente the sayle with hokes lyke a sythe
He brigeth the cuppe/ & byddeth hem be blythe
He poureth pesen upon the hatches slyder
With pottes ful of lyme/ they gon to gyder
And thus the longe day in fyght they spende
Tyl at the laste/ as euery thing hath ende
Antony is shent/ and put him to the flyght
And al his folke to go/ that best go myght
Fleeth eke the quene/ withal her purpre sayle
For strokes/ which yͤ went as thicke as hayle
No wonder was/ she might it nat endure
And whan that Antony sawe that auenture
Alas (qd he) the day that I was borne
My worshyp in this day thus haue I lorne
And for dispayre/ out of his wytte he sterte
And rofe him selfe anon throughout the herte

R.r. Er that

Er that he ferther went out of the place
His wyfe/that coulde of Cesar haue no grace
To Egypte is fled/for drede and for distresse
But herkeneth ye that speken of kyndenesse
Ye men that falsly swearen many an othe
That ye wol dye/if that your loue be wrothe
Here may ye sene of women suche a trouthe
This woful Cleopatre hath made such routh
That there nys tonge none that may it tell
But on the morowe/ she wol no lenger dwell
But made her subtyl werkmen make a shryne
Of al the rubyes and the stones fyne
In al Egypte/that she coulde espye
And put ful the shryne of spycerie
And lete the corse enbaume/and forth she fette
This deed corse/and in the shryne it shette
And next the shryne a pyt than doth she graue
And al the serpentes that she might haue
She put hem in that graue/ & thus she seyde
Now loue/ to whom my sorouful hert obeyde
So ferforthly/that fro that blysful houre
That I you swore/to ben al frely your
I meane you/ Antonius my knyght
That neuer wakyng in the day or nyght
Ye nere out of myn hertes remembraunce
For wel or wo/for carole/or for daunce
And in my selfe/this couenaunt made I tho
That right suche as ye felten wele or wo
As ferforthe as it in my power laye
Vnreprouable vnto my wyfehod aye
The same wolde I felen/ lyfe or dethe
And thilke couenaunt/ whyle me lasteth brethe
I wol fulfyl/and that shal wel be sene
Was neuer vnto her loue a trewer quene
And with ye worde/naked with ful good herte
Amonge the serpentes in the pytte she sterte
And there she chese to haue her buryeng
Anon the nedders gonne her for to stynge
And she her dethe receyueth with good chere
For loue of Antony that was her so dere
And this is storial/sothe it is no fable
Now er I fynde a man thus trewe & stable
And wol for loue his dethe so frely take
I pray god let our heedes neuer ake.

¶ Here endeth the legende of Cleopatras/ and here foloweth the legende of Tysbe of Babylone.

At Babiloyne whylom fyl it thus
The which toun ye quene Semyramus
Lete dychen al aboute/and walles make
Ful hye/of harde tyles wel ybake
There were dwellyng in this noble town
Two lordes/which that were of gret renown
And woneden so nygh vpon a grene
That there nas but a stone wal hem bytwene
As ofte in great townes is the wonne
And sothe to sayne/that one man had a sonne
Of al that londe/one of the lustyest
That other had a doughter/the fayrest
That estwarde in ye world was tho dwellyng
The name of eueryche/gan to other spryng
By women that were neyghbours aboute
For in that countrey yet withouten doute
Maydens ben ykept for ielousye
Ful strayte/leste they dydden some folye
This yonge man was cleped Piramus
Tysbe hyght the mayde (Naso sayth thus)
And thus by reporte/was her name yshoue
That as they woxe in age/so woxe her loue
And certayne/as by reason of her age
There might haue ben bytwixt hem mariage
But that her fathers nolde it nat assente
And bothe in loue ylike sore they brente
That none of al her frendes might it lette
But priuely somtyme yet they mette
By sleyght/and spaken some of her desyre
As wrie the glede/and hotter is the fyre
Forbyd a loue/and it is ten tymes so wode
This wal/which ye betwixt hem both stode
Was clouen a two/right fro the toppe adoun
Of olde tyme/of his foundacioun
But yet this clyfte was so narowe and lyte
It was nat sene/ dere ynough a myte
But what is that/ that loue can nat espye
Ye louers two/if that I shal nat lye
Ye founden first this lytel narowe clyfte
And with a sounde/as softe as any shrifte
They lete her wordes through the clyfte pace
And tolden/whyle ye they stoden in the place
Al her complaynte of loue/and al her wo
At euery tyme whan they durste so
On that one syde of the wal stode he
And on that other syde stode Tysbe
The swete sowne of other to receyue
And thus her wardeyns wolde they disceyue
And

And euery day this wal they wolde threte
And wysshe to god/that it were downe ybete
Thus wold they sayne/alas thou wicked wal
Through thyn enuye/ thou vs lettest al
Why nylt thou cleaue/or fallen al a two
Or at the leste/but thou woldest so
Yet woldest thou but ones let vs mete
Or ones that we might kyssen swete
Than were we cured of our cares colde
But nathelesse/yet be we to the holde
In as moche as thou suffrest for to gone
Our wordes through thy lyme & eke thy stone
Yet ought we with the ben wel apayde
 And whan these ydel wordes weren sayde
The colde wall they wolden kysse of stone
And take her leaue/& forthe they wolden gone
And this was gladly in the euentyde
Or wonder erly/leste men it espyde
And longe tyme they wrought in this manere
Tyl on a day/whan Phebus gan to clere
Aurora with the stremes of her hete
Had dried vp the dewe of herbes wete
Unto this clyfte/as it was wonte to be
Come Piramus/and after come Tysbe
And plighten trouthe/fully in her fay
That ylke same night to steale away
And to begyle her wardeyns euerychone
And forthe out of the cyte for to gone
And for the feldes ben so brode and wyde
For to mete in o place at o tyde
They set markes/her metynges shulde be
There kyng Ninus was grauen/ vnder a tre
For olde paynems/ that ydolles heryed
Useden tho in feldes to ben buryed
And faste by this graue was a well
And shortly of this tale for to tell
This couenaunt was affyrmed wonder faste
And longe hem thought that the sonne laste
That it nere gone vnder the see adoun
 This Tisbe hath so great affectioun
And so great lykyng Piramus to se
That whan she sawe her tyme might be
At nyght she stale away ful priuely
With her face ywympled subtelly
For al her frendes (for to saue her trouth)
She hath forsake alas/and that is routhe
That euer woman wolde be so trewe
To trusten man/but she the bet him knewe
And to the tree she gothe a ful good pace
For loue made her so hardy in this case
And by the welle/adowne she gan her dresse
Alas/ than cometh a wylde lyonesse
Out of the wodde/withouten more arrest
With bloody mouthe/of stranglyng of a best
To drinken of the well there as she sat
And whan that Tisby had espyed that
She ryst her vp/with a ful drery herte
And in a caue/with dredeful foote she sterte
For by the moone she sawe it wel withall
And as she ran/her wymple let she fall
And toke none hede/so sore she was a whaped
And eke so glad that she was escaped
And thus she sate/and lurketh wonder styll
Whan that this lyonesse hath dronke her fyll
Aboute the well gan she for to wynde
And right anon the wymple gan she fynde
And with her bloody mouthe it al to rente
Whan this was done/no lenger she ne stente
But to the wodde her way thā hath she nome
 And at the laste this Piramus is come
But al to longe (alas) at home was he
The moone shone/men might wel yse
And in his way/as that he come ful faste
His eyen to the grounde adowne he caste
And in the sonde/as he behelde adoun
He sawe the steppes brode of a lyoun
And in his herte he sodainly agrose
And pale he wext/therwith his herte arose
And nere he came/& founde the wymple torne
Alas (quod he) the day that I was borne
This o nyght wol bothe vs louers slee
Howe shulde I asken mercy of Tisbee
Whan I am he that haue you slayne/alas
My byddyng hath you slayne in this caas
Alas/to bydde a woman gone by nyght
In place there as peryll fallen myght
And I so slowe/ alas I ne had be
Here in this place/a furlonge way er ye
Nowe what lyon that is in this forest
My body mote he rente/or what beste
That wylde is/gnawen mote he myn herte
And with that worde/ he to the wymple sterte
And kyste it ofte/& wepte on it ful sore
And sayd wymple alas/there nys no more
But thou shalt fele as wel the bloode of me
As thou haste felte the bledyng of Tysbe

R.r.ii. And

And with that worde/ he smote him to the hert
The bloode out of the wounde as brode sterte
As water/ whan the condupt broken is
  Nowe Tisbe/ whiche that wyste nat this
But syttyng in her drede/ she thought thus
If it so fall that my Piramus
Be comen hyther/ and may me nat yfynde
He may me holden false/ and eke vnkynde
And out she cometh/ & after him gan espyen
Bothe with her herte/ and with her eyen
And thought/ I wol him tellen of my drede
Bothe of the lyonesse and of my dede
And at the laste her loue than hath she founde
Beatyng with his heles on the grounde
Al bloody/ and therwithal abacke she sterte
And lyke the wawes/ quappe gan her herte
And pale as boxe she woxe/ and in a throwe
Auysed her/ and gan him wel to knowe
That it was Piramus her herte dere
  Who coulde write whiche a deedly chere
Hath Tisbe nowe/ & howe her heere she rente
And howe she gan her selfe to turmente
And howe she lyeth & swouneth on the groũde
And howe she wept of teeres ful his wounde
How medleth she his blode/ with her cõplainte
How wt her bloode/ her seluen gan she paynte
Howe clyppeth she the deed corse/ alas
Howe dothe this woful Tisbe in this caas
Howe kysseth she his frosty mouthe so colde
Who hath don this? & who hath ben so bolde?
To sleen my lefe/ o speke Piramus
I am thy Tisbe/ that the calleth thus
And therwithal she lysteth vp his heed
  This woful man/ that was nat fully deed
Whan that he herde the name of Tisbe cryen
On her he cast his heuy deedly eyen
And downe agayne/ & yeldeth vp the goste
  Tisbe ryst vp/ without noyse or boste
And sawe her wymple and his empty sheth
And eke his swerde/ that him hath don to deth
Than spake she thus/ thy woful hãde (qđ she)
Is stronge ynough in suche a werke to me
For loue shal yeue me strength & hardynesse
To make my wounde large ynough I gesse
I wol the folowen deed/ and I wol be
Felawe/ & cause eke of thy dethe (quod she)
And though that nothyng saue the dethe only
Might the fro me departe trewly
Thou shalte no more departe nowe fro me
Than to the dethe/ for I wol go with the
  And nowe ye wretched ielouse fathers our
We that weren whylom children your
We prayen you/ withouten more enuye
That in o graue we moten lye
Sens loue hath brought vs this pytous ende
And rightwyse god/ to euery louer sende
That loueth trewly more prosperite
Than euer had Piramus and Tisbe
And let no gentyl woman her assure
To putten her in suche an auenture
But god forbyd but a woman can
Ben as trewe and louyng as a man
And for my parte/ I shal anon it kythe
And with ye worde/ his swerde she toke swyth
That warme was of her loues bloode/ & hote
And to the herte she her seluen smote
  And thus are Tisbe and Piramus ago
Of trewe men I fynde but fewe mo
In al my bokes/ saue this Piramus
And therfore haue I spoken of him thus
For it is deynte to vs men to fynde
A man that can in loue be trewe and kynde
  Here may ye sene/ what louer so he be
A woman dare/ and can as wel as he.

¶ Here endeth the legende of Tysbe of Babylone/ and here foloweth the legende of Dido quene of Cartage.

GLorie and honour Virgyle Mantuan
Be to thy name/ and I shal as I can
Folowe thy lanterne/ as thou gost byforne
Howe Eneas to Dido was forsworne
In thyn Eneyde/ and Naso wol I take
The tenour and the great effectes make
Whan Troye brought was to distruction
By grekes sleyght/ and namely by Synon
Faynyng the horse offred vnto Mynerue
Through which ye many a troyan must sterue
And Hector had after his dethe apered
And fyre so wode/ it might nat ben stered
In al the noble tour of Ilion
That of the cyte was the chefe dongeon
And al the countre was so lowe ybrought
And Priamus the kyng fordone and nought
And

And Eneas was charged by Venus
To flyen away/ he toke Ascanyus
That was his son/in his right hande & fledde
And on his backe he bare/and with him ledde
His olde father/cleped Anchyses
And by the way his wyfe Creusa he lees
And mokell sorowe had he in his mynde
Er that he coulde his felawshyp fynde
But at the laste/whan he had hem founde
He made him redy/in a certayne stounde
And to the see ful faste he gan him hye
And sayleth forthe/with al his companye
Towarde Ytayle/as wolde destynee
But of his auentures in the see
Nys nat to purpose for to speke of here
For it acordeth nat to my matere
But as I sayd/of him and of Dido
Shal be my tale/tyl that I haue do
So longe he sayled in the salte see
Tyl in Libye vnneth aryued he
So was he with the tempest al to shake
And whan that he the hauen had ytake
He had a knyght was called Achates
And him of al his felawshyp he chees
To gone with him/the countrey for tespye
He toke with him nomore companye
But forthe they gone/ & lefte his shyppes ryde
His feere and he/withouten any gyde
So longe he walketh in this wyldernesse
Tyl at the laste he mette an hunteresse
A bowe in honde/and arowes had she
Her clothes cutted were vnto the knee
But she was yet the fayrest creature
That euer was yformed by nature
And Eneas and Achates she grette
And thus she to hem spake/whā she hem mette
Sawe ye (q̄d she) as ye han walked wyde
Any of my sustren walke you besyde
With any wylde bore/or other beest
That they haue hunted to in this forest
Ytucked vp/with arowes in her caas
Nay sothly lady (quod this Eneas)
But by thy beautie/as it thynketh me
Thou myghtest neuer erthely woman be
But Phebus suster arte thou/as I gesse
And if so be that thou be a goddesse
Haue mercy on our labour and our wo
I nam no goddesse sothly (q̄d she) tho
For maydens walken in this countre here
With arowes & with bowe/in this manere
This is the realme of Libye/there ye bene
Of whiche that Dido lady is and quene
And shortly tolde al the occasyon
Why Dido came in to that regyon
Of whiche as nowe me lysteth nat to ryme
It nedeth nat/it nere but losse of tyme
For this is al and some/it was Venus
His owne mother/that spake with him thus
And to Cartage she bade he shulde him dight
And vanisshed anon out of his syght
I coulde folowe worde for worde Vergyle
But it wolde lasten al to longe whyle
This noble quene/that cleped was Dido
That whylom was the wyfe of Sytheo
That fayrer was than the bright sonne
This noble towne of Cartage hath begonne
In whiche she reigneth in so great honour
That she was holde of al quenes flour
Of gentyllesse/of fredom/ & of beautee
That wel was him/that might ones see
Of kynges and lordes so desyred
That al the worlde her beautie had yfyred
She stode so wel in euery wightes grace
Whan Eneas was come vnto the place
Vnto the mayster temple of al the toun
There Dido was in her deuocioun
Ful priuely his way than hath he nome
Whan he was in the large temple come
I can nat sayne/if that it be possyble
But Venus had him maked inuisible
Thus sayth the boke/withouten any lees
And whan this Eneas and Achates
Hadden in this temple ben ouer all
Than founde they depaynted on a wall
Howe Troye and al the lande distroyed was
Alas that I was borne (quod Eneas)
Through ẏ worlde our shame is kyd so wyde
Nowe it is paynted vpon euery syde
We that weren in prosperyte
Ben nowe disclaundred/and in suche degre
No lenger for to lyuen I ne kepe
And with that worde/ he brast out for to wepe
So tenderly/that routhe it was to sene
This fresshe lady/of the cyte quene
Stode in the temple/in her estate royal
So richely/and eke so fayre with al

R.r.iii. So

Of Dido quene of Cartage.

So yonge/ so lusty/ with her eyen glade
That if that god/ that heuen and erthe made
Wolde haue a loue/ for beaute and goodnesse
And womanhede/ trouthe/ and semelynesse
Whom shulde he louen/ but this lady swete ?
There nys no woman to him halfe so mete
Fortune/ that hath the worlde in gouernaunce
Hath sodaynly brought in so newe a chaunce
That neuer was there yet so strened a caas
For al the company of Eneas
Whiche that we wende haue lorne in the see
Arrived is nought ferre fro that cyte
For whiche the greattest of his lordes/ some
By auenture ben to the cyte come
Unto that same temple for to seke
The quene/ and of her socour her beseke
Such renõe was ther sprõg of her goodnesse
  And whan they had tolde al her distresse
And al her tempest and al her harde caas
Unto the quene appered Eneas
And openly beknewe that it was he
Who had ioye than/ but his meyne
That hadden founde her lorde/ her gouernour
  The quene sawe they dyd him such honour
And had herde ofte of Eneas/ er tho
And in her herte had routhe and wo
That euer suche a noble man as he
Shal ben disherited in suche degree
And sawe the man/ that he was lyke a knyght
And suffysaunt of persone and of myght
And lyke to ben a very gentylman
And wel his wordes he besette can
And had a noble visage for the nones
And formed wel of brawne and of bones
And after Venus/ had suche fayrnesse
That no man myght be half so fayre I gesse
And wel a lorde him semed for to be
And for he was a straunger/ somwhat she
Lyked him the bette/ as god do boote
To some folke/ often newe thynge is swote
Anon her herte hath pyte of his wo
And with pyte/ loue came also
And thus for pyte and for gentylnesse
Refresshed must he ben of his distresse
  She sayde: certes/ that she sory was
That he hath had suche peryl and suche caas
And in her frendly speche/ in this manere
She to him spake/ and sayd as ye may here.
  Be ye nat Venus sonne and Anchises
In good faythe/ al the worshyp and encrees
That I may goodly done you/ ye shal haue
Your shyppes and your meyne shal I saue
And many a gentyl worde she spake him to
And cõmaunded her messangers to go
The same day withouten any fayle
His shyppes for to seke/ and hem vitayle
Ful many a beest she to the shyppes sent
And with the wyne she gan hem to present
And to her royal paleys she her spedde
And Eneas alway with her she ledde
  What nedeth you the feestes to discryue
He neuer better at ease was in his lyue
Ful was the feest of deynties and rychesse
Of instrumentes of songe/ and of gladnesse
And many an amorous lokyng and deuyse
  This Eneas is come to Paradyse
Out of the swolowẽ of hel/ and thus in ioye
Remembreth him of his estate in Troye
  To daunsyng chambres ful of paramentes
Of ryche beddes/ and of pauementes
This Eneas is ledde after the mete
And with the quene whan that he had sete
And spyces parted/ and the wyne agon
Unto his chambre was he ladde anon
To take his ease/ and for to haue his reste
With al his folke/ to done what so hem leste
  There nas courser wel ybridled none
Ne stede for the iustyng wel to gone
Ne large palfrey/ easy for the nones
Ne iuwel fret ful of ryche stones
Ne sackes ful of golde/ of large wyght
Ne ruby none that shyneth by nyght
Ne gentyl hauten faukon heronere
Ne hounde for herte/ wylde bore/ or dere
Ne cuppe of golde/ with floreyns newe ybette
That in the londe of Lybye may ben gette
That Dido ne hath it Eneas ysent
And al is payed/ what that he hath spent
Thus can this honorable quene her gestes cal
As she that can in fredom passen al
  Eneas sothely eke/ without lees
Hath sent to his shyppe by Achates
After his sonne/ and after ryche thynges
Bothe ceptre/ clothes/ broches/ and eke rynges
Some for to weare/ and some to presente
To her/ that al these noble thynges him sente
And

And bade his sonne how that he shulde make
The presentyng/ and to the quene it take
Repayred is this Achates agayne
And Eneas ful blysful is and fayne
To seen his yonge sonne Ascanyus
For to him it was reported thus
That Cupido/ that is the god of loue
At prayer of his mother hye aboue
Had the lykenesse of the childe ytake
This noble quene enamoured for to make
On Eneas/ but of that scripture
Be as be may/ I make of it no cure
But soth is this/ ye quene hath made such chere
Unto this childe/ that wonder is to here
And of the presente that his father sent
She thanked him ofte in good entent
Thus is this quene in plesaunce and ioye
With al these newe lusty folke of Troye
And of the dedes hath she more enquired
Of Eneas/ and al the story lered
Of Troy/ and al the longe day they twey
Entendeden for to speke and for to pley
Of whiche there gan to breden suche a fyre
That sely Dido hath nowe suche desyre
With Eneas her newe geste to deale
That she lofte her hewe and eke her heale
Nowe to theffecte/ nowe to the frute of al
Why I haue tolde this storie/ and tellen shall
Thus I begynne/ it fell vpon a nyght
Whan that the moone vpreysed had her lyght
This noble quene vnto her reste wente
She sygheth sore/ and gan her selfe turmente
She waketh/ waloweth/ & made many braide
As done these louers/ as I haue herde sayde
And at the laste/ vnto her suster Anne
She made her mone/ & rizt thus spake she thā
Nowe dere suster myn/ what may it be
That me agasteth in my dreme (quod she)
This ylke newe troyan is so in my thought
For that me thynketh he is so wel ywrought
And eke so lykely to ben a man
And therwith so mykel good he can
That al my loue and lyfe lythe in his cure
Haue ye nat herde him tel his aueuture ?
Nowe certes Anne/ if that ye rede me
I wol fayne to him ywedded be
This is the effecte/ what shulde I more seyne
In him lythe al/ to do me lyue or deyne

Her suster Anne/ as she that coulde her good
Sayd as her thought/ & somdele it withstode
But here of was so longe a sermonyng
It were to longe to make rehersyng
But fynally/ it may nat be withstonde
Loue wol loue/ for no wight wol it wonde
The dawnyng vp ryst/ out of the see
This amerous quene chargeth her meyne
The nettes dresse/ and speares brode & kene
An huntyng wol this lusty fresshe quene
So pricketh her this newe ioly wo
To horse is al her lusty folke ygo
Unto the courte the houndes ben ybrought
And vp on courser swyfte as any thought
Her yonge knyghtes heuen al aboute
And of her women eke an huge route
Upon a thicke palfray/ paper whyte
With sadell reed/ enbrouded with delyte
Of golde the barres/ vp enbossed hygh
Sate Dido/ al in golde and perrey wrigh
And she is fayre/ as is the bright morowe
That healeth sicke folkes of nightes sorowe
Upon a courser/ startlyng as the fyre
Men myght turne him with a lytel wyre
But Eneas/ lyke Phebus to deuyse
So was he fresshe arayed in his wyse
The fomy bridel/ with the bytte of golde
Gouerneth he right as him selfe hath wolde
And forthe this noble quene/ this lady ryde
On huntyng/ with this troyan by her syde
The herde of hartes/ founden is anon
With hey gobet/ pricke thou/ let gon/ let gon
Why nyl the lyon comen or the beare
That I myght him ones meten wt this speare
Thus sayne this yonge folke/ & vp they kyl
The wylde hartes/ and haue hem at her wyl
Amonge al this/ to romblen gan the heuen
The thonder rored with a grisly steuen
Down come ye rayne/ with hayle & slet so fast
With heuens fyre/ that made so sore agast
This noble quene/ and also her meyne
That eche of hem was glad away to flye
And shortly fro the tempest her to saue
She fledde her selfe/ in to a lytel caue
And with her went this Eneas also
I not with hem if there wente any mo
The auctoure maketh of it no mencion
And here began the depe affection

Betwyxt

Bytwixt hem two this was the first morowe
Of her gladnesse/& gynnyng of her sorowe
For there hath Eneas ykneled so
And tolde her al his hurte and al his wo
And sworne so depe to her to be trewe
For wel or wo/and chaunge for no newe
And as a false louer/so wel can playne
That sely Dido rewed on his payne
And toke hym for husbõde/& became his wyfe
For euer more/whyle that hem laste lyfe
And after this/whan that the tempest stente
With myrth out as they came/hom they wente
The wicked fame vp rose/and that anon
Howe Eneas hath with the quene ygon
In to the caue/and demed as hem leste
And whan the king (ẏ Yarbas hyght) it wyst
As he that had her loued euer his lyfe
And wowed her to haue to his wyfe
Such sorowe as he hath maked/& suche chere
It is a ruthe and pyte for to here
But as in loue/alday it happeth so
That one shal laughen at anothers wo
Nowe laugheth Eneas/and is in ioye
And more rychesse/than euer was in Troye
O sely woman/ful of innocence
Ful of pyte/of truthe/and contynence
What maked you to men to trusten so?
Haue ye suche routhe vpon her fayned wo
And haue suche olde ensamples you before
Se ye nat al howe they ben forswo[r]ne
Where se ye one/that he ne hath lafte his lefe
Or ben vnkynde/or done her some mischefe
Or pylled her/or bosted of his dede
Ye may as wel it sene/as ye may rede
Take hede nowe of this great gentylman
This troyan/that so wel her please can
That fayneth hym so trewe and obeysyng
So gentyl/and so priuy of his doyng
And can so wel done al his obeysaunce
To her/at feestes and at daunce
And whan she gothe to temple/& home agayn
And fasten tyl he hath his lady seyn
And bearen in his deuyses for her sake
Not I nat what/and songes wolde he make
Justen/and don of armes many thynges
Sende her letters/tokens/broches/& rynges
Now herkeneth howe he shal his lady serue
There as he was in peryll for to sterue
For hunger and for mischefe in the see
And desolate/and fledde fro his countree
And al his folke with tempest al to driuen
She hath her body and eke her realme yeuen
In to his honde/there she might haue bene
Of other lande than of Cartage a quene
And lyued in ioy ynough/what wold ye more
This Eneas/ that hath thus depe yswore
Is wery of his crafte within a throwe
The hote ernest is al ouer blowe
And priuely he dothe his shyppes dight
And shapeth hym to steale away by night
This Dido hath suspection of this
And thought wel that it was al amys
For in his bedde he lythe a night and syketh
She asketh hym anon/what hym mislyketh
My dere herte/whiche that I loue moste
Certes (qd̄ he) this nyght my fathers goste
Hath in my slepe/me so sore turmented
And eke Marcury his message hath presented
That nedes to the conquest of Itayle
My destyne is sone for to sayle
For whiche me thynketh/broken is myn herte
Ther with his false teeres out they sterte
And taketh her within his armes two
Is that in ernest (qd̄ she) wol ye so
Haue ye nat sworne/to wyfe me to take
Alas/what woman wol ye of me make?
I am a gentyl woman/and a quene
Ye wol not fro your wyfe thus foule flene
That I was borne alas/what shal I do?
To tellen in shorte/this noble quene Dido
She seketh halowes/and dothe sacryfyce
She kneleth/cryeth/that routhe is to deuyse
Coniureth hym/and profereth hym to be
His thral/his seruaunt/in the best degre
She falleth hym to foote/ and swouneth there
Dischevyle with her bright gylte heere
And sayth/ haue mercy/let me with you ryde
These lordes/ whiche that wonnen me besyde
Wol me distroyen onely for your sake
And ye wol me nowe to wyfe take
As ye haue sworne/ than wol I yeue you leue
To sleen me with your swerde/now sone at eue
For than yet shal I dyen as your wyfe
I am with childe/and yeue my childe his lyfe
Mercy lorde/haue pyte in your thought
But al this thing auayleth her right nought
For

And as a traytour forthe gan to sayle
Towarde the large countre of Itayle
And thus hath he lafte Dido in wo & pyne
And wedded there a lady hyght Lauyne
A clothe he laft/ and eke his swerde stōdyng
Whan he fro Dido stale in her slepyng
Right at her beddes heed/ so gan he hye
Whan that he stale away to his nauye
Whiche clothe/ whan sely Dido gan awake
She hath it kyste ful ofte for his sake
And said/ o swete clothe/ whyle Jupiter it leste
Take my soule/ unbynde me of this unreste
I haue fulfylled of fortune al the course
And thus alas/ withouten his socourse
Twenty tyme yswouned hath she thanne
And whan that she unto her suster Anne
Complayned had/ of which I may nat write
So great routhe I haue it for to endyte
And bade her norice and her sustren gon
To fetchen fyre/ and other thynges anon
And sayd that she wolde sacryfye
And whan she might her tyme wel aspye
Upon the fyre of sacrifyce she sterte
And with his swerde she rofe her to the herte
But as myn auctour sayth/ yet thus she seyde
Or she was hurte/ beforne or she deyde
She wrote a letter anon/ and thus began
Right so (quod she) as the whyte swan
Ayenst his dethe begynneth for to synge
Right so to you I make my complaynyng
Not that I trowe to getten you agayne
For wel I wote it is al in vayne
Sens that the goddes ben cōtraryous to me
But syn my name is lost thrugh you (q̄d she)
I may wel lese a worde on you or letter
Al be it/ I shal be neuer the better
For thilke wynde that blewe your shyp away
The same wynde hath blowe away your fay
But who so wol al this lettre haue in mynde
Rede Ouyde/ and in him he shal it fynde.

¶ Here endeth the legende of Dido quene of Cartage: And here foloweth the legende of Hypsiphile and Medea.

Thou rote of false louers/ duke Jason
Thou sleer/ deuourer/ and confusyon
Of gentyl women/ gentyl creatures
Thou madest thy reclaymyng and thy lures
To ladyes of thy statelyche aparaunce
And of thy wordes farsed with plesaunce
And of thy fayned trouthe/ and thy manere
With thyn obeysaunce and humble chere
And with thyn counterfeyted payne and wo
There other falsen one/ thou falsed two
O ofte swore thou/ that thou woldest dye
For loue/ whan thou ne feltest maladye
Saue foule delyte/ whiche thou callest loue
If that I lyue/ thy name shal be shoue
In englysshe/ that thy discepte shal be knowe
Haue at ye Jason/ now thyn honour is blowe
But certes/ it is bothe routhe and wo
That loue with false louers werketh so
For they shal haue wel better loue and chere
Than he that hath bought loue ful dere
Or had in armes many a blody boxe
For euer as tender a capon eateth the foxe
Though he be false/ & hath the foule betrayde
As shal the good man that therfore payde
Although he haue to the capon skyl and right
The false foxe wol haue his parte at nyght
On Jason this ensample is wel ysene
By Hypsiphile/ and Medea the quene
In Thessalye/ as Ouyde telleth us
There was a kynge that hight Pellias
That had a brother/ whiche that hight Eson
And whan for age he mighte unnethes gon
He yaue to Pellias the gouernyng
Of al his reigne/ and made him lorde & king
Of whiche Eson/ this Jason getten was
That in his tyme/ in al that lande there nas
Nat suche a famous knyght of gentyllesse
Of fredom/ of strength/ and of lustynesse
After his fathers dethe he bare him so
That there nas none that lyste ben his foe
But dyd him al honour and companye
Of whiche this Pellias hath great enuye
Imagynyng/ that Jason might be
Enhaunsed so/ and put in suche degre
With loue of lordes of his regyoun
That from his reigne/ he may be put adoun
And in his wytte a nyght compassed he
Howe Jason might best distroyed be

With

Withouten sclaunder of his compasment
And at the laste he toke auysement
That to senden him in to some ferre countre
There as this Jason maye distroyed be
This was his wytte/ al made he to Jason
Great chere of loke/ and of affection
For drede lest his lordes it espyde
So fyl it/ as fame renneth wyde
There was suche tydyng ouer al/ & suche loos
That in an Ile/ that called was Colcos
Beyonde Troye estwarde in the see
That there was a ram/ that men might se
That had a flees of golde/ that shone so bright
That no where was there suche another syght
But it was kepte alway with a dragoun
And many other meruayles vp and doun
And with two bulles/ maked al of bras
That spytten fyre/ & moche thyng there was
But this was eke the tale natheles
That who so wolde wynnen thylke flees
He muste bothe/ or he it wynne myght
With the bulles and the dragon fyght
  And kyng Otes/ lorde was of that yle
This Pelleus bethought vpon this wyle
That he his neuewe Jason wolde exhorte
To saylen to that londe/ him to disporte
And sayd/ neuewe if it myght be
That suche worshyp might fall the
That thou this famous tresore myght wyn
And bring it my region within
It were to me great plesaunce and honour
Than were I holde to quyte thy labour
And al the costes I wol my selfe make
And chose what folke thou wolt with the take
Let se nowe/ darste thou taken this voyage
  Jason was yonge/ and lusty of corage
And vndertoke to done this ylke emprise
Anon Argus his shyppes gan deuyse
  With Jason wente the stronge Hercules
And many another/ that he with him ches
But who so asketh/ who is with him gon
Let him rede Argonautycon
For he wyl tel a tale longe ynough
Philoctetes anon the sayle vp drough
Whan the wynde was good/ & gan him hye
Out of his countre/ called Thessalye
So longe he sayled in the salte see
Tyl in the yle of Lemnon arryued he
Al be this not rehersed of Guydo
yet sayth Ouyde in his epystles so
And of this yle lady was and quene
The fayre yonge Hypsiphile the shene
That whilom Thoas doughter was the king
  Hypsiphile was gon in her playeng
And romyng on the cleuys by the see
Vnder a banke anon espyed she
Where lay the shyppe/ that Jason gan aryue
Of her goodnesse adowne she sendeth blyue
To weten/ if that any straunge wyght
With tempest thyder were yblowe anyght
To done him socoure/ as was her vsaunce
To furtheren euery wight/ and don plesaūce
Of very bountie/ and of curtesye
  This messanger adowne him gan to hye
And founde Jason and Hercules also
That in a cogge to londe were ygo
Hem to refresshen/ and to take the ayre
The mornyng attempre was and fayre
And in her way this messanger hem mette
Ful connyngly these lordes two he grette
And dyd his message/ askyng hem anon
If that they were broken/ or aught wo begon
Or had nede of lodesmen/ or vitayle
For socoure they shulde nothyng fayle
For it was vtterly the quenes wyll
  Jason answerde mekely and styll
My lady (quod he) thanke I hertely
Of her goodnesse/ vs nedeth trewly
Nothyng as nowe/ but that we wery be
And come for to play out of the see
Tyl that the wynde be better in our way
  This lady rometh by the clyffe to play
With her meyne/ endlonge the stronde
And fyndeth this Jason/ & this other stonde
In spekyng of this thyng/ as I you tolde
  This Hercules and Jason gan beholde
Howe that the quene it was/ & fayre her grette
Anon right as they with this lady mette
And she toke hede/ and knewe by her manere
By her array/ by wordes/ and by chere
That it were gentyl men of great degre
And to the castel with her ledeth she
These straūge folke/ & doth hem great honour
And asketh hem of trauayle and of labour
That they haue suffred in the salte see
So that within a daye/ two or thre

She

She knewe by the folke ẏ in his shyppes be
That it was Iason/ ful of renomee
And Hercules/that had the great loos
That soughten the auentures of Colcos
And dyd hem honour/more than before
And with hem deled euer longer the more
For they ben worthy folke withouten lees
And namely moste she spake with Hercules
To him her herte bare/he shulde be
Sadde/ wyse/ and trewe/ of wordes auysee
Withouten any other affection
Of loue/or any other ymagynacion
  This Hercules hath this Iason praysed
That to the sonne he hath it vp reysed
That halfe so trewe a man there nas of loue
Under the cope of heuen /that is aboue
And he was wyse/hardy/secrete/and ryche
Of these thre poyntes/ther nas non him lyche
Of fredom passed he/and lustyhede
Al tho that lyuen/or ben deed
Therto so great a gentyl man was he
And of Thessalye/lykely kyng to be
There nas no lacke/but that he was agaste
To loue/and for to speke shamefaste
Him had leauer him selfe to murdre and dye
Than that men shulde a louer him espye
As wolde god that I had yeue
My blode and flesshe/so that I might lyue
With ẏ nones/that he had aught wher a wyfe
For his astate/for suche a lusty lyfe
She shulden lede/ with this lusty knyght
And al this was compassed on the nyght
Betwyxe him Iason/and this Hercules
Of these two here was a shrewde lees
To come to house/vpon an innocent
For to be dote this quene was her entent
And Iason is as coye as is a mayde
He loketh pitously/but naught he sayde
But frely yaue he to her counsaylers
Yeftes great/and to her offycers
As wolde god that I leyser had and tyme
By processe/al his wowynge for to ryme
But in this house/ if any false louer be
Right as him selfe nowe dothe/right so dyd he
With faynyng/and with euery suttyl dede
Ye get no more of me/but ye wol rede
Thorygnal/that telleth al the caas
  The sothe is this/that Iason wedded was
Unto this quene/and toke of her substaunce
What so him lyst/vnto his purueyaunce
And vpon her begate children two
And drough his sayle/and sawe her neuer mo
A letter sent she him certayne
Whiche were to longe to writen and to sayne
And him reproueth of his great vntrouthe
And prayeth him on her to haue some routhe
And on his children two/she sayd him this
That they be lyke of al thyng ywis
To Iason/saue they couthe nat begyle
And prayed god/or it were longe whyle
That she that had his herte yreft her fro
Muste fynden him vntrewe also
And that she muste bothe her children spyl
And al tho that suffreth him his wyl
And trewe to Iason was she al her lyfe
And euer kepte her chaste/ as for his wyfe
Ne neuer had she ioye at her herte
But dyed for his loue of sorowes smerte
  To Colcos come is this duke Iason
That is of loue deuourer and dragon
As Matyre appeteth forme alwaye
And from forme to forme it passen may
Or as a welle that were botomles
Right so can Iason haue no pees
For to desyren through his appetyte
To done with gentyl women his delyte
This is his luste/ and his felycite
Iason is roomed forthe to the cyte
That whylom cleped was Iasonycos
That was the maister towne of al Colcos
And hath tolde the cause of his comyng
Unto Otes/ of that countrey kyng
Prayeng him that he muste done his assay
To gete the fleece of golde/ if that he may
Of whiche the kyng assenteth to his boone
And dothe him honour/ as it is to doone
So ferforth/ that his doughter and his heyre
Medea/ whiche that was so wyse and fayre
That fayrer saugh there neuer man with eye
He made her done to Iason companye
At meate/ and sytte by him in the hal
  Nowe was Iason a semely man with al
And lyke a lorde/ and had a great renoun
And of his loke as royal as a lyoun
And goodly of his speche/and famylier
And coude of loue al the crafte & arte plener

Withouten booke/ with euerich obseruaunce
And as fortune her ought a foule myschaunce
She woxe enamored vpon this man
 Iason (qd she) for ought I se or can
As of this thyng/ the whiche ye ben about
Ye and your selfe I putte in moche doute
For who so wol this auenture atcheue
He maye nat wele asterten/ as I leue
Withouten dethe/ but I his helpe be
But nathelesse/ it is my wyl (quod she)
To forthren you/ so that ye shal nat dye
But tournen sounde home to your Thessaly
 My right lady (quod this Iason) tho
That ye haue of my dethe or my wo
Any regarde/ and done me this honour
I wote wel that my myght/ ne my labour
Maye nat deserue it in my lyues day
God thanke you/ there I ne can ne may
Your man am I/ and lowly you beseche
To ben my helpe/ withouten more speche
But certes for my dethe shal I nat spare
 Tho gan this Medea to hym declare
The peryl of this case/ fro poynt to poynt
Of his batayle/ and in what disioynt
He mote stonde/ of whiche no creature
Saue onely she/ ne myght his lyfe assure
And shortely/ right to the poynt for to go
They ben accorded fully betwyxe hem two
That Iason shal her wedde/ as trewe knight
And terme y set to come soone at nyght
Vnto her chambre/ and make there his othe
Vpon the goddes/ that he for lefe or lothe
Ne shulde her neuer falsen nyght ne day
To ben her husbonde whyle he lyue may
As she that from his dethe hym saued here
And herupon at nyght they mette y fere
And doth his othe/ and goth with her to bedde
And on the morowe vpwarde he hym spedde
For she hath taught hi how he shal nat faile
The flese to wynne/ and stynten his bataile
And saued hym his lyfe/ and his honour
And gate hym a name/ as a conquerour
Right through the sleight of her enchantment
 Now hath Iason the fleese/ & home is went
With Medea/ and treasours ful great wonne
But vnwyst of her father she is gonne
To Thessalye/ with duke Iason her lefe
That afterwarde hath brouzt her to mischefe
For as a traytour he is from her go
And with her lefte yonge chyldren two
And falsely hath betrayed her/ alas
And euer in loue a chefe traytour he was
And wedded yet the thirde wyfe anon
That was the doughter of kynge Creon
 This is the meede of louynge and guerdon
That Medea receyued of duke Iason
Right for her trouth/ and for her kyndnesse
That loued hym better than her selfe I gesse
And lefte her father/ and her heritage
And of Iason this is the vassalage
That in his dayes nas neuer none y founde
So false a louer/ goynge on the grounde
And therfore in her letter thus she sayde
 First whan she of his falsnesse hi vmbraid
Why lyked me thy yelowe heer to se
More than the boundes of myne honeste?
Why lyked me thy youth and thy fairnesse
And of thy tonge/ the infynite gracyousnesse
 O haddest thou in thy conquest deed ybe
Ful mykel vntrouth had there dyed with the
Wel can Ouyde her letter in verse endyte
Whiche were as nowe to longe for to write.

Here endeth the legende of Hipsyphile and Medea: And here foloweth the legende of Lucrece of Rome.

Now mote I sayn the exilyng of kiges
Of Rome/ for her horrible doynges
Of the laste kynge Tarquinius
As saith Ouyd/ and Tytus Lyuius
But for that cause tel I nat this storye
But for to praysen/ and drawen in memorye
The very wyfe/ the very Lucresse
That for her wyfehode/ and her stedfastnesse
Nat onely that these paynyms her comende
But that eleped is in our legende
The great Austyn/ that hath compassyoun
Of this Lucrece that starfe in Rome toun
And in what wyse/ I wol but shortly treat
And of this thyng I touche but the great
Whan Ardea besiege was about
With Romayns/ that ful sterne were & stout
Ful longe laye the siege and lytel wroughten
So y they were half ydel/ as hem thoughten
And

And in his playe Tarquinius the yonge
Gan for to rape/ for he was lyght of tonge
And sayd/ that it was an ydel lyfe
No man dyd there more than his wyfe
And let vs speke of wyues/ that is best
Prayse euery man his owne as him leste
And with our speche let vs ease our herte
A knyght (that hyght Colatyn) vp sterte
And sayd thus/ nay sir it is no nede
To trowen on the worde/ but on the dede
I haue a wyfe (qd he) that as I trowe
Is holden good of al that euer her knowe
Go we to Rome to nyght/ and we shul se
Tarquynius answerde/ that lyketh me
To Rome be they come/ and fast hem dight
To Colatyns house/ and downe they light
Tarquynius/ and eke this Colatyne
The husbonde knewe the esters wel and fyne
And ful priuely in to the house they gone
Nor at the gate/ porter was there none
And at the chambre doore they abyde
This noble wyfe sate by her beddes syde
Discheueled/ for no malyce she ne thought
And soft woll saith Liui that she wrought
To kepen her fro slouthe and ydelnesse
And bade her seruauntes done her besynesse
And asketh hem/ what tydinges heren ye?
Howe sayth men of the siege/ howe shal it be?
God wolde the walles were fallen adowne
Myn husbonde is to longe out of this towne
For whiche drede dothe me so to smerte
Right as a swerde/ it styngeth to myn herte
Whan I thynke on this or of that place
God saue my lorde/ I pray him for his grace
And therwithal ful tenderly she gan wepe
And of her werke she toke no more kepe
But mekely she let her eyen fall
And thylke semblante sate her wel withal
And eke her teeres ful of heuynesse
Embelesed her wyfely chastnesse
Her countenaunce is to herte digne
For they acordeden in dede and signe
And with that worde her husbōde Colatyn
Or she of him was ware/ came sterlyng in
And sayd/ drede the nat for I am here
And she anon vp rose/ with blyssful chere
And kyssed him/ as of wyues is the wonne
Tarquinius/ this proude kynges sonne
Conceyued hath her beautie and her chere
Her yelowe heere/ her bountie/ ⁊ her manere
Her hew/ her wordes/ that she hath cōplayned
And by no crafte her beautie was nat fayned
And caught to this lady suche desyre
That in his herte he brent as any fyre
So woodly/ that his wytte was al forgoten
For wel thought he she shulde nat be goten
And aye the more he was in dispayre
The more coueyteth/ and thought her fayre
His blynde lust was al his coueytyng
On morowe/ whan the byrde began to synge
Vnto the siege he cometh ful priuely
And by him selfe he walketh soberly
The ymage of her recordyng alway newe
Thus lay her heer/ ⁊ thus fressh was her hewe
Thus sate/ thus span/ this was her chere
Thus fayre she was/ ⁊ this was her manere
Al this conceyte his herte hath newe ytake
And as the see/ with tempest al to shake
That after whan the storme is al ago
Yet wol the water quappe a day or two
Right so/ though that her forme were absente
The plesaunce of her forme was presente
But nathelesse nat plesaunce/ but delyte
Or an vnrightful talent with dispyte
For maugre her/ she shal my leman be
Hap helpeth hardy man alway (quod he)
What ende that I make/ it shal be so
And gyrte him with his swerde/ ⁊ gan to go
And he forthe right/ tyll to Rome he come
And al alone his way that he hath nome
Vnto the house of Colatyne ful ryght
Down was the sōne/ ⁊ day hath lost his lyght
And in he come/ vnto a preuy halke
And in the night ful thefely gan he stalke
Whan euery wight was to his rest brought
Ne no wight had of treason suche a thought
Whether by wyndowe/ or by other gyn
With swerde ydrawe/ shortly he cometh in
There as she lay/ this noble wyfe Lucrese
And as she woke/ her bedde she felte presse
What beest is that (qd she) that wayteth thus
I am the kynges sonne Tarquynius
(Qd he) but ⁊ thou crye/ or any noyse make
Or if thou any creature awake
By thilke god/ that formed man of lyue
This swerde through thyn herte shal I ryue

And therwithal/vnto her throte he sterte
And sette the swerde al sharpe on her herte
No worde she spake/she hath no myght therto
What shal she sayne/her wytte is al ago
Right as a wolfe that fayneth a lambe alone
To whom shal she cōplayne or make mone
What/shal she fyght with an hardy knyght
Wele wotte men a woman hath no myght
What/shal she crye/ or howe shal she astert ?
That hath her by the throte wt swerd at herte
She asketh grace/ and sayd al that she can
  No wolte thou nat (qd this cruel man)
As wisely Jupiter my soule saue
I shal in the stable slee thy knaue
And laye him in thy bedde/ and loude crye
That I the fynde in suche auoutry
And thus thou shalt be deed/and also lese
Thy name/for thou shalt nat chese
  This romayns wyues loueden so her name
At thilke tyme/and dredden so the shame
That what for fere of slaūder/& drede of deth
She loste bothe at ones wytte and brethe
And in a swoughe she lay/ & woxe so deed
Men mighten smyte of her arme or heed
She feleth nothing/ neyther foule ne fayre
  Tarquinius/that arte a kynges heyre
And shuldest/as by lynage and by right
Done as a lorde/and a very knyght
Why haste thou don dispyte to chiualrye ?
Why hast thou done thy lady vilanye ?
Alas/of the this was a villaynous dede
But nowe to the purpose/in the story I rede
Whan he was gone/& this mischaūce is fall
This lady sent after her frendes all
Father/mother/ & husbonde/ al yfere
And discheueled with her heere clere
In habyt suche as women vsed tho
Vnto the buryeng of her frendes go
She sate in hall/with a sorouful syght
Her frendes asken what her aylen might
And who was deed/and she sate aye wepyng
A worde for shame ne maye she forthout brig
Ne vpon hem she durste nat beholde
But at the laste of Tarquiny she hem tolde
This ruful case/and al this thyng horrible
The wo to tel/ were impossible
That she and al her frendes make at ones
Al had folkes hertes ben of stones
It might haue maked hem vpon her rewe
Her herte was so wisely and so trewe
She sayd/that for her gylt ne for her blame
Her husbonde shulde nat haue the foule name
That wolde she nat suffren by no waye
And they answerde al vnto her saye
That they foryaue it her/for it was right
It was no gylt/it lay nat in her might
And sayden her samples many one
But al for naught/for thus she sayd anone
Be as be may (quod she) of forgyuyng
I wyl nat haue no forgyfte for nothyng
But priuely she caught forth a knyfe
And therwithal she rafte her selfe her lyfe
And as she fell adowne/she caste her loke
And of her clothes/yet hede she toke
For in her fallyng/yet she had a care
Leste that her fete/or suche thynges lay bare
So wel she loued clennesse/and eke trouthe
Of her had al the towne of Rome routhe
And Brutus hath by her chaste bloode swore
That Tarquyn shulde ybanisshed be therfore
And al his kynne/and let the people call
And openly the tale he tolde hem all
And openly let cary her on a bere
Through al the town/ that men may se & here
The horryble dede of her oppressyoun
Ne neuer was there kyng in Rome toun
Sens thilke day/and she was holden there
A saynte/and euer her day yhalowed dere
As in her lawe:and thus endeth Lucresse
The noble wyfe/ Tytus bereth wytnesse
I tell it for she was of loue so trewe.
Ne in her wyl she chaunged for no newe
And in her stable herte/sadde and kynde
That in these women men may alday fynde
There as they caste her herte/ there it dwelleth
For wel I wote/that Christ him selfe telleth
That in Israel/as wyde as is the londe
That so gret fayth in al the londe he ne fonde
As in a woman/and this is no lye
And as for men/loke ye suche tyrannye
They done alday/assay hem who so lyste
The trewest is ful brotel for to tryste.

¶ Here endeth the legende of Lucrece of Rome/& here foloweth the legende of Ariadne of Athenes.

Iudge infernal Mynos / of Crete kyng
Now cometh thy lot / yͧ comest on ÿ rig
Nat for thy sake onely written is this storie
But for to cleape ayen vnto memorie
Of Theseus the great vntrouth of loue
For whiche the goddes of heuen aboue
Ben wroth / & wrathe haue take for thy synne
Be reed for shame / nowe I thy lyfe begynne
  Mynos that was the myghty kyng of Crete
That had an hundred cyties stronge & grete
To schole hath sent his sonne Androgeus
To Athenes / of the whiche it happed thus
That he was slayne / lernyng phylosophye
Right in that cyte / nat but for enuye
  The great Mynos / of the whiche I speke
His sonnes dethe is come for to wreke
Alcathoe he besieged harde and longe
But nathelesse the walles be so stronge
And Nisus / that was kyng of that cyte
So chyualrous / that lytel dredeth he
Of Mynos or his hoste / toke he no cure
Tyl on a day befyl an auenture
That Nisus doughter stode vpon the wall
And of the siege sawe the maner all
So happed it / that at scarmusshyng
She caste her herte vpon Mynos the kyng
For his beautie / and his chiualrye
So sore / that she wende for to dye
And shortly of this processe for to pace
She made Mynos wynnen thilke place
So that the cyte was al at his wyll
To sauen whom him lyste / or els spyll
But wickedly he quyt her kyndnesse
And let her drenche in sorowe and distresse
Nere that the goddes had of her pyte
But that tale were to longe as nowe for me
Athenes wan this kyng Mynos also
As Alcathoe / and other townes mo
And this the effect / that Mynos hath so driuen
Hem of Athenes / that they mote him yeuen
Fro yere to yere / her owne children dere
For to be slayne / as ye shal after here
  This Mynos hath a monster / a wicked beest
That was so cruel / that without arreest
Whan yͭ a man was brought in to his presẽce
He wolde him eate / there helpeth no defence
And euery thirde yere / withouten doute
They casten lotte / as it came aboute
On ryche and poore / he muste his sonne take
And of his childe he muste present make
To Mynos / to saue him or to spyll
Or let his beest deuour him at his wyll
And this hath Mynos don right in dispyte
To wreke his sonne was set al his delyte
And make hem of Athenes his thrall
Fro yere to yere / whyle he lyuen shall
And whom he sayleth whan this toun is won
This wicked custome is so longe yronne
Tyl of Athenes kynge Egeus
Mote senden his owne sonne Theseus
Sens that the lotte is fallen him vpon
To ben deuoured / for grace is there non
And forthe is ladde this woful yonge knyght
Vnto the coūtre of king Mynos ful of might
And in a prison fettred faste is he
Tyl the tyme he shulde yfreten be
  Wel mayste thou wepe / o woful Theseus
That art a kynges sonne / and dampned thus
Me thynketh this / that thou arte depe yholde
To whom that saued the fro cares colde
And nowe if any woman helpe the
Wel oughtest thou her seruaunt for to be
And ben her trewe louer yere by yere
But nowe to come ayen to my matere
  The toure / there this Theseus is throwe
Downe in the bottome derke / & wonder lowe
Was ioynyng to the wall of a foreyne
Longyng vnto the doughtren tweyne
Of Mynos / that in her chambres grete
Dwelten aboue the mayster strete
Of the towne / in ioye and in solas
Not I nat howe / it happed par caas
As Theseus complayned him by nyght
The kynges doughter / that Ariadne hight
And eke her suster Phedra / herden all
His complaynte / as they stode on the wall
And loked vpon the bright moone
Hem lyste nat to go to bedde so soone
And of his wo they had compassyon
A kynges sonne to be in suche prison
And ben deuoured / thought hem great pyte
Than Ariadne spake to her suster fre
And sayd: Phedra leue suster dere
This woful lordes sonne may ye nat here
Howe pitously he complayneth his kynne
And eke his poore estate that he is inne.

S.f.ii. And

And gyltlesse/certes nowe it is routhe
And if ye wol assent by my trouthe
He shal ben holpen howe so that we do
  Phedra answerde/ ywis me is as wo
For him/ as euer I was for any man
And to his helpe the beste rede I can
Is/that we done the gayler priuely
To come and speke with vs hastely
And don this woful man with him to come
For if he may this monster ouercome
Than were he quyte/there is none other boote
Let vs wel taste him at his herte roote
That if so be/that he a weapen haue
Where that he is lyfe dare kepe or saue
Fyghten with this fende/and him defende
For in the prison/ there as he shal discende
Ye wote wel/that the beest is in a place
That is nat derke/ & hath rōme and eke space
To welde an axe/or swerde/ staffe/or knyfe
So that me thynketh he shulde saue his lyfe
If that he be a man/he shal do so
And we shal make him balles eke also
Of wexe and towe/that whan he gapeth fast
In to the beestes throte he shal hem caste
To sleke his honger/and encomber his tethe
And right anon/whan that Theseus sethe
The beest acheked/he shal on him lepe
To sleen him/or they comen more to hepe
This weapen shal the gayler/or that tyde
Ful priuely within the prison hyde
And for the house is crencled to and fro
And hath so queynt wayes for to go
For it is shapen as the mase is wrought
Therto haue I a remedye in my thought
That by a clewe of twyne/as he hath gone
The same way he may returne anon
Folowyng alway the threde/ as he hath come
And whan this beest is ouercome
Than may he flyen away out of this stede
And eke the gayler may he with him lede
And him auaunce at home in his countre
Sens that so great a lordes sonne is he
  This is my rede/if that ye dare it take
What shulde I lenger sermon of it make
The gayler cometh/and with him Theseus
Whan these thynges ben accorded thus
  Downe sate Theseus vpon his kne
The right lady of my lyfe (quod he)
I sorouful man/ydampned to the dethe
Fro you/whyles that me lasteth brethe
I wol nat twynne/after this auenture
But in your seruyce/thus I wol endure
That as a wretch vnknowe/ I wol you serue
For euer more/tyl that myn herte sterue
Forsake I wol at home myn herytage
And as I sayd/ben of your courte a page
If that ye vouchsafe that in this place
Ye graunt me to haue suche a grace
That I may haue/nat but my meate & drinke
And for my sustynaunce yet wol I swynke
Right as you lyste/that Mynos ne no wight
Sens that he sawe me neuer with eyen sight
Ne no man els shal me espye
So slyly/and so wel I shal me gye
And me so wel dissfygure/and so lowe (we
That in this worlde ther shal no man me kno
To haue my lyfe/and to haue presence
Of you/that done to me this excellence
And to my father shal I sende here
This worthy man/that is your gaylere
And him so guerdon/that he shal wel be
One of the greatest men of my countre
And if I durst sayne/my lady bright
I am a kynges sonne/and eke a knyght
As wolde god/ if that it might be
Ye weren in my countrey al thre
And I with you/to beare you companye
Than shulde ye sene if that I therof lye
And if that I profer you in lowe manere
To ben your page/& seruen you right here
But I you serue as lowly in that place
I pray to Mars to yeue me suche grace
That shames dethe on me there mote fall
And dethe and pouerte to my frendes al
And that my spyrit by night mote go
After my dethe/and walke to and fro
That I mote of traytour haue a name
For which my spyrit mote go/to do me shame
And if I clayme euer other degre
But ye vouchsafe to yeue it me
As I haue sayd/of shames dethe I dey
And mercy lady/I can naught els sey
  A semely knyght was this Theseus to se
And yonge/but of twenty yere and thre
But who so had ysene his countenaunce
He wolde haue wept/ for routh of his penaũce
For

For whiche this Ariadne in this manere
Answerde to his profre and to his chere
  A kynges sonne/ & eke a knyght (q̃d she)
To ben my seruaunt in so lowe degree
God shilde it/ for the shame of women al
And lene me neuer suche a case befal
And sende you grace/ and sleyght of hert also
You to defende/ & knyghtly to sleen your foe
And lene here after I maye you fynde
To me/ and to my suster here so kynde
That I ne repent nat to yeue you lyfe
Yet were it better I were your wyfe
Sithe ye ben as gentyl borne as I
And haue a realme nat but faste by
Than that I suffred your gẽtylnesse to sterue
Or that I lette you as a page serue
It is no profyte/ as vnto your kynrede
But what is that/ yͤ man wol nat do for dre-
And to my suster syth that it is so (de
That she mote gone with me/ if that I go
Or els suffre dethe as wel as I
That ye vnto your sonne as trewly
Done her be wedded/ at your home comynge
This is the fynall ende of al this thyng
Ye swere it here/ vpon al that may be sworne.
  Ye lady myn (quod he) or els to torne
Mote I be/ with the mynotaure or to morowe
And haueth here of myn hert blode to borowe
If that ye wol/ if I had knyfe or speare
I wolde it letten out/ and theron sweare
For than at erste/ I wotte ye wolde me leue
By Mars/ that is chefe of my beleue
So that I might lyuen/ and nat fayle
To morowe for to taken my batayle
I nolde neuer fro this place flye
Tyl that ye shulde the very profe se
For nowe/ if that the sothe I shal you say
I haue loued you ful many a day
Though ye ne wyst nat/ in my countre
And aldermoste desyred you to se
Of any erthly lyuyng creature
Vpon my trouthe I sweare/ and you assure
This seuen yere I haue your seruaunt be
Nowe haue I you/ and also haue ye me
My dere herte/ of Athenes duchesse
  This lady smyleth at his stedfastnesse
And at his hertely wordes/ and at his chere
And to her suster sayd in this manere
  And sothly suster myn (quod she)
Nowe be we duchesses bothe I and ye
And sykerde to the regals of Athenes
And bothe herafter lykely to be quenes
And saued fro his dethe a kynges sonne
As euer of gentyl women is the wonne
To saue a gentyl man/ enforthe her might
In honest cause/ and namely in his right
Me thinketh no wight ought vs herof blame
Ne bearen vs therfore an yuel name
And shortly of this mater for to make
This Theseus of her hath leaue ytake
And euery poynt was performed in dede
As ye haue in this couenaunt herde me rede
His wepen/ his clewe/ his thig yͤ I haue sayde
Was by the gayler in the house layde
There as the Mynotaure hath his dwellyng
Right faste by the dore/ at his entryng
And Theseus is ladde vnto his dethe
And forthe vnto this Mynotaure he gethe
And by the teachyng of this Adriane
He ouercame this beest/ and was his bane
And out he cometh by the clewe agayne
Ful priuely/ whan he this beest hath slayne
And the gayler gotten hath a barge
And of his wyues treasure gan it charge
And toke his wyfe/ and eke her suster fre
And by the gayler/ and with hem al thre
Is stole away out of the londe by night
And to the countre of Enuppe hym dight
There as he had a frende of his knowyng
There festen they/ there daunsen they & synge
And in his armes hath this Adriane
That of the beest hath kept him fro his bane
And get hym there a noble barge anone
And of his countrey folke a ful great wone
And taketh his leaue/ & homwarde sayleth he
And in an yle/ amydde the wylde see
There as there dwelte creature none
Saue wylde beestes/ and that ful many one
He made his shyppe a londe for to sette
And in that yle/ halfe a day he lette
And sayd/ yͤ on the londe he must hym reste
His maryners haue done right as hym leste
And for to tell shortly in this case
Whan Ariadne his wyfe a slepe was
For that her suster fayrer was than she
He taketh her in his honde/ and forth gothe he

S.j.iii. To

To shyppe/and as a traytour stale away
Whyle that this Ariadne a slepe lay
And to his countreywarde he sayleth blyue
A twenty dyuel way/the wynde him driue
And founde his father drenched in the see
Me lyste no more to speke of him parde
These false louers/poyson be her bane
But I wol turne agayne to Adriane
That is with slepe for werynesse ytake
Ful sorowfully her herte may awake
Alas/for the myn herte hath pyte
Right in the dawnyng awaketh she
And gropeth in the bed/& fonde right nought
Alas (qd she) that euer I was wrought
I am betrayed/and her heere to rente
And to the stronde barefote faste she wente
And cryed: Theseus myn herte swete
Where be ye/ that I may nat with you mete?
And might thus with beestes ben yslayne
The holowe rockes answerde her agayne
No man she sawe/and yet shone the moone
And hye vpon a rocke she went soone
And sawe his barge/saylyng in the see
Colde woxe her herte/and right thus sayd she
Meker than ye/ fynde I the beestes wylde
Hath he nat synne/that he her thus begylde
She cryed/o turne agayne for routh & synne
Thy barge hath nat al his meyne inne
Her kerchefe on a pole stycked she
Ascaunce he shulde it wele yse
And him remembre that she was behynde
And turne agayne/& on the stronde her fynde
But al for naught/ his way he is gone
And downe she fel a swowne on a stone
And vp she ryst/ and kyssed in al her care
The steppes of his fete/there he hath fare
And to her bedde right thus she speketh tho
Thou bedde (qd she) that hast receyued two
Thou shalt answere of two/and not of one
Where is the greater parte/ away gone
Alas/wher shal I wretched wight become?
For though so be that bote none here come
Home to my countrey dare I nat for drede
I can my selfe in this case nat rede
What shulde I tel more her complaynyng
It is so long? it were an heauy thyng
In her epystle/Naso telleth all
But shortly to the ende tell I shal
The goddes haue her holpen for pyte
And in the signe of Taurus men may se
The stones of her crowne shyne clere
I wyl no more speke of this matere
But thus this false louer can begyle
His trewe loue/the dyuel quyt him his whyle.

¶ Here endeth the legende of Ariadne and here foloweth the legende of Phylomene.

Thou yeuer of the formes/ỷ hast wrought
The fayre worlde/& bare it in thy thought
Eternally/er thou thy werke began
Why madest thou vnto the slaunder of man;
Or al be that it was nat thy doyng
As for that fende/to make suche a thyng
Why suffredest thou that Tereus was bore?
That is in loue so false and so forswore
That fro this worlde vp to the first heuen
Corrumpeth/whā that folke his name neuen
And as to me/so grisly was his dede
That whan that I this foule storie rede
Myn eyen wexen foule/and sore also
Yet lasteth the venyme of so longe ago
That infecteth him/ that wolde beholde
The storie of Tereus/of whiche I tolde
Of Trace was he lorde/and kyn to Marte
The cruel god that stante with blody darte
And wedded had he with blyssful chere
Kyng Pandyonis fayre doughter dere
That hight Progne/floure of her countre
Though Juno lyste nat at the feest be
Ne Hymeneus/ that god of weddyng is
But at the feest redy ben iwys
The furys thre/with al her mortal bronde
The oule al nyght aboute the balkes wonde
That prophete is of wo/and of mischaunce
This reuel/ ful of songe and ful of daunce
Laste a fourtenyght/or lytel lasse
But shortly of this storie for to passe
(For I am wery of him for to tel)
Fyue yere his wyfe and he togyther dwel
Tyl on a day she gan so sore longe
To sene her suster that she sawe nat longe
That for desyre she nyst what to say
But to her husbonde gan she for to pray
For goddes loue/that she mote ones gone

Her

Her suster for to sene/and come ayen anon
Or els but she mote to her wende
She prayed him that he wolde after her sende
And this was day by day al her prayere
With al humblesse of wyfehode/worde & chere
 This Tereus let make his shyppes yare
And in to Grece him selfe is forthe yfare
Unto his father in lawe gan he pray
To vouche safe/that for a moneth or tway
That Philomene his wyues suster myght
On Progne his wyfe/but ones haue a syghe
And she shal come to you agayne anon
My selfe with her/I wyl bothe come & gon
And as my hertes lyfe I wyl her kepe
 This olde Pandion/this kyng gan wepe
For tendernesse of herte/ for to leue
His doughter gon/and for to yeue her leue
Of al this worlde he loued nothyng so
But at the laste leaue hath she to go
For Philomene with salte teeres eke
Gan of her father grace to beseke
To sene her suster/that her longeth so
And him embraceth/with her armes two
And there also yonge and fayre was she
That whan that Tereus sawe her beaute
And of array/that there was none her lyche
And yet of beaute was she to so ryche
He caste his firy herte upon her so
That he wol haue her/howe so that it go
And with his wyles kneled/and so prayed
Tyl at the laste Pandion thus sayde
 Nowe sonne (quod he) that arte to me so dere
I the betake my yonge doughter dere
That beareth the key of al myn hertes lyfe
And grete wel my doughter/and thy wyfe
And yeue her leaue somtyme for to pley
That she may sene me ones or I dey
And sothly he hath made him ryche feest
And to his folke/the moste and eke the leste
That with him came/& yafe him yeftes grete
And him conueyeth through the maister streete
Of Athenes/and to the see him brought
And turneth home/no malyce he ne thought
The ores pulleth forthe the vessel faste
And in to Trace arryueth at the laste
And up in to a forest he her ledde
And to a caue priuely him spedde
And in this derke caue/if her lyste
Or lyste nought/ he badde her for to rest
Of whiche her herte agrose/ and sayd thus
 Where is my suster/ brother Tereus?
And there withal she wepte tenderly
And quoke for feare pale and pitously
Right as the lambe/ that of the wolfe is bytten
Or as the culuer/ that of the Egle is smytten
And is out of his clawes forth escaped
Yet it is a ferde/ and a waped
Lest it be hente estsones: so sate she
But utterly it maye none other be
By force hath this traytour done a dede
That he hath refte her of her maydenhede
Maugre her heed/ by strength & by his might
 Lo here a dede of men/and that a right
She cryeth suster with ful loude steuen
And father dere helpe me god in heuen
Al helpeth nat/ and yet this false thefe
Hath done this lady yet a more myschefe
For feare/ leste she shulde his shame crye
And done him openly a vilanye
And with his swerde her tonge of kerfe he
And in a castel made her for to be
Ful priuely in prison euermore
And kepte her to his usage and to his store
So that she ne might neuer more asterte
 O sely Philomene/ wo is in thyne hert
Huge ben thy sorowes/and wonder smert
God wreke the/ and sende the thy bone
Nowe is tyme I make an ende soone
 This Tereus is to his wyfe ycome
And in his armes hath his wyfe ynome
And pitously he wepte/ and shoke his heed
And swore her/ that he founde her suster deed
For whiche this sely Progne hath suche wo
That nygh her sorouful herte brake a two
And thus in teeres lette I Progne dwel
And of her suster forthe I wol you tel
 This woful lady ylerned had in youth
So that she worken and enbrauden couth
And weauen in stole the radenore
And it of women hath be woned yore
And sothly for to sayne/she hath her fyll
Of mete and drinke/of clothyng at her wyll
And couthe eke rede wel ynough and endyte
But with a penne she coulde nat write
But letters can she weaue/to and fro
So that by the yere was al a go

She

She had wouen in a stames large
How she was brought fro Athenes in a barge
And in a caue howe that she was brought
And al the thyng that Tereus hath wrought
She waue it wel/and wrote the storie aboue
Howe she was serued for her susters loue
And to a man a rynge she yaue anon
And prayde him by signes for to gon
Unto the quene/and bearen her that clothe
And by signe swore many an othe
She shulde him yeue what she getten myght
This man anon unto the quene him dyght
And toke it her/and al the maner tolde
And whan ẏ Progne hath this thyng beholde
No worde she spake/for sorowe & eke for rage
But fayned her to gone on pilgrymage
To Baccus temple/ and in a lytel stounde
Her dombe suster syttyng hath she founde
Weppynge in the castel her selfe alone
Alas the wo/constraynte/and the mone
That Progne upon her dombe suster maketh
In armes eueryche of hem other taketh
And thus I let hem in her sorowe dwell
The remenaunt is no charge to tell
For this is al and some/thus was she serued
That neuer agylte/ne deserued
Unto this crewel man/that she of wyste
ye may beware of men if that you lyste
For al be that he wol nat for shame
Done as Tereus/to lese his name
Ne serue you as a murtherer or a knaue
Ful lytel whyle shul ye trewe him haue
That wol I sayn/al were he now my brother
But it so be that he may haue a nother.

Here endeth the legende of Phylomene/ & here foloweth the legende of Phillis.

By proue/as wel as by auctorite
That wicked frute cometh of a wicked (tre
That may ye fynde/if that it lyketh you
But for this ende/I speke this as now
To tel you of false Demophon
In loue a falser herde I neuer non
But it were his father Theseus
God for his grace fro suche one kepe us
Thus these women prayen/that it here
Nowe to the effecte turne I of my matere
Distroyed is of Troye the cyte
This Demophon came saylyng in the see
Towarde Athenes/to his paleys large
With him came many a shyp/& many a barge
Ful of folke/of whiche ful many one
Is wounded sore/and sicke/and wo begone
And they haue at the siege longe layne
Behynde him came a wynde/and eke a rayne
That shofe so sore/his sayle might nat stonde
Him were leuer than al the worlde alonde.
So hunteth him the tempest to and fro
So derke it was/he coulde no where go
And with a waue brusten was his stere
His shyp was rente so lowe/in suche manere
That carpenter coulde it nat amende
The see by nyght as any torche brende
For woode/and posseth him up and down
Tyl Neptune hath of him compassyoun
And Thetis Chorus/ Tryton/ and they al
And maden him up a londe to fall
Wherof that Phillis lady was and quene
Lycurgus doughter/ fayrer unto sene
Than is the floure agayne the bright sonne
Unneth is Demophon to londe ywonne
Weake and eke wery/and his folke forpyned
Of werynesse/ and also enfamyned
And to the dethe he was almoste ydriuen
His wyse folke counsayle haue him yeuen
To seken helpe and socoure of the quene
And loken what his grace might bene
And maken in that lande some cheuesaunce
And kepen him fro wo/and fro mischaunce
For sicke he was/and almoste at the dethe
Unneth might he speke/or drawe brethe
And lythe in Rodopeya him for to reste
Whã he may walke/him thought it was beste
Unto the countre to seken for socour
Men knewe him wele/and dyd him honour
For at Athenes duke and lorde was he
As Theseus his father hath ybe
That in his tyme was great of renoun
No man so great in al his regyoun
And lyke his father of face and of stature
And false of loue/it came him of nature
As dothe the foxe Renarde/the foxes sonne
Of kynde he coulde his olde fathers wonne
Without lore/as can a drake swymme

Whan

Whan it is caught/ and carped to the brymme
This honorable quene Phillis doth him chere
Her lyketh wel his porte and his manere
But I am agroted here beforne
To write of hem that in loue ben forsworne
And eke to haste me in my legende
Whiche to performe/god me grace sende
Therfore I passe shortly in this wyse
Ye haue wel herde of Theseus the gyse
In the betrayeng of fayre Adriane
That of her pyte kepte him fro his bane
At shorte wordes/right so Demophon
The same way/& the same pathe hath gone
That dyd his false father Theseus
For vnto Phillis hath he sworne thus
To wedden her/and her his trouthe plyght
And pyked of her al the good he myght
Whan he was hole & sounde/and had his reste
And dothe with Phillis/what so þ him leste
As wel I coulde/if that me lyste so
Tellen al his doyng to and fro
He sayd to his countrey mote him sayle
For there he wolde her weddyng apparayle
As fyl to her honour/and his also
And openly he toke his leaue tho
And to her swore he wolde nat soiourne
But in a moneth agayne he wolde retourne
And in that londe lete make his ordynaunce
As very lorde/and toke the obeysaunce
Wel and homblye/and his shyppes dyght
And home he gothe the next way he myght
For vnto Phillis yet came he nought
And that hath she so harde and sore ybought
Alas/as the storie dothe vs recorde
She was her owne dethe with a corde
Whan she sawe that Demophon her traped
But first wrote she to him/& faste him prayed
He wolde come/and delyuer her of payne
As I reherce shal a worde or twayne
Me lyste nat vouchsafe on him to swynke
Dispenden on him a penne ful of ynke
For false in loue was he/right as his syre
The dyuel sette her soules bothe on a fyre
But of the letter of Phylles wol I write
A worde or twayne/al though it be but lyte
Thyn hostesse (quod she) O Demophon
Thy Phillis/whiche that is so wo begon
Of Rhodopeye/ vpon you mote complayne
Ouer the terme sette betwyxt vs twayne
That ye ne holden forwarde/as ye sayde
Your ancre/ whiche ye in our hauen layde
Hight vs/that ye wolde comen out of doute
Or that the moone ones went aboute
But tymes four/the moone hath hyd her face
Sens thylke day ye wente fro this place
And four tymes lyght the worlde agayne
But for al that/yet shal I sothly sayne
Yet hath the streme of Scython nat brought
From Athenes the shyp/yet came it nought
And if that ye the terme reken wolde
As I or other trewe louers do sholde
I playne nat (god wot) beforne my day
But al her letter writen I ne may
By order/for it were to me a charge
Her letter was right longe/and therto large
But here and there/in ryme I haue it layde
There as me thought that she hath wel sayde
She sayd/thy sayles cometh nat agayne
Ne to the worde/there nys no fey certayne
But I wot why ye come nat (quod she)
For I was of my loue to you so fre
And of the goddes that ye haue swore
That her vengeaunce fal on you therfore
Ye be nat suffysaunt to beare the payne
To moche trusted I/wel may I sayne
Vpon your lynage/and your fayre tonge
And on your teeres/falsly out wronge
How coude ye wepe so by crafte? (quod she)
Maye there suche teeres fayned be?
Nowe certes/ if ye wolde haue in memorie
It ought be to you but lytel glorie
To haue a sely mayde thus betrayde
To god (qd she) pray I/and ofte haue prayde
That it be nowe the greatest price of all
And moste honour/that euer you shal befall
And whan thyn olde auncestres paynted be
In whiche men may her worthynesse se
Than pray I god/thou paynted be also
That folke may reden/ forthe by as they go
Lo this is he/that with his flatterye
Betrayed hath/and done her villanye
That was his trewe loue/in thought & dede
But sothly of o poynt yet may they rede
That ye ben lyke your father/as in this
For he begyled Ariadne ywis
With suche an arte/and suche subtelte

As

As thou thy seluen haste begyled me
As in that poynt/al though it be nat feyre
Thou folowest certayne/and arte his heyre
But sens thus synfully ye me begyle
My body mote ye sene/within a whyle
Right in the hauen of Athenes fletyng
Withouten sepulture and buryeng
Though ye ben harder than is any stone
  And whan this letter was forthe sent anone
And knewe howe brotel & howe false he was
She for dispayre fordyd her selfe/alas
Suche sorowe hath she/for she beset her so
Beware ye women of your subtyll foe
Sens yet this day/ men may ensample se
And trusteth nowe in loue no man but me.

Here endeth the legende of Phillis/ and here foloweth the legende of Hypermestre.

  In Grece whylom weren brethern two
Of whiche that one was called Danao
That many a sonne hath of his body wonne
As suche false louers ofte conne
  Amonge his sonnes al there was one
That aldermoste he loued of euerychone
And whan this childe was borne/this Danao
Shope hym a name/and called hym Lyno
That other brother called was Egyste
That was of loue as false as euer hym lyste
And many a doughter gate he in his lyfe
Of whiche he gate upon his right wyfe
A doughter dere/and dyd her for to call
Hypermestra/ yongest of hem all
The whiche childe of her natyuite
To al good thewes borne was she
As lyked to the goddes or she was borne
That of the shefe she shulde be the corne
The werdes that we clepen destyne
Hath shapen her/that she muste nedes be
Pytous/sadde/wyse/trewe as stele
And to this woman it acordeth wele
For though that Venus yaue her gret beaute
With Jupiter compowned so was she
That conscience/trouthe/and drede of shame
And of her wyfehode for to kepe her name
This thought her was felycite as here
And reed Mars/was that tyme of the yere
So feble/ that his malyce is hym rafte
Represled hath Venus his cruell crafte
And what with Venus/and other oppressyon
Of houses/Mars his venym is a don
That Hypermestre dare nat handle a knyfe
In malyce/ though she shulde lese her lyfe
But natheles/as heuen gan tho turne
To badde aspectes/ hath she of Saturne
That made her to dye in prison
And I shal after make mention
Of Danao and Egystes also
And though so be that they were brethern two
For thilke tyme nas spared no lynage
It lyked hem to maken maryage
Betwyxt Hypermistre/ and hym Lyno
And casten suche a day it shal be so
And ful acorded was it utterly
The aray is wrought/the tyme is faste by
And thus Lyno hath of his fathers brother
The doughter wedded/& eche of hem hath other
The torches brennen/& the lampes bright
The sacrifyce ben ful redy dight
Thencense out of the fyre reketh soote
The flour the lefe/is rent up by the roote
To maken garlandes and crownes hye
Ful is the place of sounde of mynstralcye
Of songes amorous of maryage
As thilke tyme was the playne usage
And this was in the paleys of Egyste
That in his house was lorde/right as hym lyste
And thus that day they dryuen to an ende
The frendes taken leue/and home they wende
The night is comen/the bride shal go to bedde
Egyste to his chambre fast hym spedde
And priuely let his doughter call
Whan that the house voyded was of hem all
He loketh on his doughter with gladde chere
And to her spake/as ye shal after here
  My right doughter/ tresour of myn herte
Sens first that day/ yͭ shapen was my sherte
Or by the fatall suster had my dome
So nye myn herte neuer thyng ne come
As thou Hypermistre/doughter dere
Take hede what thy father sayth the here
And werke after thy wyser euer mo
For alderfirst doughter/I loue the so
That al the worlde to me nys halfe so lefe
Ne walde rede the to thy mischefe
For

For al the good vnder the colde moone
And what I mene/ it shal be sayd right soone
With protestacion/ as sayne these wyse
That but thou do/ as I shal the deuyse
Thou shalt be deed/ by him yͭ al hath wrouzt
At shorte wordes thou ne scapest nought
Out of my paleys/ or that thou be deed
But thou consent/ and werke after my reed
Take this to the fearful conclusyoun
This Hypermister caste her eyen doun
And quoke as dothe the leefe of aske grene
Deed weyt her hewe/ ⁊ lyke as asshen to sene
And sayd: lorde and father al your wyll
After my might/ god wote I shal fulfyll
So it be to me no confusyon
  I nyl (quod he) haue none exception
And out he caught a knyfe/ as rasour kene
Hyde this (q̄d he) that it be nat ꝑsene
And whan thyn husbonde is to bedde go
Whyle that he slepeth/ cutte his throte a two
For in my dremes it is warned me
Howe that my neuewe shal my bane be
But whiche I not/ wherfore I wol be syker
If thou say nay/ we two shal haue a byker
As I haue sayde/ by him that I haue sworne
This Hypermister hath nigh her wyt forlorn
And for to passen harmlesse out of that place
She granted him/ ther was none other grace
And withal a costrel taketh he tho
And sayd/ herof a draught or two
Yeue him drinke/ whan he gothe to reste
As he shal slepe as longe as euer the leste
The narcotikes and apies ben so stronge
And go thy way/ leste that him thinke to lōge
  Out cometh the bride/ ⁊ with ful sobre chere
As is of maydens ofte the manere
To chambre brought/ with reuel ⁊ with songe
And shortly/ leste this tale be to longe
This Lino and she bethe brought to bedde
And euery wight out at the dore him spedde
The night is wasted/ and he fel a slepe
Ful tenderly begynneth she to wepe
She ryst her vp/ and dredefully she quaketh
As dothe the braunche/ that zephirus shaketh
And hushte were al in Argone that cyte
As colde as any froste nowe weyeth she
For pyte by the herte strayned her so
And drede of dethe dothe her so moche wo
That thrise downe she fyl/ in suche a were
She ryste her vp/ and stakereth here ⁊ there
And on her handes faste loketh she
Alas/ shal myn handes bloody be
I am a mayde/ and as by my nature
And by my semblaunt/ and by my vesture
Myn hondes ben nat shapen for a knyfe
As for to reue no man fro his lyfe
What dyuel haue I with the knyfe to do?
And shal I haue my throte corue a two?
Than shal I blede alas/ and be shende
And nedes this thing mote haue an ende
Or he or I mote nedes lese our lyfe
Nowe certes (quod she) sens I am his wyfe
And hath my faythe/ yet is it bette for me
For to be deed/ in wifely honeste
Than be a traytour/ lyuyng in my shame
Be as be may/ for ernest or for game
He shal awake/ and ryse and go his way
Out at this gutter/ er that it be day
And wept ful tenderly vpon his face
And in her armes gan him to embrace
And him she roggeth/ and awaketh softe
And at the wyndowe lepe he fro the lofte
Whan she hath warned him/ ⁊ don him boote
This Lyno swyfte was/ and light of foote
And from her ran/ a ful good paas
This sely woman is so weake/ alas
And helpelesse/ so that er she ferre wente
Her cruel father dyd her for to hente
Alas Lyno/ why arte thou so vnkynde
Why ne haste thou remembred in thy mynde
And taken her/ ⁊ ledde her forthe with the
For whan she sawe that gon away was he
And that she might not so faste go
Ne folowen him/ she sate downe right tho
And tyl she was caught/ ⁊ fettred in prison
This tale is sayd for this conclusyon.

¶ Thus endeth the legendes of good women/ and here foloweth a balade of Chaucer.

A balade.

¶ A goodly balade of Chaucer.

Mother of norture/ best beloued of al
And fresshest flour/ to whom good thrift god
Your childe/ if it lust you me so to cal (sende
Al be I vnable my selfe so to pretende
To your discrecion I recomende
Myn herte and al/ with euery circumstaunce
Al holy to be vnder your gouernaunce

Moste desyre I/ and haue/ and euer shal
Thyng/ whiche might your hertes ease amēde
Haue me excused/ my power is but small
Natheles of right ye ought to cōmende
My good wyll/ whiche fayne wolde entende
To do you seruyce/ for al my suffysaunce
Is holy to be vnder your gouernaunce

Meusy vn: in herte/ whiche neuer shal apal
Aye fresshe & newe/ & right glad to dispende
My tyme in your seruyce/ what so befall
Besechyng your excellence to defende
My symplenesse/ if ignoraunce offende
In any wyse/ sythe that myn affyaunce
Is holy to ben vnder your gouernaunce

Daisy of lyght/ very grounde of comforte
The Sonnes doughter (ye hight) as I rede
For whan he westreth/ farwel your disporte
By your nature anon right for pure drede
Of ẏ rude night/ that with his boystous wede
Of derkenesse/ shadoweth our emyspere
Than closen ye/ my lyues lady dere

Dawyng the day/ to his kynde resorte
And Phebus yo[r] father/ with his stremes rede
Adorneth the morowe/ consumyng the sorte
Of misty cloudes/ that wolden ouerlede
Trewe humble hertes/ with her mistyhede
Nere comforte a dayes/ whan eyen clere
Disclose and sprede my lyues lady dere

Je voudray: but great god disposeth
And maketh casuel by his prouydence
Suche thyng/ as mans frele witte purposeth
Al for the best/ if that our conscience
Nat grutche it/ but in humble pacience
It receyue/ for god sayth without fable
A faythful herte euer is acceptable

Cauteles/ who so vseth gladly gloseth
To eschewe suche it is right high prudence
What ye sayd ones/ myn herte opposeth
That my wrytyng iapes in your absence
Pleased you moche better than my presence
Yet can I more/ ye be nat excusable
A faythful herte euer is acceptable

Quaketh my penne/ my spirit supposeth
That in my wrytyng ye fynde wol some offēce
Myn hert welkeneth thus sone/ anon it ryseth
Nowe hotte/ nowe colde/ and efte in feruence
That mysse is/ is caused of neglygence
And not of malyce/ therfore bethe mercyable
A faythful herte euer is acceptable.

¶ Lenuoye.

¶ For the cōplaynt/ for the lackyng eloquence
For the lytel lettre of endytyng lame
I haue besought my ladyes sapyence
Of thy behalfe/ to accept in game
Thyn inabylite/ do thou the same
Abyde/ haue more yet: Je serue Jouesse
Nowe forth/ I close the in holy Venus name
The shal vnclose my hertes gouernouresse.

¶ Finis.

¶ Thus endeth this balade: And here foloweth the boke of Boecius De cōsolatione philosophie.

A Goodly Balade (wrongly assigned to Chaucer)

Boetius de con-
solatione philo-
sophie.

Carmina qui quōdam studio florēte pegi
Flebilis heu mestos cogor i ire modos.

ALas/ I weppyng am cōstrayned to begyn vers of sorousful mater/ that whilom in flourisshyng studye made delytable dytees. For so/ rendyng muses of poetes/ endyten to me thynges to be written/ & drery teeres. At last no drede ne might ouercome tho muses/ that they ne weren felowes & folouden my way/ that is to say: whan I was exyled/ they yͭ weren of my youthe whylom weleful and grene/ comforten nowe sorousful wierdes of me olde man: for elde is comen vnwarely vpon me/ hasted by the harmes that I haue/ and sorowe hath cōmaunded his age to be in me. Heeres hore arne shadde ouertymely the vpon my heed: and the slacke skynne trembleth of myn empted body. Thylke dethe of men is weleful/ yͭ ne cometh nat in yeres that be swete/ but cometh to wretches often ycleped. Alas/ alas/ with how deefe an eere dethe cruel turneth away fro wretches/ and nayeth for to close weppyng eyen. Whil fortune vnfaythful fauoured me with lyght goodes/ the sorouful houre/ that is to saye/ the dethe/ had almoste drepnt myn heed: But nowe for fortune cloudy hath chaunged her deceyuable chere to mewarde/ myne vnpytous lyfe draweth a longe vnagreable dwellīges. O ye my frēdes/ what or wherto auaunted ye me to ben weleful? for he that hath fallen/ stode in no stedfast degre.

Hec dum mecū tacitus ipse reputarem/ queremoniāq; lachrimabilem stili officio designarem: astitisse mihi supra uerticem visa est mulier reuerēdi admodū vultus/ oculis ardentibus/ et vltra cōmunem. &c.

IN the meane whyle that I styl recorded these thynges with my selfe / and marked my wepely cōplaynt with offyce of poyntel: I saugh stondynge abouen the hyght of myne heed/ a woman of ful great reuerence by semblaunt / Her eyen brennyng/ and clere seyng ouer the cōmen myght of men/ with a lyuely colour/ & with suche vigour & strēgth/ that it ne might nat ben nēpned/ al were it so that she were ful of so great age/ that men ne wolden nat trowen i no maner that she were of our elde. The stature of her was of doutous iugement/ for somtyme she constrayned and shronke her seluen lyke to the cōmen mesure of men: And somtyme it semed that she touched the heuen with the height of her heed. And whan she houe her heed hyer / she perced the selfe heuen/ so that the syght of men loking was in ydel: her clothes were maked of right delyce thredes and subtyl crafte of perdurable matiere. The whiche clothes she had wouen with her owne handes / as I knewe wel after by her selfe declaryng/ and shewyng to me the beaute: the which clothes a derknesse of a forleten and dispysed elde had dusked and derked/ as it is wonte to derke by smoked ymages. In the netherest hēme or bordure of these clothes/ men redde ywouen therin a grekysshe A. that signefieth the lyfe Actyue/ and aboue that letter in the hyest bordoure a grekysshe C. that sygnyfyeth the lyfe Contemplatyfe. And bytwene these two letters there were sene degrees nobly wrought in maner of ladders/ by which degrees men might clymben from the netherest lettre to the vpperest: Nathelesse handes of some men hadden kerue that clothe by violence or by strength/ and euerych man of hem had borne away such peces as he might geten. And forsoth this foresayd woman bare smale bookes in her right hande/ & in her lyfte hande she bare a sceptre. And whan she sawe these poetycal muses approchyng aboute my bed/ and enditynge wordes to my wepynges/ she was a lytel amoued/ and glowed with cruel eyen. Who (quod she) hath suffred approchen to this sicke man these comen strompettes/ of whiche is the place/ that men callen Theatre/ the whiche onely ne aswagen nat his sorowes with remedies/ but they wolde feden and nourisshe him with swete venym? Forsothe that ben tho that with thornes and prickynges of talētes of affections/ whiche that ben nothing fructuous nor profytable/ distroyen the corne plentuous of fruites of reason. For they holden hertes of men in vsage/ but they ne delyuer no folke fro maladye. But if the muses

T.t.ii. had

had withdrawen fro me with your flatteryes any an vnconnynge and vnprofytable man/ as ben wonte to fynde comenly amonge the people/ I wold wel suffre the lasse greuously. For why/ in such an vnprofytable man/ myn ententes were nothyng endamaged. But ye withdrawen fro me this man/ that hath ben nourysshed in my studyes or scholes of Eleaticis and of Achademicis in Grece. But goth nowe rather awaye ye mermaydens/ whiche that ben swete tyl it be at the laste/ & suffreth this man to be cured and heled by my muses/ that is to saye/ by my noteful sciences. And thus this companye of muses blamed/ casten wrothly the chere downwarde to the erthe/ and shewing by reednesse her shame/ they passeden sorowfully the thresshold. And I of whome the syght plounged in teeres was derked/ so that I ne might nat know/ what that woman was of so imperyal auctorite/ I woxe al abasshed and stonyed/ and cast my sight down to the erthe/ and began styll for to abyde what she wolde done afterwarde. Than came she nere/ & set her downe vpon the vttrest corner of my bedde/ and she beholdyng my chere that was caste to the erthe/ heauy and greuous of wepyng/ cōplayned with these wordes (that I shal sayne) the perturbacion of my thought.

Heu ꝙ precipiti mersa profundo Mens hebet/ et propria luce relicta Tendit ad externas ire tenebras: Terrenis quoties flatibus acta Crescit in immensum noxia cura. Hic quondā celo liber aperto. &c.

Alas/ howe the thought of this man dreynt in ouerthrowyng depnesse/ dulleth and forletteth his propre clerenesse/ myntyng to gone in to forayne derknesse/ as ofte as his anoyous busynes weyeth without mesure/ that is driuen with worldely wyndes. This man that whylom was free/ to whome the heuen was open and knowen/ and was wonte to gone in heuenly pathes/ and sawe the lyghtnesse of the reed sonne/ and beheld the sterres of the colde moone/ & whiche sterre in heuen vseth wandringe recourses flytte by dyuers spheres. This man ouercomer had comprehended al this thynge by nombre of acomptyng in astronomye. And ouer this he was wont to seken the causes/ whence the sownynge wyndes mouen/ and besyen the smothe water of the see. And what spyrite tourneth the stable heuen. And why the sterre riseth out of the reed este/ to fallen in yͤ westren wawes. And what attempreth the lusty houres of the first sōmer season/ and hyghteth and apparayleth the erthe with rosy floures. And who maketh the plentuous Autumpne in ful yeres fleten with heuy grapes. And eke this man was wonte to tel the dyuers causes of nature that were hydde. Alas howe lightly is empted the syght of his thought/ and his necke is pressed with heuy cheynes/ and beareth his chere enclyned adowne for the great weight/ and is cōstrayned to loken on the fole erthe.

Sed magis medicine (inquit) tempus est ꝙ querele. Boe. Tum vero totis in me intenta luminibus. Philo. Tune ille es (ait) qui nostro quondam lacte nutritus/ nostris educatus alimentis/ in virilis animi robur euaserat? &c.

But tyme is nowe of medycine (qđ she) more than complaynte. Forsothe than she entendyng to me warde with al the lokyng of her eyen sayde. Arte not thou he (qđ she) that whylom I nourysshed with my mylkes/ and fostred with my metes/ were escaped and comen to the corage of a parfayte man? Certes I yaue the suche armures/ that if thou thy selfe ne haddest first cast hem away/ they shulden haue defended the in sykernesse/ that may not be ouercomen. Knowest thou not me? Why arte thou styl? is it for shame or for astonyeng? It were me leuer it were for shame/ but it semeth me that astonyeng hath oppressed the. And whan she sawe me not onely styll/ but rather without offyce of tong & al dombe/ she layde her hande softely vpon my breste/ and sayde: Here is no peryll (quod she) he is fallen in to a lytarge/ which that is a commune sickenesse to hertes that ben disceyued. He hath a lytel forgeten him selfe. But certes he shall lyghtly lightly remembren him selfe/ if so be that he hath knowen me or nowe. And that he maye doone so/ I wyl wype his eyen a lytel that ben derked by the cloude of mortal thinges. These wordes sayd she/ and with the lappe of her garnement yplited in a frounce she dryed myn eyen that weren ful of ye wawes of my wepynges.

Tunc me discussa liquerunt nocte tenebre/ Luminibusq; prior redit vigor. Ut cum precipiti glomerantur sidera choro/ Nimbosisq; polus stetit imbribus/ Sol latet/ ac non dū celo venientibus astris &c.

Thus whan that nyght was discussed awaye/ derkenesse forlete me/ and to myn eyen repayred agayne her firste strength. And right as by ensample/ as the sonne is hydde whan the sterres ben couerde with cloudes/ by a swyfte wynde that hyght Chorus/ and the firmament stante derked by wete plungy cloudes. And that the sterres not aperen vpon the heuen/ so that the nyght semeth sprad vpon the erthe. If than the wynde that hyght Boreas/ ysent out of ye caue of the countrey of Trace/ beateth this nyght/ that is to sayne/ chaseth it awaye/ and discouereth the closed day. Than shyneth Phebus yshaken with sodayne lyght/ and smyteth with his beames in marueylyng eyen.

Haud aliter tristicie nebulis dissolutis/ hausi celum/ et ad cognoscendam medicantis faciem/ mentem recepi. Itaq; vbi in eā deduxi oculos/ intuitumq; defixi/ respicio nutricem meam/ i cuius ab adolescētia. &c.

Ryght so and none other wyse/ the cloudes of sorowe dissolued & done away/ I toke heuen and receyued mynde to knowen the face of my physycien: so that I sette myne eyen vpon her and fastned my lokyng. I behelde my norice Philosophie in whose house I had conuersed fro my youthe/ and I sayde thus. O thou maystresse of al vertues discended from the souerayne sete/ why art thou comen in to this solitary place of myn exile? Arte thou comen for thou arte made coulpable with me of false blames. O (quod she) my norice/ shulde I forsake the nowe/ & shulde I not parten with the by comen trauayle the charge that thou haste suffred for enuye of my name? Certes it were not leful ne fyttyng to Philosophie to leten without companye the way of him that is innocent: Shulde I than redoute my blame/ and agrise as though there were befallen a newe thing. For trowest thou that Philosophie be nowe alder first assayled in peryls by folke of wicked maner? Haue I not stryuen with ful great stryfe in olde tyme before the age of my Plato/ ayenst the foolehardynesse of folye? And eke the same Plato lyuyng/ his mayster Socrates deserued victorye of vnrightful dethe in my presence. The herytage of the whiche Socrates/ the heritage is to sayne the doctryne/ of the whiche Socrates in his opinyon of felycite/ that I clepe welefulnesse: whan that the people of Epycuriens and Stoiciens/ and many other enforced hem to go rauysshe/ euery man for his parte/ that is to sayne: that eueryche of hem wolde drawen to the defence of his opinyon the wordes of Socrates. They as in partye of their praye to drowen me cryeng and debatynge therayenst/ and coruen and renten my clothes that I had wouen with myne owne handes. And with tho clothes that they had araced out of my clothes they wenten awaye/ wening that I had gone with hem euery dele. In whiche Epicuriens and Stoiciens for as moche as there semed some traces and steppes of my habyte/ The folye of wenyng tho Epicuriens and Stoiciens my famylers/ peruerted some through the errour of the wicked multytude of hem: This is to sayne/ for they semed philosophers/ they weren pursued to the dethe and slayne. So if thou haste not knowen the exilynge of Anaxagoras/ ne the enpoysonyng of Socrates/ ne the turmentes of Zeno/ for they weren straungers/ yet mightest thou haue knowen the Senecas/ the Canios/ and the Soranos: Of whiche folke the renōme is neyther ouer olde ne vnsolempne. The whiche men no thynge els ne brought to the dethe/ but onely for they were enfourmed of my maners/and semeden moste vnlyke to the studyes of wicked folke. And for thy thou oughtest not to wondren/though that I in the bytter see be driuen with tempestes blowynge aboute. In the whiche this is my moste purpose/ that is to sayne to displesen wicked men. Of whiche shrewes al be the hooste neuer so great/ it is to dispyse/ for it is not gouerned with no leader of reason/ but it is rauysshed onely by fleetynge errour/ folily and lightly. And if they somtyme make an hoost ayenst vs/assayle vs as strenger: our leder draweth togyther his rychesses in to his tour/ and they ben ententyfe aboute sarpleris or sachelles vnprofytable for to taken. But we that ben hygh abouen/syker from al tumulte & woode noyse/ warnestored and enclosed in suche a paleys/ whither as that clateryng or anoyeng foly may not attayne/ we scorne suche raueners and henters of foulest thynges.

Quisquis composito serenus euo Fatum sub pedibus egit superbum: Fortunamqꝫ tuens vtramqꝫ rectus Inuictum potuit tenere vultum. &c.

Who so it be that clere of vertue/sad/ and wel ordynate of lyuynge/ that hath put vnderfoote the proude werdes/and loketh vpright vpon eyther fortune/ he maye holden his chere vndiscomfyted. The rages ne the manaces of the see cōmouynge and chasynge vnware heate from the bottome/ ne shal nat moue ỷ man/ ne the vnstable mountayne that hyght Veseuus/that writheth out through his broken chymeneyes smokyng fyres/ ne the way of thonder leyte/that is wonte to smyten hygh toures ne shal nat moue that man. Wherto than wretches drede ye tyrauntes / that ben woode and felonnous with any strength? Hope after nothynge/ ne drede thou not: and so shalte thou disarmen the ire of thilke vnmighty tyraunte. But who that quakynge dredeth or desyreth thyng that is not stable of his right/ that man that so dothe hath caste awaye his shylde/ and is remoued fro his place/ and enlaseth hym in the chayne / with the whiche he may be drawen.

Sentis ne (inquit) hec? atqꝫ animo illabuntur tuo? Expers ne es lyre? Quid fles? Quid lachrimis manas? Si operã medicantis expectas/ oportet vt vulnus detegas tuum. &c.

HEryst thou (quod she) these thynges? and entren they aught in thy corage? Art thou lyke an asse to the harpe? Why wepest thou? Why spyllest thou teeres? If thou abydest after helpe of thy leche/ the behoueth discouer thy woūde. Tho I had gathered strength in my corage and answerd and said. & nedeth it (qd I) of rehersyng or of amonicion/ & sheweth it not ynough by him selfe the sharpnesse that wexeth woode ayenst me. Ne moueth it not the to se the face or the maner of this place? Is this the librarye that thou haddest chosen for a right certayne siege to the in myn house / there as thou disputest oft with me of the science of thinges/touching dyuinite and touching mākynde? Was than myn habite suche as it is nowe? Was my face or chere such as is now/ whan I sought with the secretes of nature/whan thou enformedest my maners and the reason of al my lyfe/ to thensample of the ordre of heuen? Is not this the guerdon that I referre to the/ to whome I haue be obeysaunt? Certes thou enformedest by the mouthe of Plato this sentence/ that is to sayne: that comen thynges or comynaltees weren blissful/if they that had studyed al fully to wisdom gouerneden thylke thynges: or els if it so befel that the gouernours of comynaltees studiden to get wisedome. Thou saydest eke by the mouthe of the sayde Plato / that it was a necessary cause/wise men to taken and desyren the gouernaunce of comen thynges/ for that the gouernementes of cytes ylefte in the handes of felonous tourmentours / cytezeins ne shulden not bringen in pestilence and distruction

distruction to good folke. And therfore I folowyng thilke auctours desyred to put forthe in execucion and in acte of comen administracion thylke thynges/ that I had lerned of the amonge my secrete restyng whiles/ thou and god that put in the thoughtes of wyse folke/ ben knowyng with me/ ẏ nothing ne brought me to maistrye or dignyte but the comen studye of al goodnesse. And therfore cometh it that bytwene wicked folke and me haue ben greuous discordes/ that ne mighten not be relesed by prayers: for this lyberte hath the fredome of conscience/ that the wrathe of more mighty folke hath alway ben dispysed of me for sauacion of right. Howe ofte haue I resysted and withstande that man that hyght Canigast/ that made alway thassaute ayenst the prosper fortunes of poore feble folke? Howe ofte eke haue I put of or caste out him Triguyl prouost of the kynges house/ bothe of the wronges that he had begonne to done/ and eke fully perfourmed? Howe often haue I couered and defended by the auctorite of me put ayenst peryls/ that is to sayne: put myn auctorite in peryl for the wretched poore folke that the couetyse of straungers vnpunysshed turmenteden alwaye with miseases and greuaunces out of nombre? Neuer man yet drowe me fro right to wronge. Whan I sawe the fortunes and the rychesses of the people of the prouynces ben harmed and amenused/ eyther by priuy raupynes or by comen trybutes or cariagee/ as sory was I as they that suffreden the harme. Glose. Whan that Theodorike kynge of Gothes in a deed yere had his garners ful of corne/ and commaunded that no man shulde bye no corne tyll his corne were solde/ and at a greuous dere price: Boece withstode that ordynaunce/ and ouercame it/ knowyng al this the kyng Theodorike him selfe. Coempcion is to saye comen achate or byeng togyther/ that were establysshed vpon the people by suche a maner imposycion/ as who so bought a busshel of corne/ he must yeuen the kynge the fyfthe parte. Textus. Whan it was in the sore hongry tyme/ there was establysshed greuous and vnprofytable coempcion/ that men sene wel it shulde greatly turmenten and endomagen al the prouynce of Campayne. I toke stryfe ayenst the Prouost of the pretorie for the comen profyte. And the knowyng of it/ I ouercame it/ so that the coempcion was not asked ne tooke effecte.

Paulyne a counsaylour of Rome/ the rychesses of the whiche Paulyne the houndes of the paleys/ that is to saye/ thoffycers wolden haue deuoured by hope & couetyse: yet drowe I out of the iowes of hem that gapeden. And for as moche as the payne of the accusacion aiudged beforne ne shulde not sodainly henten ne punysshen wrongfully Albyn a counsaylour of Rome/ I put me ayenst the hates and indignacions of the accusour Ciprian. Is it not than ynough sene that I haue purchased great discordes ayenst my selfe? But I ought be more assured ayenst other folke/ that for the loue of rightwysnesse I neuer reserued nothynge to my selfe/ to hemwarde of the kynges hall/ by whiche I were the more syker. But through tho same accusours accusyng I am condempned. Of the nombre of whiche accusours one Basilius that whylome was chased out of the kynges seruyce/ is nowe compelled in accusyng of my name/ for nede of forayne money. Also Opilion and Gaudencius haue accused me: Al be it so that the iustyce regall had whylom demed them bothe to gone in to exyle for her trecheryes and fraudes without nombre. To which iudgement they nolden not obey/ but defended hem by the sykernesse of holy houses/ that is to sayne/ fledden in to seyntewary: And than whan this was apperceyued by the kynge/ he cōmaunded but if they voyded the cyte of Rauenne by certayne daye assigned/ that menne shulde marken hem on ẏ forheed with an hote yron/ and chasen hem out of the towne. Nowe what thynge semeth myght be lykened to this cruelte/ for certes this same daye was receyued the accusyng of my name by thylke same accusours? What may be sayd herto? Hath my studye and my connynge deserued thus/ or els the foresayde dampnacion of me made them ryghtfull accusours or no? Was not for-not fortune a shamed of this. Certes al had nat fortune ben asshamed that innocence was accused/ yet ought she haue had shame of the fylthe of myne accusours. But aske thou in some of what gylte I am accused. Men sayne that I wolde sauen the companye of the senatours. And desyrest thou to heren in what maner I am accused/ that I shulde haue distourbed the accusoure to bearen letters/ by whiche he shulde haue made the senatours giltye ayēst the kynges royal maieste. O maystresse/ what demest thou of this: shal I forsake this blame/ that I ne be no shame to the: Certes I haue wolde it (that is to saye) the sauacion of the senate/ ne I shal neuer lette to wylne it/ and that I confesse and am a knowe/ but thentente of the accusoure to ben distourbed shal cease. Shal I cleape that a felonye or a synne that I haue desyred the sauacyon of the ordre of the senate. And certes had thylke same senate doone through her decretes and her iugemētes as though it were a synne and a felonye/ that is to wylne the sauacyon of them. But folye that lyeth alwaye to hym selfe/ may not chaunge the meryte of thynges/ ne I trowe not by the iugement of Socrates that it were leful to me to hyde the sothe/ ne assente to leasynges: vut certes howe so euer it be of this/ I put it to gessen or prisen of the iugement of the and of wyse folke/ of whiche thynge al the ordynaunce and the sothe (for as moche as folke that ben to comen after our dayes shal knowen it) I haue put it in scripture and in remembraunce. For touchyng the letters falsely made/ by whiche letters I am accused to haue hoped the fredome of Rome/ what apertayneth me to speken therof. Of whiche letters the fraude had ben shewed apertely/ if I had had lybertie for to haue vsed and ben at confessyon of myne accusours/ the whiche thynge in al nedes hath great strength. For what other fredome may men hopen: Certes I wolde that some other fredom might be hoped/ I wolde than haue answerde by the wordes of a man that hyght Camus: for whan he was accused of Canyus/ Cesar Germanes sonne/ that he was knowynge and consentynge of a coniuracion ymade agaynste hym. This Canius answerde thus: if I had wyste it/ thou haddest not wyst it. In whiche thynge sorowe hath not so dulled my wytte/ that I playne onely that shrewde folke apparaylen felonyes agaynst vertue/ but I wonder greatly howe that they maye perfourme thynges that they haue hoped for to doone/ for why ne wyl ne shrewdnesse that cometh perauenture of our defaute. But it is lyke a monstre and a meruayle howe that in the presente syght of god/ maye ben acheued and perfourmed suche thynges/ as euery felonous manne hath conceyued in his thought ayenst innocentes. For whiche thynge one of thy famylyers not vnskylfully asked thus. If god is: whence comen wicked thynges. But al had it ben leful that felonous folke/ that nowe desyren the bloode and the dethe of al good men/ And eke of the Senate/ haue wylned to gone distroyen me/ whome they haue sene alwaye batayllen and defenden good men/ and eke al the senate/ that had not deserued of the fathers (that is to sayne of the senatours) that they shulden wyl my distruction. Thou remembrest wel as I gesse/ yͭ whan I wolde done or sayne any thynge/ thou thy selfe alwaye presente ruledest me. At the cytie of Verone whan that the kynge/ gredy of comen slaughter/ caste hym to transporten vpon al the order of the senate the gylte of his royal maiestie/ of the whiche gylte that Albyn was accused/ with howe great sykernesse of peryl to me/ defended I al the senate: Thou wottest wel that I saye sothe/ ne I ne auaunted me neuer in praysynge of my selfe. For alwaye whan any wight receyueth precyous renome in auauntynge of hym selfe or his werkes/ he amenuseth the secree of his conscience. But nowe thou mayste well sene to what ende I am comen for myne innocencie/ I receyue payne of false felonye/ for gwerdone of very vertue. And what open confessyon of felonye had euer iudges so accordaunte in cruelte/ that is to sayne/ as myne accusynge hath/ that eyther errour of mannes wytte/ or els cōdicion of fortune/ that is vncertayn to al mortal folke ne submytted some of hem/ that

is to

is to say/that it ne enclyned some iuge to haue pyte or compassyon. For al though I had ben accused that I wolde brenne holy houses/and strangle preestes with wicked swerde/ or that I had greythed dethe to al good men/ algates the sentence shulde haue punisshed me present confessed & conuicte. But nowe I am remoued from the cyte of Rome almost.v.C.M. paas/I am without defence dampned to proscripcion and to dethe/ for the studies & bounties that I haue done to the senate. But o wel ben they worthy of meryte/ as who sayth: nay there might yet neuer none of hem be conuicte of suche a blame as myne is. Of whiche trespace myn accusours seen ful wel the dignite/for they wolde derken it with medlyng of some felonye. They baren me on honde and sayd/ that I had polute and defouled my conscience with sacrilege for couetise of dignyte: and certes thou thy selfe that arte planted in me/chacedest out of the siege of my corage al couetyse of mortal thynges/ ne sacrilege ne had no leaue to haue a place in me before thyn eyen. For thou droppedest euery day in myn eeres & in my thought thylke comaundement of Pythagoras/ that is to say: Men shal seruen to god/and not to goddes. Ne it was not conuenient ne none nede to taken helpe of the foulest spyrites/ I that thou haste ordeigned and sette in suche excellence/that thou madest me lyke to god/ and ouer this the right cleane secrete chambre of myn house/ that is to saye my wyfe/ and the companye of myn honeste frendes/and my wyues father/as wel holy as worthy to be reuerensed for his dedes/ defenden me from al suspeccyon of suche blame. But oh malyce. For they that accusen me taken of the philosophie feyth of so gret blame/ for they trowen that I haue had affynite to malefyce or enchauntement/bicause that I am replenisshed and fulfylled with thy techynges and enformed of thy maners. And thus it suffiseth not onely that thy reuerence ne aucile me naught/ but if thou of thy frewyl rather be blemysshed with myne offencyon. But certes to the harmes that I haue/ there betydeth yet this encrease of harme/ that the gessynge and the iugement of moche folke ne loken no thyng to the desertes of thynges/ but onely to the auenture of fortune/and iuggen that only such thinges ben purueyed of god/ whiche that temporal wylfulnesse comaundeth. Glosa. As thus/that if a wight haue prosperite/he is a good man/ and worthy to haue that prosperyte/ & who so hath aduersyte/ he is a wicked man/ and god hath forsake him/ ⁊ he is worthy to haue ẏ aduersyte. This is the opynion of some folke/ and therof cometh that good gessyng first of al thynge forsaked wretches. Certes it greueth me to thinke right nowe in dyuers sentences that the people sayth of me: And thus moche I say/that the last charge of contraryous fortune is this/ that when any blame is layde vpō a caytife/men wenen that he hath deserued that he suffreth. And I that am put away from good men/ and dispoyled of dignytes/and defouled of my name by gessyng haue suffred turmentes for my good dedes. Certes me semeth that I se the felonous couynes of wicked men habounden in ioy and in gladnesse: and I se that euery lorel shapeth him to fynde newe fraudes for to accuse good folke/ ⁊ I se that good folke be ouerthrowen for drede of my peryl/ and euery luxuryous turmentour dare done al felony vnpunysshed/ and be excited therto by yeftes/ & innocentes be not only dispoyled of sykernes/ but of defēce. and therto me list to crien to god ī this maner.

O stelliferi conditor orbis/ Qui perpetuo nixus solio Rapido celū turbine versas/ Legemq; pati sidera cogis/ Ut nūc pleno lucida cornu Totis fratris obuia flammis Condat stellas luna minores: Nunc obscuro pallida cornu Phebo propior lumina perdat. ⁊c.

Thou maker of the whele that beareth the sterres/ whiche that arte fastned to thy perdurable chayre/ and turnest the heuen with a rauesshyng sweygh/ and constraynest the sterres to suffre thy lawe: so ẏ the moone somtyme shinyng with her ful hornes/meting with al the beames of the sonne her brother/ hydeth the sterres that ben lesse. And somtyme whan the moone pale/ with her derke hornes appro-

approcheth the sonne/ leseth her lightes: and that the euyn sterre Hesperus/ whiche that in the firste tyme of the nyght bringeth first her colde arysig/ cometh eft ayen her vsed course/ and is pale by the morowe at rysinge of the sonne/ and is than ycleped Lucifer. Thou restraynest the daye by shorter dwellynge in the tyme of the colde wynter/ that maketh the leaues fal. Thou deuydest the swyfte tydes of the night/ whan the hote somer is comen. Thy might attempreth the variaunt seasons of the yere/ so that zepherus the debonaire wynde bringeth ayen in the first sommer season/ the leues that the wynde that hyght Boreas/ hath refte away in Autumpne/ that is to saye/ the last ende of somer/ and the sedes that the sterre that hight Arcitures sewe/ ben woxen hygh cornes/ whan the sterre Sirius enchaseth hem. There is nothyng vnbounden from this olde lawe/ ne forleteth ŷ werke of his propre estate.

O thou gouernour/ gouernīg al thynges by certayne ende/ why refusest thou onely to gouerne ŷ werkes of men by dewe maner: Why suffrest thou/ that slyding fortune tourneth so great enterchaūges of thynges/ so that anoyous payne that shulde dulye punisshe felons/ punissheth innocentes: And folke of wicked maners sytten in hygh chayres/ and annoyeng folke treden (and that vnrightfully) on the neckes of holy men. And vertue clere and shynynge naturelly/ is hydde in derke derkenesses/ and the ryghtful man bereth the payn and the blame of the felons. Ne the forsweryng/ ne the fraude couerde and kempte with a false coloure/ ne annoyeth not to shrewdenesse/ the whiche shrewdnesse/ whan hem lyste vsen her strength/ they reioysen hem to put vnder hem the souerayne kynges/ whiche that the people without nombre dreden. O thou what so euer thou be that knyttest al bondes of thynges/ loke on these wretches/ erthes/ we men that ben not a foule partie/ but a fayre parte of so great a werke: we ben tourmented in this see of fortune. Thou gouernour/ withdrawe and restreyne the rauisshyng fledes/ and fasten and ferme these erthes stable/ with thilke bonde/ with which thou gouernest heuen that is so large.

Hec vbi continuato dolore delatraui: illa vultu placido/ nihilqꝫ meis questubus mota. Phi. Cum te (inquit) mestū/ lacrimantemqꝫ vidissem: ilico miserū exulemqꝫ cognoui. Sed ꝙ id lōginquū esset exiliū.

Whan I had with a contynual sorowe sobbed or broken oute these thynges/ she with her chere pesible/ and nothyng amoued with my cōplayntes/ sayd thus. Whan I saye the (qđ she) sorouful and weppyng/ I wyst anon that thou were a wretch and exiled: But I wyste neuer howe ferre thyne exile was/ if thy tale ne had yshewed it me. But certes al be thou ferre fro thy countrey/ thou nart nat put out of it/ but thou hast fayled of thy way ⁊ gone a mysse. And if thou haste leuer for to wene that thou be put out of thy countre/ than hast thou put out thy selfe/ rather than any other wyght hath/ for no wight (but thou thy self) ne might neuer haue doone that to the: For if thou remembre the of what countrey thou art borne/ it nys not gouerned by emperours ne by gouernement of multitude/ as weren the countreys of hem of Athenes/ but one lorde and one kyng/ and that is god/ that is lorde of thy countrey/ whiche that reioyseth him of the dwellyng of his cytezyns/ and not for to put hem in exyle. Of the whiche lorde it is a fredome to be gouerned by the bridle of him and obey to his iustyce. Hast thou forgoten thilke olde lawe of thy cyte/ in the whiche cyte it is ordayned and establysshed/ that what wyght hath leuer founde therin his seete or his house than els where/ he maye not be exyled by no right from that place: For who so that is conteyned within the paleys of thylke cyte/ there is no drede that he maye deserue to be exiled. But who that letteth the wyl tenhabyte there/ he forletteth also to deserue to be a cytezeyn of thilke cyte. So that I say/ that the face of this place ne moueth me not so myke/ as thyne owne face. Ne I ne aske not rather the walles of thy lybrarye/ apparayled and wrought with yuorie ⁊ with glasse/ than after the seete of thy thought/ in whiche I put nat whylom bookes/ but I put that/ that maketh bookes worthy

worthy of price or precious: ẏ is to say sentence of my bookes. And certainly of thy desertes bestowed in comen good/ thou hast said soth: But after ẏ multytude of thy good dedes thou hast sayd fewe. And of the honestie or of the falsenesse of thynges that ben opposed ayenst the/ thou haste remēbred thynges that be knowen to al folke. And of the felonyes ⁊ fraudes of thyn accusours/ it semeth ẏ to haue touched it forsothe rightfully ⁊ shortly: al mighten tho same thynges better and more plentuously ben couthe in the mouthe of the people that knoweth al this. Thou haste eke blamed greatly and cōplayned of the wrongful dede of the Senate. And thou haste sorowed for my blame/ ⁊ thou hast wopen for the domage of thy renoun ẏ is apeyred: ⁊ thy last sorowe enchased ayen fortune/ complaynest the guerdons ne be not euenly yolden to the desertes of folke. And in thy latter ende of thy woode muse/ thou praydest that thylke peace that gouerneth the heuen shulde gouerne the erthe. But for that many trybulacions of affections haue assayled the/ and sorowe ⁊ yre and weppyng to drawen the dyuersly/ as thou arte nowe feble of thought/ mightyer remedyes ne shullen not yet touchen the/ for whiche we wyllen somdele usen lyghter medicynes/ so that thylke passyons that be waxen harde in swellyng by perturbacions flowynge in to thy thought/ mowen waxe easy and softe to receyue the strength of a more mighty ⁊ more egre medycine by an easier touchyng.

Cum phebi radiis graue Cancri sidus inestuat/ Tum qui larga negantibus Sulcis semina credidit Elusus Cereris fide/ Quernas pergat ad arbores. Nūq̄ purpureū nem⁹ Lectur⁹ violas petas. ⁊c.

When that the heuy sterre of the Cancre enchaseth by the beames of Phebus: that is to sayne/ Whan that Phebus the sonne is in the signe of the Cancre/ who so yeueth than largely his sedes to the feldes that refusen to receyue hem/ let him gone begyled of trust that he had to his corne/ to akehornes of okes. If thou wylte gather violettes/ ne go thou nat to the purple wodde/ whan the felde chirkynge agryseth of colde/ by the felnesse of the wynde that hyght Aquilone. If thou desyrest or wilt usen grapes/ ne seke thou not a gloutons honde to strayn and presse the stalkes of the vyne in the first sōmer season/ For Baccus the god of wyne/ hath rather yeuen his yeftes to Autumpne the latter ende of sōmer. God tokeneth and assigneth the tymes ablynge hem to her propre offyces/ ne he suffreth not the stoundes/ which that him selfe hath deuyded and constrayned to ben ymedled togyder: and for thy he that forletteth certayne ordynaunce of doyng by ouerthrowing way/ he ne hath no glad issue or ende of his werkes.

Primum igitur/ pateris ne me pauculis rogationibus statum tue mētis attingere/ atq; tentare? ut quis modus sit tue curacionis intelligam. ⁊c.

Firste woldest ẏ suffre me to touche and assay the estate of thy thought by a fewe demaundes/ so ẏ I may understande by/ the maner of thy curacion? Aske me (qđ I) at thy wyl/ that thou wolte/ and I shal answere. Tho sayd she thus: Whether wenest thou (qđ she) that this worlde be gouerned folysshly by happes and fortunes/ or els wenest thou that there be in it any gouernement of reason? B. Certes (qđ I) I ne trowe nat in no maner that so certayne thynges shulde be moued by fortunous fortune/ but I wote wel that god/ maker and mayster is gouernour of his werke/ ne was neuer yet daye that might put me out of the sothnesse of that sentēce. P. So is it (qđ she) for the same thyng sange thou a lytel here beforne/ and bewayledest and weptest/ that onely men were put out of ẏ cure of god/ for of al other thinges thou ne doutest not/ that they nere gouerned by reason. But ough/ I wonder certes gretly why that thou arte sicke/ sens that thou arte put in so holsome a sentence: But let us seken deper. I coniecte that there lacketh I not what. But say me this. Sens ẏ thou ne doutest not ẏ this world be gouerned by god/ with whiche gouernayle takest thou hede that it is it is gouerned? Unneth (qd I) knowe I the sentence of thy questyon / so that I ne maye not yet answeren to thy demaundes. I was not disceyued (qd she) that ther ne fayled som what / by whiche the malady of perturbacion is crepte in to thy thought / so as the strength of thy paleys shynyng is open: but saye me this. Remēbrest thou what is thende of thinges? and whider thentencion of al kynde tendeth. I haue herde tolde it somtyme (qd I) but drerynesse hath dulled my memorie. Certes (qd she) thou wotest wel whence al thynges be comen & proceden. I wote wel (qd I) and answerde / that god is begynnynge of al. And howe may this be (qd she) that sens thou knowest the begynnyng of thynges / that thou ne knowest nat what is the ende of thynges / but suche ben the customes of perturbacion / and this power they han / that they may moue a man from his place / that is to say / from the stablenesse and perfection of his knowynge / but certes they may nat al arace him / ne alien him in al: but I wolde that thou woldest answere to this. Remēbrest thou that thou arte a man? B. Why shuld I not remembre that (qd I) Phi. Mayst thou not tel me than (qd she) what thynge is a man? Askest thou not me (qd I) whether that I be a resonable mortal beest / I wote wel and confesse that I am it. Wyste thou neuer yet that thou were any other thing (qd she). No (qd I). Nowe wel knowe I (qd she) other cause of thy maladie / and that ryght great: Thou haste lefte for to knowen thy selfe what thou art / through whiche I haue plainly founden the cause of thy maladie / or els the entre of recoueryng of thy heale. For why? For thou art confoūded with foryetynge of thy selfe: For thou sorowdest that thou art exiled of thy propre goodes. And for thou ne wyste what is thende of thynges / for thy demest thou that felonous and wicked men / bē mighty and welful: and for thou hast foryeten by whiche gouernementes the worlde is gouerned / for thy wenest thou yͭ these mutacions of fortune fleten without gouernour. These ben the causes not only to maladie / but certes great causes to dethe: But I thanke the auctour and the maker of heale / that nature hath not al forleten the. I haue great nourisshyng of thyn heale / and that is the sothe sentence of gouernaunce of the worlde / that thou byleuest that the gouernynge of it is not subiecte ne vnderput to the folye of these happes auenturous / but to the reason of god / & therfore doute the nothyng / for of this lytel sparke thyne heete of lyfe shal shyne. But for as moche as it is not tyme yet of faster remedies / and yͭ nature is of thoughtes thus disceyued / that as ofte as they caste awaye sothe oppinions / they clothen hem in false opynions. Of the whiche false opinyons the derknesse of perturbacion wexeth vp / that confoundeth the very insight. And that derkenesse shal I somwhat assaye to maken thynne and weake / by lyght and meanelyche remedies / so that after that the derkenesse of disceyuynge thynges be done awaye / thou maye knowe the shyninge of very lyght.

Nubibus atris Condita nullum Fundere possunt Sydera lumen. Si mare voluens Turbidus auster Misceat estū: Vitrea dudum / Parque serenis. &c.

THe sterres couered with blacke cloudes ne mowe yetē adoun no light / if the trouble wynde yͭ hyght Auster / turnyng & walowing the see medleth the hete / that is to sayne the boylyng vp from the bottome. The wawes that were whilom clere as glasse / & lyke to the fayre bright dayes / withstante anon the syghtes of men / by the fylthe and ordure that is resolued. And the fletynge streme that royleth downe dyuersly from high moūtaignes is arrested and resysted oft tyme by thencountryng of a stone / that is departed and fallen from some roche. And for thy / if thou wylt loken & deme sothe with clere light / and holden the way with a right pathe / weyue thou ioy / driue fro drede / fleme thou hope / ne let no sorowe approche / yͭ is to sayne: Let non of these four passyons ouercome or blēde the. For cloudy & derke is thylke thought & boūde with bridels / wher as these thinges reignen.

Explicit liber primus.

Post hec paulisper obticuit/ atq; vbi attētionem meam modesta taciturnitate collegit/ sic exorsa est. Si penitus egritudinis tue causas/ habitumq;. &c.

After this she stynt a lytel/ & after that she had gadered vp a temper stylnesse myne attention/ as who so might sayne thus. After these thynges she stynt a lytel/ & whan she aperceyued by a temper stylnesse/ that I was ententyf to heren her/ she began to speke in this wyse. yf I (qđ she) haue vnderstonden and knowen vtterly/ the causes and ye habite of thy malady/ thou languysshest & arte defeted for desyre and talent of thy rather fortune. She ye ylke fortune onely that is chaūged as thou saynest to the warde/ hath peruerted the clerenesse and the estate of thy corage. I vnderstōdyng ye fele or manyfolde colours and disceytes of thylke merueylous monstre fortune/ and howe she vseth ful flateryng famyliaryte with hem that she enforceth to begyle/ so longe/ tyl that she confoūde with vnsufferable sorowe/ hem that she hath lefte in dispayre vnpurueyed. And if thou remembrest wel the kynde/ the maners/ and the deserte of thylke fortune/ thou shalte wel knowe that as in her thou neuer ne haddest/ ne haste ylost any fayre thynge: But (as I trowe) I shal not greatly trauaylen to done the remembren on these thynges. For thou were wonte to hurtelen and dispysen her with many wordes/ whan she was blādisshyng and presente/ and pursudest her with sentences that weren drawen out of myn entre/ that is to saye/ of myn enformacion: But no sodayne mutacion ne betydeth not without a maner chaungyng of corages. And so it is befal/ that thou arte a lytel departed fro the peace of thy thought/ but nowe is tyme that thou drinke and ataste some soft and delytable thinges/ so that whan they be entred within the/ it mowen make way to strenger drinkes of medycins. Come nowe forthe therfore the suasyon of swetnesse rethoryen/ whiche that gothe onely the right way/ whyle she forsaketh nat myn estatutes. And with Rethorike come forthe musyke a damosel of our house/ that syngeth nowe lyghter modes or prolacions and nowe heauyer.

What eyleth the man? What is it yt hath caste the in to mournyng & in to weppyng? I trowe that thou haste sene some newe thing and vncouthe? Thou wenest that fortune be chaunged ayen me/ but thou wenest wronge if that thou wene alwaye tho ben her maners. She hath rather kepte as to the warde/ her propre stablenesse in the chaūgyng of her selfe: right suche was she whan she flatterde the and disceyued the/ with vnleful lykinges and false welefulnesse. Thou haste nowe knowen and atteynte ye doubtous or double visage of thilke blynde goddesse Fortune. She that yet couereth and wympleth her to other folke/ hath shewed her selfe euerydele to the: If thou approuest her and thynkest that she is good/ vse her maners and playne the not/ and if thou agrysest her false trecherye/ dispyse and caste away her that playeth so harmefully/ for she that is nowe cause of so moche sorowe to the/ shulde be to the cause of peace & of ioye. She hath forsaken the for sothe/ the whiche that neuer man maye be syker that she ne shal forsaken hym. Glose. But natheless some bokes haue the texte thus. Forsothe she hath forsaken the/ ne there nys no man syker that she ne hath not forsaken. Holdest thou than thylke welefulnesse precious to the that shal passen/ and is present fortune dereworth to the/ which that nys not faythful for to dwel/ and whan she gothe awaye that she bryngeth a wight in sorowe. for sens she maye not be with holden at a mannes wyl/ she maketh hym a wretche whan she departeth fro hym. What other thinge is flyttynge fortune/ but a maner shewyng of wretchydnesse that is to come. Ne it suffyseth not onely to loken on thinge that is present before the eyen of a man/ but wysdom loketh and mesureth thende of thynges/ and the same chaūgyng from one to another/ that is to sayne/ from aduersyte in to prosperyte/ maketh that ye manaces of fortune ne ben not for to dreden/ ne the flaterynge to be desyred. Thus at laste it behoueth the to suffren with euen wyl in pacience/ al that is doone within the floore of fortune/ that is to saye in this worlde/ sithe thou hast ones put thy necke under the yoke of her. For if thou wolt writen a lawe of wẽdyng and of dwelling to fortune/ whiche that thou haste chosen frely to ben thy lady: Arte thou nat wrongful in that/ ⁊ makest Fortune wroth and asper by thyne impacience/ and yet thou mayst nat chaungen her?

If thou cõmyttest and betakest thy sayles to the wynde/ thou shalte be shouen/ nat thyder that thou woldest/ but whider that the wynde shoueth the. If thou castest thy seedes in the feldes/ thou shuldest haue in mynde that the yeres been amonges otherwhyle plentuous/ and otherwhile bareyn. Thou haste betaken thy selfe to the gouernaunce of fortune/ ⁊ for thy it behoueth the to ben obeysaunt to yͤ maners of thy lady. Enforcest thou the to aresten or withholden the swyftnesse and the sweygh of her tournyng whele? O thou fole of al mortal fooles/ if fortune began to dwel stable/ she cessed than to ben fortune.

Hec cum superba verterit vices dextra/ Exestuantis more fertur Euripi. Dudũ tremendos seua proterit reges/ Humilẽq; victi subleuat fallax vultũ. Non illa dura miseros audit/ haud curat fletus. ⁊c.

When Fortune with a proude ryght hande hath tourned her chaungyng stoundes/ she fareth lyke the maners of the boilynge Eurype.

Glosa. Euripe is an arme of the see/ that ebbeth and floweth/ and somtyme the streme is on o syde and somtyme on that other.

Texte. She crewel fortune casteth adoun kynges/ that whylom weeren ydrad/ and she disceyuable enhaunceth up the humble cheer of him that is discomfyted: ne she neyther hereth ne recketh of wretched weppynges. And she is so harde/ that she laugheth and scorneth the weppynge of hem/ the whiche she hath maked to wepe with her free wyl. Thus she playeth and thus she proueth her strengthes/ and sheweth a great wonder to al her seruauntes/ if that a wyght is seen welefful/ and ouerthrowe in an hour.

Vellem autem pauca tecum Fortune ipsius verbis agitare. Tu igitur an ius postulet animaduerte. P. Quid tu o homo ream me agis cottidianis querelis. ⁊c.

Certes I wolde pleden with the a fewe thinges/ usyng the wordes of fortune: take hede now thy selfe/ if that she aske right.

O thou man/ wherfore makest thou me giltye by thyne euery dayes playnynges? What wronge haue I done the? What goodes haue I berafte yͤ that were thyn? Stryue or pleate with me before what iuge that thou wylt/ of the possession/ of rychesses/ or of dignites/ and if thou mayst shewen me/ that euer any mortal man hath receyued any of tho thinges to ben his in propre/ than wyl I graunt frely/ that thylke thynges were thyn/ whiche that thou askest. Whan that nature brought the forthe out of thy mothers wombe/ I receyued the naked and nedy of al thynges/ and I nourisshed the with al my rychesses/ and was redy and ententyfe through my fauour to sustayn the: and that maketh the nowe impacient ayenst me. And I enuyroned the with al habondaunce and shynynge of al goodes/ that ben in my right: nowe it lyketh me to withdrawe myn honde. Thou hast had grace as he that hath used forayne goodes. Thou haste no right to playne the/ as thoughe thou haddest utterly forlorne al thy thynges. Why playnest thou thanne? I haue doone the no wronge. Rychesses/ honours/ and suche other thiges ben of my right. My seruauntes knowen me for her lady: they come with me/ ⁊ departen whan I wende. I dare wel affirme hardely/ that if tho thynges/ of whiche thou playnest that thou hast forlorn had ben thyn/ thou ne haddest not lorne hem. Shal I than be defended only to use my right? Certes it is leful to the heuen to make clere dayes/ and after yͭ to ouercome tho same dayes with derke nyghtes. The yere hath eke leaue to apparayle the visage of the erthe/ nowe with floures/ and nowe with fruite/ and to confounde hem somtyme with raynes and with colde.

The see hath eke his ryght to ben somtyme calme and blãdisshyng/ with smothe water/ and

and somtyme to be horryble with wawes and with tempestes. But couetyse of men/ ye may not be staunched/ shal it bynde me to be stedfaste/ sythen that stedfastnesse is vncouthe to my maners. Suche is my strength/ and suche play I play comenly. I tourne the whirlyng whele with the turnyng cercle. I am glad to chaungen ye lowest to the heyest/ & the heyest to ye lowest. Worthe vp if thou wolte/ so it be by this lawe/ that thou ne holde nat that I do the wrong/ though thou descende adowne/ whan the reason of my play asketh it. Wyste thou nat howe Cresus kyng of Lydiens/ of which kynge Cyrus was ful sore agaste/ a lytel beforne that this Cresus was caught of Cirus/ and ledde to the fyre to be brende/ but that a rayne descended from heuen ye rescowed him? And is it out of mynde howe that Paulus consul of Rome/ whan he had taken the king of Perciens/ weped pitously for the captiuyte of the selfe kyng? What other thynge bewaylen the cryenges of tragedyes/ but onely the dedes of fortune/ ye with an awkewarde stroke ouertourneth the realmes of great nobley. Glose. Tragedie is to sayne a dite of a prosperite for a tyme/ that endeth i wretchydnesse. Lernedest not thou in Grece whan thou were yonge/ that in the entre or in the seller of Iupiter there ben couched two tonnes/ that one is ful of good/ that other is ful of harme?

What right hast thou to playne/ if thou hast taken more plenteously of the good syde/ that is to sayne of richesse & prosperite? And what eke if I be not al departed fro the? what eke if my mutabylite yeueth the rightful cause of hope to haue yet better thingz? Nathelesse dismaye the not in thy thought. And thou that arte put in the commune realme of al/ ne desyre not to lyuen by thyn owne propre right.

Si quãtas rapidis flatibus incitus Põtus versat arenas/ Aut quot stelliferis edita noctibus Celo sidera fulgẽt: Tãtas fũdat opes nec retrahat manũ Pleno copia cornu/ Humanum miseras haud ideo genus Cessẽt flere querelas. &c.

Though plenty goddesse of riches/ hylde adowne with a ful horne/ & withdrawe not her hande/ as many richesse as the see turneth vpwarde sandes/ whan it is moued with rauisshyng blastes/ or els as many rychesses as there shynen bright sterres in the heuen on the sterry nightes: yet for al that mankynde nolde not cesse to wepe wretched playntz. And al be it so that god receyued her prayers/ and yeueth hem as fool large moche golde/ & apparayleth couetous folke with noble or clere honours: yet semeth him haue gotten nothig. But alway cruel rauyne deuouryng al that they haue gotten/ sheweth other gapinges/ that is to saye/ gapen and desyren yet after mo rychesses. What bridels myght withholden to any certayne ende the disordynate couetyse of men/ whan euer the rather ye it fleteth in large yeftes/ the more brenneth in hem the lust of hauing? Certes he ye quakyng & dredful weneth him selfe nedy/ he ne lyueth neuermore ryche.

His igitur/ si pro se tecũ/ verbis fortuna loqueretur/ quid profecto cõtrahisceres/ non haberes. At si quid est/ quo querelã tuam iure tuearis/ proferas oportet. &c.

Therfore if that fortune spake with the for her selfe in this maner/ forsothe thou ne haddest not what thou mightest answere. And if thou haste any thyng/ wherwith thou mayste rightfully defenden thy compleynte/ it behoueth the to shewen/ & I wol yeuen to the space to tellen it. Boece. Certainly (qd I) than/ these ben fayre thinges/ & anoynted with hony swetenesse of rethorike and musike/ and onely whyle they be herde and sowne in eeres/ they ben delicious. but to wretches it is a deper felyng of harme/ this is to sayne/ that wretches felen ye harmes ye they suffre more greuously/ than the remedies or the delytes of these wordes may gladden or comforten hem. So that whan these thinges stynten for to sowñ in eares/ the sorow that is inset greueth the thought. P. Right so it dothe (qd she) For these ne ben yet no remedies of the maladie/ but they ben a maner nourisshynge of thy sorowes/ that rebel ayẽst thy curacion. For whan tyme is/ I shal moue & aiuste suche thinges/ that percen hem ful depe. But nathelesse that thou shalte not

D. D. ii. wylne

wylne to seten thy selfe a wretche. Hast thou foryeten the nombre and ye maner of thy welefulnesse. I speake nat howe that the soueraygne men of the cytie tooke the in cure and kepynge/ whan thou were orphelyn of father and of mother / and were chosen in affynite of princes of the cytee. And thou began rather to be lefe and dere/than for to be a neyghbour/the whiche thynge is the moste precious kynde of any propynquite or alyaunce yt may ben. Who is it that ne sayde tho that thou ne were right weleful / with so great nobley as thy fathers in lawe/ and with the chastyte of thy wyfe/and with thoportunyte and noblesse of thy masculyne children/that is to sayne/thy sonnes. And ouer al this (me lyste to passen of comen thynges) howe thou haddest in thy youthe dignitees/ yt were warned to olde men/ but it delyteth me nowe to comen to the singuler upheapynge of thy welefulnesse. If any frute of mortal thinges may haue any wight or price of welefulnesse / myghtest thou euer foryeten for any charge of harme that might befall/the remembraunce of thylke day/ that thou sawe thy two sonnes made cousailours/ and ladde togyther from thy house/ vnder so great assemble of senatours/ and vnder the blythnesse of the people: and whan thou sawe hem sette in the courte in hye chapers of dignitees. Thou rethoren or pronouncer of kinges praysinges deseruedest glorie of wytte and of eloquence/ whan thou sittynge bytwene thy two sonnes counsaylours/ in the place that hyght Cyrco/and fulfylledest the byddyng of the moultytude of people that was spradde aboute the with so large praysinge and laude/ as men synge in victories. Tho yaue thou to fortune as I trowe/that is to saye/ tho feoffedest thou fortune with glorious wordes/ and deceyuedest her/ whan she acoyed & norisshed the as her owne delyces. Thou bare away of fortune a yefte/ that is to saye suche guerdon that she neuer yafe to priuate man. Wilt thou therfore laye a rekenynge with fortune: She hath nowe first twynkled vpon ye with a wicked eye. If thou consyder the nombre and the maner of thy blisses and of thy sorowes/thou mayst nat forsaken that nart yet blyssful. For if therfore thou wenest thy selfe not weleful/ for tho thiges that semeden ioyful ben passed/ there nys not why thou shuldest seme thy selfe a wretche/for thynges yt seme nowe sory/ passen also. Art thou nowe comen a sodayne gest in to the sadowe or tabernacle of this lyfe: or trowest thou that any stedfastnesse be in mannes thinges: whan ofte a swyfte houre dissolueth the same man/ that is to saye/ whan the soule departed from the body. For al though that selde is there any faythe that fortunous thynges wolde dwellen/ yet nathelesse the last day of a mannes lyfe is a maner dethe to fortune/and also to thilke that hath dwelte. And therfore what wenest thou dare recke/ if thou forlete her in dyeng/or els that she fortune forlete the in fleyng awaye.

Cũ polo phebus roseis quadrigis Lucem spergere ceperit/ Pallet albentes hebetata vultus Flãmis stella prementibus. &c.

Whan Phebus the sonne begynneth to sprede his clerenesse with rosen charioltes/ than the sterre dymmed paleth her whyte cheres by the flambes of the sonne that ouercometh ye sterre light/that is to sayne whan the sonne is rysen/the day sterre weyeth pale & leseth her lyght. for the great lightnesse of the sonne/ whan the wodde weyeth rody of rosen floures in the first sõmer ceason/thrugh the brethe of the wynde zepherus that weyeth warme/if the cloudy wynde Auster blowe felyche/than gothe away fayrenesse of thornes. Ofte the see is clere and calme with mouyng floodes/and ofte the horryble wynde Aquilon moueth boyling tempestes and ouerwheleth the see. If the fourme of this worlde is so selde stable/& if it turneth by so many entrechaunges: wylt thou than trusten in the tomblyng fortunes of men: Wylte thou trowen on flyttyng goodes: It is certayne and establysshed by lawe perdurable/ that nothyng that is engendred is stedfast ne stable.

Cũ ego/ vera/ inq/ cõmemoras o virtutũ oim nutrix: nec inficiari possũ psperitatis mee velocissimũ cursũ. Sed hoc est/ qd. &c.

Than

THan sayd I thus: O noryce of al vertues thou sayest fulle sothe/ ne I may nat forsake the ryght swyfte course of my prosperite/ that is to sayne/ that the prosperite ne be comen to me wonder swyftly and soone. But this is a thynge that greatly smarteth me/ whan it remembreth me. For in al aduersytees of fortune/ the moost vnsely kynde of contrarious fortune/ is to haue ben weleful. Philo. But that thou abyest thus (quod she) The tourment of thy false opynyon/ that mayst thou nat rightfully blamen ne aretten to thinges/ as who sayth: that thou haste yet many haboundaunces of thynges.

Textus. For al be it so that the ydel name of auēturous welefulnesse moueth the nowe/ it is leful that thou reken with me/ of howe many thynges thou haste yet plentye. And therfore/ if that thylke thynge that thou haddest for more precious in al the rychesse of fortune be kepte to the/ yet by the grace of god vnwemmed and vndefouled: Mayst thou than playne rightfully vpon the myscheife of fortune/ sythen thou haste yet thy best thynges? Certes yet lyueth in good poynt the pike precious honoure of mankynde Symahcus thy wyues father/ whiche that is a manne made of al sappyence and vertue/ the whiche manne thou woldest bye with the price of thyne owne lyfe/ he bewayleth the wronges that men done to the/ and nat for him selfe. For he lyueth in sykernesse of any sentence putte ayenst him. And yet lyueth thy wyfe/ that is attempre of wytte/ and passyng other women in clennesse of chastyte. And for I wolde closen shortely her bounties/ she is lyke her father: I tel the that she lyueth lothe of this lyfe/ and kepeth to the onely her goost/ and is al mate and ouercome by weppyng and sorowe for desyre of the. In the whiche thynge onely I mote graunten the/ that thy welefulnesse is amenused.

What shal I sayne eke of thy two sonnes counsayloures/ of whiche as of children of her age/ there shyneth the lykenesse of the wytte of her father and of her elde father? And sythen the souerayn cure of al mortal folke is to sauen her owne lyues/ if thou knowe thy selfe thy goodes make the more weleful. For yet ben there thynges dwelled to the warde/ that no man douteth that they ne been more dereworthe to the than thyne owne lyfe. And for thy drie thy teeres/ for yet is nat euery fortune hateful to the warde: ne ouer great tempest ne hath nat yet fallen vpon the/ whan thyne ancres cleuen faste: that neyther wol suffren the comforte of this tyme present/ ne the hope of tyme comynge to passen ne to faylen.

Boe. And I praye (quod I) that fast mote they holden/ for the whyles that they holden/ howe so euer that thynges ben I shal wel fleten forthe and escapen. But thou mayst wel seen/ howe great apparelles and araye that me lacketh/ that be passed awaye from me.

Philo. I haue somwhat auaunced and forthered the (quod she) if thou anoye nat or forthynke nat of al thy fortune/ as who sayth/ I haue somwhat comforted the/ so that thou tempest nat the thus with al thy fortune/ sythen thou haste yet thy best thynges. But I maye nat suffren thy delyces/ that playnest so weppynge and anguysshous/ for that there lacketh somwhat to thy welefulnesse. For what man is he that is so sadde or of so great parfyte welefulnesse/ that he ne stryueth and playneth on some halfe/ agayne the qualyte of his estate? For why/ ful anguysshous thynge is the condycion of mannes goodes. For eyther it cometh nat al togyder to a wyght/ or els it ne lasteth nat parpetuel. For some man hath great rychesse/ but he is ashamed of his vngentyl lynnage. And some manne is renoumed of noblesse of kynred/ but he is enclosed in so great anguysshe of nede of thynges/ that hym were leauer that he were vnknowe. And some manne haboundeth bothe in rychesse and noblesse/ but yet he bewayleth his chaste lyfe/ for he ne hath no wyfe. And some man is/ and selyly maryed/ but he hath no chyldren/ and nouryssheth his rychesses to straunge folke. And some manne is gladed with chyldren/ but he wepeth ful sore for the trespace of his sonne or of his doughter. And for this/ there ne accordeth no wight lyghtly/

W. V. iii. to the

to the condicyon of his fortune. For alwaye to euery manne there is in somwhat that vnassayde he ne wotte nought/ or els he dredeth that he hath assayde. And adde this also/ that euery weleful manne hath a ful delycate felynge: so that but if al thynges be fallen at his owne wyl he is impacient/ or is nat vsed to haue none aduersyte/ anon he is throwen adowne for euery lytel thyng. And ful lytel thynges bene tho / that withdrawen the somme or the perfectyon of blyssfulnesse / fro them that ben moost fortunate. Howe many menne trowest thou wolde demen hem selfe to bene almoost in heuen / if they mighten attaygne to the leest partie of the rimenaunt of thy fortune? This same place that thou cleapest exyle / is countrey to hem that enhabiten here. And for thy nothynge wretchid/ but whan thou wenest it / as who saythe: Thou thy selfe ne no wight elles nys a wretche/ but whanne he weneth hym selfe he is a wretche by reputatioun of his courage. And agaynwarde: Al fortune is blyssful to a man by the agreabilyte / or by the egalyte of hym that suffreth it. What manne is that that is so welefull / that nolde chaungen his estate/ whan he hath loste his pacyence? The swetnesse of mannes welefulnesse is spraynt with many bytternesses. The whiche welefulnesse/ althoughe it seme swete and ioyful to hym that vseth it/ yet maye it nat bene withholden/ that it ne gothe awaye whan it wol.

Than it is wel seene/ howe wretched is the blyssfulnesse of mortal thynges/ that neyther it dureth perpetuel with hem/ that euery fortune receyuen agreably or equally/ ne it delyteth nat in al to hem that bene anguysshous.

O ye mortal folke/ what seke ye than blyssfulnesse out of your owne selfe: whiche is putte in your selfe? Errour and foly confoundeth you. I shal shewe the shortely/ the poynt of soueraygne blyssfulnesse.

Is there any thynge to the more precious thanne thy lyfe? Thou wolte answere nay.

Thanne/ if it so be that thou arte myghtye ouer thy selfe/ that is to sayne / by tranquyllyte of thy soule / than haste thou thynge in thy power/ that thou noldest neuer lesen: Ne fortune maye nat benempne it the. And that thou mayest knowe that blyssfulnesse ne may nat stande in thynges that bene fortunous & temporel/ nowe vnderstande and gather it togyther thus. If blyssfulnesse be the soueraygne good of nature that lyueth by reason: ne the ylke thynge is nat soueraygne good / that maye be takenne awaye in any wyse. For more worthy thynge is and more digne thilke thynge/ that maye nat be taken away. Than sheweth it wel / that the vnstablenesse of fortune maye nat attaygne to receyue very blyssfulnesse. And yet more ouer/ what man that this tomblynge welefulnesse leadeth / eyther he wote that it is chaungeable / or els he wote it nat? And if he wote it nat / what blyssful fortune maye there bene in the blyndenesse of ignoraunce? And if he wote that it is chaungeable/ he mote alwaye been a dradde that he ne lese that thyng/ that he ne douteth nat/ but that he maye lesen it: As who sayth/ he mote alwaye be agaste/ lest he lese that that he wotteth right wel he maye lese: For whiche the contynuel drede that he hath/ ne suffreth hym nat to be weleful. Or els if he lese it/ he weneth to be dispysed and forleten. Certes eke that is a ful lytel good/ that is borne with euyn herte whanne it is loste/ that is to sayne/ that menne do no more force of the losse than of the hauynge. And for as moche as thou thy selfe arte he/ to whom it hath be shewed & preued by ful many demonstratyons / as I wotte wel/ that the soules of menne ne mowen nat dyen in no wyse. And eke sithe it is clere and certayne/ that fortunous welfulnes endeth by the dethe of the body: it may nat be douted/ that if dethe maye take awaye blyssfulnesse / that al the kynde of mortal thynge ne discendeth in to wretchednesse by the ende of dethe. And sythen we knowe wel/ that many a man hath sought the fruite of blyssfulnesse/ nat onely with suffrynge of dethe/ but eke with suffryng of paynes and tourmentes howe myght than this present lyfe make men blyssful/ sith that the ylke selfe lyfe ended/ it ne maketh folke no wretchesse.

¶ Quisquis

¶ Quisquis volet perennem
Cautus ponere sedem/
Stabilisq; nec sonori
Sterni flatibus Euri/
Et fluctibus minantem.
Curat spernere pontum/
Montis cacumen alti/
Bibulas vitet arenas. &c.

W Hat maner of folke / ware and stable that wyl founden hem a perdurable seate/ and ne wol nat be caste downe with the loude blastes of the wynde Eurus/ and wol dispise the see menasynge with floodes: Lette hym eschewe to buylden on the coppe of the mountaygne/ or in the moyste sandes. For if the fel wynde Auster/ tourmēteth the coppe of the mountaygnes with al her strengthes/ and the lose sandes refusen to beare the heauy weightes. And for thy/ if thou wolte flyen the peryllous auenture/ that is to saye / of the worlde: haue mynde certaynly to sette thyne house of a mery seate in a lowe stone. For al thoughe the wynde troublyng the see/ thunder with ouerthrowynge/ thou that arte putte in quiete and weleful by strength of thy palais shalte leade a clere age/ scornynge the woodnesse and the yres of the ayre/

Sed quoniam rationum iam in te mearum fomenta descendunt/ paulo validioribus vtendum puto. Age enim. Si iam caduca ac momentaria fortune. &c.

B Ut for as moche as the nourisshynges of my reason discēden nowe in to the/ I trowe it were tyme to vsen a lytel strōger medicēs. Now vnderstāde here/ al were it so ỹ the yestes of fortune ne were nat brutel ne trāsitorie/ what is there in hem that may be thyn in any tyme/ or els that it ne is foule/ if that it be loked and consydred perfitely. Richesses ben they precious by the nature of thē self or els by the nature of the: What is most worthe of richesse/ is it nat golde or might of money assembled: Certes that golde and that money shyneth and yeueth better renoume to hem that dispēden it/ than to thylke folke that mokeren it / for auarice maketh alway muckerers to bene hated / and largesse maketh folke clere of renoume. For sithe that suche thynges as ben transferred from one man to another/ ne maye nat dwel with no manne: Certes than is that money precious / whan it is translated in to other folke / and styntyn to be had by vsage of large yeuyng of him that hath yeuen it. And also if al the money that is oueral in al the worlde were gathered toward one man/ it shulde make al other men to be nedy as of that. And certes a voice al hole/ that is to say without amenusynge/ fulfylleth togider the heryng of moche folke. And whan they ben apassed/ nedes they maken hē poorer that forgone tho richesses. O strayte & nedy clepe I these richesses/ sith that many folke ne maye nat haue it al/ ne al maye it nat comen to one man without pouerte of al other folke And the shynynge of gemmes that I cal precious stones/ draweth it nat the eyen of folke to hemwarde/ that is to sayne for the beautie. But certes/ if there were beautie or bountie in shinig of stones/ thilke clerenesse is of the stones hē selfe & nat of men. For whiche I wonder gretly ỹ men marueylen on suche thīges. For why/ what thyng is it ỹ if it wāteth mouinge & ioynture of soule & body/ ỹ by rizt might seme a faire creature to hī ỹ hath a soule of reason. For

For al be it so / that gemmes drawen to hem selfe a lytel of the laste beautie of the worlde / thorowe the entente of her creatour / and the distynctioun of hem selfe: Yet for as mokel as they ben putte vnder your excellence / they ne haue nat deserued by no way / that ye shulde marueylen on hem. And the beautie of feldes delyteth it nat mykel vnto you? Boe.

Why shulde it nat delyten vs / sythe that it is a ryght fayre porcyoun of the ryght fayre werke / that is to sayne / of this worlde.

And right so ben we gladed somtyme of the face of the see whan it is clere: And also marueylen we on the heuen and on the sterres / & on the sonne and on the moone? Philoso.

Apertayneth (quod she) any of the ylke thynges to the? Why darest thou glorifye the in the shynynge of any suche thynges? Arte thou distyngued and embelysed by the spryngynge floures of the fyrste somer season?

Or swelleth thy plentie in fruites of somer?

Why arte thou rauysshed with ydel ioyes?

Why embracest thou straunge goodes as they were thyne? Fortune ne shal neuer make that suche thynges be thyne / that nature of thynges hath maked forayne fro the? Sothe it is / that withouten doute the fruites of the erthe oughten to be to the nourisshynge of beestes. And if thou wolte fulfyl thy nede / after that it suffyseth to nature / than it is no nede that thou seke after the superfluite of Fortune. For with ful fewe thynges and with ful lytel thynges / nature hath her apayde.

And if thou wolte achoken the fulfyllyng of nature with superfluitees: Certes the ylke thynges that thou wolte thresten or pouren in to nature / shullen ben vnioyful to the / or els anoyous. Wenest thou eke / that it be a fayre thynge to shyne with dyuers clothynges?

Of whiche clothynge if the beautie be agreable to loken vpon / I wol marueylen on the nature of the mater of the ylke clothes / or els on the worke man that wrought hem. Dothe also a longe route of meyny make the a blysful manne? The whiche seruauntes if they ben vicious of conditions / it is a great charge and distruction to the house / and a great enemy to the lorde hym selfe. And if they been good menne / howe shal straunge and forayn goodnesse be putte in the nombre of thy richesses? So that by al these foresayd thynges / it is clerely shewed / that neuer one of the ylke thynges that thou accomptedest for thy goodesse / nas nat thy good. In whiche thynges if there be no beautie to be desyred / why shuldest thou be sorie to lese them? or why shuldest thou reioyce the to holde hem? For if they ben fayre of their owne kynde / what appertayneth that to the? For also wel shulden they haue ben fayre by them selfe / though they were departed from al thy richesses.

For why / fayre ne precious were they nat / for that they comen amonge thy richesses.

But for they semed fayre and precious / therfore thou haddest leauer recken hem amonges thy richesses. But what desyrest thou of fortune with so great a fare? I trowe thou sekest to dryue awaye nede with habundaunce of thynges. But certes it tourneth you al in to the contrary. For why / certes it nedeth of ful many helpynges to kepen the dyuersite of precious hostylmentes. And sothe it is / that of many thynges they haue nede / that many thynges haue. And agaynwarde / of lytell thynge nedeth hym that measureth his fyl after the nede of kynde / and nat after the outrage of couetyse. It is so than / that ye men haue no proper good sette in you / for suche ye moten seke outwarde in forayne and subiecte thynges. So is than the condicion of thynges tourned vp so downe / that a manne that is a diuyne beest / by merite of his reason / thinketh that hym selfe nys neither fayre ne noble but if it be through possessyoun of hostylmentes / that ne han no soules. And certes al other thynges ben apayde of her owne beauties:

But ye men that be semblable to god by your resonable thought / desyren to apparelen your excellent kynde of the lowest thynges. Ne ye vnderstāden nat howe great a wronge is don to your creatour / for he wolde that mākynde were moost worthy and noble of any erthely thynge / and ye thresten downe your dignitees

bynethen

be nethen yͤ lowest thynges. For if that al the good of euery thynge be more precious/ than is thylke thynge/ whose that the good is/ sithe ye demen that the foulest thynges been your goodesse: than submytten ye and putte your seluen vnder the foulest thynges by your estymation. and certes this betydeth nat without your deserte. For certes suche is the cōdytion of al mankynde/ that onely whan it hath knowynge of it selfe/ than passeth it in noblesse al other thynges. And whan it forletteth the knowyng of it selfe/ than it is brought be nethen al beestes. For why/ al other lyuynge beestis han of kynde to knowen nat hem self/ but whan that men leten yͤ knowyng of hem selfe/ it cometh hem of vyce. But how brode sheweth the errour and the foly of you men/ that wenen that any thyng maye ben apparelled with straunge apparelmētes: but forsoth that may nat be done. For if a wight shyneth with thynges that ben put to hym: As thus. If thilke thynges shynen with/ whiche a man is apparelled: Certes thylke thynges ben cōmended and praysed/ with whiche he is apparelled: but nathelesse/ thynge that is couered and wrapped vnder yͭ/ dwelleth in his fylth. And I deny that thylke thynge be good/ that anoyeth him that hath it. Gabbe I of this: Thou wolte saye nay. Certes rychesse haue anoyed ful ofte hem/ yͭ han had tho rychesse. sithe that euery wycked shrewe is for his wickednesse the more gredy after other folkes rychesses/ where so euer it be in any place/ be it golde or precious stones/ and weneth him onlye most worthy that hath hem. Thou than that so besy dredest nowe the swerde and the speare/ if thou haddest entred in the pathe of this lyfe a uoyde wayfaryng man/ than woldest thou syng beforne the these/ as who saith a poore man that beareth no rychesse on hym by the waye/ may boldly synge beforne theues/ for he hath nat wherof to be robbed. O precious and ryght clere is the blyssfulnesse of mortal richesses/ that whan thou hast goten it/ than hast thou lorne thy sekernesse.

Felix nimiū prior etas Contenta fidelibus aruis/ Nec inerti perdita luxu: Facili que sera solebat Ieiunia soluere glande/ Nec bacchia munera norat Liquido confūdere melle/ Nec lucida vellera serū. &c.

BLyssful was the firste age of men/ they helden hem apayde with the metes that the trewe feldes broughten forthe/ they ne dystroyed nor disceyued nat hem selfe with outrage/ they weren wonte lyghtly to slaken her hunger at euyn with akehornes of okes/ they ne coude nat medel the yefte of Baccus to the clere hony/ that is to sayne/ they coulde make no piement or clarre: Ne they coude nat medel the bright fleeces of the countre of Seriens with the venym of Tiry/ this is to sayn/ they coude nat dyen white flees of Syrien cōtre with the blode of a maner shelfyssh/ that men fynden in Tyrie/ with whiche blode men dyen purple. they slepten holsome slepes vpon the grasse/ and dronken of the rennyng waters/ and lyen vnder the shadowes of the hye Pyne trees. Ne no geste or straunger ne carfe yet the hye see with oores or with shippes/ ne they ne hadden seyn yet no newe strondes to leden marchandise in to dyuers countrees. tho weren the cruel claryons ful husht and ful styl. Ne blode yshad by egre hate/ ne had deyed yet armures. For where to/ or whiche woodnesse of enemyes wolde fyrst mouen armes/ whan they sawen cruel woūdes/ ne none meedes be of blode yshad: I wolde yͭ our tymes shulde turne ayen to tholde maners. But the anguisshous loue of hauig in fole burneth more cruelly than yͤ moūtain of Ethna/ yͭ ay brēneth. Alas/ what was he that fyrst dalfe vp yͤ gobbettes or the weightes of golde/ couered vnder erthe/ & the precious stones yͭ wolden haue be hydde: He dalfe vp precious peryls/ that is to sayn/ that he yͭ hem first vp dalfe/ he dalfe vp a precious peryl/ for why/ for the preciousnesse of suche thyng hath many man ben in peryl.

Quid autem de dignitatibus/ potētiaqꝫ disseram/ quas vos/ vere dignitatꝫ/ ac potestatis inscii/ celo exequatis: Que si in improbissimū quemqꝫ ceciderint. &c.

But

But what shal I saye of dignitees and powers / the whiche ye men that neyther knowen very dignite ne very power / areysen hem as high as the heuen? the which dignites and powers / if they comē to any wicked man / they don as great domages and distructions / as dothe the flambe of the moūtayne Ethna / whan the flambe waloweth vp / ne no deluuy ne dothe so cruel harmes. Certes ye remembre wel (as I trowe) that thylke dignyte that men cleape the imperye of counsaylours / the whiche whylom was begynnyng of fredom / your elders coueyted to haue done away that dignite for the pride of the counsaylours. And ryght for that same your elders before that tyme had done away out of the cyte of Rome the kynges name / that is to sayne / they nolde haue no lenger no kyng. But nowe / if so be that dignitees and powers ben yeuen to good men / the whiche thing is ful selde / what agreable thynges is there in tho dignitees and powers / but onely the goodnesse of folke that vsen hem? And therfore is it thus / that honour cometh not to vertue bycause of dignyte: and ayenwarde / honoure cometh to dignyte for cause of vertue. But whiche is thilke your dereworth power that is so clere and so requirable? O ye erthly beestes / consyder ye not ouer whiche thyng that it semeth that ye haue power? Nowe if thou sawe a mouse amonge other myce / that chalenged to him selfwarde right & power ouer al other myce / howe great scorne woldest thou haue of it? Glosa. So fareth it by men / the body hath power ouer the body: for if thou loke wel vpon the body of a wight / what thing shalt thou fynde more freel than is mākynde? the whiche men ful ofte be slayne by byting of flyes / or els with entryng or creppyng wormes in to the priuytees of mānes body. But where shal men fynden any man that may exercisen or haunten any right vpon an other man / but onely on his body / or els vpon thynges that ben lower than the body / the whiche I clepe fortunes possessyons?

Mayste thou haue euer any cōmaundement ouer a free corage? Mayste thou remeue fro the estate of his propre reste / a thought that is cleuing togyder in him selfe by stedfast reson?

As whylom a tyraunt wened to confounde a free man of corage / & he wende to constrayn him by tourmentes / to maken him discoueren and accusen folke / that wysten of a coniuracion / whiche I cleape a confederacie that was caste ayenst this tyraūt: but this freman bote of his owne tonge / and caste it in the vysage of thylke woode tyraunt. So that the turmentes that this woode tyraunt wende to haue made mater of crueltie / this wyse man made it mater of vertue. But what thynge is it that a man maye do to an other man / that he ne maye receyuen the same thyng of other folke in him selfe? Or thus: What may a man don to folke / that folke ne maye doone to him the same? I haue herde tolde of Busirides that was wonte to sleen his gestes / that herboroden in his house: and he was slayne him selfe by Hercules that was his geste. Regulus had taken in batayle many men of Affryke / and caste hem in to fetters: but sone after he must yeuen his handes to be bounde with the cheynes of hem that he had whylom ouercomen. Wenest thou than / that he be mighty that hath power to doone a thyng / that other ne maye done in him ẏ he hath in other? And yet more ouer / if so were that these dignytes or powers hadden any ꝑpre or naturel goodnes in hem / neuer nolde they comen to shrewes. For cōtraryous thinges ne ben wont to ben yfeloushipped togythers. Na[illegible]re refuseth that contraryous thynges ben ioyned. And so as I am in certayne that wicked folke haue dignytees ofte tyme / than sheweth it wel that dignytees & powers ne ben not good of her owne kynde / sens that they suffren hem selfe to cleauen or ioynen hem selfe to shrewes. And certayne the same thyng may I most dignely iugen and sayne of al the yeftes of fortune / that moste plenteously comen to shrewes / of whiche yeftes I trowe it ought be consydred that no man douteth that he is stronge / in whome he seeth strength: and in whom swyftnesse is / sothe it is that he is swyfte. Also musyke maketh musyciens / and physike maketh physiciens / and rethorike eke rethoriciēs. For why / the nature of euery thynge maketh his propertie /

ne it

ne it is not entremedled with theffecte of contraryous thynges. But certes rychesses may not restrayne auarice vnstanched. Ne power ne maketh nat a man mighty ouer him selfe/ whiche that vycious lustes holden distrayned with chaynes that ne mowen not be vnbounden. And dignitees/ that be yeuen to shrewde folke/ not onely ne maketh hem not digne/ but sheweth rather al openly/ that they ven vnworthy and indigne. And it is thus. for certes ye haue ioye to cleape thynges with false names/ that bearen hem in al the countraye/ the whiche names ben ful ofte reproued by the effecte of the same thynges. So that these ylke rychesses ne oughten not by right to be cleped rychesses/ ne suche power ne ought not to be cleped power/ ne such dignyte ne ought not to be cleaped dignyte. And at laste I maye conclude the same thynge of al the yestes of fortune: In whiche there nys nothynge to be desyred/ ne that hath in him selfe naturel bountie/ as it is wel ysene/ for neyther they ioynen hem not alwaye to good men/ ne maken hem alwaye good/ to whom they ben ioyned.

Nouimus/ quātas dederit ruinas Urbe flāmata/ patribusq; cesis/ Fratre q̄ quondam ferus interēpto Matris effuso maduit cruore. Corpus et visu gelidum pererrans Ora non tinxit lachrimis: sed esse Censor extincti potuit decoris. &c.

We haue wel knowen/ how many gret harmes & distructions were doone by themperour Nero. He lete brennen the cyte of Rome/ and made slee the senatours/ and he cruel whylom slough his brother. And he was made moyste with the bloode of his mother/ that is to say/ he let sleen & slytten the wombe of his mother/ to sene where he was conceyued/ and he loked on euery halue of her deed colde body/ ne no teere wette his face/ but he was so harde herted that he myght be domes man or iuge of her deed beautie. And nathelesse yet gouerned this Nero by ceptre al the people that Phebus may sene commyng fro his vttrest arysinge/ tyl he hyde his beames vnder the wawes/ that is to sayne/ he gouerned al the peoples by ceptre imperyal/ that the sonne gothe aboute fro Eest to west. And eke this Nero gouerned by ceptre al the peoples that be vnder the colde sterris/ that highten the Septentrions: that is to sayne/ he gouerned al the peoples that be vnder the partye of the North. And eke Nero gouerned al the peoples that the violent wynde Nothus skorchyth and baketh the brennyng sandes by his drie heate/ that is to saye/ al the peoples in the Southe. But yet ne might not al his power tourne the woodnesse of this wicked Nero. Alas it is a greuous fortune/ as ofte as a wicked swerde is ioyned to cruel venym/ that is to saye/ venemous crueltе to lordshyppe.

Tū ego. Scis (inq̄) ipsa/ mihi minū nobis ambicionem mortaliū rerum fuisse dominatam. Sed materiā gerendis rebus optauimus/ quo ne virtus tacita consenesceret. P. Et illa. Atqui hoc vnum est. &c.

Than said I thus. thou woteſt wel thy selfe/ that the couetise of mortal thynges ne hadden neuer lordshyp in me. But I haue wel desyred mater of thynges to doone/ as who sayth/ I desyre to haue mater of gouernaūces ouer comynaltees/ for vertue styl shulde not elden: that is to sayne/ that leste er that he wexe olde/ his vertue that laye nowe styl/ ne shulde not perisshe vnexercysed in gouernaunce of cōmune: for whiche men might speken or writen of his good gouernemēt. P.

Forsothe (quod she) and that is a thing that may drawen to gouernaunce suche hertes as ben worthy and noble of her nature: But nathelesse it maye not drawen or tollen suche hertes as ben ybrought to the ful perfection of vertue/ that is to sayne couetyse of glorie and renome/ to haue wel administred the commune thynges/ or doone good desertes to profyte of the cōmune. For se nowe and consyder/ howe lytel and howe voyde of al price is thylke glorie/ certayne thyng is as thou haste lerned by the demonstracion of Astronomye/ that al the enuyronnyng of the erthe aboute/ ne haste but the reason of a pricke/ at the regarde of the greatnesse of the heuen/ that is to sayne/

to sayne/that if ther were maked comparison of the erth to ye gretnesse of heuen/ men wolde iudgen in al that ne helde no space. Of the whiche lytel region of this worlde/ the fourth parte of the erthe is inhabyted with lyuynge beestes that we knowen/ as thou haste thy selfe ylerned by Ptholome that proueth it. And if thou haddest withdrawen and abated in thy thought for thylke fourthe partye/ as moche space as the see and the mareys conteynen and ouergone: as moche space as the region of drought ouerstretcheth/that is to sayn sandes and desertes/ wel vnneth shulde there dwellen a right strayte place to the habitacion of men. And ye that be enuyrouned and closed with the leste prycke of thylke prycke/ thynken ye manifesten or publisshen your renome and doone your name for to ben borne forthe. But your glorie that is so narow & so strayte throngen in to so lytel boundes/ howe mykel conteyneth it in larges and in great doynge. And also sette therto/ that many a nacyon diuers of tonge and of maners/ and eke of reason of her lyuynge/ ben inhabyted in the close of thylke habytacle/the whiche nacyons what for diffyculte of wayes/ and what for dyuersyte of langage/and what for defaulte of vnusage/ and entrecomunyng of marchandyse: not onely the names of synguler men ne may not stretchen/but eke the fame of cyties maye not stretchen. At the last/ certes in the tyme of Marcus Tullius as hym selfe writte in his boke ye the renome of the comune of Rome ne had not yet passed ne clomben ouer the mountayne that hyght Caucasus/ & yet was Rome wel waxen and redoubted of the Parthes/ and eke of other folke enhabytinge aboute. Seest thou not than howe strayte and howe compressed is thilke glorie that ye trauaylen aboute to shewen and to multeplye? Maye than the glorie of a synguler romayne stretchen thyder as the fame of the name of Rome maye not clymben ne passen? And eke seest thou not that the maners of dyuers folke and her lawes ben discordante amonges hem selfe/ so that thylke thyng that some men iuge worthy of praysing/ other folke iugen that/ that is worthy of tourment. And herof cometh it that though a man delyteth him in praysinge of his renome/he may not in no wyse bringen forthe ne spreden his name to many maner peoples/ and therfore euery man ought to be apayde of his glorie ye is publysshed amonge his owne neyghbours/ and thylke noble renome shal be restrayned within the boundes of tho maner folke. But howe many a man that was ful noble in his tyme/hath the wretches and nedy forgetyng of writers put out of mynde and done away/ al be it so that certes thylke thinges profyten lytel/ the whiche thinges and wrytynges longe and derke elde do away bothe hem and eke her auctours. But ye men semen to getten you a perdurabylite whan ye thynken in tyme comynge your fame shal lasten. But nathelesse/ if thou wylte make comparyson to the endlesse spaces of eternyte. What thing haste thou/by whiche thou mayst reioysen the of longe lastynge of thy name? For if there were made comparyson of the abydyng of a moment to ten thousande wynter/ for as moche as bothe tho spaces ben ended/ for yet hath the momente some porcion of it/al though it be lytel? But nathelesse thylke selfe nombre of yeres/ and eke as many yeres as therto may be multyplied/ ne may not certes be comparisoned to the perdurabylite that is endelesse. For of thynges whiche that haue ende may be made comparyson/ but of thynges whiche that ben withouten ende/ to thynges that haue ende may be maked no comparyson. And for thy is it that al though renome as of longe tyme as euer the lyste to thynken/ were thought/to ye regarde of the eternyte that is vnstauncheable and infynite/ it ne shulde not only seme lytel/but playnly right nought. But ye semen certes ye can do nothing a right but if it be for the audyence of the people/ and for ydle rumours. And ye forsaken the great worthynesse of conscience and of vertue/ and ye seken your guerdones of the small wordes of straunge folke. Haue nowe here and vnderstande in the lyghtnesse of suche pride and veyne glorie/howe a man skorned festyually and meryly suche vanyte. Whylome there was a man that had assayed with stryuynge wordes an other man/the which not for vsage of very of very vertue/ but for proude vayne glorie/ had taken upon him falsely ye name of a philosophre. This rather man that I spake of/ thought he wolde assay/ wheder he thilke were a philosophre or no/ that is to saye/ if that he wolde haue suffred lightly in pacyence/ the wronges that were done to him. This fayned philosophre toke pacience a lytel whyle: and whan he had receyued wordes of outrage/ he as in stryuynge ayen & reioysing of him selfe/ sayde at laste thus. Understandest thou not/ that I am a philosophre? That other man answerde agayne bytingly and sayd: I had wel understāde it/ if thou haddest holden thy tonge styl. But what is it to these noble worthy mē/ for certes of suche folke speke I ye seken glorie with vertue? What is it (q͞d she) what atteyneth fame to suche folke/ whan the body is resolued by the dethe at the last? for if so be that men dyen in al/ that is to say body and soule/ the whiche thyng our reason defendeth us to byleue: than is there no glorie in no wyse. For what shulde thilke glorie be/ whan he/ of whom thilke glorie is sayde to be/ nys ryght naught in no wyse. And if the soule whiche that hath in it selfe science of good werkes/ unbounden from the prison of therthe/ wendeth frely to the heuen/ dispyseth it not than al erthly occupacion/ and beynge in heuen reioyseth that it is exempt from al erthly thynges? as who sayth/ than recketh the soule neuer of no glorie of renome of this worlde.

Quicunq; solam mente precipiti petit/ Sūmumq; credit gloriam/ Late patētes etheris cernat plagas/ Artumq; terrarum sitū Breuē replere nō valētis ambitū. &c.

Who so that with ouerthrowynge thought only seketh glorie of fame/ and weneth ye it be souerayn good/ let hym loken upon the brode shewynge countreys of the heuen/ and upon the strayte sete of this erthe/ and he shal be asshamed of thencrease of his name/ that maye not fulfyl the lytel compas of the erthe. O what coueyten proude folke to lyften up her neckes in ydle in the deedly yoke of this worlde? For al though that renome ysprad passyng to fowe peoples/ goth by diuers tonges/ and al though great houses of kynredes shynen by clere tytles of honours/ yet nathelesse dethe dispyseth al high glorie of fame/ and dethe wrappeth togythers the hygh heedes and the lowe/ & maketh egal and euen the hyest with the lowest.

Where wonen nowe the bones of trewe Fabricius? What is nowe Brutus/ or sterne Caton? The thynne fame yet lastyng of her ydle names/ is marked with a fewe letters. But although that we haue knowen the fayre wordes of ye fame of hem/ it is not yeuen to know hem that ben deed and cōsumpt. Lyggeth than styl al utterly unknowable/ ne fame ne maketh you not knowe. And if ye wene to lyue the lenger for wynde of your mortal name/ whan one cruel day shal rauissh you: than is the seconde dwellyng to you close. The firste dethe he clepeth here the departing of the body/ and the seconde dethe here the styntynge of the renome of fame.

Sed ne me inexorabile contra fortunam gerere bellum putes/ est aliquādo/ cum de hominib9 fallax illa non nihil bene mereatur: tum scilicet cum se aperit. &c.

But for as moche as thou shalt not wenen (q͞d she) that I beare an untretable batayle ayenst fortune/ yet somtyme it befalleth that she (disceyuable) deserueth to haue right good thanke of men: and that is whan she her self openeth/ and whan she discouereth her fronte/ and sheweth her maners. Parauenture yet understādest thou not that I shal say. It is a wondre that I desyre to tel/ and therfore unneth may I unplyten my sentence with wordes. for I deme that cōtraryous fortune profyteth more to men than fortune debonayre. For alwaye whan fortune semeth debonayre/ than she lyeth falsly/ byhetyng the hope of welfulnesse. But forsothe contraryous fortune is alway sothfaste/ whan she sheweth her selfe unstable through her chaungyng. The amiable fortune disceyueth folke: the contrarye fortune teacheth. Thamyable fortune blyndeth with the beautie of her false

X.v. goodes

goodes/ the herles of folkes that usen hem. The contrarye fortune unbyndeth hem/ with the knowyng of freele welefulnesse. Thamyable fortune mayste thou sene alway wyndy and flowyng/ & euer misknowing of her selfe. The cōtrary fortune is attempre and restrayned and wyse/ thorowe exercise of her aduersyte. At the laste amyable fortune with her flaterynges/ draweth myswandring men fro the souerayne good: the contraryous fortune leadeth ofte folke ayen to sothefaste goodes/ and haleth hem ayen as with an hoke. Wenest thou than that thou oughtest to leten this a lytel thyng/ that this aspre and horryble fortune hath discouered to the/the thoughtes of thy trewe frendes? For why/this ylke fortune hath departed and uncouered to the bothe the certayne vysages/and eke the doutous visages of thy felawes. Whan she departed away fro the/she toke away her frendes and last the thy frendes. Nowe whan thou were ryche and weleful/ as the semed/ with howe mykel woldest thou haue bought the ful knowynge of this/ that is to sayne/ the knowyng of thy very frendes? Nowe playne ỹ not than of rychesse lorne/ sythe thou haste founde the moste precious kynde of rychesse/ that is to sayne/ thy very frendes.

Quod mundus stabili fide Concordes variat vices/ Quod pugnancia semina Fedus perpetuū tenent. &c.

That the worlde with stable faythe varyeth accordable chaungynges/ that the contraryous qualytees of elementes holden amonge hem selfe alyaunce perdurable/ that Phebus the sonne with his golden charyot bringeth forth ỹ rosy day/that the moone hath cōmaundement ouer the nyghtes: which nyghtes Esperus the euen sterre hath/ that the see gredy to flowen constrayneth with a certayne ende his floodes/so that it is not leful to stretche his brode termes or boūdes upon the erthe: Al this ordynaūce of thynges is boūden with loue/ ỹ gouerneth erthe & see/& also hath cōmaundement to the heuen. And if this loue slaked the brideles/al thynges that nowe louen hem togythers wolden make batayle contynuelly/& stryuen to fordone the facion of this worlde/the whiche they now leden in accordable fayth/by fayre mouynges. This loue holdeth togyder people ioyned wt an holy bonde/ and knytteth sacrament of mariage of chaste loues. And loue endeth lawes to true felawes. O weleful were mankynde if thilke loue that gouerneth the heuen/gouerned your corages.

Here endeth the seconde boke/ and foloweth the thirde.

Iam cantum illa finierat/cum me audiendi auidum/ stupentemqꝫ arrectis adhuc auribus carminis mulcedo defixerat. Itaqꝫ paulo post/ O inquam summum lassorū solamē animorū/quantū me. &c.

By this she had ended her songe: whan the swetenesse of her dyte had through perced me/that was desyrous of herkenyng. And I astonyed had yet streyght myn eeres/ that is to sayne/ to herken the bette what she shulde saye/ so that a lytel here after I sayde thus. O thou that arte souerayne comforte of corages anguisshous/ so thou hast remounted and nourisshed me with the weight of thy sentences/and with delyte of syngyng/so that I trowe not that I be unpereygal to the strokes of fortune: as who sayth/I dare wel now suffren al thassautes of fortune/ and wel defende me from her. And tho remedies/ whiche that thou saydest here beforn/that weren right sharpe/ not onely that I am not agrysen of hem nowe/ but I desyrous of herynge/ aske greatly to heren the remedyes. Than sayde she thus. That feled I wel (quod she) whan that thou ententyfe and styl/ rauysshedest my wordes: and I abode tyl thou haddest suche habyte of thy thought/as thou haste nowe/ or els tyl that I my selfe had maked it to ỹ same habyte/ whiche that is a more very thynge. And certes the remenante of thynges that ben yet to say ben suche/that first whan men taste hem/ they ben bytynge: But whan they ben receyued within a wight/than ben they swete. But for thou sayest that thou art so desyrous to herto herken hem/ with howe great brenning wolдest thou glowen/ if thou wystes whyder I wolde leden the? B. Whider is that (qd I) P. To thilke very blyssfulnesse (qd she) of which thyn herte dremeth. But for as moche as thy sight is occupyed & distourbed of erthly thynges/ thou mayste not yet seue thilke selfe welefulnesse. B. Do (qd I) and shewe me what thilke very welfulnesse is/ I pray the without taryeng. P. That wol I gladly don (qd she) for cause of the. But I wol firste marken by wordes/ & I wyl enforcen me to enforme the thilk false cause of blyssfulnesse/ which ẏ thou more knowest: so that whan thou haste beholden thilke false goodes/ and turned thyn eyen so to that other syde/ thou maye knowen the clerenesse of very blyssfulnesse.

Qui serere ingenuũ volet agrum/ Liberat arua prius fruticibus/ Falce rubos/ filicemq̃ resecat. &c.

Who so wol sowe a felde plẽteous/ let him first delyueren it of thornes/ and kerue a sonder with his hoke the bussshes & the ferne/ so that ẏ corne may comen heuy of eres & of greynes. Hony is ẏ more swete if mouthes haue first tasted sauours that be wycke. The sterres shinen more agreably/ whã the wynde Nothus leteth his plungy blastes. And after that Lucifer the day sterre hath chased awaye the darke nyght/ the daye the fayrer leadeth the rosen horse of the sonne. And right so thou/ beholdyng first the false goodes begyn to withdrawe thy necke fro the erthly affections/ and afterwardes the very goodes shullen entren in to thy corage.

Tum defixo paululum visu/ et velut in angustam sue mentis sedem recepta/ sic cepit. P. Omnis mortalium cura quã multiplicium studiorũ labor exercet. &c.

Tho fastened she a lytel the syght of her eyen/ & she withdrewe her right as it were in to ẏ streyte sete of her thought: and beganne to speake ryght thus.

Al the cures (qd she) of mortal folke/ whiche that trauaylen hem in many maner studyes/ gone certes by dyuers wayes: but natheles they enforcen hem al to comen onely to the ende of blyssfulnesse. And blissfulnesse is suche a good/ that who so hath goten it/ he ne maye ouer that thynge more desyre. And this thyng forsoth is so soueraynе good/ that it conteyneth in him selfe al maner of goodes/ to the whiche good if there fayled any thynge/ it might not ben souerayn good. for than were some good out of this soueraynе good/ that might be desyred. Nowe is it clere and certayne/ that blysfulnesse is a parfyte state/ by the congregacion of al goodes/ the whiche blyssfulnesse (as I haue sayd) al mortal folke enforcen hem to gette by dyuers wayes. For why/ the couetyse of euery good is naturelly planted in the hertes of men: but the miswandring errour/ misledeth hem in to false goodes. Of the whiche men/ some of hem wenen that souerayn good be to lyuen without nede of any thynge. And other men demen/ that souerayn good be right digne of reuerence/ and enforcen hem to be reuerenced amonge her neyghbours by the honours that they haue goten. And some folke there ben that holden that right hye power be soueraynе good/ and enforcen hem for to reignen/ or els to ioynen hem to hem that reygnen. And it semeth to other folke/ that noblesse of renome be the souerayn good/ and hasten hem to getten hem glorious name by the artes of werre or of peace. And many folke mesuren and gessen/ that soueraynе good be ioye and gladnesse/ and wenen that it be ryght blyssful thing to plungen in volupt uous delytes. And there ben some folke/ that entrechaungen the causes and the endes of these forsayd goodes: As they that desyren rychesses to haue power and delytes/ or els they desyre power for to haue money/ or for cause of renõme. In these thynges and suche other is tourned al the entencion of desyringes and werkes of men/ as thus: Noblesse and fauoure of people/ whiche that yeueth to al men/ as it semeth hem/ a maner clerenesse of renomme: and wyfe and chyldren/ that men desyren/ for cause of delyte and meryнesse. But forsoth frendes ne

X.y.ii. shullen

shullen not be rekened amonge the goodes of fortune/ but of vertue/ for it is a ful holy maner thyng. Al these other thynges forsothe be taken for cause of power/ or els for cause of delyte. Certes nowe am I redy to referren the goodes of the body/ to these foresayd thynges abouen: For it semeth that strength and gretnesse of body yeuen power and worthynesse/ and that beaute and swyftnesse yeuen glorie and renõme: and helth of body semeth to yeuen delyte. In al these thynges it semeth only that blyssfulnesse is desyred: for why/ thylke thynge that euery man desyreth moste ouer al thynges/ he demeth that it be souerayne good. But I haue diffined/ that blyssfulnesse is souerayn good/ for which euery wight demeth that thilke astate that he desyreth ouer al thynges/ that it be blyssfulnesse. Nowe haste thou than before thyn eyen almost al the purposed forme of the welefulnesse of mankynde/ that is to sayne/ richesse/ honours/ power/ glorie and delytes/ the whiche delite only considred he Epicurus/ and iuged and establysshed that delyte is the souerayne good: for as moche as al other thynges/ as him thought/ byreft away ioye and myrthe from the hert. But I returne agayne to the studyes of men/ of whiche men the corage alway reherseth and seketh the souerayne good/ al be it so that it be with a dyrked memorie/ but he note by whiche pathe/ right as a dronken man note nouȝt by which pathe he may retourne home to his house. Semeth it than that folke folyen and erren to enforcen hem to haue nede of nothing. Certes there is none other thyng/ that maye so moche performen blyssfulnesse/ as an estate plẽteous of al goodes/ that ne hath nede of none other thyng/ but that is suffysaũt of him selfe vnto him selfe. And folyen suche folke than ye wenen/ that thilke thyng that is right good/ that it is eke right worthy of honour & of reuerẽce: certes nay. For that thyng nys neyther foule ne worthy to be dispysed/ that wel nygh al the entencion of mortal folke trauaylen to get it. And power eke ought not to be rekened amõges goodes. What els? For it nis not to wene/ that thilke thynge that is moste worthy of al thynges be feble and without strength. And clerenesse of renome/ ought that to ben dispysed? Certes ther may no man forsake/ that al thyng that is right excellent and noble/ that it ne semeth be right clere and renomed. For certes it nedeth not to say/ that blyssfulnesse be anguysshous ne drery/ ne subiect to greuaunces ne sorowes/ sens that in right lytel thynges folke seken to haue and to vsen that maye delyten hem. Certes these ben the thynges that men wyllen and desyren to geten: and for this cause desyren they richesses/ dignitees/ regnes/ glorie/ and delytes. For therby wenen they to haue suffysaunce/ honour/ power/ renomme/ and gladnesse. Than is it good/ that men seken thus by so many dyuers studyes/ in whiche desyre it maye not lightly be shewed/ howe great is the strength of nature. For howe so men haue diuers sentences and discordynges/ algates men accorden al in louynge the ende of good.

Quantas rerum flectit habenas Natura potens/ quibus immensum Legibus orbem prouida seruet/ Stringatq; ligãs irresoluto Singula nexu/ placet arguto Fidelibus lentis promere cantu. &c.

IT lyketh me to shewe by subtyll songe with slacke & delytable sowne of strynges/ howe that nature myghtly enclyneth and flytteth the gouernement of thinges/ and by suche lawes she puruayable kepeth the great worlde/ and howe she byndyng restrayneth al thynges by a bonde that may not be vnbounden. Al be it so that the lyons of the countraye of Pene beren the fayre chaynes/ and taken meates of the handes of folke/ that yeuen it hem/ and dreden her sturdy maysters/ of whiche they be wonte to suffre beatynges/ if that her horrible mouthes ben bledde/ that is to sayne/ of beestes deuoured: her corage of tyme passed that hath ben ydle & rested repayreth ayen/ and they roren greuously/ and remembren on her nature/ and slaken her neckes from her chaynes vnbounde/ and her maistre first to torne with blody tethe/ assayeth ye woode wrathes of hem/ that is to sayne/ they fretten her maister.

maister. And the iangkyng birde that syngeth on the hye braunches/ that is to sayne/ in the wodde/and after is enclosed in a strayte cage/ al though the plyeng besynesse of men yeue hem honyed drinkes/ and large meates with swete studye: yet natheles if thilke byrde skyppyng out of her strayte cage/ seeth the agreable shadowes of ye woddes/she defouleth with her fete her meate yshadde/and seketh on mornyng only the wodde/and twytereth desyring the wodde with her swete wyse. The yerde of a tre that is haled adown by mighty strength boweth redyly the croppe adowne: but if that the hande that is bente let it gone agayne/ anon the croppe loketh vpright to the heuen. The sonne Phebus that falleth at euen in the westren wawes/retourneth ayen estsones his carte by a priuy pathe there as it is wonte aryse. Al thiges seken ayen to her ppre course/ and al thynges reioysen on her retournyng agayne to her nature: ne none ordynaunce is betaken to thynges/ but that hath ioyned the ende to the begynnynge/ and hath made the course it selfe stable/ that it chaunge not fro his propre kynde.

Vos quoq; o terrena animalia/ tenui licet imagine/vestrū tamen principium somniatis. Verumq; illū beatitudinis finem/ licet minime perspicaci. &c.

Certes also ye men that ben erthly beestes dreamen alway your begynnyng/ al though it be with a thynne ymagynacion/ and by a maner thought/ al be it not clerely ne perfetly/ ye loken from a ferre to thilke very fyne of blyssfulnesse. And therfore naturel entencion leadeth you to thilke very good/but many maner errours mistourneth you therfro. Consyder nowe if that be thilk thynges/ by which a mā weneth to get him blissfulnesse if that he may comen to thilk ende/ that he weneth to come to by nature. For if that money/ honours/or these other forsayde thinges bringen to men such a thing that no good ne fayle them ne semeth to fayle: Certes than wol I graunt that they be maked blissful by thinges that they haue goten. But if so be that thylke thinges ne mowen not performe that they byheten/and that there be defaute of many goodes/sheweth it not than clerely ye false beaute of blissfulnesse is knowen and attaynt in thilk thiges? First and forwarde thou thy self/ that haddest habundaunce of richesse not longe agon/ I aske the ye in thabundaunce of al thilke riches/ if thou were neuer anguisshous or sorye in thy corage of any wronge or greuaunce/ that betyd the in any syde. B. Certes (qd I) it ne remembreth me not/ that euer I was so free of my thought/that I ne was alwaye in anguisshe of somwhat. P. And was that not (qd she) for that the lacked somwhat that thou noldest not haue lacked? or els thou haddest that thou noldest haue had? B. Right so it is (qd I) P. Than desyredist thou ye presence of ye one/and thabsence of that other? B. I graunt wel (qd I) P. Forsothe (qd she) than nedeth ther somwhat that euery man desyreth. B. Ye there nedeth (qd I) P. Certes (qd she) and he that hath lacke or nede of aught/nys not in euery way suffisaūt to him selfe. B. No (qd I) P. And thou (qd she) in al the plente of thy richesse haddest thilke lacke of suffysaunce? B. What els (qd I) P. Than may not riches maken that a man nys nedy/ne that he be sufficient to him selfe: and yet that was it that they beheten as it semed. And eke certes I trowe that this be gretly to cōsyder/that money hath not in his owne kynde/that it ne may ben bynomed of hem that haue it maugre hem. B. I knowe it wel (qd I) P. Why shuldest ye not beknowen it (qd she) whan euery day ye strenger folke bynomen it from the febler maugre hem? Fro whence come els al these forayn cōplayntes/quarels/or pledynges/ but for that men asken her money that hath ben bynomed hem by strength or by gyle/ & alway maugre hem? B. Right so it is (qd I) P. Than hath a man nede (qd she) to seken him forayn helpe/ by which he may defende his money. B. Who may saye nay (qd I) P. Certes (qd she) and him neded none helpe/ if he ne had no money that he might lese. B. That is doutelees (qd I) P. Than is this thyng turned in to ye cōtrary (qd she) for rychesse/ that men wenen shulde maken suffisaunce/ they maken a man rather

X. y. iii. haue

haue nede of forayne helpe. Whiche is the maner or the gyse (qđ she) that richesse maye driuen away nede? Riche folke may they neither haue honger ne thurste? These riche men may they fele no colde on their lymmes i wynter? But thou wylt answere ẏ riche men haue ynough / wherwith they may stauchen her honger / and slaken her thurst / & done awaye colde. In this wyse may nede ben comforted by rychesse / but certes nede ne maye not al vtterly be done away. For if this nede that alway is gapynge and gredy / be fulfylled with richesse and any other thing / yet dwelleth than a nede that mote be fulfylled. I holde me styl / and tel not howe that lytel thing suffyseth to nature: but certes to auarice suffyseth not ynough of nothynge. For syn that richesse ne may not al oon away nede / and they maken their owne nede / what maye it than be / that ye wenen that richesses mowen yeuen you suffysaunce?

Quamuis fluente diues auri gurgite
Non expleturas cogat auarus opes. &c.

AL were it so / ẏ a noble couetous man had a ryuer or a gutter fletynge al of golde / yet shulde it neuer stauche his couetyse: and al though he had his necke charged with precious stones of the reed see: & though he do eere his feldes plenteous with an hũdred oxen / neuer ne shal his byting besynes forleten him whyle he lyueth / ne the lyght rychesses ne shal not bearen him companye whan he is deed.

Sed dignitates honorabilem / reuerendũq; cui prouenerint / reddunt. Num vis ea est magistratibus / vt vtentiũ mentibus virtutes inserant / vicia depellant? &c.

BUt dignytees to whom they be comen / maken they him honourable and reuerent? haue they not so great strẽgth that they may putten vertue in hertes of folkes / ẏ vsen the lordship of hem / or els may they don away the vyces. Certes they be not wonte to done away wickydnesse / but they be wonte rather to shewe wickednesse. And therof cometh it that I haue right gret disdayn / that dignitees ben yeuen to wicked men. For whiche thyng Catullus cleped a cõsul of Rome (that hight Nonyus) postome of boche / as who saith / he cleped him a congregacion of vyces in his brest / as a postome is ful of corrupcion: al were Nonius set in a chayre of dignite. Seest thou not than / howe great vylonies dignitees done to wicked men? certes vnworthynesse of wicked men shulde be the lasse sene / if they nere renomed of none honour. Certes thou thy selfe ne mightest not be brought with as many perils as thou mightest suffre / that thou woldest beare the magistrate with decorate / that is to sayne / that for peryl that might befal the by offence of the kynge Theodrike / thou noldest not be felawe in gouernaunce with Decorate / whan thou sawe that he had wicked corage of a lycorous shrewe and of an accusour. Ne I may not for such honours iugen hem worthy of reuerẽce / that I deme and holde vnworthy to haue thilke same honours. Nowe if thou sawe a man that were fulfylde of wysdome / certes thou ne mightest not deme that he were vnworthy to ẏ honour / or els to the wysdom of whiche he is fulfylled. B. No (quod I) P. Certes (qđ she) dignitees aperteynen properly to vertue / and vertue transporteth dignyte anon to thylke man / to whiche she her selfe is conioyned. And for as moche as honours of people ne maye not make folke digne of honour / it is wel sene clerly / that they ne haue no propre beautie of dignyte. And yet men oughten take more hede in this: for if a wight be in so moche the more outcast / that he is dispysed of moste folke / so as dignyte ne may not maken shrewes worthy of no reuerence / than maketh dignite shrewes rather dispysed thã praysed / the whiche shrewes dignite sheweth to moche folke. And forsothe not vnpunisshed / that is to sayne / that shrewes reuengen hem ayenwarde vpon dignitees. For they yelden ayen to dignitees as gret guerdons / whan they dispotten & defoulen dignitees with her vilonye. And for as moch as thou nowe knowest / that thilke very reuerence ne maye not comen by these shadowy transytorie dignitees / vnderstonde nowe thus: that if a man had vsed and had many maner dignitees of consuls / & were

pera-

peraventure comen among straunge nacions/ shulde thilke honour maken him worshypful and redouted of straunge folke? Certes if that honour of people were a naturel yefte to dignitees/ it ne might never cessen nowher amõg no maner folke to done his offyce. Right as a fyre in every countrey ne stynteth not to enchaufen & maken hote. But for as moche as for to ben honourable or reverent/ ne cometh not to folke of her propre strength of nature/ but onely of the false opinion of folke/ that is to sayne/ that wenen yͭ dignitees maken folke digne of honours: anon therfore whan they comen ther as folke ne knowen not thilke dignytes/ her honours vanisshen away and that anon. But yͭ is among straunge folke mayst thou sayne. Ne amonges hem there they were borne/ ne dured not thilke dignitees alwaye. Certes the dignite of the provostry of Rome was whilom a great power: nowe is it nothyng but an ydle name/ and the rente of the senatorie a great charge. And if a wight whylom had thoffyce to taken hede to the vitayles of the people/ as of corne and of other thyngz/ he was holden amõges hem great. But what thyng is more nowe outcast than thilke provostrie. As I have sayd a lytel here beforne/ that thilke thing that hath no propre beaute of it selfe/ receyveth somtyme price & shynynge/ and somtyme leseth it by thoppinion of usaunces. Nowe if that dignitees than ne mowe not make folke digne of reverence/ & if that dignitees wexe foule of her wyl/ by yͤ fylthe of shrewes. And if dignytees lesen her shyninge by chaũgyng of tymes/ & if they wexen foule by estymation of people/ what is it that they han in hem selfe of beaute/ yͭ ought to be desyred? as who sayth/ none: than ne mowen they yeven no beaute of dignite to none other.

Quamvis se tyrio superbus ostro Comeret et niveis lapillis. &c.

AL be it so/ that the proude Nero with al his wode luxure/ kembe him and apparelled hym with fayre purpure of Tyrie/ and with whyte peerles. Algates yet therof he hateful to al folke/ this is to say that al was he behated of al folkes/ yet this wicked Nero had great lordshyppe. And yaf whylom to the reverent Senatours the unworshipful seates of dignytees. Unworship ful seates he clepeth heere/ for that Nero that was so wicked yave the dignytees.

Who wolde than resonably wenen/ that blyssfulnesse were in suche honours/ as ben yeven by vycious shrewes.

An vero regna/ regumqꝫ familiaritas efficere potentem valent? Quidni? &c.

BUt reignes and famylyaritees of kynges/ maye they maken a man to bene myghty? Howe els? Whan his blyssfulnesse dureth perpetually. But certes the olde age of tyme passed/ and eke of present tyme now/ is ful of ensamples/ howe that kynges have chaunged in to wretchednesse/ out of her welfulnesse. O/ a noble thyng and a clere thynge is power/ that nys nat founden myghty to kepe it selfe. And if that power of reaumes be authour & maker of blyssfulnesse/ if thylke power lacketh on any syde/ amenuseth it nat thylke blyssfulnesse/ and bryngeth in wretchednesse? But yet al be it so/ that the reaumes of mankynde stretchen brode/ yet mote there nede ben moche folke/ over which that every kyng ne hath no lordshyppe ne cõmaundement. And certes upon thylke syde that power falleth/ whiche that maketh folke blyssful. Right on that same syde no power entreth undnethe that maketh hem wretches. In this maner than moten kynges have more porcioun of wretchednesse than of welefulnesse.

A tyraunt that was kynge of Cecyle/ that had assayed the peryl of his estate/ shewed by symilytude the dredz of reaumes by gastnesse of a swerde/ that honge over the heed of his famyler. What thynge is than this power/ that maye nat done awaye the bytynges of besynesse/ ne eschewe the prickes of drede?

And certes yet wolden they lyven in sykernesse/ but they maye nat. And yet they glorifien hem in her power. Holdest thou than that thilk man be mighty/ yͭ thou seest that he wolde done that he may nat done? And holdest thou

dest thou than him a myghtie man/ that hath
enuyroned his sydes with men of armes or
sergeauntes/ and dredeth more hem that he ma
keth agast/ than they dreden hym/ and that is
putte in the handes of his seruauntes/ for he
shulde seme mightye? But of famylyers or
seruauntes of kynges/ why shulde I tel the
any thyng/ sithe that I my selfe haue shewed
the/ that realmes hem selfe ben ful of great fe
blesse? The whiche famylyers certes the roy-
al power of kynges in hoole estate and in e-
state abated/ ful ofte throweth adowne.

Nero constrayned Senecke his famylyer
and his mayster/ to chesen on what dethe he
wolde dye. Antonius cõmaunded ỷ knyghtes
tes slowen with her swordes Papinian his fa
mylyer/ whiche Papinyan hadde ben long-
tyme ful mighty amonges hem of the courte.
and yet certes they wolden bothe haue renoun-
ced her power. Of whiche two Senick en-
forced him to yeuen to Nero his rychesse/ and
also to haue gone in to solytarye exile. But
whan the great weight/ that is to sayn/ of lor
des power or of Fortune/ draweth hem that
shullen fal/ neither of hem ne myght do that
he wolde. What thyng is than thylke power/
that though men haue it/ yet they ben agaste/
& whan thou woldest haue it/ thou narte nat
syker? And if thou woldest forleten it/ thou
mayst nat eschewen it. But wheder such men
ben frendes at nede/ as ben counsayled by for
tune/ and nat by vertue? Certes suche folke
as welful fortune maketh frẽdes/ cõtrarious
fortune maketh hem enemyes. And what pe-
stylence is more myghty for to anoy a wight/
than a famylyer enemy?

Qui se volet esse potẽtẽ/ Animos domet
ille feroces: Nec victa libidine colla. &c.

Who so wol be myghty/ he mote daũ
ten his cruel corages/ ne putte nat
his necke ouercomen/ vnder ỷ fou
le raynes of lechery. For al be it
so/ that the lordshyppe strecche so ferre/ that
the countrey of Inde quaketh at thy cõmaun
dementes/ or at thy lawes. And that the last
yle in the see/ that hight Tyle/ be thrale to the:
yet if thou mayst nat putten awaye thy foule
derke desyres/ and dryuen out fro the/ wret-
ched complayntes: Certes it nys no power
that thou haste.

Gloria vero q̃ fallax sepe/ q̃ turpis est:
Unde non iniuria tragicus exclamat.
O gloria gloria millibus mortalium: nihil
aliud facta/ nisi auriũ inflatio magna. &c.

But glory/ howe disceyuable and howe
foule is it ofte? For whiche thynge/
nat vnskylfully a tragedyen/ that is to sayne a
maker of dytees that highten tragedies/ cryed
and sayd. O glory glory (qđ he) thou nart
no thynge els to thousandes of folkes/ but a
sweller of eares. For many haue ful great
renome by the false opynyon of the peple.

And what thynge may ben thought fouler
than suche praysynge? For thylke folke that
ben praysed falsely/ they mooten nedes haue
shame of her praysynges. And if that folke
haue getten hem thanke or praysynge by her
desertes: What thynge hath thylke prise eched
or encreased to the conscyence of wyse folke/
that measuren her good/ nat by the rumoure
of the peple/ but by the sothfastnesse of con-
scyence? And if it seme a fayre thyng/ a man
to haue encreased and sprad his name/ than
foloweth it/ ỷ it is demed to ben a foule thĩg/
if it ne be yspradde and encreased. But as I
sayd a lytel here before/ that sith ther mote ne-
des ben many folkes/ to whiche folke the re-
nome of a man ne maye nat comen/ it befal-
leth/ that he that thou wenest be glorious and
renomed/ semeth in the next parte of therthes/
to ben without glorye and without renome.
And certes amõges these thynges I ne trowe
nat that the prise and the grace of the peple/
nys neither worthy to ben remembred/ ne co-
meth of wyse iugemẽt/ ne is ferme perdurably.
But nowe of this name of gentylesse: what
man is it that ne may wel sene howe vayne &
howe flyttĩg it is? For if ỷ name of gẽtylesse
be referred to renome & clerenesse of lynage/
than is gentyl name but a forain thyng/ ỷ is
to say/ to hem ỷ glorifien hem of her lynage.
For it semeth ỷ gentyles be a maner praysĩg/
that

that cometh of the desertz of auncesters. And if praysynge maketh gentylnesse/ than moten they nedes ben gentyl/ that ben praysed. For whiche thynge it foloweth/ that if thou ne haue no gentylnesse of thy selfe/ that is to sayne prise/ that cometh of thy deserte. Forayn gentylnesse ne maketh the nat gentyl. But certes if there be any good in gentylnesse/ I trowe it be al onely this: that it semeth as that a maner necessyte be imposed to gētylmen/ for that they ne shulde nat outragen or forleauen fro the vertues of her noble kynred.

Omne hominū genus in terris Simili surgit ab ortu. Unus enim rerum pater est/ Unus cuncta ministrat. &c.

AL the lynage of men/ that ben in erthe ben of semblable byrthe. One alone is father of thynges: one alone mynistreth al thynges: He yafe to the sonne his beames: he yafe to the moone her hornes: he yafe to men the erthe: he yafe the sterres to the heuen: he enclosed with membres the soules that comen from his hye seate. Than comen al mortal folke of noble seed. Why noysen ye or bosten of your elders? For if ye loke your begynnīg and god your father authour and your maker/ Than nys there no forlyued wyght or vngentyl/ but if he nourysshe his corage vnto vyces/ and forlete his proper byrthe.

Quid autem de corporis voluptatibus loquar? quarum appetentia quidem plena est anxietatis. &c.

BUt what shal I sayne of delyces of body/ of whiche delices the desyringes ben ful of anguisshes/ and the fulfyllinges of hem ben ful of penaunce? Howe great sicknesses and how great sorowes vnsuffrable/ right as a maner fruite of wickydnesse ben thilke delyces wonte to bringen to the bodies of folkes that vsen hem? of whiche delyces I not what ioye may ben had of her mouynge. But this wote I wel/ that who so euer wol remembren hym of his luxures/ he shal wel vnderstonde/ that the issues of delyces ben sorouful & sorye. And if thilke delyces mowe maken folke blisful/ than by ye same cause moten these beestes ben cleped blyssful. of whiche beestes al the entēcion hasteth to fulfyl her bodely iolyte. And the gladnesse of wife and children were an honeste thyng/ but it hath ben said that it is ouer mokel ayenst kynde/ that children haue ben founden tourmentours to her fathers/ I not howe many. Of whiche children howe bytyng is euery cōdycion/ it nedeth not to tellen it thee/ that haste er this tyme assayed it/ and arte yet nowe anguisshous. In this tyme aproue I ye sentēce of my disciple Euripidis/ y^t sayd/ that he y^t hath no children is weleful by infortune.

Habet hoc voluptas omnis Stimulis agit fruentes/ Apiumque par volantum Ubi grata mella fudit/ Fugit/ et nimis tenaci Ferit icta corda morsu. &c.

EUery delite hath this/ that it anguissheth hem with prickes that vsen it. It resembleth to these fleyng flyes that we clepen bees/ that after that he hath shedde his agreable honyes/ he flyeth away/ and styngeth the hertes of hem that ben smytten with bytynge ouerlonge holden.

Nihil igitur dubium est/ quin he ad beatitudinem vie devia quedam sint: nec perducere eo quemque valeant. &c.

NOwe is it no doute than/ that these wayes ne ben a maner mysledingz to blyssfulnesse: ne that they ne mowen nat leaden folke thider/ as they beheten to leden hem. But with howe great harmes these forsayde wayes ben enlaced/ I shal shewe you shortly. For why/ if thou enforcest the to assēble money/ thou must byreuen hym his money that hath it. And if thou wolte shynen with dignitees/ thou muste besechen and supplyen hem/ that yeuen tho dignytees. And if thou coueytest by honour to gone beforne other folkes/ thou shalte defoule thy self thorowe hublesse of askig. If thou desyrest power/ thou shalt by awaytes of thy subiectz anoyously be cast vnder by many paryls. Askest thou glorie?

thou

thou shalte ben so distracte by aspre thynges/
that thou shalt forgone likernesse. And if thou
woldest leden thy lyfe in delytes/ euery wight
shal dispysen the and forleten the/ as thou that
arte thral to thyng/ that is right foule and bri=
tel/ that is to sayne/ seruaunt to thy bodye.
Nowe is it than wel ysene/ howe lytel & howe
britel possessyon they coueyten/ that putten
the goodes of the body aboue her owne rea=
son. For mayste thou surmounten these olyf=
auntes in greatnesse or in weight of body: or
mayste thou be strenger than the bul: mayste
thou be swyfter than the tygre? Beholde the
spaces & the stablenesse/ and the swyfte course
of heuen/ and stynte somtyme to wondren on
foule thynges. The whiche heuen certes nys
not rather for these thynges to be wondred
vpon/ than for the reason by whiche it is go=
uerned. But the shynynge of thy forme/ that
is to sayne/ the beaute of thy body/ how swyfte=
ly passyng is it/ and howe transytorie/ certes
it is more flyttyng than ẏ mutabylite of flou=
res of the somer season. For so as Aristotel
telleth/ that if ẏ men had eyen of a beest that
hight Lynx/ so that the lokyng of folke myzt
percen through tho thynges that withstoden
it. Who so loked than in thentrayles of the bo=
dy of Alcibiades/ that was ful fayre in the su=
perficie without/ it shulde seme right foule.
And for thy/ if thou semest fayre/ thy nature
ne maketh nat that/ but the disceyuaunce of
feblenesse of the eyen that loken. But prayse
the goodes of the body as moche as euer the
lyst/ so that thou knowe algatz that what so
it be/ that is to sayne/ of the goodes of the bo=
dye/ whiche that thou wondrest vpon/ maye
ben distroyed or els dissolued by the heete of a
feuer of thre dayes. Of whiche forsayd thyn=
ges I may reducen this shortly in a somme/ that
these worldly goodes/ whiche that ne mowen
yeuen that they behyghten/ ne ben not parfyte
by the congregacion of al goodes/ that they
ne ben not wayes ne pathes that bringen men
to blissfulnesse/ ne maken men to be blisful.

Heu heu quam miseros tramite deuios Ab=
ducit ignorantia: Non aurum in viridi
queritis arbore. &c.

Alas/ whiche folye/ and whiche igno=
raunce missledeth wandring wretches
fro the pathe of very good. Certes ye seken
no golde in grene trees/ ne ye gadren nat pre=
cious stones in vynes: ne ye ne hyden not yo=
gynnes in hye mountayns to catchen fysshe:
of the whiche ye maye maken riche feestes.

And if you lyke to hunte to Roes/ ye ne go
nat to the fordes of the water that hight Tyr=
rene. And ouer this men knowe wel the cre=
kes and the cauernes of the see yhid in the flo=
des/ and knowen eke whiche water is moost
plenteous of whyte perles/ & knowen whiche
water haboundeth most of reed purpure/ that
is to sayne/ of a maner shelfyssh/ with whiche
men dyen purpure: and knowen whiche stro=
des haboundeth moste of tendre fysshes/ or of
sharpe fysshes/ ẏ hight Echynes. But folke
suffren hem selfe to ben so blynde/ that hem ne
retchen not to knowe where thilke goodes ben
yhydde/ whiche that they coueyten/ but plun=
gen hem in erthe/ and seken there thilke good/
that surmounteth the heuen that beareth the
sterres. What prayer maye I maken that be
digne to the nyce thoughtes of men? But I
pray that they coueyten richesse and honours/
so that whan they haue goten tho false goodes
with great trauayle that therby they mowen
knowen the very goodes.

Hactenus mendacis formam felicitatis
ostendisse suffecerit/ quod si perspicaciter in=
tuearis/ ordo est deinceps. &c.

It suffyseth that I haue sayde hyderto/
the forme of false welefulnesse: so that
if thou loke nowe clerely: the order of myne
entention requyreth from hens forthe/ to she=
wen the very welefulnesse. B. For soth (quod
I) I se wel nowe/ ẏ suffysaunce may nat co=
men by richesse/ ne power by realmes/ ne re=
uerence by dignytees/ ne gentylesse by glory/
ne ioye by delyces. Phi. And haste thou wel
knowen the causes (quod she) why it is? Boe.
Certes me semeth (quod I) that I se hem/ right
as though it were through a lytel clyfte: But
me were leauer knowen hem more openly of
the. P. Certes (quod she) the reason is al redy.
For thilke

For thilke thynge that symply is one thynge without any deuysion / the errour and folie of mankynde deuydeth and departeth it & misledeth it / and transporteth from very & parfyte good / to goodes that be false & vnparfyt. But say me this: wenest thou that he that hath nede of power / ŷ him ne lacketh nothing? B. Nay (qd I) P. Certes (qd she) thou sayest aright: for if so be that there is a thynge that in any partie be febler of power / certes as in that it mote nedes be nedy of forayn helpe. B. Right so it is (qd I) Phi. Suffysaunce and power ben of one kynde. Boece. So semeth (qd I) Philo. And demest thou (quod she) that a thynge that is of this maner / that is to saye / suffysaunt and myghty / ought ben dispysed / or els that it be right digne of reuerence aboue al thynges? B. Certes (qd I) it is no doute that it is right worthy to be reuerenced. P. Let vs adden (qd she) reuerence to suffysaunce and to power / so that we demen ŷ these thre thynges be al one thinge. B. Certes (qd I) let vs adden it if we wyl graunt the sothe. P. What demest thou (qd she) thā is that a derke thing and not noble / that is suffysaūt / reuerent / and mighty? or els that it is right noble and right clere by celebrate of renōme? Consyder than (qd she) as we haue graunted here byforne / that he that ne hath no nede of no thyng / & is moste mighty and moste digne of honour / if him nedeth any clerenesse of renome / whiche clerenesse he might not graunten of him selfe: so for lacke of thilke clerenesse he might semen the febler on any syde / or the more out caste. Glose. That is to say / naye: For who so that is suffisaunt / mighty / and reuerent / clerenesse of renome foloweth of the forsayde thinges: he hath it al redy of his suffysaunce. Boece. I maye not (quod I) denye it / but I mote graunten as it is / that this thynge is right celebrable by clerenesse of renōme and noblesse. Phi. Than foloweth (quod she) that we adden clerenesse of renomme to the foresayde thynges / so that there be amonges hem no difference. Boece. This is a consequence (qd I) Philo. This thynge than (quod she) that ne hath nede of no forayne thynge / and that maye do al thynge by his strengthes / and that is noble and honourable / is it not a mery thynge and ioyful? Boe. But whence (quod I) that any sorow might come to this thyng that is suche / certes I may not thinke. Philoso. Than mote we graunten (qd she) that this thynge be ful of gladnesse / if the foresayde thynges be sothe. And certes / also mote we graunten / that suffysaunce / power / noblesse / reuerence / and gladnesse be onely dyuers by names / but her substaunce hath no dyuersyte. Boece. It mote nedely be so (quod I) Philosophia. Thylke thynge than (quod she) that is one and symple in his nature / the wickednesse of men departeth and deuydeth it: And whan they enforcen hem to getten partye of a thynge / that ne hath no parte / they ne geten hem neyther thylke partie that nys none / ne the thynge al hole that they desyre. Boece. In whiche manere (quod I) Philosophia. Thylke man (quod she) that secheth rychesse to flyen pouertie: he ne trauayleth him not for to get power / for he hath leauer be derke and vyle / and eke withdraweth from hym selfe many naturel delytes / for he nolde lese the money that he hath assembled. But certes in this maner he ne getteth him no suffysaunce / that power forleteth and that molestie pricketh / and that fylthe maketh outcaste / and that derkenesse hydeth. And certes he that desyreth onely power / wasteth and scattereth rychesse / and dispyseth delyces and eke honour ŷ is without power / ne he ne prayseth glorie nothyng. Certes thus seest thou wel that many thinges faylen to him: For he hath somtyme defaute of many necessytees / & many anguysshes byten him. And whan he may not done tho defautes away / he forletteth to be mighty / and that is the thyng that he most desyreth. And right thus maye I make semblable reasons of honour / of glorie / & of delyces. For so euery of these forsaid thinges is ŷ same that these other thinges ben / that is to sayne / al one thyng. Who so euer seketh to geten that one of these & not ŷ other / he ne geteth not that he desyreth. B. What sayest ŷ thā / if that a man coueyte to geten al these thīgꝭ togyder. P. Certes (qd she) I wold say ŷ he wolde get him souerayn blisfulnes / but ŷ shal he not fynde in tho thynges

thynges that I haue shewed/ that mowe not yeuen that they behcten. B. Certes no (qd I) Phi. Than (quod she) ne shullen men not by no way seken blissfulnesse in suche thynges as men wenen that they ne mowe gyuen but one thynge synglerly of al that men seken. Boc. I graūt wel (qd I) ne non other thyng may be sayd. Phi. Nowe haste thou than (qd she) the forme and the cause of false welefulnesse: Nowe turne and flytte agayn to thy thought/ for there shal thou sene anon thilke very blysfulnesse/ that I haue behyght the. B. Certes (quod I) it is clere and open / though it were to a blynde man: And that shewdest thou me a lytel here beforne/ whan thou enforcedest the to shew me ye causes of the false welefulnesse. For (but if I be begiled) than is ye thilke very blyssfulnesse and parfyte/ that parfytely maketh a man suffysaunt/ mighty/ honourable/ noble/ and ful of gladnes. And for thou shalt wel knowe/ that I haue wel vnderstāden these thynges within my herte: I knowe wel that thilke blyssfulnesse that men verily yeuen one of the forsayd thynges/ sens they ben al one: I knowe doutlesse that thylke thyng is ful of blyssfulnesse. P. O my norice (qd she) by this opinyon I say that thou arte blysful/ if thou put this therto that I shal sayne. B. What is that (qd I). P. Trowest thou that there be any thyng in this erthely mortal tomblynge thynges / that maye bringen this estate? Bo. Certes (qd I) I trowe it not: and thou haste shewed me wel/ that ouer thilke good ther nys nothyng more to ben desyred. P. These thinges than (qd she) that is to sayne/ erthly suffisaunce & power/ and suche thinges erthly/ they semen lykenesse of very good/ or els it semeth that they yeuen to mortal folke a maner of goodnesse/ that ne be not parfyte: but thylke good that is very and parfyte/ that may they not yeuen. B. I accorde me wel (qd I). P. Than (qd she) for as moch as thou hast knowen/ which is thilk very blissfulnes/ & eke which thilk thīges ben/ ye lyen falsely blissfulnes/ that is to say/ that they by disceyte semen very goodes: Nowe behoueth ye to knowe whēre & wher thou mow seke thilke very blissfulnesse. B. Certes (qd I) ye desyre I gretly / & haue abyden longe tyme to herken it. P. But for as moche (qd she) as it lyketh to my dysciple Plato in his boke of Thimeo / that in ryght lytel thynges menne shulden beseche the helpe of god: What iugest thou ye be nowe to done so that we maye deserue to fynde the seate of thylke soueraygne god? B. Certes (qd I) I deme ye we shullen clepe to the father of al goddes/ for withouten him nys ther nothyng foūded a right. P. Thou sayest a right (qd she) and began anon to syngen right thus.

O qui perpetua mundū ractiōe gubernas Terrarū/ celiq3 sator/ qui tēpus ab euo Ire iubes/ stabilisq3 manens das cuncta moueri. Quem non externe pepulerunt fingere cause. &c.

O Thou father/ soueraygne and creatoure of heuen and of erthes/ that gouernest this worlde by pardurable reason/ that commaūdest the tymes to gone/ syth that age had begynnyng. Thou that dwellest thy self aye stedfast and stable/ and yeuest al other thynges to be meued/ ne foreyne causes ne cesseden the neuer to compoun werke of floteryng mater/ but onely the forme of soueraygne good ysette within the without enuy/ that meued the frely. Thou that arte alderfayrest/ bearyng the fayre worlde i thy thought: formedest this worlde to thy lykenesse semblable/ of ye fayre worlde in thy thought. Thou drawest al thinge on thy soueraygne ensampler/ and cōmaundist that this worlde parfetlich ymaked/ haue frely and absolute his perfite parties. Thou byndest the elementes by nombres proporcionables/ that the colde thynges mowen accorden with the hote thynges/ and the drye thīges with the moyst: That the fyre/ that is purest/ ne flye nat ouerhye / ne that the heuynesse ne drawe nat adoun ouerlowe the erthes that be plonged in the waters. Thou knyttest togyder/ the meane soule of treble kynde mouyng al thynges/ & deuydest it by mēbres acordīg. And whan it is thus deuyded/ it hath assembledde a mouynge in to roundes/ it gothe to turne agayne to him selfe/ and enuyronneth a ful depe thought/ and turneth the heuen by semblable

semblable ymage. Thou by euen lyke causes enhauncest the soules and the lesse lyues/ and auyng hem to height by lyghe waynes or cartes. Thou sowest hem in to heuen and in to erthe/ and whan they be couerted to the by thy benigne lawe/ thou makest hem returne ayen to the by ayen ledyng fyre. O father yeue thou to ye thought to styen vp in to thy strayte sete/ and graut him to enuyronne the wel of good. And the lyght founde graunt him to fyxen the clere syghtes of his corage in the: and scatter thou and tobreake the weightes & the cloudes of erthely heuynesse/ and shyne thou by thy brightnesse. For thou arte clerenesse/ thou arte pesyble reste to debonayre folke/ thou thy selfe arte begynnyng/ bearer/ leder/ pathe/ and terme to loke on the that is our ende.

Quoniā igit/ q̄ sit imperfecti/ que etiam perfecti boni forma vidisti/ nunc demonstrandum reor. &c.

FOrasmoche thā/ as thou hast sene whiche is the fourme of good/ that nys not parfyte/ and the forme of good/ whiche ye is pfyte. Nowe trowe I that it were good to shewe in what this perfection of blissfulnesse is set. And i this thyng I trow that we shal first enquire for to weten/ if that any suche maner good as thilke good as thou haste diffynisshed a lytel here beforne/ that is to sayne/ soueraygne good/ maye be founde in the nature of thyngꝫ. For that vayne ymaginacion of thought ne disceyue vs not/ and put vs out of the sothfastnesse of thilke thing that is submytted to vs. But it may not be denyed that thylke ne is/ and that is right as a wel of al goodes. For al thyng that is cleped imparfite is proued imparfyte/ by the amenusing of perfection of thyng that is parfyte. And herof cometh it that in euery thinge general/ if that men sene any thyng that is imparfyte/ certes in thilke thynge general/ there mote be some thynge that is parfyte. For if so be that pfection is don away/ men may not thike ne say from whence thilke thyng is/ ye is cleped impfyte. For ye nature ne toke not her begynnyng of thynges amenused and imparfyte/ but it procedeth of thinges that ben al hole absolute/ and discendeth so down in to the vttrest thynges/ and in to thynges empty & without frute. But as I haue shewed a lytel here beforne/ that if that there be a blissfulnesse that be freel and vayne/ & imparfyte/ there maye no man doute that there nys some blyssfulnesse/ that there is sadde stedfaste and parfyte. B. This is concluded (qd I) fermely and sothfastly. P. But consyder also (qd she) in whom this blissfulnesse inhabyteth. The comune acorde and concepte of the corage of men proueth and graunteth/ that god prince of al thynges is good. For so as nothing may be thouȝt better than good/ it may not be douted than ye he that no thyng nys better than he nys good. Certes reason sheweth that god is so good/ that it proueth by very force/ that pfyte good is in him. For if god nys such he ne may not ben prince of al thyng. For certes sōthyng possessyng in it selfe parfyte good/ shulde be more worthy than god: and it shuld semen that thilke thing were firste and older than god. For we haue shewed appertly/ that al thinges that ben parfyte/ ben firste/ or thynges that ben impfyte. And forthy/ for as moche as that my reason or my processe ne go not awaye without an ende/ we owen to graunten/ that the souerayn good is right ful of soueraygne parfyte good. And we haue establysshed/ that the soueraygne good is very blissfulnesse: than mote it nedes be/ that very blyssfulnesse is sette in soueraygne good. B. This take I wel (qd I) ne this ne may not be withsayd in no maner. P. But I praye the (qd she) se nowe howe thou mayste prouen holily/ and withouten corrupcion/ this that we haue sayde/ that the soueraygne god is ful of right soueraygne good. B. In whiche maner (qd I) P. Wenest thou aught (qd she) that the father of al thynges hath taken thilke soueraygne good any where out of him selfe? Of whiche souerayn good/ men proueth that he is ful. Right as thou mightest thynken/ that god/ that hath blyssfulnesse in hym selfe/ and thylke blyssfulnesse that is in him were dyuers in substaunce. For if thou wene/ that god hath receyued thilke good out of him selfe/ thou mayste wene/ that he ye yaue thilke good

X.y. to god

to god be more worthy than god. But I am beknowe and cõfesse/ and that right digneli/ that god is right worthy aboue al thynges: And if so be that this good be in him by nature/ but that is dyuers from him by weninge reason/ sens we speken of god prince of al thinges. Fayne who so fayne maye/ who was he that conioyned these thynges togyther. And eke at the laste se wel/ that a thyng that is dyuers fro any thyng/ that thilke thyng nys not that same thynge/ for whiche it is understonden to ben dyuers. Than folowth it wel/ that thilke thing that by his nature is dyuers from soueraygne good/ that thynge is not soueraygne good. But certes it were a felonous cursydnesse to thynken that of hym that nothynge nys more worthe. For alwaye of al thynges the nature of hem, ne maye not ben better than her begynner. For whiche I maye concluden by right very reason/ that thylke that is begynnyng of al thynges/ thilke same thynge is soueraygn god in his substance. B. Thou hast sayde rightfully (quod I) Philoso. But we haue graunted (quod she) that the soueraygne good is blyssfulnesse. Boece. That is sothe (qd I) Philoso. Than (quod she) we moten nedes granten and confessen that thilke same soueraygn good be god. Boece. Certes (qd I) I ne maye not denye ne withstande the reasons purposed/ and I se wel that it folowith by strength of the premisses. Ph. Loke nowe (quod she) if this be proued yet more fermely thus/ that there ne mowen not ben to soueraygne goodes that ben dyuers amonge hem selfe. For certes the goodes that ben dyuers amonge hem selfe/ that one is not that the other is. Than ne mowen neyther of hem be parfyte/ so as eyther of hem lacketh to other/ but that that nys not parfyte/ men maye sene apertly that it nys not soueraygne. The thynges than that be soueraynly good/ ne mowen by no waye be dyuers. But I haue wel concluded/ that blyssfulnesse and god ben the soueraygne good/ for whiche it mote nedes ben that soueraygne blyssfulnesse is soueraygne dignyte. Boece. Nothynge (qd I) is more sothfaste than this/ ne more ferme by reason/ ne a more worthy thynge than god maye not be concluded. Philosophie. Upon these thynges than (quod she) right as these geometriciens whan they haue shewed their proposycions/ ben wonte to bringen in thynges that they clepen porrismes or declaracions of forsayde thynges/ ryght so wol I yeue the here as a corallarye or a mede of Crowne. For why/ for as moche as by the gettyng of blissfulnesse men ben maked blyssful/ and blyssfulnesse is dignyte. Than it is manyfest and open/ that by the gettynge of dignyte men ben maked blissful/ right as by the gettynge of iustyce. And by the gettynge of sapyence they be maked wyse/ right so nedes by the semblable reason/ whan they haue goten diuynite they be made goddes. Than is euery blissful man a god. But certes by nature there nys but one god/ but by the partycipacion of the diuynite there ne letteth ne distourbeth nothynge/ that there ne be many goddes. Boece. This is (quod I) a fayre thynge and a precious/ clepe it as thou wylt/ be it Corallarie or porrisme/ or mede of crowne/ or declarynge. Philoso. Certes (quod she) no thynge nys fayrer than is the thynge that by reason shulde be added to these forsayde thynges. Boece. What thing (quod I) Philoso. So (quod she) as it semeth that blyssfulnesse cõtayneth many thynges/ it were for to weten whether that al these thynges maken or conioynen as a maner body of blyssfulnesse/ by the dyuersyte of partyes of membres/ or els if any of al these thinges be suche that it accomplysshe by him selfe the substaunce of blyssfulnesse. So al these other thynges ben referred and brought to blisfulnesse/ that is to say/ as to the chefe of hem. Boece. I wolde (quod I) that thou madest me clerely to understande what thou sayest/ and what thou recordest me the forsayd thyn- Philosophia. Haue I not iuged (quod she) that blyssfulnesse is good? Boece. Yes forsoth (quod I) and that soueraygne good. Philoso. Adde than (qd she) thylke good that is made blyssfulnesse to al the forsayde thynges. For thylke same blyssfulnesse/ that is demed to be soueraygne suffysaunce/ thylke selfe is soueraygne power/ soueraygne reuerence/ soueraygne clerenesse or noblesse/ and soueraygne delyte.

What

what sayest thou than of al these thynges / that is to saye suffysaunce / power / and these other thynges? Ben they than as membres of blysfulnesse / or ben they referred and brought to soueraygne good / right as al thynges that ben brought to the chefe of hem? Boece. I understonde wel (quod I) what thou purposest to seke: but I desyre for to herken / that thou shewe it to me. Phi. Take nowe thus the discrecion of this questyon (quod she) If al these thynges (quod she) weren membres to felycite / tha weren they dyuers that one from that other: and suche is the nature of parties or of membres / that dyuers membres compowen a body. Boece. Certes (quod I) it hath wel ben shewed here byforne / that al these thynges ben al one thyng. Philo. Than ben they no membres (quod she) For els it shulde seme that blysfulnesse were conioyned al of o membre alone / but that is a thynge that maye not be done. Boece. This thyng (qd I than) nys not doutous / but I abyde to herken the remenaunt of thy questyon. Philo. This is open and clere (quod she) that al other thynges ben referred and brought to good. For therfore is suffisaunce requyred / for it is demed to be good: and for thy is power required / for me trowen also that it be good. and this same thynge mowen we thynken & coniecten of reuerence / of noblesse / and of delyte. Than is souerayne good the somme and the cause of al that ought to ben desyred. For why thilke thyng that witholdeth no good in it selfe / ne semblaunce of good / it ne may nat wel in no maner be desyred ne requyred. And the cotrary: For though that thynges by her nature ne ben not good / algates if men wenen that they ben good / yet ben they desyred as though they were verily good. And therfore it is said that men ought to wene by right / that bountie be the souerayn fyne and the cause of al the thynges that ben to requiren. But certes thilke that is cause for whiche men requiren any thing / it semeth that thylke same thing be most desyred / as thus: If that a wight wolde riden for cause of heale / he ne desyreth not so moche the mouyng to ryden as the effecte of his heale. Nowe than sens that al thynges ben required for the grace of good / they ne ben not desyred of al folke more than the same good. But we haue graunted that blyssfulnesse is that same thyng / for whiche that al these other thynges ben desyred. Than is it thus / that certes only blyssfulnesse is required and desyred. By whiche thynge it sheweth clerely / that of good and blyssfulnesse is al one and the same substaunce. Boece. I se not (quod I) wherfore that men myght discorden in this. Philosoph. And we haue shewed / that god and very blyssfulnesse is al one thyng. Boece. That is sothe (qd I) Philoso. Than mowe we conclude sykerly / that the substaunce of god is sette in thylke same good / and in none other place.

Huc omnes pariter venite capti / Quos fallax ligat improbis catenis Terrenas habitans libido mentes. Hic erit vobis requies laborum. &c.

COmeth al togyther nowe ye that ben ycaught & bounde with wicked chaynes / by the deceyuable delyte of erthly thynges inhabyting in your thought. Here shal be the reste of your laboure: here is the hauen stable in quyete pesyble. This alone is the open refute to wretches / that is to sayne / that ye that be combred and disceyued with worldely affections / cometh nowe to this souerayn good / that is god: that is refute to hem that wylen comen to hym. Al the thynges that the ryuer Tagus yeueth you with his golden grauels / Or els al the thynges that the ryuer Hermus yeueth with his reed brinke: or that Indus yeueth / that is nexte the hote partye of the worlde / that medleth the grene stones with the whyte: ne shulde not cleren the lokynge of your thought / but hyden rather your blynde corage within her derkenesse.
Al that lyketh you here and excyteth and moueth your thoughtes / the erthe hath nourysshed it within his lowe caues. But the shynynge / by whiche the heuen is gouerned / and whence that his strengthe / that escheweth the derke ouerthrowyng of the soule / and who so

Y.y.ii. euer

euer may knowen thilke light of blyssfulnesse/ he wyl sayne/ that the whyte beames of the sonne ne be not clere.

Assentior (inq̄) cunca enim firmissimis nexa rationibus constant. Tum illa. Quanti/ inquit/ tu estimabis/ si bonum ipsum/ quid sit/ agnoueris? &c.

BOece. I assente me (quod I) for al thinges ben strōgly bou̅den with right ferme reasons. Philoso. Howe moche wylte thou praysen it (quod she) if that thou knowe what thilke good is? Boece. I wol prayse it (quod I) by price without ende/ if it shal betyde me to knowe also togyther god that is good. Philoso. Certes (quod she) that shal I do the by very reason/ if that tho thinges/ that I haue concluded a lytel here beforne/ dwellen onely in her grauntyng. Boece. They dwellen graunted to the (quod I) that is to sayne/ as who sayth/ I graunt to thy forsayd conclusyons. Philo. I haue shewed the (qd she) that the thynges/ that ben required of many folke/ ne ben not very goodes ne parfyte. For they ben dyuers that one from that other. and so as eche of hem is lackynge to other/ they ne haue no power to bringe a good/ that is ful and absolute. But than at erste ben they very good/ whan they ben gathered togyder al in to one forme/ & in to one werkyng: so that thilke thynge that is suffysaunt/ thilke same is power/ and reuerence/ noblesse/ and myrthe.
And forsothe but if al these thynges be al one same thynge/ they ne haue not wherby that they mowe be put in the nombre of thynges that ought to be required and desyred. Boece. It is shewed (quod I) ne herof may there no man douten. Phi. The thynges than (qd she) that ne ben no goodes/ whan they ben dyuers/ and whan they begynnen to be al one thyng/ than ben they goodes/ ne cometh it not than by the gettynge of vnyte/ that they be maked goodes? Boece. So semeth it (quod I) Phi. but al thynge that is good (quod she) grauntest thou that it be good by the partycipacion of good or no? Boece. I graunt it (quod I) Philoso. Than muste thou graunted (qd she) by semblable reason that one and good be one same thyng. For of thynges/ of whiche the effecte nys not naturelly dyuers/ nedes her substaunce must be one same thyng. Boece. I ne maye not denye it (quod I) Philo. Hast thou not knowen wel (quod she) that al thing that is/ hath so longe his dwellynge and his substaunce/ as longe as it is one/ but whan it forletteth to ben one/ it muste nedes dyen and corrumpen togyder? B. In which maner (qd I) Philoso. Right as in beestes (quod she) whan the soule and the body ben conioyned in one/ and dwellen togyther/ it is cleped a beest: and whan her vnyte is distroyed) by the disceueraunce of that one from that other/ than sheweth it wel that it is a deed thynge/ and it is no lenger no beest. And the body of a wight whyle it dwelleth in one fourme by coniunction of membres/ it is wel sene that it is a fygure of mankynde: And if the partyes of the body be deuyded and disceuered that one from that other/ that they distroye the vnyte/ the bodye forleteth to be/ that it was beforne. And who so wolde renne in the same maner by al thynges/ he shulde sene that without doute euery thynge is in his substaunce/ as longe as it is one. And whan it forleteth to be one/ it dyeth and perissheth. Boece. Whan I consyder (quod I) many thynges/ I se none other. Philoso. Is there any thynge (quod she) that in as moche as it lyueth naturelly/ that forleteth the talente or the appetyte of his beynge/ and desyreth to come to dethe and to corrupcion? Boece. If I consyder (quod I) the beestes that haue any maner nature of wyllyng and of nyllyng/ I ne fynde no beest/ but if it be constrayned fro without forthe/ that forleteth or dispyseth the entencion to lyuen and to duren/ or that wyl his thankes hasten him to dyen. For euery beest trauayleth hym to defende and kepe the sauacion of his lyfe/ and escheweth dethe and distruction. But certes I doute me of herbes and trees/ that ne haue no felynge soules/ ne no naturel workynges/ seruynge to appetytes/ as beestes haue: whether they haue appetyte to dwellen/ and to duren. Philoso. Certes (quod she) therof dare the not doute. Now loke vpon the herbes and trees/

trees/ for they weyen firste in suche places as ben couenable to hem: in whiche places they mowe not dyen ne drien/ as longe as her nature maye defende hem. For some of hem weyen in feldes/ and some weyen in mountaignes/ and other weye in mareys/ and other cleauen on rockes/ and some weyen plenteous in sondes. And if any wight enforce hym to beare hem in to other places/ they weyen drie. For nature yeueth to euery thing that is conuenyent to hym/ and trauayleth that they ne dye/ as longe as they haue power to dwellen and to lyuen. What wylte thou sayne of this/ that they drawen al her nourysshynges by her rootes/ ryght as they hadden her mouthes yplounged within the erthes/ and sheaden by her maryes her wodde and her barke? And what wylte thou sayne of this/ that thylke thynge that is right softe/ as the marye is/ that is alwaye hydde in the seete al within/ and that is defended from withoute by the stedfastnesse of wodde/ and that the vtterest barke is put ayenst the distemperaunce of the heuen/ as a defendoure/ mighty to suffren harme? And thus certes mayste thou wel sene/ howe great is the dyligence of nature: For al thynges renouelen and publysshen hem with sede ymultiplyed. Ne there nys no man/ that ne wote wel that they ne ben right as a foundement and edefyce/ for to duren not onely for a tyme/ but ryght as for to dure perdurably by generacion. And the thynges eke/ that men wenen ne haue no soules/ ne desyre they not by semblable reason to kepen that is his/ that is to sayn/ that is accordynge to her nature in conseruacion of her beynge and enduryng? For wherfore els beareth lyghtnesse the flambes vp/ and the weyght presseth the erthe adown/ but for as moche as thylke places and thilke mouynges be couenable to euerych of hem. And forsothe euery thynge kepeth thylke/ that is accordynge and propre to hym/ ryght as thynges that ben contraryous and enemyes corrumpen hem. And yet ŷ harde thynges (as stones) cleauen and holden her partyes togyther right faste and harde/ and defenden hem in withstādyng/ that they ne departen lightly/ and yeuen place to hem/ that breaken or deuyden hem: but nathelesse they retournen ayen soone in to the same thynges/ from whence they be araced. But fyre fleeth and refuseth al dyuisyon. Ne I ne treate not nowe here of wylful mouynges of the soule that is knowyng/ but of naturel entencyon of thynges/ as thus: Right as we swalowen the meate that we receyuen/ and ne thynke not on it/ and as we drawe our breathe in slepyng/ that we wete not whyle we slepen. For certes in the beestes the loue of her lyuynges ne of her beynges/ ne cometh not of the wylnynges of the soule/ but of the begynnynges of nature. For certes thorough constraynynge causes wyll desyreth and embraceth ful oft tymes the deth/ that nature dredeth/ that is to sayne/ as thus: That a man maye be constrayned so by some cause/ that his wyll desyreth and taketh the dethe/ whiche that nature hateth and dredeth ful sore. And somtyme we sene the contrary/ as thus: that the wyl of a wight distourbeth and constrayneth that/ that nature alwaye desyreth and requireth/ that is to say the werkes of generacion/ by the whiche generacion onely dwelleth and is sustayned the longe durabylite of mortal thynges/ as thus. This charyte and this loue that euery thynge hath to hym selfe/ ne cometh not of the mouyng of the soule/ but of the entencion of nature. For the pourueyaunce of god hath yeuen to thynges/ that ben create of hym this/ that is a ful great cause to lyuen and to duren/ for whiche they desyren naturelly her lyfe/ as longe as euer they mowen: for whiche thou mayste not dreden by no maner/ that al thynges that ben any where/ that they ne requyren naturelly the ferme stablenesse of perdurable dwelling/ and eke the eschewynge of distruction.

Boece. I confesse (quod I) that I se wel nowe/ & certainly withouten dout/ the thynges that a while ago semeden vncertayne to me. Philoso. But (quod she) thylke thynge that desyreth to be and dwell perdurably/ he desyreth to ben one: for if that one were distroyed/ certes beynge shulde there none dwellen to no wyght. Boece. That is sothe (quod I) Phi. Than (quod she) desyren al thynges one.

Bocce. I assent (quod I) Phi. And I haue shewed (qd she) that ylke same one is/ thylke that is good. Bo. ye forsothe (qd I) Phi. Al thynges than (quod she) requiren good/ and thylke mayste thou discryuen thus: Good is thylke thyng that euery wight desyreth. Bo. There ne may be thought no more very thing (qd I) for eyther al thynges be referred and brought to nought/ & floteren without gouernour dispoyled of one/ as of her propre heed/ or els if there be any thynge/ to whiche that al thynges tenden and hyen to/ that thyng must be the soueraygne good of al goodes. Philoso. Than sayd she thus: O my norice (quod she) I haue great gladnesse of the/ for thou haste fyxed in thy herte the myddel sothfastnesse/ that is to sayne the pricke/ But this thyng hath be discouered to the/ in that thou saydest/ that thou wystest not a lytel here beforne. Boe. What is that (quod I) Philo. That thou ne wystest not (quod she) whiche was thende of thynges/ and certes that is the thing that euery wight desyreth. And for as moche as we haue gathered and compreheded/ that good is thylke thynge that is desyred of al/ than mote we nedes confessen/ that good is the fyne of al thynges.

Quisquis profunda mente vestigat verũ/ Cupitqz nullis ille deuiis falli/ In se reuoluat intimi lucem visus. &c.

Who so seketh sothe by a depe thought/ and coueyteth to ben disceyued by no mis wayes/ let him rollen and treaten within him selfe/ ỹ light of his inwarde sight: and let him gatheren ayen enclynyng in to a compace the longe mouynges of his thoughtes. And lette hym teachen his corage/ that he hath enclosed and hydde in his treasours/ al that he hath compassed or sought fro without: And than thilke thynge that the blacke cloudes of errour whylom had couered/ shal light more clerely than Phebus hym selfe ne shyneth. Glosa. Who so wol seke the depe groundes of sothe in his thought/ and wol not be disceyued by false preposycions/ that gone amysse from the trouthe/ let him wel examyne and rolle within him selfe/ the nature and proprietes of the thynge. And let him yet efte sones examyne & rollen his thoughtes by good delyberacion/ or that he deme. And lette hym teachen his soule/ that it hath by naturel principles kyndlyche yhydde within it selfe/ al the trouthe/ the whiche he ymagyneth to ben in thynges without: and than al the derknesse of his misknowing/ shal seme more euydently to the syght of his Vnderstadyng/ than the sonne ne semeth to the syght without forthe. For certes the body bringynge the weight of foryetyng/ ne hath not chaced out of your thought al the clerenesse of your knowynge/ for certainly/ the seede of sothe holdeth and cleueth within your corage/ and it is awaked and excyted by the wyndes and by the blastes of doctryne. For wherfore els demen ye of your owne wyl the ryghtes whan ye be asked/ but if so were that the norisshyng of reason ne lyued/ yplunged in the depe of your herte/ that is to sayne/ howe shulde men demen the sothe of any thynge that were asked/ and if there nere a rote of sothfastnesse/ that were yplunged and hyd in naturel principles/ the whiche sothfastnesse lyued within the depenesse of the thought. And if so be/ that the muse and the doctryne of Plato syngeth sothe/ al that euery wight lerneth/ he ne dothe nothynge els than/ but recordeth/ as men recorden thynges that ben foryeten.

Tum ego/ Platoni/ inq̃/ vehementer assencior. Nam me horum iam secundo commemoras. Primum quod memoriam corporea contagione. &c.

Than sayd I thus. I accorde me gretly to Plato/ for thou recordest and remebrest me these thynges yet the secode tyme/ that is to saye/ first whan I lest my memory by the contraryous coniunctyon of the body with the soule: & eftsones afterwarde/ whan I loste it confouded/ by thy charge and by the burdone of my sorowe/ & than sayd she thus. If thou loke (quod she) firste the thynges that

that thou haste graunted/ it ne shal nat been
right ferre/ that thou ne shalt remembren the
ylke thynge/ that thou saydest that thou ny-
stest nat. B. What thyng (qd I) P. By whi
che gouernement (qd she) that this worlde is
gouerned. B. I remembre it wel (qd I) and
I confesse wel/ that I ne wist it naught. But
al be it so/ that I se nowe from a ferre/ what
thou purposest/ algates I desyre yet to her-
ken it of the more playnly. P. Thou ne we-
dest nat (qd she) a lytel here beforn/ that men
shulde doute/ that this worlde is gouerned by
god. B. Certes (qd I) ne yet ne dout I it nat
ne I nyl neuer wene that it were to doute/ as
who saith/ but I wot wel that god gouerneth
this worlde. And I shal answeren ÿ by what
reasons I am brought to this. This worlde
(qd I) of so many dyuers and contraryous
parties/ ne myght neuer haue ben assembled
in o forme/ but if there were one/ that conioy-
ned so many dyuers thynges. And the same
diuersite of her natures that so discorden/ that
one fro that other muste depten/ and vnioy-
nen the thynges that ben conioyned/ if there
ne were one that conteyned/ that he hath con-
ioyned and ybounde. Ne the certayne order
of nature ne shulde nat bryng forth so ordey-
ne mouynges/ by places/ by tymes/ by doyn
ges/ by spaces/ by qualytees/ if there ne were
one that were aye stedfast dwellyng/ that or-
dayned and disposed these dyuersytees of mo-
uynges. And thilke thyng what so euer it be/
by whiche that al thynges ben ymaked & lad/
I clepe hym god/ that is a worde that is vsed
to al folkes. Philo. Than sayd she: Sithe
thou felyste thus these thynges/ I trowe that
I haue lytell more to done/ that thou myghty
of welfulnes/ hole and sounde/ ne se eftsones
thy countree. But let vs loken the thynges ÿ
we haue purposed here beforne. Haue I not
nombred & sayde (qd she) that suffysaunce is
in blyssfulnesse. And we haue accorded ÿ god
is thylke same blyssfulnes. B. yes forsoth (qd
I). P. & that to gouerne this worlde (qd she)
ne shall he neuer haue nede of none helpe fro
without. For els yf he had nede of any helpe/
he ne shulde not haue no ful suffysaunce. B.
yes thus it mote nedes be (qd I). P. Then or-

deyned he by hym selfe alone al thynges (qd
she) B. That may not be denyed (qd I). P.
And I haue shewed that god is ÿ same good.
B. It remembreth me wel (qd I) P. Than
ordeyneth he al thynges by thilke good (quod
she) syth he which we han accorded to be good
gouerneth al thynges by hym selfe. And he is
a key and a steyre/ by which the edifice of this
worlde is kepte stable & without corrũpyng.
B. I accorde me gretely (qd I). And I haue
apperceyued a lytel here beforne/ ÿ thou wol-
dest saye thus/ Al were it so/ that it were by a
thynne suspeccyon. P. I trowe wel (qd she)
For as I trowe/ thou ledest nowe more enten
tifly thyne eye/ to loken the very goodes. But
natheles/ the thynge that I shal tel the/ yet ne
sheweth not lasse to loken. B. What is ÿ (qd
I) P. So as men trow (qd she) & that right-
fully/ ÿ god gouerneth al thynges by the key
of his goodnesse. And al these same thynges
that I haue taughte the hasten hem by natu-
rell entencyon to come to good/ there maye no
man doubten that they ne ben gouerned vo-
luntaryly. And that they ne conuerten hem of
her owne good wyl to her ordeynour. As that
they ben accordynge and enclynyng to her go-
uernour and to her kynge. B. It mote nedes
be so (qd I) for the realme ne shulde not seme
blyssful/ yf there were a yoke of mysdrawyn-
ges in dyuers parties/ ne the sauynge of obe-
dient thinges/ ne shulde not be then P. Is ther
nothynge (qd she) that kepeth his nature/ that
enforceth him to gone ayenst god? B. No (qd
I) P. & if ÿ any thyng enforced hym to with
stande god/ might it auaylen at last ayen him
that we haue graunted to be almyghty by the
right of blyssfulnes? B. Certes (qd I) al vt-
terly it ne myght not auayle hym. P. Then is
there nothyng (quod she) that eyther maye or
wyll withstanden to his soueraygne god. B. I
trowe not (qd I) P. then (quod she) is thilke
the soueraygne god/ that al thynges gouerneth
strongly/ and ordeyneth hem softly. Boece.
Then sayd I thus/ I delyte me (quod I) not
onely in thendes or ĩ the sõm of the resons that
thou hast concluded and proued/ but thylke
wordes that thou vsest/ delyten me moche mo
re/ so that at laste fooles/ that somtyme ren-
den

den great thynges/ oughten ben asshamed of hem selfe/ that is to sayne/that we fooles that reprehenden wickedly the thynges that touchen goddes gouernaunce / we oughten ben asshamed of our selfe. As I/ that sayde that god refuseth onely the werkes of men/ and ne entermeteth not of it. Philo. Thou haste wel herde (qd she) the fables of the poetes/ howe the gyauntes assayleden heuen/ with the goddes; but forsothe the debonayre force of god disposed hem as it was worthy/ ỳ is to sayne/ distroyed the gyauntes as it was worthy. But wylte thou that we reioynen togyther thylke same reasons? For perauenture of suche coniunction may sterten vp some fayre sparke of sothe. Boece. Do (qd I) as the lyste. Philo. Wenest thou (qd she) that god ne be almighty? B. No man is in doute of it certes (qd I) P. No wight ne douteth it/ if he be in his mynde (quod she) But he that is almighty/there nys nothyng that he ne may. Boe. That is sothe (qd I) Phi. May god do yuel (qd she)? B. Naye forsothe (qd I) Philo. Than is yuel nothing (qd she) sythe that he may done none yuel/that may done al thinges. Boece. Scornest thou me (qd I) or els playest thou/ or discepuest thou me/ that haste so wonnen with thy reasons / the house of Dedalus so entrelasyng that it is vnable to be vnlaced/ ỳ thou otherwhyle entrest ther thou issuest/and otherwhyle issuest there thou entrest. Ne foldest thou not togyther by replycacion of wordes a maner wonderful cercle or enuyronnyng of the symplycite dyuine? For certes a lytel here beforn whan thou began at blissfulnesse/thou saydest that it is souerayn good/ and that god is the blyssfulnesse/ for whiche thou yaue me as a couenable yefte/ that is to sayne/ that no wight nys blyssful/ but if he be god also therwith. and saydest eke/that the form of good is the substaunce of god and of blyssfulnesse. And saydest ỳ thilke one is thylke same good/ that is required and desyred of al the kynde of thynges. And thou prouedest in disputynge/ that god gouerneth al ỳ thinges of the world/ by the gouernaunce of bountie: And saydest that al thinges wolde obeyen to him/and saydest that the nature of yuel is nothynge. And these thynges shewdest thou not with no reasons taken fro without/but by proues in cercles and homlich knowyng. The whiche proues drawen to hem selfe her faythe and her acorde eueriche of hem of other. Phi. Than said she thus: I ne scorne not/ ne play/ne discepue the: but I haue shewed the thing that is greatest ouer al thynges/ by the yefte of god/ that we whylom prayden. For this is the fourme of diuyne substaunce/ that is suche/ that it ne slydeth not in to vtterest forayne thynges/ ne receyueth not no straunge thynges in hym. But right as Permenides sayde in greke/ of thilke diuyne substaunce: He sayd thus/ that thylke dyuyne substaunce tourneth the world and the mouable cercle of thynges/ whyle the ilke diuyne substaunce kepeth it selfe without mouynges/ that is to sayne/ that he moueth neuer mo/and yet it moueth al other thynges. But nathelesse/ if I haue styred reasons that be not taken fro withont the compace of the thyng/of the whiche we treaten / but reasons that ben bestowed within compace: there nys not why thou shuldest meruaylen/ sythe thou haste lerned by the sentence of Plato/ that nedes the wordes mote ben cosyns to the thynges/ of whiche they speken.

Felix qui potuit boni Fontem visere lucidum. Felix qui potuit grauis. &c.

BLyssed is that man that maye sene the clere welle of good: Blyssful is he that may vnbynden him from the boundes of heuy erth. The poete of Thrace Orpheus/that whilom had ryght great sorowe/ for the dethe of his wyfe. After that he had maked a constrayned by his wepely songes/the wodes mouable to renne/ and had maked the ryuers to stonden styl / and had maked the hartes and hyndes to ioynen dredelesse her sydes to cruel lyons/to herken his songe / and had maked ỳ the hare was nat agast of the hounde/whiche was pleased by songe: So whan the moost ardaunt loue of his wyfe/ brende the entrayles of his breste / ne the songes that hadde ouercomen all thynges / ne myghten nat aswagen her lorde Orpheus. He playned him hym of the heuen goddes/ whiche that were cruel to hym/ he wente hym to the houses of the hell: And he tempered his blandisshynge songes/ by resounyng of strynges/ and spake and songe in wepynge/ al that euer he had receyued and laued out of the noble welles of his mother Caliope the goddesse. And he sange with as moche as he might of wepyng/ and with as moche as loue/ that doubled his sorowe might yeuen hym and teache hym/ and cōmoued the hell/ and required and besought by swete prayer/ the lordes of soules in hell of releasynge/ that is to saye/ to yelden hym his wyfe. Cerberus the porter of hell/ with his thre heedes was caught/ and al abasshed of the newe songe. And the thre goddesses/ Furyes and vengeresses of felonyes/ that tourmenten & agasten the soules/ by anoye woxen sorouful and sore/ and teeres wepten for pite. Tho was not the heed of Ixion tourmented/ by the ouerthrowynge whele. And Tantalus/ that was distroyed by the woodnesse of longe thurste/ dispysed the floodes to drinke. The foule that hyght Vultur/ that eateth the stomake or the gysern of Tityus is so fulfylled of his songe/ that it nyl eaten ne tyren no more. At the laste the lorde and iuge of soules was moued to mysericordyes/ and cryed: We ben ouercomen (quod he) yeue we to Orpheus his wyfe to beare hym companye/ he hath wel ybought her by his songes and his dytees: but we wyl putten a lawe in this/ and couenaūt in the yefte/ that is to sayne/ that tyl he be out of hell/ if he loke behynde hym/ that his wyfe shal come agayne vnto vs. But what is he that maye yeue a lawe to louers: loue is a greater lawe and a stronger to hym selfe than any lawe that men maye yeuen. Alas/ whan Orpheus and his wyfe were almoste at the termes of the nyght/ that is to sayne/ at the laste boundes of hell/ Orpheus loked backwarde on Euridice his wyfe/ and lost her/ & was deed. This fable apertayneth to you al/ who so euer desyreth or seketh to lede his thought in to the souerayne daye/ that is to saye to clerenesse of souerayne good. For who so euer be so ouercomen that he fyxe his eyen in to the pytte of hell/ that is to sayne: who so euer sette his thoughtes in erthly thynges/ al that euer he hath drawen of the noble good celestyal/ he leseth it/ whan he loketh to the helles/ this is to sayne/ in to lowe thynges of the erthe.

¶ Thus endeth the thirde boke of Boece/ and here after foloweth the fourthe.

HEc cum philosophia dignitate vultus/ et oris grauitate seruata/ leniter/ suauiterque cecinisset/ Cum ego nondum penitus insiti meroris oblitus. &c.

WHan Philosophye had songen softlye and delectablye the forsaid thinges/ keppynge the dignyte of her chere/ and the weyght of her wordes. I than that ne had al vtterly forgeten the wepyng and the mournynge that was set in myn herte/ forbrake the entencion of her/ that entended yet to sayn some other thynges.

O (quod I) thou that arte gyderesse of verye lyght/ the thynges that thou haste sayde me hytherto/ ben to me so clere and shewynge by the dyuyne lokyng of hem/ and by thy reasons/ that they ne mowen ben ouercomen. And thylke thynges/ that thou toldest me/ al be it so that I had whylome forgeten hem/ for the sorowe of the wronge that hath be done to me: yet neuertelesse they ne weren not vtterly vnknowen to me. But this same is namely a ryght great cause of my sorowe/ so that as the gouernour of thynges is good/ if that yuels mowen ben by any waies: or els if that yuels passen without punisshynge/ the whiche thyng onely/ howe worthy is it to ben wondred vpon. Thou consydrest it wel thy selfe certainly. But yet to this thynge there is yet another thynge ioyned more to be wondred vpon. For felonye is emperesse/ and floureth full of rychesses/ and vertue nys not al onlye without meedes/ but it is caste downe/ and eke fortroden vnder the fete of felonous folke: and it abyeth the tourmentes in stede of wicked felons. Of al whiche thynges there

is no

is no wight may maruaylen ynough ne com-playnen/ that suche thynges be doone in the reigne of god/ that al thynges wote/ and al thynges may/ and ne wyl not onely but good thynges. Than sayd she thus: Certes (quod she) that were a great maruayle/ and an abasshyng without ende/ and wel more horryble than al the monsters/ if it were as thou wenest/ that is to sayne/ that in the ryght ordayne house of so moche a father and an ordaynour of meyne/ that the vessels that ben foule and vyle/ shulde ben honoured and heryed/ and the precious vessels shulde ben defouled and vyle. But it is not so/ for if the thynges/ that I haue concluded a lytel here beforne/ ben kepte hole and vnaraced/ thou shalt wel knowe by yͭ auctorite of god (of the whose reigne I speke) that certes the good folke be alwaye mighty/ and shrewes ben alway outcaste and feble. Ne the vyces be neuer more without payne/ ne the vertues ne be not without mede. And that blissfulnesse cometh alway to good folke/ and infortune cometh alwaye to wicked folke. And thou shalt wel knowen many thynges of this kynde/ that shulde ceasen thy playntes/ and strengthen the with stedfaste sadnesse. And for thou haste sene the forme of very blyssfulnesse by me that haue whylom shewed it the/ and thou hast knowen in whome blissfulnesse is set: al thynge treated/ that I trowe be necessarye to put forthe/ I shal shewen the the waye/ that shal bringen the ayen vnto thyn house: and I shal fyche fethers in thy thought/ by whiche it may arysen in heyght/ so that al trybulacion ydone away/ thou by my gydyng and by my pathe/ and by my sledes/ shalte mowen retourne hole and sounde in to thy countrey.

Sunt etenim penne volucres michi/ Que celsa conscendunt poli/ Quas sibi cū velox mens induit. &c.

Than for thy swyfte fethers that sourmounten the heyghte of the heuen/ whan the swyfte thought hath clothed it in tho feathers/ it dispyseth the hateful erthes/ and surmounteth the roundenesse of the great ayre/ & it seeth the cloudes behynde his backe/ and passeth the heyght of the regyon of the fyre/ that enchauseth by the swyfte mouynge of the firmament/ tyl that he aryseth in to the houses/ that bearen the sterres/ and ioyneth the waye with the sonne Phebus/ and felawshyppeth the waye of the olde colde Saturnus/ & he ymaked a knyght of the clere sterre/ that is to sayne/ whan the thought is made goddes knight/ by the sekynge of clere trouthe to comen to the very knowlege of god. And thilke soule renneth by the cerkle of sterres/ in al the places there as the shynynge nyght is ypaynted/ that is to sayne/ the nyght that is cloudelesse. For on nyghtes that be cloudelesse/ it semeth that the heuen were paynted with dyuers ymages of sterres. And whan he hath done there ynoughe/ he shal forleten the laste heuen/ and he shal presen and wenden on the backe of the swyfte fyrmament/ and he shal be maked parfyte of the worshypful lyght of god. There holdeth the lorde of thynges the ceptre of his might/ and attempreth the gouernementes of the worlde/ and the shynynge iuge of thynges/ stable in him selfe/ gouerneth the swyfte carte or wayne/ that is to sayne/ the circuler mouyng of the sonne. And if thy waye ledeth the ayen/ so that thou be brought thyder/ than wylte thou saye/ that is the countraye that thou requirest/ of whiche thou ne haddest no mynde: but nowe it remembreth me wel/ here was I borne/ here wol I fasten my degree/ here wol I dwel. But if the lyketh than to loken on the derkenesses of the erthe/ that thou haste forleten/ than shalte thou sene/ that these felonous tyrauntes/ that the wretched people dredeth nowe/ shullen be exyled from thilke fayre countrey.

Tū ego pape inquā/ vt magna pmittis. Nec dubito/ quin possis efficere: tu modo quem excitaueris/ ne moreris. &c.

Than sayd I thus. O I wonder me that yͭ behetest me so great thinges. Ne I ne doute not yͭ thou ne maist wel parforme yͭ thou behetest: but I pray the this

this that thou ne tary not/ to tel me thilke thinges/ that thou hast moued. Ph. First (qd she) thou muste nedes knowe/ that good folke ben alwaye stronge and mighty/ and the shrewes ben feble and deserte/ and naked of al strengthes. And of these thynges certes eueryche of hem is declared and shewed by other. For as good and yuel ben two contraryes/ if so be that good be stedfaste/ than sheweth the feblesse al openly. And if thou knowe clerely the freelnesse of yuel/ the stedfastnesse of good is knowen. But for as moche as the faythe of my sentence shal be the more ferme and haboundante/ I wol gone by that one way and by that other/ and I wol conferme the thynges that ben purposed nowe on this syde/ and nowe on that syde. Two thynges ther ben/ in whiche the effecte of al the dedes of mankynde standeth/ that is to sayne/ wyll and power: and if that one of these two fayleth/ there nys no thyng that may be doone. For if that wyl lacketh/ there nys no wight that undertaketh to do that he wol not done: And if power fayleth/ the wyll nys but ydle/ and stante for naught. And therof cometh it/ that if thou se a wight that wolde getten that he maye not getten/ thou mayst not doute that power ne fayleth him to hauen that he wolde. Boece. This is open and clere (qd I) ne it ne may not ben denyed in no maner. Philo. And if thou se a wight (quod she) that hath done that he wolde done/ thou nyst not doute/ that he ne hath had power to done it. B. No (quod I) P. And in that that euery wight maye/ in that men holden hem mighty to done a thyng. In somoche as a man is mighty to done a thĩg/ in so moch men holde him mighty: and in that that he ne may/ in that men demen him to be feble. Bo. I confesse it wel (qd I) Phi. Remembre the (quod she) that I haue gathered and shewed by the forsayde reasons/ that al the entencion of the wyl of mankynde/ whiche that is lad by dyuers studyes/ hasteth to comen to blysfulnesse. Boe. It remembreth me wel (qd I) that it hath ben shewed. Philoso. And recordeth the nought than (quod she) that blysfulnesse is thylke same good that men requiren/ so that whan blysfulnesse is requyred of al=

Boece. It recordeth me nat (quod I) For I haue it alwaye in my memorie fyxed. Philo. Al folke than (quod she) good and eke badde enforcen hem without difference of entencion to comen to good. Boece. This is very consequence (qd I) Phi. And certayne is (qd she) that by gettyng of good be men maked good. Boece. That is certayne (quod I) P. Than getten good men that they desyren. Boece. So it semeth (quod I) Philo. But wicked folke (quod she) if they getten the good that they desyren/ they ne mowen not be wicked. Boe. So it is (quod I) Phi. Than so as that one and that other (quod she) desyren the good/ and the good folke getten the good/ and not the wicked folke: Than it is no doute that the good folke ne be mighty/ and wicked folke be feble. Boe. Who so that euer douteth of this/ he ne maye not consyder the nature of thynges ne the consequence of reasons. Philoso. And ouer this (quod she) if that there ben two thynges that haue one same purpose by kynde/ And that one of hem pursueth and perfourmeth that same thyng by naturel offyce/ and that other ne may not done thilke offyce naturel/ but foloweth by other maner/ than is couenable to nature/ hym that accomplyssheth his purpose kyndely/ and yet he ne accomplyssheth not his owne purpose: whether of these two demest thou for more mighty? Boece. If that I coniecte (quod I) that thou woldest say/ algates I desyre yet to herken it more plainly of the. Philo. Thou nyste not than denye (quod she) that the mouement of goynge nys in men by kynde. Boece. No forsothe (quod I) Philo. Ne thou doutest not (quod she) that thylke naturell offyce of goynge/ ne be the offyce of fete. Boece. I ne doute it not (quod I) Phi. Than (quod she) if that a wight be mightye to moue and gothe upon his fete/ and another/ to whome thylke naturel offyce of fete lacketh/ enforseth hym to go crepynge on his hande/ whiche of these two ought to be holden the more mighty by right. Boece. Knytte forthe (quod I) the remenante. Philosophie. For no wyght ne douteth/ that he that maye gon by naturel office of fete/ ne be more mightye thanne he that ne maye not. But the soue=

souerayne good (quod she) that is euen lyke purposed to the good and to the badde. The good folke seken it by naturel offyce of vertues/ and shrewes enforcen hem to getten it by dyuers couetyses of erthly thynges/ whiche that nys no naturel offyce to getten thylke souerayne good. Trowest thou that it be any otherwyse? Bo. Naye (quod I) For the consequence is open/ and shewynge of thynges that I haue graunted/ that nedes good folke moten ben mighty/ and shrewes moten ben feble and vnmighty. Philo. Thou rennest a ryght beforne me (q̄d she) and this is the iugement/ that is to sayne/ I iuge of right/ as these leches ben wonte to hopen of sicke folke/ whan they apperceyuen/ that nature is redressed and withstandeth to the maladie. But for I se the nowe al redy to the withstandynge/ I shal shewe the more thilke and contynuel reasons. For loke howe gretly sheweth the feblenesse and infirmyte of wicked folke/ that ne mowen not comen to that her naturel entencion leadeth hem: And yet almoste thilke naturel entencion constrayneth hem. And what were to demen than of shrewes/ if thilke naturel helpe had forleten hem/ the whiche naturel helpe of entencion gothe alwaye beforne hem/ and is so great/ that vnneth it may be ouercomen? Consyder than how great defaute of power/ and howe great feblesse there is in wicked felonous folke/ as who sayth/ the gretter thynge that is coueyted/ and the desyre not accõplysshed/ of the lasse might is he that coueyteth it/ and may not acomplysshe. And for thy philosophie sayth thus by souerayn good: Ne shrewes ne requiren not lyght medes ne vayne games/ whiche they ne maye not folowen ne holden/ but they faylen of thilke sõme of the heyght of thynges/ that is to sayne/ souerayne good. Ne these wretches ne comen not to theffecte of souerayne good/ the whiche they enforcen hem onely to getten by nightes & by dayes/ in gettyng of whiche good/ the strẽgth of good folke is ful wel ysene. For right as thou myghtest demen him mighty of goynge/ that gothe on his fete tyl he might comen to thylke place/ fro the whiche place there ne laye no way further to be gone: right so must thou nedes demen him for right mighty/ which that getteth and atteyneth to the ende of al thynges/ whiche that ben to desyren/ beyonde the whiche ende there nys nothynge to desyre. Of the whiche power of good folke men maye conclude/ that we wicked men semen to be barayne and naked of al strength. For why forleten they vertues and folowen vyces/ nys it not for that they ne knowen not the goodes? But what thyng is more feble and more caytif/ than is the blyndnesse of ignoraũce? or els they knowen wel/ whiche thynges they oughten folowen/ but lechery and couetyse ouerthroweth hem mistourned. And certes so dothe distemperaunce to feble men/ that mowe not wrastlen ayen these vyces. Ne knowe they not wel that they forleten the good wylfully/ and tournen hem wilfully to vyces. And in this wyse they ne forleten not onely to be mighty/ but they forleten al vtterly in any wyse for to ben. For they that forleten the comune fyne of al thynges that ben/ they forleten also therwithal for to bene. And perauentureit shulde semen to some folk/ that this were a meruaile to sayne/ that shrewes/ whiche that conteynen the more ptes of men/ ne ben not/ ne haue no beyng. But natheless it is so/ and thus stante this thynge. For they that be shrewes/ I denye not/ but that they be shrewes/ but I deny symplye and playnly that they ne be not/ ne haue no beyng. For right as thou mightest sayne of the carayne of a man/ that it were a deed man: so graunt I wel forsothe/ that vycious folke ben wicked/ but I ne may not absolutely and symplie grãt that they ben. For thilke thyng that with holdeth ordre and kepeth nature/ thilke thynge is and hath beyng. But what thyng fayleth that/ that is to say/ he that forleteth naturel ordre/ he forleteth thilke beynge that is set in his nature? But thou wolt sayne/ the shrewes mowen. Certes that ne denye I not: but certes her power ne discendeth not of strẽgth/ but of feblesse/ for they mowen doone wickydnesse/ the whiche they ne might not/ if they mighten dwellen in the forme and in the doyng of good people. And thilk power sheweth auydently/ that they mowen ryght naught. For so as I haue gadred & proued a

lytel

lytel here beforne/ that yuel is not/ and so as shrewes may only but shreudnesse. This conclusyon is al clere/ yͭ shrewes ne mowen right naught/ ne haue no power. And for as moche as thou understondest which is the strength of this power/ I haue desynisshed a lytel here beforne/ that no thyng nys so mighty as souerayne good. Boece. That is sothe (qd I) P. And thylke same soueraygne good maye done none yuel. Boece. Certes no (qd I) Philo. Is there any wight than (qd she) that weneth that men mowen done al thynges. Boe. No man (qd I) but if he be out of his wyt. Phi. But certes shrewes mowen don yuels (qd she) Boece. Ye wolde god (quod I) that they ne mighten done none. Phi. Than (quod she) so as he that is mightye to done onely good thynges/ he maye done al thynges/ and they that ben mighty to done yuel thynges/ ne mowen not al thynges. Than is it open thynge and manyfest/ that they that mowen don yuel ben of lasse power. And yet to proue this conclusyon there helpeth me this/ that I haue shewed here beforne/ that al power is to be nombred amonge thynges that men oughten requyre. And I haue shewed that al thynges that oughten ben desyred be referred to good/ ryght as to a maner heyght of her nature: but for to mowen done yuel and felonye/ ne maye not ben referred to god. Than is not yuel of the nombre of thynges that oughten to ben desyred and required. Than is it open and clere that the power ne the mouyng of shrewes nys no power. And of al these thynges it sheweth wel that the good folke ben certaynly mighty/ and the shrewes doutlesse unmighty. And it is clere and open that thilke sentence of Plato is very and sothe/ that sayth that onely wisemen may done that they desyren/ and shrewes mowen hauten that hem lyketh/ but that they desyren/ that is to sayne to come to soueraygne good/ they ne haue no power to accomplisshe that. For shrewes done what hem lyste/ whan by tho thynges in which they delyten/ they wenen to attayne to thilke good that they desyren/ but they ne getten ne attayne not therto/ for vyces ne comen not to blyssfulnesse.

Quos vides sedere celsos Solii culmine reges Purpura claros nitente. &c.

Who so that the couertures of her vayne apparayles might strypen of these proude kynges/ that thou seest sytten an hygh in her chayres/ glytteryng in shynynge purpure/ enuyronned with sorowful armures/ manassynge with cruel mouthe/ blowyng by woodnesse of hert/ he shulde sene that thilke lordes bearen within her corages ful strayte chaynes: for lechery tourmenteth hem on that on syde with gredy venymes and troublable ire/ that arayseth in hem the floode of troublynges/ tourmenteth on that other syde/ her thought or sorowe halt hem wery and ycaught/ or slyding and disceyuynge hope tourmenteth hem. And therfore sythe thou seest one heed/ that is to sayne/ one tyraunt bearen so many tyrannyes/ than ne dothe thilke tyraunt not that he desyreth/ sythe he is caste down with so many wicked lordes/ that is to sayne/ so many vyces that haue so wickedly lordshyps ouer hym.

Vides ne igitur quãdo in ceno ꝓbra voluantur/ q̃ probitas luce resplẽdeat: in quo perspicuũ est nunq̃ bonis p̃mia. &c.

Seest thou not than in howe great fylthe these shrewes ben ywrapped/ and with whiche clerenesse these good folke shynen. In this sheweth it wel that to good folke ne lacketh neuer mo her medes/ ne shrewes lacken neuer more tourmentes. For of al thynges that be done/ thilke thing for whiche any thinge is done/ it semeth as by right/ that thilke thing be yͤ mede of that/ as thus: If a man renneth in the stady or in the forlonge for the crowne: than lyeth the mede in the crowne for whiche he renneth. And I haue shewed that blyssfulnesse is thilke same good/ for whiche yͤ al thynges ben done. Than is thilke same good purposed to yͤ werkes of mankynde/ right as a cõmune mede/ whiche mede ne maye not be disceuered from good folke: For no wight as by right/ from thensforth that him lacketh goodnesse/ ne shal be cleped good: for which thyng folke of good

3.3. maners

maners her medes ne forsaken hem neuer mo. For albeit so that shrewes wayen as wode as hem lyst ayenst good folke / yet neuerthelesse the crowne of wysemen/ ne shal not fallen ne faden fro forayne shreudnesse/ ne benymmen not fro the corage of good people her propre honour. But if any wyght reioysed him of goodnesse/that he had taken fro without/ as who sayth/if a man had his goodnesse of any other man than of him selfe: certes he ỹ yaue him thilke goodnesse/or els some other wight myght bynome it him. But for as moche as to euery wight his propre bounte yeueth him his mede/ than at erste shal he faylen of mede whan he forleteth to be good. And at the last/ so as al medes ben requyred/ for men wenen that they be good/ who is he that nolde deme/ that he ỹ is right mighty of good/ were partelesse of mede? And of what mede shal he be reguerdoned. Certes of right fayre mede and right great/ abouen al medes. Remembre the of thilke noble corallarie that I yaue the a lytel here beforne/and gather it togyther in this maner. So as god him selfe is blissfulnesse/ than is it clere and certayn/ that al good people ben maked blissful/ for they ben good/ and thylke people that ben blissful/ it alowbeth and is couenable to be goddes. Than is the mede of people suche/that no daye ne shal enpayren it/ne no wickednesse shal dyrken it/ ne power of no wight ne shal not amenuse it/that is to sayne/ that ben maked goddes. And sythe it is thus/that good men ne faylen neuer more of her mede/certes no man ne may doute of ỹ vndepartable payne of shrewes/ that is to sayn/ that the payne of shrewes departeth not from hem selfe neuer mo. For so as good and yuel/ and payne and medes be contrarye / it mote nedes be/ that right as we se betyden in guerdone of good/ that also mote the payne of the yuel answere by the cõtrarie ꝑties to shrewes. Nowe than so as bountie and prowesse ben mede to good folke/ also is shreudnesse it selfe tourmente to shrewes. Than who so euer is entetched and defouled with payne/he ne douteth not/that he is entetched and defouled with yuel. If shrewes than wolden praysen hem selfe/ may it semen to hem that they ben withouten partie of tourment/sythe they ben suche that the vttrest wickednesse/ ỹ is to saye/ wicked thewes/ which is the vttrest & worst kynde of shreudnesse/ ne defouleth ne entetcheth not hem only/but enfecteth and enuenymeth greatly. And also loke on shrewes/that ben the contrarie partie of good men/ howe great payne feloushyppeth and fouleth hem: for thou hast lerned a lytel here beforne/ that al thyng that is and hath beyng/is one/and thilke same one is good: than is this the consequence/ that it semeth wel/ that al thyng that is and hath beynge/ is good/ that is to sayne/as who sayth/ that beynge/ vnyte and goodnesse is al one. And in this maner it foloweth than/ that al thynge that fayleth to be good/ it stynteth for to be and for to haue any maner beyng: wherfore it is that shrewes stynten for to be that they weren. But thilke other forme of mankynde/ that is to sayne/ the fourme of the body without/shewеth that these shrewes weren whylom men/ wherfore whan they ben peruerted and tourned in to malyce/ certes than they haue forlorne the nature of mankynde: But so as onely bountie and prowesse maye enhaunsen euery man/ ouer men: than mote it nedes be that shrewes/ whiche that shreudenesse hath caste out of the condycion of mankynde/ ben put vnder the meryte and deserte of men. Than betydeth it/ that if thou seest a wight whiche that is transfourmed in to vyces/thou mayest not wene that he be a man: For if he be ardaunt in auaryce/ and that he be a rauenour by violẽce of forayne rychesse/ thou shalte sayne that he is lyke a wolfe. And if he be felonous and withouten reste/and exercyse his tonge to chydinges/ thou shalte lyken him to the hounde. And if he be a pryuy awaytour hydde/ and reioyseth him to rauisshe by wyles/ thou shalte sayne him lyke to the foxe whelpes. And if be distempred and quaketh for ire/ men shal wenen that he beareth the corage of a lyon. And if he be dredeful and flyeng/ and dredeth thynges whiche that ne oughten not to be dredde/ men shal holde him lyke to the hart. And if he be slowe and astonyed and lache/ men shal holde him lyke to an asse. And if he be lyght and vnstedfaste of cou-

of corage/and chaungeth aye his studies/men shal holde him lyke to the byrdes. And if he be plounged in foule and uncleue luxuryes/ he is withholden in the foule delyces of the foule sowe. Than foloweth it/that he that forleteth bounte and prowesse/ he forleteth to be a man/ sythe he ne may not passen in the condycion of god/he is turned in to a beest.

Vela Naricii ducis/ Et vagas pelago rates Eurus appulit insule/ Pulchra qua residens dea Solis edita semine.&c.

EVrus the wynde aryued the sayles of Ulixes duke of the contre of Natice and his wandryng shyppes by the see in to the yle there as Circes the fayre goddesse doughter of the sonne dwelleth / that medleth to her newe gestes/drynkes that ben touched & maked with enchauntementes. And after that hyr hande myghty over the herbes had chaunged hyr gestes in to dyvers maners / that one of hem is covered his face with forme of a Boor/that other is chaunged in to a Lyon of the countre of Marmouke / and his nayles & his tethe wexen. That other of hem is newlyche chaunged in to a wolfe / & howlyth whan he wolde wepe/that other goth debonayrly in the house as a Tygre of Inde. But all be it so that the godheed of Mercury that is cleped the byrde of Archadie hath had mercy of the duke Ulysses byseged with dyverse yvelles / & hath unbounden him fro ẏ pestilence of his hostesse/ algates the rowers and the maryners hadden by this ydrawen in to hyr monthes/and dronken the wicked drinkes. They ẏ weren woxen swyne/hadden by this ychaunged hyr mete of breed/ for to eten akorne of Okes. None of hyr lymmes ne dwelleth with hem hoole / but they han lost the voyce and the body/ only her thought dwelleth with hem stable / ẏ wepeth and bywayleth the monstruous chaungynge that they suffren. O over lyght hande/as who sayth feble and lyght is the hande of Circes ẏ enchaunteresse/ that chaungeth the bodyes of folke in to beestes to regarde and to comparyson of mutacyon that is maked by vyces / ne the herbes of Circes ne be not myghty/ for all be it soo that they may chaungen the lymmes of the body/algate yet they may not chaunge the hertes/for within is hyd the strength and the vigoure of men in the secretour of hyr hertes/that is to sayn/the strength of reason/ But thylke venyms of vyces to drawen a man to hem more myghtely thā the venym of Circes/ for vyces ben so cruell that they persen & thorowe passen the courage within/and though they ne anoye not the body/yet vyces wooden to destroyen men by wounde of thought.

Tu ego fateor / inquit / nec iniuria dici video vitiosos/tam et si humani corporis speciem seruent.&c.

THan sayd I thus: I confesse and am aknowe it (quod I) ne I ne se not that men maye saye/ as by right/that shrewes ben chaunged in to beestes/ by the qualyte of her soules/al be it so that they kepen yet the forme of the body of mankynde: but I wolde not of shrewes/of whiche the thought cruel & woode/ woodeth alwaye to the dystruction of good men/ that it were leful to hem to doone that.

Certes (quod she) ne it is not leful to hem/ as I shal wel shewe the in covenable place: But natheless if so were that thylke that men wene ben leful to shrewes/ were bynommed hem/so that they ne might not anoyen or done harme to good men/ certes a great partye of the payne to shrewes shulde ben alleged and releved. For al be it so that it ne seme credyble thynge peraventure to some folke/ that it mote nedes be that the shrewes ben more wretches and sely/whan they maye ful doone and parfourme that they coveyten / than if they myght not accomplysshe that they coveyten: For if so be that it be wretchydnesse to wylnen to done yvel/ than is it more wretchednesse to mowen done yvel/ without whiche mowyng/ the wretched wyl shulde languysshe without effecte. Then sythe every of these thynges hath his wretchydnesse/ that is to sayne/ wyl to done yvel/and mowynge to doone yvel / it mote nedes be that they shrewes be constrayned by her unselynesses/that wolen & mowen and parfourmen felonyes and shreudnesses. Bo. I acorde me (qd I) but I desyre gretly/ that shrewes losten soone thylke unselynesse/ that is to sayn/ that shrewes weren dispoyled of mowynge to done yuel. Phi. So shullen they (quod she) soner perauenture than thou woldest/ or soner than they hem selfe wene: for there nys nothyng so late in so shorte boundes of this lyfe/ that is longe to abyde/ namely to a courage immortel. Of whiche shrewes the great hope & the hye compassinges of shrewdnesse/ is oft destroyed by a sodeyn ende or they be ware. And that thyng establyssheth to shrewes/ yͤ ende of her shrewdnes/ for if yͤ shrewdnes maketh wretches / than must he nedes be most wretche yͭ longest is a shrewe/ the which wycked shrewes wolde I demyn aldermoost captyfes and unsely/ if her shrewdnes ne were fynysshed at leest way by utterest dethe/ for if I haue concluded sothe of the unselynesse of shrewdnes/ thā sheweth it playnly/ that thilke wretchednes is withouten ende / the whiche is certayne to be perdurable. Boece. Certes (qd I) this conclusyon is harde and wonderful to graunte. But I knowe wel that it accordeth moche to thynges that I haue graunted here beforne. Philo. Thou hast (quod she) ryght estymacyon of this. But who so euer wene that it be a harde thynge to accorde hym to a conclusyon/ it is right that he shewe that sōme of yͤ premysses ben false/ or els he mote shewe that the collacyon of proposycyons nys not spedeful to a necessary conclusyon. And if it ne be not so/ but that the premisses ben ygraūted/ there nys not why he shulde blame the argument. For this thing yͭ I shal tel the nowe/ ne shall not seme lasse wonderful / but of the thinges that ben taken. Also it is necessary/ as who sayth it foloweth of that whiche that is purposed beforne. Boece. What is yͭ (quod I) Phi. Certes (quod she) yͭ is/ yͭ these wycked shrewes be more blissful or elles lasse wretches that abyen yͤ tourmentes that they haue deserued/ than if no payne of Iustyce ne chastysed hem. Ne this ne say I not nowe / for that any man myght thynke yͭ the maners of shrewes ben coryged and chastysed by vengeaunce / & that they be brought to the ryght waye by the drede of tourment / ne for that they yeuen to other folkes ensample to flyen fro vyces. But I understande yet in another maner / yͭ shrewes ben more unsely whan they ne be not punysshed/ al be it so that there ne be had no reason or lawe of correctyon ne none ensample of lokynge. Boece. And what maner shal that ben (qd I) other than hath be tolde here beforne? Philo. Haue we not graunted than (quod she) that good folke ben blyssful / and shrewes ben wretches? Boece. yes (quod I) Phylo. Than (quod she) yf yͭ any good were added to the wretchednesse of any wyght/ nys he not more weleful/ than he that ne hath no medlyng of good in his solitary wretchednes? Boe. So semyth it (quod I). Phi. And what sayest thou than (quod she) of thylke wretche that lacketh all goodes / so that no good nys medled in his wretchednesse / and yet ouer al his wickednesse/ for which he is a wretch/ that there be yet another yuel anexed and knyt to hym/ shal not men denien hym more unsely/ than thylke wretche/ of which the unselinesse is releued by the participacion of some good? Boece. Why shold he not (quod I) Phi. Than certes (quod she) han shrewes whan they ben punysshed somwhat of good anexed to hyr shrewdnesse/ that is to sayne/ the same payne that they suffren/ which that is good/ by yͤ reason of Iustyce. And whā thilke same shrewes escapen without tourment/ than haue they sō what more of yuel/ yet ouer the wyckednesse that they han done/ that is to sayn/ defaute of paynes / whiche defaute of payne thou haste graunted is yuel/ for the deserte of felony. Boece. I ne may not denye it (quod I) Phi. Moche more than (qd she) ben shrewes unsely whan they ben wrongfully delyuered fro payne/ than whan they ben punysshed by ryghtful vengeaunce. But this is open thyng and clere/ that it is right that shrewes ben punysshed/ and it is wyckednesse & wronge that they escapen unpunisshed. Boece. who might denye it (quod I) Philoso. But (quod she) may any man deny that al that is right ne is good: and also the contrarye/ that al that is wronge is wicked. Boece. Certes (quod I) these

these thynges ben clere ynoughe/ and that we haue concluded a lytell here before. But I pray the that thou tel me yf thou accordest to letten no tourment to the soules/ after that the body is ended by the dethe/ that is to sayn: vnderstandest thou aught/ that soules haue any tourment after the dethe of the body. Philo. Certes (quod she) ye/ and that ryght great/ of whiche soules (quod she) I trowe that some ben tourmented by asprenesse of payne/ and some soules I trowe ben excercysed by a pourgynge mekenesse/ but my counsayle nys nat to determyne of this paynes. But I haue trauayled and tolde yet hyderto/ for thou shuldest know that the mowyng of shrewes/ whiche mowynge the semeth to be vnworthy/ nys no mowynge/ and eke of shrewes/ of whiche thou playnedest yt they ne were nat punisshed that thou woldest se that they ne weren neuer mo withouten the tourmentes of her wyckednesse. And of the lycence of the mowynge to don yuel/ that thou praydest yt it myght sone be ended/ and that thou woldest fayne lernen that it ne shulde nat longe endure. And that shrewes ben more vnsely yf they were of lenger durynge/ and moost vnsely if they weren perdurable. And after this I haue shewed the/ that more vnsely ben shrewes whan they escapen without her ryghtful payne/ than whan they ben punysshed by ryghtful vengeaunce. And of this sentence foloweth it/ that thā ben shrewes constrayned at the laste with moost greuous tourment/ whan men wene that they ne be nat punysshed. Boece. Whan I consyder thy reasons (quod I) I ne trowe nat that men sayn any thynge more verely. And yf I tourne ayen to the studyes of men/ who is he to whom it shulde seme/ that he ne shulde nat onely leuen these thynges/ but eke gladly herken hem. Philo. Certes (quod she) so it is/ but mē may nat/ for they haue theyr eyen so wont to the derknesse of erthely thynges/ that they ne may nat lyfte hem vp to ye light of clere sothfastnesse. But they ben lyke to byrdes/ of whiche the nyght lyghtneth her lokynges/ and the day blyndeth hem. For whan men loken nat the ordre of thynges/ but her lustes and talentes/ they wene that eyther the leue or the mowynge to done wyckednesse/ or els the scapynge without payne be weleful. But consyder the iugement of the perdurable lawe/ for yf thou cōferme thy courage to the best thynges/ thou ne hast no nede of no Iuge to yeuen the pryce or mede/ for thou haste ioyned thy selfe to the moost excellent thynges. And if thou haue enclined thy studies to the wycked thynges/ ne seke no foreyne wrekery out of thy selfe/ for yt thy selfe hast thrust thy selfe in to wycked thinges/ right as thou myghtest loken by diuers tymes the foule erthe and the heuen/ and that al other thīges stynten fro without/ so that thou were in neyther/ ne se nothynge more. Than sholde it semen to the/ as by only reason of lokynge/ that thou were nowe in the sterres and nowe in the erthe/ but the people loketh nat on these thynges. What than/ shal we than aproche vs to hem that I haue shewed that ben lyke to beestes? And what woldest thou sayn of this/ if that a man had al forlorne his sight/ & had foryeten yt he euer sawe/ & wened that no thing fayled him of perfection of mankynde? Nowe we whiche mighten sene the same thinges/ wolde we nat sayne that he were blynde/ ne also ne accordeth nat the people to that I shal sayn/ the which thinge is susteyned by as stronge foundementes of reason/ that is to sayn/ that more vnsely ben they that don wrōges to other folke/ than they that the wronge suffren. Boe. I wolde heren thilke same reasons (quod I) Phi. Denyest thou (quod she) that al shrewes ne ben worthy to haue tourment? Nay (qd I) Philo. But (quod she) I am certayne by many reasons/ that shrewes ben vnsely. Boece. It accordeth (quod I) Philo. Than ne doutest thou not (quod she) that thilk folke that ben worthy of tourment/ that they ne be wretches. Boece. It accordeth wel (quod I) Philoso. If thou were than sette a iuge or a knower of thinges/ whether trowest thou that men shulde tourmenten hem that hath done wronge/ or els hem that suffred the wronge? Boece. I doute not (quod I) that I nolde do suffycient satisfaction/ to hem that haue suffred wronge/ by the sorowe of hem that hath doone wronge. Phi. Than semeth it (quod she) that the doer of wronge is more wretche / than he that suffred wronge. Boece. That foloweth wel (quod I) Philo. Than (quod she) by these causes and by other causes / that ben enforced by the same rote / ẏ filth or synne by ẏ propre nature of it maketh men wretches / ⁊ it sheweth wel / that ẏ wronges that men don nys nat the wretchednesse of him that receyueth the wronge / but the wretchednesse of hym that doth ẏ wrong. But certes (quod she) these oratours or aduocates don al the contrarye / for they enforcen hem to commoue the Iuges to haue pyte of hem that don the greuaunces and ẏ wronges / the whiche shrewes it were a more couenable thinge / that the accusours or aduocates / nat wroth / but pyteous and debonayre ledden tho shrewes that haue don wronges to the iugement / right as men leden syke folke to the leche / for that they shulden sekyn out the maladyes of synne by tourment. And by this couenaunt eyther ẏ entente of aduocates shulde cessen in al / or els if the office of the aduocates wold better profyten to men / it shulde be tourned in to the habyte of accusacyon / that is to sayn / they shulden accuse shrewes and nat excusen hem. And eke the shrewes hem selfe / if it were leful to hem to sen at any clyfte ẏ vertue that they haue forletten / ⁊ sawen ẏ they shulde putten adowne the filthes of her vices by ẏ tourmentes of paynes / they ne oughten nat ryght for ẏ recompensacyon / for to geten hem bounte and prowesse / whiche that they haue loste / demen and holde that the ylke paynes weren tourmentes to hem / and eke they wolden refuse the attendaunce of her aduocates / and taken hem selfe to her Iuges and to her accusours / for the which it betydeth / that as to the wyse folkes / there nys no place yletten to hate / that is to sayn / that hate ne hath no place among wyse men. For no wyght nyl haten good men / but yf he were ouer moche a foole / and for to haten shrewes / it nys no reason / for ryght as languysshynge is maladie of body / right so ben vyces and synne maladye of courage. And so as we ne deme nat ẏ they which that ben syke of her body / ben worthy to ben hated / but rather worthy of pyte. Wel more worthy nat to ben hated / but for to ben had in pyte ben they / of whiche the thoughtes ben constrayned by felonous wyckednesse / ẏ is more cruel than any languysshynge of body.

Quid tantos iuuat excitare motus / Et propria fatum sollicitare manu: Si mortem petitis / propinquat ipsa Sponte sua / volucres nec remoratur equos. ⁊c.

What delyteth you to exciten so gret mouynge of hatredes / and to hasten and busyen the fatal dysposycyon of your dethe with your propre handes / ẏ is to sayn / by batayls or conteke: For if ye axen the deth / it hasteth hym of his owne wyl / ne dethe ne taryeth nat his swyfte horse. And the men that the serpentes / and the lyon / and the tygre / and the beere / and the bore / seken to sleen with theyr tethe / yet thilke same men seken to sleen eueryche of hem other with swerde. Lo / for her maners ben dyuers and discordaunt / they mouen vnryghtful hostes ⁊ cruel batayles / and wylnen to perysshe by entrechaungynge of dartes / but the reason of cruelte nys nat ynough rightful. Wylte thou than yelden a couenable guerdon to the desertes of men: loue ryghtfully good folkes / and haue pyte on shrewes.

Hinc ego video inq̄ / que sit vel felicitas vel miseria in ipsis proborum atq̄ improborum meritis constituta. Sed in hac ipsa fortuna populari. ⁊c.

This I se wel (quod I) eyther what blyssfulnesse / or els what vnselynesse is establysshed in the desertes of good men and of shrewes. But in this ylke fortune of ẏ people I se somwhat of good / and somwhat of yuel. For no wyse man had not leuer be exyled poore and nedy / and namelesse / than for to dwellen in his cyte / and flouren of rychesse / and be redoutable of honour / and stronge of power. For in this wise more clerely and wytnessfully is the office of wyse men treated / than the blyssfulnesse of power / and gouernours / is

as it

as it were shadde amonges the people/ that be neyghbours and subiectes/ sythe that namely prison/ lawe/ and these other tourmentes of lauful paynes/ be rather owed to felonous cytezyns: for the whiche felonous cytezyns the paynes be establysshed/ more than for good people. B. Than I meruayle greatly (qd I) why that the thynges be so mysse entrechaunged/ that tourmentes of felonyes pressen and confounden good people/ and shrewes rauisshen medes of vertue/ & ben in honours and great estates. And I desyre eke for to weten of the/ what semeth the to be the reason of this so wrongful a conclusyon. For I wold wonder wel the lasse/ if I trowed that al thynges were medled with fortunous hap. But nowe crepeth and encreaseth myn astonyenges god gouernour of thynges/ that so as god yeueth ofte tymes to good men goodes and myrthes/ and to shrewes yuels and aspre thynges: and yeueth ayen to good folke hardnesse/ and to shrewes he graunteth hem her wyl/ and that they desyren. What difference may there be bytwene that that god dothe/ and happe of fortune/ if men knowe not the cause why it is. Philo. Neit is no meruayle (qd she) though that men wenen/ that there be somwhat folysshe and confuse/ whan the reason of the ordre is unknowen: but although that thou ne knowe not the cause of so great a disposycion/ Nathelesse/ for as moche as god the good gouernour attempreth & gouerneth ẏ worlde/ ne doute the not but al thinges ben don aright.

Si quis Arcturi sidera nescit. Mergatque seras equore flammas. Propinqua summo cardine labi. Cũ nimis celeres explicet ortus Cur legat tard⁹ plaustra Bootes. &c.

W Ho so that knowe not the sterres of Arcture/ turned to ẏ soueraygn centre or poynte/ that is to sayne/ tourned nyghe to the soueraygne pole of the fyrmamẽt/ and wote not why the sterre Bootes passeth or gathereth his waynes/ and drencheth his late flambes in the see/ and why that Bootes the sterre unfoldeth his ouerswyfte arysynges/ than shal he wondren of the lawe of the hygh ayre. And eke/ if that he ne knowe not why that the hornes of the ful moone waxen pale and infecte/ by the boundes of the derke night: and howe the moone derke and confuse/ discouereth the sterres that she had couered by her clere vysage. The commune errour moueth folkes and maketh wery her basyns of brasse by thikke strokes/ that is to say/ that there is a maner people that hight Corybantes/ that wenen that whan the moone is in the eclypse that it be enchaunted/ and therfore for to rescue the moone/ they beaten her basyns with thykke strokes. Ne no man ne wondreth whan the blastes of the wynde Chorus/ beten the strondes of the see/ by quakyng flodes. Ne no man ne wondreth whan the weight of the snowe/ harded by the colde/ is resolued by the brennyng heate of Phebus the sonne/ for here sene men redily the causes. But the causes yhydde/ that is to sayne in heuen/ troublen the brestes of mẽ. The mouable people is astonyed of al thinges that comen selde and sodaynly in our age/ but the troubly errour of our ignorau̇ce departeth fro us/ so ẏ if they wysten the cause why that suche thynges betyden/ certes they shulden cease to seme wonders.

Ita est inquam. Sed cum tui muneris sit latentium rerum causas euoluere/ velatasque caligine explicare rationes: queso uti hinc decernas. &c.

T Hus it is (quod I) but so as thou haste yeuen or behyght me to unwrappe the hydde causes of thynges/ and to discouer me the reasons couered with derkenesse/ I praye the/ that thou deuyse and iuge me of this mater/ and that thou do me to understande it/ for this myracle of this wondre troubleth me right greatly. And than she a lytel what smylynge sayd. Thou clepest me (quod she) to tel that is greatest of al thynges/ that mowen ben asked/ and to the which question unneth is there aught ynough to lauen it/ as who sayth/ unneth is there any thyng thinge to answere perfetely to thy questyon/ for the mater of it is suche/that whan o doute is determyned and cutte awaye/ there waxen other doutes without nombre/ right as the heedes of Idre the serpent waxen/ the whiche serpent Hercules slough: ne there ne were no manere ne none ende/but if a wight constrayned the doutes/ by a right lyuely and quicke fyre of thought/ that is to sayne/ by vygour and strength of wytte. For in this mater men weren wonte to maken questyons of the symplicite of the purueyaunce of god/and of ẏ ordre of destyne/⁊ of sodeyne hap/⁊ of knowing of predestynacyon dyuyne. And of the lyberte of frewyl/ the whiche thynges thou thy selfe apperceyuedest wel/of what weyght they ben. But for as moche as the knowynges of these thynges is a maner porcyon or medycine to the/al be it so that I haue lytel tyme to doone it/ yet neuerthelesse I wolde enforcen me to shewen somwhat of it: but al though the norisshynges of dyte of musike delyteth the/thou muste suffren and forbearen a lytel of thylke delyte/whyle that I weue to the resons knytte by ordre. Bo. As it lyketh to the (qđ I) so do. Philo. Tho spake she right as by another begynnynge/ and sayd right thus. The engendring of al thynges (quod she) and al the progressions of mouable nature/and al that moueth in any maner/taketh his causes/his ordre and his fourmes/of the stablenesse of diuyne thought: And thylke diuyne thought that is set and put in the toure/that is to sayne/ in the heyght of the symplycite of god/ stablyssheth many maner gyses to the thynges that ben to done/ the whiche maner whan that men loken it/ in the pure clennesse of the diuyne intellygence/ is cleaped purueyaunce. But whan thylke maner is referred by men/ to thynges that it moueth or disponeth/ than of olde men it was cleped destenye/ the whiche thynges/ if that any wight loketh wel in his thought/the strength of that one and of that other/ he shal lyghtly mowe sene/ that these two thynges ben dyuers. For pourueyaunce is thilke diuyne reason/ that is establysshed in the souerayne prince of thynges/ the whiche pourueyaunce disponeth al thynges. But certes destynye is the disposycion and the ordynaunce cleuynge to mouable thynges/by the whiche disposycion the pourueyaunce knytteth al thynges in her ordre: For pourueyaunce enbraceth al thynges to heape/al though they be dyuers/ and al though they be infynite/ but destenye certayne departeth and ordayneth al thynges syngulerly/and deuydeth in mouyng/ in places/ in formes/and in tymes/ as thus: Let the vnfoldynge of temporal ordynaunce assembled and oned in the lokynge of the diuyne thought be cleaped purueyaunce/ and thylke same assemblynge and onynge deuyded and vnfolden/ lette that be called destenye. And al be it so that these thynges ben dyuers/ yet neuerthelesse hanged that one on that other/ for why/ the ordre destynable procedeth of the symplicyte of purueyaunce. For right as a werkeman perceyueth in his thought/ẏ forme of a thynge that he wol make/and moueth the effecte of the werke/and leadeth that he had loked beforne in his thought symply and presently by corporal ordynaunce: certes ryght so god in his purueyaunce disponeth syngulerly and stably/ the thynges that be to done/ but he admynistreth in maners and in dyuers tymes by destenye/thilke same thinges that he hath disponed/ than whether destenye be exercysed eyther by some diuyne spirites/seruantes to the diuyne purueyaunce/ or els by some soule/ or els by al nature seruynge to god/ or els by the celestyal mouynges of sterres/ or els by the vertue of angels/ or els by dyuers subtylte of dyuels/or els by any of hem/or els by hem al/ the destynable ordynaunce is wouen and accōplisshed. Certes it is open thing that the pourueyaunce is an vnmouable and symple fourme of thynges to doone/ and the mouable bonde and the temporal ordynaunce of thynges/ whiche that the diuyne symplicite of pourueyaunce hath ordayned to done/ that is destenye. For whiche it is that al thynges that ben put vnder destenye/ben certes subiectes vnto pourueyaunce/ to whiche pourueyaunce destenye it selfe is subiecte and vnder/ but some thinges ben put vnder purueyaūce/ that surmounten the ordynaunce of destenye: And tho ben thylke that stablye ben fyxed nyghe

nyghe to the firste godheed/ they surmounten the ordre of destynable mouablyte. For right as cercles turnen aboute a same centre or aboute a poynte/ thilke cercle that is innerest or moste within/ he ioyneth to the symplesse of the myddle/ & is as it were a centre or a poynte to that other cercles/ that tournen about him: and thilke that is vtterest/ compassed by a larger enuyronnyng/ is vnfolde by larger spaces/ in somoche as it is fertherest fro the myddelest symplycite of the poynte. And if there be any thing that knytteth and feloushyppeth him selfe to thylke myddle poynte/ it is constrayned in to symplycite/ that is to saye/ in to vnmouablite/ and it ceaseth to ben shadde and flytte dyuersly. Right so by semblable reason/ thilke thynge that departeth furtherest fro the firste thought of god/ it is vnfolden and also submytted to greater bondes of destyne/ and in so moche is the thynge more free and lose fro dignyte/ as it asketh and holdeth nerre to thylke centre of thynges/ that is to sayne/ to god. And if the thyng cleaueth to the stedfastnesse of the thought of god/ & be without mouynge/ certes it surmounteth the necessyte of destenye. Than suche comparyson as is skylyng to vnderstandynge/ and of thynge that was engendred to thing that is of tyme to eternyte/ and of the cercle to the centre/ right so is the ordre of mouable destyne/ to the stable simplycite of purueyaunce. Thilke ordynaunce moueth the heuen and the sterres/ and attempreth the elemētes togyder amonge hem selfe/ and transformeth hem by entrechaungeable mutacion. And thilke same ordre neweth ayen al thynges growyng and fallyng adowne/ by semblable progressions of sedes and of sexus/ that is to sayne/ male and female: and this ylke ordre constrayneth the fortunes and the dedes of men by a bonde of causes/ not able to be vnbounden: the whiche destynable causes whan they passen out fro the begynnynges of vnmouable purueyance/ it mote nedes be that they ne be not mutable/ as thus: Be the thynges wel gouerned/ if that the symplicite dwellyng in the diuyne thought/ sheweth forthe the ordre of causes vnable to be bowed. And this ordre constrayneth by the propre stablyte the mouable thynges/ or els they shulden flete folily. For whiche it is/ that thynges semen confuse and trouble to vs men/ for we ne mowen not consyder thilke ordynaunce. Neuertheles/ the propre maner of euery thyng/ dressynge hem to good disponeth hem al/ for there nys nothyng done for yuel/ for thilke thynge that is done by wicked folke/ nys not done for yuel. The whiche shrewes/ as I haue shewed ful plenteously seke good/ but wicked errour misturneth hem/ ne the ordre comyng fro the poynte of souerayne good/ ne enclyneth not fro his begynnyng. But thou mayste saye/ what vnrest may ben a worse cōfusyon/ than that good men haue somtyme aduersyte/ and somtyme prosperyte: and shrewes haue nowe also thynges that they desyren/ and now thynges that they haten. Whether men lyue nowe in suche holynesse of thought/ as who sayth/ be men nowe so wyse/ that suche folke as they demen to be good folke or shrewes/ that it mote nedes be/ ÿ folke be such as they wenen? But in this maner domes of men discorden/ that thylke men that some folke demen worthy of mede/ other folke deme hem worthy of tourment/ but let vs graunt: I suppose that some man may wel deme or knowe the good people and the badde/ may he than knowe & se thilke innerest attemperance of corage/ as it hath be wonte to be sayde of bodyes/ as who sayth: may a man speken of complexions & attempraūce of bodies/ ne it ne is not/ as who sayth/ but it is lyke a maruayle or a myracle to hem that ne knowen it not/ why that swete thinges be couenable to some bodies that ben hole/ & to some people bytter thīges be couenable: & also why some people ben holpen with light medicines/ and some people ben holpen with bytter medicines: but nathelesse tho that knowen the maner & the attempraūce of hele and of maladie/ ne meruayleth it nothyng. But what other thyng semeth helth of corages but boūte: and what other thīg semeth maladie of corage but vices? Who is els keper of good & driuer away of yuel/ but god the gouernour and leder of thoughtes: the whiche god/ whan he hath beholden from the hygh toure of his purueyaunce/ he knoweth what is couenable to any wight/

wight/and leaneth hem that he wote wel that is couenable to hem. Lo/herof cometh & herof is doone this myracle of the ordre destynable/ whan god that al knoweth dothe suche thyng/ of whiche thyng vnknowynge folke ben astonyed/but for to constrayne/as who sayth/but for to comprehende and tel a fewe thynges of the dyuine depenesse/the whiche that mannes reason maye vnderstande. Thilke man that thou wenest to ben right iuste & right kepynge of equite/ the contrarye of that semeth to the dyuine puruepaūce that al wote. And Lucan my famylier telleth/that the victorious cause lyked to the goddes / and the causes ouercome lyketh to Caton. Thanne what so euer thou mayste sene yͭ is done in this worlde vnhoped or els vnknowen/certes it is the right ordre of thynges/ but as to thy wicked opynion/it is a confusyon. But I suppose that some man be so wel thewed/that the diuyne iugement & the iugement of mankynde accorden hem togyther of him: but he is so vnstedfaste of corage/ that if any aduersyte come to him/ he wol forleten perauenture to continue innocencie/ by the whiche he ne may not withholden fortune: than the wyse dispēsacion of god spareth him/ the whiche man aduersite might enpayren/for that god wyl not him to trauayle/ to whome that trauayle nys not couenable. An other man is parfyte in al vertues/and is an holy man and nyghe to god/ so that the poueruey-aunce of god wold deme /that it were a felony that he were touched with any aduersytees/ so that he wol not suffre / that such a mā be with any bodily maladye moued. But so (as sayd the philosophre) the more excellent is by me sayde in great/ that vertues haue edifyed the body of the holy man. And ofte tyme it betydeth/that the sōme of thinges that ben to done is taken to gouerne to good folke/ for that the malyce haboundaunt of shrewes shulde ben abated. And god yeueth and departeth to other folke prosperytees and aduersytees medled to heape/ after the qualyte of her corages/ and remordeth some folke by aduersytees/ for they ne shulde not waxen prowde by longe welefulnesse. And other folke he suffreth to be trauayled with harde thynges/for that they shulde confermen the vertues of corage/ by the exercitacion of vsage of pacyence. And other folke dreden more than they oughten / yͭ whiche they myghten wel bearen/ and some dispyse that they mowe not beare/ and thilke folke god leadeth in to experience of hem selfe by aspre and sorouful thynges. And many other folke haue bought honourable renome of this worlde/ by the price of glorious dethe. And some men that ne mowe not ben ouercomen by tourment/ haue yeuen ensample to other folke/ that vertue maye not ben ouercomen by aduersyties. And of al these thynges there nys no doute/ that they ne ben done rightfully and ordaynly/ to the parfyte good of hem/to whome we sene these thynges betyde. For certes that aduersytees cometh somtyme to shrewes / and somtyme that they desyren/it cometh of these foresayd causes. And of sorouful thynges that betyden to shrewes/ certes no man ne wondreth/ for al men wene that they haue deserued it/ and that they ben of wicke merite. Of whiche shrewes the turmente agasteth somtyme other to doone felonyes: and somtyme it amendeth hem that suffreth the tourmentes. And the prosperyte that is yeuen to shrewes/ sheweth a great argumente to good people / what thynge they shulde demen of thylke welfulnesse / whiche prosperyte men sene ofte serue to shrewes: In whiche thing I trowe that god dispenseth/for parauenture yͭ nature of some man is so ouerthrowynge to yuel and so vncouenable/that the nedy pouerte of his housholde might rather agreue him to done felonyes/ and to the maladye of him god putteth remedie to yeuen him rychesse. And some other man beholdeth his conscyence defouled with synnes/and maketh comparyson of this fortune and of hym selfe/ and dredeth parauenture that the blysfulnesse/ of whiche the vsage is ioyful to him/ that the lesyng of thylke blissfulnesse ne be not sorouful to him/and therfore he wolde chaūge his maners: and for he dredeth to lese his fortune/he forleteth his wickednesse. To other folkes welfulnes is yeuen vnworthily / the whiche ouerthroweth hem in to destructyon that they han deserued / and to some other folke is

yeuen

yeuen power to punysshen / for that it shal be cause of contynuacyon & exercysyng to good folkes/ and cause of turment to shrewes. For so as there nys none alyaunce bytwene good folkes and shrewes/ ne shrewes ne mowen not accorden among hem selfe: and why not? For that shrewes discorden of hem selfe by her vyces/ the whiche vyces al to renden her consciences/ and done oft tyme thynges/ the whiche thynges whan they haue done hem/ they deme that tho thynges ne shulde not haue be done/ for whiche thyng the soueraygne purueyaunce hath maked oft tyme myracle: so that shrewes haue maked shrewes to ben good men. For whan that some shrewes sene that they suffre wrongfully felonyes of other shrewes/ they waxen eschaufed in to hate of hem that anoyed hem/ and retournen to the fruite of vertue. Than they studyen to be unlyke to hem that they haue hated. Certes onely is this the dyuine myght/ to the whiche might yuels ben than good/ whan it useth the yuels couenably/ and draweth out the effecte of any good/ as who sayth/ that yuel is good onely to the might of god/ for the might of god ordeyneth thilke yuel to good: For one ordre enbraceth al thynges/ so that what wight departeth from the reason of thylke ordre that is assigned to hym/ algates yet he slydeth in to another ordre/ so that nothyng is leful to folye in the realme of diuyne purueyaunce/ as who sayth/ nothyng is without ordynaunce in the realme of diuyne purueyaūce/ syth that the right stronge god gouerneth al thynges in this worlde/ for it is not leful for men to comprehende by wyt ne unfolden by worde al the subtyl ordynaūce and the disposycion of the diuyne entent/ for only it ought to suffyse to haue loked that god hym selfe/ maker of al natures/ ordayneth al thynges to good/ whyle that he hasteth to withholde the thynges that he hath maked in to his semblaunce/ that is to say/ for to with holden the thinges in to good/ for he hym selfe is good. He chaseth out al yuels fro the bounde of his comynalties/ by the ordre of the necessyte destynable: for whiche it foloweth/ that if thou loke the purueyaunce/ ordeynyng the thynges that men wenen be outragyous or haboundaunt in erthes/ thou shalt not sene in no place no thynge of yuel. But I se nowe that thou arte charged with the weight of the questyon/ and wery with length of my reason/ and that thou abydest some sweetenesse of songe/ take than this draught/ and whan thou arte wel refresshed & refecte/ thou shalt be more stedfaste to stye in to hygher questyons or thynges.

Si vis celsi iura tonantis. Pura solers cernere mente Aspice sūmi culmina celi.

If thou wyse wolte demen in thy pure thought/ the rightes or the lawes of the hye thonder/ that is to sayn of god/ loke thou and beholde the heightes of the soueraygne heuen: There kepen the sterres by rightful alyaunce of thynges her olde peace: The Sonne ymoued by his roody fyre/ ne distourbeth nat the colde cercle of the moone/ ne the sterre ycleped the Beer/ that enclyneth his rauysshynge courses/ abouten the soueraygne height of this worlde. Ne the same sterre Ursa/ nys neuer mo wasshen ī ẏ depe westren see/ ne coueyteth nat to deyen his flambes in the see of the Occian/ al though it se other sterres yplonged in the see: And Hesperus the sterre bodeth and telleth alwaye the late nyghtes: and Lucyfer the sterre bryngeth ayen the clere daye. And thus maketh loue enterchaungeable/ the perdurable courses/ and thus is discordable batayle yput out of the countrey of the sterres. This accordaunce atempreth by euynlyke maners the Elementes/ that the moyst thynges stryuynge with the drye thynges/ yeuen place by stoundes: and that the colde thynges joynen hem by faythe to the hote thynges/ & that the lyght fyre aryseth in to height/ and the heuy erthes aualen by her weightes: by ẏ same causes the floury yere yeldeth swete smelles/ in the first somer season warmynge/ and the hote somer dryeth the cornes/ and Autumpne cometh ayen heuy of apples/ and the fletyng rayne bedeweth the wynter/ this attēperaūce nourysshed & bryngeth forth al thynges that bereth lyfe in this worlde/ and thylke same attemperaūce rauisshing/ hideth/ benymeth/ and drencheth under the last deth al thinges yborne.

Amonge

Amonges these thynges sytteth the highe maker/ kynge and lorde/ welle and begynnynge/ lawe & wyse iuge/ to done equite/ & gouerneth & enclyneth the brydels of thynges: And tho thynges that he stereth to gone by mouynge/ he withdraweth and aresteth/ and affyrmeth the mouable or wandryng thynges. For if ẏ he ne called nat ayen the right goyng of thynges. And if that he ne cõstrayned hem nat eftsones in to roundnesses enclyned/ the thynges that ben nowe cõtynued by stable ordynance/ they shulde departen from her welle/ that is to sayn from her begynnyng and fallen/ that is to sayne/ tournen in to nought. This is the cõmune loue to al thynges: and al thynges asken to ben holden by the fyne of good/ for els ne myghten they nat lasten/ if they ne cõe nat eftsones ayen by loue retourned to ẏ cause ẏ hath yeuen hem beyng/ ẏ is to sayn god.

Iamne igitur vides quid hec omnia que diximus cõsequantur. Quid nam inquit. Omnem inquit. &c.

SEyst thou nat than/ what thyng foloweth al the thynges that I haue sayd. B. What thyng (qđ I) P. Certes (qđ she) al vtterly/ that al fortune is good. B. And howe maye that be (qđ I. P. Nowe vnderstande (qđ she) So as al fortune/ whether so it be ioyful fortune or aspre fortune/ is yeuen either bycause of guerdonyng/ or els of exercisyng of good folkes/ or els bycause to punysshen/ or els chastysen shrewes: Than is al fortune good/ the which fortune is certayne/ that it be either rightful/ or els profytable. Bo. Forsoth this is a ful very reason (qđ I) And if I consyder the purueyaunce and the destyne that thou taughtest me a lytel here beforn/ this sentẽce is sustayned by stedfast reasons. But if it lyke vnto the/ lette vs nombren hem amonges thylke thynges/ of whiche thou saydest a lytel here beforne/ that they ne were nat able to ben wened to the people. P. Why so (qđ she). B. For that the cõmune worde of men (qđ I) mysuseth this maner speche of fortune/ and sayne ofte tymes/ that the fortune of some wight is wicked. P. Wylt thou than (qđ. she) that I aproche a lytel to ẏ wordes of the people/ so that it seme nat to hem/ that I be ouer moche departed/ as fro the vsage of mankynde. B. As thou wolte (qđ I) P. Wenest thou not (qđ she) that al thynge that profyteth is good. B. Yes (qđ I) Phi. Certes al thynge that exerceth or correcteth/ it profyteth. Bo. I confesse wel (qđ I) Phi. Than is it good (qđ she) Bo. Why not (qđ I) Phi. But this is the fortune (quod she) of hem that eyther be put in vertue/ and batayllen ayenst aspre thinges/ or els of hem that eschewen and declynen fro vices/ and taken the way of vertue. Bo. This ne may I not denye (quod I) Phi. But what sayest thou of the mery fortune that is yeuen to good people in guerdon/ demeth aught the people that it be wicked: B. Naye forsothe (quod I) but they demen as it is soth/ that it is right good. Phi. What sayest thou of the other fortune (quod she) that al thoughe that it be aspre and restrayneth the shrewes by rightful turment/ weneth aught the people that it be good: B. Nay (quod I) But the people demeth that it is most wretched of al thynges that may be thought. P. Ware nowe and loke wel (quod she) leste we in folowynge the oppinyon of the people/ haue confessed and concluded thynge whiche that is vnable to ben wened to the people. Boece. What is that (qđ I) P. Certes (qđ she) it foloweth or cometh of thynges that ben graunted/ that al fortune what so euer it be/ of hem that ben eyther in possessyon of vertue/ or in the encrease of vertue/ or els in the purchasing of vertue/ that thylke fortune is good/ & that al fortune is right wycked to hem that dwellen in shrewednesse/ as who saithe/ and thus weneth nat the people. B. That is soth (qđ I) Al be it so that no man dare confesse it/ ne knowe it. P. Why so (qđ she) For ryght as the stronge man ne semeth nat to abasshen or disdaynen/ as oft tyme as he hereth the noyse of the batayle: Ne also it semeth not to ẏ wise man to bearen it greuously/ as ofte as he is ledde in to stryfe of fortune. For bothe to that one man and eke to that other/ thilke difficulte is the mater to that one man of encrease of his glorious renome/ and to that other men to confserue conserue his sappence/ that is to saye/ to the asprenesse of his estate/ for therfore is it called vertue/ for that it susteyneth and enforceth by his strēgthes/ so that it nys not ouercomen by aduersytees. Ne certes thou that arte put in encrease or in the heyght of vertue/ ne hast not comen to fleten with delyces/ and for to wasken in bodily luste. Thou sowest or plantest a ful egre batayle in thy corage ayenst euery fortune: For that the sorouful fortune confoūde the not/ ne that the mery fortune ne corrumpe the not/ occuppye the meane by stedfast strengthes. For al ỷ euer is vnder the meane/ or al that ouerpasseth the meane/ dispyseth welefulnesse/ as who sayth/ it is vycious/ and ne hath no mede of his trauayle/ for it is sette in your hande/ as who sayth/ it lyeth in your power what fortune you is leuest/ ỷ is to say good or yuel/ for al fortune ỷ semeth sharpe or aspre/ if it ne exercyse not the good folke/ ne chastyse the wicked folke/ it punyssheth.

Bella bis binis operatus annis. Ultor atrides phrigie ruinis. &c.

The wreker atrides/ ỷ is to sayne Agamemnon/ that wrought & contynued the batayles by ten yere/ recouered and purged in wrekyng/ by the distruction of Troye/ the loste chambres of maryage in his brother/ that is to saye/ that Agamemnon wan ayen Heleyne/ that was Menelaus wyfe/ his brother. In the meane while that thilke Agamemnon desyred to yeuen sayles to the grekes nauye/ and brought ayen the wyndes by bloode: He vnclothed hym of pyte of father/ and the sorie preest yeueth in sacrifyeng/ the wretched cuttynge of the throte of the doughter/ that is to say/ that Agamemnon let cutte the throte of his doughter by the preest/ to maken alyaunce with his goddes/ and for to haue wynde/ with whiche he might wenden to Troye. Itacus/ that is to say Ulixes/ bewepte his felowes ylorne/ the whiche felowes the fers Polyphemus lyggynge in his great caue/ had fretten and drenkt in his empty wombe: But natheles Poliphemus woode for his blynde vysage yelde to Ulixes ioye/ by his sorouful teres/ that is to say/ that Ulixes smote out the eye of Poliphemus/ that stode in ỷ forheed/ for which Ulixes had ioye/ whan he sawe Poliphemus weping and blynde. Hercules is celebrable for his harde trauayle/ he daunted the proude Centaurus/ halfe horse halfe man/ & berafte the dispoyling fro ỷ cruel lyon/ that is to say/ he slough the lyon/ and birafte him his skynne. He smote the byrdes that hyght Arpyes with certayne arowes. He rauisshed apples fro the waking dragon: and his hande was the more heauy for the golden metal. He droughe Cerberus the hounde of hell by the triple chaynes. He ouercomer/ as it is sayd/ hath put an vnmeke lorde fodder to his cruel horse/ that is to say/ Hercules slough Dyomedes/ & made his horse to fretten him: and he Hercules sloughe Idra the serpent/ and brent the venym. And Acheleus the floode defoulled in his forheed/ drenkt his shamfaste vysage in his strondes/ that is to say/ that Acheleus coulde trāsfygure him selfe in to dyuers lykenesse/ & as he faught with Hercules/ at laste he tourned him in to a bull/ & Hercules brake one of his hornes: and he for shame hydde him in his ryuer. And ouer that he Hercules caste adown Antheus the gyaunt in the strōdes of Lybie. And Cacus apeysed the wrathes of Euander/ that is to say that Hercules slough the monstre Cacus/ and apeysed with that orthe the wrathe of Euander. And the bristled bore marked with somes the sholders of Hercules/ the whiche sholders the hye cercle of heuen shulde thrist. And the last of his labours was/ that he susteyned the heuen vpon his necke vnbowed/ and he deserued eftsones the heuen to be the last ende of trauayle. Gothe now than ye stronge men there as the gret ensample ledeth you. Nyce men why make ye your backes/ as who saith: o ye slowe & delycate men/ why fle ye aduersytees/ and ne fyght not ayenst hem by vertu/ to wynnen the mede of heuen: for the mede ouercomen/ yeueth the sterres/ that is to sayne/ that whan that erthely luste is ouercomen/ a man is maked worthy to the heuen.

¶Here endeth the fourthe booke of Boece/ & foloweth the fyfthe.

A. a. a. Dixerat

¶ Dixerat / orationisq̄ cursum ad alia quedam tractanda atq̄ expedienda vertebat. B. Tum ego / recta quidem inq̄. ⁊c.

SHe had sayd and tourned the course of her reason to some other thinges / to be treated and to be sped. B. Than said I / certes rightful is thyn amonesting and ful digne by auctorite. But that thou saydest whilom / that the questyon of the deuyne pouruepaunce / is enlaced with many other questyons / I vnderstande wel and proue it / by the same thinge. But I aske / if that thou wenest ÿ hap be any thynge in any wayes / and if thou wenest that hap be any thynge / what is it: Philo. Than (quod she) I haste me to yelden and assoylen to the det of my behest / and to shewen ⁊ open ÿ way / by whiche way thou mayst come ayen to thy countree: but al be it so that the thinges whiche that thou askest / ben right profytable to knowe / yet ben they dyuers / so̅ what fro ÿ path of my purpose / ⁊ it is to doute / that thou ne be maked wery by mysse wayes / so ÿ thou ne mayst nat suffyse to measure ÿ right way. Boece. Ne doute the therof nothyng (quod I) For for to knowen thilk thi̅ges togider / in the whiche thinges I delyte me greatly / that shal ben to me in stede of reste / syth it nys nat to douten of the thynges folowynge / whan euery thi̅g of thy disputacyon shal haue ben stedfast to me / by vndoutous fayth. Phi. Than (sayd she) that maner wol I done to the / and began to speaken right thus. Certes (quod she) if any wyght defenisshe hap in this maner / that is to sayn / ÿ hap is betidynge ybrought forth by folysshe mouynge / ⁊ by no knyttynge of causes / I conferme that hap nys right naught in no wyse / and I deme al vtterly / that hap nys / ne dwelleth but a voyce / as who sayth / but an ydel worde / without any signification of thing co̅mitted to that voyce. For what place might ben lefte or dwellynge in folie and to disordenaunce / sythe that god leadeth and constrayneth al thinges by ordre / for this sentence is very sothe / that nothynge hath his beinge of naught / to the whiche sentence / none of these olde folke ne withsayd neuer / al be it so ÿ they ne vnderstanden it nat / by god / prince and begynner of workynge / but they casten / as a maner foundement of subiecte material / that is to sayn / of the nature of al reason. And if that any thing is waxe̅ or comen of no causes / than shal it seme / that thilke thinge is comen or woxen of naught. But if this ne may nat be done / than is it nat possyble ÿ hap be any suche thing / as I haue defynisshed a lytel here beforne. Boece. Howe shal it than be (quod I) nys there tha̅ nothing that by right may ben cleped eyther hap or eis aduenture or fortune / or is there aught / al be it so that it is hyd fro ÿ people / to which thing these wordes ben couenable: Phi. Myne Aristotle (quod she) in the boke of his phisike / defenissheth this thinge by shorte reason / ⁊ nighe to the soth. Boece. In which maner (quod I) P. As ofte (quod she) as men done any thing for grace of any other thing / ⁊ another thinge tha̅ thilke thing that men ente̅den to don betydeth by some causee / it is ycleped hap / right as a man dalfe the erthe bycause of tyllynge of ÿ felde / and founde there a gobet of golde bedoluen / than wenen folke that it is befal by fortunous betydynge. But forsothe it nys nat of naught / for it hath his propre causes / of which causes ÿ course vnforeseen ⁊ vnware / semeth to haue maked hap. For if the tyller of ÿ felde ne dolue nat in ÿ erthe / and if the hyder of the golde ne had hyd the golde in that place / the golde ne had not ben founde. These ben than the causes of ÿ abredgynge of fortuit hap / the whiche abredgynge of fortuit hap cometh / of causes of encountryng and flowyng togyder to hem selfe / and nat by the entencyon of the doer. For neyther the hyder of the golde / ne the deluer of the felde / ne vnderstoden nat / that ÿ golde shuld haue ben founde. But as I sayd / it betyd and ran togider / that he dalfe there as that other had hyd the golde. Nowe maye I thus defynysshe hap. Hap is an vnware betydyng of causes / assembled in thinges that ben don for some other thing. But thilke ordre proceding by an vneschuable betyding togyder / whiche ÿ discendeth from the well of purueyaunce / that ordeyneth al thynges in her places and in her tymes maketh / that the causes rennen and assemblen togyther.

Rupis Achemence scopulis ubi versa sequentum. Pectoribus figit spicula. &c.

Tigris and Eufrates resoluen & spryngen of o wel / in the cragges of the roche of the countre of Achemenec / there as the fleynge batayle fichen her dartes returnyng / in the brestes of hem that folowen hem. And soone after the same ryuers Tigris and Eufrates / unioynen and departen her waters / & if they comen togider / and ben assembled and cleped togyder in to o course / thā moten thilke thynges fleten togider / whiche that the water of the entrechaungynge flood bryngeth. The shyppes and the stockes araced with the flood moten assemblen / and the waters ymedled / wrappeth or implyeth many fortunel happes or maners / the whiche wandryng happes natheles / thilke declinynge lownesse of the erthe / and the flowynge ordre of the slydynge water gouerneth. Right so fortune that semeth / as it fleteth with slaked or ungouerned brydles / it suffreth brydles / that is to sayn / to ben gouerned / & passeth by thilke lawe / that is to sayn / by the deuyne ordenaunce.

Animaduerto inquam / idque uti tu dicis ita esse / consencio. Sed in hac herentium. &c.

This understande I wel (quod I) & I acorde me that it is right as thou sayst. But I aske if ther be any lyberte of fre wyl in this ordre of causes / that cleuen thus togider in hem self / or els I wolde wyten / if that the destinal cheyn constrayneth the mouynge of the courages of men. Philo. Yes (qd she) ther is lyberte of fre wyl / ne ther ne was neuer no nature of reason / that it ne had liberte or fre wyl. For euery thynge that may naturally usen reason / it hath dome / by whiche it decerneth and demeth euery thinge / Than knoweth it by it selfe thinges that ben to flyen / and thinges that ben to desyren / and thilke thinge that any wight demeth to ben desyred / that asketh or desyreth he / & flyeth thilke thing that he troweth be to flyen. Wherfore in al thinges that reason is / in him also is leberte of wyllynge and of nyllynge / but I ne ordeyne nat / as who sayth / I ne graunt nat / yt this liberte be euen like in al thinges. For why in the souereynes deuynes substaunces / that is to sayn / in spirites / iugement is more clere & wyl nat corrumpe / and mighty redy to speden thinges that ben desyred. But ye soules of mē moten nedes ben more fre / whan they loken hem in the speculacyon or lokynge of the deuyne thought / and lasse fre whan they slyden in to the bodyes / and yet lasse fre whan they ben gadered togider & comprehended in erthlȳ membres / but the last seruage / is whan that they ben yeuen to vices / & haue yfal from the possessyon of her propre reason. For after that they haue cast away her eyen fro the light of the souerayn sothfastnesse / to lowe thinges and darke / anone they darken by the clowde of ygnoraunce / and be troubled by felonous talentes / to the which talētes whan they aprochen and assenten / they heapen and encreasen the seruage whiche they haue ioyned to hem selfe. And in this maner they ben captiues fro her propre liberte / the whiche thinge natheles the lokyng of the deuyne pourueyaunce seeth / that al thinges beholdeth and seeth fro eterne / and ordeyneth hem euerych in her merites / as they ben predestynate / and it is sayd in greke / that al thinges he seeth / & al thinges he hereth.

Puro clarum lumine phebum Melliflui canit oris Homerus. &c.

Homer with the hony mouthe / that is to sayn / Homer with the swete dytees singeth / that the sonne is clere by pure light. Natheles yet ne may it nat by the infirme light of his bemes / breken or percen the inwarde entrayles of the erthe / or els of ye see. So ne seeth nat god maker of the great worlde / to hym yt loketh al thinges from an high / ne understandeth no thinges by heuynesse of erthe / ne the night ne withstandeth nat to him by ye blacke clowdes / thilke god seeth i o stroke of thought al thinges that ben / weren / or shul come : and thilke god / for he loketh and seeth al thinges alone / thou mayst sayne yt he is the very sonne.

Cum ego en inquam difficiliore rursus ambiguitate confundor. &c.

A.a.a.ii. Than

The fyfthe boke of Boecius.

Than sayd I thus/ nowe am I cōfounded by a more harde doute thā I was. Philo. What doute is that (quod she) for certes I coniecte nowe by suche thinges thou art troubled. Boe. It semeth (qd I) to repugnen and to contrary gretly / that god knoweth beforne al thinges/ and that there is any fredom or liberte / for if so be that god loketh al thinges beforne/ ne god ne may not ben deceyued in no maner. Than mote it nedes be/ that al thinges the which that ẏ purueyaunce of god hath sene beforne to come / for whiche if that god knoweth toforne/ nat onely the werkes of men/ but also her counsayls and her wylles/ than ne shal there be no liberte of arbytre / ne certes there ne may be none other dede / ne no wyl/ but thilke whiche that the deuyne purueyaunce (that ne may nat ben deceyued) hath feled beforn/ for if ẏ they mighten writhen awey in other maner than they ben purueyed / than ne shulde there be no stedfast p̄science of thing to comen/ but rather an vncertayn opynion/ the whiche thinge to trowen of god / I deme it felony and vnleful. Ne I ne proue nat thilke same reason/ as who sayth/ I ne alowe nat/ or I ne prayse nat thilke same reason/ by whiche that some men wenen ẏ they mowen assoylen and vnknytten the knotte of this questyon.

For certes they seyn/ that thyng nys nat to comen/ for that ẏ purueyaunce of god hath seen beforne that it is to comen/ but rather the contrary/ and that is this/ that for that ẏ thinges is to comen/ that therfore ne maye it nat ben hyd fro the purueyaunce of god. And in this maner this necessyte slydeth ayen in to the contrary party/ ne it ne behoueth nat nedes / that thinges betyden that ben ypurueyed/ but it behoueth nedes that thinges that ben to comen ben ypurueyed/ but as it were ytrauayled/ as who sayth that thilke answere procedeth right as though men trauayleden or weren busy to enquyren/ the which thing is cause of ẏ which thinges. As whether the prescience is cause of the necessyte of thinges to comen/ or els that ẏ necessyte of thinges to comen is cause of the purueyaunce. But I ne enforce me nat nowe to shewen it/ ẏ the betidynge of thinges ywyst before is necessary/ howe so or in what maner/ ẏ the ordre of causes hath it selfe/ al thoughe that it ne seme nat that ẏ prescyence bring in necessyte of betydyng/ to thinges to comen. For certes if that any wight sytteth / it behoueth by necessyte that the opynyon be sothe of hym that coniecteth that he sytteth/ and ayenwarde also is it of ẏ cōtrary/ for if ẏ opinion be soth of any wight for that he sytteth/ it behoueth by necessyte that he syt. Than is here necessite in that one and in that other: for in that one is necessite of syttynge / and certes in that other is necessyte of soth. But therfore ne sytteth nat a wyght/ for that the opynyon of the syttynge is sothe / but the oppynyon is rather soth for that a wight sytteth beforn. And thus al though that the cause of the sothe cometh of that other syde/ as who sayth/ that althoughe the cause of sothe cometh of the syttyng / and nat of the trewe opinyon/ algates yet is ther a cōmune necessyte in that one & in that other.

Thus seweth it/ that I may make semblable skylles of ẏ purueyaunce of god/ and of thinges to comen. For al though that for that thinges ben to comen/ therfore ben they purueyed/ and nat certes for they ben purueyed/ therfore ne betyde they nat / nathelesse it behoueth by necessyte/ that eyther the thinges to comen ben ypurueyed of god/ or els that the thinges that ben purueyed of god betyden. And this thynges onely suffyseth ynoughe to destroyen the fredom of our arbytre/ that is to sayn/ of our fre wyl. But certes nowe sheweth it wel howe ferre fro the soth/ & howe vp so downe is this thinge/ that we sene that the betidynge of temporal thinges is cause of the eterne prescience. But for to wenen ẏ god purueyeth the thynges to comen / for they ben to comen / What other thinge is it but for to wene / that thylke thinges ẏ betyde whylom/ ben causes of thilk soucrayne purueyaunce that is in god. And here to adde I yet this thynges / that ryght as whan that I wote that a thing is/ it behoueth by necessyte that thilke selfe thinge be; and eke whan I haue knowen that any thinge shall betyden so behoueth it by necessyte that thilke same thinges betyde. So foloweth it than/ that the betydyng of ẏ thinges ywyst beforne ne may nat be eschued/ and at the last / if that

any

any wight wene a thīg to ben otherwyse than it is / [illegible]nys nat onely vnsciēce / but it is deceyuable oppinyon / ful dyuers and ferre fro the soth of science. Wherfore if any thinge be so to comen / that the betydynge of it ne be not certeyne ne necessary / who may weten beforne yͭ thilke thinge is to comen. For right as science ne may nat be medled with falsnesse / as who sayth / that if I wote a thing / it ne may nat be false that I ne wote it / right so thilke thinge yͭ is conceyued by science / ne maye nat be none otherwyse than as it is conceyued / for that is the cause why that science wanteth lesyng / as who sayth / why that wetyng ne receyueth nat lesynge of that it wote / for it behoueth by necessyte that euery thing be right / as science cōprehendeth it to be. What shal I than sayn / in which maner knoweth god beforn al the thynges to comen / if they ne be nat certeyne / for yf yͭ he deme / that they ben to comen vneschuably / and so may be that it is possible yͭ they ne shullen nat comen / god is deceyued / but nat onely to trowen that god is deceyued / but for to speke it with mouth / it is a felonous synne. But if that god wote / that right so as thinges ben to comen / so shullen thy comen / so that he wote egally / as who sayth indifferētly / that thinges may be done / or els nat ydone. What is thilke prescience that ne comprehendeth no certeyne thing ne stable / or els what difference is there bytwene the prescience of thylke iape worthy deuynynge of Tiresie deuynour / that said. Al that I say (quod he) either it shal be / or els it ne shal nat be / or els howe moche is worth the deuyne prescience more than the oppynyon of mankynde / if so be that it demeth the thinges vncerteyne / as men done. Of the whiche domes of men / the betydynge nys nat certeyne. But if so be / yͭ none vncerteyne thinges ne may ben in hym / that is right certeyne wel of al thinges / than is yͭ betydyng certeyne of thilke thinges / whiche that he hath wyst beforne fermely to comen / for which it foloweth that the fredom of the counsayls ⁊ of the werkes of mākynde nys none / syth yͭ the thought of god that seeth al thinges without errour of falsnesse / byndeth and constreyneth hem to a betydynge by necessyte. And if this thinge be ones ygraunted and receyued / this is to sayn / that there nys no fre wyl / than sheweth it wel howe great destructyon ⁊ howe great domages there folowen of thinges of mākynde / for in ydel ben there than purposed and behyght medes to good folke and paines to bad folke / syth that no mouynge of fre courage voluntary / ne hath not deserued hem / that is to sayn neyther mede ne payn. And it shulde seme thā that thilke thinge is alderworst / whiche that is nowe demed for aldermost iust ⁊ most ryghtful. That is to sayne / yͭ shrewes ben punysshed / or els that good folke be yguerdoned / the whiche folkes sene that her propre wyl ne sent hem to that one / ne to that other. That is to sayn / neyther to good ne harme / but constreyneth hem certeyn necessyte of thinges to comē / than ne shullen there neuer ben ne neuer weren vyce ne vertue / but it shullen rather be confusyon of al desertes medled without discrecyon. And yet there foloweth another incōuenience / of yͭ whiche there ne may be thought no more felonous ne more wycked / and that is thus / that so as the ordre of thinges is ysed ⁊ cometh of the purueyaunce of god / ne that no thinge nys leful to the counsayls of mankynde / as who sayth / yͭ men haue no power to don nothīg ne wyl nothīg / than foloweth it yͭ our vices ben referred to yͭ maker of al good / as who saith / than foloweth it yͭ god ought to haue the blame of our vices / syth he constrayneth vs by necessyte to done vyces / than nys there no reason to hoopen in god ne to prayen to god / for what shulde any wyght hopen to god / or why shulde he prayen to god / syth that the ordenaunce of destyne / which that ne may nat ben enclyned / knytteth ⁊ streyneth al thinges that men may desyren. Than shulde there be don away thylke onely alyaunce bytwene god and man / that is to sayn / to hopen and to prayen. But by the pryce of rightwysnesse ⁊ of very mekenesse / we deseruen yͭ guerdon of diuyne grace / whiche that is inestymable / that is to say / that is so gret that it ne may not ben ful praysed / ⁊ this is only the maner / that is to say / hope ⁊ prayers. For whiche it semeth that men wol speke with god / and by reson of supplycacion ben conioyned to thylke clerenesse /

A.a.a.iii. that

that nys nat approched no rather or that men seken it and impetren it. And if men ne wene nat ẏ hope ne prayers/ ne haue no strengthes by the necessyte of thinges to comen receyued/ what thing is ther than/ by which we mowen ben cõioyned & cleuen to thilke souerayn prince of thinges. For which it behoueth by necessyte that the lygnage of mankynde/ as thou song a lytel here beforn/ be departed and vnioyned from his wel/ and faylen of his begynnynge/ that is to sayn god.

Que nam discors federa rerum
Causa resoluit: quis tanta deus. &c.

What discordable cause hath to rente and vnioyned the byndynge or the alyaũce of thinges/ that is to sayn/ the coniunctyons of god & of man: Which god hath establisshed so great batayle bytwene these two sothfast or very thynges/ that is to sayn/ bytwene the purueyaunce of god and fre wyl/ that they ben synguler and deuided/ ne that they ne wolen nat ben medled ne coupled togider: But ther nys no discorde to the very thynges/ but they cleuen alwaye certeyne to hem selfe. But the thought of man confounded & ouerthrowen by the darke membres of ẏ body/ ne may nat by fyre of his darked lokyng/ that is to sayn/ by the vigour of his insight/ whyle ẏ soule is in ẏ body/ knowe the thyn subtel knyttynges of thynges. But wherfore eschaufeth it so by so great loue/ to fynden thilke notes of soth prouered/ that is to sayn/ wherfore eschaufeth the thought of man by so great desyre/ to knowe thilke notificacions that ben yhyd vnder the couertures of soth: wote it ought thilke thing that it anguysshous desyreth to knowe: As who sayth nay. For no man ne trauayleth for to weten thinges that he wote. & therfore ẏ texte sayth thus. But who trauayleth to weten thynges yknowe: and if that he ne knoweth hem nat/ what seketh thilk blynde thought: what is he ẏ desyreth any thinges/ of which he wot right naught: As who sayth/ who so desyreth any thinges/ nedes somwhat he knoweth of it/ or els he ne coude nat desyren it. or who may folowe thinges that ne ben nat ywyst/ & though that he seke the thinges/ where shal he fynde hem: what wight that is al vnconnyng and ygnoraunt may know ẏ forme ẏ is yfoũde. But whan the soule beholdeth & seeth the hye thought/ ẏ is to sayn god/ than knoweth it togyder the some & singularites/ that is to sayn/ the principles/ & eueriche of hem by hym selfe. But now whyle the soule is hyd in the cloude & in the darknesse of the mẽbres of the body/ it ne hath nat al forgeten it selfe/ but it withholdeth the somme of thinges/ and lesyth the syngularites. Than who so that seketh sothnesse/ he nys in neyther nother habyte/ for he wot nat al/ ne he ne hath nat al forgeten/ but yet hym remembreth the sõme of thinges that he withholdeth/ and asketh counsayle/ and retreateth deplych thnyges ysene beforn/ that is to sayn/ the great somme in his mynde/ so that he mowe adden the partes that he hath forgeten to thilke parties that he hath withholden.

Tum illa. Vetus inquit/ hec est de prouidencia querela: Marcoque Tullio. &c.

Than sayd she/ this is (quod she) the olde q̃styon of ẏ purueyãce of god. And Marcus Tullius whan he deuyded the deuinacions/ that is to sayn/ in his bokes that he wrote of deuinacions/ he moued greatly this question/ and thou thy selfe haste ysought it moche/ and vtterly and longe/ but yet ne hath it nat ben determined ne isped fermely and dilygently of any of you/ & ẏ cause of this darknesse and of this difficulte is/ for that the mouinge of the reason of mankynde ne may nat mouen to/ that is to sayn applien or ioynen to the symplicite of the deuine prescience/ the whiche simplicite of the deuine prescience/ if ẏ mẽ mighten thinkẽ it in any maner. That is to sain/ ẏ if men mighten thinke and comprehẽden the thinges ẏ god seeth him self/ than there dwelled vtterly no doute/ the which reason & cause of diffycultees/ I shal assaye at last to shewe & to speden whan I haue first yspended & answered to thy reasons/ by which thou arte moued/ for I aske why thou wenest ẏ thilke reasons of hem ẏ assoylen this q̃stion ne be ne be nat spedefull ynoughe ne suffycyent / the whiche solucion or the whiche reason / for that it demeth / that the prescience is not of necessyte of thynges to come / as who sayth / any other way than thus / but that thilke thynges that the prescience wote beforne / ne maye not unbetyden / that is to sayne / that they moten betyde. But than / if that prescience ne putteth none necessyte to thynges to comen / as thou thy selfe hast confessed it and beknowe a lytel here beforne / what cause or what is it / as who sayth / there may no cause be / by whiche that the endes voluntary of thynges myghten be cōstrayned to certayn betyding. For by grace of posycion / so that thou maye the better understande this that foloweth / I suppose that there ne be no presciēce: Than aske I (qđ she) in as moche as aperteyneth to that / shulden than thynges that comen of fre wyl be constrayned to betyding by necessyte? Bo. Naye (quod I) Phi. Than ayenwarde (qđ she) I suppose that there be prescience / but that it ne putteth no necessyte to thynges / than trowe I that thilke same fredome of wyl shal dwellen al hole and absolute / and unbounden. But thou wylte sayne / that al be it so that prescience nys not cause of the necessyte of betyding to thynges to comen / algates yet it is a signe that the thynges ben to betyden by necessyte. By this maner than although ẏ presciēce had never be / yet algates or at lest way / it is certen thing that endes of betidinges of thīges to comen shulden be necessarye. For every thynge sheweth and signyfyeth onely what the thyng is / but it ne maketh not the thyng that it signifyeth. For whiche it behoveth first to shewe that nothynge ne betydeth / that it ne betydeth by necessyte: so that it may apere that the prescience is signe of necessyte / or els if there nere no necessyte / certes thilke prescience ne myght not be signe of thyng that nys not. But certes it is nowe certayne / that the prove of this yfustened by stedfast reason / ne shal nat ben lad ne proved by signes ne by argumentes / taken fro without / but by causes covenable and necessarye. But thou mayste sayne / howe maye it be that the thynges ne betyden not / that ben purveyed to comen? But certes right as we trowen that the thynges / whiche that the purveyaunce wote beforne / to comen ne be not to betyden. But that ne shulde we not demen / but rather although they shal betyden / yet ne have they no necessite of her kynde to betyden: and this mayste thou lightly aperceyven by this that I shal sayne. For we sene many thynges whan they ben beforn our eyen / right as men sene the carter worchyng in the tournyng & in the attempring or adressyng of his cartes or chariottes / & by this maner / as who sayth / mayste thou understande of al other werkemen. Is ther than any necessite / as who sayth in our lokyng / that constrayneth or compelleth any of thylke thynges to be doone so? Boece. Nay (quod I) for in ydel & in vayne were al the effecte of crafte / if that al thynges weren moved by constraynynge of our eyen or of our syght. Philoso. The thynges than (quod she) that whan that men done hem / ne have no necessyte that men done hem / eke tho same thynges first or they be done / they ben to comen without necessyte: for why there ben some thynges to betyden / of whiche the endes and the betydinges of hem ben absolute and quyte of al necessyte. For certes I ne trowe not that any man wolde sayne this / that the thinges that men done now / that they ne were to betyden first / er they were done. And thilke same thynges / althoughe men hadden wyste hem beforne / yet they have fre betynges. For right as science of thynges present ne bringeth in no necessite to thinges that men done / right so to the prescience of thynges to comen / ne bringeth in none necessyte to thynges to betyden. But thou mayst sayn / that of thilk same it is douted / as whether that of thilke thynges / that ne have none issues and betydinges necessaryes / if therof may ben any prescience. For certes they semen to discorden / for thou wenest that if that thynges ben sene before that necessyte foloweth hem / and if necessyte fayleth hem / they ne mizt not ben wyst before / and that nothyng maye be comprehended by sciēce but certayne. And if tho thinges ne have no certayn betydingz / be purveyed as certayn it shuld be derkenesse of opinion / not sothfastnesse of sciēce. And thou wenest ẏ it be dyvers

fro the

for ŷ holenesse of science/ that any man shulde
deme a thing to be otherwyse than it is it selfe/
and the cause of this errour is/ that of al the
thynges that euery wight hath knowe/ they
wene that tho thynges ben knowe only by the
strength and by the nature of the thynges that
ben wyste or knowe/ and it is al the contrary:
for al that euer is knowe/ it is rather compre-
hended and knowe/ not after his strength and
his nature/ but after the facultie/ that is to
sayne/ the power and the nature of hem that
knowen. And for that this thyng shulde now
shewe by a shorte ensample the roundnesse of
a body/ otherwyse than the syght of the eye
knoweth it/ ⁊ otherwyse than the touchynge.
The lokyng/ by castyng of his beames/ way-
teth and seeth from a ferre al ŷ body togyther/
without mouyng of it selfe/ but the touchyng
cleaueth to the rounde body/ and moueth a-
boute the enuyronnynge/ and comprehendeth
the parties by roundnesse/ and the man hym
selfe otherwyse beholdeth him/ ⁊ otherwayes
ymagynacion/ and otherwyse reason/ ⁊ other-
wyse intelligence: for the wytte comprehen-
deth without forthe the fygure of the body of
man/ that is vnstablysshed in the mater sub-
iecte. But the ymagynacion comprehendeth
only the figure without the mater. Reson sur-
mounteth ymagynacion/ and comprehendeth
by vniuersal lokynge the cōmune spece/ but
the eye of intelligence is higher/ for it surmoū-
teth the enuyronnyng of the vniuersyte/ ⁊ lo-
keth ouer that/ by pure subtylite of thought.
Thilke same symple fourme of man/ that is
perdurable in the diuyne thought/ in whiche
this ought greatly to be consydred/ ŷ the hyest
strength for to comprehenden thinges/ embra-
seth and contayneth the lower strength/ but
the lower strength ne aryseth nat in no maner
to the hyer strength. For wytte ne may com-
prehēde nothyng out of mater/ ne ŷ ymagina-
cion ne loketh not the vniuersal speces/ ne rea-
son ne taketh not the symple forme/ so as in-
telligence taketh it. But intelligence that lo-
keth al abouen/ whan it hath comprehēded the
fourme/ it knoweth ⁊ demeth al the thynges
that ben vnder ŷ forme/ but she knoweth hem
in thylke maner/ in whiche it comprehendeth
thilke same symple forme/ that ne may neuer
ben knowen of none of ŷ other/ that is to say/
to none of tho thre forsayde strengthes of the
soule/ for it knoweth the vnyuersite of reason
and the fygure of ymaginacion/ ⁊ the sensyble
materyal cōceyued by wytte/ ne it ne vseth not
ne of reason/ ne of ymagynacion/ ne of wytte
without forthe/ but it beholdeth al thynges/ so
as I shal say/ by a stroke of thought formely
without discours of collacion. Certes reason
whā it loketh any thing vnyuersal/ it ne vseth
not of ymaginacion ne wytte/ and algates yet
it comprehēdeth the thynges ymagynable and
sensible/ for reason is she that diffynissheth the
vnyuersal of her conceyte right thus. Man is
a resonable two foted beest/ and howe so that
this knowyng is vnyuersal/ yet nys there no
wight that ne wote wel that a man is a thing
ymagynable and sensyble/ and this same con-
sydreth wel reason/ but that nys not by yma-
gynacion/ nor by wytte/ but it loketh it by rea-
sonable conception. Also ymagynacion/ al be
it so that it taketh of wytte the begynnyng/ to
sene ⁊ fourmen the fygures/ algates although
that wytte ne were not present/ yet it enuyron-
neth ⁊ comprehendeth al thynges sensyble/ not
by reason sensyble of demyng/ but by reason
ymagynatife. Seest thou not than that al the
thynges in knowyng vsen more of her faculte
or of her power/ than they done of the faculte
or power of thīges that ben to knowen: ne that
is no wrong/ for so as euery iugemēt is ŷ dede
or doyng of him that demeth/ it behoueth that
euery wight performe his werke ⁊ his entēcion
not of forayn power/ but of his propre power.

Quondam porticus attulit. Obscuros nimium senes. ⁊c.

Whan the porche/ that is to say a gate of
the town of Athenes/ there as philoso-
phers hadden congregacion to dispute/ thilke
porche brought somtyme olde mē ful derke in
her sentences/ that is to say philosophers/ that
hyghten stoiciēs/ that wende that ymages and
sensibylites/ ŷ is to say/ sēsible ymaginacions
or els ymaginacions of sensible thinges/ were
enprīted in to soules fro bodies withoutforth/
as who

as who sayth/thilke stoiciens wenden that the soule had be naked of hym selfe/ as a myrrour or a cleane perchemyne/ so that al fygures musten firste comen fro thynges fro without in to soules/ and ben emprinted in to soules/ ryght as we ben wonte somtyme by a swyfte poyntel to fychen letters emprinted in ẏ smothnesse or in the playnesse of the table of waxe/ or in the parchemyne/ that hath no fygure ne note in it. Glose. But nowe argueth Boece agaynst that opynion/and sayth thus. But if the thriuyng soule ne vnplyteth nothynge/ that is to sayne/ ne dothe thyng by his propre mouyng/but suffreth and lyeth subiecte to the fygures and to the notes of bodyes withoutforth/and yeldeth ymages ydel/yuel & vayne/ in the maner of a myrrour. Whence thriueth than or whence cometh thilke knowyng in our soule/ that discerneth and beholdeth al thynges/ and whence is thilke strength that beholdeth the syngular thynges/or els whence is the strength that diuydeth thynges yknowe/ and thilke strength that gathered togyther thynges deuyded/and strength that choseth the entrechaũged way: For somtyme it heaueth the heed/that is to saye/ that it heaueth vp the entencion to ryght hygh thynges/ and somtyme it discendeth in to right lowe thynges/ & whan it retourneth in to hym selfe/ it reproueth and distroyeth the false thynges by the true thynges. Certes this strength is cause more effycient and moche more myghty/ to sene and to knowen thynges/ than thylke cause that suffreth and receyueth the notes and fygures impressed in maner of mater. Algates the passyon/that is to say/the suffrance or the wytte in the quicke body gothe before excitynge & mouyng the strẽgthes of the thought/ right so as whan that clernesse smyteth the eyen/and moueth hem to sene/ or right so as voyce or sown hurleth to the eeres/and cõmoueth hem to herken/ than is the strengthe of the thought moued & excited/ clepeth forthe to semblable mouynges the speces that it halte within it selfe/ and addeth the speces to the nootes/ and to thynges withoutforth/ and medleth the ymages of thynges without forth/ to thynges hyd within hym selfe.

Quod si in corporibus senciẽdis quamuis efficiant instrumenta sensuum. &c.

BUt what is that in bodyes to be feled/ that is to say/in the takynge and in the knowynge of bodily thynges. And al be it so that the qualitees of bodyes that be obiecte fro without forth/mouen & entalenten the instrumentes of the wyttes/ and al be it so that the passyon of the body/that is to sayne/the wytte or the suffraunce gothe beforne the strength or the worchynge corage/ the whiche passyon or suffraũce clepeth forth the dede of the thought in it selfe/and moueth & exciteth in this meane whyle/ ẏ fourmes that resten within forthe/ & insensible bodies/as I haue said/our corage nys not taught or emprinted by passyon to know these thynges/but demeth & knoweth of his own strength ẏ passion or suffraũce/subiecte to the body: moche more than tho thinges ben absolute and quyte fro al talentes or affections of bodyes/as god or his angels/ ne folowen not in discernyng thinges obiecte fro without forthe/ but they accomplisshen and speden the dedes of her thought. By this reason than there comen many maner of knowynges to dyuers and to differyng substaunces. For the wytte of the body/ the whiche wyt is naked and dispoyled of al other knowyng/ thylke wytte cometh to beestes/ the whiche ne mowen not mouen hem selfe here and there/ as oysters and muskels/ and other suche shelfysshe of the see/that cleuen & ben norisshed to rockes/ but the ymagynacion cometh of remuable beestes/ that semen to haue talent to flyen or to desyren any thyng: But reason is alonely the lynage of mankynde/ ryght as intellygence is alonely the dyuyne nature/ of whiche it foloweth/ that thylke knowynge is more worthe than is eyther/ sens it knoweth by his propre nature not onely his subiecte/as who sayth/it ne knoweth not alonly that appertayneth properly to his knowynge/ but it knoweth the subiectes of al other knowynges. But howe shal it than be/if that witte & ymagynacion stryuen ayen reasonyng/ and sayne that of thylke vniuersal thynge that reason weneth to sene/ that it nys ryght naught/ for

wytte

wytte and ymagynacion sayne/ that that is sesyble or ymaginable/it ne may not ben Vniuersal. Than is there eyther the iugement of reason sothe/ne that there nys nothyng sensyble/or els for that reason wote wel/that many thynges ben subiecte to wytte and to ymagynacion: than is the conception of reson vayne and false/ whiche that loketh and comprehendeth/ that that is sensyble & synguler/ as Vniuersal. And if that the reason wolde answere ayenst these two/ that is to saye/ to wytte and ymaginacion/and say that sothly she her selfe that is to sayne reason/ loketh and comprehendeth by reason of Vniuersalite/bothe that that is sensyble/ and that that is ymaginable/and thilke two/that is to sayne/ wytte and ymaginacion/ ne mowen not stretchen hem selfe to the knowing of Vniuersalite/for that the knowyng of hem ne may not exceden ne surmoūten yͭ bodily fygures. Certes of the knowyng of thynges men oughten rather yeuen more credence to the more stedfaste and to the more perfyte iugement in this maner stryuynge/ than we that haue strength of reasonyng and of ymagynacion/and of wytte/that is to say/ by reason and by ymaginacion/ we wolde rather prayse the cause of reason/ as who sayth/ than the cause of wytte and of ymagynacion. Semblable thyng is it/that the reason of mākynde ne weneth not that the diuyne intellygence/beholdeth or knoweth thynges to come/ but right as the reason of mākynde knoweth hem: for thou arguyst thus/ that if that it ne seme not to men/ that some thynges haue certayne betydinges/ they ne maye not be wyste before certainly to betyden/ and than is there no prescience of thilke thynges: & if we trowe that presciēce be in these thynges/ than is there nothynge that betydeth by necessyte. But if we myght haue the iugement of the diuyne thought/as we ben parteners of reason/right so as we haue demed/ that it behoueth by ymagynacion and wytte/ & beneth reason/ ryght so wold we demen that it were rightful thing/ that mans reason ought to submypt it selfe to be beneth the diuyne thought/for whiche if we may/as who saith/that if we may I coūsayle that we enhaunce vs in the height of thilke souerayne intelligence/for there shal reason wel sene that yͭ it ne may not behold in it self/ and certes that is thus/ in what maner the prescience of god seeth al thynges and diffynissheth/ al though they haue no certayne betydinges: ne this is non opinyon/but rather the symplicite of the souerayne science/ that is not shette within no maner of boundes.

Quā variis terras animalia permeant figuris. Namq; alia extento sūt corpe. &c.

The beestes passen by the erthes by ful dyuers fygures/for some of hem haue her bodyes straught/ and crepen in the duste/& drawen after hem a trace or a forough contynued/ that is to say/ as nedders & snaysles/and other beestes/ by the wandring lightnesse of her wynges beaten the wyndes/& ouer swymmen the spaces of yͤ longe ayre/by moist flyeng. And other beestes gladen hem selfe/to dyggen her traces or her steppes in the erthe with her goynge or with her fete/ and to gone eyther by the grene feldes/or els to walken vnder the woodes. And al be it so that thou seest that they discorden by dyuers fourmes/ algates her faces enclyned heauyeth her dul wyttes/ onely the lynage of man heaueth hyghest his hye heed/ & standeth light with his vpright body/& beholdeth the erthes vnder him. And but if thou erthly man waxest yuel out of thy wytte/this fygure amonesteth the/ that askest the heuen with thy right visage/& hast areysed thy forheed to bearen vp on hygh thy corage/ so yͭ thy thought ne be not heuyed ne put lowe vnder fote/syth yͭ thy body is so high areysed.

Quoniam igitur vti paulo ante monstratum est/omne quod scitur.&c.

Therfore than/as I haue shewed a lytel here beforne. that al thing that is wyst nys not knowen by his nature propre/but by the nature of hem that comprehēden it. Let vs loken nowe/ in as moche as it is leful to vs/ as who sayth/let vs loken nowe as we maye/ whiche yͭ is the estate of the diuyne substaūce/ so yͭ we may wel knowe eke what his sciēce is.

The

The cōmune iugement of al creatures reasonables than is/that god is eterne. Let vs cōsydre than what is eternite/for certes that shal shewen vs togyder the diuyne nature and the diuyne science. Eternyte than is perfyte possessyon/and al togyder of lyfe intermynable/ and that sheweth the more clerely by the comparyson or collacyon of temporal thynges. For al thyng that lyueth in tyme/it is present/ and proceedeth fro preterites in to futures/that is to sayne/ from tyme passed in to tyme comyng: ne there nys no thyng establysshed in tyme/that may enbracen togyther al the space of this lyfe/ for certes yet ne hath it not taken the tyme of to morowe/and it hath lost that of yesterday. And certes in the lyfe of this daye/ ye ne lyuen nomore/ but right as in this mouable and transytorie moment. Than thilke thynge that suffreth temporal condycion/ al though that it neuer began to be/ ne though it neuer cease to be (as Aristoteles demed of the worlde) and although the life of it be stretched with infynite of tyme/ yet algates nys it no suche thynge/ as men myght trowen by right that it is eterne. For al thought that it comprehende and embrace the space of the lyfe infynite/yet algates ne embraseth it not yͭ space of the lyfe al togyther/ for it ne hath not the futures that be not yet: ne it ne hath no lenger the preterites that ben don or passed. But thylke thyng than/that hath and comprehendeth togyder al the plentie of the lyfe intermynable/to whom there ne fayleth naught of the future/ and to whom there nys naught of the preterite escaped or passed/ thilke same is ywitnessed and proued by right to ben eterne. And it behoueth by necessyte that thylke thynge be alway present to him selfe/and competent/ as who sayth/ alway present to him selfe/ and so mighty/ that al be right at his plesaunce/ and that he haue al present yͭ infynite of the mouable tyme. Wherfore some men trowen wrongfully/ that whan they heren that it semed to Plato/that this worlde had neuer begynnyng of tyme/ that it neuer shal haue faylyng: they wene in thilke maner/that this worlde be maked eterne/ with his maker/ as who sayth/ they wene that this worlde and god be maked togyther eterne. And yͭ is a wrongful wenyng/ for other thyng it is to be ladde by the lyfe intermynable/ as Plato grāted to the worlde/ and other thynge it is to embrace togyther/ al the presence of the lyfe that is intermynable/ whiche thyng is clere and manyfest to the diuyne thought. Ne it ne shulde not seme to vs that god is elder than thinges that ben maked by quantyte of tyme/but rather by the proprete of his symple nature. For this ylke infynyte mouynges of tēporal thynges foloweth this presentary estate of this lyfe unmouable/ and so as it ne may not cōtrefayten ne fayne it/ne be euenlyke to it for the inmobilyte/that is to say/ that is in the eternyte of god/ it fayleth & falleth in to mouyng fro the symplycite of the presence of god/ & disencreaseth in the infynite quātyte of future and preterite. And so as it maye not haue togyther al the plentie of the lyfe/ algates yet for as moche as it ceaseth neuer for to ben in some maner/ yet it semeth somdele to vs/that it foloweth and resembleth thylke thyng/ that it ne may not attayne to ne fulfyllen/ and byndeth it selfe to some maner presence of this lytel moment: the whiche presence of this lytel and swyft moment/ for that it beareth a maner ymage or lykenesse of the aye dwellyng of god: it grāteth to suche maner thynges/ as it betydeth to/ that it semeth hem/as these thynges haue ben/and ben. And for that the presence of suche lytel moment ne maye not dwel/therfore it rauysshed and toke th'infynite way of tyme/ yͭ is to saye/ by successyon/ and by this maner it is done/ for that it shulde contynue the lyfe in goyng/ of yͭ whiche lyfe it ne might not enbrace the plentie of dwellyng. And for thy if we wollen put worthy names to thinges that folowen Plato/ let vs saye than sothly/ that god is eterne/ and that the worlde is ꝑpetuel. Than sythe euery iugement knoweth and comprehendeth by his owne nature/thynges that ben subiecte vnto hym/ there is to god alwayes an eterne and a presentarye estate. And the scyence of him that ouerpasseth al temporal moment/ dwelleth in symplicite of his presence/ and enbraseth and considereth al the infynyte spaces of tymes preterytes/ and of tymes futures/ and

And loketh in his symple knowynge al thin-
ges of preterite/ right as they weren ydon pre-
sently right nowe. If thou wylte than thyn-
ken ⁊ aduyse the prescyence/ by whiche it kno-
weth al thinges/thou ne shalt nat demen it as
prescience of thinges to comen/ but thou shalt
demen more rightfully that it is scyence of pre
sence or of instaunce that neuer ne fayleth/for
which it nys not cleped prudence/but it shuld
rather ben cleped puruey aunce/ which is esta-
blysshed ful ferre fro right lowe thinges / and
beholdeth from a ferre al thynges/ right as it
were fro the hye heyght of thynges. Why as-
kest thou than / or why dysputist thou than/
that thilke thynges ben don by necessyte/ whi-
che that ben ysene and yknowen by the deuine
syght/syth ẏ forsoth men ne maken nat thilke
thynges necessary/ whiche that they sene ben
ydon in her syght/ for addeth thy beholdynge
any necessyte/to thylke thyngꝫ which thou be-
holdest present? Bo. Naye (quod I) Philo.
Certes (qđ she) than/ if men mighten maken
any digne comparyson or collacion of the pre-
sence diuyne / and of the presence of man-
kynde: right so as ye sene some thinges in this
temporal presence/ ryght so seeth god al thing
by his eterne presence. Wherfore this diuyne
prescience ne chaungeth not the nature of the
propertie of thynges/but beholdeth such thyn-
ges present to him warde/ as they shulden be-
tyden to you warde in tyme to comen. Ne it
ne confoundeth not the iugementes of thinges/
but by one syght of his thought he knoweth
the thinges to comen/ as wel necessary as not
necessarie. Right so whan ye sene togyther a
man walke on the erthe/and the sonne arysen
in the heuen/ al be it so that ye sene togyther
that one and that other: yet neuerthelesse ye de-
men and discernen / that that one is volunta-
ry/ and that other is necessary: Right so than
the diuyne lokyng/beholdyng al thynges vn-
der hym/ne troubleth nat the qualite of thyn-
ges that ben certeynly present to hymwarde/
but as to the condycyon of tyme / forsoth they
ben future/ for whiche it foloweth/ ẏ this nys
none oppynyon / but rather a stedfast kno-
wynge ystrengthed by sothnesse/ that whan ẏ
god knoweth any thynge to be/ he ne vnwote
nat that thylke thyng wanteth necessyte to be:
this is to sayn / that whan that god knoweth
any thinge to betyde/ he wote wel ẏ it ne hath
no necessyte to betyde. And if thou seyst here
that thilke thing that god seeth to betyde/ it ne
may nat vnbetyde / as who sayth it mote be-
tyde/and thilke thinge that ne may nat vnbe-
tyde/ it mote betyden by necessyte / ⁊ that thou
streyn me to this name of ẏ necessyte. Certes
I wyl wel confessen and beknowen a thynge
of ful sad trouthe / but vnneth shal there any
wight mowe sene it or come therto/but if that
he be beholder of ẏ deuyne thought/for I wyl
answere the thus/that thilke thyng that is fu-
tur/whā it is referred to the deuine knowing/
than it is necessary. But certes whan it is vn-
derstanden in his owne kynde/men sene it vt-
terly fre and absolute fro al necessyte. For cer-
tes there ben two maners of necessyteꝭs / that
one necessyte is simple/as thus / ẏ it behoueth
by necessyte/that al men ben mortal or dedly.
Another necessyte is condycyonel/as thus / yf
thou wost that a man walketh/it behoueth by
necessyte that he walke/thilke thing than that
any wight hath yknowe to be / it ne may nat
be none other wyse than he knoweth it to be.
But this condicion ne draweth nat with her
thilke necessyte simple/for certes this necessyte
condicionel/the propre nature of it ne maketh
it nat/but the adiection of the condycyon ma-
keth it. For no necessyte ne constrayneth a mā
to gon/that goth by his propre wyl/ al be it so
that whan he goth/that it is necessary that he
goth. Ryght on this same maner than/if that
the purueyaunce of god seeth any thyng pre-
sent/than mote thilke thinge ben by necessyte/
al thoughe that it ne haue no necessyte of his
owne nature. But certes the futures that be-
tyden by fredom of arbytrie/ god seeth hem al
togyder present. These thinges thā if they ben
referred to the deuyne syght/thā ben they ma-
ked necessary by the condicyon of the deuyne
knowynge. But certes/if thilke thynges ben
consydered by hem selfe / they ben absolute of
necessyte/and ne forleten not/ ne cessen nat of
the lyberte of her owne nature. Than certes
without doute al the thinges shullen ben don/
whiche that god woot beforne that they ben to
comen

comen and betyden of free arbytrie/or of frewyl/that al be it so that they betyden/ yet algates ne lese they not her propre nature in beynge/ by the whiche first or they weren done/ they hadden power not to haue betydde. Bo. What is this to sayne than (qđ I) that thynges ne be not necessarye by her propre nature/ so that they comen in al maners in the lykenesse of necessyte/ by condycion of the diuyne science: Philo. This is the difference (qđ she) that tho thynges whiche that I purposed the a lytel here beforne/ that is to sayne/ sonne arysyng/and the man walkyng/that therwhyles that thilke thynges ben don/they ne might not ben vndone. Nathelesse that one of hem or it was done/it behoueth by necessyte that it was doone/ but not that other. Right so it is here that the thynges which that god hath present/ withouten doute they shullen ben/ but some of hem discendeth of the nature of thynges/ as the sonne arysynge/ and some discendeth of the power of the doers/ as the man walkyng. Boece. Than sayd I/ no wronge/ that if these thynges be referred to the diuyne knowynge/ than ben they necessarye/ and if they ben consydred by hem selfe/than ben they absolute fro the bonde of necessyte. Right so as al thynges that apereth or sheweth to the wittes/if thou referre hem to reason it is vnyuersal/and if thou loke it or refer it to it selfe/ than is it synguler. But nowe if thou sayest thus/ that if that it be in my power to chaungen my purpose/than shal I voyden the purueyaunce of god/ whan perauenture I shal haue chaunged the thynges whiche ẏ he knoweth beforne. Philo. Than shal I answeren the thus: Certes thou mayste wel chaunge thy purpose/but for as moche as the present sothnesse of the diuyne purueyaūce beholdeth that thou mayste chaunge thy purpose/ and whether thou chaunge it or no/ and whyderwarde that thou tourne it/thou ne mayste not eschue the diuyne prescience: right so thou ne mayste not flye the syght of the present eye/ al though that thou tourne thy selfe by thy fre wyl in to dyuers actions. But thou mayste sayne ayen to this thus: Howe shal it than be/shal not the diuyne science ben chaunged by my disposytion/ whan that I wyl one thyng nowe/ and nowe another thyng: And thilke prescience ne semeth it not to entrechaūge stoundes of knowynge/as who sayth/ ne shal it not semen to vs/ that the diuyne prescience entrechaungeth his dyuers stoundes of knowynge/ so that it knowe somtyme one thynge/ and somtyme it knoweth the contrarie of that thyng: Philo.

No forsothe (quod she) for the diuyne syght renneth beforne and seeth al the futures/ and clepeth hem ayen/ and retourneth hem to the propre prescience of his propre knowynge/ ne he entrechaungeth not/ so as thou wenest the stoundes of his foreknowyng/ as nowe this/ nowe that: but he dwellynge aye cometh beforne/ and enbraseth at o stroke al the mutacions. And this prescience to comprehenden and to sene al thinges/ god ne hath not taken it of the betydinges of thinges to comen/ but of his propre symplicite. And hereby is assoyled thilke thinges that thou puttest a lytel here beforne/ that is to sayne/ that it is vnworthy thyng to sayn that our futures yeuen cause of the prescience of god. For certes strength of the diuyne science/ whiche that enbraseth al thinges by his presentarie knowyng/establissheth maner to al thynges/ and it ne oweth not to latter thynges. And sythe ẏ these thynges ben thus/that is to sayne/ that necessyte is not in thynges by the diuyne prescience/ than is there fredom of arbytrie that dwelleth hole and vnwemmed to mortal men/ ne the lawes ne pourposen not wicked medes and paynes to the wyllinges of men/that ben vnbounden and quyte of al necessyte: And god beholder and foreweter of al thynges dwelleth aboue/ and the presente eternyte of syght/ renneth alwaye with the dyuers qualyte of our dedes/ dispensyng or ordeynyng medes to good men/ and tourmētes to wicked men. Ne in ydel ne in vayne ne ben there not put in god hope and prayers/that ne mowen not ben vnspedeful/ ne without effecte/ whan they ben rightful.

Withstande than and eschewe thou vyces/ worshyppe and loue thou vertues/ areyse thy corage to rightful hopes/ yelde thou humble prayers and hyghe. Great necessyte of prowesse and of vertue is encharged and com-

B.b.b. maūd

maunded to you if ye nyl not diſſimulen/ ſyth that ye worchen and doone/ that is to ſayne/ your dedes and your werkes beforne the eyen of the iuge/ that ſeeth and alſo that demeth al thynges. Deo gracias.

¶ Thus endeth the boke of Boecius of the conſolacion of philoſophie/ and hereafter foloweth the dreame of Chaucer.

The dreame of Chaucer.

I Haue great wonder by this light
Howe I lyue/for day ne nyght
I may not slepe/ welny nought
I haue so many an ydle thought
Purely for defaute of slepe
That by my trouthe/ I take no kepe
Of nothyng/howe it cometh or gothe
Ne me nys nothyng lefe nor lothe
Al is ilyche good to me
Joye or sorowe/ where so it be
For I haue felyng in no thyng
But as it were a mased thyng
Alday in poynte to fal adoun
For sorouful ymagynacioun
Is alway holy in my mynde
And wel ye wote/agaynst kynde
It were to lyuen in this wyse
For nature wolde not suffyse
To none erthly creature
Not longe tyme to endure
Without slepe/and be in sorowe
And I ne maye, ne nyght ne morowe
Slepe/and this melancolye
And drede I haue for to dye
Defaute of slepe and heuynesse
Hath slayne my spyrite of quicknesse
That I haue loste al lustyheed
Suche fantasyes ben in myn heed
So I not what is beste to do
But men might aske me why so
I may not slepe/and what me is
But nathelesse/ who aske this
Leseth his askyng trewly
My seluen can not tel why
The sothe/ but trewly as I gesse
I holde it be a sicknesse
That I haue suffred this eyght yere
And yet my boote is neuer the nere
For there is phisycien but one
That may me heale/but that is done
Passe we ouer untyl efte
That wyl not be/mote nede be lefte
Our first mater is good to kepe
So whan I sawe I might not slepe
Tyl nowe late/this other nyght
Upon my bedde I sate upright
And bade one reche me a booke
A romaunce/and he it me toke
To rede/and driue the nyght away
For me thought it better play
Than play eyther at Chesse or tables
And in this boke were written fables
That clerkes had in olde tyme
And other poetes/put in ryme
To rede/and for to be in mynde
Whyle men loued the lawe of kynde
This boke ne spake/but of suche thynges
Of quenes lyues/and of kynges
And many other thinges smale
Amonge al this I fonde a tale
That me thought a wonder thyng.
This was the tale: There was a kyng
That hyght Seys/and had a wyfe
The beste that myght beare lyfe
And this quene hyght Alcyone
So it befyl/therafter sone
This kyng wol wenden ouer see
To tellen shortly/whan that he
Was in the see/thus in this wyse
Suche a tempest gan to ryse
That brake her maste/and made it fal
And clefte her shyp/and dreynt hem al
That neuer was founde/as it telles
Borde ne man/ne nothyng elles
Right thus this kyng Seys loste his lyfe
Nowe for to speke of Alcyone his wyfe
This lady that was lefte at home
Hath wonder/ that the kyng ne come
Home/for it was a longe terme
Anon her herte began to yerne
And for that her thought euermo
It was not wele/her thought so
She longed so after the kyng
That certes it were a pytous thyng
To tel her hertely sorouful lyfe
That she had/this noble wyfe
For him alas/she loued alderbest
Anon she sent bothe eest and west
To seke him/but they founde nought
Alas (quod she) that I was wrought
And wher my lorde my loue be deed?
Certes I nyl neuer eate breed
I make a vowe to my god here
But I mowe of my lorde here
Suche sorowe this lady to her toke
That trewly/I that made this boke

V.b.b.ii. Had

Had suche pyte/and suche routhe
To rede her sorowe/that by my trouthe
I farde the worse al the morowe
After to thinken on her sorowe
  So whan this lady coude here no worde
That no man myght fynde her lorde
Ful ofte she swowned/ and sayd alas
For sorowe/ ful nighe woode she was
Ne she coude no rede but one
But downe on knees she sate anone
And wepte/that pyte was to here
  A mercy swete lady dere
(Quod she) to Juno her goddesse
Helpe me out of this distresse
And yeue me grace my lorde to se
Soone/ or wete where so he be
Or howe he fareth/or in what wyse
And I shal make you sacrifyse
And holy yours become I shal
With good wyl/body/herte and al
And but thou wolte this/lady swete
Sende me grace to slepe and mete
In my slepe some certayne sweuen
Where through that I may knowe euen
Whether my lorde be quicke or deed
  With that worde she hynge downe the heed
And fel in a swoune/ as colde as stone
Her women caught her vp anone
And brought her in bed al naked
And she forweped and forwaked
Was wery/and thus the deed slepe
Fel on her/ or she toke kepe
Through Juno/ that had herde her boone
That made her to slepe soone
For as she prayde/right so was don
In dede/for Juno right anon
Called thus her messangere
To do her erande/ and he come nere
Whan he was come/she bad hym thus
  Go bet (quod Juno) to Morpheus
Thou knowest hym wel/ the god of slepe
Nowe vnderstande wel/and take kepe
Saye thus on my halfe/ that he
Go fast in to the great see
And byd hym that on al thynge
He take vp Seys body the kynge
That lyeth ful pale/ and nothynge rody
Byd hym crepe in to the body
And do it gone to Alcyone
The quene/ there she lyeth alone
And shewe her shortely it is no nay
Howe it was dreynt this other day
And do the body speke right so
Right as it was woned to do
The whyles that it was alyue
Go nowe fast/ and hye the blyue.
  This messanger toke leue and wente
Vpon his way/ and neuer he stente
Tyl he came to the darke valey
That stante bytwene rockes twey
There neuer yet grewe corne ne gras
Ne tree/ne naught that ought was
Beest ne man/ ne nought elles
Saue that there were a fewe welles
Came rennynge fro the clyffes adowne
That made a deedly slepynge sowne
And rennen downe right by a caue
That was vnder a rocke ygraue
Amyd the valey wonder depe
There these goddes lay aslepe
Morpheus and Eclympasteyre
That was the god of slepes heyre
That slepte/ and dyd none other werke
  This caue was also as derke
As hel pytte/ ouer al aboute
They had good leyser for to route
To vye who might slepe best
Some hynge her chynne vpon her brest
And slepte vpright her heed yhed
And some lay naked in her bed
And slepte whyles theyr dayes last
  This messanger come rennyng fast
And cryed ho ho/ awake anone
It was for nought/ there herde hym none
Awake (quod he) who lyeth there
And blewe his horne right in her eere
And cryed awaketh wonder hye
  This god of slepe/ with his one eye
Cast vp/and asked who clepeth there
It am I (quod this messangere)
Juno bade thou shuldest gone
And tolde hym what he shulde done
As I haue tolde you here before
It is no nede reherse it more
And wente his way whan he had sayde
  Anone this god of slepe abrayde

Out

Out of his slepe and gan to go
And dyd as he had bydde hym do
Toke up the dede body soone
And bare it forthe to Alcione
His wyfe the quene/there as she lay
Right euen a quarter before day
And stode right at her beddes fete
And called her right as she hete
By name/ and sayd: My swete wyfe
Awake/let be your sorowful lyfe
For in your sorowe /there lyth no rede
For certes swete loue/I am but dede
Ye shal me neuer on lyue yse
But good swete herte that ye
Bury my body/for suche a tyde
ye mowe it fynde/the see besyde
And farewel swete/my worldes blysse
I praye god your sorowe lysse
To lytel whyle our blysse lasteth
  With that her eyen up she casteth
And sawe naught/alas(quod she) for sorowe
And dyed within the thyrde morowe
  But what she sayd more in that swowe
I may nat tel you as nowe
It were to longe for to dwel
My fyrst matere I wyl you tel
Wherfore I haue tolde this thynge
Of Alcione/and Seys the kynge
  For thus moche dare I say wel
I had be doluen euerydel
And deed/ right through defaute of slepe
If I ne had red/and take kepe
Of this tale nexte before
And I wyl tel you wherfore
For I ne myght for bote ne bale
Slepe/ or I had redde this tale
Of this dreynte Seys the kynge
And of the goddes of sleppynge
  Whan I had red this tale wele
And ouerloked it euerydele
Me thought wonder/if it were so
For I had neuer herde speke or tho
Of no goddes/that coude make
Men to slepe/ne for to wake
For I ne knewe neuer god but one
And in my game/I sayd anone
And yet me lyst ryght euyl to pley
Rather than that I shulde dey

 Through defaute of sleppynge thus
I wolde gyue thylke Morpheus
Or that goddesse dame Juno
Or some wyght els/I ne rought who
To make me slepe/and haue some rest
I wyl gyue hym the alther best
yefte/that euer he abode his lyue
And here onwarde/ ryght nowe as blyue
If he wol make me slepe a lyte
Of downe of pure dowues whyte
I wol gyue hym a fether bed
Rayed with golde/ and right wel cled
In fyne blacke Sattyn doutremere
And many a pylowe/and euery bere
Of clothe of raynes to slepe on softe
Hym thare nat nede to tourne ofte
And I wol yeue hym al that falles
To his chambre and to his halles
I wol do paynte with pure golde
And tappyte hem ful many folde
Of one sute this shal he haue
If I wyst where were his caue
If he can make me slepe sone
As dyd the goddesse/ quene Alcione
And thus this ylke god Morpheus
May wynne of me mo fees thus
Than euer he wanne/and to Juno
That is his goddesse/I shal so do
I trowe that she shal holde her payde.
  I had unneth that worde ysayde
Ryght thus as I haue tolde you
That sodeynly I nyst howe
Suche a lust anone me toke
To slepe/that ryght upon my boke
I fel a slepe/ and therwith euen
Me mette so inly suche a sweuen
So wonderful/ that neuer yet
I trowe no man had the wyt
To conne wel my sweuen rede
  No nought Joseph without drede
Of Egypte/he that rad so
The kynges metynge Pharao
No more than coude the lest of us
 Ne nat scarsly Macrobeus
He that wrote al the auysyon
That he met kynge Scipion
The noble man the Affrican
Suche meruayles fortuned than

B.B.b.iii. I trowe

The dreame of Chaucer.

I trowe a rede my dremes even
Lo thus it was/ this was my sweven.
Me thought thus/that it was Maye
And in the dawnynge there I laye
Me met thus in my bed al naked
And loked forthe/for I was waked
With smale foules a great hepe
That had afrayed me out of my slepe
Through noyse/ and swetnesse of her songe
And as me met/they sate amonge
Vpon my chambre rose without
Vpon the tyles over al about
And everyche songe in his wyse
The most solempne servyse
Be note/that ever man I trowe
Had herde/for some of hem songe lowe
Some hygh/ and al of one acorde
To tel shortly at o worde
Was never herde so swete steven
But it had be a thynge of heven
So mery a sowne/ so swete entunes
That certes for the towne of Tewnes
I nolde/but I had herde hem synge
For al my chambre gan to rynge
Throughe syngynge of her ermony
For instrument/nor melody
Was no where herde/yet halfe so swete
Nor of acorde halfe so mete
For there was none of hem that fayned
To synge/for eche of hem hym payned
To fynde out many crafty notes
They ne spared nat her throtes
And sothe to sayne/my chambre was
Ful wel depaynted/and with glas
Were al the wyndowes/ wel yglased
Ful clere/and nat an hole crased
That to beholde it was great ioy
For holly al the story of Troy
Was in the glasynge ywrought thus
Of Hector/ and of kynge Priamus
Of Achylles/ and of kynge Lamedon
And eke of Medea/and of Iason
Of Paris/ Heleyne/ and of Lavyne
And al the walles with colours fyne
Were paynte/bothe texte and glose
And al the Romaunce of the rose
My wyndowes weren shyt echone
And throughe the glasse the sonne shone
Vpon my bedde with bryght bemes
With many glad gyldy stremes
And eke the welkyn was so fayre
Blewe/bryght/clere was the ayre
And ful atempre /forsothe it was
For neyther to colde/ ne hote it nas
Ne in al the welkyn was no clowde
And as I lay thus wonder lowde
Me thought I herde an hunte blowe
Tassay his great horne/ and for to knowe
Whether it was clere/or horse of sowne
And I herde goynge bothe vp and downe
Men/horse/houndes/and other thynge
And al men speke of huntynge
Howe they wolde slee the harte with strength
And howe the harte had vpon length
So moche embosed/ I not nowe what
Anone ryght whan I herde that
Howe that they wolde/on huntynge gone
I was ryght glad/and vp anone
Toke my horse/ and forthe I wente
Out of my chambre/ I never stente
Tyl I come to the felde without
There over toke I a grete route
Of hunters/and eke of forsters
And many relayes and lymers
And hyed hem to the forest fast
And I with hem/so at the last
I asked one ladde/ a lymere
Say felowe/ who shal hunte here
(Quod I) and he answered ayen
Syr/ the Emperour Octoyen
(Quod he)and is here fast by
A goddes halfe/ in good tyme (quod I)
Go we fast/and gan to ryde
Whan we come to the forest syde
Every man dyd ryght soone
As to huntynge fel to done
The mayster hunte/anone fote hote
With his horne blewe thre mote
At the vncouplynge of his houndes
Within a whyle/the harte founde is
Ihalowed/ and rechased fast
Longe tyme/and so at the last
This harte rused and stale away
Fro al the houndes a prevy way
The houndes had over shot hym al
And were vpon a defaulte yfal.

Ther-

Therwith the hunte/wonder faste
Blewe a forloyn at the laste
I was go walked fro my tre
And as I went/there came by me
A whelpe/that fawned me as I stoode
That had yfolowed/ and coude no goode
It came and crepte to me as lowe
Right as it had me yknowe
Helde downe his heed/and ioyned his eeres
And layde al smothe downe his heeres
 I wolde haue caught it anone
It fledde/and was fro me gone
As I him folowed/and it forthe went
Downe by a floury grene it went
Ful thycke of grasse/ful softe and swete
With floures fele/fayre vnder fete
And lytel vsed/it semed thus
For bothe Flora/and zepherus
They two/that make floures growe
Had made her dwellyng there I trowe
For it was on to beholde
As though the erthe enuye wolde
To be gayer than the heuen
To haue mo floures/suche seuen
As in the welken sterres be
It had forget the pouerte
That wynter/through his colde morowes
Had made it suffre/and his sorowes
Al was foryeten/and that was sene
For al the woode was woxen grene
Swetnesse of dewe/had made it waxe
 It is no nede eke for to axe
Where there were many grene greues
Of thycke of trees/so ful of leues
And euery tree stode by him selue
Fro other/ wel ten foote or twelue
So great trees/so huge of strength
Of fourty or fyfty fedome length
Cleane without bowe or stycke
With croppes brode/and eke as thycke
They were not an ynche a sonder
That it was shadde ouer al vnder
And many an hart/ and many an hynde
Was bothe before me/and behynde
Of fawnes/ sowers/ buckes/ does
Was ful the wodde/and many roes
And many squyrels/that sete
Ful hygh vpon the trees and ete
And in her maner made feestes
Shortly/it was so ful of beestes
That though Argus/the noble countour
Sate to reken in his countour
And reken with his fygures ten
For by tho fygures newe al ken
If they be crafty/reken and nombre
And tel of euery thyng the nombre
Yet shulde he fayle to reken euen
The wonders me met in my sweuen
But forthe I romed/right wonder faste
Downe the woode/so at the laste
I was ware of a man in blacke
That sate/and had yturned his backe
To an ooke/an huge tree
Lorde thought I/who may that be
What ayleth him to sytten here
Anon right/I went nere
Than founde I sytte/euen vpright
A wonder welfaryng knyght
By the maner me thought so
Of good mokel/and right yonge therto
Of the age of foure and twenty yere
Vpon his berde/but lytel heere
And he was clothed al in blacke
I stalked euen vnto his backe
And there I stode/as styl as ought
The sothe to say/he sawe me nought
For why he hynge his heed adowne
And with a dedly/sorouful sowne
He made of ryme/ten verses or twelue
Of a complaynt/to him selue
The moste pyte/the moste routhe
That euer I herde/for by my trouthe
It was great wonder that nature
Myght suffre any creature
To haue suche sorowe/and he not deed
Ful pytous pale/and nothyng reed
He sayd a lay/a maner songe
Without note/ without songe
And was this/for ful wel I can
Reherse it/right thus it began
 I haue of sorowe so great wone
That ioye gette I neuer none
Nowe that I se my lady bright
Whiche I haue loued/withal my myght
Is fro me deed/and is agone
And thus in sorowe/lefte me alone

Alas

Alas dethe/ what ayleth the
That thou noldest haue taken me
Whan that thou toke my lady swete
Of al goodnesse/ she had none mete
That was so fayre/ so fresshe/ so fre
So good/ that men may wel se
  Whan he had made thus his complaynte
His sorouful herte/ gan faste faynte
And his spyrites weyen dede
The bloode was fledde/ for pure drede
Downe to his herte/ to maken him warme
For wel it feled the herte had harme
To wete eke/ why it was adradde
By kynde/ and for to make it gladde
For it is membre principal
Of the body/ and that made al
His hewe chaunge/ and weye grene
And pale/ for there no bloode is sene
In no maner lymme of his
  Anon therwith/ whan I sawe this
He farde thus yuel/ there he sete
I went and stode right at his fete
And grette him/ but he spake nought
But argued with his owne thought
And in his wytte/ disputed faste
Why/ and howe his lyfe might laste
Him thought his sorowes were so smerte
And lay so colde vpon his herte
  So through his sorowe/ and holy thought
Made hym that he herde me nought
For he had welnye loste his mynde
Though Pan/ that men clepeth god of kynde
Were for his sorowes neuer so wrothe
  But at the laste/ to sayne right sothe
He was ware of me/ howe I stoode
Before him/ and dyd of my hoode
And had ygret him/ as I best coude
Debonairly/ and nothyng loude
He sayd/ I pray the be not wrothe
I herde the not/ to sayne the sothe
Ne I sawe the not/ sir trewly
  Ah good sir/ no force (quod I)
I am right sory/ if I haue ought
Distroubled you/ out of your thought
Foryeue me/ if I haue mysse take
  Yes/ thamendes is lyght to make
(Quod he) for there lyth none therto
There is nothyng missayde/ nor do
  Lo howe goodly spake this knyght
As it had be another wyght
And made it neyther tough ne queynt
And I sawe that/ and gan me aqueynt
With him/ and founde him so tretable
Right wonder skylful/ and resonable
As me thought/ for al his bale
Anon right/ I gan fynde a tale
To hym/ to loke where I might ought
Haue more knowlegyng of his thought
  Sir (quod I) this game is done
I holde that this herte be gone
These huntes can him no where se
  I do no force therof (quod he)
My thought is theron neuer a dele
  By our lorde (quod I) I trowe you wele
Right so me thynketh by your chere
But sir/ o thyng wol ye here
Me thynketh in great sorowe I you se
But certes sir/ if that ye
Wolde aught discure me your wo
I wolde/ as wyse god helpe me so
Amende it/ if I can or may
Ye mowe proue it by assay
For by my trouthe/ to make you hole
I wol do al my power hole
And telleth me/ of your sorowes smerte
Parauenter it may ease your herte
That semeth ful syke vnder your syde
  With that he loked on me a syde
As who sayth nay/ that wyl not be
  Graunt mercy good frende (quod he)
I thanke the/ that thou woldest so
But it may neuer the rather be do
No man may my sorowe glade
That maketh my hewe to fal and fade
And hath myn vnderstondyng lorne
That me is wo/ that I was borne
May naught make my sorowes slyde
Not al the remedyes of Ouyde
Ne Orpheus/ god of melodye
Ne Dedalus/ with his playes slye
Ne heale me/ may no phisycien
Naught Ipocras/ ne Galyen
Me is wo/ that I lyue houres twelue
But who so wol assay him selue
Whether his herte can haue pyte
Of any sorowe/ lette him se me

I wretche

I wretche/that dethe hath made al naked
Of al the blysse that euer was maked
I wrothe/ werste of al wightes
That hate my dayes/ and my nightes
My lyfe/ my lustes/be me lothe
For al fare and I be wrothe
The pure deth is so ful my foe
That I wolde dye/it wyl nat so
For whan I folowe it/it wyl flye
I wolde haue hym/it nyl nat me
This is payne without reed
Alway dyenge/and be nat deed
That Tesyphus that lyeth in hel
May nat of more sorowe tel
And who so wyste al/ by my trouthe
My sorowe/but he had routhe
And pyte of my sorowes smerte
That man hath a fendely herte
For who so seeth me first on morowe
May sayne he hath mette with sorowe
For I am sorowe/and sorowe is I
Alas/and I wyl tel the why
My sorowe is turned to playnyng
And al my laughter to wepyng
My glad thoughtes/to heuynesse
In trauayle is myn ydlenesse
And eke my rest/my wele is wo
My good is harme/and euermo
In wrathe is turned my playeng
And my delyte in to sorowyng
Myn heale is turned in to sicknesse
In drede is al my sykernesse
To derke is turned al my lyght
My wytte is foly/ my day is nyght
My loue is hate/my slepe wakyng
My myrthe and meles/is fastyng
My countenaunce is nycete
And al abawed/ where so I be
My peace pledyng/ and in werre
Alas/ howe might I fare werre
My boldenesse is turned to shame
For false fortune/hath played a game
At the Chesse with me/alas the whyle
The trayteresse false/and ful of gyle
That al behoteth/and nothyng halte
She gothe vpright/and yet she halte
That baggeth foule/and loketh fayre
The dispytous debonayre
That scorneth many a creature
An ydole of false purtrayture
Is she/for she wol sone wryen
She is the monstres heed ywryen
As fylthe/ouer ystrowed with floures
Her moste worshyp and her floures
To lyen/for that is her nature
Without faythe/lawe/ or mesure
She false is/and euer laughyng
With one eye/ and that other wepyng
That is brought vp/she set al downe
I lyken her to the Scorpiowne
That is a false flatterynge beest
For with his heed he maketh feest
But al amyd his flaterynge
With his tayle he wyl stynge
And enuenym/ and so wyl she
She is the enuyous charyte
That is aye false/ and semeth wele
So turneth she her false whele
Aboute/for it is nothinge stable
Nowe by the fyre/ nowe at table
Ful many one hath she thus yblent
She is playe of enchauntement
That semeth one/and is nat so
The false thefe/what hath she do
Trowest thou/ by our lorde I wyl the say
At the Chesse with me she gan to play
With her false draughtes ful dyuers
She stale on me/ and toke my feers
And whan I sawe my feers away
Alas/I couthe no lenger play
But sayd/fare wel swete ywys
And fare wel al that euer there is
Therwith fortune sayd/checke here
And mate in the mydde poynte of ye checkere
With a paune errant/ alas
Ful craftyer to play she was
Than Athalus that made the game
Fyrst of the Chesse/ so was his name
But god wolde I had ones or twyse
Ycoude/ and knowe the ieoperdyse
That coude the Greke Pithagores
I shulde haue playde the bet at ches
And kepte my feers the bet therby
And though wherto/ for truely
I holde that wysshe nat worth a stre
It had be neuer the bet for me

For

For fortune can so many a wyle
There be but fewe/can her begyle
And eke she is the lasse to blame
My selfe I wolde haue do the same
Before god/had I ben as she
She ought the more excused be
For this I say/yet more therto
Had I be god/and myght haue do
My wyl/whan she my feers caught
I wolde haue drawe the same draught
For al so wyse/god gyue me rest
I dare wel swere/ she toke the best
But throughe that draught I haue lorne
My blysse/alas that I was borne
For euermore I trowe truely
For al my wyl/ my lust holy
Is tourned/but ye/ what to done
By our lorde it is to dye sone
For nothynge I leaue it nought
But lyue and dye/right in this thought
For there nys planet in fyrmament
Ne in ayre ne in erthe none element
That they ne yeue me a yefte echone
Of weppynge whan I am alone
For whan that I aduyse me wele
And bethynke me euery dele
Howe that there lyeth in rekenynge
In my sorowe for nothynge
And howe there lyueth no gladnesse
May glad me of my dystresse
And howe I haue lost suffysaunce
And therto I haue no plesaunce
Than may I say/I haue right nought
And whan al this falleth in my thought
Alas/than am I ouercome
For that is don/is nat to come
I haue more sorowe than Tantale
  And whan I herde hym tel this tale
Thus pytuously/as I you tel
Vnnethe myght I lenger dwel
It dyd myne herte so moche wo
  A good syr (quod I) say nat so
Haue some pyte on your nature
That formed you to creature
Remembreth you of Socrates
For he ne counted nat thre strees
Of nought that fortune coude do
  No (quod he) I can nat so.
Why so good syr/ yes perde (quod I)
Ne say not so/for truely
Though ye had lost the ferses twelue
And ye for sorowe murdred your selue
Ye shulde be dampned in this case
By as good right as Medea was
That slough her chyldren for Iason
And Phyllis also/for Demophon
Hynge her selfe/so welaway
For he had broke his terme day
To come to her: Another rage
Had Dido/ the quene eke of Cartage
That slough her selfe/for Eneas
Was false/whiche a foole she was:
And Ecquo dyed/for Narcisus
Nolde nat loue her/and right thus
Hath many another foly done
And for Dalida dyed Sampson
That slough hym selfe with a pylere
But there is no man alyue here
Wolde for her feers make this wo
  Why so (quod he) it is nat so.
Thou wotest ful lytel what thou menest
I haue lost more than thou wenest
  Howe that may be (quod I)
Good syr/tel me al holy
In what wyse/howe/why/and wherfore
That ye haue thus your blysse lore
  Blythely (quod he) come syt doun
I tel the vpon a condycyoun
That thou shalte holy with al thy wyt
Do thyne entente to herken it
  Yes syr: Swere thy trouth therto
Gladly do than holde here to
I shal right blythely/ so god me saue
Holy with al the wyt I haue
Here you as wel as I can
A goddes halfe (quod he) and began
  Syr (quod he) syth fyrst I couthe
Haue any maner wyt fro youthe
Or kyndely vnderstandynge
To comprehende in any thynge
What loue was/in myne owne wyt
Dredelesse I haue euer yet
Be trybutary/and yeue rente
To loue holy/with good entente
And through plesaunce/become his thral
With good wyl/body/ herte and al

Al this

Al this I put in his seruage
As to my lorde/and dyd homage
And ful deuoutely I prayde him to
He shulde beset myn herte so
That it plesaunce to him were
And worshyp to my lady dere
And this was longe/and many a yere
(Er that myn herte was set owhere)
That I dyd thus/and nyste why
I trowe it came me kyndely
Paraunter I was therto moste able
As a whyte wal/ or a table
For it is redy to kecche and take
Al that men wyl therin make
Whether so men wol portrey or paynte
Be the werkes neuer so quaynte.
And thylke tyme I fared right so
I was able to haue lerned tho
And to haue conde/as wel or better
Paraunter/ eyther arte or letter
But for loue came first in my thought
Therfore I forgate it nought
I chees loue to my first crafte
Therfore it is with me lafte
For why/ I toke it of so yonge age
That malyce had my corage
Not that tyme/turned to no thyng
Through to mokel knowlegyng
For that tyme/youthe my maystresse
Gouerned me in ydelnesse
For it was in my first youthe
And tho ful lytel good I couthe
For al my werkes were flyttyng
That tyme/and al my thought varyeng
Al were to me lyche goode
That I knewe tho/ but thus it stode.
It happed that I came on a day
In to a place/there that I sey
Trewly the fayrest companye
Of ladyes/that euer man with eye
Had sene togythers in o place
Shal I clepe it happe/eyther grace
That brought me there/not but fortune
That is to syen ful comune
The false traytresse peruerse
God wolde I coulde clepe her werse
For nowe she worcheth me ful wo
And I wol tel sone why so.
Amonge these ladyes thus echone
Sothe to sayne/I sawe one
That was lyke none of the route
For I dare swere/ without doute
That as the somers sonne bright
Is fayrer/clerer/and hath more lyght
Than any other planet in heuen
The moone/or the sterres seuen
For al the worlde/so had she
Surmounted hem al of beaute
Of maner/and of comlynesse
Of stature/and of wel set gladnesse
Of goodlyhede/and so wel besey
Shortly/ what shal I more sey
By god and by his halowes twelue
It was my swete/ right al her selue
She had so stedfast countenaunce
So noble porte/and mayntenaunce
And Loue/that wel herde my bone
Had espyed me thus sone
That she ful sone in my thought
As helpe me god/so was I caught
So sodaynly/that I ne toke
No maner counsayle/but at her loke
And at myn herte/ for why her eyen
So gladly I trowe myn herte seyne
That purely tho/myn owne thought
Sayd/ it were better serue her for nought
Than with another to be wele
And it was sothe/for euerydele
I wyl anon right tel the why
I sawe her daunce so comely
Carol and synge so swetely
Laughe/and playe so womanly
And loke so debonairly
So goodly speke and so frendly
That certes I trowe that neuermore
Nas sene so blysful a tresore
For euery heer on her heed
Sothe to saye it was nat reed
Ne neyther yelowe ne browne it nas
Me thought most lyke golde it was
And whiche eyen my lady had
Debonayre/ good/ glad/ and sad
Symple/of good mokel/not to wyde
Therto her loke nas nat asyde
Ne ouerthwart/ but beset so wele
It drewe and toke vp euerydele

Al that

Al that on her gan beholde
Her eyen semed anone she wolde
Haue mercy/ folly wenden so
But it was neuer the rather do
It nas no countrefeted thynge
It was her owne pure lokynge
That the goddesse dame Nature
Had made hem open by measure
And close/ for were she neuer so glad
Her lokynge was nat folyche sprad
Ne wyldely/though that she playde
But euer me thought her eyen sayde
By god my wrath is al foryeue
Therwith her lyst so wel to lyue
That dulnesse was of her a drad
She nas to sobre ne to glad
In al thynges more measure
Had neuer I trowe creature
But many one with her loke she herte
And that sate her ful lytel at herte
For she knewe nothynge of her thought
But whether she knewe/ or knewe it nought
Algate she ne rought of hem a stree
To gete her loue no nere nas he
That wõned at hom/ than he in Inde
The formest was alway behynde
But good folke ouer al other
She loued/ as man may do his brother
Of whiche loue she was wonder large
In skylful places that bere charge
But whiche a visage had she therto
Alas my herte is wonder wo
That I ne can discriuen it
Me lacketh bothe Englysshe and wyt
For to vndo it at the ful
And eke my spyrytes ben so dul
So grete a thynge for to deuyse
I haue no wyt that can suffise
To comprehende her beaute
But thus moche I dare sayn that she
Was whyte/rody/fresshe/and lyfely hewed
And euery day her beaute newed
And nyghe her face was alderbest
For certes nature had suche lest
To make that fayre/that truely she
Was her chefe patron of beaute
And chefe ensample of al her werke
And moustre/for be it neuer so derke

Me thynketh I se her euermo
And yet more ouer/though al tho
That euer lyued/were nowe a lyue
Ne wolde haue founde to discryue
In al her face/a wicked signe
For it was sad/symple/and benigne
And suche a goodly swete speche
Had that swete/my lyues leche
So frendly/and so wel ygrounded
Vpon al reason/so wel yfounded
And so tretable to al good
That I dare sweare wel by the rood
Of eloquence was neuer founde
So swete a sownyng facounde
Ne trewer tonged/ne scorned lasse
Ne bet coulde heale: That by the masse
I durste sweare/ though the Pope it songe
That there was neuer yet/through her tonge
Man ne woman greatly harmyd
As for her/was al harme hyd
Ne lasse flateryng in her worde
That purely her symple recorde
Was founde as trewe as any bonde
Or trouthe/of any mannes honde
Ne chyde she coulde neuer a dele
That knoweth al the worlde ful wele
But suche a fayrenesse of a necke
Had that swete/that bone nor brecke
Nas there none sene/that myssatte
It was whyte/smothe/streyght/a pure flatte
Without hole/or canel bone
And by semyng/she had none
Her throte/ as I haue nowe memoire
Semed as a rounde tour of yuoire
Of good greatnesse/and not to grete
And Fayre whyte she hete
That was my ladyes name right
She was therto fayre and bright
She had not her name wronge
Right fayre sholders/ and body longe
She had/and armes euery lyth
Fattysshe flesshy/nat great therwith
Right whyte handes/and nayles rede
Rounde brestes: And of good brede
Her hyppes were/a streight flatte backe
I knewe on her none other lacke
That al her lymmes nere pure sewyng
In as ferre as I had knowyng.

Therto

Therto she coulde so wel playe
What that her lyst/ that I dare saye
That was lyke to torche bright
That every man may take of syght
Ynough/ and it hath never the lesse
Of maner and of comlynesse
  Right so farde my lady dere
For every wight of her manere
Myght catche ynough/ if that he wolde
If he had eyen her to beholde
For I dare sweare wel/ if that she
Had amonge ten thousande be
She wolde have be at the beste
A chefe myrrour of al the feste
Though they had stonde in a rowe
To mennes eyen/ that coulde have knowe
For where so men had playde/ or waked
Me thought the felaushyp as naked
Without her/ that I sawe ones
As a crowne without stones
Trewly she was to myn eye
The soleyn Fenix of Arabye
For there lyveth never but one
Ne suche as she/ ne knowe I none
To speke of goodnesse/ trewly she
Had as moche debonayrte
As ever had Hester in the Byble
And more/ if more were possyble
And sothe to sayne/ therwithal
She had a wytte so general
So hole enclyned to al goode
That al her wytte was set by the roode
Without malyce/ upon gladnesse
And therto I sawe never yet a lesse
Harmful/ than she was in doyng
I say not that she ne had knowyng
What harme was/ or els she
Had coulde no good/ so thynketh me
And trewly/ for to speke of trouthe
But she had had/ it had be routhe
Therof she had so moche her dele
And I dare sayne/ and swere it wele
That trouthe hym selfe/ over al and al
Had chose his maner principal
In her/ that was his restyng place
Therto she had the moste grace
To have stedfast perseveraunce
And easy attempre governaunce
That ever I knewe/ or wyste yet
So pure suffraunt was her wytte
And reason gladly she understoode
It folowed wel/ she coulde goode
She used gladly to do wele
These were her maners everydele
  Therwith she loved so wel right
She wronge do wolde to no wight
No wight might do her no shame
She loved so wel her owne name
  Her lust to holde no wight in honde
Ne be thou syker/ she wolde not fonde
To holde no wight in balaunce
By halfe worde/ ne by countenaunce
But if men wolde upon her lye
Ne sende men in to Walakye
To Pruyse/ and to Tartarie
To Alisaundrie/ ne in to Turkie
And bydde hym faste/ anon that he
Go hoodlesse in to the drie see
And come home by the Carrenare
  And sir/ be nowe right ware
That I may of you here sayne
Worshyp/ or that ye come agayne
  She ne used no suche knackes smale
But therfore that I tel my tale
Right on this same/ I have sayde
Was holy al my love layde
For certes she was that swete wyfe
My suffysaunce/ my luste/ my lyfe
Myn hope/ myn heale/ and al blesse
My worldes welfare/ and my goddesse
And I holy hers/ and everydele
  By our lorde (quod I) I trowe you wele
Hardly your love was wel beset
I not howe ye myght have do bet
  Bet/ ne not so wel (quod he)
I trowe sir (quod I) parde.
  Nay leve it wel: Sir so do I
I leve you wel/ that trewly
You thought that she was the beste
And to beholde/ the alderfayrest
Who so had loked her with your eyen
  With myn/ nay al that her seyen
Sayd and swore/ it was so
And though they ne had/ I wolde tho
Have loved best my lady fre
Though I had had al the beaute

C.iii. That

That euer had Alcippades
And al the strength of Hercules
And therto had the worthynesse
Of Alisaundre/and al the rychesse
That euer was in Babilopne
In Cartage/or in Macedopne
Or in Rome/or in Nynyue
And therto al so hardy be
As was Hector/so haue I iope
That Achilles slough at Troye
And therfore was he slayne also
In a temple/for bothe two
Were slayne/he and Antilegius
And so sayth Dares Frigius
For loue of Polixyena
Or ben as wyse as Mynerua
I wolde euer/without drede
Haue loued her/ for I muste nede
  Nede? nay trewly I gabbe nowe
Naught nede/and I wol tellen howe
For of good wyl myn herte it wolde
And eke to loue her/ I was holde
As for the fayrest and the beste
She was as good/so haue I reste
As euer was Penelope of Grece
Or as the noble wyfe Lucrece
That was the beste/he telleth thus
The romayne Tytus Lyuius
She was as good/and nothyng lyke
Though her stories be autentyke
Algate she was as trewe as she
  But wherfore that I tel the
Whan I first my lady sey
I was right yonge/sothe to say
And ful great nede I had to lerne
Whan myn herte wolde yerne
To loue it was a great emprise
But as my wytte wolde beste suffyse
After my yonge childely wyt
Without drede I beset it
To loue her in my best wyse
To do her worshyp/and the seruyse
That I coude tho/ by my trouthe
Without faynyng/ eyther slouthe
For wonder fayne/I wolde her se
So mokel it amended me
That whan I sawe her a morowe
I was waryshed of al my sorowe
Of alday after/tyl it were eue
Me thought nothyng might me greue
Were my sorowes neuer so smerte
And yet she syt so in myn herte
That by my trouthe/ I nolde nought
For al this worlde/out of my thought
Leaue my lady/no trewly
  Nowe by my trouthe sir (quod I)
Me thynketh ye haue suche a chaunce
As shrifte/without repentaunce
  Repentaunce/nay fye (quod he)
Shulde I nowe repente me
To loue/nay certes than were I wel
Werse than was Achytofel
Or Antenor/so haue I iope
The traytour that betrayed Troye
Or the false Genelion
He that purchased the trayson
Of Roulande/and of Olyuere
Nay/whyle I am alyue here
I nyl foryet her neuer mo
  Nowe good sir (quod I) tho
Ye haue wel tolde me here before
It is no nede to reherse it more
Howe ye sawe her first/and where
But wolde ye tel me the manere
To her/ whiche was your first speche
Therof I wolde you beseche
And howe she knewe first your thought
Whether ye loued her/or nought
And telleth me eke/what ye haue lore
I herde you tel here before
Ye sayd/thou notest what thou menest
I haue loste more than thou wenest
What losse is that (quod I tho)
Nyl she not loue you/ is it so
Or haue ye aught done amys
That she hath lefte you/is it this
For goddes loue tel me al
  Before god (quod he) and I shal
I say right as I haue sayde
On her was al my loue layde
And yet she nyst it not neuer a dele
Not longe tyme/leue it wele
For be right syker/I durst nought
For al this worlde/tel her my thought
Ne I wolde haue wrathed her trewly
For woste thou why/she was lady

Of the

Of the body that had the herte
And who so hath that may not asterte
But for to kepe me fro ydlenesse
Trewly I dyd my busynesse.
To make songes as I best coude
And ofte tyme I songe hem loude
And made songes/this a great dele
Although I coude not make so wele
Songes/ne knewe the arte al
As coude Lamekes sonne Tubal
That founde out first the arte of songe
For as his brothers hamers ronge
Upon his anuelt up and downe
Therof he toke the first sowne
But grekes sayne of Pithagoras
That he the first fynder was
Of the arte/Aurora telleth so
But therof no force of hem two
Algates songes thus I made
Of my felyng/myn herte to glade
And so/this was alther ferst
I not where it were the werst
Lorde it maketh myne herte lyght
Whan I thynke on that swete wyght
That is so semely on to se
And wysshe to god it might so be
That she wolde holde me for her knight
My lady/ that is so fayre and bright
Nowe haue I tolde the/sothe to say
My first songe upon a day
I bethought me what wo
And sorowe that I suffred tho
For her/and yet she wyst it nought
Ne tel her durst I not my thought
Alas thought I/I can no rede
And but I tel her/I am but dede
And if I tel her/to say right sothe
I am a dradde she wol be wrothe
Alas/what shal I than do
In this debate I was so wo
Me thought myn herte braste atwayne
So at the laste/sothe for to sayne
I be thought me that Nature
Ne formed neuer in creature
So moche beaute trewly
And bountie/without mercy
In hope of that/my tale I tolde
With sorowe/as that I neuer sholde
For nedes/and maugre myn heed
I muste haue tolde her/or be deed
I not wel howe that I began
Ful yuel reherce it I can
And eke as helpe me god withal
I trowe it was in the dismal
That was the ten woundes of Egypte
For many a worde I ouer skypte
In my tale for pure fere
Leste my wordes mysse set were
With sorouful herte/and woundes dede
Softe and quakyng for pure drede
And shame/and styntyng in my tale
For ferde/and myn hewe al pale
Ful ofte I weyt bothe pale and reed
Bowyng to her I henge the heed
I durste not ones loke her on
For wyt/maner/and al was gone
I said: mercy/and no more
It nas no game/it sate me sore.
So at the laste/sothe to sayne
Whan that myn herte was come agayne.
To tel shortly al my speche
With hole herte/I gan her beseche
That she wolde be my lady swete
And swore/and hertely gan her hete
Euer to be stedfast and trewe
And loue her alway fresshly newe
And neuer other lady haue
And al her worshyp for to saue
As I best coude/I swere her this
For yours is al that euer there is
For euermore/myn herte swete
And neuer to false you/but I mete
I nyl/as wyse god helpe me so
And whan I had my tale ydo
God wote she acompted not a stre
Of al my tale/so thought me
To tel shortly/right as it is
Trewly her answere it was this
I can not nowe wel countrefete
Her wordes/but this was the grete
Of her answere/she sayd nay
Al utterly/alas that day
The sorowe I suffred and the wo
That trewly Cassandra/that so
Bewayled the distruction
Of Troye/and of Ilion

Had neuer suche sorowe as I tho
I durst no more say therto
For pure feare/but stale away
And thus I lyued ful many a day
That trewly I had no nede
Ferther than my beddes hede
Neuer a day to seche sorowe
I founde it redy euery morowe
For why/I loued her in no gere
  So it befel another yere
I thought ones I wolde fonde
To do her knowe/and vnderstonde
My wo/and she wel vnderstoode
That I ne wylned thyng but goode
And worshyp/and to kepe her name
Ouer al thynges/and drede her shame
And was so besy her to serue
And pyte were I shulde sterue
Sythe that I wylned none harme ywis
  So whan my lady knewe al this
My lady yaue me al holy
The noble yest of her mercy
Sauyng her worshyp by al wayes
Dredelesse/ I mene none other wayes
And therwith she yaue me a rynge
I trowe it was the first thyng
But if myn herte was ywaye
Glad/that it is no nede to aye
  As helpe me god/ I was as blyue
Reysed/as fro dethe to lyue
Of al happes the alder best
The gladdest/ and the moste at rest
For trewly that swete wight
Whan I had wronge/and she the right
She wolde alway so goodly
Foryeue me so debonairly
In al my youthe/in al chaunce
She toke me in her gouernaunce
Therwith she was alway so trewe
Our ioy was euer lyche newe
Our hertes werne so euen a payre
That neuer nas that one contrayre
To that other/ for no wo
For sothe ilyche they suffred tho
  O blysse/ and eke o sorowe bothe
Ilyche they were bothe glad and wrothe
Al was vs one/ without were
And thus we lyued ful many a yere
So wel/ I can not tel howe.
  Sir (quod I) where is she nowe
Nowe (quod he) and stynte anone
Therwith he woye as deed as stone
And sayd/ alas that I was bore
That was the losse/ that here before
I tolde the/ that I had lorne
  Bethynke the howe I sayd here beforne
Thou woste ful lytel what thou menest
I haue loste more than thou wenest
  God wot alas/right that was she
Alas sir howe/what may that be
She is deed: Nay/ Yes by my trouthe
  Is that your losse/by god it is routhe.
¶ And with that worde right anone
They gan to strake forthe/al was done
For that tyme/the hart huntynge
  With that me thought that this kynge
Gan homwarde for to ryde
Vnto a place was there besyde
Whiche was from vs but a lyte
A longe castel with walles whyte
By sayn Iohan/on a ryche hyl
As me mette/but thus it fyl
  Right thus me mette/as I you tel
That in the castel there was a bel
As it had smytte houres twelue
Therwith I awoke my selue
And founde me lyeng in my bedde
And the boke that I had redde
Of Alcyone/and Seys the kyng
And of the goddes of slepyng
I founde it in myn honde ful euyn
Thought I/this is so queynt a sweuyn
That I wolde by processe of tyme
Fonde/to put this sweuen in ryme
As I can best/and that anone
This was my sweuen/nowe it is done.

¶ Explicit.

  My mayster &c. Whan of Christ our kyng
Was asked/ what is trouthe or sothfastnesse
He not a worde answerde to that askyng
As who sayth/no man is al trewe I gesse
And therfore/ though I hyght to expresse
The sorowe and wo that is in maryage
I dare not writen of it no wickednesse
Leste I my selfe fal efte in suche dotage

I wel

I wol not saye howe that it is the chayne
Of Sathanas/on whiche he knaweth euer
But I dare sayne/were he out of his payne
As by his wyl/ he wolde be bounden neuer
But thylke doted foole/that efte hath leuer
Ychayned be/than out of prison crepe
God let him neuer fro his wo disceuer
Ne no man hym bewayle/though he wepe

But yet leste thou do worse/take a wyfe
Bet is to wedde/than brenne in worse wyse
But ȳ shalt haue sorowe on thy flessh thy lyfe
And ben thy wyues thral/ as sayn these wyse
And if that holy writte may not suffyse
Experyence shal the teache/so may happe
Take the way leuer to be take in Fryse
Than efte to fal of weddyng in the trappe

This lytel writ/prouerbes or fygures
I sende you/take kepe of it I rede
Unwyse is he/that can no wele endure
If thou be syker/put the not in drede
The wyfe of Bathe/I pray you that ye rede
Of this mater/that we haue on honde
God graunt you your lyfe frely to lede
In fredome/ for foule is to be bonde.

¶Explicit.

The assemble of Foules.

The lyfe so short/ȳ craft so lōg to lerne
Thassay so harde/so sharp the cōque-(ring
The dredeful ioy/alway ȳ slyt so yern
Al this meane I by loue/that my felyng
Astonyeth/with his wonderful werkyng
So sore iwys/that whan I on him thynke
Naught wete I wel/ whether I flete or synke

For al be that I/ knowe not loue in dede
Ne wot howe that he quyteth folke her hyre
Yet happeth me ful ofte in bokes rede
Of his myracles/and of his cruel yre
There rede I wel/ he wol be lorde and syre
I dare not sayne/his strokes be sore
But god saue suche a lorde/I can no more

Of usage/what for luste & what for lore
On bokes rede I ofte/as I you tolde
But wherfore I speke al this/naught yore
Agon/it happed me to beholde
Upon a boke/ was ywritten with letters olde
And therupon/a certayne thyng to lerne
The longe day/ ful fast I radde and yerne

For out of olde feldes/as men sayth
Cometh al this newe corne/fro yere to yere
And out of olde bokes/in good fayth
Cometh al this newe science/that men lere
But nowe to purpose/as of this matere
To rede forthe/it gan me so delyte
That al that day/me thought it but a lyte

This boke/of whiche I make mencion
Entytled was right thus/as I shal tel
Tullius/of the dreame of Scipion
Chapiters seuen it had/of heuen and hel
And erthe/and soules that therin dwel
Of whiche/as shortly as I can it treate
Of his sentence/I wol you sayne the greate

First telleth it/whan Scipion was come
In Affrike/howe he meteth Massynysse
That hym for ioy/in armes hath ynome
Than telleth he her speche/and al the blysse
That was betwyxe hem/ tyl ȳ day gan mysse
And howe his auncestre Affrikan so dere
Gan in his slepe that night tyl him apere

Than telleth it/that from a sterry place
Howe Affrikan hath him Cartage shewed
And warned him before/of al his grace
And sayd him what man/lered eyther lewde
That loueth comune profyte/wel ythewde
He shulde in to a blyssful place wende
There as the ioye is withouten any ende

Than asked he/if folke that here ben dede
Haue lyfe/and dwellyng in another place
And Affrikan sayd ye/ without any drede
And howe our present lyues space
Ment but a maner dethe/what way we trace
And rightful folke/shul gon after they dye
To heuen/and shewed him the Galaxye

C.c.c.iii. Than

Than shewed he him / the lytel erthe yͤ here is
To regarde of the heuens quantyte
And after shewed he him the nyne speris
And after that the melodye herde he
That cometh of thilke speres thrise thre
That welles of musyke ben / and melodye
In this worlde here / and cause of armonye

Than sayd he him / sens erthe was so lyte
And ful of turment / and of harde grace
That he ne shulde him in this worlde delyte
Than tolde he him / in certayne yeres space
That euery sterre / shulde come in to his place
There it was first / and al shuld out of mynde
That in this worlde is done / of al mankynde

Than prayde him Scipion / to tel him al
The way to come in to that heuen blysse
And he sayde: First knowe thy selfe immortal
And loke aye besely / that thou werche ⁊ wysse
To comune profyte / and thou shalt not mysse
To come swyftly / unto that place dere
That ful of blysse is / and of soules clere

And brekers of the lawe / sothe to sayne
And lyberous folke / after that they ben dede
Shul whirle about yͤ worlde / alway in payne
Tyl many a worlde be passed / out of drede
And than foryeuen al her wicked dede
Than shullen they come / to that blyssful place
To whiche to comen / god sende the grace.

The day gan faylen / and the derke nyght
That reueth beestes from her besynesse
Berafte me my boke for lacke of syght
And to my bedde I gan me for to dresse
Fulfylled of thought / and besy heuynesse
For bothe I had thyng / whiche that I nolde
And eke I ne had that thyng that I wolde

But fynally my spyrite at laste
For wery of my labour al that day
Toke rest / that made me to slepe faste
And in my slepe I mette / as that I lay
Howe Affrikan / right in the selfe aray
That Scipion him sawe / before that tyde
Was come / and stode right at my beddes syde

The wery hunter / slepyng in his bedde
To wodde ayen his mynde gothe anone
The iuge dremeth / howe his plees be spedde
The carter dremeth / howe his cartes gone
The ryche of golde / yͤ knight fight wͭ his fone
The sicke mette he drinketh of the tonne
The louer met / he hath his lady wonne

Can I not sayne / if that the cause were
For I had radde of Affrikan beforne
That made me to mete that he stode there
But thus sayd he: thou haste the so wel borne
In lokyng of myn olde boke al to torne
Of whiche Macrobie raught not a lyte
That somdele of thy labour wolde I quyte

Citherea / thou blyssful lady swete
That with thy fyre brōde / daūtest whan yͤ lest
That madest me this sweuen for to mete
Be thou my helpe in this / for thou mayst best
As wisely as I seygh the northe north west
Whan I began my sweuen for to write
So yeue me might / to ryme it and endyte

This foresayd Affrikan me hente anone
And forthe with him to a gate brought
Right of a parke / walled with grene stone
And ouer yͤ gate / with letters large ywrought
There were verse ywritten / as me thought
On eyther halfe / of ful great difference
Of whiche I shal you say / the playn sentence

Through me men gon in to that blissful place
Of hertes heale / and deedly woundes cure
Through me men gon in to the wel of grace
There grene and lusty May / shal euer endure
This is the way to al good auenture
Be glad thou reder / and thy sorowe of caste
Al open am I / passe in and spede the faste

Through me men gon / thā spake yͤ other syde
Unto the mortal strokes of the speere
Of whiche disdayne and daunger is the gyde
There neuer tree shal frute / ne leaues beere
This streme you ledeth to the sorouful weere
There as the fysshe in prison is al drie
The eschewyng is onely the remedye

These

These verses of golde & asure ywrytten were
Of whiche I gan/astonyed to beholde
For with that one/encreased al my feare
And with that other gan my herte to bolde
That one me hette/that other dyd me colde
No wytte had I/for errour for to chese
To entre or flye/or me to saue or lese

Ryght as bytwene Adamantes two
Of euyn weyght/ a pece of yron set
Ne hath no myght to moue to ne fro
For what that one may hale/that other let
So fared I/that I nyst where me was bet
To entre or leaue/tyl Affrycan my gyde
Me hent and shoue in/ at the gates wyde

And sayd/ it standeth wrytten in thy face
Thyne errour/ though thou tel it nat me
But drede the nat/to come in to this place
For this wrytynge is nothynge ment by the
Ne by none/but he loues seruaunt be
For thou of loue/hast lost thy tast I gesse
As sycke man hath/ of swete and bytternesse

But natheles/although thou be dul
That thou canst nat do/yet mayst thou se
For many a man/that may nat stande a pul
yet lyketh it hym/at the wrestlyng for to be
And demeth yet/ whether he do bet/ or he
And if thou haddest connynge for tendyte
I shal the shewe matter of to wryte

And with that my hande in his he toke anone
Of whiche I comforte caught/& went in fast
But lorde so I was glad/and wel begon
For ouer al/ where I myne eyen cast
Were trees clad with leues/ y aye shal last
Eche in his kynde/with colour fresshe & grene
As Emeraude/ that ioye it was to sene

The bylder Oke/ and eke the hardy Asshe
The pyller elme/ the coffer vnto carayne
The boxe pype tre/holme to whyppes lasshe
The saylynge fyrre/the cypres dethe to playne
The shoter ewe/the aspe for shaftes playne
The Olyue of peace/and eke y dronken vyne
The victor Palme/ the laurer to dyuyne

A gardeyne sawe I/ful of blosomed bowis
Vpon a ryuer/in a grene mede
There as swetnesse/euermore ynoughe is
With floures whyte/blewe/yelowe/and rede
And colde wel stremes/nothynge dede
That swommen ful of smale fysshes lyght
With fynnes rede/and scales syluer bryght

On euery bough the byrdes herde I synge
With voyce of aungel/ in her ermony
That busyed hem/her byrdes forth to brynge.
The lytel prety conyes/ to her play gan hy
And further al aboute/ I gan espy
The dredeful Roe/ y bucke/ the herte/ & hynde
Squyrels/ and beestes smal of gentyl kynde

Of instrumentes/ of strynges in acorde
Herde I so playe/ a rauysshynge swetnesse
That god/ that maker is of al and lorde
Ne herde neuer better/as I gesse
Therwith a wynde/ vnneth it myght be lesse
Made in the leues grene/a noyse softe
Accordant to the foules songe on lofte

The ayre of the place/ so attempre was (de
That neuer was there greuance of hote ne col
There was eke euery holsome spyce & gras
Ne no man may there waxe sicke ne olde
yet was there more ioy a thousande folde
Than I can tel/or euer coude or myght
There is euer clere day/and neuer nyght

Vnder a tree/ besyde a wel I sey
Cupyde our lorde/his arowes forge and fyle
And at his fete/his bowe al redy lay
And wel his doughter tempred al the whyle
The heedes in the wel/ with her wyle
She couched hem after/as they shulde serue
Some to slee/& some to wounde and karue

Tho was I ware of Plesaunce anone right
And of aray/lust/beaute/and curtesy
And of the crafte/that can and hath the might
To done beforce/ a wyght to done foly
Dyssygured was she/I wyl nat lye
And by hym selfe/vnder an oke I gesse
Sawe I Delyte/that stode with gentylnesse
Than

The assemble of Foules.

Than sawe I Beaute/ with a nyce atyre
And youthe/ ful of game and iolyte
Folehardynesse/ flatery/ and desyre
Messagery/ mede/ and other thre
Her names shal nat here be tolde for me
And vpon pyllers great of Jasper longe
I sawe a temple of Brasse yfounded stronge

And aboute the temple/ daunced alway
Women ynowe/ of whiche some there were
Fayre of hem selfe/ ⁊ some of hem were gay
In kyrtyls al dysheueled went they there
That was theyr offyce euer/ fro yere to yere
And on the temple/ sawe I whyte and fayre
Of dowues sittyng/ many a thousande payre

And before the temple dore ful soberly
Dame Peace satte/ a curteyne in her honde
And her besyde/ wonder dyscretly
Dame Pacience syttynge there I fonde
With face pale/ vpon an hyl of sonde
And alther nexte/ within and without
Behest and Arte/ and of her folke a route

Within the temple/ of syghes hote as fyre
I herde a swough/ that gan aboute ren
Whiche syghes were engendred with desyre
That made euery herte for to bren
Of newe flambe/ and wel espyed I then
That al the cause of sorowes/ that they drye
Come of the bytter goddes ialousye

The god Pryiapus/ sawe I as I wente
Within the temple/ in souerayne place stonde
In suche array/ as whan the asse hym shent
With crye by night/ and with ceptre in honde
Ful besely men gan assay and fonde
Vpon his heed to sette of sondry hewe
Garlandes/ ful of fresshe floures newe

And in a preuy corner/ in dysporte
Founde I Venus/ and her porter Rychesse
That was ful noble/ and hauten of her porte
Derke was that place/ but after lyghtnesse
I sawe a lyte/ vnnethes it myght be lesse
And on a bed of golde/ she lay to rest
Tyl that the hote sonne gan to west

Her gylte heeres/ with a golde threde
ybounde were/ vntressed as she lay
And naked from the brest vnto the hede
Men myght her se/ and sothely for to say
The remnaunt/ couered wel to my pay
Right with a lytel kerchefe of Valence
There was no thycker cloth of defence

The place gaue a thousande sauours sote
And Bacchus god of wyne/ sate her besyde
And Ceres nexte/ that dothe of hunger bote
And as I sayd/ a myddes lay Cupyde
To whom on knees/ the yonge folkes cryde
To be theyr helpe/ but thus I let her lye
And farther in the temple/ I gan espye

That in dispyte of Diane the chaste
Ful many a bowe ybroke/ hynge on the wal
Of maydens/ suche as gon her tymes waste
In her seruyce/ and paynted ouer al
Of many a storie/ of whiche I touche shal
A fewe/ as of Calixte and Athalante
And many a mayde/ of which yͤ name I wāte

Semyramus/ Candace/ and Hercules
Byblis/ Dido/ Tysbe/ and Piramus
Tristram/ Isoude/ Parys/ and Achilles
Helayne/ Cleopatre/ and Troylus
Sylla/ and eke the mother of Romulus
Al these were paynted on that other syde
And al her loue/ and in what plyte they dyde

Whan I was comen ayen in to the place
That I of spake/ that was so sote and grene
Forthe walked I tho/ my seluen to solace
Tho was I ware/ where there sate a quene
That as of lyght/ the sōmer sonne shene
Passeth the sterre/ right so ouer mesure
She fayrer was than any creature

And in a launde/ vpon an hyl of floures
Was set this noble goddesse Nature
Of braunches were her halles ⁊ her boures
Iwrought/ after her crafte and her mesure
Ne there nas foule/ that cometh of engendrure
That there ne were prest/ in her presence
To take her dome/ and yeue her audyence

For

For this was on saynt Valentynes day
Whan euery foule cometh to chese her make
Of euery kynde/that men thynke may
And that so huge a noyse gan they make
That erthe/ see/ and tree/ and euery lake
So ful was/that vnneth there was space
For me to stande/ so ful was al the place

And right as Alayne/ in the playnt of kynde
Deuyseth Nature/of suche aray and face
In suche aray/men myght her there fynde
This noble Emperesse ful of al grace
Bad euery foule to take her owne place
As they were wonte alway/fro yere to yere
On saynt Valentynes day/ to standen there

That is to saye/the foules of raupyne
Were hyghest set/and than the foules smale
That eaten/as that nature wolde enclyne
As worme or thynge/ of whiche I tel no tale
But water foule/sat lowest in the dale
And foules yͭ lyueth be sede/ sate on the grene
And that so many/that wonder was to sene

There myght men the royal Egle fynde
That with his sharpe loke/perseth the son
And other Egles/ of a lower kynde
Of whiche that clerkes wel deuysen con
There was the tyrant with his fethers don
And grene/ I mene yͭ goshauke yͭ doth pyne
To byrdes/ for his outragyous raupyne

The gẽtyl faucon/ yͭ with his fete distreyneth
The kynges hande/ the hardy sperhauke eke
The quayles foe/ the merlyon that peyneth
Hym selfe ful ofte/the larke for to seke
There was the doue/ with her eyen meke
The ielous swan/ayenst his dethe yͭ syngeth
The oule eke/that of dethe the bode bryngeth

The crane/the geant/ wͭ his trompes sowne
The thefe the choughe/ & the chatterynge pye
The scornyng Iape/the Eles foe the herowne
The false lapwynge/ful of trechery
The stare/ that the counsayle can bewry
The tame Ruddocke/and the cowarde kyte
The Cocke/that horiloge is of thorpes lyte

The sparowe Venus son/ & the nyghtyngale
That clepeth forth the fresshe leaues newe
The swalowe murdrer of the flyes smale
That maken hony/of floures fresshe of hewe
The wedded turtel/ with his herte trewe
The pecocke/with his aungel fethers bryght
The Fesaunt/scorner of the cocke by nyght

The waker gose/the cuckowe euer vnkynde
The poppyngey/ful of delycasy
The drake/stroyer of his owne kynde
The storke/ wreker of auoutry
The hote cormerant/ ful of glotony
The rauyn & the crowe/ with her voice of care
The throstel olde/and the frosty feldefare

What shulde I say/of foules of euery kynde
That in this worlde haue fethers and stature
Men myght in that place assembled fynde
Before that noble goddes of Nature
And eche of them dyd his busy cure
Benygnely to chese/or for to take
By her acorde/his formel or his make

But to the poynt/ Nature helde on her honde
A formal Egle/of shap the gentyllest
That euer she amonge her werkes fonde
The most benygne/ and eke the goodlyest
In her was euery vertue/at his rest
So farforth/that nature herselfe had blysse
To loke on her/ and ofte her becke to kysse

Nature/the vycar of the almyghty lorde
That hote/colde/ heuy/lyght/moyst/and drey
Hath knytte/by euen nombre of acorde
In esy voyce/began to speke and say
Foules take hede of my sentence I pray
And for yoͬ own ease/ in fordrĩg of your nede
As fast as I may speke/I wyl me spede

Ye knowe wel/how on saynt Valentynes day
By my statute/and throughe my gouernauce
Ye do chese your makes/and after flye awaye
With hem/ as I prycke you with plesaunce
But nathelesse/as by ryghtful ordenaunce
May I nat let/for al this worlde to wyn
But he that most worthyest is/shal begyn

The

The assemble of Foules.

The tercel Egle/as ye knowe ful wele
The foule royal/aboue you al in degre
The wyse and worthy/the secrete true as stele
The whiche I haue formed/as ye may se
In euery parte/as it best lyketh me
It nedeth nat his shappe you to deuyse
He shal fyrst chese/and speken in his gyse

And after hym/by order shal ye chese
After your kynde/eueryche as you lyketh
And as your hap is/shal ye wynne or lese
But whiche of you/that loue most entriketh
God sende hym her/that sorest for hym syketh
And there withal/the Tercel gan she cal
And sayd/my sonne the choyce is to the fal

But nathelesse/ in this condycion
Must be the choyce/of everyche that is here
That she agree to his election
Who so he be/that shulde ben her fere
This is our vsage alway/ fro yere to yere
And who so may at this tyme haue his grace
In blyssful tyme he came in to this place

With heed enclyned/& with ful humble chere
This royal Tercel spake/and taryed nought
Vnto my soueraygne lady/and nat my fere
I chose & chese/with wyl/herte/and thought
The formel on your hande/ so wel ywrought
Whose I am al/and euer wyl her serue
Do what her lust/to do me lyue or sterue

Besechynge her of mercy/ and of grace
As she that is my lady soueraygne
Or let me dye/here present in this place
For certes/longe may I nat lyue in payne
For in my herte is coruen euery vayne
Hauynge regarde onely to my trouthe
My dere herte/haue on my wo some routhe

And if I be founde to her vntrewe
Dysobeysaunt/or wylful neglygent
A vauntour/or in processe loue a newe
I pray to you this be my iugement
That with these foules I be al to rent
That ylke day/that she me euer fynde
To her vntrue/or in my gylte vnkynde

And syth that none loueth her so wel as I
Al though she neuer of loue me behet
Than ought she be myne/through her mercy
For other bonde/can I none on her knet
For wele nor wo/neuer shal I let
To serue her/howe farre so that she wende
Say what you lyst/my tale is at an ende.

Right as the fresshe reed Rose newe
Agaynst the somer sonne coloured is
Ryght so for shame/al waxen gan the hewe
Of this formel/whan she herde al this
Neyther she answerde wel/ne sayd amys
So sore abasshed was she/tyl that Nature
Sayd/ doughter drede you nat/ I you assure

Another tercel Egle spake anone
Of lower kynde/and sayd that shulde nat be
I loue her better than ye do/by saynt John
Or at lest/I loue her as wel as ye
And lenger haue serued her in my degre
And if she shulde haue loued for long louyng
To me alone had be the guerdonyng

I dare eke say/if she me fynde false
Vnkynde/ iangler/or rebel in any wyse
Or ielous/do me hange by the halse
And but I beare me in her seruyse
As wel as my wyt can me suffyse
Fro poynt to poynt/her honour for to saue
Take she my lyfe/and al the good I haue

The thyrde tercel Egle/answerde tho
Nowe syrs/ ye se the lytel leyser here
For euery foule cryeth out to be ago
Forth with his make/or with his lady dere
And eke Nature her selfe/ ne wyl not here
For taryeng her/nat halfe that I wolde sey
And but I speke/ I must for sorowe dey

Of longe seruyce/ auaunt I me no thynge
But as possyble is me to dye to day
For wo/as he that hath be languysshynge
This twenty wynter/and wel it happen may
A man may serue better/and more to pay
In halfe a yere/ al though it were no more
Than some man dothe/ ẏ hath serued ful yore

I ne

I ne say nat this by me/ for I ne can
Do no seruyce/ that may my lady please
But I dare say/ I am her trewest man
As to my dome/ and faynest wolde her please
At shorte wordes/ tyl that dethe me cease
I wyl be hers/ whether I wake or wynke
And trewe/ in al that herte may bethynke

Of al my lyfe/ syth that day I was borne
So gentyl plee/ in loue or other thynge
Ne herde neuer no man me beforne
Who that had leyser and connynge
For to reherce theyr chere/ & theyr spekynge
And from the morowe gan this speche last
Tyl downwarde went the son wonder fast

The noyse of foules for to be delyuerde
So loude range/ haue done and let vs wende
That wel wende I/ the woo had al to shyuerd
Come of they cryed/ alas ye wyl vs shende
Whan shal your cursed pleding haue an ende
Howe shulde a iuge/ eyther partye leue
For ye or nay/ without any preue

The gose/ the ducke/ and the cuckowe also
So cryed keke keke/ cuckowe/ queke queke hy
That thrughe myne eares/ the noyse went tho
The gose sayd than/ al this nys worth a flye
But I can shape herof a remedy
And wyl say my verdyte/ fayre and swythe
For water foule/ who so be wroth or blythe

And I for wormfoule/ sayd the fole cuckowe
For I wyl of myne owne authoryte
For cōmon spede/ take on me the charge nowe
For to delyuer vs/ it is great charyte
Ye may abyde a whyle/ yet perde
(Quod the Turtel) if it be your wyl
A wight may speke/ it were as good be styl.

I am a sede foule/ one the vnworthyest
That wote I wel/ and leest of connynge
But better is/ that a wyghtes tonge rest
Than entremete hym of suche doynge
Of whiche he neyther rede can nor synge
And who so it doth/ ful foule hi selfe acloyeth
For offyce vncōmytted/ ofte anoyeth

Nature/ whiche that alway had an eare
To murmure of the leudnesse behynde
Wͭ faconde voyce sayd/ hold your tong there
And I shal soone/ I hope a counsayle fynde
You for to delyuer/ & fro this noyse vnbynde
I charge/ of euery flocke ye shal one cal
To say the verdyte of you foules al

Assented were/ to this conclusyon
The byrdes al/ and foules of rauyne
Haue chosen fyrst/ by playne electyon
The Tercelet of the faucon to dyffyne
Al her sentence/ and as hym lust to termyne
And to Nature/ hym they dyd present
And she accepteth hym with glad entent

The tercelet sayd than/ in this manere
Ful harde it were/ to preue it by reason
Who loueth best/ this gentyl formel here
For euery che hath suche replycatyon
That by skylles may none be brought adoun
I can nat se/ that argumentes auayle
Than semeth it/ there must be batayle

Al redy quod these Egles tercelles tho
Nay syrs (quod he) if that I durst it say
Ye do me wronge/ my tale is nat ydo
For syrs/ taketh nat agrefe I pray
It may nat be as ye wolde/ in this way
Ours is the voyce/ yͭ haue yͤ charge in hande
And to the Iuges dome/ ye must stande

And therfore peace I saye/ as to my wyt
Me wolde thynke/ howe that the worthyest
Of knyghthode/ and lengest had vsed it
Moost of estate/ of blode the gentyllest
Were syttynge for her/ if that her lest
And of these thre/ she wote her selfe I trowe
Whiche that he be/ for it is lyght to knowe

The water foules/ haue theyr heedes layde
Togyder/ and of shorte auysement
Whan euery che had his verdyte sayde
They sayd sothely/ al by one assent
Howe that the goos/ with the faconde gent
That so desyreth/ to pronounce our nede
Shal tel our tale/ and prayed to god her spede
And

The assemble of Foules.

And for these water foules/tho began
The goose to speke/and in her cakelynge
She said/ peace nowe/ take kepe euery man
And herken which a reson I shal forth bryng
My wytte is sharpe/ I loue no taryenge
I say I rede hym/tho he were my brother
But she wyl loue hym/let hym loue another

Lo here a parfyte reason of a gose
(Quod the sperhauke) neuer mote she the
Lo/suche a thynge it is to haue a tonge lose
Nowe parde foole/yet were it better for the
Haue holde thy peace/ than shewde thy nycete
It lyeth nat in his wyt/no. in his wyl
But sothe is sayd/a fole can nat be styl

The laughter arose/ of gentyl foules al
And ryght anone/ the sede foules chosen had
The Turtel trewe/ and gan her to hem cal
And prayed her to say/the sothe sad
Of this mater/and asked what she rad
And she answered/that playnly her entent
She wolde shewe/and sothely what she ment

Nay/god forbede a louer shulde chaunge
The turtel sayd/ I weyre for shame al red
Though that his lady/euermore be straunge
Yet let hym serue her alway/tyl he be deed
For sothe/I prayse nat the goses reed
For tho she dyed/I wolde non other make
I wyl be hers/tyl that the dethe me take

Wel bourded (qd the ducke) by my hat
That men shulde loue alway causelesse
Who can a reason fynde/ or wyt in that
Daunceth he mery/that is myrthlesse
Who shulde recke/of that is rechelesse
Ye queke yet (qd the ducke) ful wel and fayre
There be mo sterres in the skye than a payre

Nowe fye churle (qd the gentyl Tercelet)
Out of the donghyl/ came that worde aryght
Thou canst not se/ whiche thynge is wel beset
Thou farest by loue/as oules do by lyght
The day hem blyndeth/ ful wel they se by nyght
Thy kynde is of so lowe wretchydnesse
That what loue is/thou canst nat se nor gesse

Tho gan the cuckowe put him forth in preace
For foule that eteth worme/and sayd blyue
So I (qd he) may haue my make in peace
I retche naught/howe longe that ye stryue
Let eche of hem be soleyn al her lyue
This is my rede/ sens they maye nat acorde
This shorte lesson/ nedeth not recorde

Ye/ haue the glutton fylde his paunche
Than are we wel/sayd the Emerlon
Thou murdrer of ye heysugge/ on the braunche
That brought the forthe/thou reuful glutton
Lyue thou soleyn/wormes corruption
For no force is/of lacke of thy nature
Go lewde be thou/ whyle the worlde may dure

Nowe peace (qd Nature) I comaunde here
For I haue herde al your opinyon
And in effecte/yet be we neuer the nere
But fynally/this is my conclusyon
That she her selfe shal haue her election
Of whom her lyst/ who so be wrothe or blythe
Hym yt she cheseth/he shal her haue as swythe

For sythe it may not here discussed be
Who loueth her beste/as sayd the Tercelet
Than wol I done this fauour to her/ yt she
Shal haue right hym/on whom her hert is set
And he her/that his herte hath on her knet
This iuge I Nature/ for I may not lye
To none estate/ I haue none other eye

But as for counsayle/for to chose a make
If I were reason/than wolde I
Counsayle you/the royal tercel take
As sayd the tercelet/ful skylfully
As for the gentillest/and moste worthy
Which I haue wrought so wel to my plesaunce
That to you it ought ben a suffysaunce

With dredeful voyce/ the formel her answerde
My rightful lady/ goddesse of Nature
Sothe is/that I am euer vnder your yerde
As is euerych other creature
And muste be yours/ whyle my lyfe may dure
And therfore graunt me my first boone
And myn entent/ you wol I say right soone

I graunt

I graunt it you (quod she) and right anone
This formel Egle spake in this degre
Almighty quene/ unto this yere be done
I aske respyte for to aupsen me
And after that to haue my choyce al fre
This al and some/that I wolde speke and sey
Ye get no more/al though ye do me dey

I wol not serue Venus/ ne Cupyde
For sothe as yet/by no maner way
Nowe sens it may none other wayes betyde
(Quod Nature) here is no more to say
Than wolde I that these foules were away
Eche with his make/for taryeng lenger here
And sayd hem thus/as ye shal after here

To you speke I/ye tercelets (qd Nature)
Bethe of good herte/and serueth al thre
A yere is not so longe to endure
And eche of you payne him in his degree
For to do wel/for god wote quyt is she
Fro you this yere/what after so befal
This entremes/is dressed fro you al

And whā this werke brought was to an ende
To euery foule/Nature yaue his make
By euen acorde/and on her way they wende
And lorde the blysse and ioy that they make
For eche of hem gan other in his wynges take
And with her neckes/eche gan other wynde
Thākyng alway/the noble goddesse of kynde

But first were chosen foules for to synge
As yere by yere/was alway her usaunce
To synge a roundel at her departyng
To do Nature honour and plesaunce
The note I trowe/maked was in Fraunce
The wordes were such/ as ye may here fynde
The next vers/as I nowe haue in mynde

Qui bien ayme tarde oublie.

Now welcom sōmer/ with thy sonnes softe
That haste this wynter wethers ouershake
Saynt Valentyne/thou arte ful hye on lofte
Whiche driuest away/the longe nightes blake
Thus syngen smale foules for thy sake
Wel haue they cause for to gladen ofte
Sens eche of hem recouered hath his make
Ful blissful may they syng whan they awake.

And wt the shoutyng whā her songe was do
That foules made/at her flyght away
I woke/and other bokes toke me to
To rede upon/and yet I rede alway
I hope iwys to rede so some day
That I shal mete some thyng for to fare
The bet/and thus to rede I nyl not spare.

Explicit.

The Floure of Curtesy.

IN Feuerier/whan the frosty moone
Was horned/ful of Phebus fyry lyght
And that she gan to reyse her streames sone
Saynt Valentyne/upon thy blisful nyght
Of dutie/whan glad is euery wight
And foules chese/ to voyde her olde sorowe
Euerych his make/upon the next morowe

The same tyme I herde a larke synge
Ful lustely/agayne the morowe gray
Awake ye louers/out of your slombrynge
This glad morowe/in al the haste ye may
Some obseruaunce dothe unto this day
Your choyse ayen of herte to renewe
In confyrmyng/ for euer to be trewe

And ye that be of chosyng at your large
This lusty day/by custome of nature
Take upon you the blissful holy charge
To serue loue/whyle your lyfe may dure
With herte/body/and al your besy cure
For euermore/as Venus and Cipryde
For you disposeth/and the god Cupyde

For ioye owe we playnly to obey
Unto this lordes mighty ordynaunce
And mercylesse rather for to dye
Than euer in you be founden varyaunce
And though your lyfe be medled wt greuaūce
And at your herte closet be your wounde
Beth alway one/there as ye are bounde

D.d.d. Tha

The Floure of curtesye.

That whan I had herde and lysted longe
With deuoute herte/the lusty melodye
Of this heuenly comfortable songe
So agreable/ as by ermonye
I rose anon/and faste gan me hye
Towarde a groue/and the way take
Foules to sene/euerychе chose his make

And yet I was ful thursty in languisshyng
Myn ague was so feruent in his hete
Whan Aurora/for drery complaynyng
Can distyl her chrystal teres wete
Vpon the soyle/with syluer dewe so swete
For she durste for shame not apere
Vnder the lyght of Phebus beames clere

And so for anguysshe of my paynes kene
And for constraynte of my syghes sore
I set me downe/vnder a laurer grene
Ful pitously/and alway more and more
As I behelde in to the holtes hore
I gan complayne myn inwarde deedly smerte
That aye so sore crampesshe at myn herte

And whyle that I in my drery payne
Sate/and behelde aboute on euery tre
The foules sytte/alway twayne & twayne
Than thought I thus/alas what may this be
That euery foule hath his lyberte
Frely to chose/after his desyre
Eueryche his make/thus fro yere to yere

The sely wrenne/the tytemose also
The lytel redbrest/ haue free election
To flyen yfere/and togyther go
Where as hem lyst/aboute enuyron
As they of kynde haue inclynacion
And as Nature/empresse and gyde
Of euery thyng lyst to prouyde

But man alone/alas the harde stounde
Ful cruelly/by kyndes ordynaunce
Constrayned is/and by statute bounde
And debarred from al suche plesaunce
What meneth this/ what is this puruеyaunce
Of god aboue/agayne al right of kynde
Without cause/so narowe man to bynde

Thus may I sene and playne/ alas
My woful houre/and my disauenture
That doulfully stonde in the same caas
So ferre behynde/from al helth and cure
My wounde abydeth lyke a sursanure
For me fortune so felly lyste dispose
My harme is hyd/that I dare not disclose

For I my herte haue set/ in suche a place
Where I am neuer lykely for to spede
So ferre I am hyndred from her grace
That saue daunger/I haue none other mede
And thus alas/I not who shal me rede
Ne for myne helpe shape remedye
For Male bouche/and for false enuye

The whiche twayne/ aye stondeth in my wey
Malyciously/and false suspection
Is very cause also that I dey
Gynnyng and rote of my distruction
So that I fele/ in conclusyon
With her traynes/that they wol me shende
Of my labour/ that dethe mote make an ende

Yet or I dye/with herte/wyl/ and thought
To god of loue/ this auowe I make
As I best can/ howe dere that it be bought
Where so it be/that I slepe or wake
Whyle Boreas dothe the leaues slake
As I haue heyght/playnly tyl I sterue
For wel or wo/that I shal her serue

And for her sake/nowe this holy tyme
Saynt Valentyne/somwhat shal I write
Al though so be/that I can not ryme
Nor curyously by no crafte endyte
Yet leuer I haue/ that she put the wyte
In vnconnyng/than in neglygence
What euer I saye/ of her excellence

What euer I say/it is of dute
In sothfastnesse/and no presumpcion
This I ensure to you that shal it se
That it is al vnder correction
What I reherce in comendacion
Of her/ that I shal to you as blyue
So as I can/her vertues here discryue.

Right

¶ Ryght by example/as the somer sonne
Passeth the sterre/with his beames shene
And Lucyfer/amonge the skyes donne
A morowe sheweth/to voyde nyghtes tene
So verily/ withouten any wene
My lady passeth/who so taketh hede
Al tho alyue/to speke of womanhede

And as the Ruby hath the souerayntie
Of ryche stones/and the regalye
And the rose of swetenesse and beaute
Of fresshe floures/without any lye
Ryght so in sothe/with her goodly eye
She passeth al/in bountie and fayrenesse
Of maner eke/and of gentylnesse

For she is bothe the fayrest and the beste
To reken al/in very sothfastnesse
For euery vertue is in her at reste
And furthermore/to speke of stedfastnesse
She is the rote/and of semelynesse
The very myrrour/and of gouernaunce
To al example/withouten varyaunce

Of porte benygne/and wonder glad of chere
Hauyng euermore her trewe aduertence
Alway to reason/so that her desyre
Is brydeled aye / by wytte and prouydence
There to of wytte/ and of hye prudence
She is the welle/aye deuoyde of pride
That vnto vertue/ her seluen is the gyde

And ouer this/in her dalyaunce
Lowly she is/discrete and wyse
And goodly gladde/by attemperaunce
That euery wight/of hygh and lowe degre
Are glad in herte/with her for to be
So that shortly/if I shal not lye
She named is/ the Floure of Curtesye

And there to speke of feminyte
The leste mannysshe in comparyson
Goodly abasshed/hauyng aye pyte
Of hem that ben in trybulacion
For she alone is consolacion
To al that arne in mischefe and in nede
To comforte hem/of her womanhede

And aye in vertue is her besy charge
Sadde and demure/and but of wordes fewe
Dredeful also of tonges that ben large
Eschewyng aye hem/ that lysten to hewe
Aboue her heed/her wordes for to shewe
Dishonestly to speke of any wight
She deedly hateth/of hem to haue a syght

The herte of whom/so honest is and clene
And her entent/so faythful and entere
That she ne may/for al the worlde sustene
To suffre her eeres any worde to here
Of frende nor foe/neyther ferre ne nere
Amysse resownig/ ẏ hynder shulde his name
And if she do/she wexeth reed for shame

So trewly in menyng she is in sette
Without chaungyng/or any doublenesse
For bountie and beautie/are togyther knette
In her persone/vnder faythfulnesse
For voyde she is of newfanglenesse
In herte aye one/for euer to perseuer
There she is sette/and neuer to disseuer

I am to rude/her vertues euerychone
Connyngly to discryue and write
For wel ye wote/colour haue I none
Lyke her discrecion/ craftely to endyte
For what I say/al it is to lyte
Wherfore to you/thus I me excuse
That I aqueynted am not with no muse

By rethorike/my style to gouerne
In her preise and cõmendacion
I am to blynde/ so hyly to discerne
Of her goodnesse/to make discrypcion
Saue thus I say in conclusyon
If that I shal shortly cõmende
In her is naught/that nature can amende

For good she is/lyke to Polycene
And in fayrenesse/to the quene Helayne
Stedfast of herte/as was Dorigene
And wysely trouthe/if I shal not fayne
In constaunce eke & faythe/she may attayne
To Cleopatre/and therto as setrone
As was of Troye/the whyte Antygone

D.d.d.ii. As

The Floure of curtesye:

As Hester meke/ lyke Iudith of prudence
Kynde as Alceste/ or Marcia Catoun
And to Grisylde lyke in pacience
And Ariadne of discrecioun
And to Lucrece/ that was of Rome toun
She may be lykened as for honeste
And for her faythe/ vnto Penelope

To fayre Phyllis/ and to Hipsyphilee
For innocence/ and for womanhede
For semelynesse vnto Canace
And ouer this/ to speke of goodlyhede
She passeth al that I can of rede
For worde and dede/ that she naught ne fal
Acorde in vertue/ and her werkes al

For though that Dydo with wytte sage
Was in her tyme stedfast to Enee
Of hastynesse yet she dyd outrage
And so for Iason dyd also Medee
But my lady is so auysee
That bountie & beautie/ bothe in her demeyne
She maketh bountie alway souerayne

This is to meane/ bountie gothe afore
Lad by prudence/ and hath the souerayntie
And beautie foloweth/ ruled by her lore
That she ne fende her in no degre
So that in one/ this goodly fresshe fre
Surmountyng al/ withouten any were
Is good and fayre/ in one persone yfere

And though that I for very ignoraunce
Ne may discryue her vertues by and by
Yet on this day for a remembraunce
Onely supported vnder her mercy
With quakyng honde/ I shal ful humbly
To her hyenesse/ my rudenesse for to quyte
A lytel balade/ here byneth endyte

Euer as I can supprise in myn herte
Alway with feare/ betwyxt drede and shame
Leste out of lose/ any worde asterte
In this metre/ to make it seme lame
Chaucer is deed/ that had suche a name
Of fayre makyng/ that without wene
Fayrest in our tonge/ as the Laurer grene

We may assay for to countrefete
His gay style/ but it wyl not be
The welle is drie/ with the lycoure swete
Bothe of Clye/ and of Caliope
And first of al/ I wol excuse me
To her that is grounde of goodlyhede
And thus I say/ vntyl her womanhede.

¶ Balade symple.

¶ With al my might/ and my best entent
With al the faythe that mighty god of kynde
Me yaue/ syth he me soule and knowyng sent
I chese/ and to this bonde euer I me bynde
To loue you best/ whyle I haue lyfe & mynde
Thus herde I foules in the dawnynge
Vpon the day of saynte Valentyne synge

Yet chese I at the begynnyng/ in this entent
To loue you/ though I no mercy fynde
And if you lyste I dyed/ I wolde assent
As euer twynne I quicke out of this lyne
Suffyseth me to sene your fethers ynde
Thus herde I foules in the mornynge
Vpon the daye of saynte Valentyne synge

And ouer this/ myne hertes luste to bente
In honour onely of the wodde bynde
Holy I yeue/ neuer to repente
In ioye or wo/ where so that I wynde
Tofore Cupyde/ with his eyen blynde
The foules al/ whan Tytan dyd springe
With deuoute hert/ me thought I herde synge.

¶ Lenuoye.

¶ Princesse of beautie/ to you I represent
This symple dyte/ rude as in makynge
Of herte and wyl/ faythful in myn entent
Lyke as this day/ foules herde I synge.

¶ Here endeth the Floure of Curtesy/ and here after foloweth/ howe pyte is deed and buryed in a gentle herte.

How pite is ded and beried in a gentyll hert.

Pyte that I haue sought so yore ago
With herte sore/and ful of besy payne
That in this worlde was neuer wight so wo
Without dethe/and if I shal not sayne
My purpose was/ pyte to complayne
Upon the crueltie and tyrannye
Of loue/that for my trouthe dothe me dye

And that I by length of certayne yeres
Had euer in one/sought a tyme to speke
To Pyte ran I/al by spreynt with teeres
To prayen her on Cruelte me awreke
But or I myght with any worde out breke
Or tel her any of my paynes smerte
I founde her deed/and buryed in an herte

Adowne I fel/whan I sawe the herse
Deed as a stone/whyle y^t the swoune me laste
But vp I rose/with colour ful dyuerse
And pytously on her myn eyen I caste
And nerer the corse I gan preasen faste
And for the soule/I shope me for to pray
I was but lorne/there was no more to say

Thus am I slayne/sythe that Pyte is deed
Alas that day that euer it shulde fal
What maner man dare now holde vp his heed
To whom shal nowe any sorouful herte cal
Nowe Cruelte hath caste to slee vs al
In ydle hope/folke redelesse of payne
Sythe she is deed/ to whom shal we cōplayne

But yet encreaseth me this wonder newe
That no wight wote that she is deed but I
So many men as in her tyme her knewe
And yet she dyde so sodaynly
For I haue sought her euer ful besily
Sythe I had first wytte or mynde
But she was deed er I coude her fynde

Aboute her herse there stoden lustely
Withouten any mo/as thought me
Bountie/ perfytly wel armed and rychely
And fresshe Beaute/Lust/ and Iolyte
Assured maner/youthe/and Honeste
Wysdome/Estate/Drede/ and Gouernaunce
Confedred bothe by bonde and alyaunce

A complaynte had I written in my honde
To haue put to Pyte/as a byl
But I there al this company fonde
That rather wolde al my cause spyl
Than do me helpe/I helde my playnte styl
For to those folke withouten fayle
Without pyte/there may no byl auayle

Than leaue al Vertues/saue onely pyte
Kepyng the corse/as ye haue herde me sayne
Confedred by bonde vnto Cruelte
And be assented whan I shal be slayne
And I haue put my complaynte vp agayne
For to my foes/ my byl I dare not shewe
The effecte/ whiche sayth thus in wordes fewe

¶ Humblest of herte/hyest of reuerence
Benigne flour/crowne of vertues al
Sheweth vnto your royal excellence
Your seruaunt/ if I durst me so cal
His mortal harme/in whiche he is yfal
And nought al onely for his woful fare
But for your renome/as he shal declare

It stondeth thus / that your cōtrary cruelte
Alyed is ayenst your regalye
Under colour of womanly beaute
For men shulde not knowe her tyrannye
With Bountie/ Gentylesse/ and Curtesy
And hath depriued you of your place
That is high beautie/ apertenant to yor grace

For kyndely/ by your herytage right
Ye be anneyed euer vnto bounte
And verily ye ought do your myght
To helpe trouthe in his aduersyte
Ye be also the corowne of beaute
And certes if ye wante in these twayne
The worlde is lore/there is no more to sayne

Eke what auayleth maner and gentylesse
Without you/benigne creature
Shal cruelte be your gouerneresse
Alas/ what herte may it longe endure
Wherfore but ye rather take cure
To breke that peryllous alyaunce
Ye sleen hem that ben in your obeysaunce

And

And further/if ye suffre thus
your renome is fordo in a throwe
There shal no man wete what pyte is
Alas/that euer your renome is fal so lowe
ye be also fro your herytage ythrowe
By crueltе/that occuppeth your place
And we dispayred/that seken your grace

Haue mercy on me/ thou Herenus quene
That you haue sought/ so tenderly and sore
Let some streme of lyght on me be sene
That loue and drede you euer lenger the more
For sothly to sayne/I beare so sore
And though I be not connyng for to playne
For goddes loue haue mercy on my payne

My payne is this/that what so I desyre
That haue I not/ne nothyng lyke therto
And euer setteth desyre myn herte on fyre
Eke on that other syde where that I go
What maner thyng that may encrease my wo
That haue I redy unsought euery where
Me lacketh but my dethe/and than my bere

What nedeth to shewe percel of my payne
Sythe euery wo/that herte may bethynke:
I suffre/and yet I dare not to you playne
For wel I wote/though I wake or wynke
ye recke not whether I flete or synke
And nathelesse yet my trouthe I shal sustene
Unto my dethe/and that shal wel be sene

This is to sayne/I wyl be yours euer
Though ye me slee by crueltе your fo
Algate my spyrite shal neuer disceuer
Fro your seruyce/for any payne or wo
Sythe ye be yet deed/alas that it is so
Thus for your dethe/I may wepe & playne
With herte sore/ and ful of besy payne.

¶ Explicit.

La belle dame sans mercy.

Halfe in a dreme / not fully wel awaked
The golde͞n slepe me wrapped under his
yet nat for thy I rose/& wel nigh naked (wing
Al sodaynly my selfe remembryng
Of a mater/leuynge al other thynge
Whiche I must do withouten more delay
For hem/ whiche I durst nat dysobey

My charge was this/ to translate by and by
Al thynge forgyue/as parte of my penaunce
A boke/called La bel dame sauns mercy
Whiche mayster Alcyne made of reme͞braunce
Chefe secratarie with the kyng of Fraunce
And herupon a whyle I stode musynge
And in my selfe greatly ymagenynge

What wyse I shulde performe ye sayd processe
Consyderynge by good aduysement
My unconnynge/and my great symplenesse
And ayenwarde the strayte co͞maundement
Whiche that I had/and thus in myne entent
I was vexed and tourned up and downe
And yet at last/ as in conclusyon

I cast my clothes on/and went my way
This foresayd charge hauyng in reme͞braunce
Tyl I came to a lusty grene valey
Ful of floures/to se a great plesaunce
And so boldly with theyr benygne suffraunce
Whiche rede this boke/ touchynge this matere
Thus I began/ if it please you to here.

Nat longe ago/ rydynge an easy paas
I fel in thought of ioy ful desperate
With great dysease & payne/ so that I was
Of al louers the most unfortunate
Syth by his darte/most cruel ful of hate
The dethe hath take my lady and maystresse
And lefte me sole/thus dyscomfyte & mate
Sore languysshynge/and in way of dystresse

Than sayd I thus/ it falleth me to cesse
Eyther to ryme/ or dytees for to make
And I surely to make a ful promesse
To laugh no more/ but wepe in clothes blake
My ioyful tyme (alas) nowe doth it slake
For in my selfe I fele no maner of ease

Let

Let it be wrytten/ suche fortune (as I take)
Whiche neyther me/ nor non other doth please

If it were so/my wyl or myne entent
Constrayned were/a ioyful thynge to wryte
My penne coude neuer knowe/ what it ment
To speke therof/my tonge hath no delyte
Tho with my mouthe I laugh/ moche or lyte
Myne eyen sholde make a coūtenaūce vntrue
My herte also/ wolde haue therof dyspyte
The wepynge teares/haue so large yssue

These sicke louers I leue/that to hem longes
Whiche lede theyr lyfe in hope of alegeaunce
That is to say/to make balades and songes
Euery of hem/as they fele theyr greuaunce
For she that was my ioy/and my plesaunce
Whose soule I pray god/ of his mercy saue
She hath my wyl/myne hertes ordynaunce
Whiche lyeth here/Within this tombe ygraue

Fro this tyme forth/tyme is to holde my pees
It weryeth me/this mater for to trete
Let other louers put hem selfe in prees
Theyr season is/my tyme is nowe forgete
Fortune by strength/the forcer hath vnshete
Wherin was sperde al my worldly richesse
And al the goodes/whiche that I haue gete
In my best tyme of youthe/and lustynesse

Loue hath me kepte vnder his gouernaunce
If I mysdyd/god graunt me forgyuenesse
Yf I dyd wel/yet felte I no plesaunce
It caused neyther ioye nor heuynesse
For whan she dyed/that was my maystres
My welfare/than made the same purchase
The dethe hath shette my bondes of wytnes
Which for nothyng myn herte shal neuer pase

In this great thought/sore troubled in mynde
Alone thus rode I/al the morowe tyde
Tyl at the last it happed me to fynde
The place/wherin I cast me to abyde
Whan that I had no further for to ryde
And as I went/my lodgynge to puruey
Ryght soone I herde/a lytel me besyde
In a garden/where mynstrels gan to play

With that anone/I went me backer more
My selfe and I/me thought we were ynowe
But twayne that were my frēdes here before
Had me espyed/and yet I wote nat howe
They came for me/awaywarde I me drowe
Somwhat by force/somwhat by her request
That in no wyse/I coude my selfe rescowe
But nedes I must come in and se the feest

At my cōmynge/the ladyes euerchone
Bad me welcome/god wote right gentylly
And made me chere/euery one by one
A great dele better than I was worthy
And of theyr grace/shewed me grete curtesy
Wt good disport/ bicause I shuld nat mourne
That day I bode styl in theyr company
Whiche was to me/a gracyous soiourne

The bordes were spred/in right lytel space
The ladyes sat/eche as hem semed best
There were no deedly seruauntes in the place
But chosen men/right of the goodlyest
And some there were/pauēture most fresshest
That sawe theyr iuges ful demure
Without semblaunt/eyther to most or lest
Natwithstandynge/they had hem vnder cure

Amonge al other/one I gan espy
Whiche in grete thought/ful oftē came & went
As one that had ben rauysshed vtterly
In his language/nat greatly dylygent
His countenaunce he kept wt great tourment
But his desyre farre passed his reason
For euer his eye/went after his entent
Ful many a tyme/whan it was no season

To make chere/ sore him selfe he payned
And outwardly he fayned great gladnesse
To synge also/byforce he was constrayned
For no plesaunce/ but very shamfastnesse
For the complaynte of his moste heuynesse
Came to his voyce/alway without request
Lyke as the sowne of byrdes dothe expresse
Whan they synge loude/in fryth or in forest

Other there were/that serued in the hal
But none lyke him/ as after myn aduyse
For he was pale/and somwhat leane withal

His

La belle dame sans mercy.

His speche also trymbled in fereful wyse
And euer alone/but whan he dyd seruyse
Al blacke he ware/& no deuyse but playne
Me thought by hym/as my wyt coude suffyse
His herte was nothyng in his owne demeyne

To feest hem al/he dyd his dylygence
And wel he coude/ryght as it semed me
But euermore/whan he was in presence
His chere was done/it wolde none other be
His schole mayster had suche authorite
That al the whyle he bode styl in the place
Speke coude he nat/but upon her beaute
He loked styl/with right a pytous face

With that his heed he tourned at the last
For to beholde the ladyes euerychone
But euer in one/he set his eye stedfast
On her/whiche his thought was most upon
For of his eyen/the shot I knewe anone
Whiche fereful was/wᵗ right hũble requestes
Than to my selfe I sayd/by god alone
Suche one was I/or that I sawe these iestes

Out of the prese he wente ful easely
To make stable his heuy countenaunce
And wote ye wel/he syghed wonderly
For his sorowes and woful remembraunce
Than in hym selfe/he made his ordynaunce
And forthwithal came to brynge in the messe
But for to iuge/his most woful penaunce
God wote it was a pytous entremesse

After dyner anone/they hem auaunced
To daunce aboue the folkes euerychone
And forthwithal/this heuy man he daunced
Somtyme with twayne/& somtyme with one
Unto hem al/his chere was after one
Nowe here nowe there/as fel by auenture
But euer amonge/he drewe to her alone
Whiche he most dred/of lyuynge creature

To myne aduyse/good was his purueyaũce
Whan he her chase/to his maystres alone
If that her herte were set to his plesaunce
As moche as was her beauteous persone
For who so euer setteth his trust upon
The reporte of the eyen/withouten more
He myght be deed/and grauen under stone
Or euer he shulde/his hertes ease restore

In her fayled nothynge/that I coude gesse
One wyse nor other/preuy nor perte
A garyson she was/of al goodlynesse
To make a frounter/for a louers herte
Right yonge & fresshe/a woman ful couerte
Assured wele of porte/and eke of chere
Wele at her ease/withouten wo or smerte
Al underneth the standerde of daungere

To se the feest/it weryed me ful sore
For heuy ioye doth sore the herte trauayle
Out of the prese/I me withdrawe therfore
And set me downe alone behynde a trayle
Ful of leues/to se a great meruayle
With grene wrethes ybounden wonderly
The leues were so thycke withouten fayle
That throughout/no man might me espy

To this lady he came ful curtesly
Whã he thought tyme to daũce wᵗ her a trace
Set in an herber/made ful plesauntly
They rested hem fro thens but a lytel space
Nygh hem were none/of a certayne compace
But onely they/as farre as I coude se
Saue the trayle/there I had chose my place
There was no more bytwene hem two & me

I harde the louer syghyng wonder sore
For aye the more/the sorer it him sought
His inwarde payne he coude not kepe in store
Nor for to speke/so hardy was he nought
His leche was nere/ꝥ gretter was his thought
He mused sore/to conquere his desyre
For no man may to more penaũce be brought
Than in his heate/to bring him to the fyre

The herte began to swel within his cheste
So sore strayned/for anguisshe & for payne
That al to peces almoste it to brest
Whan bothe at ones/so sore it dyd constrayne
Desyre was bolde/but shame it gan restrayne
That one was large/the other was ful close
No lytel charge was layde on him certayne
To kepe suche werre/and haue so many fose

Ful

Ful often tymes to speke/ him selfe he payned
But shamfastnesse & drede/sayd euer nay
yet at the last/so sore he was constrayned
Whan he ful longe had put it in delay
To his lady/right thus than gan he say
With dredeful voyce/weppyng/halfe in a rage
For me was purueyed/an vnhappy day
Whan I fyrst had a sight of your vysage

I suffre payne god wote / ful hote brennynge
To cause my dethe/al for my true seruyse
And I se wel/ye recke therof nothynge
Nor take no hede of it/ in no kynde wyse
But whan I speke after my best aduyse
ye set it at nought/but make therof a game
And thoughe I sewe/so great an entrepryse
yet peyreth not your worshyp nor your fame

Alas/what shulde it be to you preiudyce
If that a man do loue you faythfully
To your worshyp/eschewynge euery vyce
So am I yours/and wyl be verely
I chalenge nought of right/and reason why
For I am hole submytt vnto your seruyce
Right as ye lyst it be/right so wyl I
To bynde my selfe/where I was in fraūchise

Lamant

Though it be so/ that I can nat deserue
To haue your grace/but alway lyue in drede
yet suffre me/you for to loue and serue
Withouten maugre/of your most goodlyhede
Both fayth & trouth I gyue your womāhede
And my seruyce without any callynge
Loue hath me bonde/ withoute wage or mede
To be your man/and leue al other thynge

La dame

Whan this lady had herde al this language
She gaue answere/ful softe and demurely
Without chaungynge of colour or courage
Nothynge in haste/out mesurably
Me thynketh syr/your thought is great foly
Purpose ye nought/your labour for to cese
For thynketh not/ whyles ye lyue and I
In this mater/to set your herte in pease

Lamant

There may none make the peace/but onely ye
Whiche are the grounde & cause of al this war
For with your eyen/ the letters written be
By whiche I am defyed and put a far
your plesaunt loke/ my very lode star
Was made heraude/ of thylke same defyaūce
Whiche vtterly behyght me for to barre
My faythful trust/and al myne affyaunce

La dame

To lyue in wo/ he hath great fantasy
And of his herte also slypper holde
That onely for beholdynge of an eye
Can nat abyde in peace/ as reason wolde
Other or me/if ye lyst ye may beholde
Our eyē are made to loke/ whi shuld we spare
I take no kepe/ neyther of yonge ne olde
Who feleth smerte/I counsayle hym beware

Lamant.

If it be so/one hurte another sore
In his defaute/that feleth the greuaunce
Of very ryght/a man may do no more
yet reason wolde it were in remembraunce
And syth fortune onely by her chaunce
Hath caused me to suffre al this payne
By your beaute/with al the cyrcumstaunce
Why lyst ye haue me/in so great dysdayne

La dame

To your persone/ne haue I no dysdayne
Nor neuer had trewly/ ne nought wyl haue
Nor right great loue/nor hatred in certayne
Nor your counsayle to know/so god me saue
yf suche loue be in your mynde ygraue
That lytel thynge/may do you dysplesaunce
you to begyle/or make you for to raue
I wyl nat cause/no suche encomberaunce

Lamant

What euer it be/ ẏ me hath thus purchased
Wenynge hath nat dysceyued me certayne
But feruent loue/ so sore hath me ychased
That I vnware / am casten in your chayne
And syth so is/ as fortune lyst ordayne
Al my welfare/is in your handes fal
In eschewynge of more myscheuous payne
Who sonest dyeth/ his care is lest of al

La dame

This sickenesse is right easy to endure
But fewe people/it causeth for to dye
But what they meane/I knowe it very sure
Of more comforte / to drawe the remedy
Suche be there now/playnyng ful pytously
That fele god wote/nat alther grettest payne

And

La belle dame sans mercy.

And if so be/loue hurte so greuously
Lesse harme it were/one sorowful thā twayn
Lamant
Alas madame/if that it myght you please
Moche better it were/by way of gentylnesse
Of one sory/to make twayne wel at ease
Than hym to destroye that lyueth in distresse
For my desyre is/neyther more nor lesse
But my seruyce/to do for your plesaunce
In eschewynge al maner doubleenesse
To make two ioyes/in stede of one greuaūce
La dame
Of loue I seke/neyther pleasaunce nor ease
Nor haue therin no great affyaunce
Though ye be sicke/it doth me nothing please
Also I take no hede of your plesaunce
Chese who so wyl/her hertes to auaunce
Fre am I nowe/and free wyl I endure
To be ruled by mannes gouernaunce
For erthely good/Nay/that I you ensure
Lamant
Loue/whiche ẏ ioy and sorowe doth departe
Hath set the ladyes out of al seruage
And largely dothe graunt hem for her parte
Lordship and rule of euery maner of age
The poore seruaūt/nought hath of auantage
But what he may gete onely by purchesse
And he that ones/to loue doth his homage
Ful often tymes/dere bought is the richesse
La dame
Ladyes be nat so symple/thus I mene
So dul of wyt/so sotted in foly
That for wordes/whiche sayd be of the splene
In fayre langage/paynted ful plesauntly
Whiche ye and mo/holde scholes of dayly
To make hem al/great wonders to suppose
But sone they can away/theyr heedes wrye
And to fayre speche/lyghtly theyr eres close
Lamant
There is no man/that iangleth busyly
And setteth his herte/& al his mynde therfore
That by reason/may playne so pytously
As he that hath moche heuynesse in store
Whose heed is hole/and sayth that it is sore
His fayned chere/is harde to kepe in mewe
But thought/whiche is unfayned euermore
The wordes preueth/as the werkes shewe
La dame
Loue is subtel/and hath a great awayte
Sharpe i workyng/i gabbing great plesaūc
And can hym venge/of suche as by dysceyte
Wolde fele and knowe/his secrete gouernaūc
And maketh hem to obey his ordynaunce
By chereful wayes/as in hem is supposed
But whan they fal in to repentaunce
Than in a rage/her counsayle is disclosed
Lamant
Sith for as moche/as god and eke nature
Hath auaunced loue/to so hye degre
Moche sharpe is the poynt/thus am I sure
yet greueth more the faute/where euer it be
Who hath no colde/of heate hath no deynte
The one for that other/asked is expresse
And of plesaunce/knoweth non certeyne
But it be one/in thought and heuynesse.
La dame
As for plesaunce/it is nat alway one
That you thike swete/I thike it bitter payne
ye may nat me cōstrayne/nor yet ryght none
After your lust to loue/that is but vayne
To chalenge loue by right/was neuer seyne
But herte assent/before bonde and promyse
For strength and force/may nat attayne
A wyl that standeth enfeffed in fraunchyse
Lamant
Ryght fayre lady/god mote I neuer please
yf I seke other right in this case
But for to shewe you playnly my dysease
And your mercy to abyde/& eke your grace
If I purpose your honour to deface
Or euer dyd/god and fortune me shende
And that I neuer unryghtfully purchace
One onely ioy/unto my lyues ende
La dame
ye and other/that swere suche othes faste
And so condempne/and cursen to and fro
Ful sykerly ye wene your othes laste
No lenger than the wordes ben ago
And god/and eke his payntes laughe also
In suche swerypng/there is no stedfastnesse
And these wretches that haue ful trust therto
After they wepe and waylen in distresse
Lamant.
He hath no corage of a man trewly
That secheth plesaunce/worshyp to dispyse
Nor to be called forthe/is not worthy

The

The erthe to touche/ ẏ ayre in no kyns wyse
A trusty herte/a mouth without feyntyse
Thus be the strength of euery maner name
And who that layeth his fayth for lytel pryse
He leseth bothe his worshyp and his fame

La dame.

A cursed herte/a mouth that is curteyse
Ful wel ye wote they be not accordynge
Yet fayned chere/right soone may hem apeyse
Where of malyce is set al her workynge
Ful false semblant they bere/ & true semynge
Her name/her fame/her tonges but fayned
Worshyp in hem is put in forgettynge
Nought repented/ nor in no wise complayned

Lamant.

Who thinketh yl/ no good may hym befal
God of his grace graunt eche man his desert
But for his loue/amonge your thoughtes al
As thynke vpon my woful sorowes smert
For of my payne/ wheder your tender herte
Of swete pyte/be not therwith agreued
And of your grace/to me were discouerte
That by your mean/ sone shulde I be rescued

La dame.

A lightsome herte/a folly of plesaunce
Are moche better/the lesse whyle they abyde
They make you thinke/& bring you i a traunce
But that sickenesse/ wyl sone be remedyde
Respite your thought/and put al this asyde
Ful good disporte werieth me al day
To helpe nor hurte/my wyl is not aplyde
Who troweth me not/ I let hem passe away

Lamant.

Who hath a byrde/a faucon/or a hounde
That foloweth him for loue in euery place
He cherissheth hym/& kepeth hym ful sounde
Out of his sight/he wyl not him enchace
And I that set my wyttes in this cace
On you alone/withouten any chaunge
Am put vnder/moche farther out of grace
And lesse set by/than other that be straunge

La dame.

Thoughe I make chere to euery man aboute
For my worshyp/& for myne owne fraũchyse
To you I nyl do so/ withouten doute
In eschewynge al maner preiudyse
For wote ye wel/loue is so lytel wyse
And in byleue/so lyghtly wyl be brought

That he taketh al at his owne deuyse
Of thinge god wote/ẏ serueth him of nought

Lamant.

Yf I by loue/and by my true seruyce
Lese ẏ good chere ẏ straungers haue alway
Wherof shal serue my trouth in any wise
Lesse than to him/that cometh & gothe al day
Whiche holdeth of you nothyng/ẏ is no nay
Also in you is lost/as to my semynge
Al curtesy/whiche of reason wyl say
That loue for loue/were lawful despringe

La dame.

Curtesy is alyed wonder nere
To worshyp/ whiche hym loueth tenderly
And he wyl nat be bounde for no prayere
Nor for no gyftes/I say you verely
But his good chere/departe ful largely
Where hym lyketh/as his concepte wyl fal
Guerdon cõstrayned a gifte done thankfully
These twayn cã neuer accorde nor neuer shal

Lamant.

As for guerdon I seke none in this cace
For that desert/to me it is to hye
Wherfore I aske your pardon & your grace
Sith me behoueth dethe/or your mercy
To gyue the good where it wanteth truely
That were reason/ and a curtyse manere
And to your owne moche better were worthy
Tha to straungers/to shewe hem louely chere

La dame.

What cal ye good/fayne wolde I that I wyst
That pleaseth one/another smerteth sore
But of his owne/to large is he that lyst
Gyue moche/and lese his good name therfore
One shulde nat make a graunt/lytel ne more
But the request were right wel accordinge
Yf worshyp be not kepte and set before
Al that is lefte/is but a lytel thynge

Lamant.

In to this worlde was founded neuer none
For vnder heuen creature ybore
Nor neuer shal/saue onely your persone
To whõ your worship toucheth halfe so sore
But me whiche haue no season lesse ne more
Of youthe ne age/but styl in your seruice
I haue no eyen/no wit/nor mouth in store
But al be gyuen to the same office

La dame.

[illegible] A ful

A ful great charge hath he withouten fayle
That his worship kepeth in sykernesse
But in daunger he setteth his trauayle
That feleth it with others busynesse
To hym that longeth/honour and noblesse
Vpon none other shulde nat be a wayte
For of his owne/so moche hath he the lesse
That of other/moche foloweth the conceyte

Lamant.

Your eyen hath set the prynt/which that I fele
Within my hert/that where so euer I go
Yf I do thynge/that sowneth vnto wele
Nedes must it come from you/ & fro no mo
Fortune wyl this/ that I for wele or wo
My lyfe endure/your mercy abydynge
And very right wyl/that I thinke also
Of your worshyp/aboue al other thynge

La dame.

To your worshyp se wel/for that is nede
That ye spende nat your season al in vayne
As touchynge myn/I rede you take no hede
By your foly/to put your selfe in payne
To ouercome is good/and to restrayne
An herte/ whiche is disceyued folyly
For worse it is to breke than bowe certayne
Better bowe/than to fal sodaynly

Lamant.

Nowe fayre lady thinke/sith it first began
That loue hath set myn herte vnder his cure
It neuer might/ne truely I ne can
None other serue/whyle I shal here endure
In most fre wyse/therof I make you sure
Whiche may not be withdrawe/this is no nay
I must abyde al maner aduenture
For I may neyther put to nor take away

La dame.

I holde it for no gyfte in sothfastnesse
That one offreth/where it is forsake
For suche a gifte is abandonynge expresse
That with worship agen may not be take
He hath an herte ful fel that lyst to make
A gifte lyghtly/ that put is to refuse
But he is wyse/that suche conceyte wyl slake
So that hym nede/neyther to study ne muse

Lamant.

He shulde nat muse/ yͭ hath his seruice spent
On her/whiche is a lady honourable
And if I spende my tyme to that entent
Yet at the lest/I am not reprouable
Of fayned herte/to thinke I am vnable
Or I mystoke/ whan I made this request
By whiche loue hath of entreprise notable
So many hertes gotten by conquest

La dame.

If that ye liste do after my counsayle
Seche a fayrer/and of more higher fame
Whiche in seruyce of loue/wyl you preuayle
After your thought/accordynge to the same
He hurteth both his worshyp & his name
That folyly/for twayne hi selfe wyl trouble
And he also leseth his after game
That surely can not set his poyntes double

Lamant.

This your counsayle/by ought that I can se
Is better said than done/to myne aduyse
Thoughe I byleue it not/forgyue it me
Myne herte is suche/ so hole without feyntyse
That I ne may giue credence in no wise
To thinge/ which is not sownyng vnto truthe
Other counsayle I se/be but fantasise
Saue of your grace/to shewe pyte and ruthe

La dame.

I holde him wise that worketh no foly
And whan him lyst/can leue & parte therfro
But in connynge/he is to lerne truely
That wolde hym selfe conduite/& can not so
And he that wyl not after counsayle do
His sute he putteth in to disperaunce
And al the good that shulde fal him to
Is lost and deed/clene out of remembraunce

Lamant.

Yet wyl I sewe this matter faythfully
Whyles I lyue/what euer be my chaunce
And if it hap/ that in my truthe I dye
Than dethe shal do me no displesaunce
But whan that I/by your harde suffraunce
Shal dye so true and with so great a payne
Yet shal it do me moche the lesse greuaunce
Than for to lyue a false louer certayne

La dame.

Of me get ye right nought/this is no fable
I wyl to you be neyther harde nor strayte
And right wyl/not no man customable
To thynke ye shulde/be sure of my conceyte
Who secheth sorowe/his be the receyte
Other counsayle can I not fele nor se

Nor

Nor for to serne/I cast me not to awayte
Who wyl therof/let hym assay for me

Lamant.

Ones must it be assayde/ that is no nay
With suche as be of reputacyon
And of true loue/the right honour to pay
Of free hertes gotten by dewe raunsome
For frewyl holdeth this opynyon
That it is great duresse and discomforte
To kepe a herte in so strayte a prison
That hath but one body for his disporte

La dame.

I knowe so many causes meruaylous
That I must nede of reason thinke certayne
That suche auenture is wonder perylous
And yet wel more/the comynge backe agayne
Good or worship/therof is seldome sene
Where I ne wyl make suche aray
As for to fynde a plesaunce/but a barayne
Whan it shal cost so dere the fyrst assay

Lamant.

Ye haue no cause to doute of this mater
Nor you to meue with no suche fantasyse
To put me farre al out as a straunger
For your goodnesse can thinke & wel aduyse
That I haue made a prise in euery wyse
By whiche my truthe sheweth open euydence
My longe abydynge/and my trewe seruyce
May wel be knowen by playne experience

La dame.

Of very right he may be called trewe
And so must he be take in euery place
That can discerne/and let as he ne knewe
And kepe the good/if he it may purchace
For who that prayeth/or swereth in any case
Right wel ye wote/ in ỹ no trouth is preued
Suche hath there ben/and are / ỹ geten grace
And lese it sone/whan they haue it acheued

Lamant.

If truthe me cause/by vertue soueraynе
To shewe good loue/& alway fynde contrary
And cherissh ỹ/ which sleeth me with ỹ payne
This is to me a louely aduersary
Whan that pite/which long on slepe doth tary
Hath set the fyne of al my heuynesse
Yet her comforte to me most necessary
Shal set my wyl more sure in stablenesse

La dame.

The woful wight/what may he thinke or say
The contrary of al ioy and gladnesse
A sycke body/his thought is alway
From hem that felen no sore nor sickenesse
Thus hurtes ben of dyuers busynesse
Whiche loue hath put to great hyndraunce
And truthe also/put in forgetfulnesse
Whan they ful sore begyn to sighe alkaunce

Lamant.

Nowe god defende/but he be harmlesse
Of al worshyp or good that may befal
That to werst tourneth by his lewdnesse
A gyfte of grace/or any thinge at al
That his lady vouchesafe vpon hym cal
Or cherissheth hym in honourable wyse
In that defaute/what euer he be that fal
Deserueth more than dethe to suffre twyse.

La dame.

There is no iuge yset on suche trespace
By whiche of right/loue may recouered be
One curseth fast/another dothe manace
yet dyeth none/as farre as I can se
But kepe her course alway in one degre
And euermore/theyr labour dothe encrease
To bringe ladyes by their great subtelte
For others gilte/in sorowe and disease

Lamant.

Albeit so/one dothe so great offence
And is not deed/nor put to no iustyce
Right wel I wote hym gayneth no defence
But he must ende in ful myscheuous wise
And al euer sayd/god wyl hym dispise
For falshed is ful of cursednesse
That his worship may neuer haue enterprise
Where it reigneth/ & hath the wylfulnesse

La dame.

Of that haue they no great fere nowe a dayse
Suche as wyl say and mayntayne it therto
That stedfast truthe is nothyng for to prayse
In hem that kepe it longe in wele or wo
Theyr busy hertes passen to and fro
They be so wel reclaymed to the lure
So wel lerned hem to withholde also
And al to chaũge/whã loue shuld best endure

Lamant.

Whan one hath set his herte in stable wyse
In suche a place / as is bothe good and trewe
He shulde not flyt/but do forth his seruice

T.t.t.ii. Alway

Alway withouten chaunge of any new
As sone as loue begynneth to remewe
Al plesaunce gothe anone in lytel space
As for my partie/that shal I eschewe
Whyle the soule abideth in his place

La dame.

To loue truely/there as it ought of right
Ye may not be mystaken doutlesse
But ye be foule disceyued in your sight
By light understandyng/as I gesse
yet may ye wel repele your businesse
And to reason haue some attendaunce
Moche better than to abide by foly simplenes
The feble socour of disperaunce

Lamant.

Reason/counsayle/wisedome/& good aduyse
Ben under loue arested euerychone
To whiche I can accorde in euery wise
For they be not rebel/but styl as a stone
Their wyl and myne/be medled al in one
And ther with bouden with so strong a cheyne
That as in hem/departynge shal be none
But pyte breke the mighty bonde atwayne

La dame.

Ye loue not your selfe/what euer ye be
That in loue stande forgete in euery place
And of your wo/if ye haue no pyte
Others pyte bileue ye not to purchace
But be fully assured/as in this case
I am alway under one ordynaunce
To haue better trust not after grace
And al that leueth/take to your plesaunce

Lamant.

I haue my hope so sure and so stedfast
That suche a lady shulde not lacke pyte
But nowe alas/it is shyt up so fast
That daunger sheweth on me his cruelte
And if she se the vertue fayle in me
Of true seruyce/thoughe she do fayle also
No wonder were/but this is my surete
I must suffre/ whiche way that euer it go

Lamant.

Leue this pupose I rede you for the best
For the lenger ye kepe/it is in vayne
The lesse ye gete/as of your hertes rest
And to reioyce it shal you neuer attayne
Whan ye abide good hope to make you fayne
Ye shal be founde asotted in dotage
And in the ende/ye shal knowe for certayne
Hope shal pay the wretches for her wage

Lamant.

Ye say as falleth most for your plesaunce
And your power is great/al this I se
But hope shal neuer out of my remembraunce
By whiche I fele so great aduersyte
For whan nature hathe set in you plente
Of al goodnesse/by vertue and by grace
He neuer assembled hem/as semed me
To put pyte out of his dwellynge place

La dame.

Pyte of right ought to be resonable
And to no wight do no great disauauntage
There as is nede/it shulde be profytable
And to the pitous shewynge no domage
If a lady wyl do so great outrage
To shewe pyte and cause her owne debate
Of suche pyte cometh dispitous rage
And of suche loue/also right deedly hate

Lamant.

To comforte hem that lyue al comfortlesse
That is no harme/but cõforte to your name
But ye that haue a herte of suche duresse
And a fayre lady I must affirme the same
If I durst say/ ye wynne al this defame
By cruelte/whiche sitteth you ful yl
But if pyte/whiche may al this attame
In your high herte may rest and tary styl

La dame.

What euer he be that sayth he loueth me
And perauenture I leue wel it be so
Ought he be wroth/or shulde I blamed be
Thoughe I dyd not as he wolde haue me do
If I medled with suche or other mo
It might be called pyte mercylesse
And afterwarde if I shulde lyue in wo
Than to repent/it were to late I gesse

Lamant.

O marble herte/and yet more harde parde
Whiche mercy may not perce for no labour
More stronge to bowe than is a myghty tre
What auayleth you to shewe so great rigour
Pleaseth it you more to se me dye this hour
Before your eyen/for your dysporte and play
Than for to shewe some comforte and socour
To respyte dethe/whiche chaseth me alway

La dame.

Of

Of your disease/ye may haue allegeaunce
And as for myne/I set it ouer slake
Also ye shal not dye for my plesaunce
Nor for your heale/I can no surety make
I wyl nat hurte my selfe for others sake
Wepe they/laugh they/or synge they/I warãt
For this mater/so wyl I vndertake
That none of hem shal make therof auaunt

Lamant.

I can nat skyl of loue by god alone
I haue more cause to wepe in your presence
And wel ye wote/auauntour am I none
For certaynly/I loue better scilence
One shulde nat loue by his hertes credence
But he were sure to kepe it secretly
For a vauntour is of no reuerence
Whan that his tonge is his most enemy

La dame.

Male bouche in courte/hath great cõmaundement
Eche man studieth to say the worst he may
These false louers/in this tyme nowe present
They serue best to iangle as a Iay
The most secrete ywis/yet some men say
Howe he mistrusted is in some partyse
Wherfore to ladies whan so men speke or say
It shulde be byleued in no wyse

Lamant.

Of good and yl shal be/and is alway
The worlde is suche/ỳ erth is not al playne
They that be good/ỳ profe sheweth euery day
And otherwise great villony certayne
It is reason/thoughe one his tonge distayne
With cursed speche/to do hym selfe a shame
That suche refuce/shuld wrõgfully remayne
Upon the good renomed in theyr fame

La dame.

Suche as be nought/whã they here tydynges newe
That eche trespas shal lightly haue pardon
They that pursuen to be good and trewe
Wyl not set by none yl disposicion
To contynue in euery good condicion
They are the first that fallen in damage
And ful frely the hertes habandon
To lytel faithe/with softe and fayre langage

Lamant.

Nowe knowe I wel of very certaynte
If one do truely/yet shal he be shente
Sith al maner of iustice and pyte
Is banysshed out of a ladyes entente
I can nat se/but al is at one stente
The good/the yl/the vice/& eke the vertue
Suche as be good/such haue the punysshmẽt
For the trespas of hem that lyue vntrue

La dame.

I haue no power you to do greuaunce
Nor to punysshe none other creature
But to eschewe the more encomberaunce
To kepe vs from you al/I holde it sure
False semblaunce/hath a face ful demure
Lightly to catche these ladyes in a wayte
Wherfore we must/if we wyl here endure
Make right good watch/lo this is my cõceyte

Lamant.

Sith that of grace/a goodly worde nat one
May nowe be had/but alway kepte in store
I appele to god/for he may here my mone
Of the duresse/whiche greueth me so sore
And of pyte/I complayne furthermore
Whiche he forgate/in al his ordynaunce
Or els my lyfe to haue ended before
Whiche so sone am put out of remembraunce

La dame.

My herte nor I haue done you no forfeyte
By which ye shulde complayne in any kynde
Nothing hurteth you/but your owne cõceyte
Be iuge your selfe/for so ye shal it fynde
Thus alway let this synke in your mynde
That your desyre shal neuer recouered be
Ye noy me sore/in wastinge al this wynde
For I haue sayd ynoughe/as semeth me

Lamant.

This woful man rose vp in al his payne
And so departed with wepynge countenaunce
His woful herte/almost to brast in twayne
Ful lyke to dye/walkynge forth in a traunce
And sayd dethe come forth/thy selfe auaunce
Or that myne herte forgete his properte
And make shorter al this woful penaunce
Of my pore lyfe/ful of aduersyte

Fro thẽs he went/but whither wist I nought
Nor to what parte he drewe in sothfastnesse
But he no more was in his ladyes thought
For to the daunce anone she gan her dresse
And afterwarde/one tolde me thus expresse
He rent his heer/for anguysshe and for payne

C.c.c.iii. And

And in hym selfe toke so great heuynesse
That he was deed within a day or twayne

¶ Lenuoy.

The true louers thus I beseche you al
Such auẽtures flie hem in euery wise
And as people defamed ye hem cal
For they truely do you great preiudyse
His castelles stronge stuffed with ordinaunce
For they haue had longe tyme by theyr offyce
The hole countre of loue in obeysaunce

And ye ladyes/or what estate ye be
Of whom worship hath chose his dwellynge
For goddes loue do no such cruelte (place
Nor in no wyse ne foule not the trace
Of her that here is named rightwisly
Whiche by reason me semeth in this cace
May be called/La belle dame sans mercy.

Go lytel boke/god sende the good passage
Chese wel thy way/be symple of manere
Loke thy clothynge be lyke thy pylgrimage
And specyally let this be thy prayere
Unto hem al/that the wyl rede or here
Where thou arte wronge after her helpe to cal
The to correcte in any parte or al

Pray hem also with thyne humble seruyce
Thy boldnesse to pardon in this cace
For els thou arte not able in no wyse
To make thy selfe appere in any place
And furthermore beseche hem of her grace
By her fauour and supportacyon
To take in gre this rude translacion

The which god wote standeth ful destytute
Of eloquence/of meter/and colours
Lyke as a beest naked without refute
Upon a playne to abyde al maner showres
I can no more/but aske of hem socours
At whose request thou were made in this wise
Commaundynge me with body and seruyse

Right thus I make an ende of this prosses
Besechynge hym/that al hath in balaunce
That no trewe man be vexed causelesse
As this man was/which is of remembraunce
And al that done her faythful obseruaunce
And in her trouth purpose hem to endure
I pray God sende hem better auenture.

¶ Explicit.

Of quene Anne- lida and false Arcite.

O Thou feirs god of armes Mars yͤ rede
That in thy frosty coũtre called Trace
Within thy grisly temples ful of drede
Honoured arte as patron of that place
With the Bellona Pallas ful of grace
Be present / and my songe contynewe ⁊ gye
At my begynnynge thus to the I crye

For it ful depe is sonken in my mynde
With pytous herte in Englysshe to endyte
This olde story /in latyn whiche I fynde
Of quene Annelyda and false Arcite
That elde / whiche al can frete and byte
And it hath freten many a noble story
Hath nyghe deuoured out of our memory

Be fauourable eke thou Polymnia
On Pernaso that hath thy systers glade
By Elycon/ not farre from Cirsa
Singest with voyce memorial in the shade
Under the laurer/ whiche that may not fade
And do that I my shyp to hauen wynne
Fyrst folowe I Stace/ ⁊ after hym Corynne

Iamqz domos patrias Cithie post aspa gen-
tis/Prelea laurigero subuente Thesea curru
Letifici plausus missusqz ad sidera vulgi.

Whan Theseus with warres longe ⁊ grete
The aspre folke of Cithe hath ouercome
The Laurer crowned in his chapre golde bete
Home to his countre houses is ycome
For whiche the people blyssful al and some
So cryden/ that to the sterres it wente
And hym to honouren dyd al her entente

Before

Before this duke/in signe of victorie
The trompes come/and in his baner large
The ymage of Mars/and in token of glorie
Men might se of tresour many a charge
Many a bright helme/& many a spere & targe
Many a fressh knight/& many a blissful route
On horse and on foote/in al the felde aboute

Ipolyta his wyfe/the hardy quene
Of Cithya/that he conquered had
With Emelie her yonge suster shene
Fayre in a chare of golde he with him lad
That al the groũde about her chare she sprad
With brightnesse of beautie in her face
Fulfylled of largesse and of grace

With his triumphe and laurer corowned thus
In al the floure of fortunes yeuyng
Lete I this noble prince Theseus
Towarde Athenes in his way rydyng
And fonde I wol in shortly to bring
The slye way of that I gan to write
Of quene Annelida and false Arcyte

Mars ẏ through his furyous course of yre
The olde wrathe of Juno to fulfyl
Hath set the peoples hertes both on fyre
Of Thebes and Grece/& euerich other to kyl
With blody speares rested neuer styl (bothe
But throng now here nowe there amõge hem
That euerych other slew/so were they wrothe

For whan Amphioray and Tydeus
Ipomedon/and Partynope also
Were deed/and slayne proude Campaneus
And whan the wretched thebans brethern two
Were slayne/and kyng Adrastus home ago
So desolate stode Thebes and so bare
That no wight coude remedye of his care

And whan the olde Creon gan espye
How ẏ the bloode royal was brought adoun
He helde the cytee by his tyrannye
And dyd the gentyls of that regyoun
To ben his frendes/and dwel in the toun
So what for loue of him/and what for awe
The noble folke were to the towne ydrawe

Amonge al these Annelyda the quene
Of Ermonye/was in that towne dwellyng
That fayrer was than the sonne shene
Throughout ẏ world so gan her name spring
That her to se had euery wight lykyng
For as of trouthe is there none her lyche
Of al the women in this worlde ryche

Yonge was this quene/of twenty yere olde
Of myddle stature/and of suche fayrenesse
That nature had a ioye her to beholde
And for to speken of her stedfastnesse
She passed hath Penelope/and Lucresse
And shortly if she shal ben comprehended
In her might nothyng ben amended

This Theban knight eke sothe to sayne
Was yonge/and therto withal a lusty knight
But he was double in loue/& nothing playne
And subtyl in that crafte ouer any wight
And with his connyng wan this lady bright
For so ferforthe he gan her trouthe assure
That she him trusteth ouer any creature

What shulde I sayne/she loueth Arcyte so
That whan that he was absent any throwe
Anon her thought her herte brast a two
For in her syght to her he bare him lowe
So that she wende haue al his herte yknowe
But he was false/it nas but fayned chere
As nedeth not suche crafte men to lere

But neuerthelesse ful mykel besynesse
Had he/er that he might his lady wynne
And swore he wolde dyen for distresse
Or from his wytte he sayd he wolde twynne
Alas the whyle/for it was routhe and synne
That she vpon his sorowes wolde rewe
But nothĩg thinketh the false as doth ẏ trewe

Her fredom founde Arcyte in suche manere
That al was his/that she hath moche or lyte
Ne to no creature made she chere
Further than it lyked to Arcyte (wyte
There was no lacke/with which he might her
She was so ferforthe yeuen him to please
That al that lyked him/dyd her ease

There

Of Annelyda and Arcyte:

There nas to her no maner letter sent
That touched loue/from any maner wight
That she ne shewed him or it was brent
So playne she was/and dyd her ful might
That she nyl hyde nothyng from her knight
Leste he of any vntrouthe her vpvreyde
Without bode his herte she obeyde

And eke he made him ialous ouer her
That what that any man had to her sayde
Anon he wolde prayen her to swere
What was yͤ worde/or make him yuel apayde
Than wende she out of her wytte haue brayde
But al was but sleyght and flaterye
Without loue he fayned ielousye

And al this toke she so debonairly
That al his wyl/her though it skylful thyng
And euer the lenger she loued him tenderly
And dyd him honour as he were a kyng
Her herte was to him wedded with a ryng
For so ferforthe vpon trouthe is her entent
That where he gothe/her herte with him went

Whan she shal eate/on him is so her thought
That wel vnneth of meate toke she kepe
And whan she was to her rest brought
On him she thought alway tyl that she slepe
Whan he was absent/priuely dothe she wepe
Thus lyueth fayre Annelyda the quene
For false Arcyte/ that dyd her al this tene

This false Arcyte/ of his newfanglenesse
For she to him so lowly was and trewe
Toke lesse deynte for her stedfastnesse
And sawe another lady proude and newe
And right anon he clad him in her hewe
Wote I not whether in whyte/reed/or grene
And falsed fayre Annelyda the quene

But neuerthelesse/great wonder was it none
Though he were false/for it is yͤ kynde of mā
Sythe Lameth was/that is so longe agone
To be in loue as false as euer he can
He was the first father that began
To louen two/ and was in bigamye
And he founde tentes first/but if men lye

This false Arcyte/somwhat muste he fayne
Whan he was false/to coueren his traytorie
Right as an horse/that can both byte ⁊ playne
For he bare her in honde of trecherye
And swore he coude her doublenesse espye
And al was falsnesse that she to him ment
Thus swore this thefe ⁊ forth his way he wēt

Alas/what herte might endure it
For routhe or wo/her sorowe for to tel
Or what man hath the connyng or the wyt
Or what man might within yͤ chambre dwel
If I to him rehersen shal the hel
That suffreth fayre Annelida the quene
For false Arcyte/that dyd al this tene

She wepeth/wayleth/⁊ swouneth pitously
To grounde deed she falleth as a stone
Crampysheth her lymmes crokedly
She speketh as her wytte were al agone
Other colour than asshen hath she none
Ne none other worde speketh she moche or lyte
But mercy cruel herte myn Arcyte

And thus endureth/tyl that she wes so mate
That she ne hath foote/ on which she may su-
But forth lãguisshing euer ĩ this estate (stene
Of whiche Arcyte hath neyther rothe ne tene
His herte was els where newe and grene
That on her wo/ne deyneth him not to thinke
Him recketh neuer whether she flete or synke

This newe lady holdeth him so narowe
Vp by the bridel/at the staues ende
That euery worde he dred it as an arowe
Her daunger made him both bowe and bende
And as her luste/made him turne or wende
For she ne graunted him in her lyuyng
No grace/ why that he hath to synge

But droue him forthe/ vnneth lyst her knowe
That he was seruaunt vnto her ladyshyp
But leste he were proude/she helde him lowe
Thus serueth he/ without meate or syp
She sente him nowe to lande/ ⁊ nowe to shyp
And for she yaue him daunger al his fyl
Therfore she had him at her owne wyl

Ensam.

Ensample of this/ye thrifty woman al
Take hede of Annelyda and false Arcyte
That for her lyst him/ her dere herte gal
And was so meke/ therfore he loued her lyte
The kynde of mannes herte is to delyte
On thing that straunge is/also god me saue
For what they may not get/ÿ wold they haue

Nowe turne we to Annelyda ayen
That pyneth day by day in languisshyng
But whan she sawe that her ne gate no geyn
Vpon a day ful sorowfully wepyng
She cast her for to make a complaynyng
And with her owne hande she gan it write
And sente it to her theban knight Arcyte.

¶ The complaynt of Anne-
lyda to false Arcyte.

So thyrled with the poynt of remembraūce
The swerde of sorowe/whet wt false plesaūce
Myn herte bare of blysse/ and blacke of hewe
That turned is to quakyng al my daunce
My sewerte in a waped countenaunce
Sens it auayleth nought to ben trewe
For who so trewe is/it shal her rewe
That serueth loue/and dothe her obseruaunce
Alway to one/and chaungeth for no newe

I wote my selfe as wel as any wight
For I loued one/with al myn hert and might
More than my selfe/an hūdred thousande syth
And called him my hertes lyfe/my knight
And was al his/as ferre as it was right
And whan ÿ he was glad/than was I blythe
And his disease was my dethe as swythe
And he ayen/his trouthe hath me plight
For euermore his lady me to kythe

Nowe is he false alas/and causeles
And of my wo he is so routhles
That with a worde him lyst not ones dayne
To bring ayen my sorouful herte in pees
For he is caught vp in an other lees
Right as him lyst he laugheth at my payne
And I ne can myn herte not restrayne
For to loue him yet alway neuertheles
And of al this I not to whom to playne

And shulde I playne/alas the harde stounde
Vnto my foe/that gaue myn herte a wounde
And yet desyreth that myn harme be more
Nowe certes ferther wol I neuer be founde
None other helpe/my sores for to sounde
My desteny hath shaped so ful yore
I wol none other medicyne ne lore
I wol ben aye there I was ones bounde
That I haue sayd/ be sayd for euermore

Alas/where is become your gentylnesse
Your wordes ful of plesaunce and humblesse
Your obseruaunce in so lowe manere
Your awayting/and your besynesse
On me/that ye called your maystresse
Your soueraygne lady in this worlde here
Alas/is there neyther worde ne chere
Ye vouchsafe vpon myn heuynesse
Alas your loue/I bye it al to dere

Nowe certes swete/though that ye
Thus causelesse the cause be
Of my dedly aduersyte
Your manly reason ought it to respyte
To slee your frende/and namely me
That neuer yet in no degre
Offended you/ as wisly he
That al wote/of wo my soule quyte

But for I was so playne Arcyte
In al my workes moche and lyte
And was so besy you to delyte
Myn honour saue/meke/ kynde/and fre
Therfore ye put in me this wyte
Alas/ye retche not a myte
Though that the swerde of sorowe byte
My woful herte/through your cruelte

My swete foe/why do ye so for shame
And thynke ye that furthered be your name
To loue a newe/and ben vntrewe aye
And put you in slaunder nowe and blame
And do to me aduersyte and grame
That loue you moste/god thou woste alwaye
Yet turne ayen/and yet be playne some daye
And than shal this ÿ nowe is mys ben game
And al foryeue/whyle I lyue maye

Lo herte

Lo herte myn/ al this is for to sayne
As whether shal I pray or els playne
Whiche is the way to done you to be trewe
For eyther mote I haue you in my chayne
Or with the dethe ye mote departe vs twayne
There bethe none other meane wayes newe
For god so wysely on my soule rewe
As verely ye sleen me with the payne
That mowe ye se on fayned on myn hewe

For thus ferforth haue I my dethe sought
My selfe I murder with my priuy thought
For sorowe and routhe of your vnkyndnesse
I wepe/ I wayle/ I faste/ al helpeth naught
I voyde ioy that is to speke of aught
I voyde company/ I flye gladnesse
Who may auaunt her better of heuynesse
Than I/ and to this plite haue ye me brought
Without gylte/ me nedeth no wytnesse

And shulde I pray/ and weyuen womanhede
Nay rather dethe/ than do so foule a dede
And aske mercy and gyltlesse/ what nede
And if I playne what lyfe I lede
you recketh not/ that knowe I out of drede
And if I vnto you myn othes bede
For myn excuse/ a scorne shal be my mede
Your chere floureth/ but it wol not sede
Ful longe agon I might haue taken hede

For though I had you to morowe agayne
I might as wel holde Apríl from rayne
As holde you to maken stedfast
Almighty god/ of trouthe the souerayne
Wher is the trouth of man/ who hath it slayne
She that hem loueth/ shal hem fynde as fast
As in a tempest is a rotten maste
Is that a tame beest/ that is aye fayne
To renne away/ whan he is leste agaste

Nowe mercy swete/ if I missay
Haue I aught sayd out of the way
I not/ my wytte is al away
I fare as dothe the songe of chaunteplure
For nowe I playne/ and nowe I pley
I am so mased that I dey
Arcyte hath borne away the key
Of al my worlde/ & my good aueuture

For in this worlde there nys no creature
Walkyng in more discomfyture
Than I/ ne more sorowe endure
For if I slepe a furlonge way or twey
Than thynketh me that your fygure
Before me stante clad in asure
Efte to profre a newe assure
For to ben trewe/ and mercy me to prey

The longe nyght/ this wonder syght ydrie
That on the day for suche affray I dye
And of al this right naught ywys ye retche
Ne neuermore myn eyen two ben drie
And to your routhe/ & to your trouthe I crye
But welaway/ to ferre ben they to fetche
Thus holdeth me my destyne a wretche
But me to rede out of this drede or gye
Ne may my wyt (so weake is it) not stretche

Than ende I thus/ sythe I may do nomore
I yeue it vp for nowe and euermore
For I shal neuer efte putten in balaunce
My sykernesse/ ne lerne of loue the lore
But as the swan/ I haue herde say ful yore
Ayenst his dethe wol synge in his penaunce
So synge I here the destenye and chaunce
Howe that Arcyte Annelyda so sore
Hath thrilled with the poynt of remembraũce

Whan that Annelyda this woful quene
Hath of her hande written in this wyse
With face deed/ betwyxe pale and grene
She fel a swoune/ and sythe she gan to ryse
And vnto Mars auoweth sacrifyse
Within the temple/ with a sorouful chere
That shapen was/ as ye may plainly here.

¶ Explicit.

The assemble of ladies.

IN Septembre at the fallyng of the lefe
The fressh ceason was al togyder doon
And of the corne was gathered the hervest
In a gardyne aboute twayne after noone
Ther were ladyes walkyng/as was her wone
Foure in nombre/as to my mynde dothe fal
And I the fyfthe/the sympiest of hem al

Of gentilwomen fayre there were also
Disportyng hem/euerychone after her gyse
In crosse aleys walkyng by two and two
And some alone/after her fantasyse
Thus occupyed we were in dyuers wyse
And yet in trouthe we were not al alone
There were knyghtes ⁊ squiers many one

Wherof I serued/one of hem asked me
I sayd ayen/as it fel in my thought
To walke aboute the mase in certaynte
As a woman that nothyng rought
He asked me ayen whom that I sought
And of my colour/why I was so pale
Forsothe (qd I) and therby lythe a tale

That must me wete (qd he) and that anone
Tel on let se/and make no taryeng
Abyde (quod I) ye ben a hasty one
I let you wete it is no lytel thyng
But for bycause ye haue a great longyng
In your desyre/this processe for to here
I shal you tel the playne of this matere

It happed thus/that in an after noone
My felawshyp and I by one assent
Whan al other besynesses were doone
To passe our tyme/in to this mase we went
And toke our wayes/eche after our entent
Some went inward/⁊ went they had gon out
Some stode in the myd/and loked al aboute

And sothe to say/some were ful ferre behynde
And right anon as ferforthe as the beste
Other there were so mased in her mynde
Al wayes were good for hem bothe est ⁊ west
Thus went they forthe/and had but lytel rest
And some her corage dyd hem sore assayle
For very wrathe/they dyd step ouer the rayle.

And as they sought hem selfe to and fro
I gate my selfe a lytel auauntage
Al for weryed/I might no further go
Though I had won right great for my vsage
So came I forthe in to a strayte passage
Whiche brought me to an herber fayre ⁊ grene
Made with benches ful crafty and clene

That as me thought/there might no creature
Deuyse a better/by dewe proporcioun
Safe it was closed wel I you ensure
With masonrye/of compace enuyroun
Ful secretly with stayres goyng doun
In myddes ye place/wt turnyng whele certayn
And vpon that a potte of Margelayne

With margarettes growyng in ordynaunce
To shewe hem selfe/as folke went to and fro
That to beholde it was a great plesaunce
And howe they were acompanyed with mo
Ne momblysnesse and souenesse also
The poure penses were not disloged there
Ne god wote her place was euery where

The flore ⁊ benche was paued fayre ⁊ smoth
With stones square/of many dyuers hewe
So wel ioyned/that for to say the sothe
Al semed one/that none other knewe
And vnderneth the streames newe ⁊ newe
As syluer bright/spryngyng in suche a wyse
That whence it came/ye coude it not deuyse

A lytel whyle was I al alone
Beholdyng wel this delectable place
My felawshyp were comyng euerychone
So muste me nedest abyde for a space
Remembryng of many dyuers cace
Of tyme passed/with syghes depe
I set me downe/and there I fel a slepe

And as I slept/me thought there came to me
A gentylwoman/metely of stature
Of great worshyp she semed for to be
Atyred wel/not hygh but by mesure
Her countenaunce ful sadde and demure
Her colours blewe/al that she had vpon
There came no mo but her selfe alone

Her

Her gowne wel was enbraudred certainly
With stones after her owne deuyse
In her pursyl/her worde by and by
(Bien et loyalment) as I coude deuyse
Than prayde I her in any maner wyse
That of her name I might haue remẽbraũce
She sayd she was called Perseueraunce

So furthermore to speke was I bolde
Where she dwelled/I prayed her for to say
And she agayne ful curtesly me tolde
My dwellyng is/and hath be many a day
With a lady: What lady I you pray?
Of great estate/thus warne I you (qd she)
What cal ye her? Her name is Loyaltie

In what offyce stande ye/or in what degre?
(Qd I to her) that wolde I were right fayne
I am (quod she) vnworthy though I be
Of her chambre her ussher in certayne
This rodde I beare/as for a token playne
Lyke as ye knowe the rule in suche seruyce
Apertaynyng is to the same offyce

She charged me by her cõmaundement
To warne you/and your felawes euerichone
That ye shulde come there as she is present
For a counsayle/whiche shal be nowe anone
Or seuen dayes be comen and gone
And furthermore/she bad that I shulde say
Excuse there might be none nor delay

Another thyng was not forget behynde
Whiche in no wyse I wolde but ye it knewe
Remembre wel/and beare it in your mynde
Al your felawes and ye muste come in blewe
Euery lyche able/your maters for to sewe
With more/whiche I pray you thynke vpon
Your wordes on your sleues euerychon

And be not abasshed in no maner wyse
As many ben/in suche an hygh presence
Make your request/as ye can best deuyse
And she gladly wol yeue you audyence
There is no grefe/nor no maner offence
Wherin ye fele that your herte is displeased
But with her helpe/right sone ye shal be eased

I am right glad (quod I) ye tel me this
But there is non of vs that knoweth the way
As of your way (qd she) ye shal not mys
Ye shal haue to gyde you day by day
Of my felawes/I can no better say
Suche one as shal tel you the waye ful right
And Dylygence this gentyl woman hight

A woman of right famous gouernaunce
And wel cherysshed/I tel you in certayne
Her felawshyp shal do you great plesaunce
Her porte is suche/her maners trewe & playne
She with glad chere wol do her besy payne
To bring you there/now farwel I haue done
Abyde sayd I/ye may not go so sone

Why so (quod she) and I haue ferre to go
To yeue warnyng in many dyuers place
To your felawes/and so to other mo
And wel ye wote I haue but lytel space
Nowe yet (qd I) ye must tel me this cace
If we shal any men vnto vs cal
Not one (qd she) may come amonges you al

Not one than sayd I/eygh benedicite
What haue I done/I pray you tel me that
Nowe by my lyfe I trowe but wel (qd she)
But euer I can byleue there is somwhat
And for to say you trouthe more can I not
In questyons I may nothyng be to large
I medle no further than my charge

Than thus (quod I) do me to vnderstande
What place is there this lady is dwellyng
Forsothe (qd she) & one sought al this lande
Fayrer is none/though it were for a kyng
Deuysed wel/and that in euery thyng
The toures hye/ful plesaunt shal ye fynde
With phanes fresshe/turnyng wt euery wynde

The chambres and parlers of a sorte
Wt bay wyndowes/goodly as may be thought
As for daunsyng/and other wyse disporte
The galeryes right wel ywrought
That wel I wot/if ye were thyder brought
And take good hede therof in euery wyse
Ye wol it thynke a very paradyse

What

What hight ye place (qd I) nowe say me that
Plesaunt regarde (qd she) to tel you playne
Of verey trouth (quod I) and wote ye what
It may right wel be called so certayne
But furthermore this wold I wyt right fayn
What I shulde do as sone as I come there
And after whom I may best enquere

A gentylwoman/a porter of the yate
There shal ye fynde/her name is Coũtenaũce
If ye so hap ye come erly or late
Of her were gode to haue some acquaintaũce
She can you tel howe ye shal you auaunce
And howe to come to her ladyes presence
To her wordes I rede ye gyue credence

Nowe it is tyme I parte you fro
For in good faythe I haue great busynesse
I wote right wel (quod I) that it is so
And I thanke you of your great gentylnesse
your comforte hath yeuen me hardynesse
That nowe I shal be bolde withouten fayle
To do after your aduyce and good counsayle

Thus parted she/and I lefte al alone
With that I sawe (as I behelde asyde)
A woman come a verey goodly one
And forth withal as I had her aspyde
Me thought anone it shulde be the gyde
And of her name anone I dyd enquere
Ful womanly she yaue me this answere

I am (quod she) a symple creature
Sent from the courte/my name is Diligence
As sone as I might come I you ensure
I taryed not after I had lycence
And nowe that I am come to your presence
Loke what seruyce I can do or may
Commaunde me/I can no further say.

I thanked her/ and prayed her to come nere
Bycause I wolde se howe she was arayde
Her gown was blewe dressed in good manere
With her deuyse/her worde also that sayde
(Tant que ie puis) and I was wel apayde
And than wyst I withouten any more
It was ful trewe that I had herde before

Though we toke nowe before a lytel space
It were ful good (quod she) as I coude gesse
Howe farre (qd I) haue we vnto the place ?
A dayes iourney (quod she) but lytel lesse
Wherfore I rede that we outwarde dresse
For I suppose our felawshyp is past
And for nothyng I wolde not we were ye last

Than departed we at the spryngyng of ye day.
And forth we wente softe and easy pace
Tyl at the last we were on our iourney
So far outwarde/ that we might se the place
Nowe let vs rest (quod I) a lytel space
And say we as deuoutly as we can
A Pater noster for saynt Iulyan

With al my herte I assent with good wyl
Moch better shal we spede/whã we haue done
Than taryed we/and sayd it euery dyl
And whan the day was past farre after none
We sawe a place/and thyder came we sone
Whiche rounde aboute was closed with a wal
Semynge to me ful lyke an hospital

There fouñde I one had brought al myn aray.
(A gentylwoman of myne acquayntaunce)
I haue meruayle (quod I) what maner way.
ye had knowlege of al this ordenaunce
yes yes (quod she) I herde Perseueraunce
Howe she warned her felawes euerychone
And what aray ye shulde haue vpon

Nowe for my lone (quod I) this I you pray.
Sith ye haue take vpon you al the payne
That ye wolde helpe me on with myne aray
For wyt ye wel I wolde be gone right fayne
Al this prayer nedeth not certayne
(Quod she) agayne/come of & hye you sone
And ye shal se anone it shal be done

But this I doute me greatly/wote ye what
That my felawes be passed vp and gone
I warne you (quod she) that are they nat
For here they shal assemble euerychone
Notwithstandynge I counsayle you anone
Make you redy/ and tary you no more
It is no harme thoughe ye be there before

F.f.i. So

So than I dressed me in myn aray
And asked her whether it were wel or no
It is right wel (quod she) unto my pay
ye nede nat care to what place euer ye go
And whyles that she and I debated so
Came Diligence and sawe me al in blewe
Syster (qd̄ she) right wel broke ye your newe
Discrecyon purueyour.
Than wente we forth and met at auenture
A yonge woman / an offycer semynge
What is your name (quod I) good creature
Dyscrecyon (quod she) without lesynge
And where (quod I) is your most abydynge
I haue (quod she) this office of purchace
Chefe purueyour that longeth to this place
Acquayntaunce herbyger.
Fayre loue (quod I) in al your ordenaunce
What is her name that is the herbygere
Forsothe (qd̄ she) her name is Acquayntaūce
A woman of right gracyous manere
Thā thus (qd̄ I) what straungers haue ye here
But fewe (quod she) of hyghe degre ne lowe
ye be the first / as ferforth as I knowe
Countenaunce porter.
Thus with tales we came streyght to the yate
This yonge woman departed was and gone
Came Diligence and knocked fast therate
Who is without (qd̄ Countenaunce) anone
Truely (quod I) fayre syster here is one
Whiche one (qd̄ she) & there withal she loughe
I Diligence / ye knowe me wel ynoughe

Than opened she the gate / and in we go
With wordes fayre she sayd ful gentylly
ye are welcome ywys / are ye no mo?
Nat one (quod she) saue this woman and I
Nowe than (quod she) I pray you hertely
Take my chambre for a whyle to rest
Tyl your felawes come / I holde it best

I thanked her / and forth we go everychone
Tyl her chambre without wordes mo
Came Diligence and toke her leaue anone
Where euer ye lyst (quod I) nowe may ye go
And I thanke you right hertely also
Of your laboure / for whiche god do you me.
I can no more / but Jesu be your spede. (de

Than Countenaunce asked me anone
your felawshyp / where ben they (quod she)
For sothe (qd̄ I) they be comyng everychone
But where they are I knowe no certaynte
Without I may hem at this wyndowe se
Here wyl I stande awaytynge euer amonge
For wel I wote they wyl nat be longe

Thus as I stode musynge ful busily
I thought to take good hede of her aray
Her gowne was blewe / this wote I verely
Of good facyon / and furred wel with gray
Upon her sleue her worde this is no nay
Whiche sayd thus / as my penne can endyte
(A moy que ie voy) writen with letters white

Than forth withal she came streyght to me
your wordes (ꝙ she) fayne wold I yͭ I knew
Forsothe (quod I) ye shal wel knowe and se
And for my worde I haue none / this is trewe
It is ynoughe that my clothynge be blewe
As here before I had commaundement
And so to do / I am right wel content
Largesse stewarde.
But tel me this I pray you hertely
The stewarde here say me / what is her name
She hight Largesse I say you surely
A fayre lady and of right noble fame
Whan ye her se ye wyl reporte the same
And under her to byd you welcome al
There is Belchier marshal of the hal

Nowe al this whyle that ye here tary styl
your own maters ye may wel haue in mynde
But tel me this / haue ye brought any byl
ye ye (quod I) and els I were behynde
Where is there one tel me that I may fynde
To whō yͭ I may shewe my matters playne
Surely (quod she) unto the Chamberlayne
Remembraunce chamberlayne
The chamberlayne (quod I) say ye trewe
ye verely (sayd she) by myne aduyse
Be nat aferde / unto her lowly sewe
It shal be done (quod I) as ye deuyse
But ye must knowe her name in any wyse
Trewly (qd̄ she) to shewe you in substaunce
Withoutē faynyng her name is Remēbraūce
This

The secretarye she may not yet be forget
For she doth right moche in euery thynge
Wherfore I rede/ whan ye haue with her mett
your matere hole tel her without faynynge
ye shal her fynde ful good and ful louynge
Tel me her name (quod I) of gentylnesse
By my good sothe (quod she) Auysenesse

That (quod I) for her is passyng good
For euery byl and cedule she must se
Nowe good (ꝙ I) come stāde there as I stode
My felawes be comyng/ yonder they be
Is it iape/ or say ye sothe (quod she)
In iape/ nay nay/ I say you for certayne
Se how they come togyder twayne ⁊ twayne

Ye say ful sothe (quod she) that is no nay
I se comynge a goodly company
They ben suche folke (quod I) dare I say
That lyst to loue/ thynke it veryly
And for my loue I pray you faythfully
At any tyme/ whan they vpon me cal
That ye wol be good frende to hem al

Of my frenshyp (q̄d she) they shal nat mysse
And for theyr ease to put therto my payne
God yelde it you (quod I) but take you this
Howe shal we know who is yͤ chamberlayne
That shal ye wel know by her worde certaine
What is her worde syster/ I pray you say
(Plus ne purroy) thus writeth she alway

Thus as we stode togyder she and I
Euen at the yate my felawes were echone
So met I hem (as me thought was goodly)
And bad hem welcome al by one and one
Than came forth Countenaunce anone
Ful hertely/ fayre systers al (quod she)
ye be ryght welcome in to this countre

I counsayle you to take a lytel rest
In my chambre/ if it be your plesaunce
Whan ye be there/ me thynke it for the best
That I go in/ and cal Perseueraunce
Bycause she is of your acquayntaunce
And she also wyl tel you euery thinge
Howe ye shal be ruled of your cominge

My felawes al and I/ by one aduyse
Were wel agreed/ to do lyke as she sayde
Than we began to dresse vs in our gyse
yͤ folke shulde say we were nat vnpurueyde
And good wagers amonge vs there we layde
Whiche of vs was atyred most goodlest
And of vs al whiche shulde be praised best

The porter came and brought Perseueraunce
She welcomed vs in curtyse manere
Thinke ye nat long (ꝙ she) of your attēdaūce
I wyl go speke vnto the herbigere
That she puruey for your lodginge here
Than wyl I go vnto the chamberlayne
To speke for you/ and come anone agayne

And whan she departed was and gone
We sawe folkes comynge without the wal
So great people/ that nombre coude we none
Ladyes they were/ and gentylwomen al
Clothed in blewe echone her worde withal
But for to knowe her worde or her deuyse
They came so thycke/ yͤ I ne might ī no wyse

With that anone came in Perseueraunce
And where I stode/ she came streyght to me
ye ben (q̄d she) of myne olde acquayntaunce
you to enquere the bolder wolde I be
What worde they bere eche after her degre
I you pray tel it me in secrete wyse
And I shal kepe it close on warantyse

We ben fyue ladyes (quod I) al in fere
And gentylwomen foure in company
Whan they begyn to open her matere
Than shal ye knowe her wordes by and by
But as for me I haue none verely
And so I tolde Countenaunce here before
Al myne aray is blewe/ what nedeth more

Nowe than (quod she) I wol go agayne
That ye may haue knowlege/ what ye shulde do
In soth (q̄d I) if ye wolde take the payne
Ye dyd right moche for vs/ if ye dyd so
The rather sped/ the soner may we go
Great cost alway there is in tarienge
And longe to sewe it is a wery thynge

F.f.f.ii. Than

Than parted she/and came agayne anone
Ye must (quod she) come to the chamberlayne
We be nowe redy (quod I) everychone
To folowe you/whan ever ye lyst certayne
We haue none eloquence to tel you playne
Besechynge you we may be so excused
Our trewe meanynge/ that it be not refused

Than wente we forth after Perseueraunce
To se the prees it was a wonder cace
There for to passe it was great combraunce
The people stode so thycke in every place
Nowe stande ye styl (quod she) a lytel space
And for your ease somwhat I shal assay
If I can make you any better way

And forth she goth/amonge hem everychone
Makyng a way/that we might thorugh passe
More at our ease/and whan she had so done
She beckende vs to come/ where as she was
So after her we folowed more and las
She brought vs streyght vnto ye chābrelayne
There lefte she vs/and than she went agayne

We salued her as reason wolde it so
Ful humbly besechyng her great goodnesse
In our maters that we had for to do
That she wolde be good lady and maystresse
Ye be welcome (quod she) in sothfastnesse
And se what I can do/you for to please
I am redy/that may be to your ease

We folowed her vnto the chambre dore
Systers (quod she) come ye in after me
But wete ye wel/there was a paued flore
The goodlyest/that any wight myght se
And furthermore aboute than loked we
On eche corner/and vpon every wal
Whiche was made of Burel and Crystal

Wherin was grauen of storyes many one
Fyrst howe Phyllis/ of womanly pyte
Dyed pyteously for loue of Demophone
Nexte after was the story of Tysbe
Howe she slewe her selfe vnder a tree
Yet sawe I more/ howe in a rixt pytous caas
For Antony was slayne Cleopatraas

That other syde was Hawes the shene
Ful vntrewly disceyued in her bayne
There was also Annelyda the quene
Upon Arcyte howe sore she dyd complayne
Al these storyes were graued there certayne
And many mo/than I reherce you here
It were to longe to tel you al in fere

And bycause the walles shone so bryght
With fyne vmple they were al ouer sprad
To ye entent folke shulde nat hurte her syght
And through it the storyes myght be rad
Than furthermore I went/ as I was lad
And there I sawe without any fayle
A chayre set/with ful ryche aparayle

And fyue stages/it was set fro the grounde
Of Cassydony ful curyously wrought
With foure pomelles of golde/& very rounde
Set wt saphirs/as good as coude be thought
That wote ye what/if it were through sought
As I suppose/fro this countrey to Inde
Another suche it were right farre to fynde

For wete ye wel/ I was right nere that
So as I durst/ beholdyng by and by
Aboue there was a riche cloth of estate
Wrought with the nedle ful straungely
Her worde theron/and thus it sayd trewly
A endure to tel you in wordes fewe
With great letters/the better I hem knewe

Thus as we stode/a dore opened anone
A gentylwoman/semely of stature
Berynge a mace/came out her selfe alone
Sothely me thought a goodly creature
She spake nothynge to lowde/I you ensure
Nor hastely/but with goodly warnynge
Make rome (quod she) my lady is comynge

With that anon I sawe Perseueraunce
Howe she helde vp the tapet in her hande
I sawe also in right goodly ordenaunce
This great lady within the tapet stande
Comynge outwarde/I wol ye vnderstande
And after her a noble company
I coude nat tel the nombre fynerly

Attem-

Of theyr names I wolde nothyng enquere
Further than suche as we wolde sewe unto
Saue a lady/ whiche was the chauncellere
Attemperaunce sothely her name was so
For us nedeth with her haue moche to do
In our maters/ and alwaye more and more
And so forthe to tel you furthermore

Of this lady/ her beaute to discryue
My connynge is to symple verely
For neuer yet the dayes of my lyue
So inly fayre I haue sene none trewly
In her estate assured utterly
There wanted naught/ I dare wel assure
That longed to a goodly creature

And furthermore to speke of her aray
I shal you tel the maner of her gowne
Of clothe of golde/ ful riche it is no nay
The coloure blewe of a right goodly facyoun
In taberde wyse/ the sleues hangyng adowne
And what purfyl there was/ & in what wyse
So as I can I shal it you deuyse

After a sorte/ the coller and the vente
Lyke as Ermynets made in purfelynge
With great perles ful fyne and orient
They were couched al after one worchynge
With diamondes in stede of powderynge
The sleues and purfel of assyse
They were made lyke in euery wyse

Aboute her necke a sorte of fayre rubyes
In whyte floures of right fyne enamayle
Upon her heed set in the fayrest wyse
A cercle of great balays of entayle
That in ernest to speke without fayle
For yonge and olde/ and euery maner age
It was a worlde to loken on her vysage

Thus comynge forthe to syt in her estate
In her presence we knelèd downe euerychone
Presentynge our byllès/ and wote ye what
Ful humbly she toke hem by one and one
Whan we had done/ than came they al anone
And dyd the same eche after her manere
Knelynge at ones/ and rysynge al in fere

And whã this was done/ & she set in her place
The chamberlayne she dyd unto her cal
And she goodly comyng unto her a pace
Of her entent knowyng nothyng at al
Voyde backe the preace (qd she) up to y wal
Make large roume/ but loke ye do not tary
And take these byllès to the secretarye

The chamberlayne dyd her cõmaundement
And came agayne/ as she was byd to do
The secretarye there beyng present
The byllès were delyuered her also
Not onely ours/ but many other mo
Than the lady with good aduyce agayne
Anon withal/ called her chamberlayne

We wol (qd she) the first thyng that ye do
The secretarye ye do make come anon
With her byllès/ and thus we wyl also
In our presence she rede hem euerychon
That we maye take good aduyce theron
Of the ladyes that ben of our counsayle
Loke this be done/ withouten any fayle

Whan the chamberlayne wyste of her entent
Anon she dyd the secretarye cal
Let your byllès (quod she) be here present
My lady it wyl: Madame (qd she) I shal
And in presence she wyl ye hem cal
With good wyl I am redy (quod she)
At her plesure/ whan she cõmaundeth me

And upon that was made an ordynaunce
They that came first her byllès shuld be redde
Ful gentelly than sayd Perseueraunce
Rayson it wyl they were sonest spedde
Anon withal/ upon a tapet spredde
The secretarie layde hem downe echone
Our byllès first she redde one by one

The first lady bearyng in her deuyse
Sans que iamays/ thus wrote she on her byl
Complaynyng sore/ and in ful pytous wyse
Of promesse made/ with faythful hert & wyl
And so broken ayenst al maner skyl
Without deserte/ alwayes on her partye
In this mater/ desyring a remedy

F.f.f.iii. Her

Her next folowing/her word was i this wise
(Ung sanz chaungier) & thus she dyd cōplayne
Though she had be guerdoned for her seruyce
Yet nothynge lyke as she that toke the payne
Wherfore she coude in no wyse her restrayne
But in this case sewe vntyl her presence
As reason wolde to haue recompence

So furthermore/to speke of other twayne
One of hem wrote after her fantasy
(Oncques plus leuer) & for to tel you playne
Her complaynt was ful pitous verely
For as she sayd/there was great reason why
As I can remembre this matere
I shal you tel the processe al in fere

Her byl was made complaynynge in her gyse
That of her ioy/her comforte and gladnesse
Was no surete/ for in no maner wyse
She sayd therin no poynt of stablenesse
Nowe yl nowe wele/ out of al sykernesse
Ful humbly desyrynge of her high grace
Soone to shewe her remedy in this cace

Her felawe made her byl/and thus she sayde
In playnynge wise there as she loued best
Whether she were wrothe or wele apayde
She might nat se whan she wolde faynest
And wrothe she was in very ernest
To tel her worde/as ferforth as I wote
(Entierment vostre) right thus she wrote

And vpon that she made a great request
With herte and wyl/& al that might be done
As vntyl her that might redresse it best
For in her mynde there might she finde it sone
The remedy of that whiche was her boone
Rehersynge that she had sayd before
Besechynge her it might be so no more

And in lyke wise as they had done before
The gentyl women of our company
Put her bylles/and for to tel you more
One of hem wrote (cest sanz dire) verely
And her matere hole to specify
With in her byl she put it in writinge
And what it sayd/ye shal haue knowynge

It sayd god wote/and that ful pytously
Lyke as she was disposed in her herte
No mysfortune that she toke greuously
Al one to her was the ioy and smerte
Somtyme no thanke for al her good deserte
Other comforte she wanted non comynge
And so vsed/it greued her nothynge

Desyrynge her/and lowly besechynge
That she wolde for her seke a better way
As she that had ben her dayes lyuynge
Stedfast and trewe/and wyl be alway
Of her felawe/ somwhat I shal you saye
Whose byl was red nexte forthe withal
And what it ment/rehersen you I shal

(En dieu est) she wrote in her deuyse
And thus she sayd withouten fayle
Her trouthe myght be take in no wyse
Like as she thouȝt/wherfore she had meruaile
For trouth sōtyme was wont to take auayle
In euery matere/but al that is ago
The more pyte that it is suffred so

Moche more there was/ wherof she shulde cō
But she thouȝt it to great encōbraūce (playn
So moche to wryte/& therfore in certayn
In god and her she put al her affiaunce
As in her worde is made a remembraunce
Beseching her/that she wolde in this cace
Shewe vnto her the fauour of her grace

The thirde she wrote rehersing her greuaunce
ye/wote ye what/a pitous thinge to here
For as me thought she felte great dysplesaūce
One might right wel perceyue it by her chere
And no wonder/ it sate her passynge nere
yet lothe she was to put it in wrytynge
But nede wol haue course in euery thinge

(Soyes ensure) this was her worde certayne
And thus she wrote in a lytel space
There she loued/her labour was in vayne
For he was set al in another place
Ful humbly desyrynge in that cace
Some good comforte her sorowe to appese
That she might lyue more at hertes ease

The

The fourthe surely me thought she liked wele
As in her porte/and in her behauynge
And (vien moneste) as farre as I coude fele
That was her worde tyl her welbelongynge
Wherfore to her she prayed aboue al thinge
Ful hertely to say you in substaunce
That she wolde sende her good continuaunce

ye haue rehersed me these byles al
But nowe lete se somwhat of your entent
It may so hap / parauenture ye shal
Nowe I pray you while I am here present
ye shal haue knowlege parde what I ment
But thus I say/in trouthe I make no fable
The case it selfe is inly lamentable

And wel I wote ye wol thinke the same
Lyke as I say/whan ye haue herde my byl
Nowe good tel on/I hate you by saynt Iame
Abyde a whyle/it is nat yet my wyl
yet must ye wete by reason and by skyl
Sith ye haue knowlege of yͭ was done before
And thus it is sayd without wordes more

Nothynge so lefe as dethe to come to me
For fynal ende of my sorowes and payne
What shulde I more desyre as seme ye
And ye knewe al aforne it for certayne
I wote ye wolde/and for to tel you playne
Without her helpe that hath al thinge in cure
I can nat thinke that it may longe endure

As for my trouthe it hath be proued wele
To say the sothe/I can say no more
Of ful longe tyme and suffred euery dele
In pacience/and kepe it al in store
Of her goodnesse/besechinge her therfore
That I might haue my thanke in suche wyse
As my deserte serueth of iustise

Whan these bylles were rad euerychone
The ladyes toke a good aduysement
And hem to answere by one and one
She thought it was to moche in her entent
Wherfore she yaue hem commaundement
In her presence to come bothe one and al
To yeue hem her answere in general

What dyd she than suppose ye verely?
She spake her selfe/ and sayd in this manere
We haue wel sene your byles by and by
And some of hem pytous for to here
We wol therfore ye knowe al this infere
Within shorte tyme/our courte of parlyment
Here shal be holde in our palayes present

And in al this/wherin ye fynde you greued
There shal ye fynde an open remedy
In suche wyse as ye shal be releued
Of al that ye reherce here throughly
As for the date ye shal knowe verely
That ye may haue a space in your comyng
For Dyligence shal it tel you by wrytyng

We thanked her in our moste humble wyse
Our felaushyp/eche one by one assente
Submyttyng vs lowly tyl her seruyse
For as we thought/ we had our trauayle spēt
In suche wyse as we helde vs contente
Than eche of vs toke other by the sleue
And forthe withal/as we shulde take our leue

Al sodainly the water sprange anone
In my visage/and therwithal I woke
Where am I nowe thought I/al this is gone
Al masedo/and vp I gan to loke
With that anon I went and made this boke
Thus symply rehersyng the sustbaunce
Bycause it shulde not be out of remembraūce

Nowe verily your dreame is passyng good
And worthy to be had in remembraunce
For though I stande here as longe as I stode
It shulde to me be none encombraunce
I toke therin so inly great plesaunce
But tel me nowe what ye the boke do cal
For I must wete: With right good wyl ye shal

As for this boke/to say you very ryght
Of the name to tel you in certaynte
Lassemble de dames/ thus it hyght
Howe thynke ye/that name is good parde
Nowe go farewel/ for they cal after me
My felawes al/and I must after sone
Rede wel my dreme/ for now my tale is done.

¶ Finis.

The conclusions of the Astro labie.

LItel Lowys my sonne/ I perceyue wel by certayne euydẽces thyn abilite to lerne sciẽces/ touching nombres & proporcions: and also wel cõsydre I thy besye prayer in especial to lerne the tretyse of the Astrolabe. Than for as moche as a philosopher sayth/ he wrapeth him in his frende/ that condiscendeth to the rightful prayers of his frende: Therfore I haue gyuen the a suffyciēt Astrolabye for our orizonte/ compowned after the latytude of Oxenforde: Vpon the whiche by medyacion of this lytel treatyse/ I purpose to teache the a certayne nombre of conclusyons/pertaynyng to this same instrumēt. I say a certayne of conclusyons for thre causes/ the first cause is this. Truste wel that al the conclusyons that haue be founden/ or els possiblye myght be founde in so noble an instrument as is the Astrolaby/ ben vnknowen perfytely to any mortal man in this regyon/ as I suppose. Another cause is this/ ẏ sothly in any cartes of the Astrolaby that I haue ysene/ there ben some conclusyons/ that wol not in al thinges perfourme her byhestes: and some of hem ben to harde to thy tender age of ten yere to conceyue. This treatyse deuyded in fyue partes wyl I shewe the wonder lyght rules & naked wordes in englysshe/ for latyn ne canste thou yet but smale/ my lytel sonne. But neuer the lesse suffyseth to the these trewe conclusyons in englysshe/ as wel as suffyseth to this noble clerkes grekes these same conclusyons in greke/ & to arabyens in arabyke/ and to iewes in Hebrewe/ and to ẏ latyn folke in latyn: whiche latyne folke had hem firste out of other dyuers langages/ and write hem in her owne tonge/ that is to sayne in latyne.

And god wote that in al these languages and in many mo / haue these conclusyons ben suffyciently lerned and taught/ and yet by dyuers rules/ right as dyuers pathes leaden dyuers folke the right waye to Rome.

Nowe wol I pray mekely euery person discrete/ that redeth or hereth this lytel treatyse/ to haue my rude entendyng excused/ and my superfluyte of wordes/ for two causes. The first cause is/ for that curyous endytyng and harde sentences is ful heuy at ones/ for suche a child to lerne. And the seconde cause is this/ that sothly me semeth better to writen vnto a childe twyse a good sentēce/ than he forgette it ones. And Lowys if it so be that I shewe the in my lyth Englisshe/ as trewe conclusyons/ touchyng this mater/ and not onely as trewe/ but as many and subtyl conclusyons as ben yshewed in latyn in any comune tretyse of the Astrolabye/ conne me the more thanke/ and praye god saue the kynge/ that is lorde of this langage/ and al that him faythe beareth/ and obeyeth eueriche in his degre/ the more and the lasse. But consydreth wel/ that I ne vsurpe not to haue founden this werke of my labour or of myne engyn / I nam but a leude compylatour of the labour of olde astrologiens / and haue it translated in myn englysshe only for thy doctryne: and with this swerde shal I slene enuy. ¶ The firste partye.

THe firste partye of this treatyse shal reherce the fygures and the membres of thyne Astrolabye/ bycause that thou shalte haue the greater knowyng of thyn owne instrument. ¶ The seconde partye.

¶ The seconde party shal teche the to werken the very practyke of the foresayd conclusyons as ferforthe and al so narowe as may be shewed in so smale an instrument portatyfe aboute. For wel wote euery astrologyen/ that smallest fractions ne wol not be shewed in so small an instrument/ as in subtyl tables calculed for a cause. ¶ The thirde partye.

¶ The thirde partye shal contayne dyuers tables of longitudes and latytudes of sterres/ fyxe in the Astrolabye/ And tables of the declynacions of the sonne/ and tables of the longitude of cytes and townes / And tables as wel for the gouernacion of the clocke/ as for to fynde the altytude meridyan/ and many an other notable conclusyon after the kalenders of the reuerent clerkes frere Iohn Som. and frere N. Lenne. ¶ The fourth partye.

¶ The fourth partye shal be a theorike to declare ẏ meanyng of the celestyal bodyes/ with the causes/ the whiche the fourth partie in special shal shewe in a table of the very meuyng of the moone from one to one euery day and

euery

euery signe/ after thyn almanake. Vpon the whiche table there foloweth a canon/ suffycient to teache as wel in maner of worchynge in the same conclusyons/ as to knowe in our orizonte/ with whiche degre of zodiac the moone aryseth in any latytude/ and the arysynge in any planete after his latytude fro the eclyptyke lyne.

¶ The fyfte partye.

¶ The fyfthe partie shal ben an introductorie after the statutes of our doctours/ on whiche thou mayste lerne a great parte of the general rules of theorike in astrologie. In whiche fyfthe partie thou shalt fynde tables of equacions of houses/ after the latytude of Oxenforde/ and tables of dignytees of planettes/ and other noteful thynges/ if god vouchsafe and his mother ye mayden/ mo than I behete.

¶ The rynge.

¶ Thy Astrolabye hath a rynge to putten on thy thombe on thy right honde/ in takynge of the heyght of thynges. And take kepe/ from hence forwarde I wol clepe the heyght of heuy thing/ that is take by the rule/ the altytude withouten mo wordes.

¶ The turet.

¶ This rynge renneth in a maner of a turet/ fastened to the moder of thyn Astrolabye/ in a roume a space that it distroubeleth not the instrument to hangen after his right centure. The moder of thyn Astrolabye is thickest by the brinkes/ that is the vtmoste rynge with degrees: and al the myddle within the rynge shal be thynner/ to receyue the plates for dyuers clymates/ and also for the rethe/ that is shape in maner of a nette/ or els after ye webbe of a loppe.

¶ The moder.

¶ The moder of thyn Astrolabye is the thickest plate perced with a large hole/ that receyueth in her wombe the thynne plates compowned of diuers clymates/ & thy reete shapen in maner of a nette or of a webbe of a loppe.

¶ Of the foure lynes.

¶ This moder is deuyded on the backhalfe with a lyne/ that cometh discendynge fro the rynge down to the netherest bordure/ the whiche lyne/ fro the foresaid ryng vnto the centre of the large hole amydde/ is cleped south lyne/ or els the lyne meridional: And the remenaunt of this lyne downe to the bordure is cleped the northe lyne/ or al the lyne of the mydnight.

¶ Of.iiii.lynes eest/ west/ northe/ & south.

¶ Ouerthwarte this forsayd long lyne/ there crosseth him another lyne of the same length/ fro eest to west/ of the whiche lyne/ from a lytel crosse in the bordure vnto the centure of the large hole/ is cleped ye eest lyne/ or els the lyne oriental: and the remenaunt of the lyne/ fro the forsayd oriental vnto the bordure/ is cleped the West lyne/ or the lyne occidental. Nowe haste thou here the foure quarters of thyn Astrolabye/ deuyded after the four principal plages or quarters of the fyrmament.

¶ Whiche is the ryght syde/ and whiche is the lyfte.

The Eest syde of the Astrolabye is cleped the right syde/ and the Weste side is cleped ye lyft syde. Forget not this lytel Lowys. Put the ryng of thyn Astrolabye vpon the thombe of thy ryght handel and than wol his right syde be towarde thy lyfte syde/ and his lyfte syde wol be towarde thy right syde. Take this rule general as wel on the backe as on the wombe syde. Vpon the ende of this Eest lyne (as I firste sayd) is ymarked a lytel crosse/ where as euermore generally is consydred the entrynge of the Eest degre/ in the whiche the sonne aryseth.

¶ The degrees fro the Eest lyne to the Southe.

Fro the lytel crosse vp to the ende of the meridyonal lyne vnder the rynge shalt thou fynde the bordure/ deuyded with. lxxxx. degrees/ and by that same proporcion is euery quarter of thyn Astrolabye deuyded/ ouer the whiche degrees there ben nombres of augrym/ that deuyden thylke same degrees fro.v.to.v. as sheweth by longe strikes bytwene. of the whiche longe strykes the space bytwene côteyneth a myle waye/ and euery degree of thilke bordure conteyneth four mynutes/ that is to say/ four mynutes of an houre.

¶ Of the twelue signes/ Aries/ Taurus/ Gemini/ Cancer/ and the other.

¶ Vnder

Under the compas of thylke degrees ben written the names of the twelue signes/as Aries/ Taurus/Gemini/ Cancer/ Leo/ Virgo / Libra/ Scorpio/ Sagitarius / Capricornius/ Aquaries/and Pisses. And the nombres of the degrees of the signes ben written in augrym aboue/and with longe diuysions from fyue to fyue/deuydeth from ẏ tyme that the signe entreth vnto the laste ende. But vnderstande wel/ that these degrees of signes ben eueryche of hem consydred of. lx. mynutes/and euery mynute of.lx.secondes/ and so forth in to smale fractions infynite/as sayth Alcabucius. And therfore knowe we wel that a degre of the bordure cōteyneth. iiii. mynutes/ and a degree of a signe contayneth. lx. mynutes/ and haue this in mynde.

¶ The cercle of the dayes.

Nexte this foloweth the cercle of the dayes/ ẏ ben fygured in maner of the degrees/that cōteynen in nombre. CCClxv. deuyded also with longe strikes from. v. to. v. and the nombres of augrym written vnder the cercle. ¶ The cercle of the .xii. monthes.

Next the cercle of dayes foloweth the cercle of the .xii. names of the monthes/ that is to say/Januarius/Febrnarius/Marcius/ April Maius/ Junius/ Julius/ August/ Septēber/ October/ Nouēber/ Decēber. The names of these monthes taken her names/ some for properties and some by statutes of emperours/ and some by other lordes of Rome. Eke of these monthes/ as lyked to Julius Cesar and Cesar Augustus/ some were ycompownde of dyuers nombres of dayes/ as July & August. Than hath Januarius .xxxi. dayes/ Feuruarius .xxviii. Marcius .xxxi. April .xxx. May .xxxi. Juni⁹ .xxx. August .xxxi. September .xxx. October .xxxi. Nouēber .xxx. December .xxxi. Nathelesse al though ẏ Julius Cesar tooke two dayes out of Feueryre and put hem in his monthe of July/ and Augustus Cesar cleped the moneth of Auguste after his name/& ordayned it of .xxxi. dayes/ yet trust wel that the sonne dwelleth therfore neuer the more ne the lasse in one sygne than in another.

¶ The names of the holy dayes.

Than foloweth the names of ẏ holy dayes in the kalender/ and next hem the letters/ A/ B/ C/ on whiche they fallen.

¶ The scale of the Astrolabye.

Next the forsayd cercle of the A/ B/ C/ vnder the crosse lyne is marked the scale/ in maner of two squiers/ or els in maner of ledders that serueth by his .xii. poyntes/ and his dyuysions of ful many a subtel conclusyon of this forsayd scale: For the crosse lyne vnto the very angle/ is cleped Umbra recta/ or els Umbra extensa/ & the neyther party Umbra versa.

¶ The rule.

Than haste thou a brode rule that hath on euery ende a square plate/ parted with certayn holes/ some more & some lesse/ to receyuen the streames of the sonne by day/ and eke by medyacion of thyn eye/ to knowe the altytude of the sterres by nyght.

¶ The pyn/ whiche is ymagyned to be pole artyke and the horse.

Than is there a large pyn in maner of an extltre/ that gothe thorowe the hole that halte the tables of the clymathes in the reethe/ in the wombe of the moder/ thorowe whiche pynne there gothe a lytel wegde/ the whiche is cleped the horse/ that strayneth al these partes togyther. This foresayd great pynne in maner of an extiltre/ is ymagende to be the pole artyke in thyn Astrolabye.

¶ For lynes on the wombe syde.

The wombe syde of thyn Astrolaby is also deuyded with a longe crosse in four quarters from Est to West/ from Southe to Northe/ from right syde to lyfte syde/ as is the backsyde.

¶ The degrees of the wombe syde.

The border of the whiche wombe syde is deuyded fro the poynte of the Est lyne vnto the poynte of the Southe lyne vnder the rynge in lxxxx. degrees/ and by the same proporcion is euery quarter deuyded/ as is the backsyde/ that amounteth. CCC.lx. degrees. And vnderstande wel that the degrees of this border ben answeryng and consentyng to the degrees of equinoctial that is deuyded in the same nombre/ as euery other cercle is in the hye heuen.

This

This border is deuyded also with .xxiiii. letters/ and a smale crosse aboue the south lyne/ that sheweth the .xxiiii. houres equales of the clocke. And I haue sayde .v. of these degrees maken a myle way/ and .iii. myle way maken an houre/ and euery degre of this border conteyneth .iiii. mynutes/ and euery mynute .lx. secondes. Nowe haue I tolde the twyse and for the more declaracion.

¶ Of the thre principal cercles.

The plate vnder the reete is discryued with thre cercles/ of whiche the leste is cleped the cercle of Cancer/ bycause ye heed of Cancer turneth euermore cōcentrike vpon the same cercle. In this halse of Cancer is the grettest declynacion northwarde of the sonne/ and therfore is he ycleped Solsticiū of sōmer/ which declinacion after ye Ptholome/ is .xxiii. degrees and .l. mynutes/ as wel in Cancer as in Capricorne. This signe of Cancer is cleped the troppke of sōmer of tropos/ that is to sayne ayenwarde. The myddle cercle in wydnesse of this .iii. is cleped the cercle equinoctial/ vpon whiche turneth euer more the heedes of Aries and Libra. And vnderstande wel/ that euermore this cercle equinoctial turneth iustly fro very Est to very West/ as I haue shewed in the sphere solide. This same cercle is cleped also the wayer of the day. for whan the sonne is in the hedde of Aries and Libra/ than ben dayes and nyghtes lyke of lengthe in al the worlde/ & therfore ben these two signes called equinoctis. And al that meueth within these heedes of Aries and Libra/ is ycalled northwarde/ and al that meueth without these heedes/ his meuyng is cleped southwarde/ as for the equinoctyal/ take kepe of the latytudes Northe & Southe/ and forget it not: By this cercle equinoctial ben consydred the .xxiiii. houres of the clocke. for euermore the arysyng of .xv. degrees of the equinoctial maketh an houre equale of the clocke. This equinoctial is cleped the mydway of the first meuynge/ or els of the sonne. And note that the firste meuyng is cleped meuynge of the first mouable of the eight sphere/ which meuyng is fro Est to West/ & agayne in to Est. Also it is cleped gyrdel of the first meuyng. for it departeth the first meuable/ that is to sayne/ ye sphere in two lyke parties euen distante fro the poles of this worlde. The wydest of these thre cercles principal is cleped the cercle of Capricorne/ & turneth euermore concentrike vpon the same cercle. In the heed of this forsayd Capricorne is the greatest declynacion southewarde of the sonne. and therfore it is cleped Solsticium of wynter. This signe of Capricorne is also cleped the tropike of wynter. for than begynneth the sonne to come agayne to vs warde.

¶ Of the almicanteras/ the signet/ and what is thyn orizonte.

Upon this forsayd plate ben compased certayne cercles/ that hyghten almicanteras: of whiche some of hem semen parfyte cercles/ and some semen imparfyte. The centure that stondeth a myddest the narowest cercle is cleped the signet. And the nethereſt cercle/ that deuydeth the two emisperies that is the partie of the heuen aboue the erthe/ and the partie bynethe. These almicanteras ben compowned by two and two/ al be it so that on dyuers astrolabies some almycanteras ben deuyded by one/ & some by two/ and some by thre/ after the quantyte of the Astrolabye. This forsayd signet is ymagyned to be the very poynt ouer the crowne of thy heed. and also this signet is the very pole of the orizonte in euery regyon.

¶ What ben thyn azimutes.

From this sygnet (as it semeth) there comen croked strykes/ lyke to the clawes of a loppe/ or els lyke to the werke of a womans calle/ in keruyng ouerthwarte the almycanteras/ and these same strykes or diuysions ben cleped Azimutes/ and they deuyden the orizontes on thyn Astrolabye in .xxiiii. dyuisyons. And these azimutes serue to knowe the costes of the fyrmament/ and to other conclusyons/ as for to know the signet of the sonne & of euery sterre.

¶ Of the .vii. houres of the planettes.

Nexte these azymutes/ vnder the cercle of Cancer/ ben the .xii. diuysions embolife/ moche like to the shap of the azymutes that shewen the spaces of houres of planettes.

¶ Thy

¶ Thy reete or els thy zodiake.

THy reete of thyn Astrolabye whiche is thy zodiake shapen in maner of a net or of a loppe webbe/ after the olde discrypcion/ whiche thou mayste turne vp and downe as thy selfe lyketh/ conteyneth certayne nombre of sterres fyxe/ with her longitudes and latytudes determinate/ if so be that yͤ maker haue not erred. The names of the sterres ben wrutten in the mergyn of thy reete there they syt/ of the whiche sterres the smale poynt is cleped the centure. And vnderstond/ that al the sterres syttyng within the zodiake of thyn astrolabye/ ben cleped sterres of the northe/ for they arysen by the northe eest lyne/ and al the remenaunt fyxes out of the zodiake/ ben ycleped sterres of the southe/ but I saye not that they arysen al by the south eest lyne/ wytnesse of Aldeberan and also Algomysa. Generally vnderstonde this rule/ that thilke sterres that ben cleped sterres of the northe/ arysen rather than the degree of her longitude/ and al the sterres of the southe/ arysen after the degree of her longitude/ that is to sayne/ sterres in thyn astrolabye. The measure of longytude of sterres ytaken in the lyne ecliptyke of heuen/ vnder the whiche lyne whan that the sonne and the moone ben lyne right/ els in the superfycie of this lyne/ than is the eclyps of the sonne or of the moone/ as I shal declare & eke the cause why: but sothly yͤ ecliptyke lyne of thy zodyake is the vtterest bordure of the zodiake there thy degrees ben marked. The zodyake of thy astrolabye is shapen as a compace/ whiche that conteyneth a large brede/ as after the quantyte of thy astrolabye/ in ensample that the zodyake of heuen is ymagyned to be a superficies/ conteynyng the latytude of 12 signes/ where as al the remenaunt of cercles in heuen ben ymagyned very lynes withouten any latytude amyddes the celestyal zodiake is ymagyned a lyne/ whiche that is cleped the ecliptyke lyne/ vnder the whiche lyne is euermore the way of yͤ son. Thus ben there 6 degrees of yͤ zodiake of that one syde of the lyne/ and 6 degrees on that other. The zodiake is deuyded in 12 principal deuisyons/ that departen the 12 signes/ and for yͤ straytnesse of thyn astrolaby/ than is euery smale deuysion in a sygne ypted by two degrees and two/ I meane degrees conteynyng 60 mynutes/ and this forsayd heuenysshe zodiake is cleped the cercle of the signes/ or the cercle of beestes. For zodiake in langage of greke sowneth beestes in laten tonge. and in the zodiak ben the 12 signes that haue names of beestes/ bycause whan the sonne entreth in any of the signes/ he taketh the propertie of suche beestes/ or els for that the sterres yͭ ben there ben fixed ben disposed in signe of beestes or shape lyke beestes/ or els whan the planettes ben vnder the signes they transmue vs by her influences/ operacions/ and effectes/ lyke to operacions of beestes. And vnderstande also/ that whan an hote planet cometh in to an hote signe/ than entreth his hete/ and if a planet be colde/ than amenuseth his coldenesse/ bycause of the hotte sygne. And by this conclusyon mayst thou taken ensample in al signes/ be they moyste or drie/ mouable or fyxe/ reckenynge the qualyte of the planettes as I firste sayd. And euerych of these 12 signes hath respecte to a certayne parcel of the body of a man/ and hath it in gouernaunce: as Aries hath thyn heed/ & Taurus thy necke and thy throte/ Gemini thyn arme holes and thyn armes/ and so forthe/ as shal be shewed more playnly in the fifth partie of this tretyse. The zodiake the whiche is partie of the eyght sphere/ ouerkerueth the equinoctial/ and he ouerkerueth him agayne in euen partes/ and that one halfe declyneth southwarde/ and that other northwarde/ as playnly declareth the treatyse of the sphere.

¶ The label.

Than hast thou a label that is shapen lyke a rule/ saue that it is streight and hath no plates on eyther ende/ but with the smale poynte of the forsaid label shalt thou calcule the equacions in the bordure of thyn astrolabye as by thyn almury.

¶ The almury/ the dentycle of Capricorne/ or els the calculere.

Thyn almury is cleped the dentycle of Capricorne/ or els yͤ calculere/ this same almury set fyxe in the heed of Capricorne/ & it serueth

G.g.g. of ma-of many a necessary conclusyon in equacion of thynges/as shal be shewed.

¶ Here begynneth the conclusyons of thyn Astrolabye to fynde the degre in the whiche the sonne is day by day/ after his course aboute.

Recken and knowe whiche is the daye of the moneth / and lay thy rule vpon the same daye/and than wol the very poynte of thy rule verily sytten on the bordure vpon the degre of the sonne. Ensample as thus. The yere of our lorde 1391 the 12 daye of Marche at myddday/I wolde knowe the degre of the sonne/I sought in the bakhalfe of myn Astrolabye/and founde the cercle of the dayes the whiche I knew by the names of the monthes writen vnder the same cercle: tho layde I my rule ouer the foresayd day/ and founde the poynte of my rule in the border vpon the first degree of Aries/a lytel within the degree: and thus knewe I this conclusyon. Another day I wolde knowe the degree of my sonne/ and this was at myddday in the 13 day of Decembre/ I founde the daye of the moneth in maner as I sayd: tho layde I my rule vpon the forsayd 13 day/and founde the poynte of my rule vpon the first degree of Capricorne/ a lytel within ye degre/ and than had I of this conclusyon the very experience.

¶ To knowe the altytude of the sonne eyther of celestyal bodyes.

Put the rynge of thyn Astrolaby vpon thy right thombe/and tourne thy lyfte syde agayne the syght of the sonne/ and remeue thy rule vp and downe tyl the streame of the sonne shyne thorowe bothe holes of the rule: loke than howe many degrees this rule is areysed fro the lytel crosse vpon the eest lyne/ and take there the altytude of thy sonne: and in this same wyse mayste thou knowe by night the altytude of the moone/or of ye bright sterres. This chapiter is so general euer in one that there nedeth no more declaracion/but forgette it not.

¶ To knowe the degree of the sonne and of thy zodiake/by the dayes in the backsyde of thyn Astrolaby.

Than if thou wyste wele the rekenynge to knowe whiche is the daye in thy calender of the moneth that thou arte in/ lay thyn Astrolaby/ that is to say the allydatha / vpon the daye in the calender of thyn Astrolabye/ and he shal shewe the thy degree of the sonne.

¶ To knowe euery tyme of the day by lyght of the sonne/and euery tyme of the nyght by the sterres fyxe/and eke to knowe by night or by day the gree of the signe ye ascendeth on the eest orizont/whiche is cleped comenly ascendent.

Take the altytude of ye sonne whan the lyst/as I haue sayd/ and set the degre of the sonne (in case that it be before the myddle of the daye) amonge thyn almycanteras on the eest syde of thyn astrolabye: and if it be after the myddle of the day/set the degre of the sonne vpon the weste syde. Take this maner of settynge for a general rule ones for euer. And whan thou haste ysette the degre of the sonne vpon as many almycānteras of heyght as was the sonne/ taken by thy rule/ lay ouer thy label vpon ye degre of the sonne/ and than wol the poynte of the label sytten in the bordure vpon the very tyde of the day. Ensample of this. The yere of our lorde 1391 the 12 day of Marche/I wolde knowe the tyde of the day/I toke the altytude of my sonne/ and founde that it was 25 degrees/ and 30 mynutes of heyght of ye bordure in the backsyde/ tho turned I myn astrolaby/& bicause it was before myddday I turned my reete/ and set the degre of the sonne/that is to say/the first degre of Aries in the right syde in myne astrolabye/ vpon the 25 degree & 30 mynutes of heyght/ amonge my almycanteras : Tho layde I my label vpon the degree of my sonne / and founde the poynte of my label in the bordure

on the

on the capitale letter/ that is cleped an X. Tho reckened I al the capital letters fro the lyne of mydnight vnto the foresayd letter X/ and founde it was 9 of the clocke of the day. Tho loked I ouer my eest orizont and founde there the 12 degre of Geminius ascendyng/ which that I tooke for myn ascendent/ and in this wyse had I the experyence for euermore in whiche maner I shulde knowe the tyde of the daye/ and eke myn ascendent. Tho wolde I wete that same nyght folowyng the houre of the nyght/ and wrought in this wyse: amonge an heape of sterres it lyked me to take the altytude of the fayre whyte sterre that is cleaped the Alhabor/ and founde her syttynge on the weste syde of the lyne of myd day 18 degrees of heyght/ taken vy my rule on the backsyde. Tho sette I the centure of this alhabor vpon 18 degrees amonge my almycantras vpon the weste syde/ bycause yͤ he was founde vpon the weste syde: Tho layde I my label ouer the degree of the sonne/ that was discended vnder the weste orizonte/ and reckened al the letters capitalles fro the lyne of myddaye vnto the poynt of my label in the bordure/ and founde that it was after noone/ passed 7 of the clocke the space of 11 degrees. Tho loked I downe vpon my eest orizonte/ and founde there 20 degrees of Libra ascendynge/ whom I toke for myn ascendent/ and thus lerned ones for euer/ to know in whiche maner I shulde come to the houre of the nyght and to myn ascendent/ as verily as maye be taken by so smale an instrument. But nathelesse this rule in general wyl I warne the for euer: Ne make thou neuer none ascēdent at noone of the day. Take a iuste ascendent of thyn Astrolabye/ and haue sette iustly a clocke/ whan any celestyal body/ by the which thou wenest gouerne thylke thynges/ ben nye the southe lyne: for trust wel/ whan the sonne is nere the meridional lyne/ the degree of the sonne remeueth so longe concentryke vpon thyn almycanteras/ that sothely thou shalte erre fro the iuste ascendent. The same conclusyon say I by my centure of my sterre fyxe by the nyght/ and moreouer by experyence I wote wel that fro our orizont fro enleuen of the clocke vnto one in takyng of the iuste ascendent in a portatyfe astrolabye/ it is to harde to knowe/ I meane from enleuen of the clocke before noone/ tyl one of the clocke next folowyng: and for the more declaracion lo here thy fygure nexte after this rule that foloweth.

¶ To knowe the degre of the sonne in thy zodiake by the dayes in the backsyde of thyn Astrolabye.

Whan thou wolte weten to recken and knowe whiche is the daye of the moneth that thou arte in/ and lay the rule of thy Astrolabye/ that is to say the alidatha vpon the day in the calender of thyn astrolabye/ and he shal shewe the thy degre of the sonne.

¶ Special declaracion of the ascendent.

The ascendent sothly/ is as wel in al natyuites as in questyons/ and as in elections of tymes is a thing/ which that these astrologiens greatly obseruen/ wherfore me semeth conuenyent/ sens I speke of the ascendent/ to make of it a special declaracion. The ascendent sothly to take it at the largest/ is thylke degree that ascendeth at any of these foresayd tymes on the eest orizont: and therfore/ if that any planet ascende at thylke same tyme in the forsaid same gre of his longitude/ men say that thilke planette is in horoscopo/ But sothly the house of that ascendent/ that is to say/ the first house or yͤ eest angle/ is a thing more brode and large/ for after the statutes of astrologiens/ what celestyal body that is 5 degrees aboue thilke degre that ascendeth on the orizont/ or within that nombre/ that is to sayn nere the degree that ascendeth/ yet recken they thilke planette in the ascendent/ and what planet that is vnder thilke degree that ascendeth the space of 15 degrees/ yet sayne they that planette is lyke to him that is the houre of the ascendent. But sothely if he passe the boundes of the forsayde spaces aboue or byneth/ they sayne that thilke planette is fallynge for

G.g.g.ii. the

fro the ascendent: yet sayne these astrologiens that the ascendent and eke the lorde of the ascendent/ may be shapen for to be fortunate or infortunate: as thus. A fortunate ascendent clepen they whan that no wycked planette of Saturne or Mars/ or els the tayle of the dragon is in the house of the ascendet/ ne that no wicked planette haue no aspecte of enemyte vpon the ascendent: but they wol caste that they haue fortunate planette in her ascendent/ and yet in his felycyte/ and than say they that it is wel. Furthermore they sayne that fortune of an ascendent is the contrarye of these foresayd thynges. The lorde of the ascendent sayne they/ that he is fortunate whan he is in good place for the ascendent/ and eke the lorde of the ascendent is in an angle or in a succedent where he is in his dignyte/ and comforted with frendely aspectes receyued / and eke that he may sene the ascendent not retrograde ne combuste/ ne ioyned with no shrewe in the same signe/ ne that he be not in his discencyon/ ne reygned with no planette in his discencions/ ne haue vpon him none aspecte infortunate/ and than they sayne that he is wel. Nathelesse these ben obseruaunces of iudycial mater and rytes of paynyms/ in whiche my spyrite hath no faythe ne knowynge of her horuscopum/ for they sayne that euery sygne is departed in 3 euen partes/ by 10 degrees and the lyke porcion they clepen a face. And although a planette haue a latytude fro the eclyptyke/ yet sayn some folke/ so that the planette aryse in that same signe/ with any degre of the foresayd face/ in whiche his longytude is reckened. And yet is the planette in horoscopo be in natyuitees or in election.

¶ To knowe the very equacion of the degrees of the sonne/ if it so be that it fal betwyxe to almycanteras.

FOr as moche as the almycanteras of thyn Astrolabye ben compouned by two and two/ wher as some almycanteras in sondue astrolabyes ben cōpowned by one or els by two/ it is necessarye to thy lernyng/ to teche the first to knowe and wyrche with thyn instrument: wherfore whan that the degre of the sonne falleth betwene two almycanteras/ or els if thyne almycanteras ben grauen with ouer great a poynt of a compace/ for bothe these thynges maye cause errour as wel in knowing of the tyde of the day as of the very ascendent. Thou muste werken in this wyse: sette the degree of the sonne vpon the hygher almycanteras as of bothe/ and wayte wel where thy almurye toucheth the bordure/ and sette there a pricke of ynke/ sette adowne agayne the degree of the sonne vpon the nether almycanteras of bothe/ and sette there a nother pricke: remeue than thy almury in the bordure euen a myddes both prickes/ and this wol leaden iustly the degre of the sonne to sytte bytwene bothe the almycāteras in his right place. Laye than the label on the degre of the sonne/ and fynde in the bordure the very tyde of the day or of the nyght. And also verely shalt thou fynde vpon thy eest orizonte thyn ascendent.

¶ To knowe the springe of the dawnyng and the ende of the euenyng/ the whiche ben cleped the two crepusculis.

SEtte the nadyr of thy sonne vpon 18 degrees of heyght amonge thyn almycanteras on the weste syde/ and laye thy label on the degree of the sonne/ and than shal the poynte of the label shewe the springe of the daye: also sette the nadyre of the sonne vpon the 18 degrees of heyght amonge thyn almycanteras on the eest syde/ and lay ouer thy label vpon the degre of the sonne/ and with the poynte of thy label fynde in the bordure the ende of thyn euenynge that is very nyght. The nadyre of the sonne is thilke degree that is opposyte to ẏ degre of the sonne in the 320 signe/ as thus. Euery degree of Aries by order/ is nadyre to euery degree of Libra by order/ and Taurus to Scorpion / Gemini to Sagittarius/ Cancer to Capricorne/ Leo to Aquary/ Virgo to Pisces. And if any degree in thy zodyake be derke/ his nadyre shal declare hym.

¶ To

¶ To knowe the arche of the daye/ that some folke callen the day artifyciall/ fro the sonne arysing tyl it go downe.

SEt the degre of the sonne upon thyn Est orizonte/ and lay thy label on the degree of the sonne/ and at the poynte of thy label in the bordure sette a pricke: turne than thy reete aboute/ tyl the degre of the sonne syt upon the Weste orizonte/ and laye the labell upon the same degree of the sonne/ and at the poynte of the label sette another pricke. Reken than the quantyte of tyme in the bordure betwyxe bothe prickes/ and take there thyne arche of thy day: the remenaũt of the bordure under the orisonte/ is the arche of the nyght. Thus mayste thou reken bothe arches of every porcion where that thou lykest/ and by this maner of werkyng mayst thou se howe longe that any sterre fyxe dwelleth above the erthe/ fro the tyme that he ryseth tyl he go to reste. But the daye naturel/ that is to sayne .24. houres/ is the revolucion of the equinoctial/ with as moche partie of the zodyake/ as the sonne of his proper mouynge passeth in the meane whyle.

¶ To turne the houres inequalles/ and the houres equalles.

Knowe the nombre of the degrees in the houres inequales/ & departe hem by .15. and take there thyn houres equales.

¶ To know the quantyte of the day vulgare/ that is to saye/ fro spryng of the day unto the very nyght.

KNowe thy quantyte of thyn crepusclys/ as I have it taught in the chapiter before/ and adde hem to the arche of the day artifyciall/ and take there thy space of al ye hole day vulgare unto the very night. In the same maner mayste thou werke to knowe the vulgare nyght.

¶ To knowe the houres inequales by daye.

UNderstonde wel that these houres inequales ben cleped houres of the planettes: and understonde wel that somtyme ben they longer by daye than they be by nyght/ and somtyme contrarye. But understonde thou wel/ that evermore generally the houres inequale of the daye/ with the houres inequale of the nyght/ conteyneth .30. degrees of the bordure/ the whiche bordure is evermore answeryng to the degrees of the equinoctial/ wherfore departe the arche of the daye artifycial in .12. and take there the quantyte of the houre inequale by daye/ and if thou abate the quantyte of the houre inequale by daye out of 360. degrees/ than shal the remenaunt that leaveth performe the hour inequale by nyght.

¶ To knowe the quantyte of houres equales.

THe quantytes of houres equales/ that is to sayne the houres of the clocke/ ben departed by .15. degrees al redy in the bordure of thy Astrolabye/ as wel by nyght as by daye generally for evermore. What nedeth any more declaracyon: wherfore whan the lyste to knowe howe many houres of the clocke ben passed/ or any parte of any of these houres ben to comen fro suche a tyme to suche a tyme/ by daye or by nyght/ knowe the degre of thy sonne/ and laye thy label on it: than turne thy reete aboute joyntly with thy label/ and with the poynt of it recken in the border fro the sonne arysing in to ye same place there thou desyrest by day as by nyght. This conclusyon wol I declare in the fourthe partye of the laste chapitre of this tretyse/ so openly that there shal lacke no worde that nedeth declaracyon.

¶ Specyal declaracion of the houres of the planettes.

Understande wel that evermore fro the arysing of the sonne tyl it go to rest/ the nadyre of the sonne shal shewe the hour of the planet/ and fro that tyme forwarde al the nyght tyl the sonne aryse/ than shal the very degre of the sonne shewe the houre of the planet. Ensample as thus. The 13 day of Marche fel upon

G.g.g.iij. a sa-a saturday paraukture/ and at the rysynge of the sonne I founde the seconde degre of Aries syttyng vpon myn eest orizonte/ al be it was but lytel. Than founde I the seconde degree of Libra nadyre of my sonne/ discendynge on my weste orizont/ vpon whiche weste orizont euery day generally at the sonne arysyng entreth the hour of any planet/ vnder the forsaid weste orizonte/ after the whiche planet the day beareth his name/ & endeth in the next stryke of the planet/ vnder the forsayd west orizont: and euer as the sonne clymbeth vpper and vpper/ so gothe his nadyre downer & downer/ & teching fro suche strikes ye houres of planettes by order as they sytten in heuen. The firste hour inequal of euery saturday is Saturne/ and the seconde to Jupiter/ the thirde to Mars the fourth to the sõne/ the fyfth to Venus/ the syxt to Mercurius/ the seuenth to the moone/ and than ayen ye eyght to Saturne/ the nynth to Jupiter/ the tenth to Mars/ the enleuenth to the sonne/ the twelfth to Venus. And nowe is my sõne gon to rest as for that saterday/ than sheweth the very degre of the sonne the houre of Mercury/ entryng vnder my weste orizont at euen. And nexte hym succedeth the moone/ and so forthe by order planet after planette/ in houre after houre al the nyght longe tyl the sonne aryse. Nowe ryseth the sonne the sonday by the morowe/ & the nadyre of the sonne vpon the west orizont/ sheweth me ye entrynge of the hour of the foresayd sonne. And in this maner succedeth planet vnder planet fro Saturne vnto the moone/ and fro the moone vp agayne to Saturne hour after hour generally: and thus knowe I this conclusyon.

¶ To knowe with whiche degree of the zodyake any sterre fyxe in thyn astrolabye aryseth vpon the Eest orizonte/ although the orizonte be in an other signe.

Sette the centure of the sterre vpon the eest orizonte/ and loke what degree of any signe that sytteth vpon the same orizonte at the same tyme: and vnderstonde wel/ that with the same degre aryseth the same sterre. And this meruayloue arysinge with a stronge degree in another signe/ is bycause that the latytude of the sterre fyxe is eyther Northe or Southe fro the equinoctial. But sothly the latytudes of planettes ben comenly reckened fro the eclyptyke/ bycause that none of hem declyneth but fewe degrees out fro the brede of the zodiake. And take good kepe of this chapiter of arysyng of celestyal bodyes/ for there trusteth wel/ that neyther moone neyther sterre in our embolyse orizonte/ that aryseth with the same degre of his longitude/ saue in one case/ and that is whan they haue no longitude fro the eclyptyke lyne. But neuer the lesse somtyme is eueryche of these planettes vnder the same lyne.

To knowe the declynacion of any degre in the zodiake/ fro the equinoctial cercle.

Sette the degree of any sygne vpon the lyne meridyonal/ and recken his altytude in the almycanteras fro the Eest orizonte vp to the same degree set in the foresayd lyne/ and sette there a pricke: Turne vp than thy recte and set the heed of Aryes or Libra in the same merydional lyne/ and set there another pricke. And whan that this is doone/ cõsyder the altytudes of hem bothe: for sothly the difference of thilke altytude is the declynacion of thylke degree fro the equinoctial. And if it so be that thilke degree be northwarde fro the equinoctial/ than is his declynacion north/ and if it be southwarde/ than is it southe.

¶ To knowe for what latytude in any regyon the almycanteras in my tables ben compowned.

Beken howe many degrees of almicãteras in the meridional line/ be from ye cercle equinoctial vnto the sygnet or els from the pole artike vnto the north orizont/ & for so great a latitude or so smale a latitude/ is the table compouned.

To knowe the latytude of the sonne in the myddes of the day/ that is cleped the altitude meridian.

Sette

Set the degre of thy sonne upon yͤ lyne meridional/and reken howe many degrees of almicantras ben bytwyxe yͤ lyne eest orizont/and the degree of thy sonne/ and take there thyne altitude meridian/that is to sayn/ the hyghest degre of the sonne as for that day. So mayste thou knowe in the same lyne the hyghest lyne that any starre fyxe clymbeth by nyght/this is to sayne/ that whan any starre fyxe is passed the lyne meridional/than begynneth it to discende/ and so doth the sonne.

To knowe the degree of the Sonne by the reet for a maner coriouste.

Seke busyly with thy rule/ the hyghest of the Sonne in myddes of the daye/ tourne than thyne astrolabye/ ⁊ with a prycke of ynke marke the nombre of yͤ same altitude in the lyne meridional. Tourne than thy reet aboute tyl thou fynde a degree of thy zodiake accordynge with the prycke/ this is to sayn/syttynge on the prycke/ and in soth thou shalte fynde but two degrees in al the zodiake of that condycyon. And yet thylke two degres ben in dyvers sygnes. Thā mayst thou lyghtly by the season of the yere knowe the sygne in whiche is the sonne.

To knowe whiche daye is lyke to other in lengthe throughe out the yere.

Loke whiche degrees ben ylyke frome the heedys of Cancer and Capricorn/ and loke whan the Sonne is in any of thylke degrees/than ben the dayes lyke of lengthe/ yͭ is to sayn/ that as longe is that day in yͭ moneth/ as was suche a day in suche a moneth/ there varyeth but lytel. Also if thou take two dayes naturelles in the yere ylyke farre from eyther poyntes of the equynoctial in the opposite parties/than as longe is the day artificial on that one day as on that other/ and eke the contrarye.

This chapitre is a maner declaracyon to conclusyons that foloweth.

Understande wel/ that thy zodiake is departed in to halfe cercles/ from the hed of Capricorne unto yͤ hed of Cancer/ and ayenwarde from the hed of Cancer unto the hed of Capricorne. The hed of Capricorne is the lowest poynt/ where as the sonne goth in Wynter/and the hed of Cancer is the hyghest poynt/ in whiche the sonne gothe in Sōmer. And therfore understande wel/ that any two degrees that ben ylike farre from any of these two heedes/trust wel that thylke two degrees ben lyke declynacyon/ be it Southwarde or Northwarde/ and the dayes of hem ben lyke of lengthe/ and the nyghtes also/ ⁊ shadowes ylike/ ⁊ the altytudꝫ ylike at myddayes for ever.

To knowe the verey degree of any maner starre straunge after his latytude/ though he be indetermynate in thyn Astrolaby/ sothly to the trouthe thus he shal be knowen.

Take the altitude of thy starre whan he is on the Est side of the lyne meridional as nyghe as thou mayste gesse/ and take an ascendent anone ryght by some maner starre fixe which thou knowest/ and forgete not the altitude of the first starre ne thyn ascēdent. And whā that this is done/ aspye diligently whan this same fyrste starre passeth any thynge to the south westwarde/ ⁊ catche hym anone ryght in the same nombre of the altitude on yͤ West syde of this lyne meridional/as he was caught on the Est syde/ ⁊ take a newe ascendent anone ryght by some maner fyxe/the which that thou knowest/and forgete not this seconde ascendent. And whan this is done/ reken than howe many degrees ben bytwyxte the first ascendent ⁊ the seconde ascendent/and reken wel the middel degre bytwyxte bothe ascendentes/and set thilke myddel degree upon thyne Eest orizont/ and than loke what degre sit upon the lyne meridional and take there the very degre of the eclyptike/ in whiche the starre standeth for the tyme. For in the ecliptyke is the longytude of a celestyal body rekened even fro the halfe of the heed of Aries unto the ende of Pisces/and his latitude is rekened after the quantite of his declynacyon Northe or Southe/towarde the poles of this werke. As thus/ if it be of yͤ sonne or any

lyͤ

fyx starre/reken his latitude or his declyna-cyon fro the equinoctyal cercle/ and if it be of a planete/reken than the quantyte of his lati-tude from the ecliptyke lyne/al be it so ye from the equinoctyal may the declinacyon or the la-titude of any body celestial be rekened/after ye syght North or South/and after the quantite of his declynacyon. And yet so may the latitu-de or the declynacyon of any body celestyal/ saue onely of the sonne/ after his syght North or South. And after the quantite of his decli-nacion be rekened from the ecliptyke lyne/fro which lyne al planetes somtyme declyne/nor-the or South/saue onely the foresayd sonne.

To knowe degrees of longitudes of fyxe sterres/after that they ben determynat in thyne astrolabye/ if it so be that they ben trewly set.

SEt the centre of the sterre vpon the line meridional/& take kepe of thy zodiake/ and loke what degree of any sygne syt vpon the same lyne merydyonal at the same tyme/and there the degree in whiche the sterre standeth/and with the same degre cometh the same sterre vnto ye same lyne from ye orizont.

To knowe in specyal the latitude of our centre/I meane after the altitude of Oxenforde & the hight of our pole.

VNderstande wel that as farre is the heed of Aries or Libra in the equinoctial from our orizont/ as is the synet from the pole artike/ & as hye as the pole artike from the oryzonte/ as the equynoctyal is ferre from the synet/I preue it thus by the latitude of Oxenforde / vnderstande wel that the heyght of our pole artike from our North orizont is .51 .degrees/ and .50. mynutes/ thã is the synet from the pole artyke .38. degrees & 10. minutes/than is the equinoctial from our synet .51. degrees and .50. mynutes/thã is our south orizonte from our equynoctyal. 38. degrees/and .10. mynutes. Vnderstãde wel this rekenyng also/forget not that the synet is .90. degrees of heyght from the orizont/ and oure equinoctial is .90 .degrees from oure pol artike. Also this shorte rule is soth that the latytude of any planet in a regyon is the distãce from the synet vnto the equynoctyal.

¶ To proue the latitude of any place in a regyon by the preffe of the heyght of the pole artyke in that same place.

IN some wynters nyght whan the fyrmament is clere & thycke sterred/wayte a tyme tyl ye euery ster fixe syt lyne rizt ypendiculer ouer the pole artike/ & clepe that sterre A. & wayte another sterre that syt lyne ryght vnder .A. and vnder the pol/& clepe that sterre F. and vnderstande wel that .F. is not consydred but onely to declare that .A. that syt euer on the pol. Take than anone ryght the altytude of .A. from the orisonte & forgete it not/ let .A. and .F. go farwel tyl agaynst the dawnyng a great whyle/ and come than agayne/ and abyde tyl that .A. is euen vnder the pol vnder .F. for sothely than wyl .F. syt ouer the pol/take thã estsones the altitude of .A. from the orisonte/and note as wel the seconde altitude as the first altytude. And whan that this is done/reken howe many degrees ye the first altitude .A. exceded his altytude / & take halfe the like porcion that is exceded & adde it to his seconde altitude/and take there the eleuacyon of the pole/ and eke the altitude of thy region. For these two ben of one nombre/ye is to sayn as many degrees as thy pol is eleuate/so moche is the latitude of thy region. Ensample as thus. Parauenture the altitude of .A. in the euenynge is .62. degrees of heyght/ than wyl the seconde altitude or the dawning be .21. that is to sayn/lesse than .92. that was his first altitude at euen. Take than the halfe of .62. & ad it to .21. that was his seconde altitude/ & than hast thou the hyght of thy pol and the latitude of thy region. But vnderstande wel to preue this conclusyon and many another fayre conclusyon/ thou mayst haue a plomet hangyng on a lyne hygher than thyn heed on a perche & that lyne mote hange euen perpendiculer bytwyxe the pole and thyn eye / and than shalte thou se yf .A. syt euen ouer the pole and ouer F. at euen. And also if .F. syt euen ouer ye pole and ouer .A. or day.

Another

¶ Another conclusyon to preue the heyght of the pole artyke from the orizonte.

TAke any sterre fyxe that euer descendeth vnder the orizonte in thylke regyon / and consyder his hyghest altitude and his lowest altitude from the orizont / and make a nombre of these altytudes / take than and abate halfe that nombre / and take there the eleuacyon of the pole artyke in that same region / and for the more declaracion. &c.

o 82. 51. o 20.

¶ Another conclusyon to preue the latitude of a regyon that ye ben in.

VNderstande wel that the latitude of any place in a regyon is verely the space bytwyxe the sygne of hem that dwellen there / and ye equinoctial cercle / north or south / takynge the measure in the merydional lyne / as sheweth in the almicantras of thyn astrolabye / and thilke space is as moche as the pole artike is hye in the same place from ye orizont And than is the depressyon of the pole artentike beneth the orizonte / the same quantite of space / neyther more ne lesse / thā if thou desyre to knowe this latitude of the regyon / take the altitude of the Sonne in the middle of the day whan the Sonne is in the heed of Aries or of Libra / for than moueth the Sonne in the lyne equinoctyal / and abate the nombre of ye same Sonnes altitude out of. 90. degrees / and thā is the remenaūt of the nombre that leueth the altitude of the region / as thus. I suppose that the Sonne is thilke day at noone. 38. degrees of heyght / abate than. 38. degrees out of. 90. so leueth there. 52. than is. 52. degrees the latytude / I say not this but for ensample / for wel I wote the latitude of Oxenforde is certayne mynutes lesse. Nowe if it so be that the thynketh to longe a taryenge to abyde tyl that the Sonne be in the heed of Aries or of Libra / thā wayte whan that the Sonne is in any other degre of the zodiake / and consider the degre of this declynacion be northward from the equinoctial / abate than from the Sonnes altitude at noon the nombre of his declinacion / & than hast thou the hyghest of the heedes of Aries & Libra / as thus. My Sonne parauenture is in the. 10. degre of Leo almoost. 56. of heyght at noone / & his declinacion is almost 18 degrees northwarde from the equinoctyal / abate than thilke. 18. degrees of declinacion out of the altitude at noone / than leueth. 38. degrees / so there the heed of Aries or Libra & thyn equinoctial in that region. Also if it so be that the Sōnes declinacion be southwarde from the equinoctial / adde than thilke declinacion to the altitude of the Sonne at noone / & take there the heedes of Aries and Libra & thyn equinoctial / abate than the heyght of the equinoctial out of. 90. degrees / & than leueth there. 38. degrees / that is the distaunce of the regyon from the equinoctyal of any sterre fyxe that thou knowest & take the nether elongacyon lengthyng from the same equinoctial lyne / and werke after the maner aforesayd.

¶ Declaracyon of the ascencyon of signes as wel in cercle directe / as in oblyque.

THe excellēce of the sphere solyde amonges other noble conclusyons sheweth manifest the dyuers ascencions of signes in dyuers places / as wel in rizt cercles as in embolyse cercle. These auctours wryten ye thilke signe is cleped of ryght ascencyon / with whiche the more parte of the cercle equinoctial and the lesse parte of the zodyake ascendeth / & thilke sygne ascendeth embolyse / with whiche the lesse of the zodiake equinoctyal & the more parte of the zodiake ascendeth / and euer mo the arche of the day and the arche of the nyght is there ylyke longe / & the Sonne twyse euery yere passynge through the signet of her heed & 2. somers and. 2. wynters in a yere haue these foresayd people / and the almycantras in her Astrolabye ben streyght as a lyne / so hathe shewed in this fygure. The vtilites to knowe the ascencyons of sygnes in the right cercle is this. Trust wel that ve mediacions of thylke ascencyons these Astrologyens by her tables and her instrumentes knowen verely the ascēcion of euery degre and mynute in al the zodiake in the embolyse cercle / as shal be shewed. And note that this foresayd ryght oryzonte ye is ycleped is pcleped orizonte rectum/deuydeth the equy-noctial in to right angles/ and embolyfe ory-zonte/where as the pole is enhaunced vpon yͤ orizonte/ouercrouneth the equinoctial in embo-life angles.

¶ This is the conclusyon to knowe the ascen-cyons of sygnes in the right cercle: that is circulus directus.*.

SEt the heed of what sygne the lyste to knowe the ascendyng on the right cer-cle vpon the lyne meridional/ & wayte where thyn almurye toucheth the bordure/ & set there a prycke/ tourne than thy rete west-warde tyl the ende of the forsayd sygne/ sette vpon the meridional lyne/and estsones waite where thyn almurye toucheth yͤ bordure/ and set there a nother pricke. Reken than the nom-bres of degrees in the bordure bytwyxe bothe prickes/ & take than the ascencyon of the sygne in the right cercle/and thus mayst thou werke with euery porcyon of the zodyake.

¶ To knowe the ascencyons of sygnes in the embolyfe cercle in euery regyon/ I mene in circulo obliquo.

SEt the heed of the signes whiche as the lyst to knowe his ascencyon vpon the Est orizonte and wayte where thyne almurye toucheth the bordure/ and set there a prycke/ tourne than thy reet vpwarde tyl the ende of the same sygne/ set vpon the Est ori-zonte and wayte estsones where as thyn al-mury toucheth the bordure/ and set there ano-ther prycke/reken than the nombre of the de-grees in the bordure bytwyxe bothe prickes/ & take there the ascencyon of the sygne in yͤ em-bolife cercle. And vnderstande wel/ that al the sygnes in the zodiake/from the heed of Aries vnto the ende of Virgo/ ben cleped sygnes of the North from the equinoctial/and these sig-nes arisen betwyxe the verey Est and the ve-rey North in our orizonte generally for euer: and al the signes from the heed of Libra vnto the ende of Pisses/ben cleped sygnes of yͤ sou-the fro the equinoctyal/and these sygnes ary-sen euermore betwyxe the verey Est and the verey south in our orizonte/ also euery sygne betwyxe the heed of Capricorne vnto the ende of Gemini aryseth in our orizonte in lesse tha two houres equalles/ and these same sygnes from the heed of Capricorne vnto the ende of Gemini ben called tortuous sygnes or croked sygnes/ for they risen embolyse in our orizont and these croked signes ben obedient to the sig-nes that ben of the right ascencion. These sig-nes of right ascecion ben fro the heed of Can-cer vnto the heed of Sagittary/and these syg-nes arysen more vpryght than dothe the other and therfore they ben called soueraygne sygnes and euery of hem aryseth in more space than in two houres/of which sygnes Gemini obey-eth to Cancer/and Taurus to Leo/and Aries to Virgo/ Pisses to Libra/ Aquarius to Scor-pio/ and Capricorne to Sagittary/ and thus euermore two signes that ben lyke ferre from the heed of Capricorne obeyeth eueryche of hem to other.

¶ To knowe iustly the foure quarters of the worlde/as Est/ West/ south/ & North.

TAke the altitude of thy sonne whan thou lyst/ and note wel the quarter of the worlde in whiche the sonne is from the tyme by the asymutes/ tourne than thyn astrolaby and set the degree of the Sonne in the almycantras of his altytude/ on thylke syde that the Sonne standeth/ as is in maner of takyng of houres/ and ley thy label on the degre of the Sonne/ and reken howe many de-grees of the Sonne ben bytwene the lyne me-ridional and the poynt of thy label/ and note wel the nombres. Tourne than agayne thyne astrolabye/and set the poynt of thy great rule there thou takest thyn altitudes vpon as ma-ny degrees in his bordure from his meridio-nal/as was the poynte of thy label from the lyne merydyonal on the wombe syde. Take than thyn astrolabye with bothe handes sad-ly and slyly/and let the sonne shyne throughe bothe holes of thy rule/ and slyly in thilke shy-nynge ley thyne astrolaby couche adoun euen vpon a playne grounde/ & than wyl the meri-dional lyne of thyn astrolaby be euen southe/ and

and the Eest lyne wyl sygnifien Eest / and the West lyne West/and the North lyne North/so that thou werke softely and avysely in ẏ couchynge/and thou hast thus the foure quarters of the fyrmament. &c.

¶ To knowe the altitude of planetes from ẏ way of the sonne/ whether they ben north or south fro the way aforesayd.

Loke whan a planet is on the lyne meridional/ if that her altytude be of the same height/that is the degre of the Sōne for that day/and than is the planet in the verey way of the sonne/ and hath no latitude. And if the altitude of the planette be hyer than the degre of the Sonne/ than is the planet North from the way of the sygne south / a quantyte of latitude as sheweth by thyne Almicantras and yf the altytude be lesse than the degre of the sonne/than is the planete south from the way of the Sonne/suche a quantyte of latytude as sheweth by thyn almycantras. This is to sayne from the way of the Sōne in every place of the zodiake/for on the morowe the sonne wyl be in another degre.

¶ For to knowe the sygnet for the arisynge of the Sonne / this is to sayne/ the partye of the orizonte in whiche the Sonne ariseth.

Thou must fyrst consider ẏ the Sōne aryseth not in the verey Eest signet/ somtyme by North est and somtyme by south eest / sothly the sonne aryseth evermore in the verey Eest in our orizont / but if he be in the heed of Aryes or Libra. Nowe is thyn orizont departed in to. 24. partes of thy mynutes in sygnifycacyon of. 24. partes of the worlde/though it be so that shipmen reken al that partyes in. 32. Than is there no more but wayte in the whiche mynute that the sōne entreth at his arysynge/and take there the signet of the rysynge of the sonne.

¶ The maner of devysyon of thyn astrolabie is thus enfourmed/as in this case.

¶ Fyrst it is devyded in foure places prynccypally with the lyne that cometh fro the Eest to the West / and than with another lyne that gothe fro the Southe to the Northe/ than is it devyded in smale parties of minutes / as eest and eest by south/ where that is ẏ first minute above the eest lyne/and so forth fro partye to partye tyl ẏ thou come agayn to the eest lyne. Thus thou myght understande the sygnet of every sterre in whiche partye he ariseth.

¶ To knowe in whiche partye of the firmament is the conjunction.

Consider the tyme of the conjunctyon by the calender/ as thus: howe many houres that the conjunctyon is fro myddaye of the day before/ as sheweth the canon of the calender. Reken than that nombre in the bordure of thyne astrolabye/as thou were wonte to do in knowyng of the houres of the day or of the night/and lay thy label over the degree of the sonne/than wyl the poynte of the label syt upon the houre of the conjunction. Loke than in whiche minute the degree of the sonne sitteth/and in that partie of the firmament is the conjunctyon.

¶ To knowe the sygnet of the altitude of the sonne.

This is no more to say/but any tyme of the day take the altitude of the sonne/ and by the minutes in whiche he ascendeth thou might se in whiche partie of the firmament he is/& in the same wyse might thou se by night of any ster wheder he syt est/ West/ or south/or any parte bitwixe/after the name of the minutes in whiche the sterre standeth.

¶ To know sothly the longitude of the mone or any planet that hath no latitude fro the tyme of the ecliptike lyne.

Take the altitude of the mone/and reken thyn altitude up amonge thyn almicātras on whiche side that the mone standeth/ &set there a pricke. Take than anon rizt upon the mones side ẏ altitude of every sterre fixe that thou knowest/and set his cercle upō his altitude amonge thyn almicantras there ẏ sterre is foūden/ wayte than of which degre the

the zodiake is/to whiche the pricke of the alti- tude of the mone / and there take the degre e in whiche the mone standeth. This conclusion is verey sothe of the sterres in thyn astrolabie/ & stāden after the trouth. Some treatyse of the astrolabie maketh none exception whether yͤ mone haue latitude or none/nor whether syde of the mone the altitude of the sterre be fonde. And note if the mone shewe her selfe by day/ than thou mayst worche the same conclusyon by the sonne as wel as by the sterre fyxe.

¶ This is the werchynge of the conclusyon to knowe whether any planet be directe or retrograde.

¶ Take the altitude of any sterre that is cle- ped a planet and note it wel/and anone right take the altitude of some sterre fyxe that thou knowest & note it wel also/ & come agayn the thirde or the fourth night nexte folowing/for than thou shalte perceyue wel the meuynge of the planet whether he meue forwarde or backwarde/& wayte wel than whan the sterre fyxe is in this same altitude yͭ she was whan thou toke her first altitude of the forsayd pla net & note it wel/for trust wel if so be yͭ yͤ pla- net be in the right syde of the meridional lyne/ so yͭ his seconde altitude be lesse than the first altitude was/thā is yͤ planet directe/& if he be in the west syde in yͭ condycyon/than is he re- trograde/ & if so be yͭ this planet be in the eest syde whan his altitude is take/so that the se- conde altitude be more than his first altitude/ than is he retrograde/ and if he be in the West syde of the lyne meridional/ than is he directe But the contrary mouynge of these parties is the course of the mone/for sothly yͤ mone mo- ueth the contrary fro eyther planettes in her eclyptyke lyne/but in none other maner.

¶ The conclusion of equacyons of houses after the astrolabye.

SEt the begynnynge of the degree that ascendeth vpon the ende of the .8. houre inequal/ than wyl the lyne of the secōde house syt vpon the lyne of mydnyght / remeue than the degre that ascendeth/and set hym vpon the ende of the 10 houre inequal/ than wyl the be- gynnynge of the 3 house sytte vpon the myd- nyght lyne/bringe vp agayne the same degree that ascendeth first/and set hym vpon the eest orizont/ and than wyl the begynnynge of the 4 house syt vpon the mydnyght lyne. Take than the nadere of the degree that ascendeth first and set him vpon the ende of the 2 houre inequal/and than wyl the begynnynge of the 5 house syt vpon the mydnyght lyne. Take than the nadere of the ascendent and set hym vpon the ende of the 4 houre inequal/ & than wyl the begynnynge of the 6 house syt vpon the mydnyght lyne. The begynnynge of the 7 house is nadere of the ascendent and the be- gynnynge of the 8 house is nadere of the se- conde/ and the begynnynge of the 9 house is nadere of the 3 and the begynnyng of the 10 house is nadere of the 4 and the begynnynge of the 11 house is nadere of the 5 & the begyn- nyng of the 12 house is nadere of yͤ 6 house.

¶ Another maner of equacyons of houses by the astrolabye.

TAke thyne ascendent / and than thou hast the 4 angles/ for wel thou wo- test that the opposite is of thyn ascen- dent/that is to saye/ the begynnynge of the 7 house syt vpon the west orizont/and the begin nynge of the 10 house vpon the lyne meridio- nal/& his opposite vpon the lyne of mydnight than lay thy label vpon the degre yͭ ascendeth and reken than fro the poynte of thy label al the degrees in the bordure tyl that thou come to the meridional lyne / and departe al thilke degrees in to 3 euen partes/ and take there the euen porcions of 3 other houses for to lay thy label ouer euery of these 3 parties / and than thou might se by the label in yͤ zodiake the be- gynnynge of these 3 houses fro the ascendēt/ that is to say the 12 nexte aboue thyne ascen- dent/ and than the 11 house and the 10 house vpon the meridional lyne/as I first sayd the same wyse wyrche fro the ascendent downe to the lyne of midnyght/and thus thou hast thre houses/ that is to saye / the beginnynge of the seconde/the thyrde/and the fourth house: than is the is the nadyre of these thre houses / the begynnyng of these 3 houses that foloweth.

¶ To fynde the lyne meridyonal / to dwel fyxe in any certayne place.

Take a rounde plate of metal for warping the border the better / and make ther vpon a iust compace a lytel within the bordure / and lay this rounde plate vpon an euen grounde / or some euen stone / or on a euen stocke fyxe in the grounde / and laye it euen by a rule in the centre of the compace / stycke an euen pynne or a wyre vpright / the smaller the better / and sette thy pynne or thy wyre by a plōme rules ende vpright euen / and let this pyn be no lenger than a quarter / of thy diameter of the compace fro the pynne / and wayte besyly aboute 10 or 11 of the clocke whan ỹ sonne sheweth / whan the shadowe of the pynne entreth any thing within the cercle of the compace one heer brede / & make there a pricke with ynke: abyde than styl waytyng on the sonne after one of the clocke / tyl that the shadowe of the pynne or of the wyre passe any thing out of the cercle or compace / be it neuer so lytel / and set there a pricke. Take than a compace and mesure euen the myddle bytwixe bothe prickes / and sette there a pricke: take than a rule and drawe a stryke euen fro the pyn vnto ỹ myddle pricke / and take there the lyne meridyonal for euermore / as in the same place. And if thou drawe a crosse ouerthwarte the compace iustely ouer the lyne meridyonal / than haste thou eest and west / and perconsequens the opposytyte / that is southe and northe.

¶ Discrypcion of the meridyonal lyne / and of the longitudes and latytudes of cytes and townes as wel as of clymates.

This lyne meridyonal is but a maner discripcion of a lyne ymagyned / ỹ passeth vpon the poles of the world / and by the signet of our heed: & it is cleped the signet / for in what place that any man is at any tyme of the yere whan the sonne by meuyng of the fyrmamēt cometh to his meridyonal place / than is it the verey myddaye that we clepe noone / and therfore it is cleped the lyne of myddaye. Than take hede that euermore of two cytes or of two townes / of which the one approcheth nerer the eest than doth the other towne / trust wel that thilke two townes haue dyuers meridyans. Take kepe also ỹ the arche of the equinoctial / that is conteyned and bounded bytwene the two meridyans / is cleped the longitude of the towne. And if so be that two townes haue meridyan lyke / or one meridyan / than is the distaunce of hem bothe lyke farre: & in this maner they chaūge not her meridyan / but sothly they chaunge her almycanteras for the haunsynge of the pole and the distaunce of the sonne. The longitude of a clymate maye be cleaped the space of the erthe / fro the begynnyng of the first clymate / vnto the laste ende of the same clymate / euen directe ayenst the pole artyke / thus saye some auctours. And some clerkes say / that if men cleape the latytude of a centre the arche meridyan / that is conteyned or intercepte betwyxe the signet and the equinoctial / than they saye that the distaunce fro the equinoctial vnto the ende of the clymate / euen ayenst the pole artyke / is the longitude of the clymate for south.

¶ To knowe with what degre of the zodyake that any planet ascendeth on the orisonte / where his latytude be north or southe.

℞ Nowe by thyn almynake the degree of the eclyptike of any signe / in whiche that the planet is reckened for to be / and that is cleped the degree of his longitude. And knowe also the degre of his latitude fro ỹ ecliptyke / northe or southe / and by these ensamples folowynge in especial / thou maist wirch with euery signe of the zodyake. The longitude perauenture of Venus or of an other planette was of Capricorne / & the latytude of him was northwarde degrees fro the eclyptike lyne / than toke I a subtyl compace / and cleped the one poynte of my compace A / & that other F / than toke I the poynt of A / and set it in ỹ eclyptike lyne / and my zodiake in the degre of the longitude of heedes / that is to say / in the heed of Capricorne / and than set I the poynt of F / vpwarde in the same signe / bycause ỹ the altytude was northe / vpon the latytude of Venus / that is to say / in the degre fro the heed of Capricorne /

H.h.h. and

and thus haue I the degrees betwyxe my two prickes/ than layde I downe softly my compace/and set the degree of the longitude vpon the orizont/ than toke I and waxed my label in maner of a payre of tables/ to receyue distinctly the pricke of my compace/than toke I this foresayd label/ and layde it fyxe ouer the degree of my longitude/ than tooke I vp my compace & the poynte of A/in the waxe of my label/as I coude gesse/ouer the ecliptyke lyne in the ende of the longitude/ I sette the poynte ouer endelonge on the label/ vpon the space of the latytude inwarde and on the zodiake/ that is to saye northwarde fro the eclyptike: Than layde I downe my compace/and loked wel in the wax vpon the eclyptike of A/ and F/ than turned I my reete tyl that the pricke of F/sate vpon the orizont: Than sawe I wel that the body of Venus in her latytude of degrees septemtrionals/ascēdeth in the ende of degree fro the heed of Capricorne. And note that in this maner thou myghtest werche with any latytude septemtrional in al signes: But southly the latytude meridyonal of a planet in Capricorne may not be take/ bycause of the lytel space betwyxe the eclyptike and the bordure of the astrolabye/and lykerly in al other signes it may be take. Also the degre peraunctur of Iubiter or of any other planette was in the firste degree of Pisces in longitude/ and his latytude was   degrees meridyonal. Than toke I the poynte of A/ and sette it in the first degree of Pisces on the eclyptike/ than sette I the poynt downwarde of F/in the same signe/ bycause that ỹ latytude was south   degrees/ that is to say/fro the heed of Pisces/ and thus haue I   degrees betwixe both prickes. Than set I the degree of the longitude vpon the orizont/than toke I my label and layde him fixe vpon the degre of longitude/ than sette I the poynte of A/ on my label euen ouer the eclyptike lyne/in the ende of the   degree of the longitude/and I sette the poynte of F/endelonge on my label the space of   degrees of the latytude outwarde fro the zodiake/ that is to saye/ southwarde fro the ecliptyke towarde the bordure/ and than tourned I my reete tyl the poynte of F/ sate vpon the orizonte/ than sawe I wel that the body of Iuppyter in his latytude of degrees meridional/ ascēdeth with the degree of Pisces in horescopo. And in this maner thou mayst wyrche with any latytude as I sayd first/saue in Capricorne. And thou wylte playe this crafte with the arysyng of the moone/ looke thou recken wel the course of houre by houre/for she dwelleth in a degree of her longitude but a lytel whyle/as thou woste wel: but neuerthelesse/ if thou legen wel her very meuyng by the tables/or after her course houre by houre/thou shalte do wel ynough.

¶ Umbra recta.

If thou wylte wirche with Umbra recta / if thou myght come to the base of the towre/ in this maner shalte thou wirche: Take the altytude of the toure with bothe holes/so that the rule lye euen on a poynte. Ensample/as thus. I se him through the poynte of + / than mete I the space betwyxe me and the tour/and I fynde it 20 foote/than beholde I howe + is to 12/and I fynde it is the thirde parte of 12. Right so the space betwyxe the and the toure is the thirde parte of the altytude of the toure: than thrise 20 foote is the hyghest of the toure/with the addycion of thyn owne body fro thyn eye. If the rule fal on 5/ than is 5 tymes 12 the hyghest of the toure.

¶ Umbra versa.

If thou mayste not come to the base of the toure/and thou syxe him through the nombre of 1/set there a pricke at thy foote/than go nere the toure/ and se him through at the poynte of 2/and set there another pricke/ & than beholde howe 1 hath him to 12/and thou shalte fynde that he hath him 12 sythes/than beholde howe 2 haue him to 12/ and thou shalt fynde it 6 sythes/ and therfore the space betwyxe 2 prickes is 6 tymes thyn altytude. And note that at the first altytude of 1 thou settest a pricke/ and afterwarde whan thou seest him through at 2/there thou settest a pricke/than thou fyndest bytwene 80 foote/than thou shalt fynde that 10 is the 6 parte of 80/than is a fote the altytude

altytude of the toure/But if it fal vpon another poynt/as thus. It falleth on 6 at the seconde takyng it/ whan it falleth on 4 / than shalte thou fynde that 6 is the seconde parte of 12 / and 4 is the thirde parte of 12 by the thirde parte/that is to say/the space betwyxe 2 prickes/ twyse the heyght of the toure/ & if the difference were 3/ than wolde it be thre tymes the height/Et sic de singulis. Another maner werchyng by vmbra recta. If thou mayste not come vp the base of ye tour/ werche in this wyse: Set thy rule vpon 1 tyl thou se the altytude/ and set at thy foote a pricke/and than set thy rule vpon 2/ and so do in the same maner: than loke what is the difference betwyxe 1 and 2 / and thou shalte fynde that it is one. Than mesure that space betwyx the two prickes/and that is the 12 parte of the altytude of the toure/ and so of al other.

¶ Umbra recta.

If thy rule fal vpon the 8 poynt on the right shadowe/than make the fygure of 8 /.than loke howe moche space of fete is betwixe the and the toure/and multiply that by 12/ and whan thou haste multiplyed it by the same nombre/than deuyde it by the nombre of 8/ and kepe the resydue/ and adde therto thy heyght vnto thyn eye/to the resydue/ and that shal be the very heyght of the toure. And thus mayste thou worche on the same syde from one to 12. &c. ¶ Umbra recta.

Another maner of worKyng vpon the same syde. Loke vpon what poynt thy rule falleth whan thou seest the toppe of the tour thorowe the two holes/ and than mete the space from thy fote to the base of the toure/ & right as the nōbre of the poynte hath him selfe to 12/ right so the mesure betwixe the and the toure/ hath him selfe to the heyght of the same toure. Ensample as thus. I set case thy rule fal vpon 8 / than is 8 two thirde partes of 12 / so is the space two thirde partes of the toure.

¶ Umbra versa.

To know the heyght by the poyntes of Umbra versa. If thy rule fal vpon 3 whan thou seest the toppe of the toure/ sette a pricke there thy foote stondeth/and go nere tyl thou mayste se the same toppe at the poynt of 4 /and set ther another pricke: than mete how many foote is betwyxe the two prickes/ & the height vppe to thyne eye / and that shal be the heyght of the toure. And note that 3 is the 4 parte of 12/and 4 is the 3 parte of 12. nowe passeth 4 the nombre of 3 by distaunce of 1 / therfore ye same space with thy heyght to thyn eye/is the heyght of the toure. And if it were so that ther were two or thre distaūces in the nōbres/so shulde the mesure betwyxe the prickes by twyse or thrise the heyght of the toure.

¶ Umbra recta.

To know the hyght if thou mayst not come to the base of the thing/set thy rule vpon what poynt thou wylt/so ye thou maiste se the toppe of the thing thorowe the two holes/ and make a marke there as thy foote stondeth/& go nere or ferther tyl thou mayst se it thorowe another poynt/and make there another marke/ & loke what difference is betwyxe the two poyntes in the scale/and right as that difference hath him to 12/ right so the spaces betwixe ye two markes/hath him to the heyght of the thyng. Ensample. I set the case ye thou seest it thorowe at the poynt of 4 / and after at the poynt of 3/ Nowe passeth the nombre of 4 the nombre of 3 the distaunce of 1/ and right as this differēce of one hath him selfe to 12/right so the mesure betwyxe bothe the markes/ hath hym to the heyght of the same thyng/ puttyng therto the height of thy selfe to thyn eye. And thus maist thou werke from 1 to 12. ¶ Umbra versa.

Ferthermore/if thou wylt knowe in Umbra versa/by the craft of vmbra recta/ I suppose to take thyn altytude at the poynt of 4 & makest a marke/and thā thou goest nere tyl thou haste it at the poynt of 3 and makest there another marke/than muste thou deuyde 144 by 4 /.the nombre that cometh therof shal be 36/ and after deuyde 144 by 3/ and ye nombre that cometh therof is 48 / than loke what difference is betwyxe 36 and 48/ and that shalte thou fynde 12 / and ryght as 12 hath hym to 12/ so the space betwyxe the two prickes/hath hym to the altytude of the thyng.

¶ Here endeth the conclusyons of the Astrolabye.

H.h.h.ii.

The complaynt of the blacke knyght.

In May whan Flora ẏ fresshe lusty quene
The soyle hath clad/in grene/reed/& whyght
And Phebus gan to shede his stremes shene
Amydde the bulle/ with al the beames bright
And Lucifer/to chace away the nyght
Ayen the morowe our orizont hath take
To bydde al louers out of her slepe awake

And hertes heuy for to recomforte
From dreryheed/ of heuy nyghtes sorowe
Nature bade hem ryse/and hem disporte
Ayen the goodly glad grey morowe
And hope also/with seynt Iohan to borowe
Bade in dispyte of Daunger and Dispayre
For to take the holsome lusty ayre

And with a syghe I gan for to abreyde
Out of my slombre/and sodaynly vp sterte
As he (alas) that nygh for sorowe deyde
My sickenesse sate aye so nye my herte
But for to fynde socour of my smerte
Or at the leste some release of my peyne
That me so sore halte in euery veyne

I rose anon/and thought I wolde gone
In to the wodde/to here the byrdes synge
Whan that the mysty vapoure was agone
And clere and fayre was the morownyng
The dewe also lyke syluer in shynyng
Vpon the leaues/as any baume swete
Tyl firy Tytan with his persaunt hete

Had dried vp the lusty lycour newe
Vpon the herbes in the grene mede
And that the floures of many dyuers hewe
Vpon her stalkes gonne for to sprede
And for to splaye out her leues in brede
Agayne the sonne/ golde burned in his spere
That downe to hem caste his beames clere

And by a ryuer forthe I gan costey
Of water clere/ as beryl or crystal
Tyl at the laste I founde a lytel wey
Towarde a parke/enclosed with a wal
In compace rounde/and by a gate smal
Who so that wolde/frely myght gone
In to this parke/walled with grene stone

And in I went to here the byrdes songe
Whiche on the braunches/bothe in playn & vale
So loude sange/that al the woode ronge
Lyke as it shulde shyuer in peces smale
And/as me thought/ that the nyghtyngale
With so great myght/ her voyce gan out wrest
Right as her herte for loue wolde brest

The soyle was playn/smothe/& wonder softe
Al ouersprad with tapettes that Nature
Had made her selfe: couered eke a lofte
With bowes grene/the floures for to cure
That in her beautie they may longe endure
From al assaute of Phebus feruent fere
Whiche in his sphere so hotte shone and clere

The eyre attempre/and the smothe wynde
Of zepherus/amonge the blosomes whyte
So holsom was/and so norisshyng by kynde
That smale buddes/and rounde blosmes lyte
In maner gan of her brethe delyte
To yeue vs hope there frute shal take
Ayenst Autumpne redy for to shake

I sawe the Daphene closed vnder rynde
Grene Laurer/and the holsome Pyne
The Myrre also/that wepeth euer of kynde
The Cedres hye/vpryght as a lyne
The Fylberte eke/that lowe dothe enclyne
Her bowes grene/ to the erthe adoun
Vnto her knyght called Demophoun

There sawe I eke the fresshe hauthorne
In whyte motley/that so swote dothe smel
Asshe/fyrre/& oke/with many a yonge acorne
And many a tree mo than I can tel
And me beforne I sawe a lytel wel
That had his course/as I gan beholde
Vnder an hyl/with quicke streames colde

The

The grauel golde/the water pure as glasse
The bankes rounde/the wel enuyronyng
And softe as veluet the yonge grasse
That therupon lustely came spryngyng
The sute of trees aboute compassyng
Her shadowe caste/closyng the wel rounde
And al the herbes growyng on the grounde

The water was so holsome/and so vertuous
Throwe might of herbes growyng besyde
Not lyke the welle where as Narcisus
Yslayne was/throwe vengeance of Cupyde
Where so couertly he dyd hyde
The grayne of dethe vpon eche brinke
That deth mote folowe/who that euer drinke

Ne lyke the pytte of the Pegace
Vnder Pernaso where poetes slepte
Nor lyke the welle of pure chastyte
Whiche ẏ Diane with her nymphes kepte
Whan she naked in to the water lepte
That slowe Acteon with her houndes fel
Onely for he came so nyghe the wel

But this welle that I here reherce
So holsome was/that it wolde aswage
Bollen hertes/and the venym peerce
Of pensyfheed/with al the cruel rage
And euermore refresshe the vysage
Of hem that were in any werynesse
Of great labour/or fallen in distresse

And I that had throwe daunger & disdayne
So drye a thrust/thought I wolde assay
To taste a draught of this welle or twayne
My bytter langour if it might alaye
And on the banke anon downe I laye
And with myn heed/vnto the welle I raught
And of the water dranke I a good draught

Wherof me thought I was refresshed wele
Of the brennyng that sate so nye my herte
That verily anon I gan to fele
An huge parte released of my smerte
And therwithal anon vp I sterte
And thought I wolde walke and se more
Forthe in the parke/and in the holtes hore

And through a launde as I yede a pace
And gan aboute faste to beholde
I founde anon a delectable place
That was beset with trees yonge and olde
Whose names here for me shal not be tolde
Amydde of whiche stode an herber grene
That benched was/with colours newe & clene

This herber was ful of floures gende
In to the whiche/as I beholde gan
Betwyxe an hulfere and a wodbende
As I was ware/I sawe where lay a man
In blacke/and whyte colour pale and wan
And wonder deedly also of his hewe
Of hurtes grene/and fresshe woundes newe

And ouermore distrayned with sickenesse
Besyde al this he was ful greuously
For vpon him he had an hote accesse
That day by day him shoke ful pytously
So that for constraynyng of his maladye
And hertly wo/thus lyenge al alone
It was a dethe for to here him grone

Wherof astonyed/my fote I gan withdrawe
Greatly wondring what it myght be
That he so lay/and had no felawe
Ne that I coude no wight with him se
Wherof I had routhe/and eke pyte
And gan anon/so softely as I coude
Amonge the busshes priuely me to shroude

If that I might in any wyse aspye
What was the cause of his deedly wo
Or why that he so pitously gan crye
On his fortune/and on vre also
With al my might I layde an eere to
Euery worde to marke what he sayde
Out of his swough amonge as he abrayde

But first/if I shulde make mencion
Of his person/and plainly him discryue
He was in sothe/without exception
To speke of manhode/one the best on lyue
There may no man ayen trouthe stryue
For of his tyme/and of his age also
He proued was/there men shulde haue ado

H.h.h.iii. For

Of the blacke knyght.

For one the best therto of brede and length
So wel ymade by good proporcion
If he had be in his delyuer strength
But thought and sicknesse were occasyon
That he thus lay in lamentacion
Gruffe on the grounde/ in place desolate
Sole by him selfe/awhaped and amate

And for me semeth that it is syttyng
His wordes al to put in remembraunce
To me that herde al his complaynyng
And al the grounde of his woful chaunce
If there withal I may you do plesaunce
I wol to you so as I can anone
Lyke as he sayd/reherce euerychone

But who shal helpe me nowe to complayne
Or who shal nowe my style gye or lede
O Niobe / let nowe thy teeres rayne
In to my penne/and helpe eke in nede
Thou woful Mirre/that felest myn hert blede
Of pytous wo/and myn hande eke quake
Whan that I write/ for this mannes sake

For unto wo accordeth complaynyng
And doleful chere unto heuynesse
To sorowe also/syghyng and wepyng
And pytous mournyng unto drerynesse
And who that shal write of distresse
In party nedeth to knowe felyngly
Cause and roote of al suche malady

But I alas/that am of wytte but dul
And haue no knowyng of suche matere
For to discryue/and write at the ful
The woful complaynte/whiche ye ye shal here
But euen lyke as dothe a skryuenere
That can no more/what that he shal write
But as his mayster besyde dothe endyte

Right so fare I/that of no sentement
Saye right naught in conclusyoun
But as I herde whan I was present
This man complayne/with a pytous soun
For euen lyke without addycioun
Or disencrease/eyther more or lesse
For to reherce anon I wol me dresse

And if that any nowe be in this place
That fele in loue brennyng or feruence
Or hyndred were to his ladyes grace
With false tonges/that with pestylence
Slee trewe men/that neuer dyd offence
In worde nor dede/ne in her entent
If any suche be here nowe present

Let him of routhe lay to audyence
With doleful chere/and sobre countenaunce
To here this man/by ful hye sentence
His mortal wo/and his perturbaunce
Complaynyng/nowe lyeng in a traunce
With lokes upcaste/and rutul chere
Theffecte of whiche was as ye shal here.

The thouzt oppressed wt inward syghes sore
The paynful lyfe/the body languisshyng
The woful goste/the herte rent and tore
The pytous chere pale in complaynyng
The dedly face/ lyke asshes in shynyng
The salte teares that from myn eyen fal
Percel declare/grounde of my paynes al

Whose herte is grounde to blede in heuynesse
The thought resceyte of wo / ⁊ of complaynte
The brest is chest of dole and drerynesse
The body eke so feble and so faynte
With hote and colde myn ayes is so maynte
That nowe I chyuer/for defaute of heate
And hote as glede/ nowe sodainly I sweate

Nowe hote as fyre/nowe colde as asshes deed
Now hote for colde/now colde for hete agayn
Nowe colde as yse/nowe as coles reed
For hete I brenne/⁊ thus betwyxe twayne
I possed am/and al forcaste in payne
So that my hete plainly as I fele
Of greuous colde is cause euery dele

This is the colde of inwarde hye disdayne
Colde of dispyte/and colde of cruel hate
This is ye colde that euer doth his besy payne
Ayenst trouthe to fyght and debate
This is the colde that the fyre abate
Of trewe meanyng/alas the harde whyle
This is the colde that wol me begyle

For

For euer the better that in trouth I mente
With al my myght faythfully to serue
With herte and al to be dilygent
The lesse thanke/ alas I can deserue
Thus for my trouthe daunger doth me sterue
For one that sholde my deth of mercy let
Hath made despite newe his swerde to whet

Agaynst me/ and his arowes to fyle
To take vengeaunce of wylful cruelte
And tonges false through her sleyghtly wyle
Han gonne a werre/ that wyl not stynted be
And false enuy/ wrathe and enmyte
Haue conspired agaynst al right and lawe
Of her malyce that trouthe shal be slawe

And male bouche/ gan first the tale tel
To sclaundre trouthe of indignacion
And False reporte so loude range the bel
That mysbyleue and false suspeccyon
Haue trouthe brought to his dampnacyon
So that alas/ wrongfully he dyeth
And falsnesse nowe his place occupyeth

And entred is in to trouthes londe
And hath therof the ful possessyon
O rightful god that first the trouthe fonde
Howe may thou suffre suche oppressyon
That falshode shulde haue iurisdiction
In trouthes right to slee him gyltles
In his fraunchyse he may not lyue in pees

Falsly accused/ and of his foone foriuged
Without answere/ while he was absent
He dampned was/ and may not be excused
For cruelte sate in iugement
Of hastynesse without auysement
And badde Disdayne do execute anone
His iugement in presence of his fone

Attourney maye none admytted been
To excuse trouth/ ne a worde to speke
To fayth or othe the iuge lyst not seen
There is no gayn/ but he wyl be wreke
O lorde of trouthe to the I cal and clepe
Howe may thou se thus in thy presence
Without mercy murdred innocence

Nowe god that arte of trouthe souerayne
And seest howe I lye for trouthe bounde
So sore knytte in loues fyrye chayne
Euē at yͤ deth through gyrte wͭ many a woūde
That lykely are neuer for to sounde
And for my trouthe am dampned to the dethe
And not abyde/ but drawe along the brethe

Consyder and se in thyne eternal right
Howe that myn herte professed whylom was
For to be trewe with al my ful myght
Onely to one/ the whiche nowe alas
Of volunte without any trespas
Myne accusours hath taken vnto grace
And cherissheth hem/ my dethe for to purchace

What meaneth this? what is this wōder vre?
Of puruey aunce if I shal it cal
Of god of loue/ that false hem so assure
And trewe alas/ downe of the whele ben fal
And yet in soth/ this is the worst of al
That falshed wrōgfully of troth hath yͤ name
And troth ayēward of falshed bereth yͤ blame

This blynde chaunce/ this stormy auenture
In loue hath most his experience
For who that doth with trouthe most his cure
Shal for his mede fynde most offence
That serueth loue with al his diligence
For who can fayne vnder lowlyhede
Ne fayleth not to fynde grace and spede

For I loued one/ ful longe syth agone
With al myne herte/ body and ful myght
And to be deed my herte can not gone
From his heste but holde that he hath hyght
Though I be banysshed out of her syght
And by her mouth dampned that I shal dey
Vnto my behest/ yet I wyl euer obey

For euer syth that the worlde began
Who so lyst loke/ and in story rede
He shal aye fynde that the trewe man
Was put abacke where as the falshede
Yfurthered was/ for loue taketh non hede
To slee the trewe/ and hath of hem no charge
Where as the false gothe frely at her large

I take

I take recorde of Palamydes
The trewe man/ the noble worthy knyght
That euer loued/ and of his payne no relees
Notwithstandyng his manhode & his myght
Loue vnto hym dyd ful great vnright
For aye the bet he dyd in cheualrye
The more he was hyndred by enuye

And aye the better he dyd in euery place
Through his knyghthode and busy payne
The ferther was he from his ladyes grace
For to her mercy myght he neuer attayne
And to his dethe he coude it not refrayne
For no daungere/ but aye obey and serue
As he best coude/ playnly tyl he sterue

What was the fyne also of Hercules
For al his conquest and his worthynesse
That was of strength alone peerles
For lyke as bokes of hym lyst expresse
He set pylers through his hye prowesse
Away at Gaddes for to sygnifye
That no man myght him passe in chiualrye

The whiche pyllers ferre beyonde Inde
Be set of golde/ for a remembraunce
And for al that was he set behynde
With hem that loue lyst febly auaunce
For hym set last vpon a daunce
Agaynst whom helpe may no stryfe
For al his trouthe he lost his lyfe

Phebus also for al his persaunt lyght
Whan that he wente here in erthe lowe
Vnto the herte with Venus syght
Ywounded was throughe Cupides bowe
And yet his lady lyst hym not to knowe
Thoughe for her loue his herte dyd blede
She lete him go/ and toke of hym no hede

What shal I saye of yonge Piramus ?
Of trewe Tristram/ for al his hye renowne
Of Achylles/ or of Antonius
Of Arcite/ or of hym Palamowne
What was the ende of her passyowne
But after sorowe deth/ and than her graue
Lo here the guerdon that these louers haue

But false Iason with his doublenesse
That was vntrewe at Colkos to Medee
And Theseus/ rote of vnkyndnesse
And with these two eke the false Enee
Lo thus the false aye in one degre
Had in loue her lust and al her wyl
And saue falshode/ there was none other skyl

Of Thebes eke the false Arcyte
And Demephoon eke for his slouthe
They had her lust & al that myght delyte
For al her falshode and great vntrouthe
Thus euer loue alas/ and that is routhe
His false lieges fortheretl what he may
And sleeth the trewe vngoodly day by day

For trewe Adon was slayne with the bore
Amydde the forest in the grene shade
For Venus loue he felte al the sore
But Vulcanus with her no mercy made
The foule chorle had many nyghtes glade
Where Mars her knyght and her man
To fynde mercy comforte none he can

Also the yonge fresshe Ypomedes
So lusty fre as of his courage
That for to serue with al his herte he ches
Athalans so fayre of her vysage
But loue alas quitte hym so his wage
With cruel daungere playnly at the last
That with the dethe guerdonlesse he past

Lo here the fyne of loues seruyse
Lo howe that loue can his seruauntes quyte
Lo howe he can his faythful men dispyse
To sle the trewe men/ and false to respite
Lo howe he dothe the swerde of sorowe byte
In hertes/ suche as moost his lust obey
To saue the false and do the trewe dey

For faythe nor othe/ worde/ ne assuraunce
Trewe meanynge/ awayte/ or busynesse
Styl porte/ ne faythful attendaunce
Manhode ne myght in armes worthynesse
Pursute of worshyp nor hye prowesse
In straunge lande rydynge ne trauayle
Ful lytel or nought in loue doth auayle

Peryl

Peryl of dethe/ nor in see ne lande
Hunger ne thurste/ sorowe ne sykenesse
Ne great empryses for to take on hande
Shedynge of blood/ ne manful hardynesse
Ne ofte woundynge at sawtes by dystresse
Nor in partynge of lyfe/ nor dethe also
Al is for nought/ loue taketh no hede therto

But lesynges with her flaterye
Through her falshede/ & with her doublenesse
With tales newe/ and many fayned lye
By false semblaunt and coūtrefet humblesse
Under colour depaynte with stedfastnesse
With fraude couered vnder a pytous face
Accepte be nowe rathest vnto grace

And can hym selfe nowe best magnifye
With fayned porte and presumpcion
They haunte her cause with false surquidrie
Under meanynge of double entencion
To thinke one in her opynion
And saye another/ to set hym selfe alofte
And hynder trouth/ as it is sene ful ofte

The whiche thynge/ I bye nowe al to dere
Thanked be Uenus/ and the god Cupide
As it is sene by myne oppressed chere
And by his arowes that sticken in my syde
That saue dethe/ I nothynge abyde
Fro day to day/ alas the harde whyle
Whan euer his darte that hym lyst to fyle

My woful herte for to ryue a two
For faute of mercy/ and lacke of pyte
Of her that causeth al my payne and wo
And lyste not ones of grace for to se
Unto my trouthe through her cruelte
And most of al I me complayne
That she hath ioy to laughe at my payne

And wylfully hath my dethe sworne
Al gyltlesse/ and wote no cause why
Saue for the trouthe that I had aforne
To her alone to serue faythfully
O god of loue/ vnto the I cry
And to thy blynde doublē deite
Of this great wronge I complayne me

And vnto thy stormy wylful variaunce
Yment with chaunge and great vnstablenesse
Now vp now downe/ so rennyng is thy chaūce
That the to trust may be no sykernesse
I wyte it nothynge but thy doublenesse
And who that is an archer and is blynde
Marketh nothynge but shoteth by wende.

And for that he hath no discrecion
Without aduyse he let his arowe go
For lacke of syght/ and also of reason
In his shotynge it happeth ofte so
To hurte his frende rather than his fo
So doth this god with his sharpe flone
The trewe sleeth/ and letteth the false gone

And of his woundyng/ this the worst of al
Whan he hurteth doth to so cruel wreche
And maketh the sicke for to crye and cal
Unto his foe for to be his leche
And harde it is for a man to seche
Upon the poynte of dethe in ieoperdye
Unto his foe to fynde remedye

Thus fareth it nowe euen by me
That to my foe that gaue myne hert a woūde
Mote aske grace/ mercy/ and pyte
And namely there where none may be founde
For nowe my sore my leche wyl confounde
And god of kynde so hath set myne vre
My lyues foe to haue my wounde in cure

Alas the whyle nowe that I was borne
Or that I euer sawe the bright sonne
For nowe I se that ful longe aforne
Or I was borne/ my desteny was sponne
By Parcas systerne to slee me if they conne
For they my dethe shopen or my sherte
Onely for trouthe I may it not asterte

The myghty goddesse also of nature
That vnder god hath the gouernaunce
Of worldly thinges cōmytted to her cure
Disposed haue through her wyse puruey aūce
To gyue my lady so moche suffysaunce
Of al vertues/ and therwithal puruyde
To murdre trouthe/ hath take daūger to gyde

For

For bounte/beaute/shappe/and semelyhede
Prudence/ wyt/ passyngly sayrnesse
Benygne porte/glad chere with lowlyhede
Of womanhede right plenteous largnesse
Nature dyd in her fully impresse
Whan she her wrought/ & alther last disdayne
To hynder trouth/ she made her chāberlayne

Whan mystrust also/and false suspectyon
With mysvylene she made for to be
Chefe of counsayle to this conclusyon
For to exyle trouthe/ and eke pyte
Out of her court to make mercy free
So that dispite nowe holdeth forthe her reyne
Through hasty bilene of tales that men feyne.

And thus I am for my trouthe/ alas
Murdred & slayne/ with wordes sharpe & kene
Gyltlesse god wote of al trespas
And lye and blede vpon this colde grene
Nowe mercy swete/mercy my lyues quene
And to your grace of mercy yet I preye
In your seruyce that your man may deye

But if so be that I shal dye algate
And that I shal none other mercy haue
Yet of my dethe let this ben the date
That by your wyl I was brouzt to my graue
Or hastely/ yf that you lyst me saue
My sharpe woundes that ake so and blede
Of mercy charme/and also of womanhede

For other charme playnly is there none
But onely mercy/ to helpe in this case
For though my woundes blede euer in one
My lyfe/ my dethe/standeth in your grace
And thoughe my gylte be nothynge/alas
I aske mercy in al my best entente
Redy to dye/ if that ye assente.

For there agaynst shal I neuer stryue
In worde ne werke/playnly I ne may
For leuer I haue than to be alyue
To dye sothly/ and it be to her paye
Ye thoughe it be this same day
Or whan that euer her lyst to deuise
Suffiseth me to dye in your seruise

And god ỷ knowest ỷ thought of euery wight
Right as it is/in euery thinge thou mayst se
Yet er I dye/ with al my ful might
Lowly I pray to graunt vnto me
That ye goodly/fayre/fresshe and fre
Whiche onely sle me for defaute of rothe
Or that I dye/ ye may knowe my trothe

For that in soth suffiseth me
And she it knowe in euery circumstaunce
And after I am wel payde that she
If that her list of dethe to do Veugeaunce
Vnto me that am vnder her ligeaunce
It sytte me not her dome to disobeye
But at her lust wylfully to deye

Without grutchinge or rebellyon
In wyl or worde/ holy I assent
Or any maner contradiction
Fully to be at her commaundement
And if I dye/ in my testament
My herte I sende/ and my spirite also
What so euer she lyste with hem to do

And alder last to her womanhede
And to her mercy/ me I recommaunde
That lye nowe here betwixe hope and drede
Abidynge playnly what she list commaunde
For vtterly this nys no demaunde
Welcome to me whise me lasteth brethe
Right at her chopse where it be lyfe or delthe

In this mater more what might I sayne
Sithe in her hande/ and in her wyl is al
Bothe life and deth/ my ioy and al my payne
And finally my heste holde I shal
Til my spirite by desteny fatal
Whan that her list fro my body wende
Haue here my trouth/ & thus I make an ende

And with that worde he gan sygh as sore
Like as his herte ryue wolde atwayne
And helde his peace/ & spake no worde more
But for to se his wo and mortal payne
The teres gonne fro myne eyen rayne
Ful pitously for very inwarde rothe
That I him sawe/ so long wisshing for troth
And

And al this whyle my selfe I kepte close
Amonge the bowes/and my selfe gonne hyde
Tyl at the last the woful man arose
And to a lodge wente there besyde
Where al the May/his custome was abyde
Sole to complayne of his paynes kene
From yere to yere under the bowes grene

And for bycause that it drewe to the nyght
And that the sonne his arke diurnal
Ypassed was/so that his persaunt sight
His bright bemes and his stremes al
Were in the waues of the water fal
Under the bordure of our occyan
His chare of golde/his course so swyftly ran

And whyle the twylyght & the rawes rede
Of Phebus lyght were deaurat alyte
A penne I toke/and gan me fast spede
The woful playnte of this man to wryte
Worde by worde as he dyd endyte
Like as I herde and coude hym tho reporte
I haue here set/your hertes to disporte

If ought be mysse/laye the wyte on me
For I am worthy for to beare the blame
If any thynge mysse reported be
To make this dytee for to seme lame
Through myn vnconnyng/but for to sayn the (same
Lyke as this mā his complaynt dyd expresse
I aske mercy and forgyuenesse

And as I wrote/me thought I sawe a ferre
Ferre in the West lustely appere
Esperus the goodly bright sterre
So glad/so fayre/so persaunt eke of chere
I meane Venus with her bemes clere
That heuy hertes onely to releue
Is wonte of custome for to shewe at eue

And I as fast fel adowne on my kne
And euen thus to her gan I to prey
O lady Venus so fayre vpon to se
Let not this man for his trouthe deye
For that ioy thou haddest whan thou leye
Wt Mars thy knyght/whan Vulcanus fonde
And with a chayne vnuysyble you bonde

Togider bothe twaye in the same whyle
That al the courte aboue celestial
At your shame gan laughe and smyle
Ah/fayre lady wylly fonde at al
Comforte to careful/o goddes inmortal
Be helpynge nowe/and do thy dilygence
To let the stremes of thyne influence

Descende downe/in fortherynge of the trouthe
Namely of hem that lye in sorowe bounde
Shew now thy myzt & on her wo haue routhe
Er false daunger sle hem and confounde
And specially let thy might be founde
For to socouer what so that thou may
The trewe man that in the herber lay

And al trewe forther for his sake
O glad sterre/o lady Venus myne
And cause his lady hym to grace take
Her herte of stele to mercy so enclyne
Er that thy bemes go vp to declyne
And er that thou nowe go fro vs adowne
For that loue thou haddest to Adowne

And whan she was gone to her rest
I rose anone/and home to bed wente
For wery me thought it for the best
Prayenge thus in al my best entente
That al trewe/that be with daunger shente
With mercy may in release of her payne
Recured be/er Maye come efte agayne

And for that I ne may no lenger wake
Farewel ye louers al that be trewe
Prayeng to god/and thus my leue I take
That er the sonne to morowe be rissen newe
And er he haue ayen rosen hewe
That eche of you may haue suche a grace
His owne lady in armes to embrace

I meane thus/in al honeste
Without more ye may togyder speke
What so ye lyst at good lyberte
That eche may to other her herte breke
On ialousyes onely to be wreke
That hath so longe of his malyce and enuye
Werred trouthe with his tyranny.

¶ Lenuoye. Pryncesse

Prynceste pleaseth it to your benygnyte
This lytel dyte to haue in mynde
Of womanhode also for to se
Your man may your mercy fynde
And pyte eke/ that long hath be behynde
Let hym agayne be prouoked to grace
For by my trouthe it is agaynst kynde
False daungere to occupye his place

Go lytel quayre vnto my lyues quene
And my very hertes soueraygne
And be right glad/ for she shal the sene
Suche is thy grace/ but I alas in payne
Am lefte behynde/ ⁊ not to whom to playne
For mercy/ ruthe/ grace/ and eke pyte
Exyled be/ that I may not attayne
Recure to fynde of myne aduersyte.

¶ Explicit.

A preyse of women.

AL tho ẏ lyste of women euyl to speke
And sayn of hem worse than they de-
I pray to god that her neckes to breke (serue
Or on some euyl deth mote tho iaglers sterue
For euery man were holden hem to serue
And do hem worshyp/ honour/ and seruyce
In euery maner that they best coude deuyse

For we ought first to thinke on what manere
They brīg vs forth/ ⁊ what payn they endure
First in our byrth/ and syth fro yere to yere
Howe besely they done theyr besy cure
To kepe vs fro euery mysauenture
In our youth whan we haue no myght
Our selfe to kepe/ neither by day nor nyght

Alas/ howe may we say on hem but wele
Of whom we were fostred and ybore
And ben al our socoure/ ⁊ euer trewe as stele
And for our sake ful ofte they suffre sore
Without women were al our ioye lore
Wherfore we ought al women to obey
In al goodnesse/ I can no more say

This is wel knowen/ and hath ben or this
That women ben cause of al lyghtnesse
Of knyghthode/ norture/ eschewyng al mysse
Encrease of worshyp/ and of al worthynesse
Therto curteys ⁊ meke/ ⁊ grounde of al good
Glad ⁊ mery/ ⁊ trewe in euery wyse (nesse
That any gentyl herte can thynke or deuyse

And though any wold trust to your vntruthe
And to your fayre wordes wold aught assent
In good fayth me thynketh it were gret ruthe
That other women shold for her gylt be shent
That neuer knew ne wyst nouȝt of her entent
Ne lyste not to here the fayre wordes ye write
Whiche ye you payne fro day to day tendyte

But who may be ware of your tales vntrewe
That ye so besyly paynt and endite
For ye wyl swere that ye neuer knewe
Ne sawe the woman/ neyther moche ne lyte
Saue onely her to whom ye had delite
As for to serue of al that euer ye sey
And for her loue must ye nedes dey

Thā wyl ye swere that ye knewe neuer before
What loue was ne his dredful obseruaunce
But nowe ye fele that he can wounde sore
Wherfore ye put you in to her gouernaunce
Whō loue hath ordeyned you to serue ⁊ do plesaunce
Wt al your myȝt your lytel lyues space (saunce
Whiche endeth sone/ but if she do you grace

And than to bedde wyl ye soone drawe
And sone sicke ye wyl you than fayne
And swere fast your lady hath you slawe
And brouȝt you sodeynly in so high a payn
That fro your deth may no mā you restrayn
With a daungerous loke of her eyen two
That to your dethe must ye nedes go

Thus wyl ye morne/ thus wyl ye sighe sore
As though your herte anon in two wold brest
And swere fast that ye may lyue no more
Myne owne lady/ that might if ye lest
Bringe myne herte somdele in to rest
As if you lyst mercy on me to haue
Thus your vntrouth wyl euer mercy craue

Thus

Thus wol ye playne/tho ye nothyng smerte
These innocent creatures for to begyle
And swere to hem/so wounded is your herte
For her loue/that ye may lyue no whyle
Scarsly so longe as one might go a myle
So hyeth dethe/to bringe you to an ende
But if your souerayn lady lyst you to amẽde

And if for routhe she cõforte you in any wyse
For pyte of your false othes sere
So that innocẽt weneth ỹ it be as you deuyse
And weneth your herte be as she may here
Thus for to comfort/⁊ somwhat do you chere
Than wol these ianglers deme of her ful yl
And sayne that ye haue her fully at your wyl

Lo howe redy her tonges ben/and prest
To speke harme of women causelesse
Alas/why might ye not as wel say the best
As for to deme hem thus gyltlesse
In your herte ywis there is no gentylnesse
That of yo[r] own gylt/lyst thus women fame
Now by my trouth/me thynke ye be to blame

For of women cometh this worldly wele
Wherfore we ought to worship hem euermore
And though it mishap one/we ouzt for to hele
For it is al through our false lore
That day and night/we payne vs euermore
With many an othe/these women to begyle
With false tales/and many a wicked wyle

And if falshede shulde be reckened and tolde
In women/iwys ful trouthe were
Not as in men/by a thousande folde
Fro al vyces iwys they stande clere
In any thing that euer I coude of here
But if entysing of these men it make
That hem to flatteren connen neuer slake

I wolde fayne wete wher euer ye coude here
Without mens tysing/what womẽ dyd amys
For ther ye may get hem/ye lye fro yere to yere
And many a gabbyng ye make to hem iwys
For I coude neuer here/ne knowen er this
Where euer ye coude fynde in any place
That euer women besought you of grace

There ye you payne/with al your ful might
With al your herte/and al your besynesse
To pleasen hem/bothe by day and night
Prayeng hem of her grace and gentylnesse
To haue pyte vpon your great distresse
And ỹ they wolde on your payne haue routhe
And slee you not/sens ye meane but trouthe

Thus may ye se that they ben fautelesse
And innocent to al your werkes slye
And al your craftes that touche falsnesse
They knowe hem not/ne maye hem not espye
So sweare ye/that ye must nedes dye
But if they wolde of her womanheed
Vpon you rewe/er that ye be deed

And than your lady/and your hertes quene
Ye cal hem/and therwith ye sygh sore
And say/my lady I trowe that it be sene
In what pyte that I haue lyued ful yore
But nowe I hope that ye wol no more
In these paynes suffre me for to dwel
For of al goodnesse/iwys ye be the wel

Lo whiche a paynted processe can ye make
These harmlesse creatures for to begyle
And whan they slepe/ye payne you to wake
And to bethinke you on many a wicked wyle
But ye shal se the day ỹ ye shal curse ỹ whyle
That ye so besily dyd your entent
Hem to begyle/that falshede neuer ment

For this ye knowe wel/though I wolde lye
In women is al trouthe and stedfastnesse
For in good faythe/I neuer of hem sye
But moche worshyp/bounte/and gentylnesse
Right comyng/fayre/and ful of mekenesse
Good and glad/and lowly I you ensure
Is this goodly angelyke creature

And if it happe a man be in disease
She dothe her busynesse/and her ful payne
With al her might/him to comforte ⁊ please
If fro his disease she might him restrayne
In worde ne dede iwys she wol not fayne
But with al her might/she dothe her besynesse
To bringe him out of his heuynesse

I.iii. Lo

Lo what gentylnesse these women haue
If we coude knowe it for our rudenesse
Howe besy they be vs to kepe and saue
Bothe in heale/and also in sicknesse
And alway right sory for our distresse
In euery maner/ thus shewe they routhe
That in hem is al goodnesse and trouthe

And syth we fynde in hem gētylnesse & trouth
Worshyp/bounte/and kyndenesse euermore
Let neuer this gentylnesse/through your slouth
In her kynde trouthe be aught forlore
That in woman is/and hath ben ful pore
For in reuerence of the heuens quene
We ought to worshyp al women that bene

For of al creatures that euer were get & borne
This wote ye wel/a woman was the best
By her was recouered ẏ blysse ẏ we had lorn
And through ẏ woman shal we come to rest
And ben ysaued/if that our selfe lest
Wherfore me thynketh/if that we had grace
We oughten honour women in euery place

Therfore I rede/that to our lyues ende
Fro this tyme forth/whyle that we haue space
That we haue trespaced/pursue to amende
Prayeng our lady/wel of al grace
To bringe vs vnto that blyssful place
There as she & al good women shal be in fere
In heuen aboue/amonge the angels clere.

¶Explicit.

The house of Fame.

God tourne vs euery dreme to good
For it is wonder thyng by the rood
To my wytte/what causeth sweuenes
On the morowe or on euenes
And why the effecte foloweth of some
And of some it shal neuer come
Why that it is an auysion
And why this a reuelacion
Why this a dreme/why that a sweuen
And nat to euery man lyche euen
Why this a fantome/why that oracles
I not: but who so of these myracles
The causes knowe bette than I
Defyne he/ for I certainly
Ne can hem nat/ne neuer thynke
To busy my wytte for to swynke
To knowe of her sygnyfycations
The gendres/ne dystynctions
Of the tymes of hem/ne the causes
Or why this is more than that is
Or yeue folkes complexions
Make hem dreme of reflexions
Or els thus/as other sayne
For the great feblenesse of her brayne
By abstynence/or by sicknesse
Prison/ stryfe/or great distresse
Or els by disordynaunce
Or natural accustomaunce
That some men be to curyous
In studye/or melancolyous
Or thus: so inly ful of drede
That no man may him bote rede
Or els that deuocion
Of some/ and contemplacion
Causen suche dremes ofte
Or that the cruel lyfe vnsofte
Of hem that loues leden
Ofte hopen moche or dreden
That purely her impressyons
Causen hem to haue visyons
Or if spyrites han the myght
To make folke to dreme on nyght
Or if the soule of proper kynde
Be so perfyte as men fynde
That it wote what is to come
And that he warneth al and some
Of euerych of her auentures
By auisyons/or by fygures
But that our flesshe hath no myght
To vnderstande it a ryght
For it is warned to derkely
But why the cause is/ not wote I
Wel worthe of this thyng clerkes
That treaten of that/ and of other werkes
For I of none opynion
Nyl as nowe make mention
But onely that the holy Rood

Tourne

Tourne vs euery dreme to good
For neuer sythe I was borne
Ne no man els me beforne
Mette I trowe stedfastly
So wonderful a dreme as I.
The tenth day nowe of Decembre
The whiche/as I can remembre
I wol you tellen euery dele
But at my begynnyng trusteth wele
I wol make inuocacion
With a deuoute special deuocion
Unto the god of slepe anone
That dwelleth in a caue of stone
Upon a streme that cometh fro Lete
That is a fludde of hel vnswete
Besyde a folke/ that men clepe Cymery
There slepeth aye this god vnmery
With his slepy thousande sonnis
That alway to slepe her won is
And to this god that I of rede
Praye I/that he wol me spede
My sweuen for to tel a ryght
If euery dreme stande in his myght
And he that mouer is of al
That is and was/and euer shal
So gyue hem ioye that it here
Of al that they dreme to yere
And for to stande al in grace
Of her loues/or in what place
That hem were leuest for to stonde
And shelde hem from pouerte and shonde
And from euery vnhappe and disease
And sende hem that may hem please
That taketh wel and scorneth nought
Ne it misdeme in her thought
Through malycious entencion
And who so through presumpcion
Or hate or scorne/or through enuy
Dispyte or iape/or felony
Mysdeme it/pray I Jesus good
Dreme he barefote or dreme he shood
That euery harme that any man
Hath had sythe the worlde began
Befal hym therof or he sterue
And graunt that he may it deserue
Lo/ with right suche a conclusyon
As had of his auisyon
Cresus/that was kyng of Lyde
That hygh vpon a gybet dyde
This prayer shal he haue of me
I am no bette in charyte.

NOwe herken/as I haue you sayde
What that I mette or I abrayde
Of Decembre the tenthe day
Whan it was nyght/to slepe I lay
Right as I was wonte to doone
And fyl a slepe wonder soone
As he that was wery forgo
On pylgrimage myles two
To the corps of saynt Leonarde
To maken lythe/that erst was harde
But as I slepte me mette I was
Within a temple ymade of glas
In whiche there were mo ymages
Of golde/standyng in sondrie stages
In mo ryche tabernacles
And with perre mo pynnacles
And mo curyous portratures
And queynt maner of fygures
Of golde worke/than I sawe euer
But certainly I nyst neuer
Where that it was/but wel wyst I
It was of Venus redely
This temple/for in purtreture
I sawe anon right her fygure
Naked fletyng in a see
And also on her heed parde
Her rose garlande whyte and rede
And her combe to kembe her hede
Her doues/and dan Cupido
Her blynde sonne/and Vulcano
That in his face was ful browne
But as I romed vp and downe
I founde that on the wal there was
Thus written on a table of bras
I wol nowe synge if that I can
The armes/and also the man
That first came through his destyne
Fugityfe fro Troye the countre
In to Itayle/with ful moche pyne
Unto the strondes of Lauyne
And tho began the storie anone
As I shal tellen you echone
First sawe I the distruction
Of Troye/through the greke Synon

Fff.ii. With

With his false untrewe forswerynges
And with his chere and his lesynges
Made a horse/brought in to Troy
By whiche Troyans loste al her ioy
And after this was graued/alas
Howe Ilyons castel assayled was
And won/and kyng Priamus slayne
And Polytes his sonne certayne
Dispytously of dan Pyrrus
And next that sawe I howe Venus
Whan that she sawe the castel brende
Downe from heuen she gan discende
And bade her sonne Eneas to flye
And howe he fledde/and howe that he
Escaped was from al the prees
And toke his father/olde Anchyses
And bare hym on his backe away
Cryeng alas and welaway
The whiche Anchises in his hande
Bare tho the goddes of the lande
Thylke that unbrenned were
Than sawe I next al in fere
Howe Crusa/dan Eneas wyfe
Whom that he loued al his lyfe
And her yonge sonne Iulo
And eke Askanyus also
Fledden eke/with drery chere
That it was pyte for to here
And in a forest as they went
At a turnyng of a went
Howe Crusa was loste/alas
That rede nat I/howe that it was
Howe he her sought/and howe her goste
Bade hym flye the grekes hoste
And sayd he muste in to Itayle
As was his destyne/sauns fayle
That it was pyte for to here
Whan her spyrite gan appere
The wordes that she to hym sayde
And for to kepe her sonne him prayde
There sawe I grauen eke howe he
His father eke/and his meyne
With his shyppes gan to sayle
To warde the countre of Itayle
As streyght as they myghten go
There sawe I eke the cruel Iuno
That arte dan Iuppyters wyfe
That haste hated al thy lyfe
Al the Troyan bloode
Ren and crye as thou were woode
On Eolus/the god of wyndes
To blowen out of al kyndes
So loude/that he shulde drenche
Lorde/lady/grome/and wenche
Of al the Troyans nacion
Without any of her sauacion
There sawe I suche tempest aryse
That euery herte myght agryse
To se it paynted on the wal
There sawe I eke grauen with al
Venus/howe ye my lady dere
Wepyng with ful woful chere
Prayeng Iuppyter on hye
To saue and kepe that nauye
Of that troyian Eneas
Sythe that he her sonne was
There sawe I Iouis Venus kysse
And graunted was of the tempest lysse
There sawe I howe the tempest stente
And howe with al pyne he wente
And priuely toke a ryuage
In to the countre of Cartage
And on the morowe howe that he
And a knyght that hyght Achate
Metten with Venus that day
Goyng in a queynte aray
As she had be an hunteresse
With wynde blowyng upon her tresse
And howe Eneas began to playne
Whan he knewe her of his payne
And howe his shyppes dreynt were
Or els lost/he nyst where
Howe she gan him comforte tho
And bade him to Cartage go
And there he shulde his folke fynde
That in the see were lefte behynde
And shortely of this thyng to pace
She made Eneas so in grace
Of Dydo/quene of that countre
That shortly for to tellen she
Became his loue/and let hym do
Al that weddyng longeth to
What shulde I speke it more quaynte
Or payne me my wordes to paynte
To speke of loue/it wol nat be
I can nat of that faculte

And

And eke to tellen of the manere
Howe they first acquaynted were
It were a longe processe to tel
And ouer longe for you to dwel
There sawe I graue howe Eneas
Tolde to Dydo euery caas
That him was tydde vpon the see
And efte grauen was howe that she
Made of him shortly at a worde
Her lyfe/her loue/her lust/her lorde
And dyd to him al reuerence
And layde on him al the dispence
That any woman myght do
Wenyng it had al be so
As he her swore/and hereby demed
That he was good/for he suche semed
Alas what harme dothe apparence
Whan it is false in existence
For he to her a traytour was
Wherfore she slowe her selfe alas
Lo/howe a woman dothe amys
To loue him that vnknowen is
For by Christ/lo thus it fareth
It is nat al golde that glareth
For also brouke I wel myn heed
There may be vnder goodlyheed
Couered many a shrewde vyce
Therfore be no wight so nyce
To take a loue onely for chere
Or speche or for frendly manere
For this shal euery woman fynde
That some man of his pure kynde
Wol shewen outwarde the fayrest
Tyl he haue caught that what him lest
And than wol he causes fynde
And swere howe she is vnkynde
Or false or priuy/or double was
Al this say I by Eneas
And Dydo/and her nyce lest
That loued al to soone a gest
Wherfore I wol say o prouerbe
That he that fully knoweth the herbe
May safely lay it to his eye
Withouten drede this is no lye
But let vs speke of Eneas
Howe he betrayed her/alas
And lefte her ful vnkyndely
So whan she sawe al vtterly
That he wolde her of trouthe fayle
And wenden from her in to Itayle
She gan to wringe her handes two
Alas (quod she) that me is wo
Alas/is euery man thus trewe
That euery yere wol haue a newe
If it so longe tyme endure
Or els thre parauenture
And thus of one he wol haue fame
In magnifyeng of his owne name
Another for frendshyp sayth he
And yet there shal the thirde be
That is taken for delyte
Lo/or els for synguler profyte
In suche wordes gan complayne
Dydo of her great payne
As me mette dremyng redyly
None other authour allege wol I
Alas (quod she) my swete herte
Haue pyte on my sorowes smerte
And slee me nat/go nat away
O woful Dydo/welaway
(Quod she) vnto her selfe tho
O Eneas what wol ye do
O that your loue ne your bonde
That ye swore with your right honde
Ne my cruel dethe (quod she)
May holde you styl here with me
O/haue ye of my dethe no pyte
Iwys myn owne dere herte ye
Knowe ful wel that neuer yet
As farre as euer I had wyt
Agylte you/in thought ne in dede
O/haue ye men suche goodlyhede
In speche/and neuer a dele of trouthe
Alas that euer had routhe
Any woman on a false man
Nowe I se wel/and tel can
We wretched women can no arte
For certayne/for the more parte
Thus we ben serued euerychone
Howe sore that ye men can grone
Anon as we haue you receyued
Certainly we ben disceyued
For though your loue lest a ceason
Wayte vpon the conclusyon
And eke howe ye determyne
And for the more parte defyne

O welaway that I was borne
For through you my name is lorne
And myn actes redde and songe
Ouer al this lande in euery tonge
  O wicked fame/ for there nys
Nothyng so swyfte lo as she is
O sothe is/euery thyng is wyst
Though it be couerde with the myst
Eke though I myght duren euer
That I haue done recouer I neuer
That it ne shal be sayd/alas
I shamed was through Eneas
And that I shal thus iuged be
  Lo right as she hath done/nowe she
Wol done eftesones hardely
Thus say the people priuely
But that is done nys nat to done
But al her complaynte ne her mone
Certayne auayled her nat a stre
And whan she wyste sothly/he
Was forthe in to his shyppe agone
She in to chambre went anone
And called on her suster Anne
And gan her to complayne thanne
And sayd/that she cause was
That she first loued hym/alas
And first counsayled her therto
But what/whan this was sayd and do
She roste her seluen to the herte
And deyde through the woundes smerte
But al the maner howe she deyde
And al the wordes howe she seyde
Who so to knowe it hath purpose
Rede Virgyle in Eneydos
Or the pystels of Ouyde
What that she wrote/or that she dyde
And nere it to longe to endyte
By god I wolde it here write
But welaway/ the harme and routhe
That hath betydde for suche vntrouthe
As men may ofte in bokes rede
And alday sene it yet in dede
That for to thynken it tene is
  Lo Demophon/duke of Athenys
Howe he forswore him falsely
And traped Phyllis wickedly
That kynges doughter was of Thrace
And falsely gan his terme pace
And whan she wyste that he was false
She honge her selfe right by the halse
For he had done her suche vntrouthe
Lo/was nat this a wo and routhe
  Eke loke howe false and recheles
Was to Briseyda Achilles
And Parys to Oenone
And Iason to Hipsyphile
And efte Iason to Medea
And Hercules to Dyanira
For he lefte her for Iolee
That made hym take his dethe parde
  Howe false was eke Theseus
That as the storie telleth vs
Howe he betrayed Adriane
The dyuel be his soules bane
For had he laughed or ploured
He muste haue ben al deuoured
If Adriane ne had be
And for she had of hym pyte
She made hym fro the dethe escape
And he made her a ful false iape
  For after this within a whyle
He lefte her slepynge in an yle
Deserte alone right in the see
And stale away and let her be
And toke her suster Phedra tho
With hym/and gan to shyp go
And yet he had sworne to here
On al that euer he coude swere
That so she saued hym his lyfe
He wolde taken her to his wyfe
For she desyred nothyng elles
In certayne/as the boke vs telles
  But for to excuse this Eneas
Fullyche of al his great trespas
The boke sayth\e sauns fayle
The goddes bade hym go to Itayle
And leauen Affriques regyoun
And fayre Dydo and her towne
  Tho sawe I graue howe to Itayle
Dan Eneas gan for to sayle
And howe the tempest al began
And howe he lost his steresman
Whiche that the sterne/or he toke kepe
Smote ouer the borde as he slepe
  And also saugh I howe Sibyle
And Eneas besyde an yle

To

To hel wente for to se
His father Anchyses the fre
And howe he there founde Palymurus
And also Dido/and Deiphebus
And eueriche tourment eke in Hel
Sawe he/whiche longe is for to tel
Whiche paynes who so lyste knowe
He must rede many a rowe
In Vergyle or in Claudian
Or Daunt/that it tellen can
  Tho sawe I eke al the arriuayle
That Eneas had made in Itayle
And with kynge Latyn his trete
And al the batayls that he
Was at hym selfe/and his knyghtes
Or he had al ywon his rightes
And howe he Turnus refte his lyfe
And wan Lauyna to his wyfe
And al the merueylous signals
Of the goddes celestials
Howe maugre Iuno/Eneas
For al her sleyght and her compas
Atcheued al his auenture
For Iupiter toke on hym cure
At the prayer of Venus
Whiche I praye alway saue vs
And vs aye/of our sorowes lyght
  Whan I had sene al this syght
In this noble temple thus
Hey lorde thought I/that madest vs
Yet sawe I neuer suche noblesse
Of ymages/nor suche richesse
As I se grauen in this churche
But naught wote I who dyd hem worche
Ne where I am/ne in what countre
But nowe wyl I out gone and se
Right at the wycket if I can
Sene ought where steryng any man
That maye me tellen where I am
  Whan I out of the dore cam
I fast aboute me behelde
Than sawe I but a large felde
As farre as euer I myght se
Without towne/house/or tre
Or busshe/or grasse/or eared lande
For al the felde was but of sande
As smal as men maye se at eye
In the deserte of Lyby
Ne no maner creature
That is yformed by nature
Ne sawe I/me to rede or wysse
O Chust thought I/that are in blysse
From fanton and illusyoun
Me saue/and with deuocyoun
Myne eyen to the heuen I cast
Tho was I ware/lo at the last
That fast by the sonne on hye
As kenne myght I with myne eye
Me thought I sawe an Egle sore
But that it semed moche more
Than I had any Egle ysfeyne
This is as sothe as dethe certeyne
It was of golde and shone so bryght
That neuer sawe men suche a syght
But if the heuen had ywonne
Al newe of god another sonne
So shone the Egles fethers bright
And som what downwarde gan it lyght.

Explicit liber primus.

NOwe herken euery maner man
That Englysshe vnderstande can
And lysteth of my dreme to here
For nowe at erst shal ye lere
So sely and so dredeful a vysyon
That I saye neyther Scipion
Ne kynge Nabugodonosore
Pharao/Turnus/ne Alcanore
Ne metten suche a dreme as this
Nowe fayre blyssful/O Cypris
So be my fauour at this tyme
That ye me endyte and ryme
Helpeth/that in Pernaso dwel
Besyde Elycon the clere wel
  O thought/that wrote al that I met
And in the tresorie it set
Of my brayne/nowe shal men se
If any vertue in the be
To tel al my dreme a right
Nowe kythe thy engyn and thy myght
  This Egle of whiche I haue you tolde
That with fethers shone al of golde
Whiche that so hye gan to sore
I gan beholde more and more
To sene her beaute and the wonder
But neuer was that dynte of thonder

Ne that

Ne that thynge that men cal foudre
That smyte somtyme a towre to poudre
And in his swyfte commynge brende
That so swythe gan downwarde discende
As this foule whan it behelde
That I a rowme was in the felde
And with his grym pawes stronge
Within his sharpe nayles longe
Me flyeng at a swappe he hente
And with his sours agayne vp wente
Me caryenge in his clawes starke
As lyghtly as I had ben a larke
Howe hye I can not tellen yowe
For I came vp/ I nyst neuer howe
For so astonyed and asweued
Was euery vertue in me heued
What with his sours and my dreed
That al my felynge gan to deed
For why/ it was a great affray
Thus I longe in his clawes lay
Tyl at last he to me spake
In mannes voyce/ and sayd awake
And be not agast so for shame
And called me tho by my name
And for I shulde better abrayde
Me to awake/ thus he sayde
Right in the same voyce and steuyn
That vseth one that I can neuyn
And with that voyce sothe to sayne
My mynde came to me agayne
For it was goodly sayd to me
So nas it neuer wonte to be
And here withal I gan to stere
As he me in his fete bere
Tyl that he felte that I had heate
And felte eke tho myne herte beate
And tho gan he me to disporte
And with gentyl wordes me comforte
And sayd twyse/ saynt Mary
Thou arte a noyous thynge to cary
And nothynge nedeth it perde
For also wyse god helpe me
As thou no harme shalte haue of this
And this case that betydde the is
Is for thy lore and for thy prowe
Lette se/ darst thou loke yet nowe
Be ful ensured boldely
I am thy frende/ and therwith I
Gan for to wonder in my mynde
O god (quod I) that madest al kynde
Shal I none other wyse dye
Wheder Ioue wyl me stellyfye
Or what thynge may this signifye
I am neyther Enocke ne Helye
Ne Romulus/ ne Ganemede
That were bore vp as men rede
To heuen with dan Iupiter
And made the goddes boteler
Lo/ this was tho my fantasy
But he that bare gan espy
That I so thought/ and sayd this
Thou demest of thy selfe amys
For Ioue is not there aboute
I dare the put ful out of doute
To make of the yet a sterre
But er I bere the moche ferre
I wyl the tel what I am
And whider thou shalte/ and why I cam
To do this/ so that thou take
Good herte/ and not for fere quake
Gladly (quod I) nowe wel (quod he)
First/ I that in my fete haue the
Of whom thou hast feare and wonder
I am dwellynge with the god of thonder
Whiche men callen Iupiter
That doth me flyen ful ofte fer
To do al his commandement
And for this cause he hath me sent
To the: herke nowe by thy trouthe
Certayne he hath of the routhe
That thou hast so truely
Longe serued ententifely
His blynde neuewe Cupido
And fayre Venus also
Without guerdon euer yet
And netheles hast set thy wyt
Al thoughe in thy heed ful lytel is
To make bokes/ songes/ and dittees
In ryme/ or els in Cadence
As thou best canst in reuerence
Of loue/ and of his seruauntes eke
That haue his seruyce sought/ and seke
And paynest the to prayse his arte
Although thou haddest neuer parte
Wherfore also god me blesse
Iouis halte it great humblesse

And

And vertue eke/ that thou wylte make
A nyght ful ofte thyne heed to ake
In thy studye so thou wrytest
And euermore of loue endytest
In honour of hym and prayshynges
And in his folkes furtherynges
And in her mater al deuysest
And not hym ne his folke dispisest
Althoughe thou mayst go in the daunce
Of hem/ that hym lyst not auaunce
Wherfore as I sayd ywys
Jupiter consydereth wel this
And also beausyre/ of other thynges
That is/ thou hast no tydynges
Of loues folke if they be glade
Ne of nothynge els that god made
And not onely fro farre countre
That no tydynges comen to the
Not of thy very neyghbours
That dwellen almost at thy dores
Thou herest neyther that ne this
For whan thy labour al done is
And hast made al thy rekenynges
In stede of rest and of newe thynges
Thou goest home to thyne house anone
And also dombe as a stone
Thou syttest at another boke
Tyl fully dased is thy loke
And lyuest thus as an Hermyte
Althoughe thyne abstynence is lyte
And therfore Jouis/ throughe his grace
Wyl that I bere the to a place
Whiche that hight the house of Fame
And to do the sporte and game
In some recompensacioun
Of thy labour and deuocioun
That thou hast had/ so causeles
To god Cupido the reccheles
And thus this god throughe his meryte
Wyl with some maner thynge the quite
So that thou wylte be of good chere
For trust wel that thou shalte here
Whan we be comen there as I say
Mo wonder thynges dare I lay
And of loues folke mo tydynges
Bothe sothsawes and lesynges
And mo loues newe begon
And longe serued tyl loue is won
And mo louers casuelly
That ben betydde/ no man wote why
But as a blynde man starteth an Hare
And more iolyte and welfare
Whyle they fynde loue of stele
As thinke men/ and ouer al wele
Mo discordes and mo ialousies
Mo murmures/ and mo nouelries
And also mo dissymulacions
And eke feyned reparacions
And mo berdes in two houres
Without rasour or sysoures
Ymade/ than graynes be of sandes
And eke mo holdynge in mo handes
And also mo renouelaunces
Of olde forleten acqueyntaunces
Mo louedayes/ and mo acordes
Than on instrumentes ben cordes
And eke of loue mo eschaunges
Than euer corne were in graunges
Unneth mayst thou trowen this
(Quod he) No so helpe me god as wys
(Quod I) No why (quod he) for it
Were impossyble to my wyt
Though Fame had al the pyes
In al a realme and al espyes
Howe that yet he sholde here al this
Or they espyen/ O yes yes
(Quod he) to me/ that can I preue
By reason/ worthy for to leue
So that thou gyue thyn aduertence
To understande my sentence
First shal thou here where she dwelleth
Right so as thyne owne boke telleth
Her palays standeth as I shal say
Right euen amyddes of the way
Bitwene heuen/ erthe/ and see
That what so euer in al these thre
Is spoken in priue or apperte
The way therto is so ouerte
And stante eke in so iuste a place
That euery sowne mote to it pace
Or what so cometh from any tonge
Be it rowned/ redde/ or songe
Or spoken in surete or drede
Certayne it mote thyder nede
Nowe herken wel/ for why I wyl
Tellen the a proper skyl

And

And a worthy demonstracyon
In myne ymagination
Geffray/thou wottest wel this
That euery kyndly thynge that is
Hath a kyndly stede there he
May best in it conserued be
Unto whiche place euery thynge
Throughe his kyndly enclynynge
Meueth for to come to
Whan that it is away therfro
As thus. Lo howe thou mayst al day se
Take any thynge that heuy be
As stone or leed/or thynge of weyght
And bere it neuer so hye on heyght
Let go thyne hande/it falleth downe
Right so say I by fyre or sowne
Or smoke/or other thinges lyght
Alway they seke vpwarde on heyght
Light thynges vp/and downwarde charge
Whyle eueriche of hem be at large
And for this cause/thou mayst wel se
That euery ryuer vnto the see
Enclyned is to go by kynde
And by these skylles as I fynde
Haue fysshes dwellynge in flode and see
And trees eke on the erthe be
Thus euery thynge by his reason
Hath his owne propre mansyon
To whiche he seketh to repeyre
There as it shulde nat appeyre
Lo/this sentence is knowen couthe
Of euery philosophers mouthe
As Aristotel/and dan Platone
And other clerkes many one
And to confirme my reason
Thou wost wel that speche is sowne
Or els no man myght it here
Nowe herke what I wyl the lere
Sowne is not but eyre ybroken
And euery speche that is spoken
Loude or priue/foule or fayre
In his substaunce is but eyre
For as flame is but lyghted smoke
Right so is sowne eyre ybroke
But this may be in many wyse
Of whiche I wyl the deuyse
As sowne cometh of pype or harpe
For whan a pype is blowen sharpe
The eyre is twyst with violence
And rent: Lo/this is my sentence
Eke/whan men harpe strynges smyte
Wheder it be moche or lyte
Lo/with the stroke the eyre to breketh
And right so breketh it whan men speketh
Thus wost thou wel what thynge is speche
Nowe hens forthe/I wyl the teche
Howe euery speche/voyce or sowne
Throughe his multiplycacyowne
Thoughe it were pyped of a mouse
Mote nedes come to Fames house
I proue it thus/take hede nowe
By experience/for if that thou
Threwe in a water nowe a stone
Wel wost thou it wyl make anone
A lytel roundel as a cercle
Parauenture/as brode as a couercle
And right anone thou shalte se wel
That whele cercle wyl cause another whele
And that the thyrde/and so forthe brother
Euery cercle causynge other
Broder than hym selfe was
And thus fro roundel to compas
Eche aboute other goynge
Causeth of others sterynge
And multiplyeng euermo
Tyl it be so farre go
That it at bothe brynkes be
Al thoughe thou may it not se
Aboue/yet gothe it alway vnder
Though thou thynke it a great wonder
And who so sayth of trouthe I vary
Bydde hym proue the contrary
And right thus euery worde ywys
That loude or pryue yspoken is
Moueth first an eyre aboute
And of his mouynge out of doute
Another eyre anone is moued
As I haue of the water proued
That euery cercle causeth other
Right so of eyre my leue brother
Euerich eyre in other stereth
More and more/and speche vp bereth
Or voyce or noyse/worde or sowne
Aye through multiplycacyowne
Tyl it be at the house of Fame
Take it in ernest or in game

Nowe

Nowe haue I tolde/if thou haue mynde
Howe speche or sowne/of pure kynde
Enclyned is vpwarde to meue
This mayst thou fele wel by preue
And that some stede ywys
That euery thynge enclyned to is
Hath his kyndlyche stede
That sheweth it without drede
That kyndly the mancyoun
Of euery speche of euery soun
Be it eyther foule or fayre
Hath his kynde place in eyre
And syth that euery thynge ywys
Out of his kynde place ywys
Moueth thyder for to go (:):)
If it away be therfro
As I haue before proued the
It seweth euery soune perde
Moueth kyndely to pace
As vp in to his kynde place
And this place of whiche I tel
There as Fame lyst to dwel
Is set a myddes of these thre
Heuen/erthe/and eke the see
As most conseruatyfe the soun
Than is this the conclusyoun (:):)
That euery speche of euery man
As I the tel first began
Moueth vp on heyght to pace
Kyndly to Fames place
Tel me this nowe faythfully
Haue I not proued thus symply
Without any subtylte
Of speche/or great prolyxite
Of termes of Philosophie
Of fygures of Poetrie (:(:):)
Or colours of rethoryke
Perde it ought the to lyke
For harde langage/and harde matere
Is encombrous for to here
At ones/wost thou not wel this
And I answered and sayd yes
Ah ha (quod he) so so I can
Leudly vnto a leude man
Speke/and shewe hym suche skylles
That he may shake hem by the bylles
So palpable they shulden be
But tel me this nowe pray I the
Howe thynketh the my conclusyon
A good persuasyon
(Quod I) it is and lyke to be
Right so as thou hast proued me
By god (quod he) and as I leue
Thou shalte haue yet or it be eue
Of euery worde of this sentence
A profe/by experyence
And with thyne eares heren wel
Toppe and tayle/and euerydel
That euery worde that spoken is
Cometh in to Fames house ywis
As I haue sayd/what wylte thou more
And with this worde vpper to sore
He began/and sayd by saynt Iame
Nowe wyl we speke al of game
Howe farest thou nowe (quod he) to me
Wel (quod I) nowe se (quod he)
By thy trouth yonde adowne
Where that thou knowest any towne
Or house/or any other thynge
And whan thou hast of aught knowynge
Loke that thou warne me
And I anone shal tel the
Howe farre that thou arte nowe therfro
And I adowne gan to loken tho
And behelde feldes and playns
Nowe hylles/and nowe mountayns
Nowe valeys/and nowe forrestes
And nowe vnneth great beestes
Nowe ryuers/nowe Citees
Nowe townes/nowe great trees
Nowe shippes saylynge in the see
But thus soone in a whyle he
Was flowen fro the grounde so hye
That al the worlde as to myne eye
No more semed than a prycke
Or els was the eyre so thycke
That I might it not decerne
With that he spake to me so yerne
And sayd: Seest thou any token
Or aught/that in this worlde is of spoken
I sayde nay/No wonder is
(Quod he) For neuer halfe so hye as this
Nas Alexander of Macedon
Kyng: Ne of Rome dan Scipion
That sawe in dreme at poynt deuyse
Heuen and erthe/hel and paradyse

Ne eke

Ne eke the wretche Dedalus
Ne his chylde nyce Icharus
That flewe so hye/that the hete
His wynges molte/and he fel wete
In mydde the see/and there he dreynte
For whom was made a great complaynte
  Nowe tourne vpwarde (quod he) thy face
And beholde this large space
This eyre/ but loke that thou ne be
Adrad of hem that thou shalte se
For in this region certeyne
Dwelleth many a cytezeyne
Of whiche speketh dan Plato
These ben the eyrysshe beestes lo
And tho sawe I al the meyne
Bothe gone and also flye
  Lo (quod he) caste vp thyne eye
Se yonder lo/the Galaxye
The whiche men clepe the mylky way
For it is whyte: And some parfay
Callen it Watlynge strete
That ones was brente with the hete
Whan the sonnes sonne the reade
That hyte Pheton wolde leade
Algate his fathers carte/and gye
  The carte horse gan wel espye
That he coude no gouernaunce
And gan for to lepe and praunce
And bere hym vp/and nowe downe
Tyl he sawe the Scorpiowne
Whiche that in heuen a sygne is yet
And he for fere lost his wyt
Of that/and let the reynes gone
Of his horse/and they anone
Soone vp to mounte/and downe discende
Tyl bothe eyre and erthe brende
Tyl Iupiter lo/at the last
Hym slewe/and fro the carte cast
  Lo/ is it not a great myschaunce
To let a fole haue gouernaunce
Of thynges that he can not demayne
  And with this worde sothe for to sayne
He gan alway vpper to sore
And gladed me than more and more
So faythfully to me spake he
  Tho gan I to loke vnder me
And behelde the eyrysshe beestes
Cloudes/mystes/and tempestes
Snowes/hayles/raynes/and wyndes
And thengendrynge in her kyndes
Al the way throughe whiche I came
  O god (quod I) that made Adam
Moche is thy myght and noblesse
  And tho thought I vpon Boece
That wryteth a thought may flye so hye
With fethers of philosophye
To passen eueriche Element
And whan he hath so farre ywent
Than may be seen behynde his bake
Cloude and erthe/and al that I of spake
  Tho gan I weye in a were
And sayd/I wote wel I am here
But whether in body or in goost
I not ywys/but god thou woost
For more clere entendement
Nas me neuer yet ysent
And than thought I on Marcyan
And eke of Anteclaudian
That sothe was her discripcion
Of al the heuens region
As farre as that I sawe the preue
And therfore I can hem leue
  With that the Egle gan to crye
Let be (quod he) thy fantasye
Wylte thou lere of sterres ought
  Naye certaynly (quod I) right nought
And why (quod he) for I am olde
Or els wolde I the haue tolde
(Quod he) the sterres names lo
And al the heuens sygnes to
And whiche they be: No force (quod I)
  Yes perde (quod he) wost thou why
For whan thou redest poetry
Howe the goddes can stellyfy
Byrde/fysshe/or hym/or her
As the Rauyn and other
Or Ariones harpe fyne
Castor/Polcye/or Delphyne
Or Athalantes doughters seuen
Howe al these are set in heuen
For thoughe thou haue hem ofte in hande
Yet nost thou nat where they stande
  No force (quod I) it is no nede
As wel I leue so god me spede
Hem that wryten of this matere
As though I knewe her places here

And

And eke thy seluen here so bryght
It shulde shenden al my syght
To loke on hem/that may wel be
(Quod he) and so forthe bare he me
A whyle/and tho began to crye
That neuer herde I thynge so hye
Holde vp thyne heed/for al is wel
Saynt Iulyan lo/ bonne hostel
Se here the house of Fame lo
Mayst thou not here that I do
What (quod I) the great sowne
(Quod he) that rombleth vp and downe
In Fames house ful of tydynges
Bothe of fayre speche and chydynges
And of false/ and sothe compowned
Herken wel it is not rowned
Herest thou not the great swough
Yes perde (quod I) wel ynough
And what sowne is it lyke (quod he)
Peter/ lyke the beatynge of the see
(Quod I) agaynst the roches holowe
Whan tempestes done her shyppes swalowe
And that a man stande out of doute
A myle thens/and here it route
Or els lyke the humblynge
After the clappe of a thundrynge
Whan Iouis hath the eyre ybete
But it dothe me for feare swete
Nay/drede the not therof (quod he)
It is nothynge that wyl byten the
Thou shalte haue no harme truely
And with that worde bothe he and I
As nyghe the place aryued were
As men myght cast with a spere
I nyste howe/ but in a strete
He set me fayre on my fete
And sayd/walke forth a pace
And tel thyne aduenture and case
That thou shalte fynde in Fames place
Nowe (quod I) whyle we haue space
To speke/or that I go fro the
For the loue of god tel me
In sothe/that I wyl of the lere
If this noyse that I here
Be as I haue herde the tel
Of folke/that downe in erthe dwel
And cometh here in the same wyse
As I the herde or this deuyse
And that here lyues body nys
In al that house that yonder is
That maketh al this loude fare
No (quod he) by saynt Clare
And also wysse god rede me
But o thynge I wyl warne the
Of the whiche thou wylte haue wonder
Lo/ to the house of Fame yonder
Thou wost howe cometh euery speche
It nedeth not the eft to teche
But vnderstande nowe right wel this
Whan any speche ycomen is
Vp to the palays anone right
It weyeth lyke the same wyght
Whiche that the worde in erthe spake
Be he clothed in reed or blake
And hath so very his lykenesse
And spake the worde that thou wylte gesse
That it the same body be
Man or woman/he or she
And is not this a wonder thynge
Yes (quod I tho) by heuen kynge
And with this worde/farewel (quod he)
And here wyl I abyde the
And god of heuen sende the grace
Some good to lerne in this place
And I of hym toke leue anone
And gan forthe to the palays gone.

¶ Explicit liber secundus.

O God of science and of lyght
Apollo throughe thy great myght
This lytel last boke nowe thou gye
Not that I wyl for maystrye
Here arte potencyal be shewde
But for the ryme is lyght and lewde
Yet make it somwhat agreable
Though some verse fayle in a syllable
And that I do no diligence
To shewe crafte/but sentence
And if deuyne vertue thou
Wylte helpe me to shewe nowe
That in my heed ymarked is
Lo/ that is for to meanen this
The house of Fame for to discryue
Thou shalte se me go as blyue
Vnto the nexte laurer I se
And kysse it/ for it is thy tree

R.v.v. Nowe

The thirde boke of Fame.

Nowe entre in my brest anone
When I was from the Egle gone
I gan beholde vpon this place
And certayne or I further pace
I wol you al the shappe deuyse
Of house and cyte/ and al the wyse
Howe I gan to this place aproche
That stode vpon so hye a roche
Hyer standeth none in Spayne
But vp I clambe with moche payne
And though to clymbe greued me
Yet I ententyfe was to se
And for to pooren wonder low
Yf I coude any wyse yknowe
What maner stone this roche was
For it was lyke a lymed glas
But that it shone ful more clere
But of what congeled matere
It was/ I nyste redely
But at the laste espyed I
And fonde that it was euerydele
A roche of yse and nat of stele
Thought I/ by saynt Thomas of Kent
This were a feble foundement
To bylden on a place hye
He ought him lytel to glorifye
That heron bylte/ god so me saue
Tho sawe I al the hal ygraue
With famous folkes names fele
That had ben in moche wele
And her fames wyde yblowe
But wel vnneth myght I knowe
Any letters for to rede
Her names by/ for out of drede
They weren almost of thawed so
That of the letters one or two
Were molte awaye of euery name
So vnfamous was weye her fame
But men saye/ what may euer laste
Tho gan I in myne herte caste
That they were molte awaye for hete
And nat away with stormes bete
For on that other syde I sey
Of this hyl/ that northwarde ley
Howe it was written ful of names
Of folke that had afore great fames
Of olde tyme/ and yet they were
As fresshe as men had written hem there
The selfe day/ or that houre
That I on hem gan to poure
But wel I wyst what it made
It was conserued with the shade
Al the wrytyng that I sye
Of a Castel that so stode on hye
And stode eke in so colde a place
That heate myght it nat deface
Tho gan I on this hyl to gone
And founde on the coppe a wone
That al the men that ben on lyue
Ne han the connyng to discryue
The beaute of that ylke place
Ne coude caste no compace
Suche another for to make
That myght of beaute be his make
Ne so wonderly ywrought
That it astonyeth yet my thought
And maketh al my wytte to swynke
On this Castel for to thynke
So that the great beaute
The caste/ crafte/ and curiosyte
Ne can I nat to you deuyse
My wytte ne may me nat suffyse
But natheless al the substaunce
I haue yet in my remembraunce
For why me thought by saynt Gyle
Al was of stone of Beryle
Bothe the castel and the tour
And eke the hal/ and euery bour
Without peces or ioynynges
But many subtel compassynges
As babeuries and pynnacles
Imageries and tabernacles
I sawe / and ful eke of wyndowes
As flakes fallen in great snowes
And eke in eche of the pynacles
Weren sondrie habytacles
In whiche stoden al withouten
Ful the castel al abouten
Of al maner of mynstrales
And iestours that tellen tales
Bothe of wepyng and of game
And of al that longeth vnto fame
There herde I play on an harpe
That sowned bothe wel and sharpe
Hym Orpheus ful craftely
And on this syde fast by

Sate

Satte the harper Orion
And Eacides Chirion
And other harpers many one
And the Bryton Glaskyrione
And smal harpers with her glees
Sat vnder hem in dyuers sees
And gon on hem vpwarde to gape
And counterfayted hem as an ape
Or as craft counterfeyte kynde
Tho sawe I standen hem behynde
A farre from hem/al by hem selue
Many a thousande tymes twelue
That made lowde mynstralsyes
In cornmuse and shalmyes
And many an other pype
That craftely began to pype
Bothe in douced and in rede
That ben at feestes with the brede
And many a floyte and lytlynge horne
And pypes made of grene corne
As haue these lytel heerd gromes
That kepen beestes in the bromes
There sawe I than dan Cytherus
And of Athenes dan Proserus
And Mercia that lost her skynne
Bothe in face/body/and chynne
For that she wolde enuyen/lo
To pypen bette than Apollo
There sawe I eke famous olde and yonge
Pypers of al the duche tonge
To lerne loue daunces/sprynges
Reyes/and the straunge thynges
Tho sawe I in another place
Standynge in a large space
Of hem that maken blody soun
In trumpe beme/ and claryoun
For in fyght and blode shedynges
Is vsed gladly clarionynges
There herde I trumpe Messenus
Of whom that speketh Vergilius
There herde I Ioab trumpe also
Theodomas and other mo
And al that vsed clarion
In Castelloygne/ and Aragon
That in her tymes famous were
To lernen sawe I trumpen there
There sawe I syt in other sees
Playenge vpon other sondry glees
Whiche that I can not neuen
Mo than sterres ben in heuen
Of whiche I nyl as nowe nat ryme
For ease of you/and losse of tyme
For tyme lost/this knowe ye.
By no way may recouered be
There sawe I playeng iogelours
Magyciens and tragetours
And Phetonysses charmeresses
Olde wytches sorceresses
That vsen exorsisacions
And eke subfumygacions
And clerkes eke whiche conne wel
Al this magyke naturel
That craftely do her ententes
To maken in certayne ascendentes
Ymages lo/through whiche magyke
To maken a man ben hole or seke
There sawe I the quene Medea
And Cyrces eke/and Caliophia
There sawe I Hermes Ballenus
Lymote/and eke Symon Magus
There sawe I/and knewe by name
That by suche arte done men haue fame
There sawe I Coll tregetour
Vpon a table of Sycamour
Play an vncouthe thyng to tel
I sawe hym cary a wynde mel
Vnder a walnote shale
What shulde I make lenger tale
Of al the people that I sey
I coude nat tel tyl domisdey
Whan I had al this folke beholde
And founde me lose and nat holde
And I amused a longe whyle
Vpon this wal of Beryle
That shone lyghter than a glas
And made wel more than it was
As kynde thyng of fame is
And than anon after this
I gan forthe romen tyl I fonde
The castel yate on my right honde
Whiche so wel coruen was
That neuer suche another nas
And yet it was by auenture
Ywrought by great and subtyl cure
It nedeth nat you more to tellen
To make you to longe dwellen

R.v.ii. Of

Of these pates florysshynges
Ne of compaces/ne of kaluynges
Ne howe the harkynge in masonries
As corbettes/and ymageries
 But lorde so fayre it was to shewe
For it was al with golde behewe
But in I wente/and that anone
There mette I cryenge many one
A larges a larges/holde up wel
God saue the lady of this pel
Our owne gentyl lady Fame
And hem that wyllen to haue a name
Of us/thus herde I cryen al
And fast comen out of the hal
And shoke nobles and starlynges
And crowned were as kynges
With crownes wrought ful of losynges
And many ribans/and many frynges
Were on her clothes truely
 Tho at the last espyed I
That purseuauntes and heraudes
That cryen riche folkes laudes
It weren/ al and euery man
Of hem/as I you tel can
Had on hym throwe a vesture
Whiche men clepe a cote armure
Embroudred wonderly riche.
As thoughe they were not ylyche
But naught wyl I so mote I thryue
Be aboute to discryue
Al these armes that there weren
That they thus on her cotes weren
For it to me were impossyble
Men myght make of hem a byble
Twenty fote thycke as I trowe
For certayne who so coude knowe
Myght there al the armes seen
Of famous folke that had been
In Affrike/Europe/ and Asye
Sithe fyrst began cheualrye
 Lo/ howe shalde I nowe tel al this
Ne of the hal eke what nede is
To tellen you that euery wal
Of it/and rose and flore with al
Was plated halfe a fote thicke
Of golde/and that nas not wycke
But for to proue in al wyse
As fyne as ducket in Venyse
Of whiche to lyte al in my pouche is
And they were set as thyke of ouches
Fyne/of the fynest stones fayre
That men reden in the lapidayre
Or as grasses growen in a mede
But it were al to longe to rede
The names; and therfore I pace
But in this lusty and riche place
That Fames hal called was
Ful moche prees of folke there nas
Ne crowdynge/for to moche prees
But al on hye aboue a dees
Satte in a see imperial
That made was of a Ruby royal
Whiche that a carbuncle is ycalled
I sawe perpetually ystalled
A feminyne creature
That neuer formed by nature
Was suche another thynge I say
For altherfirst/sothe to say
Me thought that she was so lyte
That the length of a cubyte
Was lenger than she semed be
But thus soone in a whyle she
Her selfe tho wonderly streyght
That with her fete she therthe reyght
And with her hed she touched heuen
There as shyneth the sterres seuen
And therto yet/as to my wyt
I sawe a great wonder yet
Upon her eyen to beholde
But certaynly I hem neuer tolde
For as fele eyen had she
As fethers upon foules be
Or weren on the beestes foure
That goddes trone can honoure
As wryteth Iohan in the Apocalyps
Her heer that was owndy and cryps
As burned golde it shone to se
 And sothe to tellen also she
Had also fele up standynge eares
And tonges/as on beest ben heares
And on her fete woxen sawe I
Partriche wynges redily
 But lorde the perry and the rychesse
I sawe syttynge on the goddesse
And the heuenly melody
Of songes ful of armony

I herde

I herde aboute her trone ysonge
That al the palays wal ronge
So songe the myghty Muse she
That cleped is Caliope
And her seuen systerne eke
That in her faces semen meke
And euermore eternally
The songe of fame tho herde I
Heryed be thou and thy name
Goddes of renoun and of fame
  Tho was I ware at the last
As I myne eyen gan vp cast
That this ylke noble quene
On her shulders gan sustene
Bothe the armes and the name
Of tho that had large fame
Alysander/and Hercules
That with a sherte his lyfe dyd lese
And thus founde I syttynge this goddesse
In noble honour and richesse
Of whiche I stynte a whyle nowe
Other thynge to tellen you
  Tho sawe I stande on thother syde
Streyght downe to the dores wyde
From the dees many a pyllere
Of metal/that shone not ful clere
But though they were of no richesse
Yet were they made for great noblesse
And in hem great sentence
And folke of hye and digne reuerence
Of whiche to tel wyl I fonde
  Upon a pyller sawe I stonde
Alderfirst there I sye
Upon a pyller stande on hye
That was of lede and of yron fyne
Hym of the secte saturnyne
The Ebrayke Josephus the olde
That of Iewes gestes tolde
And he bare on his shulders hye
The fame vp of the Iurye
And by hym stoden other seuen
Wyse and worthy for to neuen
To helpen hym bere vp the charge
It was so heuy and so large
And for they wryten of batayles
As wel as of other meruayles
Therfore was lo/this pyllere
Of whiche I you tel here
Of leed and yron bothe ywis
For yron Martes metal is
Whiche that god is of batayle
And the leed withouten fayle
Is lo/the metal of Saturne
That hath ful large whele to turne
To stande forthe on eyther rowe
Of hem/whiche I coude knowe
Thoughe I by ordre hem not tel
To make you to longe to dwel
  These/of whiche I gan rede
There sawe I stande out of drede
Upon an yron pyller stronge
That paynted was al endlonge
With Tygres blode in euery place
The Tholason that hyght Stace
That bare of Thebes vp the name
Upon his shulders/and the fame
Also of cruel Achylles
And by hym stode withouten lees
Ful wonder highe vpon a pyller
Of yron/he the great Omer
And with hym Dares and Tytus
Before/and eke he Lollyus
And Guydo eke de Colempnis
And Englysshe Galfride eke ywis
And eche of these as I haue ioye
Was busy to beare vp Troye
So heuy therof was the fame
That for to beare it was no game
But yet I gan ful wel espye
Bytwene hem was a lytel enuye
One sayd that Omer made lyes
Feynynge in his poetris
And was to the Grekes fauourable
Therfore helde he it but fable
  Tho sawe I stande on a pyllere
That was of tynned yron clere
The latyn poete Vergyle
That hath bore vp a longe whyle
The fame of Pius Eneas
  And nexte hym on a pyller was
Of copper/Venus clerke Ouyde
That hath sowen wonders wyde
The great god of loues fame
And there he bare vp wel his name
Upon this pyller also hye
As I myght se it with myne eye

K.k.k.iii. Fo

The thirde boke of Fame.

For why this hal wherof I rede
Was woxe on heyght/length/ and brede
Wel more by a thousande dele
Than it was erst/that sawe I wele
  Tho sawe I on a pyller by
Of yron wrought ful sternely
The great poete dan Lucan
That on his sholders bare vp than
As hye as that I myght se
The fame of Iulyus and Pompee
And by hym stoden al these clerkes
That write of Romes mighty werkes
That if I wolde her names tel
Al to longe must I dwel
  And nexte hym on a pyller stode
Of sulphure/lyche as he were wode
Dan Claudian/sothe for to tel
That bare vp al the fame of Hel
Of Pluto/ and of Proserpyne
That quene is of the derke pyne
  What shulde I more tel of this
The hal was al ful ywis
Of hem that wryten olde iestes
As ben on trees rokes nestes
But it a ful confuse matere
Were al these iestes for to here
That they of wryte/and howe they hyght
But whyle that I behelde this syght
I herde a noyse approchen blyue
That fareth as bees done in an hyue
Agaynst her tyme of out flyenge
Ryght suche a maner murmurynge
For al the worlde it semed me
  Tho gan I loke aboute and se
That there come entrynge in to the hal
A right great company withal
And that of sondry regyons
Of al kyns condicyons
That dwel in erthe vnder the moone
Poore and ryche/and also soone
As they were come in to the hal
They gan on knees downe to fal
Before this ilke noble quene
And sayd/graunt vs lady shene
Eche of vs of thy grace abone
And some of hem she graunted soone
And some she warned wel and fayre
And some she graunted the contrayre
Of her askynge vtterly
But this I say you trewly
What her grace was I nyst
For of these folke ful wel I wyst
They had good fame eche deserued
Al though they were dyuersly serued
Right as her syster dame Fortune
Is wonte to serue in commune
  Nowe herken howe she gan to paye
Hem that gan her of grace praye
And yet lo/ al this company
Seyden sothe/and not a lye
  Madame sayd they/we be
Folke that here besechen the
That thou graunt vs nowe good fame
And let our workes haue good name
In ful recompensacioun
Of good worke/ gyue vs good renoun
  I warne it you (quod she) anone
Ye gete of me good fame none
By god/and therfore go your way
  Alas (quod they) and welaway
Tel vs what your cause may be
  For me lyste it not (quod she)
No wyght shal speke of you ywis
Good ne harme/ne that ne this
  And with that worde she gan to cal
Her messenger that was in hal
And bad that he shulde fast gone
Vpon payne to be blynde anone
For Eolus the god of wynde
In Trace there ye shal hym fynde
And byd hym brynge his clarioun
That is ful dyuers of his sowne
And it is cleped clere Laude
With whiche he wont is to heraude
Hem that me lyst ypraysed be
And also byd hym howe that he
Brynge eke his other claryoun
That hight Sclaundre in euery towne
With whiche he wont is to diffame
Hem that me lyst and do hem shame
  This messenger gan fast to gone
And founde where in a caue of stone
In a countre that hight Trace
This Eolus with harde grace
Helde the wyndes in distresse
And gan hem vnder hym to presse

That they gone as the beres rore
He bounde and pressed hem so sore
This messenger gan fast crye
Ryse vp (quod he) and fast the hye
Tyl thou at my lady be
And take thy clarions eke with the
And spede the fast/and he anone
Toke to one that hyght Tritone
His clarions to beren tho
And let a certayne wynde go
That blewe so hydously and hye
That it ne lefte not a skye
In al the welken longe and brode
This Eolus no where abode
Tyl he was come to Fames fete
And eke the man that Triton hete
And there he stode as styl as stone
And here withal there came anone
Another huge company
Of good folke and gan to crye
Lady/graunt vs nowe good fame
And let our werkes haue that name
Nowe in honour of gentylnesse
And also god your soule blesse
For we han wel deserued it
Therfore is right that we be quyt
As thryue I (quod she) ye shal fayle
Good workes shal you not auayle
To haue of me good fame as nowe
But wote ye what/I graunt yowe
That ye shal haue a shrewde name
And wycked loos/and worse fame
Though ye good loos haue wel deserued
Nowe gothe your way for ye ben serued
And thou dan Eolus (quod she)
Take forthe thy trumpe anone let se
That is ycleped Sklaundre lyght
And blowe her loos/that euery wyght
Speke of hem harme and shrewdnesse
In stede of good and worthynesse
For thou shalte trumpe al the contrarye
Of that they haue done/wel or fayre
Alas thought I what auentures
Haue these sory creatures
That they amonge al the prees
Shulde thus be shamed gyltles
But what/it must nedes be
What dyd this Eolus/but he
Toke out his blacke trumpe of bras
That fouler than the deuyl was
And gan this trumpe for to blowe
As al the worlde sholde ouerthrowe
Throughout euery regioun
Wente this foule trumpes soun
As swyfte as a pellet out of a gonne
Whan fyre is in the pouder ronne
And suche a smoke gan out wende
Out of the foule trumpes ende
Blacke/blo/greuysshe/swartysshe rede
As dothe where that men melte lede
Lo/al on hye from the tewel
And therto one thynge sawe I wel
That the ferther that it ranne
The gretter weyen it began
As dothe the ryuer from a wel
And it stanke as the pytte of hel
Alas/thus was her shame yronge
And gyltlesse on euery tonge
Tho came the thirde company
And gon vp to the dees to hye
And downe on knees they fel anon
And sayden/we ben euerychon
Folke that han ful trewly
Deserued fame rightfully
And prayde you it mught be knowe
Right as it is/and forthe blowe
I graunt (quod she) for nowe me lyste
That your good workes shal be wyst
And yet ye shal haue better loos
Right in dispyte of al your foos
Than worthy is/and that anone
Lette nowe (quod she) thy trumpe gone
Thou Eolus/that is so blake
And out thyn other trumpe take
That hyght Laude/and blowe it so
That through the worlde her fame go
Al easely and nat to fast
That it be knowen at the last
Ful gladly lady myn he sayde
And out his trumpe of golde he brayde
Anon/and sette it to his mouthe
And blewe it eest/west/and southe
And northe/as loude as any thonder
That euery wight hath of it wonder
So brode it ran or that it stent
And certes al the brethe that went
Out of his trumpes mouthe smelde
As men a potte ful of baume helde Amōg

The thirde boke of Fame.

Amonge a basket ful of roses
This fauour dyd he to her loses
  And right with this I gan espy
There came the fourth company
But certayne they were wonder fewe
And gonne to standen on a rewe
And sayden/ certes lady bright
We haue done wel with al our myght
But we ne kepe to haue fame
Hyde our workes and our name
For goddes loue/for certes we
Haue surely done it for bounte
And for no maner other thyng
  I graunt you al your askyng
(Quod she) let your workes be deed
  With that aboute I tourned my heed
And sawe anon the fyfte route
That to this lady gan loute
And downe on knees anon to fal
And to her tho besoughten al
To hyden her good werkes eke
And sayd/they yeue nat a leke
For no fame/ne suche renoun
For they for contemplacioun
And goddes loue had it wrought
Ne of fame wolde they nought
  What (quod she) and be ye woode
And wene ye for to do good
And for to haue of that no fame
Haue ye dispyte to haue my name
Nay ye shal lyen euerychone
Blowe thy trumpe and that anone
(Quod she) thou Eolus I hote
And rynge these folkes workes by note
That al the worlde may of it here
And he gan blowe her loos so clere
In his golden clarioun
That through the worlde went the soun
Al so kyndly/and eke so softe
That their fame was blowe a lofte
  Tho came the syxt companye
And gan fast to Fame crye
Right verily in this manere
They sayden/ mercy lady dere
To tel certayne as it is
We haue done neyther that ne this
But ydel al our lyfe hath be
But natheless yet pray we
That we may haue as good a fame
And great renome and knowen name
As they that haue do noble iestes
And acheued al her questes
As wel of loue as other thyng
Al was vs neuer broche ne ryng
Ne els what fro women sent
Ne ones in her herte yment
To maken vs onely frendly chere
But mought temen vs on bere
Yet let vs to the people seme
Suche as the worlde may of vs deme
That women louen vs for woode
It shal do vs as moche good
And to our herte as moche auayle
The counterpeyse/ease/and trauayle
As we had won with labour
For that is dere bought honour
At regarde of our great ease
And yet ye muste vs more please
Let vs be holde eke therto
Worthy/wyse/and good also
And ryche/and happy vnto loue
For goddes loue that sytteth aboue
Though we may nat the body haue
Of women/yet so god me saue
Lette men glewe on vs the name
Suffyseth that we haue the fame
  I graunt (quod she) by my trouthe
Nowe Eolus withouten slouthe
Take out thy trumpe of golde (quod she)
And blowe as they haue asked me
That euery man wene hem at ease
Though they go in ful badde lease
This Eolus gan it so blowe
That through the worlde it was yknowe
  Tho came the seuenth route anon
And fyl on knees euerychon
And sayd/lady graunt vs soone
The same thyng/the same boone
That this next folke haue done
  Fye on you (quod she) euerychone
Ye masty swyne/ye ydel wretches
Ful of roten slowe tetches
What false theues/ where ye wolde
Ben famed good/and nothyng nolde
Deserue why/ne neuer thought
Men rather you to hangen ought
For ye be lyke the slepy catte
That wolde haue fysh: but wost thou what:

He wol nothyng were his clawes
Euel thrifte come to your iawes
And on myne if I it graunt
Or do fauour you to auaunt
  Thou Eolus/ thou kyng of Trace
Go blowe this folke a sory grace
(Quod she) anon/and wost thou howe
As I shal tel the right nowe
Say these ben they that wolde honour
Haue/and do no kyns labour
Ne do no good/and yet haue laude
And that men wende that belle Isaude
Ne coude hem nat of loue werne
And yet she that grynt at querne
Is al to good to ease her herte
  This Eolus anon vp sterte
And with his blacke clarioun
He gan to blasen out a soun
As lounde as belleth wynde in hel
And eke therwith sothe to tel
This sowne was so ful of iapes
As euer mowes were in apes
And that went al the worlde aboute
That euery wight gan on hem shoute
And for to laugh as they were wode
Suche game founde they in her hode
  Tho came another company
That had ydone the trechery
The harme and great wickednesse
That any herte couden gesse
And prayed her to haue good fame
And that she nolde do hem no shame
But gyue hem loos and good renoun
And do it blowe in claryoun
  Nay wys (quod she) it were a vyce
Al be there in me no iustyce
Me lyst nat to do it nowe
Ne this I nyl graunt it you
  Tho came there leapyng in a route
And gan clappen al aboute
Euery man vpon the crowne
That al the hall gan to sowne
And sayd/lady lefe and dere
We ben suche folkes as ye may here
To tel al the tale a ryght
We ben shrewes euery wyght
And haue delyte in wickednesse
As good folke haue in goodnesse
And ioye to be knowen shrewes
And ful of vyce and wicked thewes
Wherfore we praye you on a rowe
That our fame be suche yknowe
In al thing ryght as it is
  I graunt it you (quod she) ywis
But what arte thou that sayest this tale
That wearest on thy hose a pale
And on thy typpet suche a bel
  Madame (quod he) sothe to tel
I am that ylke shrewe ywis
That brent the temple of Isydis
In Athenes/lo that cyte
And wherfore dyddest thou so (quod she)
By my trouthe (quod he) madame
I wolde fayne haue had a name
As other folke had in the towne
Although they were of great renowne
For her vertue and her thewes
Thought I/as great fame haue shrewes
(Though it be naught) for shrewdnesse
As good folke haue for goodnesse
And sythen I may nat haue that one
That other nyl I nat forgone
As for to get a fame here
The temple sette I al on fyre
  Nowe don our loos be blowe swythe
As wysly be thou euer blythe
  Gladly (quod she) thou Eolus
Herest thou not what they prayen vs
  Madame yes/ful wel (quod he)
And I wyl trumpen it parde
And toke his blacke trumpe fast
And gan to puffen and to blaste
Tyl it was at the worldes ende
  With that I gan aboute wende
For one that stode right at my bake
Me thought ful goodly to me spake
And sayd/frende what is thy name
Arte thou come hyder to haue fame?
  Nay for sothe frende (quod I)
I come nat hyther grant mercy
For no suche cause by my heed
Suffyseth me/as I were deed
That no wight haue my name in honde
I wotte my selfe best howe I stonde
For what I drie/or what I thynke
I wol my selfe al it drinke
Certayne for the more parte
As ferforthe as I can myn arte
What

The thirde boke of Fame.

What doest thou here than (quod he)
(Quod I) that wol I tel the
The cause why I stande here
Some newe tydynges for to lere
Some newe thyng I not what
Tydinges eyther this or that
Of loue/or suche thynges glade
For certainly he that me made
To come hyder/sayd to me
I shulde bothe here and se
In this place wonder thynges
But these be no suche tidynges
As I ment of: No (quod he)
And I answerde/no parde
For wel I wote euer yet
Sythe that first I had wyt
That some folke han desyred fame
Diuersly/and loos and name
But certainly I nyst howe
Ne where that Fame dwelled or nowe
Ne eke of her discripcion
Ne also her condycion
Ne the order of her dome
Knewe I nat tyl I hyder come
Why than be so these tydynges
That thou nowe hyther bringes
That thou haste herde (quod he) to me
But nowe no force/for wel I se
What thou desyrest for to lere
Come forthe and stande no lenger here
And I wol the without drede
In to suche another place lede
There thou shalt here many one
Tho gan I forthe with him gone
Out of the castel sothe to sey
Tho sawe I stande in a valey
Vnder the castel faste by
An house/ that domus Dedaly
That Laborintus ycleped is
Nas made so wonderly iwys
Ne halfe so queyntly ywrought
And euermo/ as swyfte as thought
This queynt house aboute went
That neuermo it styl stent
And there came out so great a noyse
That had it stonde vpon Oyse
Men might haue herde it esyly
To Rome/ I trowe sikerly
And the noyse whiche that I herde
For al the worlde right so it ferde
As dothe the routyng of the stone
That fro thengyn is letyn gone
And al this house of whiche I rede
Was made of twygges falowe rede
And grene eke/and some were whyte
Suche as men to these cages twhyte
Or maken of these panyers
Or els hutches or dossers
That for the swough and for the twygges
This house was also ful of gygges
And also ful eke of chyrkynges
And of many other workynges
And eke this house hath of entrees
As many as leues ben on trees
In somer whan they ben grene
And on the rofe yet men may sene
A thousande holes/and wel mo
To letten the sowne out go
And by day in euery tyde
Ben al the dores open wyde
And by nyght eche one vnshette
Ne porte is there none to lette
No maner tydinges in to pace
Ne neuer rest is in that place
That it nys fylled ful of tidynges
Eyther loude or of whysperynges
And euer al the houses angles
Is ful of rownynges and of iangles
Of werres/of peace/of maryages
Of restes/and of labour of vyages
Of abode of dethe/and of lyfe
Of loue/of hate/accorde/ of stryfe
Of losse/of lore/and of wynnynges
Of heale/of sicknesse/or of lesynges
Of fayre wether/and eke of tempestes
Of qualme of folke/ and of beestes
Of dyuers transmutacions
Of estates/and eke of regyons
Of trust/of drede/of ialousy
Of wytte/of wynnyng/of foly
Of plentie/and of great famyne
Of chepe/of derthe/and of ruyne
Of good or misgouernment
Of fyre/and of dyuers accydent
And so/ this house of whiche I write
Syker be ye it nas nat lyte
For it was sixtie myle of length
Al was the tymbre of no strength

Yet

Yet it is founded to endure
Whyle that it lyst to Auenture
That is the mother of tydinges
As the see of welles and sprynges
And it was shapen lyke a cage
  Certes (quod I) in al myn age
Ne sawe I suche an house as this
And as I wondred me ywis
Vpon this house/tho ware was I
Howe myne Egle faste by
Was perched hye vpon a stone
And I gan streight to hym gone
And sayd thus/I pray the
That thou a whyle abyde me
For goddes loue/and let me sene
What wonders in that place bene
For yet peraunter I may lere
Some good therin/or somwhat here
That lefe me were/or that I went
  Peter/that is nowe myn entent
(Quod he to me) therfore I dwel
But certayne one thyng I the tel
That but I bringe the therin
Ne shal thou neuer conne the gyn
To come in to it/out of doute
So faste it whyrleth lo aboute
But sythe that Ioues of his grace
As I haue sayd/wyl the solace
Finally with these thynges
Vncouthe syghtes and tidynges
To passe with thyne heuynesse
Suche routhe hath he of thy distresse
That thou suffredest debonairly
And woste thy seluen vtterly
Desperate of al blysse
Sythe that fortune hath made a mysse
The swote of al thyn hertes rest
Languysshe/and eke in poynte to brest
But he through his myghtie meryte
Wyl do the ease/al be it lyte
And gaue in expresse cōmaundement
To whiche I am obedyent
To forther the with al my might
And wysse and teche the a right
Where thou mayste moste tidynges here
Thou shalte here many one lere
  With this worde he right anone
Hent me vp bytwene his tone
And at a wyndowe in me brought
That in this house was/as me thought
And there withal me thought it stent
And nothyng it aboute went
And me sette in the floore adoun
But suche a great congregacioun
Of folke/as I sawe rome aboute
Some within and some without
Nas neuer sene/ne shal be efte
That certes in this worlde nys lefte
So many formed by nature
Ne deed so many a creature
That wel vnneth in that place
Had I a foote brede of space
And euery wight that I sawe there
Rowned eueryche in others eere
A newe tidyng priuely
Or els it tolde al openly
Right thus/and sayd: Nost nat thou
That is betydde/lo right now
  No (quod he) tel me what
And than he tolde him this and that
And swore therto/that it was sothe
Thus hath he sayd/and thus he dothe
And this shal be/and thus herde I say
That shal be founde/that dare I saye
That al the folke that is on lyue
Ne haue the connyng to discryue
Tho thynges that I herde there
What a loude/and what in eere
But al the wonder moste was this
Whan one had herde a thyng ywis
He came streyght to another wyght
And gan hym tellen anon right
The same that hym was tolde
Or it a furlonge way was olde
And gan somwhat for to eche
To this tydyng in this speche
More than euer it spoken was
And nat so sone departed nas
Tho fro hym that he ne mette
With the thirde/and er he lette
Any stounde/he tolde hym alse
Were the tydynges sothe or falle
Yet wolde he tel it natheles
And euer mo with more encrees
Than it was erst: thus northe and southe
Went euery tydyng/fro mouthe to mouthe
And

The thirde boke of Fame.

And that encreasyng euermo
As fyre is wonte to quicken and go
From a sparcle sprongen amps
Tyl al a cyte brent vp is
  And whan that was ful vp spronge
And waxen more on euery tonge
Than euer it was/and went anone
Vp to a wyndowe out to gone
Or but it might out there passe
It gan out crepe at some creuasse
And flewe forthe faste for the nones
  And somtyme I sawe there at ones
A leasyng/ and a sadde sothe sawe
That gonnen of auenture drawe
Out at a wyndowe for to pace
And whan they metten in that place
They were a checked bothe two
And neyther of hem might out go
For eche other they gonne so croude
Tyl eche of hem gan cryen loude
Let me gon first/nay but let me
And here I wol ensuren the
With nones that thou wolte do so
That I shal neuer fro the go
But be thyn owne sworne brother
We wol meddle vs eche in other
That no man be he neuer so wrothe
Shal haue one two/but bothe
At ones/ al besyde his leue
Come we amorowe or on eue
Be we cryde or styl prowned
Thus sawe I false and sothe compowned
Togyder flye for o tydynge
Thus out at holes gonne wringe
Euery tydyng streyght to Fame
And she gan yeue eche his name
After her disposycion
And yeue hem eke duracion
Some to wexe and wane soone
As dothe the fayre whyte moone
And let hem gone/there might I seen
Wynged wonders faste flyen
Twenty thousande in a route
As Eolus hem blewe aboute
And lorde this house in al tymes
Was ful of shypmen and pylgrymes
With scrippes brette ful of leasynges
Entremelled with tidynges
And eke alone by hem selue
O many thousande tymes twelue
Sawe I eke of these pardoners
Currours/and eke messangers
With boxes crōmed ful of lyes
As euer vessel was with lyes
And as I alther fastest went
Aboute / and dyd al myn entent
Me for to playen and for to lere
And eke a tyding for to here
That I had herde of some countre
That shal nat nowe be tolde for me
For it no nede is redily
Folke can synge it bet than I
For al mote out late or rathe
Al the sheues in the rathe
  I herde a great noyse withal
In a corner of the hal
There men of loue tydinges tolde
And I gan thyderwarde beholde
For I sawe rennyng euery wyght
As faste as that they hadden myght
And eueryche cryde/what thing is that
And some sayd I not neuer what
And whan they were al on an hepe
Tho behynde gonne vp lepe
And clamben vp on other faste
And vp the noyse on hyghen caste
And treden faste on others heles
And stampe as men don after eles
  At the laste I sawe a man
Whiche that I naught ne can
But he semed for to be
A man of great auctorite
  And therwithal I abrayde
Out of my slepe halfe a frayde
Rememberyng wel what I had sene
And howe hye and ferre I had ben:
In my goost/ and had great wonder
Of that the god of thonder
Had let me knowen/and began to write
Lyke as ye haue herde me endyte
Wherfore to studye and rede alway
I purpose to do day by day
  Thus in dreamyng and in game
Endeth this lytel boke of Fame.

¶ Here foloweth the Testament of Loue.

The testament of loue.

MAny men there ben/ that wᵗ eeres openly sprad so moche swalowen the delyciousnesse of iestes and of ryme/ by queynt knyttyng coloures/ that of the goodnesse or of the badnesse of the sentence take they lytel hede or els none. Sothely dul wytte and a thoughtful soule/ so sore haue myned and graffed in my spyrites/ that suche craft of endytyng wol not ben of myn acqueyntaūce. And for rude wordes and boystous percen the herte of the herer to the inrest poynte/ and planten there the sentence of thynges/ so that with lytel helpe it is able to spring. This boke that nothyng hath of the great floode of wyt/ ne of semelych colours/ is doluen with rude wordes and boystous/ and so drawe togyder to maken the catchers therof ben the more redy to hent sentēce.

Some men there ben that peynten with colours ryche/ and some with vers/ as with red ynke/ and some with coles and chalke: and yet is there good matere to the leude people of thilke chalky purtreyture/ as hem thynketh for the tyme/ and afterwarde the syght of the better colours yeuen to hem more ioye for the first leudenesse. So sothly this leude clowdy occupacion is not to prayse/ but by the leude: for comenly leude leudenesse cōmendeth. Eke it shal yeue syght that other precious thynges shal be the more in reuerence. In latyn and frenche hath many soueraygne wyttes had gret delyte to endyte/ and haue many no[illegible]ynges fulfylde/ but certes there ben so[illegible] speken their poysye mater in frenche/ of whiche speche the frenche men haue as good a fantasye as we haue in heryng of frenche mennes englysshe. And many termes there ben in englysshe/ whiche vnneth we englysshmen connen declare the knowlegynge: howe shulde than a frenche man borne/ suche termes conne iumpere in his mater/ but as the iay chatereth englysshe. Right so trewly the vnderstandyng of englysshmen wol not stretche to the priuy termes in frenche/ what so euer we bosten of straunge langage. Let than clerkes endyten in latyn/ for they haue the propertie of science and the knowynge in that facultie: and lette frenchmen in their frenche also endyten their queynt termes/ for it is kyndely to their mouthes/ and let vs shewe our fantasyes in suche wordes as we lerneden of our dames tonge. And although this boke be lytel thanke worthy for the leudnesse in trauaile/ yet suche writynges exciten men to thilke thynges that ben necessarie: for euery man therby may as by a perpetual myrrour sene the vyces or vertues of other/ in whiche thyng lightely may be conceyued to eschewe perylls/ and necessaryes to catche/ after as auentures haue fallen to other people or psons. Certes the soueraynst thyng of desyre and moste creature reasonable/ haue or els shulde haue ful appetyte to their perfection: vnresonable beestes mowen not/ sythe reason hath in hem no werkyng. Than reasonable that wol not/ is comparysoned to vnresonable/ and made lyke hem. Forsothe the most soueraygne and fynal perfection of man is in knowyng of a sothe/ withouten any entent disceyuable/ and in loue of one very god/ that is inchaungeable/ that is to knowe and loue his creatour. ¶ Nowe principally the meane to bringe in knowlegyng and louyng his creatour/ is the consyderacion of thynges made by the creatour/ wherthrough be thilke thynges that ben made vnderstondyng here to our wyttes/ arne the vnsene priuytees of god made to vs sightful and knowyng/ in our cōtemplacion & vnderstōdyng. These thynges than forsoth moche bringen vs to yͤ ful knowlegynge sothe/ and to the parfyte loue of the maker of heuenly thynges. Lo Dauid sayth: thou haste delyted me in makynge/ as who sayth/ to haue delyte in the tyme how god hath lent me in consyderacion of thy makynge. Wherof Aristotle in the boke de Animalibus/ sayth to naturel phylosophers: It is a great lykyng in loue of knowynge their creatour: and also in knowynge of causes in kyndely thynges cōsydred. Forsoth the formes of kyndly thynges and the shap/ a great kyndely loue me shulde haue to the werkman yͤ hem made. The crafte of a werkman is shewed in the werke. Herfore truly the phylosophers with a lyuely studye many noble thynges/ ryght

L.l.l.ii. preci=

precious and worthy to memory writen / ⁊ by a great swetande trauayle to us lesten of causes the propertyes in natures of thynges. To whiche therfore· Phylosophers it was more ioy/more lykynge / more herty lust in kyndely vertues and matters of reason the perfection by busy study to knowe / than to haue had al the treasour/al the richesse/al the vaynglory ye the passed Emperours / prynces / or kynges hadden. Therfore the names of hem in ye boke of perpetual memory in vertue and peace arn wryten/and in the contrarye/that is to sayne/ in stixe the foule pytte of helle arn thilke pressed that suche goodnesse hated. And bycause this boke shal be of loue / and the pryme causes of sterynge in that doynge with passyons and dyseases for wantynge of desyre / I wyl that this boke be cleped ye Testament of loue.

But nowe thou reder/ who is thylke that wyl not in scorne laughe / to here a dwarfe or els halfe a man/say he wyl rende out the swerde of Hercules handes/and also he shulde set Hercules gades a myle yet ferther/ and ouer that he had power of strengthe to pul up the spere/ that Alisander the noble might neuer wagge.

And that passyng al thynge to ben mayster of Fraunce by myght/there as the noble gracyous Edwarde the thyrde for al his great prowesse in victories ne myght al yet cõquere.

Certes I wote wel/ there shal be made more scorne ⁊ iape of me/that I so unworthely clothed al togyder in the cloudy cloude of unconnynge wyl putten me in prees to speke of loue/or els of the causes in that matter/sythen al the grettest clerkes han had ynough to don/ and as who sayth gathered up clene toforne hem/and with theyr sharpe sythes of connyng al mowen and made therof great rekes and noble/ful of al plentyes to fede me and many another. Enuye forsothe cõmendeth nought his reason/that he hath in hayn/ be it neuer so trusty. And al thoughe these noble repers/ as good workmen and worthy theyr hyer / han al drawe and bounde up in ye sheues/ ⁊ made many shockes / yet haue I ensample to gader the smale crõmes/and fullyn my walet of tho that fallen from the borde amonge the smale houndes / notwithstandynge the trauayle of the almoygner / that hath drawe up in ye cloth al the remyssayles/as trenchours/ and the relyef to bere to the almesse. Yet also haue I leue of the noble husbande Boece/ al though I be a straunger of connynge to come after his doctryne/and these great workmen/and glene my handfuls of the shedynge after theyr handes/⁊ if me fayle ought of my ful/ to encrease my porcyon with that I shal drawe by pryuytyes out of the shocke / a slye seruaunt in his owne helpe is often moche cõmended/ knowyng of trouth in causes of thynges/ was more hardyer in the first sechers/and so sayth Aristotle/ ⁊ lyghter in us that han folowed after. For theyr passyng study han fresshed our wyttes/and our understandynge han excyted in consideracion of trouth by sharpnesse of theyr reasons. Utterly these thynges be no dremes ne iapes/to throwe to hogges / it is lyfelyche meate for chyldren of trouthe/and as they me betiden whan I pilgrymaged out of my kyth in wynter / whan the wether out of measure was boystous/⁊ the wylde wynde Borias as his kynde asketh with dryenge coldes/ maked the wawes of the occian see so to aryse unkyndely ouer the cõmune bankes that it was in poynte to spyl al the erthe.

¶ Thus endeth the prologue/ and here after foloweth the fyrst boke of the Testament of Loue.

ALas Fortune alas/ I that somtyme in delycyous houres was wont to enioy blyssful stoundes/ am nowe dryue by unhappy heuynesse to bewayle my sondrye yuels in tene. Trewly I leue/ in myn herte is writte of perdurable letters al the entencyons of lamentacion that nowe ben ynempned/ for any maner disease outwarde in sobbyng maner/ sheweth sorowful yexynge from within. Thus from my comforte I gynne to spylle/ syth she that shulde me solace/ is ferre fro my presence. Certes her absence is to me an hell/ my sternyng dethe thus in wo it myneth/ that endelesse care is throughout myne herte clenched/ blysse of my ioye/ that ofte me murthed is turned in to galle/ to thynke on thyng that may not at my wyl in armes me hent. Myrth is chaunged in to tene/ whan swynke is there contynually/ that reste was wont to soiourne and haue dwellynge place. Thus wytlesse thoughtful/ syghtlesse lokynge/ I endure my penaunce in this derke prisone/ caytisned fro frendshippe and acquayntaunce/ and forsaken of al that any wode dare speke. Straunge hath by waye of intrucyoun made his home/ there me shulde be/ if reason were herde as he shulde. Neuer the later yet hertly lady precious Margarit/ haue mynde on thy seruaunt/ and thynke on his disease/ how lyghtles he lyueth/ sithe the beames brennende in loue of thyn eyen arn so bewent/ that worldes & cloudes atwene betwey wol nat suffre my thoughtes of hem to be enlumyned. Thynke that one vertue of a Margarite precious is amonges many other the sorouful to comforte yet wyl of that me sorouful to comforte is my luste to haue nought els at this tyme/ dede ne dethe/ ne no maner trauayle hath no power myne herte so moche to fade/ as shulde to here of a twynckelynge in your disease. Ah/ god forbede that/ but yet lette me dey/ lette me sterue withouten any measure of penaunce/ rather than myne hertely thynking comforte in ought were diseased. What maye my seruyce auayle in absence of her/ that my seruyce shulde accepte? is this nat endlesse sorowe to thynke? Yes/ yes god wote/ myne hert breaketh nygh a sonder/ howe shulde the grounde without kyndly norture bringen forthe any frutes? howe shulde a shippe withouten a sterne in the great see be gouerned? Howe shulde I withouten my blysse/ my herte/ my desyre/ my ioye/ my goodnesse/ endure in this contrarious prison/ that thynke euery hour in the day an hundred wynter? Wel may nowe Eue sayne to me Adam/ in sorowe fallen from welth/ driuen arte thou out of paradise/ with sweate thy sustenaunce to be swynke. Depe in this pynynge pytte with wo I lygge ystocked/ with chaynes lynked of care & of tene. It is so hye from thens I lye and the comune erth/ there ne is cable in no londe maked/ that myght streche to me to drawe me unto blysse/ ne steyers to step on is none/ so that without recouer endlesse here to endure I wotte wel I purueyde. O/ where arte thou nowe frenshyppe/ that somtyme with laughande chere/ madest bothe face and countenaunce to me wardes? truely nowe arte thou went out of towne/ but euer me thynketh he weareth his olde clothes/ & that ẏ soule in the whiche the lyfe of frendshyppe was in/ is drawen out from his other spyrites. Nowe than farewel frendshyp/ and farewel felawes/ me thynketh ye al han taken your leaue: no force of you al at ones. But lady of loue ye wote what I mene/ yet thinke on thy seruaunt/ that for thy loue spylleth/ al thynges haue I forsake to folowen thyn hestes: rewarde me with a thought/ though ye do naught els. Remembraunce of loue lythe so sore under my brest/ that other thought cometh not in my mynde/ but gladnesse to thynke on your goodnesse and your mery chere/ frendes and sorowe to thynke on your wrethe and your daunger/ from whiche Christe me saue. My great ioye it is to haue in meditacion the bounties/ the vertues/ the nobley in you printed: sorowe and hel comen at ones/ to suppose that I be veyned. Thus with care/ sorowe/ and tene am I shapte myn ende with dethe to make. Nowe good goodly thynke on this. O wretched foole that I am fallen in to so lowe/ the heate of my brennyng tene hath me al defased: how shulde ye lady sette prise on so foule fylthe? My connynge is thynne/ my wytte is exiled/

L.l.l.iii. lyke

The Testament of Love: I. i. 1–67 (A)

lyke to a foole naturel am I comparysoned. Trewly lady but your mercy the more were/ I wote wel al my labour were in ydel: your mercy than passeth right. God graunt that proposycion to be verifyed in me/ so that by truste of good hope/ I mowe come to the hauen of ease/ and sythe it is impossyble/ the colours of your qualyties to chaunge: and forsothe I wote wel wemme ne spotte maye not abyde/ there so noble vertue haboundeth/ so that the defasyng to you is verily ymagynable/ as countenaunce of goodnesse with encresynge vertue/ is so in you knytte to abyde by necessary maner/ yet if the revers might fal/ whiche is ayenst kynde/ I wol wel myn herte ne shulde therfore naught flytte by the leste poynt of gemetrye/ so sadly is it fonded/ that away from your servyce in loue maye he not departe. O loue/ whan shal I ben pleased? O charyte/ whan shal I ben eased? O good goodly/ whan shal the dyce turne? O ful of vertue do the chaunce of comforte upwarde to fal. O loue/ whan wolt thou thynke on thy seruaunt? I can no more but here out caste of al welfare/ abyde the daye of my dethe/ or els to se the syght that might al my wellynge sorowes voyde/ and of the flodde make an ebbe. These diseases mowen wel by duresse of sorowe/ make my lyfe to unbodye/ and so for to dye: but certes ye lady in a ful perfectyon of loue ben so knytte with my soule/ that dethe may not thilke knotte unbynde ne departe/ so that ye and my soule togyther is endelesse/ in blysse shulde dwel/ and there shal my soule at the ful ben eased/ that he may haue your presence to shewe thentent of his desyres: Ah dere god/ that shal be a great ioye. Nowe erthely goddesse take regarde of thy seruant/ though I be feble/ for thou arte wonte to prayse them better/ that wolde conne serue in loue/ al be he ful mener than kynges or princes/ that wol not haue that vertue in mynde. Nowe precious Margaryte/ that with thy noble vertue haste drawen me in to loue first/ me weyynge therof to haue blysse/ as galle and aloes are so moche spronge/ that sauour of swetnesse may I not ataste. Alas that your benigne eyen/ in whiche that mercy semeth to haue al his norture/ nyl by no waye tourne the clerenesse of mercy to mewardes. Alas that your brennande vertues/ shynyng amonges al folke/ and enlumynynge al other people by haboundaunce of encreasing/ sheweth to me but smoke and no light. These thynges to thinke in myn herte maketh every day weping in myn eyen to renne. These lyggen on my backe so sore/ that importable burthen me semeth on my backe to be charged/ it maketh me backwarde to meue/ whan my steppes by comune course even forthe pretende: These thynges also on right syde and lyft/ haue me so envolued with care/ that wanhope of helpe is throughout me ronne/ trewly and leue that gracelesse is my fortune/ whiche that ever sheweth it mewardes by a cloudy disease/ al redy to make stormes of tene/ and the blysful syde halte styl awayward/ and wol it not suffre to mewardes to turne: no force/ yet wol I not ben cõquered.

O/ alas that your nobley so moche among al other creatures cõmended by folowynge streme by al maner vertues/ but ther ben wõderful/ I not whiche that let the flode to come in to my soule/ wherfore purely mated with sorowe thorough sought/ my selfe I crye on your goodnesse to haue pyte on this captife/ that in the inrest degre of sorowe and disease is lefte/ & without your goodly wyl from any helpe and recouery. These sorowes maye I not sustene/ but if my sorowe shulde be tolde and to you wardes shewed/ although moche space is bytwene us twayne/ yet me thynketh that by suche ioleynynge wordes/ my disease gynneth ebbe. Trewly me thynketh that the sowne of my lamentacious weping/ is right nowe flowe in to your presence/ & there cryeth after mercy & grace/ to which thing me semeth the lyst none answere to yeue/ but with a deynous chere ye cõmaunden it to auoyde/ but god forbyd that any worde shuld of you springe to haue so lytel routh. Parde pyte & mercy in euery Margarite is closed by kynde amõges many other vertues/ by qualites of comforte/ but comfort is to me right naught worthe/ withouten mercy and pyte of you alone/ whiche thynges hastely god me graũt for his mercy.

¶ Reher-

REhersynge these thynges and many other/ without tyme or moment of rest me semed for anguysshe of disease/ that al togyder I was rauysshed/ I can not tel howe/ but holy al my passyons and felynges weren loste/ as it semed for the tyme/ and sodaynly a maner of drede light in me al at ones/ nought suche feare as folke haue of an enemy that were myghty/ and wolde hem greue or done hem disease: For I trowe this is wel knowe to many persones/ that otherwhyle if a man be in his soueraygnes presence/ a maner of ferdenesse crepeth in his herte/ not for harme/ but of goodly subjection: namely as men reden that aungels ben aferde of our sauyour in heuen. And parde there ne is/ ne maye no passyon of disease be/ but it is to meane that angels ben adradde/ not by frendes of drede/ sythen they ben perfytely blyssed/ as affection of wonderfulnesse & by seruyce of obedyence/ suche ferde also han these louers in presence of their loues/ and subiectes afore their souerayndes: Right so with ferdenesse myn herte was caught. And I sodaynly astonyed/ there entred in to the place there I was lodged a lady/ the semelyest and moste goodly to my syght/ that euer to forne apered to any creature/ and trewly in the blustrynge of her looke/ she yaue gladnesse and comforte sodaynely to al my wyttes/ and ryght so she dothe to euery wyght that cometh in her presence. And for she was so goodly (as me thought) myne herte beganne somdele to be enbolded/ and wexte a lytel hardy to speke/ but yet with a quakynge voyce/ as I durste/ I salued her/ and enquired what she was/ and why she so worthy to syght/ dayned to entre in to so foule a dongeon/ and namely a prisone/ without leaue of my kepers. For certes al thoughe the vertue of dedes of mercy stretchen to vysyten the poore prisoners/ and hem after that faculties ben had to comforte/ me semed that I was so ferre fallen in to myserye and wretched hyd captifnesse/ that me shulde no precyous thynge neyghe: and also that for my sorowe euery wyght shulde ben heauy/ and wysshe my recouery. But whan this lady had somdele apperceyued/ as wel by my wordes as by my chere/ what thought besyed me within/ with a good womanly countenaunce she sayde these wordes.

O my nory/ wenyst thou that my maner be/ to forget my frendes or my seruauntes? nay (quod she) it is my ful entente to vysyte and comforte al my frenshippes and allyes/ as wel in tyme of perturbation/ as of moost propertye of blysse/ in me shal vnkyndnesse neuer be founden. And also sithen I haue so fewe especial trewe nowe in these dayes/ wherfore I maye wel at more leysar come to hem that me deseruen/ and if my comynge maye in any thynge auayle/ wete wel I wol come often.

Nowe good lady (quod I) that art so fayre on to loke/ reynynge hony by thy wordes/ blysse of paradise arn thy lokynges/ ioye and comforte are thy mouynges. What is thy name? howe is it that in you is so mokel werkynge vertues enpight/ as me semeth/ and in none other creature yͤ euer sawe I with myne eyen? My disciple (quod she) me wondreth of thy wordes and on the/ yͤ for a lytel disease hast forgeten my name: Woste thou not wel that I am Loue/ that first the brought to thy seruyce? O good lady (qđ I) is this worshyppe to the or to thyne excellence for to come in to so foule a place? Parde somtyme tho I was in prosperyte/ and with forayne goodes enuolued/ I had mokyl to done to drawe the to myn hostel/ and yet many wernynges thou madest er thou lyste fully to graunt/ thyne home to make at my dwellyng place: & nowe thou comest goodly by thyne owne vyse/ to comforte me with wordes/ and so there thoroughe I gynne remembre on passed gladnesse. Trewly lady I ne wotte whether I shal say welcome or none/ sythen thy comyng wol as moche do me tene and sorowe/ as gladnesse and myrthe: se why. For that me comforteth to thynke on passed gladnesse/ that me anoyeth efte to be in doynge. Thus thy comynge bothe gladdeth and teneth/ and that is cause of moche sorowe: Lo lady/ howe than

than I am comforted by your companye/ and with that I gan in teeres to distylle/ and tenderly wepe. Nowe certes (quod Loue) I se wel (and that me ouerthynketh) that wytte in the fayleth/ and arte in poynte to dote.

Trewly (quod I) that haue ye maked/ and that euer wol I rue. Wottest thou not wel (quod she) that euery shepeherde ought by reson to seke his sperkelande shepe that arne ronne in to wyldernesse/ amonge busshes and peryls/ and hem to their pasture ayen bringe/ and take on hem pyny besy cure of keppyng? and tho the vnconnynge shepe scattred wolde ben loste/ rennyng to wyldernesse/ and to desertes drawe/ or els wolden put hem selfe to the swalowyng wolfe/ yet shal the shepeherde by busynesse and trauayle so put him forthe/ that he shal not let hem be loste by no waye. A good shepeherde putteth rather his lyfe to ben loste for his shepe. But for thou shalte not wene me beyng of werse condycion/ trewly for euerych of my folke/ and for al tho that to mewarde ben knyt in any condycion/ I wol rather dye than suffre hem throughe errour to ben spylte. For me lyste/ and it me lyketh/ of al myne a shepherdesse to be cleped. Wost thou not wel I fayled neuer wight/ but he me refused/ & wolde neglygently go with vnkyndenesse? and yet parde haue I many such holpe and rescued/ and they haue ofte me begyled/ but euer at the ende it discendeth in their owne neckes. Haste thou not radde howe kynde I was to Paris/ Priamus sone of Troy? How Iason me falsed for al his false behest? howe Cesars sonke/ I lefte it for no tene tyl he was troned in my blysse for his seruyce. What (qd she) most of al/ maked I not a louedaye bytwene god and mankynde/ and chese a mayde to be nompere/ to put the quarel at ende? Lo/ howe I haue trauayled to haue thanke on al sydes/ & yet lyst me not to rest/ & I mi3t fynde on home I shulde werche. But trewly myn owne disciple/ bycause I haue the founde at al assayes in thy wyl to be redy myn hestes to haue folowed/ & haste ben trewe to that Margaryte perle/ that ones I the shewed/ and she alwaye ayenwarde hath made but daunge-rous chere/ I am come in propre person to put the out of errours/ and make the gladde by wayes of reason/ so that sorowne disease shal no more hereafter the amaistry. Wherthrough I hope thou shalte lyghtly come to the grace/ that thou longe haste desyred/ of thylke iewel. Haste thou not herde many ensamples/ howe I haue comforted and rescued the scholers of my lore? Who hath worthyed kynges in the felde? Who hath honoured ladyes in boure by a perpetuel myrrour of their truthe in my seruyce? Who hath caused worthy folke to voyde vyce and shame? Who hath holde cyties and realmes in prosperyte? if the lyste cleape ayen thyn olde remembraunce/ thou coudest euery poynte of this declare in especial/ and say that I thy maystresse haue be cause/ causyng these thynges and many mo other. Nowe iwys madame (quod I) al these thynges I knowe wel my selfe/ and that thyn excellence passeth the vnderstandyng of vs beestes/ and that no mannes wytte erthely may comprehende thy vertues. Wel than (quod she) for I se the in disease and sorowe/ I wote wel thou arte one of myn nories/ I maye not suffre the so to make sorowe/ thyn owne selfe to shende: but I my selfe come to be thy fere/ thyne heuy charge to make to seme the lesse/ for wo is him that is alone: And to the sorye to ben moned by a sorouful wight it is great gladnesse. Right so with my sycke freendes I am sicke/ and with sorie I can not els but sorowe make/ tyl whan I haue hem releued/ in suche wyse that gladnesse in a maner of counterpaysyng shal restore as mokyl in ioye as the passed heuynesse byforne dyd in tene. And also (qd she) whan any of my seruauntes ben alone in solytary place/ I haue yet euer besyed me to be with hem/ in comforte of their hertes/ and taught hem to make songes of playnte and of blysse/ and to endyten letters of rethorike in queynt vnderstondynges/ & to bethynke hem in what wyse they might best their ladyes in good seruyce please/ and also to serue maner in coūtenaūce/ in wordes/ & in bearyng/ & to ben meke and lowly to euery wight/ his name & fame to encrease/ and to yeue gret yeftes & large/ yͤ his renome

renome maye springen/ but the therof haue I excused for thy losse and thy great costages/ wherthroughe thou arte nedy/ arne nothinge to me vnknowen/ but I hope to god somtyme it shal ben amended/ as thus as I sayd. In norture haue I taught al myne/ and in curtesye made hem expert their ladyes hertes to wynne/ and if any wolde endeynous or proude or be enuyous/ or of wretches acqueyntaunce/ hastelyche haue I suche voyded out of my schole: for al vyces trewly I hate: vertues and worthynesse in al my power I auaunce. Ah worthy creature (quod I) and by iuste cause the name of goddesse dignely ye mowe beare: In the sythe the grace thorough whiche any creature in this worlde hath any goodnesse/ trewly al maner of blysse and preciousnesse in vertue out of the springen/ and wellen/ as brokes and ryuers proceden from their springes/ and lyke as al waters by kynde drawen to the see/ so al kyndely thynges thresten by ful appetyte of desyre to drawe after thy steppes/ and to thy presence aproche/ as to their kyndely perfection: Howe dare than beestes in this worlde aught forfete ayenst thy deuyne purueyaunce? Also lady ye knowen al the priuy thoughtes/ in hertes no counsayle maye ben hydde from your knowyng. Wherfore I wote wel lady that ye knowe your selfe that I in my conscie̅ce am and haue ben wyllynge to your seruyce/ al coude I neuer do as I shulde/ yet forsothe fayned I neuer to loue otherwyse than was in myn herte: and if I coude haue made chere to one/ and ythought another/ as many other doone aldaye afore myn eyen/ I trowe it wolde not me haue vayled. Certes (quod she) haddest thou so done/ I wolde not nowe haue the here vysited. Ye were wel lady eke (quod I) that I haue not playde raket/ nettyl in/ docke out/ and with the wethercocke waued/ and trewly there ye me sette/ by acorde of my conscience/ I wolde not flye/ tyl ye and reason by aperte strength maden myn herte to tourne. In good faythe (quod she) I haue knowe the euer of tho condycions/ and sythen thou woldest (in as moche as in the was) a made me priuy of thy counsayle/ and iuge of thy conscie̅ce/ though I forsoke it in tho dayes/ tyl I saw better my tyme/ wolde neuer god that I shuld nowe fayle/ but euer I wol be redy wytnessyng thy sothe/ in what place that euer I shal/ ayenst al tho that wol the contrary susteyne: And for as moche as to me is naught vnknowen ne hyd of thy priuy hert/ but al hast thou tho thynges made to me open at the ful/ that hath caused my comynge in to this prison to voyde the webbes of thyne eyen/ to make the clerely to se the errours thou hast ben in/ and bycause that men ben of dyuers condycions/ some a dradde to saye a sothe/ and some for a sothe anone redy to fyght/ and also that I maye not my selfe ben in place to withsay thilke men that of the speken/ other wyse than the sothe/ I wol and I charge the in vertue of obedyence/ that thou to me owest/ to writen my wordes/ and sette hem in writynges that they mowe as my witnessynge ben noted amonge the people. For bookes written neyther dreden ne shamen/ ne stryue conne/ but onely shewen the entente of the writer/ and yeue remembraunce to the herer: and if any wol in thy presence saye any thynge to tho writers/ loke boldely/ truste on Marc to answere at the ful. For certes I shal hym enfourme of al the trouthe in thy loue/ with thy conscience/ so that of his helpe thou shalte not varye at thy nede. I trowe the strongest and the beste that maye be founde/ wol not transuers thy wordes/ wherof than woldest thou drede.

Certly was I tho gladed of these wordz/ and as who sayth wexen somdele light in herte/ both for the auctorite of witnesse/ and also for sykernesse of helpe of the forsayd beheste/ and sayd. Trewly lady nowe am I wel gladded through comforte of your wordes: be it nowe lykynge vnto your nobley to shewe whiche folke diffame your seruauntes/ sythe your seruyce ought aboue al other thynges to ben co̅mended. Yet (quod she) I se wel thy soule is not al out of the amased cloude: the were better to here thyng that the myght lighte out of thyn heuy charge/ and after knowyng of thyn owne helpe/ than to styrre swete wordes and des/ and such resons to here: for in a thoughtful soule (and namely suche one as thou arte) wol not yet suche thynges synken. Come of therfore and let me sene thy heuy charge/ that I may the lyghtlyer for thy comforte puruey.

Nowe certes lady (quod I) the moste comforte I myght haue/ were vtterly to wete me be sure in herte of that Margaryte I serue/ and so I thinke to don with al mightes whyle my lyfe dureth. Than (qd she) mayste thou therafter/ in suche wyse that my plesaunce ne entre? In good fayth (quod I) there shal no misplesaunce be caused through trespace on my syde. And I do the to weten (quod she) I set neuer yet person to serue in no place (but if he caused the cōtrary in defautes and trespaces) that he ne spedde of his seruyce. Myn owne erthly lady (quod I tho) and yet remembre to your worthynesse howe long sythen by many reuolupng of yeres/ in tyme whan October his leaue gynneth take/ & Nouembre shewеth hym to syght/ whan bernes ben ful of goodes as is the nutte on euery halke/ and than good londe tyllers gynne shape for the erthe/ with great trauayle to bringe forthe more corne to mannes sustenaunce/ ayenst the nexte yeres folowyng. In suche tyme of plentie/ he that hath an home/ and is wyse/ lyste not to wander meruayles to seche/ but he be constrayned or excited: oft the sothe thyng is doone by excytacion of other mannes opynyon/ whiche wolden fayne haue myn abydynge/ take in herte of luste to trauayle and se the wyndyng of the erthe in that tyme of wynter/ by woodes that large stretes werne in/ by smale pathes that swyne and hogges hadden made/ as lanes with ladels their maste to seche/ I walked thynkynge alone a wonder great whyle/ and the great beestes that the woode haunten and adorneth al maner forestes / and heerdes gone to wylde: than er I was ware I neyghed to a see banke/ and for ferde of the beestes shypcrafte I crydе: For lady I trowe ye wete wel your selfe nothyng is werse than the beestes that shulden ben tame/ if they catche her wyldenesse/ and gynne ayen waxe ramage: thus forsothe was I a ferde/ and to shyppe me hyed. Than were there ynowe to lache myn handes and drawe me to shyppe/ of whiche many I knewe wel the names. Syght was the first/ lust was a nother/ thought was the thirde/ and wyl eke was there a mayster: these broughten me within borde of this shyppe of trauayle. So whan the sayle was sprad and this shyppe gan to moue/ the wynde and water gan for to ryse/ and ouertwhartly to turne the welken/ the wawes semeden as they kyste togyder/ but often vnder colour of kyssynge is mokel olde hate priuely closed and kepte. The storme so straungely and in a deuouring maner gan so faste vs assayle/ that I supposed the date of my deth shulde haue made there his gynnyng/ nowe vp nowe downe/ nowe vnder the wawe and nowe abouen was my shyppe a great whyle. And so by mokel duresse of wethers & of stormes/ and with great auowyng pylgrimages I was driuen to an yle/ where vtterly I wende first to haue be rescowed/ but trewly as the first gynnyng it semed me so perillous the hauen to catche/ that but thorowe grace I had ben comforted/ of lyfe I was ful dispayred. Trewly lady if ye remembre a right of al maner thynges/ your selfe came hastely to sene vs see driuen/ and to weten what we weren: but first ye were deynous of chere/ after whiche ye gonne better alyght/ & euer as me thought ye lyued in great drede of disease/ it semed so by your chere. And whan I was certifyed of your name/ the lenger I loked in you / the more I you goodly drad/ and euer myn herte on you opened the more/ and so in a lytel tyme my shyppe was out of mynde. But lady as ye me lad I was ware bothe of beestes and of fysshes a great nombre throngyng togyder: amonge whiche a muskel in a blewe shel had enclosed a Margaryte perle/ the moste precious and best that euer to forne came in my syght/ and ye tolden your selfe that ylke iewel in his kynde was so good and so vertuous/ that her better shulde I neuer fynde/ al sought I therafter to the worldes ende/ and with that I helde my peace a great whyle: and euer sythen I haue me bethought on the man that sought the precious Margarytes/ and whan he had founden one to his lykyng/ he solde al his good to bye that iewel.

iewel: I wys thought I and yet so I thynke/ nowe haue I founden the iewel/ that myne herte desyreth/ wherto shulde I seche further/ trewly nowe wol I stynte/ and on this Margaryte I sette me for euer. Nowe than also sythen I wyste wel it was your wyl that I shulde so suche a seruyce me take/ and so to desyre that thing/ of whiche I neuer haue blisse/ there lyueth none/ but he hath disease: your might than that brought me to suche seruyce/ that to me is cause of sorowe and of ioye/ I wõder of your worde that ye sayne/ to bringen men in to ioye/ and parde ye wete wel that defaut ne trespace may not reasonably ben put to me wardes/ as ferre as my conscience knoweth: But of my disease me lyst now a whyle to speke/ & to enforme you in what maner of blysse ye haue me thronge. For truly I wene that al gladnesse/ al ioye/ and al myrthe is beshet vnder locke/ and the keye throwe in suche place that it may not be founde: my brennyng wo hath altred al my hewe. Whan I shulde slepe/ I walowe & I thynke/ and me disporte. Thus combred/ I seme that al folke had me mased. Also lady myne/ desyre hath longe dured/ some speking to haue/ or els at yͤ lest haue ben enmoysed with syght: and for wantynge of these thinges/ my mouthe wolde & hẽ durst/ pleyne right sore/ sythen yuels for my goodnesse arne manyfolde to me yolden. I wonder lady trewly/ saue euermore your reuerẽce/ howe ye mowe for shame suche thynges suffre on your seruaunt to be so multyplied: Wheron your seruaunt to be so multyplied: Wherfore knelyng with a lowe herte I pray you to rue on this caytife/ that of nothyng now may serue. Good lady if ye lyste nowe your helpe to me shewe/ that am of your priuyest seruantes at al assayes in this tyme/ and vnder your wynges of protection. No helpe to me wardes is shapen/ howe shal than straungers in any wyse after socoure loke/ whan I that am so priuy/ yet of helpe I do fayle? Further maye I not/ but thus in this prison abyde: what bondes and chaynes me holden/ lady ye se wel your selfe? A renyant forjuged hath not halfe the care. But thus syghyng and sobbyng I wayle here alone/ and nere it for comforte of your presence/ right here wolde I sterue. And yet a lytel am I gladed/ that so goodly suche grace and none hap haue I hente/ graciously to fynde the precious Margarite/ that al other leste men shulde bye/ if they shulde therfore sel al her substaunce. Wo is me that so many let games and purpose brekers ben maked wayters/ suche prisoners as I am euermore to ouerloke and to hynder/ and for suche lettours it is harde any suche iewel to wynne. Is this lady an honour to thy deytie? me thynketh by right/ suche people shulde haue no maistrye/ ne ben ouerlokers ouer none of thy seruauntes. Trewly were it leful vnto you/ to al the goddes wolde I playne/ that ye rule your deuyne puruueyaunce amonges your seruantes nothyng as ye shulde. Also lady my moeble is insuffysaunt to coũteruayle the price of this iewel/ or els to make theschange: eke no wight is worthy suche perles to weare/ but kynges or prices/ or els their peres: this iewel for vertue wold adorne & make fayre al a realme/ the nobley of vertue is so moche yͭ her goodnesse ouer al is cõmended. Who is it that wolde not wayle but he might suche rychesse haue at his wyl/ the vertue therof out of this prison may me delyuer/ & naught els. And if I be not ther thorowe holpen/ I se my selfe withouten recouery: Although I might hẽce voyde/ yet wolde I not/ I wolde abyde the daye that destenye hath me ordeyned/ whiche I suppose is without amendement/ so sore is myn herte bounden/ that I maye thynken none other. Thus strayte (lady) hath sir Daunger laced me in stockes/ I leue it be not your wyl: and for I se you taken so lytel hede/ as me thynketh/ and wol not maken by your might the vertue in mercy of yͤ Margaryte on me for to stretche/ so as ye mowe wel/ in case that you lyste: my blysse and my mirthe arne feld/ sickenesse and sorowe ben alwaye redy/ the cope of tene is wounde aboute al my body/ that stondyng is me best/ vnneth maye I lygge for pure miseasy sorowe/ and yet al this is lytel ynoughe to be the ernest sylver/ in forwarde of this bargayne/ for treble folde/ so mokel muste I suffer/ er tyme come of myn ease. For he is worthy no welthe/ that maye no wo suffer. And certes I am heuy to thynke on these thynges/

But

But who shal yeue me water ynough to dulke/ lest myn eyen drie for rennyng stremes of teares: Who shal waylen with me myne owne happy heuynesse: who shal coūsaile me nowe in my lykyng tene/ and in my goodly harme: I not. For euer the more I brenne/ the more I coueyte: the more that I sorow/ the more thurst I in gladnesse. Who shal than yeue me a contraryous drinke/ to staunche the thurste of my blysful bytternesse: Lo thus I brenne and I drenche/ I shyuer and I sweate/ to this reuersed yuel was neuer yet ordeyned salue; for soth al leches ben unconnyng/ saue the Margaryte alone/ any suche remedye to puruey.

And with these wordes I brast out to wepe/ that euery teere of myne eyen for greatnesse semed they boren out the bal of my syght/ and that al the water had ben out ronne. Than thought me/ that loue gan a lytel to heauy for miscomfort of my chere/ and gan soberly and in easy maner speke/ wel auysinge what she sayd. Comenly the wyse speken easyly and softe for many skylles: One is/ their wordes are the better byleued/ and also in easy speakynge/ auysement men may catche/ what to put forthe/ and what to holden in. And also the auctorite of easy wordes is the more/ and eke they yeuen the more understandynge to other intencion of the mater. Right so this lady easely and in a softe maner gan say these wordes. ¶ Meruayle (quod she) great it is/ that by no maner of semblaunt/ as ferre as I can espye/ thou lyst not to haue any recour/ but euer thou playnest and sorowest/ & wayes of remedye for folysshe wylfulnesse the lyste not to seche: but enquyre of thy next frendes/ that is thyne inwytte/ and me that haue ben thy maystresse and the recour and lyne of thy disease/ or of disease is gladnesse and ioy/ with a ful nessel so helded/ that it quencheth the felynge of the firste tenes. But thou that were wonte not onely these thynges remembre in thyne herte/ but also fooles therof to enfourmen/ in adnullynge of their errours/ and distroyeng of their derke opynions/ and in comforte of their feare thoughtes: now canst thou not ben comforte of thyn owne soule/ in thynkyng of these thynges. O where haste thou be so longe cōmensal/ that hast so mykel eten of the potages of foryetfulnesse/ and dronken so of ignorance: that the olde soukyng whiche thou haddest of me/ arne a maystred and lorn fro al maner of knowyng: O this is a worthy person to helpe other/ that can not counsayle him selfe. And with these wordes for pure and stronge shame I woxe al reed.

And she than seyng me so astonyed by dyuers stoundes/ sodainly (whiche thynge kynde hateth) gan deliciously me comforte with sugred wordes/ puttyng me in ful hope that I shulde the Margarite getten/ if I folowed her hestes/ and gan with a fayre clothe to wypen the teares that hyngen on my chekes: and than sayd I in this wyse. Nowe wel of wysedom and of al welthe/ withouten the may nothyng ben lerned/ thou bearest the keyes of al priuy thinges. In vayne trauayle men to catche any stedshyp/ but if ye lady first the locke unshet/ ye lady lerne us the wayes and the by pathes to heuen: ye lady maken al the heuenly bodyes goodly and benignely to done her course/ that gouernen us beestes here on erthe. Ye armen your seruauntes ayenst al debates/ with imperciable harneys/ ye setten in her hertes insuperable blode of hardynesse/ ye leaden hem to the parfyte good. Yet al thynge desyreth/ ye wern no man of helpe yͭ wole done your lore/ graunt me nowe a lytel of your grace/ al my sorowes to cease. Myne owne seruaunt (q̄d she) trewly thou syttest nye myne herte/ & thy badde chere gan sorily me greue: but amonge thy playnyng wordes me thought thou allegest thynges to be lettyng of thyne helpynge/ and thy grace to hynder/ wherthroughe me thynketh that wāhope is crope thorough thyn hert: God forbyd that nyse unthristy thought shulde come in thy mynde thy wyttes to trouble/ sythen euery thyng in comyng is contyngent/ wherfore make no more thy proposycion by an impossyble. But nowe I praye the reherse me ayen tho thynges/ that thy mistrust causen/ and thylke thynges I thynke by reason to distroyen/ & put ful hope in thyn herte. What understondest thou there (quod she) by that thou saydest/ many lette games are thyn ouer-

ouerlokers. And also by that thy morble is unsuffysant/ I not what thou therof meanest.

Trewly (qd I) by the first/ I say that iangleres euermore arne spekynge rather of yuel than of good/ for euery age of man rather enclyneth to wickednesse/ than any goodnesse to auaunce. Also false wordes spryngen so wyde/ by the sterryng of false lyeng tonges/ that fame als swiftely flyeth to her eares/ & sayth many wicked tales/ and as soone shal falsenesse ben leued as truthe/ for al his gret sothnesse. Now by that other (qd I) me thynketh thilke iewel so precious/ that to no suche wretche as I am/ wolde vertue therof extende/ & also I am to feble in worldly ioyes/ any suche iewel to countreuayle. For suche people that worldly ioyes han at her wyl/ ben sette at the highest degree/ and most in reuerence ben accepted/ for false wenyng maketh felycite therin to be supposed: but suche caytiues as I am euermore ben hyndred. Certes (qd she) take good hede & I shal by reason to the shewen/ ẏ al these thynges mowe nat let thy purpose/ by the leest poynt that any wight coude pricke.

Remembrest nat (qd she) ensample is one of the strongest maner/ as for to preue a mānes purpose. Than if I nowe by ensample enduce the to any proposytion/ is it nat proued by strength? Yes forsothe (qd I) Wel (qd she) raddest thou neuer howe Paris of Troye and Heleyne loued togyder/ and yet had they not entrecomuned of speche? Also Acrisyus shette Dane his doughter in a tour/ for suerte that no wight shulde of her haue no maistry in my seruyce/ and yet Jupiter by signes without any speche had al his purpose ayenst her fathers wyl. And many suche mo haue ben knytte in trouthe and yet spake they neuer togyder/ for that is a thyng enclosed vnder secretnesse of pryuite/ why twey ꝑsons entremellen hertes after a sight. The power in knowyng of such thynges so preuen/ shal nat al vtterly be yeuen to you beestes/ for many thynges in suche precious maters/ ben reserued to iugement of deuyne pureueyance/ for amōg lyueng people/ by mānes cōsyderation moun they nat be determyned. Wherfore I saye/ al the enuy/ al the ianglynge/ that welny people vpon my seruauntes maken efte/ is rather cause of esployte/ than of any hyndrynge. Why than (qd I) suffre ye such wrong/ and moun whan ye lyst/ lightly al such yuels abate/ me semeth to you it is a great vnworship. O (qd she) holde nowe thy peace/ I haue founden to many that han ben to me vnkynde/ that trewly I wol suffre euery wight in that wyse to haue disease/ & who that contynueth to the ende wel and trewly/ hem wol I helpen/ & as for one of myne in to blysse to wende/ as martial doyng in Grece. Who was ycrowned/ by god nat the strōgest/ but he that rathest come and lengest abode & contynued in the iourney/ and spared nat to trauayle as long as ẏ play lest. But thilke person ẏ profred hym nowe to my seruyce therin is a while/ & anon voydeth and redy to another/ & so nowe one he thynketh & nowe another/ and in to water entreth and anon respireth/ such one lyst me nat in to ꝑfyte blysse of my seruyce brynge. A tree ofte set in dyuers places wol nat by kynde endure to brynge forth frutes. Loke nowe I pray the/ howe myne olde seruauntes of tyme passed contynued in her seruyce/ & folowe thou after their steppes/ and than myght thou not fayle/ in case thou worche in this wyse. Certes (qd I) it is nothyng lyche/ this worlde to tyme passed/ eke this countre hath one maner/ and another countre hath another. And so may nat a man alway put to his eye the salue that he healed with his hele. For this is sothe/ betwixe two thynges lyche/ ofte dyuersite is required.

Nowe (qd she) that is sothe/ dyuersite of nation/ dyuersite of lawe/ as was maked by many reasons/ for that dyuersyte cometh in by ẏ contrarious malyce of wicked people/ ẏ han enuyous hertes ayēst other. But trewly my lawe to my seruauntes euer hath ben in generall/ whiche may nat fayle/ for right as mannes lawes/ that is ordayned by many determinatiōs/ may nat be knowe for good or badde/ tyl assay of the people han proued it/ & to what ende it draweth/ & than it sheweth the necessite therof/ or els the impossibilyte. Right so the lawe of my seruauntes so wel hath ben proued in general/ that hytherto hath it not fayled.

Vu.iii. Wyste

Wyste thou not wel that al the lawe of kynde is my lawe/and by god ordayned & stablisshed to dure by kynde reasoun / wherfore al lawe by mannes wytte purueyde/ought to be vnderputte to lawe of kynde/ whiche yet hath be cõmune to euery kyndely creature/that my statutes and my lawe that ben kyndely/ arne general to al peoples. Olde doynges/and by many turnynges of yeres vsed/ and with the peoples maner proued/ mowen nat so lightly ben defaced/ but newe doynges contrariauntes suche olde/ often causen diseases and breaken many purposes. Yet saye I nat therfore/ that ayen newe mischefe / men shulde nat ordaynen a newe remedye/ but alwaye looke it contrary not the olde/no ferther than the malyce stretcheth. Than foloweth/it the olde doynges in loue han ben vnyuersal/as for most eyxsoyte forthe vsed: wherfore I wol not yet that of my lawes nothynge be adnulled. But thanne to thy purpose / suche iangelers and lokers / and wayters of games / if the thynke in aught they mowe dere/ yet loue wel alwaye/ and sette hem at naught / and sette thy porte ben lowe in euery wightes presence/ and redy in thyne herte to mayntayne that thou hast begonne/and a lytel the fayne with mekenesse in wordes/ and thus with sleyght shalt thou surmount and dequace the yuel in their hertes. And wysdome yet is to seme flye otherwhyle there a man wol fyght. Thus with suche thynges / the tonges of yuel shal ben stylled: els fully to graunt thy ful meanynge/ for sothe euer was and euer it shalbe/ that myn enemyes ben aferde to truste to any fightynge: and therfore haue thou no cowardes herte in my seruyce/ no more than somtyme thou haddest in the contrarye/for if thou drede suche ianglerres thy viage to make: vnderstande wel that he that dredeth any rayne to sowe his cornes/ he shal haue than bernes. also he ẏ is aferde of his clothes/let him dãuce naked. Who nothyng vndertaketh/ & namely in my seruyce/nothyng acheueth. After great stormes ẏ wether is often mery & smothe. After moche clatering/there is mokyl rownyng: thus after iangling wordes cometh huysshte/ peace/ & be styl. O good lady (qđ I than) se nowe howe seuen yere passed & more/ haue I graffed and groubed a vyne/ and with al the wayes that I coude I sought to a fed me of the grape/but fruite haue I none founde. Also I haue this seuen yere serued Laban to a wedded Rachel his doughter / but blere eyed Lya is brought to my bedde/whiche alway engendreth my tene/ and is ful of chyldren in trybulacion & in care: and although the clippynges and kyssynges of Rachel shulde seme to me swete/yet is she so barayne/that gladnesse ne ioye by no way wol springe/so that I may wepe with Rachel/I may not ben counsayled with solace/sythen issue of myn hertely desyre is fayled. Nowe than I pray that to me sone fredom and grace/in this eyght yere/this eighteth mowe to me bothe be kynrest and masseday after the seuen werkedayes of trauayle/ to folowe the christen lawe: and what euer ye do els/that thilke Margaryte be holden so lady in your priuy chambre/that she in this case to none other person be cõmytted. Loke than (quod she) in this case to none other person be cõmytted: Loke than (qđ she) thou perseuer in my seruyce/in whiche I haue the grouded/ that thilke skorne in thyn enemyes mowe this on thy person be not lothed: so this mã began to edefye/but for his foundemẽt is bad/ to the ende may he it not bringe. For mekenesse in coũtenaunce/with a manly hert in dedes/ and in longe cõtynuaunce/is the conysaunce of my lyuery/to al my retynue delyuered. What wenyst thou ẏ me lyst auaunce suche persone as louen the first syttynges at feestes/the highest stoles in churches & in hal/ loutynges of peoples in markettes and fayres/ vnstedfaste to byde in one place any whyle togyder/wenyng his owne wyt more excellent than other/ scornyng al maner deuyse but his own: Nay nay god wot/these shul nothing yten of my blysse. Truly my maner here toforne hath ben/worshyp with my blysse/ Lyons in the felde/ and lambes in chambre/ Egles at assaute & maydens in halle/ foxes in counsayle/ styl in their dedes/& their protection is graũted redy to ben a bridge/& their baner is arered like wolues in the felde. Thus by these wayes shul men ben auaunced: ensãple of Dauid ẏ from kepyng of shepe of shepe/ was drawen vp in to the order of kyngly gouernaūce/ and Jupiter from a bole to ben Europes fere/ and Julius Cesar from the lowest degre in Rome/ to be mayster of al erthly prīces/ and Eneas from hel/ to be king of the countre there Rome is nowe stondyng. And so to the I say/ thy grace vp beryng therafter/ may set the in suche plyght/ that no iangglyng may greue the lest tucke of thy hemes/ that are their ianghes / is not to counte at a cresse in thy disauauntage.

EVer (quod she) hath the people in this worlde desyred to haue had great name in worthynesse/ and hated foule to beare any fame/ and that is one of the obiections thou alegest to be ayen thyne hertely desyre. Ye forsothe (qd I) and that so comenly the people wol lye/ & bring aboute suche enfame. Nowe (qd she) if men with leasynges put on the enfame/ wenest thy selfe therby ben enpeyred? that wenyng is wronge/ se why: for as moche as they lyen thy meryte encreaseth/ and maketh the ben more worthy to hem that knowen of ȳ the soth/ by what thyng thou art apeyred/ ȳ in so mokyl thou arte encreased of thy beloued frendes: and sothly a wounde of thy frende to the lasse harme/ ye sir/ and better than a false kyssyng in disceyuable glosyng of thyne enemye/ aboue that than to be wel with thy frēde maketh suche enfame. Ergo thou arte encresed and not apeyred. Lady (qd I) somtyme yet if a man be in disease/ thestymacion of the enuyous people ne loketh nothyng to desertes of men/ ne to the merytes of their doynges/ but only to the auenture of fortune/ and therafter they yeuen their sentence: and some loken the voluntary wyl in his herte/ and therafter telleth his iugement/ not takyng hede to reason ne to the qualite of the doyng/ as thus. If a man be ryche and fulfylde with worldly welfulnesse / some cōmenden it/ and sayne it is so lente by iuste cause: and he that hath aduersyte/ they sayne he is weaked/ and hath deserued thilke anoye. The contrarye of these thinges some men holden also/ and sayne that to the ryche prosperyte is puruayed in to his confusyon/ and vpon this mater/ many autorites of many and great wytted clerkes they alegen. And some men sayn/ though al good estymacion forsaken folk that han aduersyte/ yet is it meryte and encrease of his blysse/ so that these purposes arne so wonderful in vnderstandyng/ that trewly for myn aduersyte nowe I not howe the sentence of the indifferent people wyl iugen my fame. Therfore (quod she) if any wyght shulde yeue a trewe sentence on suche maters/ the cause of the disease maist thou se wel/ vnderstande ther vpon after what ende it draweth/ that is to sayne good or badde/ so ought it to haue his fame/ or by goodnesse enfame by badnesse: for euery reasonable person/ & namely of a wyse man/ his wytte ought not without reason to forne herde/ sodainly in a mater to iuge. After the sawes of the wise/ thou shalt not iuge ne deme toforne thou knowe. Lady (quod I) ye remembre wel that in moste laude and praysyng of certayne sayntes in holy churche/ is to rehersen their conuercion from badde in to good/ & that is so rehersed/ as by a perpetual myrrour of remembraunce in worshyppynge of tho sayntes/ and good ensample to other misdoers in amendement. Howe turned the romayne zedeoreys fro the romaynes/ to be with Hanybal ayenst his kynde nacion: and afterwardes him semyng the romayns to be at the next degre of confusyon/ turned to his olde alyes/ by whose wytte after was Hanybal discomfyted. Wherfore to enfourme you lady the maner why I meane/ se nowe in my youth I was drawe to ben assentaunt and in my mightes helpyng to certayn cōiuracions/ and other great maters of rulyng of cytezins/ and thilke thynges ben my drawers in/ & exitours to tho maters werne so paynted and coloured/ that at the prime face/ me semed them noble and glorious to al the people: I than wenyng mykel meryte haue deserued in furtheryng and mayntenaunce of tho thynges/ besyed and laboured with al my dyligence/ in werkynge of thylke maters to the ende. And trewly lady to tel you the sothe/ me rought lytel of any hate of the mighty senatours in thilke cyte/ ne of comunee malyce/ for two skylles: One was I had comforte to ben in

M.m.m.ii. suche

suche plyte/that bothe profyte were to me and to my frendes. Another was for cōmen profyte in comynaltie is not but peace and tranquylite/with iust gouernaunce proceden from thylke profyte/ sythen by counsayle of myne inwytte/ me thought the firste paynted thynges/ malyce and yuel meanynge/ withouten any good auaylyng to any people: and of tyrannye purposed/and so for pure sorowe and of my medlynge and badde infame that I was in come/ tho teeres lasshed out of myne eyen/ were thus awaye wasshe/ than the vnder hydde malyce and the rancoure of purposynge enuye forecaste and ymagyned/ in distruction of mokyl people/shewed so openly/ that had I ben blynde/ with myne hondes al the circumstaunce I myght wel haue feled.

Nowe than tho persones that suche thynges haue caste to redresse/ for wrathe of my first medlynge/ shopen me to dwel in this pynande prison / tyl Lachases my threde no lenger wolde twyne. And euer I was sought/if me lyste to haue grace of my lyfe/and frenesse of that prison/ I shulde openly confesse howe peace myght ben endused to enden al the firste rancours. It was fully supposed my knowyng to be ful in tho maters. Than lady I thought that euery man that by any waye of right/ rightfully done/ maye helpe any commune helpe to ben saued/ whiche thynge to kepe aboue al thynges I am holde to mayntayne/and namely in distroyeng of a wrong/ al shulde I therthrough enpeche myn owne fere/if he were gylty/and to do misdede assentaunt. And mayster ne frende maye nought auayle to the soule of him that in falsnesse deyeth/and also that I nere desyred wrathe of the people/ ne indignacion of the worthy/ for nothynge that euer I wrought or dyd/in any doyng my selfe els/ but in the mayntenaunce of these foresayd errours/ and in hydynge of the priuytees therof. And that al the peoples hertes holdynge on the errours syde/ weren blynde and of elde so ferforthe begyled/ that debate and stryfe they maynteyned / and in distruction on that other syde/by whiche cause the peace/that moste in comunaltie shulde be desyred/ was in poynte to be broken and adnulled. Also the cytie of London/ that is to me so dere and swete/ in whiche I was forthe growen/ and more kyndely loue haue I to that place than to any other in erthe/as euery kyndely creature hath ful appetyte to that place of his kyndly engendrure/ and to wylne reste and peace in that stede to abyde: thylke peace shulde thus there haue ben broken/ and of al wyse it is cōmended and desyred. For knowe thynge it is / al men that desyren to comen to the perfyte peace euer lastyng/ must the peace by god cōmended/ bothe mayntayne and kepe. This peace by angels voyce was confyrmed/ our god entrynge in this worlde. This as for his Testamēt he left to al his frēdes/ whanne he retourned to the place from whence he came: this his Apostel amonesteth to holden/ without whiche man perfytely may haue none insyght. Also this god by his comyng/ made not peace alone betwene heuenly and erthly bodyes/ but also amonge vs on erthe/ so he peace confyrmed/ that in one heed of loue/one body we shulde perfourme. Also I reēmbre me wel howe the name of Athenes was rather after the god of peace than of batayle/ shewynge that peace moste is necessarye to comunalties and cytes. I than so styred by al these wayes toforne nempned/ declared certayne poyntes in this wyse. Firste that thilke persones that hadden me drawen to their purposes/and me not wetyng the priuy entent of their meanynge/drawen also the feoble wytted people/ that haue none insyght of gubernatyfe prudence/ to clamure and to crye on maters that they styred / and vnder poyntes for comune auauntage/ they enbolded the passyfe to take in the actyues doynge/ and also styred innocentes of connyng to crye after thynges / whiche (quod they) may not stande but we ben executours of tho maters/ and auctorite of execucion by comen election to vs be delyuered/ and that muste entre by strength of your mayntenaunce/ for we out of suche degree put/ oppressyon of these olde hynderers shal agayne surmounten and putten you in such subiection/ that ī endelesse wo ye shul complayne. The gouernementes (qd they) of your cyte lefte in the handes of tor-

cencitencious cytezyns shal bringe in pestylence and distruction to you good men/ and therfore let vs haue the comune admynistracion to abate suche yuels. Also (quod they) it is worthy the good to cõmende/ and the gylty desertes to chastice. There ben cytezens many for ferde of execucion that shal be doone/ for extorcions by hem commytted/ ben euer more ayenst these purposes/ and al other good meanynges. Neuer the latter lady/ trewly the meanynge vnder these wordes/ was fully to haue apeched the mighty senatoures/ whiche hadden heauy herte for the misgouernaunce that they seen. And so lady whan it fel that free election/ by great clamour of moche people/ for great disease of misgouernaunce so feruently stoden in her election/ that they hem submytted to euery maner face/ rather than haue suffred the maner and the rule of the hated gouernours/ not withstandynge that in the contrary helden moche comune meyny that haue no consyderacion/ but onely to voluntary lustes/ withouten reason. But than thylke gouernour so forsaken/ faynynge to forne his vndoynge for mistruse in his tyme/ shope to haue letted thilke electyon/ and haue made a newe him selfe to haue ben chosen/ and vnder ẏ mokyl roze haue arered. These thynges lady knowen amonge the princes/ and made open to the people/ draweth in amendement/ that euery degree shal ben ordayned to stande there as he shulde/ and that of errours comyng herafter/ men may lightly to forne hande purvaye remedye/ in this wyse peace and rest to be furthered and holde. Of the whiche thynges lady/ thylke persones broughten in answere to forne their moste souerayne iuge/ not coarted by paynynge dures/ openly knowlegeden/ and asked therof grace/ so that apertely it preueth my wordes ben sothe/ without forgynge of leasynges.

But nowe it greueth me to remembre these dyuers sentences/ in ianglynge of these shepy people: certes me thynketh they oughten to maken ioye that a sothe maye be knowe. For my trouthe and my conscience ben wytnesse to me bothe/ that this knowynge sothe haue I sayde for no harme ne malyce of tho persones/ but onely for trouthe of my sacrament in my leigeaunce/ by whiche I was charged on my kynges behalfe. But se ye not nowe lady/ how the felonous thoughtes of this people/ and couyns of wicked men/ conspyren ayen my sothfast trouth. Se ye not euery wight that to these erronyous opinyõs were assentaunt and helpes to the noyse/ and knewen al these thynges better than I my seluen/ apparaylen to fynden newe frendes/ and cleapen me false/ and studyen howe they mowen in her mouthes werse plyte nempne. O god what maye this be/ that thylke folke whiche that in tyme of my mayntenaũce/ and whan my might auayled to stretch to ẏ forsayd maters/ tho me cõmended/ and yave me name of trouth/ in so manyfolde maners that it was nyghe in euery wightes eere/ there as any of thilke people weren: and on the other syde/ thilke company somtyme passed/ yeuynge me name of badde loos. Nowe bothe tho peoples turned the good in to badde/ and badde in to good/ whiche thyng is wonder/ that they knowynge me sayng but sothe/ arne nowe tempted to reply her olde praysynges/ and knowen me wel in al doynges to ben trewe/ and sayne openly that I false haue sayd many thynges. And they aleged nothynge me to ben false or vntrewe/ saue thilke mater knowleged by the parties hem selfe: and god wote other mater is none. Ye also lady knowe these thynges for trewe/ I auaunte not in praysyng of my selfe/ therby shulde I lese the precious secre of my conscience. But ye se wel that false opinyon of the people for my trouthe/ in tellyng out of false conspyred maters/ and after the iugement of these clerkes/ I shulde not hyde the sothe of no maner person/ mayster ne other/ Wherfore I wolde not drede/ were it put in the consyderacion of trewe and of wyse. And for comers hereafter shullen fully out of denwere/ al the sothe knowe of these thinges in acte/ but as they werne I haue put it in scripture/ in perpetuel remembraunce of true meanynge. For trewly lady me semeth/ that I ought to beare the name of trouthe/ that for

M.m.m.iii. the

the loue of rightwysnesse haue thus me submytten: But nowe than the false fame which that clerkes sayne flyeth as faste as dothe the fame of trouthe, shal so wyde sprede/ tyl it be brought to the iewel that I of meane/ and so shal I ben hyndred withouten any measure of trouthe.

Than gan Loue sadly me beholde/ and sayd in a chaūged voyce/ lower than she had spoken in any tyme. Fayne wolde I (qd̄ she) that thou were holpen/ but haste thou sayd any thynge whiche thou myght not prouen? Parde (quod I) the persones/ euery thyng as I haue sayd/ han knowleged hem selfe. Yea (qd̄ she) but what if they hadden nayed/ howe woldest thou haue maynteyned it. Sothely (quod I) it is wel wyste bothe amongest the greatest/ and other of the realme/ ŷ I profered my body so largely in to prouynge of tho thynges/ that Mars shulde haue iuged the ende: but for sothnesse of my wordes they durste not to thylke iuge truste. Nowe certes (quod she) aboue al fames in this worlde/ the name of marcial doynges moste pleasen to ladyes of my lore/ but sythen thou were redy/ and thyne aduersaryes in thy presence refused thilke doyng/ thy fame ought to be so borne/ as if in dede it had take to the ende. And therfore euery wight that any droppe of reason hath/ and hereth of the infame/ for these thynges hath this answere to saye: trewly thou saydest for thyne aduersaryes thy wordes affirmed. And if thou haddest lyed/ yet are they discomfyted/ the prise leaned on thy syde/ so that fame shal holde down infame/ he shal bringe vpon none halfe. What greueth the thyne enemye to sayne their owne shame/ as thus: We arne discomfyted/ and yet our quarel is trewe. Shal not the loos of thy frendes ayenward dequace thilke enfame/ and saye they graunted a sothe without a stroke or fightīg. Many men in batayle ben discomfyted and ouercome in a right ful quarel/ that is goddes priuy iugement in heuen: but yet although the partie be yolden/ he may with wordes saye his quarel is trewe/ and to yelde him in the contrarye for drede of dethe/ he is compelled: and he that graunteth and no stroke hath feled/ he maye not crepe away in this wyse/ by none excusacion. Indifferent folke wyl say/ ye who is trewe/ who is false/ him selfe knowlegeth tho thīges. Thus in euery syde fame sheweth to the good and no badde. But yet (qd̄ I) some wyl say I ne shulde for no dethe haue discouered my maystresse/ and so by vnkyndnesse they wol knette infame to pursue me aboute: thus enemyes of wyl in manyfolde maner wol seche priuy serpentynes queyntyses/ to quenche and distroye by venym of many besynesses the light of truthe/ to make hertes to murmure ayenst my persone/ to haue me in hayne withouten any cause. Nowe (quod she) here me a fewe wordes/ and thou shalte fully ben answerde I trowe. Me thynketh (quod she) right nowe by thy wordes/ that sacrament of swearyng/ ŷ is to say/ chargyng by othe was one of the causes to make ŷ discouer the malicious ymaginatyons tofore nempned/ euery othe by knyttynge of copulation muste haue these lawes/ That is trewe iugement & rightwysenesse/ in whiche thynge if any of these lacke/ the othe is tourned in to the name of periury: than to make a trewe serment/ most nedes these thynges folowe/ for ofte tymes a man to saye sothe/ but iugement and iustyce folowe he is forsworne: ensample of Herodes for holdynge of his serment was dampned.

Also to saye truthe rightfullyche but in iugement otherwhile is forboden/ by that al sothes be nat to sayne. Therfore in iugement in truthe and right wisenesse is euery creature bounden vp payne of periury ful knowyng to make/ tho it were of his owne persone for drede of synne/ after that worde better is it to dey than lyue false/ and al wolde peruerted people false reporte make in vnkyndnesse/ in that entent thy fame to reyse/ whan lyght of truthe in these maters is forthe sprongen/ and openly publysshed among cōmens/ than shal nat suche derke enfame dare appere for pure shame of his falsnesse/ as some mē ther ben ŷ their owne enfame can none otherwyse voide or els excuse/ but be hyndringe of other men-

nes

nes fame/ which that by non other cause/ clea-
pen other men false/ but for with their owne
falsnesse mowen they nat ben auaunsed / or
els by false sklaundynge wordes/ other men
shenden their owne trewe sklaunder / to ma-
ke seme the lasse/ for if such men wolden their
eyen of their conscience reuoluen/ shulden sene
the same sentence they legen on other/ springe
out of their sydes/ with so many braunches, it
were impossyble to nombre. To whiche ther-
fore maye it be sayd in that thynge/ this man
thou demest/ therin thy selfe thou cõdempnest
But (quod she) vnderstãde nat by these wor-
des/ that thou wene me saye the to be worthy
sclaunder/ for any mater tofore written/ true
ly I wolde wytnesse the contrary / but I saye
that the beames of sclaundryng wordes/ may
nat be done awaye tyl the daye of dome. For
howe shulde it nat yet amonges so great plen
tie of people ben many shrewes/ sithen whan
no mo but eight persons in Noes shippe were
closed/ yet one was a shrewe and skorned his
father. These thynges (quod she) I trowe/
shewen that false fame is nat to drede / ne of
wyse persons to accepte / and namely nat of
thy Margarite / whose wysedom here after I
thynke to declare/ wherfore I wotte wel suche
thynge shal nat her asterte/ than of vnkynd-
nesse thyne othe hath the excused at the fulle.
But nowe if thou woldest nat greue/ me lyst
a fewe thynges to shewe. Say on (quod I)
what ye wol/ I trowe ye meane but trouthe/
and my profyte in tyme comynge. Trewly
(quod she) that is sothe/ so thou con wel kepe
these wordes / and in the inrest secre chambre
of thyne herte/ so faste hem close that they ne-
uer flytte/ than shalte thou fynde hem auay-
lyng. Loke nowe what people haste thou ser-
ued/ whiche of hem al in tyme of thyne exile
euer the refresshed / by the valewe of the leste
coyned plate that walketh in money. Who
was sorye or made any rewth for thy disease?
if they hadden getten their purpose of thy mis
auenture sette they nat an hawe. Lo whan
thou were enprisonned/ howe faste they hyed
in helpe of thy delyueraunce. I wene of thy
dethe they yeue but lyte: They loked after no
thynge/ but after their owne lustes. And if
thou lyste say the sothe/ al that meyny that in
this bugge the broughten / loked rather af-
ter thyne helpes/ than the to haue releued.

Owen nat yet some of hem money for his
cõmens? Paydest nat thou for some of her
dispences/ tyl they were tourned out of Se-
lande? Who paue the euer ought for any ty-
dynge thou madest? yet pardye some of hem
token money for thy chambre / and putte tho
pens in his purse vnwetynge of the renter.

Lo for which a company thou medlest/ that
neyther the ne them selfe myghten helpe of vn
kyndnesse/ nowe they beare the name þ thou
supposest of hem for to haue. What myght
thou more haue done than thou dyddest / but
if thou woldest in a false quarel haue been a
stynkynge martyr? I wene thou fleddest as
longe as thou myght / their pryuite to coun-
sayle / whiche thynge thou helest lenger than
thou shuldest. And thilke þ ought the money
no penny wolde paye/ they wende thy returne
hadde ben an impossyble. Howe might thou
better haue hem proued / but thus in thy nedy
diseases? Nowe haste thou ensaumple for
whom thou shalte meddle: trewly this lore is
worthe many goodes.

Ofte gan Loue to sterne me these wor-
des / thynke on my speche / for trewly
here after it wol do the lykynge / and howe
so euer thou se Fortune shape her wheele to
tourne/ this meditation by no waye reuolue.
For certes fortune sheweth her fayrest/ whan
she thynketh to begyle. And as me thought
here tofore thou saydest thy loos in loue/ for
thy rightwyseness ought to be raysed/ shulde
be alowed in tyme comynge. Thou myght
in loue so the haue/ that loos and fame shul
so ben raysed/ that to thy frendes cõforte/ and
sorowe to thyne enemys endlesse shul endure.

But if thou were þ one shepe amonges the
hundred were loste in deserte / and out of the
way hadde erred/ and nowe to the flocke arte
restoored / the shepeheerd hath in the no ioye/
and thou ayen to the forrest tourne. But that
right as the sorowe and anguysshe was great
in tyme of thyne out waye goynge/ ryght so
ioye

ioye and gladnesse shal be doubled to sene the conuerted/ and nat as Lothes wyfe ayen lokynge / but hoole counsayle with the shepe folowynge/ and with them grasse and herbes gadre. Neuer the later (quod she) I saye nat these thynges for no wantrust that I haue in supposynge of the other wyse thanne I shulde / For trewly I wotte wel/ that nowe thou arte sette in suche a purpose/ out of whiche the lyste nat to parte. But I saye it/ for many men there bene/ that to knowyng of other mēnes doynges setten al their cure/ and lightly desyren the badde to clatter rather than the good/ and haue no wyl their owne mater to amende. They also hate of olde rancoure lightly hauen/ and there that suche thynge abydeth / sodaynly in their mouthes procedeth the habundaunce of the herte/ and wordes as stones/ stones out throwe. Wherfore my counsayle is euer more openly and apertely / in what place thou sytte/ countreplete therrours and meanynges/ in as ferre as thou hem wystyst false/ and leaue for no wyght to make hem be knowe in euery bodyes eare/ and be alwaye pacient and vse Jacobes wordes/ what so euer menne of the clappen/ I shal sustayne my ladyes wrathe whiche I haue deserued/ so longe as my Margarite hath right wysed my cause. And certes (quod she) I wytnesse my selfe/ if thou thus conuerted sorowest in good meanynge in thyne herte/ wolte from al vanyte parfitely departe/ in consolatyoun of al good pleasaunce of that Margaryte / whiche that thou desyrest after wyl of thyne hert/ in a maner of a mothers pyte / shul fully accepte the in to grace. For ryght as thou rentest clothes in open syghte / so openly to sowe hem at his worshippe withouten reprofe commended. Also right as thou were ensample of moche folde errour/ right so thou must be ensample of manyfolde correctioun/ so good sauour to forgoyng al errour distroyeng causeth dilygent loue/ with many playted prayinges to folowe/ and than shal al the fyrste errours make the folowynge worshyppes to seme hugely encreased/ blacke and white sette togyder/ euery for other more semeth/ and so dothe euery thynges contrary in kynde. But infame that gothe alwaye tofore/ and praysynge worshippe by any cause folowynge after/ maketh to ryse the lyke honour in double of welth/ and that quencheth the spotte of the fyrst enfame. Why wenyste I saye these thinges/ in hyndringe of thy name? Naye nay god wotte/ but for pure encreasyng worshypp thy rightwysenesse to cōmende/ & thy trouthe to seme the more. Wost nat wel thy selfe/ that thou in fourme of making passeth nat Adam that ete of the apple. Thou passeth nat the stedfastnesse of Noe/ that eatynge of the grape become dronke. Thou passyst nat the chastyte of Lothe/ that lay by his doughter. Eke the nobley of Abraham/ whom god reproued by his pride. Also Dauydes mekenesse/ whiche for a woman made Urye be slawe. What also Hector of Troye/ in whome no defaute myght be founde / yet is he reproued that he ne hadde with manhode nat suffred the warre begon/ ne Paris to haue went in to Grece/ by whom ganne al the sorowe: for trewly hym lacketh no venym of pryue consentyng/ whiche that openly leaueth a wronge to withsay.

Lo eke an olde prouerbe amonges many other/ He that is stylle semeth as he graunted.

Nowe by these ensamples/ thou myght fully vnderstonde/ that these thynges ben wrytte to your lernyng/ and in right wysenesse of tho persones / as thus: To euery wight his defaute cōmytted/ made goodnesse afterwardes done / be the more in reuerēce and in open shewyng/ for ensāple is it nat song in holy churche. Lo howe necessary was Adams synne/ Dauyd the kyng gate Salomon the kyng/ of her that was Uryes wyfe. Truly for reprofe is none of these thynges wrytte: Right so tho I reherce thy before dede / I repreue the neuer the more/ ne for no vyllany of the are they rehersed/ but for worshippe/ so thou contynewe wel here after/ and for profyte of thy selfe / I rede thou on hem thynke.

Than sayde I right thus. Lady of vnyte and accorde / enuy and wrathe lurken there thou comest in place / ye weten wel your selue and so done many other/ that whyle I admynystred

nystred the offyce of cōmen doynge/ as in ru-
lyng of the stablysshmentes amonges the peo
ple / I defouled neuer my conscyence for no
maner dede/ but euer by wytte and by coun-
sayle of the wysest/ the maters weren drawen
to their right endes . And thus trewly for you
lady I haue desyred suche cure/ and certes in
your seruyce was I nat ydel/ as ferre as su-
che doynge of my cure stretcheth . That is a
thyng (quod she) that may drawe many her-
tes of noble/and voice of cōmune in to glory/
and fame is nat but wretched and fyckle .

Alas that mākynde coueyteth in so leude a
wyse/ to be rewarded of any good dede / sithe
glorie of fame in this worlde/ is nat but hyn-
dringe of glorye in tyme cōmynge . And cer-
tes (quod she) yet at the hardest suche fame in
to heuen/is nat the erthe but a centre to the cer
cle of heuen . A pricke is wonder lytel in re-
specte of al the cercle/ and yet in al this pricke
may no name be borne in maner of peersyng
for many obstacles/ as waters and wylder-
nesse/ and straunge langages/ and nat onely
names of men ben stylled and holden out of
knowlegynge by these obstacles / but also cy-
tees and realmes of prosperite ben letted to be
knowe/ and their reason hyndred/ so that they
mowe nat ben parfitely in mennes proper vn
derstandynge . Howe shulde than the name
of a synguler londenoys passe the gloryous
name of London/ whiche by many it is com-
mended/and by many it is lacked/and in ma-
ny mo places in erthe nat knowen/ than kno-
wen : for in many countrees lytel is London
in knowyng or in spech/ & yet among one ma
ner of people may nat such fame in goodnes
cōe/for as many as praysen cōmenly as ma-
ny lacken . Fye thā on such maner fame/slepe
& suffre hym yͭ knoweth pryue of hertz/ to dele
suche fame/ in thylke place there nothynge a-
yenst a sothe shal neyther speke ne dare apere/
by attourney ne by other maner . Howe ma-
ny great named and many great in worthy-
nesse losed/han be tofore this tyme/that nowe
out of memorie are slydden and clenely for ge
ten/for defaute of writynges/and yet scriptu-
res for great elde so ben defased/ that no per-
petualte maye in hem ben iuged . But if thou
wolte make comparisoun to euer/ what ioye
mayst thou haue in erthly name/ it is a fayre
lykenesse/ a pees or one grayne of wheate / to
a thousande shippes ful of corne charged .
What nombre is betwene the one and thother/
and yet mowe bothe they be nombred/ & ende
in rekenynge haue . But trewly al that may
be nombred/is nothyng to recken/as to thilke
that maye nat be nombred/ for ofte thynges
ended is made comparison/ as one lytel/ano-
ther great/ but in thynges to haue an ende/ &
another no ende/suche comparisoun may nat
be founden . Wherfore in heuen to ben losed
with god hath none ende/ but endlesse endu-
reth/ and thou canste nothynge done aright/
but thou desyre the rumoure therof be heared
and in euery wightes eare/ & that dureth but a
pricke/in respecte of the other . And so thou se-
kest rewarde of folkes smale wordes / and of
vayne praysynges . Trewly therin thou le-
sest the guerdon of vertue/ and lesest the gret-
test valoure of consyence/ and vphap thy re-
nome euerlastyng . Therfore boldely renome
of fame of the erthe shulde be hated/ and fame
after deth shulde be desyred/ of werkes of ver-
tue asketh guerdonyng/ and the soule causeth
al vertue . Than the soule delyuered out of pri
sone of erthe/ is most worthy suche guerdone
among to haue in the euerlastynge fame/and
nat the body that causeth al mannes yuels .

Of twey thynges arte thou answered as
me thynketh (quod Loue) and if any
thynge be in doute in thy soule/ shewe it forth
thyne ignoraunce to clere/ and leaue it for no
shame . Certes (quod I) there ne is no body
in this worlde/ that aught coude saye by rea-
son ayenst any of your skylles/as I leue/and
by my wytte nowe lele I wel/ that yuel spe-
kers or bearers of enfame/may lytel greue or
lette my purpose/ but rather by suche thynge
my quarel to be forthered . Yea (qd she) and
it is proued also/ that the ilke iewel in my ke-
pynge shal nat there thorowe be steered/ of the
lest moment yͭ myght be ymagyned . That is
soth (qd I) Wel (qd she) than leneth there/to
declare yͭ thy insuffysance is no maner letting
as

as thus/ for that she is so worthy. thou shuldest not clymbe so highe/ for thy moebles and thyne estate arne voyded/ thou thynkest fallen in suche myserie/ that gladnesse of thy pursute wol nat on the discende. Certes (quod I) that is sothe: right suche thought is in myne hert/ for cōmenly it is spoken/ & for an olde prouerbe it is leged: He that heweth to hye/ with chyppes he maye lese his syght. Wherfore I haue ben about in al that euer I myght/ to studye wayes of remedye by one syde or by another. Nowe (quod she) god forbede are thou seke any other doynges/ but suche as I haue lerned the in our restynge whyles/ and suche herbes as ben planted in oure gardyns. Thou shalte wel vnderstāde/ that aboue man is but one god alone. Howe (qđ I) han men to forne this tyme trusted in writtes and chauntementes/ and in helpes of spirites that dwellen in the ayre/ and therby they han getten their desyres/ where as first for al his manly power he daunced behynde.

O (quod she) fye on suche maters/ for trewly that is sacrilege/ and that shal haue no sort with any of my seruauntes/ in myne eyen shal suche thynge nat be loked after. Howe often is it cōmaunded by these passed wyse/ that to one god shal men serue/ and nat to goddes. And who that lyste to haue myne helpes/ shal aske none helpe of foule spirites. Alas/ is nat man maked semblable to god: wost thou nat wel that al vertue of lyuelych werkynge by goddes puruegaunce is vnderputte to resonable creature in erthe/ is nat euery thynge a thishalfe god: made buxome to mānes cōtemplation/ vnderstandynge in heuen and in erthe/ and in helle. Hath not manne beynge with stones/ soule of wexyng with trees and herbes. Hath he nat soule of felynge/ with beestes/ fysshes/ and foules/ and he hath soule of reason and vnderstandyng with aungels/ so that in him is knytte al maner of lyuenges by a reasonable proporcioun. Also man is made of al the foure elementes. Al vnyuersytee is rekened in hym alone: he hath vnder god pryncipalite aboue al thynges. Nowe is his soule here/ nowe a thousande myle hence/ nowe ferre nowe nygh/ nowe hye nowe lowe/ as ferre in a momente/ as in mountenaunce of tenne wynter/ and al this is in mannes gouernaunce and disposytion. Than sheweth it/ that men ben lyche vnto goddes/ and chyldren of moost heyght. But nowe sythen al thynges vnderputte to the wyl of reasonable creatures/ god forbede any man to wynne that lordshippe/ and aske helpe of any thynge lower than him selfe/ & than namely of foule thyngꝫ innominable. Now thā why shuldest thou wene to loue to highe/ sythen nothynge is the aboue but god alone. Trewly I wote wel/ that thylke iewel is in a maner euyn in lyne of degree there thou arte thy selue/ and nought aboue/ saue thus. Aungel vpon angel/ manne vpon manne/ and deuyl vpon deuyl/ han a maner of soueraygntie/ and that shal cease at the daye of dome: and so I say/ thoughe thou be putte to serue the ylke iewel. durynge thy lyfe/ yet is that no seruage of vnderputtynge/ but a maner of trauaylyng plesaunce/ to conquere and gette that thou haste not. I sette nowe the hardest/ in my seruice nowe thou deydest for sorowe of wantynge in thy desyres: trewly al heuenly bodyes with one voyce shul come and make melody in thy comynge/ and saye welcome our fere/ and worthy to entre in to Iupyters ioye/ for thou with myght haste ouercome dethe/ thou woldest neuer flytte out of thy seruyce/ and we al shul nowe pray to the goddes rowe by rowe to make thilk Margarite ꝥ no routh had in this persone/ but vnkyndely without comforte lette the deye/ shal besette her selfe in suche wyse/ that in erthe for parte of vengeaunce/ shal she no ioye haue in loues seruyce/ and whan she is deed/ than shal her soule ben broght vp in to thy presence/ and whyder thou wylte chese/ thilke soule shal ben commytted. Or els after thy dethe anone al the forsayd heuenly bodyes by one acorde/ shal benōmen from thylke perle/ al the vertues that firste her were taken/ for she hath hem forfeyted/ by that on the my seruaunt in thy lyue she wolde not suffre to worche al vertues withdrawen/ by might of the hygh bodyes: Why than shuldest thou wene so any more. And if the lyste to loke vpon the lawe of kynde/

of kynde/ and with order whiche to me was
ordayned/ sothely none age / none ouertour-
nynge tyme / but hytherto had no tyme ne
power to chaunge the weddyng/ne the knotte
to vnbynde of two hertes thorowe one assent
in my presence/togyther accorden to enduren
tyl dethe hem departe. What trowest thou
euery ydeot wotte the menynge and the priuy
entent of these thynges : they wene forsothe
that suche accorde may not be/ but the rose of
maydenhede be plucked/ do waye do waye /
they knowe nothyng of this: for consente of
two hertes alone/ maketh the fastenynge of
the knotte/ neyther lawe of kynde ne mannes
lawe/ determyneth neyther the age ne the qua
lyte of persones/ but onely accorde bytwene
thylke twaye. And trewly after tyme that
suche accorde by their consent in hert/is ensea-
led and put in my tresorye amonges my pri-
uy thynges: than gynneth the name of spou-
sayle/ and although they breaken forwarde
bothe/ yet suche mater ensealed is kepte in re-
membrauce for euer. And se nowe that spou-
ses haue the name anon after accorde/though
the rose be not take. The aungel bade Io-
seph take Marye his spouse/ and to Egypte
wende : Lo she was cleped spouse/and yet to-
forne ne after neyther of hem bothe mente no
flesshly luste knowe / wherfore the wordes of
trouthe acorden/ that my seruauntes shulden
forsake bothe father and mother/ and be ad-
herande to his spouse/ and they two in vnyte
of one flesshe shulden accorde. And this wyse
two that werne firste in a lytel maner disa-
cordaunt/ hygher that one and lower that o-
ther/ ben made euenlyche in gree to stonde.
But nowe to enfourme the that ye ben lyche
to goddes / these clerkes sayne/and in deter-
mynacion shewen / that thre thynges hauen ye
names of goddes ben cleaped/ that is to sayn:
man/ dyuel/ and ymages/ but yet is there but
one god/ of whom al goodnesse/al grace/and
al vertue cometh/ and he his louyng & trewe/
and euerlastyng/and prime cause of al beyng
thynges: but men ben goddes/ louynge and
trewe/but not euerlastyng/and that is by ad-
opcyoun of the euerlastynge god. Dyuels
ben goddes/styrynge by a maner of lyueng/
but neyther ben they trewe ne euerlastynge/
and their name of godlyheed thy han by vsur
pacion/ as the prophete sayth: Al goddes of
gentyles/that is to say paynyms/are dyuels.
But ymages ben goddes by nuncupacion /
and they ben neyther lyuynge ne trewe/ ne e-
uerlastynge : After these wordes they cleapen
goddes ymages wrought with mennes han-
des. But nowe reasonable creature/ that by
adopcion alone arte to the great god euerla-
stynge/and therby thou arte god cleped: lette
thy fathers maners so entre thy wyttes/ that
thou myght folowe/ in as moche as longeth
to the thy fathers worshyppe/ so that in no-
thynge thy kynde from his wyl declyne/ ne
from his nobley peruerte. In this wyse if
thou werche/ thou arte aboue al other thyn-
ges saue god alone/ and so say no more thyn
herte to serue in to hye a place.

Fully haue I nowe declared thyn estate to
be good/so thou folow therafter/ and that the
abiection first be the aleged in worthynesse of
thy Margaryte shal not the lette/ as it shal
forther the/ and encrease the/ it is nowe to de-
clare/ ye last obiection in nothing may greue.
Yes certes (qđ I) bothe greue and let muste
it nedes/ the contrarye maye not ben proued/
and se nowe why. Whyle I was glorious in
worldly welfulnesse/and had suche goodes in
welth as maken men ryche/ tho was I drawe
in to companyes that loos/ prise/ and name
yeuen: tho louteden blasours/ tho curreyden
glosours/tho welcomeden flatterers/ tho wor
shypped thylke/that nowe deynen nat to loke.
Euery wight in such erthly wele habundant/
is holde noble/precious/benigne/and wyse to
do what he shal/ in any degree that men hym
set/al be it that the sothe be in the contrarye of
al tho thynges: But he that can/ne neuer so
wel him behaue/and hath vertue habundaunt
in manyfolde maners/ & be not welthed with
suche erthly goodes/ is holde for a foole/ and
sayd his wytte is but sotted. Lo how false for
auer is holde trewe. Lo howe trewe is clea-
ped false for wantyng of goodes. Also lady/
dignytees of office maken men mykel comen-
ded as thus:he is so good/ were he out his pere
shul

shulde men not fynde. Trewly I trowe of some suche that are so praysed/ were they out ones/ another shulde make hym so be knowe/ he shulde of no wyse no more ben loked after: but onely fooles wel I wotte/ desyren suche newthynges. Wherfore I wonder that thilke gouernour/ out of whome alone the causes proceden/ that gouernen al thynges/ whiche that hath ordeyned this worlde in werkes of the kyndely bodyes so be gouerned/ not with unstedfast or happyous thyng/ but with rules of reason/ whiche shewen the course of certayne thynges: why suffreth he suche slydyng chaunges/ that misturnen suche noble thynges as ben we men/ that arne a fayre parsel of the erthe/ and holden the upperest degre under god of benigne thinges/ as ye sayden right nowe your selfe/ shulde neuer man haue ben set in so worthy a place/ but if his degre were ordayned noble. Alas/ thou that knyttest the purueyaunce of al thynges/ why lokest thou not to amenden these defautes: I se shrewes that han wicked maners/ sytten in chayres of domes/ lambes to punysshen/ there wolues shulden ben punisshed. Lo vertue shynende naturelly/ for pouertie lurketh and is hydde under cloude: but the moone false forsworne/ as I knowe my selfe/ for auer & yestes hath usurped to shyne by day light/ with peynture of other mens praysinges: and trewly thilke forged lyȝt fouly shulde fade/ were the trouth away of colours feyned. Thus is nyght turned in to daye/ and daye in to night/ wynter in to sōmer/ and sōmer in to wynter/ not in dede/ but in miscleappyng of folyche people.

Nowe (quod she) what wenest thou of these thinges? how felest thou in thyn hert/ by what gouernaunce that this cometh aboute?

Certes (q̄d I) that wotte I neuer/ but if it be that fortune hath graunt from aboue/ to lede the ende of men as her lyketh. Ah nowe I se (quod she) thentent of thy meanyng: Lo bycause thy worldly goodes ben fullyche dispent/ thou berafte out of dignite of office/ in whiche thou madest the gatherynge of thilke goodes/ and yet dyddest in that office by counsayle of wyse/ any thing were ended: and true were unto hem/ whose prosp̄te thou shuldest loke/ and seest nowe many that in thilke heruest made of the mokel/ and nowe for glosing of other/ deyneth the nought to forther/ but enhaunsen false shrewes/ by wytnessynge of trouthe. These thynges greueth thyn herte to sene thy selfe thus abated/ and than fraylte of mankynde ne setteth but lytel by the lesers of suche rychesse/ haue he neuer so moche vertue/ and so thou wenest of thy iewel to renne in dispyte/ and not ben accepted in to grace: Al this shal the nothing hynder. Nowe (q̄d she) first thou woste wel thou lostest nothyng that euer mightest thou chalenge for thyn owne: Whan nature brought the forthe/ come thou not naked out of thy mothers wombe? thou haddest no rychesse/ and whan thou shalt entre in to the ende of euery flesshly body/ what shalt thou haue with the than? So euery rychesse thou haste in tyme of thy lyuynge/ nys but lente/ thou might therin chalenge no propertie. And se nowe euery thing that is a mannes owne/ he may do therwith what him lyketh/ to yeue or to kepe: but richesse thou playnest from the lost/ if thy might had stretched so ferforth/ fayne thou woldest haue hem kept multyplied with mo other: and so ayenst thy wyl ben they dep̄ted from the/ wherfore they were neuer thyn. And if thou laudest & ioyest any wight/ for he is stuffed with suche maner richesse/ ẏ arte in that beleue begiled/ for thou wenest thilke ioye to be selynesse or els ease/ & he that hath loste suche happes to ben unsely. Ye forsoth (q̄d I). Wel (q̄d she) than wol I proue that unsely in that wise is to preise/ & so the tother is the cōtrary to be lacked. Howe so (q̄d I) For unsely (q̄d she) begyleth nat/ but sheweth thentent of her workyng. Et ecōtra. Selynesse begyleth/ for in prosperite she maketh a iape in blyndnesse/ that is she wyndeth him to make sorowe whan she withdraweth. Woste thou nat (q̄d she) preise him better that sheweth to the his herte/ tho it be with bytande wordes & dispitous/ thā him that gloseth & thīketh in their absence to do the many harmes. Certes (q̄d I) the one is to cōmende/ & the other to lacke & dispice. A ha (q̄d she) right so ease while he lasteth/ gloseth & flatereth/ & lyȝtly voydeth whan she most plesauntly sheweth/ and

and euer in her absence she is aboute to do the tene and sorowe in herte: but vnsely al be it with vptande chere / sheweth what she is / and so doth not that other / wherfore vnsely dothe not begyle. Selynesse disceyueth: vnsely put awaye doute. That one maketh men blynde / that other openeth their eyen in shewynge of wretchydnesse. The one is ful of drede to lese that is not his owne: that other is sobre and maketh men discharged of mokel heuynesse in burthen. The one draweth a man from very good / the other haleth hym to vertue by the hookes of thoughtes. And wenyst thou nat that thy disease hath done the mokel more to wynne / than euer yet thou lostest? and more than euer the contrary made the wynne. Is nat a great good to thy thynkyng / for to knowe the hertes of thy sothfast frendes. Pardy they ben proued to the ful / and the trewe haue disceuered from the false. Trewly at the goynge of the lyke brotel ioye / ther yede no more awaye / than the lyke that was nat thyne proper: He was neuer from that lyghtly departed / thyne owne good therfore leaueth it styll with the. Nowe good (quod she) for howe moche woldest thou somtyme haue bought / this verry knowyng of thy frendes / from the flatterynge flyes that the glosed / whan thou thought thy selfe sely. But thou that playnest of losse in rychesse / hast founden the most dere worthy thynge that thou escapest vnsely / hath made the moche thynge to wynnen. And also for conclusyoun of al / he is frende that nowe leaueth nat his hert from thyne helpes. And if that Margarite denyeth nowe nat to suffre her vertues shyne to the wardes / with spreadynge beames / as farre or farther than if thou were sely in worldly ioye: trewly I saye nat els but she is somdele to blame.

Ah / peace (quod I) and speke no more of this / myne herte breaketh / nowe thou touchest any suche wordes. A wel (quod she) thanne lette vs syngen / thou herest no more of these thynges at this tyme.

¶ Thus endeth the firste booke of the Testament of Loue / and herafter foloweth the seconde.

VEry welth may not be founden in al this worlde / and that is wel sene: Lo howe in my mooste comforte / as I wende and moost supposed to haue hadde ful answere of my contrary thoughtes / sodaynly it was vanysshed. And al the workes of man faren in the same wyse / whan folke wenen best her entent for to haue / and wylles to perfourme / anone chaungyng of the lyft syde to the ryght halue / tourneth it so clene in to another kynde / ẏ neuer shal it come to the fyrst plyte in doynge.

O this wrongful steeryng so soone otherwysed out of knowynge / but for my purpose was at my begynnynge / and so dureth yet / if god of his grace tyme wol me graunt / I thynke to perfourme this worke / as I haue begonne in loue / after as my thynne wytte / with inspyracion of hym that hyldeth al grace wol suffre. Greuously god wotte haue I suffred a great throwe that the romayne emperour / whiche in vnyte of loue shulde acorde and euery with other / in cause of other to auaunce / and namely sythe this empyre to be corrected of so many sectes in heresie / of faith / of seruyce / of rule in loues relygion. Trewly al were it but to shende erronyous opinyons / I maye it no lenger suffre: for many menne there ben that sayne loue to ben in grauel and sande / that with see ebbynge and flowynge woweth / as riches that sodaynly vanyssheth. And some sayn that loue shulde be in wyndy blastes / that stoundmele turneth as a phane / and glorie of renome / whiche after lustes of the varyaunt people is areysed or stylled. Many also wenen that in the sonne and the moone / and other sterres / loue shulde ben founden / for amonge al other planettes moste souerainly they shynen / as dignytees in reuerence of estates rather than good han and occupyen. Ful many also there ben that in okes and in huge postes supposen loue to ben grounded / as in strength & in might / whiche mowen not helpen their owne wretchydnesse / whan they gynne to fal. But suche dyuersyte of

N.n.ii. sectes

sectes ayenst the rightful byleue of loue/ these errours ben forthe spredde/ that loues seruauntes in trewe rule and stedfaste faythe/ in no place darne apere: Thus irrecuperable ioy is went/ and anoy endlesse is entred. For no man aright reproueth suche errours/ but confyrmen their wordes/ and sayn that badde is noble good/ and goodnesse is badde: to whiche folke the prophete byddeth/ Wo without ende.

Also manye tonges of great false techynges in gylynge maner/ principally in my tymes/ not onely with wordes/ but also with armes/ loues seruauntes and professe in his relygion of trewe rule/ pursewen to confounden and to distroyen. And for as moche as holy fathers/ that our christen fayth aproued and strengthed to the iewes/ as to men resonable/ and of diuynite lerned/ proued thilke faythe with resones/ and with auctorites of the olde testament & of the newe/ her pertynacie to distroy: But to paynyms/ that for beestes and houndes were holde/ to put hem out of their errour/ was myracles of god shewed. These thynges were fygured by comynge of thangel to the shepeherdes/ and by the sterre to paynyms kynges/ as who sayth: angel resonable to resonable creature/ and sterre of myracle to people bestyal not lerned/ werne sent to enforme. But I louers clerke in al my connyng and with al my myghtes/ trewly I haue no suche grace in vertue of myracles/ ne for no discomfyte falsheedes/ suffyseth not auctorytes alone/ sythen that suche heretykes and maintaynours of falsytes. Wherfore I wotte wel sythen that they ben men/ and reason is approued in hem/ the clowde of errour hath her reason bewonde probable resons/ whiche that catchende wytte rightfully may not withsytte. By my trauaylynge studye I haue ordeyned hem/ with that auctorite misglosed by mannes reason/ to graunt shal be enduced.

Nowe gynneth my penne to quake/ to thinken on the sentences of the enuyous people/ whiche alwaye ben redy/ bothe ryder and goer to skorne and to iape this leude booke/ and me for rancoure and hate in their hertes they shullen so dispyse/ that although my booke be leude/ yet shal it ben more leude holden/ and by wicked wordes in many maner apayred. Certes me thynketh the sowne of their badde speche/ ryght nowe is ful bothe myne eeres. O good precious Margaryte/ myne herte shulde wepe if I wyste ye token hede of suche maner speche/ but trewly I wotte wel in that your wysdome shal not asterte. For of god maker of kynde wytnesse I take/ that for none enuy ne yuel haue I drawe this mater togyder/ but onely for goodnesse to maintayn/ and errours in falsetees to distroy. Wherfore (as I sayd) with reason I thynke/ thylke forsayd errours to distroye and dequace.

These reasons and suche other/ if they enduce men in loues seruyce/ trewe to beleue of parfyte blysse/ yet to ful faithe in credence of deserte/ fully mowe they nat suffyse/ sithen faith hath no meryte of mede/ whan mannes reason sheweth experyence in doyng. For vtterly no reason the parfyte blysse of loue by no waye maye make to be comprehended. Lo what is a persel of louers ioye/ parfyte science in good seruyce/ of their desyre to comprehende in bodily doynge the lykynge of the soule/ not as by a glasse to haue contemplacion of tyme comynge/ but thilke first ymagyned and thought/ after face to face in beholdyng: what herte/ what reason/ what vnderstandynge can make his heuen to be feled and knowe without assaye in doynge? certes none. Sythen thanne of loue cometh suche fruite in blysse/ and loue in hym selfe is the most amonge other vertues/ as clerkes sayne: The sede of suche springynge in al places/ in al countreys/ in al worldes shulde ben sowe.

But o welawaye thilke sede is forsake/ and mowen not ben suffred the londe tyllers to sette a werke/ without medlynge of cockle/ badde wedes whiche somtyme stonken/ hath caught the name of loue amonge ydiotes and badde meanynge people. Neuer the later/ yet howe so it be that menne cleape thilke kynge preciousest in kynde/ with many eke names/ that other thynges/ that the loue yeuen the ylke noble name/ it sheweth wel that in a maner men haue a great lykynge in worshyppynge of thilke of thilke name/ wherfore this worke haue I writte/ and to the tytled of loues name/ I haue it auowed in a maner of sacrifyse/ that where euer it be radde/ it mowe in merpte by the excellence of thilke name the more weye in authorite and worshyppe of takynge in hede/ and to what entent it was ordayned/ the inferres mowen ben moued: Euery thynge to whom is owande occasyon done as for his ende/ Aristotle supposeth that the actes of euery thynge ben in a maner his fynal cause. A fynal cause is noblerer or els euen as noble as thilke thynge that is fynally to thilke ende/ wherfore accion of thynge euerlastyng/ is demed to be eternal/ and not temporal/ sythen it is his fynal cause: Ryght so the actes of my boke Loue/ and loue is noble/ wherfore though my boke be leude/ the cause with whiche I am stered/ & for whom I ought it done/ noble forsothe ben bothe. But bycause that in connynge I am yonge/ and canne yet but crepe/ this leude A/b/c/ haue I sette in to lernyng/ for I can not passen the tellyng of thre as yet: and if god wyl in shorte tyme I shal amende this leudnesse in ioynynge syllables/ whiche thynge for dulnesse of wytte I maye not in thre letters declare. For trewly I saye the goodnesse of my Margaryte perle wolde yeue mater in endityng to many clerkes: certes her mercy is more to me swetter than any lyuynges/ wherfore my lyppes mowen not suffyse in spekyng of her ful laude and worshyppe as they shulde. But who is that in knowyng of the orders of heuen/ & putteth his resones in the erthe: I forsothe may not with blere eyen/ yͤ shynyng sone of vertue in bright whele of this Margaryte beholde/ therfore as yet I maye her not discryue in vertue as I wolde. In tyme comynge in another tretyse thorowe goddes grace/ this sonne in clerenesse of vertue to be knowe/ and howe she enlumyneth al this day/ I thynke to declare.

IN this meane whyle this comfortable lady ganne synge/ a wonder mater of endityng in latyn/ but trewly the noble colours in rethorik wyse knytte were so craftely/ that my connyng wol not stretche to remembre/ but the sentence I trowe somdele haue I in mynde. Certes they were wonder swete of sowne/ and they were touched al in lamentacion wyse/ and by no werbles of myrthe: Lo thus ganne she synge in latyn/ as I may constrewe it in our englysshe tonge.

Alas that these heuenly bodyes their lyght and course shewen/ as nature yaue hem in commaundement at the gynnyng of the first age/ but these thynges in free choyce of reson han none vnderstondynge: but man that ought to passe al thynge of doynge/ of right course in kynde/ ouer whelmed sothnesse by wrongful tyt.e/ and hath drawen the sterre of enuye to gon by his syde/ that the clyps of me that shulde be his shynande sonne/ so ofte is seyl that it wened thilke errour thorowe hem come in/ shulde ben myn owne defaute. Trewly therfore I haue me withdrawe/ and made my dwellynge out of lande in an yle by my selfe/ in the occian closed/ and yet sayne there many they haue me harberowed/ but god wote they faylen. These thynges me greuen to thynke/ and namely on passed gladnesse/ that in this worlde was wonte me disporte of hyghe and lowe/ and nowe it is fayled: they that wolden maystries me haue in thilke stoundes. In heuen on hyghe aboue Saturnes sphere/ in seasonable tyme were they lodged/ but now wͭ come queynte counsaylours that in no house wol suffre me soiourne/ wherof is pyte: and yet sayne some that they me haue in celler with wyne shed/ in gernere there corne is layde/ couered with whete/ in sacke sowed with wolle/ in purse with money faste knytte/ amonge pannes moulded in a wyche/ in presse amonge clothes layde with ryche pelure arayed/ in stable amonge horse & other beestes/ as hogges/ shepe/ and nete/ and in other many wyse. But thou maker of lyght (in wynkyng of thyn eye the sonne is queynt) woste right wel that I in trewe name was neuer thus herberowed. Somtyme toforn the sonne in yͤ seuenth partie was smyten/ I bare both crosse & mytre/ to yeue it where I wolde. With me yͤ pope went a fote/ & I tho was worshypped of al holy church Kynges baden me their crownes holden. The lawe was set as it shulde: tofore yͤ iuge as wel yͤ

N.ii.iii. poore

poore durste shewe his grefe as the ryche/ for al his money. I defended tho taylages/ and was redy for the poore to pay. I made great feestes in my tyme/ and noble songes/ and maryed damoselles of gentyl feture/ withouten golde or other rychesse. Poore clerkes for wytte of schole/ I sette in churches/ and made suche persones to preache: and tho was seruyce in holy churche honest and deuoute/ in plesaunce bothe of god and of the people. But nowe the leude for symonye is auaunced/ and shendeth al holy churche. Nowe is stewarde for his achates/ nowe is courtyour for his debates/ nowe is eschetoure for his wronges/ nowe is losel for his songes/ personer and prouendre alone/ with whiche manye thrifty shulde encrease. And yet is this shrewe behynde/ free herte is forsake/ and losengeour is take. Lo it acordeth/ for suche there ben that voluntarye lustes haunten in courte with rybaudye/ that tyl mydnight and more wol playe and wake/ but in the churche at matyns he is behynde/ for yuel disposycion of his stomake: therfore he shulde eate beane breed/ and so dyd his syre/ his estate therwith to strenghthen. His auter is broke/ and lowe lythe in poynte to gone to the erthe/ but his horse muste ben easy and hye to beare him ouer great waters. His chalyce poore/ but he hath ryche cuppes. No towayle but a shete there god shal ben handled. And on his meate borde there shal ben borde clothes and towelles many payre. At masse serueth but a clergyon: fyue squiers in hal. Poore chauncel/ open holes in euery syde: beddes of sylke with tappytes goyng al aboute his chambre. Poore masse boke and leude chapelayne/ and broken surplyce with many an hole: good houndes and many/ to hunte after harte and hare/ to fede in their feestes. Of poore men haue they great care/ for they euer craue/ and nothynge offren/ they wolden haue hem doluen. But amonge legystres there dare I not come/ my doynge they sayne maken hem nedy/ they ne wolde for nothyng haue me in town/ for than were tort and forthe nought worthe an hawe about and pleasen no men/ but thilk greuous and torcious ben in might and in doyng: these thynges to forne sayd mowe wel if men lyste ryme/ trewly they acorde nothynge. And for as moch as al thynges by me shulden of right ben gouerned/ I am sorye to se that gouernaunce fayleth/ as thus: to sene smale and lowe gouerne the hye/ and bodies aboue. Certes ye polesye is naught/ it is forbode by them that of gouernaunce treaten & enformen. And right as beestly wytte shulde ben subiecte to reason/ so erthly power in it selfe/ the lower shulde ben subiect to ye hygher. What is worth thy body/ but it be gouerned with thy soule: right so lytel or naught is worthe erthely power/ but if reignatyfe prudence in heedes gouerne the smale/ to whiche heedes the smale owen to obey/ and suffre in their gouernaunce. But souerainnesse ayenwarde shulde thynke in this wyse: I am seruaunt of these creatures to me delyuered/ not lorde but defendour/ not mayster but enfourmer/ not possessoure but in possessyon/ and to hem lyche a tree in whiche sparowes shullen stelen/ her byrdes to norisshe and forthe bring vnder suretie ayenst al rauenous foules and beestes/ and not to be tyraunt them selfe. And than the smale in reste and quyete/ by the heedes wel disposed/ owen for their souerayntes helth and prosperyte to pray/ and in other doynges/ in maintenaunce therof performe/ withouten other admynistracion in rule of any maner gouernaunce. And they wyt haue in hem/ and grace to come to suche thynges/ yet shulde they cease tyl their heedes them cleped/ although profyte and pleasaunce shulde folowe. But trewly other gouernaunce ne other medlynge ought they not to clayme/ ne ye heedes on hem to put. Trewly amonges cosynage dare I not come/ but if rychesse be my meane/ sothly she & other bodely goodes maketh nigh cosinage/ ther neuer propynquite ne alyaunce in lyue was/ ne shuld haue be/ nere it for her medling maners/ wherfore kyndly am I not ther leged. Pouert of kynred is behynde/ rychesse suffreth him to passe: truely he saith he com neuer of Iaphetes children. Wherof I am sory ye Iaphetes children for pouert/ in no linage ben rekened/ & Caymes children for riches be maked Iaphetes heires. Alas this is a wonder chaunge bytwene tho

two

two Noes chyldren/ sythen that of Japhetes offspring comeden knightes/ & of Cayn discended the lyne of seruage to his brothers childre. Lo howe gentylesse and seruage as cosyns/ bothe discended out of two bretherne of one body: Wherfore I saye in sothnesse/ that gentylesse in kynrede maken not gentyl lynage in successyon/ without deserte of a mans own selfe. Where is nowe the lyne of Alysaundre the noble/ or els of Hector of Troye: Who is discended of right bloode of lyne fro king Artour? Parde sir Perdicas/ whom that kynge Alysādre made to ben his heire in Grece/ was of no kynges bloode/ his dame was a tombystere. Of what kynred ben the gentyles in our dayes: I trow therfore if any good be in gentylesse/ it is onely that it semeth a maner of necessyte be input to gentylmen/ that they shulden not varyen fro the vertues of their auncestres. Certes al maner lynage of men ben euen liche in byrth/ for one father maker of al goodnes enformed hem al/ & al mortal folke of one sede arne greyned. Wherto auaūt men of her lynage/ in cosynage or in elde fathers. Loke now the gynnyng/ and to god maker of mans person/ there is no clerke ne no worthy in gentilesse: and he that norissheth his corage with vyces & vnresonable lustes/ and leaueth the kynde course/ to whiche ende hym brought forthe his byrthe/ trewly he is vngentyl/ and amonge clerkes may ben nempned. And therfore he that wol ben gentyl/ he mote daunten his flesshe fro vyces ŷ causen vngentylnesse/ and leaue also reignes of wicked lustes/ and drawe to hym vertue/ that in al places gentylnesse gentylmen maketh. And so speke I in feminyne gendre in general/ of tho persones at the reuerence of one/ whom euery wight honoureth/ for her bountie and her noblesse ymade her to god so dere/ that his moder she became/ and she me hath had so great in worshyp/ that I nyl for nothyng in open declare/ that in any thynge ayenst her secte maye so wene: for al vertue and al worthynesse of plesaunce in hem haboundeth. And although I wolde any thing speke/ trewly I can not/ I may fynde in yuel of hem no maner mater.

Ryght with these wordes she stynte of that lamentable melodye/ and I ganne with a lyuely herte to praye/ if that it were lykyng vnto her noble grace/ she wolde her deyne to declare me the mater that firste was begonne/ in whiche she leste and stynte to speke beforne she gan to synge.

O (quod she) this is no newe thynge to me/ to sene you menne desyren after mater/ whiche your selfe caused to voyde.

Ah good lady (qd I) in whom victorie of strength is proued aboue al other thynge/ after the iugement of Esdram/ whose lordshyp al lignes: who is that right as emperour hem cōmaundeth/ whether thilke ben not women/ in whose lykenesse to me ye aperen. For right as man halte the principalte of al thyng vnder his beynge/ in the masculyne gender/ and no mo genders ben there but masculyn and femenyne/ al the remenaunt ben no gendres but of grace/ in facultie of grammer. Right so in the femenyne/ the women holden the vpperest degree of al thynges vnder thilke gendre conteyned. Who bringeth forthe kynges/ whiche that ben lordes of see and of erthe/ and al peoples of women ben borne: they norysshe hem that graffen vynes/ they maken men comforte in their gladde cheres. Her sorowe is dethe to mannes herte. Without women the beyng of men were impossyble. They conne with their swetnesse the crewel herte rauysshe and make it meke/ buxome/ and benigne/ without vyolence meuynge. In beautie of their eyen/ or els of other maner fetures is al mens desyres/ ye more than in golde/ precious stones/ eyther any rychesse. And in this degree lady your selfe many hertes of men haue so bounden/ that parfyte blysse in womankynde to ben men wenen/ and in nothynge els. Also lady the goodnesse/ the vertue of women/ by properte of discrecion/ is so wel knowen/ by lytelnesse of malyce/ that desyre to a good asker by no waye conne they warne: and ye thanne that wol not passe the kynde werchynge of your sectes by general discrecion/ I wotte wel ye wol so enclyne to my prayere/ that grace of my requeste shal

K.k.k.iii. fully

fully ben graunted. Certes (qd she) thus for
the more parte fareth al mankynde to praye/
and to crye after womans grace/ and fayne
many fãtasies to make hertes enclyne to your
desyres: & whan these sely women for freelte
of their kynde beleuen your wordes / and we-
nen al be gospel the promise of your behestes/
than graunt they to you their hertes/and ful-
fyllen your lustes/ wherthrough their lyberte
in maystresshyp that they toforne had is thral-
led/ & so maked souerayn and to be prayed/ ye
first was seruaunt/ & voice of prayer used.
Anon as fylled is your lust/ many of you be
so trewe/ that lytel hede take ye of suche kynd-
nesse/ but with traysoun anon ye thynke hem
begyle/ & let lyght of that thyng whiche firste
ye maked to you wonders dere/ so what thing
to women it is to loue any wight er she hym
wel knowe/ & haue him ꝓued in many halfe/
for euery glytteryng thyng is nat golde/ & vn-
der colour of fayre speche many vices may be
hyd & conseled. Therfore I rede no wyght to
trust on you to rathe/ mens chere & her speche
right gyleful is ful ofte/ Wherfore without
good assay/ it is nat worthe on many on you
to truste: Trewly it is right kyndely to euery
man that thynketh women betraye/ & shewen
outwarde al goodnesse/ tyl he haue his wyl ꝑ-
formed. Lo the birde is begyled with the me-
ry voice of the foulers whistel. Whan a wo-
man is closed in your nette/ than wol ye cau-
ses fynden/ & beare vnkyndnesse her vnhãde/
or falsete vpon her putte/ your owne malyci-
ous trayson with suche thynge to excuse. Lo
than han women none other wreche in vẽge-
aunce/ but bloder & wepe tyl hem lyst stynt/ &
sorily her mishap cõplayne/ & is put in to we-
nyng that al men ben so vntrewe. Howe of-
ten haue men chaunged her loues in a lytel
while/ or els for faylyng their wyl in their pla
ces hem sette: for frenship shal be one/ & same
with another him lyste for to haue/ & a thirde
for delyte/ or els were he lost bothe in packe &
in clothes: Is this faire/ nay god wot. I may
nat tel by thousande partes/ the wrõges in tre
chery of suche false people/ for make they ne-
uer so good a bõde/ al sette ye at a myte whan
your hert tourneth: And they that wenen for
sorowe of you dey/ the pite of your false herte
is flowe out of towne. Alas therfore/ ye euer
any woman wolde take any wyght in her
grace/ tyl she knowe at the ful on whom she
might at al assayes trust. Womẽ con no more
crafte in queynt knowynge/ to vnderstande
the false disceyuable conectementes of man-
nes begilynges. Lo howe it fareth/ though ye
men gronen and cryen/ certes it is but discept/
and that preueth wel by thendes in your wer-
kynge. Howe many women haue ben lorne/
and with shame foule shent by longe lastyn-
ge tyme/ whiche thorowe mennes gyle haue
ben disceyued? euer their fame shal dure/ and
their dedes radde and songe in many londes/
that they han done recoueren shal they neuer/
but alway ben demed lightly/ in suche plyte a
yen shulde they fal/ of whiche slaunders and
tenes ye false men and wicked ben the verey
causes/ on you by right ought these shames
and these reproues al holy discende. Thus
arne ye al nyghe vntrewe/ for al your fayre
speche your herte is ful fyckel. What cause
han ye women to dispyse? better fruite than
they ben / ne swetter spyces to your behoue
mowe ye not fynde/ as farre as worldly bo-
dyes stretchen. Loke to their formynge at the
makyng of their persones by god in ioye of
paradyce/ for goodnesse of mans propre body
were they maked/ after the sawes of the byble/
rehersyng goddes wordes in this wyse: It is
good to mankynde that we make to him an
helper. Lo in paradyse for your helpe was
this tree graffed/ out of whiche al lynage of
man discendeth: if a man be noble frute/ of
noble frute it is sprongen: the blysse of para-
dyse to mennes sory hertes/ yet in this tree a-
bydeth. O noble helpes ben these trees/ and
gentyl iewel to ben worshypped of euery good
creature: He that hem anoyeth dothe his owne
shame/ it is a comfortable perle ayenst al te-
nes. Euery company is myrthed by their pre-
sent beyng. Trewly I wyst neuer vertue/ but
a woman were therof ye rote. What is heuen
the worse though sarazins on it lyen? Is your
faythe vntrewe though rennogates maken
theron leasynges. If the fyre doth any wight
brenne/ blame his owne wytte that put him
selfe

selfe so farre in the heate. Is not fyre gentyl-lest and moste element comfortable amonges al other: fyre is chefe werker in fortherynge sustenaunce to mankynde: shal fyre ben blamed for it brēde a foole naturelly/ by his own stulty wytte in sterynge. Ah wicked folkes/ for your propre malyce/ and shreudnesse of your selfe: ye blame and dispyse the precioust thyng of your kynde/ and whiche thynges amonge other moste ye desyren. Trewly Nero and his children ben shrewes/ that dispysen so their dames. The wickednesse and gylyng of men/ in disclaundring of thilke that moste hath hem gladed and pleased/ were impossyble to write or to nempne. Neuer the later yet I say he that knoweth a way/ may it lightly passe: eke an herbe proued may safely to smertande sores ben layde: So I say/ in hym that is proued is nothyng suche peuels to gesse. But these thynges haue I rehersed to warne you women al at ones/ that to lyghtly without good assaye ye assenten not to mannes speche. The sonne in the day lyght/ is to knowen from the moone that shyneth in the nyght. Nowe to the thy selfe (quod she) as I haue ofte sayd/ I knowe wel thyne herte/ thou arte none of al the tofore nempned people/ for I knowe wel the contynuaunce of thy seruyce/ that neuer sythen I set the a werke/ myght thy Margaryte for plesaunce/ frendeshyp/ ne fayrehede of none other/ be in poynte moued from thyne herte/ wherfore in to myne housholde hastely I wol that thou entre/ and al the parfyte priuyte of my werkyng make it be knowe in thy vnderstondyng/ as one of my priuy famyliers. Thou desyrest (qđ she) fayne to here of tho thynges there I lefte. Ye forsothe (qđ I) that were to me a great blysse. Nowe (qđ she) for thou shalt not wene that womans condycions for fayre speche suche thyng belongeth.

Thou shalte (qđ she) vnderstonde first amonge al other thynges/ that al the cure of my seruyce to me in the parfyte blysse in doyng is desyred in euery mannes herte/ be he neuer so moche a wretche/ but euery man trauayleth by dyuers studye/ and seke thylke blysse by dyuers wayes/ but al the endes are knyt in selynesse of desyre in the ꝑfyte blysse/ that is suche ioye/ whan men it haue gotten/ there lyueth no thynge more to ben coueyted: But howe that desyre of suche perfection in my seruyce be kyndely set in louers hertes/ yet her erronyous opinyons misturne it by falsenesse of wenyng. And although mennes vnderstandyng be misturned/ to knowe whiche shuld ben the way vnto my person/ and whyther it abydeth: yet wote they there is a loue in euery wight/ weneth by that thyng that he coueyteth moste/ he shulde come to thilke loue/ and that is parfyte blysse of my seruauntes/ but than fulle blysse maye not be/ and there lacke any thynge of that blysse in any syde. Eke it foloweth than/ that he that must haue ful blysse/ lacke no blysse in loue on no syde.

Therfore lady (quod I tho) thylke blysse I haue desyred/ and sothe tofore this my selfe by wayes of riches/ of dignite/ of power/ and of renome/ wenyng me in tho thinges had ben thilke blysse/ but ayenst the heere it turneth. Whan I supposed beste thilke blysse haue get and come to the ful purpose of your seruyce/ sodaynly was I hyndred/ and throwen so fer abacke/ yͤ me thynketh an impossyble to come there I lefte. I wol wel (qđ she) and therfore hast thou fayled/ for thou wentist not by the hye way: a lytel misgoyng in the gynnyng causeth mykyl errour in the ende/ wherfore of thilke blysse thou fayledest for hauyng of rychesse/ ne non of the other thyngꝫ thou nēpnedest/ mowen nat make suche ꝑfite blisse ī loue as I shal shewe. Therfore they be nat worthy to thilke blysse/ ꝛ yet somwhat must be cause and way to thilke blysse: Ergo there is some suche thing ꝛ some way/ but it is lytel ī vsage and that is nat openly iknowe. But what felest in thyne hert of yͤ seruice/ in whiche by me thou art entred: Wenest aught thy selfe yet be in the hye way to my blisse: I shal so shewe it to the/ thou shalte nat con saye the contrary.

Good lady (qđ I) altho I suppose it in my herte/ yet wolde I here thyn wordes/ howe ye meanen in this mater. (Qđ she) that I shal with my good wyl. Thilke blysse desyred/ som deale ye knowen/ altho it be nat parfitly/ for kyndly entention ledeth you therto/ but in thre maner

maner lyuenges is al suche wayes shewed. Euery wight in this world to haue this blisse one of thilke thre wayes of lyues must ꝓcede/ whiche after oppynions of great clerkes arne by names cleaped/ bestiallich/ resonablich/ is vertuous: manlych is worldlich/ bestialliche is lustes & delytable/ nothynge restrayned by bridel of reason/ al that ioyeth & yeueth gladnesse to the hert/ and it be ayenst reason/ is lykened to bestial lyueng/ whiche thynge foloweth lustes & delytes/ wherfore in suche thīge maye nat that pcious blysse that is maister of al vertues abyde. your fathers toforne you haue cleped such lusty lyuenges after ẏ flessh passions of desyre/ which are innominable tofore god & mā both. Thā after determination of suche wyse/ we accorden that suche passiōs of desyre shul nat be nempned/ but holden for absolute from al other lyuēges & prouynges/ and so lyueth in to lyuenges/ manlich & resonable to declare the maters begonne. But to make the fully haue vnderstādyng in mālich lyuenges/ whiche is holden worldlich in these thynges/ so that ignorance be made no letter. I wol (qd̄ she) nēpne these forsayd wayes be names & cōclusions. First riches/ dignite/ renome/ & power/ shul in this worke be cleaped bodily goodes/ for in hē hath ben a gret throw mānes trust of selynesse in loue/ as in riches/ suffisance to haue maintayned that was begon/ by worldly catel in dignite/ honour/ & reuerence of hem that werne vnderput by maistry therby to obey. In renome glorie of peoples praysyng/ after lustes in their hert/ without hede takyng to qualite & maner of doing/ and in power/ by trouth of lordships mayntenaunce/ thyng to ꝓcede forth in doyng. In al whiche thynges a longe tyme mānes coueytise in cōmune hath ben greatly grounded/ to cōe to the blysse of my seruice/ but trewly they were begyled/ & for the principal muste nedes fayle & in helping mowe nat auaile. Se why for holdest him not poore ẏ is nedy? Yes parde (qd̄ I) And him for dishonored that moche folke deyne nat to reuerēce. That is soth (qd̄ I) & what him ẏ his mightes faylen & mowe nat helpen. Certes (qd̄ I) me semeth of al mē he shulde be holden a wretch. And wenest nat (qd̄ she) that he that is lytel in renome/ but rather is out of the praysynges of mo men than a fewe be nat in shame? For soth (qd̄ I) it is shame & villany to him that coueyteth rende/ that more folk nat prayse in name than preise. Soth (qd̄ she) thou sayst soth/ but al these thīges are folowed of suche maner doynge/ and wenden in riches suffisaūce/ in power might/ in dignyte worship/ & in renome glorie/ wherfore they discēded in to discreyuable wenyng/ & in that seruice disceite is folowed. And thus in general/ thou & al suche other that so worchen faylen of my blysse that ye long han desyred/ wherfore truly ī lyfe of reason is the hye way to this blysse/ as I thynke more openly to declare herafter. Neuer the later/ yet in a lytel to cōforte thy herte/ in shewyng of what waye thou arte entred thy selfe/ & that thy Margarite may knowe the set in the hye way/ I wol enforme the in this wise. Thou hast fayled of thy first purpose/ bicause thou wentest wrōge and leftest the hye waye on thy right syde/ as thus/ thou lokedest on worldly lyueng & that thyng the begyled/ & lightly therfore as a lytel assay thou songedest/ but whan I turned thy purpose/ & shewed the a parte of the hye waye tho thou abode therin/ and no dethe ne ferdnesse of non enemy might ẏ out of thilk way reue/ but euer one in thyne hert/ to come to the ilke blysse whan thou were arested and fyrste tyme enprisoned/ thou were loth to chaūge thy way/ for in thy hert thou wendest to haue ben there thou shuldest/ & for I had routhe to sene the myscaried/ & wyst wel thyne absenesse my seruyce to forther & encrease/ I come my selfe without other mean to visyt thy person/ in cōforte of thy hert: & ꝑdy in my cōmyng ẏ were greatly gladed/ after whiche tyme/ no disease/ no care/ no tene/ miȝt moue me out of thy hert And yet am I gladde & greatly eupited/ howe contynually thou haddest me in mynde/ with good auysement of thy conscience/ whan thy kyng & his princes by huge wordes & great loked after variaunce in thy speche/ & euer thou were redy for my sake in plesaunce of ẏ Margarite peerle/ and many mo other/ thy body to oblyge in to Marces doyng/ if any contraried thy sawes/ stedfast way maketh stedfast hert/ with

with good hope in the ende. Trewly I wol that thou ikt wel knowe/ for I se the so set and not chaungynge herte haddest in my seruyce/ and I made thou haddest grace of thy kynge/ in foryeuenesse of mykel misdede: to ye gracious kyng arte thou mykel holden/ of whose grace & goodnesse somtyme herafter I thinke the enforme/ whan I shew the grounde where as moral Vertue groweth. Who brought the to werke? Who brought this grace aboute? Who made thy hert hardy? Trewly it was I/ for haddest thou of me fayled/ than of this purpose had neuer taken in this wyse. And therfore I say thou might wel truste to come to thy blysse/ sythen thy gynnynge hath ben harde/ but euer graciously after thy hertes desyre hath proceded. Syluer fyned with many heates men knowen for trew/ and safely men may trust to the alay in werkynge. This diseases hath proued what waye hence forwarde thou thynkest to holde. Nowe in good fayth lady (quod I tho) I am nowe in/ me semeth it is the hye way and the ryght. Ye forsothe (quod she) and nowe I wol disproue thy first wayes/ by whiche many men wenen to gette thilke blysse. But for as moche as euery herte that hath caught ful loue/ is tyed with queynt knyttynges/ thou shalt vnderstande that loue and thilke forsayd blysse toforne declared in this prouynges/ shal hote the knot in the hert.

Wel (qd I) this inpossession I wol wel vnderstande. Nowe also (qd she) for the knotte in the herte muste ben from one to an other/ and I knowe thy desyre: I wol thou vnderstande these maters to ben sayd of thy selfe in disprouyng of thy first seruyce/ and in strẽghthynge of thilke that thou haste vndertake to thy Margaryte perle. A goddes halfe (qd I) ryght wel I fele that al this case is possyble and trewe/ and therfore I admytted al togyther. Vnderstanden wel (quod she) these termes/ and loke no contradyction thou graunt.

If god wol (qd I) of al these thynges wol I not fayle/ and if I graunt contradyction/ I shulde graunte an impossyble/ and that were a foule inconuenyẽce/ for whiche thynges lady twys herafter I thinke me to kepe.

WEl (qd she) thou knowest that euery thynge is a cause wherthroughe any thyng hath beyng/ that is cleped caused/ than if richesse causen knot in herte/ thilke rychesse arne cause of thilke precious thynge beyng: but after the sentẽce of Aristotle/ euery cause is more in dignyte than his thynge caused/ wherthrough it foloweth rychesse to ben more in dignyte thã thilke knot/ but rychesses arne kyndely naughty/ badde/ and nedy/ and thilke knotte is thynge kyndely good/ moste praysed and desyred: Ergo thynge naughty/ badde/ and nedy/ in kyndely vnderstandynge is more worthy than thynge kyndely good/ moste desyred and praysed: the consequence is false/ nedes the antecedent mote ben of the same condycion. But that rychesses ben bad/ naughty/ and nedy/ that wol I proue/ wherfore they mowe cause no suche thyng/ that is so glorious and good: The more richesse thou haste/ the more nede hast thou of helpe hem to kepe. Ergo thou nedest in rychesse/ whiche nede thou shuldest not haue if thou hem wantest. Than muste rychesse ben nedy/ that in their hauyng maken ye nedy to helpes in suretie thy rychesse to kepen/ wherthrough foloweth rychesse to ben nedy. Euery thing causynge yuels is badde & naughty: but rychesse in one causen misease/ in another they mowen not euenly stretchen al about. Wherof cometh plee/ debate/ thefte/ begylinges/ but rychesse to wynne/ whiche thynges ben badde/ and by richesse arne caused: Ergo thylke rychesse ben badde/ whiche badnesse and nede ben knyt in to rychesse by a maner of kyndely propertie/ and euery cause and caused accorden/ so that it foloweth thilke richesse to haue the same accordaunce with badnesse and nede/ that their cause asketh. Also euery thynge hath his beyng by his cause/ than if ye cause be distroyed/ the beyng of caused is vanysshed: And so if rychesse causen loue/ and rychesse weren distroyed/ the loue shulde vanysshe/ but thylke knotte and it be trewe may not vanysshe for no goyng of no rychesse: Ergo rychesse is no cause of the knot. And many men as I sayd/ setten the cause of the knotte in rychesse/ thilke knytten the rychesse/ and nothynge the yuel: thilke

thilke persons what euer they ben / wenen that ryches is most worthy to be had / & that make they the cause: & so wene they thilke ryches be better than the person. Cōmenly suche asken rather after the quantyte that after the qualyte / and suche wenen as wel by hem selfe as by other / that conjunction of his lyfe and of his soule is no more precious / but in as mykel as he hath of rychesse. Alas howe maye he holden suche thynges precious or noble / that neyther han lyfe ne soule / ne ordynaunce of werchynge lymmes: suche rychesse ben more worthy whan they ben in gatheryng / in departing gynneth his lone of other mens praysyng. And auaryce gatheryng maketh be hated and nedy to many out helpes: and whan leueth the possessyon of such goodes / and they gynne vanyssh / than entreth sorowe and tene in their hertes. O badde & strayte ben thilke that at their departynge maketh men teneful and sory / and in the gatheryng of hem make men nedy: Moche folke at ones mowen not togyder moche therof haue. A good gest gladdeth his hoste and al his meyny / but he is a badde gest that maketh his hoste nedy / & to be aferde of his gistes goyng. Certes (qd I) me wondreth therfore that the comune opynyon is thus: He is worthe no more than that he hath in catel. O (qd she) loke thou be not of that opynion / for if golde or money / or other maner of riches shynen in thy sight / Whose is that? nat thyn: & tho they haue a lytel beautie / they be nothyng in cōparison of our kynde / & therfore ye shulde nat set your worthynesse in thyng lower than your selfe / for the riches / the fairnesse / the worthynesse of thilke goodes / if ther be any suche preciousnesse in hem are nat thyne; thou madest hem so neuer / from other they come to the / & to other they shul from the: wherfore enbracest thou other wightes good, as tho they were thyn? kynde hath drawe hem by hem selfe. It is sothe the goodes of the erth ben ordayned in your fode & norisshynge / but if thou wolte holde the apayde with that suffiseth to thy kynde / thou shalt nat be in daūger of no suche riches / to kynde suffiseth lytel thīg who that taketh hede. And if thou wolt algates with superfluite of riches be a throted / thou shalt hastelych be anoyed / or els yuel at ease. And fairnesse of feldes ne of habytations / ne multytude of meyne / maye nat be rekened as riches that are thyn owne / for if they be badde it is great sclaunder & villany to the ocupyer / and if they be good or faire / the mater of the workeman that hem made is to prayse. Howe shulde other wyse bountie be cōpted for thyne / thilke goodnesse & fairnesse be ꝓper to tho thīges hem selfe / than if they be nat thyne sorowe nat whan they wende / ne glad the nat in pōpe and ī pride whan thou hem hast / for their boūtie and their beautes cometh out of their owne kynde / & nat of thyne owne ꝑson: as faire ben they in their not hauyng as whan thou haste hem / they be nat faire for thou haste hem / but thou haste geten hem for the fairnesse of them selfe. & there the vaylance of men is demed in richesse outforth / wenen me to haue no proper good in them selfe / but seche it in straunge thīges. Trewly the cōdytion of good wenyng is in þ mystourned / to wene your noblesse be not in your selfe / but in the goodes & beautie of other thynges. Pardy the beestes that han but felyng soules / haue suffisaunce in their owne selfe: & ye that ben lyke to god / seken encrease of suffisaunce from so excellent a kynde of so lowe thynges / ye do great wrong to him that you made lordes ouer al erthly thynges / & ye put your worthynesse vnder the nōbre of the fete of lower thynges & foule / whan ye iuge thilke riches to be your worthynesse / than put ye your selfe by estimacion vnder thilke foule thynges / & than leue ye the knowyng of your selfe / so be ye viler than any dombe beest / that cometh of shrewde vice. Right so thilke persons that louen non yuel for dere worthynesse of the persone / but for straūge goodes / & saith the adornement in the knot lyth in such thing / his errour is perilous & shrewde / and he wrieth moche venym with moche welth / & that knot maye nat be good whan he hath it getten.

Certes thus hath riches with flyckering sight anoyed many: & often whan there is a throwe out shrewe / he coueteth al the golde / al the precious stones that mowen be founden to haue in his bandon / he weneth no wight be worthy to haue suche thynges but he alone. Howe many haste

ny haste

nye haste thou knowe nowe in late tyme/that in their rychesse supposed suffysance haue folowed/& nowe it is al fayled. Ye lady (qd I) that is for misse medlyng/and other wyse gouerned thilke rychesse than they shulde. Ye (qd she tho) had not the floode greatly areysed/and throwe to hemwarde both grauel and sande/he had made no medlynge. And right as see yeueth floode/so draweth see ebbe/and pulleth ayen vnder wawe al the firste out throw/but if good pyles of noble gouernau̇ce in loue/in wel meanynge maner/ben fadly grounded/to whiche holde thilke grauel as for a whyle/that ayen lightly mowe not it turne: and if the pyles ben trewe/the grauel and sande wol abyde. And certes ful warnyng in loue shalte thou neuer thorowe hem get ne couer/that lightly with an ebbe er thou beware it wol ayen meue. In rychesse many men haue had tenes and diseases/whiche they shulde not haue had/if therof they had fayled. Thorowe whiche nowe declared partely it is shewed/that for rychesse shulde the knotte in herte neyther ben caused in one ne in other: trewly knotte maye ben knytte/and I trowe more stedfast in loue though rychesse fayled/and els in rychesse is the knotte & not in herte. And than suche a knotte is false/whan the see ebbeth and withdraweth the grauel/that such rychesse voydeth/thilke knotte wol vnknytte. Wherfore no trust/no way/no cause/no parfyte beyng is in rychesse of no suche knotte/therfore another way muste we haue.

HOnour in dignyte is wened to yeuen a ful knot. Ye certes (qd I) and of that opinyon ben many/for they sayne dignyte/with honour/and reuerence/causen hertes to encheynen/and so abled to be knytte togyther/for ẏ excellence in soueraynte of such degrees.

Nowe (qd she) if dignyte/honour/and reuerence causen thilke knotte in herte/this knot is good and profytable. For euery cause of a cause/is cause of thyng caused: Than thus/good thynges and profytable ben by dignyte/honour/and reuerence caused. Ergo they accorden/and dignytes ben good with reuerences and honour/but contraryes mowen not accorden: Wherfore by reason there shulde no dignytee/no reuerence/none honour acorde with shrewes/but that is false: they haue ben cause to shrewes in many shrewdnes/for with hem they accorden. Ergo from begynnyng to argue ayenwarde tyl it come to the laste conclusyon/they are not cause of the knot. Lo al day at eye/arne shrewes not in reuerence/in honour/and in dignyte: yes forsothe/rather than the good. Than foloweth it that shrewes rather than good shul ben cause of this knot. But of this contrarie of al louers is byleued/and for a sothe openly determyned to holde.

Nowe (quod I) fayne wolde I here/howe suche dignytees acorden with shrewes.

O (qd she) that wol I shewe in manyfolde wise. Ye wene (qd she) that dignytes of offyce here in your cyte is as the sonne/it shyneth bright withouten any cloude: whiche thynge whan they comen in the handes of malycious tyrauntes/there cometh moche harme/& more greuau̇ce therof/than of ẏ wylde fyre/though it brende al a strete. Certes in dignyte of offyce/the werkes of the occupyer shewen the malyce and the badnesse in the person/with shrewes they maken manyfolde harmes/and moche people shamen. Howe often han rancours for malyce of the gouernour shulde ben maynteyned: Hath not than suche dignytees caused debate/rumoures/and yuels: yes god wote/by suche thynges haue ben trusted to make mens vnderstandyng enclyne to many queynte thynges. Thou wottest wel what I meane. Ye (qd I) therfore as dignyte suche thynge in tene ywrought/so ayenwarde the substaunce in dignite chau̇ged/relyed to bring ayen good plyte in doyng. Do way/do way (qd she) if it so betyde/but that is selde/that suche dignyte is betake in a good mannes gouernaunce. What thynge is to rekken in the dignytees goodnesse: parde the bountie and goodnesse is hers/that vsen it in good gouernaunce/and therfore cometh it that honoure and reuerence shulde ben done to dignyte/bycause of encreasynge vertue in the occupyer/and not to the ruler/bycause of soueraynte in dignite. Sythen dignite may no vertue cause/who is worthy worshyp for suche goodnesse: not

not dignyte/ but person ẏ maketh goodnesse
in dignyte to shyne. This is wonder thyng
(qđ I) for me thynketh/as the person in dig-
nite is worthy honour for goodnesse/ so tho a
person for badnesse magre hath deserued/ yet
the dignite seneth to be cõmended. Let be (qđ
she) thou errest right foule/ dignite with bad-
nesse is helper to pforme the felonous doyng:
pardy were it kyndly good or any properte of
kyndly vertue hadden in hem selfe / shrewes
shulde hem neuer haue/ with hem shulde they
neuer accorde. water & fire that ben contrari-
ous mowen nat togider ben assembled/kynde
wol nat suffre such cõtraries to ioyn. & sithen
at eye by experiẽce in doyng/ we sene that shre-
wes haue hem more often than good menne/
syker mayste thou be/that kyndly good in su-
che thyngz is nat appropred. Pardy were they
kyndly good/ as wel one as other shulden eue-
lych in vertue of gouernaũce ben worthe: but
one sayleth in goodnesse another dothe the cõ-
trary/ & so it sheweth kyndly goodnesse in di-
gnyte nat be groũded. And this same reason
(qđ she) may be made in general on al the bo
dily goodes/for they comen ofte to throwe out
shrewes. After this he is strong that hath mizt
to haue great burthyns/ & he is lyght & swifte
that hath souerainte in rõnyng to passe other
right so he is a shrewe on whom shrewde thyn-
ges & badde han most werchynge. & right as
philosophy maketh philosophers/ & my secui-
ce maketh louers: Right so if dignytes weren
good or vertuous/they shulde maken shrewes
good/ & turne her malyce & make hem be ver-
tuous/but that do they nat/as it is pued/ but
causen rãcour & debate. ergo they be nat good
but vtterly badde. Had Nero neuer ben Em
perour/shulde neuer his dame haue be slayn/
to maken open the priuyte of his engẽdrure.
Herodes for his dignyte slewe many children.
The dignite of kyng Iohn wolde haue distro-
ped al Englãde. Therfore mokel wysedom &
goodnesse both/ nedeth in a person/the malice
in dignite slyly to vndel/ & with a good bytte
of arest to withdrawe/ in case it wolde praũce
otherwise than it shulde: trewly ye yeue to di-
gnites wrõgful names ĩ your cleppyng. They
shulde hete nat dignite / but mõstre of bad-
nesse & mayntenour of shrewes. Pardy shyne
the sonne neuer so bright/ & it bring forthe no
heate/ ne sesonably the herbes out bringe of ẏ
erthe/but suffre frostes & colde/ & the erthe ba-
rayne to lygge by tyme of his compas in cyr-
cute about/ ye wolde wonder & dispreyse that
son. If the Mone be at ful & sheweth no lyzt
but derke & dymme to your syght appereth/ &
make distruction of ẏ waters/ wol ye nat sup
pose it be vnder cloude or in clips: & that some
preuy thing vnknowen to your wittes/is cau
se of suche cõtrarious doynge. Than if cler-
kes that han ful insyght & knowyng of suche
impedimentes enforme you of the sothe/ very
idiottes ye ben/ but if ye yeuen credẽce to thilk
clerkes wordz. & yet it doth me tene/to sene ma
ny wretches reioycen in such maner planettes
Trewly lytel con they on philosophy or els on
my lore/ ẏ any desyre hauen suche lyghtynge
planettes in that wyse any more to shewe.
Good lady (qđ I) tel ye me howe ye mean in
these thynges. Lo (qđ she) the dignites of po-
erte/ Sonne & Mone/nothyng in kynde shew
their shynyng as they shulde. For the Sonne
made no brenyng hete in loue/ but freesed en-
vye in mẽnes hertes for feblenesse of shynyng
hete: & the Moone was about vnder an olde
cloude/ the lyuenges by waters to distroye.

Lady (qđ I) it is supposed they had shyned
as they shulde. ye (qđ she) but nowe it is pro-
ued at the ful their beaute in kyndly shynyng
fayled/ wherfore dignyte of hym seluen hath
no beautie in fairnesse/ne dryueth nat awaye
vices but encreaseth/ & so be they no cause of
the knotte. Nowe se in good trouth/ holde ye
nat such sonnes worthy of no reuerence & dig
nites/ worthy of no worshyp/ ẏ maketh men
to do the more harmes? I not (qđ I) No (qđ
she) & thou se a wyse good man/for his good-
nesse & wysenesse wolte thou nat do hym wor-
ship? Therof he is worthy. That is good skil
(qđ I) it is dewe to suche/ bothe reuerẽce and
worship to haue. Than (qđ she) a shrewe for
his shrewdnesse/ altho he be put forthe to some
other for ferde / yet is he worthy for shrewd-
nesse to be vnworshipped: of reuerence no pte
is he worthy to haue/ to cõtrarious doyng be
longeth & that is good skyl. for right as he be-
smyteth

smyteth the dignites/ thilke same thyng ayenwarde him smyteth/ or els shulde smyte. And ouer this thou woste wel (quod she) that fyre in euery place heateth where it be/ and water maketh wete: why? for kyndely werkyng is so yput in hem to do suche thynges: for euery kyndely in werkyng sheweth his kynde. But though a wight had ben mayre of your cytie many wynter togyder/ and come in a straūge place there he were not knowen/ he shulde for his dignyte haue no reuerence. Than neyther worshyppe ne reuerence is kyndely propre in no dignite/ sythen they shulden don their kynde/ in suche doynge if any were. And if reuerence ne worshyppe kyndely be not set in dignytees/ and they more therin ben shewed than goodnesse/ for that in dignyte is shewed but it proueth that goodnesse kyndely in hem is not grounded. Iwys neyther worshyppe ne reuerence ne goodnesse in dignyte/ done none offyce of kynde/ for they haue none suche propertie in nature of doynge/ but by false opinyon of the people. Lo howe somtyme thilke that in your cytie werne in dignyte noble/ if thou lyste hem nempne/ they ben nowe ouerturned/ bothe in worshyp/ in name/ and in reuerēce: wherfore such dignites haue no kyndely werchyng of worshyppe and of reuerence/ he that hath no worthynesse on it selfe. nowe it ryseth and nowe it vanissheth after the varyaunt opinyon in false hertes of vnstable people. Wherfore if thou desyre the knotte of this iewel/ or els if thou woldest suppose she shulde sette the knotte on the for suche maner dignyte/ than thou wenest beautie or goodnesse of thilke somwhat encreaseth the goodnesse or vertue in the body? But dignyte of hem selfe ben not good/ ne yeuen reuerence ne worshyppe by their owne kynde/ howe shulde they than yeue to any other a thynge/ that by no waye mowe they haue hem selfe? It is sene in dignyte of the emperour and of many mo other/ that they mowe not of hem selue kepe their worshyppe ne their reuerence/ that that in a lytel whyle it is nowe vp & nowe downe/ by vnstedfaste hertes of the people. What bountie mowe they yeue that with cloude lightly leaueth his shynynge? Certes to the occupier is mokel appeyred/ sythen suche doynge dothe villanye to him that maye it not mayntayne/ wherfore thilke waye to the knotte is croked: and if any desyre to come to the knott, he must leaue this waye on his lefte syde/ or els shal he neuer come there.

Avayleth aught (quod she) power of might in mayntenaunce of worthy to come to this knot. Parde (quod I) ye/ for hertes ben rauysshed from suche maner thinges. Certes (quod she) though a fooles herte is with thyng rauysshed/ yet therfore is no general cause of ẏ powers/ ne of a syker parfyte herte to be loked after. Was not Nero the moste shrewe one of thilke that men rede/ and yet had he power to make senatours iustyces/ and princes of many landes? Was not that great power? Yes certes (quod I). Wel (q͞d she) yet might he not helpe him selfe out of disease/ whan he gan fal. Howe many ensamples canste thou remembre of kynges great and noble/ and huge power holden/ and yet they might not kepe hem selue from wretchydnesse. Howe wretched was kyng Henry Curtmantyl er he deyde? he had not so moche as to couer with his membres: and yet was he one of the greatest kynges of al the Normandes offspring/ and moste possessyon had. O/ a noble thynge and clere is power/ that is not founden myghty to kepe him selfe. Nowe trewly a great fole is he/ that for suche thyng wolde sette the knotte in thyne herte. Also power of realmes is not thylke greatest power amonges the worldly powers reckened? And if suche powers han wretchydnesse in hem selfe/ it foloweth other powers of febler condycion to ben wretched/ and than that wretchydnesse shulde be cause of suche a knotte. But euery wyght that hath reason wote wel that wretchydnesse by no way may ben cause of none suche knotte/ wherfore suche power is no cause. That powers haue wretchydnesse in hem selfe/ may right lyghtly ben preued. If power lacke on any syde/ on that

O.o.o. syde

syde is no power/ But no power is wretchyd-
nesse: for al be it so the power of emperours
or kynges/ or els of their realmes (whiche is
the power of the prince) stretchen wyde and
brode/ yet besydes is ther mokel folke of whi-
che he hath no cōmaundement ne lordshyppe/
and there as lacketh his power/ his nonpower
entreth/ where under springeth that maketh
hem wretches. No power is wretchydnesse/
and nothing els: But in this maner hath kyn-
ges more porcion of wretchydnesse than of po-
wer. Trewly suche powers ben unmighty/
for euer they ben in drede howe thilke power
frō lesyng may be keped of sorow/ so drede so-
rily prickes euer ī their hertes: litel is yͭ power
whiche careth and ferdeth it selfe to mayn-
tayne. Unmighty is that wretchydnesse whi-
che is entred by the ferdful weenynge of the
wretche him selfe: and knot ymaked by wret-
chydnesse is betwene wretches/ and wretches
al thyng bewaylen: wherfore the knot shulde
be bewayled/ and there is no suche parfyte
blysse that we supposed at yͤ gynnyng. Ergo
power in nothyng shulde cause suche knottes.
Wretchydnesse is a kyndely propertie in suche
power/ as by way of drede/ whiche they mowe
not eschewe ne by no way lyue in sykernesse.
For thou woste wel (quod she) he is nought
mighty that wolde done that he may not done
ne perfourme. Therfore (quod I) these kyn-
ges and lordes that han suffysaunce at the ful
of men and other thynges/ mowen wel ben
holden mighty: their comaundementes ben
done/ it is neuermore denyed. Foole (qd she)
or he wotte him selfe mighty or wotte it not:
for he is nought mighty/ that is blynde of his
might and wote it not. That is sothe (qd I)
Than if he wot it/ he must nedes ben adradde
to lesen it. He that wotte of his might is in
doute that he mote nedes lese/ and so leadeth
him drede to ben unmighty. And if he retche
not to lese/ lytel is that worthe that of the le-
syng reason retcheth nothyng: and if it were
mighty in power or in strength/ yͭ lesyng shulde
ben withset/ and whan it cometh to the lesyng
he may it not withsytte. Ergo thilke might is
leude and naughty. Such mightes arne ilyke
to postes and pyllers that upright stonden/
and great might han to beare many charges/
and if they croke on any syde/ lytel thynge
maketh hem ouerthrowe. This is a good en-
sample (quod I) to pyllers and postes that I
haue sene ouerthrowed my selfe/ and hadden
they ben underput with any helpes/ they had
not so lightly fal. Than holdest thou him
mighty that hath many men armed and ma-
ny seruauntes/ and euer he is adradde of hem
in his herte/ and for he gasteth hem/ somtyme
he mote the more feare haue. Comenly he that
other agasteth/ other in him ayenwarde wer-
chen the same: and thus warnisshed mote he
be/ and of warnysshe the hour drede: Lytel is
that might & right leude/ who so taketh hede.
Than semeth it (quod I) that suche famulers
aboute kynges and great lordes/ shulde great
might haue. Althoughe a sypher in augrym
haue no might in signifycacion of it selue/ yet
he yeueth power in signifycacion to other/ and
these clepe I the helpes to a poste to kepe him
from fallyng. Certes (quod she) thilke skyl-
les ben leude. Why? but if the shorers ben wel
grounded/ the helpes shullen slyden and suffre
the charge to fal/ her myght lytel auayleth.
And so me thynketh (quod I) that a poste a-
lone stonding upright upon a basse/ may len-
ger in graet burthen endure/ than croken py-
lers for al their helpes/ and her groūde be not
syker. That is soth (qd she) for as the blynde
in bearyng of the same gynne stomble/ bothe
shulde fal/ right so suche pyllers so enuyroned
with helpes in fallyng of the grounde/ fayleth
al togyther/ howe ofte than suche famulers
in their moste pride of prosperyte ben sodainly
ouerthrowen. Thou haste knowe many in a
momēt so ferre ouerthrowe/ that couer might
they neuer/ Whan the heuynesse of suche fay-
lyng cometh by case of fortune/ they mowe it
not eschue: and might and power/ if ther were
any/ shulde of strēgth such thinges voyde and
weyue/ & so it is not. Lo than whiche thing is
this power/ yͭ tho men han it they ben agast/ &
in no tyme of ful hauīg be they syker: & if they
wold weyue drede/ as they mow not/ litel is in
worthynes. Fye therfore on so naughty thing
any knot to cause. Lo ī aduersite/ thilk ben his
foes yͭ glosed & semed frēdes ī welth: thus arn
his

his sampliers his foes and his enemyes: and nothyng is werse ne more mighty for to anoy than is a samplier enemye/ and these thynges may they not weyue: so trewly their might is not worthe a cresse. And ouer al thynge/ he that maye not withdrawe the bridel of his flesshly lustes and his wretched complayntes (nowe thynke on thy selfe) trewly he is not mighty: I can sene no waye that lythe to the knotte. Thilke people than that setten their hertes vpon suche mightes and powers/ often ben begyled. Parde he is not mighty that may do any thyng/ that another maye doone hym the selue/ and that men haue as great power ouer him as he ouer other. A iustyce that demeth men/ ayenwarde hath ben often demed. Buserus slewe his gestes/ and he was slayne of Hercules his geste. Hugest betrayshed many men/ and of Collo was he betrayed. He that with swerde smyteth/ with swerde shal be smytten. Than gan I to studyen a whyle on these thinges/ and made a countenaunce with my hande in maner to ben huyshte. Nowe let sene (qd she) me thynketh somwhat there is within thy soule/ that troubleth thy vnderstandyng/ saye on what it is. (Quod I tho) me thynketh that although a man by power haue suche might ouer me/ as I haue ouer other/ that disproueth no myght in my person/ but yet may I haue power and myght neuer the later. Se nowe (quod she) thyne owne leudenesse: He is mighty that maye without wretchydnesse/ and he is vnmyghty that may it not withsytte: but than he that might ouer the/ and he wol put on the wretchydnesse/ thou might it not withsytte. Ergo thou seest thy selfe what foloweth. But nowe (quod she) woldest thou not skorne and thou se a flye han power to done harme to an other flye/ & thilke haue no myght ne ayenturnyng him selfe to defende. Yes certes (quod I) Who is a frayler thyng (quod she) than the fleshly body of a man/ ouer whiche haue oftentyme flyes/ and yet lasse thyng than a flye/ mokel might in greuaunce and anoyeng withouten any withsyttynge/ for al thilke mannes mightes. And sythen thou seest thyne flesshly body in kyndely power fayle/ howe shulde than the accydent of a thynge ben in more surete of beynge than substancial: Wherfore thilke thynges that we clepe power/ is but accident to the flesshly body/ and so they may not haue that surete in might/ whiche wanteth in the substancial body. Why there is no waye to the knotte/ that loketh aright after the hye waye as he shulde.

Verily it is proued that rychesse/ dignyte/ and power/ ben not trewe waye to the knotte/ but as rathe by suche thynges the knotte to be vnbounde: wherfore on these thynges I rede no wight truste/ to gette any good knotte. But what shal we saye of renome in the peoples mouthes/ shulde that ben any cause: what supposest thou in thyn herte?

Certes (quod I) yes I trowe/ for your fiye resons I dare not safely it saye. Than (quod she) wol I preue that shrewes as rathe shul ben in the knotte as the good/ and that were ayenst kynde. Fayne (quod I) wolde I that here/ me thinketh wonder howe renome shuld as wel knytte a shrewe as a good person: renome in euery degre hath auaunced/ yet wyst I neuer the contrarye: shulde than renome acorde with a shrewe: it maye not synke in my stomake tyl I here more. Nowe (quod she) haue I not sayd alwayes/ ye shrewes shul not haue the knotte. What nedeth (quod I) to reherse that any more/ I wotte wel euery wight by kyndely reason/ shrewes in knyttyng wol eschewe. Than (qd she) the good ought thilke knotte to haue. Howe els (quod I) It were great harme (quod she) that the good were weyued and put out of espoire of the knotte/ if he it desyred. O (qd I) alas/ on suche thing to thinke I wene that heuen wepeth to se suche wronges here ben suffred on erthe: the good ought it to haue and no wight els. The goodnesse (qd she) of a person may not ben knowe outforth/ but by renome of ye knowers/ wherfore he must be renomed of goodnesse to come to ye knot. So must it be (qd I) or els al lost that we carpen. Sothly (qd she) yt were great harme/ but if a good man myght haue his desyres in seruyce of thilke knot/ & a shrewe to be werned/ & they ben not knowen in general but

O.o.o.ii. by

vy lackyng and praysing and in renome/ and so by the consequence it foloweth/ a shrewe to ben praysed and knyt/ & a good to be forsake and vnknyt. Ah (qd̄ I tho) haue ye lady ben here abouten/ yet wolde I se by grace of our argumentes better declared/ howe good & bad do acorden by lacking and praysyng/ me thynketh it ayenst kynde. Nay (qd̄ she) and that shalt thou se as yerne: these elementes han cõtraryous qualytes in kynde/ by whiche they mowe not acorde no more than good & badde: and in qualytees they acorde/ so that cõtraries by qualyte/ acorden by qualyte. Is not erthe drie/ and water yͤ is next and bytwene therthe is wete: drie and wete ben contrarie & mowen not acorde/ and yet this discordaunce is bounde to acorde by cloudes/ for bothe elementes ben colde. Right so the eyre that is next the water is wete/ & eke it is hotte. This eyre by his hete contraryeth water that is colde/ but thilke cõtrariousty is oned in my moysture/ for bothe be they moyst. Also the fyre that is next the erth/ and it encloseth al about/ is drie: wherthrough it contraryeth erthe yͤ is wete: and in hete they acorde/ for bothe they ben hote. Thus by these acordaunces/ discordantes ben ioyned and in a maner of acordaunce they acorden by connection/ that is knyttyng togyther: of that acorde cometh a maner of melodye that is right noble. Right so good and bad arne contrarie in doynges/ by lacking and praysyng: good is bothe lacked and praysed of some/ and badde is bothe lacked and praysed of some: wherfore their contraryoustie acorde bothe by lackyng and praysing. Than foloweth it/ though good be neuer so mokel praysed/ oweth more to ben knyt than the badde: or els bad for the renome that he hath/ must be taken as wel as yͤ good/ and that oweth not. No forsothe (quod I) Wel (qd̄ she) than is renome no waye to the knot: Lo foole (qd̄ she) howe clerkes writen of suche glorie of renome. O glorie/ glorie/ thou arte none other thynge to thousandes of folke/ but a great sweller of eeres. Many one hath had ful great renome by false opinyon of varyaunt people: And what is fouler than folke wrongfully to ben praysed/ or by malyce of yͤ people gyltlesse lacked: nedes shame foloweth therof to hem that with wrong prayseth/ and also to the desertes praysed/ and vyllanye and reprofe of hym that disclaundreth.

Good chylde (quod she) what echeth suche renome to the conscience of a wyse man/ that loketh and measureth his goodnesse/ not by slevelesse wordes of yͤ people/ but by sothfastnesse of conscience: by god nothyng. And if it be fayre a mans name be eched by moche folkes praysing/ and fouler thyng that mo folke not praysen. I sayd to the a lytel here beforne/ that no folke in straunge countreyes nought praysen/ suche renome may not comen to their eeres/ bycause of vnknowyng/ and other obstacles/ as I sayde: wherfore more folke not praysen/ and that is right foule to him that renome despyseth/ to wete lesse folke praisen than renome enhaunce. I trowe the thanke of a people is naught worthe in remembraunce to take/ ne it procedeth of no wyse iugement/ neuer is it stedfast pardurable: It is veyne and fleyng/ with wynde wasteth and encreaseth. Trewly suche glorie ought to be hated. If gentyllesse be a clere thynge/ renome and glorie to enhaũce/ as in reckenyng of thy lynage/ than is gentylesse of thy kynne/ for why it semeth that gentylesse of thy kynne/ is but praysynge and renome that come of thyne auncestres desertes: and if so be that praysyng and renome of their desertes make their clere gentylesse/ than mote they nedes ben gentyl for their gentyl dedes/ and not thou: for of thy selfe cometh not such maner gentylesse/ praysynge of thy desertes. Than gentyllesse of thyne auncesters that forayne is to the/ maketh the not gentyl/ but vngentyl and reproued/ and if thou contynuest not their gentylesse. And therfore a wyse man ones sayde: Better is it thy kynne to ben by the gentylled/ than thou to glorifye of thy kynnes gentylesse/ and haste no deserte therof thy selfe.

Howe passynge is the beautie of fleshly bodyes: more flyttynge than mouable floures of sõmer. And if thyne eyen weren as good as the Lynx/ that maye sene thorowe many stone walles/ bothe fayre and foule in their entrayles/ of no maner hewe shulde apere to thy syght/ that were a foule syght. Than is

sapienesse

fayrnesse by feblesse of eyen/ but of no kynde/ wherfore thilke shulde be no way to the knot: whan thilke is went the knotte wendeth after. Lo nowe at al proues/ none of al these thynges mowe parfytly ben in vnderstandyng/ to ben waye to the durying blysse of the knotte. But nowe to conclusyon of these maters/ herkeneth these wordes. Very somer is knowe from the wynter: in shorter cours draweth the dayes of Decembre/ than in the moneth of June: The springes of Maye faden and forsowen in Octobre. These thinges ben not vnbounden from their olde kynde/ they haue not loste her werke of their propre estate. Men of voluntarious wyl/ withsytte that heuens gouerneth. Other thynges suffren thynges paciently to werche: Man in what estate he be/ yet wolde he ben chaunged. Thus by queynt thynges blysse is desyred/ and the fruite that cometh of these springes/ nys but anguys and bytter/ al though it be a whyle swete/ it maye not be with holde/ hastely they departe: thus al daye fayleth thynges that fooles wende. Right thus haste thou fayled in thy first wenyng. He that thynketh to sayle/ and drawe after the course of the sterre/ de polo antartico/ shal he neuer come northwarde to the contrarye sterre of polus articus: of whiche thynges if thou take kepe/ thy first out waye goynge/ prison and exile may be escaped. The grounde falsed vnderneth/ and so hast thou fayled. No wyght I wene blameth him that stynteth in mysgoyng/ and secheth redy way of his blisse.

Nowe me thynketh (quod she) that it
suffiseth in my shewyng the wayes/
by dignete/ rychesse/ renome/
and power/ if thou loke
clerely arn no wayes
to the knotte.

Euery argument lady (quod I tho) that ye han maked in these fore nempned maters/ me thynketh hem in my ful wytte conceyued/ shal I no more if god wyl in the contrarye be begyled: But fayne wolde I and it were your wyl/ blysse of the knotte to me were declared/ I might fele the better howe my herte myght assente to pursue the ende in seruyce/ as he hath begonne. O (quod she) there is a melodye in heuen/ whiche clerkes clepen armony/ but that is not in brekynge of voyce/ but it is a maner swete thing of kyndely werchyng/ that causeth ioye out of nombre to recken/ and that is ioyned by reason and by wysdome/ in a quantyte of proporcion of knyttyng. God made al thyng in reason and in wytte of proporcion of melody/ we mowe not suffyse to shewe. It is written by great clerkes and wise/ that in erthly thynges lightly by studye and by trauayle/ the knowynge may be getten: but of suche heuenly melody/ mokel trauayle wol bringe out in knowyng right lyte. Swetenesse of this paradyse hath you rauisshed/ it semeth ye slepten/ rested from al other diseases/ so kyndely is your hertes therin ygrounded. Blysse of two hertes in ful loue knytte/ may not aright ben ymagyned: euer is their contemplacion in ful of thoughty studye to plesaunce/ mater in bryngynge/ comforte eueryche to other. And therfore of erthly thinges/ mokel mater lightly cometh in your lernyng. Knowlege of vnderstondinge that is nyghe after eye/ but not so nyghe the couetyse of knyttynge in your hertes: More souerayne desyre hath euery wight in lytel herynge of heuenly connynge/ than of mokel materyal purposes in erthe. Right so it is in propertie of my seruauntes/ that they ben more affyched in sterynge of lytel thynge in his desyre/ then of mokel other mater/ lasse in his conscience. This blysse is a maner of sowne delycious/ in a queynte voyce touched/ and no dynne of notes: there is none impressyon of breakynge laboure. I canne it not otherwyse nempne/ for wantynge of propre wordes/ but paradyse terrestre ful of delycious melody/ withouten trauayle in sowne/ perpetual seruyce in ful ioye couepted to endure. Onely kynde maketh hertes in vnderstondinge so to slepe/ that otherwyse may it nat be nempned/ ne in other maner names for lykyng swetnesse can I nat it declare/ al sugre and hony/ al mynstralsy and melody ben but soote and galle in comparison by no maner proporcion to reken/

D.o.o.iii. in

in respecte of this blyssful ioye. This armony this melody/ this ꝑdurable ioye may nat be in doynge / but betwene heuens & elementes/ or twey kyndly hertes/ ful knyt in trouth of naturel vnderstōdyng/ withouten weyuynge and disceit/ as heuens & planettes/ whiche thynges cōtynually for kyndly accordaūces/ foryeteth al contrarious meuynges/ that in to passyue diseases may sowne/ euermore it thyrsteth after more werkyng. These thynges in proporcion be so wel ioyned/ that it vndooth al thyng/ whiche in to badnesse by any way may be accōpted. Certes (qd̄ I) this is a thyng p̄cious and noble. Alas that falsnesse euer or wantrust shulde euer be mayntened/ this ioye to voyde. Alas that euer any wretch shulde thorowe wrath or enuy/ ianglynge dare make to shoue this melody so farre a backe/ that opēly dare it nat ben vsed: trewly wretches ben ful fylled with enuy & wrathe/ and no wight els. Flebring & tales in such wretches dare appere openly in euery wightes eare/ with ful mouth so charged/ mokel malyce moued many innocētes to shende/ god wolde their soule therwith were strāgled. Lo/ trouth in this blysse is hyd and oueral vnder couert him hydeth: he dare nat come a place for waytynge of shrewes. Cōmenly badnesse/ goodnesse amaistreth/ wt my selfe & my soule this ioye wolde I bye/ if the goodnesse were as moche as the nobley in melody. O (qd̄ she) what goodnesse may be acōpted more ī this material worlde/ truly non that shalt thou vnderstōde. Is nat euery thīg good that is cōtrariant and distroyeng yuel? Howe els (qd̄ I) Enuy/ wrathe/ & falsnesse ben general (ꝙ she) & that wot euery man beyng in his ryght mynde/ the knotte the whiche we haue in this blysse/ is contraryaunt and distroyeth such maner yuels. Ergo it is good. What hath caused any wight to don any good dede? Fynde me any good/ but if this knotte be the chefe cause: Nedes mote it be good/ that causeth so many good dedes. Euery cause is more and worthyer than thynge caused/ and in that mores possessyon/ al thinges lesse ben compted. As the king is more than his people and hath in possessyon al his realme after: Right so the knot is more than al other goodes/ thou myght recken al thynges lasse/ and that to hym longeth oweth in to his mores cause of worshyp and of wyl do turne/ it is els rebel and out of his mores defendyng to voyde. Right so of euery goodnesse in to the knot and in to the cause of his worshyp oweth to tourne. And trewly euery thyng that hath beyng profytably is good/ but nothyng hath to ben more profytably than this knot: kynges it maintayneth/ and hem their powers to mayntayne: It maketh mysse to ben amended with good gouernaunce in doyng. It closeth hertes so togyder/ that rācour is out thresten. Who that it lengest kepeth/ lengest is gladed. I trowe (qd̄ I) heretykes and mysse meanyng people hence forwarde wol maintayne this knotte/ for therthorough shul they ben maintayned/ and vtterly wol turne and leaue their olde yuel vnderstandyng/ & knytte this goodnesse/ and profer so ferre in seruyce/ that name of seruauntes myght they haue. Their iangles shal cease/ me thynketh hem lacketh mater nowe to alege. Certes (quod Loue) if they of good wil thus turned as thou sayst wolen trewly perfourme/ yet shul they be abled party of this blysse to haue: and they wol not/ yet shul my seruaūtes the werre wel susteyne in myn helpe of maintenaunce to the ende. And they for their good trauayle shullen in rewarde so ben meded/ that endelesse ioye body and soule togyther in this shullen abyden/ there is euer action of blysse withouten possyble corrupcion/ there is action ꝑpetuel in werke without trauayle/ there is euerlastyng passyfe/ withouten any of labour: contynuel plyte without ceasynge coueyted to endure. No tonge may tel ne hert may thinke the leest poynte of this blysse. God bring me thyder (qd̄ I than) Contynueth wel (qd̄ she) to the ende/ & thou might not fayle than/ for though thou spede not here/ yet shal the passyon of thy martred lyfe ben writen/ and radde toforne the great Iuppyter that god is of routhe/ an hygh in the holownesse of heuen/ there he sytte in his trone: and euer thou shalt forwarde ben holden amonge al these heuyns for a knyght/ that mightest with no penaunce ben discomfyted. He is a very martyr that lyuyngly goynge

ynge is gnawen to the bones. Certes (qd I) these ben good wordes of cōforte/ a lytel myne herte is reioyced in a mery wyse. Ye (qd she) and he that is in heuen felyth more ioye/ than whan he firste herde therof speke. So it is (qd I) but wyst I the sothe/ that after disease comforte wolde folowe with blysse/ so as ye haue often declared/ I wolde wel suffre this passyon with the better chere/ but my thoughtful sorowe is endelesse/ to thinke howe I am cast out of a welfare/ & yet dayneth not this yuel none herte none hede to mewarde throwe/ which thynges wolde greatly me by wayes of comforte disporte/ to weten in my selfe a lytel with other me ben pinoned: and my sorowes peysen not in her balaunce the weyght of a peese: Slynges of her daunger so heuyly peysen/ they drawe my causes so hye/ that in her eyen they semen but lyght and right lytel.

O/ for (qd she) heuen with skyes that foule cloudes maken and darke wethers/ with gret tempestes and huge/ maketh the mery dayes with softe shynyng sonnes. Also the yere with draweth floures and beautie of herbes and of erth. The same yeres maketh sprynges and iolyte in Vere so to renouel with peynted coloures/ that erthe semeth as gay as heuen. Sees that blasteth and with wawes throweth shyppes/ of whiche the lyuyng creatures for great peryl for hem dreden: right so ẏ same sees maketh smothe waters and golden saylyng/ and comforteth hem with noble hauen that firste were so ferde. Hast thou not (qd she) lerned in thy youth/ that Iuppyter hath in his warderobe bothe garmentes of ioye and of sorowe? What wost thou howe soone he wol turne of the ẏ garment of care/ & clothe the in blysse? parde it is not ferre fro the. Lo an olde prouerbe aleged by many wyse: Whan bale is greatest/ than is bote a nye bore. Wherof wylte thou dismaye? hope wel and serue wel/ and that shal the saue/ with thy good byleue.

Ye/ ye (quod I) yet se I not by reason howe this blysse is comyng/ I wote it is contyngēt/ it may fal on other. O (qd she) I haue mokel to done to clere thyne vnderstandyng and voyde these errours out of thy mynde/ I wol proue it by reason thy wo may not alway enduren. Euery thyng kyndely (qd she) is gouerned & ruled by the heuenly bodyes/ whiche hauen ful werchynge here on erthe/ and after course of these bodyes/ al course of your doynges here ben gouerned and ruled by kynde.

Thou wost wel by cours of planettes al yo dayes proceden/ & to euerich of synguler houres be enterchaūged stondmele about/ by submytted worchyng naturally to suffre/ of whiche changes cometh these trāsitory tymes that maketh reuoluyng of your yeres thus stondmele/ euery hath ful might of worchynge/ tyl al seuen han had her cours about. Of which worchynges & possessyon of houres/ ẏ dayes of the weke haue take her names/ after denomination ī these seuen planettes. Lo your sonday gynneth at ẏ first hour after noon on the saturday/ in whiche hour is than the sonne in ful might of worchyng/ of whom sonday taketh his name. Next him foloweth Venus/ & after Mercurius/ & than the Moone/ so than Saturnus/ after whō Iouis/ & than Mars and ayen thā the Sonne/ & so forth be .xxiiii. houres togider/ in whiche hour gynnyng in ẏ seconde day stante the Moone/ as maister for that tyme to rule/ of whom mōday taketh his name/ and this course foloweth of al other dayes generally in doyng. This course of nature of these bodyes chaungyng/ stynten at a certayne terme/ lymytted by their iust kyndel and of hem al gouernementes in this elemented worlde proceden/ as in sprynges/ constellacions/ engendrures/ & al that folowen kynde and reson/ wherfore the course that foloweth sorowe and ioy/ kyndely moten entrechangen their tymes/ so that alway on wele as alway on wo may not endure. Thus seest thou apertly thy sorowe in to wele mote ben chaunged/ wherfore in suche case to better syde euermore enclyne thou shuldest. Trewly next the ende of sorowe anon entreth ioy/ by maner of necessyte it wol ne may non other betyde/ and so thy contygence is disproued: if thou holde this opinion any more/ thy wyt is right lewde. Wherfore in ful conclusyon of al this/ thilke Margaryte thou despyrest/ hath ben to the dere in thy herte/ and for her hast thou suffred many thoughtful diseases/ herafter shal be cause of moche of mokel myrth and ioye/ and loke howe glad causte thou ben/ and cease al thy passed heuynesse with manyfolde ioyes. And than wol I as blythly here the speken thy myrthes in ioy/ as I nowe haue yherde thy sorowes and thy complayntes. And if I mowe in aught thy ioye encrease/ by my trouthe on my syde shal nat be leaued for no maner trauayle / that I with al my myghtes right blythly wol helpe/ and euer ben redy you bothe to plese. And thā thanked I that lady with al goodly maner ye I worthely coude / and trewly I was greatly reioysed in myne hert / of her fayre behestes / & profered me to be slawe in al that she me wolde ordeyne while my lyfe lested.

ME thynketh (qd I) that ye haue right wel declared/ that way to ye knot shuld not ben in none of these disprouynge thynges/ and nowe order of our purpose this asketh/ that ye shulde me shewe if any way be thyther/ and whiche thilke way shulde ben/ so that openly maye be sey / the verry hye waye in ful confusyoun of these other thynges.

Thou shalt (quod she) vnderstande/ that one of thre lyues (as I fyrst sayd) euery creature of mankynde is spronge/ and so forth procedeth. These lyues ben thorowe names departed in thre maner of kyndes / as bestiallyche/ manlyche/ and resonablyche / of whiche two ben vsed by flesshely body/ and the thirde by his soule. Bestial among resonables is forboden in euery lawe and euery secte/ bothe in christen and other / for euery wight dispyseth hem that lyueth by lustes and delytes/ as hym that is thral and bounden seruaunt to thynges right foule/ suche ben compted werse than men/ he shal nat in their degre ben rekened/ ne for suche one alowed. Heritykes sayne they/ chosen lyfe bestial/ that volupteously lyuen/ so that (as I first sayde to the) in manly and resonable lyueng/ our mater was to declare/ but manly lyfe in lyueng after flesshe or els flesshly wayes to chese/ may nat blysse in this knotte be cōquered/ as by reason it is proued. Wherfore by resonable lyfe he must nedes it haue/ sithe a way is to this knotte/ but nat by the firste tway lyues/ wherfore nedes mote it ben to the thirde/ and for to lyue in flesshe but nat after flessh/ is more resonablich thā man lyche rekened by clerkes. Therfore howe this waye cometh in/ I wol it blythely declare.

Se nowe (quod she) that these bodily goodes of manliche lyuenges/ yelden sorousfully stoundes and smertāde houres / Who so wele remembre him to their endes/ in their worchinges they ben thoughtful and sorie. Right as a bee that hath hadde his hony/ anone at his flyght begynneth to stynge: So thilke bodily goodes at the laste mote awaye/ and than stynge they at her goynge/ wherthrough entreth and clene voydeth al blisse of this knot.

Forsothe (quod I) me thynketh I am wel serued/ in shewyng of these wordes. although I hadde lytel in respecte amonge other great and worthy/ yet had I a faire parcel / as me thought for the tyme/ in fortheryng of my sustenaūce/ whiche while it dured/ I thought me hauynge mokel hony to myne estate. I had richesse suffisauntly to weyue nede/ I had dignite to be reuerenced in worship. Power me thought that I had to kepe fro myne enemyes and me semed to shyne in glorie of renome as manhode asketh in meane / for no wight in myne admynistration coude non yuels ne trechery by sothe cause on me putte. Lady your selue weten wel/ that of tho confederacies maked by my souerayns I nas but a seruaunt/ and yet mokel meane folke wol fully ayenst reason thilke maters mayntayne / in whiche mayntenaunce glorien them selfe/ and as often ye hauen sayde/ therof ought nothynge in yuel to be sayde to me wardes/ sythen as repentaunt I am tourned/ and no more I thynke/ neither tho thynges ne none suche other to sustene/ but vtterly distroye without medlynge maner/ in al my mightes. Howe am I nowe caste out of al swetnesse of blysse/ and myschevously stongen my passed ioye: sorousfully muste I bewayle/ and lyue as a wretche.

Euery of tho ioyes is tourned in to his contrary: For richesse nowe haue I pouertie/ for dignite nowe am I enprisoned/ in stede of power wretchednesse I suffre/ and for glorye of renome I am nowe dispised/ and foulych hated: thus hath farn fortune/ that sodaynly am I ouerthrowen/ & out of al welth dispoyled.

Trewly

trewly me thynketh this way in entre is right harde/ god graunt me better grace er it be al passed/ the other way lady me thought right swete. Nowe certes (qd̄ Loue) me lyst for to chide. What ayleth thy darke duinesse? wol it nat in clerenesse ben sharped. Haue I nat by many reasons to the shewed suche bodily goodes faylen to yeue blysse/ their might so ferforthe wol nat stretche? Shame (qd̄ she it is to say) thou lyest in thy wordz. Thou ne hast wyst but right fewe/ that these bodily goodes had al atones/ cōmenly they dwellen nat togider. He that plente hath in riches/ of his kynne is a shamed: another of lynage right noble & wel knowe/ but pouert hym hādleth he were leuer unknowe. Another hath these/ but rendē of peoples praysyng may he nat haue/ oueral he is hated & defamed of thynges right foule. Another is faire & semely but dignite hym fayleth: & he that hath dignyte is croked or lame/ or els misshapen & foully dispysed. thus ꝑtable these goodes dwellen cōmenly ī one housholde ben they but lyde. Lo howe reetched is your truste/ on thyng that wol nat accorde. Me thīketh thou clepest thilke plyte thou were in selynesse of fortune/ & thou sayest for that ye selynesse is deꝑted/ thou arte a wretch. Than foloweth this vpon thy wordes/ euery soule resonable of man/ may nat dye/ & if dethe endeth selynesse & maketh wretches/ as nedes of fortune maketh it an ende/ Than soules after dethe of ye body in wretchednesse shulde lyuen But we knowe many that han geten ye blysse of heuen after their dethe. Howe thā may this lyfe maken men blyssful/ that whan it passeth it yeueth no wretchednesse/ and many tymes blysse/ if in this lyfe he con lyue as he shulde. And wolte thou acōpt with fortune/ yt nowe at he first she hath done the tene & sorowe: if yu loke to the maner of al glad thynges & sorouful/ thou mayst nat nay it/ that yet/ & namely nowe thou stādest in noble plyte in a good gīnyng/ with good forth goyng herafter. And if thou wene to be a wretch for such welth is passed/ why than art thou nat wel fortunate for badde thynges & anguys wretchednesse bē passed? Art thou nowe come first in to the hostry of this lyfe/ or els the both of this worlde/ art thou nowe a sodayne gest in to this wretched exile? Wenest there be any thynge in this erthe stable? Is nat thy first areest passed/ yt brouȝt the in mortal sorowe? Ben these nat mortal thynges agon with ignorance of beestial wyt and hast receyued reason in knowyng of vertue? What cōforte is in thy hert? the knowinge sykerly in my seruyce be groūded. And woste thou nat wel as I said/ that deth maketh ende of al fortune? What than/ stādest thou in noble plyte/ lytel hede or reekyng to take/ if thou let fortune passe dyeng/ or els that she fly whā her lyst/ now by thy lyue. Pardy a man hath nothyng so lefe as his lyfe/ & for to holde that he doth al his cure & dilygent trauayle. Than say I thou art blyssful & fortunat sely/ if thou knowe thy goodes that thou hast yet beloued which nothynge may doute/ that they ne ben more worthy than thy lyfe? What is that (qd̄ I) Good contēplation (qd̄ she) of wel doing in vertue in tyme comyng/ bothe in plesaunce of me & of thy Margarit peerle: Hastely thyn hert in ful blysse with her shalbe eased. Therfore dismay the nat/ fortune ī hate greuously ayenst thy bodily ꝑson/ ne yet to gret tempest hath she nat sent to the/ sithen the holdyng cables & ankers of thy lyfe/ holden by knyttyng so faste/ that thou discomforte the nought of tyme that is now/ ne dispayre the not of tyme to come/ but yeuen the comforte in hope of wel doyng/ and of gettyng agayne the double of thy lesyng/ with encreasyng loue of thy Margarite perle therto. For this hyderto thou hast had al her ful daunger/ and so thou myght amende al that is mysse/ and al defautes that somtyme thou dyddest/ and that now in al thy tyme to that ilke Margaryte in ful seruyce of my lore thyne herte hath contynued/ wherfore she ought moche the rather enclyne fro her daungerous lete. These thynges ben yet knyt by the holdyng anker in thy lyue/ and holden mote they: To god I pray al these thynges at ful ben performed. For whyle this anker holdeth I hope thou shalte safely escape/ & whyle thy trewe meanyng seruyce aboute bringe/ in dispyte of al false meaners/ that the of newe haten/ for this trewe seruyce thou arte nowe entred.

Certayne

Certayn (ꝙ I) amonge thynges I asked a question/ whiche was the way to the knot. Trewly lady howe so it be/ I tempt you with questions & answers/ in spekyng of my first seruice/ I am nowe in ful purpose in the pricke of ẏ hert/ that thilke seruice was an enprisonment/ & alway bad & naughty in no maner to be desyred. Ne that in gettyng of the knot/ may it nothyng aueyle. A wyse gentyl hert loketh after vertue/ & none other bodily toyes alone. And bycause toforne this/ in tho wayes I was sette/ I wote wel my selfe I haue erred/ & of the blysse fayled/ & so out of my way hugely haue I gon. Certes (ꝙ she) that is sothe/ & there thou hast myswent/ eschewe ẏ pathe from hens forwarde I rede. Wonder I trewly why the mortal folke of this worlde seche these wayes outforth / & it is ꝓued ī your selfe. Lo howe ye ben confounded with errour and folly. The knowing of very cause & way is goodnesse & vertue. Is there any thynge to the more precious than thy selfe? Thou shalt haue ī thy power/ that thou woldest neuer lese and that in no way may be taken fro the/ and thilke thyng is that is cause of this knot. And if dethe mowe it nat reue more than an erthly creature/ thilke thynge than abydeth with thy selfe soule. & so our conclusion to make suche a knot thus getten/ abydeth with this thynge and with ẏ soule/ as long as they last. a soule dieth neuer/ vertu & goodnesse euermore with the soule endureth/ & this knot is ꝑfite blysse. Than this soule in this blysse endlesse shal enduren. Thus shul hertes of a trewe knot ben eased: thus shul their soules ben pleased: thus perpetually in ioye shul they synge. In good trouth (qd I) here is a good beginnyng/ yeue vs more of this way. (Qd she) I said to the nat longe sithen/ that resonable lyfe was one of thre thynges/ & it was proued to the soule. euery soule of reason hath two thynges of steryng lyfe/ one in vertue & another in the bodily workynge: & whan the soule is the maister ouer the body / than is a man maister of him selfe: & a man to be a maister ouer him selfe/ lyueth in vertue & in goodnesse/ & as reson of vertue techeth. so the soule & the body worchīg [illegible] togider lyuen resonable lyfe/ whiche clerkes clepen felycite ī lyueng/ & therin is the hye way to this knot. these olde philosophers that hadden no knowing of diuine grace of kyndely reason alone/ wenden that of pure nature/ withouten any helpe of grace / me might haue ꝑshoned thother lyuenges/ resonably haue I lyued: & for I thynke herafter / if god wol (& I haue space) thilke grace after my leude knowyng declare: I leaue it as at this tyme. But (as I said) he that outforth loketh after the wayes of this knot/ conning with whiche he shulde knowe ẏ way inforth slepeth for the tyme/ wherfore he that wol this way knowe/ must leaue the lokyng after false wayes outforth / & open the eyen of his conscience & vnclose his herte. Seest nat he that hath trust in the bodily lyfe is so besy bodily woundes to anoynt in keping from smert (for al out may they nat be healed) that of woundes in his true vnderstādīg he taketh no hede/ the knowing euerforth slepeth so harde/ but anon as ī knowing a wake/ than gynneth the preuy medicines for healyng of his trewe entent / inwarde lightly healeth cōscience if it be wel handled. Than must nedes these wayes come out of ẏ soule by steryng lyfe of the body/ & els maye no man come to ꝑfite blysse of this knotte: & thus by this waye he shal come to the knotte/ and to the ꝑfyte selynesse that he wende haue had in bodily goodes outforth? Ye (ꝙ I) shal he haue both knot/ riches/ power/ dignite/ & renome in this maner waye? Ye (qd she) ẏ shal I shewe the. Is he nat riche that hath suffisaūce/ & hath the power that no man may amaistrien? Is nat great dignite to haue worshyp and reuerence? & hath he nat glorie of renome whose name ꝑpetual is duryng/ & out of nōbre in cōparation? These be thynges that men wenen to getten outforth (qd I). Ye (ꝙ she) they that loken after a thynge that nought is therof in al ne in ꝑtie/ longe mowe they gapen after? That is sothe (qd I): therfore (qd she) they that sechen golde in grene trees / & wene to gader precious stones amonge vynes/ and layne her nettes in mountayns to fysshe/ and thinken to hunt ī depe sees after hart & hynde/ and sechen in erth thilke thynges that surmounteth heuen/ What may I of hem say? but folysshe

lysshe ignoraunce mysledeth wandring wretches by uncouth wayes that shulden be forleten/ & maketh hem blynde fro the right pathe of trewe way that shulde ben used. Therfore in general errour in mankynde/ departeth thilke goodes by mysse sechyng/ whiche he shulde haue hole & he sought by reason. Thus goth he begyled of that he sought/ in his hode men haue blowe a jape. Nowe (qd I) if a man be vertuous & al in vertue lyueth/ howe hath he al these thynges? That shal I prouen (qd she) What power hath any man to let another of lyueng in vertue? for prisonment or any other disese/ he take it paciently/ disconfiteth he nat/ the tyraunt ouer his soule no power maye haue? Than hath that man so tourmented suche power/ that he nyl be disconfit/ ne ouercome may he nat ben/ sithen pacience in his soule ouercometh/ and is nat ouercomen. Suche thyng that may nat be amaistred/ he hath nede to nothing/ for he hath suffisaunce ynowe to helpe him selfe. And thilke thyng that thus hath power & suffysance/ & no tyrant may it reue/ & hath dignite to sette at nought al thynges/ here it is a great dignite that deth may a maistry. Wherfore thilke power suffisaunce so enclosed with dignite/ by al reson renome must haue. This is thilke riches with suffisance ye shulde loke after: this is thilke worshipful dignite ye shulde coueyt: this is thilke power of myght/ in whiche ye shulde truste: this is the ilke renome of glorie that endlesse endureth/ & al nys but substaunce in vertuous lyuyng. Certes (qd I) al this is sothe/ & so I se wel that vertue with ful gripe encloseth al these thynges. Wherfore in sothe I may saye/ by my trouth/ vertue of my Margarite brought me first in to your seruice/ to haue knyttyng with that iewel/ nat so dayn longynges ne lokes smale wordes/ but onely our conuersation togider: & than I seige thentent of her trewe menyng with flourisshing vertue of pacience/ that she used nothynge in yuel/ to quyte the wicked leasynges that false tonges ofte in her haue sayde/ I haue sey it my selfe/ goodly foryeuenesse hath spronge out of her hert/ unite & accorde aboue al other thinges she desyreth in a good meke maner/ and suffereth many wicked tales.

TRewly lady to you it were a gret worship/ that suche thynges by due chastysment were amended. Ye (qd she) I haue the excused/ al suche thynges as yet mowe nat be redressed: thy Margarites vertue I commende wel the more that paciently suche anoyes suffreth. Dauid kyng was meke & suffred mokel hate & many yuel speches: no despite ne shame that his enemys him deden/ might nat moue pacience out of his herte/ but euer in one plyte mercy he used. Werfore god him selfe toke rewarde to the thynges/ & theron suche punysshment let fal. Trewly by reason it ought be ensample of drede to al maner peoples myrth A man begcable in wrath no gouernance in punisshment ought to haue. Plato had a cause his seruaunt to scoure/ & yet cleped he his neibour to performe the doynge/ him selfe wolde nat/ lest wrath had him a maistred/ & so myght he haue layde on to moche: euermore grounded vertue sheweth thentent fro within. & trewly I wotte wel for her goodnesse & vertue/ thou hast desyred my seruice to her plesance wel the more/ & thy selfe therto fully hast profered. Good lady (qd I) is vertue the hye waye to this knot/ that long we haue yhandled? ye forsoth (qd she) and without vertue goodly this knot may nat be goten. Ah nowe I se (quod I) howe vertu in me fayleth/ & I as a seer tre without burionyng or fruite alwaye welke/ & so I stonde in dispeyre of this noble knot/ for vertue in me hath no maner workynge. A wyde where aboute haue I traueyled. Peace (qd she) of thy first way thy traueyle is in ydel/ & as touchynge the seconde way/ I se wel thy meanyng. Thou woldest conclude me if thou coudest/ bycause I brought the to seruice/ and euery of my seruantes I helpe to come to this blysse/ as I sayd here beforne: & thou saydest thy selfe/ thou mightest nat be holpen as thou wenyst/ bycause that vertue in the fayleth. & this blysse parfitly without vertue maye nat be goten/ thou wenest of these wordes contradiction to folowe. Parde, at the hardest I haue no seruant but he be vertuous in dede & thought I brought the in my seruice/ yet arte thou nat my seruant: but I say/ thou might so werche in vertue herafter/ that than shalt thou be my seruant seruaunt/ and as for my seruant acompted. For habyte maketh no monke/ ne wearynge of gylte spurres maketh no knyght. Neuer the later/ in conforte of thyne herte/ yet wol I other wyse answere. Certes lady (qd I tho) so ye muste nedes/ or els I had nyghe caught suche a cordiacle for sorowe/ I wotte it wel I shulde it neuer haue recouered. And therfore nowe I praye to enforme me in this/ or els I holde me without recouerye. I may nat long endure tyl this lesson be lerned/ and of this mysesese the remedy knowen. Nowe (quod she) be nat wrothe/ for there is no man on lyue that maye come to a precious thyng longe coueyted/ but he somtyme suffre teneful diseases/ and wenyst thy selfe to ben vnlyche to al other: that maye nat ben: And with the more sorowe that a thynge is getten/ the more he hath ioye/ the ilke thyng afterwardes to kepe/ as it fareth by chyldren in schole that for lernynge arne beaten/ whan their lesson they forgetten/ comenly after a good disciplynyng with a yerde/ they kepe right wel doctryne of their schole.

Right with these wordes/ on this lady I threwe vp myne eyen to se her countenaunce and her chere/ and she aperceyuyng this fantasye in myne herte/ gan her semblaunt goodly on me caste/ and sayde in this wyse.

It is wel knowe/ bothe to Reason and experience in doynge/ euery actyue worcheth on his passyue/ and whan they ben togider/ actyue and passyue ben ycleaped by these philosophers/ if fyre be in place chasynge thynge able to be chased or hete/ and thilke thynges ben sette in suche a distaunce that the one may werche/ the other shal suffre. Thilke Margarite thou desyrest is ful of vertue/ and able to be actyue in goodnesse: but euery herbe sheweth his vertue outforthe from within/ the sonne yeueth lyght that thynges may be sey. Euery fyre heteth thilke thyng that it neighed and it be able to be hete/ vertue of this Margarite outforth wrethe/ and nothynge is more able to suffre worching or worke catche of the actyse/ but passyse of the same actyse/ and no passyse to vertues of this Margaryte/ but the in al my donet can I fynde/ so that her vertue muste nedes on the werche/ in what place euer thou be/ within distaunce of her worthynesse/ as her very passyse thou arte closed: but vertue may the nothynge profyte/ but thy desyre be perfourmed and al thy sorowes ceased. Ergo through werchynge of her vertue thou shalte easely ben holpen and driuen out of al care/ and welcome to this longe by the desyred. Lady (quod I) this is a good lesson in gynnyng of my ioye: but wete ye wel forsothe/ thoughe I suppose she haue meche vertue/ I wolde my spousayle were proued/ and than maye I lyue out of doute/ and reioyce me greatly in thynkyng of tho vertues so shewed. I herde the say (quod she) at my begynnyng whan I receyued the firste for to serue that thy iewel/ thilke Margaryte thou desyrest/ was closed in a muskle with a blewe shel. Ye forsothe (quod I) so I sayd/ and so it is. Wel (quod she) euery thing kyndly sheweth it selfe: this iewel closed in a blewe shel/ excellence of coloures sheweth vertue from within/ and so euery wight shulde rather loke to the propre vertue of thynges/ than to his forayne goodes. If a thyng be engendred of good mater/ comenly and for the more parte it foloweth after the congelement vertue of the first mater/ and it be not corrupt with vyces/ to procede with encrease of good vertues: eke right so it fareth of badde. Trewly great excellence in vertue of lynage/ for the more parte discendeth by kynde to the successyon in vertues to folowe. Wherfore I saye/ the colours of euery Margarit sheweth from within the fynesse in vertue. Kyndely heuen whan mery wether is a lofte/ apereth in mannes eye of coloure in blewe/ stedfastnesse in peace betokenyng within and without: Margaryte is engendred by heuenly dewe/ and sheweth in it selfe by fynenesse of coloure/ whether the engendrure were maked on morowe or on eue: thus sayth kynde of this perle. This precious Margaryte that thou seruest/ sheweth it selfe discended by nobley of vertue from this heuenlych dewe/ norisshed and congeled in mekenesse/ that mother is of al vertues/ and by

werkes

werkes that men sene withouten the signyfication of the coloures / ben shewed mercy and pytie in the herte with peace to al other / and al this is pclosed in a muskle / who so redily these vertues loken. Al thyng that hath soule is reduced in to good by meane thynges / as thus: In to god man is reduced by soules resonable / and so forthe beestes or bodyes that mowe not mouen / after place ben reduced in to manne / by beestes meue that mouyn from place to place: so that thilke bodyes that han felynge soules / and moue not from places / holden the lowest degree of soulynge thynges in felynge / and suche ben reduced in to man by meanes. So it foloweth / the muskle as mother of al vertues / halte the place of mekenesse to his lowest degree discendeth downe of heuen / and there by a maner of virgyne engendrure arne these Margarytes engendred / and afterwarde congeled. Made not mekenesse so lowe the hye heuen to enclose & catche out therof so noble a dewe / that after congelement a Margaryte with endelesse vertue and euerlastyng ioy was with ful vessel of grace yeuen to euery creature / that goodly wolde it receyue. Certes (quod I) these thynges ben right noble / I haue er this herde these same sawes. Than (quod she) thou woste wel these thynges ben sothe? ye forsothe (qd I) at the ful. Nowe (quod she) that this Margaryte is ful of vertue it is wel proued / wherfore some grace / some mercy amonge other vertues / I wotte ryght wel on the shal discende? ye (quod I) yet wolde I haue better declared vertues in this Margaryte / kyndely to ben grounded. That shal I shew the (qd she) and thou woldest it lerne? Lerne (quod I) what nedeth suche wordes: Wete ye nat wel lady your selfe that al my cure / al my dyligence / and al my myght haue turned by your counsayle / in plesaunce of that perle / al my thought and al my studye / with your helpe desyreth / in worshyppe thilke iewel to encrease al my trauayle and al my besynesse in your seruyce / this Margaryte to gladde in somehalue: me were leauer her honour / her pleasaunce / and her good chere thorowe me for to be mayntayned and kepte / and I of suche thynge in her lykynge to be cause / than al the welthe of bodyly goodes ye coude recken. And wolde neuer god / but I put my selfe in great ieoperdye of al that I wolde / that is nowe no more but my lyfe alone / rather than I shulde suffre thylke iewel in any poynte ben blemisshed / as ferre as I may suffre / and with my mightes stretche. Suche thyng (qd she) maye mokel further thy grace / and the in my seruyce auaunce. But nowe (quod Loue) wylte thou graunte me thilke Margaryte to ben good? O good good (qd I) why tempte ye me and tene with suche maner speche: I wolde graunt that / thoughe I shulde anone dye / and by my trouthe fyght in the quarel if any wight wolde coutreplede. It is so moche the lyghter (quod Loue) to proue our entent.

Ye (quod I) but yet wolde I here howe ye wolde proue that she were good by reasonable skyl / that it mowe not ben denyed / for althoughe I knowe and so dothe many other / manyfolde goodnesse and vertue in this Margaryte ben printed / yet some men there ben that no goodnesse speken: and wher euer your wordes ben herde and your reasons ben shewed / suche yuel spekers lady by auctorite of your excellence / shullen ben stopped and ashamed. And more they that han none acquayntaunce in her persone / yet mowe they knowe her vertues / and ben the more enfourmed in what wyse they mowe sette their hertes / whan hem lyste in to your seruyce any entre make: for trewly al this to begynne / I wote wel my selfe that thilke iewel is so precious perle / as a womanly woman in her kynde / in whome of goodnesse / of vertue / and also of answerynge / shappe of lymmes / and fetures so wel in al poyntes acordyng / nothynge fayleth: I leue that kynde her made with great studye / for kynde in her person nothyng hath foryet / and that is wel sene. In euery good wyghtes herte she hath grace of comendyng and of vertuous praysyng. Alas that euer kynde made her deedly / saue onely in that I wot wel / that

Nature in fourmynge of
her in no thynge
hath erred.

P.p.p. ¶ Certes

CErtes (quod Loue) thou haste wel begonne / and I aske the this questyon: Is not in general euery thynge good? I not (quod I) No (quod she) saue not god euery thynge that he made / and werne right good. Than is wonder (qd̄ I) howe yuel thynges comen a place / sythen that al thynges weren right good. Thus (qd̄ she) I wol declare euerych qualyte and euery action / and euery thyng that hath any maner of beynge it is of god / and god it made / of whom is al goodnesse ⁊ al beyng / of him is no badnesse: badde to be is naught: good to be is somwhat / and therfore good and beyng is one in vnderstandyng. Howe may this be (quod I) for often han shrewes me assailed / and mokel badnesse therin haue I founden / and so me semeth bad to be somwhat in kynde. Thou shalt (qd̄ she) vnderstande ẏ suche maner badnesse / whiche is vsed to punysshe wronge doers is somwhat / and god it made and beyng hath / and that is good: other badnesse no beyng hath vtterly / it is in the negatyue of somwhat / and that is naught / and nothyng beyng. The parties essencial of beyng arne sayd in double wyse / as that it is / and these parties ben foūde in euery creature / for al thyng a this halfe the first beyng is beyng through partycipacion / takyng partie of beyng / so that euery creature is difference bytwene beynge and of him through whom it is and his own beyng: right as euery good is a maner of beyng / so is it good thorowe beyng / for it is naught other to be: and euery thyng though it be good it is not of him selfe good / but it is good by that it is ordynable to the great goodnesse. This dualyte after clerkes determission is founden in euery creature / be it neuer so syngle of onhed. ye (qd̄ I) but there as it is ysayde that god saue euery thynge of his makyng / and were right good / as your selfe sayd to me not longe tyme sythen. I aske whether euery creature is ysayde good / throughe goodnesse vnfourmed eyther els fourmed / and afterwarde if it be accepte vtterly good? I shal say the (quod she) these great passed clerkes han deuyded good in to good beyng alone / and that is nothynge but good / for nothynge is good in that wyse but god. Also in good by partycipacion / and that is ycleped good / for farre sette and representatyue of goodly goodnesse / and after this manyfolde good is sayd / that is to saye / good in kynde and good in gendre / and good of grace / and good of ioy. Of good in kynde Austen sayth / al that ben ben good: but peraunter thou woldest wete whether of hem selfe it be good / or els of anothers goodnesse / for naturel goodnesse of euery substaunce is nothing els than his substancial beyng / whiche is ycleaped goodnesse / after comparyson that he hath to his first goodnesse / so as it is inductatyfe by meanes ī to the first goodnesse. Boece sheweth this thynge at the ful / that this name good is in general name in kynde / as it is cōparysoned generally to his principal ende / whiche is god knotte of al goodnesse. Euery creature cryeth god vs made / and so they han ful apeted to thilke god by affection / suche as to hem longeth: and in this wyse al thynges ben good of ẏ gret god / whiche is good alone. This wonder thyng (quod I) howe ye haue by many reasons proued my first waye to be errour and misgoyng / and cause of baddesse and feble menynge in the grounde ye aleged to be roted: whence is it that suche badnesse hath springes / sythen al thynges thus in general ben good / and badnesse hath no beyng / as ye haue declared: I wene if al thynges ben good / I might than with the first way in that good haue ended / and so by goodnesse haue comen to blysse in your seruyce desyred. Al thyng (quod she) is good by beyng in partycipacion out of the firste goodnesse / whiche goodnesse is corrupte by badnesse / and badde meanyng maners: god hath in good thynges that they ben good by beyng / and not in yuel / for there is absence of rightful loue / for badnesse is nothynge but onely yuel wyl of the vser / and through giftes of the doer / wherfore at the gynnyng of the worlde / euery thyng by him selfe was good / and in vnyuersal they werne right good. An eye or a hande is fayrer and betterer in a body sette in his kyndely place / than from the body disceuered. Euery thyng in his kyndly place being kyndly / good dothe werche / and out of that place voyded / it disit dissolueth and is defouled him selue. Our noble god in glyterande wyse by armony this worlde ordeyned/ as in purtreytures stoured with colours medled/ in whiche blacke and other derke coloures comenden the golden and the asured paynture/ euery putte in kyndely place one besyde another/ more for other glytereth: ryght so lytle fayre maketh right fayre more glorious/ and right so of goodnesse and of other thynges in vertue. Wherfore other badde/ and not so good perles as this Margaryte that we han of this matier/ yeuen by the ayre lytel goodnesse and lytel vertue/ ryght mokel goodnesse and vertue in thy Margaryte to ben proued/ in shynynge wyse to be founde and shewed. Howe shulde euer goodnesse of peace haue ben knowe/ but if unpeace somtyme reigne/ and mokel yuel wrothe? Howe shulde mercy ben proued and no trespeace were/ by due iustifycacion to be punysshed? Therfore grace & goodnesse of a wight is founde/ the sorouful hertes in good meanynge to endure/ ben comforted/ unyte and acorde bytwene hertes knytte in ioye to abyde. What wenest thou I reioyce or els accompte hym amonge my seruauntes that pleaseth Pallas/ in undoynge of Mercurye/ al be it that to Pallas he be knytte by tytle of lawe/ not accordyng to reasonable conscience: and Mercurie in doynge haue grace to ben suffered: or els hym that weneth the moone for fayrenesse of the eue sterre. Lo otherwhyle by nyghtes lyght of the moone/ greatly comforteth in derke thoughtes and blynde. Understandyng of loue yeueth great gladnesse: Who so lyste not byleue whan a sothe tale is shewed/ adewe and a debLys his name is entred. Wyse folke and worthy in gentylesse bothe of vertue and of lyuynge/ yeuen ful credence in sothnesse of loue with a good hert/ there as good euydence or experyence in doynge sheweth not the contrarye. Thus myghtest thou haue ful prefe in thy Margaryte goodnesse/ by comendement of other iewels badnesse/ and yuelnesse in doyng. Stoundemele diseases yeueth seueral houres in ioye.

Nowe by my trouthe (quod I) this is wel declared that my Margaryte is good/ for sythen other ben good/ and she passeth manye other in goodnesse and vertue/ wherthroughe by maner necessarye she muste be good: and goodnesse of this Margaryte is no thynge els but vertue/ wherfore she is vertuous/ and if there fayled any vertue in any syde/ there were lacke of vertue: badde nothynge els is ne may be/ but lacke and wante of good and goodnesse/ and so shulde she haue that same lacke/ that is to saye badde/ and that maye not be/ for she is good/ and that is good methynketh al good: and so by consequence me semeth vertuous and no lacke of vertue to haue. But the sonne is not knowe but he shyne/ ne vertuous herbes but they haue her kynde werchynge/ ne vertue but it stretche in goodnesse or profyte to another/ is no vertue. Than by al wayes of reason/ sythen mercy and pytie ben moste commended amonge other vertues/ and they myght neuer ben shewed refresshement of helpe and of comforte/ but nowe at my moste nede/ and that is the kynde werkynge of these vertues: trewly I wene I shal not varye from these helpes. Fyre and if he yeue none heate/ for fyre is not demed. The sonne but he shyne/ for sonne is not accompted. Water but it wete/ the name shal ben chaunged. Vertue but it werche/ of goodnesse dothe it fayle/ and in to his contrarye the name shal ben reuersed/ and these ben impossyble: wherfore the contradictorie that is necessarye/ nedes muste I leue.

Certes (quod she) in thy person and out of thy mouthe these wordes lyen wel to ben said/ and in thyne understandyng to be leued/ as in entent of this Margaryte alone: and here nowe my speche in conclusyon of these wordes.

IN these thinges (quod she) that me lyst nowe to shewe openly/ shal be founde the mater of thy sicknesse/ & what shal ben the medicyn ye may be thy sorowes lysse & comfort/

P.p.p.ii. as

as wel the as al other that amysse haue erred/ and out of the way walked/ so that any drope of good wyl in amendement ben dwelled in their hertes. Prouerbes of Salomon openly teacheth/ howe somtyme an innocent walkyd by ye way in blyndnesse of a derke night/ whom mette a woman (if it be lefely to saye) as a strumpet araped/ redily purueyed in turnynge of thoughtes with veyne ianglynges/ and of rest inpacient by dissymulacion of my termes/ sayeng in this wyse: Come and be we dronken of our swete pappes/ use we coueytous collynges. And thus drawen was this innocent/ as an oxe to the larder. Lady (qd I) to me this is a queynte thynge to understonde: I praye you of this parable declare me the entent. This innocent (quod she) is a scholer lernynge of my lore/ in sechyng of my blysse/ in whiche thynge the daye of his thought turnyng enclyneth in to eue/ and the sonne of very lyght faylinge/ maketh derke nyght in his connynge. Thus in derknesse of many doutes he walketh/ and for blyndenesse of understandynge/ he ne wote in what waye he is in: forsothe suche one may lightly ben begyled. To whome came loue fayned/ not clothed of my lyuery/ but unleful lustye habyte/ with softe speche and mery/ and with fayre houped wordes heretykes and misse menynge people skleren and wymplen their errours. Austen wytnesseth of an heretyke that in his first begynnynge he was a man right experte in resones/ and swete in his wordes/ and the werkes miscorden. Thus fareth fayned loue in her firste werchynges: thou knowest these thynges for trewe/ thou haste hem proued by experience. Somtyme in doyng to thyne owne person/ in whiche thyng thou hast founde mater of mokel disease/ Was not fayned loue redily purueyed thy wyttes to catche and tourne thy good thoughtes? trewly she hath wounded the conscience of many with flourysshynge of mokel ianglyng wordes: and goodworthe thanked I it for no glose/ I am gladde of my prudence thou haste so manly her veyned. To me arte thou moche holden/ that in thy kynde course of good meanyng I returne thy mynde: I trowe ne had I shewed the thy Margaryte/ thou haddest neuer returned. Of first in good parfyte ioye was euer fayned loue impacient/ as the water of Nyloe/ whiche euermore floweth with stylnesse and pryuy noyse/ tyl it come nyghe the brinke/ and than gynneth it so out of measure to bolne/ with nouelleries of chaungyng stormes/ that in course of euery rennyng it is in poynte to spyl al his circuite of bankes. Thus fayned loue priuely at the fullest of his flowynge/ newe stormes debate to arayse. And al be it that Mercurius often with hole understandynge knowen suche peryllous maters/ yet Veneriens so lusty ben and so leude in their wyttes/ that in suche thynges right lytel or naught don they fele/ and writen and cryen to their felawes: here is blysse/ here is ioye/ and thus in to one same errour/ mokel folke they drawen. Come they sayne/ and be we dronken of our pappes/ that ben fallas and lyeng glose/ of whiche mowe they not souke mylke of helthe/ but deedly venym and poyson corrupcion of sorowe. Mylke of fallas/ is venym of disceyte: Mylke of lyeng glose is venym of corrupcion. Lo what thynge cometh out of these pappes: use we coueyted collynges/ desyre we and meddle we false wordes with sote/ and sote with false/ trewly this is the forynesse of fayned loue/ nedes of these surfettes sicknesse must folowe. Thus as an oxe to thy langoring deth were thou drawen/ the sote of the smoke hath the al defased. Euer the deper thou somtyme wadest the soner thou it founde: if it had the kylled it had be lytel wonder. But on that other syde my trewe seruaunt not faynen ne disceyue conne/ sothly their doynge is open/ my foundement endureth/ be the burthen neuer so great/ euer in one it lasteth: it yeueth lyfe and blyssful goodnesse in the laste endee/ though the gynnynges ben sharpe. Thus of two contraries/ contrarye ben the effectes. And so thylke Margaryte thou seruest shal leue the by her seruyce out of peryllous trybulacion delyuered/ bycause of her seruyce in to newe disease fallen/ by hope of amendement in the laste ende/ with ioye to be gladded/ wherfore of kynde pure/ her mercy with grace of good helpe shal she graunt graūt/and els I shal her so strayne/that with pyte shal she ben amaystred. Remembre in thyne herte howe horrybly somtyme to thyne Margaryte thou trespasest/ and in a great wyse ayenst her thou forfeytest: clepe ayen thy mynde/and knowe thyne owne gyltes. What goodnesse/ what bountie/ with mokel folowynge pyte founde thou in that tyme? Were thou not goodly accepted in to grace? by my pluckynge was she to foryeuenesse enclyned. And after I her styred to drawe the to house/ and yet wendest thou utterly for euer haue ben refused. But wel thou wost/ sythen that I in suche sharpe disease myght so greatly auayle/ what thynkest in thy wyt? howe ferre maye my wytte stretche? And thou lacke not on thy syde I wol make the knotte: Certes in thy good beryng I wol acorde with the psauter. I haue fonde Dauid in my seruyce true/ and with holy oyle of peace and of rest longe by him desyred/ utterly he shal be anoynted. Truste wel to me/ and I wol the not fayle. The leauyng of the first way with good herte of contynuaunce/ that I se in the grounded/ this purpose to parfourme/ draweth me by maner of costraynyng/ that nedes must I ben thyne helper: although myrthe a whyle be tarye d/ it shal come at suche season/ that thy thought shal ben ioyed. And wolde neuer god/ sythen thyne herte to my reasones arne assented/ and openly haste confessed thyne amysse goynge/ and nowe cryest after mercy/ but if mercy folowed: thy blysse shal ben redy iwys/ thou ne wost how sone. Now be a good chylde I rede. The kynde of uertues in thy Margaryte rehersed/ by strength of me in thy person shul werche. Comforte the in this/ for thou mayst not miscary. And these wordes sayde/ she streyght her on length and rested a whyle.

Thus endeth the seconde booke/ and here after foloweth the thirde boke.

IN nombre sayne these clerkes that it is naturel sōme of discrete thynges/ as in tellynge one/ two/ thre and so forth: but amonge al nombres thre is determyned for moste certayne. Wherfore in nombre certayne this/ werke of my besy lewdnesse I thynke to ende and parfourme. Ensample by this worlde in thre tymes is deuyded: of whiche the firste is cleped Deuiacion/ that is to say/ goyng out of trewe way/ and al that tho dyeden/ in hel were they punysshed for a mans synne/ tyl grace & mercy fette hem thence/ and there ended the firste tyme. The seconde tyme lasteth from the comyng of mercyable grace/ untyl the ende of transytorie tyme/ in whiche is shewed the true way in fordoynge of the badde/ and that is ycleped tyme of grace: and that thynge is not yeuen by deserte of yeldynge one benefyte for another/ but onely through goodnesse of the yeuer of grace in thilke tyme. Who so can wel understande/ is shapen to be saued in soule d blysse. The thirde tyme shal gyn whan trāsytorie thynges of worldes han made their ende/ and that shal ben in ioye/ glorie/ and rest/ both body and soule/ that wel han deserued in the tyme of grace. And thus in that heuen togyther shul they dwel perpetuelly without any ymaginatyfe yuel in any halue. These tymes are fygured by tho thre dayes that our god was closed in erthe/ and in the thirde arose/ shewyng our resurrection/ to ioye and blysse of tho that it deseruen/ by his mercyable grace. So this lewde boke in thre maters accordaunt to tho tymes/ lyghtly by a good inseer maye ben understonde/ as in the firste errour of mysse goynge is shewed/ with sorowful pyne punysshed is cryed after mercy. In the seconde is grace in good waye proued/ whiche is faylinge without deserte/ thylke first mysse amendynge in correction of tho errours and euen waye to bringe/ with comforte of welfare in to amendement weyynge. And in the thirde ioye and blysse graunted to hym that wel canne deserue it/ and hath sauour of understandynge in the tyme of grace. Thus in ioye of my thirde boke shal the mater be tyl it ende.

P.p.p.in.

ende. But special cause I haue in my hert to make this processe of a Margarit perle/ that is so precious a gēme with clere & lytel/ of whiche stones or iewel/ the tonges of vs Englissh people tourneth the rizt names/ & clepeth hem Margery perles: thus varyeth our speche frō many other langages. For trewly latyn/ frenche/ and many mo other langages clepeth hem Margery perles/ the name Margarites or Margarite perles: wherfore in that denomynacion I wol me acorde to other mens tonges/ in that name clepyng. These clerkes that treaten of kyndes/ & studyen out the propertie there of thynges/ sayne the Margarite is a lytel whyte perle/ throughout holowe and rounde/ and vertuous/ and on the see sydes in the more Britayne in muskle shelles of ẏ heuenly dewe the best ben engendred: in whiche by experience ben founde thre fayre vertues. One is/ it yeueth comforte to the felyng spyrites in bodily persones of reason. Another is good/ it is profytable helthe ayenst passyons of sorie mens hertes. And the thirde it is nedeful and noble in staunchyng of bloode/ there els to moche wolde out ren. To whiche perle and vertues me lyst to liken at this tyme Philosophie with her thre speces/ that is natural and moral/ and resonable: of whiche thynges hereth what sayne these great clerkes. Philosophie is knowyng of deuynly & manly thinges ioyned with studye of good lyuyng/ and this stant in two thynges/ that is connynge and opinyon: connynge is whan a thyng by certayne reson is cōceyued. But wretches and fooles and leude men/ many wyl conceyue a thyng and mayntayne it as for sothe/ though reson be in the contrarye/ wherfore connynge is a straunger. Opinyon is whyle a thyng is in non certayne/ and hydde from mens very knowlegyng/ and by no parfyte reason fully declared/ as thus: if the sonne be so mokel as men wenen/ or els if it be more than the erthe. For in sothnesse the certayne quantyte of that planet is vnknowen to erthly dwellers/ and yet by opinyon of some men it is holden for more than myddel erth. The first spece of philosophie is naturel/ whiche in kyndely thynges treten/ and sheweth causes of heuen/ and strength of kyndely course: as by arsmetrike/ geometry/ musyke/ & by astronomye/ techeth wayes and course of heuens/ of planetes/ and of sterres aboute heuen and erthe/ and other elemētes. The seconde spece is moral/ whiche in order of lyuyng maners techeth/ and by reson proueth vertues of soule moste worthy in our lyueng/ whiche ben prudence/ iustyce/ temperaunce/ and strength. Prudence is goodly wysdome in knowyng of thynges. Strength voydeth al aduersitees alyche euen. Temperaunce distroyeth beestyal lyueng/ with easy bearyng. And iustyce rightfully iugeth/ and iugyng departeth to euery wight that is his owne. The thirde spece turneth in to reason of vnderstandyng/ al thynges to be sayd soth and discussed/ & that in two thynges is deuyded: one is arte/ another is rethorike/ in whiche two al lawes of mans reason ben grounded or els maintayned. And for this booke is al of loue/ and therafter beareth his name/ and phylosophie and lawe muste here to acorden by their clergyal discripcions: as phylosophie for loue of wisdome is declared: Lawe for mainteynaunce of peace is holden/ and these with loue must nedes acorden/ therfore of hem in this place haue I touched. Ordre of homly thinges & honest maner of lyuynge in vertue/ with right ful iugemēt in causes and profitable administration in cōmynalties of realmes & cytes/ by euenhed profitably to raigne/ nat by singuler auaūtage ne by priue enuy/ ne by soleyn purpose in coueitise of worship or of goodes/ ben disposed in open rule shewed/ by loue philosophy/ & lawe/ & yet loue toforn al other. Wherfore as susterne in vnite they accorden & one ende that is peace & rest/ they causen norishinge/ & in the ioye mayntenen to endure.

Nowe than/ as I haue declared: my boke acordeth with discription of thre thynges/ & the Margarit in vertue is lykened to philosophy/ with her thre speces. In whiche maters euer twey ben acordaunt with bodily reason/ & the thirde with the soule: But in cōclusyon of my boke & of this Margarite peerle in knyttynge togider lawe by thre sondrie maners shal be lykened/ that is to saye/ lawe/ right/ & custome/ whiche I wol declare: al that is lawe cometh of of goddes ordynance by kyndly worchyng/ & thilke thynges ordayned by mānes wyttꝭ arn ycleped right/ which is ordayned by many maners & in cōstitution written: but custome is a thyng that is accepted for right or for lawe/ there as lawe & right faylen/ & there is no difference/ whether it come of scripture or of reason. Wherfore it sheweth that lawe is kyndly gouernaunce: Right cometh out of mānes ꝓuable reson: & custome is of cōmen vsage by length of tyme vsed/ & custome nat writte is vsage/ & if it be writte cōstitutyon it is ywritten & ycleped: But lawe of kynde is cōmen to euery nation/ as cōiunction of man and woman in loue/ succession of children in heritāce restitution of thyng by strength taken or lent/ and this lawe among al other halte the souerayneſt gree in worship/ Whiche lawe began at the begynnyng of reasonable creature/ it varyed yet neuer for no chaungyng of tyme: cause forsothe in ordaynyng of lawe/ was to constrayne mens hardynesse in to peace/ and withdrawing his yuel wyl/ and turnyng malyce in to gooonesse/ and that innocence sykerly withouten teneful anoye amonge shrewes safely might inhabyte by protection of safeconducte/ so that the shrewes harme for harme by bridle of ferdenesse shulden restrayne. But forsothe in kyndely lawe nothynge is cōmended/ but such as goddes wyl hath confyrmed/ ne nothyng denyed but cōtraryoustie of goddes wyl in heuen: eke than al lawes or custome/ or els cōstitucion by vsage or writyng that cōtraryen lawe of kynde/ vtterly ben repugnaunt and aduersarye to our goddes wyl of heuen. Trewly lawe of kynde for goddes own lusty wyl is verily to maintayne/ vnder which lawe (& vnworthy) bothe professe and reguler arne obedyencer and bounden to this Margarite perle/ as by knotte of loues statutes and stablysshment in kynde/ whiche that goodly maye not ben withsetten. Lo vnder this bonde am I constrayned to abyde/ and man vnder lyueng lawe ruled: by that lawe oweth after desertes to ben rewarded by payn or by mede/ but if mercy weyue the payne: so than be parte/ reasonfully may be sey/ that mercy bothe right and lawe passeth/ thentent of al these maters is the lest clere vnderstanding/ to weten at thende of this thirde boke ful knowing thorowe goddes grace/ I thynke to make neuerthelater/ yet if these thynges han a good and a sleight inseer/ whiche that can louke hony of the harde stone/ oyle of the drye rocke/ may lyghtly fele nobley of mater i my leude ymagination closed. But for my boke shal be of ioye (as I said) & I so ferre set fro thilke place/ fro whens gladnesse shulde come my corde is to short to let my boket ou3t catch of that water/ & fewe men be abouten my corde to eche/ & many in ful purpose ben redy it shorter to make/ & to enclose thentre/ that my boket of ioye nothing shulde catch/ but empty returne/ my careful sorowes to encrese. & if I dye for payne/ that were gladnesse at their hertes. Good lorde sende me water in to the cop of these mountayns/ & I shal drynke therof/ my thurstes to stāch: & sey these be cōfortable welles in to helth of goodnesse of my sauiour am I holpen. And yet I saye more/ the house of ioye to me is nat opened. How dare my sorouful goost than in any mater of gladnesse thynken to trete: for euer sobbynges & complayntes be redy refrete in his meditatiōs/ as werbles in manyfold stoudes cōmyng about I not than. And therfore what maner of ioye coude endite/ but yet at dore shal I knocke/ if the key of Dauid wolde the locke vnshypt/ & he bring me in/ whiche that childrens tōges both openeth & closeth. Whose spirite/ where he wel worcheth/ departyng goodly as him lyketh.

Nowe to goddes laude & reuerence/ ꝓfite of the reders/ amēdement of maners of yͤ herers encresyng of worship among loues seruauntes/ releuyng of my hert in to grace of my iewel/ & frenship plesance of this perle. I am stered in this makyng/ & for nothyng els: & if any good thyng to mēnes lyking in this scripture be founde/ thanketh the maister of grace/ whiche yͤ of that good & al other is authour/ & principal doer. And if any thing be insufficiēt or els myslyking/ with that yͤ the leudnesse of myne vnable cōnyng/ for body in disese anoyeth the vnderstāding in soule. A disesely habitation letteth yͤ wyttes many thinges/ & namely in sorowe. The custome neuer the later of

loue

loue/ be long tyme of seruice in termes I thinke to pursue/ whiche ben lyuely to yeue vnderstãdyng in other thynges. But nowe to enforme the of this Margarites goodnesse/ I may her nat halse preyse. Wherfore nat she for my boke/ but this boke for her is worthy to be cõmended/ tho my boke be leude: right as thiges nat for places/ but places for thynges ought to be desyred and praysed.

Nowe (qd Loue) trewly thy wordes I haue wel vnderstõde. Certes me thynketh hem right good/ & me wõdreth why thou so lightly passist in the lawe. Sothly (qd I) my wyt is leude & I am right blynde & that mater depe/ howe shulde I than haue waded/ lightly mizt I haue drenched & spilte ther my selfe. Yea (qd she) I shal helpe ẏ to swym. For rizt as lawe punyssheth brekers of preceptes/ & the cõtrary doers of the written constitucions: right so ayẽwarde/ lawe rewardeth & yeueth mede to hẽ that lawe strengthen. By one lawe this rebel is punisshed/ & this innocẽt is meded/ ẏ shrewe is enprisoned & this riztful is corowned. The same lawe that ioyneth by wedlocke without forsakyng/ the same lawe yeueth lybel of departicion bycause of deuorse both demed & declared. Ye ye (qd I) I fynde in no lawe to mede and rewarde in goodnes/ ẏ gylte of desertes. Lo (qd she) gylte couerted i your lawe/ mykel merite deserueth. Also Paulyn of Rome was crowned/ ẏ by him the mayntenours of Pompeus weren knowen & distroyed: & yet to forne was this Paulyn chefe of Põpeus coũsaile. This lawe in Rome hath yet his name of mesuring in mede/ the bewrayeng of the cõspiracy/ ordayned by tho senatours the dethe. Iulyus Cesar is acõpted in to Catons right wisnesse/ for euer in trouth florissheth his name amonge the knowers of reason. Perdicas was crowned in the heritage of Alexãder the great/ for tellynge of a preuy hate that kynge Porrus to Alexander hadde. Wherfore euery wight by reason of lawe after his rightwysenesse apertely his mede may chalenge: & so thou that mayntaynest lawe of kynde/ & therfore disease hast suffred in ẏ lawe/ rewarde is worthy to be rewarded & ordayned/ & apertly thy mede might thou chalenge. Certes (qd I) this haue I wel lerned/ & euer hensforwarde I shal drawe me therafter in ouched of wyl to auoide this lawe bothe mayntene & kepe/ & so hope I best entre in to your grace/ wel deseruynge in to worship of a wight/ without nedeful compulsion/ ought medefully to be rewarded. Truly (qd Loue) that is sothe/ & tho by constitucion good seruice in to profite & auauntage strecheth/ vtterly many men it demen to haue more desert of mede/ than good wyl nat cõpelled. Ye now (qd I) howe may men holden of this the contrary. And what is good seruice? of you wolde I here this question declared. I shal say the (qd she) in a fewe wordes/ resonable werkynges in plesaunce & profite of thy souerayne. Howe shulde I this perfourme (qd I) Rizt wel (qd she) & here me nowe a lytel. It is hardely (qd she to vnderstãde) that right as mater by due ouerchaungynges foloweth his perfection & his forme: Right so euery man by riztful werkynges ought to folowe the leful desyres i his hert/ & se toforn to what ende he deserueth/ for many tymes he that loketh nat after thẽdes/ but vtterly therof is vnknowen/ befalleth often many perils to done/ wherthrough er he be ware shamefully he is confoũded/ thende therof neden to be before loked to euery desirer of suche foresight i good seruice thre thynges specially nedeth to be rulers in his werkes. First that he do good/ next ẏ he do by electyon i his owne hert/ & the thirde that he do godly withouten any surquidry in thoughtes. That your werkes shulden be good in seruyce or in any other actes/ auctorites many may be aleged neuerthelater/ by reason thus maye it be shewed. Al your werkes be cleped seconde/ & mouen in vertue of the firste wercher/ whiche in good werkes wrought you to procede/ & right so your werkes mouen i to vertue of the laste ende/ & right in the first werkynge were nat/ no man shulde in the secõde werche. Right so but ye feled to what ende & seen their goodnes closed/ ye shuld no more recche what ye wrouzt but the gynnyng gan with good/ & there shal it cease in the last ende/ if it be wel consydred. Wherfore the myddle/ if other wayes it drawe than accordant to the endes/ there stynteth the course

course of good / ⁊ another maner course entreth / ⁊ so it is a ꝑtie by him selue / ⁊ euery ꝑte be nat accordant to his al / is foule ⁊ ought to be eschewed. wherfore euery thīge ẏ is wrouȝt and be nat good / is nat accordant to thendes of his al hole / it is foule / ⁊ ought to be withdrawe. Thus the ꝑsons that neither don good ne harme / shamen foule their makyng: Wherfore without workyng of good actes in good seruice / may no man ben accepted. Truely the ilke that han might to do good ⁊ done it nat / ẏ crowne of worship shal be take from hem / ⁊ with shame shul they be anulled. ⁊ so to make one werke acordant wᵗ his endes / euery good seruaunt by reason of consequence muste do good nedes. Certes it suffiseth nat alone to do good / but goodly withal folowe / the thãke of goodnesse els in nought he deserueth: For riȝt as al your being come from the greatest good in whom al goodnesse is closed. Right so yoᵘʳ endes ben directe to the same good. Aristotel determyneth that ende ⁊ good ben one / and cõuertible in vnderstãding / and he that in wyl doth away good / ⁊ he that loketh nat to thẽde loketh nat to good / but he that doth good and doth nat goodly / draweth away the direction of thende nat goodly / must nedes be bad. Lo badde is nothing els / but absence or negatyfe of good / as derkenesse is absence or negatyue of lyght. Than he that doth goodly / directeth thilke good in to thende of badde: So muste thyng nat good folowe / eke badnesse to suche folke ofte foloweth. Thus cõtrariaunt workers of thende that is good / ben worthy the cõtrary of thende that is good to haue. How (qđ I) may any good dede be done / but if goodly it helpe. Yes (qđ Loue) the deuyl dothe many good dedes / but goodly he leueth be hynde / for euen badly ⁊ in disceyuable wyse he worketh / Wherfore the cõtrary of thende him foloweth. And do he neuer so many good dedes / bicause goodly is away / his goodnes is nat rekened. Lo than tho a man do good / but he do goodly thende in goodnesse wol nat folowe / ⁊ thus in good seruice both good dede ⁊ goodly done musten ioyne togider / ⁊ that it be done with free choise in hert: ⁊ els deserueth he nat ẏ merite in goodnes / that wol I proue. for if thou do any thyng good by chaũce or by happe / in what thyng art thou therof worthy to be commẽded? for nothing by reason of that turneth in to thy praysing ne lackyng. Lo thilke thīg done by hap by thy wyl is nat caused / ⁊ therby shulde I thanke or lacke deserue: ⁊ sythen that fayleth / thende which that wel shulde rewarde / must nedes faile. clerkes sayn / no man but wyllynge is blessed a good dede ẏ he hath done is nat done of free choice wyllyng / without whiche blyssednesse may nat folowe. Ergo neither thãke of goodnesse ne seruice ī that is cõtrary of the good ende / so than to good ꝑuice lõgeth good dede goodly don / thorowe fre choice ī hert. Truely (qđ I) this haue I wel vnderstande. Wel (qđ she) euery thyng thus done sufficiẽtly by lawe / that is cleped iustice / after rewarde clayn. For lawe ⁊ iustice was ordayned in this wise / suche desertes in goodnesse after quantite in doynge / by mede to rewarde / ⁊ of necessyte of suche iustyce / ẏ is to say / riȝtwysenesse was free choice in deꝑtyng of wel or of yuel grauñted to resonable creatures. Euery man hath free arbitremẽt to chose good or yuel to ꝑforme. Nowe (qđ I tho) if I by my good wyl deserue this Margarit ꝑle and am nat therto cõpelled / ⁊ haue free choice to do what me lyketh: She is than holden as me thynketh to rewarde thentent of my good wyl. Goddes forbode els (qđ Loue) no wiȝt meaneth otherwise I trowe / free wyl of good hert after mede deserueth. Hath euery man (qđ I) fre choice by necessary maner of wyl ī euery of his doynges / that him lyketh by goddes proper puruyaũce. I wolde se that wel declared to my leude vnderstãding / for necessary ⁊ necessyte ben wordes of mokel entẽtion / closyng (as to saye) so mote it be nedes / ⁊ otherwyse may it nat betyde. This shalt thou lern (qđ she) so thou take hede in my speche. If it were nat in mãnes owne lyberte of fre wyl to do good or bad / but to the one keped by bonde of goddes preordynaũce: Than do he neuer so wel it were by nedeful cõpulsion of thilk bõde and nat by fre choice / wherby nothyng he desyreth / ⁊ do he neuer so yuel it were nat man for to wyte / but onelych to him ẏ suche thyng ordayned him to done. Wherfore he ne ought for

for bad be punisshed/ ne for no good dede be rewarded/ but of necessite of riztwisnesse was therfore fre choice of arbitremēt put in mans proper disposition: truely if it were otherwise it cōtraried goddes charite/ yͭ badnesse & goodnesse rewardeth after desert of payn or of mede. Me thynketh this wōder (ꝙ I) for god by necessite forwote al thynges cōmyng/ and so mote it nedes be: & thilke thīges that ben don be our fre choice comen nothīg of necessite but onely be wyl: Howe may this stonde togyther? and so me thynketh truely/ that fre choyce fully repugneth goddes forwetyng. Trewly lady me semeth they mowe nat stande togyther.

Than gan loue nygh me nere/ & with a noble countenaunce of visage & lymmes/ dressed her nigh my sytting place. Take forth (ꝙ she) thy pen & redily write these wordes/ for if god wol/ I shal hem so enforme to the/ yͭ thy leudnesse whiche I haue vnderstād in that mater/ shal openly be clered/ & thy sight in ful loking therin amēded. First if thou thynke that goddes prescīēce repugne lyberte of arbetry of arbitrement/ it is impossible that they shulde accorde in onheed of sothe to vnderstōding. Ye (qd I) forsothe so I it cōceyue. Wel (qd she) if thilke impossible were a way/ the repugnaunce that semeth to be therin/ were vtterly remoued. Shewe me the absence of that impossibilyte (qd I) So (qd she I shal). Nowe I suppose that they mowe stāde togider/ p̄science of god whō foloweth necessite of thīges cōmyng and lyberte of arbitremēt/ thorowe whiche yͭ beleuest many thīges to be without necessite. Bothe these ꝑporcions be sothe (qd I) & wel mowe stāde togider/ wherfore this case as possyble I admpt. Truely (qd she) & this case is impossible. Howe so (qd I) For herof (ꝙ she) foloweth & weyeth another ī possyble. Proue me that (ꝙ I). that I shal (ꝙ she) for sōthing is cōmyng without necessyte/ & god wot that toforn/ for al thīg cōmyng he before wot/ and that he beforn wot of necessyte is cōmyng: as he beforne wot be the case by necessary maner than/ or els thorowe necessite is sōthyng to be without necessite/ & whēdto euery wizt yͭ hath good vnderstanding/ is seen these thynges to be repugnaunt. Prescīēce of god/ whiche that foloweth necessyte & lyberte of arbytrement/ fro whiche is remoued necessyte/ for truely it is necessary that god haue forwetyng of thīg withouten any necessite cōmynge. Ye (qd I) but yet remeue ye nat away fro myne vnderstandyng/ the necessyte folowyng goddes beforewetyng/ as thus. God beforne wote me in seruice of loue to be bounden to this Margarite perle/ & therfore by necessite thus to loue am I bounde/ & if I nat had loued/ thorowe necessyte had I ben kepte from al loue dedes. Certes (qd Loue) bicause this mater is good & necessary to declare/ I thynke here in wel to abyde and not lyghtly to passe. Thou shalte not (quod she) say al onely god beforne wote me to be a louer or no louer/ but thus: god beforne wote me to be a louer without necessyte. And so it foloweth whether thou loue or not loue/ euery of hem is and shal be. But nowe thou seest the impossibylite of the case/ and the possibylite of thilke that thou wendest had ben impossyble/ wherfore the repugnaūce is adnulled. Ye (quod I) and yet do ye not awaye the strength of necessyte whan it is said/ though necessyte it is me in loue to abyde/ or not to loue without necessyte for god beforne wote it. This maner of necessyte forsothe semeth to some men in to coaction/ that is to sayne/ constraynyng or els prohibycion that is defendynge/ wherfore necessyte is me to loue of wyl. I vnderstande me to be constrayned by some pryuy strength to the wyl of louynge/ and if no loue to be defended from the wyl of louynge/ and so thorowe necessyte me semeth to loue/ for I loue/ or els not to loue/ if I not loue/ wherthrough neyther thāke ne maugre in tho thynges maye I deserue.

Nowe (quod she) thou shalte wel vnderstande that often we sayne thynge thorowe necessyte to be: that by no strength to be neyther is coarted ne constrayned/ and throughe necessyte not to be/ that with no defendynge is remoued/ for we sayne it is thorowe necessyte god to be vnmortal nought deedlyche/ and it is necessyte god to be rightful/ but not

that

that any strẽgth of violente maner cõstray-
neth him to be immortal/ or defendeth him to
be vnrightful/ for nothĩg may make him ded-
ly or vnrightful. Right so if I say thorowe ne
cessyte is ŷ to be a louer or els none/ onely tho
rowe wyl/ as god beforne wete/ It is nat to
vnderstõde that any thyng defẽdeth or forbit/
the thy wyl/ whiche shal nat be/ or els cõstray
neth it to be whiche shalbe: that same thynge
forsoth god before wot/ whiche he beforn seeth
any thyng cõmende of onely wyl/ ŷ wyl ney-
ther is cõstrayned ne defẽded thorowe any o-
ther thing. & so thorowe lyberte of arbitremẽt
it is do/ that is done of wyl. And trewly my
good childe/ if these thynges be wel vnderstõd
I wene that non inconuenyent shalt thou fyn-
de betwene goddes forwetyng & lyberte of ar-
bitremẽt/ wherfore I wot wel they may stãde
togider. Also farthermore/ who that vnderstã
dyng of prescience proprelych cõsyde reth/ thorowe
the same wyse that any thyng be afore wyst/
is said for to be cõmyng it is pronounced/ there
is nothing toforn wist/ but thĩg comyng/ fore
wetĩg is but of trouth dout may nat be wyst:
wherfore whan I sey that god toforn wote a-
ny thyng/ thorowe necessyte is thilke thyng to
be cõmyng/ al is one if I sey/ if it shalbe/ but
this necessyte neither cõstrayneth ne defẽdeth
any thyng to be or nat to be. Therfore sothly
if loue is put to be/ it is said of necessyte to be/
or els for it is put nat to be/ it is affirmed nat
to be of necessyte: nat for ŷ necessite cõstray-
neth or defendeth loue to be or nat to be. For
whan I say/ if loue shal be of necessite it shal
be/ here folowe th necessyte. the thyng toforne
put/ it is as moch to say/ as if it were thus p-
nõũced/ that thyng shalbe: None other thyng
signifyeth this necessyte but onely thus/ that
shalbe may nat togider be & nat be. Euẽlych
also it is soth/ loue was & is/ & shalbe/ nat of
necessyte/ & nede is to haue be al that was/ &
nedeful is to be al that is/ & cõmyng to al that
shalbe: & it is nat the same to saye/ loue to be
passed/ and loue passed to be passed/ or loue
present to be present/ and loue to be present/
or els loue to be commynge/ and loue com-
mynge to be cõmyng: dyuersite in settyng of
wordes/ maketh dyuersite in vnderstãdynge/

altho in the same sentẽce they accorden of sig-
nification/ right as it is nat al one: loue swete
to be swete/ & loue to be swete: for moch loue
is bytter & sorouful er hertes ben eased/ & yet
it gladeth thilke sorouful hert on suche loue to
thynke. Forsothe (qd I) outher whise I haue
had mokel blysse in hert of loue/ ŷ stoũdmele
hath me sorily anoyed: & certes lady/ for I se
my selfe thus knit with this Margarite peerle
as by bonde of your seruyce/ & of no lyberte
of wyl/ my hert wyl nowe nat acorde this ser
uyce to loue. I can deme in my selfe non o-
therwise/ but thorowe necessite am I cõstray-
ned in this seruice to abyde. But alas than/ if
I thorowe nedeful cõpulsioun maugre me be
with holde/ lytel thãke for al my great trauel
haue I than deserued. Nowe (qd this lady) I
saye as I sayde: We lyketh this mater to de-
clare at the ful/ & why: for many men haue
had dyuers fantasyes & reasons/ both on one
syde therof & in the other. Of whiche rixt lone
I trowe if thou wost vnderstõde/ thou shalte
con peue the sentẽce/ to the ptie more probable
by reason/ & in soth knowing/ by that I haue
of this mater maked an ende. Certes (qd I)
of these thynges longe haue I had great luste
to be lerned/ for yet I wene goddes wyl & his
prescience acordeth with my seruice/ in louynge
of this pcious Margarite perle. After whom
euer in my hert with thurstyng desire weere I
do brenne: vnwastyng I lãgour & fade/ and
the day of my desteny in dethe or in ioye I vn-
byde/ but yet in thende I am comforted be my
supposaile in blysse/ & in ioye to determyne af
ter my desyres. That thyng (qd Loue) haste-
ly to ŷ neigh/ god graũt of his grace & mercy/
and this shalbe my prayer tyl thou be lykende
in herte at thyne owne wyl. But nowe to en-
forme the in this mater (qd this lady) thou
wost where I lefte/ that was loue to be swete
and loue swete to be swete/ is nat al one for to
say: for a tree is nat alway by necessite white
sõtyme er it were white/ it myght haue be nat
white: & after tyme it is white/ it maye be nat
white: But a whyte tree euermore nedeful is
to be white: for neither toforn ne after it was
white/ myght it be togider white & nat white.
Also loue by necessyte is nat present as nowe
in the

in the/ for er it were present it myght haue be
that it shulde nowe nat haue be/ & yet it maye
be that it shal nat be present: but thy loue pre-
sent whiche to her Margarite the hath bounde/
nedeful is to be present. Trewly some doyng
of action nat by necessyte is comynge ferre to
forn it be/it may be that it shal nat be comyn-
ge: thyng forsoth comyng nedeful is to be co-
ming/for it may nat be that comyng shal nat
be comyng. & right as I haue sayd of present
and of future tymes/the same sentēce in soth-
nesse is of the preterit/ ẏ is to say tyme passed
for thyng passed must nedes be passed / & er it
were it might haue nat be/ wherfore it shulde
nat haue passed. Right so whan loue coming
is said of loue that is to come/ nedeful is to be
that is said/for thing comyng neuer is nat cō
mynge/ & so ofte the same thynge we sayn of
the same/ as whan we sayne euery man is a
man/ or euery louer is a louer/ so muste it be
nedes / in no waye may he be man & no man
togider. And if it be nat by necessite/that is to
say/nedeful al thyng comyng to be comyng/
than somthyng comyng is nat comynge/and
that is impossible/right as these termes nede-
ful/necessite/ & necessary betoken and signify
thyng nedes to be/ & it may nat otherwise be.
Right these termes impossible signifieth/ that
thyng is nat & by no way may it be/ than tho
rowe pert necessite/al thyng comyng is com-
myng/ but that is by necessite/ foloweth with
nothyng to be cōstrayned. so whan that com-
myng is said of thynge/ nat alway thyng tho
rowe necessite is/altho it be comyng. For if I
say to morowe loue is comyng ī this Marga
ritz hert/ nat therfore thorow necessite shal the
ilke loue be/ yet it may be that it shal nat be/
altho it were comyng. Neuerthelater/sōtyme
it is soth that somthyng be of necessite/ that is
sayd to come: as if I say to morowe by com-
mynge the risynge of the sonne. If therfore
with necessite I pronounce comyng of thyng
to come/in this maner loue to morne comyn-
ge in thyne Margarite to the warde by neces-
site is comynge/ or els the risyng of the sonne
to morne comynge / through necessite is com-
mynge. Loue sothely/ whiche may nat be of
necessyte alone folowynge/ thorowe necessyte
comyng it is made certayne. For futur of fu-
ture is said/that is to sayn comyng of comyn
ge is said: as if to morowe comyng is thorow
necessite comynge it is. Arisyng of the sonne
thorowe two necessites in comyng/ it is to vn
derstāde/that one is to forgoing necessite/ whi
che maketh thyng to be/ therfore it shalbe/ for
nedeful is that it be. Another is folowyng ne
cessite/ whiche nothyng cōstrayneth to be/and
so by necessyte it is to come / why: for it is to
come. Nowe than/ whan we sayn / that god
beforn wot thyng comyng nedeful is to be cō
myng/ yet therfore make we nat in certayne/
euermore thynge to be thorowe necessite com-
mynge. Sothly thyng comyng maye nat be
nat comyng by no way/for it is the same sen-
tence of vnderstādyng: as if we say thus. If
god beforn wot any thyng/ nedeful is that to
be comyng. But yet therfore foloweth nat ẏ
prescıēce of god/ thyng thorowe necessite to be
comyng: for al tho god toforn wote al thīges
comyng/ yet nat therfore he beforn wot euery
thyng comyng thorowe necessite. Sōe thīges
he beforn wot comyng of fre wyl out of reso-
nable creature. Certes (qd I) these termes/
nede & necessite/ haue a queynt maner of vn-
derstādyng/they wolden dullen many mēnes
wyttes. Therfore (qd she) I wol hem openly
declare/ & more clerely than I haue toforn
er I departe hense.

Here of this mater (qd she) thou shalte vn-
derstāde/that right as it is nat nedeful god to
wylne that he wyl/ no more in many thynges
is nat nedeful a man to wylne that he wol.
And euer right as nedeful is to be what that
god wol/ right so to be it is nedeful that man
wol in tho thynges/ whiche that god hath put
in to mannes subiection of wyllynge: as if a
mā wol loue/that he loue: & if he ne wol loue/
that he loue nat/ & of suche other thynges in
mānes disposition. For why/ nowe than that
god wol may nat be/ whan he wol the wyl of
man thorowe no necessyte to be cōstrayned or
els defended for to wylne/ & he wol theffecte to
folow the wyl/ than is it nedeful wyl of man
to be fre/ & also to be that he wol. In this ma-
ner it is soth/ that thorowe necessite is mānes
werke in louyng/ that he wol do altho he wol
it nat

it not with necessyte. (Quod I than) howe
stante it in loue of thilke wyl/ sythen men lo-
uen wyllyng of free choyce in herte. wherfore
if it be thorowe necessyte/ I praye you lady of
an answere this questyon to assoyle. I wol
(qd she) answere the openly: Right as men
wyl not thorowe necessyte/ right so is not loue
of wyl thorowe necessyte/ ne thorowe neces-
syte wrought thilke same wyl: for if he wolde
it not with good wyl/ it shulde not haue ben
wrought/ although that he dothe it is nedeful
to be doone. But if a man do synne it is no-
thyng els but to wyl/ that he shulde not: right
so synne of wyl is not to be maner necessary
done/ no more than wyl is necessarye. Neuer
the later this is sothe/ if a man wol synne/ it
is necessarye him to synne/ but though thilke
necessyte nothyng is constrayned ne defended
in the wyl/ right so thilke thynge that frewyl
wol and maye/ and not may/ not wylne/ and
nedeful is that to wylne he maye not wylne/
but thilke to wylne nedeful is/ for impossyble
to him it is one thyng/ and the same to wylne
he may not wylne/ but thilk to wylne nedeful
is: for impossyble to him it is one thyng/ and
the same to wylne and not to wylne. The
werke forsothe of wyl/ to whome it is yeue
that it be that he hath in wyl/ and that he wol
not/ volūtarie of spontanye it is/ for by spon-
tanye wyl it is do/ that is to saye with good
wyl/ not constrayned: than by wyl not con-
strayned/ it is constrayned to be/ and that is it
may not togyther be. If this necessyte ma-
keth lybertie of wyl/ whiche that afore they
weren they might haue ben eschewed & shon-
ned: God than/ whiche ẏ knoweth al truthe/
and nothynge but truthe/ al these thynges as
they arne spontanye or necessarie syght/ and
as he seeth so they ben: and so with these thyn-
ges wel consydred it is open at the ful/ that
without al maner repugnaunce/ god beforne
wote al maner thynges ben done by frewyl/
whiche afore they weren might haue ben ne-
uer they shulde be/ and yet ben they thorowe a
maner necessyte from frewyl discendeth.
Hereby maye (quod she) lightly ben knowe
that not al thīges to be is of necessyte/ though
god haue hem in his prescience/ for somthyn-
ges to be is of lybertie of wyl: and to make
the to haue ful knowynge of goddes beforne
wetyng/ here me (quod she) what I shal say.
Blythly lady (quod I) me lyst this mater en-
tyrely to understande. Thou shalte (qd she)
understande/ that in heuen is goddes beynge/
although he be ouer al by power/ yet there is
abydinge of deuyne persone/ in whiche heuen
is euerlastynge presence/ withouten any mo-
uable tyme there/ fole haue I not sayd toforn
this/ as tyme hurteth/ right so ayenward tyme
heleth and rewardeth: and a tree oft sapled/
is holde more in deyntie whan it frute forthe
bringeth. A marchaunt that for ones lesynge
in the see no more to auenture thynketh/ he
shal neuer with auenture come to rychesse: so
ofte must men on the oke smyte/ tyl the happy
dent haue entred/ whiche with the okes owne
swaye maketh it to come al at ones. So ofte
falleth the lethy water on the harde rocke/ tyl
it haue thorowe persed it. The euen draught
of the wyre drawer/ maketh the wyre to ben
euen and supple werchynge/ and if he stynted
in his draught/ the wyre breaketh a sonder.
Euery tre wel springeth/ whan it is wel groū-
ded and not often remoued. What shal this
frute be (qd I) nowe it gynneth rype? Grace
(quod she) in parfyte ioy to endure/ and ther-
with thou begon. Grace (quod I) me thyn-
keth I shulde haue a rewarde for my longe
trauayle? I shal tel the (quod she) retrybu-
cion of thy good wylles to haue of thy Mar-
garyte perle/ it beareth not the name of mede/
but onely of good grace/ and that cometh not
of thy deserte/ but of thy Margarytes good-
nesse/ and vertue alone. (Quod I) shulde al
my longe trauayle haue no rewarde but tho-
rowe grace/ and somtyme your seluen sayd/
rightwysnesse euenlyche rewardeth to quyte
one benefyte for another. That is sothe
(quod Loue) euer as I sayde/ as to him that
dothe good/ whiche to done he were neyther
holden ne yet constrayned. That is sothe
(quod I). Trewly (quod she) al that e-
uer thou doest to thyne Margaryte perle/ of
wyl/ of loue/ and of reson thou owest to done

D.q.q. it/ it is

The Testament of Love: III. iv. 15–56; vii. 94 (*fole*, col. 2, l. 11)—124

it/ yet is nothyng els but yeldyng of thy dette in quitynge of thy grace/ whiche she the sent whan ye first mette. I wene (quod I) right lytle grace to me she delyuered. Certes it was harde grace/ it hath nyghe me astrangled. That it was good grace I wot wel thou wylt it graunt er thou departe hence. If any man yeue to another wight to whom that he ought not/ and whiche that of him selfe nothynge maye haue/ a garnement or a cote/ though he weare the cote or els thilke clothyng/ it is not to put to him that was naked the cause of his clothynge/ but onely to him that was yeuer of the garnement. Wherfore I saye/ thou that were naked of loue/ and of thy selfe non haue mightest/ it is not to put to thyne owne persone/ sythen thy loue came thorowe thy Margaryte perle. Ergo she was yeuer of the loue although thou it vse/ and there sent she the grace thy seruyce to begynne. She is worthy the thanke of this grace/ for she was the yeuer. Al the thoughtes/ besy doynges/ and plesaunce in thy might and in thy wordes that thou canste deuyse/ ben but right lytel in quitynge of thy dette: had she not ben/ suche thing hadde not ben studyed. So al these maters kyndely drawen homewarde to this Margaryte perle/ for from thence were they borowed/ al is holy her to wyte the loue that thou hauest: and thus quytest thou thy dette/ in that thou stedfastly seruest. And kepe wel that loue I the rede/ that of her thou hast borowed/ and vse it in her seruyce thy dette to quite/ and than arte thou able right sone to haue grace/ wherfore after mede in none halue maist thou loke. Thus thy gynnyng and endyng is but grace alone/ and in thy good deseruynge thy dette thou aquitest: without grace is nothyng worthe what so euer thou werche. Thanke thy Margaryte of her great grace that hytherto the hath gyded/ and praye her of contynuaunce forthe in thy werkes herafter/ and that for no misshappe thy grace ouerthwartly tourne. Grace/ glorie/ and ioye/ is comyng thorowe good folkes desertes/ and by gettyng of grace therin shullen ende. And what is more glorie or more ioye than wysdome and loue in parfyte charite/ whiche god hath grau̅ted to al tho that wel canne deserue. And with that this lady al at ones sterte in to myn hert: here wol I onbyde (quod she) for euer/ and neuer wol I gon hence/ and I wol kepe the from medlynge while me lyste here onbyde: thyne entermetyng maners in to stedfastnesse shullen be chaunged.

SOberlyche tho threwe I vp myn eyen/ and hugely tho was I astonyed of this sodayne adventure/ and fayne wolde I haue lerned howe vertues shulden ben knowen/ in whiche thynges I hope to god here after she shal me enfourmen/ and namely sythen her restynge place is nowe so nyghe at my wyl: and anon al these thynges that this lady said/ I remembred me by my selfe/ and reuolued the lyues of myne vnderstondynge wyttes. Tho founde I fully al these maters parfytely there written/ howe mysse rule by fayned loue bothe realmes and cytes hath gouerned a great throwe. Howe lightly me might the fautes espye/ howe rules in loue shulde ben vsed/ howe somtyme with fayned loue foule I was begyled/ howe I shulde loue haue knowe/ and howe I shal in loue with my seruyce procede. Also furthermore I founde of perdurable letters wōderly there grauen/ these maters whiche I shal nempne. Certes none age ne other thynge in erthe maye the leest syllable of this in no poynte deface/ but clerely as the sonne in myne vnderstandynge soule they shynen. This maye neuer out of my mynde/ howe I maye not my loue kepe/ but thorowe wylsynge in herte: Wylne to loue maye I not/ but I louynge haue. Loue haue I none but thorowe grace of this Margarite perle. It is no maner doute/ that wyl wol not loue but for it is louynge/ as wyl wol not rightfully/ but for it is rightful it selue. Also wyl is not louynge for he wol loue/ but he wol loue for he is louynge: it is al one to wyl to be louynge/ and louynges in possessyon to haue. Right so wyl wol not loue/ for of loue hath he no partie/ ⁊ yet I denye not louynge wyl wylne more loue to haue/ whiche that he hath not whan he wolde more than he hath/ but

But I saye he maye no loue wysne/ if he no loue haue/ through which thilke loue he shuld wysne: but to haue this louyng wyl may no man of hym selfe/ but onely through grace toforne goyng: Right so maye no man it kepe/ but by grace folowynge. Consyder nowe euery man aright/ and let sene if þ any wight of hym selfe mowe this louyng wel get/ and he therof first nothynge haue: for if it shulde of hym selfe spring/ eyther it muste be wyllyng or not wyllyng. Wyllyng by hym selfe may he it not haue/ sythen hym fayleth the mater that shulde it forthe bring/ the mater hym fayleth: Why? he maye therof haue no knowyng/ tyl whan grace put it in his herte. Thus willyng by him selfe may he it not haue/ and not wyllyng may he it not haue. Parde euery consent of euery reasonable creature otherwyse wyl not graunt: Wyl in affyrmatife with not wyllyng by no way mowe acorde. And although this louyng wol come in myn hert by frenesse of arbytrement/ as in this booke fully is shewed/ yet owe I not therfore as moche alowe my frewyl/ as grace of that Margaryte to me leaned/ for neyther might I without grace to forn goyng/ and afterwarde folowyng/ thilke grace get ne kepe/ and lese shal I it neuer but if frewyl it make/ as in wyllynge otherwyse than grace hath me graunted. For right as whan any person taketh wyllyng to be sobre/ and throweth þ away/ willyng to be dronke/ or els taketh wyl of drinkyng out of mesure: whiche thyng anon as it is done/ maketh thorowe his owne gylte by frewyl that leseth his grace. In whiche thing therfore vpon the nobley of grace I mote trusten/ & my besy cure set thilke grace to kepe/ that my frewyl otherwyse than by reason it shulde werche/ cause not my grace to voyde: for thus must I bothe loke to frewyl and to grace. For right as naturel vsage in engendring of children maye not ben without father/ ne also but with the mother/ for neyther father ne mother in begettyng maye it lacke: right so grace and frewyl accorden/ and without hem bothe maye not louynge wyl in no partie ben getten. But yet is not frewyl in gettynge of that thyng so mokel thāke worthy as is grace/ ne in the kepynge therof/ so moche thanke deserueth/ and yet in gettynge and kepyng bothe done they accorde. Trewly often tyme grace frewyl helpeth in fordoynge of contrarye thinges/ that to wyllynge loue not accorden/ and strength wyl aduersytees to withsytte/ wherfore al togyther to grace oweth to ben accepted/ that my wullyng deserueth: Frewyl to louyng in this wyse is accorded. I remembre me wel howe al this booke (who so hede taketh) consydereth al thynges to werchynges of mankynde euenly accordeth/ as in turnyng of this worde loue in to trouthe/ or els rightwysnesse/ whether that it lyke. For what thyng that falleth to man in helpyng of free arbytrement/ thilke rightwysnesse to take or els to kepe/ thorowe whiche a man shal be saued/ of whiche thyng al this booke mencion hath maked/ in euery poynte therof grace oweth to be thanked. Wherfore I saye/ euery wight hauynge this rightwysnesse rightful is/ and yet therfore I fele not in my conscience/ that to al rightful is bihoten the blysse euerlastynge/ but to hem that ben rightful withouten any vnrightfulnesse. Some man after some degree maye rightfully ben accompted: as chaste men in lyuyng/ and yet ben they ianglers and ful of enuy pressed: to hem shal this blysse neuer ben delyuered. For right as very blisse is with out al maner nede/ rizt so to no man shal it be yeuen but to the rightful/ voyde from al maner vnrightfulnesse founde/ so no man to her blysse shal ben folowed/ but he be rightful/ and with vnrightfulnesse not bounde/ and in that degree fully be knowe. This rightfulnesse in as moche as in hym selfe is/ of none yuel is it cause/ and of al maner goodnesse trewly it is mother. This helpeth the spyrit to withsytte the leude lustes of fleshly lykinge: This strengtheth and maintayneth the lawe of kynde/ and if that otherwhyle me weneth harme of this precious thyng to folowe/ therthorough is nothynge the cause/ of somwhat els cometh it aboute who so taketh hede. By rightfulnesse forsothe werne many holy sayntes good sauour & swetenesse to god almighty. But that to some folkes they weren sauour of dethe in to deedly ende/ that come not of the

Q.q.q.ii. sayntes

sayntes rightwysnesse/ but of other wycked mennes badnesse hath proceded. Trewly the ilke wyl/ whiche that the lady of loue me lerned/ affectyon of wyl to nempne/ whiche is in wyllyng of profytable thynges/ yuel is it not/ but whan to fleisshly lustes it cōsenteth/ ayenst reason of soule: But that this thynge more clerely be vnderstād/ it is for to knowe/ whēce and howe thylke wyl is so vycious and so redy/ yuel dedes to perfourme. Grace at the gynnynge/ ordeyned thilke wyl in goodnesse euer to haue endured/ and neuer to badnesse haue assented: Men shulde not byleue/ that god thilke wyl maked to be vycious. Our firste father as Adam and Eue/ for vycious appetytes and vycious wyl to suche appetytes consentynge/ ben not on thynge in kynde/ other thyng is done for the other. And howe this wyl fyrst in to man first assented I holde it profytable to shewe: but if the first condycion of reasonable creature wol be consydred and apertly loked/ lightly the cause of suche wyl may ben shewed. Intencion of god was that rightfully and blyssed shulde reasonable nature ben maked/ him selfe for to kepe/ but neyther blyssful ne rightful might it not be/ withouten wyl in them bothe. Wyl of rightfulnesse is thilke same rightfulnesse/ as here toforne is shewed: but wyl of blysse is not thilke blysse/ for euery man hath not thilke blysse/ in whom the wyl therof is abydynge. In this blysse after euery vnderstandynge is suffysaunce of couenable comodytees without any maner nede/ whether it be blysse of aungels or els thilke/ that grace first in paradise suffred Adam to haue. For al though angels blysse be more than Adams was in paradyse/ yet maye it not be denyded/ that Adam in paradyse ne had suffysaunce of blysse: for ryght as great herte is without al maner of coldenesse/ and yet maye another herte more heate haue/ right so nothynge defended Adam in paradyse to ben blessed/ without al maner nede. Al thoughe aungels blysse be moche more/ forsothe it foloweth not lasse than another to haue therfore hym nedeth/ but for to wante a thynge whiche that behoueth to ben had/ that maye nede ben cleped/ and that was not in Adam at the first gynnyng. God and the Margaryte weten what I meane. Forsothe where as is nede/ there is wretchydnesse/ good without cause to forngoyng made not reasonable creature wretched/ for hym to vnderstande and loue had he firste maked. God made therfore man blyssed without al maner indygence/ togyther and at ones toke reasonable creature blysse/ and wyl of blyssednesse/ and wyl of rightfulnesse/ whiche is rightfulnesse it selue/ and lyberte of arbytrement/ that is fre wyl/ with whiche thilke rightfulnesse may he kepe and lese. So and in that wyse ordayned thylke two/ that wyl whiche that instrument is cleaped/ as here toforne mencion is maked/ shulde vse thilke rightfulnesse/ by teachyng of his soule to good maner of gouernaunce/ in thought and in wordes/ and that it shulde vse the blysse in obedyent maner/ withouten any incōmodyte. Blysse forsothe in to mannes profyte/ and rightwysnesse in to his worshyp god delyuered at ones: but rightfulnesse so was yeuen ẏ man might it lese/ whiche if he not loste had not/ but contynuelly haue it kepte/ he shulde haue deserued the auauncement in to the felowshyppe of angels/ in whiche thyng if he that loste/ neuer by him selfe forwarde shulde he it mowe ayenwarde recouer: and as wel the blysse that he was in/ as aungels blysse that to himwardes was comyng/ shulde be nome at ones/ and he depriued of them bothe. And thus fyl man vn to lykenesse of vnreasonable bestes/ and with hem to corrupciō and vnlusty apetytes was he vnder throwen/ but yet wyl of blysse dwelleth/ that by indygence of goodes whiche that he loste through great wretchydnesse/ by right shulde he ben punysshed. And thus for he weyued rightfulnesse/ loste hath he his blysse: but fayle of his desyre in his owne comodyte may he not/ and were comodytes to his reasonable nature whiche he hath loste may he not haue. To false lustes/ whiche ben bestyal appetytes he is turned: folye of vnconnyng hath him begyled/ in wenyng ẏ thilke ben the comoditees that owen to ben desyred. This affection of wyl by lyberte of arbitrement is enduced to wylne thus thing that he shulde not/ and so is

wyl

wyl not maked yuel but vnrightful/ by absēce of rightfulnesse/ whiche thing by reason euer shulde he haue. And frenesse of arbytrement may he not wylne/ whan he it not haueth/ for whyle he it had/ thilke halpe it not to kepe: so that without grace may it not ben recouered. Wyl of cōmodyte/ in as moche as vnrightful it is maked/ by wyllynge of yuel lustes/ wyllyng of goodnesse may he not wylne: for wyl of instrument to affection of wyl is thralled/ sythen that other thyng may it not wylne/ for wyl of instrument to affection desyreth/ & yet ben bothe they wyl cleped: for that instrument wol/ through affection it wylneth/ & affection desyreth thilke thyng wherto instrument him ledeth. And so frewyl to vnlusty affection ful seruaunt is maked/ for vnrightfulnesse maye he not releue/ & without rightfulnesse ful fredome may it neuer haue. For kyndly lybertie of arbytrement without it/ veyne and ydel is forsothe. Wherfore yet I say/ as often haue I sayd the same/ whan instrument of wyl loste hath rightfulnesse/ in no maner but by grace may he ayen retourne rightfulnesse to wylne. For sythen nothyng but rightfulnesse alone shulde he wylne/ what yͭ euer he wylneth with out rightfulnesse/ vnrightfully he it wylneth. These than vnrightful appetytes & vnthusty lustes which the flyes desyreth/ in as mokel as they ben in kynde/ ben they not bad/ but they ben vnrightful and badde/ for they ben in resonable creature/ where as they beyng in no waye shulde ben suffred. In vnreasonable beestes neyther ben they yuel ne vnrightful/ for there is their kynde beyng.

KNowen may it wel ben nowe/ of these thynges toforne declared/ yͭ man hath not alway thilke rightfulnesse/ which by dute of right euermore hauen he shulde/ and by no way by him selfe may he it get ne kepe/ & after he it hath if he it lese/ recouer shal he it neuer/ without especial grace: Wherfore the commune sentence of the people in opinyon/ that euery thynge after destenye is ruled/ false and wicked is to byleue: For thoughe predestynacion be as wel of good as of badde/ sythen that it is sayde god hadnest made/ whiche he neuer ne wrought/ but for he suffreth hem to be maked/ as that he hardeth whan he naught missaythe/ or ledde in to temptacion whan he not delyuereth/ wherfore it is none inconuenyent if in that maner be sayd/ god toforne haue destenyed bothe badde/ and her badde werkes/ whan hem ne their yuel dedes neyther amendeth/ ne therto hem grace leueth. But specyallyche predestynacion of goodnesse alone/ is sayde by these great clerkes/ for in hym god dothe that they ben/ and that in goodnesse they werchen. But the negatyfe herof in badnesse is holden/ as the lady of loue hath me lerned/ who so aright in this booke loketh. And vtterly it is to weten/ that predestynacion properly i god may not ben demed/ no more than beforne wetyng. For in the chapitre of goddes beforne wetyng/ as Loue me rehersed/ al these maters apertely maye ben founden. Al thynges to god ben nowe togyther and in presence durynge. Trewly presence and predestynacion in nothynge disacorden/ wherfore as I was lerned howe goddes beforewetyng and free choyce of wyl mowe stonden togyther/ me thynketh the same reason me ledeth/ that destenye and frewyl accorden/ so that neyther of hem bothe to other in nothing contraryeth. And reasonablyche may it not ben denyed/ as often as any thyng falleth frewyl werchynge as if a man another man wrongfully anoyeth/ wherfore he him sleeth/ that it be constrayned to that ende/ as mokel folke cryeth and sayth: Lo/ as it was destenyed of god toforne know/ so it is thorowe necessyte fal/ and other wyse might it not betyde. Trewly neyther he that the wronge wrought/ ne he that him selfe venged/ none of thilke thinges thorowe necessyte wrought: for if that with frewyl there had it not wylled/ neyther had wrought that he persourmed: and so vtterly grace that frewyl in goodnesse bringeth and kepeth/ and fro badnesse it tourneth/ in al thynge moste thanke deserueth. This grace maketh sentēce in vertue to abyde/ wherfore in body and in soule in ful plentie of connynge after their good deseruyng in the euerlastynge ioy/ after the day of dome shul they endelesse dwel/ and they shul ben lerned in that kyngdome with

Q.q.iii. so mo-so mokel affecte of loue and of grace/ that the leste ioye shal of the greatest in glorie reioyce and ben gladded/ as if he the same ioye had. What wonder syth god is ẏ greatest loue/ and the ne ought to loke thynges with resonnyng to prue/ and so is instrumēt of wyl/ wyl: and yet varyeth he from effecte & vsing bothe. Affection of wyl also for wyl is cleped/ but it varyeth from instrument in this maner wise/ by that name/ lyche whan it cometh in to mynde anon right it is in wyllynge desyred/ and the negatyfe therof with wyllyng nyl not acorde: this is closed in herte/ thoughe vsage and instrument slepe. This slepeth whan instrumēt and vs waken: and of suche maner affection trewly some man hath more and some man lesse. Certes trewe louers wenen euer therof to lytel to haue. False louers in lytel wenen haue right mokel: Lo instrument of wyl in false and trewe bothe euen lyche is proporcioned/ but affection is more in some place than in some/ bycause of the goodnesse ẏ foloweth/ and that I thynke herafter to declare. Vse of this instrumēt is wyl/ but it taketh his name whan wylned thyng is in doyng. but vtterly grace to catche in thy blysse/ desyred to ben rewarded/ Thou muste haue than affection of wyl at the ful/ and vse whan his tyme asketh wylely to ben gouerned. Sothly my disciple without feruent affection of wil may no man ben saued: this affection of good seruyce in good loue/ may not ben grounded/ without feruent desyre to the thyng in wyl coueyted. But he that neuer retcheth to haue or not to haue/ affection of wyl in that hath no restyng place. Why? for whan thing cometh to mynde and it be not taken in hede to comyn or not come/ therfore in that place affection fayleth: and for thilke affection is so lytel/ thorow whiche in goodnesse he shulde come to his grace/ the lytelnesse wyl it not suffre to auayle by no way in to his helpes: Certes grace and reason thilke affection foloweth. This affection with reason knytte/ dureth in eueryche trewe herte/ and euermore is encreasyng/ no ferdnesse/ no strength maye it remoue whyle truthe in herte abydeth. Sothly whan falsheed gynneth entre/ truthe draweth away/ grace/ and ioy both: but than thilke falsheed that trouth hath thus voyded/ hath vnknyt the bonde of vnderstandyng reason/ bytwene wyl and the herte. And who so that bonde vndothe/ and vnknytteth wyl to be in other purpose than to the first acorde/ knytteth him with contrarye of reason/ and that is vnreason. Lo/ than wyl and vnreson bringeth a man from the blisse of grace/ which thyng of pure kynde/ euery man ought to shonne & to eschewe/ and to the knot of wyl and reason confyrme. Me thynketh (qd she) by thy studyēt lokes/ thou wenest in these wordes me to cōtrarien/ from other sayenges here toforne in other place/ as whan thou were sōtyme in affection of wyl/ to thinges that nowe han brought the in disease/ whiche I haue the counsayled to voyde/ and thyn herte discouer/ and there I made thy wyl to ben chaunged/ whiche now thou wenest I argue to witholde and to kepe. Shortly I say ẏ reuers in these wordes may not ben foūde: for though dronkēnesse be forboden/ men shul not alway ben drinklesse. I trowe right for thou thy wyl out of reason shulde not tourne/ thy wyl in one reason shulde not vnbyde/ I say thy wyl in thy first purpose with vnreason was closed: Constrewe forthe of the remenante what the good lyketh. Trewly that wyl & reson shulde be knyt togyder was fre wyl of reason/ after tyme thyne herte is assentaunt to them bothe/ thou might not chaūge/ but if thou from rule of reason varye/ in whiche variaunce to come to thilke blysse desyred/ cōtrariously thou werchest: and nothyng may knowe wyl & reason but loue alone. Than if thou voide loue/ than weuest the bonde that knytteth/ and so nedes or els right lightly/ that other gone a sondre/ wherfore thou seest apertly that loue holdeth this knot/ and amaystreth hem to be bounde. These thinges/ as a ringe in cyrcuit of wrethe ben knyt in thy soule without departyng. A let be/ let be (qd I) it nedeth not of this no rehersayle to make/ my soule is yet in parfyte blysse/ in thynkyng of that knotte.

NOwe trewly lady I haue my groūde wel vnderstonde/ but what thynge is thilke spire that in to a tree shulde wexe: expowne

The Testament of Love: III. ix. 43–46: (col. i, l. 5) vi. 97–161; v. 8, 9

yowne me that thing/ what ye therof meane. That shal I (qd she) blithly/ and take good hede to the wordes I the rede. Contynuaunce in thy good seruyce/ by longe processe of tyme in ful hope abydyng/ without any chaunge to wylne in thyne herte: this is the spire/ whiche if it be wel kept and gouerned/ shal so hugely springe/ tyl the fruite of grace is plentuously out sprongen: for al though thy wyl be good/ yet may not therfore thilk blysse desyred hastely on the discēden/ it must abyde his seasonable tyme. & so by ꝓcesse of growyng/ with thy good traueyle/ it shal in to more & more wexe/ tyl it be founde so mighty/ that wyndes of yuel speche/ ne stormes of enuy/ make nat the traueyle ouerthrowe/ ne frostes of mystrust/ ne hayles of ielousy right lytel myght haue in harmynge of suche springes. Euery yonge setlyng lightly with smale stormes is apeyred/ but whan it is woxen somwhat in gretnesse/ than han great blastes & wethers but lytel might/ any disauantage to them for to werche. Myne owne souerayne lady (qd I) and welth of myne hert/ and it were lykyng vnto your noble grace/ therthrough nat to be displeased/ I suppose ye erren/ nowe ye maken ielousy enuy/ & distourbour to hem that ben your seruauntes. I haue serued ofte toforne this tyme/ that in euery louers hert/ great plētie of ielousies greues ben sowe/ wherfore me thynketh ye ne ought in no maner accompte/ thilke thynge among these other welked wyners and venomous serpētes/ as enuy/ mystrust/ & yuel speche. O fole (qd she) mystrust with foly with yuel wil medled/ engendreth that welked padde. Truely if they were distroyed ielousy vndone were for euer/ & yet some maner of ielousy I wot wel is euer redy in al the hertes of my trewe seruauntes/ as thus: to be ielous ouer hī selfe/ lest he be cause of his own disease. This ielousy in ful thought euer shulde be kept for ferdnesse to lese his loue by miskepyng/ thorowe his owne doyng in leudnesse/ or els thus: Lest she that thou seruest so feruently is beset there her better lyketh/ that of al thy good seruice she compteth nat a cresse. These ielousies in herte for acceptable qualytees ben demed: these oughten euery trewe louer by kyndly/ euermore hauen in his mynde/ tyl fully the grace & blysse of my seruice be on him discēded at wyl. & he that than ielousy catcheth/ or els by weenyng of his owne folysshe wylfulnesse mystrusteth/ truely with fantasy of venyme/ he is foule begyled. Yuel wyl hath grounded thilke mater of sorowe in his leude soule/ & yet nat for than to euery wight shulde me nat trust/ ne euery wight fully mystrust/ the meane of these thynges owen to be vsed. Sothly without causeful euydence/ mistrust in ielousy shulde nat be weued in no wyse person comenly/ suche leude wickednesse shulde me nat fynde. He that is wise & with yuel wil nat be acombred/ can abyde wel his tyme/ tyl grace & blisse of his seruice folowyng haue hī so mokel eased/ as his abydynge toforn hath hī diseased. Certes lady (qd I tho) of nothyng me wondreth/ sythen thilke blysse so precious is & kyndly good/ & wel is & worthy in kynde/ whan it is medled with loue & reason/ as ye toforn haue declared. Why/ anon as the one is sprong/ why springeth nat the tother? & anone as the one cometh/ why receyueth nat the other? For euery thynge that is out of his kyndely place/ by ful appetite/ euer cometh thiderwarde kyndely to drawe/ & his kyndly beyng therto him constrayneth. & the kyndly stede of this blysse/ is in suche wyl medled to vnbyde/ & nedes in that it shulde haue his kyndly beyng. Wherfore me thinketh anon as that wyl to be shewed & kydde him ꝓfreth/ thilke blysse shulde hī hye thilk wyl to receyue/ or els kynde of goodnesse worchen nat in hē as they shulde. Lo/ be the sonne neuer so ferre/ euer it hath his kynde werching in erthe: great weyght on hye vnsofte caried/ stynteth neuer tyl it cōe to his restyng place. Waters to the see warde euer ben they drawing/ thīg that is lyght blithly wyl nat synke/ but euer ascēdeth & vpward draweth. Thus kynde ī euery thyng his kyndly course/ & his beynge place sheweth: Wherfore be kide on this good wil/ anon as it were spronge/ this blysse shulde theron discēde/ her kynde wolde they dwelleden togider/ & so haue ye sayde your selfe. Certes (qd she) thyne hert sytteth wōder sore this blysse for to haue/ thyne hert is sore agreued yͭ it tarieth so lōge/ and

and if thou durstest/ as me thynketh by thyne wordes/ this blysse woldest thou blame. But yet I saye/ thilke blysse is kyndly good/ and his kyndely place in that wyl to unbyde. Never the later/ their cõmyng togider after kyndes ordynaunce nat sodaynly maye betyde/ it muste abyde tyme/ as kynde yeueth him leave for if a man/ as this wyl medled gonne hym shewe/ and thilke blysse in haste folowed/ so lyghtly cõmynge shulde lyghtly cause going/ longe tyme of thurstyng/ causeth ounke to be the more delycious whan it is atasted. Howe is it (quod I than) that so many blysses se I al daye at myne eye/ in the firste moment of a syght with suche wyl accorde. ye/ and yet other whyle with wyl assenteth/ syngulerly by him selfe there reason sayleth/ traveyle was none/ servyce had no tyme. This is a queynt maner thynge/ howe suche doynge cometh aboute. O (quod she) that is thus/ the erthe kyndely after seasons and tymes of the yere/ bryngeth forthe innumerable herbes and trees bothe profytable and other/ but suche as men might leave/ though they were nought in norisshynge to mannes kynde serven/ or els suche as tournen soone unto mẽnes confusyon in case that therof they atasle/ comen so the out of the erthe by their owne kynde/ withouten any mannes cure or any busynesse in traveyle: and the lyke herbes that to mẽnes lyve fode necessarily serven/ without whiche goodly in this lyfe creatures mowen nat enduren/ and most ben nourisshen to mankynde/ without great traveyle/ great tylthe/ and longe abydynge tyme/ comen nat out of the erthe/ and it with seede to some ordayned suche herbes to make spring and forthe growe. Right so the parfyte blysse/ that we have in meanynge of durynge tyme to abyde may nat come so lyztly/ but with great traveyle & right besy tylth/ and yet good seed to be sowe/ for ofte ye croppe fayleth of badde seede/ be it never so wel traveyled. And thilke blysse thou spoke of so liztly in cõmyng/ trewly is nat necessary ne abydynge: and but it the better be stamped/ & the venomous iuse out wrongen/ it is lykely to enpoysonen al tho that therof tasten. Certes right bytter ben ye herbes that shewen first the yere of her own kynde. Wel the more is the harvest that yeldeth many graynes/ tho longe and sore it hath ben traveyled. What woldest thou demen if a man wold yeve thre quarters of nobles of golde/ that were a precious gyft? ye certes (qd I). And what (qd she) thre quarters ful of perles? Certes (qd I) that were a riche gifte. And what (qd she) of as mokel azure? (qd I) a precious gifte at ful. Were nat (qd she) a noble gifte of al these atones? In good faith (qd I) for wãtyng of englysshe namyng of so noble a worde/ I can nat for preciousnesse yeve it a name. Rightfully (qd she) haste thou demed/ and yet love knytte in vertue/ passeth al the golde in this erthe. Good wyl accordant to reason/ with no maner properte may be countrevayled/ al the azure i the worlde is nat to accõpte in respecte of reason/ love that with good wyl & reason accordeth/ with non erthly riches may nat ben amẽded. This yest hast thou yeven I know it my selfe and thy margarite thilke gift hath receyved/ i whiche thynge to rewarde she hath her selfe bounde. But thy gifte as I said/ by no maner riches may be amended/ wherfore with thynge that may nat be amẽded/ yu shalt of thy margarites riztwisenesse be rewarded. Right suffred yet never but every good dede sõtyme to be yolde. al wolde thy Margarite with no rewarde the quyte/ Right that never more dieth thy mede in merit wol purvey. Certes such sodayne blisse as thou first nẽpnest/ ryzt wil hẽ rewarde as ye wel is worthy/ & though at thyn eye it semeth the rewarde ye desert to passe/ rizt can after sende suche bytternesse evenly it to rewarde: so ye sodayne blysse by alwayes of reson in gret goodnesse may not ben acompted/ but blisse long/ both long it abideth/ & endlesse it wol last. Se why thy wyl is endelesse/ for if thou lovedest ever/ thy wyl is ever ther tabyde and nevermore to chaũge: evenhed of rewarde must ben don by right: than muste nedes thy grace & this blysse endelesse in ioy to unbyde. Evenlyche disese asketh evenlyche ioy/ whiche hastely thou shalt have. A (qd I) it suffyseth not than alone good wyl/ be it never so wel wt reson medled/ but if it be in good servyce longe travayled. And so through servyce shul men come to the ioye/ & this me thynketh shulde be the weppyng tre of whiche ye first meued.

VEry trouth (qd she) hast thou nowe cōceyued of these thīges in thyne hert hastely shalt thou be able very ioye & parfyte blysse to receyue. & nowe I wot wel thou desyrest to knowe the maner of braunches/ that out of the tree shulde spring. Therof lady (qd I) hertely I you pray: for than leue I wol/ that right soone after I shal atast of the frute that I so long haue desyred. Thou hast herde (qd she) in what wyse this tre toforn this haue I declared/ as in groūde & in stocke of wexyng. First the groūde shulde be thy frewyl ful in thyne hert/ & the stocke (as I sayde) shulde be cōtynuaunce in good seruice/ by long tyme in traueyle/ tyl it were in greatnesse right wel woxen. & whan this tree suche gretnesse hath caught/ as I haue rehersed: the braūches than that the frute shulde forth bringe/ speche must they be nedes in voice of prayer/ in cōplaynīg wise vsed. But alas (qd I tho) he is sorowfully woūded that hydeth his speche & spareth his cōplayntes to make/ What shal I speke ye care: but payne euen lyke to hel/ sore hath me assayled/ & so ferforth in payne me thronge/ that I leue my tre is seer/ & neuer shal it frute forth bring. Certes he is greatly eased/ ye dare his preuy mone discouer to a true felowe/ that cōnyng hath & might/ wherthrough his pleint in any thynge may be amēded. & mokel more is he ioyed that with herte of hardynesse dare cōplayne to his lady/ what cares that he suffreth/ by hope of mercy with grace to be auaūced. Truely I saye for me/ sythe I came this Margarit to serue/ durst I neuer me discouer of no maner disease/ & wel the later hath myn herte hardyed suche thynges to done/ for the great bounties & worthy refresshmentes that she of her grace goodly without any desert on my halue ofte hath me rekened/ and nere her goodnesse the more with grace & with mercy medled/ whiche passen al desertes/ trauayls/ and seruynges/ that I in any degre might endure/ I wolde wene I shulde be without recouer/ in gettyng of this blysse for euer. Thus haue I stylled my disease/ thus haue I couered my care/ that I bren in sorouful anoy/ as gledes & coles wasten a fyre vnd deed asshen. Wel the hoter is the fyre/ that with asshen it is ouerleyn: right longe this wo haue I suffred. Lo (qd Loue) howe thou farest: me thynketh the palasy yuel hath acombred thy wittes/ as faste as thou hiest forwarde/ anon sodaynly backwarde thou mouest: Shal nat yet al thy leudnesse out of thy braynes? dul ben thy skilful vnderstādinges/ thy wyl hath thy wyt so amaistred. Wost thou nat wel (qd she) but euery tree in his sesonable tyme of burionynge shewe his blomes fro within/ ī signe of what frute shulde out of him spring/ els ye frute for that yere men haste desyuered/ be the grounde neuer so good. & though the stocke be mighty at the ful/ & the braunches seer & no burions shewe/ farwel the gardyner he may pype with an yue lefe his frute is fayled. Wherfore thy braūches must burionen ī presēce of thy lady/ if thou desyre any frute of thy ladies grace/ but beware of thy lyfe/ that thou no wodelay vse/ as in askyng of thynges that stretchen in to shame/ for tha myght thou nat spede by no way that I can espy. Vertue wol nat suffre villany out of him selfe to spring. Thy wordes may nat be queynt ne of subtel maner vnderstādinge. Freel witted people supposen in suche poesies to be begyled/ in open vnderstādinge must euery worde be vsed. Voice without clere vnderstādyng of sentēce saith Aristotel/ right nouȝt prīteth ī hert. Thy wordes thā to abide in hert/ & clene in ful sentēce of trewe menyng platly must thou shewe & euer be obedient/ her hestes & her wyls to performe/ and be thou set in suche a wyt to wete by a loke euermore what she meaneth. And he that lyst nat to speke/ but styly his disease suffre: what wōder is it tho he come neuer to his blysse. Who that traueyleth vnwist/ & coueyteth thyng vnknowe/ vnwetyng he shal be quyted/ & with vnknowe thyng rewarded. Good lady (qd I than) it hath ofte be sene/ that wethers & stormes so hugely haue fal in burionyng tyme/ & by perte duresse han beaten of the springes so clene/ wherthrough ye frute of thilke yere hath fayled. It is a great grace whan burions han good wethers/ their frutes forthe to bringe. Alas/ than after suche stormes howe harde is it to auoyde/ tyl efte wedring & yeres han maked her circute cours al about/ er any frute be able

able to be lasted he is shent for shame/ ye soule
is rebuked of his speche. He that is in fyre bren-
nyng sore smarteth for disease. Hym thynketh
ful long er the water come/ that shulde ye fyre
quenche. While men gone after a leche/ the bo-
dy is buryed. Lo howe semely this frute wey-
eth/ me thynketh that of tho frutes maye no
man atast/ for pure bytternesse in sauoure.
In this wyse bothe frute and the tree wasten
away togider/ though mokel besy occupation
haue be spente to brynge it so ferforthe/ that it
was able to spryng. A lyte speche hath maked
that al this labour is in ydel. I not (qd she)
wherof it serueth thy questyon to assoyle/ me
thynketh the nowe duller i wittes/ than whan
I with the first mette/ although a man be ru-
de/ cõmenly for a foole he is nat demed/ but
if he no good wol lerne/ sottes and fooles lette
lyghtly out of mynde/ the good that men tea-
cheth hem. I sayd therfore thy stocke must be
stronge/ & in greatnesse wel herted/ the tree is
ful feble that at the firste dent falleth: and al
though frute fayleth one yere or two/ yet shal
suche a season come one tyme or other/ that
shal bringe out frute that is nothyng preterit
ne passed there is nothyng future ne comyng/
but al thynges togider in that place ben pre-
sent euerlastyng without any meuyng/ wher-
fore to god al thynge is as nowe: & though a
thynge be nat in kyndly nature of thynges as
yet/ and if it shulde be herafter/ yet euermore
we shul saye god it maketh be tyme present/ &
nowe for no future ne preterit in hym may be
founde. Wherfore his wetyng & his before we-
tyng/ is al one in vnderstãdyng. Than if we-
tyng & before wetyng of god putteth in neces-
site to al thynges whiche he wot or before wot
ne thyng after eternyte/ or els after any tyme
he wol or dothe of lyberte but al of necessyte/
whiche thyng if thou wene it be ayenst reason
nat thorowe necessyte to be or nat to be/ al thi-
ge that god wot or before wot/ to be or nat to
be/ & yet nothynge defendeth any thynge to be
wyst or to be before wist of al in our wylles or
our doynges to be done/ or els cõmynge to be
for free arbitrement. Whan thou haste these
declarations wel vnderstãde/ than shalt thou
fynde it resonable at proue/ & that many thi-
ges be nat thorowe necessyte/ but thorowe ly-
berte of wyl/ saue necessyte of free wyl/ as I
tofore sayd: & as me thynketh al vtterly decla-
red. Me thynketh lady (qd I) so I shulde you
nat displease/ & euermore your reuerẽce to ke-
pe/ that these thynges cõtraryen in any vnder
stãdyng/ for ye sayne somtyme is thorowe ly-
berte of wyl & also thorowe necessite. Of this
haue I yet no sauour/ without better declara
tion. What wonder (qd she) is there in these
thynges/ sithen al day thou shalte se at thyne
eye/ in many thynges receyuen in hem selfe re
uers/ thorow dyuers reasons/ as thus. I pray
the (qd she) which thĩges ben more reuers thã
comen & gone: For if I bydde the come to me/
and thou come/ after whan I bydde the go &
thou go/ thou reuersest fro thy first cõmyng.
That is soth (qd I) & yet (qd she) in thy first
acome by dyuers reasone was ful reuersynge
to vnderstãde. As howe (qd I) That shal I
shewe the (qd she) by ensãple of thynges that
haue kyndly mouyng. Is there any thyng ye
meueth more kyndly than doth the heuens eye
whiche I clepe the sonne. Sothly (qd I) me
semeth it most kyndly to moue. Thou sayest
soth (qd she) Than if thou loke to the sonne/
in what parte he be vnder heuen/ euermore he
heygheth him in mouyng fro thilke place/ and
higheth meuyng towarde the lyke same place/
to thylke place from whiche he gothe he heig-
heth cõmynge/ and without any ceasynge to
that place he neigheth from whiche he is chaũ
ged & withdrawe. But nowe in these thynges
after dyuersite of reason/ reuers in one thinge
may be sey without repugnaunce. Wherfore
in the same wyse/ without any repugnaunce
by my reasons tofore maked/ al is one to be-
leue/ somthyng to be thorowe necessyte cõmin
ge for it is cõmyng/ & yet with no necessite cõ-
strayned to be cõmyng/ but with necessite that
cometh out of free wyl/ as I haue sayd. Tho
lyst me a lytel to speke/ & gan stynt my penne
of my wrytyng/ & sayd in this wyse. Trewly
lady as me thynketh/ I can allege authorities
gret that cõtrarien your sayenges. Job saith
of mannes person/ thou hast putte his terme/
whiche thou might nat passe. Than saye I
that no man may shorte ne length the day or-
ordayned

The Testament of Love: III. vii. 76–94; iv. 56 (*is*, col. 1, l. 25)—113

dayned of his doyng/ altho somtyme to vs it
semeth some man to do a thynge of free wyl/
wherthorowe his dethe he henteth. Naye for-
sothe (qd she) it is nothing ayenst my sayeng
for god is nat begiled/ne he seeth nothing whe
der it shal come of lyberte or els of necessyte/
yet it is sayd to be ordayned at god immoua-
ble/ whiche at man or it be done may be chaũ-
ged. Suche thyng also is that Poule the apo-
stel saithe of hem that tofore werne purposed
to be sayntes/as thus/ whiche that god before
wyst/ & hath predestyned/ cõformes of yma-
ges of his sonne/ that he shulde ben the firste
begeten/ that is to saye/ here amonges many
bretheren/ & whom he hath predestyned/hem he
hath cleped/ and whom he hath cleped/ hem he
hath iustifyed/ & whom he hath iustifyed/hem
he hath magnifyed. This purpose after whi-
che they ben cleped sayntes or holy in the euer-
lasting present/ wher is neither tyme passed ne
tyme cõmynge/ but euer it is onely present/ &
nowe as mokel a momẽt as seuyn thousande
wynter/ & so ayenwarde withouten any me-
uyng is nothyng lyche tẽporel presence/ for thĩ
ge that there is euer present. Yet amõges you
men er it be in your presence it is mouable tho
rowe lyberte of arbytrement. And right as in
the euerlastyng present no maner thyng was
ne shalbe/but onely is/ & nowe here in your tẽ
porel tyme/ somthyng was & is/ & shalbe/but
mouynge stoundes/ & in this is no maner re-
pugnaunce. Right so in the euerlastynge pre-
sence nothyng may be chaũged: & in your tẽ-
porel tyme other while it is ꝑued mouable by
lyberte of wyl or it be do/ withouten any incõ
uenyence therof to folowe. In your temporel
tyme is no suche presence as in the tother/ for
your present is done/ whan passed & to come
gynnen entre/ whiche tymes here amõges you
euerych easely foloweth other/ but the presẽce
euerlastyng dureth in onehed/ withouten any
ymaginable chaũgyng/ & euer is present and
nowe. Trewly the course of the planettes & o-
uerwhelmynges of the sonne in dayes & nigh
tes/ with a newe gynnyng of his circute after
it is ended/ that is to sayn/ one yere to folowe
another. These maken your trãsitory tymes
with chaũgynge of lyues & mutation of peo-

ple. But right as your tẽporel presence coueу
teth euery place/ & al thinges in euery of your
tymes be cõtayned/ & as nowe both sey & wist
to goddes very knowynge. Than (qd I) me
wondreth why Poule spake these wordes/ by
voice of signification ĩ tyme passed/ that god
his sayntes before wist/hath predestined/hath
cleped/ hath iustifyed/ & hath magnified: Me
thynketh he shulde haue sayde tho wordes in
tyme present/ & that had ben more accordaunt
to the euerlastyng present/than to haue spoke
in preterit voice of passed vnderstandyng.
O (qd Loue) by these wordes I se wel thou
hast lytel vnderstãdyng of the euerlastyng p̃-
sence/ or els of my before spoken wordes/ for
neuer a thing of tho thou hast nẽpned was to
fore other or after other/but al atones euẽlych
at the god ben/ & al togider in the euerlastyng
present be nowe to vnderstãdyng/ the eternal
presence/as I sayd/hath inclose togider ĩ one/
al tymes/ in which close & one al thynges that
ben in dyuers tymes & in dyuers places tem-
porel without posteriorite or priorite bẽ closed
therin ꝑpetual nowe/ & maked to dwel in pre-
sent sight. But there thou sayest that Poule
shulde haue spoke thilke forsaid sentence be ty
me present/ & that most shulde haue ben acor-
daunt to the euerlastynge presence/ why gab-
best thou to thy wordes? Sothly I say Poule
moued ÿ wordes by signification of tyme pas
sed/to shewe fully that thilk wordes were nat
put for tẽporel signification/for al thilk tyme
were nat thilke sentẽce tẽporallych borne/whi
che that Poule pronounced god haue tofore
knowe/ & haue cleped than magnified/ wher-
thorowe it may wel be know that Poule vsed
tho wordes of passed signification/ for nede &
lacke of a worde in mãnes bodily speche to-
kenynge the euerlastyng presence. And ther-
fore worde is moste semelyche in lykenesse to
euerlastyng presence/ he toke his sentence for
thynges that here beforne ben passed/ vtterly
be unmouable/ lyke to ÿ euerlasting presẽce.
As thilke that ben there neuer mowe not ben
present/so thynges of tyme passed ne mowe in
no wyse not ben passed: but al thĩges in your
temporal presence that passen in a lytel while/
shullen ben not present. So than in that it is
more

more symilytude to the euerlastyng presence / signification of tyme passed / than of tyme temporal present / & so more in accordaunce. In this maner what thynge of these that ben done thorowe fre arbitrement / or els as necessary / holy writte pronoũceth / after eternyte he speketh / in whiche presēce is euerlastyng sothe and nothyng but sothe immouable / nat after tyme / in whiche naught alway ben your wylles & your actes. & right as whyle they be nat / it is nat nedeful hem to be: so ofte it is nat nedeful that somtyme they shulde be. As how (quod I) for yet must I be lerned by some ensample. Of loue (quod she) wol I nowe ensample make / sithen I knowe the heed knotte in that yelke. Lo / somtyme thou wrytest no arte / ne arte than in no wyl to write. & right as whyle yu writest nat / or els wolt nat write / it is nat nedeful the to write / or els wylne to write. And for to make ȳ knowe utterly / that thynges ben other wise in the euerlastyng presence / than in temporal tyme: se nowe my good childe / for somthyng is in the euerlastynge presence / than in temporal tyme / it was nat in eternyte tyme / in eterne presence shal it nat be. Than no reason defendeth / that sōthynge ne may be in tyme temporal mouyng / that in eterne is immouable. Forsothe it is no more contrary ne reuers for to be mouable in tyme temporel / and mouable in eternyte / than nat to be in any tyme / and to be alway in eternite and haue to be or els to come in tyme temporel / & nat haue be ne nought cōmyng to be in eternyte. Yet neuer the later / I say nat somthyng to be neuer in tyme temporel / that euer is eternyte / but al onely in somtyme nat to be For I saye nat thy loue to morne in no tyme to be / but to day alone I deny ne it to be / and yet neuer the later it is alwaye in eternyte.

A so (quod I) it semeth to me that cōmyng thyng or els passed here in your tēporal tyme to be / in eternite euer nowe and present oweth nat to be demed / and yet foloweth nat thylke thynge / that was or els shal be / in no maner therto ben passed / or els cōmyng: than utterly shul we deny / for there without ceasyng / it is in his present maner. O (quod she) myne own disciple / nowe gynnest thou able to haue the name of my seruaunt. Thy wytte is clered / away is nowe errour of cloude in unconnyng / awaye is blyndnesse of loue / awaye is thoughtful study / of medlyng maners hastely shalte thou entre in to the ioye of me / that am thyne owne maistres. Thou haste (quod she) in a fewe wordes / wel and clerely concluded mokel of my mater. And right as there is no reuers ne contrarioustie in tho thynges / right so withouten any repugnaũce / it is sayd somthyng to be mouable in tyme temporel / & for it be / that in eternyte dwelleth immouable nat afore it be or after that it is / but without cessyng / for right naught is there after tyme / that same is there euerlastynge / that tēporallyche somtyme nys / and toforne it be it maye not be / as I haue sayd. Nowe sothly (qd I) this haue I wel understāde / so that nowe me thynketh that prescience of god and fre arbytremēt withouten any repugnaunce acorden / and ȳ maketh the strength of eternyte / whiche encloseth by presence duryng al tymes / and al thinges that ben / han ben / and shul ben in any tyme. I wolde nowe (qd I) a lytel understande sythen that al thyng thus beforne wot / whether thilke wetynge be of tho thynges / or els thilke thynges ben to ben of goddes wetyng / and so of god nothynge is: and if euery thyng be thorowe goddes wetyng / and therof take his beyng / than shulde god be maker and auctour of badde werkes / and so he shulde not ryghtfully punysshe yuel doynges of mankynde. (Qd Loue) I shal tel the / this lesson to lerne myne owne trewe seruaunt / the noble philosophical poete / in Englissh / whiche euermore hym besyeth and trauayleth right sore my name to encrease / wherfore al that wyllen me good / owe to do him worshyp & reuerence bothe / trewly his better ne his pere in schole of my rules coude I neuer fynde: He (qd she) in a treatise ȳ he made of my seruant Troylus / hath this mater touched / and at the ful this questyon assoyled. Certaynly his noble sayenges can I not amende: In goodnes of gentyl manlyche speche / without any maner of nycite of starieres ymagynacion in wytte and in good reason of sentence he passeth al other makers. In the boke of Troylus / the answere to thy